Galloping Thunder

GALLOPING THUNDER

The Story of the Stuart Horse Artillery Battalion

Robert J. Trout

STACKPOLE BOOKS

Published by
STACKPOLE BOOKS
5067 Ritter Road
Mechanicsburg, PA 17055
www.stackpolebooks.com

Printed in the United States of America

10 9 8 7 6 5 4 3 2 1

FIRST EDITION

Library of Congress Cataloging-in-Publication Data
Trout, Robert J., 1947–
Galloping thunder : the Stuart Horse Artillery Battalion / Robert J. Trout.—1st ed.
p. cm.
Includes bibliographical references and index.
ISBN 0-8117-0707-5
1. Confederate States of America. Army. Stuart Horse Artillery Battalion. 2. Virginia—History—Civil War, 1861–1865—Regimental histories. 3. United States—History—Civil War, 1861–1865—Regimental histories. 4. Virginia—History—Civil War, 1861–1865—Artillery operations. 5. United States—History—Civil War, 1861–1865—Artillery operations, Confederate. I. Title.

E581.4.S85 T76 2002
973.7'455—dc21

2002020520

To the John Pelham Historical Association
for
its untiring efforts in preserving the memory of the
Stuart Horse Artillery

CONTENTS

PART THREE: The Chew Era

Appendixes

ACKNOWLEDGMENTS

Though I would like to acknowledge all the individuals and institutions who have aided me over the last fourteen years during my work on the Stuart Horse Artillery, space limitations and a failing memory make such recognition impossible. However, there are a few who cannot go unheralded, for they were instrumental in bringing the story of the battalion to life.

This volume would not have been written had not John Ingalls answered my inquiry concerning the Chew Papers back in April 1986. John opened the archives to a virtual amateur and allowed me to stare in wonder at a treasure trove of raw material—rosters, letters, tributes, personal accounts, and more. The realization that I had bitten off more than I could chew rapidly became clear. All I could think of was having copies made of the material and getting it home, where I could explore it at my leisure. To that, John had no objection. We quickly struck a deal: the copies in exchange for transcripts as I completed them. Over the years, John continued to answer my inquiries and send additional material, while I sporadically forwarded the transcriptions I had promised. Both of us realized that what I was trying to do would take time, years in fact, and I had other projects going as well. Sadly, John did not live to see the results of his kindness and willingness to share Chew's Papers. He will not have the opportunity to read the story of the battalion. But then, knowing John, he's probably interviewing Chew, Beckham, Pelham, et al. even as I write. John, take good notes in a clear hand; I may have to transcribe them someday.

My wife, Judy, not only was a computer widow, but she willingly participated in numerous research trips and battlefield tours over the past fourteen years as well. She also aided in the transcribing of dozens of letters and other documents that appear on the following pages. Without her continued support, this work would not have been completed.

To Jennifer Young and Scott Mauger I owe a debt I scarcely know how to repay. Their expertise and advice over the years have been of immense assistance in editing my manuscript on several levels. Their knowledge of the horse artillery and of the war in general provided numerous clues and insights to various aspects of the battalion's history that I might have overlooked.

The assistance of the John Pelham Historical Association, especially its founder, Peggy Vogtsberger, was greatly appreciated. Through her various contacts, Peggy brought to light numerous letters that gave the human side of the story and tracked down descendants of members of the battalion who provided information on their gallant ancestors. The resources of the JPHA were always at my disposal and never failed to surprise me with some new bit of information.

Fellow researchers, historians, and writers Patricia Andrews, Gardner D. Beach, Chris Calkins, John Coski, Robert J. Driver, Jr., Bruce Gregory, Clark B. Hall, Robert K. Krick, Don Richard Lauter, Terry Lowry, Horace Mewborn, Robert O'Neill, Gordon Rhea, Ben Ritter, John W. Thompson IV, Eric Wittenberg, and the late John Divine gave unselfishly of their expertise and advice. I extend to them my sincere gratitude.

A special note of thanks is also due to Ms. Kyra C. Moore of Lorraine Park Cemetery in Baltimore, Maryland.

To the descendants of a number of the battalion's officers, I am indebted for their willingness to share material on their ancestors, which permitted a closer look at the battalion through the eyes of its men. Thanks to Mrs. Anne Edwards Inglis, Ph.D., Mr. William B. Edwards, and David A. Edwards (Lt. William B. Bean); Mrs. Elizabeth A. Tait (Maj. James Breathed); Mrs. Ollie M. Lunsford and Mrs. Carolyn Respess (Lt. Parkison Collett); Mr. Lee W. Henslee (Capt. Wiley H. Griffin); Mrs. Richard P. Thomsen and Mr. A. R. Hoxton, Jr. (Lt. William Hoxton); Mrs. Lucy McKinstry and Mr. John Pelham Johnston (Maj. Philip Preston Johnston); Mr. Karl Grier Hudson, Jr. (Lt. Lorenzo D. Lorentz); Mr. Lewis T. Nunnelee II (Lt. Lewis T. Nunnelee); Mr. David Prentiss Shreve (Lt. Richard S. Shreve); Mrs. Julia B. Davis, Mr. Peter T. Chew, Mr. Robert P. Chew, Mr. James M. Thomson, and Mr. Paul H. Thomson (Maj. James W. Thomson); Mr. T. Hartley Marshall (Lt. Francis Halsey Wigfall); and Mrs. Sallie R. Witten (Lt. Edwin Duke Yancy).

Several descendants of enlisted men also contributed information and material on their ancestors. My thanks to Mrs. Glenna Shurtleff (Pvt. Calvin L. Caplinger); Mrs. Carolyn Respess (Sgt. Andrew J. Collett); Mr. Virgil S. Hart (Pvt. Calvin C. Hart); Mrs. Bruce D. Seldon (Pvt. Charles W. McVicar); Mr. Parke C. Bogle (Pvt. Estel C. Mustard and Pvt. John J. Mustard); Mr. David Prentiss Shreve (Pvt. George W. Shreve); and Mr. Sharon Bell (Pvt. William P. Walters and Pvt. William A. Simpson).

The compilation of material appearing in this work would not have been possible without the cooperation of the institutions mentioned below.

The letters of Francis Halsey Wigfall are part of Louis Trezevant Wigfall Family Papers in the Library of Congress.

John Pelham's report on Evelynton Heights is from the Department of Rare Books, William R. Perkins Library at Duke University, which graciously granted permission for its publication.

James H. Williams's letters are found in the Williams Family Papers at the Virginia Historical Society.

Excerpts from the Louis Sherfesee Papers appear with the kind permission of the South Carolina Relic Room.

The "History of Hart's Battery," by Maj. James F. Hart, Dr. L. C. Stephens, Louis Sherfesee, and Charles H. Schwing, is part of the collection of the South Carolina Library of the University of South Carolina.

The Roger Preston Chew Papers are housed in the Jefferson County Museum.

William Hoxton's letters are part of the Randolph Family Papers in the Virginia Historical Society.

The Charles Richard Phelps Letters are preserved at the University of Virginia.

The Hairston-Wilson Papers and the R. Channing Price Papers are located in the Southern Historical Collection of the University of North Carolina at Chapel Hill.

J. E. B. Stuart's letter to Dr. Atkinson Pelham appears through the courtesy of the Anniston and Calhoun County Public Library.

The Blain Family Papers, 1860–69, were provided by Washington and Lee University.

Charles McVicar's letters and diary excerpts appear with the kind permission of the Winchester-Frederick County Historical Society.

The George E. Robertson papers are part of the Grinnan Family Papers in the Virginia Historical Society.

To all of these individuals and institutions, and to those I may have unintentionally omitted, I extend my sincere gratitude.

PREFACE

Almost twenty years ago, I happened upon a footnote written at the bottom of page 774 of Jennings Cropper Wise's *The Long Arm of Lee.* It read, "Col. Chew now resides in Charles Town, West Virginia. He tells the writer that he is engaged in writing the history of the Horse Artillery. May God spare him until he has completed the priceless record he alone is now capable of preparing, and for many years to come."

The "Col. Chew" whom Wise referred to was none other than Lt. Col. Roger Preston Chew, the last commander of the Stuart Horse Artillery Battalion. My attention was piqued immediately. More than anything, I wanted to read Chew's book. This was long before my research led me into countless libraries and book repositories, and I naively began a search for a volume that I soon discovered did not exist. Obviously Chew had died before finishing the task he had set for himself. There the matter rested for a number of years. Then, while researching the staff officers of Maj. Gen. J. E. B. Stuart, of which Chew as commander of the horse artillery was one, my curiosity was stimulated once more concerning the unwritten history of the battalion. I decided to add to my already busy research schedule and take time to pursue both Chew the staff officer and Chew the would-be chronicler of the battalion's history. A letter to the Jefferson County Museum in Charles Town in April 1986 brought a response from then curator John Ingalls. The many pages that follow are a result of John's return letter, which opened the Chew Papers to a novice researcher-writer with the dream of writing the history Chew never finished.

The papers revealed that Chew had begun to gather a considerable amount of material on the various batteries of the battalion. Rosters, lists of engagements, biographical material, articles, testimonials, and reminiscences abounded, but there was no evidence that he had begun to write. References to other "histories" at first raised my hopes that unpublished manuscripts by other battalion members existed. Again I was disappointed to discover that most of these were lost or beyond my ability to uncover them. Still, I believed that a history of the men who fought under Pelham, Beckham, and Chew was needed, so I expanded my search. In the end, material was uncovered in large repositories and small, in private collections, and in the hands of descendants of the men who fought the guns. Virtually all of it has found its way, in one form or another, into this work.

Among my first realizations when I began the task of writing was that this would not be a small tale shortly told. Almost four years of writing have confirmed that perception. The story of the battalion is vast and encompasses almost every campaign of the Army of Northern Virginia and a few others besides. From skirmishes in which a couple of rounds were fired to full-scale battles in which the guns went through hundreds of rounds, the horse artillery was engaged from the outskirts of Harrisburg, Pennsylvania, to the battle at Bentonville, North Carolina. But the history of the battalion was more than just the battles it fought. The men had their own stories to tell.

The letters, diaries, and reminiscences left behind by the soldiers of the battalion proved to be priceless. The war was of major concern to most, but family and home proved to be subjects always in the forefront of the minds of many. The decision to include in the text entire letters, in most instances, rather than excerpts came directly from the fact that the men told their story better than anyone else could have. The whole man is revealed, not just the soldier. To capture a true view of the battalion, one must gain as complete an understanding of its men as is possible with the limited amount of material available. To them, having their long underwear as the weather turned cold was just as important as, and in some cases more than, whipping the Yanks in a fight.

The contributions of the Stuart Horse Artillery Battalion during the four years of the war should not be underestimated or ignored—as, for the most part, they have been—by historians. Had Chew completed his work, the battalion's story would have been available to the last generation of readers and writers during a time of rising interest in this dramatic period of our nation's history. Now that "Chew's" history of the battalion is finished, it is hoped that the next generation of historians will come to recognize what the battalion accomplished as it fought under Pelham, Beckham, and Chew and include its deeds in their writings for the next generation of readers.

Robert J. Trout
Myerstown, PA

The Pelham Era

CHAPTER 1

Of Horses and Thunderbolts

"The ever-glorious and gallant Stuart Horse Artillery"

> Down the crowded highway galloped a battery, withdrawn from some other position to save ours. The field fence is scattered while you could count thirty, and the guns rush for the hills behind us, six horses to a piece, three riders to each gun, over dry ditches where a farmer would not drive a wagon, through clumps of bushes, over logs a foot thick, every horse on the gallop, every rider lashing his team and yelling. The sight behind us makes us forget the foe in front. The guns jump two feet high as the heavy wheels strike rock or log, but not a horse slackens his pace, the cannoneer leaning forward in his saddle. Six guns, six caissons, six horses each, eighty men race for the brow of the hill, as if he who reached it first was to be knighted. A moment ago the battery was a confused mob; we look again, and the six guns are in position, the detached horses hurrying away, the ammunition chest open, and along our lines the command, "Give them one more volley and fall back and support the guns."
>
> We have scarcely obeyed when "Boom, boom!" opens the battery, and jets of fire jump down to scorch the green trees under which we fought and despaired. What grim, cool fellows those cannoneers are! Every man is a perfect machine. Bullets splash dust in their faces, but they do not wince; bullets sing over and around them, but they do not dodge. There goes one to the earth, shot through the head as he sponged the gun. The machinery loses just one beat, misses just one cog in the wheel, and then works away again as before. Every gun is using short-fuse shells. The ground shakes and trembles.[1]

Pvt. David Cardwell's description of a horse artillery battery in action may seem melodramatic, but in reality, much of what he wrote was close to the truth. Serving with Capt. William M. McGregor's Battery of the Stuart Horse Artillery Battalion gave Cardwell ample opportunity to witness such events as a participant. Once seen, the charge of a horse artillery battery was not something the viewer forgot. How much more thrilling and heart-stopping to be a part of it!

For Cardwell and over 2,200 officers and men who were part of the Stuart Horse Artillery Battalion during the four years that the Civil War raged, such moments became embedded in their consciousness for the remainder of their lives. Years after the war, the old veterans were still reminiscing about Chew's charge at Middletown, Pelham's defiant Napoleon at Fredericksburg, Breathed's daring escape at Spotsylvania, and Graham's mad dash through Petersburg. Chests swelled with pride; tears flowed for parted comrades; voices cracked with emotion. But there was fire in the eyes and the souls. Gray-bearded Gunner George M. Neese volunteered to accompany his old captain, Chew, if he went to fight the Spanish in 1898.[2] In the end, Neese did not go, but it should never be doubted that he would have. Being a part of the horse artillery was something that set a man apart, something special. The old cannoneers were proud to have served under the likes of Pelham, Beckham, and Chew.

Lt. Theodore S. Garnett, aide-de-camp to Maj. Gen. J. E. B. Stuart, once stated, "The honor of firing the first gun at Fort Sumter is no longer in doubt. The proud distinction of firing the last gun at Appomattox is claimed by many, but the command that fired the most shot and shell, first, last, and all the time, is perhaps, without doubt, the ever-glorious and gallant Stuart Horse Artillery."[3] Even if this were not true—and there is a distinct possibility that it was true, as subsequent chapters will reveal—the record of Stuart Horse Artillery Battalion can stand with any artillery organization in any army, Northern or Southern. This is not to say that the batteries of the battalion were never driven from the field, never lost guns to the enemy, or never failed to silence an opposing battery, but it does say that they carved for themselves a reputation other batteries or artillery battalions would have been proud to claim as their own.

The heritage left behind by the officers and men of the Stuart Horse Artillery Battalion began to take shape in late 1861. However, the roots of the battalion went much deeper into the past. The guns the men fought could be traced back to 1624, when Gustavus Adolphus had the first practical field pieces cast. These iron four-pounders weighed in at only 400 pounds, which gave them the mobility other cannons of the time lacked. From this humble beginning came the twelve-pound Napoleons, three-inch ordnance rifles, and twelve-pound Blakelys used by Pelham, Chew, Breathed, and others during the battalion's four-year history.

Gustavus's light pieces were pulled by men using ropes or one or two horses, but the cannoneers walked into battle beside their guns. Not until Frederick the Great did horse artillery make its first appearance on the field of battle.[4] Later, in the American colonies' struggle for independence, the artillery arm of the fledging country's armies made some significant contributions to the war effort, especially at Yorktown. Once the new country was founded, it set about creating a permanent army, albeit a small one. The Act of March 3, 1799, created the "Corps of Artillerists and Engineers" as part of the army. From this organization grew the artillery arm of the U.S. Army and eventually the horse artillery. But what exactly is horse artillery, and how does it compare with light artillery, field artillery, heavy artillery, foot artillery, flying artillery, and mounted artillery? During the Civil War, these terms were flung about like cannonballs on a battlefield and as a result require some explanation.

Civil War artillery was divided into two kinds. The first of these was foot artillery, or heavy artillery, as it was sometimes called. This type of artillery was used in a siege, in coastal batteries, and garrison batteries. It also included mountain artillery and rocket batteries. The second kind was light artillery, or field artillery, which maneuvered with the troops in the field. This included two types: the mounted artillery and the horse artillery. The mounted artillery fought with the infantry. The cannoneers walked beside the pieces but when necessary "mounted" the ammunition chests and rode from one position to another. Horse artillery, on the other hand, was attached to the cavalry, though it could and did fight with the infantry when needed. Because it was designed to accompany the cavalry, it had to be even more maneuverable than a mounted battery. In order to achieve this, all the cannoneers who did not ride the limbers, caissons, or the horses pulling them rode their own mounts. In other words, no one in the horse artillery walked when the guns were in motion. As a result, it had significantly more mobility than other artillery of its time and was able to fulfill the demanding role of maneuvering and fighting with the cavalry.[5] The term "flying artillery" was used to describe the practice of keeping the guns moving from position to position to confuse the enemy. No Union or Confederate section or battery of artillery was ever listed officially as a "flying battery," though a number of batteries adopted the name informally.

By 1860, the role of artillery was well defined. That year's edition of *The Artillerist's Manual,* by 1st Lt. John Gibbon of the 4th U.S. Artillery, who later rose to the rank of major general in the Union army, defined it quite succinctly:

> The principal objective of artillery is, to sustain the troops in attack and defense; to facilitate their movements and oppose the enemy's; to destroy his forces as well as the obstacles which protect them; and to keep up the combat until an opportunity is offered for a decisive blow. Our mounted batteries have been so much perfected and increased in mobility, that they can move almost with as much celerity as horse artillery; and the latter has been practically abandoned in the United States. The men should be mounted on the boxes only when it is absolutely necessary, to avoid breaking down the horses. This rapid gait cannot, however, be kept up any length of time, as it can in horse artillery.[6]

Gibbon's conclusion that the mounted artillery was equal to the horse artillery in mobility over reasonably short distances had merit. His qualifier concerning the length of time a mounted battery could sustain such movement was a critical observation, especially where cavalry was concerned. Fortunately, Gibbon did not dismiss the horse artillery with the above curt statement but expanded on its use and capabilities:

> Horse artillery is, in France, considered indispensably necessary for service with cavalry, which having but little or no fire of its own, and acting simply by the shock of its charge, requires that the enemy should be kept at a distance, and first broken by the fire of artillery in order that the charges made may result in any practical good. Instances might be cited where the absence of its co-operation resulted in inflicting upon the enemy simply a few sabre cuts, when he ought to have been annihilated. This kind of artillery is, however, very costly, consuming a large number of horses, and should therefore be proportionally small in quantity. It should, however, be excellent in quality, bold, well maneuvered, ever venturesome, appearing at and disappearing from different points, and multiplying, as it were, its action, which should be short and decisive.[7]

In summarizing what horse artillery could contribute to the cavalry, Gibbon could not have visualized what cavalry would become in the next five years. Much would change. But Gibbon did define accurately how horse artillery should be fought, and that didn't change. "Bold" and "venturesome" would be some of the milder adjectives applied to what Pelham, Chew, Pennington, and others did with their guns.

So how was Civil War horse artillery utilized? In battle, it provided the offensive punch, which more and more meant being in the thick of the fight, not just standing off and throwing shells, though it was called upon to fulfill this role on numerous occasions as well. It created a defensive strong point on which the cavalry could rally when repulsed. It supported pickets, often being placed just in the rear of the most advanced positions. Horse batteries were able to accompany the cavalry on raids or reconnaissances, but in this it failed more than it succeeded simply because of its inability to keep up. The batteries of the Stuart Horse Artillery Battalion had their greatest success in the Chambersburg Raid, but on other raids they were only partially successful. In the Chickahominy Raid, the artillery failed to contribute anything useful.

How efficiently the horse artillery performed these various tasks depended on the officers and men in it and on horseflesh. Not all of the batteries in the Stuart Horse Artillery Battalion were of the same quality. Of the ten that eventually made up the battalion, the Ashby Battery (the Chew-Thomson-Carter Battery), the 1st Stuart Horse Artillery (the Pelham-Breathed-Johnston-Shanks

Battery), the 2nd Stuart Horse Artillery (the Pelham-Henry-McGregor-Brown Battery), the Washington South Carolina Battery (the Hart-Halsey Battery), and the Lynchburg Battery (the Moorman-Shoemaker Battery) were the premier batteries, simply because they saw more hard service and performed at a more consistently high level as horse artillery than the other batteries. Ranking just behind them were the Petersburg Battery (Graham's Battery), the 2nd Maryland Artillery or the Baltimore Light Artillery (Griffin's Battery), and the Staunton Battery (McClanahan's Battery). The remaining two batteries, the Charlottesville Battery (Jackson's Battery) and the Roanoke Battery (Lurty's Battery), performed well on a number of occasions but were often hampered by inferior guns and, in the case of the latter, a shortage of men.

Regardless of their status or reputation, the performance of any of these batteries could be severely curtailed by inferior or exhausted horses. While the fighting prowess of the battery depended on its human element, its mobility was directly linked to the quality and quantity of its horseflesh. Selection of the proper horses was an art in itself. The characteristics that made a good saddle horse were not the same as those required for a good draft horse. Pelham quickly found out on the Chambersburg Raid that all draft horses were not created equal, either. The huge plow horses used by the Pennsylvania Dutch farmers had the strength to pull the guns but wore out rapidly and had little "get up and go." They were handed over to the Transport Department of the army soon after the raid.

Even though securing the right animals was vitally important, as the war continued the batteries had to take what they could get. It became apparent early in the war that the Quartermaster Department of the army would not be able to supply completely the needs of the batteries. Official efforts were made to alleviate the problem. One was to reduce the teams from six horses to four horses per gun, even though it was accepted that this would further hamper the batteries' capabilities. Another was to limit the number of guns in a battery to no more than four. While these endeavors worked to some extent, the problem remained a serious one right to the war's end. The captains of the batteries often took on the additional duty of seeking out sources of horses on their own to supplement what the Quartermaster Department could supply. They well knew that no matter how good their guns and crews were, if they could not reach the field, they were almost useless. The struggle to secure suitable horses and maintain those already in the batteries became, next to fighting, the main focus of the batteries' commanders.

The armament used by the Stuart Horse Artillery Battalion and the Federal horse artillery contradicted Gibbon's conclusion that horse artillery should receive "the lightest guns."[8] Though this was true in part for some of the Confederate batteries early in the war, the trend soon changed. The light pieces were no match for the enemy's Napoleons, three-inch ordnance rifles, and ten-pound Parrotts that the batteries faced on virtually every field. As quickly as these and other heavier guns could be obtained, many through capture, the inferior pieces were abandoned. Stuart made every effort to see that his horse batteries had the best guns available, to the point of ignoring orders to turn over all captured pieces to the army's ordnance officers. The addition of these heavier cannons was a two-edged sword for the Confederates. While the heavier ordnance enabled the horse artillery to fight on more equal footing with their opponents, though they were still outranged and outgunned on many occasions, the added weight put a strain on the ever-dwindling horse pool. When the teams were cut from six to four horses, the batteries' mobility was hampered to a greater degree than if lighter guns had still been in use. Federal horse artillery batteries contained six guns pulled by six horses throughout the war, allowing them both greater firepower and superior mobility. Still, the Confederates gave a good account of themselves right up until the last months of the war.

Along with the problem of being unable to match the Federals in the quantity and quality of their guns, the Confederate horse artillery was plagued with inferior ammunition. Time and again, when any advantage was gained through position or number of guns, it frequently was negated by the poor quality of the Confederate-manufactured ammunition, which exploded too early, too late, or not at all. Captured ammunition helped overcome this to some extent but never enough to alter the situation significantly. Throughout the war, this lack of good ammunition proved to be just one more difficulty that Pelham, Beckham, Chew, and their faithful cannoneers had to face. Fortunately, except for ammunition that needed to be imported for exotic pieces like the Whitworth or Blakely guns, quantity was never really a serious problem. There was always a supply of something to throw at the enemy, even if it didn't always explode on target.

In the third component of the batteries, the men, the Confederates were able to match their adversaries and in some actions to surpass the Federals' performance. Even with the inferior horses and armament, the cannoneers of the battalion could stand toe to toe with the best the enemy had to offer. Superior guns, better position, greater numbers might beat them, but not a lack of courage, steadfastness, or training. What enabled the batteries to contend with the Federals was the quality of their personnel.

The men who served the guns came from all walks of life. Few were professional soldiers, even among the officers. Farmers, carpenters, students, doctors, teachers, stonemasons, and a myriad of other professions filled the ranks. For every Pelham and Beckham who thoroughly understood the function and use of artillery, there were a hundred officers and men who knew next to nothing and a good number who knew nothing. It was up to the Pelhams and Beckhams to transform the raw recruits into the machines Cardwell described above. That this task, for the most part, was accomplished will be seen in the following chapters.

In his book *Mohun,* John Esten Cooke, at one time ordnance officer of the cavalry on the staff of Maj. Gen. J. E. B. "Jeb" Stuart, wrote a passage about these men of the horse artillery. Though presented in a fictional setting, Cooke captured some of the essence of these men who were the heart and soul of the battalion.

> Around me, in light of the camp-fire, were grouped the tigers who had fought with Pelham, in the old battles of Stuart. Here were the heroes of a hundred combats; the men who had held their ground desperately in the most desperate encounters—the bulldogs who had showed their teeth and sprung to the death-grapple at Cold Harbor, Manassas, Sharpsburg, Fredericksburg, Chancellorsville, Fleetwood, Gettysburg, in the Wilderness, at Trevilian's, at Sappony, in a thousand bitter conflicts with the cavalry. Scarred faces, limping bodies, the one-armed, the one-legged,—these I saw around me; the frames slashed and mutilated, but the eyes flashing and full of fight, as in the days when Pelham thundered, loosing his war-hounds on the enemy. I had seen brave commands, in these long years of combat—had touched the hands of heroic men, whose souls fear never entered—but I never saw braver fighters than the horse artillery—soldiers more reckless than Pelham's bloodhounds. They went to battle laughing. There was something of the tiger in them.[9]

The romanticism of Cooke's words aside, the men he wrote of with such passion must have impressed him with their devotion to duty, their courage, and their tenacity in battle. Cooke certainly was in a position from which to gauge their performance. Under Stuart and then Wade Hampton, Cooke witnessed many engagements, large and small. His appraisal should not be dismissed as mere artistic musings.

Yet, more importantly, it should be remembered that these men were simply human beings caught up in a titanic struggle, the scope of which few of them comprehended. Once drawn into the conflict, most of them endeavored to do what duty required and made every effort to stay alive while doing so. Hearth and home were never far from their thoughts, as their letters illustrated. To end the war and return to their loved ones was their ultimate goal. As to victory, most never doubted it until the last few terrible months of the war. But in the beginning, there was nothing but high hopes and an eagerness to meet the enemy and gain the victory.

CHAPTER 2

The Beginning

"Young men, now that you have your company, what are you going to do with it?"

Few would dispute the statement that the graduates of the United States Military Academy and the Virginia Military Institute made up the heart and soul of the officer corps of the Army of Northern Virginia. Accepting this, it then should be no surprise that the story of the Stuart Horse Artillery begins at these two hallowed institutions with two of the men who would command the battalion: John Pelham and Roger Preston Chew.

An Alabamian by birth, John Pelham, one day to be called "the Gallant Pelham," entered West Point on July 1, 1856, at the age of seventeen years and nine months. History paints him as modest and easily embarrassed when the topic of conversation focused on his exploits. Those of his classmates who wrote of him after the war remembered that everyone liked him and he probably was the most popular cadet at the academy.[1] Many of the cadets who walked, talked, and ate with Pelham would become officers on both sides of the coming struggle. With seeming ease, Pelham made friends of all he met. A few would be connected with him in his service in the horse artillery. His roommate was Thomas Lafayette Rosser, a future Confederate cavalry general under Jeb Stuart. Mathis Winston Henry, another classmate, would serve under him in the Stuart Horse Artillery and command the 2nd Stuart Horse Artillery Battery for a time. Two years ahead of Pelham was Robert Franklin Beckham, who would succeed Pelham in command of the Stuart Horse Artillery Battalion.

During his final year, Pelham faced the rising tide of turmoil that was spreading across the nation. Inexorably, the country slipped toward a conflict that most of its people did not want yet could not seem to avoid. For some time, the cadets at the academy managed to remain above the divisive issues that were splitting their country into two sections. Then came the election of Abraham Lincoln and the secession of South Carolina, quickly followed out of the Union by six more states, including Alabama. The time had come. Pelham and his classmates had to choose. On February 27, 1861, Pelham sat down and wrote to Jefferson Davis, newly inaugurated president of the Confederate States of America. Recognizing that he could not offer his services to the new government since he was still a cadet, Pelham asked for the president's advice as to whether he should resign or not. He assured Davis that soon as his ties to the academy were broken he was ready to report for duty, whatever it might be.[2]

Afraid that if he sent the letter directly to the Confederate president, it might be intercepted and opened along the way, Pelham enclosed it with one to his father. The elder Pelham forwarded it to Montgomery, Alabama, then the Confederate capital. The letter brought a swift reaction. A commission as first lieutenant of artillery was issued in Pelham's name.

The future artillery officer now faced a difficult decision. He could resign and leave West Point or hold on until after graduation, which was what his father urged. The days passed slowly, expectantly. Other cadets were resigning and heading south, but obeying his father, Pelham waited and talked with his roommate Rosser about their situation. Patience ruled, and the two continued attending classes, though it is doubtful they absorbed much.

Roger Preston Chew entered the Virginia Military Institute on July 30, 1859, at age sixteen. He had hardly settled into the routine of classes and drills when, on October 16, 1859, the shocking news of John Brown's raid on Harpers Ferry swept through Virginia and the South. The cadets of the academy, under one of their more enigmatic professors, Thomas J. Jackson, were called out in December to witness Brown's execution at Charles Town. They were to assure that the prisoner would not be rescued by other abolitionists. At the grim scene, Chew stood with two of the artillery pieces that had been brought by Jackson from the institute. Jackson had drilled the crews in the streets of the town in preparation for what thankfully never came.[3] After marching back to the institute, Chew resumed his studies. He had the honor (or misfortune, depending on one's view) to recite for Jackson in class. All appeared normal again. All knew it was not.

Like the cadets at West Point, the young men of the Virginia Military Institute would soon have decisions to make regarding their allegiance. Chew, a Virginian, harbored no doubt as to what he would do. Some, like William C. Cuyler of New York, faced the same problem as Pelham. As the new year dawned, choices were made; lines were drawn. Cuyler bade farewell to his best friend, Jimmy Thomson, another future horse artillery officer, and returned to New York. Others went on with their studies and waited.

April 1861 arrived, but the joy that usually accompanied spring's gentle rains was lost amid drumbeats and bugle calls that signaled war. On the twelfth, Fort Sumter was fired on, and on the seventeenth, Virginia left the Union. At both West Point and VMI, young men prepared as best they could for what was to come.

On April 22, Pelham learned that Virginia had seceded, and with Rosser and thirty-one others, he submitted his resignation. Their last ties to the academy severed, Pelham and Rosser walked away from the institution that had been their home for nearly five years and set out for Pelham's home in Alabama. Artillery commissions awaited both of them. All they had to do was pass through a couple of Northern states and a good portion of the Confederacy to pick them up.

That same day, Thomas J. Jackson boarded a train in Staunton that would take him to Richmond. He had left VMI on the twenty-first, accompanied by a number of cadets from the institute, Chew among them. They crowded into stagecoaches for the trip to Staunton. Jackson also took with him the cadet battery. Milton Rouss, one of the cadets, recalled the journey in 1903:

> When we left Lexington for Richmond about the middle of April 1861 I was one of the color guard Chew being color-sergeant. E. M. McDonnell of Savannah, Georgia; C. C. Floweree of Vicksburg, Miss. & John K. Thompson of Charlestown, W.Va. [then still Virginia] were also of the color guard & in my class.[4] Our ride to Staunton in one of the old fashioned stages was enjoyed to the full as we were going to war and saw only the glittering prospect of glory & fame with none of the terrible accompaniment of Civil strife in view. Stonewall Jackson was with us too & he had the old cadet Battery that was his special charge. There was only one man among the cadets who really seemed to appreciate the seriousness of the undertaking upon which we were venturing. Henry Burgwyn[5] who went down with more than half of his immortal North Carolinians at Gettysburg—he commanded a regiment there—seemed grave and thoughtful as I noticed him on our march that day and I wondered at it for he was usually one of the happiest and cheeriest of his class.[6]

Within a week, Jackson had been commissioned a colonel and sent to Harpers Ferry. The cadets became drill instructors at Camp Lee in Richmond, where they remained until orders sent a small group of them to join Jackson. Among the select few were Chew and Rouss, who were greatly pleased by the prospect as their new assignment took them very close to their homes. Visions of visits home and reunions with friend and relatives danced in their heads. "Old Jack" had other ideas.

Meanwhile, Pelham and Rosser had made their way slowly through Yankee territory and finally arrived in Jacksonville, Alabama, on May 1. The trip had its adventurous moments. The train on which they were riding from New York to Philadelphia was searched twice. Questioned, Pelham responded with a bit of subterfuge, claiming that he and Rosser were on their way to Washington to report for duty. Afterward, the two decided that a more circuitous route might be safer, and they headed west before turning south through Kentucky. The *Jacksonville Republican* did not allow them to proceed on their way without first claiming and getting an interview, which appeared in the May 2 edition.

> Lieutenants Pelham of this county and Rosser of Texas, arrived here last night, on their way from West Point to Montgomery. They have both received appointments in the Confederate Army, and are hastening on to Montgomery for orders, and a "place in the picture."
>
> We had the pleasure of a long interview with them. They were compelled to come all the way round by Harrisburg, Pennsylvania, to avoid being arrested and detained by the abolitionists.
>
> They report that the populace all through Pennsylvania are worked up to the last degree of frenzy and madness by their abolition leaders. They talk of nothing but shooting, and gibbeting the "traitors of the South." At one place they saw a number of ropes hung up in regular hangman style, with a placard "for Southern Traitors." They were, themselves, narrowly watched, & scrutinized, and questioned as to their destination, but managed by a little finesse to pass unmolested.
>
> All Southern officers who offer to resign now are being arrested before they can get out of the country, if possible.
>
> Lieuts. Pelham and Rosser are a couple of handsome, well educated and promising young officers; and will be quite an acquisition to our army at this time. We predict for them a brilliant future.[7]

The rush to Montgomery was interrupted by a week in Alexandria, Pelham's home. The time was well spent in enjoying the hospitality of the people, who were thrilled to have not one, but two West Point cadets among them. Hunting, attending parties, and drilling the local militia, which was more for the military pomp and circumstance for the locals than for instruction from the two cadets, made the week slip by quickly. On May 10, Pelham and Rosser headed for Montgomery. On the fifteenth, Pelham accepted his commission and left immediately for his assignment—ordnance officer at Lynchburg, Virginia, an unglamorous but important post. Rosser, too, was commissioned and was ordered to North Carolina for coast duty. It was just a short stop on his journey to First Manassas. Pelham would not be far behind.

When Chew and Rouss arrived at Harpers Ferry, one of the first things they did was to apply for a furlough to visit their homes. Undoubtedly, they counted on the close proximity of their families and their acquaintance with the commanding officer to land them a pass. Jackson thought otherwise, as Rouss recounted:

> We were reckoning without our host for when on a Saturday evening we applied for permission to spend Sunday at home we were told by

> Major [John T. L.] Preston[8] that Col. Jackson declined to allow us to leave camp as he wanted us to set an example for the raw recruits and stay at our posts. This did not at all chime in with our ideas of the proper thing and so we went home any how and upon our return on Monday morning were met by our messmates who sorrowfully told us that old Jack was mad and had ordered us back to V.M.I. We knew there was no appeal from this decision and sadly enough went back with Col. John Ross[9] in charge and that beautiful May day I remember as one of the very saddest of all my life.[10]

John Pelham was equally displeased with his posting at Lynchburg. He would do his duty, but he didn't have to like it. Fortunately, the winds of change were blowing through Harpers Ferry, and those same winds would soon sweep through Lynchburg and carry away the young lieutenant to duties more to his taste.

On May 24, Brig. Gen. Joseph E. Johnston arrived at Harpers Ferry and took command of the troops there from Jackson. One thing became clear to Johnston immediately. Though Jackson had done his best to organize and discipline the regiments, under his command the condition of the "army" was deplorable. Try as he might, Jackson had been unable to overcome the lack of proper instructors for the raw recruits, who were officered by individuals more concerned with appearance than with military discipline or duties.

The problem existed because the Virginia militia forces had yet to be incorporated into the army of the Confederacy. When that finally occurred about two weeks later, Johnston acted swiftly. Orders were issued to bring in responsible officers to train and discipline the men. Among the orders was one to a certain lieutenant of artillery stationed at Lynchburg. Pelham wasted little time answering the summons. He arrived at Harpers Ferry on June 15 and was immediately assigned as drillmaster to the Henry A. Wise Battery. What followed was an intense period of training and drill that put Pelham's mark on the battery. He worked his charges long and hard for over a month, until he was satisfied that they would perform up to his satisfaction—and then he worked them some more. Only one thing was lacking: the test of battle.

Pelham had not been the only one suffering from exile to a rear echelon assignment. Chew and Rouss, who had been on the front lines of the war at Harpers Ferry, albeit briefly, languished at VMI for several weeks. Then, unable to stand the boredom any longer, they set out for Richmond to secure a position with the army. Much to their frustration, no one in the capital would sign them up. Determined to get into the war before it ended, the two cadets marched off to join Robert S. Garnett's army in western Virginia. They got as far as Monterey in Highland County, where they encountered the remnants of Garnett's forces straggling in from their defeat at Rich Mountain on July 11. Garnett was dead, having been killed at Corrick's Ford on the Cheat River during the retreat, and his command was a shambles. At first it did not appear that Chew and Rouss could be of much use, but with the discovery that the Lee Battery, from Lynchburg, was minus its officers, an order was issued. Chew and Rouss were placed in charge of the men.[11] It wasn't until early September that they were again out of a job.

Things had been going poorly for the Confederates in the East ever since Johnston abandoned Harpers Ferry on June 16. Since that time, the constant maneuvering between Johnston's forces and those of Federal general Robert Patterson had resulted in little fighting. Now, in mid-July, came word of Rich Mountain and Corrick's Ford. With Union morale soaring, Lincoln's government pushed its "On to Richmond" campaign on Brig. Gen. Irvin McDowell, who commanded the Federal army around Washington. McDowell felt his men were ill prepared for offensive operations. Nevertheless, he formed a plan and marched toward the Confederate army under Brig. Gen. Pierre G. T. Beauregard in the vicinity of Manassas. While McDowell was dealing with Beauregard, Patterson was to strike at Johnston. If all went well, the Federals would be in Richmond before the Rebels knew what hit them.

Neither Johnston nor Beauregard, however, was inclined to sit around and wait for the Federals to carry out their plans. Since the army at Manassas had to hold its position athwart the road to the Confederate capital, Johnston would have to do the maneuvering. His infantry started out for Manassas on July 18, leaving Stuart's cavalry to cover the withdrawal and keep Patterson guessing. The artillery, including Pelham and the Alburtis Wise Battery, was to follow with the cavalry after it had fulfilled its role.

The march began late in the afternoon of July 18 and continued through the night and the next morning. Bad roads, darkness, and exhausted men and horses conspired to delay the column, but it pressed on. Around 2:00 on the afternoon of the twentieth, Pelham arrived at Manassas. By the next morning, the Alburtis Battery had taken up a position in rear of Brig. Gen. Milledge L. Bonham's left flank, guarding the area between Mitchell's and McLean's Fords on the Confederate right. There it remained until Beauregard, realizing that the main Federal thrust was against his left flank, issued orders bringing most of his troops and guns on the right into the battle to save his left.

Pelham finally had his baptism of fire as he brought his guns into position on Henry House Hill. In a letter to his father dated July 23, 1861, he recounted some of his actions, feelings, and observations:

> I just write to let you know that we have had one of the most desperate battles ever fought on American soil. It was the most desperate—the enemy fought long and well, but victory is ours; it was a

splendid victory too. Jeff Davis made his appearance on the field, just as the last of the Yankees were in full retreat. I was under a heavy fire of musketry and cannon for about seven hours, how I escaped or why I was spared a just God only knows. Rifle balls fell like hail around me. Shells bursted and scattered their fragments through my Battery—my horse was shot under me, but did not give out till the fight was almost over. I was compelled to take one of my Sergeant's horses and ride through. At one time I dismounted and directed the guns—one of the gunners asked me to dismount and shoot the Federals' flag down. I did so—you ought to have heard the cheers they gave me. I directed all my guns three or four times apiece. My men were cool and brave and made terrible havoc on the enemy. They fought better than I expected they would. The highest praise is due them. We shot down three U.S. flags and dislodged the enemy from several positions. I was complimented several times on the field of battle by general officers and a great many times after the battle was over by other officers.

You may want to know my feelings—I felt cool and deliberate under the shower of lead and iron as if I had been at home by our fireside—I did not feel fear at any moment; I can't see how I escaped—a merciful Providence must have been watching over us and our cause. We slept on our arms last night but were not disturbed. The battle began about 8 o'clock but did not become general until 10 o'clock. We fought desperately about 9½ hours, but I was under fire only about 7½ hours; the enemy attacked our left flank and then tried to turn it. We had to change our line of battle and fight them on their own ground.

We whipped old [Winfield] Scott on Sunday—his great fighting fortunate day, on ground of their own choosing in open field. They poured down overwhelming numbers on us. I firmly believe they had three to our one—but I don't know positively how many they had—certainly between 50,000 and 100,000 men. A great many prisoners told us, they expected confidently to whip us here and then go to Richmond. We have got about 1000 prisoners and the cavalry are bringing them in continually. We took the celebrated Rhode Island battery of rifled cannon, also Sherman's[12] great battery of the same kind of guns—also the West Point battery that I have drilled with so often.

They say we have taken 90 pieces of Artillery[13]—I have not seen all of them, but I have seen a great many. They had the best Artillery trains and equipage I ever beheld, but <u>We</u> have them now: I have no idea how many small arms we took, a great many. The victory was splendid and complete. Col. [John H.] Forney's Reg't[14] was not

> engaged—but the 4th Ala. Reg't was cut to pieces. They fought desperately. The Col., the Lieut. Col. and Major were all shot down but neither of them are mortally wounded.[15] I don't know what the intention of our General is but I hope I will be able to write to you from Washington City before many weeks. Johnston's forces were encamped at Winchester, but we all moved down here on getting a dispatch from Beauregard. We got here the evening before the fight—Beauregard repulsed them with considerable loss a few days ago.
>
> I have seen what Romancers call glorious war. I have seen it in all its phases. I have heard the booming of cannon, and the more deadly rattle of musketry at a distance—I have it all nearby and have been under its destructive showers; I have seen men and horses fall thick and fast around me. I have seen our own men bloody and frightened flying before the enemy—I have seen them bravely charge the enemy's lines and heard the shout of triumph as they carried the position. I have heard the agonizing shrieks of the wounded and dying—I have passed over the battle field and seen the mangled forms of men and horses in frightful abundance—men without heads, without arms, and others without legs. All this I have witnessed and more, till my heart sickens; and war is not glorious as novelists would have us believe. It is only when we are in the heat and flush of battle that it is fascinating and interesting. It is only then that we enjoy it. When we forget ourselves and revel in the destruction we are dealing around us. I am now ashamed of the feelings I had in those hours of danger. The whistling of bullets and shells was music to me, I gloried in it—it delighted and fascinated me—I feared not death in any form; but when the battle was won and I visited the field a change came over me, I see the horrors of war, but it is necessary: We are battling for our rights and our homes. Ours is a just war, a holy cause. The invader must meet the fate he deserves and we must meet him as becomes us, as becomes men.[16]

In the aftermath of the battle, when reports were submitted, Pelham's name was mentioned in only one, but it was an important one. Brig. Gen. Thomas J. Jackson, newly christened "Stonewall," wrote in his account of the fighting on Henry House Hill:

> I also ordered forward the other two pieces of Captain [Robert C.] Stanard's and all of Colonel [William N.] Pendleton's battery. They, as well as the battery under Lieutenant Pelham, came into action on the same line as the others; and nobly did the artillery maintain its position for hours against the enemy's advancing thousands. Great praise is due to Colonel Pendleton and the other officers and men.[17]

Jackson would come to know and appreciate Pelham's unique gifts much more in the coming months.

With the big battle that all had expected finally fought, the victorious Confederates spent the next several months watching the Federals from the hills overlooking the fortifications of Alexandria and Washington City. There were reconnaissances and counterreconnaissances, skirmishes, the debacle at Ball's Bluff, the clash at Dranesville, and the usual picket firing between the lines that involved various units. But the majority of the Confederates who had fought at Bull Run remained in their camps, occupied with drilling and becoming better soldiers. Pelham and the men of the Alburtis Battery were among the latter. The lessons of Bull Run had fallen on fertile ground in John Pelham. When called forth again, he wanted his command ready.

Farther west, all was quiet after Chew and Rouss assumed command of the remnants of the Lee Battery. The campaign had ended before they arrived, and nothing had transpired since. Their duties centered around maintaining order and discipline among the men and perhaps a little drilling. As the days passed, their thoughts turned to what their next move should be, since both realized that their present positions were temporary. Plans were made, but necessity prompted an intermediate step.

> "Camp Baslow" Aug. 28
>
> Mr Polk
> Dear Sir
>
> Having concluded to remain in the service until the 1st of Oct. next, when we will return to the Institute, and being very much in need of clothing, we would be very much obliged to you, if you would get Mr. Vanderslice to make us a pair of pants each, and also two sack coats, like your own. We would prefer these of blue cloth if possible, but if not of Cadet cloth.
>
> We would like these articles sent by "Express" to Staunton by the 7th of Sept., as we expect to be there at that time on our way to Manassas. You will please send the bill for the coats, and we will remit the amount from that place. By accommodating us you will very much oblige.
>
> Your friends
> M. Rouss & R. P. Chew
>
> N.B.
>
> Please request Mr. V. to make pants a little larger and longer than the last measure.
>
> R. P. Chew[18]

Whether Mr. Polk had the uniforms ready and waiting in Staunton is unknown. What is known is that on September 5, as they had predicted, Chew and Rouss took their leave of the Lee Battery. The unit's officers having returned, there was no further need for the cadets, and so they set out for the Valley once more. The two cadets had conceived a plan to form a battery of artillery and hoped to lay it before Lt. Col. Turner Ashby, who was commanding cavalry in the lower Valley. First, however, came the matter of payment for services rendered.

Passing through Staunton, Chew and Rouss arrived at Richmond and made application for pay as acting lieutenants of artillery. Told there were no such officers on the payroll, they took their case before Secretary of War Leroy P. Walker, who ordered them paid. Turning around, they headed back to their homes in the Valley. Rouss told of the next steps the pair took:

> On our arrival at home Ashby was very much in favor of our scheme of raising a battery to serve with him and we found that we would have to get the men from the militia which necessitated a trip to Manassas where Gen. Joseph E. Johnston was in command. . . . I saw Gen. Johnston who declined to act in regard to our battery saying that Gen. Jackson "Stonewall" would soon be placed in command of the Valley and we would have to apply to him which made us feel a little dubious after what had happened.[19]

Johnston was right. Jackson was assigned to the Valley and arrived at Winchester on November 5, 1861, to take command. Chew and Rouss applied to Stonewall concerning their battery and received his approval. The battery was granted permission to form on November 11 and was formally organized on the thirteenth at Flowing Spring, Jefferson County, Virginia, as a horse battery, the first in the Confederacy. A total of thirty-three enlisted men and four officers—Roger Preston Chew, captain; Milton Rouss, first lieutenant; and James William McCarty and James Walton Thomson, second lieutenants—made up the roster. The battery's initial armament was a Blakely and a three-inch iron rifle.[20] Chew and Rouss reported their successful organization to Jackson. Chew recalled the incident:

> After we raised the company, Rouss and I called on General Jackson, and told him we had organized a battery. His face wore a quizzical expression, as he said: "Young men, now that you have your company, what are you going to do with it?" There was no reply to make to this as the question was more of a puzzle to Rouss and myself than to him.[21]

Jackson gave Chew little time to ponder an answer to his question. Not even a month passed before the battery was called from its camp at Martinsburg with orders to march north to Dam No. 5 on the upper Potomac at Hollywood Mills. Jackson wanted the dam destroyed in order to cut off the water supply to the Chesapeake and Ohio Canal. On the evening of December 8 and the following day, the Confederate force, with the two guns from Chew's Battery, made an abortive attempt to break up the dam. Failing to accomplish their objective, the Confederates returned to their camps around Martinsburg.[22] On the fourteenth, Quartermaster Sgt. James H. Williams wrote to his future wife, Cora Pritchartt, from Martinsburg about his duties with the battery and the brief engagement at Dam No. 5:

> I am now regularly in camp & am for the present the Quartermaster Sergeant. The Co. [Company], The Ashby Artillery, Capt. Chew, the Lieut's are all young men & I mess with the officers. My position exempts me from drill & service at the guns. I will drill for my own amusement & improvement & will take part with the men in any fight we may have. I mean for your sake to be prudent, & not needlessly expose myself, but prudence with me can not mean cowardice.
>
> You have heard of the fight at Dam No. 5 on the Canal last Saturday night & Sunday. We had 3 men wounded. One was shot in the forehead, the ball passing out at the jaw. Strange to say he lives & may recover. One man in our Co. [Pvt. George W. Hooffmaster] was wounded, leg badly broken. The expedition was designed to destroy the Dam. The Yanks let the water out & shot so well with their long range small arms at 800 yds [yards] that the artillerists were obliged to leave. We had two guns in the fight & the Rockbridge Co. 4. They left one of their guns on the field & got it at night. The fire was hot.
>
> We will in all probability renew the attack on Monday [the fifteenth]. I will have an opportunity to take part, which I will gladly do.[23]

Williams was right about another attempt on the dam, but wrong about when it would take place. Jackson wasn't ready on the fifteenth. There were a few more pieces he needed to place on the board before he made his next move.

In the meantime, Chew's Battery drilled and recruited in the Martinsburg area. Williams not only performed the duties of quartermaster sergeant, but also doubled as recruiting officer. One man he persuaded to join the battery was George M. Neese, who signed up on the eleventh. In his diary, he recorded that Chew was ill, though the captain did offer a few words of greeting. Neese had barely settled into camp when, on the seventeenth, the battery once again limbered and marched in the direction of Dam No. 5.

The battery camped in the woods about a half mile from the dam. Neese reported some skirmisher fire taking place that night, but Chew was not

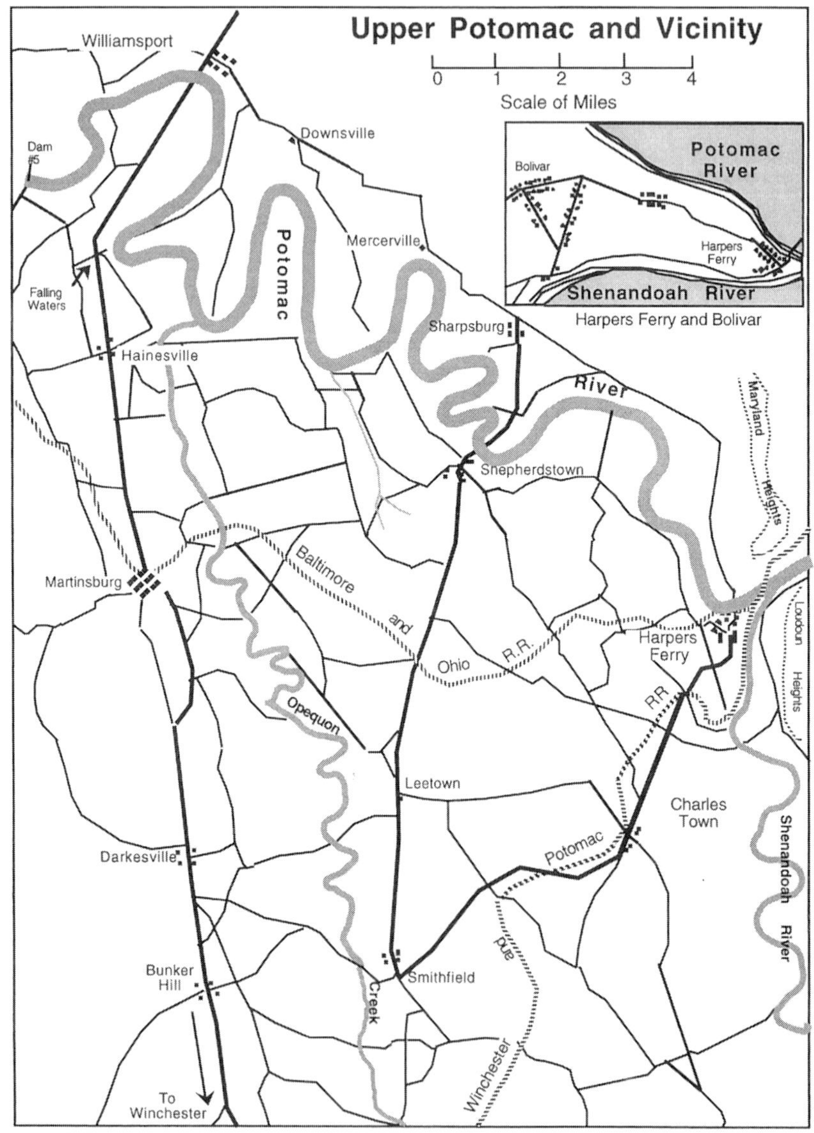
Upper Potomac and Vicinity
0 1 2 3 4
Scale of Miles
Williamsport
Dam #5
Downsville
Mercerville
Potomac
Falling Waters
Sharpsburg
Hainesville
River
Maryland Heights
Shepherdstown
Baltimore and Ohio R.R.
Martinsburg
Harpers Ferry
Loudoun Heights
Opequon
RR
Leetown
Charles Town
Potomac
Darkesville
Shenandoah River
Winchester and
Bunker Hill
Smithfield
Creek
To Winchester
Potomac River
Bolivar
Harpers Ferry
Shenandoah River
Harpers Ferry and Bolivar

engaged until the eighteenth. Brig. Gen. James H. Carson, commanding a brigade of Virginia militia, rode into Chew's camp and requested support for his pickets at Falling Waters some five miles distant. Federal artillery was threatening them, and Carson wanted the enemy driven away. On approaching the position, the men sighted the Federal piece. Chew unlimbered one gun and fired six rounds, which were sufficient to chase off the opposing piece. General Carson thanked Chew, and the battery returned to Dam No. 5 that evening.

While Chew had been scattering Federals at Falling Waters, Jackson, with the able assistance of Capt. Raleigh T. Colston of the 2nd Virginia Infantry, had begun destroying Dam No. 5. Colston, well acquainted with the area and the structure of the dam, had volunteered to take charge of the work party assigned to accomplish the task. On the morning of the nineteenth, the Confederate effort began in earnest. Chew's Battery moved into a large field a short distance below the dam. The enemy artillery had begun firing before Chew was in position, but their shells arched over the battery and landed among the 2nd Virginia Infantry's camp. After remaining in the field for an hour without returning fire, Chew limbered up and returned to camp.

The dam was still standing on the twentieth, and once again Jackson set Colston and his men to work. Chew unlimbered near his previous day's location and had a duel with an opposing battery. One man, Pvt. John H. Lewis, was slightly wounded before the firing broke off. Jackson called off the attack and in his report stated that "a breach, supposed to be sufficiently large for the object in view, was effected."[24] In actuality, the expedition failed to accomplish its goal of disrupting the canal traffic. A telegram dated the twenty-second from Col. Samuel H. Leonard to Maj. Gen. Nathaniel P. Banks stated, "Canal-boats were running today both ways."[25] Chew's Battery marched back to Martinsburg and went into winter quarters. The respite was only momentary. Jackson had another little excursion in mind.

In early September, when Chew and Rouss were proposing their plans for a horse artillery battery to Turner Ashby, another officer also was contemplating how he might have a horse battery for his command. Col. J. E. B. Stuart had recognized the value of such a battery to his cavalry and had begun a campaign to secure one. On September 18, he wrote to Virginia governor John Letcher, asking for two pieces of artillery in order to form a horse battery.[26]

On the twenty-fifth, Stuart was promoted to brigadier general and put in command of a brigade of cavalry, but no guns were forthcoming for his horse artillery. However, a series of events were already in motion that would in time bring the guns, Stuart, and a young Alabamian together.

The months from September through December 1861 brought many changes for John Pelham. Col. William N. Pendleton, Gen. Joseph E. Johnston's chief of artillery, took Pelham away from the Alburtis Battery and assigned him to Capt. George A. Groves's Culpeper Battery. The young Alabamian replaced Lt. Robert F. Beckham, who was transferred to the staff of Maj. Gen. Gustavus W. Smith. Pelham reported in early September, and Beckham left on October 1.

What Pelham saw when he arrived can only be surmised, but the condition of the battery could not have been very good. Whether this was Beckham's fault or Groves's is uncertain. Nevertheless, Pelham's first return, dated October 31, showed only twenty-four officers and men present for duty, sixteen others marked as having deserted, and six on sick leave. Pelham had resurrected one battery, and it appeared he was going to have to do it again. The records for the next several weeks are hazy, but one document to survive indicates that Pelham had some knowledge of his future assignment.[27] On November 26, 1861, he signed a receipt for ordnance stores as the commander of the Stuart Horse Artillery.[28] Despite this, Pelham was not officially attached to Stuart and the cavalry until November 29, 1861, when he received an order from Gen. Joe Johnston to report to Stuart.[29]

At one time, Stuart had put forth James Breathed, a young doctor from Maryland, as his choice to command the battery. He had met Breathed on a train ride east after Stuart had resigned from the U.S. Army. The two sat and talked. Stuart liked what he saw and heard. He also had considered John Esten Cooke, his wife's cousin, and had written the adjutant general concerning Cooke's appointment as captain.[30] Although Pendleton gave Pelham a captain's rank in the order, the young Alabamian would have to wait for some time before he wore the three horizontal bars denoting that rank.

But Johnston's order superseded Stuart's personal wishes, and Breathed joined the battery as a lieutenant while Cooke later ended up on Stuart's staff as ordnance officer. There was no opposition from Stuart, who had known of Pelham's interest in securing the appointment.[31] Pelham was welcomed and set to work. In the way of guns, the battery had the 6-pounders Beckham had fought with at Bull Run and the 6-pound field gun and two 12-pound mountain howitzers Pelham had requisitioned in late November. They would have to do for the present, but Stuart, looking to upgrade as soon as possible, sent out some feelers among his friends and acquaintances. He had some influence and made use of it for the battery's sake.

This maneuvering behind the scenes was matched by maneuvering in the field. Though the vast majority of the troops were settled in for the winter, small contingents of cavalry and infantry made forays into no man's land to slash at picket posts, attempt to capture prisoners, or secure information. One such thrust occurred on December 17, when Stuart sent out a party to attack Annandale. With it went Capt. John Pelham and one of his guns.[32] The success or failure of the expedition went unrecorded, but for the first time, the newly christened Stuart Horse Artillery had been part of a movement against the enemy. Although he must have been proud to participate, Pelham knew that much remained to be done if his battery was to become an integral part of the cavalry. He was well aware that moving one gun did not make his battery "horse artillery."

If Pelham was to have a true "horse artillery" battery, he needed horses not just to haul his guns, but to carry his gunners as well. Pelham made strenuous efforts to acquire the number of horses he needed to outfit his battery. As men and guns were added, he would require more. On December 21, he drew corn for ninety-four horses.[33] He was off to a good start.

But Pelham's main concern was men. Guns were certainly important if one was to have a battery. However, without the men to serve them, the guns became just so much ornamentation around cavalry headquarters. Among the first contingents was a company of men originally known as the Beauregard Rifles, which had been attached to the 1st Virginia Infantry. The company was subsequently relieved from duty and mustered as Company C of the 1st Regiment of Virginia Artillery. On November 13, it was mustered out.[34] At this time, the men of the company heard that Pelham was organizing a battery of horse artillery, and a large number requested that they be allowed to join it.[35]

A few recruits also came from the cavalry. One was a most colorful fellow named Thomas Kinloch Fauntleroy, from Clarke County, Virginia. Freckle-faced, red-haired, and cross-eyed, Fauntleroy had an irrepressible personality and an abundance of self-assurance despite his appearance, which must have been striking. He became a lieutenant and the ordnance officer of the battery.[36]

Others came from around Pelham's home in Alabama. William M. McGregor, who became a lieutenant and eventually captain of the battery, and his younger brother, Jesse, were two who found their way to the battery. Pelham journeyed home to recruit sometime in late December 1861 or early January 1862. Before this visit, the advertisement below appeared in the *Jacksonville Republican.*

> Mounted Flying Artillery
>
> CAPT. JOHN PELHAM, of Calhoun county, who is now in the Confederate army at Manassas, temporarily in command of the Jeff Davis Artillery, is authorized to raise two hundred volunteers for mounted Artillerists, to serve during the war. The Confederate States will furnish 240 horses, and eight splendid brass cannon, wagons, caissons and equipments complete for men and horses.
>
> This flying artillery, when raised and organized, is to have one Captain, 3 first and a second Lieutenants, and non-commissioned officers in proportion, and will be attached to General J. E. B. Stewart's [*sic*] Cavalry.
>
> The artillery of 8 splendid brass guns—200 men rank and file, and 250 horses, has the novelty of being the only one in our service—in fact the only one in America. All the men or cannoneers are mounted on horses furnished by the government.

This doubtless will be the most desirable, pleasant, and efficient service in our entire Army. The service will be active and energetic; the men will never be detailed to guard forts, fortifications, baggage or prisoners; neither will they be quartered in one place long at a time. The career of this company is destined to be a brilliant one; and whenever or where ever there is likely to be a fight, they are bound to be in the front—sustained by the gallant General Stewart who commanded the Virginia "Black Horse Cavalry" which struck such terror to the Yankee army, on the plains of Manassas on the 21st of July last.

If there be any young men who desire to enlist for the defense of their native sunny South—who desire eminent distinction, glory or renown, here is no doubt the finest opening that has yet been offered.

It may be asked, who is John Pelham. It is with pride and pleasure we say he is the son of Dr. A. [Atkinson] Pelham, and was raised in this county, near Alexandria. He was educated at the military school at West Point—was five years there—has been in the military service ever since—was in the battle of Manassas on the 21st July, had command of a battery that day and did gallant service, having his horse shot under him in the midst of the fierce conflict: He is a young man of fine attainments—high military culture—has been tried on the field of battle, and found equal to the emergency. If he has the honor to command this splendid company, we are satisfied that his men, his native State, and his Country will have cause to be proud of him.

We are informed by private letters, that Capt. Pelham could not be spared at present, to come home to aid in raising this company: he has sent out in his place, Lieut. [James F.] Brown, who comes among us highly recommended.[37] He is a native of Maryland, and is one of the gallant and patriotic young men, who at the commencement of hostilities, nobly left his native land, and joined General Stewart "Black Horse Cavalry"—as it was called by the terror stricken "Bull-runners."

Lieut. Brown was in the battle of Manassas, and distinguished himself on that day. He will make his headquarters at Dr. Pelham's in Alexandria, and at Jacksonville, where he may be consulted in reference to this important service.

We will close this article with an extract from a private letter from Capt. Pelham to a friend:

"Now is the time to serve your country—enlist the interest of the Ladies—tell them I want to do something to render myself worthy of them, and they must aid me in furnishing men. I have got the finest equipment and the finest guns in the service, and I want good men to man them."[38]

As with much of the recruiting literature of the period (or any period, for that matter) the advertisement embellished some facts, invented others, and failed to mention some at all. One has to wonder if the portion of the "letter" that was included even was written by Pelham, since at the time he had anything but the "finest equipment and the finest guns in the service." In any event, the appeal worked, and men were added to the roll. Pelham's name appears as the enrolling officer on recruiting papers from January 7 to March 1, 1862. After having spent much of the blustery winter in the sunny warmth of his home state, Pelham was back in Virginia by March 10, recruiting men in Culpeper and drilling those he had already enrolled.[39] There was still much to be done before his battery could take the field.

Chew and his men were not so fortunate as to have had the opportunity to spend some time in a warmer clime. Upon their return to Martinsburg following the fruitless attack on Dam No. 5, the men sought their winter quarters to settle in for the cold months ahead. At least one member of the battery was pleased with his accommodations. George Neese found himself a "good house in the southeastern suburbs of town, and near a good spring."[40] On December 30, he was called from his comfortable surroundings and ordered to go to Winchester to pick up a new gun, a twelve-pound howitzer, which brought the battery's armament up to three guns.[41]

On New Year's Day 1862, the battery was again ordered to take up a position near Dam No. 5. Sergeant Williams arrived with the battery's new gun at nightfall and spent the night sleeping on the porch of Capt. Raleigh Colston's home.[42] The second passed peacefully enough, although Williams was sent back to Martinsburg to draw provisions and pack baggage.[43] On the third, Chew set out to join Jackson, whose Romney expedition had begun on the first. Traveling through North Mountain Depot and Hedgesville, the men spent a cold, snowy night in a pine thicket at Johnson's Crossroads in Morgan County. The battery moved out at noon on the fourth and marched to Bath, where they encountered the enemy and sent them scurrying toward Hancock.

January 5 and 6 saw some sanguinary skirmishing in and about the town, which gave no advantage to either side. A snowfall of five or six inches covered the sleeping men.[44] Chew's Battery fired not a round and began its march back to Bath on the seventh. The conditions of the roads were such that the horses fell every few yards.[45] The men continued their march the following day, camping along Sleepy Creek for the night. From the afternoon of the ninth to the morning of the thirteenth, Chew's men were encamped near Unger's Store. One of the battery's guns had been sent back to Martinsburg on the eleventh. Sergeant Williams wrote to his beloved Cora from that town:

Martinsburg Jany 11/62

My Dear Cora,

I have come through mud, snow & rain 22 miles today, my official business is to see after some men, horses & gun. Some one else could have come as well, but I thought I would be paid & more for the fatigue & exposure by a letter from you, but I have been disappointed. It is now three weeks since I have heard from you, owing to peculiar circumstances, I suppose. I return to my company tomorrow, which is on the Romney Road 22 miles from here & Winchester where Genl Jackson's entire army is. I have seen all kinds of hardships, laid out in the snow, rain, cold, mud, etc. For the last two nights we have had our tents. I have stood the expedition pretty well, have been suffering since night before last with rheumatism in my left shoulder & arm, but will go with company.

We drove the Yanks across the River at Hancock, captured some stores, 15 prisoners, killed a few & lost some 15 or 20 men. They ambushed our men & then ran. I made some narrow escapes.

This is all the paper I have & am too tired to write even to you . . . I hope to see you soon.

Mispah
James[46]

Back at Unger's Store, Chew received orders to proceed to Romney. After they went about five miles, the orders were countermanded, and the battery headed back toward Martinsburg. Williams had left Martinsburg on the twelfth and rejoined the battery on the Romney Road just in time to be ordered back to Martinsburg. He spent his last night of the campaign trying to sleep on a hillside but found it impossible as he constantly rolled out of his bed.[47] With horses and men cold and exhausted, and caissons still full, the battery arrived in Martinsburg on the afternoon of the fifteenth.[48] Everyone gratefully went back into winter quarters.[49]

Turner Ashby established his picket line along the Potomac River and from time to time conducted little forays to gather information and harass the enemy's pickets. Between January 26 and 29, Ashby made a scout to Harpers Ferry. Chew's Battery accompanied him and on the twenty-eighth fired five rounds into a camp of Federals on the Maryland side before limbering and retreating.[50] This brief exercise was followed by an extended and welcomed rest in winter quarters. Chew took advantage of the respite to attempt to secure something very important to him.

Martinsburg
Jan 29th –62

Col. F. H. Smith[51]
Dear Sir

Having concluded to make application for an office in the regular army I write to you to request a recommendation and certificate of graduation as I understand my class has been graduated. I have but little hope of success but with the recommendations of Genls Johnston, Jackson and Col. Ashby I may succeed.

I am now connected with Ashby's Regt as Capt. of Artillery which position I expect to hold during the war. I would prefer recommendation for this branch of the service.

Yours Respectfully
R. P. Chew[52]

With recommendations from Johnston, Jackson, and Ashby, Chew's success was almost guaranteed, if he performed up to their expectations of him. He received his graduation certificate and did nothing in his long career to disappoint those who stood behind him at its inception.

In the early months of the new year, the battery lost two of its officers to the cavalry. On February 1, Chew said good-bye to the man who had helped him create the Ashby Battery. Together they had formed the plan, placed it before Ashby, and confronted Jackson. Milton Rouss had been offered a lieutenancy in the 12th Virginia Cavalry, which was then in the process of organizing. He decided to take it, and the battery lost an excellent officer. Around the same time, Lt. James W. McCarty also left to join the 7th Virginia Cavalry, becoming its adjutant in April. With his resignation, only two officers remained, Chew and Thomson. Chew took steps to correct the situation and on the fifteenth offered a lieutenancy to James H. Williams, who was soon acting as orderly and recruiting officer.[53]

On February 22, Chew had to summon his men from their peaceful repose to go marching up and down the roads of the lower Valley, but not until the second week of March did they wheel their guns into firing position. Sergeant Williams wrote his Cora about some of the fighting that week and described the tactics the battery would employ when the Yanks advanced again:

Woodstock March 10th '62

Dear Cora,

. . . Let me tell you of our army movements first leaving the more important matters for the latter pages. All seemed moving on quietly up to Friday night [March 7], when the enemy's cavalry in considerable force charged several companions of our reg't [Ashby's Cavalry] about six miles below Winchester. They were driven back some

> three miles upon their infantry some 5,000 strong, who tried their favorite movement, the flank movement. Immediately the news spread from camp to camp and our entire force was seen pouring forth eager for the conflict, all cheerful and resolute. The line of battle was formed some two miles below town. All the baggage was started for Strasburg. I never saw such commotion. But no enemy came. We about nightfall returned to our encampments. Since that time all has been quiet. I don't think it is expected that we will hold Winchester, but we will retire only after a bloody fight. Our battery is in advance, some four miles from Winchester. We open the ball, falling slowly back, contesting every inch. . . . In the fight of Friday we had one man badly wounded by pistol shot. We killed a Lt. Col. and wounded eight. The enemy never allowed us to get in saber reach. Our company [Chew's Battery] were near Winchester and got out too late to participate in the skirmish. We have some 90 men for the new company and my place I regard as certain. I have told all, except that before the week shall have ended we may be retreating up the Valley. I, as you may know, am losing confidence in our authorities, but will try to do my duty as a soldier, meeting my fate as becomes a man.[54]

Williams was right about the Yankees trying for Winchester. On the eleventh, the Federals were encountered two miles north of Winchester on the Martinsburg Pike. Maj. Gen. Nathaniel P. Banks had crossed the Potomac back on February 26 with the intention of pushing Jackson out of the Valley. Now he was closing in on Winchester. Up until this time, Chew's Battery had caught only a glimpse of "the elephant." Over the next several months, they were to see the rogue in all his majesty and fury. The real war was about to begin in earnest.

By early March, Pelham's Battery had begun to fill out. Added firepower in the form of two 12-pound howitzers arrived, and by the middle of the month enough men had been added to the roster to officially organize the battery and hold elections. The voting was almost a formality. Pelham was elected captain; Jim Breathed, first lieutenant; William M. McGregor, second lieutenant; William C. Elston, another Alabamian, third lieutenant; James S. T. Shepherd, from Charles Town, Virginia, fourth lieutenant; and Charles E. Ford, from Fairfax, Virginia, sergeant. With the election over, attention focused on drilling and filling out the battery's quota of men. On the fifteenth, Pelham drew $600 from Lt. Col. Larkin Smith, assistant quartermaster general of the army, to pay bounties to new recruits.[55]

By the beginning of April, rumors blew through the camps like spring breezes. The army pulled up stakes and marched south to Richmond, Pelham's Battery with it. Its baptism of fire lay a month away.

CHAPTER 3

Forging a Weapon

"We have taken down all the batteries and won more reputation than any."

Stonewall Jackson was not the type of commander who willingly retreated from an enemy, even one superior in numbers and equipment. The Federal army's push across the Potomac had not ebbed as an ocean tide, like some earlier maneuvers. Instead, it was a rising flood that threatened to engulf both Winchester and Jackson's smaller force. Though Banks was slow and methodical in his approach, he drew ever closer, and Jackson, much to his frustration, could only slow, not stop, the oncoming blue wave. Grudgingly, he was forced to abandon the city.

Among the troops that sought to delay Banks's capture of the city was Chew's Battery, which found itself, along with other elements of Ashby's cavalry, slowly withdrawing before the advancing Union host. By the evening of March 11, 1862, having had the opportunity to fire but two rounds from the battery's howitzer, Chew retreated to the fairgrounds just north of the city. The entire battery remained in position there until after dark, when it limbered and marched dejectedly through the quiet streets, stopping first at Milltown Mills, then passing through Kernstown, and finally encamping for the night at Bartonsville, six miles from Winchester.[1]

On the twelfth, the retreat continued up the Valley. After a brief march of about two miles, Chew drew rein on a hill half a mile south of Newtown and went into camp. Picket duty, two miles north of Newtown, occupied the next few days. The Federal pursuit was plodding and subject to intimidation, which Ashby gladly provided. However, the morning of the fifteenth saw blue cavalry and artillery challenge the "Knight of the Valley," forcing him back to Chew's camp south of Newtown. Chew fired eight to ten rounds, limbered, and retreated to the Cedar Creek bridge two miles south of Middletown. The following day, the battery crossed the creek and marched two miles up the Valley before going into camp.[2]

In a letter to his girl back home, Sgt. James H. Williams described the fighting the battery had passed through:

Camp at Cedar Creek Bridge
Saturday March 15, 1862

Miss Cora,

We are as you will see from the caption at Cedar Creek about three miles from Strasburg. Genl Jackson has fallen back beyond Strasburg. Where we are going to, I don't know. The best opinion seems to be that we will meet reinforcements as we retire up the Valley. I reached Winchester the day after I wrote you (last Tuesday) just in time to get my dinner and start for Mrs. Carter's three miles below town and take part in the skirmish. I found my gun in position. The enemy came in force and although we offered them battle as we fell back inch by inch, they would not fight, but threw out their flanking columns which made it necessary for us to retreat. We left Winchester at nightfall and came just this side of Newtown, where we remained until this morning. We had skirmishes with them every day and although out numbered we drove them back. This morning they came out in force, with several pieces of artillery and infantry in force. We gave them a brisk cannonade, & then fell back to Mrs. ——— [name not given] place. They then fell some distance below town. Our battery fared splendidly. The enemy were very cautious. We could only fire at their artillery. They killed some of the cavalry horses 92 I believe. We killed some 3 or 4 of their men. The shells flew fast and some came pretty near us. I have thus passed unhurt through several skirmishes for which I ought to be grateful.[3]

The Federals' next target was Strasburg, and Banks pushed his columns toward that goal on the eighteenth. At Cedar Creek, he ran into Jackson's ever-ready rear guard. Chew's Battery, still encamped two miles south of the creek, received orders to move to the front as rapidly as possible. The men of the battery, having become accustomed to the fine art of limbering and unlimbering their guns, more through practice brought on by service in the field than by formal drilling, were soon galloping along the Valley Turnpike, urging their horses to the top of their speed.

Arriving within a half mile of the creek, Chew wheeled his guns onto a small hill to the west of the road, where he could command the bridge. Before long he opened fire with his rifled pieces on the blue columns about a mile distant. Answering echoes were soon heard from a Federal four-gun battery that had taken position on the face of a hill on the other side of the creek opposite Chew. The duel lasted twenty-five minutes, until the Federal officer concluded that his exposed position was untenable and limbered his guns to seek a more favorable location. With night approaching, Chew chose not to renew the contest. He fell back toward Strasburg four miles in his rear.[4]

In the early hours of the nineteenth, Chew's Battery left camp and marched two miles south to Fisher's Hill, where, with Ashby's cavalry, they awaited the pursuing Federals. From their vantage point, the men of Ashby and Chew saw Strasburg fall to the enemy without a shot being fired in its defense. Once in the town, the Yanks split into two columns and continued their advance up the Valley Pike and along the line of the Manassas Gap Railroad. As soon as the column on the pike came within range, Chew opened with all his guns. His fire turned the advance into a retreat, but only momentarily. The second Federal column had brought with it eight rifled pieces, which were brought into position about a mile northwest of Chew on a hill owned by a Mrs. Kendrick.[5] The fire of these guns soon gave the young captain cause to worry, as flying metal vied with air for space above his guns. Unable to reply effectively, he was forced to abandon the hill and fall back about a mile before again going into battery.

There the previous scenario was played out again with the same result. For six miles, the retreat continued in like fashion. Chew and his men stopped to fire from every hilltop, but the Federals kept coming on. Finally, with night falling, the weary cannoneers went into camp three miles south of Woodstock. Their persistent adversaries withdrew to the comforting surroundings of Strasburg. Miraculously, there had been no casualties.[6]

The twentieth opened with Chew's tired but now seasoned battery doing picket duty just north of Woodstock. They looked in vain for the return of long, blue columns. The Federal offensive had lost its impetus, and Banks was falling back to Winchester. On the twenty-first, the ever-alert Ashby notified Jackson of the Union force's change of direction. The following day, the Confederate infantry was again on the move, this time down the Valley. Chew's Battery abruptly reversed its roll from rear guard to advance guard and pursued the retreating Federals. By afternoon, Winchester came into view.

Ashby pushed his horse artillery to within a mile of Winchester, where it took up position and shelled the few visible Yanks in the fields south of the town. One of the rounds wounded Brig. Gen. James Shields, removing him from command of his 11,000-man division.[7] Chew's next target was some infantry on the edge of town. He continued to harass them until an eight-gun Federal battery took a commanding position on a hill west of town. Its fire proved to be accurate and forced Ashby to pull his cavalry and Chew back. As the sun set, the Confederates fell back to Newtown and camped for the night.[8]

Under the cloak of darkness, Ashby's scouts entered the city, took in the sights, and returned with information that Banks would be withdrawing his rear guard the next day.[9] Ashby believed that Winchester could be taken with a small force and sent word to Jackson, who forwarded four companies from the 2nd Virginia Infantry of the Stonewall Brigade, under Capt. John Q. A. Nadenbousch, to assist the cavalry. For once Ashby was mistaken. There were many more Federal troops within striking distance of Winchester than he supposed, and the Union high command had no intention of giving up the city without a fight.[10]

On the morning of March 23, Chew's Battery enjoyed a 4:00 breakfast before moving down the pike toward Kernstown. After a two-hour rest in Bartonsville, the battery proceeded to within a half mile of Kernstown and halted. A single gun was sent forward a short distance but still south of town. Taking position in front of a brick house owned by the Mahaney family on the west side of the road, the lone gun opened fire. The artillery's job was to support Ashby's men as they engaged the Federal skirmishers beyond Kernstown.[11]

As the battle escalated, the Confederates encountered increasing resistance. Chew's single gun became the target for the Federal artillery stationed on Pritchard's Hill about a half mile northwest of Kernstown. The enemy's sharpshooters and skirmishers began to pay their compliments to the gun crew as well. Ashby held on for two hours, but with the pressure mounting, he was forced to pull back. Chew retreated about a half mile, joined the rest of his battery, and unlimbered, this time east of the pike. Two guns were located just off the pike, and the third about 200 yards farther to the right.[12] Here Chew stayed, supporting Ashby's threat to the Federal front and left as Jackson had ordered. The Yanks had other ideas. They were not about to allow Chew to get off that easily. Federal artillery thundered up the pike and wheeled into position almost at the spot that Chew had just abandoned.[13] Shells were soon screaming over the heads of the Confederate gunners. A few exploded directly above them, but fortunately not a man was wounded. Chew responded in kind and saw one of his twelve-pound howitzer shells explode amidst the Federal battery, which decided it had had enough and withdrew.[14]

Shortly after the enemy battery retreated, Jackson's infantry began to arrive and file off the pike to the west. Union regiments also could be seen maneuvering in the distance. Ashby rode up to Chew and directed him to fire on one of the blue columns. The battery continued its fire until the Federals disappeared behind a ridge. With the infantry battle now taking center stage, Chew's gunners slackened their fire, though they maintained their support of the cavalry east of the pike. As the battle drew to a close, Ashby and Chew covered the infantry's retreat. His day's work done, Chew limbered to the rear, encamping on the first hill south of Newtown. He had not lost a man or gun, but the army had been beaten. Chew did not need a crystal ball to tell him what the next day would bring.

The sun had barely risen above the horizon when the echoes of artillery fire reverberated through Chew's camp. At 9:00, Chew sighted the enemy from his position about a mile south of Newtown. When they came within range, he opened fire. The same pattern of combat that had occurred during the Confederates' first retreat from Winchester was again played out along the pike. From every hill, Chew fired, then limbered, galloped up the pike to the next hill, unlimbered, and fired again, repeating the process until the old position at

Cedar Creek was reached. On one occasion, his guns were charged, but a combination of the battery's fire and a well-timed cavalry charge led by the ever-present Ashby proved too much for the Federals to stand. They pulled back without the prize they sought.[15]

At Cedar Creek, the Yanks put a battery in the same location as they had on the eighteenth, and the artillery duel commenced. Shot and shell kicked up clods of earth all around Chew's guns. Many overshot their target and landed in the midst of Jackson's retreating wagon train and infantry rear guard, causing some casualties. Still Chew tenaciously held on, reinforced by two guns from the Rockbridge Artillery, until Stonewall was satisfied that the Yanks would be left nothing useful. After Ashby destroyed the bridge, Chew limbered to the rear. The column did not stop until it reached Woodstock. On the twenty-fifth, Chew continued on to Taylorsville, four miles south of Woodstock.[16]

Sergeant Williams took time while the battery was in Woodstock to write to his Cora and tell her of the exciting events at Kernstown and after.

Woodstock March 25th 1862

My Dear Cora,

Feeling that I have something to write about in which I have no doubt you feel an interest I will dispatch this although my letters multiply with fearful rapidity. Sunday was a day of carnage and a day of disaster to our arms. Jackson's command marched for Winchester on Saturday. Everybody thought the enemy had left the place. Our Regiment in advance, we ran a piece almost into Winchester and after firing for about an hour fell back, the enemy bringing out four pieces. In the firing we broke Genl Shields' arm. On Sunday morning early we opened on the enemy about four miles from Winchester on the Turnpike. Jackson came up about noon with perhaps 2,500 men, and attacked the enemy on the left. The impression was that the enemy were in small force. It turned out that they had some 12 or 15,000 men. Our Regiment held the right all day.

The fight on the left was warm. About nightfall our forces fell slowly back to Newtown, the infantry having exhausted their ammunition. The enemy had the advantage of position. The cannonading was awful, and the men fought within seventy yards of each other at times. We lost two pieces of artillery & 3 caissons, one in the Rockbridge, the other in the West Augusta Battery. The horses were shot and the guns had to be left.[17]

Our company has not had a single man or horse hurt, although under fire for almost two weeks. We have taken down all the batteries and won more reputation than any.

Not dreaming of any fight I went to New Market recruiting on Saturday and thus missed the fight. I have exhausted my stock of

> regrets, have been angry with myself, but I was not to blame. I got to Cedar Creek just in time to see the hottest firing yet had. The enemy pressed us hard and came near capturing our train. We covered the retreat until we had shot all our ammunition away. The little English piece [the Blakely], I have a name for it, played sad havoc with the enemy, but was brought off the field.
>
> The army is encamped near here and all is quiet. The cavalry [is] on Fisher's Hill. You will hear many rumors, but I have given you the gist of the matter.[18]

The quiet described by Williams came from a lack of a Federal pursuit, and its absence brought the Confederate retreat to a halt. Jackson had ordered his army to Mount Jackson, but on the twenty-sixth, Chew's Battery turned around and reoccupied Woodstock, where the men were quartered in the courthouse. The next day, Chew picketed the pike a few miles north of Woodstock near Maurertown, where a few shots were fired.[19] That evening, he retraced his hoofprints through Woodstock and established his camp in a woods about two miles south of that place. He remained there throughout the twenty-ninth. Each day, however, he reestablished his picket post two miles north of Woodstock. Only the minor skirmish on the twenty-seventh had interrupted the tranquillity of the countryside. The thirtieth brought an advance of the picket to Maurertown, three and a half miles north of Woodstock, though the battery returned to its old camp that night.[20]

Stonewall was preparing to take up the initiative that Banks, in spite of his victory, seemed to be willing to relinquish. Though Jackson could not risk another battle, he wanted to let Banks know that the Valley Army still had some sting left in it. But the Federal general wasn't quite ready to go over to the defensive and allow Jackson the freedom to do as he wished. His lack of pursuit had been just a pause while he regrouped his forces for another thrust at the Confederates. On April 1, the Yanks again pushed south along the Valley Pike.

A few hours after sunrise, word of the renewed Federal offensive reached Chew's Battery in its camp two miles south of Woodstock. Ashby hoped to delay the capture of the town, but by the time Chew and his guns arrived, the Yanks were almost in possession of the place. A lone gun of the Rockbridge Artillery and some of Ashby's cavalry offered resistance. The fire from two sections of Battery M, 1st New York Artillery, and five companies of the 2nd Massachusetts Infantry, deployed as skirmishers, quickly persuaded the Rebels to abandon their position. Ashby withdrew up the pike to Narrow Passage, three miles above Woodstock, where he made a stand.[21]

As Neese remembered the brief skirmish, Chew put two of his guns into position and engaged four of the enemy. As Col. George H. Gordon of the 2nd Massachusetts Infantry recalled it, he was opposed by "three 10-pounder and one 24-pounder rifled guns."[22] While the artillery duel continued, Ashby tried to burn the bridge over the creek. The Yanks came on in earnest and drove the Confederates off, saving the structure.[23] Chew limbered to the rear, falling back to a small rise south of Edenburg that lay on the north side of Stony Creek. Here Jackson reinforced Ashby with a brigade of infantry and told him to hold. Chew fought the New York Battery for a half hour until his inferior position caused him to fall back and go into camp at Red Banks on the north fork of the Shenandoah River. The two bridges over Stony Creek were burned, and the Federals were brought to a halt. They established their line north of the creek.[24]

Chew and his battery returned to the ever-popular picket duty. From April 2 to 17, the Confederates had the opportunity to rest and regroup. Ashby kept the Yankees busy as from time to time he had Chew fire a few rounds across Stony Creek into their camps or among their pickets, just "to apprise them of the fact that there is life in the old land yet," as Neese put it.[25] Every three days, two Parrott guns from the Rockbridge Artillery relieved Chew's Battery while it replenished its ammunition.[26]

On the fifth, the battery moved its camp to Mount Jackson. There, on the morning of the seventeenth, the men were roused and ordered to stand to their guns. The Yanks were again on the march. Taking position on the pike, Chew and his cannoneers waited. In the pale light of the approaching dawn, the Federal skirmish line could be distinguished slowly advancing through the fields on both sides of the road. Cavalry, in column on the pike, provided support. It also provided a prime target for Chew's guns. As the blue troopers rode through Hawkinstown, the young captain opened fire with his howitzer. The Union skirmishers to the right of the pike were brought to a halt, but those on the left continued to advance while the cavalry sought shelter in a ravine. Federal artillery soon careened into view, and with its appearance, Chew recognized the earnestness of the enemy's intentions and limbered his guns to the rear.[27]

Ashby ordered the battery to fall back to Rude's Hill, two miles south of Mount Jackson.[28] During the retreat, Gunner Neese had the opportunity to watch Ashby burn the bridge over Mill Creek south of Mount Jackson. The "Knight of the Valley" additionally had intended to burn the bridge over the north fork of the Shenandoah River, which lay just south of Mill Creek. The bridge was actually aflame, but the Yankee cavalry charged and captured the bridge after a brief but deadly melee. Ashby, on his famous white horse, was in the midst of the fight and was saved only by the devotion of his men, who charged to his rescue.[29] He managed to escape, and though his horse was mortally wounded, it had the strength to gallop past Chew's guns while its rider shouted, "Good-by, boys; they will get you this time."[30] They didn't, but it was a tight race.

After finally reaching Rude's Hill, Chew put his guns into battery under the fire of Federal artillery, which had not been slow to follow in the wake of the successful charge of their cavalry. Chew returned fire but soon gave up, as the enemy's guns were beyond the range of his pieces. Nevertheless, the battery stayed in position, the gun crews watching their Union counterparts go through the motions of serving their guns and firing. In the afternoon, the Federals added a battery of Parrott guns to those already shelling Chew, who fired a few rounds in a return salute before limbering and retreating through New Market to Sparta, eleven miles farther up the Valley.[31]

On the eighteenth, Chew moved his battery a little south of Sparta, where he placed his guns and awaited the enemy. The Federals appeared and put a battery into action too far away for Chew to effectively respond. Being continually outgunned did not alter Ashby's mode of retreat, which was to offer opposition at every practical location along the line of withdrawal. This time, however, the Yanks moved so leisurely that Chew and the cavalry marched at a comfortable rate and did not pause to offer any resistance. By nightfall, Chew's men were encamped five miles east of Harrisonburg on the road to Swift Run Gap.[32] It had been a long two days.

April 19 brought another day of marching but no fighting. Chew's Battery did not leave its camp until 10:00 in the morning, and then proceeded to Conrad's Store and camped. Banks's army ground to a halt. The Federal commander gave a lack of supplies as the reason for calling off the pursuit.[33] Whatever the cause, Jackson welcomed and put to good use the days of rest that followed. By the twenty-second, Stonewall's retreat had convinced Banks that the Confederates were giving up the Valley and heading for Gordonsville.[34] On the thirtieth, Banks reported that the Valley Army's commander was marching toward Richmond.[35] Contrary to what Banks believed, Jackson was very much close at hand and about to take back the Valley in spectacular fashion.

The short lull in operations gave Chew's Battery the opportunity to hold an election of officers. The battery had been functioning without a full complement of officers since the transfers of Rouss and McCarty. Now James H. Williams, to whom Chew earlier had offered a lieutenancy, was elected to fill one of the vacant posts. Williams briefly noted in his diary that he spent 25 cents for braiding for his jacket.[36]

During this same period, Jackson, being somewhat dissatisfied with what he perceived as a lack of discipline in his mounted arm, made an attempt to reorganize his cavalry. He divided the companies and assigned half of them to Brig. Gen. William B. Taliaferro's division and the remainder to Brig. Gen. Charles S. Winder's division. Ashby would command the advance or the rear of the army as needed but would have to apply to these officers for the necessary troops. In effect, Jackson's order left Ashby a commander without a command. In a letter written on April 24 and 25, newly elected Lt. James H. Williams expressed his discontent and recorded the actions taken by the officers in the cavalry and the battery in opposition to Jackson's order:

> The work of demoralization goes bravely on. An order was issued this evening dividing one Reg't, putting our battery and the new

> companies of cavalry in Taliaferro's Brigade under Major Funsten & Col. Ashby with others in Garnett's [Winder's]. Ashby, Funsten, Chew & almost all the officers have resigned. Never saw such discontent. Resignations not accepted. Order countermanded & matters little more quiet this morning.
>
> Note Friday Morning 25 Apr 62
>
> Matters are not settled. Ashby insists on resigning. Oh for a tongue that was free to speak, or a pen to write. You may expect the worst of news from this quarter, and now that we are put into a brigade you will never hear of us again—I forgot my manhood for the present, must [be] brave. My very soul seems burning up, but there is no redress.[37]

Jackson could not afford to lose Ashby and so many other officers at this crucial time. Accustomed to victory, he recognized defeat when he saw it. A long talk with Ashby and a revoking of the order prevented what might have been a disaster. The war was about to heat up again, and Stonewall needed every man.

There had been intermittent sparring between the Federal cavalry and Ashby's troopers from the nineteenth to the end of the month. A sharp skirmish in the vicinity of McGaheysville occurred on the twenty-seventh, but Chew's guns were not involved. On the twenty-eighth, the battery moved toward McGaheysville. No Federals were encountered. Again on the thirtieth, Chew's men left their camp to go on picket duty. After riding within ten miles of Harrisonburg without meeting a single bluecoat, the battery returned at noon. In the afternoon, it marched two miles up river and encamped for the night.[38]

As April gave way to May, a heavy downpour soaked the roads and filled the streams. At dawn on May 1, Chew's men rolled out of their wet blankets and set off through the mud toward Port Republic, which they reached on the third. The march was difficult. The battery's caissons and guns frequently became mired in muddy holes, requiring the men to pull, push, and pry them free. Horses sank to their shoulders in the sticky, gluelike mud. They, too, were saved, but the toll on both man and beast was telling.[39] A rest was needed, and the battery remained camped a mile beyond Port Republic until the sixth. Several of the men from the battery took the opportunity to visit Weyer's Cave, a nearby cavern, and enjoy nature's geologic wonders.

Chew's Battery had not suffered from the Virginia mud alone. Jackson's infantry had left its camps the morning of April 30 and set out for a destination known only to its close-lipped chief. When, on May 3, the footsore troops found themselves leaving the Valley via Brown's Gap, there was murmuring throughout the ranks. Stonewall's popularity plummeted.[40] When the weary column reached Mecham River Station at the eastern base of the Blue Ridge, the infantry boarded a ramshackle collection of trains, which pulled out of the station not eastward but westward. The question of Jackson's popularity now took a backseat to the question of his sanity. But at least the men were riding, not marching, and some gave their commander points for that. Not all, however. The Rockbridge Artillery was not directed onto railroad cars at the station. Instead, it had to return to the Valley in the same manner it had left it—on foot, this time through Rockfish Gap.[41] For the artillery, the excursion through the mud and over the mountains, twice, had been exhausting.

Upon reaching Staunton, the Valley Army rendezvoused with Maj. Gen. Edward Johnson's command, which had fallen back from West Virginia through Buffalo Gap. Jackson's plan was to return through the gap and strike at the Federals under Brig. Gen. Robert H. Milroy at McDowell, which lay just on the other side of the Shenandoah Mountains. Meanwhile, Maj. Gen. Richard S. Ewell's division, with the help of Ashby and Chew's Battery, would keep Banks occupied. The horse artillery left its camp near Port Republic and resumed its march eastward on the sixth. Striking the Valley Turnpike at Mount Sidney, Chew turned north and camped a half mile south of Mount Crawford.[42]

From the eighth through the fourteenth, Chew was twice called to picket a hill southeast of the North River that overlooked a ford in the river. Otherwise, the men of the battery lay about camp enjoying the beauty of the Valley in springtime. On the fifteenth, they marched eighteen miles down the Valley through Harrisonburg and camped at Lacey Spring. The Confederate advance came as a result of Shield's 11,000 troops leaving the Valley. With only 8,000 men, Banks fell back through New Market to Strasburg.

Still anchored near Swift Run Gap, Ewell chaffed at being unable to strike a blow at either Shields or Banks. He was receiving suggestions and orders from Robert E. Lee, Joe Johnston, and Jackson as to what he should do if the Federals left the Valley. Conflicting information also plagued him. The seventeenth brought him a report from Ashby, which stated that neither Shields nor Banks had left the Valley, while one from Col. Thomas T. Munford of the 2nd Virginia Cavalry reported that Shields had crossed the Blue Ridge, marching east.[43] Ewell had had enough and determined to seek out Jackson and settle what he should do. It was to be a long night ride, with the fate of the Valley and Richmond possibly hanging in the balance.

Meanwhile, Ashby with Chew's Battery set out the same day and marched to New Market, where the battery turned east on the Luray Pike. Two miles from the town, Chew halted the men, and the battery went into camp along Smith's Creek. There it stayed as Jackson and Ewell plotted their strategy. At this time, on May 19, the battery held an election of officers and appointment of noncommissioned officers. This was in accordance with the reorganization of all the Confederate forces that was then taking place. Chew was reelected captain. Neese had this to say about his commander:

> We might search over the whole State, and it is very doubtful whether we could find his equal in every respect as a commander of artillery. For competency and skill in handling a battery on the field his equals, according to my judgement, formed by observation, are few and difficult to find. He is gallant and brave, a strict disciplinarian without the least sign or flavor of arrogance or overbearing haughtiness, as calm and cool on the battle-field as on dress parade, and generous and impartial to his men, always manifesting a care for their welfare on the battle-field as well as in the camp and bivouac. All these characteristics are of much importance to men on the field and in camp, and hardly ever found in one bunch, consequently he has now the esteem and utter confidence of every man in the battery.[44]

Young Jim Thomson was elected first lieutenant. James H. Williams and John W. Carter became the second lieutenants.[45] Neese was appointed corporal and first gunner, a position he did not covet and, in fact, felt inadequate to fill. Time would prove him wrong. With these changes, the battery faced the coming campaign.

Ewell and Jackson's conference of the night of May 18–19 resulted in immediate action. The following day, the Confederates began their movement to strike Banks before Shields could be summoned to return and reinforce him. Chew's Battery still lay in its camp two miles east of New Market, on the road to Luray, when on the twenty-first Jackson's grizzled veterans tramped by. The battery hadn't seen Old Stonewall or his boys since April 30, and Neese speculated that Jackson was "going down the Luray Valley to give General Banks, who is at Strasburg, his first object lesson in flanking."[46]

It had been a long time since Ashby's artillery had been in the rear of Jackson's advancing army. Chew did not move out until the twenty-second and camped at Luray that evening. The next day, the battery continued its march down the Luray Valley, passing some of Jackson's infantry and camping eight miles from Front Royal. At 3:00 A.M. on the twenty-fourth, Chew had his men up and in the saddle. Ashby's cavalry had encountered the Federals on the twenty-third, and Chew was needed. After crossing the Shenandoah River and marching along the Winchester Pike for about six miles, Chew was recalled to the river and ordered north to Middletown on the Valley Pike. Accompanying him were two guns from the Rockbridge Artillery and at least one company of Louisiana Tigers.[47]

By the time Chew caught up with Ashby, he was pushing rapidly toward the Valley Pike intent on cutting off the enemy's retreat and damaging or capturing as much men and materiel as he could. The gray cavalry advanced against heavy enemy fire but slowly managed to push the Federal line back toward the road. Ashby now determined to strike hard and break through. He told Chew to ride with the cavalry and charge the enemy line that had withdrawn into an open field near Middletown. Chew obeyed and soon his guns were tearing across the field. Within about 100 yards of the Federal line the cannoneers reined in their horses, unlimbered their guns, and opened fire. The bluecoats scattered, completely surprised by the audacious move. As the enemy fled up the pike Ashby's troopers and Chew's guns pursued. At Crisman's Ashby and Chew repeated the maneuver with the same results. It was a glorious moment for Chew and his gunners. Intentionally or unintentionally a new style of fighting horse artillery had been born.[48]

This was the first instance of artillery charging in the midst of cavalry during the war. Although some horse artillery units in Europe had practiced such a maneuver, it was used to silence enemy artillery before a charge or to shield friendly units during a withdrawal and not, as in this instance, as an offensive tactic against enemy troops. What had been done was something new—shock tactics using artillery with cavalry. Chew admitted that the whole incident happened so fast that he had no time to consider what Ashby had ordered him to do.[49] Doubt exists as to whether Ashby had given the matter much thought when he rode up to Chew and gave him the command. Most likely it was a natural outgrowth of Ashby's aggressive nature and not a preconceived, calculated maneuver. However it occurred, the results could not be denied.

Wagons, ambulances, artillery, cavalry, and infantry moved through a dust storm that rose from beneath hundreds of wheels, hooves, and feet. A torrent of men and equipment poured north toward Winchester and safety. Chew's shells tore gaps in the snakelike column, which increased its speed in the hope of getting out of range. At Newtown, the Federals rallied and turned on their tormentors. Chew's men were feeding their horses in the town when the Federals sent a line of sharpshooters toward them. At first the artillerymen tried to hold their position by firing one of their guns from the middle of the town, but a lack of infantry or cavalry support forced them to limber up and make a hasty exit. Gunner Neese found himself in a most uncomfortable location. Turning toward the enemy, "I saw a sharpshooter in the middle of the street drop on one knee and shoot at us at a distance of nearly half a mile. When he fired I heard the bullet whiz close by my head. It struck the lead driver to my team and went clear through him, from back to breast, but it did not kill him."[50] The driver, George McWilliams, was carried to a nearby farmhouse. He survived his wound and returned to the battery.

As Chew was withdrawing, Jackson's infantry came up and pushed back the Federals. The fighting ended as night engulfed the two armies. Several of Chew's men, Neese included, received permission to go foraging among the numerous abandoned wagons and piles of debris that lay all along the pike. Lieutenant Williams managed to find two pistols. He had captured a horse earlier and was most pleased with his new acquisitions.[51] When the men returned, they found that camp had been established at Newtown.

On the morning of May 25, Chew's Battery was on the road to Winchester. Though they had gotten an early start, the men heard cannonading from the north, which told them that others had been up earlier and had opened the battle. So quickly did the soldiers of Jackson and Ewell decide the issue that Chew did not have the opportunity to fire a shot. The Federals failed to hold on long enough to destroy many of their supplies, which fell into the hands of the Confederates. The horse artillery followed in the wake of Banks's army and camped for the night at Darkesville about nine miles from Winchester. The men reached Martinsburg the next day, but Yankees were long gone. Chew directed his command back to Winchester on the twenty-seventh.[52]

The next day, the battery marched back to Martinsburg and camped north of the town. A day of rest was enjoyed by all. Chew apparently was not with the battery at this time. He may have been visiting friends or attempting to reach his home in Charles Town. In any event, he ended up volunteering to do a little scouting for Brig. Gen. Charles Winder. The general had been ordered to march from his camp about four and a half miles outside of Winchester to Charles Town via Summit Point. All went well until he was within five miles of Charles Town, when he learned that the Federals were in possession of the place. Although Winder had four infantry regiments and two batteries of artillery, he had no cavalry. His report described Chew's involvement in the expedition:

> Being without cavalry, I pressed into service all stragglers of that arm I met on the road, some 15 in number, which the gallant Capt. R. P. Chew, whom I met, volunteered to command and advise me of the enemy's movements in front.
>
> I moved forward cautiously. Captain Chew soon informed me he had met the enemy's pickets (cavalry) and charged them, and they had taken cover in a woods. I ordered two companies of the Fifth Regiment, Lieutenant-Colonel [John H. S.] Funk commanding, to be thrown forward, which was rapidly done, under Captain [Thomas J.] Burke. The enemy's pickets retired after a few shots.[53]

Winder went on to rout the 1,500-man Federal force at Charles Town and was most grateful to Chew, stating at the end of his report, "My thanks are eminently due, and the same are hereby tendered, to Captain Chew for his able assistance and to the great amount of information given me as to the country, thus enabling me to press forward rapidly when totally ignorant of the country myself."[54] The two men would meet each other again on the field of Port Republic.

Orders were received on the thirtieth that sent Chew's Battery back to Winchester and into camp at the point where the Front Royal Road entered the town. Jackson had been apprised that Shields's division was marching back to the Valley with the object of cutting the Confederate line of retreat up the Valley Pike. On the thirty-first, Chew's Battery was sent out on the Front Royal Road to delay the approaching Federals. When within only a few miles of Front Royal, Chew put his guns into battery and opened on the enemy with his two rifled pieces. It was but a brief show of force to bluff the Federals and gain time. Once the bluecoats disappeared into a nearby ravine, Chew limbered his guns and set out across county for the Valley Pike. The race was on.[55]

The Federal pincers that were to cut off Jackson's escape route drew closer to each other as the weary column of Confederates trudged south on the Valley Pike. When Chew's Battery finally intersected the pike, the horse artillerymen caught sight of Jackson's wagon train. Merging with it, they retreated to within a mile of Cedar Creek and established camp.

The first of June saw a resumption of the march. Near Strasburg, Chew entered a fort on a hill northwest of the town and unlimbered. Banks had constructed the fort several weeks earlier. Scarcely had the guns been rolled into position when artillery fire was heard to the northwest. Fremont, the western jaw of the Union trap, was closing in on Strasburg. Chew was moved to Fisher's Hill, and as the setting sun cast long shadows across the Valley, skirmishers from Shields's Division could be seen toward the east, while those of Fremont were visible to the west. The race had been close, but as Chew trotted away from Fisher's Hill at dusk, he knew that Jackson had won.[56]

The battery went into camp four miles above Strasburg but received orders after dark to proceed to Tom's Brook, another two miles up the Valley Pike. As the tired artillerymen finally settled down for the night, it began to rain. Without tents, they made themselves as comfortable as possible and went to sleep. June 2 brought a continuation of the retreat. During the march, the battery overtook Jackson's wagon train, which crawled along at a slow pace. Neese believed that "a shell or two in the right place would increase the speed of his trains, which would be highly beneficial just now to all concerned, as the Yanks are pressing our rear and itching for a fight."[57] Just south of Edenburg, Chew turned from the column and unlimbered on Rude's Hill.[58] The Federals were indeed "pressing the rear" of the Confederates, and cannon fire could be heard to the north.

On the third, the battery marched to Hawkinstown. Sighting the enemy, Chew unlimbered. After a half hour, he fell back about a half mile and again went into battery, holding this position until Jackson had safely crossed the north fork of the Shenandoah River. Chew followed and set fire to the bridge. On the south side of the river, he unlimbered to guard the bridge until it collapsed.[59]

Hot on the heels of the retreating Rebels, the 1st Pennsylvania Cavalry rode up on the bluff overlooking the river. As soon as they appeared, Chew opened fire with his howitzer. The blue cavalry scattered, but not before Neese managed to lob a shell into the head of the column. The smoke cleared to reveal a riderless horse galloping away.[60] The Pennsylvanians called off the pursuit. Unlike the fight at Newtown, Neese had the better of this one. When the burned-out bridge tumbled into the water, Chew limbered, withdrew to New Market, and camped for the night.[61]

The rain came again on that night and lasted through the fourth. In the late afternoon, a report that the Yankees were advancing sent Chew's Battery into position a half mile below New Market. Nothing developed, and near dark, the guns were withdrawn and pulled back to a mile south of town. The bluecoats had crossed the river in boats near the location of the burnt bridge but had not pushed on to make contact with the Rebels. The next day, Chew fell back to Harrisonburg and camped a half mile below the town.[62]

Jackson had almost escaped the trap but was still not quite out of harm's way. June 6 saw the Federals take Harrisonburg while Stonewall's army struggled through the mud toward Port Republic. Chew's Battery had broken camp, ridden through Harrisonburg, and turned off the pike onto the road to Port Republic.[63] A mile outside of Harrisonburg, the company halted and put its guns into position on a hill with other batteries to support the 58th Virginia Infantry, commanded by Col. Samuel H. Letcher, and the 1st Maryland Infantry, under Col. Bradley T. Johnson. Their opponents were 104 men of the 13th Pennsylvania Reserves, also known as the Kane Rifle Battalion. The swatches of deer hide or deer tail they wore on their caps earned them the name "Bucktails."[64]

The infantry fight had been preceded by a clash between Ashby's cavalry and the 1st New Jersey Cavalry under Col. Sir Percy Wyndham, which had resulted in Wyndham's capture. With the repulse of the Federal cavalry, Ashby had called for infantry, as had Brig. Gen. George D. Bayard commanding the Union advance force. Chew and the rest of the artillerymen on the hill watched the smoke from the battle rise through the trees. They could do little else. The Bucktails gave a good account of themselves, although they were heavily outnumbered. The 58th Virginia was hard-pressed to budge the Pennsylvanians and was thrown back. Ashby rode into the midst of the retreating regiment to rally the men, only to have his horse shot from under him. He stepped from the fallen animal and, waving his sword above his head, took a few steps toward the enemy. At that moment, he was struck in the body and killed instantly. Shortly after Ashby fell, the 1st Maryland attacked. Colonel Johnson's horse fell with three wounds, and two of the regiment's color bearers were struck down. The last man to grab the standard and carry it forward was Color Corp. Daniel Shanks, a future captain in the 1st Stuart Horse Artillery.[65]

Chew's Battery did not sit completely idle while the infantry tore at each other. Some Federal cavalrymen made the mistake of riding out from the protection of the woods and were quickly sent scurrying back under cover with a shower of shells. When the infantry lines broke apart, the artillery shelled the Federals until dark, when all became quiet. Chew's gunners stood by their pieces, tensed, listening for any movement from the enemy's lines. The silence was broken by the cracking of rifle shots and the whizzing of bullets "clipping through the rye like frightened grasshoppers."[66] Yankee sharpshooters had been listening as well and had evidently heard or thought they heard something. The battery limbered to the rear and followed the rest of Jackson's retreating army.

Ashby's death had a profound effect on Jackson's whole command. The men of the cavalry and Chew's Battery were among those who felt the loss more deeply than the rest of the army. Lieutenant Williams recounted how the battery first learned of Ashby's death and his own feelings in a letter he wrote on June 21, 1862:

> During that fatal engagement no order came to us. Never had he in a fight been absent so long. His place where we were firing was near us. I could but wonder at this. As we were leaving the field, I rode ahead to pick the road. A number of horsemen passed me. I reproved them for leaving us to bring up the rear and told them to fall in behind the Battery. Someone spoke saying we are sent forward with Gen. Ashby's body. This was the first we knew of his death. I could not realize it. I saw his body pass, rolled in his blanket. This was the last I saw of our beloved Leader. I have his picture taken after death. He seems not to be dead but sleepeth, but alas each day brings new evidence that we have no Ashby now. I almost thought he could not be killed. I was in charge of the Battery as he left Harrisonburg and remember well his last order, and the last words he spoke in my hearing as he passed along his brigade.[67]

Lt. James W. Thomson, Chew's second in command, expressed his grief in a letter he wrote in July 1862 to Daniel M. Lee,[68] a fellow cadet and friend at VMI:

> I have been through some mighty tight places since I saw you. I wish so much that you were with me, for I get so lonesome now since we lost our general. When he was living there was always something to keep a man's mind employed. Oh, Dan! You have no idea what a loss he was to us. It has cast a gloom over our whole command.[69]

The gloom would take time to dissipate, and the Yankees would see to it that Thomson's and the rest of the Confederates' minds were employed to their fullest. The war continued.

On the seventh, the battery moved three miles on the road to Port Republic. It remained in marching order for the rest of the day but was not called forward. The next day, Chew led his guns toward the sound of battle. He placed them with the Rockbridge Artillery and Carpenter's Battery on a hill overlooking the North Fork of the Shenandoah River.[70] Later Chew was ordered two miles upriver to guard a ford. After a couple hours, he was directed to take his battery farther upriver and guard another ford. All day the men heard the rumbling of cannons coming from the battle at Cross Keys, but they had no way of knowing its outcome. Darkness already had fallen when Chew left his position and marched to Middle River to camp for the night.[71]

Early on the morning of the ninth, the battery received 150 rounds of ammunition. It was an omen. After filling their ammunition chests, the men mounted and trotted downriver to Port Republic. An aide of Jackson's met Chew on the road and told him to hurry forward. Without hesitating, the battery galloped into the battle. Chew reported to Brig. Gen. Charles S. Winder, who immediately ordered him to place his guns into battery. The target was a Yankee battery that occupied an excellent position on a coaling, from which it was raking the Confederates. For the next half hour, though Chew's gunners traded shot for shot with the Union guns, they could not silence them or even diminish their fire. Not until the Louisiana infantry stormed the guns did they cease their devastating fire. The battle then turned in favor of the Confederates.

Once the guns on the coaling were taken, the Federals began to fall back, and the pursuit was on. After four miles, Jackson ordered Winder to halt all the artillery except for two of Chew's guns, which continued to chase the enemy for another five miles before returning to Port Republic.[72] At ten o'clock that night, Chew pitched his camp halfway up the Blue Ridge on the road to Brown's Gap. Remarkably, the battery had not suffered a single casualty. The men and their commander had much to be thankful for. Lieutenant Williams slept in the rain that night on blankets he had picked up while chasing the Yankees over the mountain.[73]

Marching, not fighting, occupied the next several days. Chew's Battery rode to Albemarle County on the tenth, marched to and camped near Weyer's Cave on the eleventh, and moved only a short distance to Vernon Forge on the twelfth. It was within five miles of Harrisonburg by the thirteenth and ended up within a half mile of the town on the fourteenth. After five days of continuous movement, the men were allowed to stay in camp and rest until the twentieth, when camp was moved. This second interlude lasted until the twenty-eighth, when the company moved just a half mile before again pitching its tents.

Not all members of the battery were allowed to recuperate from the rigorous campaign. There were always individuals required to see after the business of keeping the battery running efficiently. In a letter to Cora, Lieutenant Williams recorded his activities, his dismay over the results of another election, and his fear of what had happened to the Valley under the Federals:

Greenwood June 17th 1862

My Dear Miss Cora,

I came here last on Company business from Harrisonburg, will return today. Reinforcements are rapidly pouring in and a forward movement will be made today or tomorrow. The enemy are in force at Mt. Jackson. We will be in the advance and I must be with the command. Capt. Chew was yesterday elected Lt. Col. of one of the Cav. Reg'ts. Thomson will be Capt. of the battery I suppose. The Company will not be so efficient again. I think of resigning. I am almost afraid to go down the Valley. Wherever that Dutch Army have been there is wide spread desolation, houses sacked, furniture, farming utensils, clothing of every description, stock, etc. destroyed. The destruction of property has been wanton in the extreme. Have heard nothing from the Valley below Mt. Jackson.[74]

Chew's election to the lieutenant colonelcy of the 7th Virginia Cavalry clearly demonstrated the regiment's high regard for the young horse artillery commander. But Williams need not to have worried. Jackson and the War Department in Richmond did not agree with the selections made by the regiment. Chew's commission was never forthcoming, and he remained with the battery. Undoubtedly his age, and not his record, had something to do with his not receiving the appointment.[75]

As June changed to July, Chew and his men enjoyed the beauty and peace of the Valley. The campaign had been a long and arduous one. There had been losses, that of Ashby the heaviest to bear. The men and horses renewed their strength. They did not accompany Jackson and his army east toward Richmond. Stonewall left his celebrated battery of horse artillery to protect what had been won. It would not have the opportunity to test itself against the Army of the Potomac and its commander Maj. Gen. George B. McClellan. That honor would fall to another battery of horse artillery and another young artillery officer named Pelham.

CHAPTER 4

Pelham's Battery on the Peninsula

"We seem to dare the nation."

On Monday, March 17, 1862, the first of the Federal army's divisions embarked for Fort Monroe at the tip of the James River Peninsula. The campaign to follow, which would come to be called the Peninsula campaign, was the brainchild of Maj. Gen. George B. McClellan, commander of the Army of the Potomac. After landing his army, his plan was to march up the Peninsula, seize Richmond, the capital of the Confederacy, and end the war in one bold stroke. The Rebels were not about to be so obliging as to allow him to do so unmolested. On March 27, Gen. Joseph E. Johnston, who commanded the Confederate army opposing Union forces in Northern Virginia, received orders to reinforce the small Confederate army on the Peninsula. He left behind Stuart and most of the cavalry at Culpeper Court House to screen his movement. Stuart did not leave to rejoin the army at Yorktown until April 8.

By the evening of the twelfth, Stuart and his cavalry were camped seven miles from Richmond on their way to Yorktown. For Capt. John Pelham, time was running out. He would soon be expected to put his battery into the field, and to compound his problems, he had just been assigned a contingent of men from Floyd County. Sending these raw, untrained men into battle was not something Pelham wanted to do, so their rapid training was paramount. Pvt. William A. Simpson, one of Pelham's Floyd County recruits, wrote to his father about his assignment to the "flying artillery" and his new captain:[1]

York Co. Va April the 22 1862

Dear Father & Mother & Sisters one and all

It is with great pleasure that I seat myself this morning to inform you that I am well and hoping when these few lines come to hand they may find you enjoying the same blessing. I reckon you have been informed that we were mustered in the Service of the Confederate States & put in a flying artillery company under Capt. Pelham. He has 8 guns. It takes six horses and 3 drivers to one gun & 8 men to load them. They have to be on horseback. The captain hasn't got horses enough for all the men yet. He put us just where he pleased. He put me & Josh Poff & Isaac Poff to drive one gun or one on the 3 near horses & so on all the rest. He put Will [William P. Walters] to [word illegible] the [word illegible]. I should like for him to drive with me, but he won't drive. All the difference there is I have to tend to two horses & he don't tend to but one. We don't get to mess together. They won't let the cannoneers & the drivers mess together. They say they want every man to his post. I like mine pretty well. I have nothing to do in action but hold my horses. The others dismount, give their horses to the horse holder, & go to work. One hands the cartridge. One holds his thumb on the touch hole. One sticks them. One rams them down. One sights. The other fires & [word illegible] they go.

Our big bugs is in the same fix the rest of us is. We all laugh to see Colonel Williams learning to ram the cannon ball. S. R. Aldridge [Staunton R. Alderidge] [is] in the same fix. We are all in our good spirits as you ever seen men, although in 5 miles of Yorktown where there are 150 thousand Yankees. We can hear the cannon constantly. I have heard several since I have been writing. H. [Henry] L. Vest went down to Yorktown yesterday. He said he could see the Yankee ships. We will have to go there as soon as we can get drilled if not before. It is expected to be one of the hardest fights that ever was fought in the United States, But they may not attack us at all. But if they do somebody is going to get hurt. The pickets are killing one another constantly. We won't have to stand guard more than mind our own battery. That's one fine thing.

I want you all to do as you think best with every thing, for I have lost all hopes of coming home till the war ends. If kind Providence permits me to return then I will be thankful though I can't say that I am afraid to risk my life to the chance of lots, not knowing who will have to fall. The strong arm of the God of battles is as able to keep us safe here as he is in our bed chambers.

We have been exposed to hard rains for the 2 or 3 days without the benefit of a tent more than pine brush & not very plentiful of provision while we were marching, but we got enough now except horse feed.

We left uncle Hi [Hiram Walters] at Camp Winder. He had the sore throat with 7 or 8 more who had measles. I don't know as I have any more news of importance to write or [if] Will want to write if he can get the chance from drill, so I will bring my letter to a close by requesting you to write to me soon & direct your letter to me at

> Williamsburg in care of Capt. Pelham, Stuart's Horse Artillery, York Co., Va., & it will be fetched to our camp. So no more at present but remain your affectionate son until death
>
> Wm A. Simpson to James Simpson[2]

That Pelham commanded the battery down to the assignment of the men to the various positions is evident from Simpson's letter. He was thorough and not an officer to permit another to perform such vital tasks. What is also obvious is that if the situation demanded, Simpson and the new men of the battery expected to be put into battle with or without an appropriate amount of drill to learn their new trade, and that battle was fast approaching.

Near the end of the month, Pelham could count 141 men in his battery.[3] This was sufficient to service his eight guns—two six-pound howitzers, four twelve-pound howitzers, one Napoleon, and one Blakely. What he needed was enough horses to mount the men and pull the guns. Like Chew, Pelham was already experiencing the lack of good horseflesh. On April 16, he had received 50 horses from the Quartermaster Department in Richmond, and by the twenty-second, he was drawing rations of corn for 131 animals, including a small number of mules.[4] He would need more.

Through the rest of April, the battery lay in camp near Yorktown at Dam No. 2. Many of the men were ill from drinking bad water. Nevertheless, drill was the order of the day, every day. Pvt. William P. Walters wrote about his experiences and those of some of the other Floyd men:

> York County, Va. April the 30th 1862
>
> Dear Wife,
>
> It is with great pleasure that I seat myself this evening to let you know that I am well [and] hoping these few lines may find you and the children enjoying the same blessing. I would like to hear from you all again. I was looking for a letter from you when we left Camp Winder, but I don't expect to get them. I have sent two letters since I left Richmond and will keep on sending whether I get answers or not.
>
> We have come back 3 miles since before, but we are yet in hearing of Yorktown. They have been throwing bombshells at one another for about a month. We can hear them plain from here. They have been shooting all day today. Some of them almost shake the ground. We can also hear the muskets of the pickets roaring for 20 minutes & some times longer, but they have not done much damage yet on our side but killed 7 hundred Yankees one night. There will be big fighting down here yet if they don't quit their fussing.

As for our part we seem to dare the nation with our 6 pound gun and 4 12 pound guns, 1 rifle cannon, [and] 2 little mountain howitzers which we was attached to. They have set Colonel Williams and all the rest of the officers down in ranks with the rest of us. They are trying to learn them how to use the sponge staff and ram cartridges.

We have a beautiful camp ground here on the bank of the James River where it is about 9 miles wide. We can see boats and ships more than I want to look at. I have seen as much of this low country as I want to see. The land is level and sandy here. Water is tolerable good, but not like Floyd water. We don't get our coffee and sugar. We had to eat parched corn and beef with out salt for 3 days, but we have provisions now. There are several of us Floyd boys with the measles and gone to the hospital. [Name illegible] stayed at Richmond sick with several more, but thanks be to kind Providence I have had my health so far.

They all say I am getting fat. I have not got no more news to write worth your attention. We will have to stay with this artillery for a while until it is filled up with volunteers, and then we will [be] sent somewhere else. They want us to volunteer in the company, but I won't do it.[5] You must do the best you can. Save what you got, for I don't expect to get home in time to make a crop this year. Write as soon as you can [and] direct your letter to Williamsburg, York County, Va. in care of Captain Pelham, Stuart's Horse Artillery. So no more at present but remain your affectionate husband till death

Wm P. Walters to Matilda E. Walters and friends

May the 1st 1862

We are both [Walters and William A. Simpson] well this morning, good by.[6]

While Walters enjoyed watching his former militia officers perform the same drill as the rest of the men, he also felt a growing sense of pride that the constant drilling fostered as the men began to see themselves becoming one unit. His comment that "we seem to dare the nation" shows that Pelham and his junior officers were beginning to instill the esprit de corps so important to a body of fighting men. The testing of that spirit was at hand.

On May 2, Pelham broke camp and, with six guns, rode to Bigler's Wharf on the York River northeast of Williamsburg, where he joined Col. Fitzhugh Lee of the 1st Virginia Cavalry. Meanwhile, Lt. James S. T. Shepherd reported to Stuart's headquarters with the two twelve-pound mountain howitzers. He was destined to fire the first shots for the battery in combat. His report recorded the event.

Near New Kent Court-House, Va.,
May 8, 1862.

Captain: May 2 I reported, with the two mountain howitzers, to General J. E. B. Stuart. At 4 p.m. on the following day I took position on a small stream which empties near Grove Landing, where I remained until 1 p.m. of the fourth, when I was moved under General Stuart's direction, on the main road toward Williamsburg. Here a skirmish took place. I fired three rounds spherical case, and then retired, following the cavalry by Grove's Landing, then up the Beach road to Williamsburg.

One of my men (Private James W. Smith), having taken sick, was sent to the rear, and was probably taken prisoner by the enemy.

Respectfully, your obedient servant,

Jas. T. Shepherd
Second Lieutenant, Stuart Horse Artillery

Capt. John Pelham
Commanding Stuart Horse Artillery[7]

Stuart was pleased with the horse artillery's brief engagement, stating that "the mountain howitzers performed well, but the effect upon the enemy concealed in the woods could not be seen."[8] Shepherd and his section were reunited with the rest of the battery later that day.

Between 10:00 and 11:00 A.M. on the fifth, Pelham received orders directing him to proceed immediately to Williamsburg. Leaving five of his guns in the town, he continued out to the field of battle with the two mountain howitzers and the Blakely. He arrived at 2:00 P.M. and reported to Stuart. Pelham modestly recounted his participation in the battle that followed:

I took position to the right and front of Fort Magruder, and opened fire on the enemy, who occupied the woods on the road to Lebanon Church. Here I detached Lieutenant [William C.] Elston, with two men, to bring off some captured artillery. In a few minutes they returned on foot, their horses having been shot down as soon as they made their appearance at the guns. I held this position under heavy fire until General Hill's brigade moved up and deployed in front of my battery, when I moved to the left and took position on the Yorktown road, to enfilade the enemy's lines. Here the metal bed of the elevating screw of my Blakely gun gave way; but it was retained on the field and did good service. I remained in this position until 5 p.m., when I withdrew for want of ammunition.

I fired 286 rounds of spherical case and 4 of canister from the 12 pounder howitzers and 40 percussion shell and 30 solid shot from the Blakely gun. Total of 360.

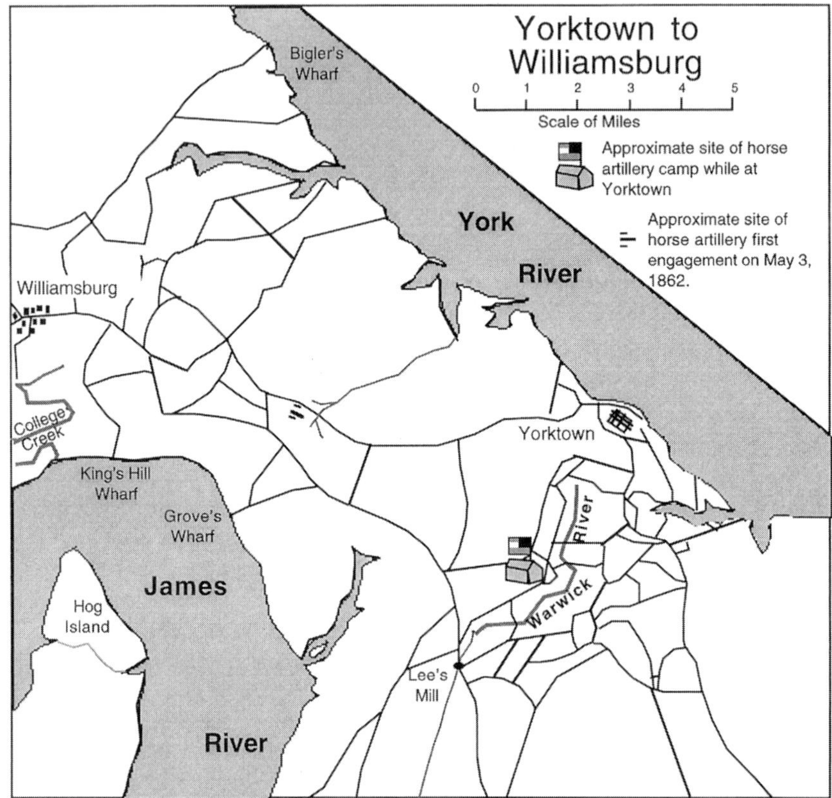
Yorktown to Williamsburg
0 1 2 3 4 5
Scale of Miles
Approximate site of horse artillery camp while at Yorktown
Approximate site of horse artillery first engagement on May 3, 1862.
Bigler's Wharf
York
River
Williamsburg
College Creek
Yorktown
King's Hill Wharf
Grove's Wharf
James
Hog Island
River
Warwick River
Lee's Mill
River

> During the entire engagement both officers and men acted with commendable calmness and courage. The example of cool, conspicuous bravery set by Lieutenants Breathed, McGregor, and Elston was emulated by my non-commissioned officers and men.
>
> Casualties as follows: 2 men wounded, Summers [T. Sumner] and Gibson;[9] 4 horses killed, 3 wounded, and 13 escaped from horse-holders, all of which have since been found except two.[10]

Pelham clinically reported his battery's role in the battle of Williamsburg but greatly understated his own involvement. This was the result of the young Alabamian's inherent shyness and humility. On the field, he could not help calling attention to himself by the manner in which he fought his guns, but these in a sense were unguarded moments when his natural abilities shone forth. Off the field, he wished to remain in the background, not in the limelight. Such was his talent, however, that the deeds he performed brought him the glory and fame he did not seek openly. Others saw, marveled, and recorded what Pelham failed to include in his reports.

According to Brig. Gen. J. E. B. Stuart's account of the battle, Pelham's Battery arrived on the field shortly after Capt. William D. Farley, one of Stuart's aides, had reported the capture of an enemy battery[11] by the 19th Mississippi and the 9th Alabama Infantry Regiments. Stuart ordered Pelham forward to help with the pursuit but stopped the guns near a wood to allow the cavalry to pass first. At that moment, the Federals opened a brisk fire to cover their withdrawal, forcing the cavalry to fall back. To counteract the enemy fire, Stuart turned to order Pelham to open with his guns.

> Before the order could be given Pelham's Battery was speaking to the enemy in thunder tones of defiance, its maiden effort on the field, thus filling its function of unexpected arrival with instantaneous execution and sustaining in gallant style the fortunes of the day, keeping up a destructive fire upon the enemy until our infantry, having reformed, rushed forward, masking the pieces.[12]

Stuart was estatic about the battery's performance. In a letter to his wife, Flora, on May 9, he praised the battery for its charge into the fight and its steadiness while under fire from the enemy infantry only 200 yards away. He also gave credit to the Floyd County militia, whose performance created a surprise because it had been so recently incorporated into the battery.[13]

The Floyd County militia had indeed stood the test. Stuart and others he knew may have been astounded by their performance. But Pelham? Pelham, who had assigned each man to a position himself? Pelham, who had drilled them? Pelham, who had bent to the task of personally demonstrating the drill of loading and firing the guns? Pelham, who had raised their morale to the point where their little battery dared a nation? No, Pelham was not surprised by what his men had accomplished. They had not failed him, because he had molded them with his own hands. They had fought as Pelham had expected them to fight.

On May 6, Johnston's army disengaged at Williamsburg and drew back toward Richmond. Stuart and the cavalry brought up the rear. The horse artillery found the trek rough going. The roads were muddy and littered with fence rails that had been used to extricate wagons from the mire.[14] Pelham and his battery went into camp at a brick schoolhouse about a half mile from Burnt Ordinary. At 10:00 on the morning of the seventh, he received orders from Stuart to return to the rear of the army with one rifled gun and one howitzer. The small column proceeded about a mile and a half beyond Burnt Ordinary to the Methodist Chapel near Slater's Store, where Pelham detached Breathed with the howitzer. Pelham continued on with the rifled gun for another mile before going into position.

The Federal cavalry made its appearance. Elements of the 3rd Pennsylvania and the 8th Illinois, under the command of Col. William W. Averell, were on a scout to pick up information, prisoners, and whatever booty made itself available. Pelham fired five shots that, according to his report, scattered the enemy. He then limbered and followed the rear of the army in its retreat.[15]

Though there are no reports of the Stuart Horse Artillery's activities over the next few days, as the army pulled back to New Kent Court House, evidence from several sources indicates that along with the cavalry, it was engaged in several rear-guard skirmishes. In his report of May 12, Maj. Gen. Gustavus W. Smith stated, "The comfort and quiet with which the march of the troops has been conducted on this line is largely due to the admirable disposition and watchfulness of the cavalry rear guard, first under Col. Fitz. Lee and more recently under Brig. Gen. J. E. B. Stuart, supported from day to day by brigades detailed for this purpose."[16] Pelham was undoubtedly with Stuart at this time and contributed much to the success of his chief.

As for the men from Floyd County, they were now veterans. A letter from Walters to his wife confirms both the battery's activity and the veteran status of the men:

> I would like to come home and see how a table and a bed looks, but I can sleep sound on the ground in the open air. I laid down the other day under my gun when we was in line of battle and went to sleep, but when they said the Yankees was coming I jumped up and rammed down the load, and they fired it off and that was the last of it and the Yankees for they turned back, and we came on about 1 mile, and we are staying here yet. People said the Floyd boys would run when we first come down here, but they have found out better, but some of the volunteers did run down at Williamsburg.[17]

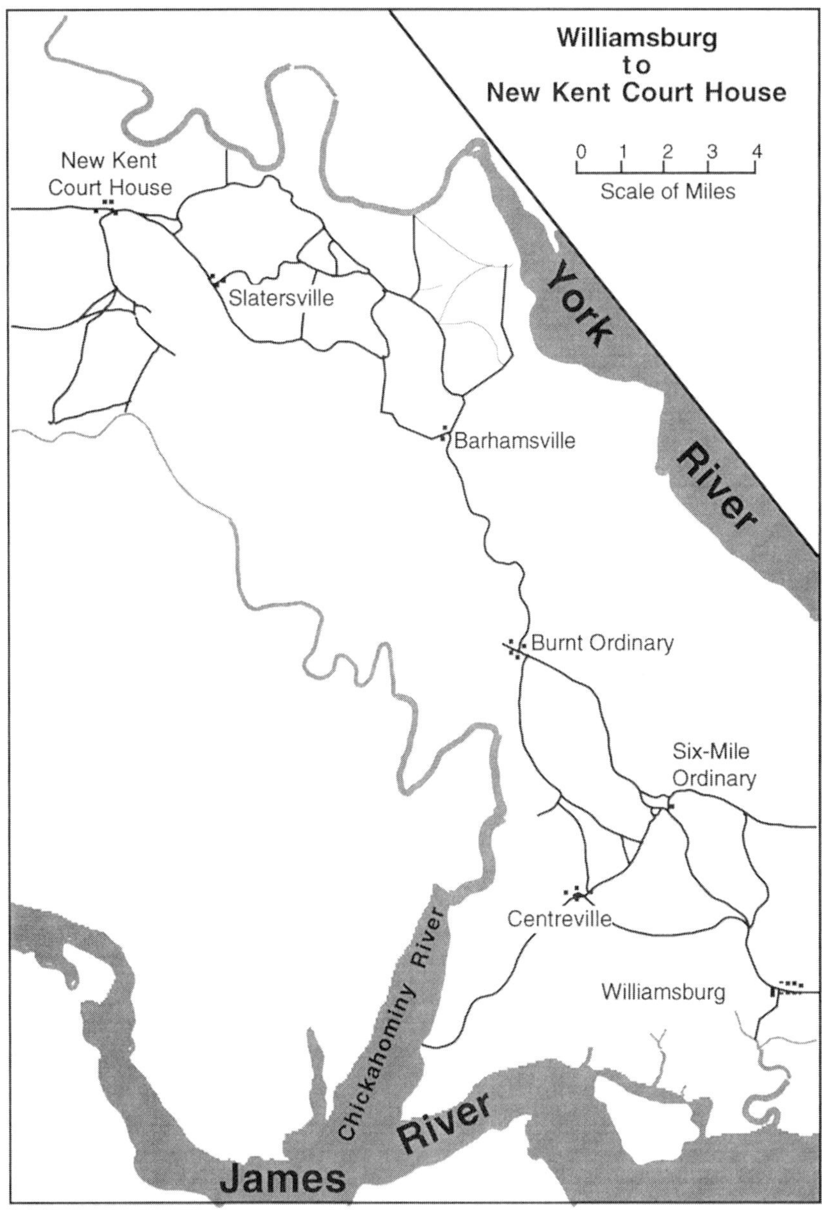
Williamsburg
to
New Kent Court House
0 1 2 3 4
Scale of Miles
New Kent
Court House
Slatersville
York
River
Barhamsville
Burnt Ordinary
Six-Mile
Ordinary
Centreville
Williamsburg
Chickahominy River
James
River

The Federal army was not the only enemy the Floyd boys and the battery faced that spring. Measles felled a number of men. At least two from Floyd County died: William Stump and Jacob Zowder.[18] Pvt. George W. Shreve also contracted the disease and missed the entire campaign while recovering.[19]

On May 14, Pelham's Battery left New Kent Court House and marched to Bottom's Bridge on the Chickahominy River. Pelham gave orders that the bridge be burned, but the recent rains made the timbers too wet to catch fire. Instead, the battery spent several days throwing up earthworks strengthened by railroad ties taken from the Richmond and York River Railroad.[20] During this time, Private Walters sent a letter to his wife.[21]

> I seat my self this morning [May 20] to let you no that me and Bill [William A. Simpson] are well and at Chickahominy Creek yet, hoping these few lines may find you all enjoying good health. I haven't got much news to write now for we have been laying here ever since I wrote before. We have not had any chance to fire on the Yankees for 2 days except some pickets which caught one Yankee this morning poking about the creek trying to see how we was fixed. He was sent to Richmond to look there where he could see something.
>
> Our forces have all been drawn to Richmond except a few. Our little battery seems to keep McClellan's whole army at bay. If they only knew that we was here with as little force as we have got they would be on us like a duck on a June bug. But if they make an attack on us we will show how it is for we are well fixed for them for we have all got horses that can run or will fall back to the main army. They fear Stuart's battery. They say they don't like to be fired on by cannons from every old field they [word illegible] in. The Yankees say that they want to get Richmond and our long shooter, but they make slow speed, but it looks like they are sure.
>
> May 22
>
> I had to stop writing yesterday to go to harder work. I wrote yesterday how we would do if the Yankees would come, but now I can tell you how we done. They come over on the other side of the creek, and we commenced firing on them with the 6 pound gun that I am working with. We fired it 8 times at them before they fired a shot or shot at us, but Oh! gracious you ought to have seen us jump about and fall down when the Yankees begun to fire their balls and shells at us. They threw some right close, but we would fall down and let them go over us. So we soon got tired of such fun and mounted our horses and run off from that field but stopped out in the woods and stayed there till they got tired of shooting at us, and then we run our six pounder up to the edge of the field and fired 6 balls at them and then run back. We had just got out of the way when they

> begun shelling us again, but we were not there. We run up and fired on them 3 times through the evening. They returned our fire every time till the last one they seemed to be still. So we went back about a mile and camped and we are here yet. We started back to take a stand on the road just now but we had not stayed on the road long before a long ranged rifled gun of another battery came and took the place of our 6 pounder, and we were sent back to the balance of our battery, and I won't write no more now.[22]

The action Walters described took place in the vicinity of Bottom's Bridge. Elements of Brig. Gen. Erasmus D. Keyes fourth Corps were ordered to scout along the Chickahominy. Keyes reported, "The enemy threw five or six shells before any of our artillery replied at all." Pelham's changing position led Keyes to believe that he had "at least one battery" opposing him.[23]

On the twenty-third, orders arrived that sent the battery to a point northwest of Richmond, where camp was established.[24] The next day, Pelham took his battery to Mechanicsville, but they arrived too late to participate in the skirmish. His West Point roommate, Rosser, now captain of the Washington Artillery, did manage to get one of his rifled guns into the fight, however, and was wounded during the action.[25] Returning to camp, the company spent the next week drilling under Pelham's watchful eye and recruiting its strength for the contest all knew lay ahead.

Not until the thirty-first was Pelham's Battery again ordered out to face the enemy. The battle of Fair Oaks, or Seven Pines, proved to be a disheartening affair for the Confederates. Pelham spent almost the entire day trying to reach the field and never fired a shot. His disappointment was echoed by the army, which had expected great things from Joe Johnston's plan. Instead, the bungling efforts of the division commanders to bring their men to grips with the Federals resulted in chaos. Johnston fell with a wound that incapacitated him for months. His successor was Robert E. Lee, and everyone from the generals down to the lowly privates wondered what the change in command would bring. Lee wasted little time showing them.

Maj. Gen. George B. McClellan failed to seize the moment fate had presented him. Johnston wounded, the Confederate army's attempt to halt the Union juggernaut frustrated, Lee's capacity to command doubted by many in the army, and Rebel morale plunging as the Federals drew within sight of Richmond created an opportunity for final victory, which Lincoln and all the North longed for. But McClellan sat on the doorstep of the capital as if awaiting an invitation to enter. Lee was not about to open the door and, in fact, took the time McClellan was obliging enough to grant him to strengthen the city's defenses and prepared to kick its unwelcome visitor off the porch.

The "King of Spades," as his men who had been put to work digging fortifications instead of fighting dubbed Lee, ordered Stuart to report to his headquarters. He had a little mission to discuss with his cavalry chieftain. Lee wanted Stuart to conduct a reconnaissance of McClellan's right flank north of the Chickahominy River. The Federal commander was extending a part of his army toward Fredericksburg to link up with reinforcements he was expecting to march south from there. The united armies would then make the final drive on Richmond. Lee desired to know if this extension would be vulnerable to an attack. Stuart left army headquarters and set to work organizing his force—a force that included two guns of the Stuart Horse Artillery but not its commander.

Just exactly what happened to John Pelham at this time is a mystery. There are three possibilities: He may have been on furlough, recruiting, or ill. Considering the first of these, it is difficult to believe that Pelham would ask for, let alone be granted, a furlough at this crucial time when the fate of the country hung on what would transpire over the next few days or weeks. His chosen profession was that of a soldier. He was well aware of what the army faced, and it can scarcely be imagined that he would want to be absent when it came to grips with its foe in what could be the final contest of the war. Furthermore, all able-bodied men were needed at their posts, and Pelham was especially needed to command a battery that had seen its first action only a little over a month before.

If Pelham had been recruiting, the records of the battery should support this. They do not. According to battery records, a total of sixteen men were added to the rolls between June 1 and June 30, but none during the dates of the raid. The recruiting officer in fifteen of the cases was Lt. James S. T. Shepherd. Pelham was the recruiting officer for one man during the month, but only the month and year are given. All the men enlisted in Richmond. There is no evidence that Pelham was away from Richmond recruiting, as these men are the only ones who joined the battery during the month.[26]

It would appear that Pelham was the victim of some illness during the period of the raid. Measles had already ravaged the battery, and other diseases were rampaging through the army as well. Several men had become ill with fever, and others had what one private called the "yellow ganders."[27] Taking this into consideration, along with the above facts, it would seem most likely that Pelham was suffering physically from some illness to the extent that he was unable to command the guns on the expedition.

Lt. James Breathed took Pelham's place and was ably seconded by Lt. William M. McGregor. During the reconnaissance, Breathed took charge of a twelve-pound howitzer, while McGregor commanded a rifled gun.[28] The column set out on June 12. The speed with which the expedition was conducted put a great strain on the artillery horses almost from the beginning. Lt. Col. William T. Martin of the Jeff Davis Legion reported that McGregor could not bring his gun forward in time to assist the cavalry in its attack at Tunstall's Station. For the most part, Breathed remained with the rear guard. Martin's report stated, "I would take occasion to mention the energy displayed by Lieutenant Breathed in overcoming the difficulties encountered in moving his piece of artillery, and the promptness shown in preparing for action on several occasions when there was reason to believe that the enemy were about to attack."[29] Stuart and his daring riders returned to Confederate lines on the fifteenth.

Although Pelham's trustworthy lieutenants had accomplished a significant feat and had brought their guns safely home, they could not have been completely satisfied. They had not had the opportunity to fire a single shot and had abandoned a limber when its pole broke on the south side of the Chickahominy River. However, the experience gained on this raid would stand them in good stead on similar expeditions in the future.

Stuart's foray provided Lee with the necessary information around which to plan his campaign to save Richmond. For several days following the raid, the horse artillery held to its camp northwest of the capital. There were new horses to train, and the men continued to drill incessantly. On the twenty-fifth, Pelham drew forage for 180 horses.[30] That same day, Stuart moved out to rendezvous with Jackson, who was coming from the Valley. The Stuart Horse Artillery and its intrepid leader were ready.

Stuart and Jackson united their commands on the twenty-fifth and bivouacked near Ashland for the night. Pelham's Battery was not needed until the twenty-seventh, when Stuart detached Lt. Col. William T. Martin with the Jeff Davis Legion and fourth Virginia Cavalry to scout in the vicinity of Old Church. Pelham and the Blakely accompanied him and assisted in determining the presence of the enemy by firing toward the church. Some cavalry was flushed but withdrew without contesting the ground. Meanwhile, Stuart pushed on past Beulah Church to Old Cold Harbor. Here at about 6:00 P.M., enemy artillery was seen moving on the road from Grapevine Bridge. The only artillery available to counter the Federal batteries was the horse artillery. Pelham was ordered forward with the Blakely and the Napoleon.[31]

Stuart's report described the fight that followed:

> The Blakely was disabled at the first fire, the enemy opening simultaneously eight pieces, proving afterward to be [Capt. Stephen H.] Weed's and [Capt. John C.] Tidball's batteries. Then ensued one of the most gallant and heroic feats of the war. The Napoleon gun, solitary and alone, received the fire of those batteries, concealed in the pines on a ridge commanding its ground, yet not a man quailed, and the noble captain directing the fire himself with a coolness and intrepidity only equaled by his previous brilliant career. The enemy's fire sensibly slackened under the determined fire of this Napoleon, which clung to its ground with unflinching tenacity. I had the opportunity of calling General Jackson's attention to the heroic conduct of the officers and men of this piece, and later he, by his personal efforts,

> re-enforced it with several batteries of rifled pieces, which, firing, advanced *en échelon* about dark and drove the enemy from his last foothold on the right.[32]

Jackson also praised Pelham in his report, stating that the young horse artillery commander had "bravely dashed forward and opened on the Federal batteries posted on the left of our infantry."[33] Pelham had again made his mark.

On July 5, Pvt. William P. Walters, who was in Richmond with the disabled Blakely, wrote to his beloved wife of his experiences during the fighting on the twenty-seventh:

> Dear wife and children and friends,
>
> I seat myself this evening to write you a few lines [to] let you know that I am tolerable well at this time, hoping these few lines may find you all well. I wrote a few days ago but will write again. I have not heard from you since Mister Hall came down here. I don't doubt but you have written, but we have been scattered so I have not got them. I have not seen Bill [Pvt. William A. Simpson] since the 26 of last month. We got with him and the rest of the boys that was gone when David Hall was here that evening and stayed with them that night and next morning [June 27] me and some of the boys started for the battle field and left him behind with some of the guns that didn't go in. George Brown was wounded and died that night. None of the rest of us got hurt as it happened, but it's only Providence that saved us for we went on the left of General Jackson's army and commenced [firing] on the Yankees with our rifle gun and Napoleon gun but our two guns was a poor show against 8 or 9 Yankee cannon [Capt. Stephen H. Weed's and Capt. John C. Tidball's batteries] which were throwing balls and shells at us fast enough but worse than all our rifle piece [the Blakely] broke its elevating screw and left us there with one gun. I rammed the balls down as fast as I could. We all worked hard. Captain Pelham helped us himself and General Stuart hollered, "Give it to them boys! You soon will have help!" And it came in good time, for we were nearly broke down when 6 guns fell in on our right and 4 guns on our left. They were fresh batteries and commenced a quick fire on the Yankees which did them as much harm as it did me good. The captain told us to quit firing and rest. Rest does good even when it is taken under a shower of ball, for we soon commenced again like a fresh set of boys and soon heard the last boom of our enemy groaning through the air but thank God its groaning and flying was like most of the rest of them. It only told us it was coming and the closer it come the louder it hollered. [Word illegible] I cannot describe the noise they make, but we all have it. They say taker, take. It was getting dark then, and after pur-

> suing them 1 mile we went back to an old field and camped for the night. The boys that was not in till the battle was over was glad to see us come out safe.
>
> Next morning [June 28] I slept till sunup when the captain and lieutenant came and told me you ought to be up to receive the honor and praise I had won the day before. I told them rest did me more good than praise. They said while the rest was falling down dozing and moving about I stood at my post like nothing was the matter. That was all true but I stood straight on the ground, for I can dodge a ball that is passing better standing, for I can tell where it is going and when it is bouncing on the ground you have a heap better chance. But it is dangerous any way.[34]

Walter's account adds one important point even Stuart failed to note. Pelham was down with his men, helping to serve the gun like a private. Obviously, Pelham's actions impressed the rank and file as much as they did the high command.

On the Federal side, Weed and Tidball told a slightly different story of the artillery duel. Their concern was not for the artillery fire they were receiving alone. The Confederate infantry was also threatening to flank them and was firing on them at the same time as Pelham and the other batteries. Weed stated:

> Between 5 and 6 o'clock a line of infantry was seen crossing the road at double-quick to gain the wood on their right. At about the same time their artillery opened fire to divert our attention from them. The artillery fire was, however, entirely disregarded. . . . About 6:30 P.M. they [the Confederate infantry] gained the open ground in their front of the wood, and opened a fire of musketry at close range upon the battery. No order had been given to retire, but it soon became very evident that the position was no longer tenable.[35]

He does not credit the fire of the Confederate artillery as being a contributing factor to his withdrawal.

Tidball, on the other hand, did give some credit to the Rebel artillery. He reported, "The ammunition of my limbers, with the exception of a few rounds which I wished to retain for an emergency, was exhausted, and being now exposed to a sharp fire of musketry as well as of artillery I thought it prudent to withdraw and seek a position where my few remaining rounds might be effective."[36] Obviously, for both officers it was the advance of the Confederate infantry that caused them to leave the field and not the *"en échelon"* advance of the Confederate artillery. Weed recorded that his battery fired 1,000 rounds and Tidball's another 600. That they were running short of ammunition should not be surprising.

Col. Stapleton Crutchfield, Jackson's artillery chief, stated in his report:

> About 5 p.m., or perhaps a little later, the batteries of Captains [John B.] Brockenbrough, [James McD.] Carrington, and [Alfred R.] Courtney were ordered in near the left to engage the enemy's guns, then firing heavily on our infantry. They went up in good style and under a hot fire; but so soon as they engaged the batteries of the enemy the fire of the latter grew wild and did very little damage.[37]

These comments indicate that Crutchfield did not believe that his artillery was the target of the Federals' guns. Interestingly, Crutchfield made no reference to Pelham's participation in the action, even though Jackson did.

None of this detracts from Pelham's performance. The Union artillery fire that fell around Pelham's, Brockenbrough's, Carrington's, and Courtney's Batteries was no less deadly if the Federals were overshooting the infantry than if they were targeting the Confederate artillery. Stuart was obviously proud of his chief of artillery. His account of Pelham's role in the battle may be criticized as being a bit overblown and romanticized, but it is understandable, considering his goal of trying to gain recognition and a promotion for Pelham.[38]

On June 28, Stuart pushed on toward White House Landing, which had been McClellan's base. The White House plantation had been the home of Martha Custis when she married George Washington. It now belonged to Col. William H. F. "Rooney" Lee of the 9th Virginia Cavalry. Stuart encountered token resistance until just past Tunstall's Station on the banks of Black Creek. Here, with the bridge destroyed, Stuart faced Federal cavalry and what appeared to be artillery. Pelham was ordered to the front, came up rapidly, unlimbered, and opened fire. The blue cavalry scattered, and the supposed guns failed to return Pelham's salute. Stuart's engineer officer, Capt. William W. Blackford, was set to repairing the bridge, but night fell before the work was completed. Everyone slept on his arms till morning, when the column moved on to the White House.

During the day, smoke had been seen rising from the direction of the landing, and at night, the sky was aglow from the flames of McClellan's burning supplies. He would leave as little to the Rebels as possible. With the morning, Stuart rode on to what was left of McClellan's base of operations. Much was desolation, including Lee's home. A gunboat was seen on the river, and Stuart ordered some sharpshooters and Pelham's howitzer forward to chase it off.[39] As the boat made its way downstream, the howitzer was sent at a gallop after it to hasten its departure.

Stuart dispatched Col. Fitz Lee's 1st Virginia Cavalry and the Napoleon gun of the horse artillery under Breathed to observe the enemy between Bottom's Bridge and Forge [Jones's] Bridge. The rest of the command drew rations and helped themselves to what was salvageable from the ruin. Fearing that the Federals might return to cart off what had not been destroyed, Stuart burned what he could not carry with him. A note from Lee had arrived that morning cautioning Stuart to be watchful of any Union move in his direction. He replied that McClellan's army was retreating not to White House Landing, but to the James River. Lee had already received information to this effect. Stuart's note confirmed it. The Confederate commander's subsequent movements culminated in the battles of White Oak Swamp and Malvern Hill, as McClellan tried to maneuver toward his new base at Harrison's Landing on the James.

As the thirtieth dawned, Stuart led the cavalry—minus the Cobb Legion, which remained at the White House—in the direction taken by the 1st Virginia the day before. Fitz Lee was at Long Bridge, so Stuart took up a position near Forge Bridge. Lee reported that enemy pickets and two pieces of artillery were visible. He opened fire with the Napoleon, but the gun's trail broke with the first shot. With both the Blakely and the Napoleon disabled and the other guns detached, Stuart had only one section of twelve-pound howitzers with him.

While the 1st Virginia grappled with the Federals without the Napoleon, Stuart engaged 200 Federal infantry, Capt. J. C. White's squadron of the 3rd Pennsylvania Cavalry, and a section of Battery M, fifth U.S. Artillery, under Lt. Valentine H. Stone at Forge Bridge. Pelham wheeled the howitzers into position and began shelling the enemy. Stone's two guns answered him. At this point, the reports of the contending sides diverge. Stone, who was conducting his first independent command with both new men and horses, thought that he was confronted by eight cannons and admitted to being under fire from 1:00 to 6:00 P.M. He stated that he completely silenced the Confederate guns for two hours, but that the enemy succeeded in crossing the river and pushing him back two miles. The lieutenant reported his horse and one cavalryman killed during the action.[40] White's superior, Col. William W. Averell, recorded that his cavalry held the bridge until night, and that White's horse was killed. He made no reference to any casualties among the men.[41]

On the Confederate side, Stuart's report is rather lacking in detail. He admitted to a spirited duel between the artillery, which resulted in a Federal withdrawal so rapid that the infantry abandoned its knapsacks. A scouting party was pushed beyond the bridge to ascertain the enemy's position, but the increasing darkness finally led Stuart to order the command to bivouac for the night. He noted that the enemy lost two men and two horses killed, while he suffered no casualties.[42]

Lt. Col. William T. Martin's Jeff Davis Legion was the vanguard of Stuart's force that day. His report stated:

> Monday, June 30, my command, with Pelham's artillery, now moved toward the Forge Bridge, encountering a few of the enemy's skirmishers. It was discovered, as the bridge was approached, that the enemy already held the position with infantry, cavalry, and artillery.

> Captain Pelham was advanced with two of his pieces to a point within 400 yards of the bridge, and opened with his pieces (howitzers). He was replied to by two rifled pieces, but soon silenced them, and they withdrew to the hills beyond the river.
>
> A reconnoitering force was crossed over the river to examine the position assumed by the enemy, and was charged upon by cavalry in the afternoon. In order to clear the road of this cavalry Captain Pelham was ordered with two twelve-pounder howitzers to take position on the bridge and shell the road. Just as he unlimbered the enemy opened upon him with two rifled pieces, one at only 400 yards' distance. As this gun had been trained upon the road occupied by the pieces of Captain Pelham its fire was very accurate and rapid, yet in fifteen minutes the enemy was driven away with a loss of 2 men and 2 horses killed and several wounded. This force of the enemy had been sent to repair the bridge, and had begun work when we attacked them. As far as could be ascertained the enemy had one regiment of infantry, a squadron of cavalry, and two pieces of artillery in the forenoon, and this force was increased toward afternoon.[43]

From all these reports, it would appear that the Federals did succeed in holding up Stuart at the bridge or its vicinity until dark, as Averell attested. However, Stone's silencing of Pelham's guns could only have come at the time Pelham was limbering forward to the bridge, a period of time somewhat less than two hours.[44] Depending on the length of time it took for Stuart to decide to push across the bridge and to organize a force for doing so, the interval may have been extended. Stone's inexperience may have lengthened the time in his mind to two hours.

As for Pelham driving off Stone on the two occasions reported, the evidence would seem to indicate that the young Union artillery officer was overmatched. He did withdraw from his first position and from his second near the end of the day. He was probably under the fire of Pelham's howitzers both times. The time factor of five hours over which the contest was fought shows that Stuart was being cautious. Not knowing the size of the force to his front, he proceeded carefully. In the end, both sides got what they wanted—the Confederates the bridge and the Federals the delay of the enemy. Pelham had proven his value to Stuart once again.

While Stuart followed up the taking of Forge Bridge on July 1, Lee and McClellan fought the battle of Malvern Hill. On the second, Lt. J. Emmett Shaw, with a twelve-pound howitzer, reported to Lt. Col. William T. Martin, commanding the Boykin Rangers, the Jeff Davis Legion, and Company H of the 4th Virginia. Martin had been ordered to picket the River Road and to advance along the road leading to Haxall's Landing. As he approached Haxall's, Martin divided his force into two sections, sending the smaller to Haxall's and proceeding with the larger and Shaw's gun to Shirley Plantation below Haxall's. As the column approached Shirley, the enemy's pickets fired on it. In pushing farther on, Martin encountered increasing sharpshooter fire and began to suspect an ambush. He called for the howitzer, which Shaw brought up in fine style. As the gun was coming forward, scouts reported a Federal infantry regiment lying behind a line of bushes on elevated ground to the right of the road. Shaw was cautioned as to the location of the enemy and effectively masked his gun. His opening shot threw the Union line into confusion and caused them to retreat rapidly toward Berkeley. Martin pursued until he came up against a brigade of infantry stretched across the road. Having only 300 men and but six rounds left for the howitzer, Martin called a halt and fell back to Haxall's. Shaw's performance in independent command reflected well on Pelham's training regimen. Both the officers and men of the battery were growing in experience and spirit.

While Martin prodded the Yanks around Haxall's Landing and Shirley Plantation, Stuart mounted a reconnaissance to Charles City Court House in the hope that he could fall on the flank of McClellan's columns if they were still in motion. The Rebel cavalry quickly discovered that the Federal commander had not ventured that far. Stuart needed more information and that night dispatched Pelham with the other howitzer and a squadron of the 1st Virginia Cavalry under Capt. Charles R. Irving on a scout toward Westover Plantation. Pelham completed his mission and sent a message to Stuart:

July 2nd 1862

Genl.

Our pickets are now below Mr. Allen Bradley's farm—I fired on the enemy's pickets and drove them in. Capt. Irving sent a scouting party out. They report the coast in front of us clear. I questioned Mr. Bradley about the position of the enemy— [sketch of Evelynton Heights appears here]. He says in Westover and Berkeley they have all their wagons and cattle. It is a beautiful plain commanded by Eventon Hills [Evelynton Heights]—one mile & 36 yards—he says that guns placed on the hill commands every thing as far as the river—the hill is two miles from our present position. He reports the road leading to this Depot blocked up with wagons & stragglers. He also says they have a considerable force there—all they have.

Mr. Turner knows this Bradley and says he is a reliable man.

Very Respt'y
Brig Genl JEB Stuart — Jno. Pelham
Comdg Cavy. — Capt. S.H.A.[45]

Pelham's report spurred Stuart to action. After forwarding it to Gen. R. E. Lee, Stuart took his command, except for the 9th Virginia Cavalry, which was stationed on his left to watch Forge Bridge, and occupied the heights, chasing off a squadron of Federal cavalry. It was 9:00 in the morning.

Stuart's next action has been controversial. Although his driving off the pickets should have served as a warning to the Federals that the Confederates now occupied the heights, they did not immediately dispute its possession. Stuart believed that Lee was in the process of sending troops to reinforce him and, in his usual aggressive style, ordered Pelham to open fire. Positioned on the River Road, the lone howitzer commenced dropping shells among the enemy camped below. Momentary panic resulted. The Federals reacted by sending infantry and artillery against Stuart's small force. By 2:00 in the afternoon, the cavalry skirmishers were down to a few rounds per man, and Pelham had but two rounds left for the howitzer. No Confederate infantry was in sight, Longstreet having become lost on the way, so Stuart pulled back off the hill.

There were those in the Confederate army who condemned Stuart's offensive posture as hasty. Many felt that he should have remained quiet and waited for the infantry to arrive. There may be some merit in this view, though mostly through hindsight. Stuart's performance throughout the campaign had been one of individual initiative and aggressiveness. The idea of taking the war to the enemy conformed to Stuart's modus operandi since the war's beginning. Stuart was unable to divine what lay in the future and therefore could not see Longstreet's delay in reaching him. All he knew was that his past experiences of aggressive action had been successful many more times than the passivity he observed on the part of the Federal high command.[46]

Pelham's role in the entire affair evidenced Stuart's growing confidence in him. The youthful artillery commander, with but one gun and a handful of men to serve it, was placed in charge of the reconnaissance over a captain leading a squadron. Pelham's note to Stuart summarized the situation and recommended the appropriate action. His questioning of a local citizen and his confirming of that citizen's reliability demonstrated his overall astuteness and affirmed Stuart's decision to give him command.

The fourth and fifth passed relatively quietly as Stuart and the cavalry engaged in scouting and watching the river. The horse artillery had been used extensively, and everyone was in need of a rest. The Blakely had returned by the afternoon of the fifth, just in time for Stuart to send it to Wilcox's Landing, about four miles below McClellan's army at Harrison's Landing. Col. Stephen D. Lee reported to Stuart with a battery of rifled cannons, Capt. Charles W. Squires's Washington Artillery. Stuart sent the Blakely along with Lee, who was under orders to attack Federal transports on the James River. Pelham did not accompany the Blakely. Instead, his fellow Alabamian Lt. William M. McGregor commanded the gun.

Colonel Lee reached Wilcox's Landing about 8:00 on the night of the fifth. Squires's Battery was placed in position, opened fire at 2:00 A.M. on the sixth, and maintained a steady cannonade until dawn. The battery was then withdrawn to the Waddell farm, where the men and horses were allowed to rest. Up to this time, the Washington Artillery had born the brunt of the fighting. According to Squires's report, McGregor had not yet been engaged.[47] Around 6:00 P.M., a section of Capt. Arthur L. Rogers's Loudoun Artillery arrived and reported to Lee, bringing the number of guns to seven. Near 8:00 P.M., accompanied by Col. Thomas L. Rosser's 5th Virginia Cavalry, the artillery left Waddell's farm and marched nine miles to Wyanoke Neck, where the guns were placed near the river on the farm of Thomas Wilcox.

At sunrise on the seventh, the combined battery opened fire on a grounded transport, the *Juniata,* which suffered some loss. The transports came under fire throughout the day. One vessel was sunk. Another was abandoned on the south shore of the river, and several were damaged. Union gunboats, which came to the aid of the transports, returned fire, which had no effect, but they were not fired upon. The transports were the sole targets of the Confederate artillery. That evening, Lee pulled the guns back to Charles City Court House, where the crews camped for the night. In all, the artillery fired 172 rounds. McGregor, who was not utilized to any great extent, expended twenty.[48]

The action against the Federal transports was the last for Pelham's Battery on the Peninsula. Along with the majority of the cavalry, it was withdrawn on July 10 and went into camp, at first near Richmond and later near Hanover Court House. The campaign had been exhausting, debilitating the men physically, mentally, and emotionally. A great many men of the battery who had been virtually raw recruits when the fighting began were now veterans. Losses in the battery had been light—one dead, three wounded, and one captured.[49] The battery had proven its value to Pelham, Stuart, Jackson, and others, and if its commander had anything to say, it would continue to do so. It wasn't long before the men were back drilling.

CHAPTER 5

From the Peninsula to the Potomac

"They are whipped this time, but I don't know whether they will stay whipped or not."

The restful days spent in the camps around Hanover Court House during the latter part of July and the early days of August 1862 would be remembered by the men of the cavalry and the horse artillery for as long as they lived. There began the process of rejuvenation of body, mind, and spirit after the grueling campaign against McClellan. The respite from the war extended over four weeks, with only an occasional brief interruption. Though the Army of the Potomac lay only a day's march away, there was none of the concern and fear that had gripped Richmond just a few weeks earlier. Instead, jubilation for the victory won by Lee and the army was felt by all, though it was tempered by the knowledge of what that victory had cost. The dead numbered in the thousands, and thousands more wounded filled the hospitals in Richmond. Many who had survived the campaign mourned for their dead comrades. More longed for an end to the war. This turmoil of emotion swirled throughout the camps of the Army of Northern Virginia. The men of the Stuart Horse Artillery were not immune to it.

> Richmond VA July the 12th 1862
>
> Dear Wife,
>
> I seat myself this evening to inform you that I [am in] tolerably good health except the rheumatism [that] is pestering me some, hoping these few lines may find you all well. We expect to leave here this evening or in the morning, but I don't know where we are going, but I expect we will go up the Valley. Our army has all fallen back to Richmond again where they were when the fight commenced, but I don't know where the Yankees are. Some say they are going down the river and some say they are following us up. The papers say old Abe is calling for 100 thousand more men and if that is the case men are plenty in the North.

The soldiers are getting tired of the fuss down here as ever a dog was of hot mush. The Yankee prisoners say they are tired too, but they are forced to fight or starve, and we will soon be forced to fight and starve both. We have gone 21 days on a six days' rations and fought and skirmished pretty nigh all the time, but we got some Yankee victuals on our way. I have got some sugar and coffee yet that I got out of a camp. I don't think there will ever be another battle as this for [both] sides have lost so many men that I think they will fight it out now like men, not take a dog fight again.

I have read histories of wars but never read of such a time as I have seen down here. One day's fight was bad enough, but when it comes to fighting a week or two I get tired of it. I never was so tired of anything in my life as I am of this foolish fuss now. When I first got down here I would sit and listen for an hour or two at a band of music, but now it makes [me] sick almost to hear them. But worse than that is the roar of the guns. Some people say after they have been in one fight they never mind it, but it isn't the case with me, for the more I fight the worse I hate it. The worst I ever dread a battle is when I am going in the field. After I get in and fire a few shots I don't mind it so bad, but the next time it is just as bad as at the first.

If I thought this war would last 3 months longer I would give 500 dollars for a substitute. I could get one any day at Richmond. A man told me so today, but I have not got the money, and I have heard that those that hired them would have to go again, but I don't reckon it is so. I will find out how things are working and if I find out they are going to fight always I will try and get the money and hire one in my place. I think I have done fighting enough for my share of the Confederacy, but I will have to wait till I can get the money. I think I can borrow it from the rest of the boys [word illegible] we draw [pay] again.

You wrote you all would hire me and Bill [Pvt. William A. Simpson] a substitute if [it] took everything you had. If we had the money here we could get one and have something left to start on maybe, but it will take me a long time to make 6 hundred dollars besides losing my summers work. But if I can get out of this war honorably with the clothes on my back I will be glad, and [if] I don't get home in time to seed this Fall you will be in a worse [word missing] than I will, for they are bound to feed me a little but nobody is bound to support you but myself and my wages is all the chance now, and if vegetables get as high there as they are here they won't half support you. But if I was at home I could make something to eat. General [Brig. Gen. John H.] Winder says we can be transferred to [Col.

> Robert C.] Trigg's regiment, but it is going to be hard work to get away from here.
>
> The New York papers acknowledge they are whipped this time, but I don't know whether they will stay whipped or not. I must quit for this time by requesting you to give my best respects to all of my friends and remember me. Write often as you can direct your letters as before. Till I write again good-bye. Tell the children I hope I will soon come home to them.
>
> Wm. P. Walters to M. E. Walters and friends[1]

Walters's rheumatism and depression were not the only things bothering him that July. On the sixteenth, he wrote that he was suffering great pain in his ears as a result of the reports of the cannons when fired. He noted further that all through the battles on the Peninsula, the pain had plagued him, and it seemed to be worsening.[2] In a letter written on the eighteenth, he elaborated on the activities in which he and the rest of the men of the battery were engaged.

> I have no news of importance to write at this time only [that] we have been resting for a while. We don't have anything to do but feed and water our horses and catch ticks and lice and chiggers which leads us a hard life. Body lice are as plentiful as dirt. We get as full of them sometimes as a dog is of fleas, but they ain't as bad as Yankees.[3]

While it would appear that Walters only had to attend the horses and fight lice, others of the battery had drawn different work. The battery was the recipient of some of the spoils taken from McClellan's army. Two Napoleons and a twelve-pound howitzer were added to the battery's armament, along with some caissons and additional equipment.[4] These pieces and the other guns and equipment of the battery needed repair and refurbishing. Even while wishing for peace, those assigned to the task of readying the guns worked with an energy fueled by pride in their unit's accomplishments.

Lt. James S. T. Shepherd, who had spent much of the campaign on recruiting duty in Richmond, was still at his post and continued to send new men to the battery. From July 9 to August 18, twenty-nine men were added to the rolls. On July 19, Pelham signed a requisition order for cooking utensils for 150 men. The battery's complement of men seemed to be growing. However, there were men whose discontentment with the war led them to hire substitutes of questionable worth, while others simply disappeared. Private Walters wrote to his wife on July 22, "Some of our boys have run off or went off, one or the other. 3 Altizers and 2 Nolleys[5] are the last that left, and they are going to send Robert Lancaster and Wall[6] after them, but I don't believe they have gone home."[7] Walters and others wanted desperately to go home and help their families work their farms. In the end most stayed. Words like honor and duty still held great meaning for some.

Stuart's performance before and throughout the Peninsula campaign was rewarded when on July 25 he was commissioned a major general. Col. Fitzhugh Lee of the 1st Virginia was promoted to brigadier general and given a brigade composed of the 1st, 3rd, 4th, 5th, and 9th Virginia. Col. Wade Hampton, commanding the Hampton Legion, was also promoted to brigadier general and given a brigade consisting of the 10th Virginia, 1st North Carolina, 2nd South Carolina, Cobb (Georgia) Legion, and Jeff Davis Legion. Pelham's Battery would have been the only horse artillery in the division, but Hampton petitioned Secretary of War George W. Randolph to be allowed to convert the Hampton Legion's Washington Artillery, commanded by Capt. James F. Hart, to horse artillery. His request was granted, and the battery began the conversion process.

None of the changes to the cavalry affected Pelham's Battery except that until Hart was able to take the field, the Stuart Horse Artillery would have to serve both cavalry brigades. Through the end of July, the war seemed far away, as McClellan's army remained relatively quiet in its camp at Harrison's Landing. These were days of reviews, dances, and pleasant social calls on families in the vicinity of Pelham's camp. Pelham made the rounds with Stuart and his staff, and if the young Alabamian was disappointed that he had not received a promotion when others of Stuart's staff did, he gave no outward sign. Stuart had campaigned mightily for him, but in the end, Richmond would only grant so many commissions. Pelham would have to wait.

While Stuart's cavalry underwent its change from one to two brigades, the rest of Lee's army was also experiencing a restructuring. The unwieldy divisional organization gave way to two wings commanded by Maj. Gen. James Longstreet and Maj. Gen. Thomas J. Jackson. Divisions and brigades were shuffled, and generals who had failed to come up to Lee's expectations were transferred or resigned. Lee was preparing for the next campaign and did not want a repetition of the failures that had occurred on the Peninsula. In the midst of implementing his reorganization plans, he received disturbing news from Northern Virginia.

Back on June 26, the Federal government had united its forces left in the Valley with those east of the mountains. The new army was christened the Army of Virginia and was placed under the command of Maj. Gen. John Pope, who had experienced some minor successes in the West. These troops, which were located in the vicinity of Fredericksburg, were charged with defending the approaches to Washington City. Pope quickly demonstrated he was not one to sit idly on the defensive. He advanced to the Rapidan River and began to threaten the Virginia Central Railroad. By July 13, Lee was concerned enough about Pope to send Jackson's and Ewell's divisions to Gordonsville. Jackson himself followed on the nineteenth and was joined by A. P. Hill's division at the end of the month. The Federal commander probed out from Fredericksburg toward Gordonsville. Lee wanted information about what the enemy was up to around Fredericksburg. Stuart was to provide it.

With Fitz Lee's Brigade and the Stuart Horse Artillery, Stuart set out on August 4 toward Bowling Green and camped a few miles east of the town. The next day, he headed straight for Port Royal on the Rappahannock River. The column arrived around 11:00 A.M. A Federal cavalry squadron had just passed through Port Royal, and a quick pursuit netted about a dozen prisoners. Around 1:00 P.M., Stuart moved on. He camped near Grace (Round Oak) Church. Early on the morning of the sixth, Stuart pushed toward the Telegraph Road, intersecting it at Massaponax Church. The leading squadron under Capt. Peyton R. Berkeley of the 3rd Virginia turned north on the Telegraph Road, charged a Federal column, and captured several wagons and a number of prisoners. The second squadron, led by Lt. Col. John T. Thornton, also of the 3rd, headed south, capturing more wagons and prisoners, until encountering the enemy's rear guard along the Po River.

Stuart soon discovered that he had barely missed running into the infantry brigades of Brigadier Generals John P. Hatch and John Gibbon, who were marching south toward Hanover Court House. It was their column's wagon train that Berkeley and Thornton had collided with. The 4th Virginia and a section of the horse artillery, including the Blakely gun, rushed to support Thornton.[8] The Federal infantry began to deploy and offered stiffer resistance. The Blakely was unlimbered and had fired only a few rounds when its elevating screw broke, rendering the piece useless.[9] At that point, Stuart determined that all had been gained that was worth gaining and began to fall back up the Telegraph Road. Pelham and the remaining gun leapfrogged from hill to hill, firing on the enemy to harass its advance. The cavalry turned off onto the Bowling Green Road about two miles south of Massaponax Church, and after a final salvo, Pelham followed. The Federals permitted Stuart to ride away, not that their infantry could effectively pursue the gray cavalry anyway, but the heat was staggering and all were content to allow the contest to end.

Stuart was pleased with his eighty-five prisoners and the fact that he had interrupted another Federal raid. He praised several officers, including Berkeley and Thornton. Strangely, Pelham's name is absent from Stuart's entire report of the affair. The horse artillery is mentioned several times, but neither its gallant commander nor any of the other officers received mention. Stuart could not have been displeased with the horse artillery's performance, except for the disabling of the Blakely, which was becoming something of a habit, so his reasons for failing to include Pelham remain a mystery.

The cavalry and artillery returned to the friendly surroundings of the camps near Hanover Court House on August 7 and settled back into a more peaceful routine. Capt. J. Hardeman Stuart, the cavalry's signal officer, put it in his diary that on the eighth, all he did was relax and sleep.[10] Similar entries followed, but events elsewhere were conspiring to bring these golden days to an end. Stuart left on the ninth for an inspection tour of Brig. Gen. Beverly H. Robertson's Brigade, which consisted of the 2nd, 6th, 7th, and 12th Virginia Cavalry, the 17th Virginia Cavalry Battalion, and Chew's Battery. This brigade had been with Jackson. Though Stuart did not have actual authority over Robertson, he would soon receive it.

Returning to Hanover Court House on the thirteenth, Stuart began preparations for the cavalry's departure. Robert E. Lee left to join Jackson that same day and would soon bring Stuart north to face Pope's cavalry. The coming campaign became the talk of the camps and the topic of letters home. On August 15, Private Walters wrote a letter to his wife recounting his service in Pelham's Battery and what he longed for in the future:

> Dear Wife and Children,
>
> It is with great pleasure that I seat myself this morning to drop you a few more lines to let you know that I am in tolerable good health at this time, hoping these few lines will find you all well. I have no news of importance to write at this time only they are fixing for a battle in [the] Valley. 5 carloads of soldiers went up from Richmond yesterday. I have heard no straight news from the last fight up there only that Major [Henry] Lane was killed.[11] I didn't hear how the rest of his company came out. I expect we will move up that way in a few days, but it can't be any worse place than I have seen, but I don't expect we will have to go through as much danger as [word illegible] for I think they are getting tired of running us in every hole where they can hear the Yankees are. This last scout was a good one but they come so my being [word illegible] that I don't think they will try another shortly.
>
> We have done our share since we have been in [the] service. If we are militia it is five months today since I left home, and we have been all over eastern Virginia and in 33 skirmishes and 2 regular fights while there are some volunteers that have been out 18 months that haven't [been in] one yet. The time flies away fast. It looks like it was only last week that I left you and home but we are always going and in a fluster that time passes, and we don't notice it. But I expect it is very different with you there at home by yourself. I wish I was there with you. Your company suits me better than the company I am in. Sometimes I think I would give every thing I am worth if I could get [to] see you and the children and stay with you the balance of my days in peace.
>
> So no more at present but remain your loving husband till death. Give my love and respects to all friends. I will send you 20 postage stamps in this letter. Tell Molly and sis I haven't forgotten them yet.
>
> Wm P Walters / M E Walters[12]

The next day, the cavalry and horse artillery saddled up and rode away from their camps, taking fond memories of the hospitality shown them by the families of Hanover County.

As Pelham's Battery made its way toward the Rapidan on the sixteenth, Chew's Battery was already there and engaging the enemy. Chew had been left in the Valley when Jackson marched east to join Lee. From June 14 until July 22, the battery had remained in the vicinity of Harrisonburg doing little more than light picket duty. On the twenty-third, camp was broken up, and the battery accompanied Col. Asher W. Harman's 12th Virginia Cavalry through New Market to the foot of the Massanutten, where everyone camped for the night.

The following day, the battery moved in the direction of Luray but encountered Yankee pickets on the east bank of the South Fork of the Shenandoah. A twelve-pound shell scattered about a dozen Federals, who retreated toward Luray. Chew pulled back about half a mile to await developments. Before too long, a four-gun battery wheeled into position on a commanding hill and answered the Rebel challenge. The bombardment produced no casualties, though Colonel Harmon had one solid shot bounce right under his horse. Since neither side wished to cross the river to get at the other, the day ended quietly, with the Confederates falling back to their camp of the previous night.[13]

Chew and his men rode back to Harrisonburg and settled down once again to picket duty until July 31, when they received orders to move east. The long march wound through Harrisonburg, Mount Crawford, Brown's Gap, Ivy Depot, Charlottesville, Keswick Depot, Barboursville, and Somerset, until the men reached Orange Court House on August 8. Here the battery went into camp. The battle of Cedar Mountain was fought on the ninth, but Chew's Battery was not engaged, though it was under fire for about twenty minutes. On the tenth, a brief scout east along the line of the Orange and Alexandria Railroad was made. A day of rest followed. On the twelfth, the battery moved about a quarter of a mile and joined Robertson's Brigade. Some Federal infantry appeared and began to advance. Chew put one gun into battery to dissuade them. The Yankee threat proved hollow, and the battery limbered and marched to Orange Court House.[14]

Picket duty first east then west of Orange Court House occupied the days between the thirteenth and fifteenth. On August 16, Chew went into battery on the south bank of the Rapidan to support the 6th Virginia Cavalry, which had crossed the river and had driven in the enemy's cavalry pickets. Federal infantry in skirmish order emerged from the woods, hastening the 6th's return. Chew opened fire with two rifled pieces, and the line of blue melted back into the trees. The battery limbered and rode back to its camp at Orange Court House. The town was abustle with troops.[15]

The troops that were arriving by rail, horse, and foot were part of Robert E. Lee's plans to trap Pope's army between the Rapidan and Rappahannock Rivers and destroy him. Jeb Stuart's role was to circle behind Pope and burn the railroad bridge near Rappahannock Station. The problem was that Stuart's cavalry was scattered. Hampton's Brigade was near Richmond, Fitz Lee's was at Hanover Court House, and Robertson's was at Orange Court House. To implement Lee's plan, Stuart chose Fitz Lee's Brigade and ordered Lee to move his brigade on the seventeenth to the vicinity of Raccoon Ford on the Rapidan, where Stuart planned to rendezvous with him. The plan went awry. Instead of marching straight for Raccoon Ford, Lee took a detour to Louisa Court House to provision his men. Meanwhile, Stuart proceeded to Verdiersville, where he expected to meet Lee. When Lee failed to materialize, Stuart dispatched his adjutant, Maj. Norman FitzHugh, to look for him. FitzHugh rode into a Federal cavalry patrol and was captured. Stuart almost suffered the same fate but managed to escape, though he lost his famed plumed hat and other articles of clothing. Worse, FitzHugh had on his person a copy of Robert E. Lee's orders. With the knowledge these revealed about Lee's plan to entrap him, Pope, who had already suspected something was up and had begun to withdraw his forces, fell back rapidly behind the Rappahannock. He was safe for the moment; Lee would have to start planning from scratch.

Fitz Lee's Brigade finally arrived on the eighteenth but was in no condition for a forced march. The following day was spent resting and preparing for action. On the twentieth, Lee's and Robertson's Brigades pushed over the Rapidan in pursuit of Pope's retreating columns. Pelham's Battery moved with Lee, though a number of men remained in camp in Orange County with the broken-down horses.[16] Chew's Battery and Col. Thomas T. Munford's 2nd Virginia Cavalry, which was detached from Robertson's Brigade, crossed the Rapidan at Mitchell's Ford and marched on the left of Jackson's advancing infantry.

Moving in advance of Longstreet's Corps, Fitz Lee collided with the Federals shortly after crossing the river. Pelham put all of his guns into action and threw two howitzers forward to press the enemy more closely. There was little resistance until near Kelly's Ford, where the blue cavalry made a brief stand and then quickly withdrew over the Rappahannock. The presence on the north bank of heavy Federal artillery with infantry support ended all pursuit.[17]

Stuart accompanied Robertson. They encountered Brig. Gen. George D. Bayard's Federal cavalry brigade between Stevensburg and Brandy Station. Bayard, under orders not to bring on a general engagement, pulled back the 1st Maine and the 1st Rhode Island while holding Stuart and Robertson with the 2nd New York, the 1st New Jersey, and the 1st Pennsylvania. Col. William E. "Grumble" Jones's 7th Virginia had some initial success, but a strong line of skirmishers thrown out by Bayard drove him back. The repulse was temporary, as Stuart hurled the remainder of Robertson's Brigade at the 2nd New York. Caught in the middle of a maneuver, the New Yorkers broke. The 1st New Jersey followed suit except for a squadron that Bayard placed in a line of woods, where their carbine fire repulsed the Confederates.

The time gained allowed Bayard to withdraw to the ford, where he was under the cover of two regiments of infantry from Brig. Gen. George L. Hartsuff's Brigade. Capt. James Thompson's 2nd Maryland Battery (Battery C, Pennsylvania Light Artillery) and Capt. Ezra W. Matthews's Battery F, 1st Pennsylvania Artillery, supported the infantry from south of the river.[18] Stuart bemoaned the fact that he had no artillery to challenge the enemy's guns. All he could do was watch Bayard's Brigade cross the river and escape. Just then, Pelham galloped up. Fitz Lee, who was at Kelly's Ford, had been sent for when it appeared that the Federals might be brought to bay. Lee dispatched the 1st and 5th Virginia with Pelham to Stuart. But before the guns could be thrown into battery, Stuart realized the opportunity had passed. Chew was unavailable, being with Munford, and Pelham arrived minutes too late. Frustrated, Stuart called off the pursuit.

On the twenty-first, the action moved to Beverly's Ford, where Col. Thomas L. Rosser's 5th Virginia pushed across the river as a prelude to the crossing of Jackson's Corps. The horse artillery was nowhere in sight, and Jackson supplied a section of guns.[19] Rosser held on until late in the afternoon, when it became apparent that Jackson wasn't going to cross. Robertson had also crossed farther upriver at Freeman's Ford but had run into a heavy force advancing to contest Rosser's crossing. At the same time, Chew's Battery had marched along the railroad south of Rosser's position at Beverly's Ford and had gone into battery in the vicinity of the railroad bridge. Shots were traded with an enemy battery for about forty minutes, [20] before Chew limbered his guns and fell back. Pelham's location during this day's actions is unclear. Stuart eventually decided that nothing more could be gained by remaining in such exposed positions and ordered Rosser and Robertson to recross to the south bank.

The scene shifted on the twenty-second to Freeman's Ford, where Stuart confronted Brig. Gen. Robert H. Milroy's Brigade and Capt. Aaron C. Johnson's 12th Ohio Battery. This time, Stuart had four of Pelham's guns with the Alabamian himself in command. Stuart decided to test Milroy and ordered Pelham to open fire. In minutes, the action escalated into a full-scale artillery duel, with the Confederates receiving more than they gave. In Stuart's own words, "Pelham tried in vain to silence the enemy's guns."[21] Even though he had a superior position, Pelham could not stop the shower of shells from Johnson's Battery that burst around his guns. Milroy's report stated:

> Too much praise cannot be awarded the captain [Johnson] for the promptness and skill exhibited in bringing his battery into position. In less than five minutes after receipt of the order he had his pieces in action amid a perfect shower of shot, shell, and canister from three of the rebel batteries, and in ten minutes after had silenced their heaviest battery. He continued engaging the enemy for about

> two hours, compelling them to constantly change the position of their guns.[22]

Pelham obviously fought quite well himself to have convinced Milroy he had three batteries instead of just four guns. Nevertheless, Johnson had a good day against Stuart's best. Pieces of one Federal shell felled Pvt. Edward McCaffrey with wounds in his chest and arm.[23] Despite the Ohioans' telling accuracy, Pelham and Stuart were not ready to throw in their cards. In fact, they were preparing to up the ante. Chew's Battery galloped onto the scene.[24]

After the previous day's fight, Chew had marched his battery across the Hazel River at Welford's Ford and had camped near the river. In the morning, the battery proceeded to the Rappahannock. Shortly after his arrival in the vicinity of the ford, Chew was met by an unknown mounted officer, who told him: "Put some of your guns in position here and fire a few shell into that piece of woods you see yonder on the other side of the river. I think perhaps there is something in there."[25] Chew complied by unlimbering a single gun and opening fire. The response was immediate. Six to eight Federal cannons answered Chew's challenge, and the fight was on. Chew added two more rifled pieces, and for the next two hours, the cannoneers fired as fast as they could load the guns. Such strenuous effort had its effect, and the rate of fire slackened as the gray cannoneers began to tire. Fitz Lee and Pelham rode up to Chew's guns to watch the fight from a different angle. Noticing the condition of the gunners, both officers dismounted and went to serving the guns with a speed and smoothness that brought smiles to the weary men they replaced.[26] The battery's shells continued to rain down on the enemy. The Yanks responded in kind, and though most of their shells either passed over the battery or failed to explode, some found their mark. Pvt. John Stewart was stuck and killed by a piece of shell, and two others were wounded.[27] Two horses were also killed.

While the artillery pounded each other, Jackson's infantry passed behind Stuart and moved farther upstream. Early in the morning, Stuart had received a dispatch from Gen. Robert E. Lee that granted permission for the cavalry chieftain to execute his planned raid on Pope's headquarters at Catlett's Station. A section of Chew's Battery was selected to accompany the cavalry and was pulled out of the fight. Guns from Jackson's command, which continued the barrage, replaced it. Other pieces were brought forward to relieve Pelham's guns, and by 12:00, the horse artillery's role in the action was over.[28]

The Federals were forced to bring up fresh batteries as well. When Johnson's ammunition eventually became exhausted, he was replaced by Capt. William L. De Beck's Battery K, 1st Ohio Light Artillery. Then Capt. Michael Wiedrich's Battery I, 1st New York Light Artillery, and finally Capt. Frank Buell's West Virginia Battery were called up by Maj. Gen. Franz Sigel and placed in support of De Beck. The bombardment continued into the afternoon. Not until 3:00 did the guns fall silent. Although Pelham's and Chew's Batteries had suffered from the accurate Yankee fire, they had inflicted damage too. Captain Buell was killed, and Wiedrich reported one killed and four wounded, along with two horses killed and ten others so badly injured that they had to be shot. In addition, one of the battery's limbers caught fire and exploded. Wiedrich stated that his guns were in exposed positions, a circumstance that he inferred was not his fault but that of General Sigel.[29] Neither Johnson nor De Beck, nor any officer from Buell's Battery, filed a report, but it could be extrapolated that their losses were in relative proportion to Wiedrich's. Milroy admitted to having two killed and thirteen wounded in his supporting infantry. Though Pelham and Chew were not involved in the entire action, they had helped turn the day around in the Confederate artillery's favor. Stuart could be satisfied with their performance.

The men of the horse artillery deserved a long rest, but not all of them were going to get one. By 10:00 A.M., Stuart set out with Robertson's Brigade, except for Jones's 7th Virginia; Fitz Lee's Brigade, minus the 3rd Virginia; and a section of Chew's Battery.[30] The column crossed the Rappahannock at Waterloo Bridge and Hart's Mill and marched toward Warrenton, which the men reached in the afternoon. Stuart called a halt to allow the column to close up. Leaving Warrenton, Stuart headed for Cedar Creek and the railroad bridge near Catlett's Station. Shortly after the raiders left the town, a violent thunderstorm engulfed them. The men were drenched to the skin in minutes, and with the road rapidly turning into a morass, Chew's guns began to fall behind. Stuart quickly decided that he had to push ahead and could not wait for the artillery. Assigning the 12th Virginia as a guard for the guns, Stuart led out the rest of his command. Night and the storm combined to create a darkness that was penetrated only by the random flashes of lightning. The artillery never made it to Catlett's Station, stopping in the road about three miles away. Neese remembered:

> The cavalry were all 'way ahead of us. We did not see or hear a sign of them anywhere, consequently toward midnight we halted in the road where the water and mud was just half knee deep. I was wet all over, and through. Cold, chilly, hungry, and sleepy all at the same time, I put myself in as small a package as I could and sat on the limber chest for three long weary hours, with wakeful dreamy visions of a good, warm, dry bed chasing one another all over me.[31]

Meanwhile, Stuart crashed upon Pope's headquarters, causing considerable turmoil but little lasting damage. The bridge, which had been the main target, remained impervious to both fire and axes, and when the Federals rallied and began firing from the darkness, the effort to destroy it had to be abandoned. Stuart recalled his midnight raiders and rode for home. The take was over 300 prisoners and an armful of "souvenirs" from Pope's headquarters tent, including the Federal general's dispatch book, which provided intelligence concerning Union troop strength and movements.

The journey back to Confederate lines was not one forgotten by any who made it. Ditches, small streams, and creeks were past overflowing. Though the rain had slackened somewhat, the heavy downpours earlier in the night and the hooves of over 1,000 horses had generated some of that famous Virginia mud. The goo, which had the consistency of peanut butter, reduced the pace to a slow walk. Every stream became an adventure. When Neese and the artillery came to Silver Run, the water was within six inches of flooding the limber chests. The gunner drew this conclusion from his experience: "Raiding with General Stuart is poor fun and a hard business. Thunder, lightning, rain, storm, mud, nor darkness can stop him when he is on the warm fresh trail of Yankee game. This morning [the twenty-third] our battery, guns, horses, and men, looks as if the whole business had passed through a shower of yellow mud last night."[32] Neese's sole consolation was that the sun was shining at last when the weary, soggy, bedraggled column entered Warrenton.

An hour's rest was all Stuart would grant before moving out on the road to Sulphur Springs. At 4:00 P.M., the advance of Robertson's Brigade reached the Springs. Before the cavalry's arrival, Federal general Robert H. Milroy was challenging Brig. Gen. Jubal A. Early for possession of the bridge across Great Run about a mile southeast of the Springs. Early was concerned because the water level in the stream was falling, and Milroy might be able to cross without using the bridge. The anxious Confederate brigadier called on Robertson for help. The section of Chew's Battery was put into position in an orchard and opened fire. The Confederate calling card was answered almost immediately by the 12th Battery, Ohio Light Artillery, commanded by Capt. Aaron C. Johnson, Pelham's nemesis at Freeman's Ford.[33] Two hours of shelling had produced no casualties when Neese's gun, the Blakely, "like a fidgety, naughty child, kicked loose from its mounting and had to be taken from the field for repairs."[34] The remaining piece, joined by a section of Capt. William D. Brown's Chesapeake (Maryland) Artillery, continued the contest until dark.[35]

Little rest was to be had on the twentieth-fourth. Neese had the Blakely repaired and then marched to Waterloo Bridge, where he joined the remainder of the battery. The Federals held the other side of the river with infantry and Capt. Michael Wiedrich's Battery. Pelham arrived with one gun from his battery and, adding one from Chew's, opened fire on the Yankee artillery. In returning fire, Captain Wiedrich displayed little talent for accuracy, at least according to Gunner Neese.[36] Later in the evening, Neese had the opportunity to show the Yanks how it should be done as he wound his way through the underbrush and unlimbered the Blakely in a concealed position.

The target Neese selected was a column of about 150 to 200 Union infantrymen standing in the road leading down to the bridge. Loaded with a percussion shell, the Blakely stood ready to fire. The order came fifteen minutes later from Fitz Lee, who had ridden up to the masked gun. Lee was not happy with the target Neese had chosen, however. Congratulating the gunner on his accurate aim, he stated that he did not wish to hurt anybody and ordered Neese to fire on a battery instead. Neese obeyed his command and had the satisfaction of watching the blue infantry break for the cover of the nearby woods. The shot unmasked the gun and brought a shower of shells down upon it. After firing three more rounds, Neese limbered the gun to the rear and put it in position to guard the bridge in case the Yankee infantry attempted a night assault. He and the rest of the men lay down to sleep next to their beloved Blakely.[37]

While Pelham traded shot and shell with the Federals at Waterloo Bridge, part of his battery was still absent in Orange County waiting for new horses or for the old ones to recover. He was minus at least one piece, which he could have used on several occasions, but without the horses to move it, he had no choice but to leave it where it was. The men left behind were plagued with a lack of information concerning their comrades. Booming cannon fire in the distance told them only that some of their friends might be in danger. The inactivity was difficult enough to bear, but wondering about their friends made the waiting worse.[38]

Dawn on the twenty-fifth found the Federals still clinging tenaciously to their side of Waterloo Bridge while the Confederates displayed equal stubbornness in maintaining their position on the south side of the river. Chew's Battery was withdrawn just before noon and pulled back to its wagon train, where it received much-needed rations. Pelham, who had taken time to issue orders bringing a gun from the camp in Orange County, remained at the bridge until later in the day, when his tired cannoneers were also relieved and sent to the rear.[39] The welcomed break was to be short-lived. At 1:00 A.M. on August 26, the shrill notes of the bugle awakened the haggard men of the horse artillery. Elsewhere, the cavalry of Fitz Lee and Robertson were also roused from their sleep and ordered to prepare to move out. Robert E. Lee's final push against Pope had been put into motion, and the cavalry and horse artillery were now to fulfill their roles.

Stuart had received his instructions from Lee the night of the twenty-fifth. He was to accompany the movement of Jackson's Corps, which had already begun its march around Pope's right flank. The gray troopers trotted in the wake of the infantry to Amissville. Here Chew's Blakely, unable to accompany the cavalry because of a lack of ammunition,[40] was detached and sent to Gaines' Crossroads west of Amissville, where many of Jackson's wagons were camped.[41] The rest of Chew's Battery, along with Pelham's, moved out with Stuart, crossed the Rappahannock at Henson's Mill four miles above Waterloo Bridge, and ran into the rear of Jackson's column at Salem. Stuart left Pelham and Chew with the ambulances and set out across country to link up with the head of Jackson's Corps. He rendezvoused with Stonewall near Gainesville on the eastern side of Thoroughfare Gap and was assigned to protect the flanks of the infantry.

Meanwhile, the two horse artillery batteries hurried along the Warrenton Turnpike in an effort to rejoin Stuart. Through the remainder of the twenty-sixth and most of the twenty-seventh, the horses pulled the guns after the cavalry, which always seemed to be just ahead and yet continually out of reach.[42] Not until the evening hours did Pelham catch up at Manassas Junction, at one time Pope's supply depot but now Jackson's.[43] Stuart placed his young horse artillery commander in charge of the captured artillery and ordered him to take it to Centreville. Two of the guns, three-inch ordnance rifles, were exchanged for two of the battery's twelve-pound howitzers.[44]

On the morning of the twenty-eighth, Pelham marched his battery from Centreville toward Groveton in the wake of Jackson's Corps. After crossing Bull Run at Lewis' Ford, Pelham became aware that Federal cavalry had moved in behind him. He detached Lt. James Breathed with one gun as rear guard. The young doctor turned artillery officer knew just what to do. Unlimbering his lone piece, he greeted the approaching blue troopers with several rounds, which caused their hasty departure. The rest of the battery continued along the Warrenton Turnpike until the rear of A. P. Hill's division was encountered near the Robinson house. The infantry was taking a right turn off the pike onto a side road. Pelham followed and halted in a field with other artillery near Sudley Church.

Just before nightfall, orders arrived that sent twenty guns to the front. Pelham, with three pieces, moved through thick woods in front of a field and rode toward the right of Ewell's division. One of the guns failed to keep pace and became lost in the gathering darkness. With his remaining two pieces, Pelham reported to Jackson, who turned him over to Maj. Lindsay M. Shumaker, chief of artillery for Brig. Gen. William B. Taliaferro's division. Shumaker guided the gallant Alabamian across the railroad and into a hail of musketry. Pelham did not have to ask the major where to put his guns. Smoothly and quickly, men long accustomed to working close to the enemy unlimbered them. In moments, Pelham opened on the 19th Indiana Infantry less than 100 yards away.

For over half an hour, the fire was maintained at a steady rate. When Shumaker ordered Pelham to withdraw, a broken pole on one of the guns prevented him from doing so. Sometime during the middle of the fight, an unknown officer rode up in the fading light and commandeered one of the guns. Pelham was unaware of what had occurred, so intensely was his attention drawn to the other gun. His command, which had numbered four guns in the morning, was now reduced to a single piece. Undaunted, Pelham continued to blast away at the enemy lines until darkness ended the contest. At the close of the fighting, Pelham began a search for his three "missing" pieces. Once he found them, he had his men settle down for the night as best they could. There would be more work in the morning.[45]

Following Jackson's orders, Stuart set out on the twenty-ninth to attempt to establish communications with Longstreet. Stuart proceeded along the Sudley Road and had just left it when he was fired on from the woods bordering the road. Surprised that the enemy had secured a position in Jackson's rear, Stuart was quick to realize the threat to Jackson's baggage train that was parked nearby. Maj. William Patrick's six companies of the 1st Virginia Cavalry stationed close by were sent for. Jackson was notified and dispatched infantry to assist Patrick. The wagon train was ordered to Aldie. Pelham had been camped in the vicinity for the night, and upon hearing the musketry, he limbered up his guns and hurried to the scene of the crisis. He arrived before Patrick and opened fire on the Federals in the woods. Patrick soon entered the fray and lost his life defending his post. Capt. Louis E. D'Aquin's Louisiana Battery came to assist Pelham, and together they drove the Federals back the way they had come.

Pelham remained in position for about an hour. Stuart eventually sent two batteries to relieve his artillery chief, who was ordered to the right of the Confederate line. Unable to locate Stuart, Pelham reported to Jackson, who gave him discretionary orders to "act as the occasion might require."[46] The occasion soon required Pelham to throw his guns into battery in support of A. P. Hill's infantry. His target was the Federal artillery, and for the next two hours, Pelham held his position 200 yards to the right of three batteries of Hill's artillery. Casualties began to mount. Pvt. Charles A. Evans had his arm so horribly mutilated that amputation at the shoulder was necessary. Privates W. W. Mangum and James Mann were wounded. Sergeants William Hoxton[47] and J. Henry Thomas also fell wounded, the latter so severely that he remained within Union lines until mid-December, when he rejoined the battery. Sgt. Wilson H. P. Turner was killed bravely serving his gun to the last. Ammunition gave out for all the guns save one of Pelham's, which continued the unequal contest until its trail was struck, forcing the young Alabamian to withdraw. He managed to find a limited amount of ammunition but did not return to the fighting then or the following day.

In his report, Pelham was generous in his praise of his officers and men. Turner was noted for behaving "with conspicuous gallantry." Others selected for individual recognition were Sergeants Robert P. P. Burwell[48] and Walter S. Dabney. Lieutenants Mathis W. Henry, Jim Breathed, and William M. McGregor also received mention for their coolness and steadfastness under fire. Pelham, himself, received accolades from both Stuart and Jackson for his performance on the twenty-eighth and early on the twenty-ninth, but their reports are strangely silent regarding the action in which his battery suffered its greatest losses.[49]

While Pelham's Battery found plenty to do and received commendations for its performance, the remaining two guns of Chew's Battery disappeared from the campaign entirely.[50] Neese was still waiting for ammunition for the Blakely on the twenty-ninth. The closest he came to the battle was to hear the cannonading in the distance. Not until 9:00 P.M. on the thirtieth did he receive marching orders. An all-night march was followed by a full day's march. Neese pitched camp at dark on the thirty-first, one mile west of Salem in Fauquier County.[51]

The pursuit of Pope began on the thirty-first. Stuart pushed toward Centreville. Pelham struggled to keep his guns up with the rapidly advancing horseman but could not maintain the pace. When the enemy was encountered moving along the Centreville and Fairfax Court House Pike, only a section of the Washington Artillery could get into the brief fight.[52] A few shells among the columns caused considerable confusion in the gathering darkness. Stuart, finally satisfied that he had chastised the Yankees enough for one day, pulled his command back two miles to Ox Hill and pitched camp for the night.

September dawned with Stuart trying to connect with Jackson's column north of Centreville. Accomplishing this, he placed Robertson's Brigade in support of Jackson's advance as Stonewall maneuvered to outflank Pope. Then Stuart went reconnoitering in person. He found Centreville abandoned, except for a few blue cavalrymen. Throwing out skirmishers, he made a drive down the turnpike toward Fairfax Court House. It soon became evident that Pope had not run all the way back to Washington. Infantry and artillery lay along the wooded ridges west of the Court House and gave every indication they were not going back without a fight. Jackson came to a halt to await Longstreet. Stuart with Fitz Lee's Brigade circled the Federal right in an attempt to secure Flint Hill. Thunderstorms drenched the men. Pelham made every effort to keep his guns available to Stuart, but the rain conspired against him. Once again he brought up the rear, wet and undoubtedly frustrated with his inability to strike at the enemy.[53]

Perhaps it was best that the horse artillery had not pushed forward heedless of men and horses. Stuart found Flint Hill well defended and was forced to retire the way he had come. A portion of a Federal infantry regiment blocked the route with the hope of capturing the bold cavalry chief and his men. Col. Williams C. Wickham, commanding Stuart's advance guard, sized up the situation in an instant and charged the daring Federals. The road was soon clear, and Stuart withdrew to Germantown and camped. The presence of the horse artillery only would have complicated the situation.

On September 2, Hampton's Brigade and Hart's Battery reported to Stuart.[54] They had been left in the vicinity of Richmond to watch the Peninsula, but with McClellan's force now in or near Washington, they had been brought north to join Lee's army. Little time was wasted in giving Hart's guns their baptism of fire as horse artillery. Shortly after sunrise, Fitz Lee's Brigade was sent to secure a deserted Fairfax Court House. Sometime past noon, Stuart sent

Hampton and Hart to attack the Union position on Flint Hill. Several guns were put into position, and shells were soon arcing across the afternoon sky while skirmishers advanced beneath.[55] The horse artillery and skirmishers drove the Federals from Flint Hill with little trouble. However, the Union force had been ordered to fall back. Had they wanted, they could have made the Confederates' job much more difficult. The Confederate offensive just quickened the Federals' pace along the road toward the defenses of Washington City. Hampton set off in pursuit with two guns of the Stuart Horse Artillery under Pelham, who placed one rifled piece in an advantageous position and fired on the blue column, scattering it.

Stuart and his assistant adjutant and inspector general, Heros von Borcke, rode forward to view the withdrawal of the Federals from Fairfax Court House. Smoke and flames from several burning farmhouses in the vicinity greeted them. Angered, Stuart turned to von Borcke and ordered him to bring up Pelham and his guns as rapidly as possible to punish the Federal arsonists.[56] Von Borcke complied, and Pelham left Hampton and brought his guns to Stuart, who watched as the young Alabamian harassed the retreating Federals. At sunset, Pelham ordered a cease-fire. The cavalry and horse artillery, with the exception of Robertson's Brigade and Chew's Battery, encamped at Fairfax Court House. These commands camped near Chantilly.[57]

Fitz Lee received orders on the third that sent his brigade and Pelham's Battery to make a demonstration in the direction of Alexandria. Meanwhile, Hampton's Brigade with Hart's Battery moved through Hunter's Mill and camped in the vicinity of Dranesville. There Hampton rendezvoused with Robertson's Brigade accompanied by Chew's Battery, now including the long-absent Blakely gun. The following day, Robertson probed toward Georgetown, Lewinsville, and Falls Church. Between Vienna and Lewinsville, the advance brushed up against Federal pickets from the 8th Illinois and the 8th Pennsylvania Cavalry.[58] These were driven in after a brief skirmish. Robertson now posted one of Chew's guns near Lewinsville to cover his flank and rode on in the direction of Falls Church to the hill above Pimmit Run. Placing the remaining two guns of Chew's Battery in position on the hill facing toward Falls Church, Robertson opened fire. His cavalry displayed itself prominently as a show of force but did not push beyond the run. Brig. Gen. Jacob D. Cox, who commanded the Federals, was not fooled by Robertson's performance, although he did dispatch a regiment of infantry and a section of artillery to reinforce the cavalry.[59] Once in position, the Federal artillery replied to Chew, and a lively exchange continued until near sunset. Once again the Blakely gave Gunner Neese problems as it kicked loose from its mounting and had to be taken from the field for repairs.[60] It proved to be the only casualty in the affair. Robertson retired in the direction of Leesburg.

As the cavalry shuffled positions in the face of the enemy before Washington, Lee's infantry and artillery shifted toward Leesburg and the Potomac. The Army of Northern Virginia was preparing to launch its first invasion of the North.

CHAPTER 6

The Maryland Campaign

"We must hold on at any cost."

Stuart's cavalry began crossing the Potomac River on the afternoon of September 5. Fitz Lee's Brigade with Pelham's Battery splashed across at White's Ford and rode toward Poolesville. Hampton's Brigade and Hart's Battery, which crossed at Conrad's Ferry, also had Poolesville as their target. Robertson's Brigade with Chew's Battery encamped at Leesburg to rest up after their skirmishing on the fourth. Earlier in the day, Robertson had been relieved and sent back to North Carolina. Col. Thomas T. Munford of the 2nd Virginia Cavalry assumed command. The greatly reduced brigade[1] had orders to bring up the rear of the army and would not ford the river until the seventh.

As Lee's Brigade approached Poolesville, it encountered a squadron of the 1st Massachusetts Cavalry. The brief skirmish that erupted ended with the Federals scattering. In this, the first cavalry clash north of the Potomac, the horse artillery's guns remained silent. The whole affair was over so quickly that Pelham's guns were not needed. Both Hampton's and Lee's Brigades camped around Poolesville that night. The next morning, with Hampton in the lead, the two brigades moved out on the road to Urbana. Reaching that place, the cavalry made itself at home and for the next several days was occupied in screening Lee's army, which was encamped in the vicinity of Frederick. Early on the seventh, Munford's Brigade with Chew's Battery rode into Urbana, having crossed the river at White's Ford. Their arrival completed the concentration of Stuart's cavalry and horse artillery.

Munford was given little opportunity to rest after his tiring march. On the morning of the eighth, Stuart sent him and Chew's Battery on a scout to Poolesville. Two of Stuart's vedettes had been captured there the day before by squadrons from the 8th Illinois and the 3rd Indiana, and Stuart wanted the Federals punished and driven out.[2] Unknown to Stuart or Munford, the Federals also were returning to Poolesville. Brig. Gen. Alfred Pleasonton had ordered Col. John F. Farnsworth to occupy the village. Farnsworth's command consisted of the 8th Illinois, the 3rd Indiana, and a section of Battery M, 2nd U.S.

Horse Artillery, under Lt. Robert H. Chapin. Col. Asher W. Harman's 12th Virginia Cavalry arrived first but was immediately challenged for possession of the place by the advancing Federals. Harman withdrew rapidly, his seventy-five troopers no match for the much larger Union regiments.[3]

Realizing he had a fight on his hands, Munford pulled back about a mile north of Poolesville and placed Chew's guns, a howitzer and a Blakely, along the edge of a woods on a hill.[4] Chew immediately opened fire on the blue troopers, who were in column with sabers drawn, preparing to charge. The shelling had its effect in breaking up the charge before it began, but it also brought Chapin's pieces forward and into battery. The Federal horse artillery proved up to the task. From a mile and a half away, it dropped several shells into the midst of Chew's guns. Gunner Neese, astonished at the accuracy of the Federals' fire, wrote: "I believe that the confounded Yankees can shoot better in the United States than they can when they come to Dixieland. They did better shooting with their artillery today than any I have seen since I have been in the service."[5] Chew's problems were just beginning.

While Chapin made things hot for Chew's men, Farnsworth was working on stoking the fire. He sent elements of the 3rd Indiana around Munford's left flank, drove in his pickets, and closed on the rear of the Confederates, cutting off their escape route. Charged from the front, flank, and rear, Munford temporarily lost his composure. Galloping in among Chew's guns, he shouted at the nineteen-year-old captain, "Cut loose from your pieces."[6] Unflustered by the surrounding chaos, and with a coolness rivaling Pelham's, Chew countermanded the order and told his men to stick to their guns. Within moments, the battery was engulfed by a torrent of pistol-firing, saber-slashing cavalrymen, blue and gray. The 7th and 12th Virginia were doing their utmost to give Chew and his men the time necessary to limber and extract their guns from what Neese rightly called "the most hazardous and eventful situation the battery was ever in."[7] Through it all, Chew and his men labored to hitch up their teams, successfully accomplishing this just as the 12th Virginia cleared the road north to Urbana. Gratefully, Chew galloped away from the near-disastrous encounter.[8]

Spared the ignominy of losing his guns along with the fight, Munford led his shaken command in a rapid retreat toward Barnesville. About one mile north of the scene of action, Chew again went into battery to offer some resistance should Farnsworth pursue. The 2nd Virginia, which had been left at the Monocacy Church two miles farther on, arrived to support the battery and its brother regiments. A half-hearted advance by the 8th Illinois was easily blunted by fire from the 2nd's sharpshooters without supporting fire from Chew. With the day's fighting at an end, Chew's men limbered up once more and fell back ten miles to the base of Sugar Loaf Mountain to bivouac for the night.[9]

Pope's Army of Virginia had been dissolved, and George B. McClellan was once again called on to save Washington. Now that Lee was across the

Potomac, McClellan was slowly moving out from Washington in an attempt to locate Lee's main force. Stuart was in his way, which set the stage for numerous cavalry clashes between Stuart's forces and those of Alfred Pleasonton. However, on the evening of the eighth, Stuart was not thinking about crossing sabers with Pleasonton. While Munford and Chew's men tried to partake of some much-needed rest, Lee's cavalry chief, with help from his gigantic Prussian staff officer, Maj. Heros von Borcke, was throwing a "Welcome to Maryland" ball. The gala affair was held in one of Urbana's largest buildings, which at one time had housed a female academy. The festivities got off to a smooth start as the 18th Mississippi Infantry's band struck up some dancing music. Stuart, members of his staff, officers of the 18th Mississippi, and local dignitaries and their ladies spun around the room as if the war were hundreds of miles away instead of just down the road.

Elsewhere, Maj. Alonzo W. Adams, with five companies of the 1st New York Cavalry, trotted toward Hyattstown, a scant three miles from Urbana. The New Yorkers, who had been dispatched on a reconnaissance mission, crested a hill overlooking the village. Adams spotted a number of pickets, who were troopers belonging to Hampton's Brigade, and promptly charged with a yell. The pickets were thrown back upon their reserve, which was in turn sent scurrying rearward as Adams and his men thundered through Hyattstown and up a hill on the other side. Discretion and not Confederate opposition brought Adams to a halt. He recognized that he had ridden as far as was prudent and withdrew to the village, leaving some pickets on the high ground.[10]

Hampton's troopers anchored themselves in a cornfield at the top of the hill and disputed its possession with the four vedettes left by Adams. At the same time, a rider sped off to inform Stuart of the incursion into his outpost line. Soon the dance was interrupted as the courier entered the hall and delivered his report in a somewhat excited fashion and with some embellishment. The officers and men left their dance partners, grabbed their weapons, and headed for their horses. Stuart shortly was leading them down the road to Hyattstown, more than a little angry that the evening's entertainment had been disrupted.

The 1st New York had stirred up a hornet's nest, as Sgt. William H. Beach discovered when he rode out to relieve the four men left on picket duty. Warned by one of the pickets that the enemy lay in ambush ahead, Beach advanced alone. Several shots rang out. As the balls whistled past his head, Beach hustled back to his three remaining pickets, and everyone hastily retreated down the hill to Hyattstown. A short while later, Stuart rode onto the scene to find the area secured by Col. Laurence S. Baker's 1st North Carolina Cavalry. Stuart, satisfied that the situation was well in hand, returned to the ball, still somewhat perturbed at the interruption. The horse artillery was not involved.[11]

The eighth had been a busy day for Chew's Battery, and Munford expected more of the same on the ninth. Chew's men were allowed to rest until about 3:00 in the afternoon, when they were alerted that Yankee cavalry was advancing. The cannoneers put their guns into battery in the road about a half mile south of Sugar Loaf. The waiting grew long, and at last all realized that the bluecoats were not coming. Writing in his diary for the day, Neese expressed some disappointment that the "reception" he and his fellow artillerymen had planned had not been attended.[12]

To the east at Hyattstown, Maj. Adams's picket came under long-range sniping fire from members of the 1st North Carolina. Pelham's horse artillery threw a few shells at the New Yorkers. But the Confederates were not willing to actually come to grips with their opponents just yet. Whatever the cause, their reluctance to drive Adams's few troopers from the village relegated the fighting to occasional potshots with both carbine and cannon.[13]

On the tenth, the 1st New York finally gave up Hyattstown to Stuart's cavalry and artillery. Elsewhere, however, it was the Federals who were the aggressors. Capt. William P. Sanders, in command of the 6th U.S. Cavalry with the 3rd Indiana, the 8th Illinois, and Chapin's two artillery pieces tried to drive the Confederates from the foot of the mountain but were unable to do so.[14] Chew's Battery, which had pulled back to Urbana earlier in the day, retraced its hoofprints "to the very same place we left this morning," as Neese reported.[15] Munford, who had calmed since his near catastrophe on the eighth, wanted the battery as support even though he had Fitz Lee's entire brigade behind him. In the end, he didn't need Chew, and only one squadron from Lee's 9th Virginia was called upon to bolster his defense. Munford's capable handling of his two regiments, the 2nd and 12th Virginia, completely frustrated the Federals. The firing died away, and as the sun dropped low in the western sky, Chew's weary cannoneers rode back to their camp at Urbana. The day had been a busy but uneventful one for the horse artillery.[16]

Out on the National Pike, Col. Tom Rosser's 5th Virginia Cavalry and a section of the Stuart Horse Artillery under Pelham were "visiting" in the vicinity of Poplar Springs. Like all soldiers, they were interested in what might be had in the way of food. However, the real focus of their foraging expedition was something of more immediate importance—horses. The campaign had been hard on the horses of both the cavalry and the artillery. Before the day was out, many a farmer in the region saw his fine horses trotted out of their stables and led away. Pelham needed those horses if his guns were to keep pace with Stuart's regiments. This above all was in the "Boy Major's" mind. The angry words and teary eyes of the farmers and their families moved the hearts of many of the Confederates, but it did not stop them from taking the horses. As the sun set, the Rebels and their prisoners disappeared westward.

At 6:00 on the morning of the eleventh, a combined infantry and cavalry force under the command of Brig. Gen. Winfield S. Hancock and Col. John F. Farnsworth moved out from Barnesville to wrest Sugar Loaf away from the stubborn Tom Munford. For the past seventy-two hours, Stuart had used every last ounce of Munford's small brigade's fighting qualities to hold back the oncoming Federals. But on this day, the blue columns advanced slowly from the south and showed a determination that was not to be denied. Munford, who was prepared to make the Yanks fight for every inch of ground, received orders from Stuart directing him to be the rear guard of the army. Reluctantly, Munford pulled his troopers back from Sugar Loaf toward Hyattstown.[17]

The Federal infantry ground to a halt once Sugar Loaf fell into their hands. Hancock plunked himself down at the base of the mountain and set out pickets. Meanwhile, the Union cavalry trailed, at a respectful distance, after Munford. A section of the Stuart Horse Artillery under Lt. Daniel Shanks supported Munford. The fire of the two guns helped scatter the oncoming Federal cavalry. Still the gray troopers lost no time in falling back through Hyattstown toward Urbana. Chew's Battery was called on again to picket the Urbana-Barnesville Road. The Yanks made an effort to move in behind them, but Chew limbered and galloped out of the trap before it could be sprung. By evening the battery was bivouacked on the banks of the Monocacy River. Munford and Shanks followed behind.[18]

Thus far in the campaign things had gone well for Lee's army, and the initiative still lay with the Confederates. McClellan was unsure what his old adversary intended, and Lee wanted to keep him in the dark as long as possible. Above all, Lee did not want to give McClellan an opportunity to land a solid blow. However, fate was conspiring to hand McClellan just such an opportunity.

News of the Maryland invasion filtered back slowly to Virginia, but since what did get back was good news, expectations for a successful outcome were high. At the horse artillery camp in Orange County, Private Walters penned a letter to his wife filled with hope:

> Orange Co. Va. September the 12th 1862
>
> Dear Wife,
>
> It is with great pleasure that I seat myself this morning to inform you that I am well, hoping these few lines may find you all well. I have heard some good news since I commenced writing. Our army is at Fredericktown in Maryland, and Baltimore has raised arms and is fighting for themselves. Stuart's cavalry was in 9 miles of there and the northern dispatch says the Confederate army will get 60 thousand soldiers out of Maryland. We have got the advantage of the Yankees one time. Our many successful battles have so weakened their forces, and the late battle at Manassas completely cut up and scattered their army that they are in no condition for fighting nor will be until they can organize and drill their recruits, and I hope against that time we pay them for the fun they had in destroying this part of Virginia. The army is on their soil now, and they will soon begin to feel the effects of war as we have done. But I am in hopes they will

soon wind up the fuss and try some other occupation. This way doesn't suit every body. I don't like it none too well myself, but I like it better than I ever thought I would.

This is a great country to live in down here. Sweet potatoes, apples, and peaches don't cost me anything, but it owing to the time I buy them. I generally buy them after night while the owner is sleeping, and we never squabble about the price. We have nothing to do here at this time, only cook and eat and that is as much as we can do for we have got so lazy we can't hardly live.

You all must do the best you can and I will do the same. Write as soon as this comes to hand. Send the letter in the envelope I send you. I will direct it myself and maybe it will get here before we leave. Every letter that is directed in care of Pelham will go to the company, but it maybe a good while before we get there. Wall has gone to the company and no doubt has got letters for us. No telling when we will get them for the company is over 100 miles from here. Give my love [to] all my connection for I can't write to them all. I remain your husband till death.

Wm P W. M E Walters[19]

While Walters raided orchards and grew lazy for lack of something to do, the rest of the men of the horse artillery were about to have plenty to do and were without any prospects of securing the fine edibles their comrades in Orange were enjoying. Meanwhile, Lee's prospects for recruiting 60,000 Marylanders to his colors were fast proving more hope than substance. Worse, the initiative that had been with the Confederate commander since the Peninsula campaign was about to change hands. McClellan was driving, albeit slowly and deliberately, toward Frederick. He wanted to know what Lee was up to. It fell to the Confederate cavalry and horse artillery to see that he didn't find out.

Stuart's job was to screen the movement of Lee's army westward through the Catoctin and South Mountains. September 12 found the cavalry regiments working hard to accomplish this task. Munford's Brigade, which had brought up the rear on the eleventh, moved from its camp three miles south of Frederick on the Buckeystown Road and with Chew's Battery rode toward Buckeystown at a pace that could only be described as slow. The twelve miles or so covered during the day brought the two commands to Jefferson. Camp was established just west of the town.[20]

The honor of being the rear guard of the army fell to Wade Hampton's Brigade and Hart's Battery. Fitz Lee, with Pelham's guns, crossed the Monocacy north of Frederick and stationed himself in the vicinity of Hamburg, but Hampton had to hold Frederick until the rest of the army had passed through. In order to have adequate warning of the Federals' approach, Hampton placed his vedettes well out from the town, covering all the roads leading to it. Two squadrons were placed at the stone bridge across the Monocacy on the Urbana-Frederick Road. Their post was a precarious one, for if their compatriots on the National Pike failed to hold their position, the men at the bridge would be cut off and captured, or worse. Hampton took steps to see that his troopers on the National Pike could delay the oncoming Federals for a sufficient length of time. A section of Hart's Battery was already guarding the pike. To it, Hampton added a rifled piece with a squadron of the 2nd South Carolina under Lt. John Meighan in support.[21]

While Hampton stiffened his forces on the pike, his opponents were not idle. The West Virginia Cavalry attached to Brig. Gen. Jacob D. Cox's Kanawha Division reached the vicinity of the bridge and began to skirmish with the Confederates still east of the river. The South Carolinians retreated across the bridge to the protection of Hart's guns and Meighan's squadron. The Federal cavalry reined in, not wishing to tangle with the Rebel horse artillery. Union reinforcements arrived. Capt. Frederick Shambeck's Chicago Dragoons joined the West Virginians on the high bank of the river. Shortly after they galloped onto the scene, Col. Augustus Moor of the 28th Ohio Infantry rode up and ordered Shambeck to charge the Confederates. The order startled the captain, but he was obliged to obey. A fence along the road slowed the blue cavalry's attack, and a blast of canister from Hart sent it careening back the way it had come.[22]

The Federals were far from finished, however. As Hart was turning the Yankee charge with his canister, Capt. Seth J. Simmonds's Kentucky Light Artillery unlimbered a section of its guns and opened fire on the Confederates. The fight appeared to be escalating, but Hampton chose not to allow it to go any further. His troopers had withdrawn from their position on the Urbana-Frederick Road, so there was no reason to slug it out east of Frederick. He ordered his squadrons to pull back and sent Hart to occupy a position west of the town that would command the road from Frederick to the mountains. But the Yanks were not about to allow Hampton to leave unmolested. They ran up a gun close to the town and began shelling the retreating Confederates. Once again Moor followed with a cavalry charge, this time down Patrick Street in the town itself. Hampton was ready and sliced into the blue column, shattering it. The Federals streamed back along the street, with Hampton's South Carolinians in hot pursuit. The lone Union artillery piece was overrun but could not be brought off because the majority of its horses had been shot. Both parties suffered a number of men killed and wounded. The impetuous Colonel Moor and several others were taken prisoner. The sharp clash ended the fighting for the day. The Federals moved into Frederick while Hampton trotted toward Middletown, where he camped for the night.

When Hampton rode through the Catoctin Mountains, he stationed Lt. Col. William T. Martin's Jeff Davis Legion to guard Braddock Pass. Early on the morning of the thirteenth, Brig. Gen. Alfred Pleasonton led the 1st Massachusetts, 3rd Indiana, and 8th Illinois west on the National Pike. He brought with him two sections of the 2nd U.S. Artillery—one from Battery B/L under Capt. James M. Robertson, and the other from Battery M under Lt. Peter C. Hains. As Pleasonton approached the pass, a solid shot screamed overhead. The report of the artillery piece that dispatched it informed him that the pass was occupied and its tenants unfriendly. The shot had come from one of the Blakely guns in a section of Hart's Battery, which Hampton had sent to support Martin.[23]

Robertson and Hains rapidly unlimbered their four guns, placing a section on each side of the road, and returned fire. Unable to elevate their guns high enough to reach Hart in the pass, the Federal artillery contented itself with making noise to bolster the cavalry's morale. The Federals' determination to take the pass became evident as the cavalry began to dismount and form skirmish lines on both sides of the pike. At the top of the pass, Stuart arrived and began to make dispositions to delay the Yanks as long as possible. The remainder of Hampton's Brigade and at least one additional artillery piece were called up from Middletown. The only part of the brigade that saw any action was a portion of the 1st North Carolina, which was dispersed as sharpshooters in support of Martin.

Pleasonton advanced his skirmishers, but Hart's fire was enough to keep them from making any real progress. The Union commander added more troopers to his line, lengthening it. Stuart dispatched Maj. Heros von Borcke with a small mountain howitzer to the left of the Confederate line. Through a tangle of brush and vines, the gunners struggled with their piece until von Borcke was satisfied it was in the proper position. Then he opened a fire that caused some scattering of the Federal cavalry below. Though von Borcke and his artillery companions enjoyed the Yankee's discomfiture, they did not fail to notice that blue infantrymen were now forming skirmish lines and advancing into the trees at the base of the mountain.[24]

Col. Edward Harland's Brigade, consisting of the 8th, 11th, and 16th Connecticut and the 4th Rhode Island Infantry regiments, had marched from its camp east of Frederick to reinforce Pleasonton. Before the brigade had a chance to deploy, a Confederate solid shot mangled the legs of three infantrymen.[25] Though most of Hart's shots had been high, a few rounds were exacting a price for the pass. Now, as von Borcke watched the Union infantry disappear among the green foliage, he became concerned. Brisk carbine and musket firing had already broken out along the line, and he feared being cut off from the North Carolinians to his right. He sent a courier to Stuart to inform the general of his situation. The cavalry chieftain soon rode up in person and ordered the howitzer withdrawn.

In fact, Stuart realized that he had held on as long as was practical. The Federals wanted the pass, and they had the men and guns to get it eventually. It was 2:00 P.M. The pass had been held for about eight hours.[26] Staying longer would gain the Confederates very little and might cost them more than they could afford. Hampton had already obstructed the road with fallen trees to discourage any rapid push by the enemy, so Stuart ordered a retreat. Hart's guns were withdrawn first, followed by the cavalry. The decrease in firing from the top of the pass told Pleasonton that his adversaries were abandoning their position. He ordered the 3rd Indiana, 8th Illinois, and 1st Massachusetts in pursuit. These regiments were brought up short by fire from Hart's Battery, posted east of Middletown.

The scenario that had played itself out in Braddock Pass was renewed on the ridges west of the mountain. The Federal cavalry stretched its lines out north and south of the pike, and a section of artillery from Capt. Horatio G. Gibson's Battery C/G, 3rd U.S. Artillery, unlimbered to oppose Hart.[27] As the Union cavalry advanced, they encountered their old nemesis from the top of the pass, the 1st North Carolina, who greeted them warmly. But once again the blue juggernaut was not to be denied. Stuart sent Hart's Battery rearward through Middletown. In the withdrawal, the North Carolinians retired too rapidly and allowed the Federal advance to block Hart's escape route. For a few anxious moments, it appeared that the guns would have to be abandoned to the enemy. Then Capt. William H. H. Cowles, in command of the rear guard, received word of Hart's predicament and charged through the town to the rescue. Crashing into the oncoming Yankees, Cowles's troopers drove them back just enough to permit Hart and his guns to gallop through the swirling mass of cavalry to safety.[28] Their mission completed, the North Carolinians raced through the town under the fire of the Federal artillery. Crossing Catoctin Creek, the regiment and Hart's guns made another stand on a hill. Gibson's Battery rolled up, took position, and traded shots with Hart's Blakelys.[29]

The fight was of short duration. Hampton fell back to Turner's Gap in the South Mountain and there turned south with Hart's Battery and his entire brigade except the Jeff Davis Legion, which stayed with Stuart. The column's destination was Crampton's Gap, where Hampton expected to rendezvous with Munford's Brigade. This command had not been idle during the day. In the early morning, Gunner Neese of Chew's Battery could see the muzzle blasts from Hart's guns on the mountain to the north as Hampton engaged Pleasonton at Braddock's Pass. Munford's command soon felt the pressure of the Union advance as well. The 6th Pennsylvania Cavalry spearheaded a column composed of Col. Harrison S. Fairchild's Brigade, which clashed with Munford. Chew's guns were soon firing on the Federals as they approached Jefferson.[30] But Munford did not linger and fell back fighting to Burkittsville. Chew limbered and retreated toward Middletown. Why Chew chose this route is unknown. Neese speculated that the battery would pick up the Middletown-Burkittsville Road at Middletown and then turn south toward Crampton's Gap, where Munford had gone.[31] In any event, Chew did not make it to Middletown or the junction of the road to Burkittsville. Federal cavalry forced the battery to take a cross-country route to the road. Chew proceeded to Burkittsville, halted briefly, and then continued on to Crampton's Gap, where he placed his guns in a position commanding the approaches to the gap from the east.[32]

Well to the north, Fitz Lee's Brigade and Pelham's Battery sat idle in the early morning. The peaceful interlude ended with the arrival of a courier from Stuart with instructions for Lee. He was to scout the Federal right north of Frederick with a view to flanking it. The 3rd, 4th, and 9th Virginia Cavalry dutifully started out, only to run into Col. Andrew T. McReynolds's Brigade, consisting of the 1st New York, the 12th Pennsylvania Cavalry,[33] and a section of Battery M, 2nd U.S. Artillery. McReynolds was on a scouting mission to Gettysburg. Lee realized his flanking maneuver could not succeed and fell back through Hamburg. Pelham commanded the section of the Stuart Horse Artillery accompanying Lee. Somehow during the encounter with McReynolds or the withdrawal, Pelham became separated.[34] He was at first thought to be captured, but the rumor proved false when on the morning of the fourteenth he showed up at Boonsboro.[35]

South at Crampton's Gap, Hampton's Brigade approached Munford's and Chew's position. The South Carolinian had already had one clash along the way in the vicinity of the Quaker School House, where Lt. Col. Pierce M. B. Young's Cobb Legion crossed swords and exchanged shots with members of the 3rd Indiana and 8th Illinois Cavalry. The fracas was over in a few minutes, leaving casualties strewn about. Hampton continued on his way to Crampton's Gap while Young, who bore a wound in his leg, gathered up his dead, wounded, and prisoners before following. As the tired column approached the gap, Munford ordered Chew to make preparations to fire on it. The colonel was understandably a bit jumpy with all the fighting that had been going on since the eighth. Fortunately, a messenger arrived from Hampton with scarcely a minute to spare. Chew's gunners stood back from their pieces, thankful that a disaster had been averted. They remained at their post until sunset, when they limbered up, crossed the mountain, and went into camp at its base. The thirteenth had been a busy day for all, but the fourteenth was to see even harder fighting.

Stuart was very busy very early on the fourteenth. His force at Boonsboro consisted of Col. Thomas L. Rosser's 5th Virginia Cavalry from Fitz Lee's Brigade, the Jeff Davis Legion from Hampton's Brigade, and at least one section of Pelham's Battery.[36] Col. Alfred Colquitt's Brigade of Maj. Gen. Daniel H. Hill's division had come up and had taken possession of Turner's Gap on the afternoon of the thirteenth.[37] These reinforcements freed Stuart of the sole responsibility of holding the gaps.[38] He was aware that Fox's Gap, a mile south of Turner's, was undefended and so dispatched Rosser and the section of guns under Pelham to hold it.[39] Stuart then rode south to Crampton's Gap. From there he accompanied Hampton's Brigade, with Hart's Battery, to Knoxville to cover the front of Maj. Gen. Lafayette McLaws's division.

Upon reaching Fox's Gap, Rosser's troopers dismounted and crouched behind a stone wall bordering a road that intersected with the Old Sharpsburg

Road. Pelham placed his section in the corner of a field just north of the end of Rosser's line.[40] As the sun rose above the horizon, Lt. Samuel N. Benjamin's Company E, 2nd U.S. Artillery, fired the opening shot of the battle of South Mountain. At about the same time, Brig. Gen. Samuel Garland was leading his brigade up the road into Turner's Gap, but he soon was sent by Hill to Fox's with orders to hold it at all costs. Rosser and Pelham understood the seriousness of the situation without orders. From his position, John Pelham was able to see that a hard day's work lay ahead for himself and his men.

Pelham's opening shot caused considerable turmoil in the ranks of the advancing Union infantry column on the road. While it deployed, Garland made use of the time to put his men into line. Capt. James W. Bondurant's Jeff Davis Artillery came onto the scene and unlimbered about 500 yards south and slightly to the front of Pelham's position. His guns appeared as a welcome addition to the defense, but they were fated not to be there very long. Meanwhile, skirmishers from the 23rd Ohio began the infantry battle in earnest. At this juncture, Pelham's involvement was minimal if he fired at all, the action being several hundred yards to his right. When Brig. Gen. George B. Anderson's Brigade came up, Rosser and Pelham fell back. Throughout the day, the fighting intensified as more reinforcements arrived for both sides. As daylight faded, a Union drive threatened to capture the Old Sharpsburg Road. With Rosser in support, Pelham's guns were "speedily placed in position a short distance in our rear on the Braddock [Old Sharpsburg] road. A few well-directed shot and shell drove the enemy up the hill, leaving the road in our possession."[41] With those rounds, Pelham's role in the battle ended, and he limbered his guns and moved slowly back toward Boonsboro.

Farther south, at Crampton's Gap, Capt. Roger P. Chew had roused his men in the early morning hours before dawn and had started them back up the road into the gap. They reached the top of the pass just as the sun lifted itself above the horizon. Shortly the rolling thunder of artillery fire alerted them to the oncoming Federal army. Chew led his battery about halfway down the mountain and put it into position. Gunner George Neese recorded:

> At about ten o'clock we saw the first of the Yankee host, about three miles away, approaching our gap cautiously and slowly. As they drew nearer the whole country seemed to be full of bluecoats. They were so numerous that it looked as if they were creeping up out of the ground—and what would or could our little force of some three hundred or four hundred available men standing halfway up a bushy, stony mountain side do with such a mighty host that was advancing on us with flying banners?[42]

The numbers of the enemy did indeed inspire awe in the few Confederates guarding the gap. Munford's two regiments contained barely 200 men, and the

16th Virginia Infantry from Col. William A. Parham's Brigade, which held the ground in front and to the right of Chew's guns, added a hundred or so more. Opposing them was Maj. Gen. William B. Franklin's VI Corps of approximately 6,500 men.[43] The 96th Pennsylvania Infantry, which numbered about 500, threw out skirmishers and began to come on.[44] Chew greeted them with several shots, which rocketed over Burkittsville and the 96th, landing on a hill to the regiment's rear. In response to Chew's guns, Lt. Leonard Martin's Battery F, 5th U.S. Artillery, wheeled its six pieces into position and fired, only to see the rounds fall well short of their intended target.

Chew now split his fire. The Blakely, Neese's gun, concentrated on the enemy's battery, while the remaining two pieces continued to bombard the Federal skirmishers. This time the rounds meant for the 96th found their mark and precipitated a hasty scramble for cover among the Pennsylvanians. Once again the Blakely was disabled when its recoil slammed its trail into the sloping bank behind it. The impact caused a couple of mounting bolts to break off, and Neese was forced to take the gun rearward for repairs. Before he rode over the top of the gap, Neese turned to look at the scene spread out below. "To observe the caution with which the Yankees, with their vast superior numbers, approached the mountain, it put one very much in mind of a lion, king of the forest, making exceeding careful preparations to spring on a plucky little mouse."[45] Without doubt, it was the roar of the mouse, produced by Chew's guns and those of Lt. John H. Thompson's Portsmouth Battery, which had joined him, that was keeping the lion at bay.[46]

Morning waned into afternoon. The 6th and 12th Virginia Infantry from Parham's Brigade and the 10th Georgia Infantry from Brig. Gen. Paul Semmes's Brigade reinforced the Confederate line along the Mountain Church Road at the base of the gap, but this did little to offset the tremendous advantage the Federals had. Chew moved his two pieces to the crossroads at the top of the pass and poured a destructive fire on the enemy.[47] Solid shot and shell tore through the ranks of the 96th Pennsylvania. The officers were forced to change the direction of the regiment's advance to escape Chew's accurate fire.[48] But the Federal attack could not be stopped. Col. Alfred T. A. Torbert's Brigade (1st, 2nd, 3rd, and 4th New Jersey Infantry) and Brig. Gen. John Newton's Brigade (18th, 31st, and 32nd New York and 95th Pennsylvania Infantry) went into line and pushed forward to support Col. Joseph J. Bartlett's Brigade (5th Maine, 16th and 27th New York, and 96th Pennsylvania Infantry). The Confederate line crumbled and streamed up into the pass. Chew's two guns fired their last rounds and joined the retreat. Munford would record in his report to Stuart, "Captain Chew used his guns with great coolness and effect, and his battery only retired when he had exhausted every round of ammunition."[49] In another report Munford sent to Jackson, he wrote, "Capt. Chew, as true as steel, and ever ready, deserves to be mentioned."[50]

September 15 was a day of retreating and regrouping for the Confederates who had fought at Turner's, Fox's, and Crampton's Gaps. With all the passes clear of defenders, the Federal juggernaut rolled up and over the mountain in what seemed like unceasing numbers. Rosser and Pelham had rejoined Fitz Lee during the night. From a masked position with his battery along the National Turnpike about a mile east of Boonsboro, Pelham watched a river of blue flow through Turner's Gap. Dismounted skirmishers from the 4th Virginia Cavalry slowly gave way before the advancing Federals. When the enemy came within range, Pelham opened fire. The shells arced across the sky, crashed down in the midst of the column, and scattered the infantry. An uncoordinated effort was made to dislodge the Rebels, but several blasts from Pelham's guns sent the bluecoats scurrying for cover. The Union infantry then began to deploy on both sides of the pike, and Pelham recognized that the next attempt would be more determined. He limbered, and the battery trotted through Boonsboro.

Pelham's withdrawal opened the door for the Federals. The 8th Illinois Cavalry, which passed through the forming Union infantry, charged into Boonsboro hot on the heels of Fitz Lee and the rear guard. For a while all was chaos. The 3rd Virginia countercharged but was roughly handled. Most of the 9th Virginia had been dismounted, lounging along the street. The troopers leaped for their horses and added to the turmoil as they made haste to escape down the Boonsboro Pike toward Sharpsburg. The 4th Virginia also found itself caught in the confusion of pistol fire and slashing sabers. A bottleneck at a covered bridge a mile south of town caused a final furious encounter, after which Fitz Lee led his exhausted and somewhat demoralized command to Keedysville. Here Pelham had his guns in place and was ready to dispute any further Union pursuit. Had he been caught between Boonsboro and the bridge during the cavalry free-for-all, he might have lost a gun or two. Fortunately he had been clear of the rout and in the end was able to support Lee.[51] When the Yanks did not come on, the grateful Confederates fell back toward Sharpsburg. As the day drew to a close, the weary column reached Antietam Creek, crossed it, and went into position to guard the fords. Pelham bivouacked his battery west of the Hagerstown Pike on a small knoll on the Nicodemus farm.[52]

Further south at Crampton's Gap, the Federals had also crossed the mountain in force early in the day. Stuart himself was present to oppose them and had his skirmishers deployed just below farmer David Arnold's peach orchard about a mile north of Brownsville. Col. William H. Irwin's Brigade of Maj. Gen. William F. Smith's 2nd Division of the VI Corps was slowly advancing toward Stuart's position. An engagement seemed imminent, when a raucous cheer rose from the Confederate troops in the vicinity of the town. Harpers Ferry had surrendered, and with its fall, the Union drive to liberate the besieged troops came to an abrupt halt. Stuart broke contact with the enemy and rode to Harpers Ferry to join the victorious Jackson.[53]

Chew's Battery had played no role in this action. The crew of the disabled Blakely, including Gunner Neese, had moved out at 1:00 A.M. to Martinsburg to have the gun repaired. They forded the Potomac at Williamsport and arrived at their destination at dusk. The gun was left at a blacksmith's while the men rode to within three miles of Shepherdstown and established camp. There was little to do but wait. Chew and the remaining two guns had taken a different route, accompanying Munford's Brigade through Harpers Ferry and crossing the Potomac into Virginia. Their time in Virginia was shorter, only long enough to obtain some ammunition, before they rode for the fords at Shepherdstown.[54]

Wade Hampton's Brigade and Hart's Battery fulfilled their mission of protecting Maj. Gen. Lafayette McLaws's division on Maryland Heights. Able to hear the firing to the north at Crampton's Gap and to their rear at Harpers Ferry, all Hampton and Hart could do was sit at Knoxville and stay vigilant. Hart's guns were quite low on ammunition, and prospects were not favorable for obtaining more. They would make do with what they had for the rest of the campaign.[55]

Pelham and his cannoneers arose on the morning of the sixteenth not knowing what to expect from the enemy who had been so eager to get at them over the previous few days. Morning stretched into afternoon without anything happening to disrupt their well-earned repose. Then, as the sun was setting, their rest was interrupted by a clash between elements of Maj. Gen. Joseph Hooker's Corps and Col. Evander Law's Brigade in the vicinity of the East Woods. Small-arms fire crackled, accompanied by the louder and deeper salvos of artillery. Col. Stephen D. Lee put a number of the guns of his battalion into action to bolster the Confederate infantry. He was supported by Capt. William Poague's Rockbridge Artillery, but the fading light and the fact that much of the fighting took place in the woods kept Pelham's guns silent.[56]

Early that same morning, the crew of Chew's Blakely gun moved from their night's bivouac to within a quarter mile of Shepherdstown, where they continued to wait for the piece to be repaired.[57] The rest of the battery had crossed the Potomac at Shepherdstown late on the fifteenth. By dawn they were in position, with Munford's Brigade on the extreme southern end of the Confederate line with orders to hold the bridge near the Antietam Iron Works.[58] All was calm, a circumstance that Chew's men must have thoroughly enjoyed after their hard fight on the fourteenth.

During the morning, Hampton's Brigade and Hart's Battery covered the crossing of McLaws's division into Harpers Ferry, which was hindered by paroled Union prisoners marching the other way.[59] The cavalry and horse artillery crossed last and followed McLaws's column to Halltown, where a halt was made. McLaws started for Shepherdstown at 3:00 P.M. and camped after dark within two miles of the Potomac.[60] Hampton's and Hart's commands trailed after the weary infantry. They had accomplished their mission but, like the footsore troops bedding down around them, wondered what tomorrow would bring.

For many of the soldiers in both armies, the bloodiest day of the war began before the sun rose above the horizon. Skirmish fire erupted at 3:00 that morning of September 17, 1862. Evidently some of the troops were eager to settle the issue and wished to get an early start. In the campsites scattered among the fields on both sides of Antietam Creek, men arose from their night's sleep, fashioned the best breakfast they could, and fell into ranks. The Federals began their attack as infantry from Hooker's Corps pushed south along the Hagerstown Pike toward the farm of Joseph Poffenberger. They were quickly within range of the Confederate artillery on Nicodemus Heights. All or part of several batteries, which Stuart placed under Pelham's command,[61] opened a devastating fire on the lines of blue that seemed to melt away in the smoke that enveloped them. Yet on they came. Fresh regiments replaced the shattered remnants of those that had gone before and continued the advance. Federal artillery replied to the Confederate bombardment with one of their own, and shells began falling thick and fast among Pelham's guns. Casualties mounted. For almost two hours, Pelham's gunners and those of the other batteries delivered withering blast after withering blast against the Union infantry. While they seriously crippled the Federal attack, neither they nor the Confederate infantry could stop it.

Shortly after 7:00 A.M., Brig. Gen. Joseph K. F. Mansfield's Corps swept forward in support of Hooker, whose corps had been decimated. The fighting swirled toward the Poffenberger farm and the Dunkard Church. The artillery on Nicodemus Heights could no longer fire without endangering the Confederate infantry.[62] Stuart determined that a change of position was necessary in order to attain a clear field of fire.[63] A number of guns were pulled from Nicodemus Heights and shifted south to another area of high ground on the Hauser farm.[64] Pvt. John W. Bryan of Capt. Ashur W. Garber's Battery gave a vivid description of Pelham once the guns reached their new position:

> This position we held the balance of the day. I wish to say that soon after taking this last position we were joined by that gallant and brave artillery officer, Major Pelham of Stuart's Horse Artillery, who remained with us throughout the day working at one of our guns as a gunner, and by his conduct and bravery greatly assisted us in repulsing every charge made against our battery, and that they were very frequent. Our battery being short of men having left about half of them asleep in the woods, all of our officers had to fill in at the guns.[65]

Once Mansfield's Corps was thrown back, it was the turn of Maj. Gen. Edwin V. Sumner's II Corps to test the Confederate line and John Pelham's guns. The Yankees walked into a slaughter pen, with Maj. Gen. John Sedgwick's division bearing the brunt of the damage. Again, Pelham's hodgepodge artillery battalion contributed in no small way to Sedgwick's discomfiture. By

11:00 A.M., the Army of the Potomac's attempts to crush Jackson's left flank had come to a bloody end. With it, Pelham's role in the day's fighting was almost finished. He had but one more scene to play.

Later in the afternoon, under instructions from Lee, Jackson ordered a probe of McClellan's right to determine whether an attack could be made to drive it back and possibly outflank it. Stuart, who was given the advance, dispatched Pelham with several guns to feel out the enemy. Capt. William Poague was one of the officers whose battery was called upon to furnish Pelham with guns for his mission. He, along with the officers of the other batteries involved, protested the move based upon the observation of thirty enemy pieces of artillery in plain view. According to Poague, Pelham wanted to shake the Federals up a bit before withdrawing.[66] The Yanks' reaction was as Poague and the others had anticipated: a thirty-gun response. Within fifteen or twenty minutes, Pelham concluded he had stirred them enough and pulled back. There would be no attack on McClellan's right flank.

Across the battlefield to the south, Chew's Battery, holding its position near the iron works, was not involved in the day's fighting. Munford was pulled north to the fields west of the Snavely farmhouse during the latter stages of the Federal drive on Sharpsburg, but Chew does not appear to have accompanied him. There is no record of the battery being engaged. As for Neese and his Blakely, they did not reach the battlefield until near sunset. When the gun finally was repaired, he and the rest of the crew set out for the Potomac. They forded the river below Shepherdstown, their pace slowed because of the number of wagons and ambulances encountered. They pitched camp in rear of the battlefield.[67]

On the sixteenth, Hart's Battery crossed the Potomac River and reported directly to Gen. Robert E. Lee. The battery was extremely low on ammunition, and Lee dispatched couriers to find what they could. Little was to be had, and Hart took a position between Lee's headquarters and the town along the turnpike. Hart supported the Confederate right but was limited by its lack of ammunition to a slow rate of fire.[68] Even so, the battery emptied its caissons except for canister rounds and was pulled back to guard the Potomac crossings. If worst came to worst, the time they purchased with their last few rounds might allow some of the army to escape across the river.[69] Hampton's cavalry, which had crossed the river and joined the army on the seventeenth, could contribute little to the fight. His brigade had marched long and hard, but Sharpsburg was not a cavalryman's battle.[70]

Sunrise on the eighteenth found the two exhausted armies staring at each other over blood-soaked fields. The night before, Lee had held a firelight conference with his generals. They reported their commands grievously wounded, some consisting of no more than a thin skirmish line.[71] Yet after each officer in turn had given his equally dismal account of his troops' number and condition, Lee told them he would remain and offer McClellan battle if he desired one.

He didn't. The "Young Napoleon" issued orders not to bring on any action. The battle was "officially" over.

Not until late in the afternoon did Robert E. Lee issue orders for the withdrawal. Stuart was given a twofold mission: cover the retreat and cause a diversion to occupy McClellan while the army withdrew. Fitz Lee's Brigade and Pelham were assigned to screen the army's retreat. Stuart with Hampton's Brigade would draw McClellan's attention. In all this activity, Munford's little brigade seems to have been forgotten. Its commander does not appear to have received any particular assignment. Neese and the Blakely rejoined Chew and the rest of the battery early in the morning and went on picket duty. Except for some skirmisher fire and the activity of Yankee burial parties, nothing much disturbed either Munford's or Chew's men.[72] Just what Hart's Battery did is unknown. It is absent from the list of units that made up Stuart's and Hampton's expedition. Two other batteries—a section from the Salem Artillery and one from the 2nd Richmond Howitzers—supplied guns for the diversion. If Hart accompanied Hampton's Brigade back to Virginia on the night of the eighteenth, he stayed there when the brigade recrossed the river at Mason's Ford.

The retreat that began on the eighteenth ended early on the morning of the nineteenth with Fitz Lee and Pelham bringing up the rear.[73] Stuart was off on his expedition, and Pelham, with nothing to do, rode to catch up with him. He took none of his guns, however. Munford's Brigade fell back and crossed the Potomac at Boteler's Ford.[74] Chew's Battery was the last to cross the river and passed through Shepherdstown on its way to Martinsburg.[75] The men and horses had profited from the lack of action on the seventeenth and eighteenth and made good time. By nightfall, they had marched through Martinsburg and were camped two miles south of the town at Snodgrass Spring.[76] Everyone in the battery—indeed, everyone in the army—was glad to be back in Old Virginia.

For some of the horse artillery who had never left the state, the long weeks of inactivity and lack of news from the front was frustrating. The men stationed at Orange Court House had been moved to Rapidan Station. They dreamed of home and worried about friends and comrades. William P. Walters's letter of the nineteenth reveals some of these mixed thoughts and emotions:

> Rapidan Station Va September the 19th 1862
>
> Dear wife,
>
> It is with great pleasure that I seat myself this evening to inform you that I am in tolerable good health, hoping these few lines will find you all well. I have no news of importance to write at this time, only we have moved from where we was to this station which is about 12 miles [north]. I have heard no news from the company nor from home, but I am looking for a letter in a few days to come to [two words illegible].

It has been so long since I have heard from you that I am getting very uneasy. I made a start to come home last Saturday but got disappointed. Our lieutenant that is with us gave me and James Gray permission to go home 10 days, but when we got to the depot we could not get a passport ticket without our permit had been signed by higher authority. But we can't blame the lieutenant, for he done all he could for us. But I am in hopes we all will get furloughs this fall and winter.

You must try and get some body to seed some for you if you can, and if you cant you must live on what you have while it lasts, and then trust to providence. Tell father's and Sol's folks that I have not forgot them yet. Tell them howdy for me, and tell them to write to me and let me no how they are getting along. Tell uncle Jim's family the same. Give my love to all and excuse my short letter. Tell Molly and Sis and the baby that I would like to see them and play with them, but I hope it won't be long till I can get to come home. So no more at present, but remain your true and loving husband till death,

Wm P Walters M E Walters[77]

Farther to the north, Walters's batterymates were receiving a well-earned rest as the horse artillery began to recuperate from its most severe testing of the war thus far. However, its commander was not recuperating with them. He had ridden off in pursuit of Stuart, and on the afternoon of the twentieth, he galloped up to Maj. Heros von Borcke with news that he had been reconnoitering the enemy and had come upon some fine peaches. He added that the peaches could be enjoyed while at the same time the enemy could be observed. Never one to miss an opportunity of mixing business with pleasure, von Borcke acceded to Pelham's suggestion, and shortly the two were perched in the branches of a peach tree within a few hundred yards of the enemy, tasting the delicious fruit. It was a strange contrast to what the two had been doing just three days earlier.[78]

Stuart accomplished all that Robert E. Lee could have desired, and late on the twentieth, he withdrew across the Potomac at Williamsport and retreated along the road to Martinsburg. He established his cavalry in a line from Williamsport to Harpers Ferry. Hampton's Brigade with Hart's Battery were stationed at Hainesville, south of Williamsport; Fitz Lee's Brigade covered Shepherdstown; Munford's Brigade took position near Charles Town. The next several days passed quietly. Chew's Battery marched from its camp at Snodgrass Spring on the twentieth to Bunker Hill and then Smithfield. By the twenty-first, it was a mile beyond Charles Town on the Harpers Ferry Road doing picket duty. There it remained until the twenty-third, when it pulled back and camped four miles from Charles Town on the Berryville Pike.[79]

At least part of the Stuart Horse Artillery encamped at Millwood near Ashby's Gap, though some sections may have been assigned to the cavalry brigades and may have camped near them.[80] Pelham is known to have visited his old commander, Capt. Ephraim G. Alburtis, in Martinsburg on the twenty-first and the twenty-third.[81] By the end of the month, Stuart had established his headquarters at "The Bower," the home of Adam Stephen Dandridge. Over the next several weeks, with a few minor interruptions and a singular major one, the cavalry and horse artillery enjoyed a quiet interlude from the war.

CHAPTER 7

Holding the Line of the Potomac

"Oh no! Oh no! They are not rebels."

During the latter days of September and the first weeks of October, Robert E. Lee set about reorganizing the Army of Northern Virginia. The first component to receive his attention was the artillery. Brig. Gen. William N. Pendleton, Lee's chief of artillery, in answer to the commander's request, submitted a report reflecting the changes he felt were necessary to streamline and make more efficient the artillery of the army. His report read in part:

> It is clear that our service is now encumbered by too many artillery companies, of which some have never been strong enough, some are commanded by inadequate officers, and some, though well officered and entitled to honor for excellent service, are so reduced in men and horses as scarcely to leave room for a hope of their restoration to efficiency. It becomes, therefore, an imperative duty to relieve the service and the Confederacy of this burden, so expensive every way, but especially in its enormous consumption of horses, if such relief can be legally and justly effected. The only practicable mode of accomplishing the object is to determine by the fairest standard that can be selected what companies should be dispensed with, to relieve from duty the officers of such, and to assign the men and equipments to other companies retained. In endeavoring to reach right conclusions in the premises, I have sought with great care the actual merit and condition of the several batteries connected with this army; and though it were vainly presumptuous to suppose that I had escaped error, I feel assured there is as little mistake as the complexity of the case and the limited time for investigation fairly admit.[1]

Pendleton proceeded to prune the artillery of its weak branches. Officers and men were to be transferred or reassigned. Equipment was to be redistributed among the surviving batteries. The report that Pendleton presented to Lee became the basis of Special Orders No. 209. It changed the artillery arm significantly, but in reading it in detail, it becomes apparent that not one word appears concerning the horse artillery. It is as if Pendleton completely overlooked it. Yet even though it was left out of Lee's special orders, the changes to the artillery arm did reach all the way down to the horse artillery. While a number of foot batteries were disbanded and the overall number of batteries reduced, the horse artillery was expanded.

On September 22, Pelham finally was promoted to major to rank from August 9. There could be little doubt about his qualifications, and certainly he was among those most deserving of promotion. The record of his achievements up to this time was among the foremost in the army. One wonders whether, if he had been in either the cavalry or the infantry, he might have been wearing the three stars and wreath of a general. But promotion in the artillery was notoriously slow, and Pelham, along with others in that branch of the service, had to make do with words of praise for his services rather than promotions.

Pelham's new rank brought about a ripple of changes throughout the Stuart Horse Artillery. The battery was split into two four-gun batteries, to be designated the 1st and 2nd Stuart Horse Artillery. This adjustment was a harbinger of a change, which would soon be made in the cavalry. Another brigade was to be formed, and the battery was divided into two so that one could remain with Fitz Lee's Brigade and one could be assigned to the new brigade. Since Pelham would now command the battalion, new battery commanders were required. Lt. James Breathed was promoted to captain of the 1st Stuart Horse Artillery, and Lt. Mathis W. Henry was made captain of the 2nd Stuart Horse Artillery. Speculation about this change ran through the battery. On the twenty-sixth, William P. Walters wrote home about what was transpiring.

> September the 26th 1862 Rapidan Station
>
> Dear wife and children,
>
> I seat myself to write you a few lines to let you know that I am not very well at this time. I have had the headache and a pain in my back and shoulders for several days but hope these will find you all well. I have not received any letter yet. I have been looking for one the last 3 mails. I expect we will leave here tomorrow, for we have orders to go to the company. It is near Winchester, and I hear they are going to divide the company and make 2 of it. It has got too large for one, and Pelham [has] been appointed major. Lieutenant Breathed will be captain of one company and Lt. Henry of the other, but neither will make as good a captain as Pelham. I will write all about it when I get there.[2]

How many others shared Walters's opinion is unknown, but the changes were coming nevertheless. Others who benefited from the wave of promotions were Moses A. Febrey and J. Emmet Shaw, who became lieutenants in Breathed's Battery, while George Wilmer Brown, William C. Elston, and Charles Edward Ford became lieutenants in Henry's. Shaw resigned on October 1 and was replaced by Philip Preston Johnston.

The changes that affected the Stuart Horse Artillery during the final week in September did not touch Chew's Battery. The only thing that changed for Chew and his men was the scenery.[3] From September 23 through October 2, the battery visited such locales as Leetown (on the twenty-fifth); Berryville (on the twenty-eighth); Purcellville, Hamilton, and Leesburg (on the twenty-ninth); and Aldie, Middleburg, and Upperville (on the thirtieth) while on a scout with about 1,000 cavalry of Munford's Brigade.[4] The marches of October 1 and 2 brought the battery back to its old camp near Charles Town.[5] All through the trek, the guns creaked and rattled along the roads, but not once did they bark at the enemy, who proved most elusive.

Chew's grand tour failed to uncover any Yankee activity, nor did the Federals north of the Potomac provide Pelham with anything much to do until October 1. On that date, Brig. Gen. Alfred Pleasonton mounted a major reconnaissance from Sharpsburg through Shepherdstown to Martinsburg. Pleasonton's force consisted of the 8th Illinois Cavalry, three squadrons each of the 8th Pennsylvania and 3rd Indiana Cavalry, and Lt. Alexander C. M. Pennington's Battery M, 2nd U.S. Artillery, in all about 700 men. The column crossed the Potomac and drove back Capt. Thomas C. Waller's Company A of the 9th Virginia Cavalry, stationed just outside of the town as pickets.

For some reason, Col. W. H. F. Lee, commanding Fitz Lee's Brigade, did not follow the plan he and Wade Hampton had discussed just the day before.[6] Lee had stated that should the enemy drive in his pickets, a stand would be made first at Williamson's Crossroads, and if that proved impossible, then at the stone bridge over Opequon Creek, which Lee promised to hold to the last extremity. When Lee's artillery, Pelham with Breathed's Battery,[7] reached him, it went into position on the west bank of the Opequon on Pleasonton's left flank.[8] The Yankee cavalry had pushed so far that Lee recognized his inability to hold the bridge and, after Pelham and Breathed fired a few rounds, withdrew southward toward Winchester.

In the morning, Lee had sent a courier to Hampton warning of Pleasonton's advance. Hampton immediately set out for the stone bridge. On nearing it, he ordered a few men ahead of his column to ascertain the situation. They returned and informed him that not only wasn't Lee there, but no pickets were stationed between the bridge and Martinsburg. Hampton quickly rode ahead with a squadron and one gun from Hart's Battery. Upon reaching the bridge, he found the enemy already across and within 600 yards of the town. Lee was nowhere in sight. Hampton fell back to Martinsburg with his entire command and put Hart's guns into battery in the town.

Pleasonton's drive toward the town caused Hampton concern for the safety of his wagon train. Such a threat had also been discussed at the previous day's meeting with Lee, so Hampton directed the train to go by the Romney Road to Darkesville on the road to Winchester as planned. He dispatched the 1st North Carolina Cavalry and two of Hart's guns to accompany it. Then, not wanting to submit the town to a bombardment, he exited by the Tuscarora Road and placed the remaining section of Hart's battery on a hill that commanded the Tuscarora, Winchester, and Romney Roads.[9] His adversary, seemingly satisfied at having captured Martinsburg, chose not to follow.

Stuart now arrived on the scene and made preparations to attack. Pleasonton made the job easier by commencing his retreat toward Shepherdstown. Hampton and Lee pursued, Breathed's and Hart's guns blazing away whenever given the opportunity. The last salvos echoed from a position within two miles of Shepherdstown, Breathed's guns getting in the final word. Neither battery suffered any casualties in the affair.

Everything returned to status quo for the next several days. The long-lost cannoneers from Orange Court House and Rapidan Station were at last brought out of exile to rejoin their batterymates in early October. Private Walters wrote his wife a long letter recapping his activities, the changes in the battery, and his hope of acquiring a substitute or a furlough:

> Clark County, Va. October the 2nd 1862
>
> Dear wife,
>
> It is with great pleasure that I seat myself this evening to inform you that I am not right well but right smarter than I was when I left Rapidan Station, hoping these few lines find you all well. I can inform you that we have got to the company last night. I was glad to see the boys but was more proud to receive a letter from you which they had kept for some time. It was dated August the 12. It gave me great satisfaction to hear you all was well and was getting along so well with your work.
>
> I can inform you that I had a very hard march, but I seen right smart of the country. We went by Culpeper CH and Woodsville, Sperryville, Luray, Front Royal, and White Post which was [a] very nice little village. We have crossed the Blue Ridge on our own side once more. We are in 12 miles of Winchester [word illegible] Shenandoah River. It is a nice river. It is about 75 yards wide where we crossed.
>
> I have no news to write about the army. They ain't fighting any at this time as I know of. Our Floyd boys has had some very hard times since they left us but all came out safe but T. Gibson. He got accidentally shot through the leg but didn't lay him up.

This morning finds me in tolerable health. We have all got straightened out in our new company. We are in Captain Henry's Company. The most of the Floyd's boys is in this company. James Gray, Isa Poff, Wm. B. Reed, D. R. Conner, T. Gibson, Wm. A. Simpson & myself is in one mess. They all are very well satisfied with their captain. I have known him ever since I have been in the service, and I think he is a very as good a captain as we could get. We have got splendid guns, but haven't got horses enough yet. I am in hopes they will make peace before we get ready for action. It is reported that our Congress has got for 60 days to try to make peace, and Lincoln wants 90 days to make peace, but I don't know whether it is so or not, but I am in hopes it is so.

There is talk of our army falling back towards Richmond again, but they had better keep the Yankees on the other side of the Potomac if they can. I have heard no news from the army in a few days. But I believe everything is still. Every[thing] looks bad up in this country. We have come from Richmond here through the country, and I have not seen more than 50 acres of plowed land and nary [an] acre seeded, and it is over 200 miles.

You wrote in your letter that I must have my substitute ready, but I don't know where I can get one now for the law requires one over 45 years and the man that hires him must stand responsible for him if he runs off. The man will have to lose his money and then go back and take his place again, and that is just what the most of the substitutes does, so you see it is a very dull chance, but if I can get one any time I will send after the money. If you haven't done sent the money, I don't think it is worth while to send it till I send after it. I think I will get a furlough before long. You must all do the best you can. Try and get some seeding done if you can. Tell father's family and uncle Jim's howdy for me. Tell them I haven't got time to write to them now, but I am in hopes I will have an opportunity to pay them for their kindness in helping you put up your grain and [word illegible]. Write soon as this comes to hand. Direct your letter to Winchester in care of Captain Henry, Stuart's Horse Artillery. Give my love and respects to all. Excuse bad writing for very nervous. Tell Molly and Sis I haven't forgot them. I remain your loving husband till death,

Wm P Walters to M E Walters[10]

Walters's belief that "everything was still" was a fair summation of the military situation following Pleasonton's little jaunt to Martinsburg and back. The horse artillery camps were quiet. Not even the sometimes-verbose George Neese had more than a sentence or two per day to record for the week after his return to Charles Town.[11] The men of all four batteries enjoyed the hospitality of the local populace, the officers somewhat more than the men. Pelham and Sallie Dandridge of The Bower renewed their acquaintance from Pelham's days as a lieutenant in the Alburtis Battery. The two shared many a quiet moment in The Bower's beautiful rose garden. Dances, parties, and other festivities helped strengthen the bond that grew between them, and Pelham's letters home spoke of an engagement and plans for the future the two would never have.[12]

Romance was also in the air at Glenvin, home of Mr. and Mrs. Nathaniel Burwell and their seventeen-year-old daughter, Susan. Her brother Robert, who had transferred to Henry's Battery, introduced her to Captain Henry. The meeting led to an engagement that would last over ten years before the two were wed in 1875.[13]

But Pelham kept an eye on his guns as well as on the lovely Miss Dandridge. Pvt. H. H. Matthews recalled Pelham visiting Breathed's camp:

> I remember Pelham bringing the ladies over to our camp, showing the guns and the men under his command. He seemed to be so proud of them. From gun to gun he would go, petting each piece as affectionately as if they were animals. He would tell them the history of each gun—how at a certain place a particular gun had wrought such terrible execution among the Yankees, and so on to the end.[14]

Pelham's choice of topics may have unnerved a lady or two but did nothing to diminish the gallant Alabamian in their eyes. He and his men were true heroes. Their accomplishments already were becoming legend throughout the South, and now the men were about to add a significant chapter to that legend.

Robert E. Lee had not been so consumed with the reorganization of his army that he neglected to plan for adding to the discomfiture of his opponent across the Potomac. McClellan was under heavy pressure from Washington to do something. His feeble jabs across the river in Lee's direction did nothing to placate Lincoln, who wanted a full offensive mounted against the Rebels.

McClellan, as was his wont, procrastinated. This passed the initiative to Lee. But Lee was not prepared to resume offensive operations either. His army needed time to recuperate, and he needed information about what McClellan was up to, if anything. Once informed, he could plan. To get that information, he turned to Jeb Stuart.

On October 8, Stuart received a communication from Lee.[15] The first sentence of the order was music to Stuart's ears: "An expedition into Maryland with a detachment of cavalry, if it can be successfully executed, is at this time desirable."[16] But there was more, much more. Chambersburg was mentioned as a target, and to Stuart that meant one thing—Pennsylvania. He would be carrying the war to the North. He wasted little time in accepting and preparing for the assignment. Stuart selected 600 men each from his three brigades. Brig. Gen. Wade Hampton and Colonels W. H. F. "Rooney" Lee and William E. "Grumble" Jones would command these contingents.[17] He also took two guns each from Hart's and Breathed's Batteries. Both Hart and Breathed, who accompanied their guns, were under the overall command of Pelham.[18]

On the night of the ninth, the column started for the Potomac. At Hedgesville, they made camp for the remainder of the night. Before dawn on the tenth, a specially picked force from the 10th Virginia Cavalry, under Lt. Hopestill R. Phillips, splashed across the river at McCoy's Ford. Its mission was to capture the Yankee pickets to prevent them from giving the alarm. Though Phillips and his men failed to grab a single picket, they did cut them off from their reserve, which brought the same result. Immediately following Phillips's men came Hampton's Brigade and Bamberg's section of Hart's Battery. Everyone struck out for the National Turnpike.[19] Next came Lee with Jones and the section of Breathed's Battery bringing up the rear.

Stuart's column did not go unobserved by the Federals, and by 10:00, the Union commanders in Williamsport and Hagerstown were both aware of the Confederates' presence. At noon, Col. Matthew C. Butler's 2nd South Carolina Cavalry and Hart with his guns entered Mercersburg. Pvt. Louis Sherfesee, guidon bearer for Hart's Battery, remembered his brief stay in the town and his subsequent search for a horse:

> In passing through Mercersburg, we noticed several ladies on the portico of a rather pretentious dwelling, and one of them as we passed by, threw her hands up, clapped them and said, "They are not rebels. They are not rebels for they look like our men. They are dressed like our men, and they ride like our men. Oh no! Oh no! They are not rebels." The boys all enjoyed the astonishment of the people as we rode along. I suppose they thought the Confederates were demons.
>
> My horse not being a very good one, I asked Captain Hart's permission to go ahead and capture one, so with four comrades went before the advance guard and left the road the command was traveling on about a half mile, and riding up to a farm house we called the farmer out and told him we wanted some horses.
>
> He said, "I am very glad to hear it, for I do not think the government has treated me right, as they have bought horses from my neighbors but not from me. I am a good Union man. I have subscribed liberally to the cause and I see no reason why they did not buy my horses."
>
> I told him that was all right. We would make amends for the past and asked him to bring his horses out, which he did. He brought out four large Percheron horses and of course we did quibble about the price, but agreed to give him what he asked for them and he was so

> well pleased with the sale that he told us his daughter had a very fine saddle horse she was very fond of, but he knew where he could get a good one that would suit her better, and if I wanted it he would sell it to me.
>
> When he brought it out, I agreed upon the price. He was satisfied, and the five horses were fastened to the hitching post with ours. The farmer was so well pleased, he asked us in to lunch. We of course could not refuse anything to eat and when through, I asked for pen and ink and wrote an order on Jeff Davis at Richmond for the amount of money due him for his horses and handed it to him. He enjoyed the joke very much and when we started to leave, asked us for a settlement. I told him we had settled, that I had given him an order on Jeff Davis at Richmond because I thought it would be easier to find him than a quartermaster (who was continually on the move) and Jeff Davis could always be found at Richmond.
>
> He even then did not see through it but laughed at the joke, and when we were in the yard and were mounting our horses, he asked me again for a settlement. I told him that I had settled with him, that he was evidently mistaken in us, and asked him who he took us for.
>
> He said, "Soldiers." "But of what army?" I asked him. He said, "The Union of course." I answered, "No sir, you are mistaken," and I raised the front of my jacket, showed him my belt buckle with C.S.A. on it. He could not take it in even then, so I took one of my jacket buttons and showed him the Palmetto Tree and S.C. on it.
>
> He then saw we were not Yankees, but Rebels, and commenced to beg very hard for the return of his horses, and I compromised by returning his daughter's horse, as we South Carolinians could not take the property of a lady. We, however, carried off the other four and you can imagine how he felt. We rejoined the command and enjoyed many laughable incidents, because the people throughout the country did not know there were any Rebels about.[20]

Even though Hart's boys were having the first crack at everything, Breathed's men, marching at the rear of the long column, were not to be outdone. They, too, searched for horses and managed to surprise more than a few of the local inhabitants. Pvt. H. H. Matthews was one who managed to secure a new mount for himself at the expense of another shocked farmer.

> My mule being very exhausted I exchanged him with an old gentleman for a sorrel mare, much against his will. Not having time to enter into an argument with the native on the rights of property in a hostile country I changed saddles and bid my angry friend an everlasting adieu. Breathed fell in love with my capture, but could not persuade

> me that my beauty would not do me as much good service as him, so I rode my mare to the end of the expedition. Nothing of any note occurred during that day except to note the astonishment depicted on the faces of the natives to see live rebels in their midst was beyond what they had ever expected to see.[21]

Despite all the side excursions, Stuart kept everyone on the move toward Chambersburg, which the men reached about an hour before dark. Hampton placed Hart's two guns in position overlooking the town and sent in Lt. Thomas C. Lee to demand its surrender, which was forthcoming. Hart's Battery then marched through the town, Private Sherfesee noting that the only store open at that time was a shoe store, which "sold out" of its goods in ten minutes.[22] The battery camped for the night on the north edge of town. Breathed led his battery into Chambersburg with colors flying and camped in the public square. The battery's flag was tied to the spoke of one of the wheels so as to leave little doubt who was in possession of the town.[23]

Stuart's rapid advance had left some disillusioned Pennsylvanians in its wake, not to mention a considerable number of embarrassed and frustrated Federal officers. Telegraph lines buzzed. Messages and orders flashed back and forth between equally confused commanders. The size of Stuart's force had grown to 3,000 men and two batteries by noon on the tenth, but by 9:30 A.M. on the eleventh, a more accurate estimate of 2,000 men and four guns had been made and Stuart's whereabouts nailed down to the vicinity of Chambersburg. Each side now had a single problem to solve. For Stuart, it was how to get back to Virginia. For the Federals, it was how to stop him.

Before Stuart departed Chambersburg, he had two parts of his mission yet to perform: destroy the railroad bridge over the Conococheague Creek and loot or burn the vast quantities of Federal stores in the town. The first task went uncompleted, the bridge wreckers returning and reporting that the bridge was of iron construction, but the second was enjoyed by all and met with considerable success.[24] It had begun to rain the evening before and had not let up all night. The downpour considerably altered the appearance of the men in Breathed's Battery, as Private Matthews recalled:

> Rain, rain, nothing but rain. Quite a number of the boys on coming through Mercersburg had provided themselves with straw hats, the kind usually worn by farmers in that region of Pennsylvania. The appearance of the battery was grotesque, indeed, so that Gen. Stuart on riding through the battery asked Pelham where he got all the farmers from. The name farmer stuck to us for quite a while. The constant rain had the tendency to make our hats quite limp, so that they resembled Shaker bonnets.[25]

When Stuart finally left Chambersburg at dawn, Pelham and Breathed, with their "Shakers" in tow, led the column with "Rooney" Lee's troopers, while Hampton and Hart's section provided the rear guard. Jones's men trotted in between. The question of how the raiders would get back to Virginia had been decided. Stuart had ridden around McClellan once before and enjoyed the trip. He decided to repeat the escapade.

The march proved long and extremely fatiguing. Stuart headed east toward Gettysburg to "prevent the inhabitants from detecting [his] real route and object."[26] Once across the Blue Ridge, he turned south toward Hagerstown for several miles, crossed the border into Maryland, and entered Emmitsburg at sunset on the eleventh. Private Matthews remembered the reception given the Rebels by the townspeople:

> We entered Emmitsburg, where we were received with open arms, the whole town turning out to greet these peerless riders of Stuart's. The ladies (God bless them) wept with joy at the sight of the dear grey jackets. Basket after basket of provisions (as an evidence of their love) was passed around until the half famished artillerymen were made to feel that they were in the land of promise and among friends. The few moments spent among those dear people were indeed happy ones, and often during the war, when I was pinched with hunger, that beautiful picture of Emmitsburg would be recalled to me. The old battle scarred boys of the battery, with their farmers' hats, were indeed an object of curiosity to those sweet, dear girls. Several of the boys could not resist the tender smiles of the fairer sex (I was one of the first victims) so we gave them our straw hats as souvenirs. I doubt not that some of those hats are still treasured by some of the dear ladies in that locality yet.[27]

The exchanges of hats and food were not allowed to slow the column. Nothing was. Pelham rode at the front in the company of Lt. Francis W. Southall of the 1st Virginia Cavalry, whose company formed Stuart's advance. Breathed's two guns trotted behind under orders to keep pace with the cavalry no matter what.[28] Keep pace they did, though it was grueling to both men and horses.

A captured dispatch from Col. Richard H. Rush, commander of the 6th Pennsylvania Cavalry, better known as Rush's Lancers, told Stuart that he had caused confusion in the ranks of his pursuers. They were unsure just what he was about. He wanted to keep it that way and pushed on through the night through Woodsboro, Liberty, and New Market to Monrovia, where the telegraph lines along the Baltimore and Ohio Railroad were cut and the tracks obstructed. The column arrived at Hyattstown at daybreak on the twelfth. Private Matthews recorded:

> At about 9 A.M., we struck a small party, of the enemy's cavalry, which evidently belonged to Pleasonton's command. This body of the enemy retired towards Mechanicstown. Everything now depended upon the rapidity of our march as Pleasonton was advised of our movements and had a shorter distance to the Ford than we had. The whole right of the column was kept in a trot and by daylight on the 12th the advance guard entered Hyattstown, which is about 33 miles from Emmitsburg. Within 24 hours we had marched, or at least trotted, 65 miles, being always up to our file leading piece. Three or four times during the night did we change horses for our old ones. When we reached the Potomac we did not have a single horse that we started with, except a few that were ridden by the cannoneers. The change was made so quickly, that there was not a moments delay. The men of the battery were unusually intelligent, and they knew that minutes to us meant a great deal. We knew that the sooner we reached the Potomac and across would our expedition cease and we could get a rest, so everybody helped the drivers to change the harness on the horses.[29]

Everyone else had begun to feel much the same. Exhaustion was a tireless enemy. Men were lulled to sleep in the saddle by the soft jangling of their accoutrements and the rhythmic sound of the horses' hooves as they struck the road. It was a night that few would remember with any clarity and that most would recall not at all. But despite everything, the troopers and artillerymen kept the pace.

Meanwhile, the Federals were closing in. Brig. Gen. George Stoneman's cavalry was guarding the area around Poolesville, and Brig. Gen. Alfred Pleasonton's forces held the ford near the mouth of the Monocacy River. Stuart just missed crossing sabers with Col. Alfred Duffié's 1st Rhode Island Cavalry at Barnesville and did clash with a company of Pleasonton's cavalry on the Poolesville Road. Stuart now called for Pelham and Breathed. The corridor to the river had to be held long enough to permit the lengthy column to cross at White's Ford. Pleasonton needed to be discouraged from interfering. That was Pelham's job. The "Boy Major" ordered up one of Breathed's guns, placed it on the ridge overlooking the Poolesville-Monocacy Road, and sent his greetings to Pleasonton. Before long, two guns of Battery M, 2nd U.S. Artillery, under Lt. Alexander C. M. Pennington, answered Pelham's challenge. The duel continued while Rooney Lee's troopers and Breathed's remaining gun headed for the ford.

Whether Lee was expecting resistance at the ford is not known, but when he arrived, he found a steep bank, located several hundred yards east and overlooking the Maryland side of the ford, dotted with the blue coats of the 99th Pennsylvania Infantry. He had Breathed unlimber his gun and sent a message to the Federal commander, Lt. Col. Edwin R. Biles, that he had fifteen minutes to surrender.[30] The time passed slowly without the desired compliance. Breathed was joined by one of Hart's guns sent on ahead by Hampton.[31] At the end of the fifteen minutes, the artillery lobbed a couple of shells toward the Federal position, and Lee's troopers advanced. To the immense surprise and great relief of Lee, the Yankees were found to be abandoning their position without a fight. The ford was opened.

Back where Pelham and Pennington traded shot and shell, Stuart watched as first Jones's Brigade and then most of Hampton's galloped behind the artillery to the ford. Only the 2nd South Carolina, the Phillips Legion, and one of Hart's pieces acting as rear guard had yet to pass. Stuart now ordered Pelham to a new position about 1,000 yards west. Again the gallant Alabamian went into battery and began to pound Pleasonton's skirmishers as they closed in. Butler, following behind, had not cleared the Poolesville-Monocacy Road and, in fact, had deployed his men and lone gun to oppose the advancing Federals. He was in danger of being cut off.

At the ford, Lee's, Jones's, and Hampton's troopers, with Hart's other gun, had crossed the river. The artillery was put into position to cover the crossing from the Virginia shore. Pelham and his piece now reached the ford. The gun splashed through the water and struggled up the slope, taking its place beside Hart's. Pelham remained on the towpath with Breathed's gun, which continued to blast away, first in one direction and then the other, at the approaching enemy. All eyes now strained to catch the first glimpse of Butler, but the road remained empty.

Stuart, who had crossed the river, dispatched several couriers with orders to Butler to ride for the ford. Not one succeeded in finding him. In a voice choked with emotion, Stuart confided in his engineer officer, Capt. William W. Blackford, that he feared the rear guard had been lost. Blackford begged to be allowed to try to bring them in. Stuart gave his consent. Blackford was mounted on his remarkable horse, Magic. While others had exchanged their horses several times during the raid, Blackford had ridden Magic the entire time. Because his staff position often required him to ride back and forth along the moving column, Blackford and Magic had actually traveled more miles than most of the command. Now he put his faith in his magnificent horse, splashed across the river, waved his hat at Pelham, who continued to hold the crossing, and raced along the road. After passing a number of couriers who had failed to locate Butler, he arrived at Pelham's first artillery position. Butler still was nowhere in sight. Riding on, he rounded a bend in the road and came upon the rear guard.

Blackford quickly informed Butler of his precarious situation and conveyed Stuart's orders to bring the gun at a gallop.[32] Butler wanted to comply but expressed his fear that Hart's gun could not be saved. The horses were in a state of exhaustion and might not be able to move the gun, much less keep up with the cavalry at such a pace. Nevertheless, they decided to attempt to bring it off. The gun had been retiring by prolonge in order to keep firing.[33] Reaching a section of the road that was somewhat sunken, the gun was limbered, and to everyone's astonishment, the horses responded.[34] The whole column went careening down the road at breakneck speed. On reaching the towpath, Blackford saw Pelham still at his post. On the Virginia shore, Stuart sent Lt. Channing Price, his aide-de-camp, with orders to have Breathed follow Butler across.[35] As this last gun came up out of the river, the pace of the horses slackened. Stuart and Hampton, who were sitting on their horses nearby, dismounted, put their shoulders to the wheels, and helped push the gun up the slope.[36] The raid had been an amazing feat in itself, but the escape had been a miracle. As the Confederates rode away from the ford, all Pleasonton and Stoneman could do was watch and begin making their excuses as to why they had failed to trap the wily Stuart.[37]

The role of Pelham, Breathed, Hart, and their guns and crews in the success of the raid should not be overlooked.[38] Unlike the Chickahominy and Catlett's Station raids, in which the horse artillery, for various reasons, failed to keep pace with the cavalry, Pelham and company were always exactly where they were supposed to be all through the Chambersburg expedition. The cost in horses was, as would be expected, high, but the results speak for themselves. Stuart most certainly would have lost considerably more men, if not his entire command, had Pleasonton, Stoneman, and Biles been more aggressive. One of the main reasons they were not was the fire of the horse artillery. Without the guns, Stuart's report of the raid, if he had had the opportunity to write one, would have had an entirely different ending.

Once across the Potomac, Stuart led his weary command toward Leesburg. Private Sherfesee of Hart's Battery left a vivid description of its condition:

> After leaving the ford, we marched about half a mile and went into a clover field; the clover was, as well as I can remember, about eighteen inches high. Reaction had taken place. The men were exhausted and they actually fell off their horses, not having enough strength to unsaddle them, and slept until next morning, just lying down and the horses loose.[39]

Even as the raiders recovered, the army celebrated their astounding accomplishment. The cavalry and horse artillery felt admiration and envy, as a portion of a letter written by Lieutenant Williams of Chew's Battery demonstrates:

> Stuart has made the entire compass of the enemy's lines, a dash more brilliant than any yet. The papers will tell you. Maj. Pelham, Chief of his Artillery, has just told me of it, many amusing incidents. Our horses were too much broken down to go or we would have been on the [raid]. What plunder.[40]

Pelham had but four days to tell his "many amusing incidents" to his comrades in the horse artillery and the ladies at The Bower. The Federals had been embarrassed, and like a horde of wasps whose nest has been disturbed, they were quick to strike back at their tormentors.

On October 16, McClellan ordered two reconnaissances across the Potomac, one from Sharpsburg through Shepherdstown to Smithfield and the other from Harpers Ferry to Charles Town. Brig. Gen. Andrew A. Humphreys led 500 cavalry, 6,000 infantry, and six guns over the river at Shepherdstown. Stuart, with Fitz Lee's Brigade and Breathed's Battery, accompanied by Pelham, first offered resistance two miles beyond Shepherdstown, but against such odds, he was forced to give ground throughout the day. The Stonewall Brigade and Capt. John C. Carpenter's Battery reinforced Stuart late in the afternoon. Only darkness halted Humphreys near Kearneysville. On the seventeenth, he pushed on to Leetown and then dispatched a small force of cavalry to Smithfield. Stuart harassed Humphreys's column with skirmisher and artillery fire and followed the Federals when they fell back to Shepherdstown. Breathed's Battery suffered no casualties; Carpenter's had one man wounded.

During the time Stuart was shadowing Humphreys's column, Col. Thomas T. Munford was likewise occupied with Brig. Gen. Winfield S. Hancock's considerable force of cavalry, infantry, and artillery. The Federals crossed the Potomac at Harpers Ferry and pushed on toward Charles Town. The 12th Virginia Cavalry, under Lt. Col. Richard H. Burks, which was on picket at Charles Town, was the first to oppose them. Supporting the picket was one gun from Chew's Battery under Lt. John W. Carter, two guns from the 3rd Richmond Howitzers under Capt. Benjamin H. Smith, and one from Capt. David Watson's 2nd Richmond Howitzers.[41]

About a mile beyond Halltown, Hancock's column ran into Smith's and Carter's guns. The artillery engagement that followed lasted a number of hours, ending only with the near exhaustion of the Confederates' ammunition and the advance of the Union infantry.[42] Early in the fighting, Carter was painfully wounded in the hand. He left his gun and went to the rear to have his wound dressed but returned and fought until the guns were withdrawn. Smith was not as lucky. While fighting with only two guns, he was struck, lost his foot, and fell into the enemy's hands when the town was captured. The artillery and its commanders were the heroes of the hour.[43] Carter's combativeness, first seen here outside Charles Town, would eventually lift him to the command of the battery. His wound would not be his last.

Like Humphreys, Hancock did not remain long in Virginia, and by the eighteenth, all the men were back to their starting points. Once again, all was quiet along the Potomac. The men of the horse artillery went back to enjoying the beauty and bounty of the area. Private Walters of Breathed's Battery wrote home on the nineteenth. He was quite satisfied with his surroundings.

> I have no news to write of importance about the army, only they had a battle down about the Potomac 3 or 4 days ago, and we heard very heavy cannonading yesterday in that direction, but haven't heard the particulars yet. There are different reports going down here. Some say the Yankees are advancing in large numbers and some say that our army is going in Maryland again, and I don't know which is the right report.
>
> We are camped in a very good place, and I don't know when we will leave. We get plenty to eat here. We get flour, beef, and mutton, the very fattest sort. But there are no sweet potatoes in this neighborhood and apples are getting scarce. There is nothing that I can press in service here but chickens. I was out last night about midnight trying to flank a hen house.[44]

Walters was not the only soldier trying to flank something. His time of reverie and a full belly were soon to be interrupted. George B. McClellan's reconnaissances west of the Shenandoah River in the middle of October confirmed the position of Robert E. Lee's army in the lower Valley. On the twenty-first, McClellan began to probe east of the river. On the twenty-sixth, he began crossing it in force. The war was about to return to Virginia in earnest.

CHAPTER 8

The Road to Fredericksburg

"A full share of the praise"

The movement of the Army of the Potomac into Virginia could not have come at a worse time for the cavalry and horse artillery of Stuart's command. At the moment that Robert E. Lee needed his mounted arm working at peak efficiency, it was severely crippled by disease. Grease heel and sore tongue[1] had reduced the number of horses in Fitz Lee's Brigade to the point that some regiments numbered scarcely 100 men.[2] In the horse artillery, the number of horses pulling each gun was lowered from six to four, a circumstance that would directly affect the artillery's mobility at crucial times.[3] Stuart responded to the problem as best he could, but the cavalry that remained would have to shoulder a larger burden.[4]

In spite of the handicap caused by the reduction of horses, Lee had to counter McClellan's move. He did so on October 28. Because McClellan's intentions were unknown, Lee divided his forces, pulling Jackson back to Winchester and sending Longstreet across the Blue Ridge into Culpeper County. Stuart screened these operations, a task that proved difficult because of the dispersion of the cavalry along the upper Potomac. Hampton, who was in the vicinity of Martinsburg, was unable to join Stuart for several days.[5] Munford's Brigade had to be left to cover Jackson's rear in the Valley. All Stuart had left was the much diminished brigade of Fitz Lee, which was under the command of Col. Williams C. Wickham.[6] Stuart would have to face the Federals with less than 1,000 men and six guns of the horse artillery under Pelham.[7]

On October 30, Stuart crossed the Blue Ridge into Loudoun County at Snicker's Gap. He turned south toward Middleburg and bivouacked for the night at Bloomfield.[8] Here Stuart received word of the presence of a Federal force at Mountville on the Snickersville Turnpike. The next morning, the 9th Virginia Cavalry, supported by the 3rd, surprised Companies I, L, and M of the 1st Rhode Island Cavalry, under Lt. Lorenzo D. Gove, which were picketing the Snicker's Gap Turnpike near Mountsville.[9] Gove was mortally wounded, and the Rhode Islanders were routed all the way back to Aldie. Pelham and his guns managed to get in a few rounds but were soon outdistanced by the cavalry.[10] As the remnants of Gove's command reached Aldie, they ran into Brig. Gen. George Bayard's Cavalry Brigade and two guns of Battery C, 3rd U.S. Artillery, under Capt. Horatio G. Gibson. Stuart's troopers were brought up short and driven out of Aldie by a charge of the 1st New Jersey Cavalry, which in turn was sent scrambling back into the village by the 4th Virginia. Carbine fire from a skirmish line of the 1st New Jersey and artillery fire from Gibson's two guns brought the 4th Virginia to a halt and drove them to cover.[11]

Stuart quickly realized that he needed to match the Federal artillery if he wished to hold his position. With Pelham nowhere in sight, Stuart ordered his ordnance officer, Capt. John Esten Cooke, to find the horse artillery commander and bring him up at the gallop. Cooke dashed rearward and found Pelham advancing at a walk, riding a huge artillery horse, his knees drawn up short by the stirrups.[12] The young Alabamian seemed quite nonplussed and assured Cooke that the guns, which had not been able to keep pace with the cavalry, were coming up at the gallop.[13] Before long, two guns were unlimbered and began shelling the enemy's battery. The fight turned into a long-range carbine and artillery duel, which ended when Bayard fell back to Chantilly. Stuart, receiving information that an enemy force was advancing on his rear from Mountville, withdrew to Middleburg.[14]

The Federals who threatened Stuart's rear on the thirty-first were led by Brig. Gen. Alfred Pleasonton. His command was made up of the 2nd Cavalry Brigade and Lt. Alexander C. M. Pennington's Battery M, 2nd U.S. Artillery. Beginning October 26, Pleasonton had crossed the Potomac at Berlin and had scouted through Leesburg, Aldie, Middleburg, and Philomont.[15] On November 1, he pushed south from Philomont toward the Ashby Gap Turnpike. Stuart left his camp at Middleburg and rode through Union,[16] about midway between the Snicker's Gap and Ashby Gap Turnpikes, and collided with the Federals just west of Philomont. The 8th Pennsylvania Cavalry, which had been ordered to scout toward Union, was ambushed and forced to retreat. The 3rd Indiana Cavalry was brought up and, with the Pennsylvanians, drove the Confederates from their position in a wood. But as the blue troopers attempted to advance further, they came under the fire of Pelham's guns. Col. David McM. Gregg noted that his men were subject to such a hail of grape and canister that he was forced to pull them back and send for Pennington.[17] The day closed with Pelham and Pennington firing at each other as the cavalries withdrew to their respective starting points.

Early on the morning of November 2, Stuart's command roused itself, saddled up, and rode back toward Union to occupy the line of the previous day.[18] Pleasonton did likewise from the other direction. A clash was inevitable. Lt. Col. J. William Hofmann's Infantry Brigade and Lt. Frederick M. Edgell's 1st Battery, New Hampshire Light Artillery, had reinforced the Yankees. Stuart, on the other hand, had to make do with Fitz Lee's depleted brigade.[19] Pelham again displayed his courage and daring in trying to stem the tide of the Federal advance. At one juncture, he took a howitzer and rode to a position where he could fire on a particularly annoying squadron of Union cavalry that was picking off the battery's horses. The enemy was unaware of his presence until Pelham opened an accurate fire and routed them. Dashing from his cover, he and his cannoneers charged forward and captured the enemy cavalry's standard and other trophies.[20]

Despite the heavy barrage from Pelham's guns, the Federals pressed the Confederates back through Union. While the "Boy Major" fought the Federal cavalry and infantry, Pennington gave Pelham his full attention and quickly proved he was a foe to be reckoned with. During his engagement with Pelham on the previous day, Pennington had taken the exact range of Breathed's guns. Now, with the Confederate horse artillery occupying the same position, Pennington's guns showered it with shot and shell. Grimly Breathed hung on. Corp. Christian Costigan and Pvt. John Phillips were killed at their posts before Pelham gave the orders to limber to the rear.[21] Pennington followed, and when Pelham again put Breathed's guns into battery, the tenacious Federal artilleryman was soon making the air around the Confederate gunners thick with iron. A well-aimed shot exploded one of Pelham's caissons, killing all the horses and wounding Privates John M. Bollman and John Culbreth. Another shell burst in front of the battery's number-two gun, heavily damaging the piece and felling three men. One of the men, Pvt. Henry H. Matthews, was struck on his left side near the hipbone.[22] Severely bruised, Matthews might not have been able to keep up with the battery on the following days had it not been for color bearer Robert L. Mackall, who helped his wounded comrade on and off his horse.

Though his men and equipment suffered much at the hands of Pennington, Pelham was only checked, not mated. His mission was to break up the waves of blue infantry and cavalry that threatened to engulf Stuart's meager force. In this task he did not falter. Under the Alabamian's direction, Breathed's guns ravaged the advancing lines. When the 7th Indiana Infantry left the protection of the houses of Union for the open fields beyond, Pelham greeted them with a shot that became legendary. Drawing a bead on the infantry regiment's color bearer, he sent a shell hurtling toward its target 800 yards away. It exploded right above the flag, killing the color sergeant and color corporal and wounding several others. But even with Pelham's heroic efforts, the Federals could not be stopped. Stuart pulled back his cavalry after giving Pelham enough time to withdraw to a new position on a rise just northeast of the junction of the Millville and Welbourne Roads known as Seaton's Hill. Unlimbering their pieces, the weary cannoneers rammed home their charges and prepared to give the enemy one last fight. As the 56th Pennsylvania Infantry moved forward from a ravine, shells burst in its midst. Casualties mounted. The regiment took shelter behind a stone wall while the Federal artillery replied to Pelham's challenge.

With darkness gathering, the firing slowly died away. Stuart moved his cavalry and artillery across Pantherskin Creek and camped for the night.

The day had been hard on Stuart's entire command, but extremely so on the horse artillery. Losses of both men and horses were high. Pelham and Breathed had fought from no less than five positions. The mobility and fighting qualities that Stuart had wanted from his horse artillery were well displayed, and he graciously praised his bold artillery commander in his report of the day's fighting. Had it not been for Pelham's guns, Fitz Lee's weakened brigade would have been handled roughly, if not crushed. The stubborn resistance of the horse artillery had been Stuart's salvation. It was precisely for such occasions that he had organized it. The battlefield laurels were Pelham's, and well deserved, but the vision of what the horse artillery could become had been Stuart's.

Though delayed by Stuart, Pleasonton had not been stopped. Indeed, he had been heavily reinforced by Brig. Gen. William W. Averell's cavalry brigade and Capt. John C. Tidball's Battery A, 2nd U.S. Artillery. The Federals were determined to renew the contest in the morning. During the night, they occupied a cornfield on the north side of Pantherskin Creek, almost exactly opposite Breathed's camp. Their intentions seemed obvious to Stuart, who heard them moving about in the darkness. The exhausted artillerymen, including Pelham, were aroused by the vigilant cavalry commander and warned in time. Color bearer Robert Mackall recounted years later that Pelham awakened the men, had them push the guns to the top of the hill, and in the morning they fired on the cornfield.[23]

Mowing the cornfield stirred up a hornets' nest of Federals. Everything indicated another day of desperate fighting on the part of the Confederates. Stuart's orders were "to move along the east side of the ridge, keeping in front of the enemy, and delaying his progress as much as possible."[24] These instructions had been followed to the letter the previous day at great cost to the horse artillery, but now Stuart received new orders from Maj. Gen. D. H. Hill, whose division was encamped at or in Ashby's Gap. Hill believed that Stuart should fall back to Ashby's Gap and resist Pleasonton there so that Jackson's Corps could get away and follow Longstreet's. Stuart agreed, but, he said, only because "I knew that I could detach part of the command to keep along east of the Blue Ridge while the rest was thus occupied, especially as Hampton's brigade was then expected."[25]

At about 9:00 A.M., Pleasonton, in answer to Pelham's earlier wakeup call, advanced his forces on all roads. The Pantherskin Creek line was held as long as possible, but not without cost. Col. Williams C. Wickham, temporarily in command of Fitz Lee's Brigade, was wounded in the neck by a shell fragment and had to turn the brigade over to Col. Thomas L. Rosser of the 5th Virginia. Breathed, with the assistance of a battery from Hill's command, fought with such vigor as to gain special mention by Stuart. Still, the Federal numbers prevailed when Pleasonton moved to turn Stuart's left flank late in the afternoon.

As planned, Stuart split his force, sending the 1st and 5th Virginia, under Maj. Beverly B. Douglas of the 5th, south toward Piedmont Station on the Manassas Gap Railroad. With the 3rd, 4th, and 9th Virginia, Stuart continued to resist Pleasonton. The fighting swirled around Upperville and along the road to the gap near Paris. There Stuart found infantry and artillery support. A single shot from one of Capt. Robert A. Hardaway's Whitworth guns positioned near Paris served to disperse an enemy battery near Upperville three or four miles away.[26]

As darkness approached, the Federals broke off the fighting. Stuart feared another flanking move in the morning and instructed Rosser, with Henry's Battery, to ride to Piedmont and rendezvous with Douglas.[27] The reunited brigade, soon to be reinforced by Hampton's Brigade, which was expected to arrive via Manassas Gap, would then be in a position to confront Pleasonton. Things did not go as planned. Rosser reached Piedmont, but Douglas, who had misunderstood Stuart's orders, was nowhere in sight. Instead, Rosser rode through the dark into the Union picket lines. Pleasonton had sent Averell to Piedmont, and it was his picket line that clashed with Rosser's advance. Rosser circled west and placed his regiments between Piedmont and Markham in order to protect the gap and be in position to meet Hampton when he arrived. Meanwhile, Stuart had left Paris to confer with Jackson at Millwood. There the cavalry chieftain learned that Robert E. Lee had changed his plans and that holding Ashby's Gap was no longer a priority.[28]

On the morning of November 4, Stuart dispatched Hampton, who had reached Millwood on the third, to Markham. Stuart intended to fight the Federals there. However, Averell's success in taking Piedmont spurred him on to attack Markham. Rosser, reunited with Douglas, moved on Markham to offer battle to Averell. The Confederates were soon hard-pressed to hold their position. Rosser concluded that he could not retake Markham and retreated south toward Barbee's Cross Roads.[29] Companies G and H of the 9th Virginia Cavalry were left with two of Capt. Mathis W. Henry's guns as rear guard. They fought overwhelming numbers for several hours. At one point, Pelham had Henry's guns firing front and rear in a desperate attempt to stem the charging Federals. Strains of the "Marseillaise," sung by the men of the "Napoleon Detachment" as they served the bronze Napoleon that had been captured on the Peninsula, could be heard above the din. Their spirit and courage would have gone for naught, however, had it not been for a timely charge by Rosser, who had turned back with his own 5th Virginia to rescue the rear guard. So close had it been that Averell reported he had 300 men and two guns in his hands at one time but couldn't keep them.[30] Pelham would have denied Averell's claim emphatically. His men had fought on when the Federals were almost among them. The guns had never been silenced. Well might Stuart have written, "Captain Henry's battery of the Stuart Horse Artillery behaved with the most signal gallantry."[31]

Averell responded to Rosser's withdrawal and pushed ahead so rapidly that Hampton barely had cleared Manassas Gap when the Union cavalry attacked him.[32] A successful countercharge cleared the road, and Hampton led his brigade on to Barbee's Cross Roads. Stuart and his staff had ridden through the night ahead of Hampton to reach Barbee's, where the hoped-for concentration of the two brigades would take place. Upon reaching the tiny hamlet, Stuart discovered that only one squadron of Fitz Lee's Brigade was present. The rest had marched south seven miles to Orlean. Stuart showed great displeasure at this circumstance and dispatched Maj. Heros von Borcke with orders for Rosser to report immediately in person and the brigade to follow.[33] Stuart had determined to give battle on the fifth, if the enemy advanced on Barbee's, and he wanted every available man.

Henry's section of the horse artillery had retreated through Barbee's and camped about three miles south of that place. It was among the first units to respond to Stuart's summons to reoccupy the crossroads, moving out sometime after midnight.[34] As the regiments of Fitz Lee's Brigade arrived, they were moved into position. Henry's two guns were placed on a hill north of the town and were supported first by the Cobb Legion and later by the 1st North Carolina Cavalry.[35] Pelham, who was commanding Henry's section, fired his first salvos when the enemy advanced shortly before 9:00. Once again Pennington's Battery answered defiantly. As had occurred at Union, Pelham targeted the blue cavalry with his fire, while Pennington was free to concentrate on the Rebel artillery. Fortunately, on this occasion, Battery M's marksmanship was not as accurate, and Henry's men escaped with no casualties. Nevertheless, Pelham had to give up his first position when the 8th Pennsylvania and the 6th U.S. Cavalry, under Col. David McM. Gregg, threatened his flank. As Pelham leapfrogged back to the crossroads, he paused long enough to deliver a few rounds of canister into Col. John F. Farnsworth's column of the 8th Illinois and the 3rd Indiana Cavalry, charging up the road. The hail of artillery fire and a barricade in the road brought the Federals to a halt.

The battle had lasted into the afternoon, when Stuart received word that Union troops were in Warrenton. Concerned that what he faced at Barbee's was only a feint, while the main enemy thrust was to come through Warrenton, Stuart ordered a withdrawal. He sent Hampton's Brigade via the Flint Hill Road to Gaines's Cross Roads, where it encamped. Stuart with Rosser rode south to Orlean and bivouacked for the night. Upon reaching Orlean, Stuart learned that the report of the enemy's presence in Warrenton was false. A portion of the 2nd North Carolina had repulsed the Federal attack.[36] He had cut his fight at Barbee's short, but it is doubtful that he would have gained any advantage had he remained longer.

The continuous fighting had taken its toll not only on the men and equipment, but also on Stuart's ammunition supply. Capt. John Esten Cooke, Stuart's ordnance officer, arrived at Lt. Col. Edward P. Alexander's headquarters at 3:00 on the afternoon of the fifth. He left with nine wagons filled with small arms and artillery ammunition for the cavalry and the horse batteries. At 6:00 P.M., a courier arrived from Stuart requesting an additional 7,300 rounds of artillery ammunition. Alexander sent what he had and added a note that he didn't think Stuart could use that much with so small an artillery force.[37] Obviously, Alexander, who had known Pelham at West Point, had never seen the Alabamian and the horse artillery in action. If he had, he would have understood Stuart's request completely.

On the morning of November 6, Stuart dispatched Rosser with a portion of his brigade to Warrenton. Stuart led the remainder south to the Rappahannock and crossed the river at Waterloo Bridge. When Rosser reached Warrenton, he found the Federals advancing and threatening his front and rear. He had little choice but to abandon the town, elude the enemy, and head for the Rappahannock and Stuart. He accomplished all without loss. Meanwhile, Hampton's Brigade spent a quiet day in the vicinity of Gaines's Cross Roads and Amissville. Pelham's guns remained silent.

Snow fell thick and fast on the morning of the seventh. Stuart rode undisturbed with Fitz Lee's Brigade to Jeffersonton, leaving pickets along the Rappahannock. Pleasonton pushed across the Rappahannock toward Amissville and Jeffersonton. Stuart offered resistance but fell back gradually.[38] Likewise for Hampton, the day began quietly enough, but the crackle of carbine fire at 3:00 in the afternoon alerted him to the approach of the enemy. His pickets were thrown back to the edge of the camp. Pressed by cavalry from the front and dismounted troopers on the flank, Col. James B. Gordon threw a portion of his 1st North Carolina Cavalry into the road and sent the remainder on foot against the Yankee skirmishers. The effort successfully drove back the Federals to their main body. Capt. James F. Hart then brought up a Blakely gun from his battery, which discouraged any further advance from the Federals.[39] As the day drew to a close, men in blue and gray did the best they could to make themselves comfortable for the night. All knew that more fighting awaited them with the coming of the new day.

The struggle with Hampton was renewed on the eighth, when Pleasonton again made a dash at the Confederates. Aimed at the Georgians of the Cobb and Phillips Legions, the blow was delivered by elements of the 5th U.S., 3rd Indiana, and 8th Illinois Cavalry. The Confederate pickets, who were encamped about three miles from Gaines's Cross Roads near Little Washington, quickly were driven in. Newly commissioned Lt. Col. William G. Delony of Cobb's Legion outdistanced his own men in trying to reinforce his pickets. He soon found himself surrounded by blue troopers and escaped being killed only by the narrowest of margins.[40] Hart's Battery was called forward and unlimbered. One shot it delivered that day was immortalized in the battery's history.

> At Little Washington a number of the enemy's skirmishers had secured a position on Hampton's right and were giving great annoyance. Under cover of a thick wood, they could not be dislodged by a charge of cavalry. One of them, armed with a Whitworth rifle, was firing explosive balls from behind a tree at the caissons with dangerous accuracy. Turning to Corporal [James R.] Blount, one of the gunners, at one of the pieces, Capt. Hart asked him if he could not punish the Whitworth rifle. Blount modestly replied—"I'll try, sir." Ranging his piece with great accuracy at the smoke from the rifle, some seven hundred yards off, he waited until another puff of smoke disclosed his position. Just as Blount gave the command "fire" another puff of smoke went up from behind the tree, and a Blakely shell from Blount's piece was accurately speeding to the same spot. As the smoke from its explosion lifted away, the Federal skirmishers were seen rapidly retiring. Gaining possession of the ground shortly afterwards, we found that Blount's shell had torn into the side of the tree, some two feet above the ground, and exploding with concussion, had literally torn in pieces the man whom had been firing the Whitworth rifle from behind its cover, and had demolished even the piece he had been firing.[41]

Both sides claimed victory, but the edge went to Hampton. Hart's Battery had played an important role in repulsing Pleasonton.

The Federal cavalry commander did not hesitate to go back on the offensive on the ninth. Pleasonton's columns pushed forward to Corbin's Cross Roads about a mile beyond Amissville. A squadron of the 8th New York was reported to have reached Flint Hill on the night of the eighth. The aggressive behavior demonstrated by the Union cavalry was bolstered by a number of infantry brigades occupying Jeffersonton and Amissville. Stuart determined to strike at the latter position and attempted to coordinate Hampton's and Fitz Lee's Brigades for just such an effort on the tenth. The attack failed when Hampton did not receive his orders in time. Fitz Lee's Brigade attacked alone and achieved some success against the Federal horse, but when they encountered the blue infantry, the Confederates broke off the engagement and fell back to their camps.

During the fighting, the horse artillery lost the services of one of its finest officers when Lt. William M. McGregor was seriously wounded.[42] Maj. Heros von Borcke gave an account of the incident in his memoirs:

> During the earlier part of the fight the Federals had been wholly without artillery, but several batteries now came to their assistance, opening a vigorous and well-directed fire upon our guns, which lost

> heavily in men and horses. I had halted near two of our pieces, and was talking with Lieutenant M'Gregor, the officer in command of them, when a shell, bursting within thirty feet of us, sent its deadly missiles in every direction, several fragments of the iron passing directly between us, and one of them shattering the leg of the brave young fellow so that it dangled loosely from his side. He insisted, however, on remaining with his guns, and it required the joint persuasions of General Stuart and myself to induce him to withdraw from the field and place himself in the hands of the surgeon.[43]

McGregor would be out of action for months, but his record of service would not be forgotten. When Capt. Mathis W. Henry later was promoted out of the horse artillery, McGregor took his place as captain of the 2nd Stuart Horse Artillery.

The brief clashes on the tenth were followed by a temporary cessation of the serious cavalry fighting that accompanied Lee's and McClellan's movements east of the mountains. How much more McClellan might have pushed at Lee will never be known, because on November 9, Maj. Gen. Ambrose Burnside assumed command of the Army of the Potomac, superseding McClellan, with whom President Abraham Lincoln had become completely frustrated.[44] With the change in command, Yankee operations ground to a halt while Burnside shook up the army. Stuart and his weary troopers welcomed the respite, as did the men of the horse artillery. They had accomplished much, and Stuart was lavish in his praise of Pelham and his command.

> In all these operations I deem it my duty to bear testimony to the gallantry and patient endurance of the cavalry, fighting every day most unequal conflicts, and successfully opposing for an extraordinary period the onward march of McClellan.
>
> The Stuart Horse Artillery comes in for a full share of this praise, and its gallant commander (Maj. John Pelham) exhibited a skill and courage which I have never seen surpassed. On this occasion I was more than ever struck with that extraordinary coolness and mastery of the situation which more eminently characterized this youthful officer than any other artillerist who has attracted my attention. His *coup d'œil* was accurate and comprehensive, his choice of ground made with the eye of military genius, and his dispositions always such in retiring as to render it impossible for the enemy to press us without being severely punished for his temerity. His guns only retired from one position to assume another, and open upon the enemy with a fire so destructive that it threw their ranks into confusion and arrested their farther progress.[45]

Though Stuart focused on Pelham in his report, the "Boy Major" would have been the first to share the accolades he received with Breathed, Henry, Hart, McGregor, and the rest of the battalion's officers and men. As gallant and courageous as he was, Pelham was well aware that he could have done little or nothing had not his junior officers and their stalwart cannoneers been of like material.

One horse battery did not have the opportunity of sharing in the glory achieved by the battalion among the hills and fields of Loudoun and Fauquier Counties. When Pelham moved Breathed's and Henry's Batteries east of the mountains, to be joined later by Hart's, Capt. Roger P. Chew's Ashby Battery had remained in the Valley. It was assigned to support Munford's Brigade as it guarded the rear of Stonewall Jackson's Corps in and around Winchester. For Chew and his men, this meant more of the tedious picket duty they had been doing since recrossing the Potomac.

October 30, the day Stuart had crossed the Blue Ridge, found two guns of the battery in the familiar position about a mile below Charles Town.[46] Jackson's headquarters was four miles south at Pendleton's.[47] On the last day of the month, three hours before daybreak, a courier alerted Chew that the Federals were advancing. The guns were rolled into battery, and the men stood to their posts until dawn without firing a shot. As it turned out, a few runaway horses had spooked the cavalry picket.[48] With considerable grumbling, the artillerymen, minus three hours' sleep, settled down to getting breakfast.

Jackson moved his headquarters to Millwood on November 3. The following day, Chew was ordered to Snicker's Ferry on the Shenandoah River, about three miles east of Berryville. Upon arrival, the artillerymen found that they were not needed because the Yanks opposite the ferry were without cannons. Chew countermarched his men to Berryville and camped for the night.[49] There the battery remained until the ninth, when at 2:00 A.M., orders were received to march to White Post. Lt. James H. Williams was in charge of the guns.[50] From White Post, the battery was sent on toward Front Royal and camped within four miles of that place for the night. Lieutenant Williams's tentmate, Quartermaster Sgt. John A. Chew, provided some warmth against the increasing cold by purchasing five gallons of brandy. All his friends were soon imbibing heavily, and the night turned somewhat raucous, with one individual delivering a "jocular speech" before the campfire. Williams participated in the drinking until he realized that he was "merry" but on his way to "drunk." He turned instead to write a letter to his beloved Cora, in which he confessed all.[51]

Chew's Battery continued its picket duty near Linden in the Manassas Gap. It arrived there on the eleventh and stayed until late in the afternoon of the fourteenth, when it marched to Clarke County, camping a little south of White Post. There was little activity for the men until the nineteenth. From early morning until evening on that date, the battery marched through Clarke County to Summit Point, where camp was established.[52] A Yankee thrust at Charles

Town on the twenty-second put Chew on the alert and in position at Rippon between Charles Town and Berryville. Nothing came of the enemy's advance, and the battery was pulled back to within a mile of Winchester on the twenty-fourth. For the next eight days, Chew remained in the vicinity of Winchester, responding every few days to the rumors of a Federal advance.[53] But December came with the Yanks still only threatening to attack. Between the wintry weather and the lack of action, the guns of the battery had grown cold indeed.

Mid-November brought several changes to the cavalry under Jeb Stuart. As had been anticipated when Pelham's Battery was split, the cavalry division was increased to four brigades, with each one having a battery of horse artillery attached: Brig. Gen. Wade Hampton's Brigade (1st North Carolina, 1st and 2nd South Carolina, the Cobb [Georgia] Legion, Phillips's [Georgia] Legion, and Hart's Battery); Brig. Gen. Fitz Lee's Brigade (1st, 2nd, 3rd, and 4th Virginia and Breathed's Battery); Brig. Gen. W. H. F. Lee's Brigade (2nd North Carolina, 5th, 9th, 10th, and 15th Virginia, and Henry's Battery); and Brig. Gen. William E. "Grumble" Jones's Brigade (6th, 7th, and 12th Virginia, the 17th and 35th (Virginia) Battalions, and Chew's Battery).[54] Jones had replaced Munford on November 8.

Chew's marching and countermarching west of the Blue Ridge were echoed in part by the activities of Stuart's cavalry and Pelham's artillery east of the mountains. Scouting and picketing the Rappahannock, along with an occasional thrust across the river to rattle the enemy, filled the latter days of November. During a reconnaissance across the river on the eighteenth and nineteenth with Fitz Lee's and Hampton's brigades, Breathed's Battery shelled the enemy at Warrenton Springs.[55] However, the actions of the horse artillery in late November are sketchy at best. Even the locations of most of the batteries cannot be determined from the available records. As the Army of Northern Virginia sidestepped toward Fredericksburg, Stuart provided a screen of picket posts along the river. Undoubtedly, Breathed's, Henry's, and Hart's batteries accompanied them, but the light brushes with the Union Cavalry were nothing compared with what had occurred earlier in the month.

Amidst the maneuvering of the horse artillery down the Rappahannock, Pelham received an addition to his command. On November 18, Capt. Marcellus N. Moorman and his Lynchburg Battery reported for duty to Stuart's artillery chief. Why Moorman's Battery was converted from a light battery to horse artillery is unknown. It had seen some hard service with the army, and its performance, while not outstanding, had been steady. The men of the battery considered the transfer a promotion and were excited about serving under Pelham.[56] The battery's arrival prompted a reshuffling of the artillery assigned to the cavalry brigades. Moorman's Battery replaced Henry's, which had been attached to Rooney Lee's Brigade. Henry's was designated the cavalry headquarters' battery under the direct command of Pelham. This gave the battalion five batteries, with one independent of any brigade, and permitted Pelham to use Henry's Battery as a roving command to go where needed. The flexibility this gave Stuart and Pelham is obvious.

The Lynchburg Battery's initiation into the horse artillery and its odyssey over the next two weeks mirrors what the rest of the batteries endured as winter began to envelop the armies. It left camp near Culpeper Court House on the nineteenth and, with snow and rain pelting the men, marched through Stephensburg, crossed the Rapidan at Germanna Ford, and rode through the Wilderness to Hamilton's Crossing. Having scarcely time to catch their breath, the men were off again at 9:00 on the morning of November 20 with orders to march to Fredericksburg and go into battery. At 1:00 P.M., the battery retraced its steps, following a Federal battery marching down river on the opposite shore. Lt. John J. Shoemaker recorded the event and his thoughts in his history of the battery:

> After marching about two hours we stopped to feed our horses and then continued until we reached Hamilton's Crossing about dark. It had been raining all day and all hands were soaking wet and it was so cold the men could hardly take the harness off the horses. The greatest trouble was to get a fire started, but we finally succeeded and managed to do a little cooking. Some of the boys managed to get a little sleep, but the most of them had to stand up around the fire all night. Oh My Country! My Country! How can you repay me for this night's suffering.[57]

The men were learning well what it meant to serve in the horse artillery.

Happily, the next few days were spent in drying out and resting. On the twenty-fourth, Moorman was ordered to the vicinity of Hick's Hill in Caroline County. A shift southeastward along the Rappahannock by portions of Robert E. Lee's army was to oppose a possible move by Burnside in the same direction. Four days later, on the twenty-eighth, Lt. Charles R. Phelps, with the battery's first section, consisting of two rifled pieces, went on picket duty at Skinker's Mill on a bluff overlooking the river. Federal gunboats stationed near Port Royal were considered a threat to Lee's flank.[58] The horse artillery was part of the move to counter that threat. Lieutenant Shoemaker, with the battery's remaining section, went into position four miles downriver at Rappahannock Academy on the thirtieth.[59]

The movement of the horse artillery had not been a hasty one. As early as November 24, Stuart had been in the area, visiting at Gay Mont, the home of the Bernard family, relatives of Capt. W. W. Blackford of his staff. On the twenty-ninth, Pelham had scouted the riverbank near Gay Mont for battery locations.[60] Such careful preparation bore fruit on December 2, when Maj. Thomas Waller of the 9th Virginia Cavalry led an expedition across the river to raid Federal pickets at Leedstown. He was supported from the southern shore by two brass guns from Capt. John Milledge's Georgia Battery, commanded by Lt. Luther R. Betts of the 9th Virginia Cavalry.[61]

This sortie met with success, but the artillery did not have the chance to contribute because there was no interference from the Federal gunboat flotilla. Despite the lack of energy on the Federal navy's part, there was still much concern among the Confederate high command over the possibility of the enemy's gunboats supporting a crossing of Federal troops below Fredericksburg, thus outflanking Lee's position. It was decided that another crack at the gunboats should be made. Accordingly, on December 3, Maj. Gen. Daniel H. Hill's division was sent to Port Royal to challenge any Yankee crossing of the Rappahannock in that vicinity. With him went Capt. Robert A. Hardaway's Battery, which included a long-range Whitworth gun. Hardaway and Pelham were about to join forces in arranging a little surprise for the Union gunboats that lay on the river opposite Port Royal.

Hardaway placed his Whitworth on Jack's Hill, some three miles below Port Royal. The remainder of his battery, along with that of Capt. William P. Carter, was located on a hill west of the town. At about 3:00 P.M. on the fourth, Hardaway and Carter opened fire at long range on the enemy gunboats and succeeded in driving them across the river and back to Port Royal, where they gained some measure of shelter from Hardaway's and Carter's guns.[62] The single Whitworth continued to pelt them. Eventually this fire became so annoying that the gunboats moved downriver. Here another surprise awaited them.

Pelham had taken Lt. Charles R. Phelps's section of Moorman's Battery and concealed it along the south bank of the river on the farm of a Mr. Pratt. When the Federal gunboats steamed into range, Pelham opened on them. The enemy was quick to reply, and a lively duel commenced as the gunboats passed by. Although Phelps's men were somewhat protected by the sloping bank of the river, the grape and canister that filled the air around them made it a dangerous place to be. But only one man fell to the enemy fire. Pvt. William A. S. Clopton had his leg taken off at the knee. He died at 1:00 A.M. on the fifth while undergoing an operation. Lieutenant Phelps discussed the fight and his section's duties in a letter to his aunt on December 8:

> On the Rappahannock
Near Port Royal Dec 8th 1862
>
> Dear Aunt
>
> Your kind letter of 16th Nov. just received yesterday. . . . Last Friday it was raining all morning. In the afternoon it changed to rain & snow. This morning it is clear, but the coldest of the season. I have however a large log fire and am quite comfortable. I wrote you on the 5th giving you an account of our attack upon the Gun Boats, &

the death of young Clopton. I had to open the letter to slip in a P.S. as Clopton died after I wrote. I sent his body to Lynchburg on Saturday in charge of Sergt. [Lewis T.] Nunnelee. Hope he has arrived safely.

I am still doing outpost duty with 2 pieces & 20 men & am detached from Capt. Moorman & his crew for the present. Hope to continue so, as I like the life & I get along with so little trouble & the men are so well satisfied. The officers whom I am under are nice, gentle, manly men, and leave everything pretty much to me, and I am more than pleased with them. Maj Pelham, Genl. [Daniel H.] Hill & others were near me at the attack on the boats and pronounced it a most bold & gallant fight.

It is not probable I shall have another chance at the boats soon. They are very well satisfied with what they got the 4th [*sic*] and our whole army is very near this point, and I expect soon to be ordered forward. This is what suits me. We are always in advance of the infantry, and generally live well. When the infantry comes up they overrun the whole country, eat up every thing they can lay hands upon. We have been daily looking for Mr. Burnside on this side of the river, (& if this weather continues he can cross without trouble as the river will freeze), and the Northern papers seem to be stirring him up for not making a forward movement, but he cannot help it, as his Pontoon Boats has not yet anchored, & he knows what kind of a reception Uncle Robert E. intends to give him. Bye the bye I intend to claim kin with my Brig. Genl. [W. H. F. Lee] as he is the nicest sort of a fellow. His kindness to Clopton has endeared me to him. He gave every attention & did every thing in his power for him. He regretted his [Clopton's] death very much as he said he [Clopton] was one of the most gallant men he ever saw. He bore his suffering so manfully etc. . . .

Hardly know where you must direct your next—

Love to all & believe your
[world illegible] Dick

Direct Care
Moorman's Battery
Genl. W. H. F. Lee's
Cavalry Brigade
—Near Fredericksburg, Va.[63]

W. H. F. Lee was indeed pleased with the performance of Phelps and his men and did not hesitate to praise their actions in his report to Stuart:

Headquarters Lee's Cavalry Brigade
Morse Neck, Va., December 5, 1862

General: I have the honor to forward Colonel Beale's report of an expedition sent into Westmoreland, which as you know, was entirely successful.

On yesterday evening I heard that General Hill had ordered the Whitworth gun to a position near Pratt's house to open on the gunboats. I ordered Major Pelham to carry the two rifled guns of Moorman's battery, under Lieutenant [Charles R.] Phelps, to the position near Pratt's house previously examined by him with yourself. After replying to the Whitworth gun for an hour, they steamed up and came down the river. Major Pelham waited until they were within 300 yards, and opened with deadly effect, putting two shot through and through one of the boats. They replied with grape, and one of the gunners had his leg carried off. I will forward the name of the man. He behaved with marked gallantry and coolness. Major Pelham superintended the guns in person.

Very respectfully,
W. H. F. Lee

Brigadier-General
(Maj. Gen. J. E. B. Stuart,
Commanding Cavalry Division.)[64]

While Pelham and Phelps added to the fighting reputation of the horse artillery, the other batteries were standing picket from the upper reaches of the Rappahannock to Fredericksburg, trying to survive the cold and damp conditions. Some weren't faring all that badly. Privates William A. Simpson and William P. Walters of Henry's Battery took time to write on December 1 and 2, respectively, to inform their loved ones back in Floyd County of what was transpiring at the front and how well they were doing despite the weather.

Spotsylvania County, Va.
December 1st, 1862

Dear father & mother & sisters,

It [is] with greatest pleasure that I avail myself of the present opportunity of writing you a few lines to inform you that I am well & hardy. I haven't got any news worth writing more than our army is all or most all close to Fredericksburg & the Yankees is just over the river, but whether they will have a fight is more than I can tell. We haven't been in any fracas since I wrote to you before, and I am in hopes we won't be called upon any more this winter, for the other company has come back to take our place, and we will stay in the rear for a while.

The last letter I had from you was dated November the 3 and we have written 2 since then. The rest of our Floyd boys are all well & in pretty good spirits, for the captain has promised to let us all go home this winter. But we can't get to come till the army gets sort of settled, and that won't be till the freeze up. I should like to get home to take Christmas with you all, but I am afraid I can't. But I will come as quick as I can. I have drawn my money since I wrote to you. I got $73 dollars, & I drew a pair of boots. You need not get uneasy about my clothes for they will last till I get to come home very well.

I must soon close for Will [Walters] wants to write. I give my best respects to Sis & the children. Write soon & give me all the news of home. We fare tolerable well for the present. You must do the best you can is all that I can say. Wishing you all the good luck that is bestowed on any one so far. Well for the present, still remaining your affectionate son until death.

Wm A Simpson to James Simpson
Direct yours to Richmond[65]

Spotsylvania Co., Va.
Dec. the 2nd 1862

Dear wife,

It is with the greatest pleasure that I seat myself this evening to let you know that I am in tolerable good health at this time, but am pestered with the rheumatism a little at times, hoping these few lines will find you all well. I have no news to write at this time, only we are living very well at this time as far as eating is concerned. But the weather is cold and cloudy, so it is very disagreeable laying in our open tents, but I hope it won't be very long till I can get to come home and spend a month with you all.

You must do the best you can. Try and hire somebody to cut and ball some wood for you before winter sets in, and if you haven't got feed enough to keep all of your stock you had better sell some, and if you have, keep them for they will be worth more than Confederate money in the spring. Everything is very high down here. Honey is worth 1 dollar per pound, but I got a half bushel bucket piled up full of the nicest honeycomb you ever saw that only cost me a mile and half walk and a heavy tote. It is [not] wrong to take the old skinflints because I know they charge us 1 dollar for a little piece of bread, and I think they can throw in the honey.

I must soon come to a close. Give my best respects to all. Do the best you can and keep in good heart. Tell Molly and Sis that I

> haven't forgotten them yet, and I will come home as quick as I can and see you all. So no more at present, but remain your loving husband till death. Tell Sole I am very glad he got out of the scrape as well as he did. We have 1 chicken and 2 ducks ready picked and cooking for dinner.
>
> Wm P Walters to M E Walters[66]

The fight Simpson thought might occur was only days away. The road to Fredericksburg had been a difficult one. The battle would be more than anyone could have imagined, and the horse artillery would play its part.

CHAPTER 9

Fredericksburg and Winter War

"Shells flew as thick as hail."

Ambrose Burnside had been placed in command of the Army of the Potomac because of Lincoln's frustration with the immobile McClellan. Cognizant of the president's strong desire to strike a blow at Robert E. Lee, Burnside had put the army in motion with the idea of maneuvering swiftly over the Rappahannock at Fredericksburg before Lee could react. The plan hadn't worked out as Burnside had envisioned. Maj. Gen. Edwin V. Sumner's Right Grand Division had reached Falmouth on November 17 but failed to cross the river into Fredericksburg because the pontoons Burnside requested did not arrive until the twenty-fifth.[1] In the interim, Lee moved onto the hills behind Fredericksburg. Burnside's plan lay in shambles. In his confusion about what to do next, he moved troops up and down the north bank of the river, only to find himself countered by Lee on the south side. By December 10, Burnside was feeling considerable pressure to do something. After some deliberation, he decided to cross the river at Skinker's Neck, about fourteen miles below Fredericksburg, but before issuing the final orders, he came to the conclusion that a crossing opposite Fredericksburg would surprise Lee more.[2] This decision brought on the battle of Fredericksburg and John Pelham's most celebrated performance.

Lee, who also was eager to come to grips with his opponent before the armies went into winter camp, anxiously awaited Burnside's next move. A flurry of Federal activity on the tenth convinced Lee that something was about to happen. On the following day, the Yanks attempted to lay the long-delayed pontoons across the river. Brig. Gen. William Barksdale's Mississippians opposed the crossing until late in the afternoon, when they began to withdraw to Marye's Heights. The Federals were coming at last. Everyone expected a battle on the twelfth, but though the artillery of both armies rumbled and roared, no blue infantry moved against the Confederate position. Burnside had put off the confrontation for one more day.

On the morning of the thirteenth, Confederate officers and men gazed into the morning fog from Marye's Heights, hoping to be the first to catch a glimpse of the advancing enemy. The mist thwarted their efforts until around 10:00, when it began to dissipate. From his position on what became known as Lee's Hill, the Confederate commander knew his wait was over. Careful observation of the Federal lines led Lee to conclude that the enemy intended to strike at his right flank. Lee and Stuart had examined that area earlier in the morning and were particularly concerned about being outflanked. Confident that the matter could be left in Stuart's capable hands, Lee had returned to the hill overlooking Fredericksburg.

As the sun cleared the valley of the low-lying clouds, the Federal lines came into view. The troops belonged to Maj. Gen. George G. Meade's 3rd Division of Maj. Gen. John F. Reynolds's I Corps. His report detailed what happened next.

> Between 9 and 10 o'clock the column of attack was formed as follows: The First Brigade in line of battle on the crest of the hollow, and facing the railroad, with the Sixth [Pennsylvania Reserves] Regiment deployed as skirmishers; the Second Brigade in rear of the First 300 paces; the Third Brigade by the flank, its right being a few rods to the rear of the first Brigade, having the Ninth [Pennsylvania Reserves] Regiment employed on its flank as skirmishers and flankers, and the batteries[3] between the First and Second Brigades. This disposition had scarcely been made when the enemy opened a brisk fire from a battery posted on the Bowling Green road, the shot from which took the command from the left and rear.[4]

The guns firing those shots belonged to a section of Capt. Mathis W. Henry's 1st Stuart Horse Artillery, and at their head was John Pelham.

Anxious to fulfill Lee's orders to protect the right flank of the army and eager to damage the beautiful blue lines before him, Stuart had told Pelham to prepare for action. The gallant artillerist wished to do more than just prepare. He asked to go forward with two pieces, place himself in advance of the Confederate line, and take such a position that would allow him to enfilade the Federal brigades as they advanced. It was a dangerous, almost foolhardy, request. The section would be alone, exposed to both enemy artillery and infantry fire, and without support. But it was in keeping with both Stuart's and Pelham's maxim of not sitting idly by when a blow could be struck. Stuart consented. Within minutes, a Blakely and "the" Napoleon were moving down the road from Hamilton's Crossing.

The two guns went into battery near the junction of Hamilton's Crossing and Bowling Green Roads.[5] The target that lay before Pelham was one that artillerymen dream of. Stretched as far as could be seen were the long, thin lines of the Yankee infantry. They were not aware of Pelham's presence. Their attention was fixed solely on the Confederate infantry, which lay along the rise of ground behind the railroad bed. Pelham ordered Henry to open fire. Solid shot began to rake the flank of the advancing brigades just 500 yards away. This barrage, from an unexpected quarter, brought them to a standstill. Their commander's reaction to the fire on his left rear was immediate. Meade faced his third brigade left to front Pelham's threat and ordered up Lt. John G. Simpson's Battery A, 1st Pennsylvania Light Artillery, Capt. James H. Cooper's Battery B, 1st Pennsylvania Light Artillery, and Capt. Dunbar R. Ransom's Battery C, 5th United States Artillery, to silence the Confederate guns.[6]

Dashing into position, the fourteen Union guns answered Pelham's two.[7] Meade's cannoneers were soon joined by Capt. John W. Wolcott's Battery A, Maryland Light Artillery, Capt. James A. Hall's 2nd Maine Battery, and a number of guns across the river, all of them trying to get the range of their tenacious adversary. Pelham continued to blast the infantry and every so often answered the enemy's artillery with a shot or two. His position was later described by Col. Charles S. Wainwright of the 1st New York Light Artillery, and chief of Reynolds's artillery, as being sheltered by cedar trees and a hedge.[8] This helped conceal Pelham's guns, though not for very long once he opened fire. He soon began to jump from position to position to avoid the storm of shot and shell that threatened to overwhelm him. Early in the exchange, the axle on one of Simpson's pieces was smashed by a well-placed solid shot, and later a limber of Hall's was blown up.[9] But Wolcott answered Pelham by bowling over the Blakely and putting it out of the action.[10] With the Napoleon alone, Pelham continued the fight.

It wasn't only the Blakely that was struck. Privates Henderson Boothe, Joseph H. Phlegar, and Samuel T. Evans suffered wounds.[11] Pvt. Hammond was killed, and Pvt. Jean Bacigalupo of the famed "Napoleon Detachment" was mortally wounded and died shortly after being carried from the field.[12] Despite the losses, Pelham somehow maintained his fire, at one point dismounting and aiding in serving the gun. For over an hour, the unequal contest continued, with twenty to thirty Federal guns pitted against Pelham's single piece. Stuart became concerned that Pelham and his men might be wiped out and dispatched Maj. Heros von Borcke with orders to withdraw. The "Boy Major" responded, "Tell the General I can hold my ground."[13] For a second time, Stuart sent orders for Pelham to withdraw. Again the messenger returned alone. Pelham would not comply until he had nothing left to hurl at the enemy. Finally, when a third order from Stuart arrived,[14] the young Alabamian limbered his lone gun and galloped rearward, his ammunition exhausted.

Though later in the battle Pelham was given command of a number of batteries and for the second time threatened the Federal flank, it was his initial action that captured the attention of the army from Lee down to the lowest private. Lee was reported to have said that it was glorious to see such courage in someone so young as Pelham. Jackson was quoted as saying that if Stuart had another Pelham, he wanted him. In fact, statements such as Lee's, Jackson's, and those of others who wrote of the action have focused so singularly on Pelham that those who were with him are seldom thought of, much less mentioned. Yet gallant as Pelham was, he was not there alone. Henry and the brave men who served the guns could lay equal claim to the sobriquet "Gallant."[15]

For those who were with Pelham that day, the battle remained a vivid memory for the rest of their lives. In his reminiscences, Sgt. George W. Shreve wrote graphically of what he and his comrades had experienced:

> A part of our battery crept slowly from Hamilton's Crossing down to a cross hedgerow, of cedar, behind which we noiselessly formed "In Battery."
>
> Beyond the hedge, we could hear the Federal Infantry (Franklin's Corps) maneuvering; distinguishing a medley of voices but could not see them. Evidently they were only a few hundred yards distant. The fog commenced to lift between nine and ten o'clock and exposed to our view, as we peered through the hedge, a grand spectacle of marshaled soldiery in readiness for the fray, spread out in vast proportions on the level plain in our immediate front. With alertness, and yet fearing annihilation at their hands in such close range of their infantry, we commenced firing.
>
> The unexpected presence of our guns so close to them seemed to paralyze them and throw them into disorder. Instead of rushing for us and overwhelming us with their numbers, they were evidently afraid of us, judging no doubt that we had a strong force concealed behind the hedge. We were far in advance of any supports, either cavalry or infantry. Our fire must have been very effective and gave them a wholesome fear of us.
>
> Immediately after our first fire and while in the act of loading the second charge, we received the fire of their artillery, showing how ready their guns were for the action.[16] No. 1 in my detachment that morning, was "Hammond," who [had] joined us in Maryland during our recent campaign there. As he stepped in with sponge staff to swab out after the first fire, a shell from the enemy's gun cut him down, and he had time only to say, "Tell mother I die bravely."
>
> We continued firing for about twenty minutes, when we were commanded to cease and to lie flat on the ground. While in this position, a shot struck squarely the head of one of our men and decapitated him as he lay prone on the ground. The rain of shot and shell upon us was terrific, both from their field batteries at close range and also from their big guns on the north bank of the river, but being concealed by

the hedge, the enemy's gunners shot high and so we escaped. We resumed firing after a short rest but were soon ordered to "limber to the rear," and we fell back under the cover of our guns, which opened from the hill in our rear and left as the enemy began to advance.[17]

Pvt. William P. Walters gave a more immediate account of the horse artillery's role in the battle in a letter to his beloved wife written just four days after the battle:

Caroline County, Va.
December the 17th 1862

Dear wife,

It is with the greatest pleasure [that] I have this opportunity to write you a few lines to inform you that I am hearty but am very near laid up with the rumatis. I have not been able for duty for 2 days.

I can inform you that we had a hard fight Saturday 13 of this month at Fredericksburg. Our battery was in all day and our loss was severe. We had 2 men killed and 8 wounded. There were 3 Floyd boys wounded, Joseph Phlegar, Samuel Evans and Henderson Boothe. The other 5 were all slightly wounded but 1 man lost his arm. Phlegar lost his right arm. Evans was struck on the breast. The doctor doesn't think he will ever get well. Boothe was struck on the shoulder but [it] did not break the skin. It was a hot fight. The cannons [opened] at daylight and went on till dark. Both sides stood their ground. We were under a shower of shells all day. Our loss was greater than all our loss before since last spring put together. Our company has been in many hard places but we always came out safe before, but we ought to be thankful that we come out [four words illegible], for it looked to me like there were cannon balls enough shot at us to kill the whole army. The shells flew as thick as hail [and] burst all around me, but thank God they never touched me yet. They struck so close to me that several times they threw my face full of dirt. We had 14 horses killed, 2 of them were killed [with]in 3 or 4 feet of me. There isn't any fun in this sort of work, so I won't say any more about it, and I expect this is more than you want to hear.

The Yankees have gone back on the other side of the river again, and we have moved 15 miles down the river to Port Royal. The Yankees and Longstreet are shelling one another every day across the river. The Yankees have knocked Fredericksburg all to pieces and burnt it very near all up.

You all must do the best you can, and I will try and get a furlough and come home this winter. It is very cold today. I think it will snow before night, so no more at present, but give my love and respects to all. Tell Molly and Sis that I want to see them very bad. Hoping these few lines will find you all well, I will quit for this time. I remain your loving husband till death. Excuse my pencil for I have no ink.

Wm P Walters M E Walters[18]

The Federal army's retreat to the north bank of the Rappahannock did not presage a furlough for Walters, only a long, hard winter encampment with his battery. For Lee, Burnside's withdrawal was a disappointment. He had wanted to further damage the Army of the Potomac and secure an even greater victory. All that could be done now was sit and await Burnside's next move, if there was to be one.

Following the battle of Fredericksburg, the various batteries of horse artillery were scattered up and down the Rappahannock in support of the cavalry that was picketing the river. Hart's Battery, encamped near Stevensburg, and Hampton's Brigade guarded the upper crossings from Beverly's to Richard's Fords.[19] Breathed's Battery was encamped near Chancellorsville on the Orange Court House and Fredericksburg Road, from where they bolstered Fitz Lee's pickets.[20] Shoemaker's Battery with Rooney Lee's Brigade returned to the vicinity of Port Royal to observe both the enemy's land and river forces.[21] Like Shoemaker's, Henry's Battery was encamped in Caroline County, somewhere near Stuart's headquarters at Hamilton's Crossing.[22]

The artillerymen took advantage of the postbattle lull to begin to settle into what they anticipated to be a winter encampment. Breathed's men spent their time grooming their horses and organizing a glee club to while away the cold evenings.[23] The run-down condition of the battery's horses and men demanded careful attention to the former and a serious effort in recruiting the latter. So depleted was the supply of manpower that Lt. Philip P. Johnston had been dispatched to Richmond even before the battle of Fredericksburg to begin recruiting for both Breathed's and Henry's Batteries.[24]

The thought of Lieutenant Johnston comfortable and warm in Richmond undoubtedly sent a wave of envy rippling through the men who remained huddled around campfires trying to fight off the cold. Time passed much the same for the men of all the batteries. A letter written on December 22 by Lt. Charles R. Phelps of Shoemaker's Battery is representative of those sent home by dozens of men at this time.

Mom's Mount on the
Rappahannock Dec. 22nd 1862

Dear Aunt

Your letter by the hands of Mr. Darnin reached me yesterday. I am truly sorry to hear of Sallie's illness and hope she may soon recover. I have been so closely confined for the last month, I have not been able to see any of my acquaintances in this neighborhood, consequently have not seen John L. and have only heard from him through the papers. I believe he is quite well. I am still with my two pieces [word illegible] along the banks of the crookedest of streams, (as I have been for the last month) seeking some villainous Gunboat to devour. I am now on the farm of a Mr. Coulter, who is in the Army having taken his family off. I am now occupying his dwelling and have very comfortable quarters, but I doubt whether it will do me any good as I may move at any moment, and have to fall back to my old tent. Everything is perfect quiet in this neighborhood. No boats, no Yanks, we occasionally get sight of a picket, which is the only thing to disturb the quiet of the scene on the opposite bank of the river. Mr. Burnside I think like all of his predecessors has run his race, and will now retire to private life to curse the rebels, & ruminate on the roughness of the road in his march "on to Richmond." We are making every preparation to give his successor a most hostile reception if he should again attempt the crossing of the Rappahannock, entrenching and fortifying the hills from Fredericksburg to Port Royal a distance of about 15 miles.

You have had through the papers full particulars of the fight. I can give you nothing more as they are [the] source through which I get most of my information. One of their pickets crossed the river the other day to have a little social chat with some of our boys. He acknowledged it to be the most thorough defeat of the War. After exchanging some sugar and coffee for tobacco he returned to his post on the opposite side of the river. I wrote you a short note by Archer the other day. Hope he has reached home safely. Tell him to be certain to hire himself and hurry back as I am much in want of his services.

I regret I cannot be able to spend a few days with you this Christmas. I expect to have a very dull time of it here, as I can see no prospect for a [word illegible] as yet. I cannot tell when I will be in a place where I can get the box you desire to send. Can only thank you for your kind intentions, & imagine to myself I have everything you desire to have as [I] sit down to my beef & bread. I wrote Miss W. a letter by A. Tell her I am still improving but do not expect to marry before Spring. Mr. Donner gave me full particulars of Miss [word illegible] marriage & trip to Richmond. Will write to her although she did not invite me as she promised.

Love to All Yours most truly Dick[25]

Indeed, "a very dull time of it" was expected by virtually everyone, although there were a few important exceptions. To Wade Hampton, the idea of having to sit around and watch the smoke rise from the campfires rankled. He had raided successfully across the Rappahannock on December 12 and decided that another "visit" behind Union lines might reap similar rewards.[26] Accordingly, from the seventeenth to the twentieth, Hampton galloped here and there along the Telegraph and Bacon Race Roads, wreaking havoc and spiriting away 150 prisoners and twenty wagons stuffed with supplies.[27] Sadly, Hart's Battery played no part in either of these stirring forays, but instead its men were occupied with that least desirable of all assignments—picket duty. Their chance at the enemy would come at the end of the month.

Hampton's expeditions, though relatively small, had revealed an apparent weakness in the Union army's dispositions. It also ably demonstrated that the blue cavalry still was inferior to Stuart's troopers. These two factors prompted Stuart to undertake one of his famous large-scale raids behind Federal lines. He selected detachments totaling 1,800 men from Hampton's, Fitz Lee's, and Rooney Lee's brigades. A section each of Hart's, Breathed's, and Henry's Batteries would accompany the cavalry to provide additional firepower.[28] The column crossed the Rappahannock at Kelly's Ford on December 26 and camped at Morrisville for the night. The next morning, Stuart split his forces. Hampton, with Hart's section, rode around the left toward Occoquan; Fitz Lee was ordered to strike the Telegraph Road between Dumfries and Aquia; and Rooney Lee advanced between the other two columns, with Dumfries as his target. Henry's section accompanied Rooney Lee's Brigade, while Breathed rode with Fitz Lee's troopers.[29]

Rooney Lee advanced without opposition until about noon, when he reached Dr. Wheat's Mill, where the Telegraph Road crossed Quantico Creek south of Dumfries. Twelve men from the 66th Ohio Infantry who were picketing the creek were captured, but others managed to escape and alert their commander, Col. Charles Candy, whose infantry threw back Lee's initial thrust on the town. Stuart called up Henry's guns and showered the enemy with canister. Candy put a section of the 6th Maine Battery, under Lt. William H. Rogers, in position near the courthouse in Dumfries. The Federal pieces zeroed in on the Confederate artillery, 800 yards away. Henry promptly changed targets and shelled Rogers's section. Neither battery's fire was very accurate, as no casualties to men or horses were recorded.[30]

Meanwhile, Fitz Lee's column was closing on Dumfries. Stuart was in need of the added firepower. The town was held by infantry, cavalry, and artillery and would not be easy pickings, if it could be picked at all. Stuart threw his left forward toward the Brentsville Road and took a few prisoners. Fitz Lee came up from the south, having struck the Telegraph Road two miles below the town. Stuart sent him across the Quantico to form for an assault. Once in position, Fitz Lee's and Rooney Lee's troopers moved forward. They were supported by Breathed's section, which had arrived with Fitz Lee. The attack was not pushed home. It became evident quite early that the loss would be too high. Pvt. H. H. Matthews of Breathed's Battery left an account of the action:

> On the arrival of Fitz Lee near Dumfries, Stuart determined to make a demonstration. The 2nd and 3rd Virginia Cavalry crossed the fords and were ordered to strike the enemy in the front, while the 1st and 5th Virginia crossed above and engaged in a mounted charge. Before this began Stuart discovered from the statements of prisoners captured that the town was held by infantry and cavalry, whose forces exceeded his own. The attack, therefore, was converted to a demonstration that would occupy the attention of the enemy until darkness might cover our withdrawal and prevent pursuit. The battery did its part, engaging a Federal battery for some time. The Federals being entrenched we could not do them much damage. The fire from their battery was very poor. They did not succeed in getting our range once. There was a frame house on our right that was occupied by a family of five people. They had just sat down to dinner when we opened on the Federal battery. One of the shells from the Federal guns passed through the house, knocking a pitcher of water into space and exploding on the outside of the house and hurting no one. They all scampered down in the cellar, remaining there until we ceased firing.[31]

Stuart withdrew along the Brentsville Road and camped for the night at Cole's Store. Breathed's section had expended its supply of ammunition during the fight and, with a squadron of the 9th Virginia Cavalry and the Federal prisoners, was sent back across the Rappahannock.[32]

On the morning of the twenty-eighth, Stuart sent his column on the road to Occoquan. Just beyond Greenwood Church, the Federals were encountered. About 300 men from the 2nd and 17th Pennsylvania Cavalry on a scout ran into Stuart's much stronger force. After a brief clash, the Pennsylvanians made a dash for Selectman's Ford on the Occoquan River. They left behind about fifty prisoners, including some wounded.[33] Stuart pursued and crossed in the face of dismounted skirmisher fire. Henry's Battery, with Pelham in command, crossed at the ford as well. It was a feat that drew praise from Stuart in his report, as the ford was reputedly impassable for wheeled vehicles. But the horse artillery made no additional contribution to the raid.

The raiders reached Annandale on the Little River Turnpike and Burke's Station on the Orange and Alexandria Railroad and caused some alarm in the vicinity. Some of Fitz Lee's troopers ventured to within a half mile of Fairfax Court House, where they were ambushed. Stuart now felt he had accomplished all he could and set off on his return. Swinging through Warrenton, Pelham and Lt. R. Channing Price of Stuart's staff stopped off at a Mrs. Lucas's for a time before moving on through Jeffersonton and Rixeyville to the cavalry's old camp at Culpeper Court House. Here they visited Lieutenant McGregor, who was recovering from his wounds at the home of Dr. Herndon.[34]

The Dumfries Raid, as it came to be called, was eminently successful for Stuart and the cavalry. The horse artillery's role was limited to shelling Dumfries and the troops protecting it. The nature of the fighting thereafter—encounter, charge, pursue—did not permit the horse artillery time to get up and deploy. Once across the Occoquan, Stuart's movements were very rapid, and considering the condition of the artillery's horses before the raid, the crossing at Selectman's Ford may have taxed their remaining strength. Not surprisingly, Pelham's name is mentioned only once in the reports of the Confederate officers. As in the pursuit of Pope after Second Manassas, when he was unable to keep pace with Stuart's flying columns, Pelham had little opportunity to display his talents. Breathed and Henry received their share of the praise but only in connection with the bombardment of Dumfries. The raid did not add to the legend of the battalion.

While Breathed, Henry, Hart, and their men went raiding, the rest of the battalion's officers and men had to content themselves with taking turns at picket duty. The men from Lt. Edwin L. Halsey's section of Hart's Battery manned their post on the road to Ellis' Ford. Their adversaries across the river had bothered them little enough, but they knew the incursions of Hampton and Stuart were bound to bring on retaliation sooner or later. It came sooner. Scarcely had Stuart returned from his expedition when the Federals struck across the river at Richard's and Ellis' Fords. Captain Hart left a record of the battery's role in the action that followed:

> Having been ordered a day or two previous to guard the crossing of the Rappahannock at Richard's Ferry, together with the First North Carolina, Jeff Davis and Cobb Legions, and First South Carolina Cavalry, these commands were on that morning [December 31] relieved, and took up their line of march at daylight up the ridge towards Kelly's Ford. Arriving opposite Ellis' Ferry one and one half miles distant, the brigade was halted to feed and rest the men and animals. The battery had moved out a short distance in the direction of Ellis' Ferry to be convenient to provender provided there. Just after the men had disposed of themselves to rest, our pickets from the First South Carolina Cavalry came from Ellis', hotly pursued by a considerable force of the enemy's cavalry.[35] The "assembly" call was instantly sounded, and the men dashed to their pieces. Capt. Hart rode to the front to gather up the scattered pickets and to endeavor to check the advancing enemy with them until the horses could be harnessed or supports reach us. The cavalry regiments were scattered at distances of half a mile or more to the rear of the battery.
>
> Lieut. [Edwin L.] Halsey, being left in command, hastily advanced two guns by hand, to bear upon the road, just as Maj. Van Buren [Capt. George M. Van Buren], in command of a regiment of New York cavalry [6th New York], dashed into view, within two hundred yards of the guns, in hot pursuit of Capt. Hart and the five pickets he

> had intercepted. As the heavy column charged forward, not a man at the guns flinched, but delivering a rapid and steady fire in the faces of the charging column, doubled it back upon itself and in less than five minutes had put it to rout.
>
> Hastily limbering to the front, these two guns started in pursuit at a gallop and, delivering their fire from every position gained, were giving them a parting salute across the river, as the gallant old First North Carolina Cavalry, under the command of Col. [Laurence S.] Baker, rode up to their aid. The courier sent to notify Col. Baker of our dangerous situation misinformed him as to the position of the battery, and he had marched his company in the opposite direction, until the roar of the guns pointed out the true position. In this daring charge, the enemy lost several of their number. Capt. Hart narrowly escaped being captured while trying to check the enemy in front. The men at the battery escaped without casualty. It was one of the few instances of the war where a battery of artillery, although surprised at the outset, and without support, fought, routed and pursued, for one and one half miles a mounted force four times its strength.[36]

Col. James Barnes, the Federal commander, made no mention of running into any artillery, though he had expected to encounter some.[37] He admitted that his cavalry chased pickets belonging to the 1st South Carolina Cavalry but did not record why he was satisfied with simply scattering the Confederate picket. Perhaps Hart's cannoneers had something to say about his decision not to go any farther.[38]

With Barnes's retreat across the Rappahannock, the war for 1862 came to a close. The various horse artillery batteries settled into their winter camp routines, which continued for the next three months with few interruptions. A number of letters from the men of several batteries recount their daily life and duties. Lt. Charles R. Phelps of Moorman's Battery wrote to his aunt in mid-January:

> Occupacia Essex Co. Va.
> Jany 20th 1863
>
> Dear Aunt
>
> Having an opportunity to send a letter, I am seated once more to inform you of my whereabouts.
>
> I arrived here from Port Royal last Thursday, & have been quite busy since fixing up temporary quarters for the winter. We are now with Genl [Rooney] Lee's Brigade and expect to be here sometime, as everything is quiet on the opposite side of the river. Our camp is about 3 miles from the Rappahannock & 1.5 miles below Fredericksburg. Capt. [Marcellus N.] Moorman left us day after [Lt. John

J.] Shoemaker arrived (about 10 days ago) for Lynchburg. It [is] reported in Camp that he goes home to enroll a conscript which he could [*sic*] succeed in enrolling when at home last summer. In short he is to be married to a cousin of his. Tho' I know but little of the lady she has my sympathies "Long May she Wave." Do not look for him for some time. I see from the Republican he has published a card explaining his course in advertising his men, but have heard nothing more from it, [word illegible] him & Dr. Owen did not have to order pistols & coffee for two.

I have no news to communicate not having seen a paper since I have been here consequently know nothing of what is going on outside of camp. John Rucker was with us last night & brought a substitute for his son Houston. His substitute was not taken and left this morning. This is the third [time] he has paid us a visit. He has a hard time getting Houston out of service.

In your last letter you spoke of getting some jeans, please send me a small sample in your next as I shall want clothes very soon. This life in the woods is awful on home made [word illegible]. Got a letter from Harvey last week. He has done nothing as yet, & expected to join his regiment soon. I hope ere this you & Cousin Sallie have recovered from your illness. There has been several cases of the smallpox in the Brigade but as yet our camp is entirely free from [it] & men all remarkably healthy. What has become of Miss Wiatt have not heard from her for sometime. Is she married yet, and who is the fortunate Gent.

Let me hear from you as soon as possible & believe me

Yours hastily
Dick

Care: Moorman's Battery
Stuart's Horse Artil'y
Gen'l W. H. F. Lee's Cavalry Brigade Occupacia near Fredericksburg[39]

Captain Moorman was successful in his recruiting efforts, but Phelps's comments concerning his commander revealed that all was not entirely well within the battery and that it had nothing to do with smallpox. The lieutenant's feelings were not shared by all, but he and others were resentful of what they considered slights by Moorman and former Lt. Blake L. Woodson. The situation did not effect the battery's fighting capability, though camp life probably was not overly congenial. Only after Moorman and Woodson left the battery did the air of contention dissipate.

Undoubtedly, Pelham tried to watch for such problems in his command with an eye to keeping things running smoothly, but he also was interested in enlarging it. Late in January, he wrote a letter to Capt. William K. Bachman of the Charleston (South Carolina) German Battery. Pelham informed the captain that Brig. Gen. Wade Hampton, who had once commanded Bachman's artillery when it was part of the Hampton Legion, wanted the battery transferred to the cavalry and converted to horse artillery, as Hart's had been. Bachman met with Pelham on the twenty-second to discuss such a possibility.[40] Nothing came of the meeting, and the battery remained with its command.

Though the battalion did not grow through the addition of another battery, it did grow with the addition of an unusual piece of equipment—a six-pound Whitworth gun.[41] Pelham turned the cannon over to Lt. William Hoxton and wrote the lieutenant's brother, Llewellyn, a letter about it. Llewellyn and Pelham had been classmates at West Point.

> Near Fredericksburg
> Feb'y 13th 1863
>
> Dear Lou:
>
> Your brother handed me a letter a few days ago to mail to you. I have concluded to enclose one also. I received your kind letter to me several weeks ago, replied to it at once, but neglected to mail it.
>
> Your brother Willie is a noble boy. He has fought with me on many a hard field and has always distinguished himself very highly. He bears a reputation for gallantry unequaled in his company, and such a reputation is not a trifling thing in such a company as my old one where all were so brave. He won his commission honestly and fairly. It is not due to any man's friendship or influence, but to his own indomitable courage and soldierly conduct. As soon as I got full command of my company I strangled the great enemy to our Service [,] "popular election" of officers, and had men promoted for distinguished gallantry. I made the recommendations, and the General [Stuart] got the commissions issued. The result is I have the most accomplished and efficient officers in service.
>
> Your brother nobly won his commission and wears it with becoming dignity and ease. I have just received a splendid 6 lb. Whitworth gun (English) and have given him the command of it. It is entirely detached from his old Battery and will act with either Brigade. He is very much pleased with it and I think will make quite a reputation for the gun. He has just been here with me but has gone over to his camp about ½ mile off. I heard him say that he had just received a letter from his sister Mrs. Randolph. He will go up to see her in a day or two.
>
> Everything is quiet along our lines at present, and necessarily so. The roads are in such condition that it is absolutely impossible for an army to move. But I hope "Fighting Joe" Hooker will come over

and give us a chance as soon as the weather will permit. This army is invincible—whenever you hear of it fighting you may add one more name to our list of victories—for will certainly be the result. . . .

Your attached friend,
Pelham[42]

The man of whom Pelham wrote in such glowing terms was as excited about receiving command of the Whitworth as Pelham was in giving it to him. Hoxton wasted little time in writing to his sister Mrs. Sarah "Sallie" Randolph to tell her of his good fortune in a letter dated February 17. He wrote, in part:

Quite a change has also of late taken place in our own condition and prospects. A most magnificent Whitworth gun had recently run the blockade, and been turned over to Genl. Stuart, and I have been detached from my company, with a detachment of men, to take command of it. Genl. Lee, who wished the gun to be held in reserve and to be altogether independent of Brigades, acting only with the Division as a whole, desired Maj. Pelham to place some lieut. of his command in charge of it, and he accordingly was kind enough to select me. I am very much pleased with my present position, and its duties, for a good many reasons principally because I think by the change, my prospects for promotion are considerably increased;—for if the gun <u>does</u> <u>good</u> and <u>gallant</u> service, being <u>immediately</u> under the Genl's eye, he will notice himself, and there being <u>no</u> <u>Captain</u> <u>over</u> <u>me</u> to receive it, I will enjoy all the credit of its performance, myself. The gun is a most beautiful piece, light, strongly made, and in every way adapted to Horse Arty. It has an extraordinarily long range of six miles, so I suppose its performance at "long view" will rather astonish our Yankee friends next summer.[43]

Both Pelham and Hoxton were confident that the gun and its commander would prove their worth. However, events were to conspire against them.

The excitement over the new gun was not necessarily shared throughout Pelham's command. For many the winter moved slowly, and the men longed for home and family. Privates William Simpson and William Walters of Henry's Battery wrote letters to their loved ones the same day and spoke of the war and their hopes for its conclusion.

Dear father & mother & sisters one & all,

It is with great pleasure that I seat myself this snowy morning to answer your kind and welcome letter which gave me great pleasure to hear from you & to hear that you were well. I am glad to inform you that I am well and doing as well as you could expect considering the snow. I haven't got any news to write to you about the army, only they say the northwestern states are raising a rumpus. They say they are going to have peace or a fuss for it. I would be very glad if they would contrive some way for peace for I am getting tired of camp life and a heap tireder of fighting.

Since I commenced writing some of the boys came from the guns that are on picket. They say the transports came down the river yesterday, and they commenced firing at them. They fired some 80 rounds at them. They hit their boats with 8 or ten balls. They said the Yankees shot several times at them, but they were behind the breast works, and they didn't hit any of them. They slept out of doors last night and got snowed under.

As I have nothing of importance to write I will bring my uninteresting letter to a close, hoping to hear from you shortly. You must do the best you can for yourselves, for I don't expect to get to come home except I run away and come and I hate the name of deserter if I can do any better. Tho' I live in hopes that they will come to some conclusion for peace this spring so we can all get to come home. I still remain your true and loving son and brother till death.

Wm A Simpson / James Simpson & family

Direct your letter to Richmond, Va. W. H. F. Lee's Brigade Stuart's Horse Artillery in care of Lee's Brigade is with us / Capt Henry / they will come sooner by so doing.[44]

Essex County Va February the 22nd 1863

Dear wife,

It is with greatest pleasure that I seat myself this morning to answer your kind letter that came to hand last Thursday bearing date 8th of this month. I was truly glad to hear that you all was well and doing well. I am well at present, hoping when these few lines reach you they will find you and the children in good health.

I have no news of importance to write at this time about the army, only the Yankees run their gunboats up the river about 10 miles from our camp and 2 of our guns were on picket now. There was some cannonading down there Friday night and yesterday, but I have not heard from them yet, but I guess they will stop now for winter has gotten here. It commenced snowing last night about bedtime, and it is snowing yet. There is a right good snow on the ground. We have had a heap of rain and warm weather, but this is a very rough day, and I am in a very bad fix. My shoes are getting very near worn out and no chance to buy here. We can make out very well. We have got a good chimney to our tent and plenty of blankets. You must not get ornery about our fare. It [is] bad it is true, but better than one would expect.

I was glad to hear that you had feed plenty and truly glad that you did not let [several words illegible] have no feed. Don't let any go, and if they press any thing from you just let me know it and that will be enough. I am in hopes that I will get to come home before long and see you all. Give my best respects to your father and mother and all the rest of them and to inquiring friends. Keep in good heart and do the best you can. Get along the easiest way you can. Don't expose yourself no more than you can help. So no more at present but remain your true and loving husband till death.

Wm P Walters to M E Walters

Tell Molly and Sis and the baby that I have not forgotten them yet and want to see them very bad and have some big fun. Tell Sis I will eat her pie.[45]

The action that Simpson and Walters mentioned took place on February 21, 1863, when Lt. Charles E. Ford, commanding two guns of Henry's Battery, opened fire from a concealed position at Ware's Point on the gunboats *Freeborn* and *Dragon.* The action lasted for fifteen or twenty minutes, as Ford poured a concentrated fire from his Napoleon and Blakely into the two boats, damaging both of them. Ford was commended for his "coolness, daring, and intrepidity" during the fight and received special mention in Gen. Robert E. Lee's General Order No. 29.[46] Ford was an officer of considerable merit, and more would be heard from him.

The Confederates countered the Federal forays with raids of their own. One conducted by Brig. Gen. Fitz Lee on February 25 resulted in a skirmish near Hartwood Church. A section of Breathed's Battery, commanded by newly promoted Lt. Daniel Shanks, accompanied Lee but did not have the opportunity to fire a single round.[47] Lee met with heavy opposition and returned to his side of the river after causing only minor damage. The Yankees were learning.

These infrequent raids were not enough to dispel the tedium of camp life or the longing for a furlough that never seemed forthcoming. There were diversions, however. Local families sent out invitations to sorghum boilings, quiltings, and dances. Privates and officers alike enjoyed these breaks from duty, but always there was the inevitable return to the cold, wet camp and the ever-popular picket duty. Once back in their humble surroundings, the men turned to reading, singing, games, and just plain talk to pass the time. Politics was a volatile subject guaranteed to heat up the chilly atmosphere of any tent, and it did not always remain just a topic of conversation. In the month of February, some powerful individuals began playing the political game for high stakes. The pot included John Pelham.

The game commenced with Stonewall Jackson's desire to promote Col. Edward P. Alexander, Lt. Gen. James Longstreet's artillery chief, to brigadier general of infantry. Such a move would leave Longstreet in need of an artillery officer. Brig. Gen. William N. Pendleton, the army's artillery commander, suggested John Pelham as Alexander's replacement.[48] The behind-the-scenes finagling continued with the mention of Maj. Lewis F. Terrell as Pelham's replacement. Terrell was already on Stuart's staff as an inspector, but he had received the appointment based on his performance as an artillery officer. In fact, his commission was in the artillery. Terrell was currently on court-martial duty, which he loathed, and wanted an artillery command. Stuart did think highly of him, but to lose Pelham was something he did not want to consider. Still, he was outranked by both Jackson and Longstreet and knew in his heart that Pelham deserved the promotion.[49]

The recommendation was sent to Richmond, but Pendleton felt that it would receive more favorable consideration if Alexander wrote some of his political friends in the capital to use their influence on his behalf. Though he was flattered by the proffered command, Alexander really had no desire to leave his position in the artillery.[50] He failed to write the letters, and the whole plan fell through. Alexander continued as Longstreet's artillery chief, and Pelham stayed with Stuart.

Other maneuvering had been going on as well. Stuart was always on the lookout for talented officers for the horse artillery, and when one crossed his path, he made every effort to secure him for the command. One such officer was Lt. Francis Halsey Wigfall. He had been serving with Bachman's South Carolina Battery but had decided to accept a staff position as an ordnance officer to Fitz Lee. He reported his "capture" by Stuart in a letter to his father, Sen. Louis T. Wigfall:

> Camp near Hamilton Xing
> Saturday Eve'g. Feb'y. 7, 1863
>
> Dear Papa,
>
> This morning after finishing my letter to you I carried Genl. Lee's application up to Genl. Stuart's to be forwarded to Genl. R. E. Lee. I handed it to him and you may well suppose I was somewhat astonished when he told me he intended to disapprove it. His endorsement, however, was highly complimentary to myself, stating that as the ground for his disapproval that my services were too valuable to be spared from the artillery, that a great many had been examined for appointment as Ordnance Officers and that one of them might be assigned to this duty and that the qualifications for an Artillery officer were more rare than those for an Ordnance Officer. The application was forwarded to Genl. Chilton with this endorsement. I then told him that the reason I had accepted it was that my present position was not a permanent one, and he asked me why I didn't come into the Horse Artillery which you know is a sort of pet of his. I did not have an opportunity of pursuing the conversation as officers were

coming in on business &c. As I was leaving he told me to see Pelham, who is now Major and Chief of Artillery on Stuart's Staff.

I went back there this afternoon. Pelham had not returned, but I saw Gen. Stuart and asked him further with regard to a position in the Horse Artillery. He said that my opportunity was a very good one and that when Pelham returned he would talk it over with us. Pelham will be back this evening and he told me to come over in the morning and he would keep him. He also told me that if he could get Rosser appointed Brig-Genl. he would give him a battery and make me a Captain of it. He said that he had made the official recommendation for Rosser's promotion in as strong terms as possible. He intends, if he can succeed in obtaining the promotion for him to take his own Regt., the 5th Va., the 15th Va. from W. H. Lee's Brigade, one Regt. from Hampton, and the Maryland Cavalry from Genl. Jones' Brigade, and give them to Rosser, thus forming a Brigade of four Regiments, and leaving Brigades of four Regts. to each of Lee's and Jones, and one of five to Hampton. He has now in his Division of four Brigades, twenty-one Regiments. Rosser has always been a very great favorite of Stuart's and since he has been in the Cavalry has very greatly distinguished himself.

The Horse Artillery is in the Provisional Army of Virginia insomuch as the appointments are made by the Governor of the State upon Genl. Stuart's recommendation. It was arranged in this manner in order to erase the right of election by the men. Genl. Stuart says that they are mostly from Maryland and Louisiana. Promotions are more by seniority except in cases of incompetency.

I shall go up to Genl. Stuart's in the morning and will let you know the result of my interview. Give my best love to Mama and Lou and kiss little Fan for me.

Ever your affectionate Son
Halsey[51]

Stuart was more successful in recruiting Wigfall for the horse artillery than Jackson had been in recruiting Alexander for the infantry. Unfortunately, Stuart also lost an officer to promotion. On February 21, Capt. Mathis W. Henry was promoted to major in command of an artillery battalion in Maj. Gen. John B. Hood's division.[52] Lt. William M. McGregor, who was promoted to captain, replaced him. McGregor, however, was still recovering from the wound he had received in November 1862 and physically would not be able to lead the battery for months. Pelham and the battery's lieutenants would have to fill the gap.

As things turned out, by the end of February, Stuart had a new officer making plans to join the horse artillery, one on his way out, one promoted, and he still had the incomparable Pelham. But not for much longer.

Battalion Flag

The Stuart Horse Artillery Battalion flag was presented to the battalion by the ladies of Charlottesville in honor of the gallant stand made at Rio Hill in defense of its camp and Charlottesville from Federal cavalry under the command of Brig. Gen. George A. Custer on February 29, 1864. Custer had his chance for revenge at Tom's Brook where he came close to capturing the flag, which was torn from its staff and hidden in the coat of one of the escaping cannoneers.

COURTESY OF THE JEFFERSON COUNTY MUSEUM

Maj. John Pelham

As commander of the original battery of Stuart Horse Artillery, Pelham was instrumental in the organization and training of what became two of the premier batteries in the battalion. His untimely death following his mortal wounding at the battle of Kelly's Ford was mourned throughout the battalion and the cavalry.

COURTESY OF THE JOHN PELHAM HISTORICAL ASSOCIATION

Maj. Robert Franklin Beckham

Called to fill the boots of the "Gallant Pelham," Beckham rose to the challenge. His reorganization and refitting of the battalion had much to do with its successes throughout 1863. A superb artillerist himself, Beckham chose to remain in the background and allow the captains of the batteries to do the fighting while he made sure they had the guns, ammunition, men, and horses to do it with.

COURTESY OF THE MUSEUM OF THE CONFEDERACY, RICHMOND, VIRGINIA

Maj. James Breathed

Breathed trained under Pelham and soon earned a reputation of utter fearlessness and bulldog tenacity that matched that of his mentor. A physician by trade, Breathed spent no time healing wounds during the war, devoting his energies to inflicting them. He rose from lieutenant to second in command of the battalion by war's end.

COURTESY OF THE MUSEUM OF THE CONFEDERACY, RICHMOND, VIRGINIA

Lt. Col. Roger Preston Chew

A cadet fresh out of the Virginia Military Institute where he trained under the stern eyes of the then unknown Thomas J. Jackson, Chew demonstrated his abilities in command of the first horse artillery in the Confederate army, the famous "Ashby Battery" of Jackson's Valley army. Chew would go on to command the entire battalion at the tender age of twenty-one.

COURTESY OF THE MUSEUM OF THE CONFEDERACY, RICHMOND, VIRGINIA

Jacket of Lt. Col. Roger Preston Chew.

COURTESY OF HARPERS FERRY NATIONAL HISTORICAL PARK

Maj. Philip Preston Johnston

Before the war Johnston had been a marble-cutter's apprentice in Baltimore, Maryland. He joined the horse artillery as a private after a year's service in the 1st Maryland Infantry. His innate abilities and his fighting prowess took him all the way to major. COURTESY OF J. P. JOHNSTON

Maj. James Walton Thomson

Like Chew, Thomson was a VMI cadet before the war. His subsequent service in the Ashby Battery eventually led to a majority and a ranking with the finest officers in the battalion. Thomson was fearless with a total disregard for his own personal safety. He enjoyed hand-to-hand combat and participated in as many cavalry charges as he could. His last one at High Bridge cost him his life.

COURTESY OF THE MUSEUM OF THE CONFEDERACY, RICHMOND, VIRGINIA

Maj. William Morrell McGregor
It was said of McGregor that he would take his guns into places where even Pelham and Breathed would not venture. His reputation as a daredevil fighter was well deserved. Those who served under his command knew that if the enemy were before them McGregor would find some way of getting at them, even if it meant pushing his guns beyond the front line. On more than one occasion he did just that. AUTHOR'S COLLECTION

Capt. John Wright "Tuck" Carter

"Tuck" Carter's presence at Fleetwood Hill at just the right moment on June 9, 1863, may have saved Stuart's cavalry from a serious defeat if not a rout. His contribution was not forgotten, and he eventually rose to command the Ashby Battery.

FROM *A HISTORY OF THE LAUREL BRIGADE*

Capt. Wiley Hunter Griffin

One of the "Immortal 600," though not of his own choosing, Griffin commanded one of the better batteries in the battalion, at least until his capture at Yellow Tavern. The Baltimore Light Artillery was a fighting battery. Griffin saw to that. Unfortunately, it did not have him during the last months of the war when it could have used his cool courage and steady control the most.

FROM THE *CONFEDERATE VETERAN*

Capt. Edward Graham
Remembered for his mad dash through Petersburg on June 9, 1864, which helped save the city and perhaps Richmond as well, Graham proved to be a steady, if not flashy, officer of horse artillery during the final year of the war.
COURTESY OF CENTRE HILL MUSEUM

Capt. Marcellus Newton Moorman

Moorman campaigned mightily to be promoted out of the horse artillery. A solid officer with some talent as an artillerist he never displayed the dash and daring required of a captain of horse artillery. Had he possessed them he may have ended up commanding the horse artillery in 1864. Instead he got his wish, was promoted, and left the battalion. He was not missed.

COURTESY OF THE VIRGINIA MILITARY INSTITUTE ARCHIVES

Capt. John Jordan Shoemaker
The true heart and soul of the Lynchburg Battery, Shoemaker's promotion to the captaincy upon the transfer of Moorman was greeted with celebration by the men of the battery. Shoemaker was a fighter and knew how to get the most from the men under his command. He got their all on the Valley Turnpike in October 1864.
FROM *SHOEMAKER'S BATTERY*

William Remsen Lyman
A man of many talents Lyman served the Confederacy as a private, lieutenant, and captain in the infantry, a staff lieutenant and drill instructor, and a courier, adjutant, and captain in the horse artillery. He proved successful in all these capacities and earned the respect of many of his fellow soldiers and officers. His career in the battalion was unfortunately too brief to gauge his true potential as an artillery officer.
FROM THE *CONFEDERATE VETERAN*

Lt. William Hoxton

Hoxton always seemed to be where the bullets and shells flew the thickest and was wounded three times during the war. Entering Virginia Theological Seminary after the war Hoxton became a minister only to die at the young age of 32, probably from the effects of his wartime wounds.

COURTESY OF MRS. RICHARD P. THOMSEN

Lt. Milton Rouss

Rouss was one of the two men, Chew being the other, responsible for the formation of the Ashby Battery. His VMI background made him a valuable commodity in and out of the horse artillery. The slow advancement in the long arm caused him to accept a captaincy in the cavalry. Captured at Brandy Station on June 9, 1863, Rouss remained a guest of the Federal government for the remainder of the war.

COURTESY OF BEN RITTER

Edward Duke Yancey

Yancey was a late addition to the Ashby Battery, having remained at VMI after graduation to teach mathematics and tactics. He did not join the battery until July 1862. Elected to a lieutenancy in the spring of 1864, he proved to be a solid, steady officer, as could have been expected of one who trained under Jackson. AUTHOR'S COLLECTION

Lt. James William McCarty

McCarty's association with the horse artillery was brief but important. He became a second lieutenant in the battery soon after its formation and played a role in its early growth and training. For reasons unknown he resigned to join the 7th Virginia Cavalry in which he served throughout the war, reaching the rank of captain. COURTESY OF THE PRAIRIE EDGE MUSEUM

Lt. William Bennett Bean
Like many of the junior officers in the battalion, Bean is virtually unknown. His contribution was that of an officer who carried out his duties in an efficient manner. However, beneath the calm, bespectacled exterior burned a fire hot enough to stand up to the irascible Jubal Early. COURTESY OF WILLIAM B. EDWARDS

CHAPTER 10

Winter and Spring in the Valley

"War is surely a stirring-up affair."

Throughout the latter part of November, the military situation in the Shenandoah Valley had been one of stalemate punctuated by rumors and the brief actions they caused. Chew's Battery had been encamped near Winchester for several days, and as December approached, there did not appear to be any prospects for a change in its routine in the near future. All was calm, though another rumor on the twenty-ninth caused the battery to limber up and move out on the Berryville Road. There seemed little to become excited about. Just another rumor. Just another short march, and then back to camp. Only this time, the rumor turned out to be true.

On the evening of December 1, Brig. Gen. John W. Geary, who was stationed at Bolivar Heights opposite Harpers Ferry, received orders to make a reconnaissance in force toward Winchester the next day. Accordingly, on the following morning, 3,200 infantry, 50 cavalry, and four guns marched for Charles Town.[1] They ran into the 12th Virginia Cavalry before reaching the town, and a running fight began. The Confederates could do little more than harass the enemy's advance guard, which pushed ahead at a slow but steady pace. On the third, Chew was ordered to Strasburg as a result of a report that other Federal troops were coming through Chester's Gap. After an all-night march, the battery reached Strasburg an hour before dawn on the fourth. Winchester fell that same day, but Chew and his men were nowhere near the city nor were they aware of what was going on. On the fifth, the battery was back on the road. It was a cold, wet, miserable day, as recorded by Pvt. George M. Neese:

> It seems that the Yankees that drove in our pickets at front Royal a few days ago went back through Chester's Gap to eastern Virginia, and early this morning we were on the march again down the valley toward Winchester. At Bartonsville [Burtonsville], six miles from Winchester, we left the pike and moved one mile east of Bartonsville and camped. This is very disagreeable weather for practical soldier-

> ing. It snowed all day and when we stopped in the woods late this evening to camp the snow was about four inches deep, and still snowing fast. This is a sort of scout we are on now, and we have no tent to shelter us from the inclemency of the wintry weather. Camping in a four inch snow, without tents, is bordering on the verge of roughing it, like Indians; but old campaigners are nearly always equal to all the demands of all kinds of emergencies, even when mixed up with snow. It was getting dark when we drove into the snowy, cheerless woods to camp. It took but a few moments to unsaddle and hitch our horses; then we divided our mess into fatigue of twos. Two went in search of straw for bedding, two chopping wood, two getting supper out of almost nothing, and two building shelter. The straw party soon got back with as much straw as they could carry, as they found a big stack not far away. Then the straw detail assisted the architects in constructing our castle for a night. In about an hour after we commenced operations supper began to smell good, and our house was finished and furnished and the bed-chamber ready for occupation. Our structure is built in the modern hog-nest style of architecture—a shed roof covered with a waterproof tarpaulin. The front is open and facing a rousing camp-fire of green hickory, and now as I am trying to write it is nearly ten o'clock. The fire is burning brightly in front of our house and flashing its cheerful dancing light all over our bed-chamber. The snow is still coming down fast and the woods are wrapped in a wintry shroud, but who cares for snow.[2]

It was good that Neese and his friends had taken so much trouble to erect their "castle." They occupied it for another eight days.

On December 13, Chew's cannoneers resumed their odyssey, marching up to Newtown and then cross-country to the Winchester and Front Royal Pike. They continued on to the north fork of the Shenandoah River and crossed, pitching camp two miles from Winchester. The next morning, Chew turned west and headed for Strasburg. Upon reaching the town, the battery passed through and camped at Locust Grove Schoolhouse, about a half mile northwest of Fisher's Hill.[3] Lt. James H. Williams left the battery for a quick visit to his home in Woodstock. While there, he penned a letter to his future wife, Cora, to tell her of his travels. He wrote, in part:

> Tonight finds me at home. I came from camp this evening afraid to hope that I might see your brother and Miss Sallie, and yet most heartily wishing to meet them. I feared the needless alarm and movement of our brigade would frighten him. I came for this reason hoping to quiet his fears. On Saturday morning [December 13] in consequence of a rumor of the approach of [Maj. Gen. Robert H.]

> Milroy by way of Moorefield and Wardensville we moved in haste to Front Royal & then the next morning early we marched to Strasburg and went into camp about noon on Fisher's Hill, where we are likely to spend the winter unless ordered by Gen. Lee or Jackson to Winchester, a place we ought never to have left. I have no particular fondness for fighting but prefer this to so much moving. There's no enemy now threatening and your brother's move needless.[4]

Williams was correct about Milroy's advance being a rumor at the time he wrote to Cora. But on the nineteenth, Chew was ordered to pack up his battery and move up the Valley toward Edenburg. Yet another rumor had the enemy heading for the Confederate rear.

From the twentieth to the twenty-fourth, Chew's men rode through New Market, across the Massanutten, back to New Market, and finally pitched camp at Tom's Brook, six miles south of Woodstock. Lieutenant Williams gave an account of how he spent his Christmas and wrote of his frustrations with the war in a letter to his Cora on the twenty-sixth:

> I have just returned from our scout (night). The Battery is encamped just above town [Woodstock]. I am too tired to write and almost sick and completely disgusted. We lost no men, and the report of the enemy will be the same. We marched to Kernstown, skirmished awhile & then returned. The enemy hold Winchester, a more perfect set of thieving rascals never scourged a country. They were without tents and stores & lived on the people. It is a shame we permitted the force to come into the Valley. It was little better than a mob. We should have captured them. I almost fret myself sick. You ought to know that I plan to get through this war with as little needless fighting & exposure as possible, as is consistent with duty, but I am afraid if opportunity offered I should forget my resolve in eagerness to wipe out the disgrace of so many retreats.[5]

Others in the battery shared Williams's frustration. Gunner Neese recorded that the fight on Christmas day involved two guns, which fired three rounds and then remained in position until sunset. As he put it, "This is Merry Christmas."[6]

From December 27 until January 1, the battery stayed in camp near New Market. If any of the men had hopes of settling in for the winter, they were sorely disappointed. On the second day of the new year, Brig. Gen. William E. "Grumble" Jones's Brigade, accompanied by the 1st Battalion of Maryland Cavalry, the 1st Battalion of Maryland Infantry, the Baltimore Light Artillery, and Chew's Battery under Lt. James W. Thomson, set out on a raid to Moorefield.[7] The long column reached its destination early on the morning of the third. The placement of the artillery was entrusted to Capt. William H. Harness of the 7th Virginia Cavalry, who had been born in Moorefield. He directed Thomson to a hill northwest of town, about two miles from the Federal camp. After reaching its position, the battery fired about thirty rounds. The effect was minimal because the distance was too great, and Thomson ordered a cease-fire.[8]

The echoes of their last rounds barely had faded when a cannon boomed in rear of the battery. A Yankee force from Petersburg had moved down behind Thomson and the 6th and 7th Virginia Cavalry, which were in position with the battery. Pinched between two fires, the Confederates sought a way to extricate themselves from what looked like a one-way ticket to Camp Chase. Fortunately, Captain Harness was with them and, knowing "every by-way and hog-path in that portion of Hardy County," guided the cavalry and artillery out of danger.[9] The trek led up a mountainside, through woods and brush, and over a horse path that had never seen a wheeled vehicle. The horses hauling Thomson's guns could not accomplish the feat without additional help. The men uncoiled ropes and tied them to the carriages, then bent their backs and strained to pull the guns over the rugged terrain. Some of the cavalry dismounted and lent their strength to the task. To Neese, it was reminiscent of Napoleon crossing the Alps, but the challenge was met as the sound of the ongoing battle at Moorefield echoed among the hills.

The Confederate force was now split and in some danger. Jones determined to hold his position at Moorefield with his half of the command, while Col. Richard H. Dulany of the 7th Virginia, in command of the other contingent, which included Thomson and his guns, made his way through the mountainous country to a place where the two could rendezvous. This was accomplished about ten miles south of Moorefield. Jones hoped to renew the attack on the fifth after resting the horses and men of Dulany's command. The horses of Chew's Battery were completely worn out. Some of the men had not eaten in twenty-four hours. Nevertheless, an attempt was made. It faltered on the news that the Yankees had been reinforced and that the Confederates' supply of food was exhausted. The battery set out on the journey back to New Market on the fifth and reached its familiar campsite the following day. The expedition achieved little, and in his report, Jones failed to commend either Thomson or the battery for their impressive performance under such severe conditions.[10]

Encamped again near New Market, Chew and his men had little to do except settle in for the winter and try out their latest capture, a large sheet-iron bake oven on wheels. It had been "liberated" when the command passed through Petersburg during the escape from Moorefield. Not until the twenty-seventh did anything occur to disturb the camp. Then a brief scout to Woodstock broke the monotony for two days. By the twenty-ninth, the battery was back in the New Market camp. There it remained until February 14, when everyone packed up and moved to Edenburg, which was described by Pvt. Charles McVicar as "a dismal looking thicket."[11] Nothing much out of the ordinary occurred for almost two weeks, except that the battery nearly lost its captain.

The situation grew out of the wounding of Capt. John B. Brockenbrough at the battle of Fredericksburg. Brockenbrough had at one time commanded the Baltimore Light Artillery, but at the time of his wound, he was the chief of artillery for Maj. Gen. William B. Taliaferro's division. Col. Stapleton Crutchfield, Stonewall Jackson's artillery commander, feared that Brockenbrough might not recover sufficiently to return to active duty. Consequently, in a report to Jackson on February 19, he recommended that Chew succeed Brockenbrough.[12] Lt. James W. Thomson would then become captain of the Ashby Battery. Jackson followed Crutchfield's suggestion and made the recommendation to Robert E. Lee in a letter of the same date.[13] The whole business hinged on Brockenbrough's health. In the end, Brockenbrough improved and was able to return to his command. The horse artillery's future commander-in-chief remained with his battery.

On exactly the same day that Crutchfield was recommending Chew as a replacement for Brockenbrough, Jones's Brigade, including Chew's Battery, underwent an inspection. The inspecting officer had this to say about the battery:

> This battery consisted at the time of the inspection of two Blakely Guns and one 24 pd. Howitzer Napoleon Gun [that] was at Staunton and has doubtless reached the Battery by this time. The Battery paraded with only four horses to the piece, but the Lt. commanding informed me that he had horses enough to turn out with six to each piece and caisson. The cannoneers are mounted on their own horses.
>
> Discipline—Very Good.
>
> Instruction—Owing to the mud I did not cause the battery to maneuver, but as Capt. Chew is an experienced artillerist I have no doubt it is well drilled.
>
> Horses—In good order.
>
> Harness—Old and rotten, but a new supply is being made in Staunton.
>
> Ammunition—The Battery is well supplied with ammunition.[14]

From this report, it is evident that Crutchfield was not the only officer Chew had impressed. His reputation was growing, and deservedly so. His battery was in fighting trim except for the harness, and steps were being taken to correct this. The winter offered time to rest and refit. If the Yanks let him alone long enough, Chew would see that his battery was ready come spring.

Up and down the Valley, the Confederates were trying to settle into winter quarters but still maintain their vigilance. One command was undergoing a period of reorganization in preparation for the opening of the 1863 campaign season. Back in December, Col. John D. Imboden had received orders to change his troops from partisan rangers to a Regular army command. In January, he was promoted to brigadier general as part of the reorganization. While carrying out this process, Imboden petitioned the Confederate War Department and was granted permission to form a battery of horse artillery. He chose to convert Capt. George W. Imboden's Company B, 1st Regiment Virginia Partisan Rangers, afterward Company K (2nd), 62nd Regiment Virginia Mounted Infantry. Captain Imboden was General Imboden's brother, but he did not want to leave the cavalry arm of the service. As a result, Captain Imboden left the company prior to its conversion, and command passed to John H. McClanahan.

While undergoing its reorganization, General Imboden's command, which consisted of the 18th Virginia Cavalry, the 62nd Regiment Virginia Mounted Infantry, and McClanahan's Battery, went into camp east of the Shenandoah Mountain. Pvt. Lantz G. Potts, who served in both the 18th Virginia Cavalry and McClanahan's Battery, recorded some of the command's winter experiences.

> We went into winter quarters east of the Shenandoah mountain in the fall of 1862, with but one regiment of infantry, 62nd Va., and one of cavalry, 18th Va., and McClanahan's Battery. There was but one house and a fairly good stable. The 62nd Va. Inf. pitched their tents up a narrow hollow to the right of the main road. McClanahan's Battery pitched on a little hill on the left side of the road. We had nothing but tents, a poor thing to winter in, so the woods being near and timber plenty we cut logs and built shanties and we stopped the cracks with mud and we built a chimney, with a food fire place and we kept good fires, consequently we suffered very little with cold.
>
> One cold night a report came to us that a force of Yankees were moving up the west side of the mountain. We were ordered to the top of the mountain with artillery and infantry. The cold wind blew a perfect gale all night and we all nearly froze, but not a Yankee came to warm us up. It was one of the hardest nights we had had since the war began. But when we got to camp the next morning we built big fires and soon were warm again.
>
> We never were attacked during the winter so we put in the time playing. Sometimes we would play ball, other times we would snowball. Sometimes the Sixty-second would come down in the bottom and divide into companies and fight a sham battle with balls. One day a man became very angry and threw a rock instead of snow and broke a man's leg and the General stopped that kind of play.
>
> It was a very healthy place at Shenandoah but sometimes a man would get sick and get a furlough and go home and stay till he would be well again.[15]

The Yankees may have left Potts and his comrades alone to enjoy their snowball fights, but they did not do likewise for Chew and his men.

On February 28, Chew received orders to march down the Valley Pike in response to a Federal advance that had struck the Confederate pickets south of Winchester on the twenty-sixth.[16] Dutifully, on March 1, the men cooked three days' rations, packed their wagons, limbered their guns, and moved out. They marched to Narrow Passage Hill and went into position. The Yanks never arrived. Jones and his cavalry had made short work of them and had driven them back to Winchester. Again on the fifth, the Federals threatened. Chew promptly responded to Jones's summons but once more failed to confront an enemy who advanced and retreated with dazzling speed. The only result was to rouse the cannoneers from their comfortable quarters and send them riding through the wet and cold for a two-hour vigil.[17]

From March 6 through 17, little occurred except for the usual forage expeditions for food and fuel. On the eighteenth, the battery left on a trek that took it through Hawkinstown and New Market, then over the Massanutten Mountain and across the Shenandoah to Luray, which it reached on the twentieth.[18] The men made camp by scraping away the snow that had been falling steadily, erecting the tents, building fires, and bedding down on the ground. On the twenty-second, all was dismantled, and the march resumed. The next day, camp was established within a mile of Front Royal. March drew to a close for Chew and his men with a battery drill along the Shenandoah on the thirtieth, followed by a heavy snowfall that produced six inches of mud throughout the camp on the last day of the month. For many of the men, to be so close to their warm homes and loving families in occupied Winchester was more difficult to bear than all the drills, snow, and mud they had endured or would in the days to come.

Early April gave testimony to the fact that March did not always go out like a lamb to make way for glorious spring. Snow began to fall on the night of the fourth and continued well into the next morning, which was Easter Sunday. Seven inches of snow greeted Chew and his men when they emerged from their slumber to celebrate the day. Tentmates McVicar and Neese were buried under an avalanche of white when their Sibley tent collapsed. All were angry and wet but not hurt. That same day, the Federals decided to brave the inclement weather and strike at Confederate cavalry two miles below the horse artillery's camp. The Yanks successfully crossed the river in company strength, marched up the west side, and fired into Chew's camp. Nothing more came of the action. Toward evening, Chew ordered Neese, who was on guard duty, that if the attack were renewed later that night, the men should be awakened and a gun unlimbered and fired as fast as possible. As it turned out, Neese did not have to disturb the men's sleep that night.[19]

April 6 saw two guns ordered out. One was sent downriver to the cavalry picket post that had been surprised on the previous day. Before it ever reached the picket, it was ordered back, as the threat appeared ended. The other gun, the howitzer, with McVicar in tow, left on a scout. Marching through Manassas

Gap, the men followed the line of the railroad. The expedition passed through Linden, Markham, and Piedmont, where camp was made. The excursion continued on the eighth to within three miles of Upperville. Foraging for supplies, the column did not set out again until the tenth, when it marched through Salem. The next day, the men visited Gaines's Cross Roads, Little Washington, and Sperryville; crossed the Rappahannock; and pitched camp. They had covered twenty-seven miles in the cold with only seven pounds of hay and no grain for the horses. On the twelfth, they crossed the Blue Ridge at Thornton's Gap and passed Luray, Hamburg, and New Market. The battery was reunited on the fourteenth, the other guns having moved out earlier on an expedition of their own.[20]

Early on the morning of April 11, Chew had received orders to break camp and march for Luray. The battery did not reach town until the twelfth, and then it moved on over the Massanutten to New Market, where it established camp. Camp was moved on the thirteenth to a mile west of town, near the North Fork of the Shenandoah. When the howitzer detachment rejoined the next day, the men turned in their tents. Winter was officially over as far as the army was concerned. As if to mock those who foresaw an early spring, it rained all day of the fifteenth while the battery marched to a position one mile east of New Market, where it rendezvoused with the 6th, 7th, and 11th Virginia Cavalry. This force had been gathered to oppose a threatened Federal advance from Fredericksburg. Chew unlimbered his guns and stood by them for two hours. When it became apparent that the Yankees were not coming, he limbered his pieces, retraced his steps to New Market, and turned south on the Valley Pike. Upon reaching Lacey Springs, the battery went into camp.[21] For Chew's men, it had been a hard winter with no real permanent camp. Being the only active horse battery in the lower Valley had put a tremendous strain on men, horses, and equipment. They had counterpunched their way through the winter, always reacting to Yankee advances or rumors of same. Now it was to be their turn. Fortunately, they were to have some help. Brig. Gen. John Imboden was at long last prepared to take on the enemy.

Gen. Robert E. Lee long had recognized the importance of striking a blow against the Federal forces threatening the Valley. Back in February, he had written to Grumble Jones to propose an advance into the Valley from the east with troops taken from Hampton's and Fitz Lee's Brigades. Jones was to have his command ready to support them.[22] In late March, Lee had sent letters to both Jones and Imboden. By then he had given up on Stuart's participation, citing the bad weather and swollen streams as major obstacles to success. He added that he had hoped this move would have presaged a thrust west of the Allegheny. Now Lee urged that simultaneous raids by Jones and Imboden should be undertaken.[23] When, on April 7, Lee again penned letters to both generals, the plan had crystallized into a double raid against the Baltimore and Ohio Railroad.[24] It was Imboden who moved first, leaving his camp on the twentieth.

Imboden's force consisted of the 22nd, 25th, and 62nd Virginia Infantry, the 18th, 19th, and 37th Virginia Cavalry, and Capt. John H. McClanahan's Battery of six guns. A large portion of the 19th and all of the 37th were dismounted and serving as infantry. The entire force numbered a little over 3,000 men, of which about 700 were mounted.[25] McClanahan's Battery had a full complement of horses and was able to take all of its guns. Pvt. L. G. Potts later wrote an account of McClanahan's Battery's first engagement at Beverly:

> The afternoon of April 23, we left the White Farm on the top of Cheat Mountain and camped in a mile of Huttonsville, arriving just at dusk.
>
> The next morning we passed on down the [Tygart's] Valley until we were at Valley Bend. We heard what we thought was our advance guard firing on Yankee Scouts and the word soon reached us that was the case and one Yankee had been shot.
>
> When we reached Daily the 18th Cavalry took the back road to the left. This was done to cut off the retreat of the enemy by gaining the road below Beverly. The 62nd Va. Inf. and McClanahan's Battery [rode] down the main road below the bridge where they could get a view of Earle Hill where the Yankees had a battery of several guns.[26] In order to get the range of that battery the Rebels had to ascend a hill to the right of the road. So they put twelve horses to one long brass piece (we had named this piece "Long Tom") and they went up hill slow but sure. Before they had gone far the Yankees began to shell them for all that was out, but they did not hit a horse or man.
>
> I at that time belonged to Co. G, 18th Va. cavalry and was on the left or back road in view of the guns, but when they saw they could not do the Rebels any damage while shooting up they turned their guns on us. While they were shooting at the Infantry we could see the smoke belch up from the guns and the shells go into the ground and burst.
>
> They kept on firing at us but soon we heard the report of our big gun that McClanahan had gotten in action and two reports silenced the Yankee guns.
>
> B. F. Potts[27] was a good gunner and his Captain stood behind him with a field glass. When the first shot was fired he said, "A little high, Orderly [Sergeant]." The second shot he said, "Pretty well, a wheel off and two men down." The Yankee battery limbered up at once, leaving the piece with the wheel off.[28]

Though only a skirmish, the action at Beverly baptized McClanahan's Battery. It was the first of thirty-eight engagements in which the battery would participate. For one of its members, the brief clash at Beverly would be remembered with bitterness.

Lt. Parkison Collett was a native of Beverly and quite familiar with the surrounding area. In one sense, he was going home, and he looked forward to seeing his family again. Climbing the hills south of Beverly, he caught his first glimpse of his home in many months. What he saw filled him with indignation. His family's house, its fencing and trees—all had disappeared. The ground was covered with the Federals' camp. Everything he had known as a boy had been destroyed. Grimly he sighted his guns and personally gave the order to fire. He soon had the satisfaction of seeing the enemy abandon its camp and retreat.[29]

Imboden's success at Beverly opened up the next phase of the campaign, which was to advance to Buckhannon and link up with Jones. By the twenty-eighth, he was within four miles of the place, and on the following morning, he entered the town. Having reached the rendezvous point, Imboden settled down to wait. He received a letter from Jones on the twenty-ninth but heard nothing further. After waiting for two days, Imboden determined to march to Philippi and set out on May 2. Just as the column began to move, a courier arrived. Jones was only six miles away and would soon join him.[30]

Jones had left on his raid on April 21.[31] With him were his own brigade, Chew's Battery, the 35th Virginia Cavalry Battalion, and elements of the Maryland Line, including the Baltimore Light Artillery, under Capt. Wiley H. Griffin.[32] Other officers of the battery were Lt. William B. Bean and Lt. James T. Wilhelm. This battery had seen some hard service, especially at Sharpsburg. It had now been refitted, recruited, and converted to horse artillery with this expedition in mind.[33]

Rain hampered the column almost from the start. The men crossed the Little North Mountains at Brock's Gap, but the roads soon turned to quagmires and streams deepened. The two horse batteries forded the South Fork three times on the twenty-third. At one ford, the rapid current nearly swept the guns and caissons downstream.[34] Camp was pitched a mile and a half above Moorefield. Here the South Branch proved unfordable for the artillery. When the rest of Jones's force rode out on the twenty-fifth, Chew's and Griffin's Batteries and the infantry of the Maryland Line were left behind under the command of Lt. Col. James R. Herbert. After resting the men and horses for two days, Herbert led his command homeward through Franklin, reaching Harrisonburg on the thirtieth.[35] Neither battery had engaged any enemy except mud and water. McClanahan's Battery would have to uphold the reputation of the horse artillery alone.

Imboden and Jones, with a part of his command, finally joined forces on May 2 and marched for Weston. The rest of Jones's force arrived there on the fifth. That same day, the Yankees struck at Imboden's pickets near Janelaw. McClanahan's Battery was engaged briefly in the fight, which nearly resulted in the capture of the entire picket. The Federals appeared to be in strength, and neither Jones nor Imboden was willing to risk a battle. They decided to split their forces. Jones was to march west to attack the Northwestern Virginia Railroad while Imboden headed for Summerville, where another rendezvous was planned.[36]

Accordingly, Imboden set out on May 6. Such were the conditions of the roads that only five and a half miles were covered that day, two and a half the next, and six more on the eighth. To make even this much progress, drastic measures had to be taken. All of McClanahan's Battery's spare wheels were destroyed, and fifty solid shot from each caisson had to be thrown away.[37] Even with such delays, the threat of Imboden's approach caused small Union garrisons at Bulltown, Suttonville, and Big Birch River to abandon their blockhouses and flee. Imboden sent his brother, Col. George W. Imboden of the 18th Virginia, ahead to Summerville. At least part of McClanahan's Battery accompanied Colonel Imboden and participated in the skirmish with the remnants of the town's Union garrison that had fled when the Confederates came too close for comfort.[38]

At this juncture, Imboden concluded that his artillery and wagon horses were worn out. The fortuitous capture of a wagon train near Summerville allowed him to replace these exhausted animals with relatively fresh mules. Jones's column arrived on the evening of the thirteenth and the next day. In his own words, "The condition and exhausted supplies rendered homeward movements necessary."[39] The return journey was without incident. The raids were not as successful as had been hoped, but damage had been done and supplies taken with comparatively little loss. Of the three batteries of horse artillery that participated, only McClanahan's had actually engaged the enemy, and even its role was of minor consequence.

Though Chew and Griffin had returned to their camps in the Valley earlier than the rest of Imboden's and Jones's commands, they were not idle. On May 5, the Federals pushed south from Winchester and reached New Market.[40] The Confederate troops in the area were called out on the seventh. Chew's Battery left its camp and marched through Harrisonburg. It took up a position two miles north of the town along the Valley Pike.[41] Private Neese described the turmoil caused by the Yankee threat:

> As we were going to the front today great excitement and stir-up prevailed among the citizens in Harrisonburg and the country around. Refugees of all descriptions, sheep, cattle, and dogs, were streaming up the Valley pike and out the Warm Springs road, conglomerated in one grand mixture of men, cattle, horses, negroes, sheep, hogs, and dogs, all fleeing from the invading foe and trying to escape the blue-coated scourge that was coming. One old citizen from down the Valley somewhere undoubtedly saw the Yankees this morning before he started, for when he passed us as we were going to the front he did

> not stop to tell us the news, but shouted, as he hastened and pressed toward the West Augusta Mountains: "Hurry up! you ought to been down there long ago."
>
> In Harrisonburg the excitement was set in the top notch. I saw men loading wagons with all kinds of furniture and household goods for removal to a more congenial clime, where war's dread alarms are not so frequent. I saw one man running through the street with a clock under his arm. I suppose he was determined to run with time. I saw another man hastily leaving town with a fine mirror, striking out toward the heart of Dixie. War is surely a stirring-up affair, especially when it breaks out in a fresh place among peace-loving citizens.[42]

One of the officers in Chew's Battery had his own stirring up. Lt. James H. Williams was at his home in Woodstock when the Yanks swept south. In a letter dated May 12, he told of his experience to his Cora:

> The Yankees saw me out of Woodstock & were within 100 yards of me at Edenburg were near capturing me.
>
> Enemy said to be evacuating Winchester. They came above New Market Thursday [May 7]. We were ready at H [Harrisonburg] for a fight, had charge of four pieces of artillery & really wanted to fight.[43]

Williams did not get his fight, and in fact, the excitement of the "invasion" proved short-lived. By the eighth, the Federals were falling back to Winchester, and Chew's Battery was marching back to its camp at Dayton. Here the battery spent the remainder of May. The only incident to disrupt the men's well-earned respite was the news of the death of Stonewall Jackson, which reached them on May 11.[44]

The end of winter campaigning meant a time of preparation for the more active military maneuvers of spring and summer. Chew, Griffin, and McClanahan were now faced with the task of getting their batteries ready for what lay ahead. Further up the Valley at Salem, Capt. Thomas E. Jackson was engaged in organizing another battery of horse artillery, which was to be attached to the cavalry brigade of Albert G. Jenkins.[45] Jackson had begun to recruit his battery on April 1. Most of his men came from three sources: Jackson's own Virginia Light Artillery, formerly Capt. John P. Hale's Kanawha Artillery, which had been broken up after its capture at Fort Donelson, Tennessee; the Virginia State Line; and transfers from the 8th Virginia Cavalry. On May 2, 1863, the battery was organized.[46] Lt. Micajah Woods gave an account of the event to his father, Dr. John R. Woods:

Jackson's Artillery Camp, near Salem, Va.
May 3rd, 1863

My dear Father:

I have been awaiting with anxious expectation a letter from you or Mother, but though I have been absent from home for 3 weeks not a word from that dear place has cheered me. I am inclined to regard this as almost inexcusable when tidings could with such ease be sent & reach their destination in less than twenty four hours I have myself written three or four letters.

Yesterday was a day they ruled high with excitement. It was the appointed time for the organization of the company & election of officers. When we first commenced recruiting, Jackson appointed to us on the muster roll our respective ranks—giving to [Randolph H.] Blain the Senr. 1st Lieu. & to me the Junr. 1st do., to [Richard B.] Wortham the Senr. 2nd do., & Harman the Junr. 2nd do., and the men enlisted under us as the officers in that order.[47] At election yesterday Capt. Jackson in person nominated Blain & passed high eulogies upon his qualifications as an officer. About 20 men came in yesterday morning who had never seen either Blain or myself & were of course (as they now boldly state) influenced by the Captain's wish & nomination. In spite of all this & without my knowledge (for we agreed not to oppose each other) the men spontaneously & without my being a candidate voted for me & to my astonishment I came within one vote of beating Blain for his place. I have heard since that of the 50 men we have had with us for two weeks I had a majority of exactly twenty—that is that out of fifty—men who have been with us for two weeks & have had an opportunity—of seeing & judging of us, 35 men for me, in spite of the terms of enlistment & in spite of the captain's whole influence being thrown for Blain.

This was done without any idea on my part of violating the original agreement. On yesterday morning I succeeded in obtaining furloughs for a few days for two of my warmest friends & if these men had been present I would have received the place over the head of Blain & without being a candidate. I was unanimously elected to the 2nd place (Junr. 1st Lt.) Harman who was to have the fourth place was defeated by a new man, [Henry J.] Norton of the Kanawha Valley by one vote.

Our commissions will date from the 2nd Inst. Jackson & Wortham will go to Richmond tomorrow after guns equipment etc. We will get four Dahlgren Boat Howitzers & two rifled six pounders Steel guns which will be a splendid battery of pieces. The material we have for working the Battery can't be surpassed in America. We have Jackson's old men who were at Donaldson [Fort Donelson], & most of the rest are old artillerists who have been transferred to us by Genl. Jenkins. 20 of these men were sent in yesterday morning to enable us to affect an organization for a six gun Battery. Between 50 & 90 men are on the rolls & in a few days our muster will be at least 130. Orders have been given to Jackson to be ready as soon as possible after the reception of his horses & pieces to move to Greenbrier Co., should not that order be countermanded, we will be sent to the army of the Rappahannock before that time or to East Tennessee, however, Jenkins' whole brigade has been sent to send for the horses of the command in N. & S. Carolina as soon as possible, & report to Stuart on the Rappahannock. We will probably go with the rest of the brigade. Some companies whose horses were near have already started for the East. Walter Preston wrote me a letter which I received yesterday stating that he was under orders to move to the front, & could not get his transfer for some time & probably not at all. We cannot delay the appointments of non Comd. officers for such a length of time, so if he joins he can get no position. In a few days, I will write a letter withdrawing my application for the 1st Lieu. of engineers.

Our expenses in the living here have been very expensive, having to pay $1.00 per pound for bacon & for everything else in proportion. I shall have my present uniform coat rimmed with red, the artillery color, red collar & cuffs & binding. Jackson & all of the officers have agreed to have new & complete uniforms made of the new English cloth, which will cost us about $40.00, the making about $100.00.

I trust that you have entirely recovered from your indisposition & that all at home are well.

With love to Mother & each one I am

Very affectionately
Your Son
Micajah Woods

Dr. Jno R Woods
Holham

P.S. I send my State Line Commission which please file away.

M. W.[48]

The animosity that Woods harbored for Jackson and Blain would continue throughout his time of service, but it would not interfere with the performance of his duties. As with Capt. Marcellus N. Moorman, Jackson was not well liked. The reasons centered on both personality and his military abilities, which were questioned by his subordinates but not by his superiors. Though at times Woods thought of leaving the battery, he never did.

Jackson was true to his word concerning the battery's uniforms—at least for the men, if not yet for the officers. On May 7 and 8, he acquired from Maj. James G. Paxton of the Quartermaster's Department forty-six jackets and thirty-nine pairs of pants, plus shirts and shoes.[49] On the seventh, Woods again wrote to his father to keep him abreast of the battery's progress as well as his own:

> Artillery Camp near Salem, Va.
> May 7th 1863
>
> My dear Father,
>
> Ever since the first tidings of the commencement of hostilities on the Rappahannock my mind has been wrought to a high pitch of anxiety and suspense. For upon result of these movements was staked the safety of our whole region. And especially when intelligence reached me of the appearance of the enemy at Trevilians, I felt almost sure that the raid would extend to Charlottesville and probably to the bridge over Mechum's River. But the Lynchburg papers of yesterday dispel all such fears & doubts from my mind, since the Raid Makers have disappeared and in the language of our glorious Lee, "We have again to thank Almighty God for a great Victory." What a splendid & invincible army we have arrayed for a defense of Virginia and her Capital! And how much I wish that I could say again that I belong to the Army of the Potomac. I have great hopes that our battery will soon be ordered to the East. Please write to me at once and give me a full account of the doings and sayings of the Albemarle people & especially of the Charlottesville Knights when the place was so imminently threatened with attack. I have no doubt but that you have heard many incidents which will be both entertain ing and amusing. Also give all the particulars of the Charlottesville Battle and how the Albemarle boys fared in the engagement. I should like also to be informed about the extent of damage done by the Yankees while in the county. Tell Men Anderson to write to me immediately if he can possibly find it convenient. I will write to him on the reception of his letter forth with.
>
> Dunn's Battalion, a portion of Gen'l Jenkins' Brigade, is under Imboden in the extreme North West. Gen'l Jenkins received intelligence by courier yesterday from Imboden who was at last accounts at Uniontown, Pennsylvania and making directly by rapid marches for Wheeling of which place he has doubtless taken possession ere this. The raid thus far is a complete success—heavy stores having been destroyed and valuable work on the Baltimore & Ohio Railroad, been burnt or blown up. My impression is that Jenkins will not be able to move before the 1st of next month as his brigade is dispersed in all parts of Va. Our Battery will be filled out & furnished with horses in a week or two and I trust that we will be able to

achieve a reputation for ourselves and the battery in the ensuing campaign.

Now some domestic talk—I will be ordered by home just before we are ordered to move to get my horse. I shall want two or three pair of thin yarn socks or cotton. I want my pants fixed everywhere they may need repair. Have a strong piece of cloth bound around the lower part of each leg as they are somewhat worn by my treading on them, they having been rather long before they were washed. This should be attended to at once as I will be able only to stay a day at home. Perhaps I hope and trust that my horse is as fat as a seal ere this. Please have my bridle sent to Charlottesville and repaired as it needs it greatly. It is important that these things be attended to as I may not go home after getting the horse till the campaign is ended next Fall or Winter.

I had my coat dressed with artillery trimming at a cost of $26.00. I have sent to Richmond by Lieut. Wortham for cloth for coat, vest, and pants and shall leave it with Westenbaker to have me a fine suit of clothes to come out in flying colors when I get a furlough in the distant future. Present my best love to Mother and each one and believe me

Very affectionately
Your Son
Micajah Woods

Dr. Jno. R. Woods
Holkham

We have just received orders to move by tomorrow's train to the Railroad bridge over New River near Central Depot where we will take up our permanent encampment—so direct all letters to me at Camp Depot

Jackson's Horse Artillery

M. Woods

In two or three weeks we will go to Greenbriar. So Jenkins said this evening.[50]

By mid-May, the battery had moved its camp to New River Bridge near Fayetteville, West Virginia. For the remainder of the month, Jackson's men mirrored the efforts of the other horse batteries in the Valley as they readied themselves for the coming campaign season. None had yet heard the word *Gettysburg,* but they would come to know it and remember it well.

CHAPTER 11

Kelly's Ford and the Death of John Pelham

"The noble, the chivalrous Pelham is no more."

Like their batterymates in the Valley, the men of Breathed's, McGregor's, Hart's, and Moorman's Batteries had little to do in the early days of March. For one thing, the abominable weather kept everyone close to their campfires. Everyone, that is, except John Mosby, who electrified the army with his capture of Brig. Gen. Edwin H. Stoughton at his headquarters in Fairfax Court House on the ninth. But toward the middle of the month, the weather improved. The Federal high command, while embarrassed by Mosby's escapade, was not stunned into inaction by any means. In fact, they planned a little countermeasure of their own.

On the sixteenth, Brig. Gen. William W. Averell began making preparations to fulfill orders he had received to destroy Fitz Lee's Brigade, which was encamped near Culpeper Court House. Averell's command was composed of Col. Alfred N. Duffié's 1st Brigade, Col. John B. McIntosh's 2nd Brigade, Capt. Marcus A. Reno's Reserve Brigade, and the 6th New York Light Battery under Lt. George Browne, Jr.[1] All told Averell had 2,100 men and six guns, a more than adequate force considering that Fitz Lee's Brigade only numbered about 800.[2]

Averell maneuvered his troopers toward Kelly's Ford early on the morning of the seventeenth. Fitz Lee was not unaware of his adversary's approach. He had received a telegram on the morning of the sixteenth informing him of the enemy's advance. Again at 6:00 in the afternoon, scouts reported to him that Federal cavalry was at Morrisville, six miles from Kelly's Ford.[3] Lee reinforced his picket at the ford to sixty men and placed Breathed's Battery on alert.[4]

John Pelham's role in the action that followed has always been filled with controversy. What time he arrived in Culpeper, where he stayed, and when he arrived on the battlefield are some of the questions that have not been answered. Officially, Pelham left cavalry headquarters on the fifteenth to inspect Moorman's Battery, which was encamped at Mount Pisgah Church, but this was just a cover. The real reason for his being in the vicinity was to pay his respects to Nannie Price of Dundee, who was visiting a friend at Orange Court House. He wished to thank her for some candy.[5] Supposedly, while waiting at the railroad station in Orange, he learned that the Federals were up to something across the Rappahannock. He took the train to Culpeper and arrived either on the evening of the sixteenth or the next morning, depending on which account is consulted. While most of this is of no importance regarding his participation in the fighting that followed, it illustrates the confusion that swirls around his final days and hours.

As fate would have it, Pelham did show up in Culpeper and did discover that a fight was brewing near Kelly's Ford. Jeb Stuart was also there to give testimony at a court-martial.[6] Stuart, Pelham, and Capt. Harry Gilmor, who offered his services as a volunteer aide to the general, rode with Fitz Lee toward Kelly's Ford. This was just after 7:30 A.M. Lee just had been informed that his pickets had been attacked about an hour earlier.[7] Accompanying the column was Breathed's Battery.[8] Pvt. H. H. Matthews recalled:

> The horse artillery up to this time had not left camp, but were hitched up awaiting orders ready to move at a moment's notice. As soon as Gen. Fitz Lee received the information that Averell had crossed he immediately ordered Breathed to report on the field with his battery. I do not think we ever traveled at a more rapid gait than on that occasion. The distance from our camp to where we met the brigade at the Wheatley House is about 3½ miles. We made the distance in about 30 minutes, not more. The horses were in a run and as the road was very slippery owing to the recent snow having melted, it made travelling at our pace very dangerous. Still we went on until we came to the line of our brigade near the Brannon House, where we were ordered into position.[9]

Matthews's account of the battery's dash to the ford failed to mention that despite the rapid pace, the cavalry outdistanced Breathed's guns and began the battle without artillery support.

The 1st Rhode Island Cavalry had forced the ford sometime before 7:00 A.M., capturing a number of the Confederate pickets who could not reach their horses and escape. Averell's success did not spur him forward. He spent the next several hours clearing the ford of obstructions and watering horses. Not until after 10:00 did the Federals push ahead in strength about a half mile. By noon, the 4th Pennsylvania and the 4th New York Cavalry were deployed to the left and right of the road, awaiting the Confederates.[10] Lieutenant Browne of the 6th New York Battery had placed one gun in position to cover the men working in the river. As soon as it was cleared, he added a second piece, and then followed the 1st Brigade across the ford with two guns. Two more marched behind the 2nd Brigade. The last two crossed and went into a supporting position on a knoll overlooking the ford.[11]

Upon hearing of the attack on his pickets, Fitz Lee had moved to within three and a half miles of the ford and halted, expecting Averell to advance toward him. When this did not happen, Lee rode for the ford. His advance regiment was the 3rd Virginia. As he approached the enemy, Lee directed the 3rd off the road and through a field. Emerging from the field, the regiment saw the enemy to the right of the road and along a stone fence to the left. Col. Thomas H. Owen gave the order to charge, and the Virginians swept forward, in a column of fours. Their opponents were the 4th Pennsylvania, in front of them on the right, and the 4th New York, which lined the stone fence to the left. As the 3rd Virginia charged forward, the Pennsylvanians wavered and fell back a short distance. Owen directed his men to the left, galloped along the wall toward the Wheatley farmhouse, and fired into the New Yorkers, who also staggered back.[12] Once the Confederates had passed, however, the Yanks recovered and returned to their positions.

Lieutenant Browne had been able to place only one gun into position near the front due to the conditions of the road. Now, as the Confederates took time to regroup and reload, he managed to put two guns on the left in support of the 4th Pennsylvania and a second gun on the right to bolster the 4th New York. Again the Confederates charged. The 3rd Virginia, reinforced by the 5th Virginia, drove forward from the woods on the other side of the field toward the stone wall. Browne had shelled the woods and now greeted the oncoming gray troopers with blasts of canister. This fire soon was interrupted because Colonel Duffié led the 1st Rhode Island, 4th New York, and 6th Ohio in a countercharge. Fighting swirled across the field before the stone wall.

Somewhere in the melee was John Pelham. He had stopped briefly and talked to Breathed when the guns were brought onto the field, but then disappeared into the turmoil of bursting shells and flashing sabers.[13] During one of the charges across the Wheatley fields to the stone wall, John Pelham was struck in the back of the head by a piece of shell. He slipped to the ground and lay motionless. The battle continued to rage around him. How long he lay there before he was noticed is unknown. It could not have been for any lengthy period of time, because the Confederates could not hold their ground. He finally was discovered, placed over the back of a horse, and taken off the field.[14] Led by two cavalrymen, the horse bearing a still-breathing Pelham slowly trudged to the rear while the battle raged on.

Meanwhile, Breathed's guns began to take a toll on the oncoming blue cavalry. The Federals had advanced another mile before crashing again into another Confederate line. The 1st Rhode Island found itself involved in a second countercharge when the Confederates made a valiant attempt to capture Browne's battery. The Union artillery had galloped forward once Fitz Lee had withdrawn from his first position. Now the guns were threatened by both the Confederate cavalry and horse artillery. But Breathed soon chose to concentrate his fire on the largest target: the enemy cavalry. As the men of the 1st Rhode Island tried to regroup after successfully fending off their opponent's thrust at their artillery, Breathed began to rain shot and shell all about them. Pvt. Joseph W. Gardner was killed by a shell that also wounded his horse. Lt. Henry L. Nicolai, who had already participated in three charges that day, was calmly sitting on his horse before his men when "a shell struck him on the side of the head, knocking it off, and his body turned a somersault and struck on the ground."[15]

Averell had pushed as far as his nerve allowed. Having an almost three-to-one numerical advantage, he had advanced only two miles during the entire day. With daylight beginning to fade, Averell began to pull his troops back to the ford. Breathed continued to shower the retreating cavalry and artillery far into the woods. By 7:30 P.M., Fitz Lee called off further pursuit. Breathed and his men had been in the saddle with the first alarm and had fought for over half the day. They rode back to their camps, their bodies slumped with fatigue, their hearts with sorrow.

John Pelham's last ride was that of one already dead. Hanging across the back of the horse, he certainly appeared to all as such. But some time into the journey he was recognized, briefly examined, and found to be still breathing, though barely. Conveyed to the home of Mr. Henry Shackelford in Culpeper Court House, he was washed and placed on a bed.[16] His wound was examined. He had been struck by a piece of shell in the back of the head. A small splinter was removed. He was made comfortable. The end approached. At 1:00 A.M. on the eighteenth, John Pelham died.

Pvt. H. H. Matthews described the scene at Pelham's bedside:

> That night the men of the battery bade their good-bye to their gallant and idolized commander as he laid in the parlor of Judge Shackelford's house. General Stuart also came. With measured step, his black plumed hat in hand, he approached the body, looked long and silently upon the smiling face, his eyes full of tears; then stooping down he pressed his bearded lips to the marble brow. As he did so the breast of the great Stuart was shaken, a sob issued from his lips, and a tear fell on the pale cheek of Pelham. Severing from his forehead a lock of the light hair, he turned away, and as he did so there was heard in low, deep tones, which seemed to force their way through tears, a single word, "Farewell."[17]

In the midst of his grief, Stuart had duties to perform. There were people who had to be informed. Among the first was Congressman J. L. M. Curry of Alabama. Stuart sent him a telegram on the eighteenth. It read:

To Hon. J. L. M. Curry:

The noble, the chivalric, the gallant Pelham is no more. he was killed in action yesterday. His remains will be sent to you today. How much he was beloved, appreciated and admired let the tears of agony we have shed and the gloom of mourning throughout every command bear witness. His loss to the country is irreparable.

J. E. B. Stuart
Maj. Genl.[18]

The man given the duty of escorting Pelham's body to Curry in Richmond was Stuart's adjutant and inspector general, Maj. Heros von Borcke. He and the rest of the staff were plunged into mourning. In Richmond, von Borcke procured an iron coffin and had the body placed in the capitol. The casket was draped with the flag of Virginia. On the afternoon of the nineteenth, the public was allowed to view the remains of the gallant Alabamian. By the time the doors were closed, the room was festooned with flowers. One of those who stood beside the still form was Miss Sallie Dandridge. On the following day, accompanied by a guard of honor, the casket was born to a waiting carriage, which conveyed it to the railroad station. Pelham was going home.

Stuart arrived in Richmond on the twenty-first, too late for the ceremonies. He had issued the following general order:

Headquarters Cavalry Division, Army Northern Va.,
March 20, 1863.

General Orders
No. 9

The Major General Commanding approaches with reluctance the painful duty of announcing to the Division its irreparable loss in the death of Major John Pelham, commanding the Horse Artillery.

He fell mortally wounded in the battle of Kellysville, (March 17th,) with the battle cry on his lips, and the light of victory beaming from his eye.

To you, his comrades, it is needless to dwell upon what you have so often witnessed—his prowess in action—already proverbial. You well know how, though young in years—a mere stripling in appearance—remarkable for his genuine modesty of deportment—he yet disclosed on the battlefield the conduct of a veteran, and displayed, in his handsome person, the most imperturbable coolness in danger.

His eye had glanced over every battle-field of this army, from the first Manassas to the moment of his death, and he was, with a single exception, a brilliant actor in all.

The memory of "THE GALLANT PELHAM," his many manly virtues, his noble nature and purity of character, is enshrined as a sacred legacy in the hearts of all who knew him.

His record has been bright and spotless; his career brilliant and successful.

He fell—the noblest of sacrifices—on the altar of his country, to whose glorious service he had dedicated his life from the beginning of the war.

In token of respect for his cherished memory, the Horse Artillery and Division Staff will wear the military badge of mourning for thirty days—and the senior officer of Staff, Major Von Borcke, will place his remains in the possession of his bereaved family—to whom is tendered in behalf of the Division the assurance of heartfelt sympathy in this deep tribulation.

In mourning his departure from his accustomed post of honor on the field, let us strive to imitate his virtues, and trust that what is loss to us, may be more than gain to him.

By command of Major General J. E. B. Stuart,

R. Channing Price,
Major and A.A.G.[19]

A more painful task awaited him. He had yet to write to the grieving parents. Not until near the end of the month did Stuart sit and write to the family expressing his sorrow.

Yet, saddened as he was, Stuart had to turn his attention to the war. Pelham was gone. The horse artillery battalion was without a commander. A successor must be named, and selecting him would not be easy.

Even before he died, Pelham's name had become legendary. The officer who would take command of the battalion would find it impossible to measure up to that legend. The best that could be hoped for would be to find an officer who had the respect of the army and the talent to lead the batteries in battle. He might not possess the dash or charisma of Pelham, but he would have to have his heart. Just when Stuart began his search is unknown, but the need was urgent. He could not have waited too long. The war would not stand still while he mourned.

Stuart had two choices: He could select an officer from the battalion or one who had no connection with it. From within the battalion, the choices were limited to the captains of the batteries, unless Stuart considered jumping a junior officer over his superiors, which was unlikely. The men who commanded the batteries then in the battalion were Capt. James Breathed, 1st Stuart Horse Artillery; Capt. William M. McGregor, 2nd Stuart Horse Artillery; Capt. Roger P. Chew, Ashby Battery; Capt. James F. Hart, Washington South Carolina Battery; and Capt. Marcellus N. Moorman, Lynchburg Battery.[20]

Of these men, Capt. Marcellus N. Moorman was the senior officer. Though he was a graduate of the Virginia Military Institute, Moorman's prewar career had not been in the military. He was an unknown to Stuart, his battery having joined the battalion only a few months previously. He had not shown any particular merit during that time. It is doubtful that Stuart ever considered him for the post.

Next in line would have been Capt. Roger P. Chew. There was no doubt that this officer had a reputation as a fighter. His had been the first horse artillery battery formed in the Confederacy. He had fought with and gained the respect of Stonewall Jackson and had been to Turner Ashby what Pelham had been to Stuart. He was attending the Virginia Military Institute when the war began and so had received his artillery training from no less a personage than Jackson himself. But he was not yet twenty years old, and as his battery had been attached to Jones's Brigade, which had remained in the Valley, it had been with the battalion only a short time. Despite his apparent abilities, Chew's youth and unfamiliarity within the battalion removed him as a candidate.

Capt. James F. Hart had received his commission in November 1861. His entire service had been with the battery he now commanded. He had been schooled at the South Carolina Military Academy but, like Moorman, had no prewar army experience. At the commencement of the war, he had served for a short time under Stephen D. Lee, from whom he had learned much. However, Stuart knew very little about Hart. The battery had converted to horse artillery only in September 1862, and though Hart's contributions up to this time had been satisfactory, they had not caught Stuart's eye. That, above everything, was essential. Stuart wanted to know his man. Hart did not fit that category.

The remaining two captains were well known to Stuart. William M. McGregor had been with Pelham almost from the beginning but was removed from consideration because of his wound. He was not now with his battery and probably would not be for several months. Jim Breathed, on the other hand, was a strong contender. He had been Stuart's choice for the command of the Stuart Horse Artillery until Pelham was assigned to it and had demonstrated his abilities on many battlefields under the eyes of both Pelham and Stuart. His lack of military training had not hindered him in the least, and his reputation among the men of the battalion was substantial. The fact that his captain's commission, along with McGregor's, only dated from August 1862 may have been the sole reason he did not receive the appointment.[21]

There were several possible officers outside the horse artillery who may have received some consideration. Capt. Mathis W. Henry might have been a logical candidate, but he had just been promoted out of the battalion. To try to bring him back into the horse artillery might prove difficult. Maj. Lewis F. Terrell of Stuart's staff may also have been considered. In his brief time as a lieutenant in Capt. William Nelson's Virginia Light Artillery, Terrell had made a reputation for himself as a resourceful and daring artillerist. He never missed an opportunity to fight the big guns and had been at Kelly's Ford assisting Breathed on the day Pelham fell. Terrell had figured prominently, though unknowingly, in the behind-the-scenes maneuvering that almost saw Pelham transferred to Longstreet's Corps. He badly wanted out of the court-martial duty Stuart had tied him to and, considering subsequent events, actually expected the assignment to the horse artillery command. He did not get it. Stuart may have believed that a year's service as a lieutenant in Nelson's Battery was not enough. Terrell had been a staff officer since he failed to gain reelection in April 1862. His prewar training was in law, and it was in this capacity that Stuart intended to use him.[22]

With all he had to consider, Stuart had little time to make his decision. He needed to settle on an individual who had the talent and reputation that could benefit the battalion. The man he chose was not in the battalion or in the cavalry in any capacity. Maj. Thomas H. Carter[23] was a graduate of the Virginia Military Institute and was serving as the chief of artillery for Maj. Gen. Daniel H. Hill's division. Of all the officers Stuart considered, Carter had the most training and experience, with the possible exception of Henry. His entire service had been with the artillery. He had earned his promotions, had experience in handling more than one battery and in administrative duties, and was a highly respected officer. Stuart offered him command of the Stuart Horse Artillery Battalion. Carter didn't accept it. He turned Stuart down because he wanted to fight artillery en masse, and the horse artillery was not organized to be fought that way.[24] Stuart had to move on to his next choice. On May 26, 1863, Stuart penned a letter requesting that Maj. Robert F. Beckham be assigned to the command of the Stuart Horse Artillery.[25]

Stuart's request for Beckham's appointment revealed little of what he had looked for in a successor to Pelham. He did know Beckham and had fought beside him. Beckham had graduated from West Point but had served in the engineers before the war. His wartime service was mostly as a staff officer. Yet Stuart was satisfied. Beckham, however, had some misgivings, which he expressed in a letter he wrote on April 5, 1863, to his old commander, Maj. Gen. Gustavus W. Smith.[26] Nevertheless, three days later, Beckham assumed command of the Stuart Horse Artillery Battalion. On the eighth, the following order was issued, not only assigning Beckham to command, but also changing the way the batteries were organized:

Headquarters Cavalry Division,
April 8, 1863.

General Orders,
No. 11.

In compliance with instructions from the commanding general, the Horse Artillery will cease to belong to brigade organizations, but will constitute a separate corps to operate with cavalry. Maj. R. F.

> Beckham, Provisional Army, C.S., is assigned to the command of the Horse Artillery of this army. Batteries will continue on duty with the brigades where now serving, subject to such change as may be hereafter thought advisable; and whenever a battery is so attached, it will be subject to the orders of the commanding officer, who will be responsible for it as for the time being part of his command.
>
> By command of Maj. Gen. J. E. B. Stuart:
>
> R. Channing Price,
> Major, and Assistant Adjutant-General.[27]

Before this order, the Stuart Horse Artillery Battalion did not exist as a military unit, though the various batteries thought of themselves as such. Pelham had commanded the batteries as part of the brigades to which they were attached. Now the batteries were to be assigned to the various brigades as necessity dictated, but they would be under a central command and organization. This would allow for greater flexibility both on and off the battlefield. Sadly, Pelham had not lived to see it.

Nothing is known of the reaction to Beckham's appointment inside the battalion. One of Stuart's staff officers, Maj. R. Channing Price, did record his thoughts:

> Major [Robert F.] Beckham from Warrenton & of the old Army succeeds Pelham as Chief of Artillery: he is a fine young man & I am glad we shall have him here: he was a devoted friend of poor Pelham & has been heretofore on Genl G. W. Smith's staff.[28]

Beckham's friendship with Pelham went back to West Point. Replacing him must have been very difficult for Beckham in more ways than one.

Twenty-two days had passed from the time of Pelham's fall until Beckham's assumption of command. The horse artillery officially would mourn the loss of their chief for eleven more days. In reality, they would mourn until the end of the war and beyond. Pelham had carved his name deeply into the soul of the battalion. How deeply Beckham would engrave his remained to be seen.

The Beckham Era

CHAPTER 12

The Chancellorsville Campaign

"Young man, I congratulate you."

Even as Stuart's command mourned Pelham's passing and Beckham entered into his new duties, the pace of the war quickened. A heavy snowstorm blanketed the camps of both armies on April 4, 1863, but winter was losing its icy grip. There was a stirring of forces both north and south of the Rappahannock. One of the units that stirred the most was the section of McGregor's Battery that had been encamped in Essex and Caroline Counties. It moved to Orange Court House, in part over roads that testified to winter's waning strength. Mud now held sway. William Simpson and William Walters wrote home on the tenth, telling their families of their battery's move, the conditions they encountered on the way, and the news that was then running through the camps.

> Orange County Va April 10th 1863
>
> Dear father & mother & sisters one and all,
>
> It is with great pleasure that I seat myself this morning to answer your kind and welcome letter, it being the first opportunity. William Reed got to camp on the 2 [of April] and fetched it & my shirt & sour apples & cakes etc. I was truly glad to receive them and to hear that you was well & doing well. He said he couldn't fetch the slips you sent there. I was glad he fetched what he did for I wouldn't take a [word illegible] for my fancy shirt.
>
> The next day [April 3] we started, that was on Friday, and on Saturday night it snowed about six inches deep. We traveled all day on Easter Sunday in the snow and mud. We reached Hanover Court House on Monday evening and by that time all the old horses that lived through the winter was on the list. We would leave one in every mudhole for a sign post. So we put the guns and all the dismounted men on the cars and started driving the remainder of the horses with

the wagons, so we reached Orange Court House last evening and joined the rest of the company. Some say we will go on to Culpeper in a few days but the lieutenant said we would stay here maybe a month, so I can't tell.

I got a letter from you this morning bearing date the 29 [of February]. I was glad to hear from you and to hear that you was well. I am well at present except a bad cold I caught sleeping in the snow. I hope this may find you all well. Still I expect you will be looking for this letter before it can get through but I can't help it. I got the ring that was in it. Tell mother that I would like to come home but there is no chance except I take the brush path. So no more but request you to write soon and give me all the news you can. I still remain your humble son and brother till death.

Wm A Simpson to James Simpson & family[1]

Orange Ch Va April 10th 1863

Dear Wife,

It is with great pleasure that I seat myself this morning to answer your letters. I received the one you sent by [William] Reed and one this morning dated the 29th [of February]. I was truly glad to hear that you was well. I was in need of my socks and shirt when they came but I have not had time to look at them hardly since they got here. We have had a long march. We are 120 miles closer [to] home than I was when I wrote before, but there is no chance to come home on furlough now, but I think I can come yet, and I hope it won't be very long until I get off.

There is no news at this time about fighting, only at Charleston, SC. They have been at work there, but I have not heard the particulars yet. Some say we drove them back but they aren't certain that it is the [word illegible].

You must do the best you can. If it is bad, you must not leave the children by themselves and you [go] off to work. Reed said you were out at work when he was there and Molly was keeping house. I know Molly is a good girl but she is too young to take care of a family yet. You must take care of the children. If you don't do anything else take care of what you have got.

Bacon is worth $1.75 cents a pound down here and everything else high. Accordingly I don't spend much money for everything is so high that I can't spare money enough to buy. I can make out on my ration. We get one fourth of a pound of bacon a day [and] one pound flour. Our mess don't hold out very well for we can eat four days rations in one very easy, but there is no use to grumble. That don't make any more sop and don't stop hunger. Give my best respects to all. Tell Molly and sis that I got the cakes and apples and ate them up and would like to come home and get some more. I am as well as [word illegible] and hope this will find you all well. I remain your loving husband till death.

Wm P Walters to M E Walters[2]

The lack of fighting lasted but four days longer. The Federal army had been under a new commander since January 25, when Maj. Gen. "Fighting Joe" Hooker had replaced Burnside. Hooker had spent two months whipping his army into shape and now was determined to strike at Lee. He selected his cavalry for the task. Accordingly, on April 12, Hooker ordered Maj. Gen. George Stoneman, his cavalry chief, to turn the Army of Northern Virginia's left flank and position himself between Lee and Richmond.[3] On the following day, Stoneman's entire corps, except for one brigade, headed for Rappahannock Bridge and Kelly's, Welford's, and Beverly Fords.[4] Opposing this impressive force was Brig. Gen. W. H. F. "Rooney" Lee's Brigade with McGregor's and Moorman's Batteries.[5]

Hooker's grandiose plan began auspiciously enough with Brig. Gen. John Buford's successful demonstration at Kelly's Ford on the fourteenth. The threat of his crossing was met by a large part of Lee's Brigade and Major Beckham with one gun from Moorman's Battery, under Lt. John J. Shoemaker.[6] Buford brought with him a section of Battery E, 4th U.S. Artillery, commanded by Lt. Samuel S. Elder. Dismounted Federal skirmishers engaged Capt. Stith Bolling's Company G, 9th Virginia Cavalry, and most of Col. John R. Chambliss's 13th Virginia Cavalry, which offered strong resistance. Shoemaker opened on the blue skirmishers and sent them scurrying for cover. Then Elder entered the fray. His two pieces began lobbing shells at Shoemaker, who was posted on an elevation south of the river about 2,000 yards from Elder.[7] The accurate Federal fire filled the air around Shoemaker's cannoneers with flying bits of hot metal, sounding much like a swarm of insects. Shoemaker hurriedly withdrew without casualties. Buford pulled back his men and guns around 4:00 P.M., his mission fulfilled.

Meanwhile, the other columns of Stoneman's cavalry were trying to execute their parts of the plan. Col. Benjamin F. "Grimes" Davis successfully pushed 1,500 men over the river at Sulphur Springs and Freeman's Ford and marched toward Beverly's Ford. Farther downstream, Brig. Gen. David McM. Gregg's division with Battery M, 2nd U.S. Artillery, under 1st Lt. Robert Clarke, approached Rappahannock Bridge. Here the Confederates were prepared to dispute the crossing with a small body of men, strongly posted in a blockhouse and a string of rifle pits. Four guns from the horse artillery—two from Moorman's Battery, under Lt. Charles R. Phelps, and two from McGregor's Battery, under Lt. Charles E. Ford, who commanded the battery in McGregor's absence—added to the defense.[8]

Upon his arrival at the bridge, Gregg made preparations to drive off the Confederates.[9] He sent two companies to cross at a nearby ford below the bridge while three more charged across the bridge itself.[10] He also ordered up a section of his artillery that was stationed two miles in the rear. Before the Union artillery arrived, Moorman, who had accompanied Phelps's section, and Ford concentrated their fire on the enemy skirmishers.[11] Both Moorman and Ford believed their fire dispersed the enemy. Clarke arrived shortly after noon and unlimbered his guns in an old earthwork 300 yards from the blockhouse. Ford noticed his approach and his intended position. He limbered his section, moved to a hill directly overlooking the river, and prepared to open on the Federal guns. Phelps, too, was ordered to change targets, and as Clarke began to unlimber, the combined fire of all four guns greeted him.[12]

The Union artillery was quick to answer. The duel lasted about forty minutes. Clarke reported that he was successful in silencing the Confederate guns and in driving the defenders from the blockhouse. Moorman and Ford reported that it was the Federal artillery that withdrew, ending the fight. Clarke admitted to being ordered to the rear after firing seventy-eight rounds. There were no casualties among Beckham's men or horses, but the Yankee artillery lost two horses wounded.[13]

Though Gregg was successful in crossing the river and securing a brief hold on the southern shore, he pulled all of his men back late in the afternoon. He briefly examined Beverly's Ford, but except for posting two squadrons on the north side of the river, he did nothing. Riding away from the ford, he went into camp between Bealton and Rappahannock Bridge. He had accomplished little.

During the action at the bridge, Lt. Edmund H. Moorman was placed in charge of the caissons for Moorman's Battery. He recalled an amusing incident involving one of men of the battery:

> John Cary was sent to me for a limber of ammunition. On his way to me Gen. Stuart met him and apparently thinking John was making a sneak to the rear, asked him where he was going. John explained and was allowed to proceed, and on his return with the ammunition he met Gen. Stuart and asked him where he was going. Stuart seemed to comprehend the situation, gave John a jolly, and they parted with a better feeling and more respect for each other. John was one of our best and bravest boys and wouldn't stand for an insinuation, no matter who it came from.[14]

The fact that Phelps called for more ammunition would indicate that his guns expended a considerable amount of ammunition in holding the bridge that day.[15]

The fighting on the fifteenth did not involve Moorman's Battery, though it was called out and posted near St. James Church. The section of McGregor's Battery under Ford was in action at Welford's Ford, but only to disperse enemy sharpshooters. Rain doused any chance of the fight escalating to more than a skirmish. That rain and the two days' fighting became topics in letters written by Privates Simpson and Walters and Lieutenant Phelps, all of whom were either engaged or in the vicinity of the fighting.

April the 16, 1863

Dear father & mother & sisters,

It is with great pleasure that I seat myself this morning to write you a few lines to inform you that I am well and hope [when] this comes to hand it may find you all enjoying the same blessing. I can inform you that we have had pretty hard times lately marching in rough weather and skirmishing with the Yankees. For my part I was with the wagons, but they had to stay in the road ready to start at any time and it rained all day. You will want to know where our guns were. They were on the cars ready to toddle for that's all the way we can go till we get horses, and I don't care if they don't get any till the spring fight goes off. Then I won't have to go in it.

I should like to get to come home but the chance seems bad without a change for everything is fight here. I wrote you a letter when I was at Orange stating that I got the things you sent by Reed and was glad to receive them. As I have no news to write you must do the best you can and I will try and dodge along some way or other till times change. It is tho't there will be pretty squally times this summer, but I am in hopes that it is misrepresented.

Write to me and let me know what you are going to do with your confederate Shucks and how many you have received. Said you was going to buy land with them. I think it would be very good policy for I don't think we can ever whip the Yankees to make it good. Let us know when you hear from Tos and what they are doing. So no more at present. I still remain your true and affectionate son & brother till death.

Wm A Simpson to James Simpson & family[16]

Culpeper Ch Va April the 16th 1863

Dear Wife,

It is with great pleasure that I have this opportunity to write you a few lines to let you know that I am well except pain in legs and shoulders, but I hope that when these few lines come to hand they will find you all well.

I have no news much to write at this time. I wrote to you when we was at Orange Courthouse and we left the same day and came to Culpeper. We have seen hard times since we left Essex. It is cold wet weather down here, and we have to lay out nearly all the time. The Yankees keep crossing the river, and we have to run them back. Two of our guns were in a hot skirmish yesterday and day before. None of them got hurt. They run them back across the river last night, but the news came to camp this morning that the Yankees were crossing again. I expect there will be some fighting today but our horses are broken down, so I don't expect we will go in, or we will have to get a stronger force here or else they will drive us back. They have 5 brigades of cavalry and we only have one. We have lost several horses and some prisoners and one man killed. We killed several of them and took 19 prisoners yesterday.

I have no more news to write about the army only I am getting tired of staying down in this country, and I don't like our company. It is filled up with rowdies, rascals, and rogues. Six of our company are in the guard house now for stealing from an old citizen that took them in and gave them their dinner and after they got their dinner they stole his watch and silver spoons and boots. We have not got but one officer that is worth a cent. I have a notion to go to the west and join the army there, but I have not come to any conclusion what I will do yet. The Floyd [County] boys are all very much dissatisfied. One half of them say they will run off.

You must do the best you can and I will do the same. You must not be uneasy about me if I go out west. I will come by home, but I will have to be very sly, but if they catch me after I get out there all they can do is bring me back, but I am not afraid of them getting me after I get there. The worst is starting.

Give my best respects to all. Tell Molly and sis and the baby that I want to see them very bad. Take good care of them. So no more, but remain your true and loving husband till death

William P Walters to Matilda E. Walters

Goodby for this time, hoping to see you soon if I have luck.[17]

Camp Near Culpeper Co. Ho.
Apl 16th 1863

Dear Aunt,

I arrived at camp at Rapidan on Sunday afternoon [12th], found all well. Got orders to leave next morning for this place arrived here on Monday afternoon, left this place at day break Thursday morn to meet the Yanks who had crossed the river at Rappahannock Bridge. Met them about 9 o'clock. Had a very brisk engagement until 5 in afternoon when we succeeded in driving them back, they retiring in very bad order—as their retreat was facilitated by several shots from my gun. Although in action nearly all day we have not lost a single man. Tuesday morning we were again ordered to meet them as they had crossed again. We moved up river some 5 miles, & met a Brigade of Cavalry & drove them across the river with considerable loss. We also took 15 prisoners, horses, etc. Yesterday was the most miserable day of the Spring. Commenced raining at 2 in the morning and continued in torrents until after dark. We were in position all day but did not fire. We are again back at our first camp, got here at day-break. You see I have commenced active service in earnest—fighting two days out of three since my arrival.

We may stay here several days, as the rains have caused the river to rise very high, & no chance for an attack for a while at least. Gen. Stuart evidently intends to keep us very busy this campaign. He has been with us in person all the time. I can hear nothing from below, presume all quiet. I am now writing in full Georgia Costume as everything I have is as wet as if I had swam the river. The sun is now out and will be all right soon. Let Miss Wiatt see this—have a chance to send mail & write in haste.

Love to All
Truly Yours
Dick[18]

Phelps proved prophetic. The river rose and remained high for the next two weeks. Military operations ground to a halt. In the interval, Lee and Hooker attempted to fathom each other's plans. The soldiers of the two armies welcomed the calm before the storm. In Beckham's Battalion, officers and men alike spent time visiting friends and writing home. Phelps, as did many others, took the opportunity during the lull to shed himself of unneeded clothing. In his bundle, he enclosed something of great value and careful instructions on how it was to be handled.

Near Culpeper Co. Ho. Apl 18th 1863

Dear Aunt

I send by Charles Gruber a bundle of clothing, more than I want. Charlie takes back all goods not wanted by the men. We expect to have a brisk time however and are not allowed to keep more than can be carried on our horses. In the bundle is our Company Flag which is in a very dilapidated condition—as we intend to have it fixed as soon as the material can be gotten. You will much oblige me by putting it away and not exposing it, & Miss Orianna might not like it if she knew her flag had left the Co. I have a pair of thin kind [of] drawers in my trunk please send them by Charlie in place of the pair I send.

I had a martingale with my saddle at Bruce's if Stephen brought it away please have it sent to Fayette Williams and it belongs to him. If he did not bring it from Bruce's, tell Uncle C. to let Williams know it was left there. Gen. Tilden arrived here last night.

Nothing new from front since I last wrote. The River is up most too high for another attempt at crossing. You may look for stirring news from this quarter soon. The Yanks are in large force on the opposite side of river.

Remember me to all Yours very truly
Dick[19]

The "stirring news" was a couple weeks away, but the Yanks were "in large force" on the north bank of the Rappahannock, and they were not going away. Things were being stirred up quite a bit in Breathed's Battery, however. Lt. Francis H. Wigfall, who had received a personal invitation from Stuart to join the horse artillery, finally reported for duty—or tried to, as he explained in a letter to his sister:

Camp near Culpeper CH
April 21 Tuesday 1863

Dear Lou

I wrote Mama on the 15th the day I reported for duty and took it over to Genl. Lee's HdQrs. that evening to Capt. Ferguson the Adjt. Genl. of the Brigade to send off. I have not yet heard from her. I told her in that how to direct my letters but will repeat for fear that she did not receive it. Direct to Breathed's Battery—Fitz Lee's Brigade—Cavalry Division—A.N.Va.

When I first reached the Battery Capt. Breathed could not put me on duty as chief of the section to which I was entitled by my rank without referring the matter to Genl. Stuart for his decision, because he said it would create dissatisfaction among the officers. I told him therefore in order to avoid difficulty that I would agree to that meanwhile would assume no command at all but await Genl. Stuart's reply. Accordingly the reference was made and on the 19th (day before yesterday) the paper returned bearing Genl. Stuart's endorsement to the effect that I would of course take command according to my rank. The Captain accordingly put me in command of the second section (12 pounder Howitzers). The first Lieutenant of the battery is named [Philip P.] Johnston and the junior second, [Daniel] Shanks. They are both as well as the Captain, Marylanders. Lieut. Johnston and I mess together.

I have not yet a horse but am riding one of those belonging to the battery until I can buy one. Genl. Lee's Hd.Qrs. are not more than fifty yards from our camp in the shell of an old house with one room and one wall of that room torn down. We are entirely al fresco having left our tents, officers, and men, at Amissville, the place from which I wrote Mama. A great many of the men have pieces of canvas with which they make shelters out <u>al</u> <u>fresco.</u> We get along very well though and the warm weather is now coming on.

On our march from Amissville we passed Gaines' X roads, Little Washington, Sperryville and Woodville, and, after reaching Gaines' X roads over the same road we marched when I was with Bachman's Battery coming down from Winchester last fall.

We are now camped about half a mile from Culpeper on the Rixeyville road. It seems to be pretty generally thought that the enemy intends trying the Peninsula again this spring. Whether he will do so or not remains to be seen. One would have supposed that the Yankees were well enough acquainted by this time with the Chickahominy Swamp to let it alone in future. Of one thing they may rest assured that whenever they do go there the A.N.Va. will be to receive them. Major Beckham is now Chief of Artillery of the Division. He was here this morning and he was talking of ordering Hoxton with his Whitworth gun to report to Capt. Breathed. He was detached last winter from this battery with a detachment of men to take command of it. I don't know whether the assignment will be permanent or not but expect it will turn out so in the end. Flap-jacks are finished and I will proceed. One of the pieces of the first section has gone off on picket four miles down the road.

Tell Fanny to write to me and kiss her for me. You have no idea how gruesome (I believe it is what the Scotch call it) I felt after first joining the battery. I was as melancholy as a March hare and was almost inclined to coincide in my opinions with "Miss Katie" who thought that "severe pain" would be an "actual relief." If it were not for parting being with those we love would be perfect happiness. I think one of the truest and most beautiful pieces in the language is Campbell's "Soldier's Dream." The first time you see a copy of his poems read it and you will think so with me. Give my best love to dear Papa and Mama and write me whenever you can. Good-bye dearest and God bless you

Ever your affectionate
Brother[20]

Wigfall was not the only officer who reported for duty to the battalion. After a long absence, Capt. William M. McGregor rode into camp sometime between the twenty-first and the twenty-fifth. His wound had sidelined him since November, but he now felt fit enough to take command of his battery. His return and other goings-on in the battalion were the topics of letters sent home by Simpson, Walters, and Wigfall on the twenty-sixth.

Culpeper Co Va April the 26 1863

Dear Father & Mother & Sisters one & all,

It is with pleasure that I seat myself this fine Sunday morning to answer your kind & welcome letter that came to hand last evening bearing the date the 21st which gave me great pleasure to hear from you, but sorry to hear that all had bad the phthisic. I am glad to inform you that I am well except a bad cold but that isn't worth complaining of.

I haven't got any news worth writing. They say there are plenty of Yankees on the other side of the river, but they haven't pestered us lately, and I am in hopes they won't. All 3 of the batteries are here together now, Captains Moorman's & Breathed's, and ours [McGregor's]. They say they are going to form a corps of artillery. We got some new horses yesterday and expect some more today. They don't intend for us to have any excuse.

You said you was done sowing oats but didn't say how much you had sowed. I expect you will raise more grain & make more money than you did when all your boys was at home by half, though I would be very glad to be there to lend a hand most especially at the table. Although old Jeff gives us a pound of flour and a quarter of a pound of bacon a day, I don't like his table. I should like to have milk and butter and a heap of other things I don't get. I am afraid I will miss my bacon and beans again this summer.

You wrote that you was working [word illegible] and wanted me to help just hold on to them till next summer for I think we will kill the last horse old Jeff's got by then, and we can work them at our leisure. If any body wants to buy tell them they are better property than shucks. So no more, but ask you to write soon. Do the best you can & I will try & do the same. I still remain your humble son & brother till death. I was sorry to hear of the death of cousin Tep Holt. You didn't state what was the matter with her.

Wm A Simpson to James Simpson & family[21]

Camp near Culpeper Ch Va April 26th 1863

Dear Wife,

It is with pleasure that I have the opportunity this morning to answer your kind letter that came to hand yesterday bearing the date the 19th of this month which gave me great pleasure to hear that you all were well and were getting along as you are. I can inform you that I am well and able to eat 3 men's rations if I could get them, truly hoping that these few lines may find you all in good health.

I have no news to write at present about the army only the horse artillery is all put in one corps and will act in no particular brigade. It is thought that there will be less fighting in this part of the state than last year but I don't know how it will be. McGregor has come back and is captain of our company. The men like him tolerable well.

You wrote that I was a long time making my furlough. I am going to try any way to get to come home that a man can, and if I can't come with out making one I want to make a good one. There is some money due me yet that I want to get before I come. We drew 24 dollars the other day. There are 2 months wages due us the first of next month, and the officers owe me 65 dollars that I must have some how before I make a furlough, or else I will not make much by cooking.

You must do the best you can. You wrote like you was above eating old Jeffs bread like your neighbor does. I will be very sorry indeed if you have to come to that, but I am afraid that old Jeff will run out of rations if he has to feed the soldiers and their wives too, but it is right that he should do so. Tell Molly to break as many hens from setting as she pleases. Tell sis not to let any of you run over her and the baby. I want to see you all very bad and would like to help you all work, but I can't do as I like for [word illegible] comes in first now and the officers next, but the poor private comes in a little before a dog. I can't tell, but I hope it won't be long till I see you all. Give my respects to all. No more, but remain your true and loving husband till death.

Wm. P. Walters to M. E. Walters

Direct your letters in care of Capt. McGregor.[22]

Camp near Culpeper C.H.
April 26 1863

Dear Mama,

I received yours of the 20th which you sent by Col. Carter on the 22d. I had written only a day or two before to Louly. We have since then moved across the Rail Road and are now part of a battalion under Major Beckham, the chief of Artillery of this division. He has at present only three of the batteries with him, McGregor's, Moorman's, and this one [Breathed's]. The other two are with their brigades, Hart with Hampton, and Chew with Jones in the Valley. As soon, however, as Fitz Lee's Brigade is ordered off on detached service we will go with him, so that unless both the Lees' brigades move together it will probably not be long before we are with Genl. Fitz Lee again.

We are camped about three miles from Culpeper on the R R in the direction of the Rappahannock. Just opposite is John Minor Botts' place given him by Stearns, the wealthy distiller in Richmond, and for which he is reported to have said he would not take all the Confederate money in the Confederacy. The afternoon we were moved over here it cleared up and we have had beautiful weather since. My overcoat has done me yeoman's service and has kept the rain from me in a way which the old one would not have been capable of.

You had better keep directing your letters to the brigade, or, which could be better, direct to Breathed's Battery, Stuart's Cavalry Division, A.N.Va. I think this last preferable because the letters will then run no risk of being missent, whether we are with the brigade or not. Everything on this line seems at a stand still. I understand that the enemy has infantry as well as cavalry on the opposite side of the Rappahannock, but as to his intentions I have not even heard a conjecture for some time past.

I rode to Culpeper the other day with Hoxton and Capt. McGregor and from there went in with Hoxton out to Genl. Stuart's. I saw Col. Carter there. Capt. Breathed had given me the letter before.

If Papa remains in Virginia this summer, I have no doubt you will have an exceedingly pleasant time. Have you thought of the country on the James River canal beyond Lynchburg. If you were to spend the summer there you would be in easy distance of Lynchburg, and from there to Richmond is not a very long journey with three lines of communication by way of Gordonsville, Petersburg, or the Danville road and the canal aforesaid. You will be in the mountains, off the line of travel, and where the army has never been. Altogether

I expect you will be more likely to find a place that you will like in that part of the state than any other. I finished reading "Shirley" this morning and like it quite well. I am now reading the "Notes of a Journey from Cornhill to Grans Caire" by Thackeray. I never cared much for books of travel but camp is a great place for wearing out old clothes and reading uninteresting books, as I have already got through more than half of those. I got "Shirley" from Capt. Ferguson, Genl. Lee's Adjt. Gen. He is a cousin of Simons and a very nice fellow. Please remember me to Mrs. Lee and tell her that I carried her letter over to Genl. Lee's immediately after getting it.

There is a rumor in camp that the brigades of the two Lees are to be ordered down to Genl. Longstreet. I think it most probably a camp rumor and merely that. They would scarcely take two out of the three brigades of cavalry on this side of the mountains to send to a force so much smaller than the army to which we now belong.

Kiss Louly and Fan, for me and give my best love to dear Papa. Write to me frequently and believe me dearest Mama as ever

Your affectionate Son
Halsey[23]

Wigfall may not have been privy to any conjectures concerning Hooker's intentions, but to anyone whose eye gazed north of the Rappahannock, it was apparent that Hooker had intentions of some kind. Even as Wigfall penned his letter, the Union army's commander was preparing to issue orders putting his corps and divisions in motion to crush Lee. The campaign season was about to begin.

For several days, Stuart had observed that Federal infantry pickets held the north bank of the Rappahannock at Kelly's Ford and Rappahannock Bridge. The question of what had happened to the cavalry became number one in his mind. He was well aware of the implications surrounding this seemingly innocent disruption of the norm. The Confederate cavalry and horse artillery were placed on the alert, but Beckham was unable to comply.

HdQrs Horse Artillery
Apr 28, 1863

Major:

Your orders are just received and will be carried into execution at once. Please say to the General that the pieces were not taken to the ford this morning as he seemed to think best. Genl Lee deeming it proper to await something like a demonstration from the enemy.

> I shall place the pieces as the General directs and with his permission will hold two or three in reserve at the position about a mile below Brandy Station. I shall so dispose of them unless otherwise directed.
>
> Very Respectfully
YrObdSvt
R. F. Beckham
Maj. Comdg S.H. Arty[24]
>
> Maj. R. Channing Price
A.A. Genl

Beckham placed his guns, and everyone waited. Hooker, expected to come calling momentarily, finally arrived the evening of the twenty-eighth at Kelly's Ford. Stuart promptly informed Lee what was happening but could not give an accurate numbering of the Yankees due to the darkness. The enemy's advance might just be another feint, and to counter the move properly, Lee needed to know the number of Federals crossing the river. Stuart ordered a concentration of his command at Brandy Station at daylight.

By morning, Rooney Lee's Brigade had taken a position between Brandy Station and Kelly's Ford to await the enemy.[25] When the Yankees failed to materialize, Lee sent forward the 13th Virginia Cavalry and a section from Moorman's Battery, under Lt. John J. Shoemaker.[26] It quickly was determined that the enemy was not pushing toward Culpeper, but to Germanna Ford on the Rapidan. Stuart left the 13th Virginia and Shoemaker's section at Kelly's Ford and with Fitz Lee's Brigade, and the 9th Virginia of Rooney Lee's Brigade rode to intercept the Federals. Breathed's and McGregor's Batteries and Phelps's section of Moorman's Battery accompanied Stuart. At Will Madden's farm, the Confederates slashed into the snaking blue columns and captured enough prisoners to confirm that three Federal corps were marching on Robert E. Lee's flank. Stuart sent off a dispatch to Lee and made preparations to offer what resistance he could. Rooney Lee's Brigade of two small regiments, with Shoemaker's section and Hart's Battery, was ordered to move through Culpeper and cover Gordonsville and the Virginia Central Railroad.[27] Fitz Lee's Brigade, with the remainder of the horse artillery, was sent to Raccoon Ford.

All during the thirtieth, Rooney Lee's small force fell back slowly toward the Rapidan. A squadron was left behind in Culpeper to offer a token resistance to Gen. George Stoneman's advancing blue cavalry, but it soon retreated and rejoined Lee at Rapidan Station that evening. The horse artillery did not have the opportunity to fire a shot during the withdrawal. The weary troopers and cannoneers were aware of what would confront them the next morning and realized that there was no chance that they could hold the river line. Stoneman was simply too strong for Lee to oppose.

Fitz Lee crossed the river at Raccoon Ford on the night of the twenty-ninth. Here Stuart ordered his regiments, except for Col. Thomas Owen's 3rd Virginia, and the horse artillery to rest. Owen was sent ahead to place himself between the enemy and Fredericksburg in the vicinity of Wilderness Run. Near midnight, he reached Locust Grove and sent scouts toward Germanna Ford to feel out the enemy. About three hours later, he rode on to Wilderness Tavern and dispatched additional scouts. At 8:00 A.M. on the thirtieth, the scouts returned. They didn't need to report their findings. The 6th New York Cavalry was right behind them. The fight for the bridge over Wilderness Run was on. Owen put up a scrap but was outmanned and fell back, still skirmishing, toward Chancellorsville.

Shortly after Owen's withdrawal, Stuart arrived on the scene with the rest of Fitz Lee's Brigade and the horse artillery.[28] Pvt. Henry H. Matthews of Breathed's Battery left an account of the fighting that day:

> We reached Wilderness Run Tavern about the same time as the 3rd Virginia did, opening fire at once upon the force that was driving the 3rd back. We advanced upon their column of infantry and artillery through a dense woods, advancing the guns by hand, with great difficulty over stumps and roots of trees; at times being close enough to the enemy to almost see the color of their eyes. We used nothing but canister, as shells would be of no service at such short range.[29]

Maj. Lansford F. Chapman, commanding the 28th Pennsylvania Infantry, who faced Breathed that day, reported that his men received grape, canister, and shell from two guns deployed against him. The fire laid down by Private Matthews and his comrades failed to make an impression on the twenty-eighth. Lansford admitted to one man killed but gave credit to the Confederate cavalry, not the artillery.[30]

Stuart battled the Union infantry from 10:00 to noon but in the end had to break off the fight. He gave orders directing the column to Todd's Tavern on a route that paralleled the Federal line of march. Breathed pulled back his two pieces, reunited his battery, and with McGregor and Phelps, who had not had the opportunity to bombard either the trees or the enemy, followed in the cavalry's wake.

McGregor's Battery was short one gun, which had been left under Lt. G. Wilmer Brown to guard Raccoon Ford.[31] Just about the time that Stuart was disengaging at Wilderness Run, Brown was desperately trying to save his gun from elements of the 5th U.S. Cavalry under Lt. Julius W. Mason. The Federals had crossed the river at Mitchell's Ford and had ranged upstream in an effort to open other crossings for Stoneman's columns. Brown had not expected trouble from the direction that Stuart had taken. When Mason's men came swooping down on him, a frantic scramble ensued. Brown and his men knew their first duty was to save their gun, and it was all they could do to limber and get it away.[32] After that, the cannoneers were on their own. Eight were captured, but they had satisfaction in the knowledge that their lieutenant and his charge were safe.[33]

Stuart reached Todd's Tavern without further incident. At that place, he ordered the cavalry and horse artillery to bivouac for the night. He and his staff proposed to ride on to Spotsylvania Court House. A short distance down the road, the small group of officers ran into the 6th New York Cavalry. The staff and the general gave way, and Stuart sent for his cavalry. Up came the 5th Virginia at the gallop. A deadly melee erupted amid the glowing shafts of moonlight that penetrated the forest canopy. The men of the horse artillery could only sit in the darkness and strain to hear the clash of arms. In the end, the enemy was driven off, and troopers and cannoneers alike sought to make themselves as comfortable as possible for the night.

On May 1, Stuart split his command in two. Fitz Lee with Breathed and two guns was ordered to maintain contact with the Federals and send back information as to Hooker's movements. Stuart would protect Stonewall Jackson's left flank. Beckham with six guns would remain with Stuart.[34] For most of the day, there was little to do except follow the cavalry from point to point. At about 4:00 P.M., Fitz Lee put Breathed's two pieces in battery at Carpenter's farm on the Brock Road. However, Federal infantry was sent forward, and Breathed had to withdraw. He could not have been in action for more than a half hour.

Meanwhile, four miles east at Catherine Furnace, Beckham had assembled his six guns and was about to engage. Stuart had been called upon by Brig. Gen. Ambrose R. Wright to support him with artillery. Wright was confronted by a Federal force of considerable size in the woods north of the Furnace. His regiments advanced and drove the Yankees back to a farmhouse. There he halted and sent for Beckham, who rode forward with four of his guns.[35] By 5:30 P.M., Beckham was in position and firing on the enemy's infantry, which fell back to their entrenchments at Hazel Grove. The Confederate success was short-lived, however. Eight Federal pieces at Fairview Cemetery responded to Beckham's fire and were soon joined by two additional guns positioned at Hazel Grove.[36]

It did not take long for the Yankees to find the range. Shells began dropping among Beckham's guns with uncanny accuracy. One piece in particular seemed to be the target of the blue cannoneers. As Lt. Robert P. P. Burwell of McGregor's Battery watched his crew serve their piece, man after man was hit and forced from the fight. An exploding shell felled Pvt. William P. Walters with a mortal wound, and soon a shell fragment struck Burwell himself. Stuart and Jackson with their staffs were sitting nearby on their horses, calmly observing the artillery duel. Federal shells burst about them. Stuart urged Jackson to withdraw to safety. Scarcely had the words left his mouth when Stuart's adjutant, Maj. R. Channing Price, was mortally wounded. As the party rode from under the rain of metal, Beckham's gunners continued their fire. Burwell had another man killed,[37] and only one man was yet unwounded. A neighboring gun had an axle nearly severed in two. Three horses were hit. It would have been insanity to remain any longer. Beckham gave the order to limber to the rear. The men hitched the horses and brought the guns off the field.

For three-quarters of an hour, Beckham and his gallant gunners had withstood the iron hailstorm. They had paid a heavy price—two killed and six wounded. Beckham praised the conduct of Captain McGregor and Lieutenants Burwell, Francis H. Wigfall, and Charles E. Ford. He noted that the men at the guns had behaved gallantly. While Beckham believed that he had inflicted some damage on the Federal batteries, his fire had actually had little effect. One man was killed and five others wounded in Brig. Gen. Charles K. Graham's Brigade, which had been in position in rear of the Union artillery, but the artillery emerged virtually unscathed.[38] Private Walters was wrapped in his blanket and quickly buried on the field. There was little time to mourn. The battery had to move on. There was still a battle to be fought.

After falling back to the Furnace, the horse artillery made camp for the night. The next morning, it became part of Jackson's flank movement. By late afternoon, the Confederate infantry was forming in the woods on either side of the turnpike and preparing for the attack on Hooker's flank. Two guns from Breathed's Battery were on the road, parallel with the first line of infantry. Breathed reported to Brig. Gen. Robert E. Rodes, who asked, "Captain will those boys stand?" "Stand!" growled Breathed, "——— ———, sir, when those boys leave their guns you will not have a man left in your division, and I am going to take them in with your skirmish line and show you d——n Tar Heels how to fight."[39]

In a letter he wrote that evening, Lt. Francis H. Wigfall described just how Breathed's boys did fight:

> May 2 1863
>
> We have had a glorious fight this afternoon. Drove the Yanks from the start and kept them going as fast as we could follow until [word illegible]. Maj. Beckham and Capt. Breathed and I were with my howitzer which was the first piece of artillery fired. The fight began about half past five. The first shot the Yankee artillery fired was a spherical case & one of the bullets struck me in the arm. It was however entirely spent—Three of our pieces and one of McGregor's were the only ones of the Horse Artillery engaged.[40]
>
> I wrote last night but don't know whether you got it. Don't look to hear from me until the fighting is over for there are no mails and it is all mere chance—as to getting a letter to you—Out of our three pieces we only lost one man. He was killed—I write by moonlight on a limber chest and on Yankee paper—Our men in the highest possible spirits—Everything is bright—Best love to dearest Mama and

> Lou, and kiss little [name illegible] for me—Good-bye dear Papa and believe me as ever
>
> Your affectionate Son
> Halsey[41]

Pvt. H. H. Matthews left a vivid account of the fighting his battery did that day:

> At 6 P.M., everything being in readiness, Breathed with the 1st section of the battery (Johnston) moved out on the turnpike in the center of Jackson's corps, at section front, Lieut. Dan Shanks being immediately in the rear with the second section. In this position we awaited the command of the immortal Stonewall Jackson to forward. The battery knew that immediately in our front, not far distant, was a Federal battery planted in the road ready to fire upon the approach of the rebs. The thought was not a pleasant one, to walk into the very jaws of a masked battery. We did not object to standing in the open and exchanging shots with any one Federal battery, but we certainly did object to walking into the jaws of death without being able to use the instruments of destruction. It seemed particularly horrible to me, as on this occasion I was driving the lead team of the 1st gun, and expecting every moment as we advanced to be hurled from the saddle by the contents of one of those guns. Fortunately we struck that battery in their rear. We [word illegible] them before they could change position and fire on us. The infantry used their guns on them with good effect. . . .
>
> We advanced on the road leading to Chancellorsville about 6 P.M., at section front, Rodes' division leading, supported by Colston's, and Hill's division being on each flank of the battery. We at once struck the enemy in his right flank and rear. Nothing stopped us. We moved on regardless of obstacles of all kinds that had been placed in the road. The enemy were thrown into the wildest confusion by the first fire from Rodes' men. Breathed, with whip in hand, would help the drivers of the pieces to force the jaded horses across the trees and other obstructions that had been placed in our way, the cannoneers at the wheels, and everybody yelling in unison. It was a sight long remembered and goes to show that nothing could keep the daring, reckless Breathed back. When he had determined to go forward, obstacles of any kind could not do it. When he said forward, he meant it.[42]

Beckham and Breathed did indeed set the pace for the guns. Breathed rode out in front to locate positions. Beckham leapfrogged the sections ahead. The cannons continually blazed away at the enemy. Hampered by obstructions in the road, the guns did not always keep up with Jackson's infantry, but their fire never slackened.

The battle raged on. The continuous serving of the guns and the strain of moving them along the debris-littered road brought the cannoneers to the brink of exhaustion. The men of Moorman's Battery voluntarily rushed forward to relieve Breathed's and McGregor's weary gunners. Five horses were shot down during the artillery's advance, but they were cut from their traces, and the guns moved ever closer to the retreating Federals. Despite their determination and gallantry, the officers and men were not immune to the enemy's shot and shell that were hurled against them. Pvt. William Evans of Breathed's Battery was killed near the end of the fight when struck in the stomach by a shell. A private from McGregor's Battery also fell with a mortal wound.[43] Pvt. John McMasters of Moorman's Battery was wounded.

For two hours, the horse artillery fought in the tangled Wilderness until, at 8:00 P.M., Beckham called a halt. Neither his men nor his horses had eaten in forty-eight hours. They had nothing left to give. As Beckham directed them rearward, Stonewall Jackson rode out of the gathering darkness and reined in his horse next to Beckham. Leaning forward, Stonewall took the young major's hand and said, "Young man I congratulate you and the brave men under you."[44] As had Pelham before him, Beckham had earned Jackson's praise by performing brilliantly under difficult circumstances. It was praise that belonged not only to Beckham, but also to all the officers and men under him. In his report of the battle, Beckham gave all the credit to Breathed, McGregor, and the other officers and men. He wrote not one word of receiving Stonewall's congratulations. However, others had heard and would make known Jackson's comment.

As Breathed's and McGregor's Batteries slowly rode back along the Plank Road, Captain Moorman unlimbered his pieces and placed them into position to renew the fight. Soon Col. Stapleton Crutchfield, Jackson's artillery chief, moved three other pieces into position and opened fire on Fairview Cemetery. Moorman's guns did not have the range and so did not have the opportunity to fire on the enemy, much to the men's frustration.[45] They were not, however, out of the action entirely. The Federal batteries bombarded the Confederates for a half hour, and a number of the shells came uncomfortably close to Phelps's men. Once Crutchfield's artillery ceased firing, the enemy's guns fell silent.

On May 3, as the infantry of the two armies struggled in the maze of trees and underbrush, the horse artillery took position to the left of the Plank Road to guard the approach from Ely's Ford should the Federals attempt to turn the Confederate flank. No such threat materialized, and as the sounds of battle slowly moved farther away, Beckham had an opportunity to assess his losses. Four men had been killed, seven wounded, and eight captured. All but one, McMasters, were from Breathed's and McGregor's Batteries. It had been a costly two days. But even as he read the casualty list, Beckham knew he might have to add to it. He still had four guns out chasing Stoneman.

On May 1, while Beckham was marching through the Wilderness to Catherine Furnace, Rooney Lee spent all day confronting part of Stoneman's force under Brig. Gen. William W. Averell at Rapidan Station. At one time, he ordered a charge across the river by the 9th Virginia Cavalry. Shoemaker's section of Moorman's Battery and Hart's Battery tried in vain to support the cavalry as it grappled with Averell's troopers.[46] Col. Richard L. T. Beale, who commanded the 9th Virginia, felt that the artillery's effort was "feeble," and nothing came of the attack.[47] Lee had received orders to burn the bridge at Rapidan Station and fall back to Gordonsville, but the torrential rains had so saturated the bridge that it withstood all efforts to set it ablaze. Finally, Lee gave up in frustration and rode for Gordonsville sometime after midnight, leaving the bridge standing.

On the second, Stoneman occupied Louisa Court House and there learned that Lee was at Gordonsville. At almost the same time, Lee was informed of Stoneman's presence at Louisa Court House and sent the 9th Virginia to ascertain the enemy's strength. A squadron of the 1st Maine routed a detachment of the 9th that was riding in advance of the regiment.[48] A charge by the entire regiment led by Colonel Beale hurried the Yanks back toward the courthouse. Gen. Lee rushed the 13th Virginia and two guns forward, only to find the fighting was over by the time he arrived. After leaving pickets on the road, he fell back to Gordonsville. The horse artillery's guns remained cold.

Both sides learned what they wanted from the brief clash. Stoneman dispatched several squadrons to destroy track and buildings of the Virginia Central Railroad and then rode on to Thompson's Crossroads, arriving about 10:00 P.M. Here Stoneman divided his forces. One contingent under Col. Percy Wyndham was to strike for Columbia on the James River and destroy the aqueduct there. Lee paralleled him, striking the river at Scottsville. Shoemaker and Hart accompanied the gray troopers. The pursuit continued to the Rivanna River's junction with the James. Only the towpath bridge was left standing. The artillerymen removed the wheels from the gun carriages and caissons and slid the guns over on the railings of the bridge. They rolled the wheels across. Men and horses walked over. Then the men replaced the wheels and renewed the chase.[49] These efforts were futile, however, as Wyndham escaped after burning five bridges, destroying a large quantity of supplies, and damaging the James River Canal. Again, the horse artillery had made a long trek for nothing.[50]

From the fourth to the seventh, the scenario was the same.[51] Though the cavalry clashed, the horse artillery was unable to bring its guns into action. Stoneman recrossed the Rapidan at Raccoon Ford in the early morning hours of the seventh. He rode for Kelly's Ford on the Rappahannock and crossed that river on the eighth. His pursuers followed wearily. The men of Shoemaker's section rejoined Moorman's Battery at Raccoon Ford on the morning of the seventh. Lt. E. H. Moorman left a description of the condition of his men:

> Here [at Raccoon Ford] we met Shoemaker with his section, and of all the dilapidated and broken down set of men and horses, they were the worst I ever saw. They had been on the march for the past week, night and day, without rest and little to eat, and they were a pitiful sight. None of them could stay awake long enough to talk; they just seemed to slip off their horses and fall asleep where they fell.[52]

In one sense, the entire army was doing the same thing. The campaign had been hard fought, and both Hooker's and Lee's troops needed a respite. Once again the Rappahannock acted as a buffer between the two adversaries.

By the middle of May, the horse artillery was encamped midway between Brandy Station and Culpeper Courthouse on the farm of John Minor Botts, a noted Unionist. Here the men and horses began to mend. The quiet hours presented Beckham with an opportunity to reflect on the several weeks of campaigning that the battalion had just passed through. There had been notable successes. Breathed's and McGregor's gallant courage and élan during the headlong charge of Jackson's infantry in the Wilderness were equal to anything the horse artillery had accomplished up to that time. This along with the valiant defense at Kelly's Ford and Rappahannock Bridge in mid-April showed the horse artillery at its best. Unfortunately, there were also some negatives: the near capture of Lieutenant Brown's gun at Raccoon Ford, coupled with the loss of eight of its crew; the disaster of May 1, which had brought heavy casualties; and Moorman's inability to participate in the fighting on the evening of May 2, a fact that highlighted the lack of long-range guns, which continued to plague the horse batteries. The futile pursuit of Stoneman's raiders by Hart's Battery and Shoemaker's section demonstrated once again the horse artillery's failure to keep pace with the cavalry during rapid marches. Taken in its entirety, the horse artillery's record for the Chancellorsville campaign laid bare both the strengths and the weaknesses of the battalion. Beckham would have to try to maintain the former and eliminate the latter. With the summer campaign season about to begin, it would not be an easy task.

CHAPTER 13

Preparation and Pageantry

"One of the most sublime scenes I ever witnessed"

Maj. Gen. J. E. B. Stuart did not subscribe to the adage that there could be too much of a good thing—at least, as far as his horse artillery was concerned. In the days following the battle of Chancellorsville, Stuart took steps to increase the size of his batteries from four to six guns. His efforts brought him into conflict with Lt. Col. Brisco G. Baldwin, the army's chief of ordnance. Stuart had not turned over to Baldwin the captured artillery (four three-inch rifles and a twelve-pound Napoleon) that had fallen into his hands during the recent campaign and which he intended to use in the horse artillery's expansion.[1] Baldwin held the responsibility of dispersing the captured pieces, and in a report to his commander, Robert E. Lee, he stated that the guns had not been "officially reported."[2] Lee wrote to Stuart. Ever the diplomat, he permitted Stuart to keep two three-inch rifled guns, ordering the remainder turned over to Baldwin. Lee also advised Stuart that increasing his batteries from four to six guns was not advisable and cited the necessity of reducing the artillery serving with the infantry because of the lack of horses. Stuart took the hint.

Beckham's part in this drama is unknown, though he probably was aware of it. However, his attention was focused on preparing his battalion for what was next. Horses were at the top of his list, but much of the equipment needed to be replaced or repaired as well. Somehow, from somewhere, Beckham succeeded in "recruiting" the number of horses he needed to put all of his batteries on an operational footing. His fighting skill and hard work did not go unnoticed. On May 21, Stuart wrote to General Cooper asking that Beckham be promoted to lieutenant colonel.[3] Though Lee endorsed the promotion, Secretary of War James Seddon did not. Like Pelham before him, Beckham would not command the horse artillery as a lieutenant colonel.

While officers of all ranks hustled and bustled about, the common soldiers took advantage of the pause in the hostilities. The men of the horse artillery seized the opportunity to "take much needed rest, to mend broken harness, and straighten out things that had been in a tangle a long while."[4] The refitting of

Hart's Battery was typical of what all the batteries went through. Hart had seen his men and equipment endure hard fighting, tedious picketing, and difficult marches. Two of the battery's brass rifled pieces were so worn that the projectiles would no longer follow the grooves. They were turned in and replaced by two imported steel Blakelys. The battery now consisted of four of these excellent guns. Fresh horses and mules were obtained, so that each gun and caisson was drawn by six horses and each wagon by four mules. The rest of the battery's equipment—four caissons, a tool wagon, two ambulances, three ordnance wagons, three forage wagons, and one baggage wagon—received careful attention to prepare them for the coming campaign. The men were issued what shoes and clothing could be supplied.[5] Harnesses and other leather equipment were checked, mended when possible, and replaced as supplies allowed. It was hard work, but there were distractions.

Officers and men used every spare moment "to become acquainted with some of Virginia's fair daughters, and to enjoy the pleasure of their sweet society."[6] The partaking of that pleasure was interrupted on May 22, when Stuart held a review of Hampton's, Fitz Lee's, and Rooney Lee's Brigades on Botts's farm. The horse batteries passed in review and contributed a brief cannonade to the festivities.[7] The glorious scene of thousands of horsemen maneuvering over a vast expanse of green sprinkled with the bright colors of spring flowers belied the fact that these same horsemen and cannoneers had just passed through a grueling campaign and would soon face another. Their closed ranks hid the gaps that had been caused by recent casualties. For some, the joy and exhilaration of the review were tempered by the loss of friends or relatives. A few still faced the sad duty of writing home to console those left behind. One such man was Pvt. William A. Simpson, whose brother-in-law, William P. Walters, had fallen on May 1.

> Camp Near Culpeper CH May the 24, 1863
>
> Dear father & mother & sisters one & all,
>
> It is with pleasure that I seat myself to write to you and to answer your letter of the 18th but with a heavy heart. You may know I wasn't disappointed last night when I received the letter to hear of the distress you were all under. I was well aware of that before I wrote but you must bear up under these losses of friends and relations for it can't be helped, for if it is God's pleasure to remove us from this world to another, He giveth and taketh to his pleasure, and we ought to content ourselves as much so as possible. The affects of this war have broken the heart of many a one.
>
> I am glad to inform you that I am well and hearty as common. I was very sorry to hear that mother and all were sick, but I hope these few lines may find you all well and more over your trouble. I haven't got any news to write. Everything seems to be in peace here. But I

hear some very heavy fights in other places. From all accounts the enemy is closing in on us at every hand or least ways trying to do so. Your letter said that mother wanted me to come home. If there is any chance I will come the first chance. Of course I will, but after 14 months fighting I hate to run away and be hunted like a deserter, but the most of the men are getting very much out of heart, not only in our company but many others. From the account of the price of grain one can't buy more than 2 bushels of corn for one month's pay now, and he won't get but one by harvest. How is a poor man's family to do when he is oblige to buy something here or go with an empty stomach himself. How it is going to be I can't tell, but I want you all to keep all the grain you can for fear of a drought, for I believe it is coming. For my part I know the feelings of one when they have to do without anything to eat for love nor money [word illegible] get it for it isn't to be had. I would advise you all to keep a sharp lookout for fear that you have to under go that trouble too. For my part I [word illegible] a week or a few grains of corn or something of the sort.

As I have no more to write I will close saying to take care of yourselves the best you can & I will try to do so too. Write soon for [word illegible] the pleasure I see. I still remain your true and affectionate son & brother till death

Wm A Simpson to James Simpson & family[8]

Dear Sister,

A few lines to you. Your sorrow and trouble I don't dispute, for I have to feel it myself. You may know I asked him [Walters] what to write to you to do. He said you had better go back to father again. The subject seemed to give him a great deal of pain. He expressed his wish to see you and the children but didn't say that he wanted to be carried home, for he knew that would be out of power at that time. When asked about his future, he frankly said in lively air he wasn't afraid to die. He only seemed troubled at the distress it would give you. I couldn't get a coffin for him, for it was out of my power, not knowing how long we could be permitted to stay there, for the battle was raging as hard as I ever heard not more than a mile off. So you may know that it was uncertain they might drive us back. The captain said to hurry and bury him, for we might have to leave, and I did so for fear that I might have to leave him to lay on the field as thousands of our poor fellows have to which would have hurt me very much. I buried him in the clothes he was killed in, as it is custom, winding him in a blanket. I would have been glad to have his new uniform to put on him which he never had worn, but it was in the ambulance in his valise, and it wasn't with us.

I was greatly relieved when I got him put away as well as I did. I would have been glad to send his things home, but it was out of my power, so I sold the pants to the captain, jacket to lieutenant, shirts & socks I have yet. He had 29 dollars in money. The officers owed him 80 dollars. They will pay for the clothes what he was charged for them. That was 20 dollars. I believe that will be 109 dollars which I will collect & send to you or fetch it soon as I can.

You asked for advice. I haven't a very good hand to give it so far away, but I think it best for you to move back to father's soon as you can make it convenient. It wouldn't be advisable to sell your stock for such money as we have now without you could turn it into something that would be of some use to you when the war is over. Maybe Uncle Mort could keep it. I don't think this war can last more than 4 or 5 more years, though I see nothing to make peace. Only them that gets killed. They are in peace I hope. I close, confident of the trouble and sorrow you have to undergo.

Wm. A. Simpson / Matilda E. Walters[9]

With his sister and family on his mind, yet sure that the war would go on, Simpson—and thousands like him—did what he could to prepare for this life and the next. With his remaining friends and comrades, he went to work mending, sewing, and polishing his equipment. One review was behind him, but plans were being laid for an even bigger one.

The day following the review of the twenty-second, Stuart received a request from Robert E. Lee for a detailed report on the cavalry, including number of regiments, their strength, officers, condition, and brigade affiliation. Brig. Gen. Beverly H. Robertson's Brigade of two regiments had joined Stuart on May 25. That happened to be the date of his report, which included Robertson's command. The concentration of so much cavalry in one place started the rumor mills churning. In a letter to his sister written near the end of the month, Lt. William Hoxton expounded on the current theories then making the rounds of the camps:

Hd. Qrs. S. H. Arty.

Dear Sallie:

I have made two or three unavailing attempts lately to hear from you by writing myself, and I can't imagine why you don't write—please do so, as soon as this reaches you. Do you recollect to whom in Richmond Mr. Randolph sent the twenty dollars which Llew left with you when he was in Fredericksburg—he told me he had sent the money out of Fredericksburg for safe-keeping. I should like to get hold of the $20 just at this time especially, and if I can find out where it is I will write for it immediately.

Our whole command is lying quiet in the vicinity of Culpeper Co. House, organizing and recruiting our horses. From everything I can gather, I am confident, however, that it will not be long before Genl. Stuart starts on a flying trip to Pennsylvania—possibly New York. We have now here three full brigades of cavalry, two very full regiments of Robertson's brigade, mounting each about eight hundred and fifty men, and a battalion of horse artillery of about sixteen pieces. Genl. Jones' brigade is also daily expected, which will give Stuart a cavalry command of about ten thousand, quite enough I know to not only put a stop to Mr. Stoneman's raids in future, but also to use him up completely should he meet Stuart face to face.

Give my best love dear Sallie to Mr. Randolph and your dear little children, and please forgive the brevity, and stupidity of my letter, and its abrupt termination—Write to me.

Your devoted brother
William Hoxton

Address Care of Genl. Stuart
Army of N. Va.[10]

Brig. Gen. William E. "Grumble" Jones was indeed bringing his entire command, including Chew's Battery, over the mountain to join Stuart. They would swell the cavalry division to almost 10,000 men and bring the horse artillery battalion up to five batteries of twenty-one guns. Well might Hoxton expect that something big was about to happen.

Jones's and Brig. Gen. John Imboden's brigades had been recuperating from their raid into West Virginia. Chew's Battery had not been able to accompany Jones on the entire raid, and for most of May the men of the battery had little to do. The boredom evidently got to Chew and Lt. Jim Thomson. On May 15, the two would-be cavalrymen joined with Lt. Gowan B. Philpot and forty-five men of the 7th Virginia Cavalry on a raid. Their target was Charles Town, where they attacked a company of Federal cavalry and captured over fifty prisoners and a large number of horses. Chew's and Thomson's taste of partisan life was bittersweet. Their initial success was followed by a rapid change of fortune that almost led to their being captured. On the afternoon of the sixteenth, while riding through a hamlet named Piedmont Station[11] in Fauquier County, Federal cavalry surprised Chew and his party. After a hard fight, the "raiders" lost their prisoners, but they managed to gallop away.[12]

The excitement of Chew's and Thomson's raid and escape had little effect on the cannoneers of the battery. Neither Neese nor McVicar gave it notice in his diary. What both did record was the news of the movement to join Stuart. The order to limber and pack came on June 1, and by the fourth, the battery was trotting through the streets of Culpeper Court House. If Chew and his company were unaware of what was to take place the following day, they were soon apprised of it. On the other hand, Lt. Francis H. Wigfall knew all about it and the other festivities that were going on throughout the cavalry division. He shared the news in a letter to his sister:

June 4, 1863

Dear Lou,

[Half of first page illegible] I found Mama and Papa both very well and in excellent quarters. I spent the night there and returned to camp. The next afternoon I rode "Gray Eagle" the horse which I bought at Orange and who by the way looks as little like an Eagle, Gazelle, or any other mare as you can imagine. I gave him the name merely as a "josh." He is [word illegible] however and will do until my ship comes in from India and arrives at a Confederate port when I intend to indulge in thoroughbreds exclusively.

There was a very pleasant picnic near Genl. Fitz Lee's Hd. Qr. on Friday gotten up by his staff at which all the young ladies from the neighborhood <u>including</u> <u>myself</u> were present. Music and refreshments were on hand and all went off very merrily. There was a Division review on Friday week and another takes place tomorrow. Reviews are very nice things for lookers on but far from pleasant for those concerned especially if the weather be hot and dusty. I wish you could be here to see it. I tried to persuade Mama to come up but she seemed to think that the pleasure would not defray the discomfort. I expect Papa up however.

I like this service a thousand times better than that in which I have been heretofore. One is not encompassed on every side by thousands of dirty infantry and the life is much more active and exciting. The service is much harder, but it has pleasures which more than compensate for the personal discomforts.

Rosser and his bride are expected on this afternoon's train, and I am going in to the C. H. to be there when the train arrives. Several young ladies also are coming up to witness the review tomorrow and I suppose the whole country round will turn out to see it. There is to be a dance in town tonight and I shall probably go to it. I expect Mama will send for you and Fanny before the end of the session as she told me she wanted you to be here in time, for the fruit and strawberries are beginning to come in now. If she remains at [name illegible] you will be delightfully situated. The situation is elevated, cool and shady and the fare, a consideration now a days, is delicious, that is, so it seems to me, though I am not perhaps a competent witness belonging as I do to the "Stuart Horse."

We have been inactive now for nearly the month, and I don't think it will continue much longer. We have now five brigades of cavalry and five batteries of Horse Artillery and I expect on review tomorrow there will be nearly ten thousand men. It will be a grand display and I wish you could be here to see it. Present my regards to Miss Anne Campbell and remember me to Miss May Deas when you write. Kiss little Fanny and tell her my next letter will be to her. You must write frequently and when you fail to hear from me lay the blame upon the mails. But in earnest the reason to my not having written of late has been that I have seen Papa and he saw you and since I have seen him and Mama and in this way I have not felt that you would miss my letters so much. Good bye dear Lou and believe me as ever

Your affectionate Brother
Halsey[13]

Wigfall may have complained somewhat about the worrisome preparations for the reviews, but that didn't stop him from glorying in the spectacle that would be created. And what a spectacle it was.

The grand and glorious review of June 5, 1863, was one that no participant or viewer ever forgot. Thousands of knights of the Southland, mounted on noble steeds whose coats glistened in the sun, galloped over the plain. The thundering of more than 30,000 hooves was accompanied by the deeper full-throated roar of the guns of the Stuart Horse Artillery Battalion, firing blank charges. The events of the day found their way into diaries and letters, along with the usual camp gossip and expectations of the coming campaign. Lt. James H. Williams of Chew's Battery had much to say to his beloved Cora:

Brandy Station
June 6th 1863

My Dear Cora,

Yesterday witnessed a grand review of Genl Stuart's Division, some 10,000 cav & 20 pieces of artillery. A grand display to gratify the vanity of one man. Had intended to comment at length on the day's transactions. Of course, many ladies were present to whom Genl S. was familiarly polite. Such days do not present him in his best light. How the times change the propriety of conduct as we passed the immense concourse of ladies that thronged around the position of the Genl. Although it was my duty to look to the front, I turned an inquiring eye [word illegible] hoping I might see a <u>Richmond</u> <u>Friend</u> shall I call her. All passed off without an accident.

Orders have just come to cook 3 days rations and strike tents, etc., etc. We reached here Thursday. Came the same road I traveled when I visited you at Hanover C. H., but the contrast of reflection struck me. This time I came reluctantly, came to take part in an active campaign. Will the result be as doubtful to say the least.

We have, much to our regret, been detached from our Brigade. Have lost our identity & been put in a Battalion commanded by Maj. Beckham. It will restrict our privileges. In future direct to Chew's Battery, care of Maj. Beckham comdg Battalion Artillery Stuart's Div. . . .

Fondly Yours
James H. Williams[14]

Lt. Charles R. Phelps of Moorman's Battery wrote to his aunt the day following the review. He was much more concerned with what was going to happen than with what he had just experienced.

Culpeper Co. Ho. June 6th 1863

Dear Aunt

I arrived at camp yesterday morning from the Rappahannock, having been on Picket since Sunday last. The Yanks are as thick as blackberries at Ely's Ford, on opposite side of river.[15] I have been in speaking distance of them day & night, but not allowed to say anything to them. They are digging rifle pits and fortifying themselves all along the river, as if to prevent our advance, but we will disappoint them as I think we will move higher up the river.

Yesterday was a grand day here. Gen'l Stuart reviewed all of his cavalry & artillery, about 15,000 cavalry & 5 Batteries Horse Artillery. It made quite a formidable display and will strike terror to Stoneman & Co.

The camp has been full of rumors of our intended movement, but I cannot give you any information. While writing we have orders to cook three days rations to move at a moments notice. We will move immediately but to what point I cannot say. My impression is that it will be a forward movement all along the line. Our Infantry seems to be moving in this direction. Hood's Division is already here and I hear of others coming. Everything is now confusion in camp, packing up & cooking rations. Will let you hear from me as soon as possible.

Remember me to Miss Wiatt, Uncle C., and all the rest

Very truly Yours
C. R. Phelps[16]

Phelps's and Shoemaker's sections had been picketing Ellis' Ford on alternate days since May 29. They returned to their camp near Brandy Station on June 1.[17] Having to come in from picket duty and within days prepare for another review probably did not sit very well with the officers and even less with the enlisted men. Charles McVicar of Chew's Battery had marched even farther than Moorman's gunners but seemed to get caught up in the thrill of the moment. He recorded his observations in his diary:

> [June] 5th—Here we are at Brandy Station in Culpeper County on review. The sound of the drums seems natural. General Stuart's Command of Cavalry is on the right and General Hood's Division of Infantry is on the left. There is a battalion of artillery here and as far as the eye can reach the cavalry are strung along in columns and a solid body. It is a magnificent sight to be on the height that we occupy and see the rapid movements of such large bodies below. There are several hundred ladies present to see us. A great many of them are riding in carriages or on horseback, loping or cantering their horses around us in every direction. The staff officers are their knights. It is one of the most sublime scenes I ever witnessed. General Stuart and his bodyguard are riding over the ground reviewing us. There are several fine brass bands from Richmond playing at intervals from one end of the line to the other. The fair sex are to be seen on every side. The weather is clear and very pleasant. Tis 4 o'clock, we are now fighting a Sham Battle. The cavalry is charging across the field; the artillery is opening. The scene is beautiful beyond description. My colt caught the bit in his teeth and ran up against the cannon or gun while the firing was going on. We commenced firing blank cartridges; fired eleven rounds while the cavalry were charging. The scene is magnificent. Our battery was ordered to join Major Beckham's Battalion of Light Horse Artillery. We are now christened Stuart's Light Horse Artillery.[18]

McVicar's fellow gunner, George M. Neese, wrote a much more detailed description of the grand review:

> June 5—General J. E. B. Stuart had a grand review today of all the cavalry and horse artillery belonging to his corps. Early this morning we started to the field where the troops were to be reviewed by passing by the eagle eye of their great commander. The place where the review was held is a beautiful and nearly level plain about four miles northeast of Culpeper Court House and a little over a mile southwest of Brandy Station, and on the west side of the Orange and Alexandria Railroad.
>
> When we arrived on the field some of the cavalry regiments were already forming in dress parade order, for the review procession. At about 10 o'clock the whole column, which was about two miles long,

was ready and in splendid trim to pass in review before its illustrious and gallant chief and his brilliant staff.

As soon as the whole line was formed General Stuart and his staff dashed on the field. He was superbly mounted. The trappings on his proud, prancing horse all looked bright and new, and his side-arms gleamed in the morning sun like burnished silver. A long black ostrich feather plume waved gracefully from a black slouch hat cocked up on one side, and was held with a golden clasp which also stayed the plume. Before the procession started General Stuart and staff rode along the front of the line from one end to the other. He is the prettiest and most graceful rider I ever saw. When he dashed past us I could not help but notice with what natural ease and comely elegance he sat his steed as it bounded over the field, and his every motion in the saddle was in such strict accord with the movements of his horse that he and his horse appeared to be but one and the same machine. Immediately after General Stuart and staff had passed along the front of the whole line he galloped to a little knoll in the southeast edge of the field near the railroad, wheeled his horse to a front face to the field, and sat there like a gallant knight effant, under his waving plume, presenting in veritable truth every characteristic of a chivalric cavalier of the first order. He was then ready for the review, and the whole cavalcade began to move and pass in review before the steady, martial, and scrutinizing gaze of the great cavalry chieftain of America.

I do not pretend to know or guess at the number of men in line, but there were thousands, and it was by far the largest body of cavalry that I ever saw on one field.

Sixteen pieces of horse artillery marched at the head of the column,[19] three bands of music were playing nearly all the time while the procession was moving, a flag was fluttering in the breeze from every regiment, and the whole army was one grand and magnificent pageant, inspiring enough to make even an old woman feel fightish.

After the whole cavalcade passed the review station, at a quick walk, the column divided up into divisions, brigades, and regiments, which maneuvered all over the field. The last and most inspiring and impressive act in the scene was a sham battle, the cavalry charging several times with drawn sabers and the horse artillery firing from four or five different positions on the field. I fired ten rounds from my gun.

Hundreds of ladies from Culpeper Court House and surrounding country stood in bunches on the hills and knolls around the field, looking at the grand military display.

A special train from Richmond stood on the track just in rear of the review stand, crowded with people, and judging from the fluttering ribbons at the car windows the most of the occupants were ladies. General Hood's division of infantry was drawn up on the north side of the field, viewing the cavalry display, and also for a support in case the Yanks would have attempted to take a hand in the show. There is a heavy force of Yankees camped on the north bank of the Rappahannock only about five miles from the review field.

By about 4 o'clock this evening the whole affair was over and the troops withdrew from the field and repaired to their respective camps. We were assigned today to Beckham's battalion of horse artillery, and we camped with it this evening. This is the first time that we have been assigned to a battalion of artillery. Heretofore our battery always operated and camped independent of any other artillery. Camped one mile south of Brandy Station.[20]

As Neese observed, there were many ladies and dignitaries present for the review. Stuart had issued a special invitation to Robert E. Lee to come and see the strength of the cavalry division. But Lee was too busy to attend—a fact that bode ill for the men of the cavalry and the horse artillery.

On the day following the review, the horse artillery battalion moved its camp to within a mile of Beverly Ford. The camp lay along the south edge of a wood on the west side of the Beverly Ford Road. All that stood between the battalion and the Yanks on the other side of the Rappahannock was a small cavalry picket. Everything remained quiet until 2:00 A.M. on June 7, when the shrill notes of a bugle called the men of the battalion from their blankets and sent them scurrying to their guns.[21] Though the enemy was expected at any moment, nothing happened. The alarm had been false. In two days it wouldn't be.

On June 8, the cavalry and horse artillery were called upon to pass in review for the third time in seventeen days. This time it was for "Marse Robert." Having missed the review of the fifth, Lee wanted to see his mounted arm before the beginning of the summer campaign. Stuart, of course, could not disobey his commander-in-chief and ordered his troopers to put on another show. However, this time it was without all the trimmings. The horse artillery quietly passed before Lee and the other officers. The entire affair came off without a hitch, except for George M. Neese and his mule.

I was trying to act in the capacity of first sergeant of our battery in the review today, and was riding at the head of the horse artillery, mounted on a mule with ears about a foot long. Just before we arrived at the reviewing stand the searching eye of General Stuart spied the waving ears of my mule, and he quickly dispatched one of his aides to Captain Chew, with the urgent request to order the mule and me with it off of the field, which was quickly done. I cared very little

> about the matter, but the mule looked a little bit surprised, and, I think, felt ashamed of himself and his waving ears, which cost him his prominent position in the grand cavalcade.
>
> No doubt General Stuart is proud of his splendid cavalry, and well he may be, for it certainly is a fine body of well mounted and tried horsemen, whose trusty blades have ofttimes flashed in the red glow of battle's fiery tide and stemmed the deadly wave of war. But my mule, too, has heard the raging battle roar and the dreadful musketry roll and seen the screaming shell tear the sod to smithers around his feet. True, a mule was not built for the purpose of ornamenting a grand review or embellishing an imposing pageant, but as mine so willingly bears the hardships and dangers of the camp and field I thought it not indiscreet to let it play a little act in some of the holiday scenes of war.[22]

Though Neese waxed tongue-in-cheek about the role of his mule, he took a more serious tone in expressing his opinion that the horse artillery had been "permitted to roost a little too near the lion's lair."[23] Indeed, the lion was about to venture from its lair with fangs bared.

CHAPTER 14

The Battle of Brandy Station

"Plenty of bullets, bloody sabers, and screaming shell"

The Federal cavalry had been considerate enough to allow Stuart and company to conduct their gala parades and dances without interruption. The lack of any kind of Federal advance permitted Lee to take the initiative from Hooker. As a result, except for the false alarm on the night of the seventh, nothing, not even Stuart's reviews, had disturbed the preparations. Despite the tumult raised by the sham battle of the fifth, the Yankee high command had little information on what was transpiring south of the Rappahannock. Though there were those who chastised Stuart for giving the enemy three opportunities to "count his sabers," the truth was that neither Hooker nor his cavalry chieftain, Brig. Gen. Alfred Pleasonton, had a clue about the location of Stuart or Lee's main forces. Hooker needed information. He believed Stuart to be near Culpeper Court House, preparing for another of his bothersome raids, and decided to kill two birds with one advance. He would send Pleasonton to destroy Stuart's cavalry and discover the disposition of Lee's army. By dark on June 8, Pleasonton had 12,000 cavalry and infantry poised to cross the Rappahannock at first light.

That same evening, the men of Beckham's battalion were bedding down in their camp about a mile from Beverly Ford on the road to Brandy Station.[1] Four of the five batteries were present—McGregor's, Moorman's, Chew's, and Hart's. The fifth, Breathed's, was split. Lt. Philip P. Johnston's section was encamped with Rooney Lee's Brigade near the Welford House, while Breathed and the remaining section camped with Fitz Lee's Brigade north of the Hazel River near Oak Shade Church. A picket from the 6th Virginia Cavalry that guarded the ford protected Beckham's camp. A mile farther toward Brandy, in the vicinity of St. James Church, lay the brigade of "Grumble" Jones. Should the pickets be overrun, the horse artillery would be on its own until Jones could reach it. If such thoughts entered anyone's head, they were dismissed as folly or were pushed aside by others that focused on the army's upcoming movement. Everyone was offensive minded. That the Yanks would take the initiative was not seriously considered.

On Fleetwood Hill, Stuart's camp had been reduced to a couple of tent flies, but in the artillery's camp, some of the officers and cannoneers made themselves comfortable inside their tents.[2] Others slept rolled in their blankets on the ground with the sky for a roof. They may have dreamed about reviews, home, the girl they left behind, or a mule with foot-long ears, but undoubtedly they did not dream about a knock-down-drag-out, all-day battle with the Yankee cavalry. Thus far, such a thing was beyond the experience of most of Stuart's cavalry. The sentinels kept watch, listened to the night sounds, and longed for the opportunity to get some much-needed sleep. It had been a long day. June 9 would be longer.

The first intimation that something was amiss came at dawn in the form of leaden missiles zipping above the slumbering cannoneers.[3] The distinctive sound soon aroused the camp.[4] Some members of Hart's Battery remembered being awakened by their sentinels, but whether by missiles or sentries, the men sprang into action.[5] Pvt. Louis Sherfesee of Hart's Battery slipped on his left boot and reached for his spectacles. Blurs in the distance became a line of Yankee skirmishers—a sight that took him completely by surprise.

> I did not wait to put on my right boot but caught it in one hand and the Guidon in the other and ran to the guns, leaving my horse, who was tied to a tree not ten feet from the tent, not having time to unhitch him. When I got to the Battery, Captain Hart with three or four men were loading one of the pieces and immediately commenced firing upon the enemy, which kept advancing.[6]

Hart's Battery had been camped closest to the road, and at first alarm, Beckham realized he needed to gain time. The cavalry pickets were already killed, captured, or headed rearward. Beckham shouted for Hart to wheel a gun into the road by hand and give covering fire, while the rest of the artillerymen scrambled to hitch up the guns, limbers, and caissons.[7] Looking toward Jones's camp, Beckham could see the high ground around St. James Church. He sent Lt. Edwin L. Halsey from Hart's Battery back to organize the new line and then turned to the business of saving his command.[8]

An escape was made, but only by the narrowest of margins and only due to the stubborn tenacity of Hart's two guns and the timely arrival of Jones.[9] The Yanks already were among the tents on Hart's left and emerging from the thickets on his right. Horses were going down. Knives flashed in the morning sun as the men cut traces. At that moment, Jones came charging by, leading the 6th and 7th Virginia Cavalry. He reined up and shouted at Hart, "All right, Captain, we will take care of them, we'll give them H——."[10] The Yanks were thrown back momentarily, gaining the artillery a few precious minutes. As blue and gray cavalrymen fought with pistol and saber, the last of the guns was hitched. Beckham headed them toward St. James Church. The ride, made at the gallop, bore little resemblance to the orderly parade of men and guns witnessed during the review the previous day. Left behind were many personal items, along with Captain Chew's tent, letters and papers, and Beckham's field desk, which contained valuable documents.[11]

Last to reach the new line were Hart and his gallant gunners. They had retreated without cavalry support. Jones had been driven back. Hart and his two remaining guns were hard-pressed by the enemy. Up to the challenge, the gallant South Carolinian pulled back one piece at a time at intervals of seventy-five yards.[12] Each gun provided covering fire for the other.[13] It had been as close as Hart had ever come to losing a piece. The bluecoats swirled toward each of his guns every time one was in firing position, only to be hurled back by a blast of canister. Cannons and cannoneers at last swung into line with the rest of the battalion. If there had been any question whether Hart belonged in the Stuart Horse Artillery Battalion, it was answered during those first harrowing minutes of battle that June morning.

Beckham was in an excellent position to command the road from the ford. His four batteries stretched from St. James Church, where Chew had his guns, eastward. Next to Chew was McGregor, then Moorman. Hart held the extreme right of the Confederate artillery line in the vicinity of the Gee house. The cavalry fight in the open ground between the artillery and the wood line sent the Federal horse back into the woods. Beckham's guns opened a hot fire, shelling the woods and Col. Thomas C. Devin's and Col. Benjamin F. "Grimes" Davis's Brigades. Maj. William S. McClure, Davis already having fallen, commanded the latter. The Reserve Brigade under Maj. Charles J. Whiting also came under this fire. Maj. Henry C. Whelan of the 6th Pennsylvania Cavalry, Rush's Lancers, stated that his regiment was bombarded heavily from the left by the enemy.[14]

Even as Jones and Beckham formed their line, Confederate reinforcements hurried to support them. Rooney Lee led his troopers from their camp around the Welford house to Yew Ridge on the left of Jones's position, while Wade Hampton came into line on Beckham's right at the Gee house. The Rebel line now resembled an obtuse angle, with Beckham's Battalion at its apex. This new line did not have to wait long to be put to the test. Brig. Gen. John Buford had adjusted his forces to better contend with the Confederates. He ordered Devin's Brigade, along with elements of Davis's, to his left to face Hampton, placed Brig. Gen. Adelbert Ames's infantry on both sides of the Beverly Ford Road in the center of his line, and brought up the Reserve Brigade on his right. Before long, Buford realized that Hampton and the Confederate horse artillery were severely testing the left of his line. To relieve the pressure, he ordered the Reserve Brigade to attack.

Major Whelan recorded that his regiment charged a whole brigade of Confederate cavalry with drawn sabers. They were met by musket fire in front and artillery fire on their left.[15] The 6th U.S. Cavalry accompanied Whelan's

6th Pennsylvania. The Regulars galloped through the leaden hail and struck Lt. Frank Bamberg's section of Hart's Battery.[16] Cannoneers sought cover while sabers flashed above them. The men jumped between the wheels of the gun carriages, while the horse holders and drivers sought safety between their horses.[17] The impetus of the charge carried the 6th U.S. through the guns. Once the Federals were past, Bamberg or Hart shouted, "Change front to rear on right pieces."[18] The gunners sprang from their places of refuge, turned their pieces, and opened fire on their tormentors. There was little time to admire the courage of the blue cavalry or the calm efficiency of the cannoneers. The battle raged while the Federals galloped back to their lines and then slackened. The action began to edge toward the Federal right.

Rooney Lee's Brigade, which held the left of the Confederate line, soon found itself being pressed by Buford, who was once again shifting his regiments in order to strike a heavier blow. Lee had placed Lt. Philip P. Johnston's section of Breathed's Battery on Yew Ridge near Dr. Daniel Green's house, with the 9th Virginia in support. Opposite Johnston was Capt. James M. Robertson with Lt. Albert O. Vincent's section of Battery B/L of the 2nd U.S. Artillery[19] and Lt. Thomas Williams, Jr.'s, section of Battery E, 4th U.S. Artillery. Robertson's initial target had been Lee's Brigade as it came into position, but soon Johnston found the range and began dropping shells among Robertson's guns.[20] The Confederate barrage proved accurate and effective. One man in Vincent's section was wounded, and several horses went down.[21] Robertson's own mount was killed under him.[22] Realizing that he could not respond effectively from his present position, Robertson ordered Williams's section behind the brow of the hill and moved Vincent's guns to the right, placing one gun on the bank of the Hazel River. During Vincent's move, Johnston showered the Federal cavalry with everything he had in his limber chests.[23] The Confederate artillery and Lee's skirmishers inflicted heavy casualties on the blue-coated horsemen.

Once Vincent was in place, Robertson ordered him to open fire. The Federal cannonade seemed to take effect, or so Robertson thought. He quickly rode back to Williams and directed him to open a slow cannonade, which appeared to slow the rate of Johnston's fire. At this time, Capt. William M. Graham arrived on the scene with Lt. William M. Maynadier's section of Battery K, 1st U.S. Artillery. Robertson sent Graham and Maynadier to relieve Vincent's section, which rejoined Williams.[24] Six pieces were now shelling Johnston. Privates Thomas D. Loudenslager, Henry F. Wegner, and William Young fell wounded. Robertson had the satisfaction of seeing Confederate artillery and the gray cavalry fall back. The Federal artillery, along with the cavalry and infantry, certainly had put pressure on Rooney Lee to withdraw, but there was another, greater reason for the Confederate retreat.

Buford's had not been the only column to ford the Rappahannock that June morning. Downstream at Kelly's Ford, Brig. Gen. David McM. Gregg had led his command, consisting of two cavalry divisions, his own and Col. Alfred N. Duffié's, and Brig. Gen. David A. Russell's Infantry Brigade, across the river. Once across, Gregg ordered Russell to push up the Kellysville Road to Brandy Station. The cavalry rode west about five miles, where Gregg again split his force, sending Duffié's division toward the station via Stevensburg while Gregg took the more direct road. If all went well, this three-pronged advance would reunite at Brandy Station and somewhat disrupt Stuart's dispositions in the process.

Stuart had taken precautions to guard his right flank. Brig. Gen. Beverly H. Robertson had been ordered down the Kellysville Road to guard the ford. Additionally, Beckham sent a section of Chew's Battery to support the cavalry. But Robertson never made it to the ford. His column ran into Capt. William White of the 5th North Carolina and his pickets, falling back from the river. Dismounting a portion of his command to resist the oncoming Federal infantry, Robertson dispatched scouting parties to his right to discover whether his flank was in danger of being turned. He quickly realized that it was not just his own flank, but Stuart's entire position that was being threatened. Confronted by an infantry force of unknown size, Robertson felt that his two regiments, large as they were, could not engage both the infantry in his front and the cavalry to his right. He sent word to Stuart of what was heading his way and then settled down to skirmish with Russell's regiments. The section of Chew's Battery that was sent to the Kellysville Road never reached Robertson. It was recalled before it had a chance to fire a single shot.[25]

Measures to defend the road from Stevensburg to Brandy Station also had been taken. Col. Matthew C. Butler's 2nd South Carolina and Col. Williams C. Wickham's 4th Virginia, along with one gun from Moorman's Battery, had been ordered to proceed to Stevensburg and oppose the enemy force encountered there.[26] Butler arrived first and was grappling with elements of the 6th Ohio, 1st Massachusetts, and the 1st Rhode Island Cavalry when Wickham rode onto the field. Moorman's lone piece was placed on a hill north of Stevensburg and opened fire. The first two shots fell near Maj. Thomas J. Lipscomb of the 2nd South Carolina, who was falling back to Mountain Run with his skirmishers. Lipscomb felt that the two errant rounds actually saved him and his men. He believed that the enemy thought his small force was one of its own columns and held its fire, permitting him to fall back across the creek.[27]

Soon Moorman's gun began a lively duel with a section of Battery M, 2nd U.S. Artillery, under Lt. Alexander C. M. Pennington.[28] While the Confederates concentrated their fire on Pennington's guns, the Yanks selected other targets besides Moorman's solitary piece. One of Pennington's rounds felled both Butler and Capt. William D. Farley of Stuart's staff. Farley would die of his wound, and Butler would lose a foot. This telling shot, coupled with the death of Butler's second-in-command, Lt. Col. Frank Hampton, and the rout of the 4th Virginia, virtually opened the road to Brandy Station. Fortunately for the

Confederates, General Gregg chose that moment to recall Duffié. Gregg's column had met no resistance. Brandy Station appeared to be free for the taking.

Maj. Henry B. McClellan, Stuart's adjutant, had been left at Stuart's headquarters on Fleetwood Hill, which dominated both the station and the surrounding terrain. McClellan was to assist with communications between the far-flung units. Except for the major and his couriers, Fleetwood Hill was deserted. By McClellan's own reckoning, two hours after Stuart had ridden off to St. James Church, a scout from General Robertson arrived and reported Gregg's advance from Kelly's Ford. The major was incredulous and sent the man back to confirm his report. Five minutes later, McClellan saw for himself that Stuart's right had been turned.[29] Immediately, a courier, the first of several, was dispatched to Stuart to alert him to the situation in his rear. Then McClellan turned to the problem of holding Fleetwood until Stuart arrived with reinforcements.

Gregg's column, with a section of Capt. Joseph W. Martin's 6th New York Battery under Lt. Moses P. Clark in the van, approached to within cannon shot of Fleetwood Hill before McClellan could offer any resistance. A howitzer from Chew's Battery, under the command of Lt. John W. "Tuck" Carter, was all McClellan had to oppose Gregg.[30] Carter had taken his gun to the rear to replenish its ammunition, having used all but a few defective shells and some round shot in the battle around St. James Church.[31] He could not have imagined that the rear was about to become the front. Carter responded quickly to McClellan's summons and wheeled his gun into position near the spot where Stuart's headquarters camp had been located that morning. The gun crew went through the loading drill as calmly as the situation permitted and fired a round at the great blue column that stretched out before them. Gregg pulled up sharply. Lt. Moses P. Clark, commanding the leading section of Martin's Battery, put his two guns into position 800 yards from Carter and opened fire.[32] The battle for Fleetwood Hill was on.

Back at St. James Church, Beckham's Battalion had continued to maintain pressure on the enemy, but not without loss. Three guns, one of Hart's and two of McGregor's, had been damaged and put out of action by recoil. In addition, one gun had been dispatched to Col. Matthew C. Butler, who was in the vicinity of Stevensburg; two more were sent down the Kellysville Road; and two had ended up near Fleetwood Hill. This left eight pieces holding the St. James Church line, and these were low on ammunition.[33] Beckham's guns had yet to be challenged by the enemy's artillery.[34]

The first intimation that there was trouble at Fleetwood came from a courier who rode up to Stuart as he was conversing with Captain Hart. The general could not bring himself to believe the man and dismissed him. Within minutes, Pvt. Frank H. Deane arrived with the same tale. Stuart knew and trusted Deane, who had served both as the general's courier and as McClellan's clerk.[35] Stuart cried out, "Where's my staff?" and sent Lt. Frank S. Robertson, the assistant engineer officer, galloping off to Jones and then Hampton.[36]

Cavalry both blue and gray raced for Fleetwood Hill. Col. Asher W. Harman's 12th Virginia of Jones's Brigade charged up one side of the hill toward the crest, while Lt. Col. Virgil Brodrick led his 1st New Jersey up the opposite side. Harman had not had an opportunity to deploy, as had Brodrick. From his position, Major McClellan, Stuart's stalwart adjutant, had seen the urgency of the situation and had galloped down the hill toward the oncoming 12th Virginia. He rode up to Harman, who was approaching at a trot, and gave the order to gallop. The regiment responded but was shattered as it crashed into the better-deployed Federals. Lt. Col. Elijah Viers White and his 35th Virginia suffered a similar fate after a gallant charge that carried them into Martin's 6th New York Battery. The 1st New Jersey, which had charged both Fleetwood and Barbour House Hill simultaneously, found itself temporarily in possession of Fleetwood's dominating heights.

Brodrick's victory was short-lived. In the wake of Harman and White came the 6th Virginia, under Maj. Cabell E. Flournoy, and a section of McGregor's Battery. The 1st New Jersey was no longer the compact fighting formation it had been when it crested the hill. Horses and men neared exhaustion. Its orderly ranks had been replaced by knots of men and horses trying to re-form or in pursuit of a fleeing foe. Losses had thinned the ranks. When Flournoy struck, Brodrick and his men realized escape was their only hope. Brodrick found himself fighting in the center of a band of Confederates determined to bring him down. His saber rose and fell, slashing at his tormentors. It was not enough. Having had two horses killed beneath him, pierced by pistol shot and slashed by sabers, he fell from his horse mortally wounded. Brodrick's second in command, Maj. John Shelmire, looked around for a way out, thought he saw one, and led those nearest him toward it. Into his path thundered the guns of McGregor and Hart.

A section of McGregor's Battery had accompanied Jones's Brigade in its mad dash between St. James Church and Fleetwood Hill. Careening up the slope, Lt. Charles E. Ford threw his guns into position to cover the hill. To his right, Hart began to unlimber his pieces. The South Carolinians had galloped alongside Hampton's Brigade as it raced toward the Federals south of Fleetwood.[37] Hart had paused and unlimbered his four guns 200 yards from the blue cavalry and opened fire.[38] He managed to get off three rounds of case shot from each piece before Hampton closed with the enemy. Unable to fire for fear of hitting his own cavalry, Hart limbered and raced up Fleetwood Hill, where he joined Ford.[39] Hart had only three guns now. The fourth piece had been disabled back at St. James, but a patchwork repair had been made there and the piece brought along on the dash to Fleetwood. The gun had managed the three rounds at the base of the hill before again breaking down.[40]

Ford's and Hart's choice of ground lay directly in the path of Major Shelmire and his troopers, who seem to come charging up out of the earth itself. Both Yankee and Rebel were somewhat shocked to behold each other only a pistol shot away. Shelmire's troopers charged on. Before the cannoneers had finished unlimbering, they found themselves fighting for their lives and their guns as the blue cavalry crashed into their flank. There was no time to load or turn the guns. It was every man for himself. Shelmire crumpled in his saddle, shot down as he rode among the guns by Pvt. LeGrand P. Guerry of Hart's Battery.[41] Lieutenant Ford and Lt. William Hoxton emptied their pistols into the swirl of bluecoats.[42] Sponge staffs dueled with sabers. Pvt. Edward Sully managed to knock one trooper from his horse and take him prisoner. Other gunners were not as successful. George W. Shreve found himself weaponless amid a windmill of sabers and a hail of lead. He shouted at one New Jersey trooper to surrender but, not to his surprise, was ignored. He wondered why the man didn't shoot him down as he dashed past.[43] Just as suddenly as they had come, the Federals were gone, leaving Ford's and Hart's men in confusion. Quickly they came to their senses, dispatched their prisoners down the hill behind them, and manned their guns. The possession of Fleetwood was still in doubt.

Beckham soon appeared, bringing with him the section of Chew's Battery that had been sent out on the Kellysville Road and Moorman's three guns from St. James Church.[44] As these unlimbered on the crest of the hill, Beckham had time to scan the battlefield before him. The plain below swarmed with Confederate and Union cavalry. Martin's 6th New York Battery lay off to the west, its guns standing ghostlike with only a few cannoneers to serve them. It had been severely handled by the 35th Virginia, but the battery's remnants steadfastly waited for one side or the other to seal their fate.[45] At last Col. Lunsford Lomax's 11th Virginia Cavalry swept over Martin's skeleton crew and captured the guns. Martin saw to it that the guns were disabled before leading what remained of his men to safety.[46]

Though Lomax's charge ended Gregg's attempts to take Fleetwood Hill, John Buford was not yet ready to concede the battle. Rooney Lee had fallen back at about 2:00 and taken position on Fleetwood Hill. His brigade, with the help of the 7th Virginia from Jones's Brigade and Lt. Philip P. Johnston's section of Breathed's Battery, had kept Buford from advancing to Brandy Station by threatening his rear. But the tenacious Buford was not willing to cut and run without taking another stab at the Confederates. He had heard the fighting around Fleetwood and was determined to help Gregg and just maybe tip the scales in the Federals' favor.[47] Buford shifted his regiments around Lee's left and launched an assault on the northern end of the hill.

The Confederate line extended along Fleetwood Hill, with Col. Thomas Marshall's 7th Virginia holding the right flank overlooking the Thompson house. To the left of that regiment was Col. Solomon Williams's 2nd North Carolina, followed by Col. Lucius Davis's 10th Virginia, Col. Richard L. T. Beale's 9th Virginia, and Col. John R. Chambliss's 13th Virginia, which anchored Lee's left flank at the hill's northern terminus. Breathed, with Wigfall's section of the battery, had joined Johnston's section around the time that Lee was withdrawing to Fleetwood. As the Confederates fell back toward the hill, Breathed's guns accompanied them, firing as they retired. When Buford launched his regiments at Lee, Breathed engaged the enemy artillery with the section of his battery that had moved into position in front of the Thompson house facing the woods.[48]

Buford ordered the 2nd U.S. Regulars and the 6th Pennsylvania to charge. They were met by the 9th Virginia, which soon found itself outflanked and in some trouble. Help arrived in the form of the 2nd North Carolina and 10th Virginia. Their counterattack brought the Federals to a standstill. Rooney Lee then committed the 7th and 13th Virginia and flung himself into the melee. The fight was a costly one for the Confederates. Col. Solomon Williams received a mortal wound, and Rooney Lee suffered a severe leg wound. This last mounted clash of the day drew to a close when the Federals retreated. Buford had received orders from Pleasonton to withdraw, and the remainder of the fighting in his sector centered on his covering his command until it was safely across the Rappahannock.

During the Federal retreat, the Confederate horse artillery continued to fire on the enemy. On the left, Breathed earned praise for his battery's performance during the enemy's withdrawal by running up three guns by hand and helping dislodge a Federal brigade and a battery. The Whitworth under Wigfall accompanied two squadrons of the 2nd Virginia in an effort to cut off the enemy's retreat by Welford's Ford.[49] Those guns with Beckham, however, were not used as effectively. Wade Hampton was critical of the batteries on Fleetwood. He tried to pursue the retreating enemy along the railroad tracks in the direction of the river but found himself under fire from his own artillery. He was forced to halt his column until he could send word back to Beckham. Hampton felt the delay gave the Federals an opportunity to escape. The rolling plains around Brandy Station finally grew quiet after fourteen hours of the tumult of war. The battle of Brandy Station was over.

During the next few days, the men of the horse artillery took time to write to friends and loved ones, describing what they had experienced during what turned out to be the largest cavalry engagement of the war. At least one artilleryman hadn't waited to record his thoughts. During the brief lulls throughout the fight, Pvt. Charles W. McVicar jotted down his thoughts about what was transpiring around him. They form a vivid picture of a horse artilleryman's day on the battleline.

> My first knowledge of daylight was the rattling of small arms and the charge of men rushing to harness and saddle their horses. The enemy was on us. They had charged across the river and surprised us in bed. We retreated about 1/2 mile as the Yanks advanced through our camp. Captain Chew's tent, clothes, letters, and papers captured. The enemy

charging up the road ahead, fortunately one of the guns ahead unlimbered and fired almost in their faces, doing terrible execution down the road.

The rest of the battery wheeled into action around the old church, and the battle raged furiously. We gave them fifty rounds. Our cavalry are charging desperately. We ceased firing for a few moments but have commenced firing again and have several shell in their column. The fight has become heavy, and we are surrounded on three sides. The Yanks are facing on our front, right, and rear. The shell are bursting above and around us thick. Two of the boys at the first piece have been slightly wounded.[50] The Yanks have all the positions of any importance. Our ammunition has given out. Sergeant [George W.] Brady sent me back to the first piece to take the place of the boys that were wounded. They have the range of our piece and are throwing the shell among us thick. We have been in the front all day, no cessation. This is fearful hard work. Part of the time we had no support. This is now getting at close range. We have just ceased firing as our guns are very hot. I am acting #4, firing the gun.

The enemy are earning every foot of ground they get. We are now back to Fleetwood Hill, firing. They have closed in on us and just burst the Blakely Gun. As I pulled the lanyard, I saw a small flame under the cascable[51] and reported [words illegible]. This is the famous Ashby Gun. I have just been sent to another detachment, 2nd section. Just after I left, both guns were captured but were retaken by a charge of the 11th and 12th [Virginia Cavalry]. We unlimbered and gave them shell faster than they could digest, causing them to check up and deploy two lines. General Pleasonton is handling his troops well, and I believe if it were not for such level headed officers as General Jones and General Stuart would today have his match.

This is a wide contrast from yesterday's Sham Battle. We have been fighting for the last hour more fiercely than ever. It is fearful. Shells are bursting around us thick. We have made it so warm for their cavalry, they brought two batteries to play on us. If my face is as black, dirty, and powder stained as most I see, I am a beauty. We have just had another hard gallop with the gun to Brandy Station for ammunition and back. We have been front all day and fired 155 rounds. Pleasonton has two brigades of regulars and certainly their movements and discipline have been fine. They have formed, wheeled, charged, and retreated in order without confusion.

Six o'clock in the evening, we are forcing them back and now have the clear front and full deep lines. Have captured a good many, and they have given up most every good position. It is sundown. The battle has ceased. Look where you will and see the dead, wounded, and no chance to relieve a great many. The ground is strewn with blankets, arms, and dead horses. The enemy crossed the Rappahannock River. Their loss must have been a full five to our one. As we move back to camp the boys were too tired to joke and were very quiet.

[Gregory] Britner and I found a regular on the side of the road. He was an Irishman with a piece of shell in his skull. Britner at his request held his head, and I pulled it out with the horseshoe pincers. We sent this Yank to the hospital in Culpeper. At 10 p.m. General Rode's Division of Infantry arrived to reinforce us but were too late for action. Have had nothing to eat all day. I have used a full large plug of tobacco since morning, probably to keep my courage up, but am sick from it tonight. This has been the hardest fought cavalry battle of the war, and many, very many, will carry the recollections of this day to their end from wounds and suffering.[52]

Lt. James H. Williams, also of Chew's Battery, found time on the day following the battle to write to his future wife. For him the panorama of battle narrowed to a personal loss. The rest seemed incidental.

Wednesday June 10th 1863

My Dear Miss Cora,

We have just buried George [Henry Williams] here.[53] He was killed in the cavalry fight just below Brandy Station and was shot in the forehead rather between the eyes. They were engaged in a hand to hand fight at the time and was shot perhaps by one on foot. I only got here in time to see him deposited in his last resting place. I was out all last night and only heard of his death a few hours since. He was shot about 12 o'clock PM. His body for awhile was in the hands of the enemy. Having laid in the sun for some hours, decomposition had taken place so rapidly that it was impossible to take his body home. No one saw him fall that I can learn. This will be a terrible shock to Ma, and I trust a useful lesson to us all. All our friends came out safely. George's horse was in no condition for service, nor had he any arms except a sabre and had permission to remain back, in fact was almost ordered. John Lovell tells me his look was stern but natural.[54]

Death so often makes for its own the noble and generous. I never had so true a companion and congenial a spirit.

Our battery had several wounded. I suppose you have or may have heard I was taken prisoner. This was correctly reported. I barely escaped but only by fighting. I know little of the details of the fight, and don't suppose they would interest you.

I wrote you on Saturday, enclosing your letters. Have not had time to answer your last and have not the heart to do so now. May write again in a few days. I must return to camp. Everything is on the move.

Our loss is about 500. Enemy's heavy.

Saw Dr. By—— [name illegible] of Abbeville [?] several times yesterday. I had nothing late from home. Good Bye. May God bless.

Yours truly,
James H. Williams[55]

McVicar's and Chew's Battery was not the only horse artillery to be busy from dawn to dusk on June 9, nor was Williams alone in his grief. Lt. Charles R. Phelps of Moorman's Battery also had stories to tell and losses to report. He wrote of his experiences in a letter to his aunt two days after the battle:

Camp near Brandy Station,
June 11th, 1863

Dear Aunt,

Tuesday last was a busy day for "Stuart's Horses." About day light the Yanks drove in our pickets stationed at Beverly Ford on the Rappahannock, and came near surprising us in bed. We had received orders last week to prepare three days rations and had moved our camp to within one mile of the Rappahannock, is why they came up so suddenly. They charged up to our camp and killed and wounded several horses before we could get out. In a few minutes we had harnessed up and took position about one-half of a mile back and commenced shelling the woods in front. They retired but soon began to show themselves in different places. About eight o'clock the engagement became general, and I had a fine opportunity of witnessing some fine cavalry fighting. Our men charged them into the woods but were met by two brigades of Infantry and had to fall back. Then the Yanks again charged our cavalry and though I do not like to say it, forced them back beyond our batteries on our left. I thought at one time I was gone, the fighting being so general that we could not use our pieces. In the meantime a large force of Yankee Cavalry had crossed at another ford and got in our rear at Brandy Station, with four pieces of artillery. Hampton's Brigade charged them and took their artillery. We then changed our position and kept up the fight until four o'clock P.M., finally driving them to their old position across the river. Our loss is very heavy for the fight but cannot say how much. I lost at my piece one killed and three wounded by one shot.

Anthony Dornin, one of the best and bravest soldiers, is no more. He was wounded about three o'clock. I immediately had him carried to Brandy Station and as I was out of ammunition and one of my pieces disabled, I went with him and gave him every attention until he died, which he did soon after his wound was dressed. I had his body enclosed in the best coffin we had and suppose ere this it has arrived in Lynchburg. William Nowlin and William Shoemaker were also slightly wounded at same time. This is the loss of our Co. except some seven or eight horses killed or wounded.[56]

Our loss is quite heavy as I hear of several of my old friends being killed. Col. Williams, 2nd N.C. and Col. Hampton killed. Gen. Lee wounded in thigh severely.

Capt. Moorman's wife and his sister arrived here last Saturday as we were ordered to march and left this morning. They had a narrow escape from being captured. The Yanks were at the same house they were staying at a few minutes after they left. Their trip could not have been a very pleasant one.

We are now under orders and expect to move momentarily to what point I have no idea. Remember me to all and believe me

Very truly yours
C. R. Phelps

Show to Miss Wiatt[57]

Phelps's account sadly recalled the loss of comrades and friends. His leaving the field to assist one of his men does not seem to have been questioned by any of his superior officers. Phelps had proven his courage on many fields. A lack of it had not prompted his going. His tenderness in the midst of such carnage was seen for what it was, a simple act of compassion. His confusion over what was to come was shared by others. One was Lt. Francis H. Wigfall, who briefly put down his battle experiences in a letter to his sister on June 13. Even after passing through such turmoil, he did not neglect to comment on the social life or his expectations of what the future held.

Starke's Ford on Hazel River
June 13, 1863

Dear Lou,

I have been in camp only a few minutes having just returned from Jeffersonton a few miles across the Hazel where we marched today in consequence of a reported advance of the enemy. We are now back at the same old place that we have occupied for nearly a week. My section only is here, Johnston's being with that of F. [Fitzhugh] Lee's brigade a few miles further above. Capt. Breathed started off before I marched to go down to Johnston's section and has not yet reached camp. My guns did not get into the fight the other day until afternoon. We had it all our own way the Yankee artillery firing on us almost literally not at all. Johnston lost three men wounded out of his section in the morning.[58] The battery is now divided between Fitz and W. H. F. Lee's brigades two guns with each. Capt. Breathed just returned and says that the alarm was a false one. Papa came up the night of the day I wrote you last and spent the next day up here returning the morning after. There was a dance at the C.H. [Culpeper Court House] that night and another the next evening (the day of the review) [June 5] which was a perfect [word illegible]. Col. and Mrs. Rosser were there and I was introduced to the bride by Papa. Expressed my regret at not having been present at the interesting ceremony, etc., etc. Miss Murray and Miss Wallis were with the party and I saw them again the next morning when I called on the happy couple.

If you expect to learn anything from this letter of army movements you will be woefully disappointed for I am as ignorant of what is going on up here as one could conveniently imagine.

June 14. I was interrupted here yesterday by the rain. We are now under orders to hold ourselves in readiness to move at a moment's notice. The Yankees I believe have driven in the pickets above Waterloo Bridge. As you may well suppose we don't have much opportunity to grow weary of remaining in one place. Papa has been up with the army within the last few days but being off at the front I have not seen him and only heard of his being here by accident. I have not received a letter from you now for nearly a month. I shall direct my next to you at Orange C.H. as I suppose by that time you will have reached there. Remember me kindly to Miss Anne. "Oh sweet Anne Page!" By the way is the aforesaid Miss Clara to be "grown up" after the expiration of this "month of battles." If so I hope she will allow me to offer my congratulation. If not say that I deeply sympathize with her. I have of late become quite pastoral, sleeping in the grass and living on milk and bread to say nothing about the [word illegible].

"My pen is good, my ink not pale.
My love for you shall not fail"

With this soul stirring sentiment I shall conclude and be still,

Your affectionate Brother
Halsey[59]

As with all the participants, McVicar, Phelps, and Wigfall saw the battle from different perspectives and carried away certain opinions of their command's performance. Undoubtedly, they were proud of their contribution to the cavalry's victory, for indeed the horse artillery battalion had more than lived up to its fine reputation. Surprised in the early hours of the morning, the battalion had received the first shock the enemy delivered and returned the favor with a blast of defiance from Hart's gun. The momentary confusion that occurred when the Federals stormed across the river quickly turned to stubborn resistance. Sometime during Beckham's rapid retreat to St. James Church, the disorganized batteries regained their equilibrium. By the time Beckham put his guns into position between the church and the Gee house, the batteries were ready to assist the cavalry in bringing the Federal advance to a halt.

After the stand at the church, Ford's and Hart's mad dash to Fleetwood Hill demonstrated the mobility horse artillery needed to be effective. The cannoneers' gallant defense of their guns proved that in a pinch, the gunners could give a good account of themselves and would not easily surrender their charges. Chew's, Moorman's, and Breathed's Batteries all contributed to the victory and in the end showed that there were no weak links in the battalion. The legacy of Pelham was upheld on the plains of Brandy Station. Stuart wrote, "The conduct of the Horse Artillery, under that gallant officer, Maj. R. F. Beckham, deserves the highest praise."[60] It was praise well earned.

However, there were smudges on the otherwise stainless performance. The firing on Hampton during his pursuit of the retreating Gregg permitted, at least in Hampton's eyes, the enemy to escape without further damage. The tendency of the guns to break down at critical moments remained a problem. Three pieces were disabled early in the morning at St. James Church and a fourth on Fleetwood near the end of the day. This was fully one-quarter of the guns Beckham had with him at the beginning of the battle. Had any others been damaged by enemy fire, the horse artillery may not have been able to perform its role as successfully. While this might seem trivial, it is more serious when viewed alongside earlier similar occurrences and in relation to the Confederacy's increasing inability to provide replacement parts.

The battle disrupted Gen. Robert E. Lee's plans for his invasion of Maryland and Pennsylvania, but only momentarily. Stuart would now be delayed in fulfilling his part of the operations. The horse artillery and the cavalry required some time to regroup, rest, and tend to the dead and wounded.[61] Their march northward would be postponed. Elsewhere, the campaign proceeded on schedule, with other batteries of horse artillery in the thick of the action.

CHAPTER 15

From Winchester to Harrisburg

"In the heart of the enemy's country"

The final weeks of May 1863 were most unpleasant for those civilians in and around Winchester who were loyal to the Confederacy. The fortunes of the Confederacy in the lower Valley were once again at a low point. In fact, Maj. Gen. Robert H. Milroy and his 2nd Division of the Federal VIII Corps had occupied Winchester since December 25, 1862. His arrival certainly had ruined Christmas, and his extended stay caused the Valley inhabitants to long for another Stonewall Jackson to liberate them. Milroy's initial opposition had come from Brig. Gen. William E. Jones's and Brig. Gen. John Imboden's cavalry forces, but they had done little more than watch the Federals sweep through Winchester and Strasburg. Jones's and Imboden's combined raid into West Virginia from mid-April through mid-May had done nothing to loosen Milroy's grip on Winchester. Then Jones was ordered east to join Stuart, and the outlook for Winchester appeared even bleaker. But there was another Stonewall on the way. In the Valley and east of the mountains, groundwork was being laid for Winchester's salvation.

Brig. Gen. Albert G. Jenkins had been organizing his brigade of cavalry in the upper Valley around Staunton. His artillery was to be the Charlottesville Artillery under Capt. Thomas E. Jackson, which was still forming near Dublin Depot. Lt. Micajah Woods was involved in his battery's organization but not so involved as to miss opportunities to visit friends and people of influence when such opportunities arose in the course of his duties. The war was a long way off, and there was time to enjoy the finer things.

Camp near New River Bridge
May 22nd 1863

My dear Father

Yesterday I returned from a very pleasant visit to Saltville on company business. I was ordered to Genl. [John S.] Williams' Hd. Quarters—but of course my business there required but a very brief period, and I had ample time to see my friends and have a good time generally at and in the vicinity of the much renowned village. As soon as I arrived I was invited by Mr. [Alexander H. H.] Stuart to make his home my home and I spent all day Wednesday at his hospitable mansion—and as is always the case his nieces and Miss Haden made themselves particularly agreeable. Not least among the circumstances that rendered the day pleasant was a splendid dinner at which the productions of more genial courses than ours graced the table in profusion. Beside the most delicious mutton flavored by exquisite seasonings were set before us tomatoes, potatoes, peas, lettuce, and numerous other vegetables and viands which only a soldier knows well how to appreciate after being dieted for weeks upon the coarse and common fare which is furnished him in the tented field. Miss Belle expressed her desire to be remembered to you especially.

I conversed with Col. [John N.] Clarkson and Mr. Stuart freely upon the subject of salt. Col. Clarkson will take charge of the State Furnaces on next Monday, and it will probably be some time before he can make any distribution of salt to the different districts. He charges $10 per bushel for his good salt and $5 for his lump. Mr. Stuart told me he would let you have as much of the lump salt as you want at $3.00 per bushel, and he will make every effort in his power to have any number of barrels you may purchase transported to you—although the difficulties of having smaller quantities than a car load carried over the road are almost insurmountable as Mr. Dodamead has positively forbidden it. This lump salt is just as good in the opinion of Mr. Stuart for salting stock and meat as the best quality, and I advise you to communicate with him as soon as possible and make a purchase as this offer is quite low. Perhaps some of our neighbors will unite with you and purchase enough to fill a car but before making any arrangements you had better get some gentleman on more friendly terms with Mr. Dodamead than yourself to ascertain from him whether he will have a car brought to Lynchburg. Mr. Ficklin, I expect, could accomplish something in this line. It is particularly important to purchase at this time as the lump salt is in great demand with the men who run wagons to Saltville from Tennessee and North Carolina, and the season is rapidly approaching when these wagons will come in great numbers and that variety of salt will be much scarcer and dearer in price, indeed a good many teams are making their appearance already.

Col. Clarkson regrets very much, I think that he made this contract with the State, but says he will stand it out for at least one year. By no means do the most kindly feelings exist between the Col. and Mr. Stuart.

I regret exceedingly that I did not go up to Fredericksburg from Richmond to see Genl. Stuart as his brother advised me, especially as he assured me that the General had promised that he would give me the first vacant place on his staff. Already two vacancies have occurred, and I would have had a far finer field in which to win my spurs as well as to be hit by a Yankee bullet—the latter fate however I have no desire to have befall me. There is no General in our Eastern army for whom I have greater admiration than Stuart and none who stands so fair a chance to win lasting laurels. His star is certainly in the ascendant and my information is that he is an officer who rewards merit and is not tainted with the abominable favoritism so prevalent in the army. And there is something glorious in belonging to the Army of Northern Virginia, whose pathway has only been strewn with victory which has literally been achieved by valor and prowess of its heroes in the deadly fray.

I saw a very intimate friend of Genl. [John B.] Floyd yesterday, Capt. Harman, who stopped a day at our encampment especially to see me on his route from Lynchburg to Wytheville. He says the old Genl. expressed great astonishment that [Capt. Thomas E.] Jackson exerted his influence in [Lt. Randolph H.] Blain's behalf and secured his election over my head and attributed it to the natural proneness of men to have weak vessels under their thumbs that they can control and make tools of at will.

Capt. Jackson received a telegram to day from Genl. Jenkins's ordnance officer informing him that our pieces had arrived in Staunton and that we must expect to follow them in a few days—and containing information which required one of us to go to the Hd.Quarters of the Dept. at Dublin. Jackson at once requested me to attend to the business as he invariably does when there is anything of import on the wing. He actually took me out the other day when he wished me to make a trip to the Salt Sulphur to see Genls Jones and Imboden and ascertain whether they could not offer us great inducements to join their commands as they have recently returned from a successful raid—after capturing many horses and urged me to go in preference to Blain or [Lt. Richard B.] Wortham on the ground that I could approach such officers so much more easily and accomplish so much more by conversing with them than my associate Lieutenants. Most consistent reasoning (don't you think?) when he made every effort in his power to give Blain a superior place to me. I did not go, however—as I said, I was requested. I proceeded to Dublin this morning and returned this evening and who do you think I met with? On entering one of the offices who should confront me but Uncle Tom. I felt really delighted to meet him—he is looking so much bet-

> ter than he has ever done since I can recollect. He had visited Lewisburg recently and reports that the inhabitants of that devoted town were miraculously rescued from a most horrible fate, threatened them by the enemy by the skill of Col. Edgar with a much inferior one. It pained me myself to learn from him that Tom Preston is a hopeless wreck. He has now a unconditional discharge from the service which he should have had eight months ago.
>
> I do most sincerely hope that my war steed may not lose an eye, as it would impair his efficiency in the field to a great extent—if it will not compel him to forego the privilege of participating in the struggle—and consign him to a position from which he can only smell the battle from afar. There is no conjecturing what a good horse will bring in the coming campaign—no one thinks asking less than $400 for a horse which in times of gentle peace would not bring more than $75.
>
> I am on quite a fair track to obtain for Mr. [name illegible] a substitute. I have addressed several letters to some of my state line friends in Tazewell and have [remainder of letter missing].[1]

Woods was unsuccessful in his attempt to secure inducements for the battery to join either Jones or Imboden. The former had Chew, the latter McClanahan. Both were proven batteries. Jackson would have to be satisfied with Jenkins.

The arrival of Jackson's guns—four howitzers and two Richmond three-inch rifles—at Staunton signaled the approach of active campaigning for the Valley troops.[2] On June 7, Robert E. Lee dispatched orders to both Imboden and Jenkins, setting the stage for a movement on Milroy at Winchester. Imboden was to distract the Federal commander by invading Hampshire County, West Virginia, west of Winchester.[3] Jenkins was to concentrate at Strasburg or Front Royal, or any point in front of either, with pickets out toward Winchester. He was to be in position by June 10 and was to cooperate with a force of infantry that would rendezvous with him.[4] That force of infantry that went unnamed in Lee's letters was the II Corps of the Army of Northern Virginia, under Lt. Gen. Richard S. Ewell.

On June 9, while Stuart struggled with Pleasonton on the fields near Brandy Station, Ewell's Corps remained encamped around Culpeper Court House. During the day, Lee ordered Ewell to send infantry to support Stuart. The division of Maj. Gen. Robert E. Rodes arrived at Brandy Station to find the enemy already retiring. On the following day, Ewell was off to the Valley. He marched without a cavalry screen, but Jenkins lay ahead of him, already in position to cover the advance on Winchester. Lee's plan was running smoothly, having lost but a step at Brandy Station.[5] Hooker knew nothing of Ewell's march, and Milroy attributed increased enemy activity in his area to Stuart's expected cavalry raid.[6]

On June 11, Ewell continued his march toward the Valley. Milroy, on the other hand, sat comfortably in Winchester, blissfully unaware of what was approaching. His immediate superior, Maj. Gen. Robert C. Schenck, commander of the VIII Corps, had repeatedly ignored General-in-Chief Henry W. Halleck's orders to pull Milroy back to guard the Baltimore & Ohio Railroad twenty miles north of Winchester. Finally, on June 11, Halleck stirred Schenck into action. The VIII Corps commander ordered Milroy back to Harpers Ferry.[7] But Milroy didn't like the thought of abandoning the loyal Union citizens of the lower Valley to what he felt would be their undoing at the hands of Confederate sympathizers. He sent back his wagon train and squatted down to hold his post.

Brig. Gen. Albert G. Jenkins's cavalry, minus Jackson's Horse Artillery, rendezvoused with Ewell on June 12 at Cedarville, just north of Front Royal. The II Corps would be blind no longer. The movement on Winchester began immediately. Ewell dispatched Rodes and Jenkins, except for the 16th Virginia Cavalry, toward Berryville, where one of Milroy's brigades under Col. Andrew T. McReynolds was guarding Milroy's left flank. It was hoped that these Federals might be scooped up before they could rejoin Milroy. The rest of Ewell's Corps, led by the 16th Virginia, headed for Winchester.

On the thirteenth, the Maryland Line under Col. James R. Herbert joined Maj. Gen. Jubal A. Early's Division at Newtown on the Valley Pike. With this command was Capt. Wiley H. Griffin's Baltimore Light Artillery. Since its conversion to horse artillery prior to the Jones-Imboden Raid, the battery had not fired a shot in anger. While the union with the other Maryland units in the Confederate army was welcomed, it had taken the battery out of the war during the Maryland Line's organization. Now every Marylander was eager to prove himself. They had a fighting reputation to live up to, and Griffin's men wanted to build on that record.

Around 5:00 P.M., Early encountered some enemy cavalry near Kernstown. Griffin was called to place his guns into battery. A single shot was enough to scatter them.[8] The Confederates quickly advanced, only to run into Brig. Gen. Washington L. Elliott's Brigade, which had been sent out by Milroy to scout toward Strasburg. At first the Confederates were surprised and driven back. Elliott's artillery, Battery L, 5th U.S. Artillery, under Lt. Wallace F. Randolph, opened a severe fire on Griffin, who responded in kind. The Confederate infantry, Brig. Gen. John B. Gordon's and Brig. Gen. Harry T. Hays's Brigades, soon rallied and pushed back Elliott. Griffin's guns fired until their targets were out of range. The men had not flinched under the enemy's hot fire. The battery's reputation had not been tarnished.

On the morning of the fourteenth, Milroy began to see the handwriting on the wall. He ordered McReynolds—Rodes and Jenkins having just missed bagging him and his command—to reunite with him at Winchester. With his last brigade in the fold, Milroy sat down in his fortifications to await the Confederate attack. Already he had given up Bowers' Hill south of Winchester, but he still held a string of forts northwest of the town. At one time Milroy had possessed complete faith in these forts, but now that he knew who and what he was facing, that faith began to waver. Ewell was not Jones or Imboden, and he had Stonewall Jackson's old corps with him.

Ewell spent the greater part of the day preparing his attack. Early's Division moved to the west and prepared to strike at Milroy's main fortifications. Maj. Gen. Edward Johnson's Division swung eastward. Brig. Gen. John B. Gordon's Brigade and Colonel Herbert's Marylanders remained at Bowers' Hill. Here too was Griffin's Battery, about a mile and a half south of Milroy's main fort. When Early's guns opened, Griffin joined in the barrage.[9] The Federal artillery tried to respond but grew silent after forty-five minutes. Then Early launched his attack. Everywhere along the line, the Confederates were successful in penetrating the enemy's defenses. Milroy's only hope to save his men was in rapid retreat to Martinsburg. During the night, Milroy led his men toward Stephenson's Depot on the Winchester & Potomac Railroad. Ewell anticipated Milroy's action and sent Johnson's division to cut him off. Through the night, the two armies marched. At 4:00 A.M., Milroy's advance clashed with Johnson's troops. When Milroy found his way blocked, he tried to fight his way out. After a valiant effort, Milroy's command was shattered. The retreat turned into a disaster. Ewell had liberated Winchester, virtually destroying Milroy's command in the process. The next obstacle was the Potomac.

To the west, Brig. Gen. John Imboden also was successfully carrying out Robert E. Lee's wishes. Imboden left his camp at Monterey in Highland County on June 8 and moved swiftly into Hampshire County. Heading for Romney, Imboden's troopers gathered up all the cattle and horses they could find and destroyed every bridge they crossed. Imboden split his forces, sending the 62nd Virginia Infantry through Pendleton and Hardy Counties while he rode with the 18th Virginia Cavalry and McClanahan's Battery. On June 15, the same day Ewell crushed Milroy at Stephenson's Depot, Imboden entered Romney, which had been held by the Federals. McClanahan's Battery did not have the opportunity to fire a shot, so swiftly had the enemy abandoned the town. Imboden received instructions from Lee to cooperate with Ewell and follow that officer's instructions.[10] As had Ewell, Imboden now turned toward the Potomac.

On the morning of June 15, elements of Brig. Gen. Albert G. Jenkins's Brigade gazed across the Potomac River near Williamsport.[11] By evening, these same troopers were across the river and headed for Chambersburg, Pennsylvania. But Jenkins rode without his artillery. Jackson's Battery had not participated in the stirring events surrounding the capture of Winchester. In a letter he wrote on June 16, Lt. Micajah Woods discussed what his battery had been doing during Ewell's rapid march north, reported Winchester's capture, and ordered his summer shirts.

Staunton, June 16th 1863

My dear Father

Timmie returns in the morning from his visit to our camp. I doubt very much whether his impressions are favorable of the soldier's life. He will be able to recount to you all the camp news, so I can afford to be brief.

The particulars of the capture of Winchester are very cheering by this evening's stage from that vicinity. Passengers report that Ewell completely invested the town with his force. Soon after his lines were established he discovered that a brigade of the enemy were approaching on the Martinsburg road. He immediately posted Early's & Rodes' Divisions on either side of the road and permitted the hostile force to march unmolested within his lines when he closed in upon them and demanded their unconditional surrender, and they complied, the whole brigade 1800 strong laying down their arms. Soon afterwards a dense smoke was discerned in the town. Genl. Ewell supposing that it was being fired, notified Milroy that if a house was burnt he would raise the black flag. This deterred the Brigand from executing his purpose if such it was. Inconsiderable fighting was done when the town was surrendered with its entire garrison consisting of 6 or 8000 men. Milroy at last accounts had not been found, but the place was being thoroughly searched in every hole and corner and it was thought he would soon be ferreted out as he can not possibly escape the town being completely encompassed by a line of pickets. The movement of our troops upon Winchester has broken the monotony of the situation in Virginia and in the future stirring scenes will be exacted on our soil till Winter again puts in its appearance.

Our Battery will not move from this neighborhood for a week or two probably. A great deal of work will have to be done before we will be on a war footing. I hope you will find it convenient to pay us a visit the latter part of the week. The train reaches here early in the evening and leaves here before 7 in the morning. You could without difficulty spare this short period of time.

I will come over in a few days for my horse. I am undetermined whether I will need my Ky. horse for Bob or not. There may be extra horses in the Battery which he can ride. We have 84 fine horses here for the Battery which besides 25 or 30 which are en route for Staunton. Lieut. [Richard B.] Wortham may accompany me home and spend a day.

Now a word to Mother. I want two white cotton shirts. I think you told me you had a roll of white cotton. They should be perfectly plain [words missing] behind to hold them. They can be cut by my new shirts which fit me very well. Please have them made as soon as possible as I shall want them immediately—indeed I need them now all my shirts being very heavy and too warm for Summer.

I called last night at Mr. Baldwin's where I was received very kindly by him & his family.

Please wrap "Fantine" up together with my Virginia buttons and gold lace & uniform pants and put it in charge of the conductor on the three o'clock train today. I will meet him at the Depot without fail, and write me also and believe me to be with love to all

Very devotedly
Your Son
Micajah Woods[12]

Even as Woods wrote about his battery's condition and speculated when it might be ready to join in the great campaign, other Confederate troops were already making their way into Maryland. By midday on the sixteenth, Jenkins was into Maryland and on his way to Chambersburg, Pennsylvania. His only opposition came from a small cavalry force that buzzed around the Confederate column like hornets, stinging and flying away. Jenkins marched through Hagerstown and pushed on into Pennsylvania. At Greencastle, he paused long enough to send out foragers into the countryside. On their return, the column moved on toward Chambersburg. It was near midnight when the Confederates entered the town. Their stay was short-lived. By the morning of the seventeenth, Jenkins had information that a large force was approaching from the north. Unnerved, he turned around and headed back to Maryland. His rapid retreat may have been prompted in part by his lack of artillery. By a strange twist, that problem was about to be remedied.

Griffin's Battery had performed well enough at Winchester to be awarded the right to claim a number of the captured artillery pieces to replace their old, worn-out guns.[13] The excited officers and men of the battery were soon fawning over four rifled Parrotts. But their excitement quickly turned to anger when they were ordered to join the reserve artillery.[14] Everyone from Captain Griffin down was insulted by the assignment, which they deemed unworthy of their reputation. They had always led the advance or covered the retreat. To be sent to the reserve was, they felt, beneath them. They quickly drew up a protest and forwarded it to General Ewell. Recognizing that such eagerness should be put to good use, Ewell ordered the battery to join Jenkins's Brigade.[15] On June 18, Griffin's men splashed across the river and rode north to join Jenkins—in the van of the army.[16]

Like Griffin's, McClanahan's Battery wished to be a part of the great movement north, but Lee's orders limited their participation early in the campaign to bridge burning and foraging for supplies. Both were important but not overly exciting. On June 16, Imboden split his command, sending the 18th Virginia Cavalry and one section of McClanahan's Battery toward Cumberland, Maryland, while the 62nd Infantry and the rest of McClanahan's Battery marched down the South Branch Valley to cut the Baltimore & Ohio Railroad near Old Town. Pvt. Lantz G. Potts wrote of the success the 18th Cavalry had in carrying out their orders:

> Early in the morning of the 16th of June, we reached Pattonsburg Depot and destroyed a railroad bridge. We then moved on to Cumberland, Md., and placed our artillery on the hill overlooking the town. Captain Ginnaman [Capt. Mathias Ginevan] took a flag of truce and rode into the town and asked them to surrender, but this they refused to do as there was a considerable squad of Yankees there and they could tell but little about our force.
>
> As soon as the captain returned our artillery opened fire and the white flags came up all over the city. The first thing that was fired on was a squad of cavalry who were forming on the left side of town. When the shell burst among them they scattered like turkeys. Some men in blue were seen going in a canal boat. A shell hit it just about the middle and the occupants came out as fast as they could and ran into town.[17]

The success of the section of McClanahan's Battery at Cumberland was mirrored by the rest of the battery at Old Town and South Branch Bridge. At the first location, a number of prisoners were taken and a railroad bridge destroyed. McClanahan had little to do in this action, but at South Branch Bridge the battery was called on to contribute in a very unusual way. One of the battery's twelve-pounders was wheeled into position and opened fire. Its target was not flesh and blood but wood and iron—the bridge. Using solid shot, the gunners blasted away and proved that their accuracy was every bit as exceptional as was their comrades at Cumberland. On the eleventh discharge, a fifty-foot span of the bridge dropped into the river.[18] The elation of the moment was somewhat tempered when the recoil dismounted the gun. Even so, the men celebrated as they worked to repair the piece.

Imboden reported his successes directly to Robert E. Lee, who, in a return letter dated June 20, encouraged Imboden to advance north of the Potomac. He was told to keep to the left of the army during the movement into Pennsylvania and to continue collecting supplies.[19] Private Potts recalled:

> The night of June 23, we passed through Hancock, Md., about midnight, and the people thought we were Yankees. They threw up the

window and cheered us in Lincoln's name, and some of our boys yelled, "Three cheers for Jeff Davis," and the windows went down like they had been shaken by an earthquake.

We marched all night, and at daylight we were in Franklin County, Pa.[20]

This invasion was just a raid. Two days later, with several hundred horses as prisoners, Imboden returned to Virginia. Including the horses captured at Cumberland, Imboden now had enough to mount the 62nd Virginia Infantry. Lee wrote to Imboden again on the twenty-third, repeating his previous injunction to stay on Ewell's left. Imboden crossed the Potomac into Maryland on the twenty-seventh, rode through Maryland, and entered Pennsylvania for the second time in three days. McClanahan's Battery trotted along with the cavalry column.

By June 30, Imboden reached Mercersburg. That morning he wrote to Lee to inform him of his progress and the loss of a large part of the 18th Cavalry's Company G, which was routed by elements of the 1st New York Cavalry at McConnellsburg.[21] Lee wrote back from Greenwood on July 1. He ordered Imboden to Chambersburg, where he was to relieve Maj. Gen. George Pickett's division, freeing it to move on to Gettysburg. Imboden was to continue to gather supplies, forward any stragglers, and watch the reserve trains of the army. On July 3, Imboden encountered Brig. Gen. William E. Jones and Brig. Gen. Beverly H. Robertson and their brigades at Chambersburg. Imboden's Brigade and McClanahan's Battery did not participate in the battle at Gettysburg. In fact, thus far they had contributed little to Lee's grand scheme. But their time was coming.

When Griffin's Battery had united with Jenkins's Brigade on the eighteenth, the men of Ewell's Corps were taking a well-earned rest. Not until the twenty-first did they again set their feet on the roads leading north. Jenkins rode through Greencastle. The invaders met only phantoms of opposition that seemed to vaporize before they could come to grips with them. Jenkins drove onward through Chambersburg to Shippensburg, where the column rested and feasted on apple butter, ham, and other Pennsylvania delicacies. While they enjoyed their repast, the cry of "Yanks" was heard. Griffin threw his guns into battery, but the enemy did not come within range and fell back toward Carlisle. Jenkins pursued but was worried enough to send back to Chambersburg for infantry support. Arriving within sight of Carlisle on the twenty-seventh, Griffin unlimbered two guns and sighted them down the main street. Jenkins demanded the town's surrender. The two gaping mouths of Griffin's Parrotts quickly persuaded the town fathers that surrender was in their best interests.[22] The march through Maryland and Pennsylvania had been steady but not taxing, so Griffin had been able to keep up with the cavalry. It was a proud moment for the men of the Baltimore Light.

But what of Jackson's Battery? It was supposed to be there—in the van of the army—challenging the enemy, intimidating towns to surrender. On paper, Jackson was Jenkins's artillery, but Griffin's Battery was reaping all the glory. Meanwhile, Jackson was far to the south, slowly making his way toward the Potomac. Lieutenant Woods explained all in a letter to his father:

Near Williamsport, Maryland
June 25th 1863

My dear Father

This evening I am again upon the soil of Maryland. I have just arrived here in advance of our Battery to report to General Lee & to receive orders. The Battery will enter the enemy's country tomorrow. In coming on today I passed by heavy columns of the Confederate Army—and such a splendid array my eye never rested on—splendidly equipped—thoroughly clad & shod the troops trod with a lighter step & are acknowledged by all to be in higher spirits than ever before upon any campaign. The greater portion of Longstreet's Corps will camp on the north bank of the Potomac this night. I crossed with the advance brigade this evening and visited Genl. Lee's Hd.Qrs. immediately where I was ordered to tell Capt. Jackson to move on by moderate marches till we reached our Brig. which is in advance of Ewell's Corps in Pennsylvania. Genl. Lee thought we could overtake it before the 30th Inst. Every eye beams with confidence and hope in the mighty army. Longstreet's crosses at this point while A. P. Hill's Corps is also crossing today at Shepherdstown. It is said by officers high in command that Longstreet has nearly 30,000 men. Hill [has] at least that number while Ewell has about 20,000. This gives Lee a powerful army which cannot be conquered by Hooker or any array of Yankees that can be raised in the United States. The greater part of the day I have ridden in rear of the army and I am sure I have not seen fifteen men going to the rear. There is no straggling & you may rely upon it that the deeds of this campaign will transcend in glory those of all other previous. Genl. Lee and his Lieutenants are said to be in a high flow of spirits.

The order from Lee to the whole army which I read today forbids any depredation upon private property in the enemy's country but confining all power of seizure to certain authorized persons as Qr. Masters-Commissaries & Generals & c. The order is rather unexpected but it will tend more to preserve the efficiency of the army than any other hundred proclamations he could have issued.

The demonstrations favorable to us in Williamsport utterly astonished me. I was here in the Maryland Campaign of last year, then every house was shut—every door & window closed and the place seemed possessed by solitude but this evening the streets were literally lined with ladies & many men—who shouted and cheered & waved their handkerchiefs to every Confederate that passed.

In riding through the army today I met with many of my Albemarle friends—among them Col. Magruder & John Watson—Lt. Michie—Capt. Wiant & numbers of others. I am spending to night at the quarters of Capt. John Cochran who is very well.

The army crossing the Potomac was a grand sight one that would tax the utmost ability of a fine painter to do the scene justice.

You can form no idea of the immense drove of cattle and horses that are being sent to the rear from our advance forces in Pennsylvania. Jenkins has been as far as Carlisle Barracks and General Rodes is pushing his infantry very near that point—and is probably there this evening—this news is brought by couriers this afternoon. The supplies in this country are represented to be nearly inexhaustible. The army moves northward at 4 o'clock to morrow morning. I shall await at this point the coming up of the Battery.

I trust you have secured Henry—about whose capture I wrote you from New Market and above all things I do hope you did not permit him to stop at home.

In great haste I am with sincere love to my dear Mother and sister & brothers

Very affectionately
Your Son
Micajah Woods

Dr. Jno R. Woods
Holkham
P.S. Write very often and direct to me thus
Lt. Micajah Woods,
Jackson's Horse Artillery,
Jenkins Cavalry Brigade
Army Northern Va.[23]

Woods awaited Jackson and the battery in Williamsport. They arrived as expected and headed north immediately. Making slow progress at first, once clear of Longstreet's infantry the battery moved on rapidly. Woods wrote to his mother on the thirtieth from his battery's camp five miles from Harrisburg and told of the ride north:

My dear Mother,

In the heart of the enemy's country, I am within five miles of the capital of a powerful state—and banishing for a while all warlike rumors & thoughts, I take occasion to address you a "few lines" to let you know my whereabouts and the incidents worthy of observation on my trip of invasion. I wrote Father a letter from Williamsport the night after crossing the waters of the broad Potomac which has ere this posted you about my movements to that place. Our march since then has been rapid on the direct macadam road to Harrisburg, passing through the Corps of Longstreet, Hill & Ewell, which gave us great trouble as they occupy the road with infantry and trains of artillery and wagons for upwards of 30 miles leaving scarcely a vacant interval. It is an array of power which may well astonish not merely our own people, but astound the population of the hostile country who could scarcely be made to believe that we had more than a hand full of men. The inhabitants of the towns through which the army has passed now declare that we have 250,000 men & that it is no wonder we have always whipped Hooker—and they have yet to see the first Pennsylvanian who expresses the least doubt about our successful invasion & ultimate victory over Hooker. They are utterly overcome with despair, & indeed they seem careless of the result, scarcely a militiaman from all this region has gone to Harrisburg and the country swarms with young men—all are unanimous for stopping the war at once on any terms, and claim that an unconditional peace Governor will succeed [Andrew] Curtin in October by an overwhelming majority. Towns line the road at distances of only four or five miles on the whole route—villages larger than Charlottesville, and invariably they are perfect models of beauty, cleanliness & taste. Oh, if our people would only imitate this people in this respect, in farming and management of their dwellings, how much more lovely our country would be. No region I have ever visited is so fertile & beautiful. Our whole army could subsist here in this village for a year. The ladies came out by hundreds all along our route to see the grand sight and have on no occasion offered us any indignity. On the other hand, they converse freely with our soldiers & seem in some circumstances to take pleasure in doing them kindnesses—all the females are remarkable for their neat and comely dresses. . . .

We treat the people very civilly. They are not only thoroughly subdued but really servile. They do every thing we demand without asking a question—we take only what is necessary for the army—horses—corn &c. generally paying current prices in Confederate money. I expect to bring one or two fine splendid horses & goods that are scarce, as many as Bob can bring. My eyes never rested on such houses, so large & in such fine condition.

We have cooked no rations since entering Penn. The Mayor of each town is being required to furnish rations. Yesterday 1500

> rations were acquired of the Mayor of Mechanicsburg which he furnished in one hour—eggs, ham, beef, apple butter, pies, and vegetables of every description.[24]

As much as Woods was enamored of the country and its people, he had little time to take in the sights. The battery had to hurry on to join Jenkins's Brigade, which had left Carlisle late on the twenty-seventh with orders from Ewell to scout toward Harrisburg. By the time Jenkins made his final approach to the Keystone State's capital on the twenty-eighth, Jackson and his six pieces had caught up. Along with Griffin's Battery, the general now had ten guns he could pit against the Pennsylvania capital and its defenders.

As Jenkins neared Mechanicsburg, which lay west of the Susquehanna River and Harrisburg, he divided his column, sending Col. Milton J. Ferguson with his own 16th Virginia Cavalry, the 36th Virginia Cavalry Battalion, and Jackson's Battery north on the Hogestown Road. Ferguson was to intersect the Carlisle-Harrisburg Pike, swing east, and proceed to a position within cannon shot of Oyster's Point near the Susquehanna River. The colonel moved out with alacrity and made good time until he arrived at Salem Church, just east of Silver Spring Creek. Here he drew rein and stopped. Ahead of him, on Sporting Hill, he could see enemy troops and artillery. These belonged to Brig. Gen. Joseph F. Knipe's Brigade, which had arrived only minutes before Ferguson. Knipe's artillery was Capt. E. Spencer Miller's Philadelphia Home Guard Artillery.[25]

Unlike Jenkins, Ferguson was not panicked by the Federals' presence, even if the Yanks did outnumber him. He called Jackson forward and ordered him to unlimber one of his guns. The captain hurried the gun into position next to the church and opened fire. In this, their initial action, Jackson's gunners proved more eager than accurate, as the rounds went wild. In addition, many of their shells failed to explode. Nevertheless, Ferguson's show of force rattled Knipe, who, having marched his men up the hill, promptly marched them down and back to Oyster's Point. The Confederates moved forward, encouraged by their easy success. Jackson's men limbered their piece and, with a sense of pride in their accomplishment, rumbled after the cavalry. Lieutenant Woods saw the action a little differently and recorded it in a portion of his June 30 letter:

> Yesterday evening[26] we overtook our Brigade in front of the fortifications this side of Harrisburg then engaged in a severe fight. Without being halted one of Lt. Blains' Howitzers and my rifle 3 inch piece were ordered to the front and I took position with my gun about 400 yds. in front the first line of works & opened fire with shell and succeeded in dislodging the enemy from his first line of works in about a half an hour. One of the horses at the gun was disabled. Nothing else was struck, the enemy overfiring with long range guns. Genl. Jenkins was standing by witnessing the action nearly the

> whole time. Our dismounted cavalry entered the works afterwards and reported several of the enemy killed & left. This was the first firing with our Battery & proved eminently successful & efficient. This is merely a feint upon Harrisburg as the whole infantry force is moving in the direction of York, and the great battle will probably be fought with Hooker in a day or two.[27]

Whether it was one gun or two, or whether Jenkins was present or not, Woods's pride in his battery's accomplishment was justified. Had they faced stiff opposition from Knipe or Miller, things might have been different, but as it happened, Jackson's men got the first-battle jitters out of the way and were prepared for more serious fighting. According to Woods's prediction, that would be soon enough. How right he proved to be!

Jenkins had watched Ferguson ride away. Then he turned the remainder of his command east to the outskirts of Mechanicsburg. He halted the column at the junction of the Trindle and Simpson Ferry Roads and stared through his field glasses at the town ahead.[28] A flag could be seen waving from a building. It wasn't Confederate. Not taking any chances, Jenkins ordered up two of Griffin's guns and put them in the road. That done, he sent a flag of truce forward. Tense minutes followed, but eventually the scouts were seen riding back, accompanied by a civilian who proved to be the mayor. Jenkins received assurances that the town was undefended. Griffin, who was becoming quite adept at persuading mayors to surrender their towns, limbered his cannon, and the column set out at a walk into the town. In a short time, the Rebels were made to feel quite at home as ladies appeared with baskets of food and drink. The only fighting the citizens saw was the gray cavalrymen and artillerymen vying for viands from the town's more enchanting inhabitants.

After a filling meal, Jenkins set out to find Ferguson. He apparently had not heard Jackson's fire, though the artillery was a scant two or three miles north of Mechanicsburg. Ferguson had moved on after Knipes's withdrawal. Jenkins found him near Orr's Bridge, where the Conodoguinet Creek loops down close to the Carlisle Pike. Two of Jackson's guns had been placed in front of a stone house occupied by the family of Samuel Eppley.[29] From there the cavalry line extended southeast across the pike. A brief inspection satisfied Jenkins that the northern flank of his line could handle whatever came its way. He turned and rode back south, stopping at the intersection of the Trindle and St. John's Church Roads.

Col. James Cochran of the 14th Virginia Cavalry had his troopers positioned near the crossroads in a grove of trees west of the Peace Church Cemetery.[30] The Baltimore Light Artillery stood nearby. Jenkins ordered it to go into battery in the road in front of the church. The ground was not very high and did not offer any advantage for the guns, but Griffin unlimbered as commanded. Jenkins found himself hampered by the restricted view and climbed the steps of the church in order to survey the clumps of trees about a mile distant. Movement there convinced him that enemy skirmishers were present. He turned to Captain Griffin and instructed him to fire a single shell at the edge of the woods. Griffin complied. Jenkins watched a troop of Federal cavalry hastily ride rearward. The infantry skirmishers, however, did not retreat. They simply took cover in a nearby limestone quarry.

For some reason, Jenkins viewed the skirmishers' dash for cover as preparation for an attack. He directed Cochran to place his men behind the cemetery wall. Griffin was ordered to open fire on the woods. Shortly, Captain Miller's Battery answered his barrage. However, the Philadelphians' accuracy was somewhat off. Their shells fell a mile short of Griffin. Seeing that he outranged his opponents, Griffin tried to locate the enemy battery, but the intervening terrain rendered it impossible. He ended up firing blindly, hoping for a lucky shot. The two batteries continued their harmless duel until dark.

On the morning of the twenty-ninth, Jackson's and Griffin's Batteries resumed their positions of the previous day. Jackson was more active, lobbing shells at regular intervals toward the Federal lines. Houses proved to be the only casualties, suffering only light damage. Around 11:00 A.M. a portion of the 16th Virginia charged toward Oyster's Point. In their wake came one of Jackson's guns. The Confederates surged up to a barricade and received a volley from some New York militia that scattered the graybacks. The cannoneers halted but did not unlimber their piece. Instead of turning the gun around, the crew rode to the rear with the retreating cavalry, leaving their piece standing, still limbered, along the north side of the pike opposite the Oyster's Point Hotel.[31] The abandoned cannon was retrieved later in the day. The humiliation felt by the men of the battery must have been great. It had had the honor of being the Confederate battery that advanced farther north than any other, only to tarnish that honor by a momentary lack of backbone. Had the gun been captured, Jackson would have had much to answer for.

On the strength of Jenkins's scouting mission, Ewell planned to attack Harrisburg on the thirtieth. On the twenty-ninth, however, Ewell received orders from Robert E. Lee to pull back toward the main army. Complying, Ewell marched south. With him went Jenkins's Brigade and Jackson's and Griffin's Batteries. Lieutenant Woods had written his mother, "We are expecting an order momentarily to move to the front to go into action. I doubt whether we will remain here [Harrisburg] very long as we will be compelled to follow the main army towards Baltimore or be gobbled up."[32] He would follow the army, but Gettysburg—not Baltimore—was to be his destination.

CHAPTER 16

Aldie, Middleburg, and Upperville

"Bullets are flying as thick as hail."

The accolades that the Stuart Horse Artillery Battalion garnered at Brandy Station were well earned, but they came at a price. Men and horses had been killed and wounded and a number of guns disabled or permanently damaged. Along with the cavalry, the horse artillery would need a few days to recover. They were granted that and more. Lee's dispatching of Ewell to the Valley required that the remainder of the army play a decoy role in front of Hooker. If Stuart's cavalry did not move, then Hooker might be lulled into a sense of false security that would allow Ewell to slip up on Winchester unmolested. The ruse worked. Not until June 15, the day after Ewell sent Milroy scurrying northward from Winchester toward the Potomac, did Lee start Longstreet's and A. P. Hill's Corps on their march toward the Valley. On the sixteenth, Stuart crossed the Rappahannock.

Stuart camped at Salem that night with Robertson's and Rooney Lee's Brigades, the latter now commanded by Col. John R. Chambliss. Fitz Lee's Brigade, temporarily under Col. Thomas T. Munford, was split, with three regiments at Piedmont Station under Col. Williams C. Wickham and two at Upperville under Munford. In the morning, Stuart sent out orders placing these three brigades into positions that would allow him to screen Longstreet's Corps as it marched north on the eastern side of the Blue Ridge. Hampton and Jones were left behind to screen Hill's Corps until it reached the mountains and then to follow in Longstreet's wake. If Hooker's cavalry rode west in search of information about Lee's infantry, it would have to go through Stuart to get it.

Both sides were busy on the seventeenth. Munford with the 2nd and 3rd Virginia rode from Upperville toward Middleburg, while Wickham with the 1st, 4th, and 5th Virginia and Breathed's Battery left Piedmont for Middleburg as well. The brigade's goal was Aldie, a small town situated in a gap of the Bull Run Mountains. Chambliss with McGregor's Battery moved to The Plains, from where Thoroughfare Gap, which lay south of Aldie Gap, could be scouted. Robertson with Moorman's Battery took up his post at Rectortown to support Lee or Chambliss as needed. Chew's and Hart's Batteries were with Jones and Hampton, respectively.[1] The Yankees were out there somewhere, but just exactly where no one knew. Stuart had no intention of stirring up a hornets' nest, but he would fight to screen the army's march. Everything depended on Pleasonton's intentions. If he was content to stay east of the Bull Run Mountains, the Confederates would leave him alone and move north with some sense of security. If he crossed the mountains, however, Stuart would have to contest his advance. All that was left was to wait.

For his part, Pleasonton seemed determined to supply Hooker with information gathered by hearsay rather than direct contact. The Federal commander-in-chief fumed at the lack of intelligence, both in Pleasonton and about Lee's army. On June 13, the blue cavalry had again crossed the Rappahannock at Beverly's Ford in search of confirmation of a report Pleasonton had received from a trusted civilian. A section of Chew's Battery had been the first to arrive on Fleetwood Hill to oppose deeper incursion, but within an hour, Beckham had two other batteries on the field.[2] Nothing further developed. The Yanks had just come for a look-see and recrossed the river without so much as getting in sight of Fleetwood.

By the sixteenth, Hooker was under increasing pressure from Washington to obtain some concrete information as to Lee's whereabouts. True to military tradition, Hooker on the following day passed the high command's displeasure down the line to Pleasonton, who was ordered: "Drive in pickets, if necessary, and get us information. It is better that we should lose men than to be without knowledge of the enemy, as we now seem to be."[3] After days of inactivity, Pleasonton at last seized the initiative and sent his troopers over the Bull Run Mountains. Brig. Gen. David McM. Gregg led his division, with Brig. Gen. Hugh Judson Kilpatrick's Brigade[4] in the advance, down the Little River Turnpike to Aldie. Accompanying the Federal cavalry was Capt. Alanson M. Randol's Battery E/G, 1st U.S. Artillery.

Stuart, riding with Munford's two regiments, reached Middleburg and decided to remain there because it was a central location from which he could better communicate with his dispersed command. Munford moved on. He sent Company A, 2nd Virginia, under Lt. Abner U. Hatcher, east along the Little River Turnpike[5] to picket the crossroads just outside of Aldie where the turnpike intersected the Old Carolina Road.[6] With the rest of the 2nd and the 3rd Virginia, Munford turned north at Middleburg in search of corn for the brigade's horses. He eventually reached the Snickersville Turnpike, which joined the Little River Turnpike at Aldie.

Following some distance behind Munford, Wickham with the 1st, 4th, and 5th Virginia and Breathed's Battery reached Middleburg and pushed on to Dover, about a mile west of Aldie. By that time, Hatcher had ridden through Aldie and sent his pickets to the crossroads. Wickham drew rein and divided his command. Tom Rosser's 5th Virginia continued on to Aldie, while the 1st,

4th, and Breathed's Battery watered their horses in the Little River, which flowed south across the turnpike.[7] The time was about 2:30 P.M., and Aldie was about to become very crowded.

Lieutenant Hatcher's pickets had barely reached their objective when the leading companies of the 2nd New York Cavalry pounded into them and chased the Virginians right through the hamlet and into Rosser's regiment. In turn, the 5th Virginia countercharged and forced the New Yorkers back through Aldie. A brief lull settled over the field as the combatants called up aid and assessed the situation. Kilpatrick sent for a section of Randol's Battery and placed it on a small hill just west of Aldie on the Snickersville Turnpike. The other regiments of Kilpatrick's Brigade now came up and took position as their commander ordered. Rosser made the grievous error of placing Capt. Reuben B. Boston's Company I on a ridge west of town. Their exposed position quickly came under pressure of Federal skirmishers and Randol's section of artillery.

Help was on the way. Munford, who had received word by courier that his pickets had been flushed and that Rosser had saved the situation for the moment, hastened over the Cobb House Road, which connected the Snickersville Turnpike to the Little River Turnpike. This vital link between the two roads, shielded from the Federals by a ridge, would prove invaluable to the Confederates. Upon reaching the turnpike, Munford saw that Wickham had things well in hand. Two guns from Breathed's Battery, under its resolute commander, were hurrying forward, while Lt. Francis H. Wigfall sought a proper position for his long-ranged Whitworth.[8] In minutes, Breathed's guns were answering Randol's in support of Boston. The Confederate artillery also forced Kilpatrick to deploy his regiments under fire. The 2nd New York, known as the Harris Light Cavalry, sitting in column in the road, received special attention from Breathed's gunners until Kilpatrick withdrew it.

Munford, satisfied that his right flank had stabilized under Wickham's firm leadership, turned his attention to his left. He realized that a Federal thrust up the Snickersville Turnpike could turn the position along the Little River Turnpike. Before riding to meet with Wickham, Munford had deployed Lt. William Walton and fifteen men from Company C, 2nd Virginia, along a stone wall north of the road near the Furr house with orders to hold until the 2nd and 3rd Virginia could come up. For the present, they composed the entire Confederate left flank. Lt. Philip P. Johnston, with one gun and the 4th and 5th Virginia, minus Boston's company, rode off with Munford to reinforce Walton.

Meanwhile, the battle to Breathed's front narrowed down to a fight for survival for Boston and his men. Although skirmishers from the 1st Virginia had moved forward to aid their beleaguered comrades, they had taken position too far in the rear to offer anything but long-range fire support. Kilpatrick launched the 2nd New York and the 6th Ohio at Boston. Breathed pounded them, but some of the Confederate artillery ammunition proved defective and burst not over advancing bluecoats, but over Boston and his men. Taken in front and flank by the Yankee cavalry and harassed by exploding shells from his own guns, Boston could do little more than surrender. The Yankees seemed content with their capture and fell back toward Aldie. For the remainder of the day, Breathed's two pieces and the 1st Virginia repulsed the few skirmishers sent their way. The Little River Turnpike was no longer the focal point of the Federal attack. Kilpatrick had shifted his attention to his right and the Snickersville Turnpike.

Lieutenant Johnston watched as his gun crew rolled their single piece into position on a small knoll overlooking a sharp bend in the road.[9] Johnston had been the battery's recruiting officer for several months in the Confederacy's capital and had enjoyed Richmond society during his off-duty hours. Such a posting was the envy of every officer and man in the battery, with the exception of its captain. Johnston's post on this day would not invoke similar feelings. Before him, the road passed through a cut on its way down to Aldie. A stone wall was but a few yards in front of the gun. The position was one that dominated the road. It also was one that could easily be spotted by the Federal artillery farther down the road near the town. Before long, Randol's Battery greeted Johnston with a welcoming shot. As the round rocketed overhead, Johnston knew it was going to be a long, hot afternoon.

As the crescendo of fighting slowly diminished on the Confederate right, it rose on the left. There had been some action along the Snickersville Turnpike from the beginning of the contest, but once Boston had been dealt with, Kilpatrick determined to try the enemy's left flank. Unfortunately, his tactics and the terrain combined to thwart his initial efforts. He launched his troopers piecemeal at the Rebels and struck up the road in column. The road's features funneled the charging bluecoats through the narrow cut to the sharp bend. Lt. Alexander D. Payne with the 3rd Squadron of the 4th Virginia prepared to meet the Federals in the road, while men from the 2nd Virginia and the remainder of the 3rd lined the stone walls in front of Johnston's gun. These skirmishers could pour their fire, bolstered by Johnston's canister, down the narrow confines of the road and decimate an approaching column.[10]

First into the maelstrom was Capt. Lucius Sargent with the lead platoon of his squadron, Companies H and F, of the 1st Massachusetts. Following him was Maj. Henry L. Higginson with the rest of the squadron. They were repulsed in bloody fighting that left Higginson, Sargent, and Lt. George M. Fillebrown crumpled in the road. After that, the remainder of the 1st Massachusetts and elements of the 4th New York and the 1st Maine took turns flinging themselves at the Confederates. Charge and countercharge swept back and forth on the road and in the fields paralleling it. The 2nd, 3rd, 4th, and 5th Virginia joined the fray, charging, retreating, rallying, and charging again as the battle escalated. Johnston's gunners alternated targets between Kilpatrick's determined cavalry and Randol's all too efficient artillery: first a shell into the charging bluecoats at a distance, then canister when up close, then back to shell and solid shot to answer Randol's iron messengers. The Union battery's fire proved more accurate. Johnston's men frequently hugged the ground to escape the iron hail passing overhead and the iron fragments that showered from bursting shells.[11] Randol's shots were not falling short, and the health of any man brave enough or foolish enough to stand was in serious jeopardy.

One of the Confederate charges almost crowned the day with success as it nearly reached Randol's guns, but it was not to be. The 1st Maine, under Col. Calvin S. Douty, turned the Rebels back and then launched a countercharge that finally uprooted the gray skirmishers along the Snickersville Turnpike. In doing so, Douty was killed, but his attack swung the fight in the Federals' favor. Lieutenant Johnston saw that he could do no more where he was, limbered his gun, and galloped rearward. Munford knew his flank was turned and that he had to pull back to a new line. Shortly, Lt. Frank S. Robertson of Stuart's staff came with an order to break off the fight and retreat due to the advance of another Federal force on Middleburg in Munford's rear. During the withdrawal, Breathed's Battery suffered a serious loss. The next day, Lieutenant Wigfall took the time to report the day's action and his battery's casualties to his mother.

> Rector's X roads June 18 1863
>
> Dear Mama
>
> I have this moment received yours of the 14th inst. and hasten to reply. I have written only twice within the past two weeks and the reason I did not write you after the fight was that you were so close I did not think you would feel uneasy at not hearing from me. The best proof you can have of my safety except hearing so positively is by hearing nothing. Moving with the cavalry, here today and there tomorrow it is impossible to keep up a regular correspondence. The wounded are always sent to the rear and if I am ever unfortunate enough to be placed in that category I shall certainly let you know. So till you hear positively to the contrary make your mind easy on my account.
>
> We marched from [word illegible] Ford the day your letter is dated and came up by Amissville, Gaines' X Roads, Flint Hill, Orleans, Piedmont on the Manassas Gap R.R., Paris, Upperville, and Middleburg to Dover Mills which we reached yesterday afternoon and where we engaged the Yankee cavalry and Artillery. I was detached from the battery in command of the Whitworth gun of my section. This piece lost now. The other pieces each lost one man killed. These were the only men of the battery lost. The drivers of the Whitworth in trotting through a gate ran against one of the posts and snapped the pole short off.[12] Only the limber of the caisson was there, the pintle-hook[13] having been broken, and the body left at

> Orange C.H. so that there was no spanpole. I had therefore to take the pole of the caisson limber to replace that of the piece and have the [word illegible] minus the pole. I hope the Yankees will derive much benefit from their capture. We were falling back at the time, so there was no chance to repair it. The enemy was flanking us so we were forced to fall back making a circuitous route and striking the turnpike between Upperville & Middleburg late last night. The battery is about to move now so good-bye. Give my best to dear Papa and Lou and kiss "Buddy's buddy" for him. You must not expect to hear from me regularly but write yourself frequently.
>
> Your affectionate,
> Halsey[14]

Wigfall's frustration at losing the services of the Whitworth undoubtedly was shared by Breathed and Stuart. The gun was valuable for its range and accuracy. The loss of the caisson meant the loss of ammunition that could not be manufactured in the Confederacy. Without that ammunition, the gun was just so much dead weight.

The Federals who precipitated Stuart's order for Munford to withdraw turned out to be a single regiment of cavalry. In his wisdom, Brig. Gen. Alfred Pleasonton had pushed a whole division through Aldie Gap, but only Col. Alfred N. Duffié's 1st Rhode Island Cavalry drew the assignment of penetrating Thoroughfare Gap. Duffié's target was Middleburg, where he was supposed to camp and communicate with Kilpatrick, his brigade commander. Pleasonton did not elaborate on Duffié's mission, which was basically an unsupported jaunt behind enemy lines. Unless Kilpatrick reached Middleburg, Duffié would be alone and have no prospect of receiving aid should he encounter Stuart's forces.

Munford's retreat from Gregg successfully avoided Middleburg and its environs, but had Duffié's column been the vanguard of a second Federal division or even a brigade, Stuart would have been in serious trouble. Munford could have been taken from behind, and there would have been little Stuart could have done about it. Chambliss, who had been instructed to watch Thoroughfare Gap, offered only a token resistance to Duffié, allowing the Rhode Islanders to reach Middleburg virtually unmolested.[15] Unlike Breathed's, McGregor's Battery, which accompanied Chambliss, does not appear to have been engaged at any time during Duffié's advance to Middleburg and his subsequent destruction.

Stuart began plotting that destruction as soon as he was safely away from Middleburg. He rode toward Rector's Crossroads, where he knew he would find Brig. Gen. Beverly H. Robertson's Brigade and Moorman's Battery. A courier sent ahead soon had the North Carolinians on the road to Middleburg. Moorman's Battery trotted along in the rear of the column without the urgency of its cavalry brethren. It would reach Middleburg on the night of the seventeenth to eighteenth, but would not contribute in the effort against Duffié.[16]

The Rhode Islanders' success on the seventeenth did not last through the morning hours of the eighteenth. Stuart had been quick to realize he was dealing with a small, isolated command with limited options—fight it out to the bitter end, scatter, or surrender. His unhesitating action in bringing Robertson forward proved his confidence in dealing with the blue interlopers. Furthermore, he knew Chambliss could not be far afield and wanted a quick end to the enemy presence in the town, especially with Gregg breathing down his neck at Aldie. Duffié came to the same conclusions about his choices as Stuart had. While some of his men fought, others did their best to escape. Assailed from all points, the troopers of the 1st Rhode Island did all they could do, which undoubtedly included uttering a few select words about General Pleasonton's parentage. It was a sad affair, paid for with the lives of gallant men.

That the horse artillery failed to participate in the rout of the 1st Rhode Island most likely was due to its lack of speed. Duffié's men had ridden hard and fast to reach Middleburg, leaving Chambliss to play catch-up. McGregor simply could not keep pace with the cavalry. The same was true of Moorman. The sense of urgency Stuart felt in bringing up Robertson caused the brigade to outmarch the artillery. Had Stuart believed he could take his time in dealing with Duffié, the horse artillery could have reduced the number of casualties on both sides. One blast down the road into the Federals' makeshift barricades might have convinced the bluecoats of their hopeless situation much earlier. As it was, Stuart reoccupied Middleburg and had his command more concentrated for whatever the rest of the day might bring. Fitz Lee's Brigade (Munford) and Breathed's Battery were stationed at Union. Robertson and Chambliss, with Moorman's and McGregor's Batteries, camped at Middleburg. "Grumble" Jones's Brigade, including Chew's Battery, was on the way and would arrive the next day. This concentration put four horse batteries within supporting distance of each other. Breathed already had gotten in his licks. McGregor, Moorman, and Chew would have their chance soon.

Hampton's Brigade and Hart's Battery had been on their way to rejoin Stuart, but Stuart received information that revealed a Federal reconnaissance to Warrenton and Culpeper was being contemplated. Hampton was directed to oppose such a move. On the seventeenth, while the Aldie fight raged, Hampton clashed with the 1st Vermont and 1st West Virginia Cavalry under Col. Othneil De Forest near Warrenton. These regiments were a part of Maj. Gen. Julius Stahel's Cavalry Brigade, stationed in Washington City. Pleasonton had drawn on them to bolster his own forces in his search for Lee's infantry. After the brief affair, De Forest reported that he had driven back Hampton to within a mile of the town, only breaking off the fight for fear of being enveloped. He claimed that Hampton had between 5,000 and 6,000 men.[17] No mention was made of encountering any artillery, so Hart's Battery most likely was not involved. It was well that they were not. They would need every shell in their caissons before too long. Once De Forest had gone his way, Hampton turned and rode north to rendezvous with Stuart.

On the morning of the eighteenth, the Confederate cavalry chieftain once again faced another enemy advance. As day dawned, Stuart had possession of Middleburg, following Duffié's ouster. Pleasonton had taken a few hours to realize that all he had won on the seventeenth was Aldie Gap. He had not one shred of information that would help Hooker fathom Lee's intentions. Still under pressure from his superiors, at 7:00 A.M. on the eighteenth Pleasonton pushed Col. J. Irvin Gregg's Brigade down the Little River Turnpike through Aldie toward Middleburg, while Col. William Gamble's Brigade rode out on the Snickersville Turnpike. Gregg ran into Stuart's pickets east of Middleburg, and a lengthy skirmish erupted. From 10:00 A.M. to 3:00 P.M., the two combatants traded shots at a distance. Mounted charges such as those of the seventeenth were not the highlights of this day's fighting. Gregg brought up a section of Battery C, 3rd U.S. Artillery, under Lt. James Lancaster, which shelled Stuart's troopers. The Confederate horse batteries remained silent.

Stuart's plan was to retire slowly before the enemy's skirmishers and avoid a general engagement. In this he succeeded, but being unwilling to submit Middleburg to a bombardment, he did not bring his artillery into action and gave the town up to the Federals. Stuart pulled back to a ridge west of town known as Mount Defiance. Late in the afternoon, the Yanks, who seemed equally reluctant to start a full-fledged ruckus with the Rebs, withdrew through Middleburg and camped about a mile and a half from town. Gamble's column returned to Aldie about 9:00 P.M., having scrapped with Munford's pickets most of the day. When the Confederate resistance had stiffened, Gamble thought it was better to retreat than push on. He was a long way from any supporting troops and did not want to end up another Duffié. As the sun slipped down behind the mountains, Stuart had the satisfaction of knowing that he had fended off prying blue eyes for one more day. Pleasonton, on the other hand, had exactly what he had started the day with—nothing. His orders remained unchanged, however. With the dawn, he would once more cross sabers with Stuart in an attempt to learn what Lee was up to.

The Union cavalry's initial movements on the nineteenth would resemble those of the previous day. Col. J. Irvin Gregg's Brigade, supported by Kilpatrick, would push through Middleburg while Brig. Gen. John Buford's division endeavored to turn Stuart's northern flank. Waiting in the wings would be elements of three Federal infantry corps should Pleasonton's troopers discover the presence of Lee's infantry. The number of troops Hooker committed to Pleasonton's advance indicated the importance the Union army's commander attached to the reconnaissance in force. Hooker could not formulate any plans to counter Lee's movements if he remained uninformed. His frustration was beginning to show.

Stuart's pickets met and threw back Gregg's first attempt to recapture Middleburg, which the Confederates had reoccupied during the night. A second, more coordinated attack succeeded in driving the Rebels back to their Mount Defiance position, which was somewhat formidable. Open fields and woods separated by stone fences checkered the ground between the town and the hill where the Confederates waited. The Little River Turnpike climbed the rise through two deep cuts. Running parallel to the road were stone fences. The northern fence was strengthened by another perpendicular fence that formed an L and gave defenders an excellent field of fire down the turnpike. The position was naturally strong, and if Stuart's troopers fought as they had at Aldie, their Union counterparts were in for another difficult day.

On the crest of Mount Defiance, south of the turnpike, stood a blacksmith's shop. Before it ran a small lane. Here, planting one gun on the turnpike, McGregor's Battery unlimbered and prepared for action. Moorman's Battery was nearby to lend support if necessary.[18] To its right, east of the lane, Robertson's two North Carolina regiments occupied a wood. The 2nd North Carolina, stationed in the rear of McGregor, supported the battery. The 9th and 13th Virginia from Chambliss's Brigade took position north of the turnpike. Stuart believed himself ready.

Once Colonel Gregg had possession of Middleburg, he pushed out his lines on either side of the road and began sniping at the Rebs to his front. Kilpatrick came up and placed Lt. William Fuller's Battery C, 3rd U.S. Artillery, in position on a ridge west of the town. McGregor's guns were already raking Gregg's skirmishers with canister. Fuller returned the favor by concentrating his fire on the Confederate skirmish line.[19] Gregg hesitated, studying the enemy's position and strength. The artillery and skirmishers continued to bang away, but no advance came from either side. Concerned for his flanks, Gregg spread out virtually his entire brigade as skirmishers.[20] Then Brig. Gen. David McM. Gregg rode onto the field. He told Colonel Gregg not to worry about his flanks and to attack Stuart's center. Before long, the Federals were advancing on both sides of the pike.

Some of Robertson's skirmishers had taken cover in a small cemetery to the right of their main line. They greeted the oncoming Federals with a concentrated fire that brought the bluecoats up short, but only for a moment. Dismounted troopers of the 4th Pennsylvania stormed the cemetery and drove out the Confederates. Some of the bluecoats took possession of the nearby Cocke house and opened fire on Robertson's men in the woods where they had retreated. The Yankees' presence rapidly came to the attention of McGregor, who turned a gun on the house. After a few well-placed rounds, the Federals tumbled out and sought cover elsewhere.

The determined attack on Robertson was gaining ground and threatened the entire Confederate position. Colonel Gregg, following General Gregg's suggestions, hurled his regiments toward the enemy's main line and McGregor's guns on the ridge. McGregor gave them shell in an effort to slow or break the blue lines. At least one piece found its mark, literally. Lt. Mark Neville of the 1st Maine tumbled to the ground, a fragment in his temple.[21] So swift was the attack, however, that McGregor's guns could not fire a second time before the Federals were in the woods on their right. Robertson's men met them but gave way. They were driven out of the woods to the stone fence that bordered the lane. Again the Federals struck, and again the North Carolinians broke. Even as Stuart's right fell apart, his left struggled to hold on.

Simultaneously with the attack on Robertson, Kilpatrick's 6th Ohio and 2nd New York charged Chambliss's men, huddled behind the stone fences north of the pike. On the road itself, elements from Gregg's 1st Maine thundered forward in a mounted charge that was hauntingly reminiscent of those at Aldie. This time, though, the outcome was different. The determined Federals absorbed the Confederates' carbine fire and surged up to McGregor's guns. The fighting swirled around the gun on the pike. The cannoneers fought with whatever was at hand. It was Fleetwood Hill all over again—cannoneers against cavalry. It appeared that McGregor was about to lose one gun, if not the whole battery.

To the rescue came the 9th Virginia.[22] Slashing into the road, portions of the regiment crashed into the enemy in the woods to the battery's right, while others met the charging Federals in a melee of flashing sabers and barking pistols around the artillery. The 9th's charge saved McGregor's guns.[23] As the gray tide swept the road clear of blue troopers and charged after them down the road, McGregor's cannoneers began to limber their pieces. They paused only long enough to deliver one blast into the onrushing 10th New York, which had repulsed the 9th and was now charging up the road. That last round trimmed the battery's escape time to a precious few seconds. Its salvation was assured when the Federals topped the ridge and saw Stuart's reserves ready to contest any further advance. McGregor galloped to safety. Stuart, minus his gigantic Prussian staff officer, Maj. Heros von Borcke, who was seriously wounded at his side, took up a new position on the next ridge to the west. Gregg chose not to pursue.

While Stuart and Gregg wrestled with each other for possession of Mount Defiance, other events were unfolding to the north. Brig. Gen. John Buford, with two of his three brigades, had ridden with Gregg as far as Middleburg. There Buford took Col. William Gamble's Brigade and Maj. Charles J. Whiting's Brigade of Regulars and turned north. His goal was to flank Stuart and come down on his rear. The first sign of resistance came at Benton's Bridge over Goose Creek, about a mile and a half from Middleburg, where Confederate pickets were encountered. The Yanks crossed the creek under fire and pushed ahead. Col. Thomas Rosser of the 5th Virginia opposed Buford's further advance at the Pot House, about two miles southeast of Union and three miles north of Middleburg.

Stuart did not want a second battle on his hands and had ordered that the Federals be delayed but not fully engaged. Breathed's Battery was not called on to assist in this tactic, nor was Chew's, which had passed through Union with Jones's Brigade late on the eighteenth.[24] The only reinforcements Rosser received were Lt. Col. Thomas Marshall's 7th Virginia from Jones's Brigade. The 7th's sharpshooters did good service, and Marshall ordered a charge, which quickly came upon Buford's main line and just as quickly retreated. The presence of three guns from Capt. William M. Graham's Battery K, 1st U.S. Artillery, convinced Marshall that he could do little more than he had done. Buford was never in any danger from the two regiments facing him but did not have the opportunity to do any further damage. Following orders he received, Buford sent the Regulars south, where they clashed briefly with Stuart in his new position west of Mount Defiance. The fighting around the Pot House came to an end as Buford led Gamble's Brigade back to Aldie. Little had been accomplished. Stuart had once more fulfilled his mission.

Wade Hampton's Brigade and Hart's Battery had a difficult march amid a drenching rain but at last joined Stuart during the night of the nineteenth. Stuart now could muster five brigades and five batteries of horse artillery. Hampton's weary troopers and those of the other brigades settled down and set themselves to the task of capturing as good a night's sleep as possible, considering the soggy conditions. Gunner Neese of Chew's Battery had the luxury of being holed up in a barn in Union. Before dropping off to sleep he noticed that "General Jones came into the barn and slept on the straw with us, just like a horse artilleryman."[25]

Neese's diary notation for the twentieth was brief and to the point: "All quiet along the lines in front. Rained hard all day and we remained in the barn here at Union."[26] The rain gave the opposing forces a respite after three days of fighting. The ground was washed of the spilt blood as if nature were cleansing itself. The opportunity of rest for the men at the front did not trickle upward. At higher echelons, officers were preparing to renew the contest once the rain abated. On a day when the guns fell silent, Pleasonton found himself still under verbal fire from his superiors. An unhappy Hooker had yet to receive what he could accept as solid information about Lee's army. The Federal commander intended to share his unhappiness with others, notably Pleasonton. Convinced that he was facing mounted infantry, the Union cavalry's commander-in-chief had asked for infantry support as early as the seventeenth. Seeking any means to break through Stuart's cavalry curtain, Hooker acceded to Pleasonton's request. Col. Strong Vincent's Brigade of Brig. Gen. James Barnes's division of Maj. Gen. George G. Meade's V Corps reported to Pleasonton on the morning of the twenty-first. Pleasonton had used up his allotment of excuses. Hooker wanted action, and he wanted it immediately. The combined Federal infantry, cavalry, and artillery force lurched forward in the darkness toward Stuart.

The Confederates waited along the Little River Turnpike about two miles west of Middleburg. Stuart had Robertson's Brigade and Hampton's, the latter missing the 1st South Carolina and the Phillips Legion. Hampton's four regiments straddled the road, with the 1st North Carolina and the Jeff Davis Legion to the south and the 2nd South Carolina and the Cobb Legion to the north. Robertson was off to Hampton's left guarding the Millville Road. Captain Hart with Lt. Frank Bamberg's section of the battery took position about seventy-five yards north of the pike.[27] Bamberg had to wait only about half an hour, when the Yankees came into range. He greeted them with a salvo from his two guns. The peaceful quietude of the beautiful Sabbath morning was shattered as Lt. H. C. Meinell's section of Lt. William Fuller's Battery C, 3rd U.S. Artillery, hurled the challenge back at Bamberg.

The Federal attack force was split by the pike, with Vincent's infantry south of the road and David McM. Gregg's cavalry to the north. As the cavalry and infantry moved into position, Pleasonton called for another section of artillery. Fuller responded by sending forward his four remaining guns. Bamberg already had dueled with Meinell long enough to have expended about seventy-five rounds. Just after Fuller's other guns came onto the field, one of Bamberg's pieces, designated the battery's number four gun, broke its axle tree from recoil. The wood around it held together so that the carriage was mobile but useless for fighting. As the gun's crew left the field, with the tube on a caisson, they passed Lt. Edwin L. Halsey's section on its way to the front.[28] The men greeted each other as they crossed Cromwell's Run 600 yards in rear of where Bamberg's lone piece continued the unequal duel with Fuller.[29] There were six guns opposing Bamberg until Halsey joined him. The three Confederate cannons barked their defiance as the infantry and cavalry skirmished beneath the arcing shells.

Hart's adventures were just beginning. He scarcely had put his three guns in line and begun to fire when the number two gun from Halsey's section broke its axle from recoil. It, too, left the field on its caisson.[30] Hart could do little more than watch his battery disintegrate. Enemy fire was one thing, but to lose two guns in the same engagement to broken axles was almost beyond belief. Still Fuller's shells kept dropping ever closer as his gunners found the range, so Hart could spend little time pondering his misfortune. The two remaining guns would have to uphold the battery's reputation.

By now Pleasonton was ready for his big push. His men had skirmished with Stuart's dismounted troopers for an hour, and the time had come to drive them off their ridge. Vincent's infantry went forward on the left and Gregg's cavalry on the right. Stuart's line was not long enough and was outflanked. Hart saw what was coming and determined to be ready for the order to withdraw. He limbered one gun and sent it rearward to find a new position from which to cover the second piece as it fell back.[31] Halsey drew the short straw and kept pounding away with his Blakely while Bamberg galloped off down the hill to the creek. The Federals almost were close enough to shake hands with when Halsey began to limber his gun.

All went as smoothly as such things can go when being bombarded by six cannons and shot at by several hundred infantrymen and cavalrymen. The horses were hitched, and the driver poised to dash from the jaws of death or capture when Fuller's artillery got the range. A shell smashed into the ammunition chest, igniting an explosion that killed or wounded every horse pulling the gun.[32] The driver, thrown to the ground and stunned but otherwise unhurt, scrambled to his feet. Miraculously, no one was killed or seriously wounded. Halsey, his beautiful military hat blown from his head, his face blackened, and his uniform singed, stayed down until the caisson that had become a volcano of bursting shells ceased erupting.[33] When he arose, he took in the situation at a glance. For a brief instant, thoughts of how the gun could be saved flashed through his mind, but he knew that with all the horses killed or disabled, there was no hope of pulling the gun to safety. He gave the order, and the crew rode off, leaving the piece to be swept over by Vincent's jubilant infantry. The battalion had lost its first gun.

In the space of half an hour, Hart had had two of his four guns disabled and one captured. Yet he had little time to wonder about his turn of luck or the tendency of the guns of the horse artillery to put themselves out of action at crucial moments. Bamberg, as tenacious as he was, could scarcely hope to oppose the Federal infantry, cavalry, and horse batteries single-handedly. Help was needed. McGregor's and Moorman's Batteries galloped up and joined the unequal contest, taking position on the ridge above Cromwell's Run to cover Stuart's and Hart's withdrawal.[34] The added firepower seemed to make little difference. Gregg and Vincent pushed ahead as Fuller's guns maintained their constant pounding. Stuart attempted to make a stand with the artillery on the high ground west of Cromwell's Run. It was futile. The fighting retreat continued.

Try as they might, McGregor's and Moorman's guns along with Hart's lone piece failed to match Fuller's accuracy. Nor would the enemy's infantry and cavalry be denied. Stuart was forced to fall back a second time. Hart and McGregor limbered up and dashed away. Moorman followed but made another brief stand near Rector's Crossroads.[35] Here, once more, the enemy horse artillery played havoc with its Confederate counterparts. Moorman's Battery was in the act of limbering to the rear when a shell dropped among the guns. The explosion tore Pvt. John T. Edmundson to pieces[36] and crushed the leg of Pvt. Charles D. Saunders, inflicting a mortal wound.[37] Miraculously under such deadly fire, the battery's horses escaped the devastation that had been inflicted on Hart's teams. Moorman managed to gallop after Hart and McGregor, who were already across the bridge over Goose Creek and hurrying to put their pieces in position on the high bank overlooking the bridge. Col. John L.

Black's 1st South Carolina Cavalry covered the artillery's flight to safety, but at a terrible price.

As Black's troopers moved in a column across the bridge, Fuller's Battery took position at Rector's Crossroads and sent a shot into the mass of horses and men. Nine horses crumpled, and Black suffered a wound. The cavalry received a taste of what the horse artillery had endured from the start of the contest. Fuller was at his best and clearly demonstrated the mobility and fire power a horse battery in the hands of a competent officer brought to a field of battle. On this day, the Union horse artillery simply outgunned and outclassed its gray brethren. Even so, the courage of Hart, McGregor, Moorman, and their men could not be questioned, and they were still full of fight.

Moorman wheeled his guns into line atop the steep hill alongside Hart and McGregor, who were preparing once again to test their mettle and their metal against Fuller. Capt. Alanson M. Randol's Batteries E/G, 1st U.S. Artillery, had arrived to reinforce Fuller, giving the Federals twelve pieces.[38] The additional help served to increase the already heated exchange between the opposing batteries. Neither side was willing to call it quits at this juncture, and officers and men alike redoubled their efforts to inflict as much punishment on their opponents as possible.

Unfortunately, the Confederate gunners soon were forced to concentrate on the Federal infantry and cavalry, trying to fight their way across the stream and to ignore the blue artillery. For their part, Fuller's and Randol's crews shifted their fire from Black's regiment to the enemy horse batteries. For upward of two hours, the big guns sent their messengers of death back and forth. At one point, one of McGregor's guns, which had been placed on the reverse slope of the hill with only its muzzle showing, recoiled and rolled 100 feet down the hill.[39] The gunners manhandled the piece back up the slope and positioned it on the crest—a more dangerous post, but one that avoided a repeat of the artillerymen's shortened version of the 100-meter dash.

Despite the Union barrage, casualties were light. Sergeant Shreve of McGregor's Battery took a piece of shrapnel in the leg but refused to leave his post.[40] Moorman's Battery had one man, Pvt. William H. Buchanan, slightly wounded in the hip.[41] Overall, however, Fuller's and Randol's cannoneers did not demonstrate the uncanny accuracy of earlier in the day. For Fuller's men, fatigue was setting in, and Randol's could not find the range. Even so, their fire did not go unnoticed by Hart, McGregor, or Moorman.[42] They knew they were in a one-sided fight as long as their targets remained the enemy's foot and horse soldiers. The unequal contest continued until Stuart recognized that he could not hold the creek line a moment longer. Most of the horse artillery limbered and, with the cavalry, trotted rearward, but one section drew a different assignment.

Lt. John J. Shoemaker and his section of Moorman's Battery received orders to ride north and assist Chambliss in his retreat.[43] A glance across the intervening fields and the knowledge of what the Federal artillery had done to them at Rector's Crossroads deepened the sobriety of the moment. The men realized that the assignment was not going to be a ride in the park. Still, orders were orders. Shoemaker trotted off into no man's land, his thoughts focused on getting through as rapidly as possible. Only 500 yards separated the opposing battle lines, so Shoemaker's move did not go unnoticed and brought immediate attention from the enemy. Whizzing shells and buzzing minié balls entertained the men's ears all the way. The cannoneers had to pause to pull down one of the omnipresent stone fences to get the guns through. Time seemed suspended, but Shoemaker's calm encouragement and the men's solid discipline withstood the test. Thankfully, not a man suffered even so much as a scratch, though nerves certainly were casualties of the experience. The section rendezvoused with Chambliss's Brigade and turned to face John Buford.

From the start, John Buford's division struggled to fulfill its orders to flank Stuart. Because of the scattered condition of his division, Buford did not begin on time. He then had to contend with the terrain and the brigades of Jones and Chambliss. Marching north from Middleburg along Pot House Road, Buford reached Goose Creek. There he took his men off the road south of the stream and led them on a cross-country trek that slowed their march and brought them into a position from which they could see Stuart's flank (Robertson) but could not get at it because of the nature of the ground. Retracing his route, Buford crossed the creek in the face of Confederate skirmishers, who now harassed his advance. The Federals pushed ahead. In a mistaken belief that he had passed Stuart's flank, Buford ordered Maj. Samuel H. Starr's Reserve Brigade and two sections of Capt. William M. Graham's Battery K, 1st U.S. Artillery, to cross the creek at Millville.[44] Too late it was realized that Stuart had already withdrawn past that point. Buford sent Starr on to Gregg and with his remaining two brigades pushed on toward Upperville in the hope of catching Stuart there.[45]

The skirmishers resisting Buford's advance were from Jones's Brigade, stationed around Union. Chambliss had been on Jones's right, connecting him with Robertson, while Jones provided the link between Chambliss and Munford on the Snickerville Turnpike. Stuart, aware that if Hampton and Robertson pulled back, Chambliss and Jones would be left in an exposed position, alerted Chambliss, who in turn notified Jones to retreat toward Upperville. The race was on. To attain the greatest possible speed, Chambliss placed his wagons in the road and his regiments in the fields on either side. Jones did likewise. The formation worked, enabling the two brigades to keep ahead of Buford, but it would exact a price before long. Jones hurried to follow Chambliss west on the Millville Road—the same road on which Buford's column marched. In between the two columns rose the constant crackle of skirmisher fire, as the gray troopers continued to resist Buford in an effort to slow him down and allow the two Confederate brigades time to unite with Stuart. Buford admitted that his advance was "disputed pretty warmly by the enemy," but they did not stop him.[46]

Col. Lunsford Lomax now commanded Chambliss's rear guard. Repeatedly he forced Buford's leading brigade, commanded by Col. William Gamble, to stop and deploy. Aided by Shoemaker's two guns, Lomax and a squadron from the 9th Virginia led by Col. Richard L. T. Beale did all in their power to keep Buford off Chambliss and Jones. The Confederates had to reach the Trappe Road before Buford cut them off. In the distance, the sounds of the fighting along the Little River Turnpike added a sense of urgency to the march. If Stuart failed to hold the intersection of the Trappe Road and the pike, Chambliss and Jones would be caught between Buford and Gregg. That thought hung like a threatening cloud over the column.

At Willisville, Buford made another attempt to aid Gregg, but the terrain played havoc with his formations. The main obstacle was Pantherskin Creek, and in trying to find his way over it to get at Stuart, Buford found instead a more accessible target. A line of wagons and troops in the distance was making for Ashby's Gap. Buford sent his brigades in that direction and shortly became engaged with the enemy. The discovery of a farm lane connecting the Trappe Road and the Green Garden Road near Kinchloe's Mill afforded an excellent opportunity to reach the Trappe Road and cut off the Confederates' retreat. Buford moved quickly to take advantage of his discovery.

The troops and wagons Buford had spotted belonged to Chambliss, who gained awareness of the Federal threat in time to take countermeasures. Like two antagonists facing each other across a chessboard, Buford and Chambliss had moved their "pieces" here and there in hopes of obtaining some advantage. Chambliss had had a long, hard day already. He had reached the point where a draw looked appealing. However, Buford's latest gambit, which held dire consequences for the Rebel cavalry, had to be met immediately and forcefully or Chambliss was checkmated.

Chambliss made his decisions in seconds. He sent the wagons off the road on a cross-country jaunt that would gain the Little River Turnpike farther west of the Trappe Road intersection. Then, as the 2nd North Carolina and 10th Virginia rode in the fields east of the Trappe Road, Gamble's skirmishers opened fire, and Gamble charged with the 3rd Indiana and 8th and 12th Illinois. Hemmed in by the stone fences and unable to retreat, the Carolinians launched themselves in a countercharge to gain their comrades a few precious minutes. Shoemaker's section, backed by the 9th Virginia, unlimbered in a field to the right of the road and opened fire.[47]

Jones's Brigade was just turning off the road to follow Chambliss when Gamble's Brigade attacked. With his regiments strung out in column, Jones could do little to help Chambliss. The only force close at hand that could avert disaster was the horse artillery. Captain Chew, riding with his battery in the road between Jones's regiments, saw at a glance what had to be done. He ordered the battery to the left off the road and down through a field for about half a mile to a stone wall, where he unlimbered. Cannon mouths protruded over the wall and belched forth flame and destruction. Even as Chew fired, the Federals swerved and came at the guns. The battery's first shells proved accurate as Gamble's horse went down, throwing its rider. Col. David Clendennin of the 8th Illinois and his horse were both wounded.[48] Pvt. Charles McVicar of the battery remembered "firing faster than [he] ever saw artillery fire."[49]

Shoemaker's section exhausted its ammunition and, accompanied by the 9th Virginia, started out after the wagon train.[50] Back at the stone wall, Chew continued the struggle. Gamble's regiments rode through the storm of iron up to the wall and fired over it into the faces of Chew's begrimed gunners. But the Federals could not get over the wall and take the guns. Chew was in trouble. Sooner or later, the Yanks might send dismounted skirmishers in the wake of their mounted regiments. Assistance came in the form of Capt. Charles T. O'Ferrall of the 12th Virginia, who was sent charging into the fray by his commander, Lt. Col. Thomas B. Massie. O'Ferrall's attack ran into a buzzsaw and was blunted and thrown back. Lt. Col. Oliver Funsten and elements of the 11th Virginia now took up the challenge. He soon received support from the 7th Virginia, which Jones sent charging this way and that across the fields in an effort to stem the Yankee onslaught. Chew knew the time had come to pull back. McVicar wrote of the fighting that swirled around him:

> John William Henry and I were ordered to open a rail fence. He was swinging the last rail when shot through the head and fell on me. He was as good and brave a young man as we had in the company. He was from Jefferson County and was anxiously expecting to go home soon. God Bless Him. I pulled his body out of the way into a fence corner. His brother-in-law from the first section got the body and said he would take it home and fight no more and we never saw John Lindsay again.
>
> The first section ran through the gap in that little field. Major Charles O'Ferrall[51] used our gap and with saber drawn, led a squad to charge the fence. He was shot through the body and several men are taking him back. We unlimbered and gave them ten rounds. The bullets are flying as thick as hail around us. The second section had turned to the right and opened. We were ordered back at a run. Our horses were sent back, passed the second section about 100 yards and opened. The second section came back under our fire.[52]

After the war, Chew described the fight in a letter to Capt. William N. McDonald:

> When we reached the hill opposite the position of the enemy a squadron of our cavalry, I think under Capt. Hatcher, had let down the fence and charged in the direction of Upperville. Our cavalry was forming on the west side of the road in considerable confusion. We put the guns on the east side of the road, but finding this position would not be supported, I had a gap let down in the fence on the west side of the road, and put my guns into position so as to command the gap and the fields in front.
>
> The enemy frequently charged up to the stone fence, but it was easy to make the gap so hot with canister that they would not venture across. Our cavalry had formed in the field behind us, and after remaining there for some time commenced to move off towards the Upperville turnpike. The guns were served with deadly effect, and kept the enemy completely in check until we had an opportunity to retire.[53]

From his new position on a knoll west of the Trappe Road, Chew continued pounding Gamble's men. The guns did fearful execution. In one instance, Lt. George W. Beale of the 9th Virginia saw a rider pass in front of the guns just as they were fired. A solid shot decapitated the trooper, whose horse continued on riderless.[54]

The charging Southern squadrons and Chew's devastating fire took their toll on Gamble's Brigade. Weary and fought out, Gamble pulled back to his jumping-off point and allowed Col. Thomas Devin's Brigade to have a go at the Rebels. Lt. Theophilus B. von Michalowski, with the third section of Graham's Battery K, 1st U.S. Artillery, also came onto the field and unlimbered. Chew was not oblivious to Devin's arrival and greeted the newcomer with a few salvos. The shells rained down among the forming Federals. Devin ordered the 17th Pennsylvania Cavalry to charge and take the enemy battery. The Keystone Staters responded but saw their gallant effort frustrated by the same stone fences that had blunted Gamble's regiments.

Chew's sweating gunners had accomplished all that could have been asked of them. It was time to get out. Limbering the still-smoking guns, the men vaulted into their saddles and galloped off on the same cross-country jaunt Chambliss's column had made before them. The artillery's work was not yet finished, however. Replenishing empty ammunition chests while bouncing on horseback or limber could not have been the favorite pastime of any of the men, but the situation demanded it, and somehow the men succeeded. The filled chests would be needed before too long. Ashby's Gap loomed ahead and still had to be held.

The struggle along the Trappe Road was mirrored on the Little River Turnpike by Stuart's fight to hold back Gregg. After the Goose Creek Bridge line was breached, Hampton and Robertson withdrew to Upperville, making a stand just east of the town. Hart, McGregor, and Moorman were pressed so hard by the oncoming enemy and became so disordered that they could not take a position. They continued on through Upperville to Ashby's Gap. Hampton would have to face the Federals without artillery.[55] Grimly, he placed his men south of the pike on Vineyard Hill. Robertson was north of the road with his flank stretched toward Pantherskin Creek.

Gregg came on with the same kind of determination he had exhibited all day. By the time he reached the outskirts of Upperville and faced Hampton and Robertson, Gregg's artillery consisted of Fuller's Battery C, 3rd U.S. Artillery; Randol's Batteries E/G, 1st U.S. Artillery; two sections of Graham's Battery K, 1st U.S. Artillery; and Lt. John H. Calef's Battery A, 2nd U.S. Artillery—a total of twenty-two guns.[56] The batteries opened an intense fire, and the cavalry went right at their graybacked foes. The smell of victory spurred the Federals to fight all the harder. They had chased Stuart for many miles and were determined to finish him.

Robertson's Brigade was still shaky. As the Federals charged, the North Carolinians turned their backs to the foe and hightailed it to the rear. Their rally along the Trappe Road was only temporary. Hampton's troopers fought with steel-eyed resolution. The odds were overwhelming, but Upperville would not be given up without exacting a price. Smoke, dust, lead, and iron engulfed the gray cavalrymen. Sabers clashed and pistols barked. Delay the enemy they might; defeat them—not this day. After fighting like a trooper among his gallant cavalry, Stuart ordered a retreat to Ashby's Gap. Upperville was abandoned to the enemy.[57] The Confederates rode for the gap, and though they did not run, most would admit they hurried.

Chew's Battery had unlimbered on a ridge near Paris, a small hamlet east of the gap, and had gone into battery. Like a bulldog, Gregg did not want to let go. His troopers snapped at Robertson's heels as the North Carolinians fought a rear-guard action to give Stuart time to reach the ridge. Robertson finally broke away. Still Gregg pursued. Charles McVicar of Chew's Battery remembered the solid blue column marching up the pike toward the gap. At three-quarters of a mile, Chew opened fire. Thirty rounds convinced Gregg it was time to call it quits. McGregor, Moorman, and Hart put their guns in line next to Chew.[58] Col. Henry C. Cabell's Artillery Battalion and Brig. Gen. Joseph B. Kershaw's Brigade of infantry of Maj. Gen. Lafayette McLaws's division stood ready to assist Beckham's exhausted cannoneers and Stuart's weary horsemen if the enemy pressed on. They did not. Where saber, pistol, shot, and shell failed to gain the victory, exhaustion conquered. Both Yankee and Rebel could fight no more.

As the firing died away, the Federals trotted back to Upperville. Pleasonton, satisfied "that the enemy had no infantry force in the Loudoun Valley," proceeded to give up all the ground he had won during the long, hot day.[59] The Federal cavalry chieftain later stated in a report to army headquarters that a large infantry camp in the Shenandoah Valley was viewed from the top of the mountain north of Ashby's Gap. Buford and a company from the 8th New York Cavalry conducted the reconnaissance. Although this would indicate that Pleasonton had succeeded in his mission and that Stuart had failed in his, the information was actually of small value to Hooker. It contained none of the vital facts that could help him determine a course of action. Pleasonton's retreat negated any chance of confirming or adding to what had already been observed. Stuart had fulfilled his orders, but the cost was high.

The battles of Aldie, Middleburg, and Upperville, coming on the heels of Brandy Station, clearly demonstrated the rise of the Federal cavalry arm. The all-day running fight of the twenty-first served to underscore that fact. Many of the men in the Confederate units that participated in the action were angry, embarrassed, and not a little ashamed of the whipping they had received. Used to wielding the whip, it was an altogether humiliating experience to have it land on their backs. For the men of Beckham's Battalion, there was the added humiliation of the loss of a gun. Beyond that, there was also the knowledge that the Federal horse batteries were in every way their equals and in at least one respect—the quality of their guns and ammunition—their superiors.

The pounding the Stuart Horse Artillery received from June 9 through June 21 might have demoralized many other units. Certainly, the loss in men, horses, and equipment was bad enough, but the manner in which those losses had occurred was galling. On many of the fields, the battalion's targets had been restricted to the blue cavalry simply because of the sheer numbers they brought on the field. Stuart's regiments could not counter such numbers without artillery support. Unfortunately, that left the Federal batteries free to concentrate on the gray horse artillery, which they did effectively. On the few occasions Beckham's gunners had opportunities to answer the enemy's fire, they had been largely ineffective.[60] Yet the batteries did fulfill their role. Without their grim determination and courage, Stuart could not have delayed Pleasonton's force as long he had. Though bruised and battered, the battalion would somehow prepare itself for what was to come. Pelham's legacy lay in the never-say-die spirit he infused into his men. That would see them through whatever lay ahead.

June 22 dawned with Stuart following up Pleasonton's retiring columns. Upperville, Goose Creek Bridge, and Rector's Crossroads were passed before the Federals turned to make a brief stand before Middleburg. Along the way, the carnage of the previous day's fighting lay on both sides of the pike. Chew's, McGregor's, and Moorman's Batteries accompanied the advance.[61] Outside Middleburg, the batteries exchanged shots with a Federal battery.[62] The contest was brief, as the Yanks were intent on pulling back to Aldie. Stuart followed them through Middleburg and had McGregor's Battery give them a few parting shots.[63] Then he let them go and rode back to Rector's Crossroads, where he established his camp, leaving Moorman's Battery on picket duty.[64]

To the north, Rosser's 5th Virginia of Munford's command began skirmishing with pickets from Col. Thomas Devin's Brigade. The Snickersville Turnpike had seen little action on the twenty-first. Breathed had not had the opportunity to use his guns since the nineteenth at Aldie. He did not get the chance this day either. Devin fed in more men, and Rosser countered with his whole regiment. The bluecoats were thrown back and chased for about a mile, when Maj. John Eells, who led the advance, was killed. Rosser pulled up and watched Devin's troopers ride out of sight. Stuart's mission to screen the movement of Lee's infantry ended almost exactly where it had started on the nineteenth. Now the time had come for Lee and Stuart to decide the cavalry's next move.

CHAPTER 17

Toward Gettysburg

"I am doing all I can to squelch this Rebellion."

Over the next few days, as the role of the cavalry in the upcoming invasion was considered and decided upon, the horse artillery made repairs and preparations for continuing the campaign. Even though there was much to be done, some of the men found time to write loved ones of the momentous events through which they had passed and their feelings about what the future held in store. One such man was Lt. Charles R. Phelps of Moorman's Battery.

On Picket Near Upperville
Fauquier Co. June 25th 1863

Dear Aunt

This is the first opportunity I have had to write you since the receipt of your letter the day I left Brandy Station (Culpeper). We left Brandy Station the 16th and arrived at Middleburg the 18th and have had several fights with the Yankee Cavalry. On Thursday 20th [18th] had a fight and run the Yankees back several miles and took about 200 prisoners. On Friday [19th] had a skirmish all day with Artillery and Cavalry. On Sunday last [21st] we commenced the fight near Middleburg and fell back to Upperville in the afternoon, a distance of 8 miles. This was the heaviest fight since the action at Brandy Station. The loss on both sides was quite heavy, but I think the Yankee loss much greater than ours. On Monday morning [22nd] we again attacked them, and ran them to beyond Middleburg where the fight commenced the day before. Everything is quiet here at this time though I believe Stuart is now engaged at Thoroughfare Gap as he left us with a Brigade to guard the Gap (Ashby's) in the mountain.

On Sunday we lost two men killed and three wounded slightly in our Co. Tho's Edmonds [Pvt. John T. Edmundson] was killed, a shell striking him literally tearing him to pieces. The shell or a portion of it struck Charlie [Pvt. Charles D.] Saunders in the leg above knee crushing it in an awful manner. I had been very unwell for several days and was not in action that day. I assisted in taking him to the rear to Upperville where he had every attention possible to be given to him. The Surgeon was with him promptly but could do nothing for him as he never rallied after he was wounded. He had lost so much blood and had sunk so low, that amputation could not be performed. I was very fortunate in making the acquaintance of the Rev. George W. Harris, a Methodist Minister, who rendered us a great service in attending to Charlie, as the Yanks charged us thru the town and we all had to leave or be taken prisoners. Mr. Harris stayed with him until he died which was about an hour after we left and had him properly shrouded and put in an elegant coffin. Fortunately the next morning we attacked the Yankees and ran them off, and Joseph Chalmers & myself stopped in Upperville and succeeded in getting a wagon to take the body to Culpeper Co. Ho. It left here on Tuesday in charge of his servant John and should reach home today. John stayed with Charlie until he died.[1] The Yankees tried hard to get him off, but he told them he was free and would not leave.

In regard to Anthony Dornin,[2] I have written a letter to Mr. George Kinnear & told him to show a portion of it to Tho's D. [Dornin] detailing the circumstances of his death. I am very sorry indeed that they did not hear of his death until he reached Lynchburg. As I wrote a dispatch and gave it to [Pvt. John] Herley who I also got to have his coffin made. After putting it on the cars he started to [the] telegraph office where he met Capt. M. [Moorman] who took my dispatch from him and substituted one of his own, which was put in the office & paid for by me. This is why it was not received, for I believe if my dispatch had been taken to office it would have reached Lynchburg, as I am well acquainted with the operator, and I know he would have put my message through. I asked Capt. M. about this. He said he telegraphed but would not say anything about my message. Why he did this I cannot tell, but it is in keeping with his whole conduct. I suppose he thought he had an opportunity of doing something for the family without costing him anything. I believe he has written to Mrs. Dornin. I hope the family are satisfied that I have done everything possible under the circumstances. I would also like to write a letter to Mrs. D. [Dornin] but I have already detailed the circumstances to Geo. Kinnear & I suppose they are known by now. I sent Anthony's pocket book containing $15 to his brother by Mrs. Isa Pettyjohn which I hope has come to hand. I would stake that Capt. M. got Mr. John Massie to take charge of the body, that is he said so.

I cannot hear anything from the various seats of war. Rumor has it here that Ewell is doing wonders in Maryland & that Johnson & Smith has whipped Grant, but we can hear nothing reliable. I think we will move in a day or two towards My Maryland as all our forces have passed the Blue Ridge on their way in that direction. Harvey was 6 miles from here Monday and quite well. I saw him at Culpeper Co. Ho. before I left. Say to Miss Wiatt I do not want to hear of her making herself sick by attending the sick. I am doing all I can to squelch this Rebellion so I can come home and have a good time generally, and I do not want her to be laid up—not even with [word illegible]. I had much rather hear of her marrying some good man, even if he cannot shake hands straight, as there would be some chance for me to get the situation or measure of plank etc. when I return. I send Sallie a valentine from a Yankee knapsack. Love to all and believe me yours truly. C. R. P.

Just ordered to Ashby's Gap to camp [word illegible]. This letter must do for both as my last [word illegible] is directed to Sister.

Do not say anything about the portion concerning Capt. Moorman as I wish to have peace in the family for the present.[3]

Phelps may have been able to keep "peace in the family" of his battery, but the war rolled on around him without pause.

Once Stuart decided on his next move, the cavalry division split up. At 1:00 A.M. on June 25, Stuart, with the brigades of Hampton, Chambliss, and Fitz Lee, who now returned and assumed command of his brigade from Munford, started out on his most controversial ride of the war. Trotting along with him were six guns of the Stuart Horse Artillery, Breathed's Battery, and a section of McGregor's Battery.[4] Proceeding through Glasscock's Gap, Stuart and company ran into elements of Maj. Gen. Winfield S. Hancock's II Corps near Haymarket. The Union infantry was marching north, and Stuart determined to harass the column and gain some information. Breathed unlimbered and dropped several shells into the unsuspecting Federals. Chaos reigned as men and horses scattered. The surprise was short-lived, however. The panicked blue soldiers soon sorted themselves out, formed lines of battle, and advanced. Stuart had seen all he needed and ordered Breathed to pull out. The gray riders retreated to Buckland, where they grazed their horses while Fitz Lee scouted for another route that was not occupied by the enemy.

The next obstacle Stuart encountered was the Potomac River. Once the decision was made to ride around the Army of the Potomac as it maneuvered northward, the necessity of finding a ford across the river between the Yankees and Washington City became paramount. Rowser's Ford appeared a likely spot for the crossing, but a brief examination of the ford showed it impassable for the artillery and ambulances that accompanied the column. Another ford was checked but was no better than Rowser's, which became Stuart's choice. When the horse artillery reached the ford, the men emptied the caissons and distributed the ammunition among the cavalry, which carried it over. The guns and caissons entered the water and were completely submerged during the entire crossing. By 3:00 A.M. on the twenty-eighth, Stuart's command was on the north shore of the Potomac.

For the greater part of Stuart's ride, the horse artillery had little to do. It was not involved in the capture of the wagon train near Rockville on the twenty-eighth or in the brief clash with elements of the 1st Delaware Cavalry at Westminster on the twenty-ninth.[5] This lack of participation could not be detected in the appearance of the men. They looked like they had seen hard campaigning, which indeed they had. Lt. Francis H. Wigfall of Breathed's Battery described his attire in a letter to his sister:

> I think that when we reached Westminster Md. on Genl. Stuart's expedition round the Yanks I was a little the richest specimen of a Confederate Officer that you, at all events, ever saw. My boots were utterly worn out, my pantaloons were all one big hole as the Irishman would say, my coat was like a beggar's and my hat was actually falling to pieces in addition to lacking its crown which has allowed my hair, not cut since some time before leaving Culpeper, to protrude and gave a highly picturesque finish to my appearance. I fortunately there got a pair of boots a pair of pantaloons and a hat which rendered my condition comparatively better.[6]

On the morning of the thirtieth, Stuart marched for Hanover, Pennsylvania. Brig. Gen. H. Judson Kilpatrick's Union cavalry division got there first. Since fighting at Aldie, Middleburg, and Upperville, Kilpatrick had been placed in command of the 3rd Cavalry Division, which consisted of two brigades, Brig. Gen. Elon J. Farnsworth's 1st Brigade and Brig. Gen. George A. Custer's 2nd Brigade. All were new to their positions. Kilpatrick had assumed command of the division the previous day but had experience in commanding a brigade. Farnsworth and Custer had jumped from captains to brigadier generals virtually overnight. They held promise, but so had many other officers in the Army of the Potomac who were now commanding handfuls of men in faraway outposts or were out of the war entirely. Time would tell if the gamble was worth the risk. The first opportunity to judge was at hand.

Kilpatrick reached Hanover around 8:00 A.M. on the thirtieth. Custer arrived first, to be greeted by the inhabitants with food and refreshments. The feasting and festivities continued for two hours, until the brigade pushed on down the road to Abbottstown. Following in Custer's wake, three of Farnsworth's regiments received equal treatment at the hands of the townspeople. The fourth, the 18th Pennsylvania Cavalry, was the division's rear guard, and while a portion of the unit was receiving its repast, the rest were being entertained in a decidedly different manner. Two small detachments had been sent south to determine if any Confederates were present. Near Gitt's Mill, three miles southwest of Hanover, one of the 18th's scouting parties ran into Confederates and exchanged shots, killing at least one Rebel. The regiment's other detachment encountered the advance of the 13th Virginia Cavalry and was taken prisoner. These two small clashes precipitated the battle of Hanover.

The fighting quickly heated up as both sides fed in reinforcements. The 13th Virginia and the 2nd North Carolina handled the Pennsylvanians roughly, giving Stuart the early advantage. The Carolinians charged into the town, throwing the Keystone Staters into confusion. The Confederates' success lasted but a few minutes. Farnsworth arrived on the scene, put himself at the head of the 5th New York and such elements of the 18th Pennsylvania as could be rallied, and charged back through the town. Their counterattack shattered the 2nd North Carolina and sent it reeling down the Westminster Road. Stuart and members of his staff suddenly found themselves trapped in a field between charging Yankees and a fifteen-foot ditch. Stuart's famed horse, Virginia, took the ditch in a magnificent jump and carried its rider back to where he had placed the two pieces of artillery that had arrived with Chambliss.

The cannoneers of McGregor's Battery had seen the troopers of the 2nd North Carolina come galloping back from the town trailing a long line of bluecoat cavalry.[7] The guns were deployed on a ridge to the right of the road facing Hanover. The position dominated the town. The gunners manned their pieces and sent several shells arcing over the retreating graybacks into the oncoming Federals.[8] This fire and the timely arrival of the rest of Chambliss's Brigade drove Farnsworth back into the streets of Hanover. A lull settled over the field as Stuart and Farnsworth aligned their forces and looked about for reinforcements.

Brig. Gen. George A. Custer, black velvet uniform and all, rode with his Michiganders to bolster Farnsworth's defense. The "Boy General" deployed his regiments on the northwestern side of the town but did nothing that would bring on a renewal of the wild cavalry fight that had rumbled through the streets of Hanover earlier in the day. For a time he was content to sit and watch. The Federal artillery, on the other hand, did not mirror Custer's spectator role. Lt. Alexander C. M. Pennington's Battery M, 2nd U.S. Artillery, and Lt. Samuel S. Elder's Battery, 4th U.S. Artillery, took position on Bunker Hill north of town and immediately commenced firing on the Confederates' position. The bombardment was more harassing fire than preparation for an attack. The long pause continued, interrupted only by the booming of the artillery and the intermittent staccato of skirmisher fire.

Stuart welcomed the delay. He was at a disadvantage because of the extended formation of his column of march. The wagon train had to be guarded, and Stuart had arranged his brigades to do just that. Chambliss had the advance; Fitz Lee guarded the left flank; Hampton brought up the rear. Chambliss's defeat forced Stuart to take a defensive posture. He needed time until Fitz Lee and Hampton could arrive. Sitting near McGregor's section, Stuart watched the gunners run through the drill of loading and firing. They were the only Confederate guns on the field, but their fire had helped turn back Farnsworth. Could they deter the enemy from attacking before Lee and Hampton were up?

The sanguinary artillery duel grew to be a half hour in length; then forty-five minutes; then an hour. During that time, Fitz Lee arrived on Chambliss's left, and at 2:00 P.M., Hampton appeared on the right. With him came Breathed's four guns, which were unlimbered on Mount Olivet.[9] The men rammed the charges home, and the pieces roared to life. Below them in the town, the men of the 1st West Virginia Cavalry of Farnsworth's Brigade soon felt the effects of Breathed's well-directed fire. A Sergeant Collins had his horse killed and his leg nearly severed by one of Breathed's shots.[10] There were other casualties in the form of the town's buildings and trees. Hanover's inhabitants huddled in their cellars, wondering how long the thunder and crash would continue.

Finally, Custer had enough of the stalemate and ordered the 6th Michigan to deploy skirmishers and move out from their position in the general direction of McGregor's section. McGregor and his boys had already welcomed this regiment to the battlefield. As the 6th had come riding along the Hanover Road in a column of fours, McGregor had dropped a few shells on the bluecoats. Several men were wounded, and a Lieutenant Potter of C Troop had his horse killed.[11] McGregor saw them coming. Switching his attention from the other Michigan regiments he had been entertaining, the Alabamian's guns fired shell into the Yanks. The 6th went to ground but did not retreat. Instead, the Westerners crawled forward until they were 300 yards from McGregor's cavalry supports to his front. The Federals rose and delivered a volley that rocked Chambliss's troopers back on their heels and precipitated an undignified skedaddle. McGregor was on his own.

The guns were saved by the tenacity of McGregor and the timely arrival of support from Fitz Lee. Twice more the 6th Michigan came on, only to be pushed back by McGregor and Lee. McGregor's two pieces had been in action since Chambliss's initial repulse. The men were hot, tired, and not a little hungry and thirsty. The suspension of the cavalry fighting in the late morning and early afternoon had given the mounted troops a breather, but the horse artillery had maintained a continuous, if slow, barrage on targets of opportunity or anything that looked menacing for upward of six hours. They were wearing a bit thin. When the 6th Michigan fell back from its third unsuccessful attack of the afternoon, McGregor and company could not have witnessed a more welcome sight. The chance to catch a breath and take a swallow of whatever was at hand did not move the men from their posts, however. If need be, the Yanks would find them ready and waiting should there be a fourth assault.

There wasn't. Custer had chosen not to involve the remainder of his brigade in any of the 6th's attacks, and after the last charge failed, he decided to call it quits. The lack of a renewed Federal offensive did not spur Stuart into opening one of his own. He was satisfied with the day's work. Until night fell, he would counter any threatened movement on Kilpatrick's part but would not attack Hanover again. All he wanted was to break away, find Ewell, deliver the wagons, and reunite with the army. Screened by the same ridge on which McGregor's and Breathed's guns stood, Stuart's wagon train rolled eastward. The firing slowly died away as the shadows lengthened. Hampton would cover the withdrawal. The guns were limbered in the early darkness and slipped away.

The march continued through Jefferson to Dover, which the men reached early on July 1. Breathed placed some guns on a ridge in front of Salem Church overlooking the town.[12] The delegation sent into Dover used the guns' presence to threaten the town's officials into surrendering. It worked, though the asked-for ransom could not be raised. The brief rest in the town's comfortable confines was used to parole prisoners and shop in the local stores. Straw hats, handkerchiefs, cloth, articles of clothing, and several horses were drafted into Confederate service, much to the consternation of the shop owners and townspeople.[13]

Stuart rode on through Dillsburg to Carlisle, where once more the horse artillery was called upon to intimidate the locals. This time, however, the citizenry was bolstered by the presence of Brig. Gen. William F. "Baldy" Smith's 1st Division of the Department of the Susquehanna. Fitz Lee ordered Breathed into battery.[14] The two officers sent to negotiate Smith's surrender threatened to shell the town if Smith refused. The plucky Federal commander replied, "Shell away." Upon receiving Smith's curt answer, Breathed promptly opened up.[15] The bombardment was more for show than effect. After the long fight at Hanover, the artillery's ammunition was running low. Smith's own artillery, Capt. Henry D. Landis's 1st Philadelphia Battery, replied. Breathed's gunners quickly found the range and on their second shot wounded a Corporal Patterson in the right hand, taking off two fingers and damaging the remainder so severely that they had to be amputated the next day.[16] Breathed's cannoneers escaped with one casualty: Pvt. Thomas F. Yates received a wound in the nose.[17]

The United States Cavalry barracks was the main casualty at Carlisle. Stuart ordered the place burned before he moved out. He had received word of the army's location through one of his staff officers and dispatched orders. Breathed limbered his battery and headed south. His destination was the small crossroads town that had suddenly become the hub of the war in the east—Gettysburg.

If nothing else, Stuart's ride was a testament to the endurance of man and horse. When put to the test, the stern character and inner strength of the cavalry had not wavered. Exhausted, saddle sore, hungry, gaunt phantoms of their former selves, Stuart's troopers rose to every challenge encountered on the seemingly endless march. Their record never had shone more brightly. So, too, for Breathed and McGregor. Direct descendants of the "Gallant Pelham," these officers and their men outdid their cavalry comrades. The guns were always where they were needed. Other rides had brought successes, but those successes had not been preceded by days of constant movement and battle. To have endured all that and then meet the demands that Stuart placed on them during this expedition was unprecedented. Critics who pointed their fingers at Stuart after Gettysburg could not do the same for the men who rode with him. They had given their all.

One of those who gave his all was Lieutenant Wigfall of Breathed's Battery. He summed up his impressions of the ride to his sister in a handful of sentences. What he chose to write about was not of the hardships and battles, but of the human element as he encountered it along the way.

> We left Union in Loudoun Co. Va. on that expedition on the morning of the 24th of June and reached the lines of our army at Gettysburg, Adams Co., Pa. late in the afternoon of the 2nd of July. During that time the harness was off the horses only twice. You should have seen the Dutch people in York Pa. turning out with water and milk and bread and butter and "apple butter" for the "rugged rebels." I was quite surprised at the tone of feeling in that part of the State. In two or three instances I found people who seemed really glad to see us and at scores of houses they had refreshments at the door for the soldiers. The people generally seemed not to know exactly what to expect and I don't think would have been at all astonished if every building had been set on fire by us as we reached it, nor would a great many have been surprised if we had concluded the business by massacring the women and children. I stopped at a house near Petersburg in Adams Co. and almost the first question addressed to me by the daughter of the house, a girl of eighteen or twenty and a perfect Yankee, was whether our men would molest the women. I told her not, and she seems to feel considerably reassured. It was this same girl who told me in all seriousness that she has heard, and I believe it, that the Southern women all wore revolvers.[18]

Wigfall's assurances to one "perfect Yankee" girl were probably echoed by other men of the horse artillery and the cavalry to the many civilians whose lives they entered, albeit briefly. They had come to make war, true enough, but not on women and children. Now that they were at last reunited with Lee's army, all they desired was a little food and rest. They managed the former, but the latter remained elusive. There was more fighting ahead.

When Stuart began his ride around Hooker's army, he left the brigades of Jones and Robertson to guard the mountain gaps and follow along after Longstreet. The batteries of horse artillery that remained behind—Chew's, Hart's, Moorman's, and half of McGregor's—were in varying condition. Hart's had been the hardest hit during the fighting around Aldie, Middleburg, and Upperville. It had left for the Valley before Stuart moved out on the twenty-fifth. The battery marched over the mountains in the wake of the army's wagon train and reached Martinsburg on the twenty-sixth.[19] There the command's artisans took possession of the Baltimore & Ohio Railroad's shops and forges. Nothing could be done about the gun that had been lost, but the two disabled pieces could be repaired.[20] Corp. William Arnot, artificers[21] David G. Enseln and John M. Phelps, blacksmith Ephraim Kissell, and Privates Robert M. Arnan, George M. Cannon, Peter Freany, Henry Kennedy, and John F. Phillips were instrumental in returning the damaged guns to service.[22]

The work of repairing the guns took six hours, after which Hart set out to catch the rear of Lee's army.[23] The battery had no escort as it passed through Williamsport, Hagerstown, and Greencastle. On reaching Chambersburg on the twenty-eighth, Hart reported to Lee for assignment. Col. John L. Black of the 1st South Carolina Cavalry, who had been slightly wounded at the Goose Creek bridge fight, had been directed by Lee to organize those of the cavalry with weak horses that Stuart had left behind with his wagons. They had been placed under Longstreet's command. The battery was assigned to Black. Hart's South Carolinians approached Gettysburg on the evening of July 1.

On June 23, Chew's Battery left the camp at Rector's Crossroads and marched north with Jones's Brigade through Union to Snickersville, where it camped in an orchard.[24] Moorman's Battery and the remaining section of McGregor's fell back on the twenty-fifth from Rector's Crossroads to Ashby's Gap with Robertson's Brigade and camped. Little more occurred, with the exception of Chew's Battery receiving its pay for the months of January, February, March, and April, until the twenty-ninth. On that date, in a soaking rain, both Jones and Robertson broke camp, crossed the Shenandoah River, and rode to Berryville. At dark, Moorman's Battery and McGregor's section found themselves about a mile and a half from the town, while Chew's Battery encamped four miles south of Berryville on the Charles Town Pike. The following morning, the column set out for the Potomac, marching through Rippon, Summit Point, Smithfield, and striking the Winchester-Martinsburg Pike at Bunker Hill. Camp was pitched at Martinsburg, where a number of men from Chew's Battery who lived in the area made quick trips home to see their loved ones before returning to the battery the next day.[25]

July 1, 1863, dawned in the lower Valley only minutes after the sun's first rays were visible to thousands of men who would soon be in mortal combat with each other near Gettysburg miles to the northeast. Shortly after crossing the Potomac, Lt. James H. Williams of Chew's Battery took time to jot a little note to his beloved Cora.

> July 1st 1863
>
> My Dear Cora,
>
> We moved from our camps near Martinsburg this morning. We will cross into Md. today. Before leaving my native state I feel as though I must take leave of my friends. When we shall return no one can tell, so good by my dear Cora. I will write as occasion offers and I am sure that did you know the pleasure your letters afford, however distasteful and unpleasant writing me may be, you would arouse yourself occasionally [and] write. Am in command this morning of the Battery[26] and can write no more.[27]

Williams's need to "take leave" of friends and family was a feeling shared throughout Chew's and Jones's commands. Many men left the marching columns for a brief visit to loved ones. Quick, joyous embraces were followed all too soon by tearful partings. For some, it would be the last.

The column crossed the Potomac at Williamsport and pushed on through Greencastle.[28] The men made camp that evening a half mile short of the Pennsylvania line.[29] On the second, the march continued through Franklin County to Chambersburg, where the troopers and artillerymen bivouacked for the night. In the evening, Charles McVicar accompanied Pvt. James M. Homerick, a batterymate, on a visit to some of Homerick's Northern relations. It was an interesting experience for all concerned.

> James Homerick, one of the Battery, and myself walked around to see an uncle of his. This uncle met him at the door, sorry enough to see him in the C.S.A. [word illegible] his cousin came out and shook hands with him with a distant grasp as if he thought the touch would contaminate his contemptible majesty. His aunt would not come out to see him. I was talking to some of the fair sex. They wanted to know why I, so gay a looking chap, came to be among the Rebels. I, of course, pleaded the cause, liberty & honor at stake, our rights trampled on by a set of Monomaniacs. They all wanted to see the war end immediately. I told them as long as 2 of us [were] together we would never give up. They allowed we would have hard fighting. That was what we were used to, of course.[30]

On their way back to their battery, the two artillerymen may have pondered just exactly how much hard fighting lay ahead before the end of the war. Once they returned to camp, only one thing, other than food, was on their minds—sleep. The cold-shoulder greeting they had experienced did not keep them from getting a night's sleep, such as it was.

The bugle blew at 1:00 on the morning of July 3.[31] A quick breakfast, a moment to pack up a few scant belongings, followed by a hitching of horses, and the column moved off at 2:00.[32] Since Robertson and Jones had united at Berryville, the two brigades had marched as one. On this day, they would begin to take different roads. While encamped at Martinsburg, Robertson had received orders to send some of his cavalry to New Guilford Court House in Pennsylvania to relieve elements of Maj. Gen. John B. Hood's infantry that had been stationed there. Upon leaving Chambersburg, Robertson dispatched a portion of his own brigade to carry out this assignment while the rest, with Jones's Brigade, rode on to Cashtown.[33]

Near this hamlet, an order from Lee reached Jones, who was temporarily in command because Robertson was absent. Lee wanted the town of Fairfield occupied to protect the right rear of the army, where Lee's supply train lay vulnerable to attack by an enterprising enemy. Jones determined to act on the order with his brigade and Chew's Battery. Before Jones could leave, Robertson returned and sanctioned the movement. Jones's column trotted off in the direction of Fairfield, not knowing what might be encountered. Chew and his gunners moved along with the troopers.[34]

A little more than half of the distance had been covered when Jones's leading regiment, the 7th Virginia Cavalry, spotted a group of about thirty Federals, who immediately turned and galloped off. This was Company F of the 6th U.S. Cavalry, under Lt. Christian Balder. The Virginians did not hesitate and increased their speed in pursuit. Two miles north of Fairfield, Jones encountered the rest of the 6th. The regiment had taken position behind a post-and-rail fence on a rise known as Mary's Hill, which intersected the Fairfield Road perpendicularly. Jones thrust the 7th Virginia forward in a charge that ended in an embarrassing run for the rear when the Federals caught the leading elements of the regiment in a crossfire. Attempts to rally the 7th were initially unsuccessful, so Jones turned to the 6th Virginia, which had arrived on the field only moments before its sister regiment's ignominious retreat. With it came Chew's Battery.[35]

Chew directed his men into a wheat field on the east side of the road, where they unlimbered the battery's three pieces. The guns opened on the enemy but fired only briefly.[36] Jones was both shocked and furious at the repulse of the 7th. He wasted little time in riding up to Maj. Cabell E. Flournoy of the 6th Virginia and ordering him forward. The 6th swept up the road, followed by rallied portions of the 7th and a small contingent of the 11th Virginia. As they catapulted past Chew's guns, the cannoneers ceased firing and watched their cavalry virtually annihilate the Federals. The artillery had little to do in the rout that ended the contest. As Chew limbered his pieces, Moorman's Battery and McGregor's section appeared in the distance with Robertson and his brigade. Together they rode toward Fairfield but stopped to camp before reaching the town.[37]

Up to this point, Robertson's and Jones's commands had failed to contribute significantly to Lee's Northern invasion. The horse artillery that had accompanied these two brigades had seen little action. The Fairfield fight barely had warmed the guns. The time wasted in guarding the gaps in Virginia could not be recouped and would become a point of controversy. Time permitted those batteries that did not participate in Stuart's ride to recover somewhat from the hard service they had been subjected to during and after Brandy Station. Even as Jones was decimating the 6th U.S. Cavalry, the final struggle at Gettysburg was drawing to a close. The bombardment preceding Picket's Charge had been heard by the men in Jones's ranks.[38] George Neese and others had caught a glimpse of the battlefield from a hill south of Cashtown.[39] The men of the battery had speculated on what the tremendous roar might portend. Circumstances had prevented them from being a part of that climactic scene. However, their brother cannoneers who had reached Gettysburg had played a greater role in the campaign but had not been able to alter its outcome.

CHAPTER 18

Gettysburg

"It was not ordained that we should always be master of the situation."

The batteries of the Stuart Horse Artillery Battalion, along with the rest of the elements of the Army of Northern Virginia, were drawn to Gettysburg like iron to a magnet. Inexorably the long, gray columns marched around and over all natural obstacles toward their date with destiny. Yet as the battle erupted in the morning hours of July 1, not one gun of the Stuart Horse Artillery Battalion was on the field. As the day lengthened and more and more troops were fed into the maelstrom of the first day's fighting, Capt. James F. Hart's Battery, marching with Longstreet's Infantry, and Capt. Thomas E. Jackson's and Capt. Wiley H. Griffin's Batteries, accompanying Brig. Gen. Albert Jenkins's Brigade, drew ever closer to the battlefield. The deep-throated rumble of artillery fire and the rolling crescendos of musket volleys told every one of the cannoneers that a major engagement was on, and they would soon be a part of it.

Not until evening did Jackson and Griffin reach the vicinity of Gettysburg. Griffin was with the advance, and Jackson's Battery brought up the rear.[1] Both went into camp with Jenkins's Brigade on the farm of John Henry Majors, which was situated about three or four miles northeast of Gettysburg along the Heidlersburg Road.[2] Majors's house became Jenkins's headquarters. Griffin, Jackson, and the cavalry remained there throughout the night of the first. The rest was welcomed by all, but it also gave the men a chance to ponder what their role might be the following day.

At sunrise on July 2, the men of Hart's Battery became the first of the horse artillery battalion to reach the battlefield.[3] They rode onto the fields west of Gettysburg and traversed the ground of the first day's fighting. What greeted the eyes of the cannoneers bore grim witness to the titanic struggle that had occurred. The battery made its way toward the right of the Confederate line and took position on the left of Longstreet's Corps in front of Seminary Ridge around 11:00 A.M.[4] Hart found little to do during the day. He was not called into action when Longstreet assaulted the Peach Orchard or Little Round Top.

The gunners spent their time resting and trying to gauge the success of Longstreet's attacks. When night fell, the men bedded down beside their guns.

Early that same morning, Jenkins received word to report to Gen. Robert E. Lee for orders. Returning to his command, Jenkins had "Boots and Saddles" sounded, and the brigade soon was moving south on the Heidlersburg Road, with the horse artillery in tow. After riding about a mile, the column turned off the road to the left and took position in a woods along Rock Creek. There it remained through the morning hours. Just before noon, Jenkins and his staff rode back to the road and turned once again toward town. After crossing a bridge over the creek, the party rode up a small hill known as Blocher's Knoll[5] to the right of the road. Jenkins was scanning the distance with his field glasses when a courier arrived. The general and the courier dismounted and were in the act of examining a map when a battery of Federal artillery positioned on Cemetery Ridge opened fire. Before long, shells began bursting around the hill. One exploded above the small mound, killing Jenkins's horse and wounding the general in the head. Whatever role Jenkins's Brigade and Griffin's and Jackson's Batteries might have had that day ended when Jenkins was struck down.[6] The day was spent in limbo until about 9:00 P.M., when orders sent the brigade and its artillery back a few miles toward Petersburg,[7] where they made camp. Before morning, Stuart added the brigade to his command.[8] He would find something for them to do before too long.

Maj. Gen. J. E. B. Stuart reached Gettysburg on the afternoon of July 2. His command trailed behind him along the road from Carlisle. On the countenance of every man was written one word: exhaustion. The artillerymen of Breathed's Battery and McGregor's section rode in with Fitz Lee's and Chambliss's troopers. Stuart placed the brigades of Lee and Chambliss on the York and Heidlersburg Roads. Hampton, who was without horse artillery, passed through Hunterstown on the York Pike toward Gettysburg. His rear guard was attacked, and Hampton was forced to turn and fight off Federal cavalry led by the intrepid George A. Custer. The "Boy General" had artillery, which punished the Confederates severely. Hampton sent a courier to Stuart asking for reinforcements and artillery. The time had come for the horse artillery to strike a blow. Shockingly, it failed to answer the call. The only artillery Stuart had with him at that time was Breathed and McGregor, neither of which was in any condition to respond to Hampton's plea.[9] Even had they been able, the meager amount of ammunition contained in their caissons and limbers scarcely would have sufficed. Stuart appealed to Lt. Col. Hilary P. Jones of Ewell's Corps for guns. Jones sent a section of Capt. Charles A. Green's Louisiana Guard Artillery, which did excellent service but suffered heavily from the enemy's guns.[10] With Green's help, Hampton held on until darkness brought an end to the fighting. At last Hampton's weary troopers could join their comrades in Lee's and Chambliss's Brigades and take a well-earned rest, albeit a short one.

In the early morning hours of July 3, the men of Stuart's cavalry and those of the horse artillery arose and ate what meager rations were available. The cavalrymen replenished their ammunition from the rapidly dwindling ordnance stores of Lee's army train. Stuart had orders to place his command on Ewell's far left and moved to fulfill them, taking position along Cress Ridge.[11] Stuart's command now included Jenkins's Brigade, led by Col. Milton J. Ferguson of the 16th Virginia Cavalry. Accompanying Ferguson was Jackson's Battery. The initial movement was made by Ferguson's and Chambliss's Brigades, which started out about noon.[12] Hampton and Fitz Lee soon moved out with Captain Green's section of guns.[13] Breathed's and McGregor's batteries were to follow as soon as they found ammunition.[14] The delay did not please Jim Breathed one bit, as one member of the battery recalled:

> The way that Breathed flew around that morning, cursing the ordnance officer for not having the ordnance on the ground, would have been shocking to a Sunday school convention. He swore up hill and down vale, and still the wagons did not make their appearance. The Jackson Battery, commanded by 1st Lt. Micajah Woods, having plenty of ammunition, moved out with Jenkins's Brigade, to which they were attached.[15] This only made Breathed more nervous than ever. Breathed did not want any other battery to get into a fight, and he waiting for ammunition. At last the wagons came in sight, and the two batteries began to refill their limbers and caissons.[16]

While Breathed fumed, Ferguson's and Chambliss's Brigades reached Cress Ridge and deployed unobserved in the woods. This stealth seemed an unnecessary precaution when Stuart ordered one of Jackson's guns to fire a few random shots in different directions.[17] The reason for this display has never been ascertained. In any event, it elicited no immediate response from the Federals. Hampton and Fitz Lee, still minus Breathed and McGregor but with Green's Battery in tow, now rode onto the field. Hampton took position on Chambliss's left, and Fitz Lee on Hampton's left but perpendicular to Hampton's line.[18] The columns inadvertently rode out of the cover of the woods, informing the enemy of their presence.

Opposite Stuart were Brig. Gen. David McM. Gregg's Cavalry Division and Brig. Gen. George A. Custer's Michigan Brigade of Kilpatrick's Division. The Yanks also had artillery—Lt. Alexander C. M. Pennington's Battery M, 2nd U.S. Artillery, and Capt. Alanson Randol's Battery E/G, 1st U.S. Artillery. The cannon fire from Cress Ridge and the large masses of Confederate horsemen had alerted Gregg that something big was brewing in the woods along Cress Ridge. Risking, at the least, censure or, at the worst, a court-martial, Gregg assumed the responsibility of ignoring Maj. Gen. Alfred Pleasonton's order that would have removed Custer's Brigade from the approaching battle.[19] This done, events escalated.

Custer deployed his brigade, which gave Jackson an inviting target.[20] The Charlottesville Battery's accurate fire began to fell men and horses among Custer's regiments. Custer countered with Pennington, who quickly proved his guns' superiority, as his shells began falling around Lieutenant Woods's guns. Woods's two pieces and Lt. Randolph H. Blain's section were unable to reach Pennington, though Woods tried, and were forced to continue to concentrate on the enemy's skirmishers and mounted columns.[21] Col. John B. McIntosh sent troopers from his brigade to support Custer. These, along with Custer's, were the skirmishers Jackson targeted. McIntosh also ordered up Lt. James Chester's section of Randol's Battery to add its fire to that of Pennington's.[22] Meanwhile, Jackson took a pounding and had to pull out of the contest.[23] Woods left two accounts of his battery's participation.[24] In a letter written on July 10, he recorded:

> On Friday early we were ordered to the advance line on the left. Lt. Blain in command of one section, of two guns and I in charge of the other. A few minutes after taking position we were charged by cavalry and threatened by infantry, which we repulsed without the aid of other Batteries as ours was the extreme one of our line on the left wing, where we were sent to check a powerful flanking force of the enemy army. Very soon Stuart's whole Cavalry Division came to our support and one of the most desperate cavalry fights of the war ensued, lasting nearly all day. Each party being sustained by infantry & artillery. Battery after battery opened upon us. By the rapid firing I had done against the cavalry and infantry,[25] in the morning, I had nearly exhausted my supply of shell and shrapnel.
>
> A splendid Yankee battery of six pieces took position immediately in my front. I opened on them slowly and with effect, but the distance was rather great for my short range guns—in less than ten minutes nearly half the horses at my gun and Caissons had been killed or disabled—four of my men had been wounded. I myself had been struck by a piece of a shell which cut my pants for three or four inches below my knee, bruising my leg considerably—but fortunately not direct enough to cause a gash—the piece entered the ground just by me. The spokes of one of my guns had been cut by the balls and the carriage of my rifled piece was so much injured that the next day it broke to pieces.
>
> During the action Maj. Terrell Commanding Battalion of Art.[26] and Capt. Jackson both galloped to me and told me they could ask me to do no better service, that I was handling my pieces splendidly. I sighted them nearly every fire myself. My ammunition soon gave

> out and I had to retire, but I never left the field til I had cut every dead horse loose and replaced him and brought off both my guns & their caissons. Lt. Blain's lost not a man or horse, nor did he have anything struck. [His] section was less exposed and suffered no loss.[27]

On July 16, Woods elaborated his account, once again writing his father, Dr. Woods:

> Among the first in the morning we were launched forward on the left wing to resist a serious demonstration in that quarter. For some time supported by infantry and cavalry we had nothing to oppose us but material of the same nature, and repeatedly we were cheered by seeing columns of infantry and cavalry retire in confusion before our guns—but it was not ordained that we should always be master of the situation. Suddenly a splendid Battery of 20 Pounder Parrotts (which I learned from prisoners was Ringgold's Baltimore Battery—Bragg's in Mexico[28]) took position about one mile in our front.
>
> The very first shell thrown burst about 40 feet from me—covering me with dirt and a fragment grazed my leg about two inches below my knee, cut my pants and passed on—only bruising the flesh, but scarcely scratching it enough to draw blood. We stood before them about ten minutes when Maj. Terrell commander of our Battalion ordered the pieces from the field. In that time four of the horses at the gun I had taken in especial charge had been killed & several had been wounded in my section. Several spokes had been cut by the balls & shells & my carriages were being so injured I could scarcely get them off the field.
>
> It is considered very remarkable by all who were near that we did not lose some men when every thing else was being struck—only four being wounded. All the casualties were in my section. I fired 23 rounds at the opposing Battery but not a shot took effect. My guns being of such short ranges that they could not carry the distance. I am confident that had our men remained ten minutes longer all my guns would have been dismounted & many of the men killed.[29]

Woods's section was lucky indeed. Pennington and Chester had the range and were making every shot count. Green's Battery finally arrived and took up the position Jackson had abandoned.[30] Having disposed of Jackson, the Federal cannoneers turned their attention to the Louisiana boys. The enemy's dismounted troopers were also zeroing in on the Confederate artillery. Stuart countered the Federal skirmishers with some of his own. Lt. Col. Vincent Witcher's 34th Virginia Cavalry Battalion moved forward into the Rummel barn to act as skirmishers. At one point, Green moved his guns forward to a small ridge near the Rummel barn, but the blue cavalry made the place too hot, and the men pulled the guns back to their initial position.[31] The battle now jumped to the next level, taking the artillery out of the contest for a while.

Back at the ordnance train, Jim Breathed had had enough.

> Breathed was just about finished loading his limber chests when he heard the firing between Pennington's and Woods's guns. If he had received an electric shock he could not have been more excited. He jumped on his horse and was on the road to the Cress Ridge in a jiffy, the battery following as fast as their jaded horses could travel. We took position on the right slope within sight of Pennington's battery and awaited orders to go into action.[32]

McGregor's section accompanied Breathed's Battery to the front and deployed next to it, but the guns remained silent.[33] What kept the anxious Breathed waiting to fire was the series of mounted charges that swept over the fields between Pennington's and Breathed's guns. Thousands of hooves stirred up their own thunder, which replaced that of the opposing artillery. The two sides crashed together in such fury that none that participated ever forgot it. The massive gray columns were met by Custer's Michiganders in front and small bodies of men on the flanks. Formations disappeared into tangled masses of struggling individuals. Quarter was neither asked nor given. The antagonists seemed bent on mutual extermination. Sabers rose and fell. Pistols barked. Horses and riders tumbled to the ground to be quickly trampled beneath flashing hooves. Hampton, in the thick of the fighting, was wounded by both blade and ball. Such fury could not last. The blue and gray lines parted, each to its own starting place.

The cannoneers of both sides had stood around their guns in awe, unable to fire for fear of hitting their own comrades. But with the separation and retreat of their cavalry's forces, the silent guns spoke again. H. H. Matthews recalled the ensuing contest between his and Pennington's batteries:

> Now was Breathed's opportunity and right glad did he avail himself of it. We opened on Pennington's guns with a vim peculiar to the old battery (the cavalry looking on) and never in the annals of warfare did two opposing batteries more ardently strain every nerve to crush each other. These two batteries had opposed each other on every battlefield of Virginia and now that they met on Northern soil, it was our ambition to hold our ground, and we did so. Shell was fired as fast as men could load. The guns became so hot that I was afraid the old 2nd gun would have a premature explosion and blow No. 1 into eternity. My thumb on my left hand became burnt from thumbing the vent so that it

> became very painful to use it. We stayed with Pennington until dark, expending every round of ammunition. Both batteries suffered heavily.[34]
>
> Darkness at last came to our relief and exhausted man and horse had a short respite from that fearful ordeal that we had passed through that day. Lt. [Francis Halsey] Wigfall, an officer of the battery, distinguished himself by his cool bravery, remaining on his horse during all of that terrible duel. In fact all the officers and men, without a single exception, added another jewel to their crown of diadem. The cannoneers, after we had ceased firing, dropped down by their pieces, tired, worn out, ready to respond to the call of their idolized captain, the peerless Breathed. We were slightly disfigured, but still in the ring. Our ammunition in this engagement was very inferior, some shell exploding at the muzzle of the guns. We usually had plenty of U.S. ammunition, but it becoming exhausted we had to use Confederate ammunition, drawing on the reserve artillery for what we wanted.[35]

Across the intervening ground, Pennington's men joined Breathed's in taking the opportunity to rest from their day's labors. They had driven one of the enemy's horse batteries from the field and had stood toe to toe with one of Stuart's best batteries without yielding. As memorable as the day was, Pennington simply reported that he engaged an enemy battery and silenced it.[36]

The Confederate artillery ammunition that gave Breathed's gunners so much trouble was only part of a larger problem facing the Confederate ordnance department. When Jackson's Battery fell back, Lieutenant Woods was anxious to refill his limber chests. What he discovered greatly surprised him: "I applied at once for ordnance to the division and corps trains, but to my astonishment found that the ammunition of the whole army had been exhausted—there being twelve rounds for each cannon in the army."[37] Between Breathed's experience with faulty ammunition and Woods's inability to refill his empty chests, the Confederate artillery was in serious difficulty.

Stuart held on to his position until after dark, when he ordered his command back to the York Road. His cavalry and his horse artillery had failed to break the Federals, who in their turn had been unable to drive the Confederates from the field. Both sides claimed victory. In reality, they had fought each other to a stalemate. Pennington had the advantage early in the fight, but Breathed and McGregor had held their own in the latter stages of the battle. This would not be the last time these batteries exchanged compliments. Two long years and many more meetings lay ahead.

One other battery of the Stuart Horse Artillery Battalion participated in the fighting on July 3. Col. John L. Black's hodgepodge cavalry command and Hart's Battery awoke to orders sending them from their post on Longstreet's left to the extreme right.[38] They were targeted as reinforcements for Brig. Gen. Evander M. Law, who anchored Lee's right flank. Black and Hart arrived a little after noon. Already, skirmishing had erupted with the dismounted troopers of Brig. Gen. Elon J. Farnsworth's Brigade of Kilpatrick's Cavalry Division. Kilpatrick's threat to Law's flank along the Emmitsburg Road developed even as the bombardment preceding Pickett's Charge rumbled in the distance. Federal reinforcements also appeared. Brig. Gen. Wesley Merritt's Brigade arrived about 3:00 P.M. and was deployed on Farnsworth's left, west of the Emmitsburg Road.[39]

Black and Hart were sent forward and occupied a position south of the Kern house along the Emmitsburg Road.[40] Black threw out a skirmish line, to the right of the road, while Hart unlimbered near a large gate on the southeastern slope of a hill beyond the Currens house.[41] The Federals attacked on foot, slowly driving back the Confederate dismounted cavalry. Black's troopers could not halt the enemy's advance. Fearing that Hart might be overrun, the colonel ordered the guns to be retired one at a time to a position nearer the Kern house, while the others maintained a continuous fire, a tactic Hart understood completely.[42] The movement was carried out successfully, with Hart occupying a new position close to the junction of the Slyder farm lane and the Emmitsburg Road. Here the battery, in immediate support of the 7th and 8th Georgia Infantry, turned its guns to face the threat of Farnsworth's Brigade east of the road.[43]

After Hart's departure, Merritt once again struck Black's exposed flank and broke through. Hart was again forced back, this time to a position near the Snyder house on the Emmitsburg Road.[44] Law had ridden back for reinforcements and had just brought forward the 11th and 59th Georgia Infantry regiments of Brig. Gen. George T. Anderson's Brigade.[45] At first Law had the Georgians face Farnsworth, but Black's rout caused Law to hurl the two regiments at Merritt. The attack swung around Merritt's flank and sent his men scurrying back to the Emmittsburg Road. His right secure, Law turned his attention to Farnsworth. Passing Hart's Battery on his way to the left flank, Law ordered the battery to support the Georgia infantry on the right. As the cannoneers went about the task of limbering their pieces, Farnsworth, at the command of Kilpatrick, was preparing to launch his suicidal charge.

The 1st Texas Infantry, which had earlier stopped an attack by the 1st West Virginia Cavalry, was the first to feel the weight of the charge. The Texans' skirmish line was overrun. Capt. George Hillyer, commander of the 9th Georgia, led his regiment forward to assist the Texans and save the guns of Capt. James Reilly's North Carolina Battery. Hart, who had moved out with the two infantry regiments to secure Law's right flank, played no part in repulsing Farnsworth's charge.[46] The gallant Federal troopers were turned back, and their leader was killed. Hart's final position was between the Kern house and Douglas house, about three-quarters of a mile from the site of Farnsworth's charge.[47] The firing slowly died away as the Federals drew back. Evening descended, bringing the battle to a close.

The Stuart Horse Artillery Battalion's contribution to the Confederate cause at Gettysburg pales in comparison with that of the other Southern batteries. There were no gallant charges with the infantry like that at Chancellorsville, no heroic stands as at St. James Church and Fleetwood Hill at Brandy Station. Breathed's and McGregor's Batteries had performed well during Stuart's ride north, but they were in no condition to render the kind of effective service they had on other occasions, despite Matthews's claim. Hart's Battery also had ridden long and hard to reach the battlefield. Along the way, the men had to repair their guns and march unprotected. Once they arrived, they were relegated to a minor role. Their efforts on July 3 were an adequate but not crucial part of Law's success against Kilpatrick.

Griffin's Battery's participation was brief and virtually undocumented. It failed to add to the reputation it had gained as a field battery. In the future, the battery would perform well, but at Gettysburg, it did nothing to add to its reputation. Lieutenant Woods summed up the role of Jackson's Battery in a letter to his father: "Our Battery is pronounced by all authorities in the army to be very inefficient—in fact the most inefficient Battery in the army on account of our short ranged guns."[48] The inefficiency was limited by the metal of the battery, not the mettle of its men. Woods's determined stand against Pennington, though brief, demonstrated that the human element of the battery would stand and fight when called upon. Considering that it had fired its first shots near Harrisburg scarcely a week before, it had done as well as could have been expected, if not better.

All in all, the horse batteries present at Gettysburg did nothing that could be labeled outstanding and, in fact, barely attained mediocrity. This harsh judgment is tempered by the fact that those batteries with experience (Breathed's, Chew's, Hart's, McGregor's, and Moorman's) could not be utilized in crucial situations because of their hard use before and during the march north or their poor positioning once they arrived. Only Breathed's, Hart's, and a portion of McGregor's Batteries, three of the finest batteries in the battalion, had even made it to Gettysburg. Brandy Station, Aldie, Middleburg, and Upperville had taken a greater toll than anyone realized at the time. The question now was, Could the batteries rise to meet the challenge of the long retreat to Virginia?

CHAPTER 19

Back to Virginia

"The danger to which I have been exposed and the excitement accompanying, have surpassed anything I have experienced."

One hour before midnight on July 3, Brig. Gen. John Imboden received an order to report to General Lee. Not until 1:00 A.M. on the fourth was Imboden met by the commander of the Army of Northern Virginia. Lee inquired what troops Imboden had. In reply, Imboden said that he had 2,100 well-mounted cavalry and McClanahan's six-gun battery of horse artillery.[1] Lee then gave Imboden command of the army's wagon train and outlined its route of march—over the mountain on the Chambersburg Road and south to Williamsport. The choice of the actual route would be Imboden's. There were to be no stops. The army could not afford even one. Lee warned Imboden that enemy cavalry would harass him. The disposition of his own troops was left to Imboden's judgment.[2] A promise of additional artillery was all Lee could offer. Imboden turned and left. A daunting responsibility had been laid on his shoulders. Time would tell if he could bear it.

By dawn, Imboden realized that the wagon train would not be assembled until afternoon. Heavy rain added further delay to an already lengthy procedure. During the wait, the guns Lee promised arrived. There was the famed Washington Artillery of New Orleans under Maj. Benjamin F. Eshleman, Capt. William A. Tanner's Courtney Artillery, and a Whitworth under Lieutenant Pegram. Hampton's Brigade, now commanded by Col. Laurence S. Baker,[3] and Hart's Battery were assigned the role of rear guard. Imboden's artillery had been increased from six to twenty-three guns. Finally, at 4:00 P.M., the column began the long trek that became a seemingly endless nightmare for the thousands of wounded carried in the wagons.

That same morning, the rest of the horse artillery batteries were scattered about the Pennsylvania countryside as the need for their services had dictated. Moorman's and Chew's Batteries and a section of McGregor's were encamped near Fairfield with Robertson's and Jones's Brigades. They limbered and marched through Fairfield, halting just beyond the Oak Grove Inn.[4] Late in the afternoon, they were still there, watching Ewell's vast train pass by.[5] Their job would be to protect that train as it wound its way over Jack and South Mountain. In addition to those troops already with Imboden, Stuart assigned Fitz Lee's Brigade with Breathed's Battery and McGregor's section to assist in guarding the rear of the train on the Cashtown Road. Jackson's and Griffin's Batteries with Chambliss's and Ferguson's Brigades under Stuart's personal command would move toward Emmitsburg, Maryland. All troopers were in motion by the evening of the fourth.

The night of the fourth was one that the entire Army of Northern Virginia would have liked to forget but could not. Pvt. Charles McVicar of Chew's Battery recorded his movements and his thoughts:

> July 4th Moving over the battlefield [Fairfield] at 6 o'clock in the evening. Traveling across the Blue Ridge towards Hagerstown. Raining very hard, crossing Mountain Gap, an awful road. Guarding the rear of the wagon train [Ewell's]. The cannon is booming in the center about 2½ miles distant and the sharpshooters are at work. The enemy attacked our long train. The firing ahead is rapid. It is near daylight, we cannot pass. The road and wagons full of dead, wounded and disabled men from yesterday's battle. Got a place for one gun and sent a few shots. Was out on the pike as day broke and opened fire. They have fallen back after cutting down a few wagons. Went to the left and took position on the heights. There are two regiments of infantry supporting us. They threw up a fine breastwork in an hour. The firing has been incessant and this has been the most horrible night I ever spent.[6]

The orders that sent Chew's Battery over that "awful road" were not carried out. Gunner Neese explained what happened:

> The cannon heard in the forepart of the night belonged to the Yanks, and they were shelling some of our wagon trains on top of the mountain. This morning [July 5] just before day Colonel [Capt. John A.] Throckmorton, commanding the Sixth Virginia Cavalry, came down the mountain with his regiment in a rather stirred-up condition, as if something wild and very dangerous had been seen in front. Captain Chew asked Colonel Throckmorton where he was going. He replied, "Down the mountain. A Yankee battery fired canister into the head of my command, and I am not going up there again until daylight." Captain Chew then remarked, "Colonel, my battery was ordered up here to support your regiment, and if you go back, I will too." Accordingly, we went back down the mountain a short distance, fed our horses and waited for day.[7]

"Grumble" Jones, who was in command of the 6th Virginia as well as the 4th North Carolina from Robertson's Brigade, admitted in his report the artillery's and cavalry's inability to reach the wagons on top of the mountain. He had proceeded with his staff to try to rally some stragglers and fight off the Federals but found only Capt. George W. Emack's company of Maryland cavalry and one gun from a North Carolina battery with two rounds left in its limber chest. Emack and his small band did steadfast service that night, but the wagon train still suffered casualties.

Even as Emack struggled to save Ewell's wagons, Stuart with Chambliss and Ferguson struggled through the darkness and rain to reach Emmitsburg. The march was so hampered that it was dawn on the fifth before the gray cavalry entered the town. Here Stuart learned that Kilpatrick had passed through on his way to threaten Ewell's wagons. Deciding that Robertson and Jones could draw support from the army if the need arose, Stuart pushed on to Cavetown. At Mount Zion Church, Stuart split his force, sending Ferguson to Smithsburg[8] and Chambliss to Leitersburg. Stuart accompanied Chambliss's Brigade and found the going tough. Col. Pennock Huey's Brigade and Lt. William D. Fuller's Battery C, 3rd U.S. Artillery, occupied the northern pass. The cavalry chieftain was forced to dismount most of his men and try to fight his way through. He sent a message to Ferguson to come down in rear of the Federals.

However, Ferguson was having his own problems. His route was blocked by Col. Nathaniel P. Richmond's Cavalry Brigade, aided by Lt. Samuel S. Elder's Battery E, 4th U.S. Artillery. Ferguson made little progress against Richmond. He finally turned around, headed back to the fork, and took the same road Stuart had. In the meantime, Stuart pushed through the pass, thanks to Kilpatrick, who pulled his troopers out of the fight. Once out of the pass, Stuart was harassed by an enemy battery positioned on the Boonsborough Road. Griffin's Battery, which had accompanied Chambliss, unlimbered its guns and, with a few well-placed rounds, persuaded its adversary to abandon his post.[9] His way clear, Stuart paused until Ferguson came up and then rode on to Leitersburg in the dark.

Imboden spent the fifth fending off Federal attacks. Reaching Waynesboro, Imboden swung the train west on the Greencastle Road. In the lead was the 18th Virginia Cavalry under Col. George W. Imboden, the general's brother, and a section of McClanahan's Battery under Lieutenants Hugh H. Fultz and Carter Berkeley. When this advance contingent was about a mile west of Waynesboro, Capt. Ulric Dahlgren and his Pennsylvanians slashed between it and the train, striking at a vulnerable spot where there were no troops. In the melee that followed, the Federals took axes and chopped at the wheels of the wagons and shot the teams.[10] Chaos reigned for some minutes. Imboden had little to fight with. He turned to the nearest troops at hand, a section of McClanahan's Battery, and opened on the raiders with canister.[11] The cannon fire failed to drive Dahlgren away. Imboden feared capture until his brother came charging back with the 18th Virginia to rescue him.

All day the attacks continued. Another bold raid on the train momentarily netted a section of McClanahan's Battery, along with Lt. Carter Berkeley and the battery's future surgeon, Dr. Charles A. Ware. Once again Colonel Imboden had to about-face his regiment and make another charge. The Federals were chased away, the guns saved, and Berkeley and Ware rescued.[12] The long train suffered many such attacks. Losses in men, horses, and wagons mounted. Still Imboden pushed ahead toward his goal. Finally, the head of the column reached Williamsport on the afternoon of the fifth. The rest of the train, including Baker's Brigade and Hart's Battery, would not arrive until the sixth.[13] Even as his command settled down for the night amidst the groans and cries of the wounded, Imboden knew the danger was far from over.

Early on the morning of the sixth, Imboden began to look to the defense of his position. He became aware of the approach of Kilpatrick's and Buford's divisions. These two officers had met in Boonsboro and decided to split their commands, with Buford attacking the trains and Kilpatrick holding off Confederate cavalry. Buford would be the first to test Imboden's makeshift defense. For that defense, Imboden had little in the way of manpower to work with. The artillery that had accompanied the wagon train would have to step to the front and bear the heaviest load.

There were many approaches that had to be guarded. McClanahan placed a section of his battery in between the Hagerstown and Boonsboro Roads, another section to the right of the Boonsboro Road, and a third section along the Clear Spring Road near the Potomac River. Other batteries were scattered along the defensive perimeter and bolstered with whatever manpower was available, including cooks, teamsters, and walking wounded. Hart's Battery arrived shortly after noon and bivouacked along the Greencastle Road. Scarcely had they settled down for some much-needed food and rest when the Federals began to make their presence felt. Hart, who had been placed in command of that part of the line to the west of the Hagerstown Road, wrote of the defense of Lee's wagon train:

> About an hour after halting, the enemy's cavalry were reported as coming in heavy columns from towards Hagerstown. Our little force of organized companies was hastily strung out over the hills, in a thin skirmish line, to oppose them. It was Kilpatrick at the head of the Federal cavalry—at least six or eight thousand strong—who had dodged Stuart by cutting through a pass in South Mountain, and was now gazing down on the richest prize a cavalry leader could aspire to—the wagon and ordnance trains of a whole army.[14]
>
> Gen. Imboden disposed his little force by placing his cavalry—some three hundred possibly—on the right,[15] and Smith's infantry

regiment of about two hundred men and some artillery, in the center, near the Hagerstown road, while Hart's battery of artillery occupied the left of the road. If Kilpatrick had pressed on as soon as he reached this little line he might have crushed it in a few minutes, and had a wagon for every two men in his command. But he paused to survey his prize and feel the strength of the defense. He dismounted his troops, threw out skirmishers, and when his preparations were completed moved steadily upon us. He was met with firmness, but it was perfectly evident that our little force, on open ground as it were, would soon melt away under the terrific fire that began to pour upon it. Even if it could have withstood the fire, our force was too small to cover the ground on the front, and it was very certain that the enemy could go around, if not over us, and possess himself of the vast acreage of wagon trains parked in behind us, down to the river banks. But a new factor entered into the problem, which had seemed so nearly solved.

Every wagon and ambulance, of course, had a teamster. True, they were not armed, but there were immense trains filled with guns, whose gallant bearers were sleeping under those little mounds we had left at Gettysburg; ammunition was equally abundant, and why not equip this new force and strengthen our fragile line with it. Gen. Imboden seems to have acted promptly upon this impulse, and officers and men were sent back to gather from the wagons all the recruits that could be had, almost as soon as the enemy came in sight.

Besides the teamsters, the trains had a miscellaneous following. Quartermasters and commissaries with their clerks, army chaplains, and officers' servants made a goodly part of it. Then the immense ambulance train contained a large number of the wounded from Gettysburg, who could bear being moved, as also the surgeons, nurses, etc. accompanying them. Then came that nondescript organization dubbed through the army as "Company Q," composed of recruits from all arms of the service. They were generally patriotic men who thought fighting necessary and had each been in one battle or a part of one at some time or other during the war, but ever thereafter battles were devoid of attraction or novelty to them. They could scent the signs afar with the accuracy with which the weather bureau foretells a storm; and on such occasions the cavalryman would have a lame or sore-backed horse, and the infantryman blistered feet or some distressing ailment that sorely puzzled the surgeons to diagnose, but the result was generally to swell the ranks of "Company Q."

But "Company Q" was cornered on this occasion. The river was an impassable torrent in front, and Kilpatrick with six or eight thousand picked horsemen was closing up on the rear, and within musket shot.

A few essayed the river but were swept away by the current. "Q" was prompt in an emergency, and now that a great emergency was upon him, he decided to fight. He had not fought to any great extent through patriotism or love of excitement, but a wagon was a different thing from a prison. It was next to home and the fireside to him, and he decided to fight for his wagons at all events. So along with the teamsters, and commissary and quartermaster's staff, surgeons and chaplains, came "Q" with a force and unanimity surprising to those who knew his ways and weaknesses. The enemy had not more than fairly closed on our original line before these recruits came along in bunches of dozens or more at a time to reinforce it.

The enemy made their first attack on that part of our line to the right of the Hagerstown road, and at first pressed in back by their overpowering numbers. A section of the Washington Artillery, of New Orleans, which had been sent back disabled, with the wagon train, suffered heavily here, and its guns were at one time almost unmanned. Recruits, coming from the wagons, went to the pieces and worked gallantly to help the little detachment. On the left of this road the attack was not so vigorous, and we held the ground easily enough, with the aid of the teamsters and "Q" men. Sergeant John Newton of Hart's Battery had been placed in charge of the wagon train of the battery and was with it near the river when the fight began. He left the wagons and hurried to the front at the fire of the first gun. Missing his own command he came upon the feeble Louisiana Battery and at once took charge of one of its guns. There for half an hour he commanded and encouraged the feeble detachment until he fell, cut in two by a shell. The remnant of brave Louisianians, touched by his conspicuous gallantry, tenderly buried him after the fight and adopted appropriate resolutions to his memory, which were forwarded to us the next morning. No more earnest patriot gave his life to "the Lost Cause" than this gallant son of Erin who fell among strangers in an unrecorded but not inglorious battle. The waters of the Potomac will chant a requiem over no more heroic dust than fills this unknown grave.[16]

Shortly after the fight began an officer with the insignia of a captain reported to me for a place with the left. I put him in command of a squad that had just preceded him and was moving into position. His coolness, self-possession and daring soon attracted attention, and his command was rapidly enlarged. After the battle was over I inquired his name, and he answered for himself, saying, "I am Manning Brown, chaplain to the 2nd South Carolina Cavalry." Many a later battle might have different results if the battalions had been commanded by such men as the Rev. Manning Brown of the Methodist Episcopal Church.

Kilpatrick was determined, however, that so rich a prey as Lee's whole transportation service should not escape him, and about six o'clock P.M. made a terrific onslaught on the right and center with dismounted cavalry and artillery. Gen. Imboden sent a message to the left for help; but while we had a solid line of wagoneers there and were holding our own easily enough, it was a matter of some difficulty to determine how to handle such a disorganized body as a reinforcing column. It was solved by advancing our left against the enemy's right as the surest way of relieving our hard pressed comrades, where away over the hills to the right the firing was heaviest.[17] The wagoneers went forward in splendid style, and the enemy fell back slowly before them. They had just begun to believe then that they were going to whip Kilpatrick, not withstanding the odds in his favor. As for advantage in numbers, I doubt if he had much on this part of the field; but he had organized troops, which we did not have.

The fire on our right began to slacken as the left advanced. About this time we heard the rattling of musketry to the rear of the enemy's right, and his retreat was observed a few minutes later all along the line. The gallant Young, of our escort, in command of the remnant of Hampton's old brigade,[18] had come in on the Mercersburg road and was threatening their right and rear opposite our left. Then the wagoneers knew that Kilpatrick was whipped. We pressed forward until we met Young, the enemy oozing out from between the two forces on the road towards Hagerstown. It was now near dusk, and the battle had lasted since two o'clock. There had been glory enough won, and neither the wagoneers nor Company "Q" felt any desire to pursue Kilpatrick's horsemen in search of more. The wagons were safe, and the teamsters went back to feed their mules and talk over the wonderful victory; and Company "Q" sought shelter from the drizzling rain under the grateful cover of a wagon, where his repose was undisturbed for the remainder of that night.[19]

The pressure put on Buford's rear came from Stuart, who had his hands almost as full of Yanks as Imboden.

The morning of the sixth found Lee's cavalry chief at Leitersburg. He had been joined there by Jones's Brigade and now had four brigades—Ferguson's, Chambliss's, Robertson's, and Jones's—under his immediate command. He also had with him Griffin's, Jackson's, Moorman's, and Chew's Batteries and a section of McGregor's. The commanding general had sent Stuart a dispatch that reached him at 6:00 A.M. Stuart was sure that Kilpatrick had moved on to Boonsboro and determined to pursue him there. Chambliss and Robertson with Moorman's Battery and McGregor's section left Leitersburg and headed straight for Hagerstown. Stuart with Jones and Ferguson rode toward Cavetown.

There Stuart divided his command. He sent Jones with Chew's Battery along the Boonsboro Road and then over byroads to Funkstown, which Stuart ordered him to hold. Stuart with Ferguson's Brigade and Griffin's and Jackson's Batteries rode to Chewsville and then toward Hagerstown.[20]

The first of these columns to contact the enemy was that of Chambliss and Robertson. As they approached the town, they were charged by elements of the 18th Pennsylvania and the 1st West Virginia of Richmond's Brigade, Kilpatrick's Division. The Confederates were caught by surprise at the onslaught. Col. James L. Davis of the 10th Virginia was captured, and Moorman's Battery came close to losing a gun. The Federals charged to within fifty yards of the lead piece before it could be unlimbered and brought into action.[21] The battery and McGregor's section were soon engaged in heavy fighting.[22] Stuart, learning of Chambliss's predicament, pushed Ferguson's Brigade forward and attacked. Jones also launched an assault down the Funkstown Road. Chew's Battery continued its habit of being in the thick of the fighting. Pvt. Charles McVicar wrote of the fight in his diary:

> Moving towards Hagerstown, cutting off a Brigade of Cavalry that was on a flank after the train came to Ringgold, Maryland. Our forces are using them up. We helped but little. On through Littlestown[23] to Hagerstown. The enemy is here and opened. We replied with two guns. We are driving them rapidly towards Boonsboro. They halted at the ridge, have been reinforced, the infantry is fronting us. General Stuart came in front. Imboden came in rear. We are running them from one position to another. 6 o'clock. Darkness is closing around the scene. They are holding their position and we have taken a stand in the pike. Our guns recoiling, bury themselves in a field of mud. Thought we were done for. The cannoneers ran to a fence, got rails and pried the wheels out. Their battery is 400 yards distant. We are under a rapidly advancing line of sharpshooters fire forty yards away. We don't mind shell but these little bees zipping by make us nervous. The cavalry charged and we are firing. It's 8½ o'clock. They are on the run. So dark we can't see what shell they are sending back. If we had two more hours of daylight it would have been a Yankee retreat. We have driven them six miles; this has been a very heavy division and certainly a hard fight. One of our men, a Mr. Wright, was mortally wounded.[24]

Chew's Battery began the fight south of Hagerstown. Once the Federals had been driven from the town, Chew changed position and swung around the town onto the Williamsport Road. Here he met opposition from Lt. Samuel S. Elder's Battery E, 4th U.S. Artillery, which unlimbered on the grounds of the Female Seminary. The cannonade was heavy for some time.[25] Toward dusk, the Federal skirmishers opened a severe fire on the battery. Pvt. James W. Wright was struck in the thigh, fracturing the bone. He was the only casualty in the horse artillery that day.

Stuart received welcomed help from Brig. Gen. Alfred Iverson's Brigade of infantry, though for a while Iverson's men mistook Ferguson's Brigade as the enemy. In the end, Richmond, abandoned by Kilpatrick, who had taken his two other brigades to help Buford, was forced back two miles or more. Elder fought magnificently, upholding the honor of the Federal horse artillery by driving back several mounted charges on his guns. On the Confederate side, Chew, Moorman, McGregor, and Griffin lent their fire to the cavalry's and infantry's advance.[26] In the distance, the battle at Williamsport could be heard. Stuart resolutely pushed ahead.

Assailed from front and rear, Buford and Kilpatrick took turns fighting with grim determination and praying for night. As Stuart's forces neared Williamsport, the going became tougher. A section of McGregor's Battery supported Chambliss's mounted attack. H. H. Matthews wrote an account of the fight and McGregor's role in it:[27]

> The first charge was made by the 9th Virginia of Chambliss's Brigade, supported by the 13th Virginia of the same brigade. The charge was a most brilliant one. McGregor aided them very much, taking position on the right of the road. Jenkins [Ferguson] was now hurried up, but owing to the many stone fences and ditches in his path did not make time, allowing the enemy an opportunity to rally along the stone fences, from which he opened, raking them with his fire. Jenkins dismounted his men and they advanced under these conditions with marked effect. McGregor engaged the enemy's battery, making him change position three times, finally driving him from the field.[28] The brigade of Chambliss, being mounted, kept them in motion. They made one countercharge but were met by Col. [James B.] Gordon, of the 5th North Carolina, and driven back. This repulse was afterwards turned into a rout by Col. L. L. Lomax of the 11th Virginia.[29]

As night fell, Kilpatrick and Buford finally extricated themselves from what had the potential of becoming a disaster. The former retreated in the direction of Boonsboro, while the latter rode toward Jones's Crossroads.

Imboden had saved the army's wagons. Stuart had provided some last-minute and much-needed assistance, but the men of Imboden's command, along with the various artillery batteries and the teamsters, were the real heroes. The arrival of Stuart and a portion of Lee's infantry meant that until Meade brought up his own infantry, the wagons were safe. The wounded could now be cared for in a more humane manner. Many had not seen a doctor since they had been wounded. Their agonized cries would haunt Imboden and his men to their dying day. But the army was not yet home. A river, raised to a rushing torrent by heavy mountain rains, stood between Lee and safety. Stuart's work was not finished.

Stuart's cavalry division was at last united. All of the brigades were in the vicinity of Williamsport, as were the batteries of the horse artillery. On the morning of July 7, Stuart set out to make sure that the Federal cavalry kept its distance. With a portion of Brig. Gen. William T. Wofford's Brigade of infantry, Stuart rode to Downsville, where he stationed the infantry. Ferguson's Brigade was thrown out in advance of Wofford. Jones's Brigade guarded the Cavetown Road, with Robertson on his left, north of Hagerstown. Chambliss, Fitz Lee, and Baker maintained their positions near Williamsport. The horse artillery batteries were still scattered about. The sections of McClanahan's Battery remained in the positions they had held during the fighting of the sixth. Part of Chew's Battery accompanied Jones through Hagerstown and into position on the Cavetown Road, while the rest rode to Williamsport to have their horses shod.[30] Moorman's Battery marched in the early morning hours from its camp near Williamsport toward Funkstown. Upon reaching Antietam Creek, the battery went into camp until the following day.[31] The locations of Hart's, Breathed's, McGregor's, Jackson's, and Griffin's Batteries cannot be given with any certainty.

On the eighth, Stuart with the brigades of Fitz Lee, Baker, Chambliss, and Jones again moved forward by different roads in the direction of Boonsboro. At Beaver Creek Bridge, Jones, in the advance, came upon the enemy in the form of Buford's Cavalry Division with Kilpatrick in support. The fight quickly drew in the other Confederate brigades. The portion of Chew's Battery that had ridden out with Jones on the seventh opened the fighting for the horse artillery.[32] It was soon joined by the other guns of the battery and Hart's, Jackson's, and McGregor's Batteries.[33] On the Federal side, Lt. John H. Calef's Battery A, 2nd U.S. Artillery; Lt. Alexander C. M. Pennington's Battery M, 2nd U.S. Artillery; and Lt. William D. Fuller's Battery C, 3rd U.S. Artillery were engaged.

With the help of a crossfire from a section of the horse artillery,[34] the Confederate dismounted skirmishers finally forced back Col. William Gamble's Brigade, which had managed to hold its position for three hours. Calef's Battery, which had arrived at the front shortly after 8:00 A.M. to assist Gamble, joined in the retreat. The battery had performed up to its usual standard, at one point forcing one of the Confederate batteries to abandon its position near a barn to the left of the road.[35] Buford's line drew back to Boonsboro. They were hurried along by the arrival of Ferguson's Brigade, advancing up the Williamsport Road. Abandoning Boonsboro, the Federals retreated toward Turner's Gap, where they made a stand. Pennington's Battery, which had also been engaged throughout the morning, found itself positioned in an unusual setting and opposed by its old enemies, Hart's and McGregor's Batteries. The ensuing fight added another chapter to the legendary confrontations between these great batteries.

> From early morning until dark, the battle raged fiercely, the enemy's cavalry giving back slowly until they were driven through Boonsboro and into Turner's gap of South Mountain. On a beautiful eminence on the west slope of this mountain, was located the Boonsboro Cemetery. Battery M, 2nd U.S. Artillery, was put in its last position just before nightfall in the cemetery.[36] For half an hour Hart's and McGregor's batteries received the plunging fire of this battery, at what seemed to us much disadvantage, returning it as best we could. To our great relief, we saw it hastily withdraw, at a moment we expected to have to do likewise. Lieut. Carle Woodruff, of this battery, after the war, humorously explained the matter thus: "Every shot you fired," he said, "that missed something in my battery, hit a marble tombstone in that graveyard, and the broken fragments of marble came like hail upon my men. You were ruining us. We did not think it fair for you to shoot tombstones at us, and we left."[37]

Hart's and McGregor's "tombstone" bombardment was the last gasp of the Confederate offensive. Stuart became aware of the arrival of Federal reinforcements and his dwindling supply of ammunition almost simultaneously. He began an effort to disengage. The Yanks were not about to allow him to go quietly.

As Lt. John Calef remembered it, his battery had scarcely reached its position during the withdrawal when he received orders to advance again. Back he went, putting his guns into action in support of the blue skirmishers, which were now pushing back their gray counterparts. The Rebels still had some bite left, despite the ammunition shortage. Calef recalled that his men came under the fire of Confederate sharpshooters holed up in a stone barn. To add to that annoyance was the fact that the enemy horse artillery had managed to approach dangerously close—for artillery—under the cover of the surrounding terrain. Their presence was not immediately noted but became apparent when Calef ordered Lt. John W. Roder to take one gun and drive the Confederate skirmishers out of the barn. The lieutenant's first fire brought a hail of shot down on him from a Confederate horse battery not 1,000 yards away.[38] The first shot severely wounded one man and killed a horse. Calef swung his guns around and returned fire as best he could. By his own admittance, the enemy's fire was "extremely warm." However, Stuart was set upon leaving Buford behind, and before long Calef had the satisfaction of seeing his adversary depart, a circumstance the young lieutenant erroneously attributed to his "accurate" fire.[39]

Stuart continued his retreat toward Funkstown.[40] He was not alone. Buford hung on to the Confederates tenaciously. After crossing Beaver Creek, the two sides were right back where their day had begun, but Buford was not yet satisfied. The lead squadron of the Federal cavalry "galloped forward as if to charge." The 1st North Carolina prepared to meet them but never got the opportunity. A Blakely from Chew's Battery barked, and a shell arced across the sky unerringly to its target. Others followed it. No matter which way the blue column turned, Chew placed a shot in its path. Finally, the Federals decided to terminate their pursuit before Chew terminated them. With this marvelous display of accuracy, the day's fighting drew to a close.[41] The gray cavalry and horse artillery settled down for the night near Funkstown.[42] Taking advantage of the moment, Lt. James H. Williams penned a short letter to his Cora back home:

> July 8th 1863
> Near Hagerstown
>
> My Dear Miss Cora,
>
> Don't suppose you care to hear of any movements, nor have I time to write them. This is the first hour of rest I have had for a week & it is I fear short-lived. For 1 week we have been going night & day. I have been sick & have only been kept up by the excitement. For the last three nights I have not slept except naps stolen on the march. I only write to assure of my safety, trust it is worth all else I could write. We have made many narrow escapes. Should we meet again may tell you of it & many adventures.
>
> We were not in the Friday's [July 3] fight, the big fight at Gettysburg but were watching the right flank & had an engagement with Cav. In it Mark Bird was wounded & I fear is in the hands of the enemy.[43] Fountaine is missing.[44] It rains as it has done every day for a week.
>
> Can write no more. Am afraid our army will soon be in Va again. Love to your Ma, Sallie & believe me
>
> Yours in haste,
> James[45]

Williams's fear that the army would soon be in Virginia again mirrored the feelings of many in the army who did not relish the thought of admitting that they had been beaten. Others, however, couldn't wait to get home but were forced to bide their time because of the high waters of the Potomac. The army had no Moses. As long as the river made its fords impassable, Robert E. Lee was stuck in Maryland, and Jeb Stuart had an important job to do. He got back to it the following day.

The ninth was a day of quiet until about 5:30 P.M., when Buford once more tested the Confederates holding the Beaver Creek line. This time the Federals were more successful. Lt. Albert O. Vincent, in command of a section of Battery B/L, 2nd U.S. Artillery, added his firepower to the three squadrons of dismounted skirmishers that advanced against the Confederates. Buford's entire mounted division followed. The initial object of this offensive was a hill held by enemy skirmishers. Chew had a section of his guns in position, supporting the Confederate skirmishers. When the Yanks attacked, Chew's guns blazed away as rapidly as they could be loaded and fired. Charles McVicar recalled that the Federal sharpshooters were hidden in the wheat and fired on the battery.[46] The juggernaut could not be stopped. Chew pulled out his guns, and the Confederate line was pushed off the hill.

Buford now decided that one hill was not enough. He forged ahead despite the lengthening shadows that foretold the coming of night. Near Funkstown, the remaining section of Chew's Battery was started toward the sound of the fighting.[47] By the time these reinforcements reached their hard-pressed comrades, night was close at hand. Chew's entire battery now faced the Federals and fired two rounds into the gathering gloom. Those were the last shots fired by the Confederate artillery. By mutual consent, the fight was postponed until morning. Chew limbered and marched back to Funkstown to camp.[48]

While Chew's Battery upheld the honor of the battalion, the other batteries were just trying to hold up. Men and equipment were worn, and ammunition was scarce. Breathed, Griffin, McClanahan, and the section of McGregor's Battery had not moved from Williamsport,[49] but during the day, Moorman's Battery had ridden to Funkstown, encamping there for the night. Hart's and Jackson's Batteries and McGregor's other section had not participated in the fighting and welcomed the opportunity to rest. Buford's push late in the day was a foreshadowing of what Stuart could expect on the tenth. Regardless of their condition, the Confederate cavalry and horse artillery still had some hard work ahead of them.

That hard work began at 8:00 A.M. Buford picked up right where he had left off the evening of the ninth. So did Chew. The Ashby Battery greeted the Federals about two miles below Funkstown. Their engagement was short and without success. After a few rounds, it became apparent that Buford was not about to be put off by a single battery of horse artillery and a few grayback skirmishers. The enemy's sharpshooters were making the air thick with lead around the guns. Chew limbered and rode back toward Funkstown. A mile short of the village, he again tried to halt the Federals. However, Chew had gone into action with little ammunition. Before long he used up what he had and was forced to withdraw.

Into the breach galloped Moorman's Lynchburg Battery. Its contribution to the campaign thus far had not been as significant as that of some of the other batteries, but it could be counted on when the need arose. The ninth had been a day of relative calm for the battery in its march to Hagerstown. Lt. Charles R. Phelps even had time to pen a quick letter to his aunt to bring her up to date on what he had seen and heard:

Hagerstown MD July 9th 1863

Dear Aunt

We arrived here yesterday and took possession of this place. We met the Yankees near the city, charged them through the streets and followed them about six miles near Williamsport. After leaving Ashby's Gap, where I wrote from last, we came to Williamsport and crossed Potomac, from thence went to Chambersburg, Pa and on to Cashtown, 6 miles from Gettysburg where we arrived on the 2nd July.[50] Our Battery was not engaged at Gettysburg as we have been bringing up the rear and guarding our flanks. I cannot give anything correct from the fight at Gettysburg. So many rumors are afloat. Our loss has been very heavy. The first and second day we whipped them badly and drove them from every position but on [the] 3rd day we attempted to storm their heights and our loss was very heavy. Picket's Division bearing the heaviest loss.

Harvey is amongst the missing, from all the information I can get from his regiment he was slightly wounded in the famous charge and as the Division did not have sufficient support our men had to fall back and he would not expose himself to the fire—which was deadly. He sat down behind a stone fence and was taken prisoner. This is all the information I can get of him. His wound I understand was a slight one, and I believe he is all right tho' a prisoner. Capt. [Hugh] Nelson & the Adjt. of 28th Regt have promised me to get all the information they can and let me know. This charge will be famous in history as one of the most gallant ever made—none excepted, & if Heth's Division had come up in time, we would have achieved the most glorious victory of the war. As it was, the Yanks reinforcements were too many for us, and we had to fall back after carrying their works. The 11th Regt from Lynchburg has suffered terribly, the Regt being now in command of a 2nd Lieut. [James R.] Hutter is prisoner—[Capt. Kirkwood] Otey wounded, in fact all the officers killed & wounded.

I cannot say what is the program now. All our forces are in this neighborhood, and we doubt we will have another heavy battle. We have done the Yanks great damage since we have been here. The Cavalry have had several heavy fights and have been very successful. Stuart had been going day and night since he left us at Ashby's

Gap. He went within 2 miles of Washington—captured 180 wagons—2000 mules—1500 prisoners etc.etc. Yesterday about 12,000 prisoners passed through the streets of Hagerstown (on their way to Richmond) singing the Star Spangled Banner. They did not seem to receive any sympathy from the citizens, though I believe more than two thirds are strong for the Union. There are a great many Copperheads about here, and they say they will resist the draft.

Will let you hear from me as soon as possible & give you all information concerning Harvey. Tell Miss Wiatt not to be uneasy about him as I believe he will turn up all right in a short time—that is the impression of all the men I have talked with.

The crops here are the finest I ever saw, but there is nothing to eat and nothing to wear—cannot buy anything for greenbacks even. Our Army had passed in front of us & stripped the country of everything that was to be had. I did not even see a horse in Pa but what were in service. The people had run off almost all they had & the Army took the balance.

I write in haste—Remember me to all & believe me Yours very truly

Dick[51]

The haste with which Phelps wrote on the ninth was echoed in his battery's dash to the front in relief of Chew. Moorman unlimbered and went right to work. Unfortunately, he had come at a bad time. Buford had his teeth into Stuart and wanted to administer a good mauling. Stuart knew he was in for a fight and proposed to give as good as he got.

Moorman's gunners found themselves in a hornets' nest. Lt. John H. Calef's Battery A, 2nd U.S. Artillery, had seen some hard service over the past few days but did not seem averse to a little more. As skirmisher fire ripped through both batteries, Moorman and Calef settled down to an old-fashioned artillery brawl. The Confederates received the worst of it. Whether from Calef's shelling or sharpshooters' fire, Moorman began to take casualties.[52] Pvt. Augustine Leftwich, Jr., crumpled to the ground with a mortal wound. Pvt. Thomas J. White, who was struck in his left leg, followed him. The wound proved so severe that he could not move with the battery and had to be left at Hagerstown, where he was captured on the thirteenth.

At this point, the Napoleon gun of Lieutenant Shoemaker's section ran out of ammunition. More was sent for, but in the meantime, the lieutenant did not see the need to expose his men. They were ordered to lie down. Before long, Stuart rode by and inquired why the men were lying on the ground. Shoemaker's explanation evidently did not strike Stuart as a plausible one. He ordered the cannoneers to stand for "moral effect." They scrambled to their feet beside their temporarily useless gun as Stuart rode off. He did not know that he had earned the new nickname of "Moral Effect," which, according to Shoemaker, was always spoken with respect and admiration. Stuart never asked anyone to do something he was not willing to do himself, and he had been on horseback while the gunners were hugging Mother Earth.[53]

The ammunition arrived, and the Napoleon once again thundered away at Calef and company,[54] though more and more the target had to be the clouds of blue skirmishers. As the day lengthened, Stuart began to see that he could not hold Buford in check without infantry help. His artillery was doing everything it could. Moorman had three additional men down, Privates Ephraim H. Parker, Samuel T. Preston, and James W. Griffin, but fought on. It was not enough. About 1:00 P.M., Stuart sent a courier to Col. William W. White, commanding the brigade of Brig. Gen. George T. Anderson, who had been severely wounded at Gettysburg. White was told to report to Fitz Lee, who gave him orders as to how he wished the infantry to deploy. There was a short delay so that Fitz Lee's horse batteries could open on the enemy. After ten minutes, White moved forward and deployed with some difficulty about 150 yards from the Federal line. As the brigade advanced, its right regiment, the 59th Georgia, came under fire from Fitz Lee's horse artillery.[55] Six men were killed or wounded by this errant fire, which brought the 59th to a halt. A short time later, Fitz Lee ordered the brigade to fall back. Eventually, Stuart retreated behind Antietam Creek, and Buford withdrew to Beaver Creek and camped.

July 10 also saw action west of Williamsport on the Clear Springs Road. On the seventh, Col. Watson A. Fox's 74th Regiment New York State National Guard had received orders to march to Clear Spring. Fox moved out on the eighth, accompanied by three companies of the 29th Pennsylvania Militia under Col. Joseph W. Hawley, and encamped on the afternoon of the ninth at the southern end of Blair's Valley in the vicinity of Gillard, about two miles from Clear Spring. Here Capt. Nathaniel Payne's company of cavalry, which had been attached to Maj. Gen. Robert H. Milroy's division, joined him. At 8:00 A.M. on the tenth, Fox and Hawley left their men in camp and rode out on a reconnaissance with Payne and his cavalry. By 10:00, they had returned, collected their commands, and marched to Clear Spring. When within half a mile of the town, Fox was informed that Payne had run into about 500 Confederate cavalry with a section of McClanahan's Battery in support. The size of the Federal force caused the Confederates to make a "precipitate retreat." McClanahan's guns barely got warm.[56]

While Chew, Moorman, and McClanahan grappled with the enemy on widely separate fields, the other batteries remained in much the same positions as they had been on the evening of the ninth. Jackson's Battery, encamped near Boonsboro, had a few precious moments when the men could think of something other than manning the guns. Lt. Micajah Woods took the opportunity to write a letter to his father, describing the momentous events that had transpired around him. He wrote, in part:

> With difficulty and after delay I find myself at a halt long enough to communicate to you, I trust, some of the res gestæ[57] in our short and yet uncompleted campaign.
>
> Never have I been so anxious to let you hear from me, because the danger to which I have been exposed and the excitement accompanying, have surpassed anything I have experienced in the other campaigns, and not since the commencement of the war have I left it incumbent upon me so much to be thankful to an Almighty Providence for shielding and protecting me during the hail storm of furious battles in which I have participated.[58]

The opening lines to Woods's letter undoubtedly reflected the feelings of many of the men, not only in the horse artillery, but throughout Lee's battered army. Almighty Providence had brought Lee's gallant veterans to the banks of a swollen Potomac—to where Virginia lay so close yet so far away. They were not yet home. Woods and others looked to Almighty Providence and "Marse" Robert to take them the rest of the way.

From the eleventh to the thirteenth, Meade's forces tightened the ring around Williamsport.[59] Stuart offered some resistance, but there was no repetition of the heavy fighting of the sixth, eighth, or tenth. Some of the horse artillery batteries were attached to the various brigades of cavalry, while others were part of the defensive lines around Williamsport. No accurate accounting of their positions over the final few days of the campaign can be given. When at long last the waters of the Potomac began to drop to fording levels, the horse artillery took its place in the columns of Lee's army and crossed once more into Virginia. Some would be back, but for most, it was their last invasion of the North.

In retrospect, from the beginning of the campaign on the battlefields of Brandy Station to the final shots fired at an enveloping Federal host around Williamsport, the Confederate horse artillery's overall performance added significantly to the battalion's already outstanding reputation. There had been bad moments when equipment or circumstance had brought about a less-than-desirable outcome. This was especially true of some of the newer batteries, Jackson's in particular, which fought with inferior armament. But the men and officers had not faltered. Stuart's long ride north tested Breathed's and McGregor's men to the utmost, but they did not fail to keep up or deliver when called upon. Gettysburg itself was not a highlight of the campaign for the horse batteries. The battalion's record on this most famous of battlefields was barely adequate. However, it could be argued that the men made the best of the opportunities presented.

The retreat to Virginia was a different story. During those fateful days, the horse artillery illustrated what men could do when asked to go above and beyond their call of duty. With their cavalry comrades, the men of the Stuart Horse Artillery Battalion stood between Lee's crippled army and the oncoming Federals. True, Meade's army was tattered and worn, but it still had the potential to inflict great damage to the Confederates by destroying Lee's wagon train. Imboden and Stuart did not permit that to happen. In the thick of the fighting was the horse artillery; its contribution helped the Army of Northern Virginia survive. Pelham would have been proud.

Lt. Parkison Collett

Wounded in action three times the former recruiting officer for Brig. Gen. John D. Imboden's brigade proved his worth as an artillery officer on more than one field. Collett earned the respect of the men under his command as well as his superiors by his devotion to duty and his courage in the face of the enemy.

AUTHOR'S COLLECTION

Lt. Micajah Woods
If not for Woods little of the history of Jackson's Battery would be known. More than a chronicler, however, Woods was a contributor to the history his pen recorded in his letters home. A solid officer in a battery that never made the upper tier of the battalion, Woods could have served successfully in any of the other batteries in the horse artillery.
FROM THE *CONFEDERATE VETERAN*

Lt. Carter Berkeley
An artilleryman in the Staunton Battery, a hospital steward, and a cavalryman before joining McClanahan's Battery as its fourth lieutenant in May 1863, Berkeley proved himself more than capable by rising to command the battery in the war's last year. His appointment came as a result of "valor and skill." He did nothing to diminish that assessment.
COURTESY OF ROBERT J. DRIVER, JR., AND THE AUGUSTA COUNTY HISTORICAL SOCIETY

Lt. Robert Powell Page Burwell

Young and enthusiastic, Burwell transferred from the infantry to take a commission in the horse artillery. His career was brief, and he was lost to the battalion after serving for less than eight months. He showed promise and was greatly mourned throughout the command.

COURTESY OF THE CLARKE COUNTY HISTORICAL ASSOCIATION, INC.

Pvt. Charles Wilson
1st Stuart Horse Artillery.
COURTESY OF NANCY P. LESURE

Pvt. Abraham Shriver Wilson

1st Stuart Horse Artillery.

COURTESY OF NANCY P. LESURE

Lt. Lewis Tune Nunnelee
Forty-one at the beginning of the war, Nunnelee showed that courage was not solely the property of the young. Promoted to a lieutenancy for gallantry, he led by example, having come up through the ranks. He never asked his men to do anything he hadn't done or wasn't willing to do.
COURTESY OF LEWIS T. NUNNELEE II

Pvt. John James Williams
Ashby Battery.
COURTESY OF BEN RITTER

Pvt. George H. Burwell
2nd Stuart Horse Artillery.

COURTESY OF THE CLARKE COUNTY HISTORICAL ASSOCIATION, INC.

Pvt. James Gray
2nd Stuart Horse Artillery.
COURTESY OF BEN RITTER

Pvt. Samuel T. Evans
2nd Stuart Horse Artillery.
FROM THE *CONFEDERATE VETERAN*

Pvt. Calvin L. Caplinger
McClanahan's Battery.
COURTESY OF BEN RITTER

Pvt. Francis T. Brook
McClanahan's Battery.
COURTESY OF ROBERT J. DRIVER, JR.,
FROM *BOY SOLDIERS OF THE CONFEDERACY*

Pvt. Robert Z. Furry
Ashby Battery.
COURTESY OF BEN RITTER

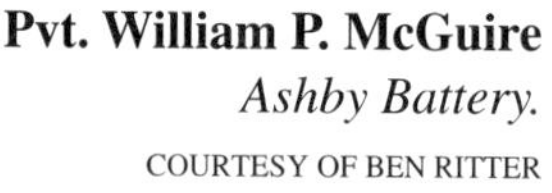

Pvt. William P. McGuire
Ashby Battery.
COURTESY OF BEN RITTER

Pvt. Thomas C. Williams
Ashby Battery.
COURTESY OF BEN RITTER

Pvt. Philip W. Boyd
Ashby Battery.
COURTESY OF BEN RITTER

Pvt. Americus J. Souder
Ashby Battery.
COURTESY OF BEN RITTER

Pvt. Francis Edward Conrad
Ashby Battery.
COURTESY OF BEN RITTER

Pvt. Edward Jackson Reed
Ashby Battery.
COURTESY OF BEN RITTER

Corp. George M. Neese
Ashby Battery.
COURTESY OF MRS. MARY R. OREBAUGH

Pvt. Marcellus Barksdale Fuqua
Lynchburg Battery.
FROM THE *CONFEDERATE VETERAN*

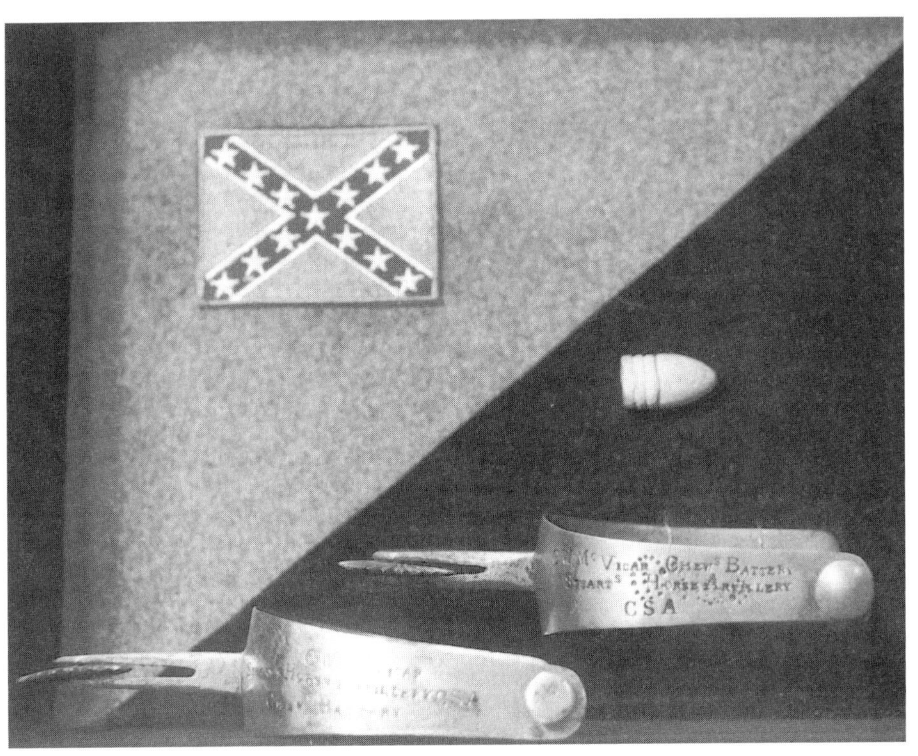

Charles McVicar's spurs.

COURTESY OF MRS. BRUCE B. SELDON

Maj. Mathis Winston Henry
Henry was a West Pointer like Pelham. He knew how to fight horse artillery and demonstrated it repeatedly, but especially so on the field of Fredericksburg. His actions that day earned him a promotion, which unfortunately took him from the battalion.
COURTESY OF THE U.S. MILITARY ACADEMY

Lt. Francis Halsey Wigfall
Halsey, as he preferred to be called, was the son of Confederate Senator Louis T. Wigfall, but it does not appear that he used his father's position to acquire high rank. He came to the horse artillery having already served in Rosser's Battery at the beginning of the war and then in Bachman's Battery. He remained a lieutenant throughout the war until April 28, 1865, when he received a promotion to major and aide-de-camp on the staff of Gen. Joe Johnston.
COURTESY OF MARTY AND JAMES ROGERS

CHAPTER 20

On Familiar Ground

"I return from Pennsylvania poorer than when I entered."

For the majority of the soldiers in the Army of Northern Virginia, the crossing of the Potomac meant safety and a chance to rest. Stuart and his cavalry had no such luxuries. To them fell the job of vigilance. Meade's army must be watched and any incursions must be met and rebuffed or delayed until Lee could bring infantry up to meet the threat. Baker's Brigade (formerly Hampton's) with Hart's Battery was assigned the duty of patrolling the river crossings between Falling Waters and Hedgesville.[1] The 18th Virginia Cavalry and McClanahan's Battery guarded the fords above Hedgesville.[2] Robertson's Brigade was sent to the fords of the Shenandoah River. Fitz Lee's and Chambliss's Brigades camped in the vicinity of Leetown, with Stuart's headquarters at The Bower nearby.[3] Jones's Brigade, which had preceded the other cavalry brigades into Virginia on July 13 to guard Lee's communications through Winchester, eventually went into camp near Charles Town on the sixteenth.[4]

The horse artillery batteries were also required to remain vigilant and were stationed with the various cavalry brigades. Upon crossing the Potomac with Jones's Brigade, Chew's Battery rode to Martinsburg, where its guns were repaired, and went into camp at Smithfield in Jefferson County.[5] Moorman's Battery passed through Martinsburg on the fifteenth and joined Fitz Lee's and Chambliss's Brigades at Leetown.[6] Breathed's and McGregor's Batteries also encamped near Leetown.[7] Griffin's Battery marched to Fredericksburg and remained there until the army crossed the mountains and entered Culpeper County.[8] Jackson's Battery moved farther south in the Valley than any of the other horse artillery batteries. It finally encamped at Bunker Hill, well below Martinsburg. Here Lt. Micajah Woods took pen in hand to write to his father. His letter covered news of the army, what was, what might have been, his battery's role in the campaign, and his and his battery's condition.

Near Bunker Hill Berkely Co. Va.
July 16th 1863

My dear Father—

At last and much to my gratification I have a prospect for a day's rest, and I shall at once devote a portion of my holiday to writing to you & those at home. I have addressed you two letters recently, but such are the uncertainties of war & mail transportation that it is more than probable that neither reached their destination. So I shall first tell you briefly the chances good and evil that have befallen our Battery in the eventful campaign which has just been completed north of the Potomac.

Constant and incessant forced marches brought us to our Brigade [Jenkins's] in front of Harrisburg where we had the good fortune to be engaged in two fights with Yankee infantry and cavalry, hence the pleasure of bursting shell & shrapnel among our enemy & creating wild confusion was unallayed by visits of like unwelcome messengers among ourselves. A battery made its appearance once in our front & fired a few shots, but ere long we forced it to be limbered up & disappear by a few well directed rounds from our guns. We lost no men, but the constant marching begins to tell upon our horses, many of which fell from sheer exhaustion in the road, & we were necessitated to supply their places from the barns of Pennsylvania farmers. These in time we soon found utterly unfit for hard service.[9] Though immensely large & generally unnaturally fat, they are so delicate & so clumsy that often a day's travel puts them out of the road in a helpless condition. Our constant service & motion which has been [word illegible] for a day till this time has caused us to make way with about 90 horses since our departure from Staunton, & today there are not 20 of the 100 horses which we started in the Battery. . . . Our Battery is in Virginia again safely with the whole army, but my section is placed hors de combat and it will be necessary for us to recruit for two weeks before being ready for action.

The entire army effected a safe & entirely orderly crossing of the Potomac night before last and yesterday at Willamsport and Falling Waters—without being pressed or harassed by the enemy. Two regiments of cavalry which charged into our rear were almost completely annihilated. The campaign we have just finished has not only been arduous & fruitless but it is useless to deny the fact that it has been terribly disastrous to our armies in as much as the men have suffered much from fatigue. They have fought the most terrible battle in the annals of war in which from fifteen to nineteen thousand of our best soldiers have been numbered among the killed and wounded. This is the view that the whole army takes of the events that have just transpired. True, we have lived for nearly a month upon the enemy's soil—we have killed as many, if not more of the foe, than we have lost, but we can look around and see no fruits of success—and this is a crisis when our cause can afford to lose nothing without heavy compensation.

Genl. Lee says had he remained in his position two hours longer, he could have claimed a great victory as the enemy did certainly evacuate their lines as soon as he did his. For three days we remained in line of battle near Hagerstown but the enemy would not attack. Had they done so in our strong position we would have utterly crushed their army. Demonstrations in our rear I presume caused the crossing of the River. The enemy held a perfect Gibraltar at Gettysburg and no one can explain why Lee attacked it of course.

I have no idea of our future movements but I would not be surprised to find the army concentrated around Richmond in a month from this time. The clouds around the Confederacy are darker & blacker than ever. This army is now regarded as the main stay & prop of the Country's cause. It is still dauntless in spirit, powerful & to be feared, but alas! How many thousand of its bravest & best will never more lift an arm or tramp the soil of their native land. They are now but a handful to cope with myriads. I hope they will do it successfully. One thing is proved beyond doubt that we are unable to carry on a war of invasion. The enemy had at Gettysburg 50,000 more men than they ever could have concentrated against us on the Rappahannock line.

Our Battery is pronounced by all authorities in the army to be very inefficient. In fact, the most inefficient Battery in the army on account of our short ranged guns and one of us Blain, Wortham, or myself, will very soon have to go to Richmond to secure better ones.

I return from Pennsylvania poorer than when I entered. I did no plundering. I bring away not a cents worth of trophy—on the contrary I am minus a fine overcoat & blanket which I carried with me but I am perfectly satisfied that I came with my body intact. If I always get out of a tight place as well I shall be fortunate. Bob is safe, healthy and hale. I have purchased for him a splendid little mule which I [about a quarter of the page illegible]. I don't think my horse at home [two words illegible] a bargain at $1000. I can sell him in his present condition for 350 or 400 dollars or more. My mule is five years old, & attracts the attention of all who see him. He carries himself well & is Lt. gray in appearance. I purchased him from the Qr. Master at cost prices I am entitled to go by for my own use or the use of my servant.

I was compelled to leave Staunton so hastily that I failed to get my splendid boots, the consequence is I am at present nearly bootless. In other words, I will be bare footed before very long if I don't supply myself from some source. Enclosed you will find the exact length of my foot. Please send it by the very next mail to Staunton, and purchase me a pair of cavalry boots at the Government shoe store. I was offered the first quality at $50 per pair. They are worth elsewhere $75 & $100. The price has probably been raised since I was there, but they would be cheap at $75. The conductor on the train or Home Peyton will take pleasure in attending to it. I generally wear (nos. 8 or 9) I think. I am particularly urgent as I know vast number of orders are being sent on. I am almost destitute of anything to wear on my head. My first hat has about a dozen holes in it which every one takes for granted have been pierced by balls. It will not last me long, so please get me a nice cap—trimmed with artillery colors if possible. One can, I suppose, be purchased in Richmond if such cannot be obtained get a nice military cap of any description. I can have it trimmed properly hereafter. My size is 7 1/8. I think of sending Bob home in a day or two to get these things or of getting an order to go to Staunton in person, but this is not probable by any means. The crown of the cap should be high so as not to touch the top of my head. The cap should have a cover.

These are all my wants at present and they are urgent & I trust they will be supplied as soon as possible. There is no room for conjecturing where our Brigade will next move. The impression is that we will remain either in the Valley or in Western Virginia. I earnestly hope so, I for one have had enough & seen enough of the grand army of Northern Virginia to satisfy all my ideas of "the pomp & circumstance of glorious war." I meet with numbers of my friends every day which affords me great pleasure.

I have about expended my fund of material for writing and with the expression of great love to my dear Mother, Sister, & brothers I am Very affectionately Yr. Son

Dr. Jno. R. Woods Micajah Woods
Holkham[10]

Jackson's Battery was effectively out of the Army of Northern Virginia and the war for some time. The remaining Confederate horse batteries were not as fortunate. While Woods relaxed far from the front, the other horse batteries were being called upon to repel the invader.

On the day before Woods wrote his letter, Col. J. Irvin Gregg's Brigade led an advance of Brig. Gen. David McM. Gregg's 2nd Cavalry Division across the Potomac and brushed up against Stuart's pickets near Charles Town. Chew's Battery was called up to bolster the Confederate defenders and arrived after the gray cavalry had been driven to a point about a mile south of the town.[11] Gunner George Neese chose not to waste his ammunition on the enemy's skirmish line, which was composed of men of the 1st Maine Cavalry. Only when the men from Maine presented a larger target in the form of a body of mounted troopers preparing to charge did Neese loose his salvos. Encountering the horse artillery halted the 1st Maine in its tracks. There was no further advance. However, it was not entirely due to Chew's few artillery shells. The rest of Colonel Gregg's Brigade and Col. John B. McIntosh's Brigade had turned off toward Shepherdstown, leaving the 1st Maine without support. General Gregg reached Shepherdstown and encamped there for the night.[12] Chew's Battery held its position until almost dark and then fell back about four miles and camped on the Berryville Pike.[13]

July 16 brought renewed fighting along Stuart's outpost lines. Fitz Lee's Brigade, followed by Chambliss's, marched on Shepherdstown from their camps near Leetown. Stuart hoped to bring Ferguson's Brigade over from Martinsburg. "Grumble" Jones was posted in front of Charles Town and informed of Stuart's intentions so he could cooperate as things developed. Going with Fitz Lee was Shoemaker's section (a Napoleon and a howitzer) of Moorman's Battery and part or all of Breathed's and McGregor's Batteries.[14] Pickets from the 10th New York Cavalry were struck and driven in by Fitz Lee's troopers. The Confederate thrust was brought up short by the 1st Maine, which had been out looking for forage and found Rebels instead.

Fitz Lee began working around the Federal flanks, but General Gregg countered with elements of the 4th and 16th Pennsylvania Cavalry. Soon Shoemaker, Breathed, and McGregor unlimbered and opened fire.[15] Lt. G. W. Beale of the 9th Virginia Cavalry remembered the horse artillery firing "by piece, one after another, again by sections, and again simultaneously."[16] Lt. Ernst L. Kinney with a section of Battery E, 1st U.S. Artillery, supplied the Federal firepower. Typically, in the end, both sides claimed a victory in what was basically a draw. Fitz Lee's men settled down for the night with the intention of starting the contest again in the morning. Gregg's forces bivouacked near the home of Col. Alexander R. Boteler but were gone come dawn.[17]

The enemy driven off for the present, the men of the horse artillery turned their attention to letter writing. Lieutenant Woods of Jackson's Battery wrote his father yet again on the seventeenth. He was not reserved in his criticism of his captain over the condition of the battery, and his letter shows that the "what [Stonewall] Jackson would have done" school of thought began classes shortly after Gettysburg.

Near Bunker Hill. July 17th 1863

My dear Father,

I wrote you a letter day before yesterday and sent it to Martinsburg to be delivered to Dr. Wm. Hoge. I am in doubt whether he received it. Our Battery has been reported unfit for duty & yesterday an order was given us to take it to the rear till we could be furnished good long ranged guns and recruit our horses sufficiently to again take the field. We will take up camp somewhere I presume above Woodstock. One of us—Wortham or myself—will go to Richmond in a day or two to procure guns & equipments. Capt. Jackson's run mad spirit of hurry and haste brought us from Staunton entirely unprovided for a campaign without a Battery wagon or forge—indispensable appendages to a Battery. We will not again join the Brigade, under any circumstances till we are thoroughly equipped in every particular, but I fear that Jackson will again hurry us to the scene of action without due preparation or rest—in a condition in which we can neither do efficient service for the country or win for ourselves credit commensurate with the danger that will imperil our lives. As soon as we reach our permanent camp I will give you my post office, where I shall expect a letter. Not a word have I heard since leaving home.

You need not purchase the articles I requested as Wortham can supply my wants, if I am not, in person, ordered to Richmond.

The wonted confidence of this army in its power & irresistibility—is now entirely restored, & the Yankee army that comes out to meet it, may well beware of its fate. I met with Nat. Osborne yesterday—he is ordnance officer in Rodes' Division he says that Genl. Rodes thinks that 16,000 will cover our entire loss at Gettysburg, three thousand of this no. are prisoners. He says that Lee aimed high & risked nearly all in his effort to storm the heights, knowing that could he once [word illegible] the enemy, he would capture the whole Artillery of their army, and the Yankee army is as helpless as a babe without that powerful arm.

The officers of the army are very prone to compare the action of Ewell on Wednesday with what Jackson would have done in a like situation. Had he moved on and followed up his magnificent success the whole Yankee Army would have been swept before us before they had seized their powerful position & fortified it. Again A. P. Hill is censured for not standing his ground as expected in support of Longstreet in his efforts to storm the heights on Thursday & Friday.

The army is in position at Bunker Hill where it will make a stand, should the enemy feel inclined to attack. It is thought that the Yankees are crossing the Potomac in two columns—one at Leesburg—the other at Shepherdstown, the former to operate immediately against Richmond—the latter to engage the attention of Genl. Lee. It is rumored this morning that our corps has been ordered to Richmond—it, joined with the force already there, will be expected to protect the Capital, while the main body of the army whips the two columns in detail. These rumors & conjectures, you can take for what they are worth. One thing is certain, that if a heavy force marches on Richmond while the main army is so far distant, the country between Charlottesville and Richmond will catch "hail Columbia"—to an extent not altogether agreeable.

I was rather surprised at hearing a day or two since, that Meri Anderson enlisted in the cavalry, he may regret it that he permitted his patriotism to impel him to such a step before it was required by law. While I try never to regret anything that is passed, I am sure it would have been wiser in me to have delayed entering the army a little longer. Bob has been unfortunate with his mule. It was stolen day before yesterday, and I have not been able to find any clue to his whereabouts and probably never will. It is not yet determined whether I will lose the $100 or not. I trust you are filing all the "Examiners" as I anticipate a great deal of pleasure in reading the accounts from the army at this [word illegible] in future. I have seen only one Southern paper since leaving Staunton.

What course did you pursue with Henry? What is "Importing & exporting stock" selling for, now? In what condition is my bay horse, and do you think he would answer to relieve my present horse for a month or two? How is the crop of peaches? I want to get home at the time they are ripe.

Give my best love to my Mother and all the household and believe me to be Very Affectionately

Your Son
Micajah Woods

Dr. Jno. R. Woods—
Holkham
Va.[18]

Lieutenant Wigfall of Breathed's Battery also took advantage of the lull to write a letter to his sister. He reported the condition of his battery and some possible movements of the army that were being talked about throughout the camps. It seemed everyone had an idea of what should be done.

Camp near Leetown
Jefferson Co. Va. July 18th 1863

Dear Louly,

I wrote a short note to Papa from near Funkstown on the other side of the river on the 9th inst. though I have very great doubts as to whether it ever reached you. The battery is in very bad condition as regards horses and is out of ammunition. Two of the guns got some of the latter before we recrossed the river leaving the other two without and I was left with them and have consequently been in the rear ever since the cavalry fight near Boonsboro Md. on the 8th inst. All the guns are now in the same condition, but the ordnance officer of the division, Capt. John Esten Cooke, perhaps better known to you as "Tristan Joyeuse, Gent." has sent to Staunton for ammunition and as [Lt. Philip P.] Johnston has gone to Richmond I shall be done for the present with "Company Q." . . .

I suppose of course by this time you have seen from the papers who has been killed wounded and captured and have very little doubt but that you know more on these points than I do myself for beyond hearing the report that Genl. Lee's Hd.Qrs. are at Bunker Hill and that the infantry are beyond Martinsburg and some little inkling of the position of the cav. Division, I am in the same condition as honest John Falstaff before he formed the acquaintance of Prince Henry and "knows nothing."

I received yesterday a double letter of the 23rd of June from you and Mama the first since I left Rector's X Roads on the 13th of that month. Genl. Lee has issued an order curtailing all transportation except that for the Corps and General Reserve Ordnance trains. He is evidently getting ready for another move but whether it is in order to cross the Potomac again or to fall back behind the Rappahannock, or merely to be in readiness for any movement of the enemy is more than your correspondent is aware of.

Present my most felicitous compliments to Miss Annie and Miss Mary Bull and remember me to Mollie Cincinnatus Warren whose Christian name is Annie, if you know her.

Give my best love to dear Papa and Mama and kiss "the duck" for me, and tell it to write. Good-bye dearest Lou and God bless you

Your affectionate Brother
Halsey[19]

While Wigfall and the rest of Breathed's Battery concerned themselves with the need for horses and the lack of ammunition for their guns, Hart's Battery had an opportunity to put its pieces to some use. On the seventeenth, Col. Bradley T. Johnson, who was commanding Brig. Gen. John M. Jones's

Brigade of infantry in that officer's absence because of wounds received at Gettysburg, had been ordered to destroy the Baltimore & Ohio Railroad in the vicinity of Martinsburg. Federal cavalry began to harass the working parties on the eighteenth and by the following day had forced them back to within a mile of Martinsburg. Hampton's Brigade, led by Col. Laurence S. Baker, failed to stifle the enemy's intrusions. Johnson countered with the 50th Virginia Infantry and a section of Hart's Battery. The South Carolinians earned plaudits from Johnson, as they "did very great service" in helping the infantry drive off the raiders.[20] The Confederates finished their work of destruction, and Hart's guns went back to picket duty.

During the time Breathed's cannons idled and Hart's barked, Jackson's Battery was simply trying to procure guns with which to fight. On this subject, Lieutenant Woods had good news to report to his mother in his third letter in five days:

Camp near Winchester Va.
July 20th 1863

My dear Mother—

At present I have a little [several words illegible] and am in camp four miles [word illegible]. It is difficult to imagine [word illegible] poor soldiers are for a [word illegible] from the constant marches and [word illegible] vigorous campaign, such as all acknowledge the Great Pennsylvania trip to have been in the highest sense. Yesterday Capt. Jackson set out for Richmond with an order from Genl. Lee to procure new guns as speedily as possible—he will be absent probably for ten days or two weeks and during that time we will remain in status quo. Our new armament will consist of two 10 Pr. Parrotts & two 3 inch Rifles—the guns combining the greatest advantages in the service.

It is my earnest hope that now since I am on a direct mail route you & the home folks generally will extend to me a little more gratification by the [word illegible] reception of letters, which [several words illegible] the circumstances are [several words illegible] number. On Examination [word illegible] Brigade mail yesterday I found two letters from home, one of July [date illegible] the other of July 12th which old as they were in date contributed much to my good cheer. I live in expectation of communications of a later date today & shall go to Winchester in person to get mail—as I can scarcely realize that none of you have written me a word since the 12th Inst. I wrote from near Harrisburg from Boonsboro the day after the Cavalry Battle in which our Battery participated so prominently, giving you full details of the great conflict at Gettysburg, and the [words illegible] enacted by different commands.

I wrote from Martinsburg [words illegible] and my last letter was mailed yesterday. My disappointment is as great as [words illegible] if these various letters have not reached their destination. Now that our line of communication is open, letters will arrive safely in the army.

Considerable reinforcements have come into the army since recrossing the Potomac—perhaps as many as ten thousand—principally troops from Western Va. and men heretofore wounded and absent who are rejoining their commands.

Many are predicting another invasion of the enemy's country ere long—and I believe the troops would hail with delight such an order—so determined and anxious are they to retrieve the day which was not won at Gettysburg. Genl. Stuart has unreservedly said that he reposes more confidence in the men of Jenkins' Brigade than in those of any other [words illegible] and the Infantry bestows [words illegible] terms of praise upon them.

The main object of this letter is to urge you & Father to write me. And dear Sister Sallie ought to find time to add something since her school is out. Give my love to all and believe me to be in great haste

Very affectionately
Yr. Son
Micajah Woods[21]

The resurgent morale of the army was quite evident in Woods's letter. Just days before, he had written of the "terribly disastrous" campaign north of the Potomac. Now the young lieutenant wrote enthusiastically of the new guns his battery was waiting to receive. For the men of the Stuart Horse Artillery Battalion, there was no waiting. They had their guns, albeit with little or no ammunition. All that was needed was an enemy to supply the targets.

The Army of the Potomac lumbered across its namesake river east of its confluence with the Shenandoah River at Harpers Ferry, threatening to isolate Lee in the Valley. Stuart became aware of the move despite the Federal attacks west of Harpers Ferry, which were executed in part to conceal the lower river crossings. Longstreet's Corps was dispatched to counter Meade's move. Stuart used Robertson's Brigade as the advance guard through Front Royal and Chester Gap. Baker was ordered to bring up the rear of the army, which was Ewell's Corps. Jones remained to picket the lower Shenandoah River. Fitz Lee, Chambliss, and Ferguson force-marched from Leetown through Millwood toward Manassas Gap to protect the flank of the army. The batteries of horse artillery moved with the cavalry toward familiar ground—Culpeper Court House and the Rappahannock River line.

The twenty-second had found Chew's Battery encamped near Berryville with a section of guns at Charles Town, or so Col. John B. McIntosh of

Buford's Cavalry Division reported on July 22.[22] Actually, Chew's guns were far from Charles Town and heading south. On the twenty-third, one section of the battery camped at Winchester, while the other section was on the road to White Post.[23] The sections reunited at Fisher's Hill on the twenty-fourth. The next day, the battery marched through Woodstock, Edenburg, and Mount Jackson and bedded down on Rude's Hill for the night. On the 26th, the battery crossed the Massanutten Mountain, passing through New Market and Luray with Jones's Brigade before bivouacking beside the Hawksbill two miles south of Luray. The following day, Chew led his men and guns through Thornton Gap and Sperryville and encamped two miles south of the latter on the Culpeper Road. On the twenty-eighth, the battery covered the twenty miles to Culpeper Court House, pitching camp there for the night.[24] There were tired hooves and tired posteriors aplenty after the grueling marches. One of the first things Pvt. Charles McVicar did once the battery settled into its new location was write a letter home chronicling his adventures:

> Camp near Hazel River[25]
> Culpeper Co. Chews Battery
> Dear Mother,
>
> It is with a thankful heart that although so far from Home I can write to you to let you know how [word illegible] getting along [and] what we are all doing. I will try and give you a rough description of our tramps for the past few days. On Friday morning last I was with you all at home little thinking that this the following Wednesday would find me in Culpeper Co. We camped near Fisher's Hill 2 miles above Strasburg on Friday night. I came by Mrs. Campbell's but did not get to see Miss Annie as she was in Newtown. Willie was not able to come after the cows and Mr. Campbell had a sore foot or he would have come after them himself. He went to a neighbors and tried to get a horse but did not succeed.
>
> I expected the Battery would camp at Newtown over night and intended to come back after the cows on a flank the next morning, but as the Battery did not stop before we were at Fisher's Hill 21 miles from home, I had not the slightest chance to come back as we moved early next day. Everything was moving very much like an evacuation. I was very sorry to leave. The cows could not help it.
>
> I bought a fine bay colt three years old. Paid 400.00 for him. [Word illegible] that was before I come to Newtown thinking that we would picket near home so Kate could have the colt to ride. The colt is a very fine mover but alas for my calculations Saturday found me at Rude's Hill near New Market. Raining hard. Laid in the barn for the rest of the night. Sunday morning at sunrise I led my colt out to Mr. Neese's 1 mile from New Market and put him in pasture. Mr.

Neese is to take care of the colt for me. I am still riding Celim, the one I traded for. Willie is the name of the colt.

The Battery passed through New Market at 10:00. I stayed awhile to see old acquaintances. We crossed the Massanutten Mountain [and] camped over night near Luray, Page Co. Monday across the Blue Ridge to Sperryville. Halted a part of the night. Moved on to Culpeper Court House. This Wednesday morning we moved 7 miles further below the court house. I saw John Chapman in Woodstock and promised to pay him 10.00 ten dollars to bring the cows to Mr. Campbell's for me. Mother you must send them out as soon as you can. You do not know how soon this enemy may dash in. Well I must close. Give my regards.

Your Affectionate Son
Charles Wm McVicar

Mother you must excuse this badly written letter as I am almost asleep. Tell Kate that I have a beautiful pony in the Valley for her. God bless you all. There are a great many troops around this place.

Mother you will please tell Mollie Stewart that George[26] is well & hearty, that he is anxious to get a letter from home, [and] that she must write as soon as possible to let him know how they are all getting along. He is sitting beside me as I am writing. I am in fine health at present.

George would have written had I not been writing. That horse that Mr. Danley sent out came to the Battery safe.[27]

McVicar's "tramps" toward Culpeper Court House were mirrored by the other batteries, though the roads over which they marched differed. For some of Beckham's battalion, Yankees, not cows, were the main concern.

On the twenty-third, Moorman's Battery[28] marched toward Chester Gap to support Brig. Gen. Ambrose R. Wright's Brigade of infantry, which was being attacked by a superior force of cavalry and infantry. It arrived too late to help.[29] Moorman turned his guns around the next day and marched for Bentonville. Riding through that place, the battery continued south. After passing Milford and Rileyville, the battery camped at Oak Hill. Here on the twenty-fourth, Captain Moorman was sent to the rear because of illness, and the battery was split.[30] Shoemaker's section and McGregor's Battery were ordered to Gaines's Cross Roads. Lieutenant Phelps's section of Moorman's Battery and Breathed's Battery were to ride on to Culpeper Court House on the twenty-fifth.[31] Both parties crossed the Blue Ridge at Thornton's Gap at different times.[32] Phelps's contingent went into camp on the farm of John Minor Botts on July 26.[33] Shoemaker and his part of the battalion arrived there about the same time.

Hart's Battery and Baker's Brigade had the greatest distance to march because of their posting in the lower Valley. The battery made excellent time, however. Marching in rear of Ewell's Corps, Hart rode south to Winchester and New Market, then across the Massanutten Mountain through the Luray Gap, to Luray, and through Thornton's Gap to Culpeper, which the battery reached on the twenty-seventh.[34] It was the last of the Stuart Horse Artillery Battalion to leave the Valley. The two batteries that remained in the Valley had fought with the battalion during the Gettysburg campaign but were not officially part of it. Jackson's and McClanahan's Batteries would become part of the battalion, but that was in the future. For the present, they were, along with the cavalry they supported, the guardians of the Valley.

On July 21, 1863, Brig. Gen. John Imboden was appointed to the command of the Valley District. On that same date, the 18th Virginia Cavalry and McClanahan's Battery attempted to capture a Federal force at Hedgesville, but the Yanks fled across the Potomac to safety. By July 25, Imboden had fallen back to Fisher's Hill. Lee's departure from the Valley threw the remaining Confederate troops on the defensive. Jackson's Battery could do little until the captain brought the guns up from Richmond. As the main armies prepared to face each other again east of the Blue Ridge, the Valley became a secondary theater of the war, but one that could at any moment affect Lee's or Meade's plans.

As July drew to a close, the cavalry and horse artillery picked up the routine that had become second nature by this time in the war—picket, skirmish, picket, skirmish. August would see heavier clashes on the familiar ground around Brandy Station, but the last days of July were somewhat quiet. Griffin's Battery rejoined the army from Fredericksburg and became the sixth member of the battalion. Beckham's responsibilities grew accordingly. His men, when not on picket duty, wrote letters home and dreamed of a furlough. Lt. Francis H. Wigfall's dreams were no exception.

> Camp near Culpeper C.H.
> July 30th 1863
>
> Dear Mama,
>
> We reached here on last Sunday afternoon [July 26] and on Monday I rode over to Gen. Stuart's to see if I could obtain two or three days leave of absence to visit you at Orange [Court House]. He told me that there was a howitzer at the C.H. which he wished brought up and he would send me down there for it. I accordingly went down next day and was greatly disappointed at not finding you there. The howitzer had been sent to Richmond and I came up again yesterday my trip having proved fruitless both as required business and pleasure. I met in the cars Mrs. [Betty Barbara Winston] Rosser on her way to Culpeper. The col. [Thomas L. Rosser] of the "5th Horse" met his bride or wife (which is correct?) at the depot and seemed very much glad to see her.[35] He has procured lodging for her in town. I believe Mrs. A. P. Hill was also in the cars and the General

waiting for her but he seemed to take things much more composedly than the other.

While at Orange I stayed at Mr. Hilden's who seemed quite glad to see me and gave me a general invitation to his house whenever I should visit the place. Mrs. Hilden fixed dinner for me earlier than usual yesterday in order to allow me full time for the cars and while at dinner presented me with Judge Tucker's argument entitled "The Bible or Atheism." While at Orange this Spring she sent over to the Battalion a bundle of them containing one for each officer.

The last I have received from you was of the 23rd of June and came to me near Leetown beyond Winchester. I wrote to Papa just after reaching Maryland on our return from Pennsylvania and to Louly from near Leetown on the 18th inst. Two couriers have come to me today with a dispatch transmitted through the signal corps from Gen. Longstreet to Genl. Stuart inquiring the whereabouts and condition of Lt. Wigfall. I am afraid from this that you have failed to receive my letters and that Papa has written to Gen. Longstreet to find out what is the reason.

Old John Minor Botts was at Maj. Beckham's Hd. Qrs. this morning again with a complaint. This time it was that the horses were in his corn field inflicting upon it the ravages of war. He says that he is inclined to resign his ownership that he is nothing more than Gen. Stuart's overseer and that he doesn't receive enough wages to compensate him for his time and trouble.

I saw Major [Edward H.] Cunningham on the train on Thursday who told me that Gen. Hood was coming to Charlottesville.[36] I was glad that he was doing so well and hope it will not be long before he returns to duty. If you see Mrs. McKensie you must remember me to her. We are at present lying entirely idle and are in a pretty badly used up condition. Our battery and McGregor's which were the only ones with Gen. Stuart in his expedition round the Yankee army have had by far the hardest marching of any artillery in the army. The horses of this battery would not, if all the corn they received had been given at once, have received (on an average) two good feeds from the time they left Papertown, five miles this side of Carlisle Pa. until they reached Culpeper C.H. They lived on wheat, green oats, & grass and received little of that. The worst time for something to eat I have ever seen was on this march. I ate supper about dark the evening of the 4th July near Gettysburg, and about 9 o'clock the morning of the 7th I got a piece of bread and two small slices of bacon from one of the men at the wagon trains at Williamsport. Between supper and breakfast I had one biscuit and five rolls. These and cherries were my sustenance. You may imagine I relished the bread and bacon.

Give my best love to dear Papa and Louly and kiss "Pansy Baby." Write frequently dearest Mama and believe me I am

Your affectionate Son
Halsey[37]

Wigfall's trip to Orange Court House, abortive though it may have been, was more of a furlough than most of the other officers and men of the battalion received in the waning days of July 1863. Lee and Meade were jockeying for position along the Rappahannock once again. Not surprisingly, Stuart's cavalry and Beckham's artillery were right in the middle.

CHAPTER 21

Brandy Station Again

"They are complimenting us with shells that come uncomfortable close."

The first day of August 1863 found Beckham's horse artillery batteries spread out along the Rappahannock doing picket duty with their cavalry comrades. Usually one section was on duty while the other rested. Chew's Battery was posted along the Hazel River, guarding the ford near Rixeyville.[1] Lt. Charles R. Phelps's section of Moorman's Battery and three guns from Breathed's Battery, all under Captain Breathed's command, left the vicinity of the John Minor Botts farm on July 31, rode to Brandy Station, and turned toward the Rapidan. They crossed the river at Ely's Ford, though the high water forced the gunners and the accompanying cavalry of Fitz Lee's Brigade to carry the ammunition across on horseback.[2] They marched on, passing through Chancellorsville and finally encamping at Salem Church, where they remained until August 18.[3] Shoemaker's section of Moorman's Battery remained at the Botts farm. McGregor's Battery probably was encamped with Shoemaker. Hart's Battery was stationed on Fleetwood Hill.[4] Griffin's Battery was somewhere in the vicinity of Culpeper Court House.

Brig. Gen. John Buford had his division of cavalry up at 3:00 A.M. on August 1. Massing his command at Rappahannock Station, he had hoped to cross there as early as possible and push on to Brandy Station. Problems developed that delayed the crossing until 11:00, and soon after crossing Buford's troopers ran into Baker's Brigade led by Stuart in person. Hart's Battery found itself on the very spot on Fleetwood Hill from which it had fought on June 9.[5] The fighting became heavy, as Stuart was determined to hold the hill. Buford had other ideas and sent troopers around both flanks. Outnumbered, Stuart was forced to fall back about 600 yards to another hill, on which stood the Kennedy house. Here Hart took position on the western side of the railroad, where McGregor's Battery joined him.[6] Baker formed his cavalry on the eastern side of the tracks. The deep railroad cut separated the artillery from the cavalry, a serious error in tactics.

Buford kept pushing his brigades forward. The blue cavalry pounded at Baker while Buford's artillery thundered at Hart and McGregor, who were endeavoring to both assist Baker and respond to the Federal guns.[7] The enemy cavalry soon began to force Baker back. At about the same time, Merritt's Brigade turned the Confederate left, coming out of the woods at the gallop almost on top of Hart and McGregor. Hart's response was swift.

> Every gun was swung around and this column checked by a rapid fire of canister. The 1st South Carolina Cavalry was nearest our position across the cut to our right and was being pressed back through a corn field some distance to the rear of us. Capt. Hart, seeing that his guns were lost unless one or the other of the Federal columns could be driven away so as to enable the railroad crossing to be reached, called on the 1st South Carolina to try to drive back the column that was pressing it. The gallant Lieut. Col. [John D.] Twiggs, of this regiment, received the message and promptly said, "Tell him I'll do it." And bravely and well this heroic old regiment responded to the command "right about fours—forward—Charge!" The enemy's line was swept back far enough beyond our front to enable the Battery to move forward to the crossing and gain the east side of the railroad.[8]

The men of McGregor's Battery remembered the close call as well. Sgt. George W. Shreve recalled fighting with canister at very short range. The danger of being overwhelmed by the numerically superior Federal cavalry continued until the order "A double charge" rang out. For the first time, McGregor's cannoneers rammed home double charges of canister and sent them hurling into the oncoming blue cavalry. The blue wave receded, allowing McGregor's men a breathing space. When Twiggs drove back the Federals on the eastern side of the railroad cut, McGregor's Battery joined Hart's in making a hasty retreat. Left behind in the hands of the enemy was Private Larking, too seriously wounded to move.[9]

The Confederates were now nearing Culpeper, but Buford was showing no signs of giving up the fight. Fortunately for Baker, Hart, and McGregor, help was close at hand. They needed it. "Grumble" Jones, with a section of Chew's Battery in tow, arrived about 3:00 P.M.[10] When the battlefield came into sight, Jones realized he was on the right flank of the enemy line and in a perfect position from which to enfilade it. Chew quickly unlimbered his guns and opened on two Federal batteries, which were at the time concentrating their fire on either Hart's or McGregor's Battery. Pvt. Charles McVicar wrote of what happened after Chew entered the fight:

> The enemy are falling back slowly. We are under a heavy fire. This is lively work. They have better range of us than usual. We are constantly changing positions to escape their range. They have in the last

> hour thrown fifteen shells and marked the ground within twenty paces of our gun. Yet we disabled their gun by striking it with one of our shells, another burst among their horses and limber chest. They are complimenting us with shells that come uncomfortable close and they are firing wild and fast. We are giving in return the best we have. We have succeeded in driving them from their position and are advancing rapidly, keeping on a line with the skirmishers. The Minie bullets are flying around us thick. Not a man sulking. They are all standing firm under this withering fire. Third position is sending a regular shower of bullets at us. The trees are literally trimmed, yet not a man of our gun has been hurt. Fourth position fired fifteen shells. Fifth position has thrown three shells within twenty paces of our gun and bursting among us, but the fragments flew harmlessly by. It is now getting too dark to fire. We succeeded in driving them back. Went to camp at Brandy Station for the rest of the night. The heaviest fighting was done on our old reviewing grounds of last month.[11]

Baker and Jones had some help from A. P. Hill's infantry, which entered the fight near Culpeper.[12] The "ease" with which Buford allowed himself to be pushed back was due in large part to both Jones's position on his flank and the infantry he ran into.

Hart's Battery had fired 250 rounds per gun and had been under a heavy fire for most of the day yet emerged without a single casualty, except for its bullet-riddled guidon and several horses, equally riddled.[13] McGregor's, in addition to Private Larking, lost Lt. Robert P. P. Burwell, who was also wounded but expected to recover. The wound, however, proved mortal, and Lieutenant Burwell died at the hospital in Staunton on August 31.[14] Chew's Battery had one man captured, Pvt. A. Edmonds, though how he managed it is unknown. An additional casualty was Lt. William Hoxton, the adjutant for the battalion, who was wounded.

Stuart, pleased with the performance of both Baker's Brigade and the horse artillery, issued the following order on August 6:

> The gallant and spirited resistance offered by Hampton's [Baker's] brigade, to a body of the enemy's cavalry greatly superior in numbers, on the 1st instant, deserves the highest commendation at the hands of the division commander.
>
> The good conduct of the officers and men of that veteran brigade, in such a conflict, reflects the highest credit on their patriotism and soldierly qualities, and is worthy the emulation of the entire division.
>
> In this contest, the Horse Artillery performed a part equal in heroism to its already brilliant prestige and but for its supply of ammuni-

tion on the field becoming exhausted, the enemy's losses, confessedly more than three times our own, would have been far greater.

J. E. B. Stuart,
Major General[15]

Stuart might have had the opportunity to write this order earlier if not for another brush with Buford closer to Kelly's Ford. This time it was the Confederates who initiated the fight, hoping to drive their blue adversaries back across the Rappahannock, or at least find out what they were up to. The fighting was the main topic of letters written home by Lt. Charles R. Phelps of Moorman's Battery and Lt. Francis H. Wigfall of Breathed's Battery.

Camp Near Culpeper CH Aug 10th 1863

Dear Aunt

Your letter of the 4th ult. to hand last night. Please accept my thanks for your kind remembrance of me also received last night by Mr. Tilden.

I received yesterday a letter from Sister informing me of the death of Harvey. This very much surprised me, as I was daily expecting to hear of his arrival at home, but such is the fate of war. I regret very much it was not in my power to have seen him before I left Penna.

I heard that you intended visiting the springs. If so I hope you will take Miss Wiatt with you. I have written her urging her to take a trip if only for a few days. I am afraid that her health is not as good as it should be, & I believe it would benefit her very much to take a trip for a short time.

"Another fight at Brandy." This has become a common saying with us here—a fight last Monday, and on Thursday and Saturday three fights in less than a week but still, Moorman's Battery does not get into any fight of any consequence according to correspondent of Lynchburg Republican. On Tuesday last I had the hottest artillery fight I have ever had for some time.[16] The Yanks had a four gun battery playing on my one gun (Napoleon) and literally ploughed up the ground all around the piece. Every man at the gun was struck & three of them badly wounded. Still we held our ground until a shell struck the wheel of carriage, disabling the piece entirely. We then had to withdraw. Genl Stuart and other officers complimented the cannoneers on the field. Garland Poindexter died at 2:00 A.M. next day of wounds received. I was with him until he died, but nothing could be done for him his wound being internal. I regret very much I could [not] have his corpse sent home, but there was no cars running regularly here, and no conveyance to be had. The Yanks were expected at the Co. Ho. [Culpeper] every minute & the weather was such he could not be kept out of the ground.

Our pickets and the Yanks are within 300 yds of each other and momentarily expect an engagement. I do not think [we] will try to hold this place but will fall back to the Rapidan.

I have nothing new to communicate, the weather here is awful hot. Will write again in a day or two. Have a chance to send this off & must close.

Remember me to all
Yours Very Truly
Dick

Hope to hear of Miss Wiatt's being well in a short time & will try and get off to see you all. I think our Capt [Marcellus N. Moorman] is entirely too much demoralized to return. We all can spare him. Some one should show him Genl Lee's last order.

D.[17]

Camp near Culpeper C.H.
Aug. 13, 1863

Dear Mama,

I received yours of the 6th inst. day before yesterday. A day or two after writing my last [letter of July 30, 1863] I rode into Culpeper and on reaching camp on my return found that Capt. Breathed was about taking two of the guns down the river with Fitz Lee's brigade. I was left in command of the other two. The next morning [August 1] Yankees made a reconnaissance in force towards Culpeper. This force greatly out-numbering ours (a division, Buford's, against Hampton's [Baker's] brigade), the cavalry was forced back. All the guns of the battalions which had ammunition were sent to the front and the rest including my own went with the wagons back to Culpeper. I here got a little for my Whitworth gun and returned to the front.[18] It was after sun-set when I reached them and about dark I fired a few rounds and withdrew.

On the 4th Capt. McGregor's two guns, one of Capt. Moorman's,[19] and mine which were together at Brandy Station were ordered down to Petty's hill about half mile from Brandy. We found the sharp shooters at work when we reached there and shortly after going into position Capt. [Wiley H.] Griffin's opened on the enemy from the plain in front.[20] I had received orders to open on them as soon as I saw them, and after a while after our skirmishers had driven them back for some distance and had been in turn driven from the ground they had gained and forced back to about their first position, I opened on a body which I supposed at the distance to be a small party of cavalry. This proved however to be a section of artillery. I had only twenty rounds when I went into action and they of course lasted a very short time when I withdrew my piece and took it back to the wagon train beyond Culpeper C.H. Next day I got my 3-inch rifle ammunition-chest full and came back to the front where I have been ever since. We have been treated shamefully in regard to ammunition but as there is now an abundance at Orange C.H. I hope in future that difficulty will not be encountered. In the fight on the 1st inst. Hoxton who is acting Adjt of the Battalion was wounded quite severely.[21] Lieut. Burwell also, of McGregor's battery was wounded seriously in the arm.

It is impossible for me to get any leave whatever at present as I am the only officer here and if Capt. Breathed does not return to the battalion Maj. Beckham intends sending me down to him to return two guns from other batteries as soon as he can get some Whitworth ammunition for me. In that case I shall be as far off from seeing you as ever, Fitz Lee's brigade being in the neighborhood of Fredericksburg.

I saw Young Green from Washington the other day. He had not heard from his father lately, but I believe the old gentleman still holds true to his principles. He has been imprisoned once but released. The son is in the 4th Cavalry of Fitz Lee's brigade.

As soon as the battery gets united and there is a probability of quiet for a while if we are up here I intend to go to Gen. Stuart to try to get three days leave of absence and come up and see you all.

Give my best love to dear Papa and Lou and kiss to Fan. You must write frequently and tell Louly to do the same. Remember me to Gen. Hood and Dr. Darby.

Good-bye dearest Mama and believe me as ever

Your loving son
Halsey[22]

The ammunition shortage that plagued Wigfall did not affect the Federal horse batteries. As the gun crew of Shoemaker's lone Napoleon had found out, their blue-clad counterparts hadn't lost anything in the accuracy department, either. In addition to Poindexter, Privates John F. Wood and Robert R. Miller were also wounded.[23] Miller's wound was so severe that he was discharged and lost to the battery a year later.

The seesaw contest finally drew to a close with Buford's picket line advanced about 800 yards from where it had been when the Confederates attacked. Those batteries that had been engaged returned to camp or picket duty. Chew's Battery, which had not seen action, had been on picket duty on Fleetwood Hill. They relieved the other section of Griffin's Battery that had been stationed there.[24] Even though fighting raged toward Kelly's Ford, Lt. James H. Williams took time to write a letter to his "Dear Cora." The close proximity of the Federal host was not uppermost on his mind.

On Picket Near Culpeper C.H.
August 6, 1863

My Dear Cora,

Yours of the 2nd reached me today while temporarily in camp where we were encamped after the Brandy Station fight. I have been on detached service ever since we came over here. Tomorrow I will rejoin the command at Brandy. Shall be glad when we leave this place. It abounds in sad reflections and thrusts home on me the realization of the loss of my best loved companion and dearest brother. Have been to the spot where we laid him. I shall see that he is laid where the hands of [word illegible] affection can pay its tributes. I have heard nothing from home. The enemy occupy Winchester, unfortunate town. When shall its final redemption come.

We hold our position (I mean the cavalry) at the sufferance of the enemy. Expect at any moment to be driven back. Of course, must make a resistance. We will be in front. I prefer to be on detached service. Have a good set of men with my guns, not a few gentlemen, and they all seem to be attached to me.

At last again the skies are bright & the waves are still. May clouds of doubt arise no more, nor may sense of duty nor ought else disturb our relation. It did seem to me that my position [word illegible] you would—must—understand. I dreaded the idea of having you think me unreasonable & exacting. Your declaration of confirmed confidence is [word illegible], not that my opinion needed confirmation for had I been uneasy, dissatisfied, or harbored misgivings you perhaps unwittingly or with higher objects in view gave many an opportunity of which I could [word illegible] have availed myself, but it is no little to put on paper for you. When we meet I, of course, must be permitted to ask for a full history of all that has passed. You will always seem an unsentimental lover. How would a less impulsive & more spirited man have succeeded. I must be persevering to say the least.

I left my letter at Mt. Jackson on our way to this place. Suppose it was forwarded to Winchester. I have not been there since June 1. Shall most cheerfully comply with your request at my earliest

> opportunity, but you would not fancy one taken now, am thin, sunburned, been in the saddle every day, marching or in line of battle for six weeks.[25] Have not worn a glove for two months. My chief beauty & pride is an enormous beard, longer by far than ever before. When has my hair seen brush or [word illegible] but these like their owner will be obliging, yielding. If you prefer it will sacrifice the former. It grows back, but thank fortune is cool. Must reserve my comments on [word illegible] for morning.
>
> [Word illegible] Miss Ella—Good night.[26]

Lieutenant Williams was to have sufficient time to attend to his tonsorial needs and have his picture taken, because the fighting on the sixth was followed by an extended period of calm as Lee's and Meade's wearied armies settled down to rest and recuperate. This, of course, did not mean that the horse artillery was free of its duties entirely. Picketing and refitting required the men to exert themselves, but not in the manner in which they had been required for almost two months.

The condition of Beckham's battalion was somewhat depressing, to say the least. A brief accounting of what Hart's Battery had passed through will stand as an example for all the other batteries.

> Since the opening of the Gettysburg Campaign, the battery had been in the most arduous service, without a day of rest. It had been engaged with the enemy twenty days out of fifty-two and had marched over four hundred miles. Its men were almost without shoes and clothing; its members diminished by casualties; and its horses worn down with service. Even its splendid steel Blakely guns had begun to show impairment from constant use. A period of rest for re-equipment was necessary, and this was now fortunately afforded us.[27]

Hart was able to secure two new guns from Richmond while disposing of one of his beloved Blakelys.[28] The officers saw personally to the mounting of the guns on strong carriages. Shoes and clothing were issued, a number of fresh horses obtained, and several new men recruited to fill the depleted ranks. The same scenario was played out in the other batteries. However, there may have been one difference. The records show that Chew's, McGregor's, Moorman's, and Griffin's Batteries each took its turn at picketing, but Hart's and Breathed's Batteries are missing from the accounts.[29]

The lull provided time for the men to lay down the tools of war and pick up the pen. Letter writing occupied the time for many a gunner. Pvt. Charles McVicar wrote home to his sister, Katie, on the eighteenth:

Chews Battery Aug 18th/63

Dear Sister,

Judge my surprise on last Friday [14th] when George Stewart [30] handed me your letter of the 7th. I was on picket when the letters came on the hill [Fleetwood] that we had such a warm time on the 9th of June last, the enemy not 1/2 mile off. Our outpost and theirs is in speaking distance of each other. I had written three letters, one for Mother, another for Aunt Minnie in Louisville. Rode down to the front and signaled to the Yanks and met them at half ways gave them the letters. They promised to forward them immediately. I gave them paper. They gave some cigars in return. We had a civil chat for some time. They were two very civil fellows belonging to the 8th Illinois Regiment [of] Cavalry.[31]

At the time I received your kind & welcome letter I was sitting near the gun thinking of home. You may judge with what feelings of delight I tore the envelope when I recognized your hand writing. I had the blues horridly. The news here was that the enemy was at New Market, advancing on towards Staunton, but I must give you a history [of] our adventure before this time. We left home on the 24th of July. . . . The Battery camped 2 miles above Strasburg at Fisher's Hill. I bought a fine Bay Colt at $400.00. 25th to Rude's hill. 26th through New Market. I left my colt here on pasture. I paid $175.00 down on the animal and gave my note for $225.00 in four months which I think I can do without any difficulty. So Katie if I have luck and do not lose the colt, you can have a gay pony as jack if we should get down there once more.

We marched down across the Massanutten Mountain to Luray. 27th crossed the Blue Ridge at Thornton's Gap, through Sperryville, Rappahannock County. 28th to Culpeper Court House. 29th to Rixeyville 7 miles from the court house. On picket there August 1st. At nine o'clock the pleasant music of the Artillery opened to our right. We did not come into action until three o'clock. Fought until dark. None of us hurt, however, that is in the company. Since then we have been on picket at Fleetwood farm near Brandy Station. So you see that is the reason why I had blues when I heard that the Yanks were at New Market. I feared they had gotten my colt, Willie. He is a pretty pony. Gentle as a lamb. Tell Henry that I have a pony for him. God bless him.

I was glad to hear definitely where Father was. I will write to John Brannon this week and see what can be done. Tell Mother that she must not grieve for me as I am living in the town of Culpeper County off the fat of the land. Kate you just ought to see this country here in eastern Virginity. The land is so poor that the killdees have to carry their haversacks along with them, also ladders to climb over the fences as they are too poor to get over otherwise.

Katie this is the third [letter] I have written home. If you knew how much good it does me to receive [a] letter from you, you would avail yourself of every opportunity. Well I must close. My love to all the children. God bless you all. My respects to my friends.

Your Brother
Chas Wm McVicar

George Stewart says you must tell Mollie that he received her letter, that he has been well & hearty since he left home, [and] almost crazy about getting home to see the family, especially that little babe. Tell her she must write often.[32]

Again on the twenty-ninth, McVicar put pen to paper and wrote to a friend. This time he revealed more of what troubled many of the men who answered their country's call.

Reserve Picket Post Culpeper
Court House Chews Battery Aug. 29 / 63

Miss Annie Campbell Dear Friend

Here we are, laying in a pine thicket near town. The scenery around here [is] very pretty indeed. One can sit for hours wrapped in mystic thoughts too powerful to mention. The beauties of nature are beyond description. The thickets we are in are large and expansive. They look as if this has been a camping ground for the war. The fields are covered with a beautiful verdure of weeds about waist high. There are no obstructions in the shape of fences. In fact it seems as if fences had vacated this section altogether.

In regard to prices for what there is left to sell, they are quite moderate. For a meal \$4.00. Flour per barrel \$50.00. Corn meal not comestible. Black-eyed peas 50 cents per pint. Rice $33^2/_3$ cents per pound. Bacon \$2.50 per lb and as for clothing, a hat is worth \$25.00 to \$35.00. Factory cloth \$25.00 per yard. Ready made overshirts \$25.00. Calico shirts \$20.00. Boots \$50.00, 75.00, 100.00. This is the country for a poor man and large family undoubtedly emigrants will choose this locality I am sure. Don't you think so.

Annie I suppose you are getting tired of this plain matter of fact business kind way of writing. I will choose the main topic. Weather for instance. It is raining. We have a blanket thrown over some poles under which I am now writing. Oh Annie, you would little think how this lazy indolent life worries me. I am not contented by any means, having been used to active labor. Labor in which I took a delight in. It was energetic and pushing work that I was engaged [in] both with my Boss and for myself and now to have no employment, nothing to occupy my mind, nothing to do but stand guard, marching, or a battle now and then, nothing in fact but the army rules to perform, I hardly know how to spend the time. I would much rather perform labor of any kind than call such a life. All my bright anticipations for the future are thus blighted. Fond imaginations picturing a neat cottage, a fine workshop, a run of customers by prompt attention to business, and a pleasant bachelor's life to lead, and none of those anticipations which life itself to dream over are left but the bachelor. That is brilliant enough of itself, but the mind and muscle both need food. But my country calls my service. I will try and content myself and hope, yes hope, against hope for better days. But this is transgressing Annie. You must look over this for I feel when writing you that I was speaking to some mean friend. . . .

On picket 7 miles below at Rixeyville August 1st. Relieved at 10 o'clock by the 2nd Section of our battery. 1 o'clock, marching towards Culpeper at a trot. The pleasant music of the cannon thundering forth. Its missiles of death were plainly to be heard in that direction. We came into battle at 3 o'clock and kept on a line and sometimes in front of our infantry skirmishers. It was a running fight. After we came in we turned the scales and drove the enemy to Brandy Station. We fought over our old reviewing ground of June.

I have heard from home twice. Kate wrote in her last letter that Father was at home. I was very glad to hear that I assure you. Well I must close. Give my kind regards to all the family. We have been picketing at Fleetwood farm ever since the fight. That farm is one mile below Brandy Station

Respectfully your Friend
Charles Wm McVicar
Chew's Battery
C.S.A.

Write when convenient.
Send word down home
that I am well if you
have an opportunity
I [have] written four letters there but they may
not have received them.[33]

The picture of the shattered dreams that McVicar revealed in this letter could be multiplied by the thousands of men in both blue and gray who lay in camp or stood picket across northern Virginia that month of August 1863. Worse, there were those who would dream no more. Lieutenant Phelps of Moorman's Battery conveyed news home about one of that growing number:

On Picket Near
Brandy Station Aug 30th

Dear Aunt,

Your letter of the 21st to hand a day or two ago, but have had no chance to answer. I am now doing picket duty at this place, every tree, hill etc. of which have become perfectly familiar to me, as we have traveled & fought for miles around me, the last being the eighth fight we have had within a circuit of ten miles. Our outer picket is within 3/4 of a mile of me in a few yards of the Yankee picket—their camp in full view about three miles off. There has been no change in their position for three weeks, and they do not seem disposed to make any forward demonstration. Their force on this side of the river consists only of Cavalry & Horse Artillery. From present indicators I do not expect any active movements in this direction shortly. I hope Uncle C. will pay me a visit. I will promise him the soft side of my blanket and will endeavor to give him an insight of camp life on the front. Will show him all the sights to be seen in this neighborhood. Do let him come, if only for a day.

Received letter from Miss W. last week, but cannot tell whether she is in Lynchburg or [word illegible]. Very glad to hear she is getting better, but sorry she would not take trip to mountains.

Capt. Moorman has reached camp much improved in health and spirits. He did not succeed in getting a transfer, and I suppose he will have to continue with his old Co. I will not be able to get a furlough as his brother [34] has applied & only one officer at a time can leave camp.

Hurrah, for the old town. It seems from the tune of the Milish, that there are some little patriotism left. I do hope they will not have a test of courage by the Yanks soon. I understand Miss Mary Jones is to be married in a few days. I wish her "good luck." The fate of Dexter Otey has been looked for by me for several years. He was a very bad man.

Heard yesterday that Aug Leftwich Jr. died at Hagerstown of his wound. Capt Moorman sent the letter to Col. I have written to [Pvt. Thomas J.] White who was with him to go to Lynchburg and see his family. White is [a] nice young man and a good soldier. [Rest of letter lost.][35]

September dawned, but the routine did not change. The Federals were content to stay in their camps, so the Confederates held to theirs. However, neither side relaxed its vigilance. Beckham's batteries continued taking turns standing picket on Fleetwood Hill. The strength of the battalion at this juncture was 18 officers and 392 men present for duty. The armament totaled fourteen guns.[36] Not all of the six batteries were present, nor did those on duty all have a full complement of guns. The effects of the Gettysburg campaign had not yet dissipated.[37]

Thankfully, the calm continued. On September 1, Charles McVicar wrote yet another letter home to his sister. It was good that he took the time to do so. The friendly atmosphere created by the decrease in hostilities was soon to change, as the military situation was about to explode.

> Reserve Picket Post Culpeper Court House Chew's Battery
>
> Sept 1st 63
>
> Well Katie,
>
> We are on picket today about 7 miles from Culpeper and one mile below Brandy Station picketing on the Hill we had such a hot time on the 9th of June last. The farm is called Fleetwood. The enemy is only one half mile from here. Their outpost and ours are in speaking distance of each other. We get their papers daily. I am at present writing on the limber chest of the cannon. The Yanks' camps are plainly in sight. We can see and hear them drilling quite plainly. Their tents make quite a comfortable display. In fact, they look more like a village in the distance. We have been gazing at each other in this way on the same lines since the 6th of last month.
>
> On 1st of last month we had a very interesting as well as a hard battle over the reviewing ground between here and Culpeper. It was a beautiful fight over a level tract of land and showed both parties off splendidly. We succeeded in driving the enemy about 6 miles in gallant style. Since then nothing of any importance has happened, excepting hard living and short rations as our wagons are some distance in the rear. We have been getting along very well considering.
>
> Kate I have met with severe misfortune since I left home. I bought a Colt at $400.00, left it in the valley on pasture, and it was stolen. If I should get home this winter you will have a poor brother to welcome. I intend to come home about the first of November on a flank if nothing happens and it is safe, so you need not be surprised to see Geo. Stewart and myself between the first of November and Christmas.
>
> Katie this is the fifth letter I have written home. I have received two letters from you, one stating that Father was free and home. It afforded me a great deal of pleasure to get that letter I assure you. Oh Katie, if only I could get letters from home regular. You little can guess how much satisfaction it would afford me.
>
> Well, I am now going down to chat [with] the Yankee pickets for awhile. I will finish when I get back. Excuse me a few moments. Adieu.

I have just returned and will finish this uninteresting letter. I have written so often and directed the letters in so many different ways and not receiving an answer to any of them that I cannot say whether you will get this, but [word illegible] you must tell Kate McCann that she must write me. I cannot find out how to get letters there yet. The scouts are among you all so often that it is an easy matter for you to send them to me. Give Lissa my kind regards. Tell them that I would like very much for her to see the scenery around our camps. It is magnificent beyond description. One can gaze on the beauties of nature here wrapped in mystic thoughts too deep to mention. In front of the camp is an undulating scene of table land as far as the eye can reach covered with a rich green verdure of weeds about waist high. Flocks of beautiful plumaged birds of the killdee description are running around so poor that they cannot fly. They have to carry their rations with them when they come here and so on. I must close.

Give my love to all the family. Kiss the children. God bless you all. My kind regards to all inquiring friends.

Respectfully Your Brother
Charles McVicar

You must excuse the [word illegible]
as I have a bad [word illegible]

Tell Mollie Stewart that George is well, and he now weighs 200 lbs. [and] is as large around the waist as a flour barrel and so on.[38]

Obviously the short rations McVicar was getting had not affected George Stewart, who must have been a better forager. Others were not concerned with foraging or picketing but with recovery, a return to duty, and promotion.

Lt. William Hoxton was not with his batterymates as they stood watch over the Federal campfires and picket posts. His wound had taken him out of the war for the present. On the fifth, he wrote his brother, Llewellyn, about his condition and other items of interest. He wrote, in part:

Danville Sept 5/63

Dear Llew,[39]

Your letter was received day before yesterday and was read with great pleasure by both Sallie and myself. My wound heals very slowly and occasions me a good deal of trouble every now and then, but I still am sufficiently improved to get out of bed sometimes, which is a most inexpressible relief to me, for the confinement to my bed I have found more disagreeable and unendurable than even the pain from the wound. . . .

It is exceedingly gratifying, Llew, to hear that the Old Dominion and our army on her soil are so highly spoken of in the South-west.

Such expressions of enthusiastic praise, as you mention, are enough to make every Virginian's heart throb with a pure and noble pride for his glorious old birth-place. The Army of Northern Virginia has undergone and suffered a great deal in its numerous bloody battles and heavy and fatiguing marches, but the officers and men comprising it are still as high strung and eager for a fight as if fighting were mere pastime, and they have become so perfectly inured to hardship and privation that I don't believe there is a better disciplined, more subordinate army of the same size to be found—even in Europe.

Llew, are you not entitled to an Adjutant? I should like exceedingly to be in your command, and if you could procure me a lieutenancy, I would be delighted to resign and come out to you. I am considerably disgusted just at present for General Stuart has assigned a young man, a son of Gen. Wigfall to my battery ranking me. Of course it is enough to discourage & disgust a young officer to take away from him all hope of promotion by putting over his head a man who has seen no service (as is the case in this instance) and whose only earthly claim to the position is his father's influence. . . .

Yr. devoted brother,
William Hoxton[40]

Hoxton's emotions over Wigfall's appointment eventually would be soothed by a transfer, not of Hoxton, but of Wigfall. Even Hoxton's pride in the Army of Northern Virginia was not enough to overcome his feelings of injustice. Fortunately, he would remain with the horse artillery, building a reputation as a fine officer and, unfortunately, receiving another severe wound.

On September 9, Stuart's cavalry underwent reorganization. The cavalry division was officially designated a corps, and the brigades were now arranged in two divisions. Wade Hampton, promoted to the rank of major general, commanded the brigades of Brig. Gen. William E. "Grumble" Jones, Brig. Gen. Laurence S. Baker, and Brig. Gen. Matthew C. Butler. Fitz Lee was commissioned major general and given a division consisting of the brigades of Brig. Gen. William H. F. "Rooney" Lee, Brig. Gen. Lunsford L. Lomax, and Brig. Gen. Williams C. Wickham. The horse artillery battalion, which remained in the capable hands of Maj. Robert F. Beckham, was still composed of Capt. James Breathed's 1st Stuart Horse Artillery, Capt. William M. McGregor's 2nd Stuart Horse Artillery, Capt. Roger P. Chew's Ashby Battery, Capt. James F. Hart's Washington South Carolina Battery, Capt. Marcellus N. Moorman's Lynchburg Battery, and Capt. Wiley H. Griffin's Baltimore Light Artillery. This new organization was soon to be put to the test, with sad results for Beckham's batteries.[41]

The idyllic scene described by McVicar on the first changed abruptly on the thirteenth. Instead of exchanging newspapers with the enemy, the cannoneers and troopers went back to exchanging lead and iron. The divisions of

Brig. Gen. John Buford and Brig. Gen. H. Judson Kilpatrick crossed the Rappahannock and slammed into Stuart's pickets.[42] The Confederate cavalry chieftain had some notice of their coming, as did some members of the horse artillery. Pvt. Benjamin T. Holliday, who had joined Chew's Battery on September 1, recalled what transpired the day and night prior to the Federal attack:

> On Saturday evening, Sept. 12, 1863, the gun detachment that I belonged to left camp with the 3-inch rifle piece for Brandy Station to do picket duty. We took position on Fleetwood Hill, the battleground of the great cavalry fight between Stuart and Averell [*sic*] on the 9th of June 1863. This hill commands an extensive view northward in the direction of the river, which is only a few miles away, where Gen'l Meade's army is camped. On this hill is a fine old Virginia mansion. The night was threatening rain and some half dozen of us Winchester boys obtained permission to sleep on the parlor floor. Late in the night we were aroused by someone trying to get in the house. Upon investigation we found the party to be a scout, who came to tell us the Yankee army was going to advance at daylight, and for us to be on the alert. We went out into the yard and could plainly see the enemy's camp fires along the Rappahannock River. Shortly afterward a thunder storm of unusual severity developed, and the rain came down in torrents, which delayed the advance of the enemy.[43]

The warning Stuart received allowed a few hasty preparations, but little else could be done. When the Yanks crossed early on the morning of the thirteenth, Jones's Brigade, led by Lomax, fought them over the familiar terrain around Brandy Station. On August 1, Stuart had denied the Federals the capture of Culpeper, but on this day, the enemy's forces were too numerous and too determined. McGregor's Battery and the lone gun of Chew's Battery made a stand on Fleetwood Hill against Kilpatrick, who had crossed the river at Kelly's Ford. Before long, an artillery duel erupted between McGregor's and Chew's guns and Lt. Jacob H. Counselman's section of Battery K, 1st U.S. Artillery.[44]

At this juncture, Kilpatrick and Buford, who had crossed the river at Rappahannock Bridge, linked up. Buford had clashed briefly with Griffin's Battery along Muddy Run but had thrown it back toward Culpeper.[45] McGregor and Chew made a precipitate retreat from Fleetwood. Private Holliday remembered the morning's confused fighting:

> We could see the enemy's cavalry vidette down the road in our front, and at the base of the hill we occupied were our cavalry pickets. Several times we saw a movement of the enemy's cavalry in the distance, working around our right. Word was sent to us to keep a sharp lookout on the Rixeyville road, which was to our right. Pretty soon an order came for us to fall back toward Culpeper C.H., about six miles

south of us.[46] There was a large body of oak woods adjoining Fleetwood hill on the south and east sides. The road to Culpeper C.H. broadened on the west side of the woods. We had gone but a short distance down the southern slope of the hill when we heard firing nearby, and in looking in the direction of the sound of it, which came from the woods, we saw the Yankee cavalry in hot pursuit of our cavalry, who were few in numbers. We were in great danger of being captured, and we left the road and took a course due west, across the fields, the four horses attached to the gun going in a full gallop, and urged to their utmost speed by the drivers on the rear and front horse. Had the enemy seen us, they could have captured us with ease, as only the officers carried side arms.

Captain Chew, realizing the peril we were in, rode out a short distance from the gun and beckoned to a squadron of our cavalry which looked to be five or six hundred yards north of us, and moving leisurely in our direction.

I had not secured a horse for myself up to this time and was riding on the limber chest of the gun, holding on to the trunnions[47] in order to retain my seat, for we were going at a lively pace, over rough ground, and at the time, I thought the gun would be overturned.

When we had gone sufficiently far westward, we turned to the south and came to the John Minor Botts estate. As we passed through his farm I saw him at his barn. We moved up to the front of his house, a fine old Colonial Mansion, which stood on a slight elevation. The ladies of the household were on the front porch, looking at the fight in the fields nearby. We unlimbered the gun and fired one shot at the Yankee cavalry, but up to this time the enemy had not appeared in force and those in front of us were too much scattered for us to do any execution. We moved southward on our way to Culpeper and made another stand at the corner of a woods. At this point they fired a shell at us which passed with a scream over our heads.

Their line of battle now came into plain view and our cavalry was retiring before them. We moved back again, passing the woods where we had been encamped and took a position in a level field some four or five hundred yards south of the woods, and we shelled the woods with the 3-inch rifle gun. Their sharpshooters began to make it warm for us. A small body of our cavalry in falling back got in the line of our fire, and we called to them to get out of the way. They divided, some going to the right and some to the left of our gun. As they did so, I heard a thud and saw a large man fall from his horse, having been shot in the back.

I had a close call here. I had to go to the caisson to get the shell and insert it in the gun, and in doing so, I felt the wind of a bullet as it passed my ear. It couldn't have missed me by more than an inch or

> two. The enemy began to flank us, and we again fell back, this time to the suburbs of Culpeper C. H. The enemy now had opened with their artillery all along the line, and shells were screaming through the air every few seconds. I passed a Confederate cavalryman who had his head tied up with a handkerchief. He said he had been cut over the head with a sabre, and the lieutenant of his company killed. I pitied the poor fellow as he seemed to be suffering a great deal of pain. We had now reached Culpeper C. H. and crossing Crooked Run, we climbed a very steep hill at the north end of the town and unlimbered the gun.
>
> From this point of view we had an unbroken view of the country in front of us. The enemy cavalry, some five or six thousand under Generals Buford, Kilpatrick, and Custer, were in plain view, and behind them came the infantry of Meade's army. We lost no time in paying our respects to their cavalry, which I judge was about three-fourths of a mile distant. Our gunner soon got the range, and at every discharge of the gun, I could see men and horses go down, but they would close up and continue to advance. Their artillery now began to pay some attention to us. The chimney of a house that had been burned, standing nearby, had the bricks knocked out of it by one of their shells. Another shell burst over the gun and a fragment of it wounded a horse.
>
> Captain Chew was with our gun, and he sat erect on his horse, looking like a statue, watching the enemy and directing the firing of the gun.[48]

Holliday's gun was just a part of the overall Confederate withdrawal to Culpeper. Lomax's outnumbered troopers had been outflanked and driven from every position they had taken. The running fight slowed near the town when Rooney Lee's Brigade, under Col. Richard L. T. Beale, reinforced Lomax. Griffin's, Moorman's, Chew's, and McGregor's Batteries made every effort to stem the Federal advance.

The situation had been no better for Baker's Brigade, commanded this day by Col. James B. Gordon, which had been stationed near Stevensburg. Hart's Battery was in the thick of things and helped the brigade to hold its own. The enemy force was composed of only one regiment, the 1st Michigan Cavalry, led by Lt. Col. Peter Stagg, but it gave Gordon and Hart all they could handle. At one point, Stagg's skirmishers came within pistol shot of Hart's guns before being driven back.[49] The Michiganders took up a defensive position and were soon ordered to join Custer at Culpeper. Gordon's men retreated as well, because Lomax's withdrawal to Culpeper exposed Gordon's left flank. In order to form a junction with Lomax, Gordon fell back to Pony Mountain.

Back at Culpeper, the state of things had turned critical for the Confederates. Private Holliday saw disaster in the making:

> Although kept busy at the gun, I observed that the enemy were overlapping our right and left flanks and getting to the rear of us. Captain Chew gave the command to cease firing, and as I had no horse I remarked to him I would go ahead and join the gun on the south side of the town. I had his permission to do so.
>
> I suppose I had gotten fifty or sixty yards from the gun when I heard a commotion and, on looking around, to my surprise I saw a Yankee cavalry regiment charging by fours in the rear of the gun. The hill on which we were located dropped off very abruptly to our right, and they crossed the railroad and came up over the hill without our seeing them. There was no support for the gun and it was captured. Those who had time to mount their horses lost no time in getting away. Captain Chew escaped. A Yankee rode up to Lieut. James Thomson and ordered him to surrender. Thomson quick as a flash of lightning shot the fellow and went away like a whirlwind. He did not kill the man, as the shot only dazed him.[50]

The charge by the 2nd New York Cavalry was well executed.[51] No Confederate cavalry units were in any condition to countercharge. The gun was doomed. For the crew, it was every man for himself. Though Chew and Thomson managed to escape, Corp. George W. Everly and Privates William Anderson, William Buck, Benjamin T. Holliday, Richard Oaks, White, and John Whitmire were captured.[52]

At the same time that Chew's gun was overrun, one of Moorman's pieces suffered the same fate. The men of the battery put up a gallant resistance, but to no avail. Pvt. Andrew H. Kirby received a saber stroke to his head and crumpled to the ground. Privates Zachariah N. Mundy and Richard A. Watts also fell wounded next to their gun. Corp. William A. Morris and Privates Charles H. Derr, James N. Feasel, William T. French, Robert A. Glenn, Kirby, Mundy, Richard J. Perkins, James S. Rucker, Leslie C. Smithson, William W. Turner, Watts, and Alexander E. Whitten were captured.[53] It had been a black day for the horse artillery, and the day wasn't over.

When Griffin had fallen back from Muddy Run, he took a position near Culpeper and unlimbered his three pieces. Beckham gave him an order: "Hold it." The men of the Baltimore Light gritted their teeth and went to work. Before long, six enemy guns were shelling them. The Confederate cavalry melted away, leaving the battery exposed to the oncoming Federal skirmishers. Griffin quickly assessed the situation and concluded he had done all he could. The time had come to save his guns, if he could. The experienced crews had the guns limbered and the teams ready to make the dash in a few minutes. Then the race through Culpeper began. The men whipped the horses into a frantic pace, and as the enemy fell behind, Griffin began to breathe more easily.[54] Suddenly, from a side street, the 1st Vermont Cavalry charged in among the galloping horses.[55] Lt. John R. McNulty; Corporals James O'Grady and William Wallace; Privates Walter Bell, James O. Cosgriff, John G. Gatchall, N. E. Ladde, William Paine, and James Roane; and musician W. Texas became prisoners.[56]

Moorman's Battery came close to losing another piece this day. Sergeant Nunnelee's gun was in position near a woods, when the enemy suddenly emerged and rode for the gun. There was no time to swing the gun around and fire, so the cannoneers prepared to defend themselves as best they could. Miraculously, a small group of gray horsemen dashed between the gun and the oncoming bluecoats. Opening up with their pistols, the Confederates sent the Federals reeling back among the trees. Nunnelee and his men had been saved by none other than Stuart himself and the members of his staff, whose timely arrival allowed them to fight another day, the battery had suffered heavily.

The gray cavalry made a stand at Pony Mountain. The horse artillery took position and again contested the advance of the enemy. In Chew's Battery, Lieutenants John W. Carter and James H. Williams suffered wounds. Pvt. Francis Asbury also fell wounded. Pvt. Hiram C. Homan spun to the ground, shot through the body. He was carried from the field but died of the wound. In the desperate fighting, Moorman's Battery suffered additional losses. Corp. John Herley and Pvt. Thomas R. Yeatman were struck as the Federals continued to press closer to the Confederate lines.

Hart's Battery joined the contest when Gordon with Baker's Brigade arrived. The Federal horse artillery added its barrage of metal to a battlefield already thick with lead. Pvt. Louis Tongers was instantly killed while serving one of the guns. Orderly Sgt. William W. Whetstone had his shoulder so badly mangled that he later died from the effects of the wound. As the enemy's skirmishers drew ever closer, their fire became intense. The bullet that lodged in Pvt. Charles W. Stewart's right hip took him out of the battle and the war, permanently disabling him.

McGregor's Battery had is own narrow escape as it hurried through Culpeper. Having stood his ground on the outskirts of the town, Lieutenant Ford watched with dismay the scattering of the Confederate cavalry. He quickly ordered the battery's guns limbered to the rear, which meant a fast ride through the town.[57] As the battery entered by one street, the enemy entered by another in an attempt to cut off the battery's escape route. Ford saw the danger, turned the guns into a side alley, and reached open ground. Having suffered a scare, Ford decided to return in kind and unlimbered his guns. A blast at close quarters coupled with a belated charge of the gray cavalry threw back the oncoming Federals. Immediately the guns were limbered, and the race to the Rapidan continued.[58] The battery escaped with only one man wounded, Pvt. Samuel McLearn.[59]

That retreat was taken up by all of Stuart's cavalry and the horse artillery. By nightfall, Stuart's weary brigades approached the waters of the Rapidan. Some of the troops crossed, while others waited until the morning of the fourteenth.[60] Hart's Battery found itself guarding Raccoon Ford. Chew's held a commanding position on Robertson's River. Moorman's was posted at Rapidan Station. Griffin's and McGregor's Batteries also guarded Rapidan River crossings. Early on the morning of the fourteenth, a section of Moorman's Battery and several other pieces[61] from the battalion recrossed the Rapidan at the railroad station and went into position between the Taliaferro and Antrim houses and, along with the cavalry, engaged the enemy. The Federals had no artillery up, so the gray batteries took a little revenge for the previous day. Several charges by the enemy were repulsed, and the Confederate cavalry made a few of their own. At the close of the fighting, the horse artillery retreated back across the river. They returned to the same position on the morning of the fifteenth, but the Federals failed to show. After withdrawing across the Rapidan, the men pitched camp near the railroad.[62] With this last show of bravado, the Confederates went to picketing the Rapidan and Robertson's Rivers. Once again, the two antagonists began to strengthen their new positions. Meade still held the initiative. Lee would have to play a wait-and-see strategy.

Among those who welcomed the opportunity to settle down, if only for the time it took to write a letter, was Lieutenant Williams of Chew's Battery. Afraid that rumors might unnerve those at home, especially a certain young lady, Williams hurried off a letter to calm the fears such rumors produce:

> Camp Near Orange C.H.
> Sept 15/63
>
> My Dear Cora,
>
> Suppose the papers have informed you of the fight our Division has had, and perhaps rumor has created some uneasiness. We had information of an advance about 3 A.M. Sunday morning [13th], contemplated to take place at 4 A.M. Had my section on picket. The enemy came in our rear at Brandy. We had to run the gauntlet to get out. We then commenced fighting & falling back slowly. After some stubborn fighting, although we had but one regiment of cavalry and two other guns besides ours, we took position with one of my guns & one or two others on the [word illegible] hill at the lower end of Culpeper C.H. Here we fought for some 1/2 hour against at least 5,000 cavalry. Here I was wounded by a ball from a shell in the right arm underpart very near the shoulder. I had injured my arm before so as almost to lose its use. This wound, though painful, was not severe, my arm is very stiff and rather painful. I have no use of it this morning. Was on foot at the time. A large piece of shell passed under my arm at the same time cutting my coat on the right side, and before I reached my horse was struck on the foot, but no injury was sustained. I had just mounted my horse as the Yankees charged the

> guns, taking mine and another. Took some [word illegible] of my men. I had a hard run to get off.
>
> My escape was narrow. Although [the] ball did little more than pass under the skin, it passed near both the bone and artery. Had it struck either it would have proved fatal perhaps.
>
> I came in to Aunt Sarah T's Sunday night and reached here last night. Should have written yesterday but had no facilities for writing. Our Battalion lost 3 guns & 25 men. Loss otherwise slight. Lt. Carter was also wounded & two others of our Company.
>
> I write with difficulty. Fingers are stiff. Must write to Ma by today's mail as have no doubt she has already heard of the fight, and I know how miserable she will be until she knows of our safety.
>
> You may have heard me speak of my dread of losing my right arm. When struck I thought my arm was broken, and all the consequences of the loss of it flashed across my mind. Should then have had to write left handed letters all the time. The enemy came up to the River last night. There may be a general fight in a day or two. Continue to direct to Army of Northern Va., Stuart Horse Artillery, Chew's Battery, only reversing the order. The division has been divided etc. & we separated from our old brigade. The loss of the guns will be the subject of investigation. But all this does not interest you & I am writing too much.
>
> Love to you, Ma, & Sallie, & believe me
>
> Yours fondly,
> James
>
> P.S. Don't think I am wounded enough to come to Richmond or get a furlough.[63]

Williams's narrow escape was one among many for the officers and men of the horse artillery that day, and Williams was right—it wasn't enough to get him, or the others, a trip to Richmond or a furlough. There was still much fighting to be done before Lee or Meade was to close shop for the winter.

The performance of Beckham's Battalion from the time the army took up the line of the Rappahannock until that line was breached on September 13 was equal to the batteries' earlier standards, as far as courage and skill were concerned. Why, then, the disaster on the thirteenth? It cannot be attributed to the superiority of the Federal horse artillery's weaponry. As on numerous occasions when Beckham's batteries fought the Federal horse batteries, they were for the most part outgunned. However, in the past they had been able to hold their own, compensating for the Federal advantage in metal with courage and skill. That did not change during the fighting of August and early September. What tipped the scales in the Federals' favor was the ever-growing need to add more and more fire support to the Confederate cavalry, which found itself increasingly unable to cope with the improved Federal horse.

In the two months following the end of the Gettysburg campaign, Stuart's legions had faced three serious challenges—August 1, August 4, and September 13. In each instance, the horse artillery fought well, but the lack of cavalry support negated whatever they accomplished. The clashes in early August were harbingers of the debacle that occurred on September 13. On that date, the cavalry failed miserably to support the horse artillery. The results were three guns captured and more casualties among the officers and men than in any other engagement up to that time, including Brandy Station. As Beckham's boys forded the Rapidan to take up their new posts, they undoubtedly were happy that the Federals had been satisfied with just three of their pieces. They knew it could have been more.

CHAPTER 22

Bristoe Station

"Shell and shrapnel shot raked the sod and tore the ground around our gun."

With the rolling waters of the Rapidan and Robertson's Rivers dividing them, the two armies were limited in their operations to picketing the crossings and probing for weak points. The saber rattling heard during Meade's advance of the thirteenth quieted, much to Lee's pleasure. Lee had dispatched Longstreet's Corps west to fight with Gen. Braxton Bragg's Army of Tennessee in the hope that a quick victory could be won there. When Meade's offensive died at the Rapidan, Lee breathed easier and began to plan. The Federals gave up their initiative, and Lee was more than willing to take it up if an opportunity presented itself.

Beckham's batteries resumed the same role they had played along the Rappahannock—support the cavalry guarding the river crossings. On September 16, Stuart made a reconnaissance across the river, taking with him one gun from Chew's Battery and at least one from Shoemaker's.[1] The Confederates' visit was brief, however, and everything remained relatively peaceful for the next few days. Moorman's Battery was moved on the sixteenth to picket the Robertson River near Locust Dale.[2] While there, Lieutenant Phelps scratched off a brief note to his aunt.

Picket Station on
Robertson's River
Orange Co. Sept 18th

Dear Aunt

I delivered Uncle Charles to Conductor on Tuesday morning & hope he has arrived safe and sound at home. I regret very much that his visit was interrupted by the Yanks on Sunday [13th] but I hope he is quite well again, and not so much dissatisfied with camp life. Thanks to your kindness our bill of fare was much better than usual, but I know he will not speak very favorably of my lodgings, particularly of the hotel we stopped at on Tuesday night. I hope you did not have him hung on the [word illegible] to Sunday when he arrived, as the Confederates are perfectly harmless tho' very troublesome occasionally & no soldier can be healthy unless he has a good stock of them at hand.

After I left him on Tuesday I was ordered to this place on picket. Shoemaker left on a scout with Genl Stuart. Meade's entire army has crossed the river and now lies near Culpeper Co. Ho. Would not be surprised at a general engagement in a few days.

I was woke up last night at 12 o'clock by a heavy shower of rain. It has been raining very hard ever since. I have found shelter in an old cabin to write this note. I left a pair of boots in my room, ask Uncle C. to have them mended immediately (half soled & heeled) and send them to me by the first one coming to the Co. My feet are on the ground, and it may be sometime before I can get those I ordered. I will send money to pay for them by Mr. Tilden. Do not like to trust to mail.

Love to Miss Wiatt and all the rest. Tell Miss W. to write. In haste Yours

Dick[3]

The general engagement Lieutenant Phelps envisioned did not materialize, at least not for the infantry. The cavalry was another matter. Stuart had shifted some of the cavalry and horse artillery behind the Robertson's and Rapidan Rivers, but so had the Federals.[4] Robert E. Lee sent Stuart a message informing him that a Federal deserter reported that the Yankee cavalry supported by a corps of infantry had moved toward the Confederate left. More ominous was that infantry had replaced the enemy's cavalry pickets along the Rapidan. Something was up.

That something turned out to be the cavalry divisions of John Buford and Judson Kilpatrick, which crossed Robertson's River on September 21. Kilpatrick occupied Madison Court House and pushed on toward Wolftown. He met little opposition. His goal was to rendezvous with Buford at Liberty Mills after examining all the fords on the upper Rapidan. Meanwhile, Buford's column would move down the Gordonsville Pike. One brigade would proceed down the road to Barnett's Ford, detaching one regiment to ride through Locust Dale and reunite with the brigade at the ford.

Stuart responded with portions of Brig. Gen. Matthew C. Butler's Brigade under Col. James B. Gordon, Brig. Gen. Laurence S. Baker's Brigade under Col. Dennis D. Ferebee, and Brig. Gen. William E. Jones's Brigade. Seven guns from Hart's,[5] McGregor's, and Moorman's Batteries accompanied the cavalry as it crossed the Rapidan at Liberty Mills and rode toward Madison Court House.[6] When Stuart reached Jack's Shop around 4:00 P.M., he collided with Buford and immediately launched mounted charges against the enemy. Buford's troopers shrugged off the attacks, demonstrating once again their ability to defy the once unstoppable Confederate mounted onslaughts. Stuart tried a dismounted assault with equal results. The artillery of both sides now became engaged.

The day was not going well for Stuart. He was in a no-holds-barred, knock-down fight with the outcome doubtful. Suddenly, the situation became worse. Kilpatrick, on his way to Liberty Mills, swung into Stuart's rear, cutting off the Confederates' escape route. The graybacks tried to break off the fight with Buford to attend to Kilpatrick's threat, but Buford would have none of that. He went over to the offensive and attacked Stuart's lines. Sitting among McGregor's section, Stuart calmly gave orders to attack Kilpatrick and hold Buford in check. Cavalry charges were executed all over the field, sometimes in opposite directions. Sgt. Charles A. Boyd of Moorman's Battery, who had ridden forward with Major Beckham when the battery's Napoleon had become disabled, joined in one of the charges, only to be mortally wounded.[7] Shoemaker's and Phelps's gun had its axle shot to pieces.[8] Hart's two sections ended up side by side, blasting in opposite directions.[9] At last Kilpatrick gave way, and Stuart beat a hasty retreat to safety behind the Rapidan. It had been a close call.

Buford's and Kilpatrick's foray over Robertson's River was not a prelude to any major offensive by Meade. The Federal commander had no immediate plans.[10] However, Lee's dispatching of Longstreet's Corps to Bragg had prompted action in Washington. On September 24, Meade was ordered to prepare the XI and XII Corps for transport west.[11] The logistics of such a move occupied Meade's attention and allowed Lee to pause and contemplate the situation. His natural aggressive tendencies soon had him looking for an opportunity to exploit the enemy's distraction. Not having Longstreet with him in May had not stopped Lee from taking the risks that had resulted in the victory at Chancellorsville. It would not stop him now.

The pause resulting from the Federal preoccupation with the troop movements was put to good use not only by Lee, but also by the rank and file of the Army of Northern Virginia. Beckham's Battalion crossed the Rapidan on the twenty-fourth and camped on the farm of James Twyman.[12] The battalion remained here, with various batteries doing picket duty along Robertson's River at various times, until October 11.[13] During this time, repair and repose took turns in the number one spot on the men's list of activities. During their repair phase, the officers and gunners gave attention to their own condition as well as that of the batteries. With winter approaching, heavier clothing was an absolute necessity, and the lapse of rigorous campaigning presented an opportunity to address this problem. As always, the batteries themselves required constant repair of harnesses, metal and wood parts, and attention to the horses. The fate of the guns might rest on their condition.

As to repose, the men had little problem finding what to do with spare moments. For many, letter writing was at the top of the chart. Lt. James H. Williams wrote once more to his beloved Cora with sad news and with a view to clarifying a "heart condition":

Gordonsville Sept. 24/63

My Dear Cora,

My place of writing may surprise you. Had thought before this shall have reached its destination to have more surprised you by having my own dispatches. I came here yesterday with John Green's body & tried to get permission to accompany it to Richmond but failed.[14] John was killed in a charge near Rochelle Shop on Tuesday [22nd]. Have just written his father an account of the particulars. He was struck in the throat, the ball passing out of the right shoulder, was killed instantly. He had been transferred to the 11th Regt., Jones's Brigade. Our Battery is now attached to Lomax's Brigade, Lee's Division. The 11th Regt. is in Hampton's. We were not in the fight. I found his body partially covered with earth. Recognized his face as I was riding across the field. His person was robbed of everything of value, ring, locket, buttons. Sent his remains by express on early train. Thus has gone another. I don't permit gloomy forebodings to make me unhappy, nor would I cause uneasiness to my friends, but I sometimes fear I can not survive this contest. I have made so many escapes. I am not rash not reckless in a fight but cool & cautious, [word illegible] to danger. My aim is to do my duty.

I have thought several times in view of this thought of suggesting that these are matters (I know you ought to tell me, would if we could meet) which might be communicated by letter. I don't mean to ask it, for so many requests are seemingly disregarded [word illegible] that I can ill bear a repetition. I only mean to suggest. Aside from the destiny of the soul thoughts of death are not unconnected with our relation. The duty I owe at home first of all would make me cling to life, hope, wish to live, but I cannot realize that you must seal so much up from me that I must or may hear so little that breathes of attachment, that subjects that concern us so nearly are never spoken of, that I am kept in the dark as to what are the real facts in reference to which others know so much. I have sometimes thought my loss would be or might be none to you. Your manner of receiving such views has deterred me from alluding to this. You seemed to doubt my motives & question what will shine above [all] else, pure & ardent, but this is foreign to my purpose. I only meant to give you an opportunity to tell what heretofore you have been unwilling to put on paper, to be freer. For we may never meet. That you have been silent may matter little to you. It cannot be so to me.

I wrote you a day or two after I was wounded. Am almost or quite well. Have had nothing from you since your hurried [word illegible] letter. Had a long letter from Ma a few days since. She spoke of dear George for the first time. Will in my next send an extract. Have not time now. Also had letter from Mollie.

Love to your Ma & Sally. Direct to the Battery, Lomax's Brigade Cav., Lee's Division, A.N.V.

Now Good Bye. Have written no army news & never write any supposing they interest you little.

Yours fondly,
James[15]

Williams's melancholy mood was not to be easily dispelled. Throughout the horse artillery, cavalry, and infantry of Lee's army, the loss of relatives and friends since the beginning of the war was slowly taking a toll on the morale of each individual soldier. News from home that at one time rekindled the patriotic flame was now more frequently drowning it with tears of sorrow over loss of loved ones and over tales of the suffering the families were enduring while their men were away fighting. Williams shared more of his inner feelings and that of his grieving family in a letter to Cora's sister:

Camp near the Rapidan Oct. 1

My Dear Miss Sallie,

Your welcome letter of [the] 22nd inst. only came to hand this morning. Since the change of brigades or rather the organization of Stuart's Corps we have had no mail. Was wondering if all my friends by concert of action had forgotten or neglected me at once. With yours came a letter from John Green's father thanking me for recovering his body & forwarding it etc.

I wrote your sister a week since of the particulars of his death. He was engaged to a lovely woman, who his father says was motherless & fatherless before the war. His family first met her around his coffin. Thus another has fallen, a dear friend & kinsman. I often fear I am not to survive this war. I don't permit it to give me any unnecessary care. Its consequences I fear to contemplate. . . .

Expect to get a horse furlough the last of the week and start for the Valley. Be absent some 10 or 12 days. I mean by all this, I have made application to go. Don't expect I shall be able to visit Richmond. There is much at home that requires my attention. Shall bring back with me George's horse. It will be safer with me.

My arm is almost well. The wound has healed. Though slight, deprived me of the use of my arm for two weeks and though at times painful was rather more of an inconvenience than anything else. I made some narrow escapes that day, & but for my wound would have been taken prisoner perhaps. So it is all for the best.

Everything is quiet here, although the Yankee army are just beyond the river from us. At any time we [can] be called to battle, but one of my guns was captured & the other broke down a day or two since, so I am now without any command. Am free for the next fight.

I wish you would drop in on us some day & try a camp meal. Sometimes it is bread & meat. This monotony is broken by occasionally having soup, potatoes, stolen corn, where it cannot be bought. On the whole the fare is pretty hard, but a cheerful heart removes all idea of complaint. The life of a soldier is [a] production of indifference & thoughtlessness. I have gathered for you some chinquepins which I will give to the mail agent at Orange to be given to Billy Haas for you. Will take them to the C.H. tomorrow. For want of employment I gathered them, send them hoping they may prove acceptable. The lion's share is for you. Miss Cora is so much of a man of business, so strong minded that I feared to engage her attentions with such small affairs. . . .

Yours truly
James H. Williams

Direct
to Chew's Battery
Lomax's Cav. Brigade
Lee's Div. A.N.V.[16]

The quiet that Williams spoke of was not dispelled by either Lee or Meade, though the former was contemplating what best could be done to pry the Federals from Culpeper. Lee was not yet ready to make a move however, so the men of Beckham's horse batteries, like the rest of the army, had some additional time to write to loved ones. Pvt. Charles McVicar was one who took advantage of the opportunity.

Chew's Battery Lomax Brigade Cav Oct 4/63
Genl Fitzhugh Lee's Dv Cavl

Dear Sister,

The sun has just set. This evening is a beautiful Sabbath evening. Kate it carries my thoughts back to scenes of pleasanter days, but hark the bugle is sounding for Roll-call. That awakes my reveries to the present and my situation as a soldier. Katie I received your answer to my note written to Katie McCann last evening. I was very glad to hear from you all as home is the only green spot left on earth for me. The life I am leading is utterly disgusting to me and were it not for stern duty I should be at home, but my country before self. My hopes, my aspirations are centered in that loved family left back. Your letter headed at home carried my mind to that spot ever dear to a soldier.

Mystic thought planted me by the fireside, Henry on my knee playfully chatting, calling me [word illegible], Bob & Minnie hanging around, but the bugle awoke me from my reveries. Stern military duty first always you know. I am sorry you was worried so much on my account. I was in hopes that my letter would reach you before you had any news of the fight as I wrote several days after. I was glad that you had forethought not to worry mother about it. I thought even uncle was a prisoner some ten days since but did not know the circumstances.

I was glad to hear Aunt Mary had returned. I thought probably she might have some difficulty in getting back but suppose she had not & John is contented & I hope that he may make a man of himself. The army would have ruined him. I wrote an answer to that long and interesting letter you wrote some five or six days ago and sent a letter to John for you to forward by some of the enemy scouting parties. John's letter is in the one I wrote last. The Sun paper you [have] seen gives fair account of the fight in Tennessee.[17] We have received about 1000 prisoners in Richmond and captured 50 pieces of artillery. Both armies are laying still near Chattanooga. Our trains of cars are running within 4 miles of that place.

Everything is quiet along the lines here. There is a great deal of talk about the recognition of the Confederacy by the French powers, yet nothing is definite as yet.

I was glad to hear that Mother had seen Father, yet sorry to hear that he was in that section. I hope he will go on to Richmond soon. I will start a letter to him when I forward this. Geo received a letter from Mollie and answered it in my last letter. He was glad to hear from them. He is well, sends his love. Katie, I would like very much to get home to get fixed for winter but cannot at present. If possible can [you] get Calico or gingham to make me a couple of shirts. You will please me very much. I cannot get any dark shirts for less than 25.00 dollars a piece, and that is more than I can pay. Make them up as soon as you get this, for I may get a chance to send for them soon. I am nearly out. We are all well here getting along fine. Well, Katie as here is a letter for you and one for Mother so you must excuse me for this time your

Affectionate Brother
Charles W McVicar
Chews Battery

Katie, direct your answer to Chew's Battery Genl Lomax Brigade Fitz Lee's Division Cavl

We have been taken away from Ashby's old brigade and put into Lomax's. Geo. & I sent 1.00 worth of stamps in the last letter we wrote to divide between you and Mollie. We would have sent more but could not get them.[18]

Letters home such as McVicar's were not the only letters written during those early autumn days, nor were families at home the only concern. Some of the men of the horse artillery were worried about the spiritual condition of their military family. A revival was sweeping through the army, and at least one member of Moorman's Battery took the time to rejoice in its impact on the battalion:

Camp Near Robertson River
October 8, 1863

Brother Bennett,

I have been much rejoiced to hear of the glorious work going on throughout our army, and the happiness it gives me to tell you that our little battalion has commenced that glorious work. God has blessed us. Many sinners have found peace with God. Forty or more have been converted in the battalion, and twenty-four in our company. Notwithstanding we are marching and countermarching and changing camp from place to place, we never forget when we stop to select some place to assemble ourselves together to worship God.

Brother J. B. Tyler and Brother [Edgar T. R.] Fripp have been conducting our meetings. But some few weeks ago I felt as if I had been sinning too long. I went up to the prayer meeting when they had assembled themselves together to worship God. Then I was blest to feel that God had pardoned me of my sins, and from that day to the present I have been trying to do what the Lord requires of me. I ask the prayers of all Christians in my behalf, that I may always do the duties required of me by my Heavenly Father.

I am glad I am fighting in this army; I am fighting the Devil and his imps as well as the Northern army. But I have a leader. Christ is our commander. He will not forsake us if we obey Him. He will lead our whole army if we will desert the Devil and his army to join the army of the Lord. Oh, sinners, desert him and join us and let us all go together. I will let you hear from us again soon.

Samuel T. Preston
Moorman Battery, Stuart Horse Artillery[19]

Private Preston's spiritual war on the Devil and his imps and the revival within the battalion would soon give way to a more physical conflict. Robert E. Lee at last had made a decision to strike at Meade. Even as Preston wrote, one of his officers, Lt. Charles R. Phelps, penned a quick note to his aunt in which he mentioned the activity around him that signaled the start of another campaign:

Camp Near Orange Co Ho
Oct 8th 1863

Dear Aunt

I wrote you a short note by Genl. Tilden, but as I have just heard he lost his carpet bag on his way home, presume you did not receive it.

The boots arrived in good time (as the frost was beginning to feel for my toes) for which accept my sincere thanks. I have endeavored to buy a cow for you, but there is not one to be had in this section of country. Everybody has moved everything moveable from here. I think the best chance would be for Uncle Charles to get one of May Johnson, as I have no doubt he has them on hand. I have been on the lookout for him but have not been able to see him.

Everything seems to indicate a forward movement by our army. The infantry has been moving all day, and we have just received orders to cook three days rations & be ready to move at a moment's notice. Everything is bustle about camp, as we expect to have a warm time of it. I am just called to inspect my ammunition and must close. Will let you hear from me by first opportunity. Love to all & believe me Truly Yours

Dick[20]

The hustle and bustle occurring in Phelps's camp also invaded the tranquil camps of the other horse artillery batteries. The army was on the move and Stuart's cavalry was, as usual, in the van. Fitz Lee's division remained along the Rapidan, leaving Stuart with Hampton's division (the brigades of Brig. Gen. Matthew C. Butler, Brig. Gen. James B. Gordon, and Brig. Gen. William E. Jones)[21] to execute the opening movements. Accompanying Hampton's division were Hart's, Griffin's, and Moorman's Batteries.

The campaign began on October 10, with Col. Oliver R. Funsten's (Jones's) Brigade leading the way, protecting the flank of Ewell's and Hill's Corps of infantry. Young's and Gordon's Brigades crossed Robertson's River at Russell's Ford and rode straight for James City. Their job was to attract the Federals' attention away from Ewell's and Hill's flanking columns.[22] A few troopers of the 5th New York Cavalry were captured when Gordon's Brigade forced the ford.[23] The rest fell back slowly toward James City. After they had passed through the town, the Confederates were brought up short by fire from Capt. Samuel S. Elder's Battery E, 4th U.S. Artillery, which was in support of Brig. Gen. Henry E. Davies's Brigade.[24]

On the Confederate side, Griffin's Battery, which was placed just outside the town,[25] was first to engage.[26] Elder and Griffin exchanged shots.[27] Stuart, not possessing the strength necessary to drive Davies from his position on the ridge, continued to hold the enemy's attention with Young's Brigade in front and Gordon's on their right flank.[28] Hart's Battery, under Lt. Edwin L. Halsey, came up to support Griffin. The brash lieutenant pushed two of his pieces beyond his supports. The guns did not appear to be in any immediate danger, but about 3:00 P.M. Custer's Brigade with Lt. Alexander C. M. Pennington's Battery M, 2nd U.S. Artillery, came onto the field to bolster Davies. Griffin began to shell the newcomers, somewhat checking Custer's advance,[29] but it was the exposed position of Halsey's guns that attracted the most attention.

Col. Russell A. Alger of the 5th Michigan, which occupied the extreme left of Custer's line, led a portion of the regiment under Maj. John E. Clark in a charge to capture the guns.[30] Halsey's gunners now had center stage and an opportunity to show their mettle. They rose to the occasion and greeted the oncoming Michiganders with canister. A few blasts were enough to bring Alger and Clark up short, 200 yards from their goal. They were hurried rearward by a volley from about 150 sharpshooters of the 1st South Carolina.[31] The failed charge did convince Halsey that it might be in his best interest to pull back closer to the cavalry, an action he quickly executed.[32]

Desultory firing continued until nightfall. Both sides tucked themselves in for the night, though the Confederates continually probed the Federal picket line in the hope of finding a weak point that could be exploited. Stuart had every intention of renewing the contest the next day, but Davies had ascertained that the gray cavalry's advance "was only made for the purpose, if possible, of masking the movement of their infantry and train along the base of the mountains to Woodville on the Sperryville pike."[33] Before sunrise, orders had come to withdraw to Culpeper. At dawn on the eleventh, when Stuart found that Davies was no longer in his front, he left Young's Brigade with Hart's and Griffin's Batteries at James City and rode with Gordon's Brigade to Griffinsburg. There he found Colonel Funsten with Jones's Brigade and began laying plans to entertain the Federal cavalry along the road to Culpeper.

While Stuart and Davies clashed at James City, Fitz Lee played out his part along the line of the Rapidan. He had with him Breathed's, McGregor's, and Chew's Batteries.[34] Chew had been in position at Raccoon Ford since the evening of the ninth.[35] On the afternoon of the tenth, Lee learned that Buford's division had crossed the river at Germanna Ford and was marching upriver to Morton's Ford, driving before him Lt. Col. Henry C. Pate's 5th Virginia, which offered what resistance it could. Buford encamped for the night at Morton's Ford. The next morning, Fitz Lee sent the brigades of Chambliss and Lomax to attack Buford and led Wickham's Brigade, under Col. Thomas H. Owen, and Brig. Gen. Robert D. Johnston's Brigade of infantry, under Col. Thomas M. Garnett, across the river at Raccoon Ford to move against Buford's rear.

When Lomax encountered the Federals, he brought up one gun of Chew's Battery. The ensuing action was described by Gunner Neese:

> General Lomax's brigade of cavalry and the first piece of our battery hurried to the rescue and were soon engaged in a spirited fight. We opened fire on their cavalry with one gun, and after an hour's fighting we drove the enemy back across the river. There they held a strong position, with two pieces of artillery in battery. We advanced our gun to within about a thousand yards of their battery and opened a rapid fire on their position. The Yankee battery had the advantage in position, as it was on higher ground than we, and their shell and shrapnel raked the sod and tore the ground around our gun; but at last they were compelled to abandon their position, both by our artillery fire and General Fitzhugh Lee's cavalry, which had crossed the river and successfully charged and routed their cavalry support, which rendered their artillery position untenable, and the two Yankee guns struck out for the Rappahannock.[36]

Charles McVicar of Chew's Battery was also in the middle of the fighting and left a vivid account of his experience that day:

> Moved to Morton's Ford. A Brigade of the enemy crossed here last night. General Wickham is charging them now. It is quite early. General Lomax and General Lee's Brigade are driving them in the river. Caught several hundred prisoners. We are firing in their flank. If we could cease firing, a dozen or more of us could charge and take in part of the fun and capture our share. General Buford has come down to cover their retreat. Our forces have captured over half of them. It is lively, and since General Buford could not cross we have held them in check. Other batteries are playing on them. They brought down a fine six gun battery and opened on us.[37] Their horses are in splendid condition, and they gave us plenty of work.
>
> I am writing while we have ceased firing and am laying down under their fire, waiting for others to come up. George Stewart was just wounded near me by a piece of shell in the head, an ugly wound. George is one of my messmates. He was sent back to Orange Court

> House. The enemy are getting a good breakfast, and we have had none. If we could get over the river we'd be glad to help them. General Fitz Lee is in sight of crossing Raccoon Ford and a part of us too. General Lomax and General W. H. F. Lee are with us. We surprised them and in their rush to get out we have picked up their breakfast, sutler wagons, plenty of rations, and delicacies. Beef and bacon thrown around and barrels of hardtack. I was modest and only took two hams. Put them and some cans of condensed milk in my limber as I had No. 6. Filled our haversacks and moved on. This was sharp and short. We fired into camp after Buford had left. A great many were wounded and killed for so short a time.[38]

Buford certainly was discomfited this day. Conflicting orders had left him somewhat in limbo. When he finally concluded to recross the river, he was caught with one boot, Col. George H. Chapman's Brigade, on one side of the river and his other boot, Col. Thomas C. Devin's Brigade, on the other. Buford admitted that Devin's troopers "suffered quite severely."[39]

North of the Rapidan, Chapman had to hold off Fitz Lee with Owen's (Wickham's) Brigade and Breathed's Battery. Lee had no sooner crossed the river than he ran into Chapman in the vicinity of the Stringfellow house.[40] Owen sent the 1st and 3rd Virginia charging up the road and ordered the 2nd and 4th Virginia to deploy in line to the left of the road, where they could support Breathed's guns that were galloping into position. Fitz Lee, noticing that the Federal artillery, Lt. Edward B. Williston's Battery D, 2nd U.S. Artillery, was more strongly supported than had been first perceived, countermanded the order to charge. This caused some disorder in the ranks, as the two regiments executed a changing front maneuver.[41]

As Owen adjusted his line and threw out skirmishers, Breathed opened fire. Federal sharpshooters began to get too close for comfort. Lt. F. Halsey Wigfall's horse was shot underneath him.[42] The pressure on the battery was becoming too great. The 4th Virginia launched a charge, which drove back the enemy. By this time, Devin had extricated himself from his perilous predicament south of the Rapidan, and Chapman began a slow withdrawal toward Stevensburg, where he linked up with Devin's Brigade. Owen and Breathed's Battery followed, harassing the bluecoats at every opportunity.

Nearing Mountain Run, Buford noticed a wagon train rolling down the Kelly's Ford Road and determined to make a stand to protect it. McVicar wrote of the brief fight that ensued:

> Came up near Stevensburg with the enemy and charged along the line. Very lively for awhile. Our forces are on their front and on their flank. We have hardly passed a mile today without galloping to action. A horrible sight here. Our gun fired into a squad of videttes,

> one shell bursting among a group and got four horses and three men. The top of one's head was gone. Part of one's spine and his bowels partly out. He begged us to give him some water and shoot him, to put him out of his misery. We gave them water but could not shoot them. One was bleeding to death from a piece of shell through his thigh.[43]

The horrid spectacle described by McVicar was soon left behind as Buford continued his retreat. With Chambliss, Lomax, and Owen, Fitz Lee pursued to Brandy Station. The Federals were hurried along by a charge of the 2nd, 3rd, and 4th Virginia regiments. The 1st Virginia was left behind to protect Breathed's guns, which were falling behind.[44]

At Brandy Station, Buford encountered the V Corps and learned of the retreat of the entire Army of the Potomac. He also was informed that Pleasonton with Kilpatrick's division of cavalry was bringing up the rear and decided to make a stand in order to link up with it. Kilpatrick was being pressed by Stuart, who had had a busy morning himself. After the Confederate cavalry chieftain had joined up with Funsten at Griffinsburg, he began to push east down the Culpeper Court House Road. The enemy fell back, stubbornly contesting the ground to allow time for the infantry to get to the Rappahannock. Arriving in the vicinity of Culpeper, Stuart was greeted by the sight of Kilpatrick's cavalry, with Lt. Alexander C. M. Pennington's Battery M, 2nd U.S. Artillery, deployed on the hills north of the town.[45]

Stuart concluded to demonstrate with Gordon's Brigade and, despite Pennington's fire, pushed the enemy beyond Mountain Run. However, Pennington claimed a new and more advantageous position, and his guns soon brought Stuart up short. Since charging them from the front would have meant heavy casualties, Stuart chose to demonstrate with his artillery and swing around Kilpatrick's right flank toward John Minor Botts's farm. Griffin's Battery unlimbered and began to fire.[46] It would not have been necessary. Pleasonton, who was now commanding in person, had no intention of holding his line for any length of time.[47] Fitz Lee's artillery could be heard in the distance, indicating he was accomplishing his task. The Federals dared not linger.

Buford and Kilpatrick at last linked their commands near Brandy Station. Even in retreat, the blue horse batteries swept the ground before Stuart with shot and shell, which discouraged any attack along the line of the railroad. Still desirous of striking at Pleasonton, Stuart sent Colonel Funsten's Brigade around to the left toward Rixeyville with the idea of occupying Fleetwood Hill and threatening the Federal line of retreat.[48] As Stuart moved past the Slaughter Bradford home and onto the Botts farm, the smoke from Fitz Lee's guns could now be seen plainly. Unable to distinguish friend from foe, Breathed and Chew were shelling their comrades in arms. Stuart's own horse artillery, Griffin's Battery, had not been able to keep up, so he could not fire on the retreating

Federals to show he was in pursuit and not part of the extended Federal columns. For his part, Lee saw Stuart's troops as enemy reinforcements, which caused him to slow his advance.[49]

The confusion allowed Pleasonton to reach Fleetwood first and crown the heights with guns.[50] In the fields below, Stuart and Fitz Lee, now combined, pressed the blue cavalry back to the protection of those guns. A series of charges and countercharges that rivaled anything that had taken place on June 9 ensued. Some regiments made as many as five separate charges, littering the ground with men, horses, and equipment. Stuart instructed Lee to sweep around the Federal right toward St. James Church in order to outflank its Fleetwood position, which was unassailable. Pleasonton saw what was coming and abandoned the high ground.

At this juncture, Stuart rode up to Chew's Battery and requested a rifled piece to follow him. Off galloped Stuart, with Neese's gun bouncing behind. The next several minutes were typical of a horse battery's engagements.

> When we put our gun in position right near the Barbour house the Yankee battery was firing on our cavalry and artillery in its immediate front, and paid no attention to us; but when we opened fire the whole Yankee battery turned its fire on my lonely gun, and before I could make my third shot a thunderbolt from a twelve-pound gun struck my piece and crushed one of the wheels to smithers, and slightly wounded two of my cannoneers. We had just loaded our gun and were ready to fire when the twelve-pound solid shot came crashing through a little house that stood near our position and struck the gun carriage, then whizzed past us at a fearful speed and unhealthily close. When I saw the debris of the little house, such as shivered weather boarding, pieces of window sash, and fractured glass flying at us, and very sensibly felt the concussion of the solid shot, I thought the hill had exploded.[51]

Despite placing Neese's gun temporarily *hors de combat,* the Federals could not hold their ground much longer. Pleasonton fought off Stuart's tiring troopers long enough to cross the Rappahannock with the majority of his command as darkness closed the fighting. Stuart's cavalry and horse artillery camped around Brandy Station for the night.

Dawn on the twelfth saw Stuart's columns in motion once again. Col. Thomas L. Rosser's 5th Virginia and one gun of Chew's Battery were placed on Fleetwood Hill to occupy Pleasonton's attention, while Stuart headed for the Hazel River to pick up his infantry screening duties. Stuart took additional precautions to protect his rear. Col. P. M. B. Young's (Butler's) Brigade with Hart's and Moorman's Batteries were ordered from James City to Culpeper

Court House. Until they arrived, however, Rosser would be on his own—a most unenviable situation, as it turned out.

The 5th Virginia's 200 troopers and the crew of Chew's lone gun watched Hampton's and Fitz Lee's regiments ride off into the distance. Some undoubtedly complained that they were going to miss out on an opportunity to fight and share in captured booty, while others simply welcomed the chance to rest themselves and their horses. Their feigned strength was not put to the test until midafternoon, when their old adversary John Buford came calling. The bold front was maintained briefly by a few rounds from Chew's gun, but the ruse that had worked at 1st Brandy Station would not work a second time. Soon Fleetwood was covered with blue, and Rosser and company were double-quicking rearward toward Culpeper Court House.

Chew's single piece unlimbered once on the retreat to make a feeble attempt to slow Buford. The Federals seemed quite determined and pushed forward, precipitating Chew's hasty departure. Near Culpeper, Young's Brigade and four pieces of artillery from Hart's and Moorman's Batteries were drawn up in line of battle on Slaughter's Hill. Rosser and Chew filtered through the welcomed reinforcements, which opened fire on Buford. The Federal commander suddenly became unsure of what lay ahead of him and halted his advance. Young was in no position to attack. To do so would have revealed his weak numbers. He was content to have stopped Buford and welcomed night, though it proved an anxious one for fear that the bluecoats would attack again the next morning. Come dawn, the Federals were gone.[52] The men of the cavalry and the horse artillery breathed a sigh of relief, and Lt. Charles R. Phelps took time to bring his aunt up-to-date on the goings-on around Culpeper:

> Near Brandy Station Oct 13th 1863
>
> Dear Aunt
>
> I arrived at Culpeper Co. Ho. yesterday at 12 PM, having been on a scout through the county Madison since Saturday last. I wrote Sister a note as soon as I arrived here and sent some Yankee papers. At 4 o'clock we were informed that a large force of Yankees were at Brandy Heights making their way to the Co. Ho. We were ordered on the road & met them near Brandy Station and engaged them until dark. We had one small Brigade of South Carolina Cavalry & 4 pieces of Artillery and held them in check without any loss on our side. Their loss is reported heavy by prisoners taken. Last night their whole force consisting of Cavalry & two Corps Infantry crossed Rappahannock & burnt the rail bridge. Our scouts are bringing in prisoners every moment. Their exit from this country was a perfect stampede. They burnt baggage, tents, etc. etc.
>
> The Yanks are at a great loss to know our movements. They have been double-quicking their Infantry all over the country for three or

four days as they could not tell what point they were to be attacked. A. P. Hill was reported at Warrenton last night. If so Mr. Meade is in a bad box. We have taken a good many prisoners since we left Orange, suppose upwards of a thousand. We are now expecting orders, and I think will move up towards Sperryville.

Since I arrived here I have been feasting on Yankee crackers & pickled pork. Nothing could have suited our boys better as we have been without rations for two days.

I have never seen such destruction in my life. Splendid dwellings whose owners had left them have either been pulled down or burnt up and the timber used to make frames for their tents. They had evidently gone into winter quarters. Many had built houses with chimneys to them, but they burnt everything they could not take off.

I will be much obliged for a reply at your earliest convenience.

I met Mr. Minor Botts & family yesterday. They had been arrested and were on their way to Richmond.

Love to all
In haste
Dick

Moorman's Battery
Stuart's Horse Artly
Richmond[53]

Phelps's casual reference to the fighting on the twelfth revealed either an ignorance of the situation's crucial nature or a callous attitude brought about by having been in so many such instances that they no longer left much of an impression. Certainly the horse artillery was accustomed to tight spots by this date, and one in which the guns were in no real danger could not have unnerved the officers or the men.

After Stuart left Rosser at Fleetwood Hill on the twelfth, Lee's cavalry chieftain set out to fulfill his orders regarding the screening of the army's movements. Fitz Lee with Breathed's Battery crossed the Hazel River at Starke's Ford and headed for the Rappahannock, while Stuart with Funsten's and Gordon's Brigades and McGregor's, Griffin's, and Chew's Batteries moved through Jeffersonton on his way to Warrenton Springs.[54] Reaching that village, the 11th Virginia, which had the advance, crashed into the pickets of the 13th Pennsylvania, and a lively skirmish erupted. Stuart suffered at least one repulse before outflanking the enemy and pushing on to Warrenton Springs, where he planned to cross the Rappahannock.

Federal dismounted cavalry and artillery guarded the river and gave every indication that they would dispute passage. Stuart sent forward some dismounted skirmishers of his own and some infantry. He turned to look for his artillery, but Beckham's three batteries had been unable to keep up. Stuart requested artillery support from Brig. Gen. Armistead L. Long, chief of artillery for Ewell's Corps. Long in turn ordered eight guns from Col. Thomas H. Carter's Battalion to assist the cavalry.[55] The crossing soon was effected, and Stuart proceeded to where Funsten's and Gordon's Brigades had camped for the night.

For the men of Fitz Lee's command and Breathed's Battery, the day was rather uneventful in comparison with that of Stuart's, Rosser's, and Young's. Lee had arrived at Fox's Mill on the Rappahannock on the afternoon of the twelfth and encamped for the night. The following day, he set out for Warrenton. Before the column got into motion, Lieutenant Wigfall of Breathed's Battery scratched a short note to his mother:

> Camp near Fox's Ford
> Rappahannock Riv.
> Oct. 13, 1863
>
> Dear Mama
>
> We are once more on the campaign. We had a running fight day before yesterday lasting all day. My little grey was killed under me at the first position we went into. The battery lost four killed and wounded, three of them from my section.[56] We crossed at Raccoon Ford that morning and camped at Brandy Station that night. We have had no fighting since. We are about to move and I must close. Love to all. Good-bye dearest Mama and God bless you.
>
> In haste
> Your affectionate
> Halsey[57]

Stuart, too, had some marching on his mind on the thirteenth. Robert E. Lee needed information on Meade's army and dispatched Stuart with Lomax's, Funsten's, and Gordon's Brigades and seven guns from McGregor's, Griffin's, and Chew's Batteries under Beckham to Catlett's Station.

With Lomax in the lead, the Confederate cavalry approached Auburn, where it halted. When Stuart was informed of Federals in strength at Warrenton Junction, he decided to leave Lomax at Auburn to guard his rear while he pushed on to Catlett's with Funsten, Gordon, and Beckham's guns. Coming into view of the station, Stuart and his troopers were greeted with a sight that set their mouths to watering. An immense wagon train lay before them, its white canvas covers gleaming in the sun like earthbound clouds. Preparations were made to strike at this treasure trove but were terminated abruptly when Stuart learned that Auburn was in the hands of the enemy. Lomax had been attacked and had retreated on the orders of Fitz Lee after some stubborn resistance.[58] Stuart whirled about and rode for Auburn. As he approached, night fell.

Skirmishing could be heard in the distance. Stuart faced the fact that he was trapped and put his mind to saving his command from capture or worse.

For one who put a good charge at the top of his tactical options list, Stuart recognized that such a move was out of the question under the circumstances. The night that enveloped him just might conceal him from the enemy. With that in mind, he led his troops off the road among some low hills. Everyone settled down to a long, very quiet vigil. Barely 300 yards away, the Federal infantry marched upon the road the gray cavalry had vacated. Some went into bivouac. Hundreds were within earshot. Stuart's troopers stood by their horses and the mules of their ordnance and ambulance train to keep the animals as quiet as possible.

Six messengers, including Sergeants Ashton Chichester and C. P. Shurley of McGregor's Battery, were dispatched by Stuart in an effort to inform Gen. R. E. Lee of his cavalry chief's predicament.[59] Stuart would need help to battle his way out in the morning—if he made it through the night without being discovered. And so the dark hours passed. Sound and the coming light became enemies. Everything hinged on whether the messengers got through and whether Lee could bring forces to bear in time. Answers to those questions were not to be had among Stuart's command, but as the eastern sky brightened, preparations were made to greet both the new day and the nearby Federals. If this was to be their last fight, Funsten's, Gordon's, and Beckham's men were not going to be taken easily.

Beckham had his seven guns rolled by hand onto a hill overlooking the camp of the enemy infantry. Discovery seemed inevitable. Then shots rang out in the direction of Warrenton. Stuart took it as a signal and gave the word to Beckham. McGregor's, Chew's, and Griffin's men leaped to their pieces and opened a barrage of shell and canister on the startled Federal troops, who had been preparing their breakfasts unaware of Stuart's presence. Momentary confusion in the ranks of the enemy was quickly replaced with advances on Stuart's flanks and the opening of artillery fire. This proved so effective that Stuart was compelled to withdraw Beckham. The situation looked particularly grim as the firing toward Warrenton died away.

The cavalry responded to the threat of annihilation with several charges. In the fighting that followed, General Gordon was wounded and Col. Thomas Ruffin of the 1st North Carolina was mortally wounded and captured. Their gallantry and that of their men finally managed to open a path to safety, and under a barrage of artillery fire, which proved more annoying than damaging, Stuart's troopers and cannoneers made their way back to Auburn. The horse artillery had been in tighter places on the battlefield, but the increasing tension of the long night had certainly been a test for the stoutest of hearts among Beckham's boys. It was an enemy their guns could not fight.

As Stuart battled his way to freedom, Fitz Lee marched his division through New Baltimore and Gainesville to the vicinity of Bristoe Station.

Breathed's Battery moved with the cavalry and managed to get in a few shots at a retreating enemy. The Yankee artillery did not reply, but there was a casualty nonetheless. A minié ball mortally wounded Pvt. John Dorsey.[60] The one gun from Chew's Battery trailed in the rear of the long columns. The cavalry's arrival was in time to hear the fighting of A. P. Hill's Corps near Bristoe Station. The attack proved a dismal failure, though the Federal retreat did not abate. Meade was on the run, and the victory over Hill was simply a rear-guard action. The tide was still running in the Confederates' favor. Stuart's cavalry and horse artillery would have more to do on the morrow.

After their clash with Buford near Culpeper on the twelfth, Young's Brigade with Hart's and Moorman's Batteries had held their position through the night. On the thirteenth, Young encamped for the night at Rixeyville, where he received orders directly from Robert E. Lee to push on to Bealeton the next day. Arriving there on the evening of the fourteenth, Young learned that Stuart was near Bristoe Station.[61] All the following day, the brigade struggled to catch up with the rest of the cavalry, but it did not do so until the night of the fifteenth at Manassas Junction.[62]

Stuart's pursuit of the Federal cavalry after his near capture took him toward the old fighting ground around Manassas. His entire division, with the exception of Young, was now concentrated, as was the majority of the horse artillery. Beckham had Breathed's, McGregor's, Griffin's, and Chew's Batteries with him, missing only Hart's and Moorman's.[63] In all, Stuart could call on eleven guns.[64] The onward rush eventually caught up with the Federals at McLean's and Blackburn's Fords on Bull Run and drove them across. For about an hour, the fighting continued across the creek. Breathed's three guns and one of Chew's went into action. The response was immediate. So violent was the barrage that Pvt. Charles McVicar of Chew's Battery thought that the enemy had thirty guns in the fight. Pvt. Hayward F. Triplett of Breathed's Battery was wounded so severely in the foot that it required amputation by the battery's surgeon, Dr. William Murray.[65] One gun was disabled when its axle was shot in two. Beckham had his horse killed beneath him and had to leave the field.[66] It fell to Chew, the senior officer present, to order Breathed out of the fight. That left Chew's lone gun to hold the position until Breathed was safely away. The few minutes that were required for the maneuver were filled with cannonballs that plowed up the ground all around the gun. Finally, the order came to fall back. The speed with which such a movement could be performed was amply demonstrated as Chew's men hurried away to safer ground.[67]

On the morning of the sixteenth, Stuart left Fitz Lee camped at Manassas and marched with Hampton's division and a section from Moorman's Battery and one from Griffin's to Groveton.[68] He hoped to swing around the Federals' flank and strike their rear at Centreville. The weather was abominable. The rain turned the roads into quagmires and doomed the expedition from the start. After crossing Bull Run, the men bedded down for the night. Back with Fitz

Lee, the men were just as wet but had not had to endure a long, exhausting march. Lieutenant Wigfall of Breathed's Battery found a dry spot and penned a few lines to his sister:

Camp at Manassas
Oct. 16, 1863

Dear Lou,

I wrote to Mama on the 13th a few lines which I hope she received. We have been marching every day since. We fired a few shots day before yesterday but were not replied to. One of the best soldiers in the battery however was mortally wounded by a stray minié ball. We had a fight yesterday taking several positions. At one of them we had three guns fighting about twelve across Bull Run at Blackburn's Ford. They were however about two thousand Yanks and only one of our men was hurt—his leg shot off. One of the guns also had its axle shot in two. It was a pretty lively place I can assure you. We have lost six men and six horses killed and disabled since crossing the Rapidan besides several other horses slightly wounded. We are now at the place we camped last night horses harnessed but not hitched and it is much later than we have been in camp for several days, usually marching shortly after sun-rise.

Good-bye my dear sister and God-bless you. Give my best love to Mama and Papa and kisses to little Fanny and believe me as ever your affec.

Brother

P.S. Jim recovered just in time to come with me, so my horse and I both receive plenty of attention. Don't fail to write and some of the letters at all events will reach. Good-bye again.

H.[69]

Wigfall must have been pleased when his late stay in camp that morning turned into an all-day rest, although there was a little excitement that night when the blue cavalry crossed Bull Run and drove in Lee's pickets. Chew's Battery was soon in line and ready for a fight.[70] Fortunately for all, the Yanks fell back, and everyone returned to his soggy bedroll.

Stuart and Hampton skirmished with the enemy on the seventeenth around Frying Pan Church, but this was the farthermost point of Stuart's advance. A message received from the commanding general caused Stuart to fall back on the eighteenth through Gainesville to Haymarket. On that day, Lee moved his infantry back to the line of the Rappahannock, his offensive having accomplished all it could. Stuart, meanwhile, learned of an intended advance of Kilpatrick's division. Early on the nineteenth, Confederate pickets were driven in around Gainesville, and Stuart responded by ordering Young's Brigade to hold the rear of the column, which retreated to Buckland. Kilpatrick followed Young closely. Stuart informed Fitz Lee, who was near Auburn, of his movement and cautioned him to watch his right flank. Upon receipt of Stuart's message, Lee formulated a plan to entrap Kilpatrick between the two Confederate cavalry divisions. What followed became known as the "Buckland Races."

Lee suggested that Stuart withdraw toward Warrenton. At the appropriate moment, Lee would attempt to interpose his division between Kilpatrick and Broad Run. When Stuart heard Lee's guns, Breathed's Battery, he should turn and attack. The plan might have worked except that when Lee descended on Broad Run, he found Custer's Michigan Brigade and Pennington's Battery in possession of the crossing.[71] Pennington had a gun in position in short order, and in the fighting that followed, Lee was unable to make any headway against the stubborn Custer. Stuart responded to Breathed's salvos and turned loose McGregor's Battery on Kilpatrick, who soon heard the firing in his rear.[72] Not knowing whether Custer could maintain his position, the Federals headed rearward. The race was on.

Back near Broad Run, Pennington was holding a clinic for Breathed's gunners. His shower of metal felled four men, including Lieutenants Daniel Shanks and Philip P. Johnston, and killed six horses. Almost before Breathed could get the range, Pennington had crippled his battery, but the stubborn captain would not yield and kept the rest of his men at their guns. Lieutenant Johnston wrote of the fight after the war:

> The battery was hotly engaged when Fitz Lee attacked Custer's brigade at Buckland Mills. The battle was of the most obstinate character. Fitz Lee exerting himself to the utmost to push Custer into Broad Run, and Custer seeming to have no thought of retiring. Suddenly a cloud arose on the road towards Warrenton, and as suddenly everything in our front gave way. The mounted men were ordered forward, and I saw no more of the enemy, although following as closely as my wounded condition would permit.[73]

What finally moved Custer and Pennington was the arrival of Stuart, preceded by Kilpatrick's panicked troopers. Breathed had not fared well during his brief but furious exchange with Pennington and in fact had inflicted no damage on his worthy foe. But with the rout of the Federals, Breathed had an opportunity to take revenge on the flying bluecoats without any interference from Pennington, who managed only a few shots in opposition from his first position on the other side of Broad Run. The gray cannoneers crossed the run in a pursuit that lasted three miles. They used their cannon with good effect until darkness obliterated their targets.

That same evening, Lieutenant Wigfall sat down and scratched off a short letter to his father about the day's activities:

Camp at Buckland
Oct. 19, 1863

Dear Papa,

We have had another fight today. We marched from between Gainesville and Bristoe Station before the day and passed that Station and Catlett's and then up the Warrenton road which we left about half-way between the two places taking the road leading to Buckland four miles from Gainesville on the Warrenton and Alexandria turn pike. We got in position about twelve hundred yards from Battery "M" 2nd U.S. Arty, six guns. We had two. We lost four wounded, Shanks and Johnston among the number, neither dangerously, however. I shall get Lt. Shanks who starts for Warrenton directly to take this. I think that the army is on the retreat and when we get back I will write a full account of our doings. Till then you must excuse brevity. Good-bye dearest Papa. Give my best love to dear Mama and Lou and a kiss to Buddy's Baby—

In haste as ever
Your affectionate Son
Halsey[74]

The scrap at Buckland closed the curtain on the Bristoe campaign for the cavalry. By the evening of the twentieth, Stuart was across the Rappahannock and encamped on the farm of Dr. Green. The men resumed the seemingly endless picket duty. As always, the chance to rest brought about an avalanche of letter writing throughout the horse artillery. Pvt. Charles McVicar of Chew's Battery was quick to put pen to paper.

Camp near the Rappahannock
Chews Battery Lomax Brigade
Cavl Oct 22nd

Dear Sister,

I have only [several words illegible] one of my messmates, as I have gone in a new mess for reasons to be explaining verbally, is about to leave for the valley. His wife came to camp this morning. He lives at Rippon, 6 miles from Charles Town, and he is going home with her. We have just [several words illegible] Manassas. We attacked Meade's army on the 11th and fought every day near to Manassas driving him. Gen. Lee tore up the railroad back to Brandy Station. I will not give a full account of our marches. We captured near three thousand 3000 prisoners, some wagons and a [several words illegible] provisions & our piece was engaged six days.

I hope to be at home in two weeks if I have to come on a flank. I am very thankful to you and mother for fixing my clothes. I would like for you to send my clothes by Sergeant [George E. S.] Phillips or George Stewart for fear I should not get there. I suppose George [Stewart] has been home before this time. I have not heard from him since he was wounded on the 11th.

I wrote a letter from Manassas last Thursday to you giving account of our fights. I suppose you have received it before this time. I received yours & mother's letters yesterday of the 8th of this month. Oh, how much pleasure one letter from home gives me I cannot describe.

I fear you overrate my abilities in giving advice to my cousin. I am sorry you did not receive my letter for Lissa[75] and yourself. I was glad to hear you had a visit to pleasant Dale. It is certainly a beautiful place as to the visit up the valley. I have promised, rest assured, no matrimonial engagement will prevent that as for my corresponding with the fair sex I am merrily in friendship, nothing farther I assure you. Well Dear Sister I must close for want of time & space Ever your Affectionate Brother

Charlie McV.

Mother,

Your note in Kates letter was welcome & joyfully received and read with scrutinizing care I devoured each word as a treat from home. . . . If I should not get home send me that new pair of shoes as I am barefooted and what clothes you think I need

Respectfully your
Son Charlie McVicar

Send me a couple pairs of socks Mother. I have seen the captain today. There is no possible chance to get home unless flanking, and he advises me not to do that. You will please send my clothes and shoes and as much Confederate money as you can conveniently spare, also some tobacco. I wish to get my boots footed and have not the funds. It will cost 25.00 to get them footed. Send those things by George or by Sergeant Phillips. Unless I get them that way I will flank and come Home Christmas. If I get comfortably fixed for winter I will stay with the army until a move that way or something should turn up. I do not wish to be court-martialed for flank. Write often give my regards to all inquiring friends, Charlie[76]

While McVicar was more concerned with flanking home and getting prepared for winter, Lieutenant Wigfall of Breathed's Battery kept his word and provided his father with an account of his most recent adventures:

Camp near Beverly's Ford
Rappahannock River
Oct. 23, 1863

Dear Papa,

We reached this side of the river on the night of the 20th inst after a pretty fatiguing march of ten days. We crossed the Rapidan at Raccoon Ford on the 11th inst and were marching and fighting all that day, camping near Brandy Station. The 12th we marched by Rixeyville crossed the Hazel River there and camped near Fox's Ford on the Rappahannock and passed Warrenton marching down the Catlett's Station Road and camping about three miles from Warrenton. The 14th we marched over to the Alexandria & Warrenton Turnpike by Gainesville to within three miles of Bristoe Station where we camped. The 15th we marched by Manassas and out to Bull Run where we had quite a brisk engagement. We camped at Manassas that night, and next day the 16th we remained there until nearly night when we were ordered out but did nothing except get soaking wet returning to camp after dark.

The 17th we marched to Gainesville and then back camping about two miles from there. The 18th we marched and camped near the camp of the 14th inst. The 19th we marched by Bristoe and Catlett's Stations and across to Buckland on the Alexandria & Warrenton turnpike where we had a fight. The 20th we marched from our camp at Buckland and crossed the Rappahannock at Beverly's Ford and camped where we are now.

From the time we crossed the Rapidan we have lost two officers and nine men killed and wounded and fourteen horses disabled. Several other horses also wounded but we have them still in service. The very first shot from the Yankee battery after we crossed at Raccoon Ford cut No. 1's arm off at the Whitworth and the sponge staff and right wheel of the gun in two. At Bull Run the axle of the first gun was nearly shot in two and broke down as the gun started to the field. The 2nd Caisson, the piece being in the rear of the rest of the battery and firing to the right, was disabled but everything was brought off the field except the end of the axle and the caisson wheel which had been shot in two. We had two other wheels disabled and an ammunition chest, fortunately without ammunition, nearly torn to pieces.

On the 13th we fired some shots at the Yankees but were not replied to though one of the very best soldiers in the battery was mortally wounded by a stray shot from their skirmishers. On the 19th Hampton's Division was on the turnpike west of Gainesville and ours about midway between Gainesville and Bristoe Station.

Before daylight we marched to Bristoe then down to Catlett's and from there across the country by Auburn which lies about half way between Catlett's and Warrenton. At Auburn we left the Warrenton road and took that leading to Buckland which is four miles from Gainesville to the west. Meanwhile Stuart with Hampton's Division had been retiring before the Yankees along the turnpike towards Warrenton. Thus while the Yankees thought everything was getting along finely the whole of Fitz Lee's Division came in on their flank and before night we had them back on their infantry supports and some even of the latter on their way to Richmond.

Gen. Hill is very much blamed in the army for slowness on the advance. It is said that Gen. Lee's intention was to throw Hill's corps in Meade's rear and make the attack simultaneously with the one in front by Ewell's corps. If such was the design and Hill had marched with the same dispatch that Ewell used nothing would have been easier than its execution.

On the 13th about four miles and a half from Catlett's on the Warrenton road our division encountered infantry who were guarding the march of a baggage train and the next morning before daylight from our camp three miles from Warrenton we could distinctly hear the rattling of the wagons over the rough road. On the 13th Ewell was at Warrenton and moved in the direction of the railroad that afternoon. The morning of the 14th we struck the [word illegible] of A. P. Hill's baggage train on the Alexandria turnpike when we reached it.

As far as we marched along the railroad it was completely destroyed. I noticed in one place where immense oak, which had stood at the side of a cut had been felled and thrown into the excavation and earth filled in from each side.

Rosser has at last been promoted. He has command of Jones' old brigade of Cavalry. Gen. Jones has been ordered I understand to the Southwest. Affairs in the artillery are as yet at a stand-still. Some time ago the arrangement was to allow two batteries this and Chew's for our division to be increased in time to four from the mounted artillery and the other four batteries of the old Battalion to Hampton's division. Capt. Breathed however saw Major Beckham yesterday who said that this arrangement was all done away with, that a new one would be made and until then that everything was as it had been and that we were considered merely on detached service and not as permanently separated from the battalion. Under the first order of things it was pretty well understood that Moorman and Chew the two senior Captains of the old battalion were to be Chiefs of Artillery in their respective divisions. Whether this new turn augurs favorably for Breathed's promotion or not, it certainly has that appearance to me.

Give my best love to dear Mama and Lou and a kiss to little Fan. I wrote on the 13, and twice afterwards—merely notes however to let you know I was well. Good-bye dear Papa and write whenever you have leisure to.

Your affectionate Son
Halsey[77]

Wigfall's quick summary of his battery's role in the campaign and its casualties gave evidence of the hard service the horse artillery was once again called upon to perform. Most importantly, the batteries had produced even though below strength.

That the proposed reorganization of the battalion and the addition of two new batteries came to naught should not be too surprising. Both horses and men were in short supply. Beckham had difficulty maintaining the guns and crews he already had and had fielded only sixteen pieces for the campaign just finished. Certainly, the new arrangement would have provided deserving promotions for a number of officers, but a corresponding increase in efficiency would not necessarily have followed. The problem would not have been with Moorman's or Chew's replacements, Lieutenants John J. Shoemaker and James W. Thomson, respectively, but with the unknowns of the two new batteries. Expansion of the horse artillery would eventually occur, but not in the immediate future. In fact, there first would be a reduction.

Lt. Charles R. Phelps of Moorman's Battery waited almost a week after taking up his old camp south of the Rappahannock to write to his beloved sister. His concerns were not with what had passed, but with preparation for what was coming.

Camp Near Brandy Oct 26th 1863

Dear Sister

Your letter by Mr. Tilden to hand, as he informs me that the box containing my boots & coat was stolen from depot at Orange Co. Ho. I do not know what the box contained but if it was my coat, it could not be replaced for less than $200 & boots 150$—making $350. Please tell him what the box contained and tell him to make out a bill against Railroad Co. in accordance with the above. I have ordered another pair of boots from Staunton to be sent me by him. You will please send me my counterpane, & a thick blanket (if I have one [word illegible]) from Aunt Mary's by Mr. Tilden next trip. It is now getting quite cool, and although [Lt. John J.] Shoemaker makes a good bedfellow, it is hard to keep warm on the damp ground.

> We are taking a resting spell after our late raid. Our Batteries have all been assigned to different Brigades for the Winter, and as I do not anticipate much work, hope to have a more pleasant time than I did last Winter. . . . I have a gun that shoots seven times that I will send home as soon as I can get some ammunition for it. I captured it in a fight the other day.
>
> Love to all & everybody
In haste
Yours truly
Dick[78]

Phelps's hope for a more pleasant winter would be dashed soon enough. For the time being, though, the men could reflect on a campaign that proved Stuart's cavalry and horse artillery still had some sting left. Beckham drew praise from Stuart, which undoubtedly was passed down to the battery commanders and their men. Nevertheless, the fighting had not gone well. Beckham was consistently outgunned, and losses in men and horses had been high. There had been no outstanding contribution by the horse artillery during the campaign. At one point, Stuart even had to "borrow" guns from Ewell's Corps to accomplish his mission. The battalion needed a complete rest and refitting if it was to continue to provide Stuart with the firepower he increasingly needed. Unfortunately, that was not to be.

CHAPTER 23

Mine Run and Winter Quarters

"A few whispering fragments of Dixie"

At the end of October 1863, the war had yet to be put to bed for the winter. There was still activity on the north side of the Rappahannock, which prevented the troops from going into winter quarters. Beckham's batteries were once again strewn across the countryside with the cavalry brigades. Some were guarding the roads from the various fords of the Rappahannock should Meade again get offensive minded, while others were just enjoying a period of rest. Several of the batteries, Chew's included, camped between Brandy Station and Culpeper Court House. Moorman's Battery camped on the farm of Col. Charles A. Wager, between Brandy Station and Welford's Ford on the Hazel River.[1] Hart, who had rejoined his battery shortly after it had recrossed the Rappahannock at the close of the Bristoe campaign, settled his men near Stevensburg, where Hampton took up his old post.[2] Griffin's Battery was about to bid farewell to the battalion.

On November 1, Robert E. Lee issued an order that removed all Maryland infantry, cavalry, and artillery units from their commands and transferred them to Col. Bradley T. Johnson. The various units were to report to Hanover Junction for duty in the Department of Richmond. Once there, they were to form what was to be called the Maryland Line. While this was greeted with enthusiasm by some, many Marylanders would have been happy to have stayed right where they were. Among those units that were moved was Griffin's Battery, which left for Hanover Junction within days of receiving Lee's order. This battery would be absent from the battalion for months but would rejoin it again at Yellow Tavern in May 1864.[3]

During the latter days of October, Lee's inspector general conducted an inspection of Beckham's batteries. The hard service had not been kind to the batteries, nor was the inspector general's report. Stuart responded by writing to Lee, who in turn reiterated the findings of his inspector in a letter to Stuart on November 2:

Headquarters Army of Northern Virginia
November 2, 1863

Maj. Gen. J. E. B. Stuart,
Commanding, &c.

General: Your letter of the 31st ultimo, with reference to the inspection report of the batteries in your command, is received.

I am aware of the difficulties under which those batteries labor, and am disposed to make proper allowances for them. The matters which I mentioned in my letter, however, are such as require only a due degree of attention on the part of the officers. As far as grease for the harness is concerned, all that is used in the artillery is made in the same way as that you refer to, and as it is impossible in our condition to have all the facilities and means that we would desire, it is necessary to exert increased effort to supply the deficiencies, and render available such as we have. We are compelled to depend upon the resources of our officers and men in making the most of what we have, and not to wait until we get what we would prefer. The subject of greasing the harness was not mentioned in the report. I only referred to its being dirty and suffered to lie on the ground for want of proper racks. This can be easily remedied.

In the case of Chew battery, the report does not mean that it has not changed camp in eight days, but only that it has not been on the march or in action during that time, so that it has had opportunity to wash and clean the guns and equipments.

The report of Gen. [Robert H.] Chilton was a simple statement of facts, and as I have extracted all that require your attention, I see no good that would result from departing from usages in such matters by sending you a copy. I know that you and the officers of your artillery will do all in your power to correct these evils, and it was only with that view they were brought to your attention.

Very respectfully, your obedient servant

R. E. Lee,
General[4]

Between his kind words of explanation and understanding, Lee basically was telling Stuart to pull his artillery into shape. Hard service or no, the officers were still responsible for keeping their equipment in repair and in fighting trim. Chew's Battery had been inspected on October 30 and had received three new guns on November 1, bringing it once again to the status of a full battery.[5] But the strain of the nearly continuous campaigning had undermined discipline from Chew downward. Lee was just reminding Stuart of this and of the need to conserve for as long as possible the resources of each battery. Nor was he through. Hart's Battery was also brought to Stuart's attention.

Headquarters Army of Northern Virginia
November 2, 1863

Maj. Gen. J. E. B. Stuart,
Commanding, &c.

General: By inspection report of Hart's battery, it appears that there will be wanted to mount the men now present for duty and for four guns and caissons, 62 horses. The wagons and forge must be supplied with mules, of which there are 19 with the battery, 1 having been condemned, and including 2 riding mules. As this company had no record of property, and no morning reports, it was impossible to ascertain how many horses it had, or what had become of them. All that could be learned was what the orderly sergeant remembered. I suppose some of the horses must have been sent back to the horse infirmary, and desire to know how many you can procure from there to supply the deficiency in this battery, as the quartermaster's department will not be able to furnish them all.

The condition of this battery is reported to be bad. I call your attention particularly to the necessity of having morning reports and a proper record, without which it is impossible to have proper responsibility in the command. The horses are said to be in worse condition, and to show more evidences of want of attention than those of the other batteries. The guns have not been washed off recently, nor the harness greased, and a chain is substituted for a pole yoke in one of the guns. The grounds about the guns and caissons are badly policed.

It is due to Captain Hart to say that he has but recently returned to the battery.

Very respectfully, your obedient servant

R. E. Lee,
General[6]

There was less of the understanding Lee and more of the commander-in-chief in this correspondence. Lee was not pleased and made reference to specific problems he expected Stuart to correct. In Hart's absence, Lt. Edwin L. Halsey had been in command, and though he had been successful on the battlefield, his inexperience in commanding a battery had quickly become evident. In Lee's mind, there had been sufficient time since the end of the Bristoe Station campaign to correct the problems the batteries faced. Neither Stuart nor Beckham had taken steps to do so. Lee was making a clear statement that they should do so, immediately.

The commanding general's eye had been on the cavalry in general for some time. In mid-September, even as Stuart fought around Brandy Station and Culpeper Court House, a new inspector had been appointed to the Cavalry

Corps. Lt. Col. George St. Leger Grenfell arrived in Stuart's camp with the purposes of tightening up the cavalry's and horse artillery's record keeping and assuring that equipment was conserved and kept in repair. Grenfell was only the second officer ever appointed to Stuart's staff that Stuart himself had not personally selected.[7] The active campaigning had not allowed Grenfell to exercise his duties to their fullest. But once the armies settled into their camps on the opposite sides of the Rappahannock, he had gone to work. His reports to Chilton had led directly to Lee's letters to Stuart.

Any actions Stuart might have taken to correct the problems facing his horse artillery batteries were set aside when hostilities resumed. The cavalry held another grand review on the John Minor Botts farm on November 5, and that evening a section of Chew's Battery set off on a scout into Rappahannock County with Rosser's Brigade. They did not encounter any Federals and returned to Culpeper on the eighth.[8] The remainder of the horse artillery was present in its camps when, on the seventh, the enemy smashed across the Rappahannock at Kelly's Ford and overwhelmed Brig. Gen. Harry T. Hays's and Brig. Gen. Robert F. Hoke's Brigades on the north side of the river at Rappahannock Station. The horse artillery contributed its mite in holding back the Federal advance.

Moorman's and Chew's Batteries, minus the section from the latter accompanying Rosser, unlimbered on Fleetwood Hill early on the morning of the eighth but withdrew to a position on the farm of a Mr. Kennedy between Brandy Station and Culpeper Court House.[9] Here they encountered the enemy and the two batteries engaged, slowing the Federals down until they brought up their own artillery. After holding on for a time under a heavy fire, Moorman and Chew fell back half a mile to a new line, where they were reinforced by some cavalry and Breathed's and McGregor's Batteries. Later, McGregor's section of Napoleons and a portion of Moorman's Battery marched out on the Rixeyville Road and engaged the Federals briefly early on the ninth before moving back to Culpeper.[10] Hart's Battery fought the oncoming bluecoats near Stevensburg but was not heavily engaged.[11]

Robert E. Lee had a line constructed north of Culpeper Court House, which his troops occupied the night of the eighth. The next day, he abandoned it and retreated to the Rapidan. Fitz Lee's division, along with Moorman's, McGregor's, and Breathed's Batteries and the section from Chew's, trotted out on the road to Sperryville. Reaching Griffinsburg, the column swung south to James City. The men pitched camp about a mile and a half from the town amidst the first snowfall of the season. On the tenth, Lee led his troopers and artillerymen through James City and Wayland's Mill, over Crooked Run, and past Cedar Mountain, to the Culpeper and Orange Court House Road about five miles south of Culpeper Court House, where he set up camp. The following day, all the horse artillery with Lee, except for Breathed's Battery, was sent across the Rapidan at Barnett's Ford and spent the night in camp on the farm of John Chapman. On the twelfth, the horse artillery moved through Orange Court House to the farm of Col. John Willis.[12] Breathed rejoined the battalion in a few days.

Hampton, who had just returned to the army after recovering from his Gettysburg wound, with Hart's Battery and Chew's other section, which had arrived on the night of the eighth, fell back toward the Rapidan on the ninth. Crossing the river on the tenth, Hampton took position on the army's right between Orange Court House and Fredericksburg. Chew's section rode all the way to Spotsylvania Court House on the twelfth before heading back to the battalion on the fourteenth. It reached the camp on the Willis farm on the sixteenth. Hart's Battery held its position until the twenty-fourth, when it was withdrawn to Victoria Furnace in Louisa County because of a lack of forage for the horses.[13]

Many of the men in Beckham's command now believed that the campaign season had drawn to a close. They began to think of building their winter quarters and settling into a more peaceful routine.[14] Among those anticipating a period of reverie was Lt. Charles R. Phelps of Moorman's Battery. During his stay on the Willis farm, he penned a letter to his aunt:

> Orange Co. Ho.
> Nov. 17th 1863
>
> Dear Aunt,
>
> I arrived here yesterday [from] Richmond. I was detailed to take thirty men and bring up 100 horses for the S.H.A. Arrived in Richmond on Wednesday, transacted my business Thursday, left on Friday, and arrived here on Monday with all but 3 horses. The greatest & most successful trip on record. I am, however, pretty well used up. I have the worst cold I ever had. Dr. [Alexander T.] Bell is now working on me, & hope to be all right in a day or two.
>
> While in Richmond Dr. Bell's trunk was sent to Uncle C. Please have it taken care of. The doctor wishes it thus as he has opportunities of getting articles from it thru Mr. Tilden and as we expect to pay you a visit this winter we want to use some of the [word illegible] clothes that it contains. We look for Shoemaker back every day. As soon as he returns we intend to apply for our furloughs and know of nothing now to prevent our getting them, unless our Captain's health may be such as to make it necessary for him to take trip to Flat Creek.
>
> Everything seems to be very quiet on our lines, nothing since Sunday the 8th when we fell back from Culpeper, except the fight at Morton's ford—where we drove the Yankees back with considerable loss. I do not think there will be a general engagement here this Winter, tho' it may be brought on any day by Meade making an advance.

I saw Capt. John L. Eubank in Richmond and on my way back stayed all night with Capt. R. S. Ellis in this county. He is a very fine old huntsman and was acquainted with your relations.

The mail is about to leave and must close. I hardly think you can read what I have written as it is so badly done.

Love to all
In Haste Yours truly
Dick[15]

Phelps's timely arrival with the horses allowed Hart's Battery to make a rapid movement to the front when the Army of the Potomac pushed across the Rapidan at Germanna Ford on November 26. Shoemaker had been lucky. Phelps and the other officers would have to wait for their furloughs.

Meade's crossing was not a complete surprise. Lee had received information on November 24 from one of his ever-alert spies that the Federals were making preparations for a move.[16] A clash on the following day at Ely's Ford between Rosser and elements of Brig. Gen. David McM. Gregg's division of cavalry also provided Lee with information of Meade's intentions.[17] On the twenty-sixth, the Confederate signal station on Clark's Mountain spotted the Army of the Potomac's movement toward the river.[18] Stuart responded to the advance by ordering Hampton to support his pickets at Germanna and Ely's Fords. Fitz Lee was to hold the river line west of Clark's Mountain with one brigade and relieve the infantry at Morton's Ford with the remainder of his command.[19] Some of the horse artillery was also put in motion. Hart rode with Gordon's and Young's Brigades of Hampton's division, while Moorman's and Chew's trotted beside Fitz Lee's troopers on their way downriver.[20] Breathed's and McGregor's Batteries also left camp but were not engaged during the campaign.[21]

Lee placed his infantry in motion on the night of November 26, marching east from Orange Court House on the Old Turnpike. By the morning of the twenty-seventh, Maj. Gen. Jubal Early's division was entrenching along Mine Run. Moorman's and Chew's Batteries had been swallowed up in the mass of infantry and artillery en route to Mine Run. At 4:00 A.M. on the twenty-seventh, they had reached Verdiersville, twelve miles east of Orange Court House, and watched Early's infantry march past on their way to intercept Meade. After a brief rest, the batteries pushed on toward Germanna Ford, but upon nearing Mine Run, they were halted. Confederate infantry to the front prevented any further advance, and for the rest of the day, Moorman and Chew awaited orders that never came.[22]

Hampton's participation in the opening phase of the campaign did not begin auspiciously. Shortly after issuing his orders on the twenty-sixth, Stuart realized that sending Hampton to support his pickets at the fords was impractical, so he decided to shift the South Carolinian across the Plank Road. The cavalry chieftain had wanted to meet Meade as far east as possible, but the first brigade from Hampton's division did not arrive until 9:00 A.M. on the twenty-seventh. Immediately Stuart pushed Gordon's Brigade down the Plank Road, where around 11:00 it ran up against elements of the 1st Massachusetts Cavalry and 3rd Pennsylvania Cavalry from Col. John P. Taylor's Brigade of Brig. Gen. David McM. Gregg's division at New Hope Church.[23] Hampton with Young's Brigade and Hart's Battery were nowhere in sight, so the job was left to Gordon's men. They performed admirably and fought with a stubbornness that belied their scanty supply of ammunition.[24]

By midafternoon, Maj. Gen. Harry Heth's division had arrived and relieved Gordon's beleaguered troopers, which Stuart split, sending a portion to Heth's right and the rest to the left along the Turnpike.[25] Hampton finally came up, and Stuart ordered Young's Brigade to dismount and strike the enemy's flank. Two guns from Hart's Battery were unlimbered on the flank as well and began blasting away at the enemy.[26] Capt. Joseph W. Martin's 6th New York Battery answered with a barrage of shot and shell that quickly demonstrated that Hart was outmatched.[27] Fortunately, help was at hand. Maj. John Cheves Haskell was summoned with four guns of the Branch Artillery and two from the Rowan Artillery.[28] The added metal soon quieted the enemy's guns, and the firing began to fall away as the sky darkened into night.

For Hampton's cavalry and horse artillery, the twenty-eighth was quiet except for the ever-present skirmisher fire. On the army's other flank, however, Fitz Lee expected increased enemy activity and ordered up Chew's Battery to Morton's Ford. The battery barely had arrived at the Morton house near the ford, when the Federals gave every indication of launching an attack. Chew threw his guns into position next to the house and awaited developments. Col. Charles H. Town's Brigade of Brig. Gen. George A. Custer's division crossed the Rapidan but did not push up against Fitz Lee's line. As dark fell, Chew moved one gun forward. Neese recorded what transpired:

> This evening at dark one of our guns advanced and shelled a piece of woods in which the Yanks had kindled their campfires and fixed to spend the night, but when our shells exploded among the tall trees and gently scattered a few whispering fragments of Dixie, casting impartially around the campfires, the enemy hastily bade us good night and disappeared toward the river.[29]

Colonel Town reported that the Confederate artillery opened at half musket range but did not even drive his skirmisher line back. He only withdrew over the river, he claimed, upon orders from Custer.[30] In any event, Neese's "few whispering fragments of Dixie" undoubtedly contributed to Custer's decision not to leave one of his brigades south of the river. The battery saw no further action and did not leave the vicinity of Morton's Ford until December 3.[31]

For Moorman's Battery, the twenty-eighth was a day of disappointment marked not by combat, but by changes in position that brought them no nearer the fighting.[32] The twenty-ninth would not be all that different. Early morning found Stuart with Rosser's Brigade riding out along the Catharpin Road.[33] The column turned west on the Plank Road toward Parker's Store at the farm of James Foster and struck the 1st Massachusetts Cavalry and 3rd Pennsylvania Cavalry of Taylor's Brigade, which were encamped along the road. The Yanks were taken completely by surprise. Before long, the Federals were routed and abandoned all their camp equipment, which was eagerly gobbled up by the Confederates. The fighting scattered Rosser's troopers, and Stuart ordered them to withdraw east to a small field and regroup. The lull in the action allowed a few squadrons of the enemy to advance to the unfinished railroad cut, from which they peppered Rosser with small-arms fire.[34]

Stuart had expected Hampton with Gordon's and Young's Brigades to follow after Rosser rapidly. For some reason, this did not occur. Had Hampton been on hand when Rosser pulled back, the pressure on the Federals could have been maintained. They would not have been able to rally and occupy the railroad cut. At this juncture, however, Hampton rode up with his two remaining brigades, accompanied by Hart's Battery and three guns from Moorman's Battery under Lieutenant Shoemaker.[35] Now Hampton's entire division threw itself at Taylor's lone brigade and sent it reeling. Hart's Battery blasted away as the attack began, but once Hampton pushed ahead, the artillery ran into difficulty. A rickety bridge prevented all but one gun of Hart's Battery, under Lieutenant Bamberg, from pursuing the fleeing enemy.[36] The remaining cannoneers could only grumble at their misfortune and hurl epitaphs rather than iron at the Federals. Once again Moorman's gunners were denied a chance to contribute to the discomfiture of their foe, but at least they had some company.

The inability of the majority of the horse artillery to accompany Hampton hampered the Confederate onslaught. Taylor's troopers skedaddled through Parker's Store, up the Plank Road, and into a column of reinforcements sent by Gregg. Three regiments from Col. J. Irvin Gregg's Brigade and a section of Battery A, 4th U.S. Artillery, under Lt. Rufus King, Jr., brought Hampton up short. King's pieces commanded the Plank Road. Bamberg's single gun could not contend with the Federal artillery. This fact, and a message that reached Stuart informing him that enemy infantry had reached the Catharpin Road in his rear, convinced the cavalry chief that it was time to go home. The withdrawal was skillfully managed, and the cavalry and artillery went into camp at Antioch Church.

At sunrise on November 30, Moorman's Battery got another crack at the enemy. Leaving its camp at Antioch Church, the battery marched about half a mile south along the road before turning left across a field. The guns were unlimbered and opened fire on the enemy's infantry skirmishers. Soon the Federals brought up their own guns, and a lively duel commenced. Moorman was forced to change position but unlimbered again behind a hill and renewed the contest. Late in the afternoon, the battery was relieved by Capt. Charles I. Raine's Battery. Moorman's only casualty was Pvt. John Murphy, who was slightly wounded. After the battery left, the enemy got the range and Captain Raine was killed.[37] That same morning, Stuart moved Hampton's division out on the right flank of Lee's lines across Terry's Creek near Jacob's Mills. Major Beckham was on hand to place Hart's guns along the creek in such a position that they could enfilade the blue infantry if Meade chose to attack Lee's lines.[38] He didn't, and December 1 passed with no significant fighting. Beckham's preparations went for naught, for on the morning of the second, Meade was gone.

A scout had informed Stuart on the night of the first that Meade would attack the next morning.[39] This had put the cavalry on the defensive, a circumstance Stuart quickly changed. First he launched Rosser's Brigade in pursuit, and then ordered Hampton to follow up with the remainder of his division. The Federals' trail led to Ely's Ford, but the head start they had prevented doing them any serious damage. Only a few prisoners were taken. Hart's Battery ended up at Hamilton's Crossing near Fredericksburg on the extreme right of the army. Moorman rode back to the old camp on the Willis farm near Orange Court House, and Chew first returned to his former camp north of the Rapidan about a mile below Barnett's Ford. His stay was brief. On the fourth, the battery wound its way to the horse artillery camp on the Willis farm, where the entire battalion was assembled—Breathed, McGregor, Chew, and Moorman—except for Hart's Battery. Everyone hoped that the year's campaigning was at an end.

After a few days of recuperation, the men allowed themselves to settle into a camp routine and exchanged their ramrods and lanyards for the pen. Lieutenant Phelps wrote to his aunt on the twelfth:

Camp Near Orange Co. Ho.
Dec. 12th 1863

Dear Aunt

I have no doubt you begin to think that I have forgotten you, as I have not written since I left here on 26th Nov. advising you that I was then ordered off in direction of Fredericksburg. Thank God, I have passed through another campaign with [no] injury.

After leaving we marched all night, (the coldest we have had this Winter) and attacked the Yankees next day & drove them from their positions capturing prisoners etc. without any loss on our side, for five days & nights we were marching & fighting, until Mr. Meade returned across the river and we were ordered to old camp.

I would have written you, but on my arrival here, our Major insisted on my sending in my furlough again, and as I fully expected it would come back approved, hoped to have seen you before this. But no Leave of Absence are being granted at this time. I wrote Sister, yesterday, that I could not leave at present as I expected a Grand Move on our part soon, but I find I am in error, we are all going into Winter Quarters, & I have just been detailed by the Major to go to Charlottesville and select a camp in that neighborhood for the Battalion. We are very much disappointed in not being able to pay you a visit at present, but Major Beckham says I must forward my leave as soon as we get settled, & I hope get to be in Lynchburg about Christmas. Dr. Bell sends his kindest regards to Uncle C. & family. I was at the Co. Ho. today and saw G. L. E. He is quite well. Nothing going on in this neighborhood. It has been raining all day & weather cold. I will leave at daylight & be absent three or four days.

Love to all
In haste Yrs truly Dick[40]

Phelps's assignment meant that the men of the battalion had at least one more move to make before they could build their winter quarters. Not having to worry about gathering building material, the men made themselves as comfortable as possible. Lieutenant Wigfall of Breathed's Battery took the time to inform his mother of his current situation:

Camp near Orange C.H.
Dec. 13 1863

Dear Mama

I am almost ashamed to write, I have been so long silent. Louly's letter of the 5th has been in my pocket several days. I have been waiting to find out what would be our destiny and probable place of abode this winter. Gen. Fitz Lee moved back on Friday to the neighborhood of Charlottesville with Wickham's and Chambliss' brigades leaving us with Gen. Lomax to picket the Robinson [Robertson's River].

Capt. Breathed, however, saw Maj. Beckham and induced him to relieve us, and we accordingly marched yesterday morning and are now at the Battn. camp about a mile from Orange C.H. just back of Col. Willis' pagoda. Chew's battery was sent to take our place, and we moved into his camp with our battery. The officers of the battery have taken possession of a fine [word illegible] chimney which Capt. Chew had had put up for his own use and are very comfortable. I think it most likely from all I can gather that we will move back in a few days into permanent winter quarters. It will be necessary I expect on account of forage. Otherwise I should prefer almost remaining where we are though the situation in some respects is not a very desirable one. Gen. Lee told me he had received Papa's letter and so sent in my application for leave the very morning I intended doing so. Although he put a very strong endorsement on it, I am rather fearful for its fate as so many have been returned disapproved. It will be sure to return, however, in one way or the other before Christmas and if Gen. Robert E. puts his fist on it favorably, I will be assured to be in Richmond on the 23rd. You must not expect me, however, until you see me for as I tell you numbers of the same sort of applications have had the life utterly crushed out of them by the aforesaid formidable fist.

The battery was absent from its camp a week during the last advance of Meade but didn't even go into position, remaining the whole time at Pisgah Church where I came very near being blown away several times. The weather was intensely cold though by dint of large fire we kept in the vital spark though terribly smoked—i.e. the spark. By the way, speaking of the cold, reminds me to ask you if you have an opportunity to send up my bedding as soon as possible.

You must excuse this short letter with a promise to do better next time. I will write again in a day or two. Give my love to Pappy and Lou and a kiss to Fan. Good-bye dearest Mama and believe me as ever

Your loving Son
Halsey[41]

The opinion of Chew and his cannoneers on Breathed's success in having his battery returned to camp was not recorded. Certainly, when Chew rode out on the thirteenth, he could not have failed to notice that his chimney was being confiscated by Breathed's officers. But orders were orders, and the battery trotted down the familiar road to Barnett's Ford. By the fifteenth, Chew was on the banks of the Rapidan, building quarters again. Neese spent part of the time constructing a chimney for his small cabin. He swore that if he had to move one more time that winter, he would not build another.[42] The rest of his batterymates probably swore as well, though their words may have been directed more at Breathed than at chimneys.

Back at the artillery camp, Phelps had accomplished his mission. A site for the battalion's winter quarters had been selected at last. Lieutenant Wigfall scratched off one more letter to let his father know of the impending move:

Camp near Orange C.H.
Dec. 20 1863

Dear Papa

Orders came this morning to be ready to march tomorrow morning. We are going back for the winter to the neighborhood of

Charlottesville. I have heard nothing from any application for leave except that it had been forwarded by Gen. Stuart approved. It had been approved by every one else so that I have no doubt it will succeed unless it has been mislaid. It is most likely however that even in the event that it returns to me it will be too late for me to be with you on Christmas. There is still a possibility though and until Christmas is really here I shall not give up hope. Gen. Stuart has recommended four of the captains of the batteries for majorities: Hart on his own application and to be assigned elsewhere and possibly Moorman. Breathed, and Chew are the other two. Gen. Stuart has made so many recommendations for promotion at different times and of different officers that it has come to be regarded as by no means an indication that an officer will be promoted because he has Gen. Stuart's recommendation.[43]

The proceedings of Congress on the currency questionnaire are very eagerly watched in the army. The finances of the country seem to be almost the only subject of discussion in one of the men's messes which is nearest our tent. I hear them every day talking of thousands, millions, bonds, & taxes & etc., as if they had had nothing else to think of during their lives. I trust that something will be done and believe that the people will submit willingly to the heaviest taxation to alleviate this evil which seems to me the greatest we have to contend against.

I saw Dr. Breckinridge in Orange the other day, and he begged to be remembered. Give my best love to dear Mama and Lou and kiss little Fan for me. Hoping that this will be my last before seeing you all I remain as ever

Affectionately your son
Halsey[44]

The orders to move were not a false alarm. On the morning of December 21, Beckham led his battalion, with the exception of Hart's Battery, from its camp near Orange Court House and rode south toward Charlottesville. Pvt. David Cardwell of McGregor's Battery wrote after the war about part of that journey:

As the command reached the Rivanna River, the lead team took the water and proceeded to the other side, but when they attempted to pull the gun up the bank of the river the horses' feet slipped on the ice which had formed from the drippings from the lead horses, and they could not budge the gun, which was yet in the river and which river was from three to four feet deep. The horses were whipped and pushed and the men shouted, but all to no purpose; the horses could

> not get a footing. When this was demonstrated, Capt. Wilmer Brown[45] turned in his saddle and gave the command: "Cannoneers, dismount; by hand to the front!" Now, there you are; get down into the icy water and put your shoulder to the wheel. Cold? Cold was no name for it. But down we got, up to our waists in the ice water. We finally had to attach prolonge ropes to the tongues of the limbers and pull them out separately by main strength of the men.[46]

Cardwell's account of the crossing of the north fork of the Rivanna was seconded by George Neese of Chew's Battery, who recorded that the fording took three hours. One of Chew's gunners even stripped off his clothes and dove into the water to save a horse from drowning.[47] A bridge over the south branch of the river eliminated the last obstacle before the batteries reached their intended campsite. By the evening of December 22, everyone was settled in camp near Rio Hill. Construction of winter quarters began the next day and was finished before the end of the month.

Hart's Battery, stuck way out on the army's right flank, was not included in the order to move to Rio Hill. The men shivered in their flimsy shelter tents pitched near Hamilton's Crossing, unable to construct more permanent structures because of the perceived threat of enemy activity. Finally, near the end of December, the battery received orders to pull back to Penola Station, on the Richmond and Fredericksburg Railroad about thirty miles south of the Rappahannock, and go into winter quarters. For the men of Hart's Battery and the rest of the battalion, it had been a long year.

The role of Beckham's Battalion in the Mine Run campaign had been minimal. Small opportunities had arisen but for one reason or another had not born fruit. Two batteries, Breathed's and McGregor's, had remained virtually idle. Of the other three, Hart's managed to get in the best licks at the enemy, with Chew's coming in second. Moorman's gunners were not at the right place at the right time during much of the campaign, though not through any fault of their own. It all may have been for the better. The condition of the battalion's men and horses was terrible. The challenge of a knock-down-drag-out fight may have been beyond the capacity of the batteries at this time. The men welcomed the cold and snow that enveloped them. Penola Station was off the beaten track, and Rio Hill was a secluded spot away from the tumult of the war. Both were places where the strength of man and beast could be renewed without fear of molestation. Or so everyone thought.

CHAPTER 24

Protecting the Valley

"We succeeded in driving the enemy's battery from the field."

When the Army of Northern Virginia marched from the Valley in late July 1863 to oppose Meade's new offensive thrust, Robert E. Lee left Brig. Gen. John D. Imboden in command of the Valley District. His command consisted of his own cavalry brigade; the 41st Battalion of Virginia Cavalry; the 18th Virginia Cavalry; Hanse McNeill's Partisan Rangers; Brig. Gen. Gabriel C. Wharton's Infantry Brigade, which was soon ordered to join Lee's army; McClanahan's Battery; two Maryland cavalry battalions; and a Signal Corps detachment. It was a small force that became even smaller with Wharton's departure. Despite this, Imboden had little to concern him. The Federal presence in the Valley was minimal, and the newly appointed commander had a little time to allow his men to regain their strength.

Brig. Gen. William W. Averell's raid into West Virginia from August 5 through August 31 initially failed to disturb Imboden's troopers. The Federals were no immediate threat to the Valley, but Imboden was called upon to ready himself if the situation warranted his intervention. To the south at Staunton, Brig. Gen. Albert Jenkins's men, still under the command of Col. Milton J. Ferguson, were rooted out of their camps and sent off to assist in turning back the invader. Not surprisingly, Jenkins's column did not include Jackson's Battery of horse artillery, which was still in the recovery stage after Gettysburg.[1] However, when word reached the town of the proximity of the enemy, both Imboden and Jackson's Battery responded. Lt. Micajah Woods wrote about the expedition and his role in it, among other things, in a letter to his mother:

Camp near Staunton
August 25th 1863

My dear Mother,

I have intended writing to you for some days past but have been so indisposed for the last three days that I have been in no humour for doing anything. My sickness was brought by imprudent eating, I suppose. Last night I took a large dose of saltz which has relieved me greatly, indeed the fever & head-ache no longer annoys me & I suffer more now from extreme weakness than from any other cause.

Having heard nothing from home since your heavy loss & affliction, I take it for granted that you have had no more sickness. I do hope that every member of our house hold will lead a different life in future. How much more we ought to love each other—how much kinder & more affectionate we should be among ourselves since we have been so fearfully warned of the uncertainty of human life by having the two dearest & most precious gems of our circle so suddenly & prematurely snatched away from our embrace. But there is no consolation to soothe our sorrow which is the belief that our Tommie & Sallie are to day happier by far than they ever could have been on this orb of misfortune and affliction. Dear Sister Sallie's letter written while I was on the Pennsylvania campaign was received two or three days ago and scarcely could I realize that it was that the last tidings I should ever hear from the sweet little creature on earth.

Yesterday at break of day our Battery was ordered to report immediately at Staunton to resist the Yankees who were reported to be only a few miles distant. The tide of excitement and panic was high. I arose out of my sick bed & accompanied the Battery. We took position & remained all day in anticipation of an attack, but towards evening the rumour was exploded—the enemy having at no time been within 10 or 20 miles of the place. Wm. L. Jackson's command is said to be in a very critical situation—the enemy in heavy force pressing him. I [word illegible] fears are outdistanced for its safety. Imboden who is in this vicinity is on the eve of starting to his assistance.

Please send me by Thursday's train some tomatoes & butter especially besides eatables which you may think acceptable. They can be put in a basket or bag & put in charge of the conductor or baggage agent. I will return the basket or bag & kettle Friday or Saturday. Give my love to my dear Father and all and believe me very affectionately in great haste

Your Son
Micajah Woods

Mrs. Jno. R. Woods
Holkham[2]

The very next day, Woods took the opportunity to elaborate on what had occurred and poured out his frustration concerning the military situation and the people of Staunton. He took no prisoners.

Camp near Staunton
August 26th 1863

My dear Mother

My letter of yesterday was very unceremoniously cut short by the approach of a shower of rain which scarcely granted me lief to sign my name on dry paper, so I shall today complete what I was forced to forego mentioning in that epistle.

The condition of my health has continued to improve and in a short time I hope to have entirely recovered my [word illegible] strength. All fears of a raid on Staunton [word illegible] have vanished and I suppose Wm. L. Jackson's safety is not as seriously threatened as at first thought, as Genl. Imboden who started to his relief yesterday returned to his old encampment during last night. It seems to me that there never was any occasion for the fright at Staunton, and that had Imboden exercised the vigilance and generalship which is demanded of one in his situation, the alarm could not only have been entirely prevented but the enemy would never have penetrated as far as they have. The Yankees are said to have reached the Warm Springs and to have caused a tremendous stampede from thence and all the adjoining places of resort in that vicinity. Every day I am more and more confirmed in the opinion that political generals whose minds have never been schooled to war are incapable & unworthy of reliance in nine cases out of ten. For my part I think it would be a blessing to the country if Staunton were destroyed and as quickly as possible for such a cowardly, niggardly close fisted population doesn't infest America as most people who are left behind in that detested village. She may have some good soldiers in the field, but I have heard of but few. The other day when the Yankees were thought to be within 12 miles & were momentarily expected to attack, Jno. Baldwin & one or two others strapped on their muskets & went from street to street appealing to the citizens old & young to turn out & strike for their homes & firesides, assuring them, if they would only report at the armory that every man would be furnished a gun and enough ammunition to last him a week's fight. But at least half of able bodied men proved craven wretches and cowards and refused to move either by the appeals of patriotism or sneers of shame, when asked their reason for such actions they would reply they would turn out as soon as some one else did upon whom they had their eye thus each waited for another & half remained at home. It is a notorious fact known to nearly every soldier in the Army of Northern Va. that no soldier ever receives a kindness or any attention from the citizens of Staunton, with few exceptions unless he be a General or some official out of whom something can be made to enhance their personal welfare. "Staunton Hospitality" is now a saying surely as well known as old Abe's expression "Nobody's hurt." For the first time since I have been in this neighborhood Mr. Baldwin came out on the street and gave me quite pressing invitation in general to visit his house. I shall not go. I met [word illegible] Neilson of Bloomfield memory a day or two since in Staunton. He is a private in one of Imboden's companies. I wish you could see him and hear some of his numerous and wonderful accounts of his own exploits and adventures. He desired to be remembered particularly to yourself and Father & expressed great sympathy for us in our affliction.

I forgot to tell you that an invitation to Miss Crockett's wedding came to hand some weeks ago which had been wrongly directed & delayed so my conjectures in some respect were unfounded.

Miss Virginia Carrington & Mrs. [name illegible] are on a visit to James Cochran who is extremely anxious I should pay him a visit which I shall probably do if we remain here when I feel perfectly able.

No orders have reached us yet to move in any direction. On the contrary Col. Ferguson, commanding Jenkins' Brigade, has sent instructions for us to remain where we are quietly as the Brigade will probably join us ere long. An order is expected daily by us to report to Wm. L. Jackson who promises to fill us out to a six gun battery immediately & give us every favor in his power. He is straining every means to have us ordered to him as he has no artillery.

I trust that my letter of yesterday reached you today as I am very anxious for you to send vegetables and butter by tomorrow's train. In this weather & in the present condition of my system I can not relish plain camp food—bacon and bread. Our bread however is a very [word illegible] better generally perhaps than our cook makes at home—nothing can be attained from the wealthiest people in the community without money. An ordinary tomato costs only 50 cents in glorious Augusta—it is considered very liberal indeed for a citizen to let any of his eatables at all go to a soldier even at these unmerciful prices. How different in Albemarle. Still we are in camped what is called my first neighborhood.

Please reserve for me enough of the same jeans of which I have a pair of pants to make another pair. A pair of gray jean pants from the factory at Government prices (which are much lower than the price to citizens) will cost me only [word illegible].

I think it probable that I will send Bob home in a day or two to get some of my winter clothing and other things that I will need in the coming campaign. Bob is complaining considerably this morning. He will take a dose of saltz tonight. Should you get this letter out in time tomorrow morning please don't forget to put a few cantaloupes if they are ripe.

When will Mr. Fabre arrive? Willie will doubtless improve himself greatly under his instructions as well as dear little Johnnie.

With best love to dear Father & each member of the family I am

Devotedly
Your Son
Micajah Woods

Mrs. Jno. R. Woods[3]

Woods's anger and frustration over what he considered ineptitude was justifiable from his point of view. Nevertheless, he was not in command. Imboden was burdened with a great responsibility: protecting the Valley, which was the breadbasket for Lee's army. His reaction to Averell's threat may have been slower than Woods would have liked, but the general had more things to consider than just Averell. Lee wished him to take the offensive, and there was always the danger of a direct Federal strike up the Valley. Command of the Valley was not as easy as Woods apparently thought.

After Imboden's troops returned to their camps, the excitement elicited over the threat to Staunton died down momentarily, but the Federal presence in West Virginia forced Maj. Gen. Samuel Jones to order Ferguson with Jenkins's Brigade and Jackson's Battery to leave Staunton and proceed to Warm Springs. Woods wrote of the expedition to his father:

Near Staunton
August 29th 1863

My dear Father,

Again have we broken up our camp to enter upon a campaign which can't be otherwise than active and arduous in the mountains of Western Virginia. Our march was taken up this morning at day light—but as yet we have progressed only a few miles owing to the delay of the Brigade [Jenkins's] in Staunton to be clothed, equipped, &c. The promises of Col. Ferguson & Paxton are very fair—inducing us to hope that in a short time the Battery will have its full complement of men & horses. At present with only three pieces & those with the caissons pulled by only four horses each should the Brigade also delay in this vicinity tomorrow, which I will ascertain this evening, I will send Bob home in the morning after some of my winter underclothing & other articles for the western seasons & he can return by the evening train. Should we however move on towards Buffalo Gap tomorrow I will not send home for two or three weeks hence.

The scene of action for the Brigade in the future will be the country from Warm Springs—Lewisburg to Princeton. Wharton's Brigade of Infantry passed up yesterday so the number of troops concentrated in Western Va. is very great—indicative of an aggressive campaign towards No. Western Va. The condition of the horses of the command is really deplorable. The number of the men surprises me, it being more than one third larger than any other Brigade on the Rappahannock under Stuart.

When we reach our new scene of action our mail will come via Dublin Depot, I presume.

You will see, I have no doubt, dispatches in today's paper from Genl. Jones, announcing the Battle at Dry Creek [Warm Springs] & repulse of the enemy with particulars. I read yesterday at the office of the past commandant, several dispatches from forces giving accounts of the fight &c, they were sent to Genl. Imboden. If Bob goes I will write by him for what I want.

With best love for Mother & all I am my dear Father,

Your affectionate son
Micajah Woods

Dr. Jno. R. Woods
Holkham[4]

The repulse of Averell at Warm Springs on August 25–26 resulted in his eventual retreat to Beverly. Jenkins's Brigade and Jackson's Battery were ordered to march for McDowell, where they encamped. Here, a problem that had been festering within Jackson's Battery for quite some time came to a head. In the midst of the war against the invader, the men of the battery still found time to war with each other. Woods sent a report of the whole sordid affair to his father:

Camp near McDowell
Highland Co. Va. Sept. 4th 1863

My dear Father,

Our present camp is removed by many a mile from the region from which I expected to date my next letter on our departure from Staunton. After a day's march on the Warm Springs road the Brigade was ordered to turn aside to the Highland County and choose a camp in the fertile valleys which lie between the numerous mountain ranges of that county where the horses of the command could be recruited. Should the Yankees leave us unmolested we will remain in this county for the next week or ten days perhaps longer. The valleys here are perfectly lovely, always beautified by babbling mountain streams—clear as crystal, bordered by meadows, green with grass of the most luxuriant growth. Our horses turned loose on these literally fatten on the richness of the sod. As I mentioned only two pieces of the Battery are now in the field—one from my section & one from Blain's. They are in very good moving condition having six horses to each carriage.

Last evening quite an unfortunate affair occurred in camp—or rather an unexpected expression of sentiment by the men to one of the lieutenants. A long petition was handed in signed by 9/10 of the men in the Battery, requesting Lieut. Blain to resign his position as 1st Lieutenant immediately as they had no further desire to have any intercourse with him whatever as an officer. It came upon him like a shock of thunder, for in the flights of his imagination he fancied that he was seated on a throne too lofty to be assailed by any authority much less by the poor insignificant privates of the Battery. A reply was requested at evening roll call. Blain however, not being able to face the music did not appear, but awaited the return of the Capt. (who was absent). He returned late at night, and Blain threw himself under the aegis of his authority for protection—as he always does when in a difficulty—never daring to extricate himself from a tight place before the men. Jackson of course took his pet lamb under his wing and this morning denounced the signers of the petition (ie. the whole company) and announced that the character of Blain was unimpeachable, that he was satisfied with him, & that he would not permit that officer to take any notice of such petitions. Of course this action has thrown the company into a blaze of excitement, and I am sorry to say dissatisfaction with both Jackson & Blain. It is a remarkable fact that every private present who voted for Blain at the organization signed the petition and that the three or four men who did not were & always have been my warmest supporters, but they have since come to me & told me that they thought they avowed their sentiment sufficiently at the organization when they warned these very men that they would soon regret their action and they determined they would let the men who had forced him on the company get rid of him the best way they could.

You can scarcely imagine the bitter feeling against him which has I am informed been brooding long & only hatched into shape yesterday afternoon. I was nearly as much astonished as Blain at seeing the petition, for not since the Pennsylvania campaign have I heard three words in any manner shape or form about Blain or his conduct, and I was nearly as ignorant as he about the extent of dissatisfaction in the Company. But this morning it has come to me like a full blown nose—for I am sure that with very few exceptions every member of the Battery has expressed himself to me in some manner regarding their treatment. Of course my duty as an officer has caused me [to] use every effort to allay the bad feeling, and I am sure I have said nothing which I could not be willing for Blain, Jackson "et id genus omne"[5] to hear for word. You can well conceive of how very much to be regretted such a state of feeling is in the command. As far as I am concerned I know I have nothing to fear from the ill will of any single man in the Battery, and by every officer I am treated with the greatest kindness & courtesy. This is perhaps owing to some degree to the fact that I have no favor to ask, and manage each day to bestow several upon those around me, thus I feel under obligation to no one. I believe firmly in the maxim of Shakespeare—"He who needs not, never lacks a friend."

Our mail comes very regularly via Staunton & my Sentinel comes to hand punctually. I consider it without exception the first paper in the Confederacy. It is able—discreet, and above all things cheerful—& displays in every issue a spirit to do justice to all whether friend or foe. I have just read from its columns Mr. Rives splendid letter, and I wish every citizen & soldier in the Confederacy could read it entire. Enclosed you will see the introductory comments of the Sentinel which I know will please you. When the term of the Enquirer expires I hope you will take the Sentinel.

I forgot to tell you that while camped near Staunton the Rev. Wm. Blain spent several days with us in camp on a visit to Randolph.[6] I found him a very pleasant old gentleman—but generally I was much disappointed. His nature seemed to me very cold—to lack that general warmth which I expected in him from what I had heard of him.

Please write me without delay and give my best love to my dear Mother & all and believe me in haste.

Very affectionately
Your Son
Micajah Woods

Dr. Jno. R. Woods
Holkham

P.S. The butter & potatoes came safely to me at Staunton I concluded to keep the bag & tin can for use in the mess. We eat the last potatoes last night—they were really a great treat—as were the splendid peaches. Genl. Jenkins is expected to be with us in a few days and to take charge of the Brigade—his resignation not having been accepted.[7]

The feeling of the men toward Lieutenant Blain, and their subsequent action against him, may have come as a shock to the officers, but the assault proved a tonic for what ailed the lieutenant. Woods wrote later that Blain underwent a dramatic change and no longer put on pompous airs.[8] With that problem rectified, everyone in the battery settled down to enjoy the bounty of the region that came rolling in with every foraging expedition. Contented stomachs led to contented dispositions. Even the war seemed farther off than usual. However, the war remained quite close for John Imboden and his command.

Robert E. Lee's urging eventually spurred Imboden into action, and the Valley commander clashed with his blue-coated adversaries several times in September.[9] Unfortunately, McClanahan's Battery played no part in these small affairs. Not until October did the gallant captain and his cannoneers have the opportunity to warm their guns. Once again Lee was the impetus, instructing Imboden to move into the northern Shenandoah Valley to provide some protection for the Army of Northern Virginia as it commenced the Bristoe Station campaign. Imboden chose Charles Town as his target and marched north with Maj. Harry Gilmor's Battalion, the 18th Virginia Cavalry, the 62nd Virginia Mounted Infantry, and McClanahan's Battery.

As Imboden approached the town on October 18, he divided his force, sending Gilmor and the 18th Virginia to cover the Harpers Ferry Road, while the 62nd Virginia and McClanahan moved to the attack. A request for surrender was refused with "Take us if you can" from the Federal commander, Col. Benjamin L. Simpson of the 9th Maryland Infantry. With the enemy holed up in the courthouse, Imboden turned to his artillery. Lt. Carter Berkeley and his section rolled up just as Imboden received Simpson's defiant response. Imboden's aides who had carried the offer to surrender urged Berkeley forward, saying, "Hurry up, Lieutenant, they have refused to surrender. The building is loopholed and you will have to be quick or they will kill your men before you can unlimber."[10]

Not knowing the way to the courthouse, Lieutenant Berkeley called to a young boy to show him the way. Once they arrived, Berkeley saw he had his work cut out for him but went at it with grim determination. He described the fight that followed:

> As we turned the corner I saw the Yankees standing at the big windows with their guns in their hands. The courtroom was in the second floor. Just as we got unlimbered I heard the Yankee officer give the command to fire, and as I gave the same command, they poured a volley into us, but, strange to say, did not kill a single man. We fired several times rapidly, and soon the courthouse was obscured by the smoke. I discovered that they had stopped firing and gave the command to my men to cease firing. When the smoke cleared away I saw that the enemy had gone. We were so close and the room was so high that our shots had gone under them and I found that we had only wounded one man, a field officer.[11] Poor fellow! he was lying, horri-

> bly wounded, on the courthouse steps. He had on a beautiful sword, which he said had been presented to him, and which he asked to be allowed to retain. We fixed him as comfortably as we could and laid the sword by his side.[12]

Pvt. Calvin C. Hart of the battery recorded that Imboden himself sighted the piece and fired the shot that blew down the door and wounded the 9th's adjutant.[13] Whether or not Imboden assisted Berkeley in his brief assault on the courthouse, the results were the same. The Marylanders lit out for Harpers Ferry.

Another of McClanahan's guns had also come under fire from the 9th Maryland before it skedaddled. Sgt. Andrew J. Collett had been ordered into position west of the town. Bluecoats in the cupola of the courthouse opened fire before Collett unlimbered, wounding the sergeant's horse. The ball tore through the neck of the unfortunate animal and exited from the shoulder. The shot almost robbed the battery of a gallant soldier who was called "one of Randolph County's bravest artillerymen."[14]

Once the Marylanders vacated the courthouse, Lieutenant Berkeley sent two men with a wagon and four horses to empty the building of anything useful to the Confederate cause. In their haste, the Federals had graciously left almost all their equipment behind. Visions of blankets, knapsacks, and clothing danced in the lieutenant's head. Such plunder would go a long way to warming the men through the coming winter. As things turned out, however, the two men sent to gather up the loot evidently had a strong affinity for martial music. When Berkeley had an opportunity to check the wagon's contents the next day, all that had been harvested were thirteen drums of various sizes. However, blessed with a true Confederate "waste-not" philosophy, Berkeley turned the drums over to the 62nd Virginia Mounted Infantry, which soon had an excellent drum corps to entertain the men on cold winter nights.[15]

Imboden's stay in Charles Town was brief. Word was received that Federal reinforcements were on the way from Harpers Ferry, and McClanahan was ordered to limber and exit the town as quickly as possible. The 434 Federal prisoners were herded together and escorted south. Even with the rapid departure, Imboden's rear guard had to fight off the enemy as far south as Berryville. As part of that guard, Lieutenant Berkeley leapfrogged his guns rearward, stopping only to fire at his tenacious pursuers. The crisis came when the Federals outflanked the guns and came within a few feet of capturing them. A last-minute turn of the pieces, a blast of canister, and a timely charge by Gilmor saved the day.[16] The successful escape crowned Imboden's achievement, which Lee called "well conceived and executed."[17]

The Confederates continued their retreat, finally stopping at Front Royal, where they camped until the twenty-eighth. October ended with Imboden's troopers enjoying their spoils. Unlike Berkeley's would-be musicians, the cavalry of Imboden's command knew good plunder when they saw it and hauled off everything not nailed down. The month ended with a sense of satisfaction and accomplishment. Unfortunately, the other Valley horse battery did not enjoy the same warm feelings of success. For the officers and men of Jackson's Battery, the months of September and October had passed without an opportunity to grapple with the enemy. Still, they had not been entirely idle.

During the early days of September, Jackson's command moved to a new campsite, which was described by Lieutenant Woods in a letter home:

> Camp in Crab Bottom, six miles
> West of Monterey, High Land Co. Va.
> September 9th 1863
>
> My dear Mother,
>
> I start Bob off to day en route for home. He can only remain there from during the interval between morning and evening trains. Please give him two or three pairs of winter socks—my two pairs winter drawers—my ordinary dark vest, lined in the back with flannel, and [words illegible]. This is all the additional thick clothing I think I shall need. My red flannel shirt, I will leave for the future. The vest is in my carpet bag—the key of which I send you.
>
> Bob himself may need a pair, of socks, but in other respects is well provided for. Should you find any other article of clothing which you may deem needful for me and which I have forgotten you can send it, but it must be very small & light, as I can with difficulty transport & provide room for my present supply of baggage.
>
> The valley we are now in, is wide, long, & fertile—and produces blue grass more luxuriantly than any region I have been in for a long time. Very little of the land is cultivated—nearly all being devoted to pasturage. The people have suffered greatly from the Yankees, who have deprived them of all horses, cattle & stock (including negroes) of every description. Most of the farmers succeeded in saving their cows from which they obtain bountiful supplies of milk & butter. I went out foraging yesterday (the day of our arrival here) and succeeding after a very short ride in purchasing onions, potatoes, and butter enough to last the mess for a considerable period. So we live well here for soldiers. Col. Ferguson (Comdg. Brigade) speaks of camping here for 10 or twelve days if the Yankees will give their consent—but of course no soldier knows where he may be 24 hours in the future.
>
> Col. Ferguson and the Brigade Staff are all very pleasant gentlemen. The other officers attached to the staff are Capt. [Nicholas] Fitzhugh of Kanawha, Lieuts. Sinclair & James of Richmond. Head Quarters and the officers of Jackson's Battery are very intimate—

> and the interchange of visits & courtesies is incessant. We have the choice of everything—nothing that the Battery asks or its officers is refused. The grand Line of the Institution—Blain, who hitherto has been notorious only for his lofty bearing & assumption of mighty authority—who could not give the simplest order to his men without all the ceremony & depth of voice which you could imagine accompanying the action of an eastern potentate, this lovely specimen of humanity (who happens to be only a Lieutenant) has been wonderfully changed in character in contact with the men by the document recently handed him. He is now with them as mild & accommodating & as reasonable as ordinary men would be in his position. Some medicines work powerfully! I failed to charge Father to let no one see my late letter as it was strictly confidential. I hope he has not.
>
> Bob takes my saddle bags & will have room to bring peaches & other eatables which will not be injured by a ride of upwards of 50 miles. You will please find a bottle of whiskey as there are two or three gentlemen at [remainder of letter lost][18]

The contentment with the camp at Crab Bottom pervaded the entire brigade. Ferguson's wish to remain in place for "ten or twelve days" was granted, as the command was not uprooted until the twenty-ninth.[19] The interval was spent fighting the occasional frost and light snowfalls. Though there was no "drum corps" to while away the tedious hours, the men of Jackson's Battery found other ways to combat camp boredom. On at least one occasion, a horse race with bets totaling $1,000 had the men at fever pitch, buoying spirits and helping weaken the effects of the frost and snow.[20]

The orders that arrived on September 29 and set Ferguson's men on the road to Lewisburg were prompted by what Imboden viewed as a threat to that place by a Federal force at Beverly. Some of Jackson's cannoneers may have been happy to leave, as Lieutenant Woods reported the temperature at Crab Bottom was averaging twenty degrees colder than in Albemarle County. The trek was made over mountainous terrain, which was not conducive to improving the condition of the battery's horses. Nevertheless, by October 7, Woods and his batterymates had made themselves comfortable, or reasonably so, in their new camp near Lewisburg. Woods held the opinion that the camp was to be the battery's winter quarters, though he did caution that it could all be rumor.[21]

The services of both McClanahan's and Jackson's Batteries in the Valley and beyond pointed out the value of horse artillery to the high command. Even with the frustrations of insufficient horses and inferior guns, the contributions of horse batteries could not be overlooked. Those contributions were a strong factor in the formation of the 9th Confederate horse artillery battery in the eastern theater of the war. Capt. Warren S. Lurty's Roanoke Battery was organized on October 8, 1863, for service with Col. William L. "Mudwall" Jackson's Cavalry Brigade. The battery was initially armed with only two guns, and many of its men were raw recruits. The men had little time to become familiar with their new weapons. Five days after its formation, the battery experienced its first action when Colonel Jackson struck Capt. William H. Mattingly's 6th West Virginia Infantry, stationed at Bulltown, West Virginia, on the thirteenth.[22] The attack failed. Lurty's cannoneers supported the Confederate advance, which was supposed to have begun with the firing of the artillery. Instead, Maj. Joseph R. Kessler of the 19th Virginia Cavalry launched his attack prematurely. Jackson's battle plan fell apart. His men were repulsed, and Lurty had to be satisfied with having engaged the enemy for the first time.

At the same time that Jackson with Lurty was approaching Bulltown and Imboden with McClanahan was preparing to advance on Charles Town, Ferguson and Jackson's Battery were expecting the return of their old commander Brig. Gen. Albert Jenkins. Lieutenant Woods found he had plenty of time to write and did so on the twelfth:

> Camp near Lewisburg Va.
> Oct. 12th 1863
>
> My dear Father,
>
> Your welcome favors of the 1st & 4th Inst. came to hand on yesterday, & I will assure you caused me much delight. I am much grieved to hear dear Mother improves slowly, having hopes that she had gathered strength more rapidly. The presence of Aunt Preston doubtless tends to cheer her greatly and I sincerely trust that she may be able to remain at Holkham for some weeks till Mother's entire recovery. I have the pleasure of seeing Johnnie & Davidella every day or two either at Mr. Price's or at home. They seem very happy & in the enjoyment of excellent health. They have received I believe several letters from their Mother—one of the 6th Inst. later than other tidings from home.
>
> Aunt P. thinks of paying Walter a visit. This I dare say will be exceedingly difficult of accomplishment. I am so well acquainted with the routine of that army that I am quite sure that she will have to encounter many & unanticipated obstacles in seeing him. If the army is on the move or on the eve of action it will be almost an impossibility. Should she go, it is important that she should be attended by a good escort; perhaps Mother's situation and the absence of an overseer at home may render it out of your power to go; if so you had better get Mr. Watson to accompany her.
>
> The action of the Quarter Master in impressing your property is nothing more than I anticipated—the shafts envenomed by malignity—low envy which are characteristics of narrow and contemptible faculties, always seek some underhanded method to

deliver themselves, some method dictated by few, which can be pressured with impunity under the pale of a little brief authority. In this manner as such men vent their spleen & secret feelings of inferiority which they have neither the courage or manliness to openly avow. There is a consolation in knowing that there is a future when the field for contest intellectually & otherwise will be open when they can be made to realize more keenly their own contemptible insignificance by me & sustained by the noble motto "sans pens et sans reproche."

I am sorry to hear of your heavy loss in sheep. Surely [name illegible] should be able to trace the abstractions of so many as 14 to some source.

I see my relatives in this vicinity quite frequently—all of whom are very kind. I spent yesterday—Sunday—at Mr. Price's where it would indeed be gratifying to you to hear & see their various ways of evidencing their high appreciation of yourself & Mother. Cousin Jane & the young ladies of the household never part with me without urging me to convey to you their kind feeling of remembrance and sympathy.

Old Mr. Edgar (father of Uncle L's wife) died very suddenly on Saturday & was buried yesterday in Lewisburg.

Genl. Jenkins is again expected to report to his Brigade in a few days. It is very acceptable to our command to be for a while in this peace establishment of Western Virginia where they are satisfied with one battle per annum, that one, however on so grand a scale that by special orders it is immediately inscribed in flaming characters on the banners of the participants.

Bob is getting on remarkably well. My horse "Stricker" has the hoof evil—he is under treatment & will be ready for duty in a day or two.

The enemy has been annoying our outposts considerably on the old national road—15 or 18 miles from Lewisburg. Nearly every report one or two have been killed. Col. Ferguson told me yesterday that he had adopted summary measures for the punishment of their impudence. They have a force of 200 infantry at one of the nearest fords on New River. It is thought this demonstration is intended to cover a retreat from Kanawha of a large body of troops reinforcing Rosecrans.

Please send by Aunt Preston when she comes two of my linen bosomed shirts and four or five of my linen collars. Having settled down, I will in the coming winter have, for the first time a chance to resume some of the luxuries of civilization. Should Willie accompany her, he could bring me a small keg of butter—as such things seem to have gone out of use in camp in this region. We have to depend almost exclusively upon the Q. Master who only furnishes beef & flour. My appetite literally yearns for butter or something rich. He could also bring a ham—a luxury not issued even to Genl. [Brig. Gen. John] Echols.

Johnnie [name illegible] had the kindness to spare the mess a half bushel of potatoes—without these I believe we would almost choke. Some say such diet will only make us love "gentle peace with her white wings" more ardently and can be induced with amazing cheerfulness when we consider that we are fighting only "pro aris et focis"[23] but for the pretty maiden of the land.

Do write soon and frequently.

With best love dear Mother, Aunt Preston & all I am,

Your devotedly attached
Son
Micajah Woods[24]

Woods's outrage against the quartermaster's impressment of foodstuffs and material from his family undoubtedly was compounded by the knowledge of what he was issued by his own quartermaster. Where were all those good things going? Certainly he could testify that the troops in his vicinity weren't the recipients. But there were other matters that soon grabbed his attention. When he wrote again on the fourteenth, his mind was focused almost entirely on the military situation, which was changing rapidly.

In Camp near Lewisburg
Wednesday Morning Oct. 14th '63

My dear Mother,

The forces which have been concentrated in this vicinity for some time past have marching orders this morning. The troops to move are the following: the 22nd Regt. [Col. George S. Patton], [Lt. Col. George M.] Edgar's [26th Virginia] Battalion & [Lt. Col. Clarence] Derrick's Infantry [23rd Virginia Battalion]—and 14th, 16th, & 17th Regts. of Cavalry [Jenkins's Brigade], [Capt. George B.] Chapman's Battery & Jackson's in all perhaps not numbering more than 2500 or 3000 men. The direction is the Kanawha Valley via Fayette Ct. House where we will first encounter the enemy in force.

I learn from Col. Ferguson that Genl. Lee has ordered that the enemy be pressed with vigor and at once by all troops in every department east of the Mississippi. The Yankees are said not to hold Kanawha in any considerable force and I trust that our march will not be fruitless of results. The troops are in buoyant spirits & enthusiastically expect to see the Ohio before their return. All equipments

& paraphernalia of camp are to be carried. I infer from this that a lengthy campaign is anticipated.

Our Battery is in good order having yesterday received a full complement of the best ammunition. We start at 11 o'clock & will march to Meadow Bluff to night. I shall communicate with you as often as possible but don't be surprised if you should hear nothing for a week or ten days.

I do earnestly pray that by this time you have sufficiently recovered to get about the house—and that I will hear from you very soon.

I have written several letters recently which I trust have reached their destination.

Best love to Father and Aunt Preston & all

I am, Your

Devotedly attached Son,
Micajah Woods

Mrs. Jno. R. Woods[25]

The high hopes held by those who entered upon the expedition were dashed when, two days after it had begun, the troops were back in their camps. Lt. Randolph H. Blain of Jackson's Battery wrote, among other things, of the abortive foray in a letter to his mother:

Camp Near Lewisburg
October 17th, 1863

My Dear Mother,

It seems to me time I was receiving a line from you to tell me that you had received my note written on leaving Crab Bottom or the letter written about two weeks before leaving there and sent about two weeks after getting here. As is my custom the last mentioned I laid aside after relieving the boredom of my mind by writing it, and the next time I heard of it Lt. [Richard Beverly] Wortham asked me why I didn't send it, the Company box having been littered up with it long enough.

Father asked me to write whenever anything occurred, so that he might know how and where I was. Well, four days ago we received orders to move at eleven o'clock on the Kanawha road. Everybody went around to tell their friends good-bye, and those who had them their sweet hearts. The whole talk was that a move was to be made on Kanawha. All the troops in these parts had marching orders. Before starting I went into town, told Aunt Ann, and the pretty Miss Ellen Lewis (just recovered from a very severe spell of sickness, first time I had seen her)—good-bye. I then rode down to the bridge, told

Aunt, Cousin Bill, & Martha Jane etc. good-bye, and after (your letter telling of sister's arrival, and altogether so cheerful had just been handed me) filling my haversack with good things, Aunt N. gave me a beef tongue & some bread, & Aunt Ann some onions, I set out to overtake the battery which by this time was several hours ahead of me. The Kanawha people were all perfectly delighted at our going down the valley. I promised to lay in any amount of things for my friends. Now for the rest of it.

The first night we camped at Meadow Bluff, 16 miles from Lewisburg, as ordered. The next morning we were notified to await orders, as we could go no further until the return of the flag of truce which had been sent in, in charge of the Irish. All day we lay there, the infantry, all coming up about 12, but no flag. I saw a good many of my friends, [H. Brown] Craig (Adj.) [26th Virginia Battalion], Maj. [William] McLaughlin [commanding the artillery], and others. Captain's brother, Ned, Col. [James] Cochran [14th Virginia Cavalry], Murphy, & Harvey & several others took dinner with us. About dark we received orders to move in the morning at 5. We rose at $^1/_2$ past 3 and moved off as soon as it was light. The morning was very threatening, it having rained enough during the night to settle the dust.

The infantry (nearly all from the Valley, 22nd, Edgar's Batt., Derrick's Batt.) set out with bands playing and from all appearances we were in for a hard day's march. In the course of an hour after, the whole command was halted and countermarched, with orders to return to our original encampments. Just as we commenced our return, the rain began to pour, and upon my word I never but once saw it rain half so hard & that I believe was on our trip here from Highland.

In the course of some hours I got back to where we were before encamped & dried myself, which was a comfortable winding up. Thus ended our great campaign. I must tell why we didn't prosecute it. Genl. Sam Jones countermanded the order because the enemy were pressing him at Bristol. Part of our cavalry has already been sent there, & I wouldn't be surprised at any time if we should receive orders.

I am really delighted to hear you have sister with you at last. Tell her to write as soon as she can. I hope Luce too, may be better. A letter from [name illegible] tells me how delighted she is with Florence & her friends. I am glad father is still with you. . . .

Dearest love to Luce, sister, Father & all others of the family, Aunt N. & hers & write soon to your most affectionate son

Randolph H. Blain[26]

Lieutenant Woods shared Blain's frustration over the botched campaign:

Camp near Lewisburg Va.
Oct. 18th 1863

My dear Father—

The grand trip to Kanawha which I mentioned in my last communication is at last only an exploded idea. Like every thing else in this unfortunate department it was noised abroad, commenced, and abandoned. Nothing better can be expected from leaders who are most noted for weakness and a plentiful lack of decision and energy of purpose. On Wednesday all the forces marched as far as Meadow Bluff. Three days before an officer with a flag of truce had been sent in charge of some Irish who wished to go through the lines. His return was expected on Wednesday but he did not make his appearance. It is a sacred maxim of war that no advance can be made while a flag of truce is pending. All day Thursday we awaited its return and hearing from a scout that it would arrive during the day Friday the whole force marched to the foot of Little Sewell by break of day that morning when a dispatch from Genl. Jones reached Genl. Echols stating that he was sorely pressed at Bristol—ordering one Regt. in that direction, and the return of the rest of the force to their old camp near Lewisburg. A march through an incessant rain Thursday, brought us where we were before. The officer in charge of the truce flag reports that one regiment and a piece of artillery could go without difficulty to Charleston that there is only a corporal's guard at Gauley Bridge and only one regiment at Fayetteville.

A rumor is current that another great battle has been fought on the classic plains of Manassas and another great victory achieved. I trust it may be true.

Direct letters as before to Lewisburg.

Best love to dear Mother who I sincerely trust is entirely well, and to Aunt Preston & all I am

Affectionately Your Son—in haste—
Micajah Woods[27]

The rumblings of discontent continued for a few days, and then the attention of the battery focused on a reassignment that removed Jackson's Battery from Jenkins's command and placed it under Maj. William McLaughlin.[28] The purpose of the move was unfathomable to Lieutenant Woods, though he supposed it had to do with remaining in the vicinity of Lewisburg while Jenkins rode elsewhere. The concerned young officer felt that his battery's horses could not be sustained in the area for more than ten days. He now longed for Crab

Bottom, where there was hay aplenty. He understood that the horses were his command's lifeblood, and without them the men could do little or nothing.[29]

November dawned with Federals on the march. On October 26, Brig. Gen. William Averell, then stationed at Beverly, was ordered by his superior, Brig. Gen. Benjamin F. Kelly, to advance and seize Lewisburg. Brig. Gen. Alfred N. Duffié, of Middleburg fame, was to lead another column from Charleston in conjunction with Averell. The threat that had hung over the heads of the Confederates for weeks was a threat no longer.

The first inkling of Averell's movement came on November 3, when Lt. George W. Siple of the 19th Virginia Cavalry clashed with the enemy at Green Bank, twenty miles north of Huntersville.[30] Siple sent word of his discovery to Col. William L. Jackson, who in turn alerted Gen. John Echols. Siple also notified nearby Confederate commands under Col. William W. Arnett and Capt. Jacob W. Marshall. Troopers were dispatched to keep an eye on the invaders. Little resistance could be offered, however, though Jackson informed Echols on the fourth that he intended to offer battle if the Federals continued their advance.[31] With only the main portion of the 19th Virginia Cavalry and Lurty's Battery at hand, Jackson would be in for a tough fight. Echols appreciated his subordinate's grit and determined to support him. On the fifth, Echols's Brigade, McLaughlin's Artillery Battalion, which included Jackson's Battery of horse artillery, and a portion of Jenkins's Brigade under Ferguson set out to reinforce Jackson.

That same day Colonel Jackson engaged the enemy at Mill Point south of Huntersville along Stamping Creek. In his report, he described the encounter with Averell and Lurty's role in it:

> As soon it became light the next morning the enemy advanced skirmishers and sharpshooters, and I directed Capt. Warren S. Lurty to open his artillery (two 12-pounder howitzers), and the skirmishers and sharpshooters fell back over the hill where the main force of the enemy was masked. Here it was evident that the cutting down of the roads, &c. had delayed the artillery of the enemy. The shells from Capt. Lurty's pieces held the enemy in check and produced some confusion in his camp. It becoming evident from the sound that the enemy was about to make some movement, Capt. L. R. Exline, with 30 men, made a successful reconnaissance, encountering and driving in the sharpshooters and returning in safety, after discovering that artillery was coming up. Knowing that with long-range guns the enemy would have decidedly the advantage, I was prepared to fall back as soon as his artillery was put in position.
>
> About 11 a.m. it was so placed, but previous thereto our shells were thrown with some effect. Accordingly my command fell back in good order under a heavy fire of five pieces of artillery and pur-

> sued by a large mounted force, Lieutenant-Colonel Thompson with cavalry bringing up the rear. Arriving at Droop Mountain, I posted my artillery and infantry on that very strong position. The effort of the enemy in pursuit seemed to be to cut off Lieutenant-Colonel Thompson, but in this he was foiled at the foot of the mountain by a few well-directed shells from Lurty's Battery.[32]

Jackson's delaying action was not even mentioned by Averell, but Capt. Ernst A. Denicke of the 68th New York Infantry credited the enemy artillery with resisting their progress.[33] Lurty's Battery, in existence for less than a month, had proved its worth to Jackson in minor affairs. How it would do in battle remained to be seen. The answer would not be long in coming.

Jackson fell back to Droop Mountain, the best defensive position between the enemy and Lewisburg. Lurty's Battery was placed on "a projecting spur of the mountain and commanding the approaches from the front."[34] Early on the morning of November 6, Confederate reinforcements under Echols arrived. Maj. William McLaughlin, who commanded the artillery, positioned Jackson's Horse Artillery on the same spur as Lurty's and posted Chapman's Battery on the hill behind them. The Confederates now had seven pieces of artillery on the field: Lurty's two, Jackson's two, and Chapman's three. McLaughlin's report of the battle tells of his command's splendid performance:

> In a short time the enemy advanced a battery of six guns to within about five-eighths of a mile of our batteries and opened fire upon the horses of the cavalry and upon our batteries. Captains Jackson and Lurty promptly replied, as also Chapman with his piece in position, and after a sharp and steady artillery duel, lasting for about half an hour, the enemy's battery was silenced and driven rapidly from the field. Captain Chapman's battery then moved to the same position as the other batteries, and desultory fire was kept up for some time upon the infantry and cavalry of the enemy as they presented themselves within range. About 1 a.m. the enemy again advanced three pieces to the position previously occupied and opened upon our batteries. Captain Jackson with his two pieces, and Captain Chapman with his rifle piece, replied with a steady and well-directed fire, and in a short time succeeded in again silencing them.
>
> In the meantime two pieces were advanced up the road and opened upon the Twenty-second Virginia Regiment, which occupied a position to the left of our front, but a few shots from Chapman's and Lurty's howitzers soon drove them off. Perceiving that we were being steadily pressed back on the left, and that our center was wavering, I ordered Captain Lurty's battery (the ammunition of which was nearly exhausted), the 24-pounder howitzer of Chap-

> man's battery and the caissons to the rear, while the remaining pieces opened upon the enemy's infantry as they advanced in front. In accordance with the instructions of the brigadier-general [Echols] commanding, I directed Lieutenant Blain, of Jackson's battery, to place the Parrott gun of his battery and the 12-pounder howitzer of Chapman's battery in position on the hill in rear, so as to cover the retreat should that be necessary. The two pieces remaining—one of Chapman's and the other of Jackson's batteries—continued to play upon the enemy's infantry, as they attempted to advance, with shell and canister, driving them back and preventing their advance in our front and up the road.[35]

The Confederate artillery's command of the field notwithstanding, the battle turned into a rout for Echols's small army. Outflanked, the Confederate left gave way. The center followed, almost permitting the capture of one of Jackson's guns. The chase was on and did not stop until Echols's demoralized command crossed the Greenbrier River between 3:00 and 4:00 on the morning of the seventh.[36] Though the infantry and cavalry suffered a humiliating defeat, the artillery had done its duty and more. Both Lieutenants Woods and Blain wrote detailed accounts of the battle and the part played by Jackson's Battery.

> Battle of Droop Mountain
> On the road borders of Craig & Monroe
> On road to Christiansburg
> Sunday, Nov. 8th 1863
>
> My dear Father—
>
> This letter bears to you mournful intelligence from this army & department. First I will state, I passed the ordeal without harm & am now safe. Last Thursday morning the approach of the enemy from Beverly was discovered and the whole force near Lewisburg—22nd Regt. Infty. (550)—Edgar's Battn. (400)—Derrick's Battn. (200)—14th Cav. (600). Chapman's Battery & ours moved at once on the Frankford road, hoping to meet and whip that force before the arrival of Scammon [Duffié] from Kanawha who we knew was also approaching.
>
> Thursday night we camped three miles behind Frankfort, leaving Friday morning at 2 o'clock A.M. and marching eleven miles to Droop Mountain just west of Little Level in Pocahantas where Jackson (W. L.) was holding the enemy in check with 600 men on a very powerful position of Droop Mountain. The position for Artillery was splendid. The enemy attacked in force at 11 o'clock and opening with artillery. Chapman has 4 pieces—W. L. Jackson [Lurty's Battery] 2 & we had our 10-pounder & 3 in. Rifle Yankee guns the only

long range guns. So Blain & myself were masters of the situation on our side.

The enemy opened on us with a six gun Parrott Battery 2250 yards from us from the only position they could get, which was much inferior to ours—we having 12 degrees natural elevation and being thoroughly protected by the brow of our position, upon which we would run our guns by hand after each rebound which put it between us & the enemy's shots & served as a complete cover for guns, men & horses. The firing was very heavy, endeavoring to draw the attention of our forces while they were massing their infantry on our left under cover of the woods. In about an hour the whole force infantry and artillery was engaged and we succeeded in driving the enemy's battery from the field entirely by our shell which were thrown beautifully.

The enemy made desperate efforts to turn our right and reach the rear & capture the artillery. While the infantry were engaged hottest, again they brought a battery of 10-pounder Parrotts and opened upon us furiously from the same position. Again we fairly knocked them from the field. Blain did good execution with his guns (ie. his gunner did/for he did not fire a single shot). My gun did most admirably. I fired myself & sited every shot, throwing 120 shell. It drew the particular attention of all.

Soon however our infantry & dismounted cavalry being overpowered commenced giving away. All the artillery left except one of Chapman's guns & mine—everything ran—the enemy pressed—the support to our guns ran ignominiously, leaving us entirely at the mercy of the enemy who were nearly in our rear. Thus we stood depending on our own resources. The enemy ran another Battery right below us & opened furiously. Then infantry approached rapidly. I shelled them to the best of my ability till within 450 yards when I gave them 12 rounds of canister well directed which threw them into great confusion. At this juncture I withdrew my gun under a heavy fire of infantry & artillery which, however, only killed one man near us our [word illegible] not being exposed very far. My gun was the very last to leave the field.

On reaching the main road we found everything in utter confusion, infantry, cavalry & all rushing pell-mell to the rear—crowding together, running over each other. Genl. Echols, seeing us return in perfect order, rode up to Capt. Jackson who was near & exclaimed, "Capt. I saw your little band of heroes standing alone and am proud that such men are in the field in all this confusion."

The rout occurred about 5 o'clock. A great run was made till we reached Frankford, the enemy pressing us hotly for several miles &

killing a large number of men & officers. A large loss was sustained by Derrick & the 22nd, Maj. Bailey of the latter being mortally wounded. At Frankford we remained for about two hours assembling the remnants of the command—then made a big run to Lewisburg to pass the place before Scammon [Duffié] arrived. The rout & run for 29 miles to Lewisburg cannot be described.

By five o'clock Saturday morning most of the men who kept to the road—all the artillery (except one piece of Chapman's which broke down) and all the wagons had passed Lewisburg in safety and took the road towards Union. About one hour after our rear left Lewisburg Scammon [Duffié] entered in force on the Kanawha pike. Our escape must only be attributed to our rapid running. The whole distance from the battle field to Greenbriar bridge—32 miles was made in a full trot and often at a full run. Hundreds of the infantry & dismounted men took to the bushes and large numbers who are missing will come up. The 22nd Regt. infty now numbers for duty only about 100 men. Their loss in killed & wounded will only amount to about 75 or 100, nearly all the rest will be up in a few days I trust. Edgar's Battn. took a different route by way of Sweet Springs, was overtaken & forced to make a very rapid march to save itself. Several hundred fugitives are with it I understand.

The troops on leaving Lewisburg to fight left all their camps standing with all their baggage—which was immense. All was burnt. The loss sustained by the men & officers in clothing and material is very heavy. I am proud to say that our Battery has come off without the loss of a pound of baggage of any description. Even our tent flies are saved. And not a man was out of his place at any time during the fight or retreat.

Averell on the Frankford road is thought to have had about 6500 men and Scammon [Duffié] about 3500. The fate of the people of Greenbriar and that whole region is much to be deplored—all the men of the country came out with us—the women are left helpless to the tyranny of the foe. I stopped for a few minutes at Mr. Price's as I came through Lewisburg. Mr. Price was with us on the battle field and came out with us. His family are all at home and intend remaining. Cousin Jane declares she will stand her ground to the last and never leave her home—but stay and protect it herself. Large numbers of cattle & horses were brought out by citizens. I regret to state that about 200 government cattle were left to the enemy. Also a considerable quantity of provisions was I believe burnt.

Soon after the enemy occupied Lewisburg they burnt the Southern Methodist church and several large houses on main street which had been devoted to government purposes. I learned that two or three private residences were also burned but whose they were I have not heard.

McCausland has also been driven from Princeton towards the Narrows. The enemy are certainly moving in force in this department for the accomplishment of plans which if effected will prove still more disastrous to us. The force operating must be at least 12 or 15000 strong. It seems to be understood that we will fall back near the Rail Road & be heavily reinforced. Make due allowance for this letter if you please, it is snowing—we are halted but a few minutes and my fingers are so cold that I can scarcely use them—I am determined however to keep up my practice of writing immediately after action—I write again in a day or two. Love to all— Affectionately Yr. Son

Micajah Woods

Dr. Jno. R. Woods
Holkham

Ten miles from Lewisburg Giles Co. Va.
Tuesday morning—Nov. 10th

We reached this camp yesterday evening after an arduous march on the mountains in terribly cold weather. The enemy have not advanced further than Union in this direction. Reinforcements are arriving on the RailRoad and we will doubtless check the enemy in any advance which I have no doubt that they will soon make towards the RailRoad. Hundreds of the fugitives are coming in & are being again organized. Our entire loss, killed wounded and missing will not be over 350 or 400. We will remain here several days. Write and direct to Jackson Battery, Dublin.[37]

Lieutenant Blain wrote on the same day:

Bivouac at foot of Middle Pond Mtn. Nov. 8th '63
My Dear Mother,

I write you a note this Sunday morn at a halt, to relieve you from any uneasiness which you may have on my account. Of course you have heard that on the 6th the force out here under Genl. Echols, consisting of 22nd Regt. & Derrick's Batt., Col. Jackson two skeleton's of Regts. & 14th Va. Cav. of our own brigade, two pieces of our, 2 of Jackson's [Lurty's Battery], 2 [four] of Chapman's, altogether about 12 or 15 hundred men & 6 [eight] pieces of Art. engaged the enemy at Droop Mtn. and were completely routed. Such is the fact, no matter what the papers may say. But the Art. did nobly, every body says. We lost in the whole affair not one single thing. One of Chapman's pieces broke down & he had to bury it.

Well to begin at the beginning, on Tuesday night I retired not dreaming of a foe (but of my love). Just before day I was awakened by Maj. McLaughlin who gave us orders to be ready to march by 8 o'clock. At that hour we started on the Frankford road, making 15 miles by dark. Here I understood that Col. Jackson had fallen back to Droop Mtn. 27 miles from Lewisburg & just this side of Hillsboro & that he could hold it with 800 men & wished that a fight should be made there. Accordingly at 2 o'clock we were aroused & marched by 10 to his position on the mountain.

At once our pieces, 1 Parrott & 1 3 in. Rifle, first commanded by myself & 2nd By Lt. Woods, were ordered on the field. In a few moments the enemy opened upon us with a battery of 4 pieces & after about 2 hours firing we drove them from the field. Our position was upon the brow of the mountain & I think a most elegant one. During the fire I observed an immense force of cavalry file past Hillsboro & towards our left. In the course of a short time skirmishing commenced on the left & I soon perceived the main attack was being made there. Again the enemy's battery took position where it was before & evidently to attract attention which we gave them & silenced their guns a 2nd time.

In the mean time I perceived another large force advancing upon our center which had been weakened by reinforcements sent to the left. Now I could perceive by the firing that our left was overpowered & being driven. When the infantry in our front were struck to my surprise & shame they turned & ran like dogs. One of our pieces remained in position & checked the enemy while the others were sent off. I saw the Genl. & several others, myself among them, try to rally the troops to protect the last piece on the field but there ensued such a rout of infantry & cavalry as I never before saw or wish to see.

Our battery was in rear & came within a hundred yards of being cut off by the flankers on the left. Everything then went pell-mell for at least 10 miles. Several times the enemy coming in sight & firing on us when Col. Ferguson gathered together 8 men & resisted the enemy's advance. By this time word came that 3,300 of the enemy [Duffié] were within 10 miles of Lewisburg, coming from Charleston & that we must hurry to get through town. So we did & by 3 we, the artillery, had passed through town & crossed the river. I stopped in town to tell Aunt good-bye.

Yesterday morning at day the enemy entered Lewisburg. Last night we halted for the night near the Salt Sulphur [Springs]. Yesterday a large smoke was seen in the direction of Lewisburg & since we have heard various rumors of the property burnt.

Upon the whole I never saw men make so poor a fight & never was before in a rout. There is some excuse though, for the enemy were in such overpowering numbers. On the field they had, as our ideas were too truly confirmed by a dispatch from Gen. Lee, 2 batteries of artillery, 4,000 cavalry & 3,000 infantry. As it was everything turned out for the best. If we had not been defeated we could only have checked the enemy when the force from Charleston would have come in our rear & captured everything. It was also fortunate that the 22nd ran so soon for as it was we just escaped being captured. The whole command is now scattered, there being some 200 infantry [with us]. Our two regiments, 16th & 14th, follow as rear guard. Our company has lost nothing, neither tents, clothing, nor any thing else. Thank God that I was again preserved amid the storm of [word illegible] lead. The command I think has lost few killed & wounded.[38] When you write direct to Dublin. I will get it.

Best love to all, your own son

in good spirits & fine health, though mightily in want of flannel & clothes

Randolph

9th Halted on the top of Salt Pond Mountain for the night. This morning we were enveloped in a snow an inch deep.

We are now at the foot of the mountain near Giles Court House.[39]

Blain's positive outlook aside, the Confederates had received a drubbing that boded ill for the surrounding area. Lieutenant Woods sat down and wrote a second, more detailed account of the battle to his mother on the eleventh:

Camp near New Port, Giles Co. Va.
Nov. 11th 1863

My dear Mother,

On yesterday I forwarded a letter to Father. So uncertain are the mails that, not trusting to the certainty of its reception, I will repeat some of its contents on today, well knowing how anxiously all of you in the east await definite intelligence from this Department—at this ill fated juncture. I shall be as brief as possible.

As soon as the advance of the enemy from Beverly was known all the forces in the neighborhood of Lewisburg—consisting of Echols' Brigade & the 14th Va. Cavalry, Chapman's Battery & Jackson's marched to meet them. All were confident that the move was a general one & that a force would cooperate on the Kanawha road. The 16th Cavalry was left on that approach to hold in check any demonstration from that direction. The plan was to meet & whip each advancing party before they could form a juncture & come near enough together to participate in the same engagement. How disastrously this plan failed can be told in a few words.

On the 6th Inst. we reached a powerful position on Droop Mountain in Pocahantas, 29 miles from Lewisburg where Wm. L. Jackson with about 500 men and Lurty's Battery of two guns was making a stand. Without halting we marched to the front and assumed position—and the battle opened at once very fiercely with artillery & the enemy bringing a Battery of four 10-pounder Parrotts in position 2300 yards distant. The guns of Lurty's and Chapman's Batteries were of not sufficient range to reach them with effect so it fell to the lot of our Parrott & 3-inch Yankee guns to return the rude messengers sent us. Lieut. Blain had charge of the Parrott and I of the 3-inch gun. Our position was several degrees higher than the enemy's and was further more advantageous in affording very complete cover behind the brow for horses, carriages, and men. Each rebound of our guns which we would run by hand to the front would bring us out of danger in loading. In one hour we fairly drove the enemy's battery from the field in great confusion & haste.

During this time the infantry had not been very hotly engaged. The enemy had been massing their troops on our left under cover of woods & ravines, intending to turn our left & reach our rear on the mountain before the artillery and the rest of the command could withdraw. In this they nearly succeeded. They attacked in heavy force and with determination bringing a Battery in position again in our front to occupy the attention of the center while their infantry did the main work on the Left. Again the distance was too great for all the guns but those of Jackson's Battery. This time also we literally knocked them from the field forcing them to leave two guns unattended by men or horses which we have good reason to believe were disabled—our shot & shell being thrown with great precision.

Unfortunately, however, all had not sustained the attack as well as the artillery. The whole left gave way. It was evident that the fates were unfavorable to us. All eight of our guns, Chapman's, Lurty's, and ours opened on the infantry which was advancing rapidly on our left. All did well—the enemy were evidently hesitating on further advance under such a fire of shell & shot. At this juncture all the guns were withdrawn except one of Chapman's and my 3-inch. The enemy still came—our supports every where were yielding in confusion until our two guns—Chapman's & mine were left entirely in rear & unsupported. The victorious foe advanced eager for their prey, but when at a distance of 400 yds., we opened rapidly with canister & so effectively that 12 rounds of double charges threw them into confusion & compelled them to retire behind a little eminence. This moment we limbered up & moved rapidly to overtake the retreating command. A few brave men even rallied by gallant officers & came to the rescue when we had gone a short distance. Here Major Bailey of the 22nd fell severely, if not mortally wounded. Lieut. Donalson and a large number of others were wounded immediately around us, besides several killed—mostly belonging to the 22nd. Fortunately, almost miraculously, we escaped and our horses were not killed.

In the main road the scene was the most disgraceful & humiliating I have ever witnessed. The infantry could not be rallied for the cavalry rushing by and few infantry could be found in the terrible panic which seemed to pervade not only men but officers. Nearly all rushed by the artillery. Genl. Echols, Col. Ferguson of Jenkins' Brigade & a few other intrepid spirits gathered around them a band of 30 or 40 men in rear & saved the entire army from utter dispersions. The enemy pressed [several words illegible] immediately on our rear. Hundreds took shelter in the forests and mountains in their fright. A literal run was made to Frankford—a distance of 19 miles. There the column of fugitives was halted & some organization effected. Intelligence came through courier after courier that Scammon [Duffié] from Kanawha was within 12 miles of Lewisburg & rapidly advancing to intercept us. Another run was made to pass Lewisburg & cross the Greenbriar before his arrival. Most of the men who kept the road succeeded in crossing the Greenbriar by 5 o'clock Saturday morning. Scammon [Duffié] entered Lewisburg about daylight—and at once commenced his work of tyranny & destruction.

In the killed and wounded will sum up 250 men. No idea can be formed of the captured as hundreds who are missing will come up & are arriving hourly. The 22nd Infty. which at Frankford could not collect 40 men, now numbers about 400—it entered the fight with nearly 600.

All the camps in the vicinity of Lewisburg—containing the tents, blankets, and baggage of several thousand men were burned. The loss sustained by this is quite large to individuals. I believe my Battery is the only command which brought off every thing—and lost none of its equipage.

Averell, in command of the force on the Beverly road, had about 7000 men it is thought and three Batteries. Scammon [Duffié] had near 3500 and one battery. So it is very natural that one should have been whipped by such overpowering numbers; no excuse however can be made for the shameful flight and panic. I am informed that upon our retreat Genl. Echols received a dispatch from Genl. Lee telling him that 7500 men were advancing on him and ordering him not to fight, but fall back before them. It came too late. The day had been fought and lost.

Nearly all the men from Greenbriar and Monroe came out with us, bringing their cattle, horses, & valuables. I called to see some of my lady friends in Lewisburg for a few minutes. Their situation—in the power of an almost barbarous foe is much to be lamented.

The enemy have not advanced as far as Union in Monroe. The 16th & 14th Cavalry being still in the vicinity.

Thanks to Heaven there is little chance for the Yankees to lord it much longer over our friends in Lewisburg. Their authority is likely to be brief.

Our command has been again placed in fighting trim and we are reinforced by two heavy brigades. Not an hour ago we received an order to take up our line of march to Lewisburg at break of day tomorrow. We will be followed by an escort sufficient to take us back to Lewisburg. Our Battery is on this trip again placed in advance and the most cherished wish of my soul will be gratified if we can only meet the enemy over Lewisburg and thoroughly beat them. Gen'l Jones is with us also and says we must have Lewisburg and at once. This is my information.

I am writing by dim light of a camp fire. You shall be informed as soon as an action occurs. You little realize how anxious I am to hear from home. I earnestly trust that you recovered your strength ere this—and how is Father? I hope he will write immediately and direct to me at Dublin Depot thus—

Jackson's Horse Artillery
Jenkins Cavalry Brigade
Dublin Depot
Va.

I saw cousin Jane Price all the family in Lewisburg a short time. I disliked very much to part with them under the circumstances.

Uncle David's sons are all safe so is Tom Preston—all in the fight. Capt. Jackson's brother Clarence just 17 years old was very severely wounded—his hand being shattered by a minié. I dined at Uncle David's the day before our march to the battle ground. I believe however I told you of that in a letter sent by Walter Preston—with whom I took tea the same night. The temperature has been bitter cold for several days—some snow has fallen. The troops have suffered severely. In your letter let me hear how little Lynn is doing, Bobbie, Johnnie & all. Excuse haste & believe me

Very devotedly Yr. Son
Mrs. J. R. Woods Micajah Woods[40]

Blain and Woods told similar tales of valor and terror, of gallant stands and ignominious rout. Pride and embarrassment welled in both, and for Woods, at least, the thought that "the most cherished wish of [his] soul" might be granted brought renewed hope. There was still plenty of fight left in Jackson's Battery.

During the battle and retreat from Droop Mountain and in the days following, Brig. Gen. John Imboden was not idle. Though unable to assist Echols directly, he did what he could to disrupt the Federal advance, skirmishing daily with the enemy from the fifth to the fourteenth. On November 9 at Covington, he struck the 8th West Virginia Mounted Infantry and scattered it with a few rounds from a section of McClanahan's Battery. When Imboden learned that Averell was marching toward Hardy County instead of Augusta, he realized that the Federals were pulling back. The campaign was over.

On the sixteenth, a section of McClanahan's Battery under Lt. Carter Berkeley was engaged at Mount Jackson in the lower Valley, when the lieutenant's Blakely twelve-pounder blew up at first fire. Imboden claimed that the gun was defective when he received it from Richmond. Berkeley had the honor of proving his general's assessment correct at the risk of his crew. Fortunately, no casualties resulted. The Federals were repulsed, and Berkeley's section rejoined the battery at Staunton.

Winter was now taking hold. Building and settling into some kind of permanent winter quarters occupied the thoughts of many Confederate soldiers who had spent the campaign season defending their beloved Shenandoah Valley. For the remainder of the month, Jackson's Battery camped near Lewisburg. Lieutenant Woods was appalled at the damage inflicted upon the community and destitution faced by many of its inhabitants. On the fifteenth, he wrote his mother, in part:

> It grieves me to tell you of the misfortune of the people of this region and especially of the damage suffered by our friends and relatives. The stay of the enemy, not long but every minute a day in horror, will long be remembered by many families once comfortable now destitute and helpless—in all this country. Fences are burnt all along their line of march, thousands of bushels of corn used and destroyed. Few people drove off their horses cattle and sheep—the enemy have taken all, even milk cows in many instances. Large numbers visited Aunt Preston & committed many depredations—none very injurious however. Edwinia and her whole family took

> deliberate leave and went off with the Yankees. This leaves her in a very unfortunate situation, having to do all her own work. I have seen her in town twice—at Mr. Prices yesterday evening and at church this morning. She seems to sustain her loss in a cheerful spirit. Uncle David lost three horses only leaving one. Cousin Jane Price lost one negro boy and a horse. Indeed every citizen had lost something valuable. Mrs. North at the Bridge suffered more than any one I have heard of. Immense numbers entered her house & seized everything that could be carried off—Blankets, parlor ornaments, daguerreotypes & watches—officers rode through her kitchen. What was not taken was destroyed. Her niece sick in the house was intruded on most shamefully—two or three rings on her fingers were wrenched off in bed. The house itself would have been burnt but for her confinement & disability— [two words illegible]. The loss of small commodities in every house nearly is very heavy. No houses burned in Lewisburg.[41]

The losses of the civilian population in Lewisburg may have weighed heavily upon the infantry and cavalry who ran at Droop Mountain, but Woods and his comrades could look the people in the eye, knowing they had done their duty to its fullest.

By December 1, Jackson's Battery was encamped at Warm Springs, West Virginia.[42] Lurty's Battery, after a brief stint with Col. John McCausland's Cavalry Brigade, was back with Col. William L. Jackson, who also had established his headquarters at Warm Springs.[43] McClanahan's Battery was located near Harrisonburg, where it received a new James rifled gun to replace the defective Blakely.[44] All probably thought they were finished chasing Yankees for the winter, but William Woods Averell had other ideas.

On December 8, Averell began another raid. Echols, Jackson, and McCausland were launched in pursuit, and with them marched Jackson's, Lurty's, and McClanahan's Batteries. McClanahan had no opportunity to engage the enemy, but Lurty's Battery managed to get into a scrap with the enemy on the nineteenth near Alum Rock, along the Jackson River on the Covington Road. Col. William Wiley Arnett of the 20th Virginia Cavalry, who was in command of the troops involved, claimed that Lurty shelled the Covington Road at a time when it was lined with enemy infantry. The result was the precipitate retreat of the Federal force, allowing the capture of twenty prisoners.[45] While not as dramatic as Arnett claimed (the troops only amounted to one company), Lurty's Battery did contribute to the small Confederate success at the Jackson River.[46]

Jackson's Battery's contribution to the campaign was relegated to Lieutenant Woods and his single gun. He recounted his brush with the invader in a letter to his father:

Near Warm Springs Allegheny Co.
Dec. 21st 1863—

My dear Father

I have long waited in vain to hear from you. I think it is really hard, almost cruel that no one at home can find time to write me a word for nearly a month. I had made up my mind not to write a syllable till I received a letter, but having been engaged in a considerable campaign—and this Department having been pretty unceremoniously handled in the past few days, I will depart from my purpose & let you know I am safe & sound.

This morning I am assured that Averell & co. have effected an escape via White Sulphur—it is entirely needless for me to say that it is a result of abject cowardice & imbecility. Enough troops were at command to have eaten the entire Yankee force—their guns & all, lock, stock, and barrel. To tell the truth [Maj. Gen. Samuel] Jones was afraid to meet him & was glad for him to escape with only a show of effort to capture him.

This Brigade—Echols with 8 pieces of Artillery was seven days marching from Lewisburg to Warm Springs—only about 26 miles. All the oaths on earth would not convince me that Maj. Genl. Sam Jones is not a complete old granny & never intended to meet Averell. On Warm Spring Mountain we have been for three days & waiting for Averell to come & attack us in fortifications when a dozen roads were open by which he could escape and all of which would have been covered by one day's march of 25 miles towards Fincastle. Every body of any [word illegible] swears at, curses & denounces the miserable mismanagement.

Last Saturday a week ago we evacuated Lewisburg in front of a force not superior to ours—disgracefully abandoned the place without a fight, when no other Yankee force was within 40 miles of us. My piece as usual was left in rear at Greenbriar Bridge—where a sharp artillery duel ensued. I fired 41 rounds—no casualty in my detachment—a battery of three guns was firing upon us from a superior position. I killed two or three of the enemy & they ceased firing first. It is easy to talk about cold weather in rooms & houses but it is terrible to experience the shivering piercing wind & blasts of these mountains. Where we go now I have no idea—perhaps to Monroe county.

Blain & [Lt. R. Beverly] Wortham go on leave of absence this morning. I send this by them—they will be absent for 20 days, when I shall go home—Wortham will visit Holkham for his clothes—treat him as well as you can & give him some of our good liquor, he can appreciate a dram.

I took breakfast at Col. Wm. Lewis this morning—had a long talk with Mrs. Lewis about the old Genl & his treatment. Yankees did not do them much damage—took a horse or two but damaged them otherwise not much. I have heard little from Lewisburg since leaving. The enemy did our relatives little damage. Aunt Preston, Aunt Francis & the rest were not disturbed. Mr. Price lost the few negroes that had remained with him before—our troops have committed immense depredations on the recent marches & done no good. Fences have been burnt for miles. I hope measure will be taken to have the officers [word illegible] of this department [several words illegible] in the eastern army & that men will be sent who can do something else than eat with ladies & invariably run from the enemy.

Where I will spend Christmas I cannot foresee. I will write again in a day or two if in the mean time I don't freeze—Excuse haste, cold weather, general disgust with the war, army & things in general—

Love to all
Affectionately Your Son
Micajah Woods

Dr. Jno. R. Woods
Holkham[47]

Woods's clash with the enemy occurred on December 13 and involved Capt. James L. McMullin's 1st Ohio Light Artillery, which was part of Brig. Gen. Eliakim P. Scammon's command. The Federal commander credited the Confederates at Lewisburg with having fifteen guns. McMullin's section of pieces fired about 100 rounds at Woods's single gun. Night ended the contest, with Scammon claiming no losses beyond two wounded.[48] Woods obviously overestimated his effectiveness in the fight.

For Jackson's and Lurty's Batteries, the 1863 campaign season had lasted almost into 1864. The men were finally allowed to settle into winter quarters, though Jackson's Battery did not officially do so until January 15, when it marched to Walker's Creek near Dublin Depot.[49] Lurty encamped at Warm Springs.[50] The men of McClanahan's Battery were not as fortunate. Imboden's responsibility for the lower Valley had meant constant vigilance. It seemed that his men had been continuously on the march. Under the circumstances, they had performed well. Imboden's reward for his efforts was the appointment of Maj. Gen. Jubal Early to the command of the troops in the Valley on December 15. "Old Jube" did not bring a peaceful winter with him. The campaign trail did not end for Imboden's command in the comfort of winter quarters.

On January 28, Early took Brig. Gen. Thomas L. Rosser's Brigade of cavalry, Brig. Gen. Edward L. Thomas's and Brig. Gen. Henry H. Walker's infantry brigades, McNeill's Partisan Rangers, Gilmor's cavalry, and four guns from McClanahan's Battery on a raid into Hardy County, West Virginia.

McClanahan's only action came on the thirtieth, near Patterson's Creek on the road to Petersburg. A single gun helped rally Rosser's troopers, who drove the enemy into the mountains. The raid proved a minor success, and before long the battery was back at Staunton. Throughout the remainder of the winter, its sections took turns serving picket duty with elements of Imboden's Brigade.

Spring seemed far off, and the officers of the batteries, along with some of the men, managed to obtain furloughs home. On leap year day, Lieutenant Woods wrote a long letter to his mother, filled with news, hopes, rumors, and questions:

> Camp Jackson's Battery Giles Co.
> February 29th 1864–,
>
> My dear Mother
>
> Father's welcome letter, enclosing Genl. [Jeb] Stuart's was received yesterday. His reply is very much of the nature I expected—it gives me to some degree a claim on his favor in future, by which I may profit should I grow very anxious to change my branch of service.
>
> Since my return to camp I am far better satisfied with my situation in the Battery than I have felt since its organization. There is a manifest determination on the part of Capt. Jackson as well as the other officers, to enter the coming campaign with our colors flying over a Battery of which we can be proud. Ere long, we will probably have our full complement of men. There is a strong disposition on the part of all the authorities in this Department to grant the Battery every favor it can ask. [Brig. Gen. Albert] Jenkins was at Dublin a few days ago preparing to assemble his force as soon as the grass pelts forth sufficiently to subsist the horses. He promises us an early and active campaign northward. A spirit animates this Department to retrieve itself this spring & summer. Wheeling & Clarksburg haunt the fancy of some of our leaders. The appointment of Breckinridge is significant of [word illegible] work. He is a Lieutenant Genl. and will be heavily reinforced. His old Kentucky Brigade, I am informed will be of the accessions to his command.
>
> Our encampment is splendidly situated in a fertile and plentiful region. We are entirely denied the privilege of modern "society" in these parts—but that deficiency is well supplied by an honest unpretending population, whose possessions are well stocked with all the substantial supports of existence, including the "soldier's partiality—onions", cabbage & other kindly productions of the earth, which are more potent by far than fine dress & exquisite entertainment to charm the soldier's appetite and thereby to enchain his affections. Our men are all domiciled in good wall tents with chim-

neys attached which render them as comfortable as they would be in plastered rooms. My own tent wears an amazingly cozy & inviting appearance on the inside. Among my ornaments are a wooden bucket—a tin basin & cup, a snug bed and a three legged stool. Hanging from various nails in the tent poles are a small looking (not mine) glass, my towel—haversack and spurs—what more than these can the heart desire or the ambition of a Confederate aspire for?

The men of the Battery were delighted with the socks and return many expressions of appreciation to yourself and the ladies who assisted in the knitting. I hope you will let Mrs. Gentry know especially how very highly I esteem her efforts in that line and how much I prize the nice gloves she presented. Say to her I know of no better way of demonstrating my appreciation of her than by selecting from her pretty scholars—a sweet heart—whom she can recommend as being trained under her eye "in the way she should go." And since this is my plan of action, you can whisper confidentially to my pretty cousin Luly that I hope that she will manage to get into the good graces of the old Lady. But seriously speaking, I do take great interest in Cousin Luly's progress and I shall be much gratified when I hear from Mrs. Gentry (as I know I shall) that she has advanced rapidly in her course of studies.

Has Willie started school yet? I suppose Father will accompany him at least as far as Richmond. I trust that he will then commence a correspondence with me. I expect he will soon become such a thorough "Tar heel" that it will be dangerous to open his letters, sealed with that commodity & filled with [word illegible] & pitch.

A most atrocious and horrible murder was committed in this immediate neighborhood night before last. A Mrs. Lucinda Carr left home to spend the night with one of her neighbors. After dark while she was sitting in company with her host by the fire a gun was run through the window behind her & fired—the load taking effect in the head of Mrs. Carr & literally blowing it to atoms. All the proof goes to show that her husband himself was the perpetrator and that the woman at whose house it happened is beyond doubt "particeps criminis."[51] Mrs. Carr was a harmless inoffensive woman who had not an enemy on this earth but her husband. She was surrounded by a large family of young children. The husband & the suspected woman (whose character is very low) were very intimate. It has been proved that Mrs. Carr was made to go to her house by her husband. Both Carr & the woman were arrested & sent to jail this morning—leaving the young children helpless & alone—no one having as yet proffered to care for them. I cannot give you the many harrowing circumstances the whole community is in a frenzy of excitement.

The murder is beyond doubt the most cold blooded, unnatural & revolting that I ever heard or read of in fiction or history.

Lieut. Blain is on a visit to Richmond & Staunton to procure guns for the Battery. He will not return for ten or twelve days. During his absence men & officers will be happy & contented. One of our men gave Blain's history connected with the Battery to Mr. Madison Allen of Giles Co. who lives only five miles from here & where Capt. Jackson's sister is teaching. Old Allen after hearing it, said he never wanted the threshold of his house darkened by such a character. Capt. Jackson heard the remark a few days before my arrival made a speech to the company & stated if he could discover the man who had spoken of Blain he would arrest him & send him in irons to Dublin. Of course this has only served to intensify the hatred of the men towards that officer. Capt. Jackson is exceedingly polite and obliging to me—nothing that I can ask is not granted. Wortham is on leave in Lynchburg & will return tomorrow. His betrothed is dangerously ill.

Edward Lampkin of this Battery of whom I have spoken in your presence has been very sick with fever. His Mother is with him. I go down to see them nearly every day. She & her family were peculiarly kind to me while in Russell—and I flatter myself that ingratitude for attentions & kindnesses bestowed is no part of my disposition.

Capt. Charles L. Minor, who taught at Bloomfield & married Miss Caznove of Alexandria has been assigned to our Brigade as ordnance officer. He was here yesterday to test our guns ammunition & c. Our target practice was very good. I wish so much you could have witnessed it—having never seen any thing of the kind. Minor's wife is with him at Dublin. Don't fail to send Walter Preston two or three pairs of socks. One of his Mother's last injunctions to me when I left was that you would supply him with such articles. The campaign will open soon in that Army & now is your opportunity to send him what you wish.

Capt. Jackson starts to Lewisburg on day after tomorrow. By him I shall send the articles I have in charge for Aunt Preston. The Captain's mission is one of love. He expects to ride six days in order to spend one day with his lady-love. Good proof that Cupid still holds sway on this earth.

Uncle Tom is now in Greenbrier—Giles Co. His station is 16 miles from our camp.

Has nothing been heard from Nelson since he left? I didn't think Father ought to support the older members of the family when all the able bodied young men desert him.

Stricker, my old standby is in good condition & fine spirits but not as fat as I hoped to find him. He has a good stable and stands completely covered by one of my largest blankets. Say to Father that the owner of the horse I wrote to him about purchasing told me today he would not take less than $2000 for him. He is a noble looking animal—not four years old till next May. Of course, he is not very nimble in his movements, but travels well for a horse so large. His eye, neck & head & whole carriage are splendid. He would bring considerably more, but I should rather depend on Stricker than pay so much.

Do write often. Love to cousin Lulie & "tell her to remember me kindly to her mother cousin Carrie & all at her house as well as Miss Hattie" How is little Maggie?

With love to dear Father & all I am
Your devoted Son
Micajah Woods[52]

Mrs. JR Woods

For Woods and the other members of his battery, along with those of Lurty's and McClanahan's, the winter passed. Spring and the war were not all that far away from the rippling waters of Walker's Creek.

CHAPTER 25

War in Winter

"A little strategy seasoned with a large proportion of the finest kind of deception"

January 1864 was an eventful month for the men of the Stuart Horse Artillery Battalion. Those batteries that had marched to Rio Hill barely had arrived in late December when Major Beckham took leave and headed for Richmond. His tenure as battalion commander was drawing to an end, though that fact was unknown at the time. Stuart had campaigned mightily for Beckham's promotion, and his efforts were about to bear fruit. Beckham would rarely be in camp with his men from this time until his promotion came through. In his absence, command fell to Capt. Marcellus N. Moorman, senior captain of the battalion.

The rest of the men made the transition from active campaigning to the mundane life of a winter encampment without too much difficulty. Indeed, there were plans circulating to enliven the men's dreary surroundings. Lt. Francis H. Wigfall mentioned those plans when he wrote to his sister to give her news of his battery and the battalion:

> Camp near Charlottesville
> Jan. 3 1864
>
> Dear Lou,
>
> I have heard nothing from you since the 9th of last month the only letter received since that gap, having been one from Mama written at Charlottesville Nov. 26. I wrote to Papa just before marching for this place and was then in hopes to be in Richmond in time to spend Christmas with you but I have been disappointed. I had set my heart on this and in order to make assurance doubly sure had sent up my application for leave more than two weeks before hand, intending should the leave arrive before Christmas to wait until the 23d and reach Richmond that night. But the 23d came and the leave

didn't, and so it is I find my self in camp this bright Sunday morning of /64. We honored the day by firing a salute on Christmas morning which I understood rather astonished the sedate citizens of Albemarle. One venerable physician was heard to remark that he didn't believe there was another battalion in the service that would have dared to do such a thing. But all rules fail in dry weather and when applied to "The Horse."

I rode into town on Christmas in order to attend church but there was no service. I saw Mr. Bird in there the other day. He was looking very well and invited me to call. I have not yet had the courage to go anywhere but think it likely I shall do something of the kind before the winter is over. You mustn't think though that I have relinquished the idea of getting to Richmond. Far from it. I sent in another official document not entirely unconnected with a leave of absence on the 30th ult. If it doesn't return within a reasonable time I shall put another on the way and continue to repeat the operation until I get an answer or the campaign opens. I have heard nothing yet from the application I made while on the Rapidan except that it had been approved by every one as far as Gen. Stuart's Hd.Qrs., including the redoubtable "Jeb."[1]

"The Horse" is to give a ball!!!

This wonderful affair is to take place on the evening of Tuesday the 5th inst. After it is over I will write more concerning it. I expect to have a good deal of fun and make up for the dull Christmas I have spent.

We are camped nearly north of Charlottesville on the road leading out from the street in front of the Farish House passing the house of your friend Miss Lydia Wood. The men have all made themselves comfortable in huts and tents and are busily at work on the stables. [Lt. William] Hoxton and I have a big fireplace to our tent and are quite comfortable. These are some of the batteries up here, Chew's, McGregor's, and Moorman's, in addition to our own. Hart's is still with Hampton's Division.

Maj. Beckham is absent on leave and told me that he would see Papa in Richmond. He went off immediately after we marched here and will be back I suppose in four or five days. Breakfast is nearly ready and I will conclude. Best love to all and a kiss to little Fan if she is not too much of a young lady to be offended at it. Good-bye dearest Lou and a happy New Year.

Your affectionate
Brother[2]

Despite his comfortable quarters, Wigfall was uncomfortable with his place in the horse artillery. Advancement in the artillery branch of the service was slow, and Wigfall evidently saw no future for himself as a part of Breathed's Battery. He had already taken steps to move onward and upward. Like Beckham, his time with the battalion was limited. Time was also running out for others in the battalion, but instead of leaving, they chose to stay.

The men of Hart's Battery, sequestered from the rest of the battalion at Penola Station on the Richmond and Fredericksburg Railroad, were nearing the end of their three-year enlistment. Without their officers, the men began to talk among themselves and on January 20, 1864, held a meeting at which they unanimously voted to reenlist for the duration of the war. They amended their vote with a resolution asking that they be allowed to maintain their organization and remain under their current officers. This was a patriotic step that precipitated an avalanche of reenlistments throughout the army. Unit after unit followed Hart's Battery's lead. So overwhelming was the result that Robert E. Lee himself expressed his gratitude in a general order, thanking Hart's cannoneers for their "noble example."[3]

Back at Rio Hill, the rest of the battalion continued to battle Old Man Winter. The men were comfortably situated in excellent log shelters that housed six men each. Even the horses had superior lodgings. Forage, however, remained a problem. There were ways of dealing with it that, unfortunately for the surrounding farm owners, were regularly put into practice. Henry H. Matthews told of Breathed's Battery's answer to the forage shortage:

> How dear those old horses were to us. It seemed they knew every man in the battery, and many a night have we started out on an expedition in quest of forage (when graveyards yawn) to visit some unsuspecting Albemarle farmer in order that we might obtain some fodder, by any means, for our dear old horses. And when in the morning our camp was visited by the aforesaid farmer, bent on finding the midnight marauders, we had been convulsed with laughter by the indignant manner in which Capt. Breathed would dismiss him, with the assurance that the men in his battery were all gentlemen, and did not do such naughty things. At the same time Bill, Breathed's horse, was quietly nibbling on some of that identical fodder.[4]

While raiding parties scattered through the night (Stuart had obviously taught them well) searching for forage, the days of January came and went. A liberal furlough policy cut down the number of men in camp, with the result that the army did not have to feed or clothe so many bodies. The morale was also bolstered tremendously. Near the end of the month, Lt. Charles R. Phelps of Moorman's Battery returned to camp. His letter home illustrates clearly the life of an officer in winter quarters:

Camp Horse Artillery
January 29th 64

Dear Aunt

Your letter of last week to hand with notes in same from Miss Wiatt. I am truly glad to hear of your being well & the frolics throughout the Christmas [word missing] did not [word illegible] you as bad as myself. I am once more installed in my old quarters and everything has quieted down to the usual routine of camp life and has become perfectly natural to me again. I have been quite busy since my return, getting up stables, cabins, &c. and have kept very close to camp—have paid no visits and made no acquaintances among the fair sex, with the exception of those made at a Ball which I attended at Charlottesville given by Gen'l Fitz Lee's Cavalry division. It was like all other Balls I have attended and everything passed off in good style. I was off at daybreak without losing my heart, & only wish I could say as much for my hat—about forty of us could be seen the next morning with handkerchiefs tied around our heads looking for a hat store.

The Doc[5] has almost entirely deserted me since my return—he is out every day visiting—the Ladies—sometimes staying several days at a time. I do not know that any particular one has taken his eye but the acquaintances he made when in Lynchburg did not make any lasting impression on him—at all events I hope none of them will take the matter seriously—and do anything desperate on account of his absence. He is playing a high game & playing it very strong.

Has the Diamond got the calves out of the yard? if not put him to driving them [word illegible] it is very healthy employment—& it is necessary they should be kept out of the front yard.

I sent you a bundle books by Express and by Capt. Moorman two packs cards—all of which has been received.

The weather for the last week has [been] more like Spring than Mid Winter & if it continues would not be surprised if we not have some work.

Nothing new here. The Major has just stepped in & must close for inspection of Battery etc.

Will write soon. Love to Sallie, Uncle Charles and all friends.

Yours most truly
Dick[6]

The "Major" was more than likely Beckham, performing one of his last inspection tours. Though things were moving a little slowly out at Rio Hill, behind the scenes at Richmond, efforts on Beckham's behalf by Stuart and others were soon to bring both promotion and separation.

That both Pelham and Beckham were deserving of high rank for their services in establishing and maintaining the horse artillery battalion as one of the premier fighting units in the Army of Northern Virginia was denied by no one. The difficulty lay, at least for the pencil pushers in Richmond, in that the battalion did not contain a sufficient number of batteries to grant the rank of lieutenant colonel to its commander. This was the story that had been given Stuart back in June 1863, when he had attempted to secure that rank for Beckham in the wake of the artilleryman's performance at Chancellorsville. Pelham had achieved the rank posthumously, though the number of the battalion's batteries had not changed. Fortunately, Beckham did not have to pay the price the "Gallant" one did to get it.

By the second week of February, Stuart knew that Beckham was leaving the battalion. The cavalry chieftain's telegraph to his artillery commander on the fifteenth congratulated him and wished him success.[7] On the following day, the promotion became official. Beckham was a colonel, assigned to the Army of Tennessee, and the Stuart Horse Artillery Battalion was without a commander. Next in line for the job was Capt. Marcellus N. Moorman, but events were transpiring elsewhere that would prevent Moorman from ever holding the position.

At the same time Beckham departed the battalion, Lt. Francis H. Wigfall was bidding farewell to his fellow officers and men. Longing for both a higher rank and a more prestigious post, Wigfall's considerable political influence through his father helped him secure an aide-de-camp position on the staff of Gen. Joseph E. Johnston. Wigfall eventually became a major, a rank he probably would not have reached had he remained in the horse artillery. By February 27, he was writing his mother from Kingsville, South Carolina, a stop on his way west. On that same day, preparations were being made behind Federal lines for a foray that was to test the mettle of the Stuart Horse Artillery Battalion. The camp at Rio Hill was soon to have unwelcome visitors.

The Federal advance that resulted in the fight at Rio Hill was actually part of a much larger offensive operation orchestrated by Brig. Gen. Hugh Judson Kilpatrick, who had developed a scheme to free Federal prisoners of war in Richmond. Kilpatrick had campaigned vigorously, going directly to President Lincoln, who had his own agenda, the distributing of his amnesty proclamation throughout the enemy countryside, and was persuaded that the plan had a chance for success.[8] The commander of the Army of the Potomac, Maj. Gen. George G. Meade, was not as easily convinced. However, with Lincoln firmly behind Kilpatrick, Meade could do little more than make every effort to see that the expedition met with success.

Part of that effort was to be an attempt at diverting the attention of the Confederate high command from Kilpatrick's proposed route of march. In order to accomplish this, Meade directed Maj. Gen. John Sedgwick to march his VI Corps, along with Maj. Gen. David B. Birney's division of the III Corps, toward Madison Court House south of Robertson's River. Moving with Sedgwick's infantry were elements of the 1st, 2nd, and 5th U.S. Cavalry, the 1st New York Cavalry (Dragoons), and the 6th Pennsylvania Cavalry, all from the Reserve Brigade of the 1st Division, and detachments of the 1st New Jersey and the 6th Ohio Cavalry regiments from the 1st Brigade, 2nd Division. One section of Battery E, 1st U.S. Artillery, under the command of Lieutenant Essex Porter, accompanied the cavalry. This force, totaling 1,500 men, was under the command of Brig. Gen. George A. Custer. By 6:00 P.M. on the twenty-eighth, Custer's troopers were bivouacked for the night around the courthouse. The infantry would be going no farther, but Custer had orders to continue south as far as Charlottesville. His target was the destruction of the Virginia Central Railroad bridge over the Rivanna River near Charlottesville. All that stood between the town and its capture were four batteries of the Stuart Horse Artillery—sixteen guns and barely 200 men. Turning out his command at 2:00 A.M. on the twenty-ninth, Custer resumed his march.

The Union raiders left Madison Court House, rode past Wolftown, across the Rapidan River, through Stanardsville and Earlysville, and approached within a mile and a half of the Rio Bridge over the Rivanna River. Custer was within striking distance of the horse artillery's camp but unaware of its existence. Meanwhile, at the battalion's camp, Privates Marcellus B. Fuqua and Littleton W. Moorman of Moorman's Battery had just returned from an early morning trip into Charlottesville, bringing with them the mail for their own battery plus that of Chew's, Breathed's, and McGregor's. Captain Moorman ordered the two privates to take their mud-splattered horses down to the river and give them a good washing. Having given the order, the captain decided that his own mount could also do with a bath, and he accompanied the two men toward the river. The trio had not gone far when Captain Moorman reined up his horse. He told Fuqua and Moorman that he had forgotten something back at the camp and that he would have to tend to his horse's cleanliness on some other occasion. While their captain returned to camp, the two privates continued on toward the river. Ten minutes later, they were prisoners on their way to see Custer.[9]

Captain Moorman's lapse of memory was a stroke of luck that saved him from sharing the fate his men suffered. Nevertheless, he would need more of that good fortune very soon. Scarcely had he arrived back at his headquarters to attend to his forgotten business when the calm of the camp was disrupted by the rapid hoofbeats of an approaching rider. Lt. James N. Cunningham of the 1st Virginia Cavalry reined his lathered horse to a stop before a startled Moorman and reported that Custer's column was almost upon the camp. Cunningham had been shadowing the raiders all the way from Madison Court House.

Since a raid on their camp had been the last thing on the minds of the cannoneers, they were completely unprepared for any sort of armed encounter. The battalion's horses grazed in nearby fields, and the guns stood silent in the artillery park adjacent to the camp. Immediately upon receiving word of the enemy's approach, Moorman ordered the cannons limbered and sent a thin line of skirmishers armed with a few pistols toward the Rio Bridge, hoping to dispute as best as possible the enemy cavalry's crossing of the Rivanna. But it was already too late. The blue troopers were in possession of the bridge, and a large number of them were across the river and deploying against the horse artillery's camp. Still, the resolute cannoneers opened fire with their meager arsenal of small arms. The close proximity of the pistol fire alerted Moorman to the fact that he could not save his camp and might not be able to save his guns unless he added more of a sting to his delaying tactics.

Once across the river, Custer had sent Capt. Joseph P. Ash of the 5th U.S. Cavalry with sixty-five men downriver to strike the enemy's right flank in order to ascertain what forces were present there. These were the men that encountered Moorman's feeble pistol-wielding skirmishers. In his report, Custer stated that he had met with a heavy concentration of graycoats prior to dispatching Ash. He estimated that there was "a superior force of the enemy's cavalry, four batteries of artillery, in position, and a heavy force of infantry (which I have since learned was Early's division)."[10] Lt. George W. Yates, aide-de-camp to Federal cavalry commander-in-chief Alfred Pleasonton, who was accompanying Custer, was also convinced that an infantry division stood between Custer and Charlottesville. He additionally claimed in his report that the enemy's infantry had been brought by trains that had been heard while the Federal column crossed the Rio Bridge. In reality, the Confederate cavalry and infantry were nonexistent, and the trains had not brought the Confederates a single soldier. The horse artillery was on its own.

Moorman's cannoneers-turned-skirmishers delayed Captain Ash but a few moments. Ash's charge, according to Custer, "drove the enemy back very gallantly, and succeeded in capturing 6 caissons filled with ammunition, 2 forges and harness complete, besides destroying the camp of the enemy."[11] Ash was soon joined by elements of the 1st U.S. Cavalry, which added their strength to the attack. The results since crossing the Rivanna should have encouraged Custer to press on to Charlottesville, but he hesitated, unsure of exactly what he was facing. Upon that hesitation hung the fate of the guns of the Stuart Horse Artillery and the town of Charlottesville. The Confederate reaction to Custer's vacillation would determine the day.

Captain Moorman watched as the men of the four batteries hurriedly rounded up grazing horses and hitched them to the guns. He realized the

Federal troopers would be among the guns before they could be hauled to safety. Something more was needed. Depending on which account is consulted, Moorman, Breathed, Chew, Shoemaker, or Phelps ordered some guns wheeled into position by hand and fired into the Union troopers, who recoiled before the blast. Moorman noted the effect the discharge had on the enemy and with a sense of relief saw the majority of the battalion's cannons being moved rapidly toward Charlottesville. Then, while the Yankee cavalry regrouped for another charge, the last of the guns was hitched to its team of horses and, under Moorman's direction, galloped to the rear. The graycoats' retreat was not a disorganized flight, however. On a hill overlooking the camp, the men unlimbered four guns and formed a makeshift line. The fight wasn't quite over.

The thin line of cannoneers was anything but substantial. Scarcely 200 men were gathered on the crest of the hill. The artillery pieces were manned by skeleton crews, and the mounted artillerymen who made up the "cavalry" of the line of battle were armed with only a few pistols and sabers. Those having nothing with which to fight picked up fence rails and other pieces of wood in order to simulate carbines and swords. Above this thin gray line flew a tattered flag. Moorman and company were bluffing with all the coolness of a riverboat gambler holding nothing but a pair of deuces.

Custer had followed his troopers across the Rivanna and rode to within a mile of the battalion's camp. Here he quizzed his prisoners—Fuqua, Moorman, and a servant who lived at the nearby home of a Dr. Cooke. The artillerymen gave the general very little information, but according to Fuqua, the servant informed Custer that the Confederates had "six pieces of artillery and that our soldiers were camped from Dr. Cooke's all the way to Charlottesville."[12] During the questioning, the fire from the front became more intense. Since he had only a single section of guns, Custer knew that most of the loud crashes of artillery were coming from the enemy's batteries. Even as he spoke to the prisoners, a few shells whistled overhead and exploded just in the rear of where he sat.[13] Custer added the servant's statement to the earlier sounds of trains and the reports that the Confederates' resistance was stiffening and concluded that, with his back to a river, he was not in a position to face any kind of heavy counterattack. Captain Ash's success aside, Custer felt threatened and, believing he had accomplished his mission, ordered a withdrawal to the north bank of the river.

At the camp, Ash's men had recovered from their initial repulse and charged into Chew's and Breathed's camp. Fire engulfed the crude cabins, and the Confederates on the hill watched solemnly as their belongings were given to the flames. The four guns on the hill, which had been dropping shells in among the Federal cavalry and around Custer, ceased fire. The enemy gathered for another charge. Just then, one of Chew's abandoned caissons caught fire and exploded, plunging the Federals into confusion. Seizing the moment, Chew and Breathed launched their "cavalry" in a charge. Ash headed for the river and joined the rest of Custer's command in putting the rolling waters of the

Rivanna between themselves and the "vast superiority of the numbers of the enemy."[14]

Following Custer's withdrawal, the men of the horse artillery returned to their camp—or what was left of it. In his report, Captain Moorman summed up the battalion's losses by battery:

> Moorman's battery, 2 men and 2 horses captured; Chew's battery, 10 sets of harness, 1 limber with canteens, 1 forge, 6 tents, 5 tent-flies, 4 tarpaulins, 60 pounds axle-grease, 15 curry-combs and brushes, 3 public horses, 40 Government bags; Breathed's battery, 9 tents, 2 horses, 3 1/2 sets harness; McGregor's battery, 6 sets harness, 3 tent-flies, 12 bridles, 6 saddles and blankets, 4 halters, 2 mules, 4 skillets, 2 camp-kettles, 4 water-buckets.[15]

The captain would seem to have been quite thorough, but Chew's report of his losses was much more detailed.[16] The other batteries may also have suffered more than Moorman's report indicated.

In spite of these losses, the battalion had something to celebrate. Pvt. George M. Neese of Chew's Battery recorded it in this fashion: "A little strategy seasoned with a large proportion of the finest kind of deception were the principal weapons and instruments with which the backbone was entirely and efficiently extracted from the great Custer's raid on destruction bent, without bloodshed on our side."[17] The horse artillery had challenged a force seven times its size led by an officer who possessed a reputation for aggressiveness second to none in the Union army, and it had emerged victorious. Lt. Charles R. Phelps of Moorman's Battery wrote about the "battle" in a letter he penned on March 2:

> Old Camp near Charlottesville
> March 2nd 1864
>
> Dear Aunt,
>
> I wrote you a short note Tuesday morning to let you know that I was still in the land of the living and not "gone up" as rumors had it in Lynchburg.
>
> Monday was a "very large" lively day, in fact the most lively we have had this Winter, the weather being fine we were all engaged, as usual doing nothing. About 10 o'clock an amateur courier rode into camp very much excited and gave us the startling intelligence that the Yanks were within six miles of us and advancing rapidly. This only created a laugh as no one thought it could be possible. A few minutes later another amateur arrived and corroborated the statement of the first. To be on the safe side we ordered the horses to be caught, they in a large field grazing.

Courier No. 3 arrived [word illegible] to let us know that the Yankees had crossed the river—only one & half mile off. By this time everything was in confusion—men & horses running every way—our object then being to save our pieces—as the first report turned out to be too true. I had one of my pieces put in position and commenced firing right & left—this held them in check and we got all the pieces hitched and moving out of camp. After we got everything out that could be taken away the Yanks advanced into Capt. Chew's camp and burnt a portion of his tents, stables, and a caisson which he had left—at this time a party about 20 men headed by Capt. Breathed charged a squadron and drove them to the river and across, where the whole force formed line of battle, awaiting our advance—but Capt. Breathed's party had no small arms they had to stop and send to Charlottesville after them. The Yanks in the meantime burnt the bridge across the river and a large mill—and commenced falling back the way they came.

Capt. Breathed and his party then followed them about 20 or 30 miles skirmishing with them several times, & wounding several—besides capturing several fine horses. Towards night the Provost Guard and some citizens of the town came out and offered their valuable services—this being the only support we had, they [were] very heartily welcomed.

In the evening I again took position in the yard of Rev. R. K. Meade and stayed all night with him. He is a very hospitable gentleman and seems to think this raid will do the citizens in this neighborhood a great deal of good. I agreed with him, and when I see some of the citizens armed here I almost regret the Yanks did not stay longer with us.

The citizens of Charlottesville are very lavish in their praise of "the Hoss" and give us credit of saving the town etc. Capt. Moorman was on hand in all his glory—his wife was at Dr. Cooke's (& is there yet). The Yanks passed through the yard and our men charged them from that point. Mrs. Moorman behaved in the most gallant manner and actually counted the Yanks as they passed. Everything was quiet all day yesterday, but today again we are expecting another advance but do not know from what point. The Yanks was at Barboursville 17 miles from here, but seem to be making their way towards Columbia, Fluvanna [Co.]. Take care not to get up as high as the Ferry.

I commenced this letter this evening but had to stop to "harness up" as the Yanks are reported advancing. It is now 10 P.M. and everything quiet and asleep—would be surprised if we were not called up before morning. Dr. B. arrived yesterday and has been complaining all day—he cannot stand a City Campaign. I will have him all right in a day or two. He sends his love. Many thanks for present received by the Dr. You must know that [name illegible] thinks a great deal of me, and can anticipate my wants. The "Camphor" could not have come in better time as Tuesday was one of the most miserable days we have had this Winter—raining & freezing all day and we were out all day moving camp. I have not as yet had the pleasure of calling upon Mrs. Cooke, & hardly think I shall now have an opportunity. I have seen them several times—Ladies of fine personal appearance. Miss Smith I would not know if I was to see her. I hardly think I shall marry her. I am not partial to the "Iae Bowens" style of music. Enclosed I send an order for the cloth. If it can be had let me know what it costs. I want enough to make a uniform—whoever gets it can fill up the blank. A uniform will cost me $775.00 in Lynchburg and that is rather over my pile.

Love to all in haste
Dick

Genl Tilden arrived this "evening" and will take command if we are attacked tomorrow.[18]

"The Hoss" was worthy of the lavish praise. Custer may have faced the unknown with 1,500 men, but Moorman, Chew, Breathed, and their boys knew what odds they were up against and stood the test despite the numbers and the surprise of the onslaught. The ladies of Charlottesville certainly felt that "the Hoss" deserved something and set out to show their appreciation. A resolution passed by the town council on March 7, 1864, thanked the men of the Stuart Horse Artillery for their actions in saving the town.[19] In addition, the ladies of the town presented a flag to the battalion, which flew over the guns for the remainder of the war.[20] Unfortunately, all the batteries did not share the battalion's proudest moment. Hart's Battery had not been on hand to help repel Custer. However, they did manage to get in a few rounds against Kilpatrick.

On the morning of the twenty-ninth, Maj. Gen. Wade Hampton received a dispatch that alerted him to Kilpatrick's movement against Richmond. He ordered Brig. Gen. James B. Gordon's North Carolina Brigade and Hart's Battery, under Lt. Edwin L. Halsey, from Penola Station to Mount Carmel Church. Hampton joined this skeleton force on March 1, and the chase was on. Night had fallen by the time Hampton caught up with the raiders near Atlee's Station, where Kilpatrick's men were encamped. Halsey rolled two guns into position but held his fire until the cavalry was deployed. Then he let loose a deadly barrage that threw the camp into the wildest confusion. Their job finished, Halsey's gunners stood by their pieces and watched their cavalry comrades charge the camp through a snowstorm. Though the attack routed the enemy, darkness permitted his escape. The condition of his command's horses prevented Hampton from properly following up his victory. Halsey led the battery to Milford Station near Hanover Junction, where it encamped until April 1.[21]

The midwinter interruption of Kilpatrick's and Custer's raids behind them, the men of the battalion settled down once again to camp life. Chew's and Breathed's men had lost many personal items, which they tried to replace. Yet even in the midst of this turmoil, matters of the heart and soul often superseded creature comforts. Gunner Charles McVicar wrote of many things, the least of which was the clash with Custer, in a letter to his sister:

> Chews Battery Horse Artillery
> Camp near Charlottesville March 7th/64
> Katie Dear Sister,
>
> I received your thrice welcome letter of the 26th, also one from Father Thursday evening last. Father's was dated the 14th. George Stewart also received two from Mollie the same evening.
>
> I had begun to think almost that you had all forgotten me. It was the 13th of January when I left that section and not to hear from any of you until the 4th of March. I had written two letters to Father and one to you and no answer. I did not know what to think. I was fearful that something was the matter, but your kind letter relieved me very much.
>
> Lissie received your letter and mine. I received an answer to mine Saturday evening just as I was getting into the saddle to ride over to parson Beachs with his son. It was a very pleasant and familiar letter, giving me a description of how she has spent the time also of her travels.
>
> Katie, you wished me to make you my confidant in that. Well I will and also elsewhere, for I am certain that I could not get a better and more honest one anywhere, but I have no secrets to reveal. I am candidly speaking "Heart" whole and Fancy "free." I think a great deal of Lissie I will admit, but just as much of Belle or Rachel Campbell or Miss Ellen [name illegible] in Bridgewater. Katie to think of going farther than an interesting friendly correspondence or controversy until this war is over is absurd. At least I think so. If any of my intimate Lady friends thinks that is too far in the future to wait they are all at perfect liberty to do otherwise. I have a great deal to do after this struggle is ended before I could possibly have any serious thought in regard to matrimony, so you see I am not likely to be ensnared by any means provided I should live.
>
> You do not fancy my accomplishment of washing and ironing. I feel very grateful to you for your kind proffer in regard to performing such service for me. Since I have become better acquainted in this neighborhood I have been getting my washing done at 25 ct apiece.

I was glad indeed to hear from you that had been so much good done by the revival in the Methodist Church. Mata, poor girl seems to have a hard time. I trust she may reap the reward that she has been so long struggling for.

Annie Campbell is in Bridgewater. I suppose by this time Sallie, that's Jim's wife, will lead her a gay time of it [if] she will let her.

Katie. You seem to be despondent of ever seeing any more happiness. You must not do that. There are many ways that you can enjoy yourself. Recollect that you are the [word illegible] support of your mother. That should be a source of pleasure to you while we are all away that this war cannot last always. I know that it must be lonesome, very lonesome, to you. Yet you must hope. Have courage. Do more visiting around among your friends. You have not much to do. You could spend a great many hours pleasantly that way. Tell mother that she must also do the [three words illegible] as pleasant as you can. Would that I could alleviate you in some way, but I cannot. I am very sorry, Katie, that you seem so downhearted.

I was sorry to hear of Aunt Ettie's illness but hope she is better by this time.

We are doing very well here. I like the neighborhood very much. I am intimately acquainted with Parson Beach's family. He very kindly proffered me the use of his library while we were in this vicinity. They are all very kind. Madam frequently sends me over delicacies that are welcomely accepted. The parson has been over and dined with me on camp fare.

I was in a light engagement with the enemy on Monday last. They rushed in on us before we were aware of it. We fought them about an hour. They burnt most of our winter quarters. The boys had not time to save anything. They lost blankets, knapsacks, and all of their clothing. Poor Nicewander[22] lost everything he had as he was not in camp when the alarm came. Our quarters were not troubled. The sound of battle was quite natural. I was fortunate enough to save everything.

Kate you must give my kind regards to all inquiring friends. Tell Marion that she must write soon and mother also. This is horrible paper.

Kiss the children for me. Did Henry get his birds or not and how does he like them. Jennie Campbell in her last letter told me that [word illegible] her mother had taken them down to Him.

Well Katie I must close hoping to
receive an answer soon
Your brother
Charles McVicar[23]

The "light engagement" had at least provided a few moments of excitement during a time when boredom had reached its zenith. Those men not fortunate enough to secure a furlough could look forward to hours of trying to keep warm and the routine of camp duty. By the third week in March, however, something was in the wind. Orders came down from above to move camp near Gordonsville. They were executed on March 20. The reasons for the move highlighted a letter Lieutenant Phelps wrote to his aunt on the twenty-second:

> Camp near Gordonsville
> March 22nd 1864
>
> Dear Aunt
>
> Your letter received Saturday last. We left Charlottesville Sunday morning and arrived here last night. Our object was to get forage for horses. We will be here but a short time as we are now fitting up for the Summer campaign—would not be surprised if I did not date a letter from MD or Penn in less than a month, that is the general impression now—if so, I will try and make my next trip pay.
>
> I am very sorry you were not at home when I was in Lynchburg. I could not let you know of my visit as it was very unexpected to me. I went to your house, knocked at the door—no answer—leaped the fence and rushed into the kitchen and no doubt frightened the old lady I saw very much. Hope you succeeded well in your foraging expedition. The weather is as cold as any we have had this winter—quite a change from comfortable winter quarters to the open air.
>
> I have not time to write mom—I have to hunt up my horse—he is either stolen or has strayed off. If you should hear of any good soldier riding him about Lynchburg please have him arrested.
>
> All well and in good spirits—too cold to be [word illegible].
>
> Love to Uncle C., Sallie, and all friends.
>
> Yours truly Dick—
>
> Many thanks to Uncle C. for his kind offer—he cannot do anything for me at present.
>
> In haste D.[24]

Others in the battalion and throughout the army shared Phelps's optimism concerning a visit to Maryland and Pennsylvania. True, some had given up; some stayed because it was their duty; some believed the Confederacy could still be victorious. There was yet hope. Marse Robert still led them. Stuart's plume still waved before them. But who would lead the men of the battalion with Beckham gone? Campaign season approached. Someone must be found to command those who had fought under Pelham and Beckham. Someone worthy. The search began.

The Chew Era

CHAPTER 26

Into the Wilderness

"The everlasting ping and thud of slugs, balls, and fragments of shell filled the air with horrid screams."

As March slowly gave way to April, the men of the Stuart Horse Artillery Battalion began to prepare themselves for the fighting they knew lay ahead. Equipment was checked, and the ravages of winter and raiders repaired. A reorganization of the battalion's command structure caused by Beckham's promotion also was under way. In this matter, Stuart faced a knotty problem. The senior officer was Capt. Marcellus N. Moorman, commander of the Lynchburg Battery. Stuart's feelings for Moorman are unknown, but this officer obviously was not in the mold of either Pelham or Beckham. He had not been an inspiring commander. While the record of his battery was commendable, it did not reflect well that Moorman's name was seldom found in the reports of the battery's actions. His contributions, whatever they may have been, had not drawn Stuart's or Beckham's attention. His succession to command of the battalion would have caused considerable discontent among the men of his battery and the battalion. Fortunately, as events unfolded, Moorman was never considered for the post.

Even prior to his battery's conversion to horse artillery, Moorman had campaigned mightily on his own behalf for a promotion to the rank of major, eliciting recommendations from several general officers and influential politicians. These repeated efforts had failed to bear fruit, probably due to the slow promotion rate in the artillery. As a result, Moorman's fate, and that of the horse artillery, eventually fell into the hands of Brig. Gen. William N. Pendleton, Robert E. Lee's chief of artillery. On November 20, 1863, Pendleton had outlined his proposed reorganization of the Army of Northern Virginia's artillery and the necessary promotions that would follow. Moorman's name, along with those of Chew and Breathed, had been listed with those who would be promoted to a majority. Beckham's promotion to lieutenant colonel was listed in the same report.[1]

True to the mysterious workings of the army and those nebulous individuals who control the fate of soldiers everywhere, Pendleton's recommendations were not implemented in their entirety or within what could be labeled as a reasonable amount of time. Not until March 1864 did Beckham, Moorman, and Chew see the results of Pendleton's plan for reorganization, and when it came, Beckham and Moorman were promoted out of the horse artillery. Beckham rode west, while Moorman assumed command of a battalion of artillery in Ewell's II Corps. That left Roger Preston Chew, whose record as a combat officer was equal to any in the battalion, as senior officer. However, Chew only assumed temporary command. Though Pendleton's report at long last had brought Chew a well-deserved promotion, it also led to another officer's rise in rank, an officer Pendleton had targeted for command of the horse artillery.

> SPECIAL ORDERS No. 80.
>
> ADJT. AND INSP. GENERAL'S OFFICE,
> Richmond, April 5, 1864.
>
> V. Lieut. Col. James Dearing, artillery, Provisional Army, C.S., will proceed without delay to the headquarters Army of Northern Virginia, and report to General R. E. Lee, commanding, for assignment to duty with horse artillery of that army.
>
> By command of the Secretary of War:
>
> JNO. WITHERS,
> Assistant Adjutant-General.[2]

With the issuing of this order, the problem of finding a commander for the Stuart Horse Artillery Battalion seemed resolved. The series of events that brought about Dearing's assignment to the horse artillery began with his artillery battalion's transfer in September 1863 from the Army of Northern Virginia to the Department of North Carolina under Maj. Gen. George E. Pickett.

In December 1863, Dearing's career began to shift away from the artillery toward the cavalry. Late in the month, Pickett recommended Dearing for the command of a proposed cavalry regiment he was hoping to organize.[3] In January 1864, Pickett gave command of the newly organized cavalry regiment to Dearing, promoting him to the temporary rank of colonel.[4] It was while Dearing served in this capacity that Pendleton's order to report to Lee for assignment to the horse artillery arrived. Dearing's response was quick and emphatic. He refused to go unless guaranteed the rank he presently held. Stuart, who knew of Dearing's satisfaction with the proffered cavalry command, responded.[5] He requested that Dearing's assignment be annulled and that Chew be given command.[6]

Robert E. Lee agreed with Stuart, and Dearing remained with his cavalry. He knew his request for a colonelcy would never be granted and would remove him from consideration for a command he never really wanted. Within months, he was a full brigadier general of cavalry, proving once again that advancement was far more rapid in the infantry and cavalry than in the artillery.

Dearing's refusal meant that Chew would command the horse artillery in the upcoming campaign. Stuart's praise of Chew virtually guaranteed his receiving the position. The general obviously was impressed with Chew's initiative in facilitating the battalion's preparations for the renewing of hostilities even though he was not officially in command. That willingness to work coupled with his combat record was enough to convince Stuart of Chew's worthiness for the command. Typically, no further promotion accompanied the posting. Dearing would have been a lieutenant colonel, but Chew had to be satisfied with a majority.

Despite having found the right man for the job of leading his artillery, Stuart was not satisfied with the battalion's command structure. Chew had been penciled in as a second in command under Dearing, and Stuart still felt that the horse artillery had reached the size where a second in command was a necessity. Of course, he already had someone in mind: Jim Breathed. Stuart's awareness of Dearing's preference for the cavalry had led to his requesting a promotion for Breathed as early as March 24.[7] His reiteration of the request in his note of April 21 confirmed his strong desire to see that Breathed received the promotion he so richly deserved. His efforts bore fruit on the following day, when Breathed was promoted to the rank of major.[8] Sadly, Stuart did not live long enough to see how well Breathed repaid his confidence in him. At the time he wrote urging Breathed's promotion, forces were already in motion that would take Stuart to Yellow Tavern and the horse artillery into some of the most desperate fighting it had yet encountered.[9]

Chew's rise to the command of the battalion affected at least one other officer. Lt. William Hoxton wrote to his sister about his new assignment:

> Hd. Qrs. Horse Artillery
> April 9th 1864
>
> My dearest Sallie,
>
> My days work is over, and I sit down to reply to your most welcome letter, which was received last Wednesday the 6th. In my letter from Richmond I neglected to tell you why I was unable to pay you a visit while on my recent leave, and will now do so. I received five days leave upon the 19th, which leave would have enabled me to stay only three days in Richmond, so that I could have only run up to Halifax [and] spent a night with you, and returned the next day. Although I would have been delighted even to do this still I didn't think it worth while to take the trip for so short a stay, and besides I really did not have the money enough to pay my expenses to Halifax and back which is in fact the true reason. The subsequent extensions of my leave were unexpected—had I known when I got to Dr. M's that I should get 5 additional days, I would certainly have managed to reach you before my return to the army.

A few days ago I was again detailed as Adj [adjutant] of the battalion by the officer recently promoted to the command of it (vice Beckham promoted) Maj. R. P. Chew, and ever since have been very differently occupied from the lazy sort of an existence as 2nd Lt in my old battery. My duties in my company gave me more spare time than I knew what to do with, but I am here constantly occupied from morning until night. I have no doubt that the more a man is usefully employed the happier he is in the army as elsewhere, so I am well satisfied with my position. . . .

Please forward my over-coat by the first opportunity. I should be very glad to get it. As it is nearly eleven o'clock I must stop. Kiss little Eliza for me. Good-night my dearest Sallie. May God bless you all.

Your devoted brother, Wm. Hoxton[10]

Hoxton may have had little to do in his battery over the long winter months of relative inactivity, so the duties of the battalion adjutant were for him a welcomed change. However, he must have known that the coming campaign would make him give up his pen and paper duties and return to his gun.

North of the Rappahannock, Lt. Gen. Ulysses S. Grant had taken over the reins of the Army of the Potomac, though Maj. Gen. George G. Meade was still in nominal command. Grant was a fighter, and his counterpart on the south side of the river, Robert E. Lee, well understood what lay in store for the Army of Northern Virginia once Grant formulated a plan and began to advance. Lee expressed himself to Gen. Braxton Bragg in a letter dated April 7, 1864: "I think every preparation should be made to meet the approaching storm, which will apparently burst on Virginia."[11] Lee began to plan his own moves, and throughout the army, everyone from general to private did his part to see that everything was in readiness. The ranks of the army swelled as men returned from furloughs. Lt. Charles R. Phelps wrote home upon his return to the horse artillery's camp:

Camp near Gordonsville
April 22nd 1864

Dear Aunt

I arrived here in due course of time and found everybody well and ready to move. We have new horses, harness, etc. and are only awaiting orders and from what I can learn it will be some days yet before the campaign opens.

A great many troops are passing here and seem to be making their way on our left. From what I can see & hear I think Uncle Bob [Robert E. Lee] will make a flank movement & get in rear of

Grant—if so the fight I think will take place near Manassas. Today was a lively day in camp a deputation came down from Charlottesville with a flag presented by the Ladies of that place to our Battalion. It was presented by Rev. Broadus in a very neat speech and received by Maj. Chew. Several other gents favored us with blood and thunder speeches and everything passed off very well. It is a beautiful flag and costs several hundred dolls.

Speaking of flags—would it be too much trouble for you to see if some red & white bunting can be bought in Lynchburg if so I want to have Miss Orianna's flag fixed up. I told Shoemaker today it was a shame it should be in my trunk, & he told me if it could be done he would have it fixed up and pay for it.

Love to Uncle C. Sallie, etc. etc.
Very truly yours
C. R. P.[12]

The new horses and harness were evident not only in Shoemaker's Battery but throughout the battalion. Chew had worked hard to bring his command up to combat standards and had been as successful as the Confederacy's limited resources allowed.[13] The new flag would soon be baptized in the coming battles. Just where and when that baptism would take place was still unknown. All that anyone could know was that it lay in the immediate future.

May 1, 1864, found Stuart's Horse Artillery Battalion ready and awaiting the opening salvos of the campaign season. Chew with McGregor's, Thomson's, Johnston's, and Shoemaker's Batteries were still encamped on the Bolling Haxall farm north of Gordonsville. Hart's Battery had been moved from Milford Station to near Fredericksburg in early April and would have a considerable amount of ground to cover to link up with Chew once the fighting commenced. Griffin's Battery, still a part of the Maryland Line, was camped at Wickham's Park near Hanover Junction. It would miss the opening phases of the spring campaign but quickly be immersed in the torrent of fighting by the eleventh. The storm that produced that torrent broke on the morning of May 4. Grant crossed the Rappahannock.

Head Quarters Chew's Battalion, horse Artillery
Near Gordonsville May 4 1864

Dear Aunt

Yours just to hand, I have only time to say we move to the front immediately. The Yanks crossed Rapidan River this morning at Ely's Ford. You may expect to hear the heavy guns in a day or two, as the fight cannot be postponed now. I have every confidence in our success tho' it will be a bloody fight. I send my trunk per Express.

There is a pair pants, pair shoes & a heavy blanket belonging to Shoemaker—please have them sent to his father.

Love to all, will let you hear from me as soon as I can write.

Yours truly
Dick[14]

Lieutenant Phelps's short note conveyed the urgency of the moment that May morning. Chew led three batteries, Johnston's, Thomson's, and Shoemaker's, toward the Wilderness. McGregor's Battery was left in camp with orders to report to Maj. Gen. W. H. F. "Rooney" Lee at Orange Court House on the fifth.[15]

Chew rode ahead of the men and guns and paused at Orange Springs, where he composed a dispatch:

ORANGE SPRINGS, May 5, 1864—4.30 A.M.

Maj. H. B. McClellan,
Assistant Adjutant-General, Cavalry Corps:

MAJOR: Your dispatches just received. The batteries—Thomson's, Shoemaker's, and Johnston's—will arrive here by 6.30 o'clock. I will reach Dr. Almond's by 9 o'clock. The trains (ordnance and quartermaster) have orders to follow the batteries today. Is it desired that they shall move to this point, or not? McGregor will equip his battery with horses from the lot, expected last night, and has orders to report to Maj. Gen. W. H. F. Lee, by daylight, at Orange Court-House.

Very respectfully, your obedient servant,
R. P. Chew,
Major, Artillery.[16]

Chew was two hours off in his estimation of the battalion's arrival time, striking the Catharpin Road at Almond's house about 11:00 A.M. Once the batteries were up, Chew quickly realized that the junglelike growth would not allow for the use of all of his guns. Leaving Breathed in charge, Chew rode off with one section of Thomson's Battery to support Rosser's troopers, who were engaged with the blue cavalry under Brig. Gen. James H. Wilson. George Neese described the fighting:

Near the Wilderness we encountered a force of the enemy consisting of cavalry and artillery. They opened fire with their artillery and fired on our cavalry at first sight and right away, without wasting any time or opportunity, and were trying to do some ugly work from the start. We put two of our rifled guns in position and replied to their battery, but they had decidedly the advantage of us, both in position and num-

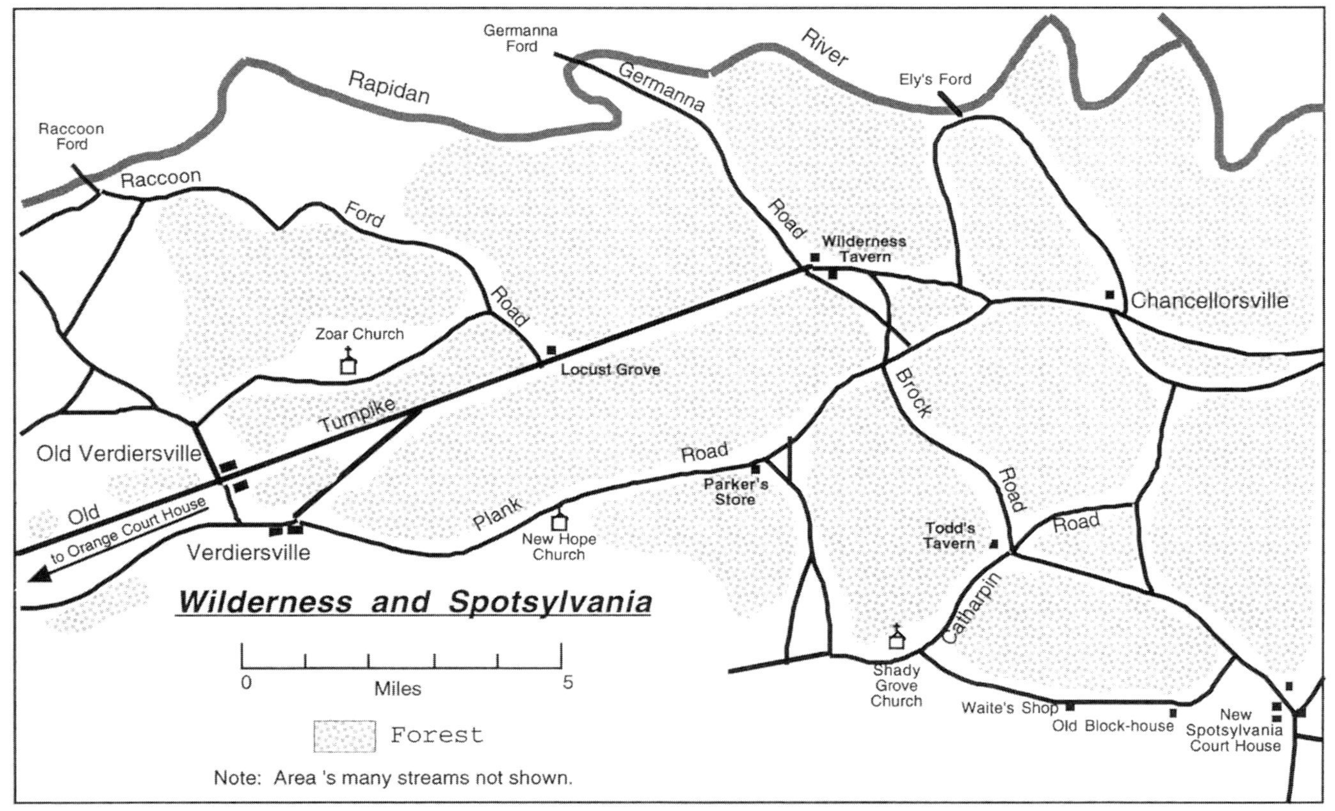

Wilderness and Spotsylvania
Rapidan
River
Germanna Ford
Germanna
Road
Ely's Ford
Raccoon Ford
Raccoon
Ford
Road
Chancellorsville
Wilderness Tavern
Locust Grove
Zoar Church
Turnpike
Old Verdiersville
Old
to Orange Court House
Verdiersville
Plank
Road
New Hope Church
Parker's Store
Brock
Road
Todd's Tavern
Road
Catharpin
Shady Grove Church
Waite's Shop
Old Block-house
New Spotsylvania Court House
0
Miles
5
Forest
Note: Area 's many streams not shown.

> ber of guns. We had only two guns engaged and the Yanks had eight, yet as unequal as the first fierce conflict was, they did not budge us from our position with our two pieces. After fighting about an hour they ceased firing and we put in the last word and remained on the field an hour after the firing ceased; then we moved our battery to their left and flanked their position, thereby causing them to retire their guns and wholly abandon their first position. Undoubtedly the Yankee batteries did the best and most accurate firing today that I have seen or been around since the war; their shrapnel shot exploded all around and over us, and the everlasting ping and thud of slugs, balls, and fragments of shell filled the air with horrid screams for an hour, and the death-dealing mixture tore and raked up the soil all around us like a raging storm of iron hail. We had three men wounded, two horses killed, and several disabled.[17]

Neese's praise of his foe, Lt. Alexander C. M. Pennington's Battery M, 2nd U.S. Artillery, and Lt. Charles L. Fitzhugh's Battery C/E, 4th U.S. Artillery, was well earned. So many of Thomson's cannoneers were disabled that the officers dismounted and helped man the guns.[18] The hard fighting continued until the Federals gave up their position. At about the same time, Breathed rode up with the rest of the guns and pursued the retiring enemy with Rosser's troopers. About a mile beyond Shady Grove Church, Johnston's and Thomson's Batteries and one gun of Shoemaker's again went to work. An attempt to outflank the Confederate line was made by some dismounted Federal cavalry, but a few blasts of canister from Shoemaker's lone piece threw them back.

Wilson reinforced his line and counterattacked, driving Rosser's advance back. The horse artillery found itself on the front line, a position of some familiarity, and threatened by the enemy, who had taken position on the hill about 150 yards to the right. The carbine fire became severe. Pvt. James A. Ryan of Johnston's Battery was knocked to the ground with a wound that would cost him his leg. His batterymates Charles A. Wilson and Edward H. O'Brien also fell wounded. Nevertheless, Chew's boys held on until Rosser rallied and drove the Federals off. Wilson withdrew toward Todd's Tavern, where Brig. Gen. David McM. Gregg's division reinforced him. Chew's guns had kept up with Rosser's pursuit of Wilson, and the daring major now placed some of his pieces on the east bank of the Po River and began to shell Wilson and Gregg. A member of the 1st Massachusetts Cavalry testified to the effectiveness of Chew's fire:

> At once the fight became lively. This was the initiation of the new battalion into real war. . . . It made the veterans smile to see these new men, and witness their various emotions, as they came under the fire of the enemy's artillery. There was no doubt about their having the

> range, as they fired down the road with shells. One went through Captain [Amos L.] Hopkins's horse, wounding the captain in the leg, and the same shot did the same for Sergeant-Major [Edward P.] Light and his horse, and the sergeant died from the wound. The shells crashed through the trees and made it appallingly lively, until for some reason they changed the direction of their fire a little, spoiling some first-rate practice.[19]

The disorganization brought about by Chew's shelling was short-lived. Gregg's fresh troopers were not willing to follow Wilson's rearward and tore into Rosser's tired men. The Confederate cavalry was also running short of ammunition and were freeing prisoners of their munitions burdens on their way to the rear.[20] It would not be enough.

The Federal cavalry aligned itself amidst the trees and underbrush and came at Rosser. Chew's guns belched canister, but the Confederate cavalry had already given their best for the day. Lt. Col. John W. Kester of the 1st New Jersey Cavalry charged forward with such determination that Chew was forced to pull out his guns rapidly to avoid being overrun.[21] Rosser now turned his back and fought a rear-guard action as his troopers, and the horse artillery, retreated across the Po toward Shady Grove Church. Chew's first fight had not been of a spectacular nature, but the horse artillery had conducted itself well. The firm handling of the batteries under new officers and old with Chew at the head proved that the battalion had not lost its edge. Beckham would be missed, but his stirrups had been amply filled.

For Hart's Battery, most of the day had been spent in marching. Lt. Edwin L. Halsey had accompanied Fitz Lee's division from the vicinity of Massaponax Church to Spotsylvania Court House and then north on the Brock Road toward Todd's Tavern. About two miles short of that place, Lee's advance ran into Federal cavalry.[22] The skirmish that erupted was of short duration but sharp nevertheless. Halsey managed to put his two guns into action briefly, but the fight was too short for him to make a significant contribution. Lee, satisfied that he had found the enemy, shifted to his left to link with Rosser. Halsey stayed where he was and awaited the morning, when he might have a better chance at the Federals.[23]

As May 6 dawned, Rosser again crossed the Po, looking for a fight. Thomson's and Shoemaker's Batteries rode with the gray troopers, while Johnston's guns remained behind at Shady Grove Church. Initially Rosser's leading unit, White's Comanches, encountered little resistance as they pushed toward the Brock Road. The Confederates were driving elements of the 1st Michigan Cavalry of Brig. Gen. George A. Custer's Brigade but were unaware that Custer's main body lay just ahead. Emerging from the woods on the Rowe farm, White's troopers were confronted by the Michigan Brigade, which charged to meet them. Only a deep ditch running down the middle of the clearing kept the two sides from smashing together. Settling for carbine and pistol fire, Rosser fed in the 11th Virginia, followed by the 12th and 7th Virginia. The two sides peppered each other across the ditch, not able to come to grips. Custer faced a flanking maneuver by Rosser and was on the verge of being forced to fall back when Col. Thomas C. Devin's Brigade arrived. The fresh Federal troopers not only thwarted Rosser's attack, but charged with such fury that the Confederates reeled back in near rout. The horse artillery saved the day.

Eight Federal guns had prepared the way for Custer's and Devin's counterattack, but not a single gun of Thomson's or Shoemaker's Batteries had reached the field in support of Rosser. At this critical juncture, Lt. John W. "Tuck" Carter, of Fleetwood Hill fame, galloped up with a single piece,[24] quickly unlimbered, and hurled several shots over the heads of the retiring Confederates and into the advancing Federals. The bluecoats paused, permitting Rosser's troopers to rally on Carter, who had been joined by the rest of Thomson's Battery and Shoemaker's four guns. For the next three hours, the rival horse batteries pounded each other. At first the Confederates seemed to have some success in silencing the enemy guns, or at least forcing them to change their position, but when a Federal battery opened an enfilading fire, things began to deteriorate. Chew ordered Thomson to move his guns to the left so as to engage the enfilading battery, leaving Shoemaker to deal with the eight pieces in his front.

What happened next the men of Shoemaker's Battery would long remember. The Federal artillery somehow spotted Thomson's movement through the thick "battle smoke that hung pall-like over the fields."[25] That, coupled with the slacking off of Confederate fire, caused the enemy to renew their efforts. A hail of shot and shell showered Shoemaker's position. However, for once the cannoneers at their pieces were relatively safe. The Federal artillery slightly overshot their mark, and instead of punishing the gunners, the iron rain wreaked havoc with the men around the battery's caissons. Newly commissioned Lt. Lewis T. Nunnelee, being the lowest-ranking officer, had charge of the battery's ammunition. Sitting on his horse, which was wounded in the face during the bombardment, Nunnelee witnessed what he called "a singular experience." While the cannoneers remained unscathed, one by one the men under his command were struck down. Pvt. Parson W. Couch crumpled to the earth, killed instantly. Corporals George W. R. McDonell and John Carey were wounded, along with Privates James A. Cobbs, John W. Hall, Robert W. Irving, James A. Musgrove, Samuel T. Preston, George H. Stump, and Joseph H. Torrence.[26] Three horses also were killed and another eight wounded and later abandoned. Physically decimated, Nunnelee's men did their duty, but the cost was high.

Beneath the flying projectiles of their artillery, the Federals sent forward dismounted men, who managed to worm their way through the smoke and underbrush and push between Thomson and Shoemaker.[27] Chew recognized that his guns were in danger of being captured and ordered them to limber to the rear. Rosser was falling back as well, but neither went far. Chew placed his pieces on an eminence a short distance from his former position. Rosser's weary, fought-out troopers formed a line on the artillery, both determined to offer what resistance was left in them. Custer and Devin would have continued the contest but had received orders not to move beyond their present position. The firing began to die away by noon. Just before dark, Custer and Devin were ordered back to the vicinity of the Furnace Road, where they encamped. Rosser's and Chew's men plopped down where they were and took what rest they could get.[28] It had been a long, long day.

Rosser's battle failed to pull Fitz Lee's cavalry into the fight. Lee did not want to bring on a general engagement and was happy just to block any threatened advance in his direction by the Federal cavalry.[29] That advance did not materialize, and in fact, the Federals abandoned Todd's Tavern and retreated north along the Brock Road. Halsey's section of Hart's Battery contented itself with sporadic supporting fire for Brig. Gen. Williams C. Wickham's tentative thrust toward Todd's Tavern. Halsey certainly must have heard the tremendous artillery fire that was Thomson's and Shoemaker's fight, but he could not have known that his comrades were involved or how roughly they were being handled. The day closed with Halsey's guns lukewarm. They would have an opportunity to heat up shortly.

Johnston's Battery had not been involved in any fighting on the sixth, but on the morning of the seventh, Chew sent it and Breathed to report to Fitz Lee. The action around Todd's Tavern on the seventh eventually involved two Federal cavalry divisions and elements of three Confederate cavalry divisions. The terrain made the use of artillery difficult but not impossible. Lt. Edward B. Williston's Battery D, 2nd U.S. Artillery, unlimbered on a high ridge and shelled the Confederate artillery, which could only have been Johnston or Halsey.[30] Breathed managed to get in his licks, too, as his guns helped smash enemy attacks with canister. In the end, Sheridan's decision to break off the engagement and fall back gave Lee the battleground and some claim of victory. Sheridan had not cleared the Brock Road of Confederates. Fitz Lee and Breathed had held on.[31]

Shoemaker's and Thomson's Batteries advanced early on the morning of the seventh from their camp on Mrs. Rowe's farm. They were intermingled with the Confederate infantry. Only one of Shoemaker's guns and an unknown number of Thomson's opened fire. The enemy's artillery did not reply. Nothing developed like the battle of the previous day. The men of both batteries had experienced a rough twenty-four hours, as Gunner Neese recalled:

> Late this evening there was some musketry on the right of General Longstreet's line, just to the left of our battery. Our orders to leave bivouac and hasten to the front this morning at daylight were urgent and pressing, and we had no time to prepare or eat any breakfast,

> which greatly ruffled some of our drivers. When we neared the enemy's line we awaited orders, and one of our drivers was still going through with the baby act about something to eat and having no breakfast. Just then General Stuart and staff came along rather on the reconnaissance order, and halted a moment in the road right where we were, and heard the gallant grumbling and childish murmuring of our hungry man, and the General rode up to him and through pure magnanimity gave our driver two biscuits out of his own haversack.[32]

Stuart's generosity may have silenced the grumbling of one horse artilleryman, but the rest of Thomson's men did not have an opportunity to halt their stomach grumbling until the battery was pulled out of the line at dusk and sent to the rear to camp along with Shoemaker's Battery.

On the night of May 7–8, Grant made his dash for Spotsylvania Court House. The Brock Road had not been cleared, but Maj. Gen. Gouverneur K. Warren's V Corps had orders, so Brig. Gen. Wesley Merritt's cavalry took another crack at Fitz Lee the morning of the eighth. The blue cavalry's attack swept back Lee's first line, but behind it lay another, with Jim Breathed and Johnston's four guns in support.[33] In the face of the horse artillery's fire and the fusillades from Lee's dismounted troopers, Merritt's onslaught came to a halt. Infantry was needed, and Warren was quick to send it in. The Confederates could not stand against the foot soldiers' attack. Breathed blasted away with canister, felling those before him, but his flanks were unguarded. His cannoneers took casualties. Pvt. Henry H. Matthews was struck and taken senseless from the field.[34] Breathed retreated.

Against these determined bluecoats, Lee grudgingly was forced to give way. Battling for every foot of ground, the Confederates fell back to the freshly plowed fields around the Alsop farmhouse. Here Breathed ordered Johnston to unlimber yet again, but Warren's regiments would not be denied. On they came, and Fitz Lee's dismounted men, deciding that resistance was futile, headed rearward. What happened next made Breathed a legend. Captain Johnston left an account of Breathed's heroism, grit, and defiance of the odds:

> Suddenly the woods in front of us were alive with Union soldiers. They had formed their line of battle under cover of the woods about half a mile from us, and we had not seen them at all until they burst into view, charging us.
>
> In battle line and yelling as they came, they swept across the field and toward us. They were pouring in volleys, and it soon became so hot where we were that we had to leave. We retreated from left to right—that is, the gun on the left was limbered up and moved to the rear, while the other guns kept firing. Then the next gun moved off.

> My gun was third, and by that time things were getting pretty lively. The Yankees were so close to us that we could hear them cursing us, but the third gun got off safely. That was mine, and as we went to the rear a musket ball struck me. I was able to sit my horse, although the ball had gone almost through my left shoulder.
>
> Major Breathed was in command of the battery, and he had stayed with the last gun. The Union soldiers were coming on fast and a perfect hailstorm of bullets swept over the gun. The horses, which had been stationed in the rear to avoid being wounded, were brought up, and a desperate effort was made to get out the last gun. The Yankees were trying to capture it, but Major Breathed went to work. As the horses were brought to the gun four of them were instantly killed, and it looked like the gun certainly would be taken. Three of the gunners were wounded in as many seconds. Major Breathed jumped off his own horse, cut loose the traces of the dead animals, sprang on the back of one of the gun horses, lashed him with his saber, and started to the rear, with hundreds of Union soldiers so close that they could have hit him with a rock. They were all shooting and shouting to him to stop, but he rode on and actually took the gun out. He escaped without a scratch.[35]

Fitz Lee's version of the fight was even more laudatory toward Breathed:

> He [Breathed] fired until their line got so close that you could hear them calling out "Surrender that gun, you rebel son of a b——h." Breathed's own horse had first been shot. The cannoneers jumped on their horses, expecting of course the gun to be captured, and retreated rapidly down the hill. Breathed was left alone. He limbered the gun up and jumped on the lead horse. It was shot from under him. Quick as lighting he drew his knife, cut the leaders out of the harness and sprang on a swing horse. It was also shot from under him just as he was turning to get into the road. He then severed the harness of the swing horse, jumped upon one of the wheel horses and again made the desperate trial for life. The ground was open between the piece and the woods; the enemy had a full view of the exploit; and Breathed at last dashed off unharmed almost miraculously escaping through a shower of bullets.[36]

Though Breathed escaped through the "shower of bullets," his gallantry and luck could not stop those bullets.[37] They may have missed him but were striking elsewhere.

Fitz Lee's beleaguered troopers staggered back to Laurel Hill and once more formed a ragged line. The end seemed near. Brig. Gen. James Wilson's division of cavalry was closing in on Lee's rear. If help did not come immediately, all would be lost, and Breathed's guns would yet be captured. At that precise moment, Maj. Gen. Richard Anderson and Jeb Stuart arrived at the head of infantry reinforcements, just in time to halt Wilson and throw back Warren. Fitz Lee's cavalry and Breathed's horse artillery had held on long enough for Anderson to reach Spotsylvania Court House. Their stubborn resistance had bought the time Robert E. Lee needed to oppose Grant's shift eastward. It had been a near-run thing, but it had been done.

For the rest of the horse artillery battalion, the day was not nearly so dramatic. Bamberg's section of Hart's Battery lay near Shady Grove Church and was not engaged. McGregor was with Rooney Lee, marching for Spotsylvania Court House after guarding the army's left flank. Thomson's Battery moved from its campsite back to the position it had held the night of the seventh, then shifted slightly eastward. A brief skirmish with the enemy forced the Confederate cavalry and Thomson to fall back to the Dobbin house. Shoemaker's Battery also took position here.[38] Nothing happened until evening, when the Federals moved forward in force. Thomson fired about forty rounds of shell and, with Shoemaker's assistance, persuaded the enemy to try another approach. Flanking skirmishers appeared, and even a blast of canister from Neese's gun could not get them to halt. Both batteries limbered to the rear, which was all the Federals seemed to have wanted. They stopped their advance and settled down for the night. Thomson and Shoemaker fell back to White Hall, then advanced again to the Dobbin farm. After dark, Thomson pulled back a short distance and bivouacked for the night.[39] Shoemaker continued on to Shady Grove Church and encamped.[40]

Dawn on May 9 found the various batteries of Chew's command scattered from one flank of Lee's army to the other. Breathed's contingent of Johnston's Battery and Halsey's section of Hart's Battery had moved to the extreme right of the line, where they passed most of the day in relative peace and quiet. Bamberg's section of Hart's Battery remained at Shady Grove Church and out of the fighting. Shoemaker stayed in the rear at Shady Grove Church except for one section that drew picket duty.[41] McGregor rumbled along with Chambliss's Brigade toward Massaponax Church on the right. Thomson's Battery broke camp before dawn, rode to Shady Grove Church, and settled down comfortably, undoubtedly happy to be out of the fight for a few hours longer. Morning gave way to early afternoon before the battery's reverie was dispelled by artillery fire from the direction of Waite's Shop. A courier galloped up with orders to make haste for the front. Thomson had his men in the saddle and his guns careening down the road in minutes.

The cause of the alarm turned out to be the fire of Capt. T. Fred Brown's Battery B, 1st Rhode Island Artillery, and Capt. Frederick M. Edgell's 1st New

Hampshire Battery, which had caused a considerable disruption in a Confederate wagon train belonging to the irascible Jubal Early. The general was none too pleased to have the tail end of his column pinched by enemy artillery. Suddenly, Thomson's guns appeared and made preparations to avenge the affront to Early's dignity. Three pieces deployed and opened fire. Gunner Neese left a vivid account of what happened next:

> When we opened we were under the impression that there was nothing there but a battery, and perhaps a few cavalry raiders, but after we fired about forty shell I saw a column of infantry debouch from a wood on our left front, headed for our position and coming right at us. When they arrived at a point for good rifle range they threw out a heavy skirmish line and opened fire, and still came on with overwhelming numbers. We had no support whatever, but we stuck to our position until the Yankee infantry commenced pouring a heavy fire into us at close range; then we left in double-quick style amid a storm of Yankee bullets and shell.[42]

The Federals did indeed come close. The last gun was almost captured, and its caisson's tongue snapped when the driver turned too sharply. Only through the valiant efforts of Sgt. Americus J. Souder and Corp. Marcus M. Rodeffer was the caisson brought off the field.[43] Though Thomson had to abandon his position abruptly, he had stayed long enough to punish Lt. Charles A. Brown's section of the 1st Rhode Island Artillery, killing two men.[44] Neese and company rode back to Shady Grove Church and camped for the night. Breathed and the cannoneers of Johnston's Battery, now under Lt. Daniel Shanks, and Halsey's section would not have that opportunity.

Jeb Stuart had seen some hard fighting throughout the battles in the Wilderness. His troopers had fought the enemy's cavalry and infantry amidst the tangle of trees and undergrowth, yet he still managed to keep his scouts and patrols functioning on the fringes of the two armies. On the morning of May 9, he had received word of a Federal cavalry column slipping around Lee's right flank. Not until midafternoon was he able to set off in pursuit of what turned out to be Phil Sheridan and practically the entire cavalry corps of the Army of the Potomac. Sending Wickham's Brigade chasing after Sheridan's column, Stuart gathered the brigades of James B. Gordon and Lunsford L. Lomax and rode south. With him trotted Breathed with Shanks and Halsey.

Rear-guard clashes between pursuer and pursued marked the rest of the ninth and much of the tenth. Breathed's guns were not involved in these brief encounters.[45] Toward evening on the tenth, Stuart arrived at Hanover Junction and turned south to Taylorsville. From here he dispatched a courier with the following request:

May 11th, 2:30 o'clock A.M., 1864

To Colonel B. T. Johnson:

Colonel,—General Stuart directs me to say that he would be glad to obtain one of your light batteries to assist him today, as he is short of artillery. Our cavalry is interposed between the enemy and Hanover Junction. General Stuart will return the battery as soon as the present emergency has passed. The enemy encamped last night at Ground Squirrel bridge. They had orders to start at 12 o'clock tonight. General Stuart is now moving down the Telegraph road, and desires you to send the battery by the same route.

Very respectfully, your old sergeant,
H. B. M'Clellan
Major and Adjutant[46]

Before Bradley Johnson acceded to Stuart's request, he wanted assurance from Stuart in person that he would get his battery back safe and sound. He rode to Taylorsville and sought Stuart out. He found the general so deep in sleep that neither he nor McClellan could awaken him. Receiving McClellan's promise that great care would be taken with the battery, Johnson trotted back to Hanover Junction.[47]

Capt. Wiley Hunter Griffin's Baltimore Light Artillery had been away from the front lines and had not fired a shot in anger for months. The battery was primed for action. Its four guns boasted complete crews and a full contingent of horses. Lt. John R. McNulty and the men captured with him at Culpeper Court House back in September had all returned. Colonel Johnson had seen to it that the battery received everything it needed to qualify as one of the finest in the army. His concern for its well-being was understandable. Still, though it was the best battery he had, he sent it to Stuart. The Baltimore Light Artillery was back in the Stuart Horse Artillery Battalion. It was to be quite a homecoming.

Stuart now had ten guns. Sheridan had over thirty. The Federal cavalry also outnumbered Stuart's two to one. Despite the odds, Stuart meant to strike Sheridan at the first opportunity. That came on the eleventh. After an exhausting ride, Stuart with Lomax's Brigade had managed to beat Sheridan to the junction of the Telegraph Road and the Mountain Road just north of Yellow Tavern. Lomax's troopers took their positions along Telegraph Road facing west. The Federals struck the Confederate picket and skirmish line in front of Lomax, driving the gray troopers back on their main line. The 6th Virginia, on Lomax's left, found itself outflanked and forced to fall back north along the Telegraph Road. Col. Henry Clay Pate's 5th Virginia was next in line. Stuart ordered Pate to hold his position in a road cut. It was a suicide mission, but Pate and his men stayed put.

Meanwhile, Wickham was deploying along a ridge north of Pate to the right of the Telegraph Road. Stuart brought up Griffin's Battery, which unlimbered to the left of the Telegraph Road at the edge of a piece of woods.[48] One gun was placed on a small hill behind three others that were positioned in the road itself.[49] Lomax's Brigade, minus Pate, extended Wickham's line to the left of the road. Halsey's section anchored Wickham's right, while Shanks moved over to Lomax's left flank.[50] While all this was transpiring on the ridge, the 5th Virginia was being overrun on the Telegraph Road. Pate fell with a bullet through his head, but his stand bought time for Stuart to put his line together.

With the crushing of Pate and his men, the Federals now turned their attention to the new Confederate position but were repulsed by a combination of small arms and artillery. A lull now settled over the field. Sheridan decided to await reinforcements before assaulting Stuart's new line. Once the additional troops were up and in place, Sheridan determined to ride over the graycoats. He gave the honor of performing the mission to George A. Custer, who recognized opportunity when he saw it. Eager as he was, Custer took his time and reconnoitered Stuart's line until he concluded that he could break it at the point occupied by the enemy's center battery. The Baltimore Light had been targeted for extermination.

Custer's regiments broke into a charge. At the same time, Brig. Gen. James Wilson attacked Wickham. Halsey and Griffin poured shell into the oncoming squadrons, but it wasn't enough. A cannoneer in Griffin's Battery wrote about what happened:

> Sheridan brought three batteries to bear on Griffin at a range of not over eight hundred yards, and the rain of shot and shrapnel became terrific, but the brave fellows never flinched, and served their guns with great effect. Hour after hour this savage fight was waged. But no man faltered at his post, though the groans of the wounded & dying, and the shrieks of maimed and disemboweled horses, were enough to appall the stoutest heart. But Genl. Stuart was there, watching with an anxious eye that little command, upon which so much depended, and they fought on, undismayed, despite the frightful scenes around them. At length the enemy massed a heavy body of cavalry determined at any sacrifice to capture the guns that were making such dreadful havoc in their ranks. A charge was made upon him, when Griffin resorted to grape & canister. At every discharge, whole companies melted away, and the enemy fell back in confusion. But again they advanced, and the Confederate cavalry giving away at the instant, the battery was left at the mercy of the enemy, who dashed upon it, but there the brave men continued to stay, determined to remain at their post to the last, for all knew the vital importance of the position; and as the enemy pressed on they were met with that never ceasing hail of canister, until they reached the guns, and rode over the men, and sabered and captured them at their pieces.[51]

The initial repulse of Custer's lead regiments came at the hands of Stuart's old 1st Virginia Cavalry. Their countercharge cleared the guns momentarily, and mounted and dismounted bluecoats retreated down the ridge. One of these turned and fired the fatal bullet into Stuart.

With Stuart down, command fell to Fitz Lee, who rapidly surmised that his position was untenable. Fresh enemy squadrons thundered up the slope toward Griffin's pieces. The time had come to go, only Griffin couldn't. Horses down, crews in disarray from the last charge, the gallant captain and Jim Breathed rallied what men they could. Lt. John R. McNulty saved the piece on the hill, its teams having suffered least.[52] Even if horses had been available, Griffin probably could not have saved his remaining guns. Pummeled by Lt. Edward Heaton's Battery B/L, 2nd U.S. Artillery, Griffin looked down the ridge to see Custer's Michiganders coming on again. A blast or two of canister was all Griffin could muster. His cavalry support gone, it was every man for himself, yet few left their pieces. The blue wave swept up and over the guns. Colonel Johnson would not be getting his battery back.

Jim Breathed had taken his post with Griffin's guns. During the fierce fighting, he became engaged in a hand-to-hand encounter with a Federal officer. Breathed managed to kill his adversary but was wounded himself. He abandoned his own exhausted mount for that of his foe and rode to safety.[53] He was not the only casualty. Privates W. H. Brown, Henry J. Edell, Adolph Frederick, James A. King, William P. Whalin, and E. Hiram McKinzie, and Sergeants Willoughby N. Brockenborough and James S. Morrison were captured, along with Captain Griffin. Sgt. John F. Hayden had a more harrowing experience:

> During the hottest of the fight private John Hayden was struck by a piece of shell, and dreadfully mangled, and would have bled to death in a few minutes had not the surgeon of the battery, Dr. [John B.] Wortham, carried him on his back into the woods and staunched the hemorrhage. In a short time the enemy had possession of the field, but carefully concealing himself and his charge until they had passed on, he that night carried Hayden to a place of safety, where he eventually recovered.[54]

Hayden's and Wortham's escape was most fortunate. Many of their cavalry brethren were not so lucky. Thankfully, though Griffin's Battery had been roughly handled, the remainder of the horse artillery left the field intact.

Out on Wickham's flank, Halsey's two guns helped to stem the enemy's attack in that quarter. Their staunch resistance drew down upon them the fire of the enemy's artillery, which caused some casualties. When the center broke, Halsey limbered his guns and brought them off the field. For Shanks, far off on the Confederate left, the battle seemed out of reach. He contributed little to the defense other than long-range fire. As the line fell apart, Shanks ordered the guns to limber and retreat. One officer, however, made an effort to come to closer grips with Custer's troopers.

Shortly after Lt. William Hoxton pulled his gun from its position, he arrived in the vicinity of the Telegraph Road and met Lt. Theodore S. Garnett of Stuart's staff. Hoxton was adamant in his desire to get into the fight and asked Garnett where he could place his gun. Garnett told Hoxton that the situation was hopeless, that there was nothing between him and the enemy, and strongly urged him to turn around before he, too, was captured. The gritty artilleryman did not want to accept what Garnett had to say, but his own eyes could see that a disaster was in the making and prudence should rule over courage. Frustrated, Hoxton turned his gun around and rode north on the Telegraph Road.[55] Shanks's other guns were already heading in that direction.

The Federals followed the retreating Confederates all the way to the bridge over the Chickahominy River near Half Sink. Here Lieutenant McNulty unlimbered the two remaining guns of the Baltimore Light and fired a few shots at the pursuers. Those shots ended the battle.[56] In reality, few of the enemy had ventured far from the battleground. Sheridan had other concerns besides chasing two shattered brigades of gray cavalry. His men bedded down for the night on the battlefield. They were still in a tight situation but were beginning to believe in their new commander. All knew more fighting lay ahead before they could close both eyes and sleep soundly.

Fitz Lee's troopers did not even enjoy one-eyed sleep. Their new commander recognized that Sheridan might still be trapped between his two brigades and forces marching out from Richmond. Fitz Lee's knowledge of the area made it easy to select where his men needed to be to assist in Sheridan's discomfiture. He ordered Lomax and Wickham to ride downstream to Meadow Bridge. Johnston's Battery and Halsey's section accompanied the column. With his much-reduced command, Lee deployed his artillery and troopers against Merritt's division.[57] After a stiff resistance, Lee was forced to give way and retired to Pole Green Church, where he again clashed with advancing Federals. This time the exhausted Confederates held, and Sheridan drew back to begin his movement to the James.[58]

On the thirteenth, Fitz Lee marched to Mechanicsville, where he rendezvoused with Gordon's Brigade, commanded by Col. Clinton M. Andrews following the mortal wounding of Gordon on the twelfth. Lee ordered McNulty to take his two guns back to Hanover Junction, from where the battery rejoined the Army of Northern Virginia.[59] Halsey's section also did not stay with Lee. Either on the thirteenth or fourteenth, it headed north to Milford Station below Fredericksburg, where it was reunited with Bamberg's section on the sixteenth. Breathed with Johnston's Battery accompanied Lee as he shadowed Sheridan. The gray cavalry reached Atlee's Station, which they occupied until the twenty-sixth.

Those batteries that had remained with the army when Stuart began his ride on May 9—Shoemaker's, Thomson's, McGregor's, and Bamberg's section of Hart's—had spent the days either in camp, on picket, or marching. Shoemaker's Battery left Shady Grove Church on the tenth and marched toward the army's right, ending up on the south side of the Mat River a few miles northwest of New Market on the farm of Edward Smith. There it stayed until the twelfth.[60] The morning of the tenth saw Thomson return to the position he had held near Waite's Shop. The guns were unlimbered and put into battery. When nothing developed by noontime, Thomson was ordered to the right, following much the same route as Shoemaker. The battery camped somewhere along the Louisa Court House Road southwest of Spotsylvania Court House. It spent most of the eleventh in camp but late in the day responded to a report of enemy movement on the army's left. Arriving at the front, Thomson found the report to be false and ordered his men to return to their camp.[61] Though neither Thomson nor Shoemaker had been idle, not until the twelfth did their guns speak in anger.

Early that morning, Chew ordered Thomson and Shoemaker to Waite's Shop in the rear of the army's left flank. Shoemaker unlimbered his guns and immediately opened fire.[62] Thomson moved farther to the left and put his guns into position but remained quiet. The men lounged amid the roar of the infantry fighting taking place near Spotsylvania Court House until General Hampton ordered Chew to fire on the two enemy batteries that had been bombarding the infantry.[63] Chew moved the three rifled guns of Shoemaker's Battery closer to the front and opened fire in unison with Thomson's guns.[64] The ensuing duel tested the cannoneers of both sides. Gunner Neese recalled the memorable fight:

> The Yankee gunners that fired on our battery certainly put in some fine work in the shooting business; nearly every shell they fired at us exploded either just in front of our guns or right over our heads, and sometimes their exploding shrapnel sowed the leaden slugs around us apparently as thick as hail.
>
> After we were firing about an hour a shell from the Yankee battery exploded right in front of my gun, and I saw a good-sized fragment that was whizzing fearfully and searching for something to kill. It came right at me as though I was its sure game, but I quickly jumped across the trail of my gun in order to clear the path for the little whirling death machine that was after me as was ready to call me its own dear Rebel. It passed me with a shrill snappish ping, and with a thud it ripped up the ground just in rear of where I had been standing; if I had not seen it coming and quickly jumped out of its path it would have struck me square in front just below the breast, which would have undoubtedly labeled me for transportation to the silent city. But

> a miss is as good as a mile, and when the fragment that was courting familiarity had passed over me I jumped back to my place at the gun, and the very next shell I fired struck and exploded a limber chest in the Yankee battery; immediately after I fired I saw a dense telltale column of smoke shoot up in the air from the enemy's position, and then I knew that my shell had done some ugly work among the ammunition boxes of our brethren in blue.[65]

Thomson's and Shoemaker's opponents were Capt. Charles A. Phillips's Battery E, Massachusetts Light Artillery, and Lt. George Breck's Batteries E and L, 1st New York Light Artillery. Their commanding officer, Col. Charles S. Wainwright, returned the compliment Neese had accorded the Federal gunners. He reported that "the fire of the enemy was very accurate, wounding several of the men and exploding one of Captain Phillips's limbers."[66]

This mutual respect did not allow for a nonpartisan view of the duel. Both sides claimed to have silenced the other. In the end, Chew's boys probably had the better of it. Thomson reported one casualty, Pvt. Edward J. Read, wounded, while Shoemaker had one man, Pvt. Robert W. Irving, who was part of the crew of the gun left behind, killed by a shell fragment that passed through the center of his body. Chew eventually pulled his guns off the field, leaving the Federals right where they had been at the start of the contest. The two batteries marched back about two miles toward Shady Grove Church and bivouacked for the night on the Pool farm.[67]

Bamberg's section of Hart's Battery did not participate in the artillery duel but somehow managed to record three casualties. Encamped at Shady Grove Church since the morning of the ninth, the section did not receive any orders to move out as had Thomson and Shoemaker. Nevertheless, some of the men did move out, probably on a food-foraging expedition. In the tangled growth of the Wilderness, the risk of being surprised by the enemy had been well documented during both the Chancellorsville campaign and the battles currently being fought. Three of Bamberg's men, Privates Jacob Belitzer, Benjamin F. Ellis, and Charles K. Ray, were captured and spent the next several months practicing their foraging skills in Northern prison camps.

On the right of Lee's lines, McGregor's Battery was drawn into the maelstrom of infantry fighting on the twelfth.[68] Chambliss's Brigade was guarding the flank, but the heavy Federal infantry attacks compelled the use of every available gun to repel them. McGregor received the call and responded, putting his guns into action. He did not go unnoticed. The enemy's return fire proved deadly. Privates John A. Donald and James A. King were both killed, and Pvt. Fielding H. Little was wounded. This was the first real action the battery had seen since the opening of the campaign, and it had proven costly.

The thirteenth passed in relative silence as Grant's and Lee's weary troops took a break from trying to exterminate each other. Chew with Thomson,

Shoemaker, and Bamberg shifted from the army's left toward Spotsylvania Court House and were not engaged.[69] McGregor's guns also remained quiet. The following day, however, McGregor had two brief clashes with the enemy in the same position as on the twelfth but suffered no loss. On the sixteenth, Thomson and Shoemaker were still in position near Spotsylvania Court House awaiting an attack that did not materialize. Lt. Charles R. Phelps of Shoemaker's Battery made good use of the lull to write a letter to his aunt:

Camp Block House
Near Spottsylvania Co. Ho.
May 16th 1864

Dear Aunt,

I have at last an opportunity of writing a few lines to you. For the last three days everything has been quiet. No heavy fighting going on. Mr. Grant has moved nearer to Fredericksburg. I began to think that he was so badly whipped that he would give up the fight and fall back, but he will hardly give it up as yet, & we expect to have some heavy fighting yet. I can give you no particulars, as I can hear nothing reliable. Uncle Bob says his people have behaved nobly. We have repulsed the Yanks in every assault they have made. Our loss is very slight and will not be 10,000 in killed, wounded & some prisoners while the Yankee surgeons say they have not lost less than 50,000 and some estimate it much higher. I have been over several battle fields & I have never seen as many dead Yanks in my life. I have not heard a word or seen a paper for two weeks. Have heard that we have repulsed them at Richmond & of [word illegible] surrender & hope soon to hear of Grant [word illegible] a fact which I believe will close the ball. Our Battery has been fortunate—2 killed & about 15 wounded tho' we were fighting almost daily for ten days.

Our people are in the best spirits & anxious for Mr. Grant to renew the fight.

Please let Miss W. know I am well as I have not time to write now.

Love to All

Yours in haste
Dick
Chew's Battalion
Stuart Horse Artly[70]

That Phelps thought his battery fortunate in sustaining only seventeen casualties illustrates how jaded many of the men had become. Such losses two years earlier would have been shocking. Now they were taken in stride.

If Thomson and Shoemaker were inactive, Chew's other batteries were not. Bamberg had marched with his section to Spotsylvania Court House on the thirteenth and had kept right on marching. He ended up near Milford Station on the sixteenth, where he met Halsey's section. Hart's Battery had been split since the beginning of the campaign but was at last reunited under its gallant commander. As for McGregor, he managed to be the only battery to entertain the Yanks with a few shots.

Taking a position near Stanard's Mill where the Telegraph Road crosses the Po River, McGregor had a brief clash with elements of the 5th New York Cavalry. Lt. Col. John Hammond admitted to pushing a reconnaissance squad across the Ny River at Smith's Mill on the Telegraph Road. About one and a half miles south, it ran into what Hammond believed to be a regiment of enemy cavalry and one gun. He reported that the gun was "used on our men and then retreated."[71] If anyone retreated, it was the Federals. McGregor's gun was still in position on the seventeenth when Hammond sent out another scouting party with the same results, though this time Sgt. George W. Shreve of McGregor's Battery admitted to having a "sharp little fight."[72] The bluecoats also came calling on the eighteenth and nineteenth, which kept McGregor's men alert, but nothing developed from these brief encounters.

During this time, Thomson and Shoemaker had little to do. All was quiet until the eighteenth, when Shoemaker's Battery was ordered to the front in the direction of Spotsylvania Court House. After firing at an enemy battery that failed to respond, Shoemaker shifted to the left and unlimbered on the Jones farm. Here the battery was not engaged, and several hours later, Shoemaker limbered up and returned to the battery's camp at the Block House.[73] On the nineteenth, Thomson was ordered out on a scout with Rosser's Brigade in support of Ewell's attack, which developed into the battle of Harris Farm. The participation of the cavalry and horse artillery was minimal. Thomson's guns fired a couple of rounds at some enemy infantry before the column returned to camp near Spotsylvania Court House. Shoemaker's Battery never left camp but did receive orders, which Lieutenant Phelps recorded in a short note to his aunt:

Camp Near Spottsylvania
Co. Ho. May 19th [1864]

Dear Aunt,

All quiet in front this morning. Yesterday the Yanks made a severe attack on our whole line, but were repulsed handsomely—our loss very slight.

We are ordered to report to Gen'l Fitz Lee near Richmond, & will leave immediately.

I think Grant is played out.

Love to All Dick[74]

Those orders spelled the end of the horse artillery's fighting in the Wilderness. Grant had taken his best shots and had been thwarted at every turn. Like Hooker before him, he was leaving the Wilderness. Unlike Hooker, Grant did not retreat across the Rappahannock. Instead, he swung his army east, then south. The Federal commander was not quite "played out." Now Lee would have to follow and try to keep his army between Grant and Richmond. The march to the James River had begun.

CHAPTER 27

To the James

"Move up closer; they have got the range, boys."

As Lee's ragtag army left its entrenchments to slowly parallel Grant's blue columns, the onerous duty of the army's rear guard fell to Brig. Gen. John R. Chambliss's Brigade of Rooney Lee's division and McGregor's Battery. Not a task to be taken lightly, the "honor" of being the rear guard was both arduous and dangerous. Constant vigilance was required—a circumstance that could weigh heavily on officers and men alike. McGregor's role in this crucial undertaking did not begin auspiciously. A brief skirmish on the evening of May 21 seemed to foretell a rocky road ahead. Once the enemy had withdrawn, McGregor received orders "to be ready to fire at any minute."[1] As a result, the men spent the night fighting, but sleep, not the Yanks, was the enemy. The battery got in a few vengeful licks at Bartlett's infantry along the Motto River on the Littleton Flippo farm on the twenty-second. Following an hour of exchanging shots, McGregor extracted his guns and rode to Beaver Dam Station. All of the following day was spent marching and countermarching. By the twenty-fourth, McGregor was on the south bank of the North Anna River, where he remained for three days. The battery's rear-guard experience thankfully turned out to be more flash than substance.

The other batteries in the battalion marched over different roads toward the same goal. Thomson's Battery left the vicinity of Spotsylvania Court House the morning of the twenty-first and wound its way toward Milford Station, which was in the possession of the enemy. The battery fired a few rounds to discourage any foray the Federals might have been contemplating. Satisfied that there would be no pursuit, Thomson limbered his guns and proceeded south on the Hanover Road, encamping about four miles from Milford. The next day, the battery went into position near its camp. When the Federals advanced, Thomson fell back across Polecat Creek and again unlimbered. This second position was strong, and the Yanks decided against attacking it. As evening fell, Thomson limbered his guns, marched to the north bank of the North Anna, and camped for the night.

Early on the twenty-third, an advance by the enemy's cavalry precipitated a short, sharp skirmish with Rosser's Brigade, which was in front of Thomson. The Federal infantry appeared after a couple hours, and by noon it became evident they meant business. Thomson hitched his teams to his guns and rode across the North Anna, taking a new position on the south side not far from the ford on the Hanover Junction Road. The enemy's cavalry and infantry continued to advance toward the river. Thomson paid them his compliments with a slow fire, while Rosser's troopers fashioned fence-rail breastworks. Before long, Thomson ceased firing to conserve ammunition. The situation was serious. If the Federals were intent on forcing a crossing, Rosser and Thomson might delay them but certainly could not stop them. Gunner Neese told what happened next:

> Then I heard the beating drums sounding the alarming thrill of the long roll in General A. P. Hill's camp, about a mile away in the direction of Hanover Junction, which meant "to the rescue" of the cavalry and horse artillery. After we had endured the nerve-trying suspense for an hour or so, and every man was standing at his post ready for the fray and to do or die, some one remarked: "Yonder comes a carriage across the field." As it was an unusual occurrence to see a carriage drive on a field that was stripped ready for fight, I looked to the rear and saw a carriage with a single horseman riding behind it, coming right toward our position where we had our guns in battery. The carriage drove up close to our guns and stopped. When the door opened who should step out but our beloved and confidence-inspiring General Robert E. Lee, and the first glimpse of the grand old chieftain instilled new life and vigor into the whole command and dispersed the gloomy mist which was gathering around the star of Hope and lifted a burden of momentous anxiety that had settled along our line; I felt like a new man all over.
>
> General Lee came right to where my gun was in position and leaned against a large pine tree not more than ten feet from my piece; he then, without the least sign of agitation, slowly drew his field glass from the case and carefully scanned the enemy's battle line; he commenced the scrutinizing gaze at the right of their line on that part which was farthest up the river. After he swept from end to end with his glass he turned around and remarked to the horseman that accompanied him, "Orderly, go back and tell General A. P. Hill to leave his men in camp; this is nothing but a feint, the enemy is preparing to cross below." Then he put his glass back in the case, got in his carriage and went back toward Hanover Junction. A single glance from the old warrior's eye, like a flash of genius, instantly penetrated and

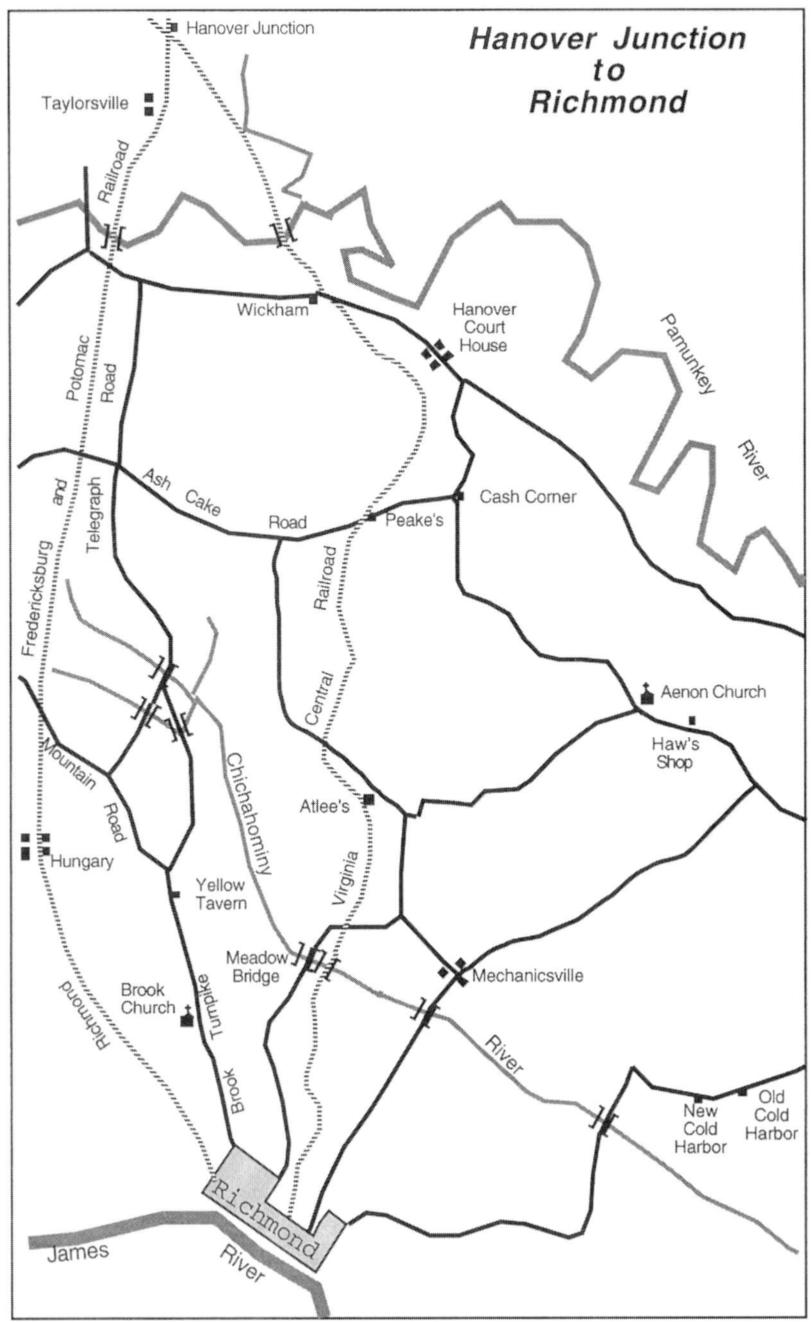
Hanover Junction
to
Richmond
Hanover Junction
Taylorsville
Railroad
Wickham
Hanover
Court
House
Pamunkey
River
Potomac
Road
Ash
Cake
Road
Cash Corner
Peake's
Telegraph
and
Fredericksburg
Railroad
Central
Aenon Church
Haw's
Shop
Mountain
Road
Chichahominy
Atlee's
Hungary
Yellow
Tavern
Virginia
Meadow
Bridge
Mechanicsville
Brook
Church
Turnpike
Richmond
River
Brook
New
Cold
Harbor
Old
Cold
Harbor
Richmond
James
River

fathomed the depths of the enemy's design, for in less than ten minutes after he left his carriage he was back in it again and on his way to some other point lower down the river.[2]

The "old warrior" proved correct in that the crossing would not test Thomson's position, but Grant did cross later that day upriver at Jericho Mills. Thomson's cannoneers held their post until late in the day, and then as night approached, they limbered and fell back to Taylorsville, where they camped.

The twenty-fourth was spent in camp, but the following day, Thomson was ordered to move toward Hanover Court House. The enemy was not engaged, and the battery encamped at Hanover Academy, where it remained until the twenty-seventh. On that day, Thomson received orders to march south. He crossed the South Anna and pushed on until after midnight. Camp was pitched at Hughes' Cross Roads, just ten miles from Richmond. The Federals were closing in, or so it seemed. A fight appeared imminent.

Johnston's Battery saw little action after Yellow Tavern. Breathed summed up both Johnston's and Shoemaker's Batteries' roles in this phase of the campaign by simply stating that all they did was march.[3] Actually, Shoemaker had spent most of the time from the thirteenth to the nineteenth in camp and did not rendezvous with Fitz Lee until the twenty-first. Thereafter, the battery accumulated a significant number of miles, marching hither and yon in search of the enemy. By the twenty-fourth, Shoemaker was camped on the farm of Brig. Gen. Williams C. Wickham, where it remained until the twenty-seventh, when it once more started in search of "raiders."[4]

Breathed's report probably was more accurate for Johnston's Battery which had ridden after Sheridan with Stuart. If Fitz Lee's cavalry did skirmish with the enemy from time to time, it is difficult not to picture Breathed getting involved in some manner. However, for the most part, Fitz Lee was inactive from the fourteenth to the twenty-first, so Breathed may not have been downplaying his part in the fighting, as was his custom.

On May 23, Lee set off with portions of Wickham's, Lomax's, and Andrew's (formerly Gordon's) Brigades and one gun from Shoemaker's Battery under Lt. Edmund H. Moorman to attack Wilson's Wharf.[5] The fortifications in the vicinity of the wharf were occupied by Brig. Gen. Edward A. Wild's Brigade, which was composed of the 1st, 10th, 22nd, and 37th U.S. Colored Infantry regiments, but only about 1,100 men from one and a half regiments were present. Lee was under orders from Gen. Braxton Bragg.[6] Lee spent May 24 trying to break through Wild's defenses but in the end was forced to give up. Moorman's lone artillery piece took fire from the enemy's batteries and gunboats for three hours but did not return fire.[7] Fortunately, there were no casualties in the artillery, though the cavalry suffered a loss of over fifty in killed and wounded. Lee fell back to Charles City Court House that evening. On the twenty-fifth, he rode north toward Atlee's Station, arriving there on the twenty-sixth, and reunited with the remainder of his division.

Hart's Battery had been busy since Halsey's and Bamberg's section had linked up at Milford Station on the sixteenth. From there, the battery helped Hampton screen Robert E. Lee's left flank on the march to the North Anna, having several minor skirmishes along the way. On reaching the river, Hart went into position to guard one of the fords until replaced by Lee's infantry and artillery. Grant's shift from the river line around Lee's flank brought both Rooney Lee's and Hampton's divisions to Atlee's Station on the twenty-seventh, where they joined Fitz Lee. The cavalry and the horse artillery were once again united.

Another battery of horse artillery made its appearance at this time. On the twenty-second, Maj. Gen. John C. Breckinridge, fresh from his victory at New Market, arrived with his division at Hanover Junction to bolster Lee's army. Maj. William McLaughlin's Battalion of artillery, including Capt. Thomas E. Jackson's Battery of horse artillery, had accopmanied the infantry east. It did not take long for McLaughlin's command to face the enemy. On the twenty-fourth, the battalion replaced Lt. Col. Carter M. Braxton's Battalion on the right of Lee's line along the North Anna. McLaughlin's Battalion returned to Hanover Junction that evening. There Lt. Micajah Woods, who had longed to be part of the Army of Northern Virginia and had at last been granted his wish, took the time to inform his father about his battery's move and what it now faced:

> Bivouac, Hanover Junction
> May 25th 1864 12 o'clock M.
>
> My dear Father,
>
> I write to you this morning to the music of musket and cannon—a hundred yards to my front is our second entrenched line of infantry—200 yards beyond is the advanced line. A few paces further are our skirmishers firing. Yesterday evening & up to this hour today the skirmishing along the whole line has been incessant. The crack of small arms and occasional booms of cannon reach my ear every minute. The last hour the firing has grown much less rapid. Having felt our position along its whole extent I presume Grant is marshalling his forces for the grand attack for which the whole Army of No. Va. shouts ready—But more of the prospects of the situation hereafter.
>
> I passed by Depot in charge of the train which contained our horses & a detachment of 35 men on the morning of the 20th leaving there a bundle of extra baggage. Great as my anxiety was to stop for a few hours, I considered it was no account to make such a request. My Division had preceded me I thought perhaps [word illegible] immediately. While the guns of my comrades were thundering in battle I would have been ashamed to be seen loitering on my way to the field even to enjoy the society of those so dear to me at home for

a few hours. I found Breckinridge's Division encamped immediately in this vicinity ready to move at a moment's notice. The next day also we were held under orders—in anticipation of an attack by Sheridan's Raiders who during the morning made a descent on the Central road at Hanover Co. Ho. During the evening the firing in our front in the direction of Milford was quite heavy leading us to believe that a general engagement was perhaps at hand between the main armies.

Early the next morning Ewell's corps bivouacked at the junction, and during the day Lee's whole army was concentrated in this vicinity. The troops were much faded from marching the previous day and the whole night. This movement was necessitated by Grant having swung around Lee's right wing and getting a march of 13 hours before our General was aware that he had vacated his position in front of Spotsylvania CtH. The denunciations of our Cavalry are unanimous throughout the army. During this campaign they have been perfect ciphers, having given the enemy free pass through the country. Genl. Lee is said to have been maneuvered out of every position—not whipped out—from the Rapidan to his present ground simply because the Cavalry have failed to watch & report the movements of the enemy on either flank. But perhaps it has all been for the best. Here we are at last in a powerful defensive position—our whole line is entrenched—the whole army is in position—and every man of this army stands anxious and determined to strike the great & crushing blow whenever the Yankee General chooses to accept the gage of battle & butts his hosts against our veterans.

Yesterday morning the enemy crossed the No. Anna in force. Our line is nearly parallel with & north of the central road, leaving a space varying in width from a half to a mile and a half between it and the River. Along this space the enemy are drawn up in lines of battle this morning. Our right is opposite the Junction held by the troops of Ewell and Breckinridge. The center is bisected by the Telegraph road held by Longstreet's corps commanded by Anderson—the left is composed of Hill's corps commanded by Early. Breckinridge is in the extreme right—our Battery is waiting with the Battalion within 100 yds. of the Depot for orders. We may not assume any position at present but be held to support any part of this wing when the enemy attacks. The main line is already well supported by artillery which can only be used at short range against infantry charges—so dense is the growth of pines & underbrush. I don't suppose there is a man in the army who permits himself to dream of giving himself an inch of ground. The sooner they come the better for us. We all feel that the crisis of our fate is nigh—and more still we feel confident that we have the will and power to decide it in our favor. Lee's reinforcements have been considerable during the past three days. I will not state whence they come or their number as this letter may be captured, but they will fill nearly all gaps in the ranks caused by recent fighting—and they are veterans. Therefore be hopeful. A Yankee Lieut. captured this morning says that they will take Richmond this time or never. He speaks confidently of course says Grant has been reinforced by 25000 troops recently.

Bob with the wagons reached the Junction safely night before last after making a narrow escape 12 miles from here. Our infantry were formed along the roadside—the enemy charging while the trains were passing—one of our Battery wagon horses was killed & three men killed immediately by them. Bob is said to have been terribly frightened but got off safely. An hour later and the whole party would have been captured. I was greatly rejoiced to receive your letter and Mother's and especially so at the deliverance of the bag of eatables which have come at the very nick of time. I am exceedingly sorry that you should be put to much inconvenience in sending me a horse. I earnestly trust that I may be able to return him before many days. I am endeavoring to purchase the horse of a wounded man from his brother as he stands no chance of sending him home. Also I may be able to capture a horse after we have whipped Grant.

Walter Preston has certainly lost an arm and is in the hands of the enemy. He wrote a note to Col. Jones from a house occupied by our skirmishers near Spotsylvania CH. stating the character of his wound & asking him to send him something to eat. Soon after the enemy's line advanced and no further communication was had with him. I have seen several of the Battery—Herndin Fife among others. A day or two since I saw Jno. Cochran—Parkinson, Billy Randalf & Capt. Pleasants—all looking well. I saw on the road yesterday while returning from the Ct. H. (whither we had been sent the day previous to protect a ford before the plans of the enemy ever developed) Dr. Bayler of Carolina a refugee for Albemarle. I hope you will pay us a visit as soon as the road is clear of obstructions in the way of Yankees. I am [word illegible] to send some additional baggage home. I have decided that I need no blankets—Two oil cloths & an overcoat shall be my campaign equipage. Also I shall send my boots home. My Yankee shoes are so much more pleasant. I don't need any others at present. Rider and Lowden seem pleased with their treatment at home. This letter will go by way of Richmond and Lynchburg. Direct to me thus—Lt. M. W. Jackson's Battery

Breckinridge Division
Army of No. Va. Lynchburg[8]

Woods was not alone in his hope that Grant would make some blunder that could open the way to victory. Every grayback in Lee's army was counting on it. Woods knew it was possible. He had seen Sigel make a mistake in the Valley, and Breckinridge's small army had beaten the bigger foe. But Grant was not Sigel. Victory over him would not come easily and would require some very hard fighting—fighting that was beyond Woods's experience. The other horse batteries already knew what fighting Grant was all about.

Up to this point in the campaign, the horse artillery battalion had seen as hard service as any unit in the army. It had fought on the front lines with the infantry, on the flanks with the cavalry, and on the fly against Sheridan's raiders. The men had given everything that had been asked of them, and more. On May 25, Capt. John Esten Cooke inspected four of the battalion's batteries. His report was reflective of what the battalion had been through.

OFFICE ASST. INSP. GEN., HORSE ARTILLERY BATT.,
May 25, 1864.

Brig. Gen. W. N. PENDLETON, Commanding Artillery:

GENERAL: I have the honor to report that, in obedience to your order, I have inspected the horses of the batteries of horse artillery serving with Maj. Gen. Fitz. Lee, viz: Johnston's and Shoemaker's batteries—seven pieces. These batteries have lost heavily in killed and wounded horses in the operations against Sheridan, and the horses are in very bad condition. In Johnston's battery 28 have been killed, or wounded so badly as to make it necessary to abandon them; 5 others wounded are with the battery. Of the other horses 6 are in very bad order, with painful galls on back and neck, and greatly broken down. Two of the gun-carriages have only 5 horses apiece and two others only 4 apiece. Shoemaker's battery is in worse order still; 16 of the horses are covered with sores, and so much broken down by heavy marches as to be unfit for active service. In this battery 4 have been killed, 6 wounded and abandoned, 2 broken down and left on the road, and 2 strayed or stolen. Thirty horses are needed to put this battery in efficient condition. Three mules in ordnance wagons are broken down and unfit for service.

The order directed an inspection to ascertain the number of horses unable to "work in harness." The horses reported are in such an exhausted condition that they are unfit for severe marching or rapid movement, but are still worked in harness. Under these circumstances, I have not directed them to be turned in. A few days of rest would make some of them efficient again. Others are totally unfit for service as horse artillery horses.

RECAPITULATION.

Johnston's battery:

Horses killed, or wounded and abandoned	28
Wounded slightly	5
Sore-backed and broken down	6
Total (cannoneers and gun horses) deficit	39

Shoemaker's battery:

Killed, or wounded and abandoned	10
Broken down and left	2
Strayed or stolen	2
Sore-backed and broken down	16
Total	30

Thomson's battery:

Killed, or wounded and abandoned	16

Hart's battery (1 piece inspected):

Sore-backed and broken down	2

McGregor's battery:

Killed, or wounded and abandoned	7
Sore-backed and broken down	5
Total	12

Aggregate	99

Many of the cannoneers have been dismounted to supply the teams. One hundred fresh horses is the least number with which the batteries will be able to perform efficient service.

Most respectfully, your obedient servant,
JNO. ESTEN COOKE,
Captain and Assistant Inspector-General.[9]

Cooke's concern that the batteris needed fresh horses in order to "perform efficient service" meant little to the men of the batteries, who had performed efficient service under like conditions too numerous to count. The simple fact was that if they were needed, they would be sent, fresh horses or no fresh horses, and on May 28, Robert E. Lee would need his cavalry and horse artillery.

By the morning of the twenty-seventh, Lee was aware that Grant had left the North Anna River line but was unsure just exactly where his adversary was going to pop up next. After waiting through the night and receiving no news of Grant's whereabouts, Lee called on Wade Hampton to secure that vital bit of information. Hampton gathered together an assortment of commands. He took Rooney Lee's division, Rosser's Brigade, and Brig. Gen. Matthew C. Butler's brand new brigade of North Carolinians from his own division; Wickham's Brigade from Fitz Lee's division; and McGregor's, Johnston's, and Shoemaker's Batteries under Chew. The column rode east from Atlee's Station.[10]

At approximately the same time, Brig. Gen. David McM. Gregg's division of Federal cavalry saddled up and rode from the vicinity of Crump's Creek and Hanovertown toward Mechanicsville. Their route took them to a country crossroads names Haw's Shop, which they reached about 10:00 A.M. on the morning of the twenty-eight. Recognizing the value of holding the road junction, Gregg halted to await reinforcements. He sent a portion of the 10th New York of Brig. Gen. Henry E. Davies's Brigade to picket the road from the west.[11] The blue cavalry barely had started out when the van of Hampton's column, led by Rosser and Wickham, trotted into view scarcely half a mile from Haw's Shop. The gray troopers charged headlong into the New Yorkers, sending them catapulting back toward the road junction. The sounds of the collision reached Gregg sometime before he caught sight of his panicked pickets' hasty retreat. His response was to send the rest of Davies's Brigade thundering into Hampton's oncoming graybacks. This time the Rebels gave way and raced rearward to a makeshift line of works that Hampton's other brigades had quickly constructed on both sides of the road near Enon Church.

Davies's pursuit of Rosser's and Wickham's fleeing men came to an abrupt halt when they slammed into Hampton's stopgap defenses. The Confederate commander had ordered his men to dismount and fight on foot, which was the growing tendency among the cavalry on both sides. The initial repulse of Davies allowed time for Hampton to stabilize his line. Rosser shifted to the left, where he could support Chew, who unlimbered McGregor's Battery and a section of Shoemaker's for the contest.[12] Wickham deployed between Rosser and the road, while Butler's boys held the right of the road. Rooney Lee was sent to the left on a country road in the hope that he could outflank the Federal right. Hampton's line was barely in place when Gregg launched Davies at it again, this time supported by Col. J. Irvin Gregg's Brigade and Capt. Joseph W. Martin's 6th New York Battery of Brandy Station fame.

The fight degenerated into a slugging match. Even though they were raw, Butler's troopers were armed with Enfield rifled muskets, which gave the Federals the impression they were facing infantry. The nattily clad South Carolinians had taken a severe drubbing at the hands of Hampton's veteran regiments, who hooted and hollered at the "new issue." There had been little doubt about what they would do the first time they "saw the elephant"—run. They didn't.

Gregg sent attack after attack at Hampton's right, but each was thrown back in turn. Chew, over on the left, could do little to help Butler's boys, but he did pour shot and shell into every available target that presented itself. The horse artillery expected and received in kind.[13] Pvt. John D. Jones of Shoemaker's Battery was killed, and Privates Andrew B. Echols and John C. Strine were wounded. In the end, Gregg threw Brig. Gen. George A. Custer's Brigade at Hampton, who was in the act of withdrawing. The Michiganders took advantage of the situation to chase Wickham's Virginians off the field and take numerous prisoners. But Hampton had what he came for—information on the whereabouts of Grant's forces—and so was content to leave the field to Gregg. He fell back to Atlee's Station, where on the twenty-ninth, Cooke again inspected the horse artillery.

> HDQRS. ARTILLERY, ARMY OF NORTHERN VIRGINIA,
> May 29, 1864.
>
> Brig. Gen. W. N. PENDLETON,
> Commanding Artillery:
> GENERAL: I have this morning inspected the Stuart Horse Artillery and find the command in tolerably efficient condition. The fresh horses (100) have not yet been supplied by Colonel [James L.] Corley, and are greatly needed. Those now in the batteries are much worn down and many of them unfit for service. They are properly groomed and cared for, grazed, and receive about 8 pounds corn. The caissons are well supplied with ammunition. The axle of a Napoleon gun in McGregor's battery is broken, and the piece has been sent to Richmond for repair. In the action yesterday 1 man was killed and 1 wounded, and 2 horses disabled. Major Chew is very anxious to effect the transfer to his battalion of the battery of horse artillery in General Breckinridge's command. He urges that General B. has now two battalions of mounted artillery, and that the horse artillery would be of more service in the cavalry, and would give two batteries to each division. Major Chew is desirous that you will direct the transfer. I shall make every exertion this morning to procure the fresh horses for the batallion.
>
> Very respectully, your obedient servant,
> JNO. ESTEN COOKE,
> Captain and Assistant Inspector-General.[14]

The battery Chew wanted transferred to his command was Jackson's. Eventually it would become part of the Stuart Horse Artillery Battalion, but not at this time. Since coming east, the battery had not seen any heavy action. That changed on the thirtieth and thirty-first.

Positioned along Totopotomy Creek near Gardner's Farm with Breckinridge's Division, Jackson's Battery became swept up in Grant's continuing attacks on Lee's lines. Over those two days, the battery suffered more casualties than it had absorbed since its inception. Lt. Randolph H. Blain was severely wounded in six places and burned about the face by a shell that exploded near him. His wounds would take him from the battery for some time. Bugler Jacob T. Black and Privates Charles Jackson and Robert A. Miller also fell wounded on the thirtieth. The following day, Corp. William Christ was killed and Corp. Lawrence E. LeTulle and Privates George Mitchell and William H. Smith were wounded. Not until June 2 was the battery withdrawn from its works and allowed to rest, and then only briefly.[15]

As for Chew's batteries, Cooke's appraisal that they were in "tolerably efficient condition" meant only one thing—there would be no break in the ongoing fighting with Grant. That general was continually sliding to his left, and in attempting to keep track of him, as well as hinder him when possible, the horse artillery would continue to be employed almost daily. In fact, Haw's Shop heralded a series of hard-fought cavalry actions that would culminate at Trevilian Station on June 11 and 12.

Following Cooke's inspection, the batteries again went their separate ways, trotting off with the various cavalry brigades to bring Lee information and harass Sheridan's troopers. Most of the thirtieth was spent marching. Thomson pitched camp near Hughes' Cross Roads; McGregor rode toward Hanover Court House with Rooney Lee's division; Johnston accompanied Fitz Lee's advance in the direction of Mechanicsville; Shoemaker moved toward Atlee's Station; and Hart remained with Hampton near Atlee's Station. The Federals were out there somewhere, maybe everywhere, and "Marse" Robert's cavalry was determined to do its part in keeping Grant away from Richmond.

Rooney Lee's division screened the army's left flank. On May 31, Rooney moved to Hanover Court House, where at about 4:00 P.M. he clashed with Brig. Gen. James H. Wilson's division. McGregor's Battery found itself right in the thick of it. Earlier in the day, the battery was in position in a large, level field just south of Hanover Court House but received orders to limber rearward. As it moved down the road, a courier dashed up with orders to return at the gallop. The battery turned into the field, which was now swept by the enemy's fire, but McGregor raced on with two dead horses in the traces. The guns were unlimbered and began firing shell, which was quickly replaced with canister as the enemy came forward. McGregor sat on his horse shouting: "Give 'em hell, boys! Pour it on, boys!"[16] Lt. Charles E. Ford walked his horse calmly up and down behind the battery. In the growing darkness, the flashes of the guns illuminated him and his mount briefly. The enemy sharpshooters were beginning to get the range. Bullets zipped through the air. Some tossed up small clods of earth as they struck the ground around the battery.

Ford turned and called out to Captain McGregor: "It is as hot as Williamsburg. Mack, you had better retire these guns." McGregor did not hear Ford above the concussions of the cannons, so the lieutenant turned and ordered, "Limber to the rear!"[17] The cannoneers did not have to hear the command twice. Pvt. David Cardwell put the pintle hook in number four gun and turned to mount his horse. As he settled into the saddle, one of the crew, a Frenchman named Antonio,[18] cried out, "Garçon, Lieutenant Ford is killed."[19] Cardwell looked to see the crewman catch Ford as he slipped from his horse, and the private rode toward the stricken officer to assist in carrying him from the field. At that instant, Cardwell's mount was hit and knocked to the ground, briefly stunning the private. Sgt. Temp Brown pulled Cardwell up behind him and galloped off.

When Brown and Cardwell reached the road, they saw one of the battery's guns stuck on a stump, its pintle hook not having been placed properly. The two raced ahead and caught the battery in time to send back a limber for the gun, which was saved from capture. Farther up the road was an ambulance. Riding up beside it, Brown and Cardwell looked in and saw Lt. G. Wilmer Brown, who told them that Ford had just died. The sad procession continued on for some time before going into camp about 10:00 P.M. That night, Ford was hurriedly buried in his blanket in a fence corner.

June 1 began with Wilson pushing Rooney Lee back toward Ashland. The Federals struck the Virginia Central Railroad and began the work of destruction. Col. John B. McIntosh's Brigade was absorbed in its task when Hampton's division and Hart's Battery slammed into it. Rooney Lee welcomed the assistance, and the combined strength of the two Confederate cavalry divisions drove McIntosh back through Ashland. Hart's Battery galloped among the forward units as they charged through the village. A number of ladies came out of their homes to cheer the cavalry and artillery.[20] Unfortunately, the onrushing guns could not be used to their fullest extent because of the heavily wooded terrain. As a result, both McGregor's and Hart's men became mostly spectators, while their cavalry comrades chased McIntosh in the direction of Hanover Court House. On the second, McGregor marched to Meadow Bridge and encamped.[21] Hart remained with Hampton's division near Ashland.

At the opposite end of the Confederate line, Fitz Lee had been charged with holding on to the important crossroads of Cold Harbor. On May 31, his troopers, along with Johnston's and Shoemaker's Batteries, reached Ellerson's Mill just beyond Mechanicsville. While halted, one of the men from Johnston's Battery noticed a wire in the road. Out of curiosity, he pulled it, setting off a torpedo that exploded right between the two lead horses of his team. The only casualty was the pole between the horses, which was broken off when the team turned away from the explosion. The booby trap had been set by other Confederates to hamper the Federal cavalry's movements.

The column moved out shortly after the excitement died down. Shoemaker pitched camp at Gaines's Mill,[22] but Johnston continued on with Fitz Lee toward Cold Harbor, where they were severely tested by Brig. Gen. Alfred T. A. Torbert's cavalry division. Backed by Custer's Michiganders, Torbert attacked Lee, who was reinforced by three regiments of infantry under Brig. Gen. Thomas L. Clingman. The Federals persisted in their attacks and threw Lee and Clingman back about a half a mile, uncovering the crossroads of Old Cold Harbor. Lee's losses were severe, and Johnston's Battery had at least three men wounded and seven horses disabled.[23]

On June 1, Fitz Lee skirmished with the enemy all day but managed to hold his position. Johnston's Battery under Breathed was engaged but suffered no loss. Having lost the vital crossroads, the cavalry now fought valiantly to keep the enemy from pushing too far beyond it. The Federals proved too strong, but just as the Confederates reached the breaking point, Maj. Gen. Robert F. Hoke arrived with reinforcements to stem the Federal tide. Strangely, Shoemaker's Battery, which had accompanied Fitz Lee and Johnston's Battery to Gaines's Mill on the thirty-first did not become involved with the fighting at Cold Harbor. At 3:00 P.M. on the first, the battery under Captain Shoemaker left Gaines's Mill and marched away from the scene of battle toward New Bridge, parking on the farm of Walker Hogan. Here Lt. Charles R. Phelps's section was detached and sent on a scout in the direction of Richmond via Mechanicsville. Though the cannonading at Cold Harbor could be heard, Shoemaker's cannoneers followed orders that did not permit them to go to Breathed's assistance.[24]

Fitz Lee spent the morning and part of the afternoon of the second holding the line near Cold Harbor. Johnston's Battery took position on the army's right flank in the vicinity of Turkey Hill.[25] Lt. Edmund H. Moorman's section of Shoemaker's Battery marched from its bivouac on the Hogan farm past Gaines's Mill to the Joseph Adams farm and joined Johnston. Breathed had overall command and shortly opened fire on the enemy. The Federals brought up a battery, which tore into the Confederate infantry at point-blank range. Immediately, Breathed turned his guns on the battery in an attempt to silence it.[26] The enemy returned the favor and changed its target from the infantry to the artillery. After an hour's bombardment, which saw Corp. Charles Branch and Pvt. Thomas D. Loudenslager, both of Johnston's Battery, suffer arm wounds, the latter so severely it required amputation, the Federals had enough and left their pieces to hide behind a hill. Later in the day, Lee was relieved by Maj. Gen. John C. Breckinridge's division and marched to Bottom's Bridge to prevent the enemy from crossing the Chickahominy River.[27] Moorman's section returned to the Hogan farm, where he also received orders to move to Bottom's Bridge. At 8:00 p.m. he encamped on the farm of Philip Watkins on Seven-Mile Road about two miles from Bottom's Bridge. After a circuitous ride, Lt. Charles R. Phelps's section of Shoemaker's Battery reached Bottom's Bridge late on the second and took position to guard the crossing.[28]

On June 3, Grant mounted furious assaults on Lee's line only to see his men slaughtered by the hundreds. Caught up in the fury of the battle was Jackson's Battery, which once more sustained a number of casualties. Lieutenant Woods received a slight wound. First Sgt. David S. Van Matre was struck in the leg, as was Pvt. Jefferson Smith. In the evening, Lt. Col. David G. McIntosh's Battalion replaced Jackson's Battery and the rest of McLaughlin's guns.[29] In a few days, Breckinridge's division and its artillery were sent back to the Valley, where the Federals were resurgent. Lieutenant Woods recorded in his diary that he boarded the train for Charlottesville on June 8.[30] This time there were no words of confidence. Grant still confronted Lee, and now the Valley again was threatened. The victory that Woods had hoped for had not materialized.

When the attacks at Cold Harbor finally died away, Grant had to admit that he could not go through Lee to get to Richmond. He sat back and weighed his options. During the horrible fighting, the Confederate cavalry and horse artillery demonstrated their versatility by performing a reconnaissance on Lee's left, holding a position on the army's right flank during the battle at Cold Harbor, and guarding a crossing of the Chickahominy River at Bottom's Bridge. In each instance, they proved once again their ability to fulfill the variety of roles Lee required of them.

During these critical days, Thomson's Battery remained at Hughes' Cross Roads, where it had been since the night of May 30, and played no part in any of the fighting. Corp. George M. Neese had little to write about in his daily journal, other than that he and his batterymates were awaiting orders. Those came on June 3, when Wade Hampton conducted a reconnaissance of the Federal army's right flank. Taking Rooney Lee's division and Thomson's Battery, Hampton pushed out toward Haw's Shop, where he encountered Wilson's cavalry division.[31] Both sides claimed victory in the action, which lasted until near dark. Thomson's Battery had an artillery duel with a section of the enemy's horse artillery that lasted for a couple of hours.[32] As the day waned, the fighting died down. Hampton fell back to Ashland. Thomson's Battery continued its march until it camped at Meadow Bridge.

A section each from Johnston's and Shoemaker's Batteries saw some action at Bottom's Bridge on the Chickahominy on the morning of the third. The Federal cavalry divisions of Brig. Gen. Alfred A. T. Torbert and Brig. Gen. David McM. Gregg were spread out along the river, probing for any weakness in the Confederate dispositions that would allow a crossing. Fitz Lee's division occupied the river line and opposed the enemy's thrusts. The Federals pushed forward a small force to test the Confederate position at Bottom's Bridge. Shoemaker's and Johnston's sections under Breathed's command became involved with four guns of the enemy. The attack amounted to very little. The only casualty was one of Shoemaker's horses, which was shot in the knee and abandoned. Shoemaker claimed that the Federals were "whipped from the field in about 1 hour."[33] Torbert summed up the importance he placed on the action by reporting "nothing of interest except some artillery firing."[34]

In fact, little of any importance happened over the next few days, as each army took time to review the past month's campaign and contemplate future strategy. The weary soldiers, blue and gray, gratefully welcomed the respite from the almost constant fighting that had engulfed them. The men of the horse artillery battalion were no exception. Thomson's Battery stayed in the area of Meadow Bridge until the eighth, when they moved back near the Brook Turnpike. Hart's Battery moved with Hampton's division to Atlee's Station, then continued on and joined Thomson's Battery at Meadow Bridge. Here Captain Cooke inspected the two batteries on the eighth.

HDQRS. ARTILLERY, ARMY OF NORTHERN VIRGINIA,
June 9, 1864.

Brig. Gen W. N. PENDLETON,
Comanding Artillery, Army of Northern Virginia:
GENERAL: I have the honor to report that I yesterday made an informal inspection of the two batteries of the Stuart Horse Artillery, Thomson's and Hart's, camped above Meadow Bridge and serving with Major-General Hampton. The general condition of the batteries is very good; Thomson's especially. Great care has been taken of his horses by this active and efficient officer, and they are in excellent order. Hart's are not so good, but are fit for active service. The horses of both batteries are regularly supplied with corn, and grazed, and well groomed. They are now commanded in person by Major Chew, and are camped on the south side of the Chickahominy, near the Brook turnpike, about 5 or 6 miles from Richmond.

The losses in these batteries since my last report have been inconsiderable, and the companies are full Thomson has 98 men for duty, and Hart about 112. The ordnance wagons are well supplied with ammunition, except Blakely. The limber chests and caissons are full, and the ammunition properly packed. The deficiencies in horses have been supplied by 100 horses recently supplied to the battalion, but some of these are indifferent. About 12 mules are much needed for the ordnance wagons. The batteries serving with Mah. Gen. Fitz. Lee will be inspected to-morrow or next day.

Most respectfully, your obedient servant,
JNO. ESTEN COOKE,
Captain and Assistant Inspector-General.[35]

The fact that both Thomson and Hart had not seen as hard service as the other batteries undoubtedly contributed to their overall good condition. As for Cooke's plans to inspect the other batteries, they were to go awry in a matter of hours.

From the third to the ninth, McGregor's, Johnston's, and Shoemaker's Batteries spent their time watching the river line. Constant skirmishing continued through the eighth, though the artillery probably was not brought into use. On the fourth, Lt. Edmund H. Moorman's section was sent to guard Couch's Ford a few miles above Bottom's Bridge. The orders came at dusk, and it was dark by the time the ford was reached. About 2:00 P.M. the following day, Gen. Robert E. Lee visited the picket post on a round of inspection. Later Moorman was relieved by a section of the Washington Artillery and marched his battery across the Seven-Mile Road, camping on the farm of John Garthright near White Oak Swamp.[36] On the eighth, Shoemaker sent one gun downriver to picket Long Bridge.

McGregor left Meadow Bridge sometime after the fourth and moved downriver to the vicinity of White Oak Swamp. The Federal cavalry under Sheridan was slowly being withdrawn in preparation for a raid that would test the resiliency of Hampton's and Fitz Lee's divisions and Hart's, Johnston's, Shoemaker's, and Thomson's Batteries.

In the meantime, the officers and men of the battalion enjoyed a few days of relative quiet. Lt. William Hoxton took the opportunity to pen a letter to his sister and fill her in on the most recent events:

> Camp near White Oak Swamp
> Charles City Road, June 6/64
>
> My dearest Sallie,
>
> Though I'm afraid there isn't much probability of my heart's being gladdened by your dear letters, still I know you feel anxious about me so I shall continue to write at every opportunity. As no one from my command has charge of our mail arrangements, I don't expect to get letters through the P.O. till we settle down again, and in the meantime I wish you would send letters for me to Mrs. Minnigerode.
>
> My section was very sharply engaged last Tuesday [May 31] near Cold Harbor in a fight Fitz Lee had with the left of the Yankee line. I lost three men wounded, one or two others hit but not hurt much, and seven horses. How true it is that in spite of our ingratitude and forgetfulness God constantly cares for us. "Mr. Binks" (my horse) was shot down but is now in a fair way to recover.
>
> I got a letter from dear Mrs. Minnigerode day before yesterday in which she said she had written to you, telling you I was safe. In addition to her other numerous loveable qualities, she certainly has as much kind, considerate thoughtfulness as any one I ever knew. I can't begin to tell you my dearest Sallie what a true friend of mine she is. You must love her for my sake.
>
> I am anxious to hear from Llew. If he has written let me know. I am obliged to use these tracts for writing paper as I have no other

stationery. Give my best love to bro. Alf and tell him if he can get me a servant to send him on as soon as practicable. Kiss the dear little people for me. I think of you and pray for you very often. Don't forget me in your prayers—but I know you don't—

Your devoted brother
William Hoxton[37]

On the same day that Lieutenant Hoxton wrote his "dearest Sallie," the Federal cavalry division of Brig. Gen. Alfred T. A. Torbert and Brig. Gen. David McM. Gregg were assembling at New Castle Ferry on the Pamunkey River. Grant was about to turn Phil Sheridan loose again behind Confederate lines. The expedition's ultimate goal was Charlottesville, but along the way, Sheridan was to tear up the Virginia Central Railroad. A possible rendezvous with Maj. Gen. David Hunter's army from the Shenandoah also was contemplated. When Sheridan began his raid on the seventh, he targeted Trevilian Station as the starting point for his railroad destruction. He had a long ride ahead of him, but at least the Rebel cavalry would not harass him. They were caught unaware, giving Sheridan a two-day head start. It would not be quite enough.

Though Robert E. Lee's cavalry had been left in Sheridan's wake, Wade Hampton was not one to give up all that easily. Taking his own division and that of Fitz Lee, Hampton set off on the eighth.[38] Trotting along with the gray troopers were Hart's, Johnston's, Shoemaker's, and Thomson's Batteries under Chew. Breathed also rode with the column, commanding Johnston's and Shoemaker's Batteries. McGregor's Battery and one gun from Shoemaker's Battery remained with Rooney Lee's division.[39] In order to get ahead of Sheridan, Hampton had to maintain a grueling pace. He pushed men and horses to the limit. By the evening of June 10, Hampton's division with Hart's and Thomson's Batteries was in position near Trevilian Station, while Fitz Lee's division with Johnston's and Shoemaker's Batteries was at Louisa Court House. Sheridan was camped around Clayton's Store northeast of Trevilian Station.

Even after such a difficult and exhausting march, Hampton had no intention of holding to the defensive and waiting for Sheridan to come to him. The South Carolinian proposed to attack. While one brigade guarded the left flank, he would push the other two brigades of his division up the road between Trevilian Station and Clayton's Store, attack, and fix Sheridan in place. Then Fitz Lee's division would advance up the road from Louisa Court House to Clayton's Store and crush Sheridan's flank. If all went as planned, the Federal cavalry could be dealt a crippling blow.

Early on the morning of the eleventh, Hampton moved Brig. Gen. Matthew C. Butler's and Brig. Gen. Pierce M. B. Young's Brigades, the latter under Col. Gilbert J. Wright of Cobb's Legion, forward on the Clayton's Store Road. About two miles above Trevilian Station, Butler's leading regiment struck Brig. Gen. Wesley Merritt's Brigade of Torbert's division. The fight was furious from the start. Hart's Battery[40] had accompanied Butler, and about a mile above the station, a section under Lt. William T. Adams went into position to the right of the road "in a field behind a pine thicket with the left gun within ten feet of the road and opened fire."[41] Major Chew had ridden forward with Butler to locate a position for a section of Thomson's Battery, the other section having been sent with Brig. Gen. Thomas L. Rosser's Brigade down the Gordonsville Road to protect Hampton's left flank.[42] As Adams's section pounded away, Chew located what he felt would be an advantageous spot for Thomson's two pieces and started back to the station to get them.[43] At this point, Hampton's plan began to unravel.

Fitz Lee dutifully began his advance up the Clayton's Store/Louisa Court House Road, but he made little headway. Brig. Gen. Williams C. Wickham's Brigade clashed with elements of Brig. Gen. George A. Custer's Michigan Brigade. A section of Shoemaker's Battery was brought forward to shell some woods.[44] Lee did not push his attack, allowing Custer to fall back and take a side road to Trevilian Station that ran between Hampton's right flank and Lee's left. When Custer came within sight of the station, his eyes fell on a marvelous prize—Hampton's wagon train, his led horses, and the caissons of Hart's and Thomson's Batteries. Within minutes, Custer's Wolverines were scooping up prisoners and booty by the armload. A Federal triumph seemed imminent, but this day held surprises for everyone.

While riding back to the station, Chew met Hampton, who informed him that the enemy had gotten into the division's rear and ordered Chew to do the best he could with his guns. Chew rode for the station at a gallop and arrived to find that Custer's troopers had completely overlooked Thomson's two guns, which were there for the taking, and attacked the lead horses and wagon train instead. Realizing that luck was with him, Chew led the section to a small eminence to the left of the Gordonsville Road that commanded the battlefield below.[45] It proved to be a key position in the battle that was unfolding right before Chew's eyes.[46] But before he could contribute signifcantly to Custer's discomfiture, he needed more firepower. Unknown to Chew, the enemy was about the help him get it.

The situation confronting Butler became serious when Fitz Lee failed to attack Torbert's left flank. Instead of dealing with a couple of brigades, Butler found himself facing the strength of two divisions with no prospect of support anytime soon. As the pressure mounted, he decided to fall back toward Trevilian Station and sent an order to Lieutenant Halsey to withdraw Hart's guns. For whatever reason, Halsey did not immediately obey the order and kept on fighting. Before long, Butler rode up to Halsey and, in language liberally sprinkled with expletives, told the lieutenant that the enemy was about to charge down the road and take his guns. That, plus the expletives, caused Halsey to give the "limber up" command, which his men did not need repeated.[47]

As the battery rolled back down the road, Lieutenant Adams and standard-bearer Louis Sherfesee heard Butler give the command to charge to the Charleston Light Dragoons. Since this would be the first mounted charge for the troop, Adams and Sherfesee decided to remain and see its execution. Both were blissfully unaware of what was transpiring about the station in their rear. Once the charge was over, the two started after the battery. Sherfesee told what happened on the way:

> After it [the charge] was over, Lieutenant Adams and I started for the Battery, having heard the order where they were to go but when we reached the place, found that it had left there, and we followed the tracks, walking our horses. While wandering among the hills, a minié ball whistled very close to us and one of us said, "That was carelessness," thinking, of course, that it was one of our men [Butler's cavalry] who had fired. We had not gone but a few steps farther when another ball struck the pommel of my saddle, and I said, "That was d—— carelessness." A few steps farther a minié ball passed between us and, looking around, we saw a line of the enemy's skirmishers not two hundred yards off. Putting spurs to our horses, we, in a few minutes, reached the Battery, which we found in position on the top of a hill. We had hardly stopped our horses when I heard "Yip" and Adams threw his hands up. I held him in my arms until some of the boys came up, and we found he had been struck in the face by a minié ball. Seeing Maj. [Theodore G.] Barker[48] a short distance off, I rode to him and asked where the rear was, telling him that Lieutenant Adams was seriously, if not mortally, wounded. Maj. Barker's reply was, "Sherfesee, there is no rear. We are surrounded." So we laid Adams in rear of the Battery which was the best we could do for him.[49]

The hill on which Sherfesee found Hart's Battery already held Thomson's section, minus his caissons, which had been left along the road that Rosser had taken to the west. When Chew placed Thomson on the hill, he opened fire on Custer's troopers, who were galloping past him, en route to capturing Hampton's wagons and Butler's lead horses. Pvt. David M. Deck, a caisson driver in Thomson's Battery, described what happened when Custer's Wolverines reached the caissons:

> Captain Thomson soon received orders to move his battery forward in the direction of the station, and from the firing which we heard a few minutes later I judged that they had taken position on the left of the road. The firing had not continued long, hardly more than a half hour; but we who had been left in the road with the caissons when the guns

> were ordered forward received orders to turn our teams as though we were preparing to fall back, which events later seemed to prove. While sitting on our horses with our backs to the enemy, patiently waiting for orders to fall back to take up another line, as we thought, a noise in our rear attracted our attention, and, looking back, we saw the Federal cavalry within fifty yards of us. The road in this part of the field passed through the woods, while a small hill close in our rear prevented our seeing them, and doubtless the roar of the artillery, mingled with the small arms, prevented our hearing the sound of the approaching enemy. So they were upon us, firing at us, and there was nothing for us to do but surrender.[50]

Thomson's teamsters and caissons were but a small part of Custer's total of captured vehicles and their drivers that day. The only problem the "Boy General" had was holding on to them.

By the time Hart's Battery reached the hill and joined Thomson's section, giving Chew a total of six guns, Butler slowly was being pushed back to the station.[51] This fact did not escape Chew, and he well knew what it meant: With Butler so heavily engaged, he could expect no support for his guns. By his own admission, he conceded that "artillery is helpless without support."[52] Fortunately, Custer's troopers were so occupied with their captures that they failed to take notice of Chew's guns or the shells those guns were dropping on them. Because of a curve in the road just below the hill, Chew found himself firing in three directions: northwest, south, and east. How long he had before the enemy took notice of him and decided to deal with him, Chew did not know. Until that time, he could only pound away and hope for succor.

The first intimation that help was indeed on the way came from the direction of Louisa Court House in the form of artillery fire. Fitz Lee's weak advance toward Clayton's Store earlier that morning had doomed Hampton's plan and forced Butler's and Young's Brigades into a fight they could not win. However, Lee was far from whipped and recognized that if he could not advance in one direction, he could march in another. Taking the Trevilian Station Road, Lee came onto the battlefield in rear of Custer's Michigan Brigade at the moment of their triumph. The 15th Virginia of Brig. Gen. Lunsford Lomax's Brigade was the first of Lee's regiments to enter the fray. Its charge recaptured a substantial number of Hampton's wagons and Butler's horses.[53] The rest of Lomax's Brigade joined the fight.

Before long, Maj. James Breathed galloped onto the field with a section each of Johnston's and Shoemaker's Batteries.[54] As usual, Breathed was ready for a fight, and as usual, Lt. Alexander C. M. Pennington's Battery M, 2nd U.S. Artillery, was more than happy to accommodate him. The two antagonists squared off for one of their familiar brawls. For about two hours, they exchanged round for round. When Pennington's shells dropped close to him,

Breathed's voice could be heard above the din: "Move up closer; they have got the range, boys."[55] One of those close rounds felled Lt. William Hoxton with a very serious wound. He would need every one of his sister's prayers. The advance made by Breathed brought on a charge by the Federal skirmishers that forced the major to fall back near his first position on the William W. Wood farm next to the railroad. During the maneuver, Pvt. Abner D. Ford of Shoemaker's Battery dropped to the ground with a wound in his side.[56] As Hoxton and Ford were moved to the rear for attention, Breathed continued his duel with Pennington, neither one willing to quit.

At almost the same time that Fitz Lee ploughed into Custer from the east, Rosser charged him from the west. Realizing that Rosser could do him no good where he was, Hampton had sent a courier to recall him. Rosser rushed his brigade back to the station, leaving the section of Thomson's Battery that had accompanied him far behind and out of the fight.[57] The first Federals Rosser's troopers met were those of the 5th Michigan who had captured Hampton's wagons, Butler's horses, and Hart's and Thomson's caissons. Liberating the teamsters and horse holders, and taking prisoners as he drove forward, Rosser soon came within range of Chew's guns on the hill. Fortunately, Chew saw them coming. He ceased fire in that direction and swung the pieces around to bear on Custer, who was now surrounded on every side.

Chew was busy directing the fire of his hilltop bettery when Maj. Theodore G. Barker galloped up and asked for all the men that could be spared from the operation of the cannons. He proposed to enter the melee in the fields below. Sixteen men rode off down the hill in a feeble attempt to emulate a cavalry charge. Arriving at the fence bordering the field of which the hill was a part, Barker's "troopers" popped away with their pistols at the Federals on the other side. A gap in the fence allowed Barker to continue his "charge." His artillery/cavalry netted eighty-one prisoners. One of them was kind enough to donate his McClellan saddle to standard-bearer Sherfesee as a replacement for the one ruined by a Yankee bullet earlier in the day.

Custer fought valiantly, holding one part of his defensive circle, for that was the formation forced upon him, while charging out from another. He shifted his artillery wherever they were needed most. Pennington and company were magnificent. But in the end, they all would have to fall unless they received aid from Sheridan. They got it. Fitz Lee and Rosser, concentrated on crushing Custer as they were, could give no help to Butler and Young, who were rapidly being pressed back to the station by Torbert. Then the Federals paused while Torbert reorganized his line in preparation for a turning movement against Butler's left. It was now about 5:00, and Hampton decided to pull his men out. Butler, Young, and Rosser, along with Thomson's and Hart's Batteries, retreated west approximately half a mile. Fitz Lee also broke off the fight and fell back toward Louisa Court House. Pvt. Charles McVicar described the last two hours of fighting and Hampton's retreat as he experienced it:

> Three o'clock, mending the lines, the Howitzer was sent forward, am with it this evening, our forces forming a strong line half mile back. We are laying down on the hot sand. Ammunition ready. Every man at his post ready to rise in action in a minute. A hot fire of grapeshot is falling on us. General Rosser and staff have been reconnoitering. Major Chew is with him. They are coming this way. Several volleys fired on them. Two aides are being steadied on their horses. Major Chew's mare badly shot, covered in front with blood. They stop by us in a small yard. The General is having their wounds dressed, when we find he is wounded and falling. Several of us run and help him off the horse, down on the grass. Find he is shot through the leg. Cut a high cavalry boot off of him filled with coagulated blood, put a rag tourniquet on him and get them all away out of danger. His energetic and anxious mind was on his brigade. His words were "that he could whip Sheridan with his Gallant brigade, that God never placed better men on earth."
>
> Britner, our gunner, and I got on top of a rail fence and sat there looking at the enemy's movements. He on one panel and I on the next. A shell cut the stakes between us. He fell on one side and I on the other, both shaken and stunned but not hurt.
>
> I saw a beautiful horse running between the lines. Like all lovers of fine horses, temptation [was] too much. Mounted and after it. Just as he leaped the fence about one length ahead, a shell passed through him. I got down and took saddle, martingale, breast strap, crupper, and a fine leather saddle valise, swung them on my mare. The enemy did not fire at me, although only about 100 yards away, until I started back. My didn't they send a hornets' nest of bullets after me. Can hear them zipping by yet.
>
> Britner sent our horses back. Enemy moving as they charged the howitzer. Only ten of us and drivers. How we worked giving them grape. They stopped to deploy and we ran the half mile to protection under the fire of the rest of our battery. Were relieved at dark and bivouacked five miles from that point. Found my captured valise a prize. Two all wool fine striped cashmere shirts, two fine undershirts, several linen shirts and drawers, socks and handkerchiefs, a useful hussey (small sewing kit), surely an officers outfit.[58]

McVicar's fortunate escape from Yankee bullets was only the beginning of his good luck. Sheridan was not willing to pack up and leave after one day's fight, especially since he held the field at the end. The battle of Trevilian Station was not over.

The morning of June 12 passed quietly. Many of Sheridan's troopers were engaged in tearing up the railroad track in the vicinity of Trevilian Station. The

Federal commander was very much aware that Hampton had not gone away and began to make preparations to attack the Confederates in their new position. Hampton's men did not waste the morning hours either. Fitz Lee was given orders to take a circuitous route around Sheridan at the station and join Hampton, which he did about noon, bringing Johnston's and Shoemaker's Batteries with him. At the same time, Hart's and Thomson's Batteries, which had spent the night at Green Springs, where forage could be had for the horses, were ordered to the front.[59]

At the close of the fighting on the eleventh, Hampton had taken up position on the Charlottesville and Gordonsville Roads about one mile west of where the roads forked. Butler's Brigade held the left along the railroad embankment with the 6th South Carolina in position where the line bent at an obtuse angle. Next came Young's Brigade, then Rosser's. A section of Thomson's Battery (two brass howitzers) was placed "just in rear of our line, not far to the right of the angle, in the open field."[60] The other section of Thomson's Battery was 300 yards south of the first section supporting Young and Rosser. On the extreme right was Hart's Battery, once again commanded by Captain Hart, who had returned from sick leave. Fitz Lee's division was at first stationed to Rosser's right. Johnston's and Shoemaker's Batteries were with Lee but were not engaged early in the fight.

Sheridan's attack began about 3:00. Almost immediately, the left gun of Thomson's section at the angle was in trouble. Pvt. Charles McVicar described what he and his fellow cannoneers endured:

> Battery ordered to the front, first section into action shortly after the firing commenced. Took a position too near a deep railroad cut, six feet or more which was rapidly filled with a brigade of dismounted Yanks. They hardly exposed a hat brim. John "Jap" Pierce, the battalion color bearer from Jefferson County, held the flag too close and was hit by six bullets. Sent him back to Charlottesville to the ladies who presented us the flag. They will take special care of him. The gun was some hundred yards from the railroad. Corporal Frank Reily, from Summit Point, Jefferson County and cousin of Captain James W. Thomson, who should have been with his caisson, acting #2 at the gun, was shot through the breast. He mechanically inserted the cartridge, it was rammed, then the shell and he fell dead without a groan. He had his eye shot out the year before at Barboursville near Brandy Station. Then George Nicewander was shot through the wrist joint. They had to abandon the gun and take shelter behind the old house.[61]

The crew was not driven from its gun by the enemy fire. True to the reputation that Thomson's Battery possessed, it would have stayed until every last man was down, but Butler could see no purpose in that. He ordered Chew to pull back the men.[62] However, Captain Thomson did not like the fact that one of his pieces remained unmanned before the enemy. McVicar recorded what happened next:

> An order was sent back to the second section to detail three men to take the place of those killed and wounded. Robert Powell,[63] [Louis B.] Morel, and I volunteered to fill their places. We mounted and rode rapidly. Was ordered to take horses back and run to shelter where the detachment was under shelter of an out building, leaving the gun some twenty paces.
>
> The Captain [Thomson] ordered me with six men to bring the gun off by hand, and I led them in that galling fire of death. Jumped over the trail [and grabbed the] handle with my left hand. Anthony Beale Burgess caught the left trail handle with his right hand. As we raised the trail, Burgess was shot over the right eye and out over the left ear. He quivered and fell forward on my breast and some of his brains and blood were on my jacket.[64] [Reuben T.] Phillips, son of a preacher from Staunton, stepped over the body and took his place. He fell but was quickly up and helped me. Corporal Carthage Kendall was struck and crazed. He was holding the trail spike. We had trouble to keep him out of the way. He recovered in half an hour and was back in action again. Then Cal Miller was shot in the back. John Hare of Baltimore was shot through the thigh. [James L.] Crawford lost his little finger. I was the only one with no loss of blood and a whole hide, but my clothes had three bullet holes. We fought in desperation, and all who helped came out but poor Beale.[65]

Small-arms fire was not all McVicar and his fellow gunners faced. A section of guns, part of Pennington's Battery, added its fire to that of the dismounted Federal cavalry. Hart's Battery was ordered to silence the enemy cannon, which was done, though Pennington reopened fire several times during the afternoon and evening. After McVicar and company rescued their abandoned piece, they again opened fire. By this time, Corp. George M. Neese had been ordered to act as gunner for one of Thomson's pieces at the angle. His accurate shooting contributed almost immediately to the defense of the angle.

> There was a large house just in rear of the Yankee line and rather to the left of the railroad cut, which was occupied by a goodly number of the enemy's sharpshooters, who were firing from the upper windows with long-range rifles and doing some damage to our dismounted sharpshooters, and causing considerable annoyance to the left of our line by now and then dropping a cavalryman dead in his tracks. I saw the house and also saw the sharpshooters firing from the

> windows, but I had no orders to fire on the house, and, moreover, I was just then firing at closer game. After I fired some eight or ten shell General Butler[66] of South Carolina came riding on the field where we were and glanced at the situation a moment, then rode up to my gun and, pointing at the house where the enemy's sharpshooters were, said to me, "Fire that house." I immediately turned my gun, and the very first shell I fired struck the house and set it ablaze; however, I sent another shell at it for quick work and good measure. Just after I fired the first shell I saw a thick volume of smoke rising from the roof; while a nice little stream of Yankee sharpshooters rolled out below, and that completely cleaned up the sharpshooting business from that point for all time to come.[67]

Though Neese's well-aimed shot solved one problem facing Butler's line, it did nothing to stop the galling fire from the Federals in the railroad cut.[68] The angle remained a hot spot for Butler's South Carolinians and Thomson's gunners. More firepower was needed. To get it, Chew looked to his right and sent for reinforcements.

Around 5:00, Lt. Charles R. Phelps's section of Shoemaker's Battery unlimbered next to Thomson's section at the angle.[69] Lt. Edwin L. Halsey's section of Hart's Battery also arrived to help.[70] One of its guns was disabled, so its crew was assigned to one of Thomson's pieces, replacing those men who had been killed and wounded.[71] These additional pieces helped throw back the Federals' renewed assaults, but the cost was high. Lieutenant Phelps had his horse killed under him, and Privates Robert A. Hamlet, John McGrath, and Henry D. Wooling were wounded. None of these men left the field but stayed with their guns and fought the rest of the day. Thomson's Battery had no additional casualties,[72] but Hart's had two men slightly wounded.[73] Butler's line repulsed no less than seven assaults, the last one coming after the sun had set.

The stalemate on Butler's front forced Sheridan to take other steps to pry the Confederates from their position. Merritt's Brigade withdrew from in front of Butler and swung around to the South Carolinian's left flank. The plan might have worked but for the fact that Hampton was able to counter it with Wickham's Brigade of Fitz Lee's division, which was pulled from Butler's right flank. Merritt's attack ground to a halt. However, neither Hampton nor Fitz Lee was through. They had one more card to play. Lomax's Brigade was also on Butler's right. The lack of Federal pressure in that sector allowed Hampton to move Lomax to Butler's left. Confederate scouts had discovered a weak point on Merritt's right flank. Fitz Lee led Lomax's Brigade and Breathed with a section each from Johnston and Shoemaker over a wooded road and into position on the Federal flank. Breathed found an advantageous position, ran his pieces forward, and opened fire. Merritt's line crumbled, and only a gallant effort on the part of the 2nd U.S. Regular Cavalry, two regiments from Col Thomas C. Devin's Brigade, and Lt. Edward B. Williston's Battery D, 2nd U.S. Artillery, stabilized the line. The halting of Lomax's attack brought the battle of Trevilian Station to an end.

With Hampton resolutely blocking his way and reports that Hunter had advanced only as far as Staunton, Sheridan decided to start back to Grant. From the thirteenth to the twentieth, the long blue column threaded its way eastward. Hampton once more took a shorter route, and on the nineteenth, Fitz Lee was in position at White House on the Pamunkey River, which had been a supply port for Grant and was still protected by troops and gunboats. Hart's, Johnston's, Shoemaker's, and Thomson's Batteries unlimbered on the farm of Dr. Macon and dueled with the Federal artillery and gunboats that were covering Sheridan.[74] Private McVicar described his role in the day's festivities:

> General Sheridan and his men are under the protection of their gunboats. The ball has opened. We have run him 120 miles since the 12th from Trevilian, skirmishing and fighting daily.[75] We have an excellent position on the high ground, three of our guns are for the first time firing on full uniformed negroes backed by whites. They are replying to our little six-pound rifle guns with twenty-pound parrots. The scenery is magnificent, looking over these broad, rich river bottoms. The Pamunkey River is stretched out wide and romantically in view. The gunboats have opened on us with 150 pound shells, crashing the trees over us, limbs falling. It looks like an angry devil as she vomits forth her fiery hail. Yet we continue to fire for some two hours into their camp of negroes and whites, firing with accuracy and rapidity.
>
> Trent Powell was wounded in the thigh. I was sent after the doctor as he had a small artery cut and we feared he would bleed to death. Rode fast between the lines, the shortest was to the ambulance train. We have been reinforced by some infantry and one battery.[76] As I was passing it, one of the caissons was blown up, a terrible sight, two men up in the air. One as he hit ran hollering fearfully, eyes burnt, clothes on fire. They caught him near the ambulance and filled his head and face with grease and wrapped his head up.
>
> I found Dr. Bell,[77] and we rode back together. Powell's wound in the thigh had coagulated and been bound. An hour later, laying under fire of the gunboats as they came up on our faces, one of those large shells burst and a piece struck and disabled the 2nd gun. I was ordered to take it back to Richmond with seven men. I struck the Cold Harbor Road, traveling across the battlefield of some weeks ago. As we neared the fortifications what a horrible sight. Had to move ten or twelve bodies. Hogs had routed them into the road. The stench was so

> fearful, the horses would hardly pass. Their clothes were good, but some heads had rotted from the bodies and rolled down into the road. Had to open the road for the gun and caisson to pass through. Our finer feelings were blunted. . . . Camped three miles from Richmond.[78]

While McVicar struggled to get his gun to Richmond for repairs, the rest of the horse artillery continued to struggle with the enemy artillery and gunboats. Hart's Battery especially was hard hit by the Federal firepower. Privates Samuel I. Joy and John Lewis were killed; Pvt. Charles B. Prentice was mortally wounded; and Privates Howell W. Cooper, Benjamin R. F. Davis, James Morris, Jesse J. Nettles, and Henry D. Simpson were wounded. The only other casualties were Corp. Demetrius A. G. Coode of Johnston's Battery, and Pvt. Pendleton P. "Pent" Powell of Thomson's Battery, who were wounded. Everything considered, the day did not go well for the battalion. As night fell, everyone was withdrawn except for Lt. Charles R. Phelps of Shoemaker's Battery, who remained on picket with his Napoleon.[79]

Dawn on the twenty-first showed that the Federals had been reinforced, which resulted in an attack that drove Hampton back for about two miles. Once out of range of the gunboats, the gray cavalry formed a line to contest any further advance. At least part of Thomson's Battery and Phelps's Napoleon opened a fire that persuaded their opponents to return to White House.[80] Hampton did not pursue but turned and marched toward Bottom's Bridge. His withdrawal marked the end of the Trevilian Station campaign.

The performance of the horse artillery from the eighth through the twentieth was equal to anything the batteries had accomplished under Pelham or Beckham. They had kept pace with the cavalry on the way to Trevilian Station and were ready for the fight on the eleventh. Caught unaware by Custer's attack, Thomson's and Hart's Batteries provided the first opposition to the Wolverine Brigade. When Johnston's and Shoemaker's Batteries entered the battle, they helped turn the tide against Custer. On the twelfth, all four batteries added their firepower to the cavalry's line and inflicted considerable damage on the attacking Federals. Breathed's offensive use of Johnston's and Shoemaker's guns in the attack on Merritt rolled up Sheridan's line and ended the battle. Then in the long pursuit, the battalion again managed to stay with the cavalry and was available for the fruitless duel with Federal artillery and gunboats at White House. For this efficiency, the batteries paid a high price. The six killed, three mortally wounded, twenty-one wounded, including two officers, and three taken prisoner made this the bloodiest campaign the battalion had fought to that time. Its toll in horses, while not recorded, must have been proportionally as high. Taken in its entirety, the Trevilian Station campaign was one of which the battalion could be proud.

During the time that Hart's, Johnston's, Shoemaker's, and Thomson's Batteries were chasing after and battling Sheridan's raiders, McGregor's Battery and the one gun of Shoemaker's Battery that had been left behind with Rooney Lee's Cavalry continued to perform picket duty. On June 13, Lee's and McGregor's position at White Oak Swamp was attacked. After four hours of fighting, Maj. Gen. Cadmus M. Wilcox's infantry finally relieved Lee.[81] The next day, McGregor moved to Malvern Hill.[82]

These were critical days for the Army of Northern Virginia. Robert E. Lee knew Grant was maneuvering toward the James River but was unsure what he would do when he reached it. Rooney Lee's cavalry was spread out guarding crossings of the Chickahominy, rendering it unavailable for a thrust at Grant to determine what was transpiring. The army's commander-in-chief resorted to sending infantry patrols forward on the fourteenth. The information they obtained did little to clarify the picture when, in fact, Grant's army had begun to cross the river that day. On the seventeenth, Rooney Lee was ordered to "push after enemy and endeavor to ascertain what has become of Grant's army."[83] The orders were unnecessary. The son had already dispatched a courier with the information the elder Lee desired.[84] A large part of the Army of Northern Virginia began crossing the river on the night of the fifteenth. On the night of the seventeenth, the rest of the army crossed the river. By the nineteenth, Rooney Lee's division with McGregor's Battery,[85] soon to be joined by Dearing with Capt. Edward Graham's Battery, was on the Jerusalem Plank Road, guarding the Weldon Railroad.[86]

When Hampton encamped at Bottom's Bridge on the night of the twenty-first, he was not oblivious to the altered situation north of the James River. R. E. Lee had written to him on June 17 that most of Grant's army had crossed the river.[87] But Sheridan was still north of the river, and if an opportunity to crush him presented itself, Hampton intended to take advantage of it. Lee was also intent on striking a crippling blow at the Federal cavalry and had placed Brig. Gen. John R. Chambliss's Brigade at Hampton's disposal.[88] Before that could happen, however, the cavalry and horse artillery needed some time to recuperate.

Chew's command was in somewhat of a shambles. Besides the loss of men and horses, the equipment itself had taken a beating. Thomson's Battery had one gun damaged at White House and on the twenty-second sent another gun to Richmond as "a worn-out gun unfit for further use in the field."[89] Shoemaker's Battery lost one gun with a broken axle on the march from White House to Bottom's Bridge, and another was sent to a camp near Richmond because the horses were so worn out they were no longer serviceable.[90] Hart's Battery had lost a caisson at White House. Johnston's Battery had all of its guns, but several of its men and horses had been sent to the rear. Lieutenant Nunnelee of Shoemaker's Battery was ordered by Major Breathed to take charge of the men, horses, and guns of this "Company Q," as it was called.[91] Chew did what he could, but fourteen days of marching and five of fighting had taken their inevitable toll.

The respite lasted until the twenty-fourth, when elements of Brig. Gen. David McM. Gregg's division drove in Hampton's pickets in the vicinity of Samaria Church. Hampton decided to strike back and met the enemy at Nance's Shop. Brig. Gen. Martin W. Gary's Brigade was joined by those of Chambliss and Wickham with Johnston's Battery and Shoemaker's single piece. Chew and Breathed were present and assisted the cavalry in breaking the Federal line and sending it scurrying for several miles toward Charles City Court House. Hart's Battery was called to the front, but because of its broken-down horses, it arrived late and never did catch up to the retreating enemy. Thomson's Battery was in camp near the Chickahominy and did not participate in the fighting on the twenty-fourth.

Hampton's and Fitz Lee's divisions crossed the James River on the twenty-sixth and rode hard for Petersburg. Hart's, Johnston's, and Thomson's Batteries crossed the same day, but because of the condition of their horses, their ride to Petersburg was conducted at a more leisurely pace. Shoemaker's Battery camped near Chaffin's Bluff on the twenty-sixth and did not cross the river until the twenty-eighth. What awaited Chew's battalion was more hard campaigning around Petersburg and, for some, in the Shenandoah Valley, where other horse batteries had been grappling with an enemy determined to exterminate every last vestige of the Confederacy. The task proved somewhat difficult.

CHAPTER 28

Cleansing the Valley

"It looked as if we were going into the very jaws of death."

March 1864 found the war in the Shenandoah Valley at low ebb. The weather was not conducive to large- or small-scale military operations. Very little was taking place around Walker's Creek, where Capt. Thomas E. Jackson's Battery had its winter quarters. Men left on furlough to visit loved ones for a short time before returning to the battery. Once they were back in their camp, they picked up pen or pencil and wrote the letters that were their lifelines to hearth and home. During the month, Lt. Micajah Woods wrote his father several letters in which he discussed the condition of his battery, its personnel, and its inner workings.

> March 7th 1864
>
> . . . Maj. Genl. Breckinridge has assumed command of this Department & has brought with him a fine reputation good looks & a numerous staff. There were at Dublin before his arrival sixteen officers who held rank as Majors. I presume this number will be increased. Genl. [William E. "Grumble"] Jones was ordered to Richmond. It is not known what disposition will be made of him. I saw at Dublin, besides Breckinridge, Genls [Albert G.] Jenkins & [John S.] Williams. The former expresses himself in high spirits about his Brigade. He hopes to collect his whole force—increased by Williams & Jackson's command & Col. [Henry S.] Bowen's Regt. [22nd Virginia Cavalry], recently organized in Tazewell—early in the spring & he assured me that we should not complain for want of work. His remarks portended a move northward in force. . . .
>
> We obtained from Tazewell 10 or 18 recruits, none as yet been assigned to us by the conscript bureau. There are a number at Dublin who wish to join us & we are daily looking for authority to receive them. Captain Jackson is on a visit to Lewisburg—leaving me in Command of the Battery. He will return on the 11th or 12th Insts. I

do not approve of your suggestion of presenting him with a pair of pants. He is as polite & kind to me as he well can be—and surely he has had sufficient reason. I have given him a fine felt saddle blanket, two pairs of socks—a splendid new towel—articles which would cost him $40 or $50 & some of them cannot be gotten for any price, & the kindnesses & favors I have done him are certainly ample to evidence to him my good will, as well as yours. When my box is sent, a pair or two of socks can be put in for him & Norton, to whom I gave two prs. of the lot I brought. I wish nothing sent at present, but when my new mess is formed, I will write a list of things I will need. Burly can make me two iron spoons & keep them "under orders." I shall want my gray jeans pants, without a stripe sent, also for Bob and be sure to reserve enough of the yellow jeans cloth to make me another pr. pants & vest, as there will be a demand for them towards the latter part of summer. . . .[1]

March 15th 1864

. . . During the last week six new men have joined us. We expect ere long to have an acquisition of 30 or 40 from Tazewell Co. & Dormann's Camp. Ge'l. Jenkins remarked to me at Dublin the other day that we need not be uneasy about horses, that he would have us by the 20th May, when every man could get a private horse. This indicated a big raid early in the campaign. . . .

Genl. Breckinridge is on a tour of inspection in this Department. Soldiers & citizens are universally charmed with him. In McCausland's Brigade he inspected every musket himself. Such condescension pleases all the troops and shows them he takes an interest in them. . . .[2]

March 24th 1864

. . . Since my last letter nine men have enlisted. The Battery is filling up rapidly, and in a few days we hope to have about one hundred men on our Rolls. A requisition has been sent in for guns for the third section. If Mr. Via has to enter the service or any others in our neighborhood I can safely recommend to them our Battery as enjoying advantages far above the cavalry or any other arm. Until the 1st of next month they will have the privilege of volunteering under a recent order. Several of the recent recruits are men of considerable wealth bringing servants with them and making applications to furnish two horses. Should any of my friends come from Albemarle they could enter very pleasant messes.

We expect about April 1st to move to the vicinity of Blacksburg if forage can be obtained in that neighborhood. We are acting upon anticipation of another year's war—a permanent farming detail has been made for farming four men. We have rented of the two Bane's about 100 acres of land—rich, black soil. Already about 40 acres are plowed. We will put in 50 acres corn—30 acres oats and an immense garden of cabbage onions, beans, potatoes &c. &c., besides all the country pledges to us its tithe tax next winter. If the war continues we at least have nothing to fear. When the campaign ends we will fall back to this place and have enough corn & forage of every description to supply the horses during the whole winter, and vegetables ample for the whole Battery will be at our command. Our course is sanctioned and approved by Genl. Breckinridge. As the news spreads through the country, it enhances our popularity amazingly even in adjoining counties and brings numbers of recruits. . . .[3]

The battery's plans for the next winter revealed the confidence the men had in the ultimate outcome of the 1864 campaign season. This outlook helped Woods and the other men endure a March and April that brought wind, rain, sleet, and snow to batter the camp at Walker's Creek.[4] Toward the end of April, Woods began to focus on the war that soon would engulf him and his batterymates again. He wrote a long letter to his father in which he expressed his feelings about what lay ahead:

Jackson's Horse Artillery
Giles Co. Va. 22nd April 1864

My dear Father

Your welcome letters of the 17th & 18th Inst. came to hand on the 20th and I hasten to reply at my earliest leisure moment, I do so more cheerfully since so long a period had elapsed since my last intelligence from home and I had been a sufferer from "hope deferred" for such an unreasonable time that I prefer replying while the glow of the sensations and feelings awakened by such acceptable messengers still possess me. I am sure that if home people could witness the joyful countenances and comprehend the pleasing emotions of a son in the army on reception of their letter, they would more frequently put pen to paper and multiply their number. They, far more than the tyrant custom, tend to make the steel & flinty couch of war a bed of down for I am inclined to disbelieve Shakespeare's "Great miscegenator" when he says that even so effective a power as habit can render such a berth entirely soft and agreeable.

My Battery is still stationary and I am happy to be able to state that it is in better condition than ever heretofore. Nearly 100 men are in camp for duty—35 fresh horses have been sent us, and nearly every cannoneer is mounted on a private horse. Our utmost energies have been taxed recently in fitting out thoroughly for the field as early as the roads and elements permit, and I fancy we could handle severely any rash enemy who may attempt "to seek the bubble reputation in "our" cannon's mouth."

I have watched the progress of events in the East with an all absorbing interest, and daily have I yearned to receive an order to proceed to that field of operations. I feel that I can scarcely reconcile myself to being absent from the noble army and not to share its dangers in the great conflict in which it will soon engage; for still my pride is great that I once belonged to the Army of Northern Va. and that I have been an humble participant in so many of its bloody and glorious achievements, and now that it is on the eve of its greatest and perhaps final trial upon the issue of which the destiny of a nation depends—as little as I love the danger of battle, and as small as is my desire to end my life on the field, even in so glorious a cause—I am yet decidedly inclined to chafe at the circumstances which retain my command in Western Va. Perhaps this feeling is somewhat intensified because my home lies in the East and there is an instinct which impels every one to prefer striking—if he has to strike—in a region and on a field where the blow will directly affect his interests and his happiness.

Nearly all, both soldiers and civilians in this region regard the impending contest the most momentous that has ever been joined on this continent. If Genl. Lee is repulsed, the result will be the blackest and most terrible that the imagination can paint; the very mind refuses to contemplate the horrible consequences that will inevitably trail upon disaster. The enemy, under their favorite leader are marshalling the heaviest columns and most stupendous resources that even in modern times has aspired to the overthrow of a people. If this army is beaten, if this concentrated essence of their hope be blasted, the sun shine will break through the hitherto black clouds of our horizon and the dawn, though bloody will, beyond the shadow of doubt, deliver among the powers of Earth a nation new but assured in its own invincible resources. Thanks to heaven, the whole power of the government seems to be exerted. Young and old, rich and poor all comprehend the mightiness of the struggle and are offering with a heart in his bosom, with an impulse of patriotism in his breast, with one sentiment of pride or self respect to animate him, who would not be willing—yes who would not burn—to lend a helping hand in such a crisis where all is at stake. That able bodied young man, without wife or child or who is not almost of superhuman usefulness in furnishing provisions, who skulks under any subterfuge at such a time, deserves to be a serf and an object of contempt and execration to a whole people. He will merit hereafter to be esteemed unworthy the association of honest men or virtuous woman.

Some of our journals are urging the perfection of arrangements for the establishment of a "battle roll" for the Army of Northern Virginia, by which to perpetrate the noble deeds and mighty achievements of its men and its leaders. I should like also to see made out a "black scroll" in which to hand down to futurity her odious and withering colors, the names of those whom neither self respect nor the sentiment of the multitude could drive into the rank of defender in the nation's greatest & extremist peril. It would be as a beacon light for coming generations to avoid contact with the most dastard blood that ever coursed through the veins of the human race. But for the honor of our country it may be said there are a few such, who have not spirit and pride enough to wish to number among the gallant defenders of the soil. The list would be short.

But I must stop. I find that I have unconsciously suffered my feelings to flow to such a length that I fear your patience is already exhausted and I will proceed to tell you things that may prove more interesting.

This Department has been literally "stuck in the mud" for the last six weeks. I find from reference to my diary that the 21st Ult. was the very first clear day we have had for more than a month. You will scarcely realize it when I tell you that up to yesterday snow has fallen nearly every day for several weeks. Such a season has not been experienced in this Valley for 30 or 40 years by the oldest inhabitants. Vegetation has made no progress. The Earth has been made glad yesterday & to day for the first time by the sun shine of Spring. The enemy are making no demonstrations. I am induced to believe that the campaign in this section will be totally inactive, unless disturbed by our own forces. Genl. Breckinridge is exerting himself greatly to place his command on a thorough war footing—he has won the hearts of his officers and men and such consciousness of ability to defend this Department has never before prevailed. Genl. [Albert G.] Jenkins has as yet taken no steps for the assemblage of his Brigade. He seems entirely engrossed by perfecting a new revolving gun that he has invented and apparently has forgotten his men of war.

This Battery cannot possibly remain in the immediate Section for more than seven days. Our horses 107 in number we find very hard to subsist. Recently we have had to resort to impressment which very disagreeable duty has devolved upon me by special order. The people however have given no trouble and the county of Giles certainly has shown a liberality which could be well copied by other counties.

I should not be at all surprised if ere long we were ordered to the Shenandoah Valley. Both man and officers would hail with delight such a movement. Four splendid rifled guns are now in our park and in a few days we expect an addition of 30 more men & two more guns. The additions to the Battery since my last letter have been numerous some very nice young men. I shall forward a roll containing all the names and residences of the men. . . .

The mail which arrived five minutes since is also the bearer to me of your letter of the 20th. . . . It also brought an order from Maj. [William] McLaughlin, Chief Artillery in this Dept. for the Battery to hold itself in readiness to march at a moment's notice. This causes me to attach some importance to a rumor I heard today that the enemy are advancing in two columns on Saltville—or perhaps it is ominous of an order sending us to the East or to the Valley. We are ready for either. . . .

My horse has given me immense trouble recently he has been almost totally blind during the last two weeks. I have been forced to ride him considerably in collecting forage & his stumbling & falling down has disgusted me with him. His eyes are now improving but he has a spell monthly. I now have in an application to Maj. Genl. Breckinridge to turn him over to the Battery & take a Battery horse to have them both valued by a board of officers & to pay the difference. Urging it on the ground that he would answer well as a draught horse by reason of his great strength. Should it succeed I will secure a hardy serviceable animal. Capt. Jackson & Maj. McLaughlin approved it & I am confident it will succeed.

Bob is doing very well—our mess is working splendidly. Lieut. Norton drew his pay $1080.00 the 1st of this month paid a visit to Lynchburg & occupied himself handsomely.

Please secure me enough leather for a good pair of boots if possible—at any rate for a pair of shoes as I shall need them before long.

And now my dear Father let me implore you to not let so long a period ever again pass without writing to me. Before your letter of the 17th you had not written me a word since March 19th. Ask dear Mother also to write me.

I shall certainly write again in a day or two—more than half this letter is written by the best fire light a camp can afford by night which is not very bright. Tell Eytell I will be very glad to have him in the Battery—that if he will forward his application for transfer,

Capt. Jackson will approve it—but there is scarcely a remote chance that it will be approved in the East. Remember me to Mrs. Gentry.

Love to dear Mother—little Maggie, Bob, Cousin Luly & the household.

Very Devotedly Your Son
Micajah Woods[5]

The month drew to a close with Jackson's Battery still in camp at Walker's Creek and Woods still speculating. He felt his battery was in excellent shape with 4 rifled guns, 103 men, and 107 horses.[6] All that was needed was the weather, which had continued to be abominable, to clear and an enemy to appear.

There were other horse artillery batteries wintering in or near the Valley that would be affected by any Federal invasion come the Spring. McClanahan's Battery was encamped on Hay's Creek in Rockingham County. But whereas Jackson's men had a winter free from any duty connected with the enemy, McClanahan's cannoneers took turns standing picket with a section of their guns. Considering that the weather Woods experienced was more than likely the weather McClanahan's men experienced, picket duty, in the best of times a rather disagreeable experience, must have verged on the intolerable. The only consolation was that somewhere their counterparts in blue were suffering equally—perhaps even more, being a little farther north. That neither side ventured to interrupt the other's boredom testified to Woods's accuracy concerning the weather conditions.

At Warm Springs, West Virginia, Lurty's Battery seemed to be drifting toward extinction. A number of the men were made prisoners when they evidently were caught by Federal patrols while visiting their homes, many of which were behind enemy lines. Such losses might not have affected a larger organization, but Lurty's Battery had never boasted of large numbers. When it stood for inspection by Breckinridge in early March it could muster only four officers and sixty-two men, while its aggregate strength was ninety-five. Fortunately, its roster never dipped low enough to warrant disbandment, and in mid-April, it moved out with the rest of Col. William L. Jackson's Brigade and marched to Jackson's River Depot. By the end of the month, elements of the brigade guarded various points in Alleghany County, covering the Virginia Central Railroad. Like the men from Jackson's and McClanahan's Batteries, Capt. Warren S. Lurty's boys greeted the month of May with renewed hope and just a bit of trepidation.

The month of flowers barely had begun to bloom when the Federals set out on the campaign trail. Lt. Gen. U.S. Grant had devised a grand strategy that coordinated the advance of the various Federal armies in all the major theaters of the war. Pressure was to be brought against the Confederate armies so that they could not detach troops to assist each other. The Federals made several thrusts in and around the Valley, achieving some successes and experiencing some failures. On one of these incursions, a portion of the Confederate horse artillery became involved in repelling the enemy. Brig. John D. Imboden led the 18th Virginia Cavalry, McNeill's Rangers, and a section of McClanahan's Battery into West Virginia and "thrashed part of three regiments" at Lost River Gap in Hardy County on May 10.[7] All of these skirmishes were just the preliminaries. The main threat to the Valley lay in the person of Maj. Gen. Franz Sigel, who brought with him 9,000 men bent on sweeping the Valley clean of Rebels.

Sigel had begun his advance up the Valley on April 29 but did not appear to be in a hurry to get anywhere. From his point of departure at Martinsburg to Winchester, it was a mere twenty-two miles. The Federals moved at a veritable snail's pace, taking three days to cover the distance. Once he entered the place, he liked what he saw and stayed until May 7. He entertained himself by having his men drill. They even fought a sham battle on the fifth. When at last the army marched, Sigel had managed to give the Confederates the time they needed to organize. As the Federals tramped south, Maj. Gen. John C. Breckinridge swept north to give them a warm Valley welcome.

The Confederate response to Sigel's invasion began to take shape even before Sigel left Martinsburg. When Breckinridge took command in the Valley, his available troops numbered about 5,000. Many of the units had deteriorated, suffering from "garrison fever," a condition brought about by a lack of campaigning.[8] From the date of his arrival in the Valley, Breckinridge had set about drilling his command into shape. The results were positive, but there was one problem all the drilling could not overcome—numbers. To meet the main Federal thrust, Breckinridge needed additional men. He would not get them from Robert E. Lee, who was preparing to face the main Federal army in the East. However, reinforcements did appear in the form of Brig. Gen. Gabriel C. Wharton's Brigade of infantry, Brig. Gen. John D. Imboden's Brigade of cavalry, the Virginia Military Institute's Corps of Cadets, and a section of the Cadet Corps's artillery. Coupled with Brig. Gen. John Echols's Brigade of infantry and other units, Breckinridge felt strong enough to confront Sigel. By May 4 Breckinridge was ready.

Marching orders reached Jackson's Battery at 1:00 P.M. on May 5. By the tenth, the battery had reached Jackson River Depot, where the cannoneers and guns boarded a train for Staunton. A small number of men led by Captain Jackson took the horses overland. The only casualty during the long trek was a caisson that suffered a broken axle. The train reached Staunton at 10:00 P.M. on the tenth, where the men waited until the horses arrived on the morning of the twelfth. The following day, the battery marched with Wharton's and Echols's Brigades, the reserve militia, the Corps of Cadets, Chapman's Battery, and the section of guns from the Institute. By the fourteenth, the column was within five miles of New Market.[9]

McClanahan's march to the battlefield was not as peaceful as Jackson's. By May 11, Imboden had returned from his expedition into Hardy County to find that the remainder of his force, which had been confronting Sigel's advance, had been pushed back from Woodstock to Mount Jackson. Here McClanahan's Battery was reunited. On the fourteenth, the 18th Virginia Cavalry, under Col. George W. Imboden, and the battery fought a delaying action at Rude's Hill. Pvt. Calvin C. Hart described the fight and subsequent events:

> On Saturday following [May 15], the main body of the enemy moved up the road. Our battery of four pieces[10] opened fire on the head of the column, and they withdrew. The Yankees set up twelve pieces of artillery in the valley opposite our station on the hill and began firing. Two of our pieces broke their axles, leaving but two against twelve pieces most of the afternoon.[11]
>
> When it was too dark for any more fighting, Imboden ordered roll call. To our surprise and joy, not a man was missing. The general then gave orders to limber up the guns and move down the hill. Not a man was allowed to speak above a whisper. We moved back up the Valley three or four miles, under the cover of General Breckinridge, who was coming to reinforce us. We stopped our battery close to the road, and with orders not to lay down our equipment, were permitted to rest until morning. The writer slept with a sponge staff for a pillow the remainder of the night. Imboden and his staff had their camp in a fence corner right behind the battery. At about midnight[12] several men rode into the field behind us and called for General Imboden. The General answered, "Here I am!" A man said then, "Is there room in your saddle for two heads?" "Yes," said Imboden. "I have a little whiskey. Do you want a drink?" said the newcomers. "You can have all the saddles!" Imboden laughingly answered. The visitors turned out to be Generals Breckinridge, Echols, and Wharton with their staffs. We all felt pretty safe with so many generals with us.[13]

Hart may have felt safe near so many generals, but he should have known that being so close might also mean being the first called upon to enter the fight.

As fate would have it, once Breckinridge had formed his line of battle, Lt. Carter Berkeley was ordered to take a section of McClanahan's Battery, including Hart, to Shirley's Hill and open fire on the enemy. Breckinridge had tried to coax Col. Augustus Moor's Federal infantry into launching an attack on the Confederate position by advancing and withdrawing Imboden's skirmishers, but Moor failed to take the bait. Berkeley's job was to develop the situation more fully. He soon had some help as Jackson's Battery, under Lt. Randolph H. Blain, Captain Jackson having been left behind in camp ill, dashed up, unlimbered, and added its fire to Berkeley's barrage.

The horse artillery pounded away until Breckinridge ordered Berkeley to move to a position east of the Valley Turnpike. The lieutenant limbered his two guns and trotted off. On the way, he passed the Corps of Cadets. Berkeley's men could not resist taunting the boys with cries of "Bomb-proof" and "Wagon Dogs!" The cadets would soon turn the jeers into cheers. Arriving at his new position, Berkeley began to ready his guns for action. Before he could fire a single shot, Capt. Alonzo Snow's Maryland Battery filled the air with shot and shell. As quickly as he could, Berkeley replied, and the artillery duel was on.

Back on Shirley's Hill, Breckinridge was making the final adjustments to his line before sending it forward. Jackson's Battery, situated below the crest of the hill, was joined by Capt. George B. Chapman's Battery, which put its six guns into position on top of the hill to Jackson's left, and the section of cadet guns, which unlimbered to the horse artillery's right. The twelve pieces rained lead and iron on the Federals below. Behind the artillery, Breckinridge formed his troops for the attack. If Moor would not come to him, he would go to Moor.

The Confederate commander had special plans for Imboden's cavalry and the other section of McClanahan's Battery, which was commanded on this day by Lt. Parkison Collett. They were dispatched to hold the right of the line and from there to cross Smith's Creek, ride north, and recross the creek in the vicinity of Mount Jackson. This would put them in rear of the enemy, trapping the Federals. Imboden and Collett galloped off. Breckinridge turned, gave a few last-minute orders, and launched his skirmish line forward. Before long the battle was raging, the cadets were advancing, and the Federals were falling back, giving up New Market in the process. Moor's troops began to form a new line north of the village. They were to hold here while Sigel put his main line of defense together on Bushong's Hill.

The rapid movement of the Confederate line had taken the guns on Shirley's Hill out of the fight for fear of hitting their own infantry. Breckinridge shifted Chapman's Battery and the cadet guns to the right to join Berkeley east of the turnpike, with orders to push forward, engage the enemy, and draw their artillery fire away from the infantry. Jackson's Battery would remain east of the pike, moving behind the infantry, taking positions of opportunity, and firing over the infantry. The batteries limbered up and raced off the hill toward their new positions. There was still much work to be done if Sigel was to be defeated.

Meanwhile, Imboden had discovered a target that he believed worth his attention. Behind the woods east of the turnpike stood "Sigel's entire cavalry force massed in very close order in the fields."[14] Nearby was a Federal battery. Imboden believed he could place his cavalry and Collett's section to enfilade these troops and immediately dispatched a courier to Breckinridge, who gave his consent. Before too long, Imboden with the 18th Virginia Cavalry and Collett's section of guns were on their way down to the bridge over Smith's Creek. Once across, Imboden led his column to a rise in rear of the Federal cavalry.

Here Collett unlimbered his pieces while the 18th Virginia rode on to carry out the original plan. Collett opened fire. As anticipated, the enemy's cavalry was caught unaware and rapidly sought shelter in retreat.

Berkeley's section of McClanahan's Battery, which had been joined by Chapman and the cadet artillery, had begun to pound away at Moor's new line. Capt. Albert von Kleiser's 30th New York Battery had been placed next to the road on the left. The battery's six Napoleons faced the ten guns that Breckinridge placed on his right. The New Yorkers took a terrible beating. Horses and men began to fall. One of Berkeley's rounds smashed a wheel on one of the guns. Then Breckinridge's infantry collided with the Federals and sent them reeling. Kleiser limbered his guns and raced toward Bushong's Hill. The blue infantry followed.

Once more Breckinridge ordered his artillery forward to a new position. Berkeley, Chapman, and the cadets limbered and surged up the Valley Pike about half a mile, where they placed their guns. Jackson's Battery moved up behind Breckinridge's advancing infantry and fired over their heads whenever it was safe to do so. The artillery managed to shell Sigel's line on the hill and drew the fire from a portion of the Federal artillery. This was what Breckinridge had hoped. With less fire directed at his infantry, they would have a better chance of coming to grips with Sigel's shaky troops. But at the moment, there was danger that Breckinridge's own line might falter. A gap had opened up in the line. If Sigel attacked immediately, the Confederate line could be shattered and thrown back. With a heavy heart, Breckinridge committed the Corps of Cadets, who plugged the hole in gallant style. Then another threat arose on the right.

Maj. Gen. Julius Stahel had extricated his cavalry from under the fire of Collett's guns. Now, from his new position east of the pike opposite Bushong's Hill, Stahel could see that the Confederates were having some difficulties and recognized that the time had come for a charge. He began to form his squadrons. This did not go unnoticed by Breckinridge, who countered the threat by moving Berkeley's, Chapman's, and the cadets' artillery farther down the road to a position behind a low stone wall to the right of the pike. By Breckinridge's order, the pieces were double-shotted with canister. When Stahel's troopers came within range, the artillery belched forth its deadly missiles, which buckled the oncoming columns and threw them into disarray. Simultaneously, Collett's guns, which were still in position east of Smith's Creek, raked the left flank of the enemy squadrons while the 22nd Virginia Infantry peppered the right flank, creating further chaos. Stahel's charge stalled. Horses and men crashed to the earth, and before too long, those that were still mounted turned and rode for the rear.

The infantry west of the turnpike now decided the battle. Repulsing a feeble advance by Sigel's infantry, Breckinridge's troops, after some initial wavering, rallied and re-formed their line. The charge that followed immortalized the

Virginia Military Institute's Corps of Cadets, which swept toward Kleiser's Battery and captured a gun that had been abandoned because too many horses had been killed. On the extreme right of the Federal line, Capt. John Carlin's 1st West Virginia Battery became the target of both the Confederate infantry and Jackson's guns. One shell from Jackson's Battery seriously damaged the wheel of a Federal piece, but the crew managed to limber and haul it away, only to see it become stuck in the mud. The gun had to be left behind.

Breckinridge knew the battle was won, but he wanted more. His plan had called for Imboden to get behind Sigel's forces and cut off their escape route. In this he was to be frustrated. Following the breaking of the Federal line, the Confederates discovered they could go no farther without a fresh supply of ammunition. While the men filled their cartridge boxes, all Breckinridge could do was wait. At this juncture, Imboden arrived and broke the news that his cavalry had failed in their mission. The commanding general knew full well that without the threat to his rear, Sigel would probably make a stand on Rude's Hill. That would give the enemy infantry a chance to rally, a circumstance that could not be allowed if the victory was to be complete. Breckinridge knew what must be done and dispatched a courier. Lieutenant Berkeley wrote after the war of what happened next:

> In a few minutes a courier dashed up and told me that General Breckinridge said I was to bring my guns to the pike and report to him at once. I followed the courier through our line and found the General sitting on a splendid Kentucky horse fresh and strong, looking like the very god of war, and as I touched my hat to him he said: "Lieutenant, are your horses fresh and strong?"
>
> I replied: "Yes, sir."
>
> He said: "I have no cavalry, unfortunately. I sent it all with General Imboden to get in the rear of the enemy on the pike beyond Mount Jackson. I fear they are taking advantage of our stop to make a stand on Rude's Hill."
>
> The rain had decreased considerably in volume and we could see the enemy on either side of the road on a hill which was, I think, about a mile off. Just about that time one of their guns opened on us. The General said: "Go at once; charge down the pike and drive them off the hill. I will follow up with the infantry as rapidly as possible." I rode at once to the pike, where I had left my guns, and found that Lieutenant Collett had joined them with another section.[15]
>
> We had six guns, but two of them had been knocked out in the fight the evening before. Our boys were highly elated at being selected to do a thing so daring and so unusual, and as soon as I gave the order we put out at a run, every man yelling at loud as he could. The enemy's battery turned the guns on us as soon as they saw us coming, but we were moving so rapidly toward them that the shells

> passed over our heads. It looked as if we were going into the very jaws of death, for the enemy seemed, as we got nearer to them, to be in considerable force on the hill. The road made a slight dip just before it began to ascend, and for a moment we were out of sight of the enemy. I anxiously rode ahead to see what we would run up against, and to my delight as I ascended the hill I saw the battery limbering up and the whole line breaking in confusion.
>
> The boldness and strangeness of the movement demoralized them. I could see the long [Meem's] bottom before us filled with fugitives, I have seen a statement from one of the enemy's artillery officers that they fired back at us as they retreated, and I remembered that they did fire several shots which passed over our heads. A squadron of cavalry on our left started toward us, and I looked back anxiously for our infantry support, but a shot or two well aimed sickened them and they joined their defeated comrades.
>
> Now we had everything our own way; the poor, panic-stricken wretches were flying before us in easy range of our guns and relentlessly we poured the shot and shell into them. It was awful; it seemed cruel, but as Sherman said, "War is hell," the truth of which saying they were experiencing. We had left all our tender feeling behind on the field covered with our dead and dying comrades.
>
> If Imboden could have gotten in their rear not a man would have escaped, but high water prevented it.
>
> We continued our deadly fire on them until they crossed the bridge and burned it behind them. We put in our deadliest shots as they were packing like frightened cattle across the bridge. This ended the fight on Sunday.[16]

When they reached Rude's Hill, the men in Jackson's Battery echoed Berkeley's lack of compassion for the routed Federals. They felt no compunction about opening up on the defenseless men below. Fortunately for Sigel's beleaguered troops, Breckinridge did not move beyond Rude's Hill. Once the Yanks crossed the bridge, they burned it to halt a pursuit that did not materialize.

As the guns fell silent, the Confederates began to celebrate a victory that brought sighs of relief throughout the upper Valley and all the way to Richmond. Certainly Breckinridge's soldiers had much to be proud of, and before long cheering filled the air and shook the very mountains to their foundations.[17] There were heroes aplenty, from the Corps of Cadets to the artillerymen standing by their smoking pieces. Jackson's and McClanahan's batteries could claim a sizable share of the glory—the latter especially so. McClanahan's boys had started the fight and were instrumental in finishing it. They had galloped with their guns all over the field, up and down hills, across creeks, and back again. It was undoubtedly McClanahan's finest hour.

Jackson's Battery, too, could be proud of its contribution to the success of the little Valley army. Its reward was a number of the captured guns, which replaced the battery's poor ones.[18] On the day following the battle, Lieutenant Woods composed a long letter to his father in which he shared his feelings on what had been accomplished by his battery and the army:

Dr. Meems Farm—Near
Mount Jackson May 16th 64

My dear Father,

In spite of the rain & wind this morning I cannot forgo the opportunity which a halt affords me of informing you of our glorious & decisive victory of yesterday. As stated in my letter from Staunton we did reach the enemy's front on the evening of the 14th and found Imboden skirmishing with them at New Market. Early yesterday we took up our line of battle about two miles above New Market. Wharton's Brigade on the right—Echols's & Imboden's forming the center and left—and the corps of cadets held in reserve—Chapman's Battery, Jackson's, McClanahan's, & a section of artillery manned by the cadets were all on the field. The infantry charged from position to position driving the enemy from every position they assumed. The enemy had about an equal number of pieces and of all regions on this continent there is none that affords such a splendid field for the maneuvering of artillery. We drove the enemy's batteries and did great execution among their infantry & keeping our pieces up with the line of infantry and very often firing over our own line into the enemy's.

Genl. Breckinridge cheered the troops during the entire action by his presence along the line. Troops never did better charging nor were they ever more successful. The enemy were driven by our continuous charge for eight miles—7 pieces of Artillery captured. Just at dark they retired across the river in great confusion at Mount Jackson, burning the bridges in their rear. So utterly routed were they that when our men charged Rude's Hill just above the Steinberger Estate and on one of the most powerful positions in the Valley—they retired without making a stand—only keeping their artillery in battery long enough to cover their crossing of the river.

Genl. Breckinridge and all compliment the action of the artillery. Our Battery was engaged on five different sites—each time charging as fast as our horses could carry the pieces taking position, firing vigorously. The whole action was probably one of the most exciting of the war. The constant charges, the rushing of the batteries from hill to hill, the rapid action, the immense cheering and utter discomfiture of the Yankees are seldom all the attendants of our field. Echols's and Wharton's brigades fought gloriously. Patton's Regt. acted with distinguished gallantry. But the most devoted band on the field was the youthful, the impetuous, the gallant corps of cadets. When charging a battery on a powerful position supported by the whole Yankee force one portion of our line wavered under a withering fire of canister & musketry—the cadets rushed gallantly to the front—their flag never paused till it was placed in the center of the battery over five splendid pieces. They are glorious boys and should be the pride of our commonwealth. About twenty of the little fellows have been killed, 7 wounded I understand. I saw four of them lying dead in one heap—one of them a son of G. A. Crockett of Wytheville, another was a son of your friend Dr. Cabell of Richmond, David Pierce, a little fellow in the artillery section and brother of my friend Miss Belle P. was slightly wounded while on our right in action.

Jackson's Battery fired about 400 rounds & was with the front line all day and exposed to the heaviest fire that 12 or 15 pieces could shower upon us—but choice of position & deliberate firing protected us. One of our men fell with his ankle shattered by a shell which exploded just under his gun.[19] Of course, it is needless for me to say that my hair breadth escapes were numerous as every one knows that shot & shell fly thick on a battlefield. Several shell exploded or passed in a few feet making a great noise but doing but little damage except occasionally throwing dirt over me. Our men stood up nobly, only one leaving his post & he will be court-martialed for cowardice.[20] Chapman had a caisson exploded killing one man & wounding three.

Our loss is comparatively small. I suppose 300 will cover the entire casualties.[21] The enemy's dead strew the field in great numbers. The men of the army have made great & valuable captures. Many horses were secured and five saddles. The earth for 7 miles was spotted with capital blankets & oil cloths—knapsacks & haversacks and all descriptions of trinkets & notions. I could readily have captured a good horse but preferred permitting our men to mount themselves and in one instance sending a man after a horse that was retained for me. I have secured a splendid McClellan saddle, equipments complete—three large green cloths—two good pair of shoes—one pr. for Bob and one for myself—and a splendid large cavalry overcoat with immense cape and extending some distance below my knees—double breasted & well furnished.

Some of our men have made their fortunes in the field nearly. Siegel commanded—their whole force was engaged. They had not anticipated any formidable resistance. I am not informed of the no. of prisoners captured but suppose they will number about 200. More would have been taken but their running was too good. We are lying on [word illegible] this morning being unable to pursue the enemy further on account of the bridge being burnt and the swollen river. I presume we will move on in an hour or two and endeavor to cross. The enemy have lost five or six field officers whose bodies have fallen into our hands. Major McLaughlin is in very high spirits about the action of his battalion and will give us a flattering report I expect.

I have been terribly annoyed the last three days—having no horse to ride—my horse was kicked a few days ago on one of his muscles and can scarcely be forced along. I have ridden a borrowed horse in action putting the owner to great inconvenience & causing him great loss in not having his servant up with him. I never want to go on another campaign without two horses—nearly all officers that can possibly afford it in the artillery have one extra horse, there being so great a liability of having a horse killed in action. Bob got several fine blankets and some other things. If he had had a horse he could have brought off enough property from the field to pay for a good horse and he could unquestionably have gotten a horse had he been up near enough in rear. I was unable to take one myself—tho' having a good opportunity because my duties with the Battery of course precluded even temporary absence. I shall have to leave my horse with some farmer, if we move further down the Valley. I made arrangements this morning to ride the horse of our wounded man for a few days. I find I lose a great deal by being so scrupulous about appropriating property in the field. I passed a splendidly furnished officers saddle on a dead horse. Blain came on a few yards afterwards & did not hesitate to take it—in spite of delay in going into action. I never saw troops in better spirits—it is the first time that many of them have ever won a victory, having served under slow coach generals in a slow coach department till Breckinridge handled them.

I send cousin Julia a little photograph I got out of a Yankee haversack in the field.

Please write me a letter by return mail—remember I get no papers & can hear nothing rumorous from Lee's main army for we consider ourselves a portion of his left wing.

I want to take a jaunt over the battlefield this morning so I will draw this hurried letter to a close.

Love to dear Mother & all–
Very affectionately
Yr. Son
Micajah Woods

Dr. Jno. R. Woods
Holkham
Va.

Bob has no word to send except that he is all right & charged gallantly over the battlefield this morning without injury making sundry captures.[22]

The victory that Breckinridge had brought to the little Valley army filled with men who had only been led by "slow coach" generals lifted spirits to a level almost equal to the heights reached when Stonewall Jackson scoured the Valley clean of the invader.[23] Like Jackson in 1862, Breckinridge had worked a miracle, though Stonewall was credited with several others as well, and like Jackson he was called east to reinforce Robert E. Lee. Four days after the battle, Breckinridge's men were boarding flatcars at Staunton bound for Hanover Junction. The small but victorious Valley army got smaller.

Sigel's threat to the Valley was not the only offensive that the Confederates had to deal with west of the Blue Ridge. Amid the mountains of West Virginia, Brigadier Generals George Crook and William W. Averell mounted an attack against the Virginia and Tennessee Railroad. Their advance eventually involved Col. William L. Jackson's command, including Lurty's Battery, which consisted of one rifled gun and one howitzer.[24] On May 13, Jackson, who had joined with a force under Col. William H. French, was engaged on Gap Mountain west of Blacksburg against Averell and Brig. Gen. Alfred N. A. Duffié, who were forced to turn back. Jackson was off in a futile pursuit the next day, leaving his wagon train and Lurty's howitzer behind with a small escort. In attempting to catch up with the main body, this detachment stumbled into Crook's column. The cannoneers abandoned the gun, the teamsters their wagons, and Crook gobbled up the whole lot. Jackson fumed and vowed to hold an investigation.[25] However, the war took precedence, and no charges were ever brought. For a while, at least, Lurty's Battery was reduced to one gun.

Back in the Valley, the days that had seemed so bright after New Market began to cloud over rapidly. Sigel's wretched performance cost him his command. On May 19, Maj. Gen. David Hunter was assigned to the command of the Department of West Virginia. His selection could not have been worse for the citizens of the Valley. Before too long, the cloudy skies would blacken with the smoke of burning crops, barns, and homes. On May 26, only eleven days after New Market, Hunter marched back up the Valley with over 8,000 men and thirty-one guns. To oppose him, Brig. Gen. John D. Imboden had a scratch force of about 1,000 men and the six guns of McClanahan's Battery. Reduced to futile harassing attacks, Imboden could only watch the Federals roll southward. He was powerless to stop Hunter's vengeful tactics.

Imboden's retreat continued through New Market on June 1 and beyond Harrisonburg to Mount Crawford on the second. Here he received word that Brig. Gen. William E. "Grumble" Jones was at Lynchburg and on his way north with 3,000 men. These reinforcements, which turned out to be only 2,200 men, began to arrive on the third. Hunter remained in Harrisonburg that day, which allowed the Confederates some time to organize their hodgepodge command. When Hunter did move on June 4, it was toward Port Republic, not Staunton. Jones's and Imboden's position at Mount Crawford was flanked. Hunter's maneuver precipitated the battle of Piedmont on June 5, though it was Jones who chose to make a stand there. Imboden wanted to fight at what he considered a stronger position on Mowry's Hill, but Jones overruled him, and the battle opened when Imboden's cavalry clashed with Hunter's advance units led by Stahel's cavalry.

Initially the Confederates were driven back, but once additional troops arrived, they were able to stop the Federals. Before long, Imboden saw enemy infantry and artillery massing and sent to Jones for the same. Lt. Carter Berkeley with a section of McClanahan's Battery galloped into position. By this time, Imboden had been forced back to Crawford's Run, about a mile from Jones's main line of battle. Pvt. Calvin C. Hart, number one to Berkeley's first gun, rammed down the first shell, which was soon on its way.[26] Berkeley's fire halted Stahel and wreaked havoc on a section of the enemy's horse artillery.[27] But the two Confederate guns soon were facing five times their number. Jones rode forward and was confronted by Imboden, who recorded the moment:

> By this time the enemy had opened a heavy artillery fire on Berkeley and had driven in my skirmish line so far that they had brought our guns under the range of their musketry. I had received a message from that part of the field saying that all Berkeley's horses would soon be killed and the section would be unable to withdraw. I turned to Jones and said, "General, you have heard the message, what orders shall I give Lieutenant Berkeley?" "Direct him to move his guns back to this point immediately, and I will put the rest of our artillery into the fight."[28]

Jones's infantry held the left of his line along the edge of a wood. Brig. Gen. John C. Vaughn and Imboden's cavalry held the right. There was a gap between Vaughn and Jones's infantry. It was to this point that Berkeley retreated and unlimbered. He was soon joined by Lt. Hugh H. Fultz's section. These two sections, along with two guns of Capt. James C. Marquis's Battery and two from Capt. Thomas A. Bryan's Battery, filled the void. Jones's makeshift line managed to throw back the first Federal infantry assault, but then Hunter's artillery commander, Capt. Henry A. Dupont, massed twenty-two pieces of artillery and concentrated their fire successively on each Confederate battery. The result tipped the scales in the Federals' favor.

Dupont's firepower silenced Marquis's, Bryan's, and McClanahan's guns. Berkeley and Fultz sustained considerable punishment. The battery suffered a number of casualties—1st Sgt. Joseph R. Merriken and Privates Joseph S. Baldwin, D. H. M. Burns, and William J. Chrisman were wounded.[29] Pvt. Calvin C. Hart recalled that when his gun finally was pulled back, only three out of its six horses were left to do the job.[30] Lieutenant Berkeley recounted what happened next:

We were soon surrounded by our own flying men [Jones's infantry], and in sight of the Yankees. Our men began to give way. Jones became desperate, rushed impetuously to the front, followed by many of [Col. Kenton] Harper's men, right on to the Yankee line of battle, which poured a deadly volley into them, killing Jones and many others. Just then Col. Robert Doyle, who with other officers was trying to rally our men, was also killed. I had just gotten my guns unlimbered and would have fired but was peremptorily ordered by a staff officer of the dead general to limber up and try to save my guns. I would have lost them I believe had I stayed a minute longer. My boys were behaving splendidly and would have stood by the guns until the last.

In our retreat, we had to pass through a piece of woods, and my intention was to make a stand as soon as I got out of the woods. Flying men were all around us, and a regiment of Yankee cavalry right behind us. This cavalry had been pushed to the front to take advantage of the break in our line and complete the victory now nearly won. As we got out of the woods I saw a section of McClanahan's Battery, commanded by Lieut. Park Collett, standing in the road limbered up and evidently oblivious of the critical condition of things. I called out to him to get into battery, that the Yankees were right behind us, intending to unlimber my section as soon as I got in line with him, but it was too late, for before we had time to get into battery the enemy burst out of the woods with yells of triumph, sabring, shooting, and riding down our poor fellows. But it was the last yell that some of them ever gave, for just in front of them were McClanahan's guns and behind the guns were men who had never been run off a battlefield. By the time I got to him Collett had unlimbered and shotted his guns, and the gunners were standing with the lanyards in their hands, hesitating to fire; and when I called out to them to do so, one of them said, "Lieutenant, we will kill our own men." There was no time to lose; they would have been over us in a minute more; so I jumped off my horse and made a grab for the lanyard in the hands of the gunner nearest me; but he anticipated me and pulled it off himself, the other gunners doing the same, and I never before saw two shots do such execution. The whole head of the Yankee column seemed to melt away. The timely and gallant action of Collett saved everything, all of our guns and wagons.[31]

Soon after Collett began firing, General Imboden came up and said, "You are doing the right thing. How long can you hold this position?" The reply was, "We have stopped here for good." He [Imboden] said that the Eighteenth Regiment was coming to our support. Soon it came, and it was suggested to the General to charge down the road that we might redeem the day; but he only threw out a line of battle, and we held the position.[32]

Private Hart, who heard another officer tell the lieutenant that his stand was "too hazardous an undertaking, that he would be killed" also witnessed Collett's brave stand. Collett fired back, "I would rather be killed fighting than to be killed running."[33]

Indeed, Collett's courageous defiance in the face of the victorious Federals saved the day for many of Jones's beaten troops, but it could not alter the outcome of the battle or change the fate of Staunton, which fell to Hunter on June 6. The Valley was being cleansed of Confederates at a rate that was appalling to its residents. Outside the Valley, there were many who were also shocked and discouraged by the turn of events in so short a time. Among them was Robert E. Lee, who recognized that drastic steps were in order if his army was to benefit from the Valley harvests for part of its sustenance. Breckinridge was dispatched back to the Valley on the seventh, but Lee realized that more troops would be needed to cope with Hunter. Ever the gambler, on June 12 the commander of the Army of Northern Virginia called Lt. Gen. Jubal A. Early, newly appointed commander of the II Corps, to his headquarters for a conference. At its close, Early emerged with orders that sent him and his corps to the Valley. Hunter was about to become the hunted.

Meanwhile, the situation in the Valley had worsened. On June 8, Generals Crook and Averell linked up with Hunter at Staunton, bringing with them 10,000 men and two batteries.[34] Two days later, Hunter marched on Lexington. Brig. Gen. John McCausland did what he could to slow down the Federal juggernaut but was driven from the town on the eleventh. Hunter took revenge for the Federal defeat at New Market by torching the Virginia Military Institute and the property of former Virginia governor John Letcher. On the thirteenth, Hunter sent Averell after McCausland and welcomed Brig. Gen. Alfred N. A. Duffié and his forces, who had been harassing Col. William L. Jackson's Brigade as it made its way to Waynesboro[35] to rendezvous with the remnants of Jones's defeated army. On June 14, Hunter left Lexington and pushed south toward Buchanan. Thus far he had faced stiff opposition only once—at Piedmont—and his men had taken every objective he set before them. But Confederate forces slowly were gathering strength and organizing themselves. The Federals' successes were all behind them.

Maj. Gen. John C. Breckinridge had arrived at Rockfish Gap several miles east of Waynesboro on the eighth. He quickly took command and began to do what he could to rally the forces at hand. He well knew that Lynchburg was Hunter's target, and on the ninth, he set out with his small army. Reports of the whereabouts and activities of Hunter's army were constantly being received. Over the next few days, both sides maneuvered into position for a test of strength at or near Lynchburg. McClanahan's Battery fought a number of skirmishes during this time, and on the seventeenth, along with Lurty's Battery and a section of the Botetort Artillery, it supported Imboden's much reduced brigade in a fight at Quaker Church along the Salem Pike five miles southwest of Lynchburg. While the battle was in progress, Jubal Early rode onto the field. His troops were not far behind him. Lynchburg was saved.

Another battery of Confederate horse artillery had arrived with Early but saw no action in the fighting around Lynchburg. Jackson's Battery had completed its trip from the vicinity of Richmond and had camped one mile from Lynchburg on the morning of the sixteenth. The next day, the battery unlimbered on Cemetery Hill and spent the day fortifying the position—unnecessarily, as events proved. On the eighteenth, the battery replaced Capt. Henry C. Douthat's Battery in a work along the Lexington Road and peppered the enemy with forty rounds from each gun.[36] Meanwhile, McClanahan and Lurty continued their battle along the Salem Road. The Federal commander had not expected to encounter such heavy opposition and was rapidly becoming unnerved at the thought of confronting what he was convinced was a superior force. Early had contributed materially to Hunter's distress by various means, not the least of which was a bold attack against the Federal left and center. In the end, Hunter decided he could not take Lynchburg. Claiming he was heavily outnumbered and short of ammunition, he fell back to Liberty. On the nineteenth, the Federals continued their retreat. That same day, Early sent off Maj. Gen. Robert Ransom, now commanding all of the cavalry with Early, in pursuit. It was now time to cleanse the Valley of the invader.

Ransom received orders that sent him, along with McClanahan's and Lurty's Batteries, over the Peaks of Otter to Bedford, in the hope of catching Hunter's column on its way back to Staunton. Early's infantry with Jackson's Battery chased down the road to Liberty. Ransom soon learned that Hunter was heading not for Staunton, but over the Catawba Mountain past Hanging Rock to New Castle. Making a dash, Ransom arrived at Hanging Rock first and, after some delay, attacked. Lt. Carter Berkeley unlimbered a piece without orders and opened fire. He was answered quickly by a single enemy gun. Berkeley's second shot dismounted the Federal cannon.[37] Ransom ordered Brig. Gen. John McCausland to charge. The result was eleven captured guns, but Hunter had made good his escape. Early's tired troops needed rest. On the twenty-second, Lt. Micajah Woods of Jackson's Battery recorded in his diary that his battery was resting at Salem.[38]

With Hunter skedaddling from the Valley, Early was free to put into operation a plan that he and Lee had discussed on June 12. If Early was able to drive Hunter from the Valley, Lee wanted him to move down the Valley, cross the Potomac, and threaten Washington.[39] With that in mind, Early turned his army northward and marched, reaching Staunton on the twenty-sixth. There he spent several days organizing his little army. Jackson's Battery arrived on the twenty-seventh. The next day, Lieutenant Woods wrote to his father, bringing him up to date on the momentous events he had witnessed and the effects of Hunter's presence on the civilian population of the Valley.

Near Staunton Va.
June 28th 1864

My dear Father

Our movements have been too constant during the past week to allow me to write you. In pursuit of the enemy we marched rapidly to Salem too late to do them material damage. The accounts of the operations of the cavalry in the vicinity you have seen. At Lynchburg our company contributed handsomely towards fortifying the heights none of which proved of service to us. On the 18th Inst. we moved to the front of the enemy on the Lexington road and relieved [Capt. Henry C.] Douthat's Battery stationed in a permanent work. His guns were inferior—the enemy's battery & columns had approached very near our lines with comparative impunity—about 40 rounds from each our guns in half an hour cleared the field of all visible Yankees and elicited from Genl. Ransom and Genl. McCausland high compliments for our battery.

The rear of our column reached this neighborhood yesterday. Today we rest and reorganize—lay in supplies &c. for what may be one [of] the most brilliant campaigns of the war. Early's corps and Breckinridge's command will make a beautiful column of invasion and five days from tomorrow will probably find us on the banks of the Potomac—no transportation whatever is allowed officers or men—all the baggage I carry is on my horse. We have been so very busy yesterday and today that it was impossible for me to leave in this morning. I could have been [word illegible] at home. Only four batteries out of 9 in Breckinridge's Division will accompany the command. The other batteries are broken up to furnish the ones that go.

I have repeatedly seen Cyrus Creigh and his brother Tom & Charlie & Tom Preston. Uncle David was certainly executed at Mr. Morrison's near Brownsburg. Cyrus as soon as he heard of it went there and had him interred properly—he has started home before this,—Everything was taken from his family as from every family in that region—all Uncle Tom's negroes left—Aunt Frances does her own cooking. Robertson Stuart's family were treated terrible. His mind is said to be affected by the scenes he & his daughter have passed.

I saw Mr. Reid who married Miss Stewart was returned a few days ago from Greenbrier. Aunt Preston has had left barely enough to subsist on.

I left at Cousin Henrietta Ruff's a tolerably good Yankee horse with a very sore back—he will probably be fit for service in a month or two. Should you know of an opportunity to have him brought home I hope you will avail yourself of it—He was shot just across the withers and may be thicker there than he should be when he recovers. The enemy did Mr. Ruff little damage except the taking of 70 sheep but captured from Cousin H. several horses & cattle.

Lt. Col. J. Floyd King of Georgia commands all the Artillery in our corps he is exceedingly unpopular among the officers (Capts.) because he makes them do their duty. He has urged me repeatedly to accept of a soft position with him as his Inspector—but I told him I preferred "the line." He will do anything for me I ask of him.

With best love to dear Mother and all I am in haste

Yr. affectionate son
Micajah Woods[40]

Lt. Col. John Floyd King did assume overall command of Early's artillery, but the horse artillery was placed in a battalion under Maj. William McLaughlin. The major's position was similar to Chew's in that the batteries under his command were dispersed among the cavalry brigades and did not fight as a battalion. Lurty's Battery would operate with Col. William L. Jackson's Brigade; Jackson's Battery would accompany Brig. Gen. John McCausland's Brigade; and McClanahan's Battery would remain with Brig. Gen. John D. Imboden's Brigade.

By the time Woods wrote his letter, another horse battery had joined Early's army. The Baltimore Light Artillery had been roughly handled at Yellow Tavern, and its subsequent service had been with Col. Bradley T. Johnson's Maryland Line, which was stationed in Richmond. When Johnson was sent west with the Maryland Battalion of cavalry, the Baltimore Light accompanied him. The command had fallen to Lt. John R. McNulty immediately after Yellow Tavern because of the absence of Capt. Wiley H. Griffin, who was still a prisoner of war, and Lt. William B. Bean, who was ill. However, Bean returned just prior to Early's move north, so the battery entered the campaign with its senior lieutenant in command.[41] Johnson assumed command of Jones's Cavalry Brigade. The Baltimore Light Artillery would operate with it.

Early's columns left Staunton on June 28. Lee's plan was about to unfold. For three years, the Confederates had heard the cries of "On to Richmond." Now they had a chance to shout, "On to Washington."

CHAPTER 29

To Washington and Back

"We brought our gun into position and threw shells into their very midst."

Jubal Early's army was not much to look at. The II Corps was greatly reduced in strength since the battles in the Wilderness and at Spotsylvania Court House. The men were ragged, dirty, and gaunt. Their Valley brethren were only slightly better off. They had seen some hard times as well. Yet the men all moved with a jaunty, if barefooted, step, as they sped up the Valley Turnpike. Few in number but mighty in spirit, they had chased Hunter from the Valley, and maybe they could chase Lincoln from Washington City. Optimism was rampant. The civilians along the pike rejoiced. They had seen enough of Sigel and Hunter. Now their boys were back and making the Federals run. There was much jubilation for old "Jubilee" Early.

As the Valley's most recent savior drove northward, Imboden's Cavalry Brigade, with McClanahan's Battery, was dispatched through Brock's Gap on a mission to destroy the Baltimore & Ohio Railroad bridge over the South Branch of the Potomac. The rest of the army continued up the turnpike and reached Winchester on July 2. The following day, Early moved on Martinsburg, where Breckinridge's old nemesis, Sigel, commanded a few regiments of cavalry and infantry. McCausland's Brigade swung west over the Little North Mountain, targeting the bridge over Back Creek and the Federal troops at North Mountain Depot. The hope was that he then could debouch from the mountains into the path of Sigel's retreat and gobble him up. One section of Jackson's Battery trotted along with McCausland's troopers.

The other pincers of Early's plan to trap Sigel was Brig. Gen. Bradley T. Johnson's Cavalry Brigade, which was sent toward Leetown. There the Confederates encountered some resistance from Col. James A. Mulligan's force of about 1,500 men and five guns.[1] At first Johnson drove the Federals back, but Mulligan counterattacked. Lt. William B. Bean and the Baltimore Light found themselves in a scrap.[2] A section of Jackson's Battery was also involved and suffered two casualties. Pvt. Marshall R. Black was mortally wounded, dying in Winchester on the tenth, and Pvt. Richard P. Price was hit in the foot. Johnson lost the ground he had gained and was pushed back on the advancing Confederate infantry under Maj. Gen. Robert E. Rodes and Maj. Gen. Stephen D. Ramseur. Their presence was enough to persuade Mulligan to retire toward Kearneysville.

Meanwhile, Sigel's cavalry clashed with advancing Confederate cavalry at Darkesville.[3] The fighting unnerved the Federal commander, and he decided to evacuate Martinsburg and retire to Harpers Ferry. This decision robbed McCausland of the chance to capture the fleeing Federals. He did manage to take some prisoners at North Mountain Depot, where the section of Jackson's Battery got themselves into the fight. While peppering the blockhouse to persuade the Federals to surrender, the gunners were peppered by the bluecoats, causing two casualties. Pvt. William S. Shilling died while undergoing amputation, and Pvt. John W. Hampton was severely wounded. Eventually Jackson's peppering won out, and McCausland captured two companies of the 135th Ohio National Guard.[4]

On July 4, Early threatened Harpers Ferry. Sigel had retreated across the Potomac on the third and had occupied Maryland Heights. Once again the Confederates' approach threw panic into the Federals, who abandoned the town on the night of the fourth. That same day saw Imboden arrive at the railroad bridge over the South Branch of the Potomac. He soon discovered that he did not have the strength to attack the bridge's defenses. McClanahan's Battery tried to rattle the defenders, who were holed up in a blockhouse, but to no avail. Unable to blast them out, Imboden chose not to waste his men in a fruitless attack and rode off toward Bath. The brigade would not rejoin Early until the ninth at Frederick, Maryland. When it did, its commander would be Col. George H. Smith. Imboden had contracted typhoid fever and was taken to Winchester.

McCausland's, Jackson's, and Johnson's Brigades crossed the Potomac at Shepherdstown on the fifth, with Jackson's, Lurty's, and Griffin's Batteries in tow. Early was now committed to an advance on Washington City and over the next several days slowly moved eastward. McCausland was sent to Hagerstown, where he extracted a "contribution of $20,000" with the help of a threatened bombardment by Jackson's guns.[5] Johnson's Brigade and Griffin's Battery occupied Boonsboro.[6] By the seventh, the cavalry was moving on Frederick. At 6:00 A.M., Johnson's Brigade ran into a portion of Lt. Col. David R. Clendenin's 8th Illinois Cavalry and a section of Capt. Frederic W. Alexander's Baltimore Battery under Lt. Peter Leary between Middletown and the Catoctin Mountains. Lt. William B. Bean unlimbered a section of the Baltimore Light Artillery, and Federal Baltimorians and Confederate Baltimorians dueled for the honor of the best battery in Baltimore.[7]

Initially, Bean had the advantage due to the longer range of his pieces—a circumstance that was a rarity for the Confederate artillery. But Clendenin slowly withdrew to the Catoctin Mountains and parked Leary's guns in the gap. Having the advantage of greater elevation, the Baltimore Battery was now able to cope with Bean's rifled guns. For five hours, Clendenin and Leary held Johnson at bay. Only the threat of being flanked pried the Federals from their position. Still, the bluecoats battled all the way back to the outskirts of Frederick, where Captain Alexander met Leary with a third gun and a supply of ammunition. Johnson was loath to use his artillery for fear of damaging the town and inflicting injury on its inhabitants. For a while, Bean remained in a commanding position south of the Hagerstown Pike unable to use his guns.[8] After enduring the enemy's fire for some time, Johnson at last gave Bean the command to open fire.[9] The artillery blasted away until dark, when Johnson withdrew to the Catoctin Mountains.[10]

July 8 saw the renewal of the contest between Johnson and Clendenin. The usual cavalry skirmishing was punctuated with a few charges, none of which brought about a favorable decision for either side. Bean's and Alexander's guns were silent, a condition that probably favored the Baltimore Light, as Alexander now had all six of his pieces at his disposal. In the end, Johnson again fell back to the mountains to await Early's infantry. McCausland spent part of the day at Hagerstown, having returned there from a foray to the Catoctin Mountains on the seventh, and then rode toward Frederick to rendezvous with Early. Jackson's guns had not fired a shot during the whole expedition.

The abandonment of Frederick by the Federals early on the ninth set the stage for the battle of Monocacy. Early pushed through the town and came face-to-face with a hastily gathered army under Maj. Gen. Lew Wallace along the Monocacy River. The Confederate commander had dispatched Johnson's Brigade and a section of Griffin's Battery under Lt. John R. McNulty on a raid to destroy the railroad near Cockeysville, Maryland, and, if feasible, to liberate the Confederate prisoners of war at Point Lookout.[11] The rest of Early's cavalry and horse artillery were somewhat scattered. Smith's Brigade with McClanahan's Battery had not yet rejoined the main army. The disposition of Jackson's Brigade and Lurty's Battery is unknown, but they may have been acting as a rear guard for the wagon train. McCausland's Brigade with Jackson's Battery took position on the army's extreme right.

The fighting along the banks of the Monocacy River proved to be short but bloody. McCausland's Brigade took an especially high number of casualties as it fought dismounted against Brig. Gen. James B. Ricketts's division of veterans. Jackson's Battery was positioned west of the river and could only fire at long range. It suffered no casualties. The day closed with Early's troops victorious but mauled. Wallace's stand against the odds bought the time that was needed to save Washington City. Early lost his campaign, if he ever had a chance of winning it, on the banks of the Monocacy River.

On July 10, the march resumed. The 62nd Virginia Mounted Infantry of McCausland's Brigade took the lead, with Lt. Carter Berkeley's section of McClanahan's Battery in support. The enemy made several stands, but each time, the 62nd dismounted and attacked, driving its opponents back. Berkeley could not maintain the pace and fell behind.[12] A final clash near Rockville ended the fighting for the day, with McCausland going into camp for the night. The next morning, the brigade and Jackson's Battery moved down the Georgetown Pike. Smith's Brigade with McClanahan's Battery marched down the Seventh Street Road. Jackson's Brigade and Lurty's Battery occupied Brookville and covered the left flank of Early's advance.

Colonel Smith's Brigade drove some enemy cavalry into defensive works along the Seventh Street Road. The gray cavalry then dismounted and went forward in skirmish order. General Early arrived in advance of his infantry and for a time harbored the hope that the works might be taken by a quick thrust. He called for Rodes's division, but before it could arrive, the Federals opened fire with their heavy artillery and demonstrated that any assault would entail considerable loss of life. The Seventh Street approach into the capital was blocked. The same proved to be true on the Georgetown Pike. McCausland pushed forward to the enemy's defensive works and even fired a few rounds from Jackson's guns to test the Federals' resolve. Pvt. Lewis C. Tickle was mortally wounded in this engagement. McCausland decided an attack was out of the question. Early concluded that his army had come to the end of its tether. It was time to go home. The retreat began on the night of the twelfth.

The decision to abandon the attempt to take Washington City was prompted in part by a dispatch from Brig. Gen. Bradley T. Johnson that contained the news that two corps from Grant's army had arrived in the capital. Johnson had accomplished part of his mission by burning the railroad bridge at Cockeysville on the tenth. Col. Harry Gilmor, at the head of a portion of the 1st Maryland Battalion, had also destroyed the railroad bridge over the Gunpowder River and captured two trains. While encamped on the night of the twelfth, a scout brought the news of the movement of the two Federal corps. Despite this knowledge, Johnson rode toward Point Lookout in an attempt to free the prisoners, but he was called back by a courier from Early. Johnson encountered a force of Federal cavalry at Beltsville. McNulty unlimbered and fired a few shots while the gray cavalry charged. The bluecoats remembered an appointment they had elsewhere and hastily retreated toward Washington. Johnson arrived at Silver Spring on the thirteenth to find the army in retreat and Jackson's cavalry hard-pressed by the 2nd Massachusetts Cavalry near Rockville. A charge by a squad of the 1st Maryland Cavalry routed the Bay Staters and relieved the pressure on Jackson, who was acting as the army's rear guard.[13]

Early's retreat was unmolested until the army reached Poolesville. Here a thrust by the 16th Pennsylvania Cavalry, supported by a section of Battery G, 1st Rhode Island Light Artillery, brought the Baltimore Light into action.[14] The fight proved to be brief, and the Confederates successfully crossed the Potomac into Virginia on July 14. After a day of rest, the army headed back to the Valley on the sixteenth. Near Purcellville, the column's wagon train was struck by Federal cavalry, which broke through Johnson's Brigade and captured a number of prisoners and wagons. Lieutenant Berkeley of McClanahan's Battery managed to unlimber a section of guns and open fire, only to have one of the pieces burst. The day had not gone well for Early or Berkeley.

By July 19, Early had brought his army across the Shenandoah River, where he felt it could be given time to regain its strength. The enemy, however, proved unwilling to let matters rest and advanced on several fronts. Sgt. Samuel T. Shank of McClanahan's Battery received orders to report to Berry's Ferry to assist the 62nd Mounted Infantry of Smith's Brigade in holding the crossing. Shank's superior, Lieutenant Berkeley, had been ordered to Staunton with the gun that had burst on the sixteenth, leaving Shank to uphold the honor of the battery. He was up to the task.

> On the morning [July 19] that Lieut. Berkeley was to start for Staunton an order was received for a commissioned officer and one gun to report to Col. [David B.] Lang, of the Sixty-Second Virginia Infantry, at Berry's Ferry for guard duty. Lieut. Berkeley told the officers in command that I could fill the place, as there would be nothing to do but lie around the ferry during the day. So he started to Staunton and I to the place designated, reaching there about 8 A.M. We were on the west side of the river, which is flanked by a low ridge of hills. The road to the ferry passes through a deep ravine of this ridge. Arriving here, I found that the enemy had thrown a skirmish line across the river, which had advanced far as the entrance to this ravine, and had just been driven back by our pickets, which consisted of only a few detachments of infantry, possibly in all one hundred men.
>
> I reported at once to Col. Lang, and he told me to select a position, and do the best I could. This was the only order I received during the day. I took my gun to the top of the hill on the south side of the ravine, and there had an opportunity for using it most effectively. On the opposite side of the river, about a mile distant, there was a stretch of bottomland literally covered with troops just in the act of crossing the river by wading. In a moment we brought our gun into position and threw shells into their very midst as rapidly as we could, until they sought shelter. During this time we had all in our own hands, as we were too far off to be reached with their smaller arms, and their artillery, it seems, had not arrived. In a short time, however, they had a battery of six rifle guns in position and opened fire on us at such a distance that we could not reach at all with our howitzer. As we could do no effective work for a while, we left the gun in position and retired behind the brow of the hill for protection. Their firing continued for some time, and whenever their infantry or cavalry would become visible I alone would load and fire our gun, not wishing to expose more than one man at a time. One or two others did this after me. After

> some time I inferred from their movements that they were preparing to charge across the river with their cavalry and capture our gun, thus opening the way for their army to cross the river.
>
> We then drew our gun by hand, not wishing to expose our horses, below the crest of the hill, limbered up and moved several hundred yards to the right, placed it in position again without being seen by the enemy, and waited developments. We had not long to wait, for soon the anticipated charge was made through the placid waters of the Shenandoah, and on through our feeble line of infantry, out through the ravine, then wheeled to the left up the ridge and over the very ground our gun had occupied all morning. Then at a short distance on their right we began firing, using first the shell with which the gun was loaded and then canister. We fired so rapidly into their midst that very few of them were able to recross the river to their friends. As soon as all this was over I went to where they had passed, and where our gun had been. Two men, whose horses had been shot, were crouching under some bushes like frightened birds. I walked up to them wholly unarmed and demanded their arms. They deliberately unbuckled their belts and gave me two new Colt's army revolvers, which had never been fired, and forty rounds of cartridges. . . . This was the last effort made to cross the river. . . . We remained upon the hill until night, then were relieved by others sent to our assistance.[15]

Despite Shanks's heroics at Berry's Ferry, Early was forced back toward Winchester after small actions on the nineteenth at Darkesville, Bunker Hill, Charles Town, Kabletown, and Ashby's Gap. Jackson's Battery participated in the fighting in the gap and suffered one casualty, Pvt. Henry Edison, Jr., who was wounded. The rout of Ramseur's division at Stephenson's Depot north of Winchester on the twentieth sealed the town's fate. Col. William L. Jackson's Brigade anchored Ramseur's right flank and, when the infantry broke and ran, covered the retreat. Lurty's Battery probably was present, but the part it played, if any, cannot be determined.

The Valley army ended up in Strasburg with its commander eager to redeem his position in the lower Valley. A skirmish at Kernstown on the twenty-third prompted Early to make a general advance the following day. A Federal force under the command of Maj. Gen. George Crook was met at Kernstown, outflanked, and beaten. Imboden's Brigade, with its commander once again leading it, and McClanahan's Battery participated in the battle. Johnson's Cavalry Brigade clashed with enemy cavalry on the Front Royal Road and drove them back.[16] Undoubtedly, the Baltimore Light Artillery contributed to the victory. Jackson's Brigade with Lurty's Battery guarded Early's left flank but was not engaged. Winchester was taken, and McCausland's Brigade with Jackson's Battery rejoined the army, having been in Front Royal since the twenty-second. The Federals were chased all the way to Martinsburg, where on the twenty-fifth, McCausland had a sharp engagement. Jackson's Battery got in a few licks before the Federals scurried toward the Potomac. By the twenty-sixth, Early's entire army was encamped at Martinsburg while his cavalry reached Williamsport. The opportunity was present for another thrust over the Potomac.

Jubal Early may have longed to take one more Confederate army across the river and into Pennsylvania, but it was not to be. The best he could do was mount a cavalry raid—specifically, a raid of retribution for the wanton destruction visited upon the citizens of the Valley by Hunter. The man chosen to lead the expedition was Brig. Gen. "Tiger John" McCausland. He would take his own brigade, that of Brig. Gen. Bradley T. Johnson, and Griffin's, Jackson's, and McClanahan's Batteries—a total of about 2,800 men.[17] The column crossed the Potomac on July 29 and arrived before Chambersburg on the morning of the thirty-first. A few rounds from one of the horse batteries announced to the residents that all was not well.[18] The occupation of the town soon followed.

McCausland made the required demand for a ransom, which was not met and was assumed to be an attempt to scare the populace. The refusal brought the order to burn the town. In this act, the horse artillery played no known part and, in fact, probably had not even entered the town. The entire occupation lasted only a short time, and McCausland was on his way before noon. His journey home began over the same route he had used to reach Chambersburg until he reached St. Thomas, when he continued west to McConnellsburg instead of turning south to Mercersburg.

The Confederates were soon being pressed by their old nemesis Brig. Gen. William W. Averell, who had been camped at Greencastle, a mere nine miles away from Chambersburg, when the town was burned. McCausland's column was led by Johnson's Brigade, which reached Hancock, Maryland, just after noon on the thirty-first. After resting, eating, and in some cases looting, the troopers' reverie was interrupted by gunfire as Averell once again clashed with the rear guard. An ironclad railroad car appeared, was greeted by fire from one of the horse batteries, and steamed back in the direction it had come, having taken two hits. But McCausland could not cross the Potomac River at this point because Averell's artillery commanded the ford. Instead, "Tiger John" rode westward toward Cumberland, Maryland, hoping that he could get his command across the river there.

The long trek home, now made even longer thanks to Averell's dogged pursuit, continued. There was one consolation—Averell's column, its horses and men thoroughly exhausted, remained in Hancock. However, if McCausland and his troopers believed themselves home free, they were in for a rude awakening. On August 1, about two miles east of Cumberland, the leading Confederate units ran into Col. Caleb Marker's 156th Ohio National Guards, a detachment of the 11th West Virginia Infantry under Maj. James L. Simpson, and Lt. John McAfee's section of Battery L, 1st Illinois Light Artillery. These troops were under the command of Maj. Gen. Benjamin F. Kelly, who was stationed in Cumberland.[19] A blast from the Federal battery was the Confederates' first intimation that their route to Cumberland would be disputed. Before long, McCausland arrived on the scene, placed four guns in position, including those of Jackson's Battery, and opened a sharp engagement that lasted until night fell. During the short fight, Sgt. James O. Choen of Jackson's Battery was mortally wounded. Under the cover of darkness, McCausland pulled back his men and took another road in the direction of Old Town, several miles downriver from Cumberland.[20]

Once again the Federals were one jump ahead of McCausland. Kelly had sent Col. Israel Stough's 153rd Ohio National Guards to block the road to Old Town. The Confederates clashed with them on the morning of the second. Johnson deployed his regiments and attacked. One of the battery's members left an account of the role played by Lieutenant McNulty's section of the Baltimore Light Artillery:

> At the dawn of day the enemy was discovered in line behind the crest of a range of hills between the canal and river, when McNulty was ordered to post his guns, and open the fight, whilst the cavalry dismounted and crossed the canal on a bridge hastily constructed by Captain Welsh of the First Maryland Cavalry when the enemy retired. But a more formidable obstacle then presented itself in the shape of an ironclad battery mounted on an engine upon the railroad, whilst the cars to which it was attached were loop-holed for musketry, and the banks of the railroad, which formed an excellent breastwork, was lined with infantry. A very strong block house that commanded every approach to the ford was also found strongly garrisoned.
>
> Colonel Harry Gilmor was at once ordered to carry the ford, which he attempted in most gallant style, but was unable to reach the opposite bank, owing to the dreadful enfilading fire opened upon him.
>
> Lieutenant McNulty was then directed to take position with his pieces, and open on the ironclad. Quickly moving his guns to an open field, and but two hundred yards from the enemy he unlimbered at this much exposed point, and called upon his best gunner, George McElwee, to bring his piece to bear upon the formidable looking mass of iron before him. The brave fellow, despite the shower of bullets to which he was exposed, coolly sighted his piece and fired, and when the smoke cleared away McNulty had the satisfaction of seeing the huge monster enveloped in steam, for the shot directed by the unerring aim of McElwee had pierced the boiler, and it lay a helpless wreck upon the track. His next shot was as effective, and entered one

> of the portholes, dismounting the guns and scattering death and destruction around, when the enemy along the bank broke and fled.
>
> But there was yet the blockhouse to dispose of before the command could resume its retreat, and minutes were becoming precious. An hour was consumed in discussing the matter before anything definite was determined upon, when Genl. Johnson suggested that an attempt be made to get a piece of the artillery across the river. The suggestion was instantly adopted, and under cover of the bank, though subjected to a severe fire, the piece was started over in a full run, and unlimbered in the river, and taken to its bank by hand, when, at the instant, a demand for the surrender of the blockhouse was complied with, and McCausland was safe.[21]

The gallant behavior of the men of the Baltimore Light, especially McAlwee, did indeed allow McCausland and his raiders, after a brief side trip to New Creek, to safely reach Moorefield and encamp on August 5.

While McCausland made good his escape over the Potomac, fate was planning a little surprise for him in the form of his tenacious adversary, Averell. The Federal cavalry commander had remained in Hancock to rest his weary brigade. There on August 3 he received reinforcements when Brig. Gen. Alfred N. A. Duffié's brigade arrived. The next day, Averell set out to find McCausland, taking 1,300 of his own men and 500 from Duffié. Knowledge of the Confederate retreat from New Creek toward Moorefield, along with the false information that McCausland was reinforced by Imboden's and Vaughn's cavalry, spurred Averell on to Romney, which he reached on the morning of August 6. Here he learned more about McCausland's route of march and later in the day captured a courier with an order that confirmed McCausland's presence in or near Moorefield. Ignoring the rumors that the Confederates had received additional troops, Averell determined to strike the raiders.

The bone-weary men of Johnson's Brigade were encamped on the north side of the South Branch of the Potomac, while McCausland's regiments were south of the river closer to Moorefield. Johnson's pickets were captured by Federals dressed as Confederates, and before any alarm could be raised, Averell's revenge-bent troopers were charging through the camp. The 1st and 2nd Maryland broke and scattered. The 36th Virginia managed to put up a fight, which gave Lieutenant McNulty time to load his two pieces with canister and turn them in the direction of the oncoming Federals. Just as the cannoneers of the Baltimore Light were about to punish the intruders, they were overwhelmed by another body of blue-coated cavalry that swept down on the section's flank. Somewhere in the melee that followed, McNulty's horse was killed beneath him, but its rider managed to escape. Not so for other members of the battery. Pvt. William C. Rogers took a cut across the nose from a saber and became a prisoner. Pvt. Joshua Hickman fell dead beside one of the guns.

Corp. George W. McAlwee, who had demonstrated his accurate gunnery at Old Town, was wounded and captured. He had plenty of company, as Corporals John Bunting and Albert Holland and Privates Martin Beane, Charles L. Beucke, J. Bukey, John A. Coleman, William A. Davis, Robert E. Fitzgerald, and Henry Wysong either threw up their arms in surrender or were run down and forced to yield. Both guns were captured as well. It was as black a day as the battery had seen since Yellow Tavern.

The Baltimore Light was not the only Confederate artillery to suffer significant losses in the surprise attack. Jackson's Battery felt the wrath of Averell's avengers as their camp was overwhelmed. Privates Stephen R. Deskins and John T. Woods were killed trying to save either their guns or themselves. Corp. John N. Smith, Jr., and Privates Wythe G. Bane, William L. Davidson, John B. Dawson, Alexander H. Elam, Thomas B. Monks, John Neel, Hezekiah Paul, Henry J. Saddler, William J. Thomas, Micajah A. Thorn, and J. N. B. Wilson suffered the humiliation of becoming prisoners.[22] Additionally, forty horses were lost to the battery, along with two guns.[23]

McClanahan's Battery also lost men in the catastrophe that engulfed McCausland's and Johnson's commands. Privates Abraham Burns, Michael J. Hinkles, David K. Landes, Henry Martin, and Samuel A. Wise were captured and started on their way to various Northern prison camps. Not until mid-March of 1865 would they be exchanged. The battery was fortunate that it did not lose as many men as Griffin's or Jackson's Batteries. Nevertheless, McClanahan's casualties would be enough to always remind the captain and his men of the near disaster visited upon them that early August morning.

Back in the Valley, Early had demonstrated vigorously to distract the Federals from McCausland's raiders, even to the point of crossing the Potomac on August 4. Jackson's Cavalry and Lurty's Battery were involved in the crossing, taking a position near Sharpsburg.[24] Vaughn's Cavalry occupied Hagerstown, while Imboden's Brigade put on a show by advancing toward Harpers Ferry.[25] The whole charade was over on the sixth, when the elements of Early's army recrossed the river. The following day, Early's troops pulled back to Martinsburg. These two days held no more significance for Early or his men than many other days. But they were to be days of great importance to the little army and its commander, as they were soon to discover. For on August 6, a new commander was placed in charge of the Federal forces in and around the Valley. His orders were to cleanse the Valley of Early and make it a place of desolation so that Robert E. Lee could no longer use it as a secondary theater of operations or as a source of supplies. On August 7, those orders were transformed into action. Maj. Gen. Philip Sheridan had come to the Valley.

CHAPTER 30

Stalemate at Petersburg

"Boys, give them Hell!"

The titanic struggles between Grant and Lee from the Rapidan to the James and between Sigel, Breckinridge, Hunter, and Early in the Valley were not the only offensive operations Grant had coordinated in Virginia in the spring of 1864. In tune with his plan to pressure the Confederacy from all sides, Grant had ordered Maj. Gen. Benjamin F. Butler with his Army of the James to advance up its namesake river and threaten either Richmond or Petersburg, depending on what circumstances it encountered. In as excellent a demonstration of bungling as could be found in military history, Butler managed to get himself bottled up on the Bermuda Hundred peninsula between the Appomattox and James Rivers. Gen. Pierre G. T. Beauregard's aggressiveness had proven too much for the North's most infamous political general. For all intents and purposes, Butler was out of the war, or so it seemed.

The situation south of the James changed dramatically in the early days of June 1864. After the bloodbath at Cold Harbor on the third, Grant formulated a strategy that would allow him to break contact with Lee and cross the James River. He orchestrated two diversions, Sheridan's raid toward Charlottesville and Butler's breakout from the Bermuda Hundred. These, along with a feint at Richmond by elements of his own army, would hopefully occupy Lee while Grant went about his real business. If all went according to plan, Grant would be across the James, Sheridan would link up with Hunter in Charlottesville, and Butler would attack and maybe capture Petersburg. Success on this scale might bring a swift end to the war. It was not to be. Hampton ended Sheridan's raid at Trevilian Station, well short of Charlottesville, and Butler, though he came within a hair's breadth of capturing Petersburg, was defeated by a combination of incompetence among his officers and unequaled courage and determination among the city's defenders. Among the heroes who saved Petersburg were the officers and men of the last battery of Confederate horse artillery to be formed in the eastern theater of the war.

Butler's plan called for the use of a pontoon bridge that had been laid over the Appomattox to City Point. Portions of Brig. Gen. Edward W. Hinks's division of infantry and Brig. Gen. August V. Kautz's division of cavalry would be combined with troops from Maj. Gen. Quincy A. Gillmore's X Corps to make up the attacking force. Butler permitted himself to be talked into allowing Gillmore to command the expedition, a decision that would haunt both Butler and Grant. Once across the river, the force would split, with Gillmore advancing directly toward Petersburg while Kautz and Hinks swung farther south. The latter was to attack up the Jordan's Point Road while Kautz continued on and launched an assault up the Jerusalem Plank Road. The plan was complicated, and Gillmore, sadly, was too simple a man to execute it.

Almost immediately the fine strategic tapestry began to unravel. Gillmore encountered the Confederate pickets and took an hour driving them back to their defensive works. Hinks reached his jumping-off point and moved along the Jordan's Point Road until he, too, came up against the Confederate entrenchments. Here in the face of Brig. Gen. Henry A. Wise's skeleton force of barely 1,000 men and a few scattered artillery pieces, the Federal drive ground to a halt. Gillmore felt he could not succeed in any assault on the works without Kautz's attack along the Jerusalem Plank Road. Hinks sent a message to Gillmore that he could advance no farther unless Gillmore attacked in unison with him. Gillmore ordered Hinks to await Kautz's attack, which he expected within a short time. The Federals' first opportunity to take the city ended with Gillmore and Hinks staring at the formidable Confederate works manned by a few hundred men.

Despite the failures of Gillmore and Hinks, the Petersburg defenders still had to deal with Kautz. Maj. Fletcher H. Archer's company of local militia, about 125 old men and boys from the city, held the Jerusalem Plank Road defenses.[1] Kautz ordered a mounted charge, which was met by a ragged volley that toppled a few of the blue-coated riders to the ground. The rest fell back. Kautz dismounted his men and formed them into a line that overlapped both of the militia's flanks and slowly moved forward. Behind the militia, Brig. Gen. Raleigh E. Colston arrived with one artillery piece and its six-man crew. A renewed Federal advance, to the accompaniment of a section of 8th New York Battery, enveloped Archer's and Colston's men and their lone gun. Outflanked and pounded by artillery, the thin line of old men and boys held on until almost surrounded and then fell back fighting, leaving over half their number in killed, wounded, or prisoners to the Federals. The price had been high, but the two hours gained were just enough to save the city—with a little help from the horse artillery.

To the northeast, Gillmore and Hinks waited for the sound of Kautz's attack. When it finally came, neither general budged. Recognizing that the real threat to Petersburg was the Federal cavalry on the Jerusalem Plank Road, Beauregard sent reinforcements to Wise. At the head of the column galloped

Capt. Edward Graham's Petersburg Artillery. Attached to Brig. Gen. James Dearing's Brigade of cavalry, which followed in its wake, Graham's Battery had been converted to horse artillery a scant two months earlier. Now, as it thundered across the bridge over the Appomattox River, the fate of Petersburg hung on every hoofbeat. Graham made what appeared a grievous error when he led his command down the wrong street, but the gallant captain whirled his guns around and retraced his steps.[2] In so doing, he almost ran down a lady who was attempting to cross the street. Angered with himself for making a wrong turn and with the woman for obstructing his way, Graham cried, "Get out of the way! Damn the women! Run over them if they don't get out of the way."[3]

Graham's drivers and mounted cannoneers missed the woman, though in doing so, there was a decrease in their frantic pace. The teams of lathered horses, with their guns and caissons trailing behind them, careened onto Sycamore Street and continued their mad dash.[4] The battery clattered past the Southern Female College, where the young ladies of the school stood on the porch waving their handkerchiefs. Not even Pelham had been so fortunate as to have the opportunity of saving the day before so lovely an audience. A cheer arose from the throats of the onrushing gunners and drivers in answer, but in a moment they were past the school, and thoughts turned to the business at hand.

As Graham emerged from the street onto Reservoir Hill, he could see the Federals in the valley below advancing in two columns. Kautz had halted his dismounted men and waited until he could mount "a squadron or two" before following up his rout of the militia.[5] The delay was fatal. Graham wasted little time in placing his guns—two just south of the reservoir and two between Sycamore and Jefferson Streets at the edge of town. He gave but one order when the guns were loaded: "Boys, give them hell."[6] The blast that echoed across the valley below, accompanied by a ragged volley from what was left of the militia, brought Kautz's cavalry up short.[7] Looking up at the hill, the Federals could see that they faced more than militia. Dearing's troopers had dismounted and were forming a line of battle in support of the artillery and the militia. The Federals drew back, seeking cover from the fire. For the second time in a month, Butler had lost an opportunity to capture Petersburg.

Graham's timely arrival had resulted from a series of fortuitous circumstances: Gillmore's and Hinks's lack of aggressiveness, Beauregard's recognition that Kautz was the main threat to the city, the gallant resistance of the old men and boys of Petersburg, the rapidity of Graham's and Dearing's movement, and Kautz's failures of command. In the end, the shock of hearing Graham's blast of defiance from Reservoir Hill tipped the scales in the Confederates' favor. Throughout the war, the horse artillery made many contributions to the victories gained by Southern arms. A reasonable argument could be made that Graham's initial volley of four guns at Petersburg on June 9, 1864, was the most significant.

Though Petersburg once again had been saved, Grant's crossing of the James in mid-June posed another threat to the city's safety. Maj. Gen. William F. "Baldy" Smith's XVIII Corps, which had previously been detached from Butler's command to assist Grant north of the James, was returned to the south side of the river and given the advance of yet a third thrust by Butler at Petersburg. For many of the men in the ranks of Kautz's cavalry and Hinks's infantry who augmented Smith's Corps, there was a sense of déjà vu about the whole operation. The Federal cavalry pushed forward on the City Point Road and at about 8:00 A.M. collided with their old adversaries from June 9—Graham's Battery and Dearing's Brigade.

The Confederates put up such stiff resistance that Kautz deployed some dismounted men to occupy the graycoats and then detoured around Dearing's right and drove up the Jordan's Point Road. Some outer works were successfully assailed, but once the main works loomed ahead, Kautz stopped his advance to reconnoiter. Smith, trailing behind the cavalry, had no desire to attack what he considered strong entrenchments without a reconnaissance. As on the ninth, delay and luck allowed the Confederates time to bring additional troops to bear on the threatened point. Once more Petersburg survived.

Over the next few days, the Confederates strengthened their position, and Lee, at last convinced that the vast majority of Grant's army was south of the James, crossed portions of the Army of Northern Virginia to deal with the rising threat to Richmond via Petersburg and the railroad lifelines that passed through the city. Grant, too, was very much aware that the railroads were the key to destroying Lee's army and taking Richmond. He wasted little time in maneuvering toward them.

The first target was the Petersburg & Weldon Railroad. Slowly but steadily, Grant stretched forth a tentacle from his vast host in an effort to cut the closest of Lee's supply lines. Maj. Gen. David B. Birney, temporarily commanding the II Corps in place of Winfield S. Hancock, was ordered to envelop the Confederate position on the Federal left flank.[8] This move would bring Birney's troops within striking distance of the railroad. On June 21, Brig. Gen. Francis C. Barlow's division dutifully set out to fulfill this mission.

Guarding that portion of the Confederate flank in the vicinity of the Davis farm was the cavalry brigade of newly promoted Brig. Gen. Rufus Barringer. His command consisted of the 1st, 2nd, 3rd, and 5th North Carolina. Attached to the brigade was McGregor's Battery. The horse artillerymen had just crossed the James River a day or two earlier and had hoped for a little respite to recoup their strength. The hope proved vain when, early on the morning of the twenty-first, cavalry pickets brought word of the Federal advance. Barringer took steps to counter what he viewed as a threat to the railroad, placing McGregor's Battery in position near the Davis house and throwing the 1st, 2nd, and 3rd North Carolina into the thick undergrowth. No battle line was formed, only a heavy cloud of skirmishers. The 5th North Carolina was ordered to support McGregor, and all settled down to await the enemy.

Barlow's troops pushed through the maze of scrub oak and pine with ever-increasing trepidation. They had no idea of what lay ahead, and when they at last brushed up against Barringer's line, their nerves were at the breaking point. The Confederates opened with a volley, and McGregor let loose with a blast from his guns.[9] The rout was on. Barlow was aghast to see his men streaming back in confusion toward the security of their original position.[10] Try as Barlow might, nothing stopped them until they had reached their old rifle pits. Here the bluecoats rallied and managed to throw back a brief assault, which Barringer launched on the entrenchments. After the repulse, the fighting died away to intermittent skirmishing.

The Confederates had successfully thwarted Barlow's golden opportunity to seize a section of the Petersburg & Weldon Railroad. With a single brigade of cavalry, Barringer had claimed a victory over three infantry brigades from one of the Federals' finest corps. McGregor's role, though limited by the terrain to his initial blast and possibly a few additional rounds, had been vital. Coming as it did on the heels of the volley from the skirmishers, the artillery's fire magnified the danger in the minds of the enemy and contributed to their demoralization. For the moment, the railroad was safe in Confederate hands.[11]

With his infantry checkmated, Grant turned to his cavalry. He decided to launch a cavalry raid against not one, but three of Lee's crucial rail supply lines: the Petersburg & Weldon Railroad, the Southside Railroad, and the Richmond & Danville Railroad. Brig. Gen. James H. Wilson, who commanded the 3rd Division of cavalry under Sheridan, would lead the expedition. The fact that Sheridan had not yet rejoined the army meant that to bolster Wilson's force, troopers would have to be pulled from Butler's Army of the James, so Kautz's division was assigned to Wilson. The Federal cavalry, consisting of 5,500 men and twelve guns, set out on June 22. Though they met with no Confederate cavalry or infantry to bar their way, a brigade of Maj. Gen. W. H. F. "Rooney" Lee's cavalry division and Dearing's Brigade did start in pursuit.[12] Lee's leading squadrons stung the rear of Wilson's column at Reams's Station on the Petersburg & Weldon Railroad. Unable to do any real damage, Lee swung away from the Federals and after a hard march caught Wilson at Blacks & Whites near Nottoway Court House on the twenty-third. A seesaw fight erupted. Col. George H. Chapman's Brigade drove Lee back, but oncoming reinforcements allowed Lee to counterattack and in turn push Chapman back to the fight's starting point.

Graham's and McGregor's Batteries were in the thick of the action. Graham quickly found himself in a predicament. His cavalry support was driven back, and with the enemy closing in, he tried to save his guns. Two limbered and escaped, but the other section was riddled. Pvt. Charles R. Hargrave was killed. Privates Walter H. Saunders and George Bauer suffered mortal wounds. Pvt. Stephen Black survived a horrible wound, having two ribs torn out. Privates Joseph P. Bailey and Lewis N. McCargo also were wounded. Sgt. William J. Acree had his horse killed beneath him. The guns had to be abandoned, but the teams were saved.[13] The two pieces stood ghostlike on the field between the two lines until Lee's counterattack reclaimed them.[14]

McGregor's Battery did not escape entirely unscathed. Lt. Richard Shreve received a serious wound while sitting on his horse with one of the sections of the battery. Not being able to travel, he was left behind at the home of Freeman Epes when Lee moved out on the morning of the twenty-fourth.[15]

Wilson and Kautz rode on to the bridge over the Staunton River near Roanoke Station, which they reached on the twenty-fifth. Along the way, they destroyed large sections of the Richmond & Danville Railroad. The bridge was held by about 900 militia, regular, and convalescent troops with six cannons under the command of Capt. Benjamin L. Fairnholt of the 53rd Virginia Infantry. The stubborn resistance of Fairnholt and Lee's attack on his rear forced Wilson to break off the engagement and turn for home. He had a long way to go, and other forces were gathering to assure that he didn't make it.

On June 27, while Wilson's raiders rested and fed both man and beast, Wade Hampton received orders from Gen. Robert E. Lee to proceed to Stony Creek Station on the Petersburg & Weldon Railroad in the hope of blocking the Federals' escape route. Hampton requested that infantry be sent to Reams's Station and that Fitz Lee's cavalry take position near that place. The trap was closing on Wilson, who was not completely unaware that his undoing was being plotted, though he believed that Hampton was not yet on the scene. In actuality, Hampton reached the station on the twenty-eighth, where he rendezvoused with Brig. Gen. John R. Chambliss's Brigade of Rooney Lee's division. Scouts were sent out and returned with the information that Wilson was near Sappony Church. Hampton determined to strike him.

The fighting erupted with the driving in of the Confederate pickets near the church by Col. John B. McIntosh's Brigade. They in turn were brought up short by Chambliss's Brigade, which dismounted and counterattacked. Lt. Col. William J. Crawley led his Holcombe Legion infantry into the fight in support of Chambliss. The lines stalemated. Wilson concluded that it would be best to pass around Hampton and consequently ordered Chapman's Brigade to reinforce McIntosh while Kautz detoured toward Reams's Station. After dark, Wilson deployed Capt. William M. Maynadier's Battery K, 1st U.S. Artillery, and Lt. William N. Dennison's Battery A, 2nd U.S. Artillery, to bolster his dismounted men. Hampton answered by ordering Maj. Roger P. Chew to bring up the only artillery he had,[16] a section of Graham's Battery commanded by Graham himself.[17] Chew and Graham got the most out of the two pieces,[18] and Hampton acknowledged, "These guns were well served and rendered me great assistance."[19]

Hampton was willing to renew the battle on the morning of the twenty-ninth and attacked with Chambliss in front and Brig. Gen. Thomas L. Rosser's and Brig. Gen. Matthew C. Butler's brigades on Chapman's left flank. The enemy's works were taken with ease, convincing Hampton that Wilson had taken the road to Reams's Station. Hampton pivoted and retraced his hoofprints to Stony Creek Station to cut off any attempt by Wilson to cross the railroad below the station by using the Halifax Road. Butler rode off for Malone's Crossing, and the other brigades were dispatched to other roads leading to the Halifax Road. Wilson was encountered at Rowanty Creek near the Perkins' house.

Confusion reigned for a time. Part of Wilson's column tried to reach the bridge over Rowanty Creek but was met by parts of the 9th and 10th Virginia. The remainder of the 10th Virginia charged another group of the enemy, just as a third column appeared. These Federals debouched from a byroad and delivered a volley into the Confederate flank at the time Hampton and one of Graham's guns was passing. Hampton whirled and yelled, "Unlimber that gun." The threat proved enough. The Federals surrendered.[20] Some of the bluecoat cavalry began to break up, with small groups riding away in what was perceived a safe direction. The remainder continued on to Reams's Station, where they found Kautz in another fight with still more gray cavalry and infantry as well.

As Wilson's troopers were fighting Hampton for their lives, Kautz reached Reams's Station, only to find his way blocked by Confederate infantry and Fitz Lee's cavalry. The horse artillery had been unable to keep pace with the cavalry because of the poor condition of its horses. However, a number of the men rode ahead of the guns and joined various cavalry units so that they could participate in the fighting. Among them was Maj. James Breathed. Pvt. Henry H. Matthews recorded what followed:

> The horse artillery did not have much chance to distinguish itself on this occasion, but individual members of Breathed's [Johnston's] Battery when they found it impossible to keep up with the flying Yankees followed with the cavalry and were in at the death. I [Matthews] was one of those individuals who took advantage of the situation to join the cavalry pro tem. Breathed when he found his artillery could not be of any use placed the artillery near Stony Creek, joining his fortunes with the 6th Virginia Cavalry, who were always glad to see him, continuing with them until he was shot down at the head of the regiment.[21] His wound was a very severe one, being hit in the stomach by a pistol ball. . . .
>
> E. H. O'Brien states that he and Corporal Al Hopkins rode on after the cavalry, as did the others. We had not seen Breathed up to this time, but knew he would give a good account of himself when we did see him. After galloping down the road a mile or two we saw a small group standing near the road. On reaching them we discovered our much loved Breathed lying on the ground severely wounded, his old battery around him as if to receive his dying benediction. His sufferings were intense and as we gazed on our hero we thought his

> hours were few: that [in] but a short time his soul would go to meet his commanders, Gen. J. E. B. Stuart and the gallant Pelham. As we bent over him he said, "Boys, they have got me this time." While we were trying to comfort him Surgeon Leigh,[22] who, after making an examination, told Breathed that the wound was not fatal, and that, by good care and nursing he would be able to worry the Yankees a good many times yet. The ball had not penetrated the bowels but was lodged in the walls of the stomach. This encouraging diagnosis cheered Breathed very much. An ambulance was procured and in it we placed him. He ordered O'Brien and Hopkins to ride on as he had heard that some of the enemy's wagons had been captured, and they could be of service there. This shows the spirit of the man. Badly wounded as he was his thoughts were [on] how to help the cause he loved so well. Riding two miles further on we found two captured cannons which were turned on the skedaddling Yankees.[23]

Breathed was the second major of horse artillery to be wounded while with a cavalry regiment, Pelham being the first. Had the guns been able to keep up, Breathed undoubtedly would have remained with them and not have been lost to the battalion for the time necessary to recover from his wound. But at least he recovered. His loss would have been felt almost as deeply as that of Pelham, his mentor.

The combined forces of Mahone, Hampton, and Fitz Lee proved too much for Wilson's and Kautz's troopers to handle. Fatigued from their long march, the Federals had not prepared for Hampton's strong counterattack at Sappony Church. Wilson was caught by surprise, as he did not believe Hampton was anywhere near him. Kautz's run-in with Mahone and Fitz Lee had an equivalent effect on him and his men. Still, the bluecoats put up enough of a fight to hold the Confederates in check until midafternoon. By then, Wilson knew it was time to save as many of his men as he could. He gave orders to abandon all wagons, ambulances, and guns, and ordered his horse artillery to fight a rear-guard action until McIntosh's Brigade, the last in his column, could get clear of the field.[24] Hampton and Fitz Lee continued a vigorous pursuit, but by dint of sheer grit and a little luck, Wilson got what was left of his command back to Grant's army. Though Kautz became separated from Wilson, he still managed to save about two-thirds of his men.

The only Confederate horse artillery praised for its part in the actions against the Wilson-Kautz raiders was Graham's Battery. Hampton wrote in his report, "Captain Graham, who had a section of his battery with me, did good service, and he was well supported by his command."[25] Its performance on June 9 at Petersburg, though significant, had not been witnessed by either the cavalry or the horse artillery of the Army of Northern Virginia. In this sense, Graham's Battery was still an unknown to Chew, Breathed, and the other batteries. After proving their worth at Nottoway Court House and Sappony Church, the men of Graham's Battery could take their place in the battalion with their heads held high.

In the days following the victory over Wilson and Kautz, the batteries of the horse artillery battalion that had not participated in the victory over the raiders began to rejoin their cavalry comrades below Petersburg. An inspection of McGregor's Battery conducted by Capt. John Esten Cooke illustrates the overall condition of the batteries at this time.

> HDQRS. ARTILLERY, ARMY OF NORTHERN VIRGINIA,
> July 4, 1864.
>
> Brig. Gen. W. N. PENDLETON,
> Commanding Artillery, Army of Northern Virginia:
>
> GENERAL: I have the honor to report that I this day inspected McGregor's battery, Stuart horse artillery, which was detached at the time of my last inspection and not included in the report. The condition of the battery does not materially differ from that of the rest of the battalion. The horses are broken down by severe marching, and many of them are badly galled on back and shoulders; but they are evidently improving from the rest, and I think will be fit in a few days for active service again, unless movements are uncommonly rapid and arduous. These and the horses of the battalion generally are excellent animals and only require rest. They are properly groomed and get full feed of oats and about five pounds of corn. Captain McGregor is using all his available transportation to haul oats.
>
> The guns and ammunition are in good order; the harness and accouterments, especially the saddles and bridles of the cannoneers, in bad order. The saddles were originally of the bad Jennifer pattern and being now nearly worn out are ruinous to the horses. All articles of this description were inspected and condemned and a certificate left for Lieutenant [Alexander R.] Boteler [Jr.], ordnance officer, who will be able to procure the excellent new saddle of the Alleghany pattern now made by the Ordnance Department, and such harness, &c., as are needed to supply deficiencies. Thomson's and Hart's batteries have moved with the quartermaster's train to a point on the Dinwiddie Court-House road about ten miles from Petersburg. McGregor's battery will probably move to the same place today or tomorrow.
>
> Very respectfully, your obedient servant,
> JNO. ESTEN COOKE,
> Captain and Assistant Inspector-General.[26]

Cooke's observation that the horses of the battalion were "broken down by severe marching" did not stop the high command from moving some of the batteries around as needed, however. Thomson's Battery had crossed the James River on June 26 and the Appomattox the following day, camping about one mile south of Petersburg.[27] On the twenty-eighth, the battery moved to a point five miles southwest of the city on the Southside Railroad.[28] Once camp was established, Pvt. Charles McVicar sat down and penned a letter to his beloved sister:

> Dinwiddie Co. Tuesday 28th/64
> Thomson's Battery Chew's Battalion
> of Horse Artillery Halted on the Southside
> of Petersburg Va
>
> Dear Sister
>
> I received yours of the 3rd on the 24th. Oh how happy it made me to hear from you all. I should have written before but knowing that the Yanks were passing through the valley and us marching daily I saw no opportunity to forward a letter but had commenced to write one the day before I received yours to Mother. I have mailed that in Petersburg.
>
> Yesterday the enemy were shelling the city with heavy siege guns as we passed through. The lower portion of the city has been deserted. Several woman & children have been killed by shell. Grant—the inhuman Monster—commenced shelling the city without giving a moment's warning to any one. Petersburg was previous to the war about 20,000 population. The Appomattox River runs through the city.
>
> Day before yesterday, Katie, I went around the Capitol square as we were passing through Richmond. Washington's Monument is a beautiful structure eight-square. His statue mounted on a superb steed on the monument. Also the statues of Henry Mason & Jefferson. The statues are all composed of Brass. It is a magnificent sight. I wish you had been there to witness some of the grandeur of Richmond.
>
> We crossed the James, passing through the town of Manchester down along the south side to Petersburg. The roar of artillery is awful. I was on guard last night and heard the firing through the night. It makes no difference now. Night affords no rest to the soldier. He builds and repairs breastworks and fights alternately night and day.
>
> I reached the Battery after an adventurous furlough on the 31st May. Have been in 4 heavy battles and am as yet spared by a merci-

ful God. Our loss in one of those engagements was three killed and five wounded. Katie I met with a sad loss last night my mare was stolen. She was getting in fine order. Was [ap]praised at 1100 dollars, but I would not have taken 1500 dollars for she was getting to be a perfect beauty. I may find her yet.

Katie things cannot last long. It will be for weal or woe in a very short time. It used to be that they measured battles by the hour but now it is by the month or campaign. I do not know of a day since the 4th of May that has not witnessed a scene of action with some portion of the army. We have killed, wounded, and taken prisoner over 100,000. Now this campaign. If we are conquered it will be by the force of numbers nothing else. I have just received a letter from Lissa. You have seen her ere this as she started home on the 23rd.

[Pvt. Edward D.] Bowly, [Pvt. Luther W.] Kohlhousen, [Pvt.] Phillip [W.] Boyd, and [Pvt. David] Henry Deahl here & well. Tell Mrs. Marstella that [Pvt.] William [Marstella] is at Charlottesville at Hospital. He had the diarrhea. [Pvt. Anthony] Beale Burgess was killed by my side at Denny's Store [Trevilian Station] in Louisa County on the 12th. George is well & hearty. We are all completely wore out from loss of sleep marching night and day.

Give my love to Grandma, Grandfather, and all of them. Kiss Katie McCann for me. Tell Marion that she must not feel slighted at me for not writing for I am too near wore out to do anything. Kiss the children for me. Tell them that they must all learn their Books that Charlie will be home this winter to see them and my pet, Henry, tell him that I say he must learn to read by the time I get there. Katie try and improve your writing. You are far more deficient in that than anything else. My regards to all inquiring friends. I have not written to Mata Lewis since I left. I wrote her a note when I was down. I must close

Your Brother
Charles William McVicar

God bless you all write often[29]

McVicar may have been worn out, but that did not mean he or his battery-mates could expect a long rest. On July 3, Thomson moved his battery toward Dinwiddie Court House, which it passed on the fourth. By the next day, the battery was encamped on the Nottoway River, one mile from where the Petersburg & Weldon Railroad crossed the river. Its assignments over the following twenty-four days included picket duty, charcoal making, and recruiting the battery's horses.[30] Private McVicar wrote to his sister again on July 18 to let her know he wasn't doing much of anything:

Camp near Stony Creek Station Sussex County Va
Thomson's Battery July 18th/64

Dear Sister,

There is nothing of importance going on in this vicinity. We are doing nothing comparatively speaking. I just came off picket last evening. We were down in Prince George Co. We are getting along very well here, and there would be general satisfaction if we were north of the James River. Grant "has or is" falling back from Petersburg is generally believed but not confirmed. They were shelling the city last night heavily. It is almost impossible for a man to raise his head above the breastworks near the city and live. To place a hat on a ramrod and elevate it above the breastwork nine chances out of ten a bullet will be sent through it immediately, so you see our infantry has no enviable position along the front.

Our cavalry have succeeded beyond the most sanguine expectations this campaign. Their battles have been principally executed in regular infantry style. This has been undoubtedly the most severe and vigorous campaign the world has ever known. How it will end I cannot form an idea but hope for the best is my way. God grant that this fall and winter may terminate the struggle in our favor is the hope and prayer of every soldier. It is the general opinion that it will.

Katie how I would love to be at home now to feel that I was free among you all once more would be happiness indeed. Yet I must forbear wishing and forego that pleasure for five months at least. We will surely get paid for the greater portion of the season by that time. I want to square up with the company before I attempt to come home again and intend to stay awhile Yank or no Yank, so you can prepare the cavity upstairs for my reception on Christmas if I live and nothing happens I will be there. I often have a line drawn in imagination, of course, eight in number but oftener seven, Mother, Katie, Marrion, Bob, Minnie, my pet Henry, & Ashby. Look at them all hope they are all well and getting along well. Father, I often see him through my minds eye and wish him well, 'tis all that I can do but then sleep vanishes the dreams that imaginations conjure up and morning brings back the regular duty of a soldier and that duty is to do anything no telling what—he does not do.

Katie I cannot describe this country to you definitely. Suffice to say it is hot, yes, to suffocation almost. No rain since I have been here. Crops are almost burnt up. Thickets of endless pines, swamp and marshes, on all sides. Tell mother here is half dozen pipe stems for her from Sussex county. Katie you have been scolding me about not writing. Now this is my sixth letter while I have received but two. Where is Gen. Early at present? Enlighten us. We are all anxi-

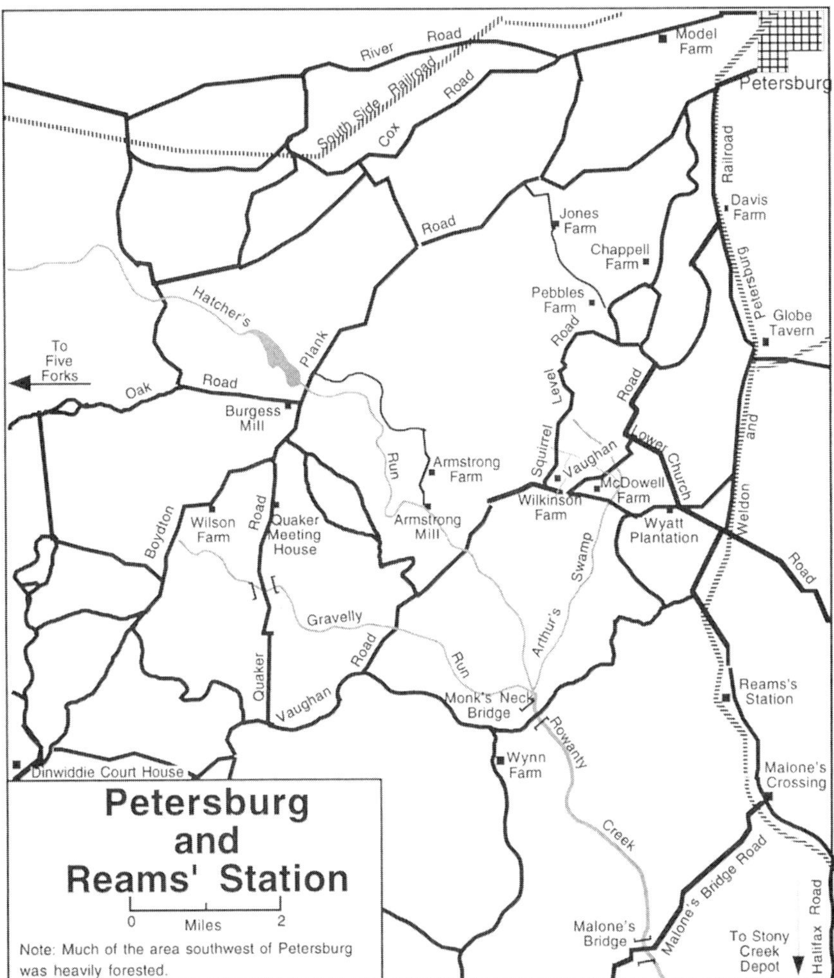
Petersburg
and
Reams' Station
0 Miles 2
Note: Much of the area southwest of Petersburg was heavily forested.
River Road
South Side Railroad
Cox Road
Model Farm
Petersburg
Railroad
Davis Farm
Jones Farm
Chappell Farm
Pebbles Farm
Road
Petersburg
Globe Tavern
Hatcher's
Plank
To Five Forks
Oak
Road
Burgess Mill
Level
Squirrel
Road
and
Run
Armstrong Farm
Vaughan
McDowell Farm
Lower Church
Wilkinson Farm
Weldon
Wilson Farm
Boydton
Road
Quaker Meeting House
Armstrong Mill
Wyatt Plantation
Road
Swamp
Arthur's
Gravelly
Road
Run
Quaker
Vaughan
Monk's Neck Bridge
Rowanty
Reams's Station
Wynn Farm
Dinwiddie Court House
Malone's Crossing
Creek
Malone's Bridge Road
Malone's Bridge
To Stony Creek Depot
Halifax Road

ety to hear from that quarter. Johnny Magson will give you all the particulars. Well, I must close. Kiss them all for me. My respects for Maggie and Jennie. What has become of Aunt Mary and Ann Haymaker? Are they still living you never mention anything about them?

Charlie[31]

McVicar was not the only artilleryman in the battalion with little to do during these warm, muggy days of mid-July 1864. The men in the other batteries took full advantage of the first real break in the fighting since the early days of May.

Lt. Lewis T. Nunnelee of Shoemaker's Battery received orders to bring "Company Q" to the front and rejoin the battery. After a march of four days, on July 6 they reached the battalion's camp on the farm of William G. Wynn, five miles from Reams's Station. Nunnelee's batterymates had arrived only a couple days before, having spent a few days camped near Petersburg to rest the horses. Lt. Charles R. Phelps of Shoemaker's Battery had been settled into his quarters for several days when he wrote to his aunt:

Head Quarters Shoemakers Battery, Stuart Horse Artillery
Near Petersburg July 10th 1864

Dear Aunt,

Your letters May 19th & June 26th handed me yesterday. We have been in camp near this place since we routed Wilson's Raiding. As the Yankee Cavalry have been so roughly handled in our late engagement with them, it is probable we may stay here several days more. In fact our horses are in such poor condition I do not think we can move.

On the 3rd I was sent to Petersburg with some captured guns to have them mounted, on my arrival there, found that the Yanks had destroyed the Government Shop by shelling & had to take them to Richmond. I met J. L. E. in Richmond and was glad to hear from home. I met in Richmond Dr. Ball's brother (who is ordered to Wytheville in Conscript Dept.) and had a very pleasant time with him. I told him to call and see you [when] he passed through Lynchburg.

I am glad to hear that the Yanks were not as bad to some of my friends as they usually are. I have heard several times they did nothing to Papa, and treated him very kindly. The people in Bedford & Cumberland can now realize what this war is, hope it will stimulate some of those who have been skulking and picking out soft places to shoulder their musket or at least give some aid to the Gov'nt in some way.

I have been in Petersburg several times. No one in the city, but a few men who can not get away—houses all closed & place looks deserted. I stayed one night with friend Capt. Nichols, no one at home but himself & two or three darkies. A shell or part of one came through the roof of the house into the room in which I slept—scattering the plastering, glass etc. all over the floor. Very little damage as yet has been done—only one fire has occurred—a great [many] houses have been struck, but only two or three deaths have occurred.

We are all speculating as to what will be Grant's next move. I do not think he will attack Uncle Bob, and he cannot stay in his present position long—unless we have heavy rains. His troops are suffering very much for want of water—fever etc. He may continue to shell Petersburg and may destroy the city. This will be all I think he will attempt. Mr. Early and his people are causing Ole Abe no little uneasiness—they are in doubt at what point he will turn up. I hope when he does so it will be with good effect. I am glad to hear that Uncle C. has become acquainted with my old friend Col. Coleman—glad to hear he is not seriously wounded. Sam was a great favorite with him. I have promised him one of his descendants.

This campaign has proved most too hard for me—tho I am in very good health. I only want rest & sleep to be all right again—you would not know me—my whiskers off. Shelton's clothes would be entirely too large for me. I weighed [word illegible] the 121 lbs. down weight. I am however picking up since I have been resting. You will oblige me by sending my boots by Express to Petersburg. Have them wrapped securely so I can send for them. Tell Uncle C. to send me some tobacco at same time. I will send in for them about Wednesday or Thursday next. Love to all in haste

Yours Dick[32]

Like Shoemaker's Battery, the other batteries of the horse artillery battalion were trying to recuperate both man and beast on the Wynn farm. Graham's, Hart's, and Johnston's Batteries marched in during the first week of July. McGregor's Battery bivouacked on the Armstrong farm, west of the Vaughn Road.[33] These camps were restful, with little to do except for the occasional picket duty until the closing days of the month, when once again the Federals bestirred themselves for another offensive.

It began with a bang. On the morning of July 30, the Federals exploded a mine under the Confederate works protecting Petersburg. The subsequent assault became bogged down in the crater left by the explosion, allowing the Confederates to seal the breach in their line and capture large numbers of the attacking troops. The horse artillery not only played no part in the momentous battle, but was nowhere near enough to witness the event. For some of the batteries, the peaceful days of camp life ended before the massive explosion. Just before midnight on July 28, orders were issued to prepare to march. McGregor's and Shoemaker's Batteries moved out at 1:00 A.M. to accompany Rooney Lee's division across the Appomattox and the James Rivers to face an enemy that was not there.[34] The Federal thrust across the James included Brig. Gen. David McM. Gregg's division of cavalry, which was what drew Rooney Lee north of the river. The cavalry and horse artillery were ordered back to their old camps on the thirty-first.[35]

McGregor's Battery returned to the Jones farm near the Boydton Plank Road, about three miles southwest of Petersburg. Pvt. David Cardwell of the battery gave an account of an incident that occurred about this time:

> One hot afternoon our battery was ordered into camp near Jones's farm. When we had spread our blankets and unsaddled—that was all we had to do, as we had no tents—some of the boys went out to see what the neighborhood afforded in the way of something to eat. Very soon one of them returned with information that Mr. Jones's watermelon crop had not been harvested, but lay in full view, and that the ground was fairly covered with luscious melons. The fellow who brought the news was asked why he did not bring in a sample, when he informed us that there was a guard over the patch.
>
> For a moment the situation was gloomy. Soon Joe Pearl, rarely ever downed by trifles, said: "Boys, I've got it; get ready to eat Jones's melons. Do you fellers join me? I will go on guard in the field myself and you boys lay along the fence in the bushes and I'll roll out the melons." We had great faith in Pearl as a manager, but did not see how he would get away with the guard already in charge.
>
> Well, we did as he directed. With a saber hanging to his belt he mounted the fence and boldly advanced on the "true, true" guard, who, in time, challenged, "Halt!" Guard Pearl did not stop, but he commanded, "Halt!" "Who are you?" "I am on guard here," he answered. "Whose command do you belong to?" demanded Pearl in haughty tones. He replied, "To Graham's Battery." "Ah! That's all right," said Pearl, "I am from McGregor's; you watch that end and I will watch this." And the goose said, "All right."
>
> In a few minutes our "guard" began to roll out the largest and best melons under the fence. We held a council of war to decide whether we should give our officers any of them or not. Finally we decided to roll a melon or two down to where they had their bivouac, and it was noticed that not one of them even cared to know where they come from.[36]

How much the cannoneers and their officers enjoyed their ill-gotten booty is unknown, but the melons probably tasted extra sweet for having been "liberated" from under the very nose of the guard from Graham's Battery. More than likely he was rolling melons out on the other side of the field for his battery-mates. Though the melons were a tasty addition to the men's scant rations, they were but a refreshing moment to be fondly remembered amid the horrors of the war that still raged before Petersburg.

Like McGregor and Shoemaker, Thomson also received marching orders. On July 29, his battery moved from its camp on the Nottoway River to near the battalion camp west of Reams's Station. Here the cannoneers heard the rumble of the mine explosion on the thirtieth. The battery was ordered out to oppose a Federal advance along the Petersburg & Weldon Railroad north of Reams's Station. When the movement proved to be rumor, the battery returned to its camp. Along the way, some members stopped to extract the gold fillings from several Federal corpses that had not been buried following the fight with Wilson and Kautz.[37]

For the other batteries of the battalion, July ended in the same manner as much of the month had passed. The restful days that were interspersed with picket duty and short marches would soon be a golden memory. Since the army had crossed the James River, the batteries of Chew's Battalion, with a few exceptions, had not been overly taxed. The men had an opportunity to heal both body and soul, and the horses regained much of their strength. Fresh recruits had joined some batteries. The men's confidence in their final victory had not yet begun to erode. They were ready to reenter the maelstrom.

CHAPTER 31

Protecting the Lifelines

"The hell I will!"

The early days of August brought little change in the posting of Chew's Battalion. Along with the cavalry, the batteries held to their camps near Reams's Station. All were poised to repel further encroachment on the vital railroad lifelines. However, events were transpiring elsewhere that would greatly affect the battalion. The deteriorating situation in the Shenandoah Valley concerned Robert E. Lee to the point that he decided to detach troops from the Army of Northern Virginia and send them to reinforce Jubal Early. Maj. Gen. Joseph B. Kershaw's division of infantry and Maj. Gen. Fitzhugh Lee's division of cavalry were dispatched to Culpeper Court House, where they could be drawn on by Early or return to Petersburg as the situation required. Johnston's[1] and Shoemaker's Batteries would make the move to the Valley with the cavalry.[2] Two other batteries began the journey north a few days later.

Hart's and Thomson's Batteries received their orders on August 10.[3] They were to accompany Hampton's division to Culpeper to threaten the Federal flank and rear. Lee hoped that the enemy would retain a significant force to protect Washington rather than reinforce Sheridan in the Valley.[4] By the fourteenth, Hampton, who had succeeded to the command of all the cavalry on the eleventh, had reached Beaver Dam Station, only to be called back to the lines north of the James.[5] All the cavalry had to do was turn around and ride south. For Hart and Thomson, things were a bit more complicated. Both batteries had put their guns and part of their crews on a train headed for Gordonsville, while the remaining men took the horses through the country.[6] To be of any use, the guns, crews, and horses had to unite, and since the plan had been to rendezvous at Gordonsville, everyone continued on to that place.

Not surprisingly, considering the state of the railroads, the horses arrived before the guns.[7] Once reunited, the two batteries settled into a period of limbo. They received no orders to return to the main army or to move on to Culpeper or the Valley.[8] From August 17 to September 10, Hart's Battery camped at Barnett's Ford on the Rapidan River.[9] Here the horses enjoyed fine pasturage, and the men found the foraging to their liking. Not until mid-September would Hart's Battery wind its way back to Hampton. Thomson's Battery had an equally idyllic time, camping with Hart's at Barnett's Ford before moving on to Madison Mills, north of the Rapidan, on September 7.[10] By the fifteenth, it was back at Gordonsville, where it remained until the twenty-seventh. Private McVicar recorded the only excitement the battery had in his diary on the nineteenth:

> The sun rose clear and pleasant; all nature seemed quiet and serene, but "alas" the enemy was near before we were aware of it, burning, pillaging, and destroying everything in his way. Our horses loose in a 100 acre field, such running, grabbing, catching, saddling up, and harnessing of horses to wagons. Everything out of place, complete confusion. Lieutenant [John W. "Tuck"] Carter ordered me as I was well mounted and armed to get the colors and carry them out of danger. An honor I wish he had conferred on someone else and let me go up front with him and the boys. [Pvt. William R.] Lyman and I moved the wagons out through byroads near Madison Courthouse. Enemy going back, six of us rode near them and fired at close range with our pistols, wounding several. Nightfall, the boys are coming in trailing us. Carter's squad captured several horses. They were not bothered with prisoners.[11]

Gordonsville, thankfully spared a visit from the Federals, was pleased to see Kershaw's division, which passed through on September 23 on its way to reinforce Early in the Valley. Despite the situation there, Thomson received no orders to follow the infantry west. Not until October 1, after brief stays in or near Charlottesville and Lynchburg, did the battery move on to the Valley.[12] Its period of idleness had proven good for man and beast. With renewed strength, the battery was ready to face the enemy. Unknown to the officers and men, disaster loomed along a quiet stream called Tom's Brook.

Of the six batteries Chew had with him at the beginning of August, only two—Graham's and McGregor's—were still with the army after the tenth. Unlike Hart's and Thomson's, they were not idle during the golden days of midsummer. McGregor was encamped at Armstrong's farm when he received orders at noon on the fourteenth to march with the cavalry across the James River. Rooney Lee's division was being sent to bolster Confederate forces there in response to a Federal threat mounted by Maj. Gen. Winfield S. Hancock's II Corps, Maj. Gen. David B. Birney's X Corps, and Brig. Gen. David McM. Gregg's 2nd Cavalry Division. Graham's Battery would stay behind with Dearing's Brigade as the only cavalry and horse artillery south of the Appomattox.

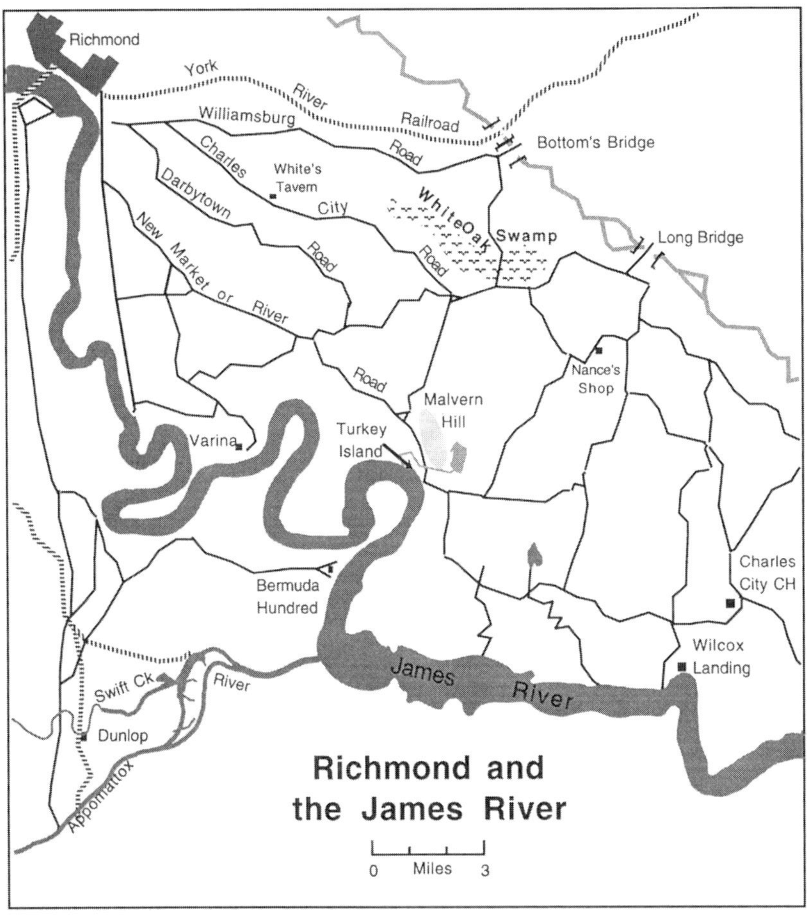
Richmond
York River Railroad
Williamsburg Road
Charles City Road
Darbytown Road
New Market or River Road
White's Tavern
White Oak Swamp
Bottom's Bridge
Long Bridge
Nance's Shop
Malvern Hill
Turkey Island
Varina
Bermuda Hundred
Charles City CH
Wilcox Landing
James River
Swift Ck
River
Dunlop
Appomattox
Richmond and the James River
0 Miles 3

Part of Hancock's force was to push up the New Market Road and drive the Confederates into their entrenchments. Gregg's cavalry was to guard this column's right flank by advancing up the Charles City Road. The Federal plan ran into some difficulties on the fifteenth that prevented Hancock from accomplishing all that he had desired. McGregor managed to bring up a section, which encountered the enemy in the vicinity of White Oak Swamp.[13] A short skirmish occurred, with neither side causing much damage.[14] When the engagement ended, McGregor fell back and joined his other section on the Jones farm six miles below Richmond.[15]

The Federals were not through. Frustrated by the lack of success on the previous day, Hancock went at the Confederates again early on the morning of the sixteenth. Gregg once more sent his cavalry up the Charles City Road. The 13th Virginia Cavalry, doing picket duty about two miles below White's Tavern, was the first Confederate unit to clash with Gregg's troopers.[16] But it was not only cavalry that the Confederates faced. Federal infantry moved forward to flank the 13th Virginia and assisted in driving them back from their position along Deep Creek. Desperately trying to stem the blue tide that threatened to overwhelm them, the 13th Virginia, now supported by elements of the 10th Virginia Cavalry, had formed a makeshift line when Brig. Gen. John R. Chambliss arrived at about 8:00 A.M. In an effort to steady his somewhat shaken men, the general rode back and forth behind the line. Within a few minutes, a small group of troopers from the 16th Pennsylvania Cavalry advancing on foot had flanked the Confederate line, which fell back. In the confusion, Chambliss was left alone to face the enemy. Called on to surrender, the general attempted to make his escape, only to be killed by a volley from the dismounted cavalry.

Chambliss's fall further demoralized his men, who streamed back toward White's Tavern. Here reinforcements, including McGregor's Battery, brought the Federals to a halt. In the fighting that followed, the Confederates slowly drove the enemy back to White Oak Swamp. McGregor was in the thick of the action, losing one man killed and two wounded.[17] At the close of the battle, McGregor limbered his guns and rode back to the Jones farm, where he encamped for the night. On the seventeenth, there was little fighting, and the Confederate high command ordered McGregor's Battery back to Petersburg. The resumption of the contest on the eighteenth did not terminate McGregor's journey south. Passing through the besieged city, the battery continued on to Stony Creek Station, where it bivouacked until the twenty-fourth.

The stalemate north of the James brought repercussions south of the Appomattox. Grant concluded that if Lee had enough troops to stop Hancock from breaking through to Richmond, he might not have enough to protect his lifelines below Petersburg. Consequently, Maj. Gen. Gouverneur K. Warren, with his V Corps, was ordered to take the offensive and see what he could accomplish. The advance began at 4:00 A.M. on August 18 toward Globe Tavern on the Petersburg & Weldon Railroad. By 8:30 A.M., the 3rd New York Cavalry from Brig. Gen. August V. Kautz's cavalry division struck pickets from Brig. Gen. James Dearing's Brigade, capturing a number of the gray troopers. The Confederates were forced back, which uncovered the railroad. Immediately some of the Federals set to tearing up track. They started fires, using the ties for fuel. The rails soon adorned trees and poles as twisted decorations.

At 11:00 A.M., Brig. Gen. Romeyn B. Ayres's 2nd Division was advancing up the railroad toward Petersburg. Resistance came from Dearing's Cavalry in the vicinity of the W. P. Davis house. Graham's Battery unlimbered near the house and opened a bothersome fire, to which Battery C, Massachusetts Light Artillery, replied.[18] Dearing had informed Gen. P. G. T. Beauregard that his small command was opposing a major Federal offensive, but until reinforcements could arrive, the cavalry and Graham would have to do the best they could. Although Dearing committed his second regiment to the battle line, the Federals continued to drive back the thin line of cavalry skirmishers. The bullets were flying thick around Graham's guns. A minié ball felled Pvt. George W. Livesey, who was mounted and acting as Captain Graham's courier. The wound proved mortal. Lt. William T. Britton's horse was shot beneath him, giving additional evidence that it was not a good day to be mounted.

The pressure eventually proved too much for Dearing's two small regiments, and they were compelled to give up their position near the Davis house. Graham limbered to the rear. Expecting the Federals to continue their advance, Dearing was pleased to see the enemy's skirmish line come to a halt. The skirmishers had outdistanced their supporting battle line and had stopped to allow it to catch up. The delay permitted Beauregard's relief column, consisting of two brigades from Maj. Gen. Henry Heth's division and Capt. Thomas A. Brander's Letcher Artillery, to reach the scene of the crisis. The infantry formed their lines of battle. Heth's skirmishers replaced Dearing's weary troopers, and then the infantry swept forward. Dearing and Graham now left the fighting to Heth.[19] The struggle lasted until the twenty-first, but the Confederates failed to regain control of the Petersburg & Weldon Railroad. Another of Lee's lifelines was severed.

The few miles of track the Federals managed to destroy before turning to deal with the Confederates was not enough for Grant. While he held the railroad, he wanted to obliterate as much of it as possible.[20] This job was given to Hancock's II Corps, which was to tear up the tracks to Reams's Station. Hancock had just marched his men from across the James River. With Brig. Gen. David McM. Gregg's 2nd Cavalry Division and Col. Samuel P. Spear's 2nd Cavalry Brigade of Kautz's division to assist him, Hancock took two of his three infantry divisions, Maj. Gen. Francis C. Barlow's and Maj. Gen. John Gibbon's, and set to work.[21] Little opposition was encountered as Gregg's cavalry forged ahead, watching out for any signs of the enemy, while Hancock's infantry carried on its knot-tying exercises.

Gregg reached Reams's Station the evening of August 22. He was aware that Col. James L. Davis's Cavalry Brigade, formerly Chambliss's Brigade, was encamped at the Tabernacle Church, south of Rowanty Creek about three miles from the station, but no threat was perceived.[22] Federal infantry arrived at the station on the twenty-third, the men pried up track, gouged railroad ties from the earth, set them afire, and commenced twisting. By now the work had become routine. However, the Confederate cavalry at last began to offer some objection to the enemy's wanton destruction. Fighting erupted along Rowanty Creek at Monk's Neck Bridge between Spear's troopers and those of Brig. Gen. Rufus Barringer's Brigade and Maj. Gen. Matthew C. Butler's division. After a seesaw contest, Butler managed to drive Spear back, though not without a momentary scare when the Confederate troopers panicked. Butler rallied them and threw in his reserves to win the day, or at least the moment.

Unfortunately for Butler's tired troopers, Brig. Gen. David McM. Gregg brought his cavalry division into the fray shortly after arriving at Reams's Station and learning of Spear's repulse. At first Gregg committed two regiments, but the fighting quickly escalated, and he soon had all but one of his regiments grappling with Butler.[23] The Confederates drove ahead resolutely but could not reach the station. Darkness failed to bring an end to the conflict, as the two antagonists grappled in the moonlight. Finally, exhaustion brought the fight to a close. Neither Graham's nor McGregor's Battery played any part in the struggle. Graham was with Dearing back toward Petersburg, watching the Federals south of the Davis house. McGregor stayed in his camp at Stony Creek Station and, though not oblivious to the meaning of the sounds of fighting to his north, awaited orders. He did not have to wait too long.

August 24 brought more Federal troops to Reams's Station. Determined to hold on to the station, the Army of the Potomac's commander, Maj. Gen. George G. Meade, dispatched Gibbon's division toward the threatened point. Meade ordered Hancock south to take charge of all the troops in the vicinity. Gibbon's footsloggers spent the day attempting to improve on some shabby, poorly planned and constructed defensive works just south of the station. Their efforts met with only moderate success. By nightfall, Gregg's cavalry had taken up positions behind the works, while Spear's troopers guarded Malone's Crossing four miles to the south.

Though the Confederates allowed the twenty-fourth to pass without testing the Federal position at Reams's Station, Maj. Gen. Wade Hampton used the time to read scouting reports and gather information on Hancock's forces. His findings led to a proposal to Lee that infantry be assigned to work with the cavalry in attacking the enemy at Reams's Station.[24] The commander-in-chief liked what he heard and directed that Lt. Gen. A. P. Hill with two brigades from Heth's division and two from Maj. Gen. William Mahone's division cooperate with Hampton. Lee later committed Maj. Gen. Cadmus Wilcox's division[25] and Brig. Gen. George T. Anderson's Brigade from Maj. Gen. Charles W. Field's division to the venture. The cavalry forces that could be brought to bear included Rooney Lee's division,[26] temporarily commanded by Brig. Gen. Rufus Barringer,[27] Butler's division, and a section of McGregor's Battery.[28]

McGregor marched up Malone's Road toward Malone's Crossing with Butler's division, which was in support of Davis's Brigade.[29] Barringer's Brigade was directed to approach the crossing using the Halifax Road. Brig. Gen. John Dunovant's Brigade, detached from Butler's division, and the 7th Virginia Cavalry, from Brig. Gen. Thomas L. Rosser's Brigade, screened Hill's infantry as it approached the station and then protected the flanks against Federal counterattacks. Davis and Butler would maneuver to strike the enemy's left flank.[30] With all in readiness, Hampton gave the order to advance.

Davis's Brigade was the first to make contact with the enemy just beyond Malone's Bridge. A sharp fight ensued between Davis's dismounted men and Spear's skirmishers. The Confederates forced the bluecoats to give way, and they reached and passed Malone's Crossing. Now McGregor galloped up with his two guns. The battle had been going on since about 8:30 A.M.[31] It was now 11:00.[32] The cannoneers unlimbered and opened fire on the enemy's skirmish line. McGregor's accurate fire helped drive Spear back toward Reams's Station and Gregg. Federal resistance stiffened as the combined forces of Spear and Gregg slowed Hampton's attack. More trouble came calling when Gibbon's division threatened both of Hampton's flanks. Gregg now pulled the cavalry out of the fight and let Gibbon handle Hampton. With pressure mounting against him, the Confederate cavalry commander communicated with Hill, telling him what he faced. Hill, who had not yet committed his troops, suggested that the cavalry fall back toward Malone's Crossing to draw the Federals out of their works. Hill would then attack them in the rear.

Hampton adopted the plan and slowly withdrew. McGregor participated in the fighting withdrawal. Sometime during this maneuver or just after the crossing was reached, one of McGregor's guns was disabled by recoil.[33] Upon reaching the crossing, Hampton was met by Barringer's Brigade, which he had ordered to join him. With these reinforcements, Hampton formed a firm line, which Gibbon's infantry ran into and could not budge. The gray cavalry's firm stand, bolstered by McGregor's remaining gun, might have brought on a full engagement with Gibbon's division but for the threat of attack back at Reams's Station. Hancock had suddenly become aware that all was not well and that a large force of Confederate infantry was about to advance.

The first attack, consisting of Wilcox's command, was repulsed. Heavy skirmishing and sharpshooting followed, riddling the Federal lines. The Confederate cavalry maintained contact with part of Gibbon's division but did not move forward. Finally, around 5:00 P.M., Hill's artillery, under the direction of Lt. Col. William J. Pegram, opened a destructive fire. It was followed by renewed infantry attacks that gained a foothold in the Federal works. Hill sent Hampton word that the infantry had gone forward. As if to verify the message, the sound of Pegram's guns reverberated through the hot August air. Hampton's troopers and McGregor's lone gun began their attack. McGregor pushed to within 200 yards of the enemy's line.[34] There the gray artillerymen were brought to a halt.

McGregor continued to pound away at the Federals. The captain, who sat mounted next to the lone gun, watched with great interest as Sgt. George W. Shreve sighted and fired the three-inch rifle. Several of the rounds found their marks, and McGregor complimented Shreve on his excellent gunnery.[35] Unfortunately, Shreve's accuracy could not compensate for the enfilading fire Hampton's regiments faced. However, Gibbon's stand was brief. Other parts of the Federal line crumpled, which allowed some of the Confederate dismounted cavalry to move around the blue infantry's flank and deliver devastating volleys into the rear of Gibbon's line. Resistance became futile. Hundreds of Federals were taken prisoner as Gibbon's troops scrambled rearward. McGregor's cannoneers played no part in the final scenes of what was a major Confederate triumph. Their contribution had been the support they gave to Hampton when he needed it most. The section advanced with the assault columns, which permitted Hampton to maintain pressure on the enemy's line even when his troopers were unable to move forward. McGregor's loss was one man wounded.[36] The captain summed up his day's work tersely: "We returned to camp late at night."[37]

The battle of Reams's Station extracted a considerable number of teeth from the Federal bite that Grant had been taking out of Lee's army both north and south of the James. The days following the fight were filled with caring for the wounded and burying the dead. Both sides welcomed the lull. McGregor's Battery shifted its camp only slightly, always keeping near Stony Creek Station, as August gave way to September. Graham's Battery's position also changed little. It remained encamped on the right of the lines around Petersburg, along with Dearing's Brigade, to which it was still attached. On September 5, Hampton's famous scout (or infamous if you take the Federal perspective) George D. Shadburne learned that about 3,000 head of cattle intended to feed Grant's army were corralled at Coggin's Point. He also learned that they were weakly guarded, the opinion being that they were safe from Confederate molesters, who would not dare venture so far in rear of the Federal lines. For good measure, Shadburne included the disposition of the troops guarding the beeves.

Hampton's interest was piqued immediately, and putting together a plan, he went to see Lee. The commander-in-chief had great faith in his new cavalry leader and listened intently to what Hampton proposed. Lee acceded to the plan and even promised an infantry movement as a diversion. His only concern was whether Hampton could get back once he had the cattle. Hampton was confident he could and added that he would move when he learned of Grant's absence. With the head away, perhaps the body might react a little slower. His plan approved, Hampton selected the forces to execute the raid: Rooney Lee's division, consisting of Barringer's and Davis's Brigades; Rosser's Brigade from Butler's division; Dearing's Brigade; and a 100-man contingent from Young's and Dunovant's Brigades, under Lt. Col. Lovick P. Miller.[38] Maj. Roger P. Chew with two guns from Graham's Battery and two from McGregor's Battery would add some punch if and when needed.[39]

Hampton's column set out before daylight on the morning of September 14. McGregor's section fell in behind the 13th Virginia Cavalry of Davis's Brigade.[40] Swinging southwest on the Boydton Plank Road to Dinwiddie Court House, the gray cavalry here made a turn and headed southeast on Flat Foot Road. About two miles northwest of Stony Creek Station, in the vicinity of Sycamore Church, Hampton turned east and passed over the Petersburg & Weldon Railroad. He made camp at Wilkinson's Bridge, which spanned Rowanty Creek.[41] The horse artillery had kept up with the cavalry and was ready when the column moved out early on the fifteenth. The riders reached the Jerusalem Plank Road and continued on to Cook's Bridge over the Blackwater River. The bridge had been destroyed earlier by the Federals, so everyone settled down to wait while engineer officer Lt. John F. Lanneau and his men set to work rebuilding the bridge. In the meantime, McGregor's cannoneers invaded nearby sweet potato fields with the idea of having some cooked rations, but being told that fires were forbidden, they had to enjoy the potatoes in their raw state.[42]

As evening fell, Lieutenant Lanneau reported the bridge finished, and some of the cavalry crossed immediately. McGregor did not cross until 10:00 P.M., and then marched with Rooney Lee's division along the Lawyers Stage Road until sunrise on the sixteenth.[43] Near Prince George Court House, McGregor unlimbered his section. He remained there until 10:00 A.M.[44] During that time, he fired a few shots, but no enemy came in sight.[45] Dearing's Brigade trotted up the Hines Road to Cocke's Mill.[46] Hampton with Rosser's Brigade and Colonel Miller's composite command moved forward to Sycamore Church. This column would make the attack at Coggin's Point and seize the cattle. At 5:00 A.M., Rosser charged the Federal pickets at Sycamore Church, routing them. The cattle were secured and started rearward before 8:00 A.M. In all this, Graham and McGregor played no part.

Now came the tough part of the raid: getting the cattle into Confederate lines. In this endeavor, the horse artillery could be of some help. McGregor received orders at Prince George Court House to retreat along the same road he had come. Neither he nor Graham fired a shot on the retreat until they came to the Jerusalem Plank Road.[47] The Federals had hurried down the road in the hope of cutting off Hampton's escape route. Rosser, who had the advance, informed Hampton of the threat. The cattle were diverted farther south to Hawkinsville, and Rosser was ordered to block the bluecoats at Ebenezer Church. Rosser fought well and was soon reinforced by Miller and Dearing.

As the sky darkened, Chew galloped up, with Graham's and McGregor's guns rumbling behind him. Thrown into position, the four pieces were soon thundering away at the enemy. Several half-hearted attacks were repulsed. The horse artillery continued to fire until about 9:00 P.M. Then the men limbered up, and the guns disappeared into the night, along with 2,468 head of cattle.[48]

The raid, which followed so closely behind Hampton's successful fight at Reams's Station, lifted Confederate morale and filled Confederate stomachs. Far from being used up, the gray cavalry demonstrated it still had a sharp edge on its sabers. As far as Chew and the horse artillery were concerned, the raid was gratifying simply because the guns had been able to contribute to the overall success of the expedition. McGregor bolstered Rooney Lee's position at Prince George Court House and, in combination with Graham, solidified Rosser's line at Ebenezer Church, permitting the cattle to escape recapture. For all of this, Graham lost one man, Pvt. Albert Ellis, who deserted,[49] and McGregor lost two men as prisoners and a few horses.[50]

Graham's and McGregor's Batteries returned to their camps and settled once more into the routine of camp life and picket duty. Within a few days of the raid, Hart's Battery rode in from its "vacation" along the Rapidan River. The arrival of Hart gave Chew a total of twelve guns and 227 men.[51] While Chew's command increased, Hampton's decreased. Rosser's Brigade was transferred to the Valley to reinforce the cavalry already there. Hampton's remaining five brigades guarded a line that ran from the Peebles farm past Reams's Station to Malone's Crossing on the Petersburg & Weldon Railroad.[52] Farther south, at Stony Creek Station, the Confederates had built a strong earthwork. Some heavy guns were mounted inside, but they were useless without crews. The decision to train some infantry as cannoneers prompted a transfer of six men from Hart's Battery to be instructors.[53] These troop dispositions were in effect as the end of September approached.

On the twenty-ninth, Rooney Lee was ordered to take Barringer's and Davis's Brigades and McGregor's Battery across the James to reinforce Confederate forces before Richmond. He never made it. Federal cavalry under Gregg pushed in Hampton's picket line between Peebles's farm and Reams's Station, which was retaken by a portion of the 1st New Jersey Cavalry.[54] Meanwhile, Col. Charles H. Smith's Brigade, led by the 13th Pennsylvania Cavalry, drove in the pickets of the 5th South Carolina Cavalry along the Vaughan Road. Hampton established a firm line paralleling Hatcher's Run, placing Maj. Henry S. Farley's foot dragoons[55] in shallow entrenchments dug out on the right bank of the stream. Not wanting to test Farley, the Federals tried to outflank him.[56] After some initial success, the bluecoats ran into Matt Butler's troopers. Gregg's determination to reach the Boydton Plank Road led him again to slide west around Butler. The South Carolinian would have none of that, and when Gregg reached Hatcher's Run near Armstrong's Mill, Butler barred his way once more. The Federal commander's final effort was squelched with the repulse of the 1st Maine Cavalry along the Lower Church Road. Gregg had enough and pulled back his troopers to the vicinity of Wyatt's plantation.[57] Now it was Hampton's turn.

The Confederate response to Gregg's advance had been immediate. Hampton countermanded Rooney Lee's orders and instructed him to send Barringer's Brigade up the Vaughan Road and keep Davis's with McGregor's Battery in position on the Boydton Plank Road near Petersburg. Once Gregg surrendered the initiative, Hampton was quick to take it up. He ordered Butler to launch an attack near the Cummings house. Driving back the Federals' thin skirmish line, Butler halted his men as they approached the Wyatt house. Now the enemy artillery opened fire. Butler's response was prompt. A section of Hart's Battery rumbled into position and unlimbered. Fresh from their extended holiday, Hart's cannoneers eagerly joined the fray. Gunner William J. Verdier showed that he had lost none of his ability while relaxing along the Rapidan when, on his third shot, he exploded one of the enemy's caissons. The rising column of fire and smoke greatly eased the humiliation of the loss of a caisson Hart had suffered at White House the previous June. The fighting trailed off as darkness approached, but the fact that neither side was satisfied with the day's outcome foreshadowed a renewal of the contest the next day.

Capt. Edward Graham and his battery, having escaped the fighting on the twenty-ninth, greeted the dawn of September 30 from the confines of Fort Archer on the Peebles farm along the Church Road. Directly in support of the battery was a portion of the 7th Confederate Cavalry, while the rest of the 7th along with the 8th Georgia Cavalry held other positions on the farm.[58] The Confederates were vastly outnumbered, but Graham opened fire, giving the impression that the Federals would have a difficult time if they chose to attack. Graham's barrage was intimidating despite being inaccurate. Nevertheless, the Federals eventually overcame their hesitancy and threw a line of skirmishers forward. Case shot from Graham's guns and enfilading fire from concealed troops to the battery's right brought the bluecoats to a halt.[59] This minor success only delayed the inevitable.

Brig. Gen. Charles Griffin reinforced his skirmish line, which led to a general advance once he had placed the remainder of his regiments. Confederate skirmishers did little to halt the oncoming wave. Graham opened up with canister. Most of it passed harmlessly over the oncoming infantry. Sometime during this phase of the fighting, the battery suffered its first casualty. Pvt. Jeremiah P. Moody was beheaded by a cannonball from Lt. Robert E. Rodgers's Battery B, 1st New York Light Artillery, the only Federal artillery engaged.[60] Graham's gunners kept to their work despite the grisly scene, but they were unable to break Griffin's determined troops. The Confederate cavalry began to filter rearward. The air around the guns became thick with flying lead. The Federals could not be stopped. Becoming aware that his support was quickly eroding, Graham gave the order to limber to the rear. The time had come to save the guns. One section managed to bring up its limbers and gallop off, but the other was too late to get away clean.

As the last two pieces were being attached to their limbers, Pvt. James G. McAllister was struck by a rifle ball and killed, falling next to Moody. The two lay together in death as they had stood together in life—beside their gun. Seeing that two cannons were still there for the taking, the enemy surged toward the fort. Casualties among the battery continued to mount. Corp. Theodorick L. Jones had his knee smashed by a minié ball yet somehow managed to get away. Pvt. Charles W. Sydnor, the flag bearer, was also wounded. He, too, galloped to safety with the battery's colors. One of the two remaining pieces was limbered. The driver, Alexander Caudle, raised his whip to strike the horses, when two Yankee officers rode up and attempted to capture the guns. One of them cried out for Caudle to surrender. The feisty driver yelled back, "The hell I will!"[61] The officers fired at Caudle several times and succeeded in wounding him. Using the only weapon at his disposal, Caudle struck at the officers with his whip and beat them back, knocking one of them out of his saddle. He brought the gun off in triumph. Pvt. George A. Wingfield captured the officer's horse.[62]

The last piece could not be saved. Lt. Albert Fernald of the 20th Maine halted the driver, who was not made of the same material as Caudle.[63] The gun and a large portion of its crew were captured.[64] Privates Stephen Black, William D. Cheatham, Chastine Dobbs, Robert W. McGuigan, John A. Partin, and John W. Watts began their journey to Point Lookout. The three-inch rifle had made a journey of a sort as well. The Confederates had captured it at Reams's Station on August 25. As happy as the Federals were in recovering it, the Confederates were disgruntled in giving such a fine piece back. However, the mourning would have to be put off for another time. Griffin's infantry was not quite through.

A number of Confederates began to rally in a small fortification back along the Church Road. Graham wheeled two of his guns into position and prepared to reopen the fight. Griffin sent his regiments forward. For a few minutes, the Confederates paused as if to make a stand, then reconsidered. Graham had already lost one gun and did not want to give up another. The cavalrymen wavered and finally decided to fight again another day. Limbering his two pieces, Graham and the last of the cavalry abandoned Peebles farm to Griffin's victorious infantry.

Having captured the entire Confederate works on Peebles farm, the Federals paused to consolidate their position. When at last things were sorted out, Brig. Gen. Robert B. Potter's 2nd Division of Maj. Gen. John G. Parke's IX Corps moved forward, Brig. Gen. Simon B. Griffin's Brigade leading the way. After passing Peebles farm and the Pegram house, the Federal skirmishers began to encounter Confederate pickets from Dearing's Brigade. Griffin's line had driven the graycoats back about a quarter of a mile, when Graham's Battery opened on them. The Federals halted to deploy the rest of the brigade into line of battle. Potter brought up his second brigade. Two hours passed before the Federals were satisfied with their deployment. Not until 5:00 P.M. did the bluecoats attack.[65]

Fortunately for the Confederates, Wade Hampton reached Dearing's headquarters just as word of the rout on the Peebles farm was coming in.[66] Recognizing the serious consequences of what had occurred, he took steps to rectify the situation. Rooney Lee's cavalry and a section of McGregor's Battery were ordered from the Boydton Plank Road into works south of that highway and on the left flank of the Federal line. Meanwhile, other Confederate reinforcements reached the threatened area. Elements of Maj. Gen. Cadmus Wilcox's and Maj. Gen. Henry Heth's divisions arrived. Hampton and Heth determined to attack. Graham's Battery lent its firepower when the infantry of Brig. Gen. James H. Lane and Brig. Gen. Samuel McGowan of Wilcox's division advanced.

In the battle that followed, the Federals found themselves attacked in front and on both flanks. Griffin's regiments crumpled under the onslaught. Col. John I. Curtain's Brigade, which was placed to support Griffin, also found itself unable to resist the gray wave. These Federals fled westward, unknowingly toward Hampton. McGregor's section greeted them as they approached. The captain pushed forward one of his pieces, which soon had to be abandoned.[67] Curtain's regiments sought an escape route, and one gun was not going to stop them. In answer, Hampton ordered Rooney Lee to charge on foot with the 9th and 10th Virginia. McGregor joined the charge with his remaining gun and the crew of the other, which was recovered and turned on the now distraught bluecoats.[68] About 900 prisoners were captured. McGregor drew praise from Hampton for his part in the fighting.[69]

The infantry of both sides now took over the battlefield and continued the carnage until dark. Even with the successful counterattack, the Confederates could not retake all of the ground they had lost. Graham's Battery contributed nothing further and drew back to rest and lick its wounds. McGregor's Battery probably would have done the same had it not been for a pesky enemy sharpshooter who had chosen a small group of Confederate officers for his target. Rooney Lee, Barringer, and a third officer of rank were sitting on their horses conversing when the sharpshooter opened fire. His first shot felled a private nearby, and his second shot almost claimed another. Lee ordered McGregor to see what he could do. The first round knocked the lone Federal from his perch.[70] McGregor reported that he was engaged until 9:00 with the enemy sharpshooters.[71]

The silencing of the enemy sharpshooter undoubtedly highlighted McGregor's day. His battery's overall execution proved that it still could fight in the old Pelham style. The men stood to their posts and once again demonstrated their courage. No more could have been asked of them. However, their commander had gotten a bit carried away. Well known for his intrepidity, McGregor had put one of his pieces in danger by pushing it too far forward without adequate support. Only Rooney Lee's timely charge saved the piece from capture. Though the battery lost but two horses all day, it could have been much worse.[72] McGregor's fighting spirit had almost caused the needless loss of men and materiel. True, risks still needed to be taken, but not foolish ones.

The day had not gone well for the Petersburg Battery, which left behind one gun and eight men, while three wounded managed to escape. Not since the fight of June 23 had the battery been so roughly handled. Graham could scarcely be happy with the performance of his command or himself. The fact that most of the battery's rounds had passed harmlessly over the heads of the enemy meant that the guns had contributed little to the defense of the fort. Graham's inability to either recognize or correct this and his tardiness in ordering the retreat contributed to the day's outcome. The results of these failures could be read on the battery's casualty list.

October 1 dawned with the threat of renewed fighting hanging heavily in the air. The infantry began tearing at each other at 7:00 A.M., when Heth's skirmishers went forward. The cavalry on both sides was not idle. Gregg's bluecoated troopers sallied forth on the Vaughan Road and slowly made their way to the Squirrel Level Road. From there, Brig. Gen. Henry E. Davies's Brigade pushed ahead out Route 673. This vanguard came within sight of some of Rooney Lee's troopers in the vicinity of Fort MacRae.[73] Hampton had placed Lee's division and Dearing's Brigade in works near the fort.[74] Having found what he had been looking for, Gregg turned back to McDowell's farm, at the intersection of the Wyatt and Vaughan Roads. Meanwhile, other Confederates moved into the area vacated by Gregg. Matthew C. Butler's division also marched toward the McDowell farm. Brig. Gen. Pierce M. B. Young's Brigade reached the key road junction and encountered the 1st Maine Cavalry. Skirmishing erupted. Young brought up a section of Hart's Battery and pushed a little harder. The Federals retreated up the road taken by Gregg, and Young took possession of the vital crossroads.

Butler ordered Young and Hart to sit tight and fortify their position and sent for Dunovant's Brigade and Farley's dismounted dragoons. Gregg was delayed in returning to the McDowell farm by the infantry fighting around the Chappell farm on Squirrel Level Road. When that sector quieted, he turned his attention to recovering the intersection of the Vaughan and Wyatt Roads. Confronted by an ever-increasing number of bluecoats, Young fell back across the bridge over the creek that ran through Arthur's Swamp to the Wilkinson farm at the junction of the Vaughan and Squirrel Level Roads. Gregg followed, and a sharp engagement ensued. Young managed to stop the Federals, and the fighting tapered off as the two antagonists worked feverishly to strengthen their lines. Dunovant arrived and immediately deployed. Hart brought up his other section and joined in what proved to be an all-day affair. To oppose him, Lt. William N. Dennison's Battery A, 2nd U.S. Artillery, unlimbered near the McDowell house.

Hampton recognized the seriousness of Gregg's attack on Butler. The cavalry commander responded by taking Brig. Gen. Lucius Davis with the 9th and 13th Virginia from Rooney Lee's division and marched to reinforce Butler. These troops did not arrive until about 3:00 P.M. The plan was to strike the Federals' unprotected right flank. However, things went awry, and Davis ended up on Butler's flank instead. Nevertheless, Davis attacked and pushed the enemy back. Simultaneously, Young and Farley, who had reached the field after Dunovant, charged. The combination proved too strong, and the Federals fell back across the bridge or waded the creek. Hart now concentrated his fire on Dennison, but the blue artillery answered shot for shot.[75] The duel lasted for less than an hour. What followed was a futile mounted charge by Dunovant that cost him his life and that of Dr. John B. Fontaine, the cavalry's chief surgeon, who raced to Dunovant's aid, not knowing that the general was already dead.

Dunovant's repulse reduced the fighting to skirmishing and artillery fire. Hampton sent orders for Rooney Lee to bring up two more regiments, but before they arrived, Hampton launched another attack. This time the results were different, as the Federals gave way. They formed a new line in the works on the hill just below the McDowell house. Dennison planted a gun almost in the road and sent the other three farther up the hill. When the Confederates came within fifty yards of the new line, the Federals opened fire and brought the graycoats to a halt. Hart galloped forward and unlimbered at close range. He began to pound away at the enemy's fortifications. Hampton's men tried to advance again, only to be met with the same fierce fire that had stopped them before. It did so again. Unable to stand the withering blasts, the Confederates fell back. As soon as they did, the bluecoats poured out of their works and took their turn at chasing their enemy back.

Hampton tried one more flank maneuver, which failed miserably. He then was informed that the enemy was in his rear, which caused him to shuffle his troops around to confront the new danger.[76] The report proved false. The time lost, however, meant that any further fighting would have to wait until the next day. After dark, Hampton fell back to the Wilkinson farm. Hart's Battery recrossed the bridge and unlimbered on the hill above the farmhouse. Although they had been in the thick of the fighting for most of the day and expended a considerable amount of ammunition, the men had little to celebrate. They had inflicted but three casualties, all wounded,[77] on Dennison's Battery with their counterbattery fire, and their efforts to assist the dismounted cavalry in breaking the enemy line on the McDowell farm failed. No matter how they looked at it, the Confederates had been bested, and that included Hart's Battery.

Happily for Chew and his horse batteries, the four days of fighting were ending. Though Graham's Battery became involved in the infantry battle on October 2, it was not heavily engaged and suffered no casualties. The next few weeks passed without any major offensive operations. Graham, Hart, and McGregor used the time to rest their men and horses, wash and mend clothes, and repair harness and other equipment. There was intermittent picket duty and some minor skirmishing that kept the batteries on alert. However, no advance of the enemy occurred until October 27, when Maj. Gen. Winfield S. Hancock's 2nd Corp and Gregg's cavalry division drove in Hampton's pickets all along his line. Gregg's goal was the destruction of the Southside Railroad. The Confederates were not found napping and responded quickly.

Hampton ordered Butler to reinforce his pickets and in so doing became heavily engaged.[78] A courier was dispatched to Rooney Lee, who was ordered to move up the military road and strike the enemy's rear. Hampton became concerned for the security of his own rear and sent his adjutant, Maj. Andrew R. Venable, to Dearing with orders to leave his position north of Hatcher's Run and move to a point on the Boydton Plank Road south of the run, where he could watch the roads from Armstrong's Mill. Venable delivered his message, but Lt. Gen. A. P. Hill countermanded Hampton's orders, sending Venable back to notify Hampton of the change. Along the way, Venable was captured, and Hampton continued with his battle plan as if Dearing were in place.

Hart's Battery was encamped near the Wilson house along the Boydton Plank Road. Aroused by the sound of heavy firing, Hart put the battery in motion. A courier rode up with orders to bring the guns to Armstrong's Mill on Hatcher's Run, where Hampton with Butler's division was tangling with Hancock's infantry. The battery started in the direction of the mill, but upon reaching the Quaker Road near the location of the Quaker Meeting House, Hart encountered some Confederate cavalrymen, who informed him that the Federals were advancing up the Quaker Road behind them. Hart realized that if the enemy reached the Boydton Plank Road, they would cut off Hampton's retreat route and capture Butler's wagon train. After conferring with Maj. Theodore G. Barker, Butler's adjutant, Hart decided to fight a delaying action with one section until Hampton could be made aware of the danger to his rear. Barker galloped off to inform Hampton of the critical situation, taking Lieutenant Bamberg's section with him. Hart also requested that Barker send him any help he could find.[79]

Hart with Lieutenant Halsey's section, temporarily under the command of Lt. William T. Adams, raced down the Quaker Road for about three-quarters of a mile to the bridge over Gravelly Run, where he unlimbered his pieces. The terrain was excellent for the kind of holding action Hart intended to fight. The bridge was about fifty yards long and traversed not only the stream, but also a thick bog that bordered it. Mounted attacks would be limited to the bridge. If the Federals chose to advance over the bog, it would have to be on foot. Hart did not have long to wait. The enemy appeared only minutes after he had placed his guns on a small hill overlooking the bridge. Adams was ordered to open fire. The time was about 7:30 A.M.[80] A courier arrived with orders from Hampton: "Hold the bridge at all hazards until I can support you."[81] Hart and his boys were in for a full day's work.

Col. Charles H. Smith's Brigade of Gregg's division came up to the bridge, having successfully scattered the Confederates guarding Monk's Neck Bridge over Hatcher's Run. That Hart's guns were well posted was not lost on Gregg. Adams's fire discouraged any mounted assault, so Smith deployed the 1st Maine and the 6th Ohio as skirmishers, putting the 21st Pennsylvania behind them as a mounted support.[82] Under a hot fire from Adams and a thin line of about sixty skirmishers from the 6th South Carolina, who had just arrived, the Federals made their way across the boggy ground. The going was slow, but they reached the far bank at last. Only 150 yards separated the bluecoats from Adams's section. From this point, the men from Maine and Ohio opened a severe fire on Adams's cannoneers. Casualties began to mount. Pvt. Daniel Morgan was killed outright, while Privates Legrand P. Guerry of Brandy Station fame and J. A. Brown were mortally wounded. Sgt. William Arnot, Corp. Robert M. Arnan, and Privates James W. Knott and William D. Robinson were wounded.

Hart and Adams had done all that could have been asked of them. With so many men down, the guns could not be served as efficiently. Still they fought on. At this critical juncture, Brig. Gen. Pierce M. B. Young's Brigade arrived and formed a line in the battery's rear. Hart had accomplished what he had set out to do. He had bought sufficient time for Hampton to fall back and take position at the Quaker Meeting House.[83] Now the time had come to save his guns. Hart had barely given the order to limber to the rear when he was struck in the leg by a rifle ball. Command fell to Lieutenant Adams as Hart was taken to the rear.

Word reached Hampton that enemy infantry had reached Burgess Tavern on the Boydton Plank Road and were advancing along the White Oak Road toward Five Forks. Abandoning his position at the Quaker Meeting House, Hampton ordered Butler to ride cross-country to the White Oak Road and stop the Federals there. Now the fighting escalated, drawing to it additional troops from both sides. Rooney Lee's division and McGregor's Battery first engaged the enemy about 10:00 A.M. near the junction of the Vaughan and Military Roads. For fifteen minutes, all of McGregor's guns maintained a brisk fire, but then the captain received orders that drew him to the Boydton Plank Road. He went into position in support of Lee's troopers near the Wilson house, where Hart's Battery had been encamped that morning, and opened fire on Gregg's cavalry.[84]

Meanwhile, Butler's cavalry and Hart's Battery, now commanded by Lieutenant Bamberg, reached the White Oak Road west of the Boydton Plank Road in time to keep the enemy's columns from moving too far westward. Up to this time, the gray cavalry had fought alone. Now Confederate infantry reinforcements finally were arriving. With them came Graham's Battery, which soon entered the fray.[85] Suddenly, the Federals found themselves in the uncomfortable position of being attacked on three sides, but Hancock and Gregg were not about to panic. They shifted their troops and fought like trapped animals, biting, slashing, and clawing in every direction. Graham's cannoneers unfortunately came within range of some of the bluecoats' sharpest teeth and claws. Since joining Hampton's cavalry, the battery had suffered heavy casualties. This day was no different.

While commanding his section, Lt. William T. Britton was struck in the left thigh. Fortunately, the wound was not as serious as Hart's had been, or the horse artillery would have lost two officers that day. Others in the battery were not as lucky. Pvt. John W. Taylor was killed while sponging number two gun, and Privates John C. Drake, Joseph W. Kendall, Joseph H. Lynch, John J. Moffit, Edward P. Walsh, and William T. Wilkinson were wounded. Pvt. John W. Kendall, the lead driver for gun number two, had a close call while leading a pair of white horses during the battle. A shell burst close by, killing both horses but leaving Kendall unscathed.

Late in the afternoon, Hampton ordered Butler and Rooney Lee to make an all-out attack in conjunction with the Confederate infantry. On hearing the infantry's guns, Butler and Lee rushed forward and drove back the enemy until Butler's right flank linked with Lee's left. In the gathering gloom, the firing gradually died away until only occasional shots disturbed the quiet. The soldiers, blue and gray, had been fighting since dawn. Commanders on both sides pulled back their troops as darkness fell. The Federals quietly marched back toward their lines, while Hampton made preparations to attack in the morning. The next day, Hampton pursued, but his lead brigade, Dearing's, could only hurry the enemy's rear guard across Hatcher's Run between Dabney's and Armstrong's Mills. The horse artillery played no part in this action.

The battle of Burgess Mill proved costly to both Graham's and Hart's Batteries. Graham's losses, coming on top of those of September 30, must have posed a serious threat to the proficiency of the battery. Twenty-four men had been lost either permanently or temporarily since June 23. If the battery was to maintain its fighting prowess, time for rest and rejuvenation was needed. The loss of Hart for what amounted to the rest of the war was a severe blow to his excellent battery. However, his successor, Lt. Edwin L. Halsey, ably filled the gap. The battery lost little, if any, of its efficiency due to this command change. Halsey had served under Hart since the battery's inception and was very familiar with the men and well acquainted with the duties that devolved upon him.[86]

The performance of the batteries was up to the usual standards. Hart's, especially, demonstrated the mobility and hard-nosed fighting quality necessary for a horse battery. Captain Hart's decision to fight a delaying action at the Gravelly Run Bridge on the Quaker Road was a key factor in Hampton's later success. The contribution of all the batteries to the victory was summed up in Hampton's report when he wrote, "Major Chew here, as in all the previous fights of the command, behaved admirably, and handled his artillery to great advantage."[87] Praise of Chew was praise of the battalion.

Except for a small foray by Gregg along the Petersburg & Weldon Railroad on November 7, which drew McGregor's Battery out on the eighth and amounted to nothing more than a reconnaissance in force, little occurred during the month. Chew's cannoneers may have allowed themselves to be lulled into believing that there would be no more campaigning for the year, but the Federals felt otherwise. If the Confederate high command thought that way, they were rudely awakened from their reverie when, on December 1, Gregg swooped down on Stony Creek Station below Reams's Station and gobbled up the garrison. Some warning of the expedition must have reached the Confederates, because McGregor's Battery was aroused at 3:00 A.M. on November 30 with orders to be ready to move at daylight. Nothing further developed, however, and the men unsaddled their horses and unlimbered the guns at noon.[88]

In this instance, the rumor that prompted the orders proved true, and the battery found itself going through the same process on December 1. Fortunately, the alarm was raised in the midst of drill, which allowed for a shorter preparation time. Before long, the guns were rumbling toward Stony Creek Station. The pursuit of the raiders turned out to be an exercise in futility for the artillery. It saw no enemy, fired no shots, and did little more than wear out its horses and men for nothing. The battery returned to its camp on the second and tried to resume the routine of a winter encampment.[89] As events proved, the Federals were not quite ready to permit it.

Not satisfied with having already destroyed significant portions of the Petersburg & Weldon Railroad, Brig. Gen. David McM. Gregg mounted another rail-bending excursion on December 7. Leading his entire division minus two regiments and one battery, Gregg struck the railroad first at Nottoway River Bridge, and then moved on to Jarratt's Station. From there the work of tearing up the track commenced and continued toward Hicksford. Wade Hampton responded to Gregg's move with Rooney Lee's and M. C. Butler's divisions. Hart's and McGregor's Batteries rode with the cavalry in what became a race to get ahead of the Federal column. Though some small skirmishing occurred along the route, the horse artillery did not get in its licks until the enemy reached Hicksford. Here Hampton determined to defend the railroad bridge over the Meherrin River.[90]

Gregg made a fight of it, chasing the Confederates to the south side of the river, where Hart and McGregor held positions. Opening fire on the approaching bluecoats, both batteries demonstrated that any further advance would be hotly contested and executed at considerable loss. Maj. Gen. Gouverneur K. Warren, who held overall command, conferred with Gregg and, deciding that tearing up the track in their rear would cause sufficient damage, brought the Federal drive to a halt. Hampton's troopers and Hart's and McGregor's guns may have had something to do with persuading the enemy to begin their retreat.[91] The horse artillery suffered no casualties from enemy fire, but the cold, snow, sleet, and freezing rain over the five days of marching and fighting brought intense suffering to the men and horses. Following Gregg's withdrawal, the horse artillery settled into winter quarters. Both Hart's and McGregor's Batteries ended up at Hicksford.[92] Graham's encamped in the vicinity of Stony Creek Station.[93]

Since May, Robert E. Lee's army had been pressed back into the defenses of Richmond and Petersburg. Unable to maneuver, Lee could only defend his lifelines and pray for a miracle. Chew and the men of Graham's, Hart's, and McGregor's Batteries had fought valiantly to preserve those lifelines.[94] They had not always been successful, but no one could deny that they had given their all. The casualty lists from the Wilderness to Hicksford testified to their courage and sacrifice. How much more of that courage and sacrifice would be needed when the campaign season opened in the spring was unknown, but the men of the horse artillery would be there to give them.

CHAPTER 32

Disaster in the Valley

"My darkest forebodings have alas been too soon fulfilled."

The success Jubal Early had experienced since coming to the Valley had lifted him into the select company of Stonewall Jackson and John C. Breckinridge, the Valley's other "saviors." Truthfully, however, their miracles had bought only time, for the Valley had continued to be imperiled and in need of a continuous string of miracles. Early had supplied another, but like those of Jackson and Breckinridge, it would not last. What was more ominous was that the time each miracle bought was less than the one before it. The day that both the time and the miracles would run out had not yet come, but the one who would end them had.

Maj. Gen. Philip Sheridan's assumption of command over the new Middle Military Division, which included the Shenandoah Valley, led to immediate action. Detailed instructions were given to the various commanders under his authority on August 9. The next day, the army set out from Harpers Ferry and marched south toward Berryville. Jubal Early and the Confederate army were encamped at Bunker Hill north of Winchester. If Sheridan moved quickly enough, he could cut Early off or at least force him to abandon his present position. "Old Jube" responded to Sheridan's advance by retreating to Winchester. The chess game for control of the Valley had begun.

During these early days of August, the various batteries of horse artillery attached or soon to be attached to Early's army were scattered to the four winds. McClanahan's Battery, which escaped Averell at Moorefield without the loss of any guns, had marched back into the Valley with McCausland's Brigade and was ready for duty when Sheridan's forces began their campaign to crush Early. Lt. Micajah Woods's section of Jackson's Battery was encamped near Mount Jackson, trying to recuperate from the loss suffered at Moorefield.[1] The other section was with Captain Jackson on duty with Early's cavalry, as was the remaining section of Lurty's Battery.[2] Maj. James Breathed was en route to the Valley with Johnston's and Shoemaker's Batteries.[3] The remnants of Griffin's Battery, now commanded by Lt. John R. McNulty,[4] withdrew from Moorefield to New Market, where it began the process of reorganizing and refitting.[5] Thomson's Battery had not yet been assigned to the Valley and was in the vicinity of Petersburg. It would begin its trek north on August 11.[6] At the time Sheridan marched from Harpers Ferry, McClanahan's Battery was the only complete battery of horse artillery with Early's cavalry.[7] Jackson and Lurty had a section each. The ten guns these units could muster between them were not much with which to confront the Federal cavalry and horse artillery.

On August 10, newly commissioned Maj. Gen. Lunsford L. Lomax succeeded to the command of Early's cavalry.[8] The brigades of William L. Jackson, Bradley T. Johnson, John D. Imboden, John McCausland, and John C. Vaughn formed Lomax's small division.[9] The horse artillery batteries that were then attached to this command were those that had served with these brigades—Griffin's, Jackson's, Lurty's, and McClanahan's.[10] The cavalry's unification under one commander was not new with Lomax. Maj. Gen. Robert Ransom had occupied the position previous to Lomax. Grouping these brigades together looked good on paper, but welding them into a solid, dependable division was an altogether different matter. For the most part, they went their separate ways unless circumstances threw them together. The deficiencies in Early's cavalry and horse artillery would remain an Achilles' heel for the little Valley army even after the arrival of reinforcements from Lee's army.[11]

Following Sheridan's opening advance, Early slowly withdrew to Fisher's Hill below Strasburg, where he arrived on the evening of the twelfth.[12] During this time, McClanahan, Lurty, and Jackson rode with the cavalry and skirmished with the enemy. On August 14, Sheridan received information that Early was about to receive reinforcements from Lee. Immediately the Federal commander issued orders that pulled his army back from its position along Cedar Creek. That same day, he dispatched Col. Thomas C. Devin's Brigade from Brig. Gen. Wesley Merritt's division of cavalry to Cedar Springs near Front Royal to shadow Maj. Gen. Joseph B. Kershaw's division of infantry and Maj. Gen. Fitz Lee's division of cavalry, which were assembling there. Breathed's Battalion of Johnston's and Shoemaker's Batteries arrived on the fourteenth and encamped.[13]

On the 15th, Merritt joined Devin with Brig. Gen. George A. Custer's Brigade, placing Col. Charles R. Lowell's Reserve Brigade to the northwest at Nineveh. The two antagonists watched each other carefully until the afternoon of the sixteenth, when Brig. Gen. Williams C. Wickham's Brigade of Fitz Lee's division, backed by Johnston's Battery and the infantry of Brig. Gen. William T. Wofford's Brigade of Kershaw's division, jumped on Devin's pickets stationed on Guard Hill about half a mile north of the North Fork of the Shenandoah River. Initially, Wickham seemed to have the upper hand, but Devin soon turned the tables on the Confederates.

While Johnston hauled his guns into position on Guard Hill, Wickham's mounted troopers dashed up the road toward Cedarville. They soon ran into a dismounted squadron of the 9th New York, which blunted Wickham's thrust long enough for Devin to lead the 4th New York in a countercharge. With Wickham repulsed, Devin looked to drive him back across the river by threatening the Confederate left. He was suddenly made aware of the Confederate infantry on his own left. The Confederates were discovered before they had an opportunity to form, and Devin quickly sent portions of the 4th and 6th New York against them. The graybacks were driven to the river, losing many prisoners and a flag. Wickham made a second charge but once more was routed. Custer joined the fight on Devin's left and succeeded in thwarting the Confederate advance.

Once Johnston had his four guns in position, he opened fire. Devin commented that "the enemy by incredible exertion, succeeded in placing his guns upon the almost perpendicular crests, and during the whole action kept an incessant rain of shot and shell upon our line, but fortunately with slight effect."[14] Merritt wrote, "The fight degenerated into an artillery duel, the enemy using vigorously a heavy battery which they had finely posted on a hill to our right front, and which had given us much trouble by its wicked fire during the battle."[15] Whether Devin's or Merritt's view is taken, Johnston's Battery provided the only high point in an otherwise dismal showing for the Confederates. The fight presaged what lay ahead for Fitz Lee's and Lomax's troopers, as well as Rosser's when he brought his famed Laurel Brigade to the Valley. The gray cavalry was a shadow of its former self and, along with the horse artillery, would suffer greatly for it.

Despite having bloodied the nose of Wickham's cavalry and Wofford's infantry, Merritt pulled back on the seventeenth, slowly retreating toward Berryville. That same morning, Early discovered that Sheridan's infantry had withdrawn from his front toward Winchester, covered by Col. Charles R. Lowell's Brigade of cavalry. The Confederates began their pursuit with McCausland's Brigade pushing down the Valley Pike, Jackson's Brigade marching on the Middle Road, and Johnson's Brigade taking the Back Road. Jackson's, Lurty's, and McClanahan's Batteries trotted along with the brigades,[16] suffering only one casualty—Captain Jackson's horse. Lowell's Reserve Brigade, supported by Col. William H. Penrose's Brigade of infantry, made a brief stand near Kernstown, but Early brought up his infantry and, in conjunction with the cavalry, drove the bluecoats back into the town.[17]

Early spent the eighteenth consolidating his forces around Winchester while Kershaw and Fitz Lee came up from Front Royal. On the nineteenth, Early moved the bulk of his army to Bunker Hill, north of Winchester. That same day, Lomax's division advanced to Martinsburg, positioning units along the line of the Opequon Creek to cover all the crossings. Kershaw and Fitz Lee remained in the vicinity of Winchester on the Front Royal and Millwood Roads. Late in the day, Wickham's Brigade with Johnston's Battery tangled with Lowell's Brigade at Spout Spring, but no major fighting occurred. The

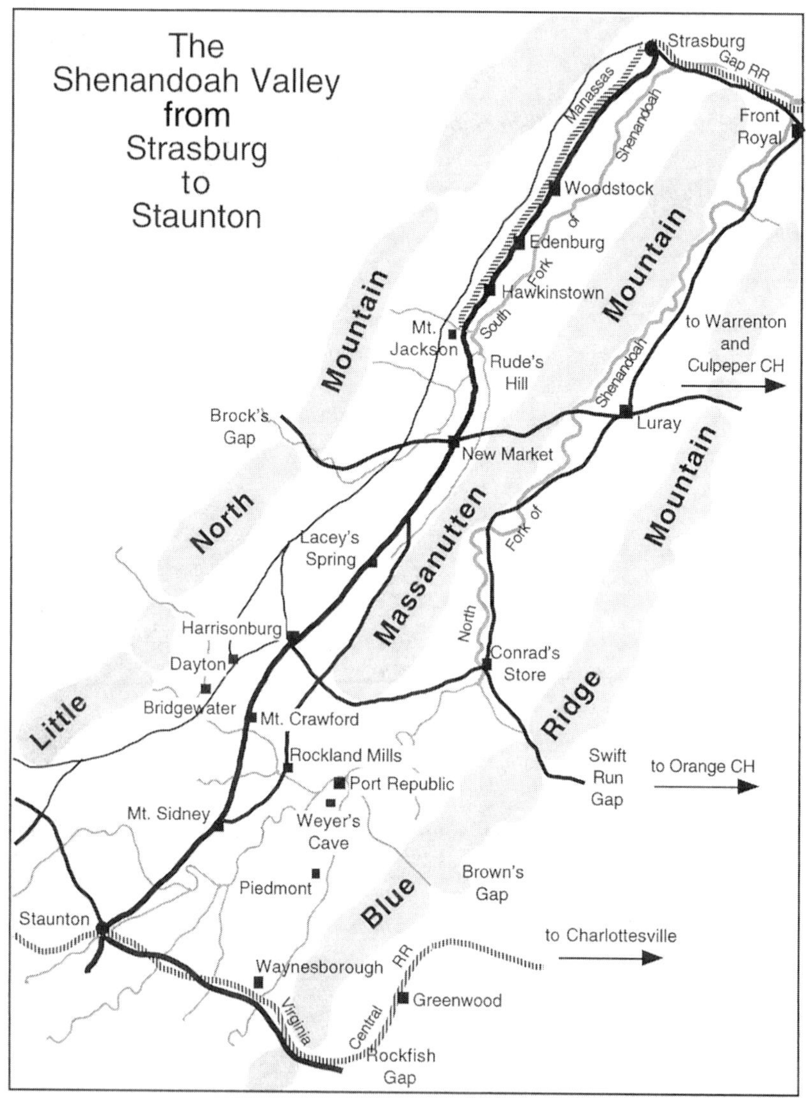
The Shenandoah Valley from Strasburg to Staunton
Strasburg
Gap RR
Manassas
Shenandoah
Front Royal
Woodstock
Edenburg
South Fork of
Hawkinstown
Mountain
Mt. Jackson
Rude's Hill
to Warrenton and Culpeper CH
Shenandoah
Luray
Mountain
Brock's Gap
New Market
North
Massanutten
Fork of
Mountain
Lacey's Spring
North
Harrisonburg
Dayton
Conrad's Store
Bridgewater
Ridge
Little
Mt. Crawford
Rockland Mills
Swift Run Gap
to Orange CH
Port Republic
Mt. Sidney
Weyer's Cave
Brown's Gap
Piedmont
Blue
Staunton
to Charlottesville
Waynesborough
RR
Greenwood
Virginia
Central
Rockfish Gap

twentieth passed with only minor skirmishing, but on the twenty-first, Early attacked Sheridan's line along the Opequon. Fitz Lee's cavalry advanced on the Berryville Road and clashed with Lowell's Brigade.

Johnston's and Shoemaker's Batteries engaged the enemy and assisted Lee's troopers in driving them back toward Berryville, often firing over the heads of the charging cavalry.[18] Lowell fell back slowly until he reached a strong position on a ridge near Berryville. Lee marshaled his forces and attacked. Under orders, Sgt. John Herley of Shoemaker's Battery took one gun into an open field in front of the enemy's line and opened a galling fire, which eventually drove the Federals back.[19] The only casualty was Pvt. George W. Covington of Johnston's Battery. Three bullets pierced Captain Shoemaker's clothes, but he emerged without a scratch.[20] The fight ended when Lowell withdrew to the north fork of Bullskin Run above Rippon.

McCausland's Brigade with McClanahan's Battery had its own scrap with the Federal cavalry as it advanced across the Opequon beyond Smithfield, where McCausland sent some of his men toward Summit Point early in the morning.[21] Backed by Early's infantry, McCausland had little trouble until the afternoon near Cameron Depot. Heavy skirmishing, including artillery fire, resulted. The gray cavalry was forced back on its infantry support, but Sheridan did not want to provoke a battle and yanked his troops out, retiring closer to Charles Town. Lomax with Jackson's, Johnson's, and Vaughn's Brigades, accompanied by Jackson's and Lurty's Batteries, marched through Leetown toward Charles Town, coming in on McCausland's left. He encountered almost no opposition.[22]

Sheridan abandoned the positions around Charles Town on the night of the twenty-first. The next day, Early sent his cavalry through the town and out the road to Halltown but did not move his infantry forward. The twenty-third was marked by a lack of movement by either army, although there was some light skirmishing. The brief respite was enjoyed by all who were able to take advantage of it. For some Confederates far away from the scene of battle, each day of inactivity that passed allowed time to reflect on what had happened and on the unknowable future. On the twenty-fifth, back at Mount Jackson, Lt. Micajah Woods wrote to his father recalling the disaster that had taken him out of the war and his efforts to get back in it:

Camp near Mt. Jackson
Aug. 24th 1864

My dear Father,

Lieut. [Richard B.] Wortham starts to the rear en route for Lynchburg tomorrow morning. He promises either to deliver this in person or to leave it at Ivy Depot.

Since my letter written from after reaching Mt. Jackson we of "The Battery" have been enjoying one of those pleasant little episodes in war so dear to the soldier, after a severe and arduous campaign—our various encampments have been selected on a back road solely with good pastures, good water, & good foraging neighborhood in view. Not a battle order or even a war rumor has ruffled the smooth quietude of our existence. Capt. Jackson has been absent during the whole time and will be for some time.

Fourteen of our very best men were killed, wounded, or captured in the stampede near Moorefield—Two are believed killed and three severely wounded, the rest captured—about 40 horses captured from us. The section now under my command has barely enough horses to move the empty carriages. In my opinion we are out of the ring for a month or two to come and perhaps for the Fall. For where are we to get the 20 horses, we need to take the field? The Government has none to spare & will they dare impress them during the busy season of seeding & garnering? Capt. Jackson wrote me a day or two ago that we would not be needed until the campaign was decided in the lower valley—When McCausland [is] expected to be made "foot loose and free" to dash into the mountains where he will winter—perhaps in Greenbrier or Monroe—while we will quietly drop down on Walker's Creek where we have 2000 bushels [of] corn & abundance of hay & oats of our own awaiting us besides the tithe of the region. I expect to be camped in this region adjacent to Mt. Jackson for a month unless our army below is driven back of which there is no likelihood.

A few days since, I started two reliable men to Salem to collect private & public horses of the Battery along the route. They are especially contracted to get my bay horse "Davy" if he can be found. They are due on Sept. 5th. Also they will bring the horse I left at Mrs. Ruff's.

Lieut. Wortham will take the train at Staunton. His negro boy "Riley" who accompanies him will take his horses to "Holkham" and stay there until Wortham returns from Lynchburg which will be about the 6th of September. By that time Lieut. [Randolph H.] Blain will have returned to duty, and I expect to join Wortham at home. Starting from camp about the 5th Inst. when my horses from Salem will have arrived. Riley the negro boy can wait on the table & do house duty or plantation work as you wish, while he stays. Five commissioned officers—our duties will be light during the Fall and without detriment to the service our commanding officers can conscientiously afford to grant us many leaves—only two officers being needed with the Battery.

Wortham will spend a day perhaps longer time with you, even if I should not succeed in joining him.

> Please don't fail to write to me immediately on the receipt of this. I shall myself attend the post office on Monday & Tuesday several miles distant with the certain expectation of receiving a letter. Direct thus. Lt. M. W. Jackson's Battery—Mt. Jackson, Shenandoah Co. Va. and it will be received. Tell the young ladies if still at Holkham that I am terribly anxious to hear from them and should write them a letter if this sheet was not the last & only one at my command this evening. Ask them if they cannot fancy I have already written them & write me a reply—They can form no idea of the pleasure [remainder of letter missing][23]

Woods's assurance that there was little likelihood of Early's army being driven from the lower Valley reflected the prevailing notion that Early could deal with Sheridan. Early, who did not have too high an opinion of Sheridan, also held this view.[24] As the campaign resumed, events were put in motion that would render a verdict not to Early's liking.

The lack of activity over the twenty-third and twenty-fourth permitted Early to reflect on his next move. He realized that Sheridan's position was too strong to attack and decided to flank him out of it by marching to Shepherdstown and threaten another crossing of the Potomac. He began his movement on the twenty-fifth, the infantry marching through Leetown directly on Shepherdstown and the cavalry to Martinsburg. On the twenty-sixth, the cavalry reached the Potomac River at Williamsport. Breathed placed a section of Johnston's Battery in position overlooking the river and the town. The Federals occupied defensive works behind the canal, their flag flying defiantly from the embankment. Breathed opened fire and rained shot and shell on them for about forty minutes.[25] Sgt. H. R. Smith shot down the flag. The affair provided good practice but was an impractical exercise and a waste of ammunition, since Early had no intention of forcing a crossing.

Failing to gain any advantage by his maneuvering, Early began to draw back his infantry to Bunker Hill on the twenty-seventh. His cavalry remained before the enemy. McCausland was ordered to Charles Town and on reaching there pushed on toward Harpers Ferry. Fitz Lee and Lomax remained near Shepherdstown. Johnston's Battery was ordered to report to Lomax at Leetown.[26] The next day, Sheridan's cavalry advanced, clashed with Lomax near Leetown, and chased him to Smithfield.[27] Here Fitz Lee joined Lomax, but little resistance was offered. A section from Shoemaker's Battery crossed the Opequon and was engaged briefly near Smithfield. In the evening, it returned as Fitz Lee withdrew across the Opequon in the direction of Brucetown and Lomax did the same toward Bunker Hill.[28]

Things got worse on the twenty-ninth. Merritt mounted a reconnaissance in force across the Opequon and drove Lomax back. He discovered what he came for—Early's infantry. With Lomax and two divisions of infantry on their heels, the Federals scurried across the Opequon and made a stand. A battery was placed in a strong position, and its fire discouraged further pursuit by the Confederates. Not one to give up quite that easily, Early called up a section of Johnston's Battery and ordered it to silence the enemy's guns. A brisk fire drove the blue cannoneers from their pieces in twenty minutes, and in twenty more they retired from the field. Early was delighted and highly praised Johnston's performance.[29] The battery suffered one casualty when Pvt. John Dullard was wounded.

The Confederate success at the Opequon left the two armies staring at each other across the creek for several days. Shoemaker reported that his battery did nothing more than picket duty through the end of August.[30] The cavalry rattled its sabers and small skirmishes flared, but nothing interrupted the overall quiet until September 2. On that date, Sheridan began a series of maneuvers to which Early responded. This jostling continued in varying degrees for over two weeks. The various horse artillery batteries that remained with the army moved hither and yon, helping the cavalry fulfill its missions of scouting, picketing, and skirmishing. Little information on the part played by the individual horse artillery batteries is available. Shoemaker's Battery was split on the seventh.[31] All the better-conditioned horses were grouped in one section, while the other section with the broken-down animals was sent to Mount Jackson[32] to rest, refit, and recruit.[33] For the section of Jackson's Battery still at Mount Jackson, the time of refit had passed. The urgency now was to return to the field.

Camp Jackson's Battery
Near Mount Jackson Va.
September 5th 1864

My dear Father,

Circumstances are such that it will be impossible for me to reach home by the 8th Inst. I hope however to get off in a few days. Lieuts. Blain or Wortham will have to return before I can be well spared. Capt. Jackson returned to camp last night will leave again tomorrow, I believe, to have a pair of boots made. He'll not return for a day or two.

The men I sent up the valley after horses are due this evening. If they bring my horses I will start Bob with them to Albemarle at once.

Your very acceptable favor of the 29th Ult. was duly received. Please let me know how my mare is doing. Has her ankle gotten entirely well? I may send the horse home I have with me. He will answer well to work but is entirely unsuitable for riding.

Enough horses have been sent for to fill our number—they are due on the 12th when we will at once report for duty. Genl. Lomax comdg. our division is very anxious to have us at once.[34] Capt. Jackson is in hot haste to return the Battery to the field. His hopes of promotion rest to a great extent on his early presence in the field. This is very [word illegible]. How does the big Pennsylvania horse stand work? The five rains we have had recently have doubtless afforded five seasons for ploughing & seeding. I regret exceedingly it is not in my power to meet Lieut. Wortham at Holkham. I wanted to show him some of our Albemarle girls. But best laid plans of men & mice oft gang agleé, and it is not the first time a soldier's anticipations have not been realized. I hope he will spend a day or two with you.

Have you heard of Lieut. Blain? If he could report I could leave.

Mother or yourself will of course write me by Lt. Wortham, giving all news. Ask William to write also. Quite a treat to hear from him as he has honored me with a letter.

Please send by Wortham 5 or 6 of the last "Chronicles." With love to dear Mother & the household I am

Most devotedly
Yr. Son
Micajah Woods

Dr. Jno. R. Woods
Holkham Va.
P.S.
Mt. Jackson Va.
Dear Father,

I have just learned direct from an officer direct from Richmond that the Government has large supplies of fine English double width cloth for officers uniforms—price $8 per yd. Will you please write at once to Col. J. A. Woods to secure me enough for a complete suit. He can get an officer in the city to go to the Dept. & purchase it or he can use the enclosed power of attorney. It is of the utmost importance that application should be made at once as the supply, however large, will be very soon exhausted & it is an opportunity not likely to rise again.[35]

Lomax's anxiousness to have Jackson's complete battery available to him was based on the simple fact that he did not have enough artillery to meet all his needs. A clash near Bunker Hill between Vaughn's and Johnson's Brigades and Averell's division resulted in the complete rout of the former with a loss of prisoners, wagons, and a battery forge.[36] The Confederate cavalry had no artillery, a situation that may have been avoided if Griffin's Battery or the absent sections of Jackson's and Lurty's Batteries had been available.[37]

Despite occasional setbacks like the cavalry's debacle at Bunker Hill, the strategic situation seemed stalemated along Opequon Creek, which provided a strong natural barrier between Early and Sheridan.[38] One of the commanders would have to commit a major mistake for the other to gain the upper hand. Early obliged Sheridan by taking the initiative and bungling first. On the fourteenth, Kershaw's division and its accompanying artillery left the Valley to return to Robert E. Lee's beleaguered army at Petersburg. As soon as confirmation could be had that Kershaw was indeed gone, Sheridan struck. The third battle of Winchester was the beginning of the end for Early in the Valley.

When Sheridan launched his offensive across Opequon Creek early on the morning of September 19, the Confederate horse artillery batteries were scattered, with the various cavalry brigades from Stephenson's Depot north of Winchester to Senseney Road southeast of the town. McClanahan's Battery supported McCausland's Brigade, which guarded the Charles Town Road crossing of the Opequon at Seiver's Ford. Imboden's Brigade, stationed near Stephenson's Depot, watched the Martinsburg Pike.[39] Lomax with Johnson's and Jackson's Brigades was positioned east of Winchester. Johnson's Brigade was split, a part being deployed north of the Berryville Road along Red Bud Run and the rest south of the road along Abram's Creek. Jackson's Brigade held the extreme right of the army near where the Senseney Road crossed Abraham's Creek. The location of Jackson's and Lurty's Batteries is unknown, though one or both may have been with Lomax.[40] Fitz Lee's cavalry with Johnston's Battery and Shoemaker's section, under Breathed's command, camped near Winchester.

The battle opened when Brig. Gen. John B. McIntosh's Brigade of Brig. Gen. James H. Wilson's division splashed across Opequon Creek at the Berryville Road crossing and, driving ahead, ran into pickets of the 23rd North Carolina Infantry at the west end of the two-mile-long Berryville Canyon. McIntosh was followed by Wilson's other brigade, under Brig. Gen. Charles H. Chapman. The predawn fight escalated as the rest of the 23rd North Carolina's brigade, under Brig. Gen. Robert D. Johnston, formed a line and Johnston's superior, Maj. Gen. Stephen D. Ramseur, fed in reinforcements. These new troops brought the Federal cavalry to a halt. Other grayjackets responded to the roar of the guns and hurried to bolster the Confederate line.

Wickham's Brigade, under Col. Thomas T. Munford, and that of Brig. Gen. William H. F. Payne scrambled from under their blankets and rode to the front.[41] Galloping in their wake came Breathed with the guns of Johnston and Shoemaker.[42] For the next three hours,[43] the gunners helped contend against Wilson's cavalry and those few portions of Sheridan's infantry that had managed to get to the front through the tangled mess at the crossing and in the narrow confines of Berryville Canyon. The fighting raged, and the Federal pressure on Ramseur mounted. Only half of Brig. Gen. Bradley T. Johnson's Brigade protected his left flank. The Marylanders fought fiercely, but the odds were against them. More troops were needed.

Though Ramseur had wasted little time marching his division to Johnston's aid, he took a moment to dispatch a courier to inform Early, who was encamped at Stephenson's Depot, of the Federal onslaught. The Valley army's commander recognized the threat Sheridan's attack posed and sent out couriers with orders for his scattered divisions to rally. Then he raced for Winchester. Behind him, Maj. Gen. Robert E. Rodes's division swung into line and tramped south. Maj. Gen. John B. Gordon's division soon followed. Early reached Ramseur and rendered what aid he could, but his eyes repeatedly turned to look toward the Martinsburg Pike. His salvation lay in the feet of Rodes's and Gordon's men. The question of whether they would arrive in time was answered, as first Rodes, then Gordon, hove into view. These veterans of the Army of Northern Virginia went about forming a new line with machine-like precision. Upon its completion, Early pulled Ramseur back to align with Rodes and Gordon.

Sheridan's plan had called for a rapid strike at Winchester and a crushing in detail of Early's army. The sheer numbers of cavalry and infantry confronting Ramseur should have overwhelmed him. But the natural bottleneck created by the crossing and the canyon robbed Sheridan of a quick victory. Early was given the time necessary to build up his force. Now Sheridan had to take the time to do the same. At this juncture, it may have appeared that Early had avoided a disaster, but to the north it was still in the making.

Like Wilson's to the south, Brig. Gen. Wesley Merritt's division approached the lower fords of Opequon Creek well before the sun had risen above the eastern horizon. Lowell's and Devin's Brigades drew rein near Seiver's Ford, while Custer's halted on the east bank of Locke's Ford about three miles downstream.[44] Opposing Merritt's division was McCausland's Brigade. To his rear along the Martinsburg Pike, Imboden's Brigade faced Averell's division advancing up the Valley from Martinsburg. The greatly outnumbered Confederates offered what resistance they could when Lowell charged across the creek. A similar scene was enacted at Locke's Ford, where Custer's Michiganders drove back the gray-jacketed pickets with relative ease.

McClanahan's Battery could do little until daylight revealed the Federals, so other than hitching the teams to the guns and caissons, the artillerymen bided their time. Lowell forged ahead, but Custer ran into a buzz saw in the form of the 22nd Virginia Cavalry and initially was thrown back.[45] Forming for another attack, the "Boy General" noticed the Confederates giving ground. Averell's push from the north and Lowell's success to the south had uncovered their flank. All they could do was retreat. Dawn found Merritt firmly established on the west side of the Opequon and chasing McCausland toward the pike. Maj. Gen. John C. Breckinridge with Brig. Gen. Gabriel C. Wharton's division of infantry presented a firm line on which McCausland could rally. Merritt chose not to come to grips with the infantry, and his regiments came to a standstill.

For about three hours, only light skirmishing and artillery fire could be heard along Merritt's front. Undoubtedly, McClanahan's Battery contributed to the Southern artillery's response, but this, too, was only sporadic. About 11:00 A.M., the Federals launched a determined charge against Wharton's position. They made a brief breakthrough but were hurled back by heavy artillery fire and musketry from the flanks. Merritt delayed further attacks until after 1:00 P.M. Averell's columns bogged down as well. Early's extreme left was holding on, but Sheridan still had the advantage to the south, where the tempo of the battle began to quicken.

Just after 11:30 A.M., Sheridan's legions finally rolled forward. The VI and XIX Corps faced Ramseur, Rodes, and Gordon, while Wilson shifted his entire command to the left against Lomax. But Wilson did not have his heart in the attack and barely nudged Lomax's line. Noticing this, Fitz Lee concluded that Lomax could deal with Wilson and hold Ramseur's right. The real danger lay on Gordon's left, where Bradley T. Johnson needed assistance. Wickham was ordered to pull out Munford's Brigade and Breathed's Battalion, pass behind the infantry, cross Red Bud Run, and take position on Johnson's left.[46] For the second time that morning, Lee's troopers and Breathed's gunners were in a race. It wouldn't be the last.

Col. Thomas T. Munford described his and Breathed's roles in the fighting that followed:

> Johnson's troops were on the left of [Brig. Gen. Clement A.] Evans's infantry brigade of Gordon's division.[47] We were dismounted and became engaged very quickly; but a few well-directed shots from our horse artillery cleared our immediate front. General Fitz Lee, taking command of the whole line, Wickham of the division, I had the brigade. Our battery was moved up to the edge of a piece of timber;[48] to our front and right was an open plateau extending for several miles. Our battery was sheltered by timber on our left. The enemy's batteries were firing obliquely to our right at our infantry and their batteries (Carter's and Braxton's). A little more than a quarter of a mile to our right was "Ash Hollow," a water shed, a deep ravine in which the enemy had formed, and Rickett's division of the Sixth corps, and Grover's division of the Nineteenth corps, were debouching to attack—this was about 12 o'clock. General Fitz Lee turned his artillery's guns upon this body of the enemy. The handling of our six guns of horse artillery was simply magnificent. Strange enough, the enemy's guns did not respond to these. Our cannoneers made their battery roar, sending their death-dealing messengers with a precision and constancy that made the earth around them seem to tremble, while their shot and shell made lanes in this mass of the enemy moving obliquely to their right to attack Evans's brigade.[49]

The Federal infantry that endured this fire were the brigades of Brig. Gen. Henry W. Birge and Col. Jacob Sharpe of Brig. Gen. Cuvier Grover's division of the XIX Corps. Emerging from the "Ash Hollow" woods, Birge and Sharpe ran into a whirlwind of shot and shell from Confederate artillery to their front and Breathed's guns on their flank. Johnston's and Shoemaker's cannoneers quickly became begrimed, as smoke and burnt powder mixed with sweat. Since no enemy battery or infantry fired on them, the men were able to work the guns with a rhythm that was beautiful yet frightening. Death leaped from each cannon's mouth at the jerking of the lanyard. The Federals were stung but not stopped.

Both brigades forged ahead. However, Birge's outraced Sharpe's and won the honor of receiving a deadly volley of musketry from Atkinson's Brigade. Breathed kept up his fire, but Birge did not break. Atkinson did, and the fleeing graybacks were chased by the intermingled men of Birge's and Sharpe's commands. Then Gordon's remaining brigades and Braxton's artillery hurled back the Federals. Munford recalled Breathed's part in the rout:

> As they [the Federals] went back over the same ground over which they had marched to attack in great disorder, having been badly broken up, our battery, if possible, excelled itself, and a more murderous fire I never witnessed than was plunged into this heterogeneous mass as they rushed back. We could see the track of the shot and shell as they would scatter the men, but the lanes closed up for another to follow. The field was strewn with their dead and wounded before they got back from whence they started.[50]

With Grover's repulse, a lull settled over that portion of the field as each side stopped to regroup and catch their collective breath. Breathed's gunners slumped down next to their pieces, thankful for the chance to rest. It did not last very long. Barely had the cannoneers made themselves as comfortable as the situation allowed when a courier dashed up and ordered Munford to mount up and return to the right flank to aid Lomax.[51] The command was given, and teams were hitched to the guns. The men jumped into their saddles and galloped off to meet yet another crisis, of which there seemed to be a growing number. A very big one was coming to a head north along the Martinsburg Road, where McCausland, Smith, and Breckinridge still confronted Averell and Merritt.

Merritt's lack of activity following his 11:00 A.M. repulse was enjoyed by McCausland's and Smith's cavalry and Breckinridge's infantry, who preferred to let sleeping dogs lie. The Federal cavalry commander was none too excited about renewing the contest either, as long as he knew he was dealing with Breckinridge's foot soldiers. Pot shots were all that anyone was willing to exchange, and this was done with care to avoid a possible eruption of heavier fighting. This impasse lasted until after noon, when two things occurred that pivoted the battle in Sheridan's favor.

The first of these came in the form of a courier who galloped up to Maj. Gen. John C. Breckinridge and handed him an order from Early. The general was directed to march south to Winchester. The battle there had used up all of the reserve troops Early had, and Breckinridge's men were needed to fill that role.[52] This decision, while necessary and wise on one hand, committed the fate of the army's left flank to the two small brigades of McCausland and Smith. Yet Early had to take the gamble. Jackson had gambled in the Valley and won. So had Breckinridge at New Market. Early could only hope the gods of war that had blessed the other Valley armies would grant one more blessing to his. Unfortunately, like an avalanche that begins small at the top of the mountain and grows as it cascades downward, Early's decision to withdraw Breckinridge began an avalanche of Federal blue.

The second decision was out of Early's hands. It rested with Averell and Merritt. They would have to decide to challenge McCausland and Smith, and at about 1:30 P.M. they did just that. Merritt plowed into McCausland and drove him back. Averell did the same to Smith. McClanahan's Battery could do little without cavalry support to stem the oncoming Federals, and soon the whole Confederate force was hightailing it rearward.[53] After a run of about a mile, McCausland and Smith met Fitz Lee with Payne's Brigade.[54] Lee made a valiant effort to stop Averell and Merritt but had his favorite horse killed beneath him and received a wound in the leg for his trouble. Confederate resistance then disintegrated. A mad dash for Winchester ensued, but at the outskirts of town, another stand was attempted.

Col. George S. Patton's Brigade of infantry and a battalion of artillery delayed the Federal cavalry's all-out pursuit. This allowed Lee some time to rally the Confederate cavalry just north of Winchester. However, Patton's troops were outflanked by Averell and fell back to a defensive position on the outskirts of Winchester, where they meshed with the rest of Early's army, driven back at last by Sheridan's infantry. In this final position, the Confederates tried to halt the Federals, who smelled victory on the wind. Aiding in this final struggle were Munford's Brigade and Shoemaker's section, hurried over from where they had been assisting Lomax on the army's right flank. Munford wrote of the cavalry's and artillery's parts in the final struggle:

> Two divisions of cavalry, Averell's and Torbert's [Merritt's] were now just ahead and in sight. Averell had sent a mounted regiment to take Fort Hill, to the north of Winchester, and a very commanding position to the west of the pike. General Early had no idea of allowing him to hold it, as that covered the pike below, and sent orders to me to take it and hold it. Up the hill we went and at them, followed by two guns of our horse artillery. We drove them from the hill, ran the two pieces in

the fort, dismounted the First, Second, and Fourth Virginia cavalry, giving the Third the protection of the led horses, and we had just gotten well into the fort when Averell charged to recapture it; but we gave them a rough welcome, and sent them back faster than they came up. A second charge was made with the same result, during which time our two guns had been doing splendid service. They had opened with such precision upon the cavalry below that it checked them.

Looking below to our right we could see our infantry falling back rapidly and in some disorder, and our little battery was now to catch it. Three of the enemy's batteries from below opened upon us with a terrific fire. I ordered the guns to retire; they limbered up and had moved out, when a shell from the enemy's battery took off the head of one of our cannoneers [Pvt. Thomas P. Cullen].[55] Sergeant Hawley [Sgt. John Herley],[56] in charge of that piece, stopped it, and as it was shotted, unlimbered and fired it while the dead man was being strapped on the limberchest, and then moved off.[57]

Captain Shoemaker provided another view of his section's gallant fight:

About 4 o'clock in the afternoon Gen. Lee gave orders for Wickham's brigade [Munford] and our battery to follow him at a gallop to our left on the Martinsburg Pike, where a strong force of the enemy's cavalry were driving our left flank back in some confusion. It was a sight to see our cavalry led across that field by Fitz Lee and Wickham, followed by my battery, at a gallop. The cavalry met the enemy on the Martinsburg Pike, and my battery went to the top of Fort Hill at an angle of nearly 45 degrees—a most extraordinary feat—and one, I believe, which could not have been accomplished under less exciting circumstances.

At any rate we went right up to the top of it and got there in time to knock a Yankee battery into pie before they could unlimber and fire a shot. Other of their batteries followed at once under our fire and soon commenced firing on us and our men. Our cavalry were not strong enough to cope successfully with the superior force of the enemy, who had already gained a point on the Pike, where they were forcing Early's left flank back, and from that time—about sundown—the fate of Winchester was sealed and Gen. Early's army retreating. My battery remained on the hill, shelling the enemy, until Sheridan's entire army came into view on the plateau in front of Winchester and fired on us with all their artillery from our left and front. The sight of 30,000 troops drawn up in line of battle with their glistening arms was a grand and impressive spectacle, but the flashing of all their artillery and the storm of shells thrown at us were more persuasive, and we had to bid them a very hasty "Good afternoon."[58]

Munford's and Shoemaker's withdrawal in the face of overwhelming odds was not an isolated incident nor an act relegated to the horse artillery and cavalry. After fighting for almost twelve hours, the small Valley army could stand the pressure no longer. The Federal cavalry simply rode over the Confederates, shattering their lines and breaking their will to resist. Early's entire army abandoned the field to Sheridan's victorious troops.

The army, though beaten, was not destroyed, as it probably should have been. One of the main reasons for this was the fact that Wilson had failed to aggressively attack Lomax and seize the Valley Pike south of Winchester. Compared with the contribution made by Averell and Merritt, Wilson's meager thrusts at Lomax did little to enhance that officer's reputation. The Confederate horse artillery with Lomax, along with Breathed's Battalion early in the day and Shoemaker's section later, helped put up enough of a front to keep Wilson from launching what could have been a devastating blow.

Little can be said concerning the overall performance of the five batteries of Confederate horse artillery on the field. No accurate account of Jackson's, Lurty's, or McClanahan's participation was recorded, although two pieces were lost from these batteries.[59] Pvt. Hendron H. Stone of McClanahan's Battery was recorded as being wounded, and Pvt. Aylett B. Coleman was mortally wounded. The other batteries were only lightly engaged, or the records failed to show the casualties suffered. On the other hand, Johnston's and Shoemaker's Batteries displayed the qualities that had made them two of the premier horse batteries in the Confederacy. While their mobility again highlighted their performance, their fighting prowess, displayed in the morning against Grover's division and in the afternoon by Shoemaker's section against Averell, cannot be overlooked. Amazingly, Johnston's Battery recorded not a single casualty for the day. Of all the batteries, Shoemaker's suffered the heaviest loss, but considering the length of time it was in action, it was not excessive.

Early's army retreated until it reached Fisher's Hill, about twenty miles south of Winchester, near daylight on the twentieth. Jackson's, Lurty's, and McClanahan's Batteries and Shoemaker's section moved with Lomax's cavalry and arrived at Fisher's Hill with the army. Shoemaker's section continued on and joined the battery's other section at Mount Jackson on the twenty-first.[60] Breathed and Johnston's Battery accompanied Wickham, now commanding Fitz Lee's division, to Front Royal in order to prevent the Federals from using the Luray Valley to outflank Early. Wilson's division pursued, capturing Front Royal the morning of the twenty-first and forcing Wickham to retreat up the Luray Valley. Torbert with Merritt's division, minus Devin's Brigade, followed Wilson. At Gooney Run, on the road between Front Royal and Milford, Wickham made a brief stand. Johnston's Battery was unlimbered, but no heavy fighting erupted, as the Confederate position was vulnerable to being outflanked, and Wickham only wanted to hold until dark. Captain Johnston had his horse killed beneath him but was unhurt. The battery suffered no casualties. That night, Wickham retreated.

By the morning of the twenty-second, Wickham had taken a new position at Milford south of Overall's Run. Torbert, with Wilson in advance, came up, and a small skirmish began. The Confederates held a very strong position. The dismounted troopers occupied defensive works that spanned the narrow valley and were backed by Johnston's Battery in a small work above them. Wilson studied Wickham's line and determined that it could not be taken without heavy loss. Still, he wanted to take a crack at trying to turn the enemy's right flank. Munford, who commanded the division, Wickham having ridden off to conference with Early, was ready for any Federal advance, as was Jim Breathed.

> Torbert, running out his artillery, commenced a furious shelling which our battery answered with vigor. His men demonstrated heavily in front of Payne, whose men were at the bridge, and they moved up in our front as if they intended to assault my lines. Payne repulsed those in front of him, and our rifles opened from behind stumps, rocks, and rail piles and trees with such a ringing fire, back they all went. This was being kept up so long I began to suspect something, and sent Captain Thomas Whitehead, of Company E, Second Virginia Cavalry, to my extreme right with a scout, who soon notified me by courier that a considerable force (he thought a brigade) were making around across the mountain to turn our position. My line had already been stretched to its greatest tension; our led horses had consumed one-fourth of the command.
>
> I was in conversation with Major Breathed when this information was brought me; I asked him if he felt safe with his battery, if I moved the squadron in his front, over whose heads his guns were firing? He smiled and said, "If 'Billy' (Colonel Payne) can hold that bridge—and it looks like he is going to do it—I'll put a pile of canister near my guns, and all h——l will never move me from this position. I'll make a horizontal shot turn in full blast for them to come through; you need not be afraid of my guns."[61]

Wilson quickly discovered Munford's preparations and chose not to test them. Torbert withdrew to McCoy's Ferry and gave up his pursuit.[62] The turning back of Torbert saved Early's army from being outflanked on their right. Wickham's and Munford's use of an excellent defensive position was textbook. If only Early had been capable of the same!

The Valley army's position at Fisher's Hill looked impregnable, and it would have been if Early had possessed enough troops to man it properly. The Confederate infantry occupied the main line of works, but all Early had to hold his left was Lomax's cavalry, which, with the exception of Jackson's and Johnson's Brigades, had received a sound drubbing at Winchester. Upon reaching Fisher's Hill on the twenty-second, Jackson's, Johnson's, and Smith's Brigades were dismounted and placed on the left of the infantry. To hold a line of over one mile, Lomax had about 1,000 men.[63] McCausland's Brigade was placed east of the North Fork of the Shenandoah River to guard the crossings there. Other portions of his command picketed the mountain gaps in rear of the army.

Interspersed behind Lomax's line was his horse artillery. Jackson's Battery[64] was on the extreme left, along with at least one gun of McClanahan's Battery. The disposition of the remainder of McClanahan's Battery and Lurty's Battery is unknown. The disaster was precipitated by an attack on Early's left flank. Maj. Gen. George Crook's Army of West Virginia began its assault about 4:00 P.M. on the twenty-second. Crook's infantry poured down from Little North Mountain and smashed into Lomax's flank and rear. In a letter to his father, Lieutenant Woods described what happened to the horse artillery on that flank:

> In the field near New Market Va.
> September 23rd 1864
>
> My dear Father,
>
> Capricious fortune makes me again the bearer to you of direful intelligence to our cause. My communication of Tuesday detailed to you the disasters of the previous day—how the intrepid Rodes & many a gallant compeer fell victims to the enemy's hail in unsuccessful battle—and the frightful intelligence that for the first & only time in the annals of the war four grand Divisions of the army of Northern Va. had been driven in confusion & discomfort from the field of conflict. This fact was then ominous to me of unexpressed evil. My darkest forebodings have alas been too soon fulfilled to an extent that is woeful to our young country & its cause. Worn out by hard work in fortifications, by hard fighting for hours, & a march of 20 miles in the dark I can scarcely summon sufficient energy to recount to you the stirring deeds & terrible disasters that fell to the fate of this army on the line of Fisher's Hill on yesterday.
>
> As I wrote you after the reverse at Winchester our forces concentrated on the strongest position in the Shenandoah Valley and immediately proceeded to strengthen the already strong natural & artificial position stretching across Fisher's Hill from the lower end of the Massanutten to the base of the North Mountain. During Tuesday & Wednesday the whole line was constructed from mountain to mountain and the troops assigned. The section of our Battery under my command (Lt. Blain being sick) occupied good works of our own construction on the extreme left of our position, held by Lomax's

cavalry all dismounted. The enemy contented himself during the morning feeling & developing our lines. Late in the evening [he] filed a column around the end of our fortifications along the base of the mountain on the left, thereby completely flanking the position. This movement through the shameful negligence of someone was not discovered till it had been actually accomplished, and the columns had not only reached the rear of our lines but had actually charged upon the rear of the position.

As soon as the enemy's position & intention were developed I opened with my two guns assisted by one of McClanahan's, giving the advancing column a furious fire of shell and canister—but terrible to behold, as well as decisive of our fate (the artillerists) the entire line on the left of dismounted cavalry upon which we had to rely rushed from the works in confusion—neither officers nor men seeming to know what to do. First they retired on a line with my guns & opened a desultory fire from a loose & huddled formation. As the enemy approached I continued my rapid discharge with such effect that twice the enemy's line was broken by shell & canister alone, but our supports vanished and fled & left us to the enemy's mercy. Lieut. Wortham with the second gun detachment heroically stood their ground along with my first piece of which [I] had taken charge, giving the enemy canister until they were in a few yards in front & actually on our flank. Then we attempted to withdraw.

Lieut. Wortham limbered up his gun but had proceeded but a few steps before two of his horses were killed [and] a driver struck, causing the abandonment of the piece. I ran my piece by hand to the rear about 50 yds. & limbered up—the enemy doing their best to overtake and we escaped after a race of over a mile—the enemy being only about 50 yds. in the rear all the time & succeeding in wounding one of my drivers and two of my horses. But to return to the "tent ensemble" of the engagement. Simultaneously with striking the left flank & turning it, capturing one of my guns & McClanahan's under the same circumstances—the foe made heavy demonstrations along the line with skirmishers & artillery—the column on the left moved down our line winding up brigade after brigade & division after division & causing them to retire in the wildest confusion—deserting artillery & small arms without compunction, until night ended the disgraceful drama.

The result may be summed up thus: our whole army was forced to give up its line—more than half of it in great confusion with the loss of fourteen cannons & many prisoners & horses. The victory was more easily won & less dearly bought by the enemy than any ever achieved on this continent. The quick advent of night alone prevented the terrible affair from being an overwhelming disaster to the army—resulting in its rout & destruction. As it is we have some artillery left and about three or four thousand men are minus small arms, having had them frightened from their grasp—not wrenched or broken in honorable combat. The entire extent of the column that tapped & turned our flank & finally wound up half the army was under my view as well as under my guns—and it is my deliberate conviction that one thousand men properly handled could at any time have repulsed its assault & changed the fate of the day. It is apparent to every man in this army, and I am grieved to say it, that there is something radically wrong in the management of this command and which if not speedily changed will result not only in its destruction but in the ultimate ruin of our cause. The enemy were doubtless far more amazed than we that they should unobserved & unmolested be permitted to occupy a position on the flank of the army & then march over two miles of our works—emptying them almost without resistance except from artillery.

I cannot find words but they are too tame to express my pride in the heroic men of my Battery. Their noble & intrepid stand yesterday has elicited not only the admiration of Capt. Jackson but of all on our part of the line. There are some among them who would be disparaged by being put upon our so called "Roll of honor" which we of the army know to be the work of favoritism & individual self-interested intrigue. As yet we are unable to form an estimate of the loss in the Battery. Several we know to be wounded, and many are missing either wounded or captured. Some may yet report. You will perhaps esteem me very silly for thus expressing myself about the men of Jackson's Battery, but you must recollect it is the honest expression of feeling of a devoted son to his father, who knows his unreserved confidence will not be abased or misinterpreted. The attack of the enemy's infantry on our left was followed by charge of cavalry which resulted in the capture of our Battery ambulance & wagon & our two caissons on a back road by which they were retiring. Jackson's Battery this morning consists of one gun & one forge manned by greatly reduced numbers.

Our army (what remains of it with arms) is in the vicinity of Mt. Jackson awaiting the enemy's advance. There has been some cannonading this morning. I take it for granted that the enemy will advance in force. If Genl. Early determines to give them another round it will be at Rude's Hill, and I will take my gun down & give him "the best in the shop." Of the prospects & condition of the army I forbear to speak. I can confidentially say to you that I regard its future career in the Valley with by no means hopeful anticipation.

After reading my accounts of Winchester & Fisher's Hill you can readily conceive my reasons. It is evident that if there is not a speedy change for the better in resisting the heavy advancing column of the enemy that Albemarle, Lynchburg, & Richmond with the very State itself is in jeopardy & should prepare for the worst. God forbid that the demonical plans of the foe under such fair headway may succeed. I write this to you & (have not said all I think) in the strictest confidence as you well know how cautious an officer in the service should be in the expression of his sentiments. I know one thing that I can maintain, my position in the field as long and shall do it as long as the most sanguine, and I pray to Heaven that our cause may be successful and shall battle for it as long as there is hope in my judgment.

Bob reached me in safety this morning with Kate & his mule. The enemy gave him a hard chase yesterday evening while endeavoring to reach me on the left. He was only about 100 yds. from the wagon when the Yankee cavalry caught it.

I should be much delighted to reach home during the visit of Mr. Foote. I have high admiration for his talents & especially for his manly & bold course in Congress.

In the recent retrograde movements & engagements I have been to some extent a sufferer, having lost all my blankets including my saddle & oilcloth. The arrival of my overcoat this morning is therefore extremely opportune. The collars that Mother was kind enough to send as Bob states were lost. My thanks for them are none the less sincere also the eatables & peaches though somewhat dilapidated were truly acceptable.

Lt. Wortham's servant & horse have not yet reported they were both probably captured.

Please let Jack wash the back of the horse I sent by Bob as I wish him in service before long.

As ever my best love to Mother and all,

Dr. Jno. R. Woods Your devoted son

Micajah Woods[65]

Of all the horse artillery engaged at Fisher's Hill, Jackson's Battery absorbed the greatest loss. In addition to losing one gun, Privates George W. Asberry, Elijah G. Davis, Clarence L. Jackson, John B. Low, F. M. Owens, and Marcellus Wood were captured. Sgt. William E. Cox and Lt. Henry P. Norton became prisoners as well. Pvt. Thomas J. Young was severely wounded in the side, and Pvt. John M. Kent was mortally wounded. Privates Thomas Malloy and Charles L. Rhodes were killed. McClanahan's Battery lost a gun, but only two men were captured—Privates William J. Griffin and Z. Isey.

The rout in which Woods was forced to participate carried Early's shattered divisions to Woodstock. Once again darkness saved the army, which actually suffered little in the way of casualties—a fact that illustrates just how quickly the men bolted. Spared to fight another day, Early began the job of saving what he had. After reestablishing some order, he directed the army to continue its retreat until it reached Mount Jackson, where it rested most of the twenty-third. That night, it crossed the river and took up position on Rude's Hill. Sheridan came up that same day and sent Devin's Brigade to outflank Early's left. Not to be caught napping a second time, Early ordered a retreat. The army, except for Jackson's Brigade of cavalry, swung toward Port Republic and pitched camp beyond the village in Brown's Gap. Sheridan let Early go and instead marched on to Harrisonburg, driving Jackson before him.[66] On the twenty-fifth, Wickham rejoined the army at Brown's Gap. His army at last united, Early awaited reinforcements and watched Sheridan burn the Valley.[67]

Little fighting occurred for the next several days. McCausland's Brigade and McClanahan's Battery tangled with Devin's Brigade near Port Republic on the twenty-sixth. The battery lost one man captured, Pvt. James M. Wood. An opportunity to strike at Col. William H. Powell's division, formerly Averell's,[68] occurred on the twenty-seventh. Wickham's division, led by Munford's Brigade, which included at least one section of Johnston's Battery, followed by Gordon's and Ramseur's infantry divisions, crossed the South Fork of the Shenandoah River at Patterson's Mill and attacked the enemy's camp. Munford unlimbered two guns of Johnston's Battery and then began to shift his troopers into a position from which to launch an assault. Before this could be accomplished, General Wickham arrived and ordered the guns to commence firing. This alerted the enemy to the Confederate presence, and in the subsequent fighting, Powell was able to retreat with little damage. The battery suffered no casualties.

Having missed the chance to seriously damage a part of the Federal cavalry, Wickham turned to stab at another. He received information that Wilson's division and Lowell's Brigade from Merritt's division were near Waynesboro, destroying the iron railroad bridge over the South Fork of the Shenandoah River. Wickham sent Munford with Johnston's Battery to deal with them and promised support from Brig. Gen. John Pegram's division of infantry. Munford wrote about the fight that followed and the role played by Johnston's Battery:

> We had to wait a little time for our artillery to come up. The blind road was filled with fallen trees and logs, but that splendid battery could follow the cavalry anywhere and overcome any reasonable obstacle. When well up, the First Virginia Cavalry was dismounted and sent down the Chesapeake and Ohio railroads towards Waynesboro and the bridge over the Shenandoah. The Fourth Virginia,

> mounted, was ordered to charge the enemy's reserve picket. Captain Johnston, commanding the battery (a gallant officer), was ordered to move up at a trot and occupy an elevated piece of ground with his guns, while the Third and Second, dismounted, supporting it and the Fourth Virginia. They were all pushed over across the Charlottesville and Staunton pike, south of and parallel with the railroad. This was promptly executed, and immediately after the move was started, the enemy started back. (Coming in behind their picket from the opposite direction from which we were expected was a complete surprise, which advantage I pressed, and was heartily seconded by the whole command. Prisoners captured told me they supposed it was Hampton's command from Gen. Lee's army, as we had come from the direction of Charlottesville, and they had heard that morning that General Early had been reinforced from Richmond.)
>
> Captain Johnston's battery was handled with great skill. He opened on the working party attempting to pull the bridge to pieces with splendid effect. They scattered and started back at a run, and as long as there was a mark to fire at, east of Waynesboro, his guns blazed at it. Arriving at the river, the First, Second, and Third were mounted, but the Fourth had pushed on, and had some sharp skirmishing in the town before the other regiments came up. Upon their arrival we soon cleared the town, and Johnston's Battery took position on the west end and was having a sharp duel with the enemy's battery. This was after sundown, when Gen. Early with his infantry appeared on their flank, and with a few shots from the artillery attached to Gen. Pegram's infantry brigade, they started to retire, and after night moved rapidly back through Staunton to join their own army.[69]

Early's arrival took the Federals completely by surprise, but they did try to put up a fight. Johnston's Battery was instrumental in breaking their resistance east of the river. Capt. George N. Bliss of the 1st Rhode Island Cavalry had been in the town when Munford's troopers attacked the wrecking party. He gathered about thirty men and charged across the river. Colonel Lowell then directed him to go to the ford, stop the stragglers from retreating, rally them, and form a line. As this was being done, Johnston's Battery dropped a few of its first shells among these men, and they broke for the rear.[70] All resistance east of the river was swept away by Johnston's accurate fire. His battery's actions well deserved Munford's praise.

The success at Waynesboro did little to alleviate the suffering in the Valley. Like the rest of the army, the men of the horse artillery batteries could only stand and watch the destruction. Lieutenant Woods wrote a letter to his father telling of the horrors he witnessed from his post with the lone gun of Jackson's Battery in Brown's Gap:

Top of Brown's Gap
30th Sept. 1864 Evening

My dear Father

I am on the highest point of Brown's Gap with my gun supported by McCausland's Brigade. The enemy have made no demonstration in our front. The road is heavily blockaded up the mountain & we are ordered to hold the gap to the last extremity.

Yesterday I witnessed a sight so atrocious that the [word illegible] dastard would become a hero in preventing in his own land. "The Valley" was in flames from dawn till the late hours of night were brightened by lurid flames. Immediately in my view were burnt not less than one hundred haystacks & barns. Nearly every farm large or small has been visited by the torch. The enemy advanced up the Valley with a skirmish line from mountain to mountain capturing all stock and negroes—and delivering to the flames every article that could subsist man or beast.

About 12 yesterday they burnt Jno. Lewis furnace and forge [name illegible] saw both his barns fired.

The whereabouts of the enemy are unknown precisely. It is my opinion that they have brought up their infantry but have been devastating & pursuing with their heavy cavalry force of three divisions. Their main force in my judgment has not yet appeared if indeed it comes at all by this route. The army is in better spirits since joined by Anderson & Kershaw with a reinforcement of 2100 men. Let us hope for the best but our prospect is bad in this region. Albemarle may escape the fire & sword.

Rejoiced to hear your stock (some of it) has been sent to the mountain farm—safer there perhaps than at home. The Valley is certainly being made untenable by an army as well as the country as they advance. The country below here burned, a great field of fire [word illegible] last night.

Bob reached us at 12 last night having missed us near Port Republic & traveled with the army to Waynesboro thence via Mechum's River to this place. Many thanks for the provisions. Capt. Harvie and myself will be down in a day or two. If our command ordered from here higher up by Mechum's River I will bring Col. Ferguson to see you. This will be taken down by Mr. Jno. Lewis.

Love to all & kind regards to Col. C. & lady.
Yr. affte son
Micajah Woods[71]

The story was the same as far as the eye could see. Smoke from burning hay, grain, barns, mills, and some houses filled the air. Those soldiers who called the Valley their home suffered most of all. They carried an almost unbearable burden. First they had failed to drive out the invader, and now, because of that failure, they were forced to watch the destruction of their friends', neighbors', and, in many instances, their own property. Veterans of a score of battles wept bitter and vengeful tears. It was all they could do. Yet as appalled as the troops of the Valley army were, they could not foresee that things would get worse.

CHAPTER 33

The Valley Lost

"The whole Yankee army with Abe Lincoln in the lead was after them."

Having driven Early's army nearly out of the Valley, Maj. Gen. Philip Sheridan had a free hand to implement Grant's command to lay waste to the "Breadbasket of the Confederacy." He did so with relish. As October dawned, the Federals continued their denuding of the upper Valley. Then on the fifth, Sheridan issued orders to fall back down the Valley. His cavalry was commanded to scorch everything behind them. Prior to the withdrawal, some of Early's cavalry and infantry had skirmished with the Federals. Johnston's Battery was engaged at Bridgewater on October 2 and had one man, Pvt. P. H. Kelcher, wounded. Such efforts were feeble and did little to stem the destruction, but until the bulk of the army gathered its strength, it was all that could be done.

Unlike Johnston's Battery, which continued to strike at the enemy, the other horse batteries spent the last days of September and the early days of October resting or marching. On September 27, Lt. John R. McNulty, still commanding Griffin's Battery, received orders to rejoin the army at Port Republic. Since the fiasco at Moorefield, the battery had been recuperating and refitting in the vicinity of New Market. As Sheridan advanced up the Valley, the battery managed to avoid capture and, when the word came, was ready to return to the struggle. Jackson's Battery remained in Brown's Gap for some time and did not follow the army when it moved out on the sixth. Lurty's and McClanahan's Batteries continued to serve with Lomax's division, which did little between September 26 and October 6. Shoemaker's Battery crossed over the mountain through Brown's Gap, on September 24. On the twenty-eighth, it received orders to return to the Valley and marched to the summit of Brown's Gap, only to find that the army had moved farther up the Valley. Turning around, Shoemaker led his men into Albemarle County. They would not link up with the army until October 9.[1] During this same time period, additional reinforcements arrived from Lee's army in the form of Brig. Gen. Thomas L. Rosser's Brigade of cavalry and Thomson's Battery of horse artillery. The battery had been whiling away its time encamped near Gordonsville and was well rested. Thomson's cannoneers were Valley men, and the sight of burning barns, mills, and houses inflamed them. They had come to help Early take back the Valley.

When Sheridan began his retrograde movement, Early was quick to respond. He ordered Lomax to send some troopers into the Luray Valley to parallel the Federals' line of march and to follow Sheridan with the rest. Smith's Brigade with McClanahan's Battery headed for the Luray Valley.[2] Lomax with Jackson's and Johnson's Brigades trailed after Sheridan. Griffin's Battery accompanied Lomax. McCausland's Brigade stayed behind to guard Brown's and Swift Run Gaps, keeping with it Jackson's and Lurty's Batteries for that purpose.[3]

Rosser, who was given command of all of Wickham's cavalry, wasted little time in crossing swords with Sheridan's mounted arm.[4] Having arrived on the fifth, he was off in pursuit on the sixth and tangled with Custer at Mill Creek on the Back Road west of Mount Jackson on the seventh. The bluecoats fell back stubbornly but were out of range before Johnston had an opportunity to unlimber his guns and give them even a parting shot. Thomson's Battery was still trailing the column, trying to catch up.[5] The cavalry scratched and clawed at each other again on the eighth, with Rosser driving Custer back to Tom's Brook. The Federals spent the night on the north side of the stream, while the Confederates settled down on its south side.

Lomax held on doggedly to the tail end of Sheridan's army as it retreated up the Valley Pike. Nipping at the bluecoats' heels, he managed to save some barns and mills from the flames, capture some prisoners, and generally make a nuisance of himself. Devin's Brigade took a swipe at Lomax on the seventh, forcing him to fall back five miles. On the eighth, Lomax went right back at the enemy. His leading brigade, Jackson's, pushed the Federal rear guard beyond Woodstock before it ran into blue-coated infantry, which caused the Confederates to retreat. Later in the day, Lomax advanced once more to prevent the Federals from concentrating their strength against Rosser. It was a bold gesture but, as events would prove, futile and costly.

Late on the night of the eighth, Brig. Gen. George A. Custer received a "brief note from the chief of cavalry, directing [him] at an early hour the following morning to move [his] command up the Back road toward Columbia Furnace, and to attack and whip the enemy."[6] Custer would have company. Merritt's division would entertain Lomax on the pike but not develop a full attack until Custer had dealt with Rosser. And deal with him he did. The brigade of Col. Alexander C. M. Pennington, late of the Federal horse artillery, led the advance early on the morning of the ninth and encountered pickets of the 4th Virginia Cavalry, which had been pushed north of Tom's Brook in the vicinity of Mount Olive. The Federals chased them back on their reserves, and the fight was on. The Confederates withdrew across the stream and took up what Custer felt was a position "well adapted for defense."[7] He faced dismounted cavalry along the base of a ridge that overlooked the brook. On the crest, Rosser had deployed his mounted cavalry and Breathed's six guns, two of Thomson's and four of Johnston's.

Capt. Charles H. Peirce's Battery B/L, 2nd U.S. Artillery, unlimbered on a small rise north of the stream and opened fire. Thomson's guns, under the "gallant Carter," replied and had the better of the exchange.[8] For a change, it was the Federal ammunition that proved faulty, and Breathed's position was superior.[9] Corp. George M. Neese of Thomson's Battery later took credit for a shot that exploded in front of Lt. Samuel B. McIntire's section of light twelve-pounders, killing one crewman, wounding five, and damaging one gun's carriage. The battery's other section had one man wounded by another shot.[10] Throughout the duel, Thomson's gunners remained unscathed. Neese's shot was the high point of the day.

Rosser's stiff resistance forced Custer to bring up another brigade and look for another way to pry the graycoats from their stronghold. He sent the 18th Pennsylvania, supported by the 8th and 22nd New York, around Rosser's left flank. As they came into position, Custer ordered an attack all along the line. Struck in front and flank, the outnumbered troopers of the 1st and 2nd Virginia bolted and the rout commenced. Despite efforts by small groups of the Confederate cavalry to save the guns of Johnston and Thomson, the horse artillerymen found themselves on their own. Attempts to limber to the rear and a brief stand made with Munford's Brigade at Pugh's Run two miles south of Tom's Brook were all to no avail. One by one the guns were overrun. Johnston lost all four of his pieces and twenty-seven men. Pvt. Lewis J. Smith was mortally wounded. Sgt. William C. Watkins and Privates Lloyd Beall, William V. Bennett, L. N. Coit, William Conner, Robert Crabb, William A. Elam, N. C. Glenn, W. A. Gruggs, Alexander Harris, William W. Harrison, Hayden Haynes, Virgil S. Haynes, James L. Higgins, W. H. Jordan, William G. Lewis, Elijah Lindsey, James S. Lindsey, W. W. Mangum, Benjamin F. Miller, Nicholas S. M. Morton, R. J. Roach, Hames A. Ryan, Jr., William G. Smith, Jacob A. Supinger, and John A. Whit were all captured.

Thomson's Battery fared little better. Corporal Neese recorded that his gun held three different positions as the cannoneers tried to extricate themselves from the danger and save their charges. While limbering up at the third position, both guns were captured. Neese with Privates William S. Frazier, Anthony Good, Joseph H. Kagey, Charles Longerbeam, William P. McGuire, George McWilliams, Lloyd Noland, Jr., Stephen Roberts, Jacob Shaffer, Francis T. Stribling, Jr., Chapman J. Thuma, John C. Williams, and James K. Wright were made prisoners.

The battalion's battle flag, which had been a present of the ladies of Charlottesville, nearly fell into the enemy's hands as well. The color bearer, Pvt. Nimrod A. Ware, was not present, and the flag had been entrusted to the care of Pvt. Charles F. Conrad. As the Federals neared the fleeing guns, and their capture seemed assured, Lt. "Tuck" Carter noticed that Conrad's horse was weakening and ordered another mounted man to take the flag.[11] The man ripped it from its staff, shoved it under his coat, and galloped off. Conrad's horse held up and carried his rider to safety, but Carter could not have known that Conrad would escape. He took action to save the flag, which was the symbol of the fighting prowess of the battalion, though on this day the cavalry had left it with little choice but to run.[12]

The catastrophe that befell Johnston's and Thomson's Batteries on the Back Road was duplicated on the pike near Woodstock. Fugitives from Rosser's broken regiments fled in all directions except north. Some reached Lomax's cavalry, warning him of the danger on his left. The men began a careful withdrawal, and all went well until they reached the open fields around Woodstock. Here a Federal column from the Back Road struck Lomax's left flank while Merritt pressed his front. Johnson's Brigade broke, and it became every man for himself. In the midst of the chaos was Griffin's Battery. The battery's historian wrote of what happened to the gallant Marylanders:

> Towards noon Rosser, on the left, was overwhelmed, and soon after the heavy columns massed in front of Lomax, attacked furiously, and drove that General back in the utmost confusion.
>
> During this time the gallant McNulty and his brave command were hurling death and destruction into the ranks of the enemy but to no avail. With the retreat of the cavalry under Lomax, McNulty limbered up and suddenly fell back, unlimbering at every available point and opening his fire upon the pursuing foe, thus enabling the cavalry to escape. In this manner the village of Woodstock was reached. Still through its streets he continued to pour into the faces of the advancing enemy destructive discharges of grape & canister. But the gallant little Battery was doomed, for the enemy pressed upon them in overwhelming numbers, and still they disdained to abandon their pieces. Beyond the town they make one more effort to stay the dense masses which almost enveloped them, but even as the gunners were ramming home the last double charge of canister, they were captured and cut down in the act.
>
> Twenty-three men & four guns fell into the hands of the enemy. Lt. McNulty who had had his horse killed under him, with the balance of his men fought their way through, and escaped.[13]

The story for McNulty and his men was the same as for Johnston and Thomson and theirs—too much blue cavalry and too little gray. In the final tally, the battery lost all four of its pieces and had nineteen men captured: Corporals Chester C. Burnett and Fayette Gibson, Bugler Charles S. Evans, and Privates Henry Arens, Hugh V. Barry, Richard C. Briscoe, George W. Clotworthy, Matthew J. Coffee, Robert Hunter, Edward Hynes, James L. Kernan, Louis W. Knight, Daniel Lynch, Robert W. McCubbin, Jr., James Rheim, William C. Rheim, G. W. Richardson, William J. Tarr, and Joseph D. Sullivan.

McNulty lost his guns singly, the last just outside Woodstock.[14] But the rout was not over, and one more battery was to be put in harm's way. Shoemaker's Battery had not accompanied Rosser's or Lomax's divisions on their ill-fated pursuit of Sheridan's barn burners.[15] The battery had been slowly making its way back to the army, albeit at an unhurried pace, which turned out to be most fortuitous. Having spent the night of the eighth near Hawkinstown, the battery resumed its march on the morning of the ninth and reached a point about halfway between Hawkinstown and Edinburg, where it met Rosser's wagon train. Here the battery halted to feed its horses.[16] Lt. Lewis T. Nunnelee described what happened next:

> While halted here there came a grand rush of our Cavalry (several hundred) & from the speed they were making we could not tell but the devil in front. The whole Yankee army with Abe Lincoln in the lead was after them. All we could tell, they were going & "Not standing on the order of their going."[17]

Nunnelee and others of the battery managed to halt a few of the fleeing men long enough to learn of the calamity and that the Federal cavalry was not far behind. Immediately the wagon train teamsters began to hitch up their horses, as did the cannoneers, but before this could be accomplished, the bluecoats galloped into view. With a small group of Confederate cavalrymen that had been persuaded to stay, Shoemaker waited until all the fugitives were clear and welcomed the Federals with a few well-placed rounds. This checked them, but only long enough for the faint-hearted gray cavalry to hightail it once more, leaving the battery alone to confront the enemy.[18]

Shoemaker gathered his officers for a hasty conference, which resulted in Lt. Edmund H. Moorman taking one section of the battery back to the next rise of ground. The other, under Phelps, stayed to turn back the next charge.[19] When the blue cavalry appeared again, a few more shots scattered them, and with some of the mounted cannoneers acting as rear guard with their pistols, Phelps limbered his section and raced for the cover of Moorman's guns. The scene was enacted over and over: fire—limber—gallop—unlimber—fire. Back mile after mile. Past Mount Jackson. Across the North Fork of the Shenandoah. Finally the men reached Rude's Hill. One last time the battery unlimbered and prepared to fire, but the enemy had given up the chase at Mount Jackson.[20] At the cost of three men captured,[21] Shoemaker had saved his guns and some honor for the battalion.

The worst day in the history of the Confederate horse artillery saw eleven guns with most of the ordnance wagons, forges, and ambulances captured.

Sixty-three men were casualties, almost all of them prisoners. For all intents and purposes, Griffin's Battery ceased to exist. It was never able to procure any guns or equipment, because the Confederate government had none to give. Lieutenant McNulty was transferred, and command of the battery devolved upon Lt. John W. Goodman. Eventually the men were sent to Petersburg, where they participated in the last campaign of the Army of Northern Virginia, helping to man the fortifications.[22] Johnston's Battery, too, became a battery on paper. With all its guns and most of its equipment captured, it would be quite some time before it could again take the field. Thomson's Battery was reduced to one gun, a howitzer,[23] which was all that prevented it from the paper extinction of Griffin's and Johnston's Batteries.[24]

Breathed's Battalion, or what was left of it—one gun of Thomson's Battery and four of Shoemaker's—remained camped at New Market until the twelfth, when it set off for the Back Road to link up with Rosser's cavalry, undoubtedly none too pleasant a thought for some of the cannoneers. Lomax marched into the Luray Valley. Breathed found Rosser near Columbia Furnace and bivouacked for the night.

More than the cavalry was on the move. Early still was determined to follow Sheridan down the Valley and, if the opportunity presented itself, strike him a crushing blow. On the thirteenth, Rosser approached Cedar Creek, as did Early's infantry. Both tangled with the enemy. Late in the day, Rosser brought up a section of Shoemaker's Battery and did some heavy skirmishing. The battery sustained two wounded, Pvt. Francis G. McNamee, who lost a leg, and Pvt. John Murphy. The late hour limited the fighting, and as darkness fell, the Confederates marched back to Fisher's Hill. The next few days were spent in position on the Middle Road, returning each night to camp on the farm of George Funkhouser.[25] On the sixteenth, all of Thomson's men, with the exception of those attached to the howitzer, were sent back to Mount Solon to recruit horses and await guns. The next day, the howitzer was ordered back as well.[26] Johnston's men made the same journey for the same reason.[27]

On the seventeenth, Shoemaker received orders to cook three days' rations and be ready to move at a moment's notice. However, the battery stayed put until late afternoon of the following day, when it moved on the Middle Road toward Winchester. On reaching the forward position it had held since the fourteenth, the battery was ordered to camp for the night. In the early hours of the nineteenth, the men were aroused, and the battery was put in motion. Arriving at the same position as the section had held during the skirmish of the thirteenth, the men unlimbered the guns and put them into battery. About this same time, Early was launching his attack on Sheridan's sleeping troops at Cedar Creek.

Rosser pushed a squad across the creek and drove back the enemy's cavalry. Shoemaker limbered his guns and followed in a chase that lasted several miles. It was fun while it lasted, but the tables were turned as quickly on Rosser as they were on Early. The infantry retreated rapidly, though still fighting, in the face of Sheridan's counterattack. Rosser's troopers also made a fighting withdrawal. Crossing Cedar Creek, Shoemaker put his four pieces in their same old position and opened on Pennington's Brigade without much effect.[28] What saved Rosser and very probably Shoemaker's guns was that Custer decided to pull most of his troopers out of the fight with Rosser and attack the right flank of the Confederate infantry, which crumpled into a mass of fugitives.[29] Early's army had a déjà vu experience. Scenes of Winchester, Fisher's Hill, and Tom's Brook flashed before the eyes of infantrymen and cavalrymen alike. The same horrors were repeated. In that moment, even though there would remain a token Confederate presence, the Valley was lost.

For Shoemaker's Battery, the battle was more like a running skirmish. Only one man, Pvt. Patrick Harper, was wounded. For the horse artillery in general, Cedar Creek was a nonbattle. Johnston's Battery was still without pieces, as was most of Thomson's. Its lone gun was nowhere near the battlefield. Jackson's Battery was still in the vicinity of Staunton. Lurty's Battery was either near Staunton or with McCausland's Brigade, which did not participate in the battle.[30] McClanahan's Battery had accompanied Lomax's division, consisting of Jackson's and Johnson's Brigades and possibly some of McCausland's, into the Luray Valley to protect Early's right as he advanced down the Valley. While the rest of the army lost forty-three pieces of artillery,[31] the horse artillery lost none. They had already supplied their share at Tom's Brook.

Early retreated to New Market, which he reached on the twentieth. Sheridan's cavalry followed behind, skirmishing at times with the Confederate rear guard. Rosser with Shoemaker's Battery marched on the Back Road to Columbia Furnace and arrived there on the morning of the twentieth after riding all night. The column finally joined Early's army at New Market late on the twenty-first. The battery moved to Forrestville southwest of Mount Jackson on the twenty-second and remained there until the twenty-seventh. Johnston's and Thomson's Batteries were still awaiting new guns at Mount Solon. Lurty's and McClanahan's Batteries continued their service with Lomax's division, which by the twenty-fifth was encamped near Milford in the Luray Valley.[32] Jackson's Battery was still in camp near Staunton. Lt. Micajah Woods wrote to his father on the twenty-sixth about events as he saw them:

> Staunton Oct. 26th 1864
>
> My dear Father,
>
> Yesterday evening after reaching the vicinity of Harrisonburg an order reached the Battery to return to Staunton to reequip & prepare for the field. So again our rendezvous is on the Rail Road—How long we will remain is undetermined—probably a week & perhaps much longer.
>
> The number of orders & their variety is such that have been given us recently shows that our Generals below are utterly undetermined what to do.

My letter which reached you today you will please reply to directed to this point. Rider's mule was killed by the train day before yesterday in the field where we were encamped—valued by three disinterested individuals at $866.66. I wrote to know what course to pursue to receive his value.

On my way from Charlottesville I saw Mr. Via & Mr. White who told me they had to enter service & stated they would come immediately to my Battery without going to Richmond if I would receive them. Send word to Mr. Via where we are & say to him if he comes with White I will muster him in & hold him. Many are being enlisted now under exactly the same circumstances to avoid going to Camp Lee & being assigned to Infantry. Tell them to come at once—there will be no difficulty about it.

Enclosed I send a pass to avoid any difficulty.

In great haste
Your attached son
Micajah Woods

Dr. John R. Woods
Holkham[33]

Whether Early and his generals were "utterly undetermined what to do," orders had to be obeyed. Jackson's Battery settled down near Staunton. The men occupied themselves by complaining about their officers, as all soldiers are wont to do at one time or another, but at least they were not ordered out to face the enemy.

Brig. Gen. William H. Powell's division of cavalry was making a pest of itself in the Luray Valley. From October 22 through 25, Powell constantly probed and attacked Lomax's position at Milford. McClanahan's Battery was kept busy helping its dismounted cavalry comrades repulse Powell's attacks. The next day, the Federals withdrew to Guard Hill, their commander boasting, "The country through which I have passed and in which I have operated has been left in such condition as to barely leave subsistence for the inhabitants."[34] At least Lomax had the satisfaction that the destruction had been held to that part of the valley north of Milford. However, he had notified Early of Powell's persistence and asked for help. Lt. Edmund H. Moorman's section of Shoemaker's Battery was dispatched to Lomax on the twenty-seventh. They were ordered back on November 4 without having engaged the enemy.[35]

Meanwhile, Phelps's section remained in Forestville near New Market. The lieutenant wrote to his aunt, giving an account of what was transpiring in the army:

Camp near New Market
Shenandoah Co.
Nov. 4th 1864

Dear Aunt,

Your letter of 26th October reached me this morning and found me in fine health. The cause of its delay was its direction. Since I wrote last we have been in camp and have had a very quiet time—neither Army seems disposed to renew the fight. Tho' today we have rumors of an advance of the Yanks & I suppose in a few days we will be once more on the War Path. Our Army has been recruited at least a third more and seem to be in fine spirits. They are heartily ashamed of their conduct on the 19th & I believe only ask another trial to redeem their character. Gen. Early's address has done much good—as it was kindly received by everyone.

I am very sorry to hear that Newman has been ordered to Camp Lee. I hope that his detail will be granted so he can remain at home. Camp life will not suit him this winter in his present state of health. I wrote him to get my blue pants from my trunk and send me by William Shoemaker who leaves home in a few days for camp. If Newman is not at home please get Tommy E. to see Shoemaker and get him to bring my pants to me as I am very much in need of them. The weather has been very disagreeable for the last week, raining daily & very cold. We have not suffered from cold as we do not spare the wood—& there is a plenty of it where we are. I often wish you could have as much as we burn a day—it would last you all winter.

We are almost shut out from the world where we are now at. I have not seen a paper since the 20th last month and am almost totally ignorant of what is going on anywhere else but our camp. I am anxious to hear from Richmond as I think there must be heavy fighting going on there at this time. The Yanks are straining every nerve to obtain a victory before the election. I am looking forward to election of [Maj. Gen. George B.] McClellan, with much interest as I believe that is our only hope for a speedy peace. In that event I believe proposition will come even from Lincoln.

I have stolen a moment to write this much. We are very busy today—making reports inspecting etc. Will let you hear from me in a day or two.

Love to Sallie and all friends
In haste Very truly Yours
Dick
Shoemaker's Battery
Stuart Horse Artly
Fitz Lee's Cav. Div.
Valley District[36]

While Phelps anticipated the advance of the enemy, which failed to materialize, back at Mount Solon, Johnston's and Shoemaker's Batteries anticipated the arrival of men, horses, and guns. On October 29, ten dismounted cavalrymen were brought in to fill out the battalion. Twenty-four horses were sent to Staunton for a section of guns that had just arrived.[37] Slowly the battalion was being reborn.

Shoemaker's Battery was aroused from its camp at Forestville on November 6 and set out for Mount Jackson. The next day, Johnston's and Thomson's Batteries left Mount Solon for the same destination. The battalion, when it reunited on the ninth on the banks of the North Branch of the Shenandoah River,[38] consisted of eight guns: Shoemaker had three, Johnston two, and Thomson three.[39] Early's army was on the move once again. The Federals had fallen back above Winchester, or so things appeared. Rosser, moving with Breathed's Battalion along the Middle Road, ran into pickets of the 2nd Ohio Cavalry of Pennington's Brigade at Mount Zion Church west of Newtown. The pickets were driven within a mile of their camp, when the rest of the brigade arrived to support them. A running fight began, which saw Rosser chased about five miles. The artillery of both sides failed to get involved. Breathed's Battalion returned to the old camp at New Market on the thirteenth with nothing but worn-out men and horses to show for their efforts.[40]

During the abbreviated offensive, McCausland's Brigade and Lurty's Battery were stationed at Cedarville on November 12 to guard the Winchester and Front Royal Pike. Col. William B. Tibbits's Brigade of Brig. Gen. William H. Powell's division, moving forward on a reconnaissance, was spotted by McCausland's scouts. Preparations were made to hold the road as ordered. Lurty's two guns were unlimbered "in position so as to command the road."[41] Tibbits's first attack was repulsed. McCausland then launched an attack of his own, which drove the Federals back. Lurty limbered and joined the pursuit.

McCausland's eagerness led him into his own version of Tom's Brook. With his attention fixed on Tibbits, he either failed to notice Powell with his other brigade or believed his men capable of handling two enemy brigades at once. Powell had his men draw sabers and charge. The gray troopers broke, and the horse artillery again was left to fend for itself. Captain Lurty was wounded and captured. Sgt. James E. Tankersley and Privates Thomas W. Harris, Allen Huffman, David M. Huffman, Giles T. Huffman, Amos N. Johnson, Charter McCrander, Henry S. Tingler, William H. Webber, and John R. Williams were taken prisoner. Both guns and their caissons fell into the hands of the enemy. Like Griffin's Battery, Lurty's now existed only on paper.[42]

The slap on the wrist that Sheridan gave to Early convinced the Confederate commander that the time had come to put the army in winter quarters. On the fifteenth, Breathed's Battalion, including Johnston's, Shoemaker's, and Thomson's Batteries, began to march south from its camp near Mount Jackson through New Market and reached Harrisonburg, where the column turned right on the Warm Springs Road. Another three miles brought the batteries to the farm of Jonas Glosser, where camp was made. The march was resumed on the sixteenth. When the horses finally were reined in, the men found themselves within four miles of Mount Solon, and their old recruiting and refitting camp. There the battalion remained until the twenty-eighth.[43]

As Breathed fell back, the men of Jackson's Battery had been preparing to move forward. Lieutenant Woods wrote to his father to tell him of the disaster that had befallen Lurty's Battery and his own battery's status:

> Staunton Va.
> 17th Nov. 1864
>
> My dear Father,
>
> We have thoroughly fitted out a section of our Battery and will start down the Valley tomorrow morning—having received orders to report as quickly as possible. Our Brigade, McCausland's, has again been very badly whipped, losing 200 men and two pieces of Lurty's Battery. This occurred a few days ago near Front Royal. The Brigade at first repulsed & drove for four miles a Division of the enemy's cavalry when another Division came up and utterly routed them, running the command for nine miles.
>
> I am grieved to say that in this affair my friend Capt. C. I. Harvie fell mortally wounded & was left in the hands of the enemy. He died probably in a few minutes.
>
> Bob reached me safely day before yesterday.
>
> Early's army is retiring from New Market in this direction with a view I suppose of going into winter quarters. Kershaw's Division takes the train for Richmond this evening at Waynesboro.
>
> With love to the household, I am,
> Most affectionately
> Your son
> Micajah Woods[44]
>
> Dr. Jno R Woods
> Holkham
>
> P.S. I have called to see Maj. Tate twice and have each time found him absent in the country. I leave a memorandum in his office this evening requesting him to address you on the subject. As soon as I am with the main army I will see Maj. Snodgrass.
>
> M. W.

Woods need not have worried if he thought that joining McCausland meant active campaigning. The drubbing at Nineveh had taken the bite out of "Tiger John" for the time being. Instead, Woods and Jackson's Battery set off on a jaunt to winter quarters, as his letter of the thirtieth to his father described:

Jackson's Battery
Near Sperryville, Rappahannock Co.
November 30th 1864

My dear Father,

Today I date my letter from a new point of our old commonwealth. Thus far it has been my fortune to make tracks in nearly every county north of the James & west of the mountains and should the war continue it is likely I will visit nearly every neighborhood in our boundaries. After leaving Staunton we came by way of New Market to the vicinity of Luray. Marching thence through Thornton's Gap with the Brigades of McCausland's and [Brig. Gen. Henry B.] Davidson's (formerly William L. Jackson's) we assumed our present encampment between Sperryville and Little Washington. There we are doing well—in a region abounding in good pastures, hay, & corn—so much for the comfort of the horses. Men are equally well suited. The people are abundantly supplied with the necessaries of life—very kind and hospitable. Our camp is about three miles from the residence of Col. Charles Green whose acquaintance I have made & whose hospitality I have enjoyed. Last Sunday I dined with him—he offered very courteously to ride with me whenever convenient to me to see your friend Col. I. Shak. Green, his relative who lives twelve miles distant. The Col. is a robust old gentleman being sixty five years old. He owns a very large and fertile estate and lives alone—his wife being dead his only son living near him and his only daughter married to Mr. Ambler of Amherst.

This is a beautiful country to live in. The lands produce splendid grass & good wheat & corn, and are well watered. I have been in no section of Eastern Va. which presents so inviting a prospect to the farmer who desires fertile soil and an honest & intelligent community.

On last Tuesday a week since we marched through Early's army and a fine opportunity was afforded me of judging the strength and efficiency of his command. The whole force was in motion towards Rude's Hill to meet the advancing force of the enemy which afterwards proved to be two divisions of cavalry. His troops present a formidable appearance having been recently clad & armed and augmented by the addition of eight or ten thousand men—viz. absentees and conscripts under the last call. His army is large enough if properly organized, handled, and fought to make a successful defense of the Upper Valley against Sheridan's present force—estimated at 50,000.

Major Snodgrass I found had been ordered to Richmond and assigned to a new field of duty. His assistant was also out of place making some arrangements about his transportation as the army was in motion. If any opportunity is given me I will get the receipt you wish, but I fear I will not be with the main army again this winter. I would advise you to write a statement of facts—the quantity of hay & oats obtained & the date and enclose it to the army directed thus—Maj. Gen. Pegram Cmdg. Division—Early's Army—Maj. Snodgrass was quartermaster of Pegram's Division & the Gen'l would lay the statement before his present Qr. M. and require him to forward the proper receipt.

I have higher hopes for the efficiency of the Valley Army than for several months. A board of competent officers has been appointed for every division with instructions to examine minutely every officer of every grade and report upon his qualifications. In anticipation of the result quite a large number of officers in this Division (Lomax) have already forwarded their resignations rather than stand the test. This order if rigidly enforced will rid the service of hundreds of inefficient, ignorant, & worthless who now hold commissions. I am sorry to say however some of the officers on the examining boards whom I know are incapable of standing a minute & thorough examination themselves. Of course when such is the case no good will result from the investigation of the claims of the officers. I will appear before the board of this Division composed of Brigadier Genl. H. B. Davidson, Col. Smith, & Major Cleburne in a day or two. I have no tactics nor a work upon Artillery to be had in the Division—yet I have no fears. I know I can stump the board oftener than they can find me ignorant on any branch of the service.

Brigadier H. B. Davidson Cmdg. Jackson's Brigade to whom we now report is an old acquaintance of mine—he having been a member of Floyd's old Brigade then ranking as major in the regular army—having attended West Point. He is very large, very lazy, and very good for nothing—in other words he is a pretty thorough specimen of a western rowdy. He is very kindly and amicably disposed towards me expressing great delight at again meeting me.

Capt. Jackson is still near Staunton retained by his wound. The chances are all in favor of his being made Major as soon as he returns—in that event Blain is our Captain. The feeling of the other men against him is terribly bitter and ere many days my impression is they will strike him a sledge hammer blow in the way of a petition—setting forth various & sundry reasons which will be forwarded through Genl. Early. This is simply my impression. I can honestly say I have neither influenced nor prejudiced any one against him. He has done his own work; and I have done my duty as far as I am able.

To speak honestly however I must say that I believe Capt. Jackson entertains under his cloak of kindness and politeness the bitterest feelings of enmity & prejudice against me. I have never found it consistent with my views of honor & independence to waive my opinions when in a conflict with his. Neither have I kissed his toe nor licked his heel as his toads have. I have never seen fit to join the chorus—all honor—all praise and all glory to Thos. E. Jackson! I believe he attributes the unpopularity of his special pet to my influence, and I have the clearest reason for believing that rather than see me promoted over the head of his tractable spaniel he would retain his position as Captain. However I have no fear of his influence or his person. I can work equally as powerful levers here in the army as he can.

At present there is little prospect for our entering permanent quarters this winter—at least till very late. After exhausting this country, including Fauquier & Culpeper—we will move into Madison. These counties will subsist this Cav. Division until the last of next month—all this, by the way, with the consent & approval of Sheridan's four divisions of splendid cavalry!

I was sent for this morning to settle a personal difficulty between Col. James Cochran and Lieut. H. W. Cox ordnance officer McCausland's Brigade from Amelia. These gentlemen deferred the arbitrament of the case to me for decision. It involved the "lie direct" in its harshest form. I succeeded in so arranging matters to satisfy the parties.

McCausland's Brigade is in a lamentable condition—the line officers being sadly deficient in all the essentials of officers—and all the flowers among the field officers being killed or captured. At Cedarville where Harvie fell—my friend Lieut. Col. Jno. Radford was also killed—a noble soldier & thorough gentleman—the last son of Dr. Radford—Willie Radford being killed at Williamsburg on McClellan's advance. Maj. [Benjamin F.] Eakle of Lewisburg—a choice officer was also captured together with Lt. Col. [John A.] Gibson. This leaves only Col. [Milton J.] Ferguson & Maj. Moorman who are confided in by all. Cochran & Bowen are brave, but stand differently from others.

I expect I will have to get Mother to have some socks knit for the Battery as the men will be very destitute. Please write me immediately giving all the news. Direct as formerly to me, thus, Lt. M. W., Jackson's Horse Artillery—Lomax Division Early's Army—without designating Brigade.

I write again soon. As always express best love to Mother and all.

Most devotedly
Your son
Micajah Woods

Dr. J. R. Woods
Holkham[45]

Jackson's Battery was not the only horse artillery in the Valley to worry about the prospects of entering permanent winter quarters. The men of Breathed's Battalion were dissatisfied with their camp near Mount Solon. Captain Thomson, who was temporarily in command, sent Lieutenant Nunnelee and a Mr. Green[46] of Johnston's Battery to locate a more suitable campsite. A two-day trek proved fruitless, but in true army tradition, the battalion moved out anyway on the thirtieth. By evening, all were trying to make themselves comfortable on the farm of Alexander Anderson, which was located four miles from Churchville and six miles from Staunton on the road to Parnassus.[47] They would be comfortable only until December 8.

Christmas 1864 came a little early for the men of Thomson's Battery. On December 1, the success of Rosser's New Creek raid brought the battery a twelve-pound brass rifle, an ambulance, and several horses. Two more brass guns were received on the fourth. On that same day, seven men from the battery who had participated in the raid returned "loaded with plunder." The fifth was spent "fixing up" the new brass battery.[48] The battalion was off again on the eighth and did not put down stakes for two days. The new camp was on the banks of the South Fork of the Shenandoah River, four miles from Port Republic on the Waynesboro–Port Republic Road on the farm of Philip Coyner.[49]

The men of Breathed's Battalion greeted the 18th with emotions that ranged from disgust to resignation. Orders to move the day before set the men to putting the guns, limbers, and caissons into marching condition. By morning, amidst the usual grumbling from the usual grumblers, all was in readiness. The subsequent march of twenty miles through mud and wet proved most disagreeable, but at least it could be seen as the last one. The purpose of the expedition was to go into permanent winter quarters, which were seven miles from Staunton near Swoope's Depot on the farms of John Sellers and Harrison H. Teaford.[50] Work began on the quarters but was interrupted on the twentieth by an advance of the enemy. Portions of each battery, Johnston's, Shoemaker's, and Thomson's, were to accompany Rosser's cavalry to confront the enemy. They hurried to ready themselves and marched off with seven out of the battalion's twelve pieces.[51]

Two days later, Breathed sent orders to Lieutenant Nunnelee, who had been left in charge, to bring the remainder of the battalion to Staunton, where the other guns had gone after a brief encounter with the enemy in which the artillery played no part. The battalion rendezvoused on the twenty-third, three and a half miles south of Staunton on the Lexington and Greenville Pike.[52] Winter quarters were again contemplated, and some of the men began construction the day before Christmas. Pvt. Charles McVicar remembered being warm on Christmas Day but celebrating the traditional meal with hardtack and pork. He complained of snow, snow, and more snow.[53] The men of Jackson's Battery had something more to complain about. In the spirit of the season, they had made a present of two of their guns to the enemy on the twenty-third. Not surprisingly, their superiors were unhappy about their generous nature.

The tragedy began to develop on the nineteenth, when Maj. Gen. Alfred T. A. Torbert marched two divisions of his cavalry from Winchester toward the Blue Ridge Mountains. Crossing the mountains through Chester Gap on the twentieth, Torbert's column skirmished with Davidson's and McCausland's Brigades of Lomax's division at Liberty Mills on the twenty-second. Jackson's Battery of two guns helped hold the position along the Rapidan River. However, Torbert was not to be denied and sent brigades both upriver and down to seek other crossings. Flanked out of his strong position, Lomax withdrew toward Gordonsville. At daylight on the twenty-third, Torbert picked up exactly where he had left off the night before. This time, darkness did not stop him from damaging Lomax, driving him to within two miles of Gordonsville and capturing Jackson's two three-inch rifled guns.[54] Only the arrival of Smith's Brigade of cavalry and McClanahan's Battery prevented the Confederates from absorbing additional casualties and embarrassment. Lieutenant Woods, who was not present, learned about the loss of the guns firsthand and reported it all to his mother:

In the field
Near Gordonsville Va.
December 27th 1864

My dear Mother,

I formed a junction with Lomax's Division at this point the morning after leaving home—escaping the previous evening another one of those grave stampedes for which Lomax cavalry & Early's army generally are so justly renowned.

On reaching Earlysville I found myself in a labyrinth of dangers—which only increased the further I rode. Rumor had Yankees everywhere & had I not been an old soldier & peculiarly incredulous of troopers tales I would have either fled or hoisted a white flag (or something less sightly) to each approaching traveler. Making a circuit by Fray's Mills and thence towards Standardsville in pursuit of my Battery, I found myself about 7 o'clock PM at Barbourville. The enemy being at Liberty Mills and at the fords in the Rapidan about four miles distant. I called to see our friend Mr. Johnson Barbour who induced me to partake of tea & spend the night. Not wishing to be captured or to endanger him by my presence at his house should the enemy come I rose before break of day & proceeded towards Liberty Mills where I knew my Battery had been the day before. Before going very far I was informed that the enemy held the ground occupied by our troops the previous evening. Lomax having been repulsed & had fallen back in [the direction of] Gordonsville. Turning my course I reached Gordonsville bright and early found the cavalry in line of Battle on the Mountain by the Madison CH. road

& Jackson's Battery acting provost Guard for the town of Gordonsville!! Oh! what a fall was there my countrymen! Jackson's Battery had come to the low status of acting provost guard in rear of the command whose van it had ever guarded on the field of battle.

At Liberty Mills the guns had been captured by the enemy. No officer nor man was either killed, wounded, or captured but both guns were gone & all the horses with them. While they were in action against the enemy in front, the enemy crossed a Division at Brooking's ford above, surprised Lomax & his whole command by a sudden flank attack about dusk, creating the greatest confusion. Genl. Lomax was rather irresponsible for either word or action, having taken four or five more drinks than his capacity justified. The cavalry command, of course, took care of themselves. Several orders were sent to the Battery of a conflicting character causing its delay in withdrawal until the enemy had possession of the only road upon which it could escape. In the darkness & without support the Battery ran into a marsh the horses became mired together with the pieces & all were abandoned. This is the long & short of it.

Lomax said the next morning that the guns were deserted unnecessarily & that Lieut. Blain would be court-martialed for cowardice. This spread through the whole command—and was freely canvassed—all agreeing that no men ever acted with more bravery & Gen'l McCausland stating the guns should have been abandoned ten minutes sooner than they were. Genl. Lomax sent for all the officers of Jackson's Battery & required an explanation of Lieut. Blain. With his explanation he expressed himself entirely satisfied. Lieut. Blain proved by members of his own staff that the orders causing the loss of Battery emanated from his own lips—he professing to have no recollection of having issued them which was probable as he was somewhat intoxicated at the time. He exculpated Lt. Blain & the men entirely—he himself having been exposed. Inst. as we were about to leave I turned toward him & said, "Genl. Lomax, it is believed & circulated in this Division that you yourself accused this Battery of cowardice & you acknowledge you expressed yourself imprudently & wrongfully. I deem it but just that you should now at once publish a general order exculpating men & officers from all blame—verbal apologies you will admit are insufficient. I was not there myself & am glad of it. Still I feel thoroughly interested in the reputation of my command and whether present or absent in person in its operations." As a result of it he issued a general order yesterday of the most satisfactory character.

He promises to refit & reequip the Battery at once.

Entre nous, I feel as perfectly confident as I do of my existence that if I had been present that affairs would have turned out differently.

Train coming—more tomorrow. Love to all

Affectly Yr Son
Micajah Woods

Mrs. J. R. Woods
Holkham

Purchased a beautiful English jacket yesterday—need nosack coat.

P.S.

Having reached the Depot and having some time I avail myself of it. I consider myself extremely fortunate in being absent from the engagement at Liberty Mills. I never yet have lost a gun & have no desire to participate in an action where they are lost. Genl. Lomax complimented me in the interview day before yesterday before Blain & Wortham for bringing off my gun at Fisher's Hill under such tragic circumstances—having our man killed—three wounded & two horses shot with the gun. Wortham lost his gun at the same time it being impossible to save it—the wheel horses having been killed. Still, I don't think he liked the remarks of Lomax to me.

There is no telling where we will rendezvous while refitting—but I expect to go to the vicinity of Fisherville in the Valley—marching by Charlottesville. All the cavalry are near here, nothing to feed horses on. Mr. Barbour lost several negroes & horses at his lower place, besides other damage done. His home place was not visited by the enemy. The Yankees released all our prisoners 40 in no. without even paroling them. Their officers said the war would certainly end in eight months. Please get my vest & pants cut out by Connor & have them made & properly trimmed—Conner will have enough trimming left for this purpose. Also get Father to speak to him about finishing my coat at once.

Have Bob's shoes made also by Inke the next two or three days as he is greatly in need of them.

Affly Yr Son
MW[55]

The Federal penchant for helping the Confederates transform their horse batteries from metal to paper had now claimed another victim. As 1864 gave way to 1865, three batteries existed only on paper as far as being a fighting force. They boasted officers and cannoneers, but without guns, their existence amounted to paper shuffling. Such shuffling would continue to the end of the war.

At long last, it became official: The batteries would enter winter quarters. Breathed's Battalion and McClanahan's Battery, which marched to Staunton after the fight near Gordonsville, settled into making the best of a situation that everyone could see was none too good. Food for man and beast was not plentiful in an area that had suffered severely at the hands of Sheridan's barnburners. On January 2, the men of Shoemaker's and Thomson's Batteries petitioned the government to be allowed to disband over the winter, promising to take forty horses with them and feed them at the expense of the men. They settled back to wait, all the while building their quarters just in case their proposal failed to receive approval.

While waiting, the Christmas dinner they had missed arrived. Shoemaker's Battery received one turkey, thirty puffs, ten loaves of bread, fifteen apples, one round of beef, and nine ginger cakes. Pvt. Jesse Pettyjohn cut them all up, and according to Pvt. William J. Black, every man received a mouthful. But their hearts were full.[56] The women of the South had done their all just to give them that. An equally welcome gift arrived on the fifteenth. The request for disbandment was approved, with the men of Shoemaker's and Thomson's Batteries being granted furloughs until March 1, 1865. That same day, the guns and equipment were loaded on trains and sent to Lynchburg.[57] Jackson's and Johnston's Batteries spent the winter on Walker's Creek in Giles County without their guns, which, like Shoemaker's and Thomson's, were sent to Lynchburg.[58] McClanahan's Battery spent the winter in Giles County as well, having been assigned to Lt. Col. J. Floyd King's Battalion of artillery, which wintered there.[59]

The year 1864 had been a tumultuous one in the Valley. From the glowing victories of New Market and Lynchburg to the crushing reverses at Winchester, Fisher's Hill, Tom's Brook, and Cedar Creek, the horse artillery had given all it was asked to give, and in many instances more. Many men and guns had been lost. Looking ahead, some men saw the inevitable. Others still hoped for victory. Most would be ready to do their duty when again called to arms for what became the final struggle for the Confederacy.

CHAPTER 34

The Last Campaigns

*"I told them that they had been good and brave soldiers;
that they had done their whole duty;
that no reproach could rest upon them."*

The horse artillery's preparation for the coming spring campaign season began early in the new year. On January 17, Brig. Gen. William N. Pendleton wrote to Lt. Gen. Jubal Early's acting chief of artillery, Col. Thomas H. Carter, concerning the movement of some artillery battalions to Lee's army at Petersburg. Pendleton also broached the subject of a reorganization of the horse artillery that was being contemplated. It would entail the creation of five battalions of two batteries each, commanded by a major. Chew would be promoted to lieutenant colonel and continue to command the entire horse artillery. Pendleton added a postscript:

> I am requested by General Lee to prepare for him a schedule of the horse artillery battalions proposed to be formed. I should adjust them by assigning together one of Lomax's and one of the old horse artillery companies. But I desire to know something of the officers and men in Lomax's companies. Will you kindly inform me, where do they come from? what can be made of them? can you send me a field return of them? Of course they will have to be thoroughly brought up and equipped. Johnston will have temporary charge of the force—Jackson's, McClanahan's, Griffin's, and Lurty's; but after the entire organization he will have only two batteries as his battalion.[1]

Carter's response to these inquiries, if he made one, may have alluded to just how much three of those batteries would have to be "thoroughly brought up and equipped." Griffin's Battery had been without guns since Tom's Brook. Where Pendleton expected to get the cannons and horses to perform this miracle he failed to say. In other quarters, plans were under way that would affect Pendleton's reorganization if they were carried out.

On January 19, Maj. Gen. Matthew C. Butler's division of cavalry was ordered to proceed to South Carolina to bolster defenses there. Wade Hampton was to accompany Butler and assist in getting the division remounts. He eventually was assigned command of the cavalry in that department.[2] In the same order, Hart's Battery was told to report to Rooney Lee. The battery wasted little time in responding and adopted the following resolutions on the twentieth:

> Whereas, we have received information of the intended departure of our old and well-beloved commander, General Wade Hampton, to another field of duty, in which are the homes of nearly all the members of this Battery, and we naturally feel an unwillingness to be separated from the leader under whose eye we have fought since the commencement of the war,
> Resolved, That we feel it to be the duty of General Hampton, with whom we have been so closely connected during the war, to exercise all his influence, as far as compatible with the public interests, to carry his old Battery with him to his new field of operations.
> Resolved, That we request Lieut. Halsey to forward a copy of these proceedings to General Hampton for his immediate attention.[3]

When the resolution was passed to Hampton, he began efforts to have the battery transferred, but for the immediate future, it would remain in Virginia. Pendleton proceeded with his plan of reorganization, which soon began to bear fruit. In the meantime, there was still an enemy to be watched and confronted.

Hart's Battery was brought out of its snug winter quarters at Hicksford in early February, when the Federals made another push along the Hatcher's Run line. The battery was engaged on both the fifth and sixth, suffering no loss.[4] The inclement weather did little to improve the men's morale, but in the middle of the month, news arrived that did. Hampton had not forgotten his old battery and had continued to work for its transfer. His efforts were crowned with success, and before long, Halsey's men were loading their guns and equipment on railroad cars bound for Charlotte, North Carolina. A few men accompanied the guns as guards, while the rest brought the horses and wagon train overland.[5] The battery began an odyssey that, after several attempts, finally ended in their reunion with Hampton just prior to the battle of Bentonville.

Back with Lee's army, the problem with arming the horse artillery was partially addressed in a letter from Brig. Gen. Edward P. Alexander, chief of artillery for Longstreet's Corps, to Pendleton on February 28:

> Cannot the cavalry take 12-pounder howitzers? I consider them the best gun for their service, and would prefer them to anything

> were I in that arm. Our 3-inch have no shrapnel; their shell are very defective and uncertain, even when they explode at all, and you know the frequent complaint on this head, and their canister is very small and inferior. The Yankees have shrapnel and canister with lead balls, and thus use them very efficiently, but our 3-inch are not their 3-inch by a great deal. The 12-pounder howitzer is lighter, its ammunition cheaper and more abundant; it fires a formidable shrapnel; its shell seldom ever fails, and its canister is but little inferior to that of Napoleons. Where guns have to protect themselves against a charge of either infantry or cavalry, I believe the 12-pounder howitzer superior to the Napoleon and worth twice its number of 3-inch rifles. Is not this gun better adapted to the service of cavalry than a gun whose only recommendation is that it has a very long range and one-half of whose projectiles never burst (and when one does burst it does not make a dozen fragments), and which is very dangerous to our own men when fired over their heads? I have entirely forbidden their use by my battalions over our infantry. . . .
>
> Cannot the horse artillery be ordered to provide themselves with 12-pounder howitzers, and report to me to be directed where to exchange them for 3-inch rifles? Please reply to me by telegraph, care of General Longstreet, if you wish the exchange to go on as you have directed in your note.[6]

At this point in time, though Alexander's comments concerning what guns the horse artillery should use were well meant, he simply demonstrated the general lack of knowledge concerning the difficulties facing some of the batteries. Major problems existed, especially in the Valley, many of which would not be solved before the opening of the spring campaign. They included not only guns, but personnel too.

After Moorefield, McClanahan's Battery had managed to escape the drubbing that all the other horse artillery batteries, save Shoemaker's, absorbed at the hands of Sheridan's mounted legions. Fate, however, was not about to favor one battery over another. When the men of McClanahan's Battery left for their winter quarters in Giles County, their captain remained behind to command in Staunton. In declining health for some time, Captain McClanahan resigned his commission effective February 27, 1865. Command of the battery fell on 1st Lt. Hugh H. Fultz, who would have been ably seconded by Lt. Carter Berkeley had he been there. Not surprisingly, considering the way lieutenants of the horse artillery had been winding up as prisoners of war in recent months, Berkeley had managed to get himself captured in Charles Town on February 1. Not only was there a shortage of guns, but of lieutenants as well.

Things only became worse for the battery as March dawned. Sheridan's long blue columns became active in late February and marched south from Winchester on the twenty-seventh. By the twenty-ninth, Staunton was in Federal hands. The Confederates had been unable to oppose the enemy's advance. Early's tiny army finally made a stand at Waynesboro east of Staunton on March 2. Among the fourteen pieces of artillery with the army was McClanahan's Battery. Captain McClanahan was present, though he had resigned and been reassigned to the Invalid Corps the day before. The battle that followed was a repeat of those the army had endured since Winchester. Sheridan occupied the Confederates in front while his cavalry swept down on the flank. For one final time, the Valley army bolted. All fourteen guns were lost, four of them belonging to McClanahan's Battery. Among the 1,602 prisoners were Captain McClanahan[7] and Privates Wingfield S. Blackburn, Alexander Colbert, John M. Garber, James H. May, Thomas N. Mitchell, Henry Snyder, T. A. Sperry, H. Stale, and Silas A. Thrayer of the battery.[8]

Another battery suffered losses during the Waynesboro debacle. Lt. William Hoxton of Johnston's Battery explained what happened in a letter to his sister:

> To Mrs. A. M. Randolph — The lines Nr. Lynchburg
> March 9th 1865
>
> My dearest Sallie,
>
> Tho' I presume you've heard of my safety ere this and tho' you still owe me a letter yet I'll avail myself of the first moments of quiet and rest which for some days have been granted me to write for as I once told you during active operations I shall make it a habit to write when I can irrespective of your communications.
>
> Today one week ago the force of about 1200 men then comprising the Army of the Valley under Gen. Early was utterly routed by a large body of the enemy some ten or fifteen thousand under it is supposed Sheridan in person. My battery which was placed on the cars at Waynesboro for transportation to a point of safety fell into the hands of the enemy. I put my Company on a train at Greenwood Depot and sent them on following in the last train that left the depot, which was surrounded by Yankee cavalry just as it was "getting underway" and while almost stationary received their fire. I thank a most merciful God for my own escape. The position in which I was placed was more trying than any I have ever before encountered—lying down in a box-car <u>filled</u> <u>with</u> <u>ammunition</u> with Yankees firing almost in our faces. Young Bev. Randolph, a fine boy of about 17, was shot through the heart and fell near me. A servant was wounded. The rest of the occupants of the car escaped.

Saturday and Sunday I spent in Richmond, enjoying a sweet Communion at St. Paul's. Dear Dr. Minnigerode was not at home, but passed down to Richmond the day I reached Burkeriver, tho' I did not get a chance to speak to him. The letter which you enclosed in your last from Mary I left with Lucy who will forward it for me, as I had not time to write to you and did not like to retain it any time for fear of losing it.

I now have charge of a battery of guns on a commanding position just in front of the city [Lynchburg], which I hear will be defended vigorously if the enemy advances. Tom Roland who is still with Gen. Lomax told me yesterday that Lomax had expressed his determination (not worth much by the way) of "going up" with Lynchburg in the event of its fall. This briefly all the news.

Buck I am glad to say will be with you before long unless he first goes to Fauquier. I met him in Richmond and enjoyed seeing him very much. I become more attached to him every time I see him. He has obtained a leave of 30 days. I hear he is engaged to Miss Judith Coleman. If you can answer the question—is it true? He told me Alfred proposed a visit to the army to see us both. I hope he may yet be able to make it. Affec. love to him, Mrs. Randolph and kiss darling baby and Bunks for me. If you write immediately upon receiving this direct to Lynchburg. If not you had better wait until you hear from me again.

May God Our Father bless and keep you and all I love in these times of trial and trouble for Christ our Savior's sake.

Affec. yr brother,
Wm. H.[9]

Johnston's guns supposedly had been sent to Lynchburg for the winter. Hoxton probably was placed in charge of them. They either had not been moved that far or were in the process of being brought forward for the coming campaign. The vast majority of the men were still in winter camp. Hoxton had with him no more than the number needed to care for the guns while in storage. In any event, the battery was once again cannonless.

The battle of Waynesboro ended all formal resistance to Sheridan in the Valley, permitting him to take most of his troops and march to rejoin Grant at Petersburg. However, Early's virtual destruction did not include many units in or near the Valley, who were in winter quarters or disbanded and had not participated in the battle. These were still viable as far as many senior Confederate officers and government officials were concerned, and efforts were begun to bring them to locations where they could be organized and regrouped for service. The horse artillery in the Valley was part of this regrouping.

Pendleton's horse artillery reorganization came to the Valley in mid-March, even though three of the batteries it included were without guns, three were without captains, one was on its way to Petersburg, and two disbanded.[10] As part of Pendleton's plan, Chew became a lieutenant colonel, and James F. Hart, Philip P. Johnston, William M. McGregor, and James W. Thomson joined Breathed as majors. Five "battalions" of two batteries each were to be organized, with a major in charge of each battalion. The individual battalions were to serve with one of the five cavalry divisions. Orders to this effect reached Chew on the twentieth.

HDQRS. ARTILLERY, ARMY OF NORTHERN VIRGINIA,
March 20, 1865.

Col. R. P. Chew,
Commanding Horse Artillery:
COLONEL: The following is the arrangement of horse artillery battalions sanctioned by General Lee:

Hart's battalion: Hart's battery, Graham's battery—to serve with General Butler's division.[11] McGregor's battalion: McGregor's battery, McClanahan's battery—to serve with General W. H. F. Lee's division.[12] Breathed's battalion: Shoemaker's battery, Griffin's battery—to serve with General Fitz Lee's division.[13] Johnston's battalion: Johnston's battery, Jackson's battery—to serve with General Lomax's division.[14] Thomson's battalion: Thomson's battery, Lurty's battery—to serve with General Rosser's division.[15]

* * * * * *

You will cause the several commanders to direct their energies to the thorough preparation of their respective commands for efficient service in the campaign soon to open and apply your own efforts to the same end. There is no time to be lost. Although horses cannot yet be called in because of insufficient forage, there are many elements of equipments and organization to be attended to at once. It is essential to get each command ready for service, so that however early or unexpectedly the enemy may advance the horse artillery battalion may on short notice repair to operate with their proper divisions.

Very respectfully, your obedient servant,
W. N. Pendleton,
Brigadier-General and Chief of Artillery[16]

Pendleton's order regarding the reorganization was followed rapidly by several others meant to guide and assist Chew in preparing his command for the coming campaign. Two more orders affecting the horse artillery were issued the same day.

HDQRS. ARTILLERY, ARMY OF NORTHERN VIRGINIA,
March 20, 1865.

Lieut. Col. R. P. Chew, Commanding Horse Artillery:

COLONEL: You will please make arrangements for recovering the guns of the horse artillery which were captured by the enemy near Greenwood, Albemarle County, Va., and subsequently abandoned with carriages disabled.[17] It may be well to commit the enterprise to Major Thomson and direct him to secure the guns and such portions of the carriages as may be useful. Let the best plan practicable be adopted as to teams and either wagons or spare gun carriages for hauling those guns to Lynchburg. You may also with advantage arrange with Colonel Cole for Major Thomson to be connected with the operations in Albemarle and Greene Counties for impressing horses, as I understand there are a good many surplus horses in portions of those counties. Major Thomson's interest in the matter would insure success in thus securing horses for his battalion if Colonel Cole will authorize his co-operating with the colonel's agents. You should also satisfy yourself concerning the transportation that will be needed for your several battalions and employ the present time in arranging with Colonel Corley and otherwise for getting it ready by the time operations may be expected.

Respectfully, your obedient servant,
W. N. Pendleton,
Brigadier-General and Chief of Artillery.[18]

The second order affected Griffin's Battery. The officers and men of Capt. Walter S. Chew's 4th Maryland Battery, also known as the Chesapeake Battery, were ordered to report to Lieutenant Colonel Chew for assignment with Griffin's Battery. This would supply the missing manpower needed to make up the full complement of men for the battery. Unfortunately, Captain Chew was to turn over his guns and equipment to Braxton's Battalion, which still left Griffin's Battery without guns.[19] With the crisis approaching, Pendleton continued to try to control the situation from afar.

HDQRS. ARTILLERY, ARMY OF NORTHERN VIRGINIA,
March 23, 1865.

Lieut. Col. R. P. Chew,
Commanding Horse Artillery, Richmond, Va.:

McClanahan must be found and gotten to his place at once. Thomson also must be made ready immediately. I cannot assign horses while the men are scattered. Johnston can have three howitzers in Lynchburg from Colonel Carter. You had better at present be nearer me than in Richmond.

W. N. Pendleton,
Brigadier-General and Chief of Artillery.[20]

Again on the twenty-fourth, he wrote:

> SPECIAL No. 14. ORDERS
>
> HDQRS. ARTY., ARMY OF NORTHERN VA.,
> March 24, 1865.
>
> Captain McClanahan having been ordered, by telegram to Lieutenant-Colonel Chew, on the 27th of February, to prepare his battery for operations and report to Major McGregor near Petersburg as soon as possible with his battery, and nothing having been yet heard from him, it becomes necessary to hasten the movement of the battery, especially as a report is heard that Captain McClanahan was captured by the enemy near Staunton. The officer commanding the battery will therefore immediately collect his men, with all the horses belonging to the company, and rendezvous at Lynchburg. He will then transport the company to Petersburg without delay, and report for orders to Capt. D. D. Pendleton, assistant adjutant-general, artillery. No time is to be lost in the execution of the order.
>
> By command of General Lee:
>
> W. N. Pendleton,
> Brigadier-General and Chief of Artillery.[21]

Now the mad rush began. The men of the horse artillery gave every effort to carry out the instructions they received, but for some the war was already over.

For most men of the horse artillery in the Valley, Lynchburg became the focal point. Toward that rail hub, the men of Jackson's, Johnston's (Shanks's), Lurty's (Lyman's), McClanahan's (Fultz's), Shoemaker's, and Thomson's (Carter's) Batteries made their way. Of these batteries, only Shoemaker's managed to become mobile in March.[22] Reuniting in Lynchburg on March 1, it remained idle until the eleventh, when it shipped out on the railroad to Farmville, but the battery was back in Lynchburg on the sixteenth. On the twenty-eighth, Shoemaker loaded his men and guns on the cars and left for Petersburg, arriving on the twenty-ninth. The battery was unloaded and parked, the men camping on the Williams lot a mile north of Petersburg on the Richmond Turnpike.[23] It had brought no horses and would have to wait until some were supplied. Even so, Shoemaker's was the only battery to leave the Valley and rejoin Lee's army. Another battery that had been part of Lee's army but was now far from the fields where it had gained its fame also became active in March.

After arriving in Charlotte, North Carolina, Hart's Battery had found itself unable to connect with Hampton because of the route taken by Maj. Gen. William T. Sherman's army, which was sweeping into the Carolinas. On March 1, the battery was in Salisbury, North Carolina, with no way of reaching Hampton, who was in Lancaster, South Carolina. The battery's horses still had not caught up with it.[24] Relocation to Raleigh, North Carolina, was followed by a move to Smithfield.[25] There, at long last, orders came, and with the long-overdue horses hitched to guns and caissons, Capt. Edwin L. Halsey marched his battery toward Bentonville, North Carolina. He linked up with Hampton on the seventeenth at Willis Cole's house, on the Goldsborough Road three miles southwest of Bentonville.[26]

Gen. Joseph E. Johnston, commanding the conglomerate Confederate forces, had decided to make a stand and strike at Sherman. The problem was that Johnston needed to concentrate his army. Hampton had selected a site for the battle near Bentonville and on the eighteenth fought a delaying action against Sherman's approaching army. Despite all he could do, Hampton watched his troopers driven back to the very ground he had selected as the place Johnston should face Sherman. The time had come to make a stand, and Hart's Battery was called to the front to help make it. Hampton wrote of this decision:

> It was vitally important that this position should be held by us during the night, so I dismounted all my men, placing them along the edge of the woods, and at great risk of losing my guns I put my artillery some distance to the right of the road, where, though exposed, it had a commanding position. I knew that if a serious attack was made on me the guns would be lost, but I determined to run this risk in hope of checking the Federal advance. As an illustration of the quick perception of our private soldiers, I recall an expression of one of them as I rode off after placing the guns in position. Turning to some of his comrades he said with a laugh, "Old Hampton is playing a bluff game, and if he don't mind Sherman will call him." He evidently understood the game of war as well as that of poker.[27]

At the least, the wag that made the remark clearly demonstrated the perception of the men of Hart's Battery. They had been on too many fields and fought in too many battles not to know when they were being hung out on a limb. Yet there they were, performing their duty, knowing all the while they were to be sacrificed if necessary. Halsey and his cannoneers stood by their pieces and gazed out across the fields. If the guns were to be lost, they would see to it that the price was high. Fortunately, the Federals chose not to test Hampton's makeshift line of tired troopers. Hart's Battery was granted a reprieve, though only a momentary one.

On the nineteenth, Johnston's army rallied on Bentonville and made preparations to meet Sherman. Hampton's plan of battle went awry almost immediately, when Lt. Gen. William J. Hardee's Corps was unable to reach its assigned position on the battlefield. As a result, a large gap in the Confederate line beckoned to the Federals. Hampton sent for Hart's Battery and the Furman

Light Artillery, commanded by Capt. William E. Earle.[28] The batteries were to plug the gap until Hardee could come up. Plug it they did, but their stubbornness and courage went for naught. Elsewhere on the battlefield, circumstances conspired against the Confederates. Because of the heavy attack on the division of Maj. Gen. Robert F. Hoke, part of Hardee's Corps was sent to Hoke's aid. This weakened Johnston's attack force. In the end, Hoke repulsed the Federals without Hardee's troops, but the opportunity was lost. Hardee's attack, though successful, did not have the punch to crush the Federals. The division sent to Hoke was greatly missed. In the end, Johnston was forced to withdraw. Hart's Battery suffered four casualties. Corp. Thomas R. Chew was killed by a shell burst, and Pvt. Marx E. Cohen, Jr., was mortally wounded.[29] Pvt. Leonidas M. Raysor had his arm torn off by a shell, and Pvt. Henry Kennedy was wounded.

Standard-bearer Louis Sherfesee recalled the battle that day:

> The whole army was in commotion, and a line of battle was formed in the shape of a crescent, and our Battery was placed in the center with orders to remain quiet until further instructions.
>
> Shortly afterwards the enemy opened on us, and we had to lie down behind our guns for several hours under a hot fire without the privilege of replying. During this time Chew, and shortly afterwards Cohen, were killed, and Raysor had his arm taken off just below the shoulder, which we thought was a mortal wound.
>
> As I said before, the fire from the enemy was a very hot one, and we could not reply. When General Joseph E. Johnston and Wade Hampton rode up, Captain Halsey asked General Hampton to allow us to reply to the enemy, saying that his men could not stand it any longer, for they had been under fire for several hours without replying. General Hampton turned to Johnston and asked if the Battery could open fire in the enemy.
>
> Johnston replied, "General, you are in charge, do as you think best." Hampton then turned to Halsey and told him to commence firing. Halsey had hardly given the command, "Attention!" when Hampton called him and asked if he thought his men would like to charge the Yankee battery that was firing on them. Halsey answered that he thought nothing would please them better, and Hampton told him to do so.
>
> Orders were given to limber up and mount, and we started for the enemy, who allowed us to get within two hundred yards without firing on us. We then halted, got into position, and gave the enemy canister.
>
> If there was ever a surprised body of men, it was they, for they thought when we were crossing the field that we were cavalry, all of our men were mounted and rode around the guns, so the enemy could

> not see them, and when we got into position and commenced firing on them, they were so surprised they could not reply but started to run.
>
> We then had things our own way and captured three pieces of artillery and about eighty men.[30]

The charge of the battery was actually part of General Hardee's attack at 2:45 P.M.. It was the infantry that captured three pieces of Lt. Clinton Keeler's 19th Indiana Battery. Keeler had already suffered several horses killed and two men wounded when Confederate artillery fire exploded an ammunition chest.[31] Obviously, batteries other than Hart's had targeted Keeler's guns. The role of Hart's Battery in the rest of the fighting on the twentieth and twenty-first was minor, but the filling of the gap and the gallant charge on the 19th had been in the true horse artillery tradition.[32]

For the remainder of March, as Johnston fell back before Sherman, Hart's Battery fought a number of rear-guard actions with Hampton's cavalry. Increasingly, it became evident that the Federals could not be stopped, but as March drew to a close, there was no question that Johnston's little army would fight on. Hart's Battery would continue to face the enemy whenever and wherever found. Farther north, some horse artillerymen were just receiving the call to arms, while others still awaited orders.

The recall for Thomson's Battery was sounded on April 1. The men began to drift into Lynchburg, as did men from McClanahan's and Lurty's Batteries. Jackson's and Johnston's Batteries over at Walker Creek seemed forgotten by Pendleton, Chew, and everyone. No orders arrived.[33] The officers and men sat and waited, which was exactly what the men who reached Lynchburg did. The guns of several batteries had been sent there, but until sufficient numbers of men arrived, not much could be done. Standing around and doing nothing were not to Jim Breathed's and Jim Thomson's liking. Since they knew that their battalions were scheduled to report to Lee's army, they chose to ride ahead and set out for Petersburg—artillerymen without their guns but ready to fight in any capacity. For one, it proved a fateful decision.

The two batteries of horse artillery—Graham's and Brown's, formerly McGregor's—that had spent the winter months with Lee and his tattered remnant were called into action in the waning days of March. Brown's Battery participated in the fighting on the thirty-first along Chamberlain's Bed at Fitzgerald's Ford. Sheridan had returned to Grant, and Rooney Lee and Rosser welcomed him in true Southern style. A seesaw fight across the ford with the cavalry of Brig. Gen. Charles H. Smith ended with the Confederates recoiling with considerable loss.[34] The Federals fortified their side of the ford. Brown's Battery entered the fray about 5:30 P.M. and immediately began to rain shot and shell on the enemy. But Smith's troopers held until near dark, when their ammunition began to give out. They then retreated toward Dinwiddie Court House. The battery's only casualty was Sgt. Ashton Chichester, who was shot through the thigh.

The first day of April found the Confederates in position around the country crossroads of Five Forks. Maj. Gen. George Pickett was in command of the infantry committed by Robert E. Lee to holding this vital position. Fitz Lee was Pickett's cavalry counterpart. The Confederate line extended along White Oak Road, with the crossroads located slightly left of the middle of the line. The left flank ended in an open field, where a small, two-sided fortification, referred to as the "Return," was constructed, one side extending north perpendicular to the White Oak Road. The right of the line ended at the junction of the White Oak and Roper Roads.

Fitz Lee's cavalry was positioned on both flanks. Col. Thomas T. Munford's Brigade held the left, with skirmishers in advance of the Return. Rooney Lee's division was positioned on the right, with some of the troopers dismounted and manning some hastily constructed works paralleling the White Oak Road. One of his brigades, commanded by Brig. Gen. William P. Roberts, was stretched tenuously between Pickett's left and the Confederate fortifications at the junction of the White Oak and Claiborne Roads, well beyond Munford's Brigade. Rosser's Brigade was guarding the wagon train across Hatcher's Run in rear of the Confederate position. Early in the morning, Brown's Battery was stationed on the extreme left of the Confederate line in the area of the "Return." Shortly after a breakfast of "corn pone cooked three days before and raw Nassau pork," the battery was "ordered to the extreme right at a gallop" to join Rooney Lee's cavalry.[35]

Late on the first, a Federal assault overwhelmed the left of Pickett's line, and part of the attacking force moved into the Confederate rear and assaulted the position at Five Forks by moving south down the Ford Road. At this critical juncture, Brown's Battery held its position near the end of Rooney Lee's line. Graham's Battery, which was stationed somewhere to the right of the forks, possibly near the brigade of Brig. Gen. Montgomery D. Corse, was ordered late in the day to support Brig. Gen. George H. Steuart's Brigade, which had been posted at Five Forks. The battery's two Napoleons were sent, and the men were attempting to go into action in knee-deep mud when they were attacked in the rear by Sheridan's cavalry as it swept over the works at the crossroads. Graham's cannoneers were driven from the guns at the point of the saber.[36] Most managed to make their escape, but Privates James Griffin and William A. Griffin became prisoners.

Brown's Battery did a little fighting on the right before making its escape, as related in part by Pvt. David Cardwell:[37]

We limbered up under order to do so, and moved out toward the right—down the road [White Oak Road]. As I attempted to follow with two other comrades, we were stopped by Col. Brien—Col. L. Tiernan Brien. . . . He told us to pull down a fence in front of the Second North Carolina Cavalry "squadron front," and we did it. By so doing, we got (after we had mounted) terribly mixed up in a charge of that regiment. We were pressed back to the road and I was looking for a way out and I was looking hard, too.

I looked west and there was a line of fire clear across the road. I knew I could not go east. The enemy were there, and south. So northwest I went. I jumped my horse over a fence. Poor old Dick Chamberlaine (of Norfolk, who was No. 2 at my gun) had all of his eyebrows, mustache and hair on the right side of his head burnt off. Half of his jacket was also burnt off by his being too slow to clear the front of the gun when the order to fire was given. Poor old Dick, my messmate, rode close behind me, and jumped the fence into the swamp also. Dick was a sight. You could not tell which army he belonged to. Your humble servant was also a sight. My face, I found out afterwards, was black with powder, and when I woke up from my excitement I had my attention called to it.

The Second North Carolina Cavalry had checked Custer's mad charge, which enabled the artillery and most of the cavalry to get away. In the melee of the charge of the Second North Carolina Cavalry, sabers and pistols were used before Custer's men recoiled. We were at very close quarters and such fights do not last long.

Henry L. Moore of our Battery, Owen O'Brien, and myself were close together. In the mix-up a color bearer was cut from his horse, and as the flag fell it was seized by Moore. A great big man made a swipe at Moore with his saber, missed his head and struck the flagstaff. Moore struck him over the head with his pistol. Moore brought the flag out. This about closed the battle of Five Forks. Night had come on before we got through, and the line of fight could easily be traced by the line of fire.

Soon after we got in the swamp we encountered the numerous wounded men who either had been taken out of the fight and laid behind the sheltering trees or had crawled out there. As we rode along in the dark woods they begged piteously to be taken up. We talked about it but could not see that we could do them any good. We knew that an ambulance corps of one army or the other would look after them in the morning.

I found I had, when I jumped the fence, a saber hanging to my wrist by a strap and a pistol in my hand. With Dick running by my side, I looked much like a man with a prisoner. Soon a man said to me, "Great God, Man, how did you get a prisoner?" I put up my saber and pistol and looked more peaceful. Dick and I floundered about in that swamp and soon were out of sight and sound of the wounded and all sound of strife.

We kept on in a northwesterly direction and just as the roosters began to crow, we emerged into an open field. We halted and in a few minutes we discovered the figure of a man standing upright holding a gun. He looked like "one in authority." In fact, he looked "on guard." So we contemplated him with interest, Dick and I. Dick says, "Davy you ride forward and challenge him." I said, "Dick, suppose you amble up and ask his name and command." We did not know where we were, nor who he was. After some more debate we both rode forward and the figure promptly presented his gun and said "H-A-L-T" in a cross tone of voice, and we halted as fast as we could. We found he was on guard and belonged to our division. We asked him where our battery was, and he said: "Way over beyond that big white house." And for over beyond the big white house we started.

Before we had gone far, however, we came upon a group of mounted men and in their midst we soon made out Maj. Gen. William Henry Fitzhugh Lee. It was broad daylight and we could see things plainly. But I must say that in the darkest part of that forest, at the darkest period of the night, we could have made out Gen. Lee. He was six feet three or four and weighed not an ounce less than 300 pounds. He was mounted on his brown war horse Frantie, a horse he always had his saddle changed to when practicable, before going into a fight. The two together, man and horse, made one of the largest establishments I ever saw.

We halted here. Meantime Moore and O'Brien had joined us, Moore still carrying the battle flag. We found Gen. Lee trying to gather together and get into some shape his scattered division. We three boys sat on our horses nearby, feeling very much at home with our division commander. The general would call out, for instance, "Any officer here from the First North Carolina Regiment? Is Col. Cowles here?" No reply. Some captain or lieutenant would ride up and say, "I am here general, Captain of troop B, Capt. So and So." "Well, captain form the First Regiment out there (pointing) and take command." And so he went through the whole list of his regiments and found what was left of that once splendid division.

Now our turn had come. The general turned in his saddle, and in the sweet, soft, courteous voice he said, seeing the red trimmings on our jackets: "Well, young gentlemen of the artillery, what is your battery?" We answered, as we always did with great pride, "McGregor's!" "Well, permit me to inquire why you are not with your

> battery?" We thought we had a splendid excuse. In fact, we felt that we had done even more than our duty. Think of that mix-up with Custer at the Forks, etc. Henry Moore rode up (with some style), and, expecting to be complimented, showed Gen. Lee the recovered flag. We told him of Col. Brien and the line of fire to the west, across the road. As our battery retired that way we thought it was captured. He answered, with more harshness than I thought him capable of, "Go to your battery; it is not captured, it is over there in that field. You should never allow yourselves to be separated from your battery." We rode off in no good humor and said about this: "He is a doggoned ungrateful old fellow and I don't like him anyway. He ain't much of a general." A courier rode up and told Gen. Lee that he was wanted at the big white house to attend a council of war. We rejoined our battery in the big field and were received with great rejoicing.[38]

The battery's dash to safety had been fraught with close calls as well. McGregor had conducted a fighting retreat and had become separated from Rooney Lee's cavalry. He rejoined Lee on the morning of the second, not long before Cardwell and his comrades made their appearance.[39]

Pickett's defeat at Five Forks led to the fall of Petersburg and Richmond. The Army of North Virginia gathered itself, broke away from Grant, and marched west. Pickett's command was cut off from Lee and had to fend for itself. Shoemaker's Battery had been stationed on the right of the Petersburg defenses across the Cox Road. Here Chew and Breathed received their orders to begin the retreat and turned Shoemaker's four guns westward. They had not fired a shot.[40]

April 2 found Major McGregor with Graham's and Brown's Batteries riding west with the enemy paralleling them. McGregor's fighting blood was up. Without orders, he pulled down a section of fence, galloped his pieces into a field, and opened fire. The barrage caused some confusion in the Federal column, but the enemy did not return fire. Orders soon arrived for the guns to cease fire. However, toward evening, when the opportunity arose to harass the blue troops who were so close, McGregor once more yielded to temptation and ordered Brown to send them the battery's compliments. His belligerent attitude brought him another "cease fire" command from some superior. The officers and men of the battery were used to tackling their enemies whenever and wherever they were encountered. This "hands-off" attitude was somewhat perplexing. Still, orders were orders. McGregor ordered the guns limbered and continued to move west.[41]

Orders came on the third that were a little more to McGregor's liking. One of Brown's pieces was detailed to support Brig. Gen. Rufus Barringer's Brigade of North Carolinians, acting as rear guard near Namozine Church. The Federal pursuit, conducted by Custer's division, was getting a bit close and needed to be slowed down. Col. William Wells's Brigade had the advance and struck the Confederate picket line, driving it with ease back on Barringer's main line. The 1st Vermont and the 8th New York Cavalry now launched attacks that brought on a counterattack by the 2nd North Carolina Cavalry. Through all this, McGregor's lone gun, which was stationed along Green Road northwest of the church, blasted away at the oncoming enemy with little effect. The crisis of the battle came with the repulse of the 2nd North Carolina and the flanking of its sister regiment, the 1st North Carolina. Suddenly the rout was on. Abandoned to their fate, the gunners of Brown's Battery fired one last round and were overwhelmed by the 1st Vermont.[42] Sgt. Owen O'Brien, Corp. George A. Pryme, and Privates George W. Hicks, John F. Lewis, Joseph Spicer, and John A. Strong were taken prisoners.

Lt. Col. Roger P. Chew and Majors Jim Breathed and Jimmy Thomson rode west with the cavalry of Fitz Lee. Cut off from the three batteries of horse artillery with Lee's army, they were technically nothing more than supernumerary officers. Chew and Breathed had been with Shoemaker's Battery but had separated from it. That battery, due to its position, did not participate in any of the serious fighting during the entire retreat.[43] These officers' tenacious personalities would not allow them to be content with watching others fight. When near Amelia Springs on the fifth, the cavalry clashed with the enemy. The three threw themselves into the fray like troopers. Thomson received a minor wound in the arm, while Chew and Breathed came through unscathed. Their performance brought two of them immediate rewards:

> Headquarters Cavalry Corps, 6th April, 1865—Special Order No. 2.
>
> The following officers of the Horse Artillery are temporarily assigned to the Regiments hereafter named, those regiments being deficient in field officers, and these gallant officers being separated from their commands, viz. Lt-Col. R. P. Chew, to command 3rd Va. Cav., Munford's Brigade; Major James Breathed to command 8th Va. Cav., Payne's Brigade.
>
> By order of Maj.-Gen. Fitz Lee.
>
> To Brig.-Gen. T. T. Munford, Com. Lee's Cav. Div.[44]

Fitz Lee could not have selected finer officers for his cavalry. They were known among the regiments and, with their reputations as fighters, had gained great respect from the cavalry. Thomson failed to obtain a command, but as long as he could fight with the cavalry as a private, he would be satisfied.

Except for some minor clashes, Graham's and Brown's Batteries had no major engagements until the sixth. That day saw one-third of the men of the Army of Northern Virginia captured at Sayler's Creek in a disaster unequaled in the proud army's history. Graham's Battery became involved in the battle as it followed the command of Lt. Gen. John B. Gordon. Pvt. George E. Robertson wrote a description of what occurred:

> At Sayler's Creek, we went into action on the west side of the creek, and after firing our last shot, and that being a solid shot, the enemy almost upon us, Capt. Graham, with a sad expression on his face, ordered the guns limbered up. Gen. Gordon, seeing this, rode up and said, "Captain, don't leave yet, the enemy are not on you." Capt. Graham replied, "General, I have fired my last shot," and then his eyes flashing fire, he said, "General, if you will only give me ammunition, I will stay right here until Hell freezes over, or I drive these Damned Yankees back," and we, who had stood by him, knew too well what that meant. We left the field with empty chests, but before reaching the High Bridge we found an abandoned caisson with ammunition; filling our chests, we were engaged at High Bridge, Farmville, Buckingham, and Appomattox.[45]

Graham's determination to fight was echoed by three other horse artillery officers on that tragic day.

Federal cavalry under Brig. Gen. Theodore Read made a bold attempt to get ahead of the Confederates and burn High Bridge, but Rosser and Dearing brought up their troopers and met the enemy the old-fashioned way—on horseback. Dearing was mortally wounded in a duel with Read, who was killed. Chew, Breathed, and Thomson were in the thick of the fighting. The Federals were badly beaten. A white flag appeared, but before the firing ceased, Thomson fell to the earth, killed by two pistol shots.

Breathed would have joined Thomson in death had it not been for the timely arrival of a companion. Entering a saber duel with two Federal officers, Breathed was hard-pressed to defend himself. He managed to mortally wound one of his antagonists and saved himself only by falling from his horse, parrying a tremendous blow from the other that left a huge nick in his saber. At that moment, another Confederate rode up and dispatched the second Federal with a pistol shot.[46] It had been a close call. Had Breathed been less experienced in the use of the saber, he probably would have fallen victim to his opponent. As it was, all those cavalry charges he had participated in had paid off.

On April 7, both Graham and Brown were engaged at Farmville. Brown was cut off for a time but fought his way through. Graham ran into the enemy on the Buckingham Court House Road. Pvt. George E. Robertson described the short fight:

> In Buckingham when we took position with our guns, the enemy brought six guns to bear on us; we had nothing but shells to give them, and very poor ones at that. The enemy seeing this ran several of their guns by hand in close range and opened on us with canister, wounding Lt. [Edward M.] Pollard and several men, and killing several horses, having the advantage of positions, guns, and men. We were forced from the field. Notwithstanding this, we brought our wounded and guns away in safety.[47]

Graham's Battery was not alone in its futile attempts to keep the pursuing Federals at bay. The whole army had the bluecoats nipping at its heels, but it continued to defend itself as best it could. Nevertheless, the noose was tightening around Lee's ragged few.

Late in the afternoon of the eighth, Brown's Battery faced a decision none of the officers or men had ever believed they would have to make. Sgt. George W. Shreve recalled what took place:

> The last position taken by our battery was on the 8th of April at about 4 P.M. We were following a large wagon train, and coming to a place where a country road or trail intersected the main road, from the direction of the enemy (south), Capt. [George W.] Brown was ordered out on this road to protect the train. The order was given by some superior officer. Capt. Brown posted one section about a quarter of a mile down this road. The section was under command of Lt. [Richard] Shreve; the writer had charge of one detachment, and I failed to remember the name of the sergeant in charge of the other.
>
> The small road led through the woods, and we were unlimbered and ready for action. All was still in front, and we could see nothing and the silence of waiting gave us time to think. We discovered we had no videttes out and no support on either flank, nor in rear, and so the situation was discussed pro and con. The Captain appealed to the Lieutenant for his opinion, [who] not caring to express his honest convictions, and so evaded a direct answer. Then he appealed to the writer. I replied that in my judgment anything that we could do would be futile; that we had always done our duty, and while there was hope we were willing to fight, but that in our present position, if the enemy advanced, his sharpshooters would flank us, and we were helpless and furthermore, I considered that every life lost from now on would be a useless sacrifice. Others had joined in the conversation.
>
> Capt. Brown said, "I agree with Sergt. Shreve. Limber to the rear." We fell back to the main road, which was full of wagons, and Gen. Lomax with his cavalry division coming up, we were ordered to follow the same. We marched by a country road leading north and west, towards the James River for several miles and bivouacked for the night.[48]

Brown's decision, which was reached without consulting Major McGregor, received no known reprimand. The truth of the situation confronting Lee's army was becoming apparent to all who took the time to look at the ever-dwindling ranks around them. The question became more of what would happen to the battery than what would happen to the army. Shreve told of the last day of the Army of Northern Virginia and Brown's Battery:

Early on the morning of April 9th, we resumed the march in the direction of Lynchburg, passing on country roads, leading through farms, and not striking the main road until Lynchburg, where we arrived about 5 P.M. and parked our guns in the outskirts of the town.[49] At once we were ordered to assemble in ranks, and an order was read to us, announcing the surrender, by General Lee on the same morning, including our command. We were dismissed from ranks for the last time.

Within a half hour, Major McGregor, mounted with other officers beside him, announced that he was going to start immediately southwest to join General Johnston's army and invited all who felt so disposed to join him forthwith. Quite a number fell in, and the party started off about dark. Many pathetic incidents occurred. Men were crying, being overcome with emotions, produced by the thought of a crushing defeat, and a doubtful future, whether they should return home or essay to join the expedition to Johnston. A young man, whom I esteemed highly, was greatly agitated, and asked me what he should do. I told him that brother [Lt. Richard Shreve] and I were going with the expedition, but that knowing him as I did I advised him to return home, that we were entering upon what would be most probably a fruitless mission.

McGregor called out, "Fall in at once, all who are going with me." My brother replied, "Go ahead. We will overtake you," being engaged just then in writing a missive to his sweetheart, standing, bridle in hand. I was also ready, waiting to accompany him. Very soon he and I started off, through the city, in pursuit of McGregor and party. Suffice it to say we never overtook them, but came up with some who had dropped out of the ranks. Being tired and hungry, we rode up to a farm house, where they received from us the first news of the surrender and gave us an abundant refreshment. We continued our march and halted and rested under some trees for the remainder of the night. The next day continuing our southwest course, we reached the vicinity of Salem, where we received news of the surrender of Gen. [John] Echols's command. We halted and relinquished our purpose of proceeding further. After a rest of a week, we started for our home in Fairfax County. We went by way of Staunton and Winchester, near which latter town we met the first picket of the enemy. They treated us with great kindness and escorted us to the officer of the Provost Marshall, not as prisoners but as companions in arms. By direction of this officer, we went to Millwood the next day and received our paroles.[50]

Major McGregor's mission was fruitless. He did rendezvous with Echols and eventually rejoined Wade Hampton, who told him that he should see General Johnston. The brief meeting ended when Johnston informed McGregor that he had been included in Lee's surrender. His war was over too.

Graham's Battery, having been roughed up on the seventh, struggled to Appomattox Court House, where it remained on the firing line until Fitz Lee cut his way out. The battery's two guns rode with him, but the wounded and those with horses in poor condition stayed behind and surrendered. Lieutenants Edwin M. Pollard and Thomas Shanks with nineteen men ended their war on the ninth. Private Robertson recounted the story of the rest:

> When we got to Lynchburg next day, we met with a sight that tried our very souls. The women of that city met us in the streets with baskets of provisions, but no cheering nor waving of handkerchiefs; but with sad and tearful faces, telling us that Gen. Lee had surrendered at Appomattox, and that the army of Northern Virginia was no more. Capt. Graham allowed us to remain long enough to finish eating, and this was the first square meal that we had had for many a weary day. We were then marched to the fair grounds, where the guns were spiked and the harness cut up. The line then formed, and we officially informed that Gen. Lee had surrendered. Capt. Graham saying tho' that as for himself, he had no idea of surrendering to the Damned Yankees, called for volunteers to go to Gen. Johnston in North Carolina. But three Virginians stepped to the front, George Wingfield, George E. Robertson, and John C. Robertson, and some eight or ten men from North and South Carolina members of the Battery; the rest were disbanded, and we, taking the best horses, started for Johnston's army. We were soon joined by Capt. Oden of Loudoun County, Va., the Quartermaster of our Battalion, and about five or six men of McGregor's [Brown's] Battery, also Virginians.
>
> After many trials and hardships, we got to Greensboro, N.C.,[51] stayed there several days, and finding conditions about the same as in Virginia, Gen. Johnston about to surrender his army, Capt. Graham disbanded his little body of men and told us to get home as best we could. We Virginians, retracing our steps, crossed the Roanoke River near Wentworth, and there separated, each going to his own home.[52]

The desire of some of the officers and men of Graham's and Brown's Batteries to join Johnston's army in North Carolina and continue the war was shared by a number of men in Shoemaker's Battery as well. This battery also arrived at Appomattox on the eighth but refused to surrender, riding out with Fitz Lee and reaching Lynchburg with all of its guns and caissons.[53]

Once there, Captain Shoemaker, Lieutenants Phelps and Moorman, and about fifty of the men chose to march south and offer their services to Johnston. They parked their guns at the fairgrounds, spiked them, cut the carriages down, and set out. But as with Graham and Brown, Johnston told them they had already been surrendered and should go to their homes. Lt. Lewis T. Nunnelee had been in Richmond when the lines at Petersburg collapsed. He had wandered through the country, trying to rejoin the battery. Failing in that, he waited for a time in Riceville and Halifax Court House until news of Lee's surrender reached him.[54] Then he, too, went home.

The horse batteries that had been with Lee's army were surrendered at Appomattox, but not one had left its guns on the field. Unwilling to quit without one more effort, Brown, Graham, McGregor, and Shoemaker had marched on until they were told that the war for them had ended at Appomattox, even if they had not been there. For the batteries that had remained in the Shenandoah Valley, the end had come as well.

* * *

The men of the batteries that had received orders to re-form at Lynchburg trickled in one by one and in small groups. With the few officers that were present, the cannoneers looked to the defense of the city. There were no orders to move or join Lee's retreating army. Everyone waited. Pvt. Charles W. McVicar recorded the last hours of Lurty's, McClanahan's, and Thomson's Batteries:

> Sunday, the 9th—Moved our section [from Carter's Battery] early to White Rock, east of the city. The stragglers coming in by hundreds. 10 o'clock. Just heard officially of general R. E. Lee's surrender of eight thousand men at arms at Appomattox. Lieutenant John Dunnington [Lurty's Battery] and I sat on our guns looking at the remains of the army coming in; a sad sight to us. Evening—We just finished spiking and burning thirty fine pieces of artillery. At sunset, most of the officers disbanding their men. We marched our battery out to New London, twelve miles from the city, with Colonel Nelson's battalion of infantry. Artillery held a consultation that night in an old barn. At daylight Captain Carter assembled us, and several spoke. He disbanded us on the 10th April 1865. A sad parting! We had been shoulder to shoulder in so many hard places.[55]

Some pushed on with a number of guns from New London, Lieutenant Colonel Chew among them. Like many of the other horse artillery officers, he wanted to join Johnston and fight on, but he took some guns with him. He struggled with these pieces, remnants of three batteries, until he reached the Staunton River. Here he decided that the guns could be transported no farther and ordered the carriages burned and the cannons buried. Symbolically, though he may not have known it, he was burying the battalion with them.[56]

The men of the two remaining batteries in the Valley, Jackson's and Shanks's, formerly Johnston's, waited patiently near Walker's Creek for orders or news of events. The news reached them first. When they learned that Petersburg and Richmond had fallen, those men with healthy horses set out for Lynchburg, where they believed their guns were located. They rode as far as Fincastle. There, on April 12, the two batteries were disbanded on their promise to join the nearest Confederate force within sixty days.[57] This scattering brought to a close the proud histories of these batteries.

The Stuart Horse Artillery Battalion ceased to exist in the days immediately following Lee's surrender at Appomattox. Some batteries had not fired a shot in anger since the closing months of 1864. Others, determined to continue the fight, had marched south to Johnston. The last vestiges of their hopes and dreams dissipated with the realization that the war had truly ended for them on April 9 when Lee laid down his sword. In the last battles of the battalion, the officers and men performed their duty to the utmost. Some tragically laid down their lives. Those remaining departed for their homes with the knowledge that they had done their part and had served in one of the finest artillery organizations in any army, North or South. But a part of that organization still lived. Hart's Battery had yet to spike its guns.

Following the battle of Bentonville, Hart's Battery formed part of Johnston's rear guard. The army retreated to Raleigh, which was abandoned to the enemy as the Confederates fell back toward Greensboro. On April 14 at High Point, southwest of Greensboro, Hart's Battery was engaged with the enemy. Orders arrived to cease firing, both sides having agreed to a suspension of hostilities. At this last moment of conflict, Sgt. Benjamin B. Cox received a wound that cost him his arm. He had the distinction of being the last member of the battalion to be wounded during the war. The battery marched east and went into camp at Machine Shops[58] to await what all knew would come.[59]

When news of the surrender on April 26 arrived, Captain Halsey, like his comrades to the north, refused to concede defeat. He determined to take two of his guns and his best men and horses and ride to the Trans-Mississippi Department and keep fighting. After making preparations, the small column set out. In a speech he gave on February 22, 1878, during a celebration of the thirty-fourth anniversary of the Washington Artillery, Gen. Wade Hampton recounted the last poignant moments of the battery and the Stuart Horse Artillery Battalion:

> When they [Hart's battery] heard that the army was to be surrendered, for the first time since their organization they turned their backs upon the enemy—not from an enemy but from a surrender. I followed them

> for twenty-five miles before I overtook them. As I rode up, and the Battery was halted by my men, the sun was just gilding the tops of our forest trees—the last sun that ever rose on the Southern Confederacy. . . .
>
> I told them that they had been good and brave soldiers; that they had done their whole duty; that no reproach could rest upon them; and that I knew they would follow me. I told them that they had been surrendered by superior authority and that it was their duty to remain where they were and obey commands.
>
> And when I had spoken this, the veterans of Hart's Battery threw themselves upon their captured guns (for they had no others) and, passionately kissing them, wept like children.[60]

And thus the last guns of the Stuart Horse Artillery Battalion were silenced.

APPENDIX I

The Death of John Pelham

The circumstances surrounding the death of Maj. John Pelham require a more detailed examination of the various versions than allowed in the chapter on the battle of Kelly's Ford. While several accounts of Pelham's mortal wounding exist, the only ones taken seriously by historians are those written by Capt. Harry Gilmor and Lt. Henry B. McClellan, who supposedly were eyewitnesses. Unfortunately, Gilmor's and McClellan's stories are so in conflict as to be irreconcilable. Historians have spent many hours attempting to fit them together, to no avail. One is left to choose between them. The other versions that presume to explain what happened to Pelham should be read with caution but should not be dismissed in their entirety. Some of the authors were present at the battle, though not with Pelham at the time he was struck down. Certain elements of their stories can contribute to a clearer understanding of what may have occurred. What follows is an attempt to present some of what has been written about the battle of Kelly's Ford and John Pelham's role in it.

The most accepted story of what happened states that Pelham fell wounded along the stone fence near the Wheatley farmhouse during the first charge of the 3rd Virginia at the very beginning of the battle. This is very close to McClellan's account, which undoubtedly was the source.

McClellan wrote that his regiment (3rd Virginia) charged the enemy at the stone wall but, finding no opening, was forced to ride left along the wall and fire its pistols at the Federals across the wall. McClellan accompanied the column and carried out his duty as adjutant, which was to see the column kept closed up. Amid all the confusion McClellan claimed he saw Pelham riding to the head of the regiment. Later near a small enclosed area in the vicinity of the Wheatley house McClellan saw a lone cavalryman placing a body, which he recognized as Pelham, across the back of a horse.[1]

McClellan's history of Stuart's cavalry was and is highly regarded. He was certainly in a position to witness the events he reported. His mentioning of the stone fence is probably most responsible for fixing that feature in historians' minds. While he does not state that Pelham fell by the stone fence, what he called a small enclosed area could only refer to an area surrounded by a fence of some type, with the possibility of a small building on one side. Pvt. Henry H. Matthews quoted another version attributed to McClellan in his account of Pelham's death that appeared in the *Southern Historical Society Papers:*

> At the moment a regiment of Federal cavalry swept down upon us. Pelham's sabre flashed from its sheath in an instant. At that moment his appearance was superb. His cheeks were burning; his bright blue eyes darted lightning, and from his lips, wreathed with a smile of joy rang, "Forward!" as he cheered on the men. He looked the perfect picture of a hero, as he was. For an instant he was standing in his stirrups, his sabre flashing in his grasp; for a moment his clarion voice rang like a bugle that sounds the charge, and then I saw him hurled from his saddle under the tramping hoofs of the horses. With a single bound of my horse I reached him. He lay with his smiling face turned upward; his eyes closed. A shell had burst above him, a fragment of which had struck him on the head. He was gone, and his young blood, sacred to the men of the battery and the entire command, had bathed Virginia's soil.[2]

There are several problems with this account, not the least of which is that it entirely refutes what McClellan wrote in his book. As if to confuse the problem even more, Matthews printed a similar version in the *St. Mary's Beacon* on February 16, 1905, and attributed the paragraph to John Esten Cooke. The *Southern Historical Society Papers* version, which is the one quoted above, was published in 1910. To anyone who has read both Cooke and McClellan, the overly romanticized style fits the former better than the latter. If the writing is McClellan's, Matthews must have received this account directly from him, because it appears nowhere else but in Matthews's writings.

Capt. Harry Gilmor's version is entirely different:

> About half an hour after [Maj. John W.] Puller was killed, Pelham and I were standing together, on the right of the 2nd Virginia, which was in line, and just then sustaining a severe fire of shell from a light battery posted near. . . . The shells continued to explode all around us, but principally in our front; and so familiar had they become, that I had ceased to regard them . . . when, just as the last files of the 2nd wheeled into column, I was deafened by the explosion of one very near. Even then I did not look back till I heard [Capt. James] Bailey exclaim, "My God, they've killed poor Pelham."
>
> I had not heard the well known "thug" of a bullet or piece of shell, which you never fail to hear when a man is struck as near as Pelham

> was to me. Turning quickly in my saddle, I saw Pelham's horse, without his rider slowly moving off, and Pelham himself lying on his back upon the ground, his eyes wide open, and looking very natural, but fatally hurt.[3]

If Gilmor is to be believed, Pelham fell far back from the stone fence and was not participating in a charge with the 3rd Virginia or any other regiment. Pelham's wounding occurred half an hour after Maj. John Puller's death, which was sometime after the 3rd Virginia's first charge. The stone fence and the Wheatley farmhouse are absent entirely from Gilmor's version. He also claims to have assisted with Pelham's body but makes no mention of McClellan.

These two views do agree on one thing: Pelham was felled by a piece of shell. Since both men found common ground on how Pelham was wounded, this has not been questioned. But there are problems with McClellan's first account concerning this point. Lt. George Browne of the 6th New York Battery stated that he was ordered to the front but could get only one gun in battery because of the condition of the road. He was trailing behind at least two full regiments and parts of two others.[4] Though Browne does not indicate his exact position when he finally reached the front, the fact that he remained on the road would put his gun at the front between the 4th Pennsylvania and the 4th New York, with the stone fence and woods to his right.

Browne failed to record whether he managed to fire once he put his gun into position. The charge of the 3rd Virginia could have passed by his point on the line by the time he manhandled his gun through the mud and into place beside the road. If he did fire, he may have opened with shell on the 3rd Virginia when it began its charge toward the Federal line, but he certainly was not firing shell once the Confederates came within 200 yards of Browne's gun. That would have been canister range, and Browne would have switched to it for greater effect. Furthermore, the position of the 4th New York along the fence to Browne's right would have placed it in danger of being hit by any shell fired down the length of the line. Finally, from Browne's location, the Wheatley farmhouse could not be seen because of the intervening woods, and Browne would not have fired blindly in that direction, not knowing the extent or deployment of the 4th New York's line. If Pelham did fall near the wall in the vicinity of the Wheatley farmhouse, as McClellan wrote, it becomes hard to envision that Browne fired the shot that felled him, at least in the opening charge.

As Browne's other pieces reached the front during the lull following the 3rd Virginia's charge, their actions would have been governed somewhat by the same conditions.[5] Again, Browne did not elaborate concerning the exact locations of his sections, but because of the woods, the guns had to be pushed fairly close to the front. Any charges made by the Confederates would have been met with shell as they came out of the woods along the western edge of the Wheatley field and as they formed for their charges in the open. Once more, Browne would have switched to canister when they approached the wall or ceased to fire for fear of hitting his own cavalry, which was more extensively deployed in and around the Wheatley farm buildings.[6] Browne reported that he expended half of his ammunition in the first phase of the fight, which would mean it lasted longer than a brief charge or two.[7] In conclusion, McClellan's claim that Pelham was felled by shellfire from Browne's battery near the Wheatley farm buildings during the first or a subsequent charge is subject to question.

This prompts other considerations. Could there have been another stone fence closer to the Confederate position along the west woods? In his report, Col. J. Irvin Gregg of the 16th Pennsylvania stated, "I dismounted the balance of my command, and threw my entire force some 300 yards in advance of the houses, under the cover of a stone wall, and drove the enemy from the position."[8] The Confederates could have been trying to hold on to this wall and were being shelled by the Federal artillery prior to Gregg's advance. At the end of its first charge, the 3rd Virginia rallied in this area, and Pelham could have fallen here trying to encourage the cavalry to charge or hold its ground. Although this would contradict McClellan as to the time and exact location that Pelham fell, it would still place him close to a stone wall.

There are other alternatives. One is that Pelham did not fall anywhere near a stone wall, but rather between the western edge of the woods and effective canister range where he would have been under fire from Browne's shells. This would be more in agreement with Gilmor's account. A second is that Pelham was wounded much later in the battle, during its second phase, when the opposing sides were two miles from the river. Gilmor's "about half an hour after Puller was killed" is a vague time reference, since he did not state when Puller fell. But if Puller was killed late in the fighting on the Wheatley farm, the Confederates may have pulled back to their second line, and Pelham could have fallen in defense of it.

The idea that Pelham fell later in the fight is supported by other sources. Fitz Lee and Browne stated in their reports that Breathed's guns did not open fire until the Federals had pushed two miles from the ford. Sgt. Robert S. Hudgins of the 3rd Virginia remembered the guns being fired before he participated in the charge in which Pelham was wounded.[9] Pvt. Henry H. Matthews of Breathed's Battery also testified that they were working the guns at the time that Pelham was there. He recalled Pelham saying to Breathed, "Captain, do not let your fire cease; drive them from their position," prior to his riding off to enter into the fatal charge.[10] This would place Pelham with Breathed after the latter opened fire during the second phase of the fight.

On a related point, could a shell fired by his own artillery have struck Pelham? This would not be plausible with McClellan's version, but the longer Pelham survived into the fight, the more it becomes a possibility. In conjunction with the recollections of Hudgins and Matthews, it should receive some consideration. Breathed may have been firing shell over his own cavalry to hinder the Federal deployment. Confederate ammunition was notorious for exploding short or long of its target. A short round might have inflicted Pelham's wound if he had been close to the Federal line.

Jeb Stuart's version of how Pelham was wounded does not appear in any of his writings. But Capt. Jedediah Hotchkiss recorded in his journal a conversation he had with Stuart about Pelham. Stuart told him Pelham had been hit by a musket ball. The wound, which was to the head, occurred near a gap in a fence as Pelham cheered the cavalry charging past him.[11]

There are certainly elements of this account that are familiar. The fence and Pelham's cheering on a regiment are in common with what McClellan wrote. The fact that Pelham was trying to return to Stuart after being with his artillery supports the view that Pelham was with his guns before his fall. However, the wounding by a musket ball is new. Did Hotchkiss receive this particular piece of information from Stuart during his lengthy conversation with the general? Is this what Stuart believed?

These are just some of the mysteries surrounding the mortal wounding of John Pelham. His personal life has remained shrouded in legend. Why should not his death? There seem to be no answers, only questions. Questions that cannot be answered from any of the known accounts. Until additional evidence is forthcoming, the spot where the gallant Alabamian fell, indeed, the very circumstances of his wounding, like much of his life, must remain a mystery.

APPENDIX II

The Baltimore Light Artillery at Gettysburg

The participation of the Baltimore Light Artillery at Gettysburg has long been a subject of controversy. The fact that it was present on the field is not in doubt, but its position and the role it played in the fighting are points of conjecture still being debated. The prevailing opinion is that the battery was placed somewhere on Seminary Ridge south of Oak Hill near the Cashtown/Chambersburg Pike. Supposedly Griffin's Battery was attached to Lt. Col. Thomas H. Carter's Artillery Battalion and participated in the bombardment prior to Pickett's Charge. This view is based on the Bachelder Papers, specifically two letters written by members of the battery, and the Bachelder maps that give the various units' positions throughout the battle.[1]

Strengthening this opinion is the conclusion drawn by Maj. Henry B. McClellan, adjutant to Maj. Gen. J. E. B. Stuart. In his book, *I Rode with Jeb Stuart,* McClellan wrote that the Baltimore Light accompanied the cavalry and participated in the cavalry battle on the afternoon and evening of July 3.[2] However, after corresponding with Bachelder and others, McClellan came to the opinion that he had mistaken Jackson's Battery for Griffin's and that what he had written in his book was in error.[3] At this point, the controversy would appear to have been settled. There are some problems with this view, however, that need to be addressed, not the least of which are the two letters that were the basis for Bachelder's conclusions regarding the position of Griffin's Battery.

Joshua Davis, a member of Griffin's Battery, wrote the first letter on March 24, 1886. He stated that the battery approached Gettysburg from the direction of Thaddeus Stevens's ironworks (Caledonia Furnace) on July 1, encamping near a bridge over a creek. The battery was eventually placed 100 or 200 yards to the right of the Whitworth guns of Hardaway's Alabama Battery, commanded by Capt. William B. Hurt, which on July 3 were stationed on Oak Hill.[4] Davis's fellow batterymate, John F. Hayden, appeared to confirm the battery's position in a letter dated April 7, 1886, in which he stated that the battery was placed in a position to the left of the Cashtown Pike.[5] With these two statements, it becomes easy to see why Griffin's Battery has been placed near Oak Hill on July 3. What have been ignored are the finer points of the letters, which cast some doubt on the position given by Bachelder.

To begin with, Davis's memory was faulty, and his story begins to unravel in his first paragraph. Thaddeus Stevens's ironworks was located ten miles east of Chambersburg on the Cashtown/Chambersburg Pike.[6] Griffin's Battery marched to the battlefield on the Heidlersburg (Harrisburg) Road and came nowhere near Caledonia Furnace. Such a grievous error raises serious doubt as to the validity of Davis's further statements.

A comparison of Davis's and Hayden's accounts uncovers other discrepancies, not the least of which is Davis's positioning of the battery near Hurt's Whitworth guns, which were part of Maj. David G. McIntosh's artillery battalion. McIntosh gave the positions of his guns in his report dated July 30, 1863:

> On the morning of Wednesday, July 1, it [McIntosh's Battalion] moved with General Pender's division into the line of battle. One battery of Napoleons (Captain [R. S.] Rice) and a section of Whitworths were placed first in position a short distance to the right of the turnpike, by the side of a portion of Major Pegram's battalion, and fire was opened slowly upon the enemy wherever they brought into view considerable bodies of troops, and occasionally upon their batteries. The Whitworth guns were used to shell the woods to the right of the town. . . .
>
> On Thursday morning, July 2, the battalion was put in position behind a stone wall, on the range of hills to the left of the town of Gettysburg, Captain Rice's battery in reserve. . . . The two Whitworth guns were moved Friday morning, by direction of Lieut. Gen. A. P. Hill, to a commanding point north of the railroad cut, to enable them to enfilade the enemy's position. They fired, it is believed, with effect from this point.[7]

McIntosh clearly states that the Whitworth guns held one position on July 2 and another on the third. However, both Davis and Hayden agree that their battery took a position upon reaching the field and did not move until after Pickett's assault on July 3.[8] If Griffin took his position on July 2, he could not have been 100 or 200 yards to the right of the Whitworths on Oak Hill on July 3, since those guns were moved there only on the morning of the third. Furthermore, even if we allow that the battery approached Gettysburg on the third along the Cashtown/Chambersburg Pike, it would not have ended up where Davis claimed.[9] Hayden and Davis recorded that the battery took a position to the left of the road, Hayden stating that it was about 200 yards from the road.[10] In this position, the guns would have been over half a mile south of the Whitworths on Oak Hill and not within the 100 to 200 yards as given by Davis.[11]

In any case, knowing that the battery approached the battlefield on the second along the Heidlersburg Road changes the situation. The battery would have had to march through Gettysburg and out either along the Mummasburg Road or on the Cashtown/Chambersburg Pike to reach the general area Bachelder gave for its position. Taking the Mummasburg Road from town, the battery would have turned left (according to Hayden) and gone into position 200 yards south of the road. But Hayden makes no reference to the Mummasburg Road, only the Cashtown Pike, and a position 200 yards south of the Mummasburg Road is almost half a mile north of the Cashtown Pike and several hundred yards from the Whitworth guns stationed on Oak Hill on July 3. If the battery marched out along the Cashtown Pike and turned left for 200 yards, it would have been over three-fourths of a mile south of the Whitworths, and not the 100 or 200 yards to the right of these guns as given by Davis. Obviously, neither of these positions agrees with what Davis and Hayden wrote in their letters to Bachelder.

Another important reference given by Davis is the crossing of the creek. This has been taken to mean Willoughby Run, which the Cashtown Pike crossed. In fact, the creek in question was Rock Creek, which was crossed by the Heidlersburg Road and both the Hanover Road and York Pike east of Gettysburg. These two roads intersect to become the Cashtown Pike, an important fact when considering the positioning of Griffin's Battery.

If a case can be made that Griffin's Battery was not in a position along the Cashtown Pike west of Gettysburg or near Oak Hill at anytime on either July 2 or 3, the question still remains, where was it? Certainly, before any conclusions can be drawn concerning the probable position of the battery, the problem of Davis's reference to the Whitworth guns must be addressed. What is evident from McIntosh's report is that the Whitworths were never in a position close to the Heidlersburg Road and therefore could not have been in the vicinity of Griffin's Battery, despite Davis's claim to the contrary. However, there were guns nearby that may have been taken for the Whitworths.

Capt. Charles I. Raine's Lee Artillery of Maj. Joseph W. Latimer's Battalion had two twenty-pound Parrott guns, which in size resembled the Whitworths more than any other gun on the field. From a distance, it would have been possible to mistake one for the other. On July 2 and 3, Raine's section of twenty-pound Parrotts was stationed behind Benner's Hill near the tollgate on the Hanover Road just east of Rock Creek.[12] Placing Griffin's Battery in proximity to these guns on the second hinges on Hayden's account that the battery was placed about 200 yards to the left of the Cashtown Pike upon its arrival on the field the evening of the second.[13]

The key to solving the problem would seem to lie with understanding the reference to the Cashtown Pike. Both Davis and Hayden mention it, as does the battery's historian who recorded "upon arriving at Gettysburg the battery was ordered to report to Major [Joseph W.] Latimer, who assigned it a position a short distance to the left of the Cashtown Pike."[14] In looking at a map of Gettysburg, it can be seen that the Cashtown Pike passes through the town, splitting and becoming the York Pike and the Hanover Road. Griffin's Battery could have entered the town on the Heidlersburg Road and turned east where the road intersected with the Cashtown Pike. Unfamiliar with the roads east of the town, the batterymen understood that they were on the Cashtown Pike, even though Cashtown was to the west. The historian's reference to Latimer and the fact that Raine's twenty-pound Parrotts were stationed east of the town on July 2 would seem to support this interpretation. Griffin could very readily have been placed 200 yards left (north) of either the York Pike or the Hanover Road and near the Parrotts. The attack to which Davis referred was not on Cemetery Hill, but on Culp's Hill, and was not on the third, but the second.

Hayden's letter contains another piece of information that has been overlooked. He wrote that after Pickett's Charge, the battery was given orders to go to the east of the town to fight the enemy cavalry.[15] While this does not confirm the battery's presence on the cavalry field, it does add some support for its positioning close to the left flank. To think that Stuart could have known where the battery was west of the town and then ordered it to march several miles to the cavalry field is extremely doubtful. More likely he knew its position east of Gettysburg and sent for it.

Finally, Griffin would have been placed under a battalion commander regardless of the position in which the battery was placed. Lt. Col. Thomas H. Carter had command of the batteries from the Mummasburg Road to the area south of the Cashtown Pike. In his report, he does not mention that Griffin was placed under his command.[16] Capt. Willis J. Dance, whose 1st Regiment of Virginia Artillery was posted south of the Cashtown Pike, reported that two rifled guns of Capt. Abraham Hupp's Salem Artillery, commanded by Lt. Charles B. Griffin, did participate in the bombardment with the rest of Carter's battalion.[17] Some writers and historians have mistaken this Griffin to be Capt. Wiley H. Griffin of the Baltimore Light Artillery, further adding to the false notion that the Baltimore Light was somewhere on Seminary Ridge under Carter's command.

The battery's historian's account claimed that the battery was attached to Latimer's battalion of artillery. Unfortunately, Latimer was mortally wounded at Gettysburg on the second and never filed a report. The actions of his battalion were recorded by his superior officer, Lt. Col. Richard Snowden Andrews, who was not present at the battle and, unless told, would not have known if Griffin's Battery was temporarily attached to the battalion. He made no mention of Griffin in his report. Factually speaking, nothing can be learned regarding Griffin's Battery from Carter's, Dance's, or Andrews's reports.

While the position of the Baltimore Light Artillery at Gettysburg may be of little significance in the overall panorama of the battle, it is important in a history of the Stuart Horse Artillery Battalion. Placing the battery among the guns along Seminary Ridge and crediting it with participating in the bombardment preceding Pickett's Charge based on the cursory reading of two letters, one written by an individual who did not even know by what route his command reached the field, would seem to be a poor examination of the facts.

What actually happened may never be known, but a more logical understanding of the events would be that Griffin arrived on the second and was assigned a position east of Gettysburg across Rock Creek, within a couple hundred yards of both the Cashtown Pike (in the form of the York Pike or the Hanover Road) and the twenty-pound Parrott guns of Raine's Battery. There the Baltimore Light Artillery contributed what it could to the bombardment of Culp's Hill throughout the afternoon and evening of the second. Following the repulse of Pickett's Charge on the third, it was recalled by Stuart and arrived in the vicinity of the cavalry fighting in the early evening. Most likely it did not participate in the cavalry action, or if it did, it was limited to the desultory firing that continued in the evening after the cavalry action ended.

NOTES

THE PELHAM ERA

Chapter 1

1. David Cardwell, "A Horse Battery," *Confederate Veteran* (hereafter cited as *CV*) 27 (1919): 7.
2. George M. Neese to Roger P. Chew, March 28, 1898, Roger Preston Chew Papers, Jefferson County Museum, Charles Town, West Virginia.
3. Theodore Stanford Garnett, *Riding with Stuart: Reminiscences of an Aide-de-Camp,* ed. Robert J. Trout (Shippensburg, PA: White Mane Publishing Company, 1994), 106.
4. Albert Manucy, *Artillery through the Ages* (Washington, DC: United States Government Printing Office, 1962), 7, 11.
5. Col. Thomas E. Griess and Jay Luvas, eds., *Instruction for Field Artillery* (New York: Greenwood Press, 1968), 1; M. C. Switlik, *The Complete Cannoneer* (Rochester, MI: Ray Russell Books, 1979), 9.
6. John Gibbon, *The Artillerist's Manual* (Glendale, NY: Benchmark Publishing Company, 1970), 389.
7. Ibid.
8. Ibid., 388.
9. John Esten Cooke, *Mohun* (Charlottesville, VA: Historical Publishing Co., 1936), 250.

Chapter 2

1. Charles G. Milham, *Gallant Pelham: American Extraordinary* (Washington, DC: Public Affairs Press, 1985), 21.
2. Unfiled Slips and Papers, Confederate Records, United States Archives, Washington, DC.
3. Roger Preston Chew, *Stonewall Jackson: Address of R. P. Chew Delivered at the Virginia Military Institute, Lexington, Virginia, on the Unveiling of Ezekiel's Statue of General T. J. Jackson, June 12, 1912* (Lexington, KY: Rockbridge County News Print, 1912), 8.
4. Edgar Mandelbert McDonell (?–September 1, 1911), Class of 1863, served as a lieutenant in the 22nd Battalion, Georgia Heavy Artillery. Robert W. Wentz, ed., *The 1989 Register of Former Cadets of the Virginia Military Institute* (Lexington, VA: VMI Alumni Association, 1989), 67.

   Charles Conway Flowerree (October 26, 1842–September 16, 1929), Class of 1863, was from Virginia. He became successively the adjutant, major, lieutenant colonel, and colonel of the 7th Virginia Infantry. Flowerree was wounded at Second Manassas and captured at Saylor's Creek. After the war, he moved to Vicksburg, Mississippi, and became president of the Vicksburg Ice Company. Robert K. Krick, *Lee's Colonels* (Dayton: Morningside House, 1991), 142.

   John Koontz Thompson (?–January 3, 1925), Class of 1863, became a captain in the 22nd Virginia Infantry. He also served as the adjutant of the regiment. Suffering four major wounds, one involving the loss of an eye, and several minor ones, Thompson survived the war to become a member of the West Virginia State Legislature, a United States marshal, and a farmer after the war. Wentz, *1989 Register,* 67; Editor, "The Last Roll," *CV* 33 (1925): 144.

5. Henry King Burgwyn, Jr. (October 3, 1841–July 1, 1863), Class of 1861, was from North Carolina. Burgwyn became lieutenant colonel and then colonel of the 26th North Carolina Infantry. Killed at Gettysburg, he is buried in Oakwood Cemetery, Raleigh, NC. Wentz, *1989 Register,* 67; Krick, *Lee's Colonels,* 76.
6. Milton Rouss File, Virginia Military Institute Archives (hereafter cited as VMIA), Lexington, Virginia.
7. *Jacksonville Republican,* May 2, 1861.
8. John Thomas Lewis Preston (?–July 1890) was professor of Latin and English literature at VMI. He served as Jackson's adjutant until February 1862, when he returned to the institute. Preston is buried in Stonewall Jackson Cemetery, Lexington, Virginia. Wentz, *1989 Register,* 46.
9. John DeHart Ross (May 1, 1840–December 12, 1912) was a graduate of VMI (Class of 1859) and had taught French and tactics there until the outbreak of the war. He became a lieutenant of engineers on the staff of Brig. Gen. William W. Loring, in which capacity he served until August 1862, when he was commissioned major in the 52nd Virginia Infantry. Promoted to lieutenant colonel, Ross resigned in December 1864 and afterward was enrolling officer in Staunton, Virginia. He was a farmer after the war. Ross is buried in Stonewall Jackson Cemetery, Lexington, Virginia. Krick, *Lee's Colonels,* 327.
10. Rouss File, VMIA.
11. The battery was commanded by Capt. Pierce Butler Anderson (?–December 13, 1861) at this time. He and the other officers had been separated from their guns during the retreat. Anderson was later killed in Federal Brig. Gen. Robert S. Milroy's attack on the Confederate position on top of Allegheny Mountain in Pocahontas County, Virginia (now West Virginia). He is buried in Tullahoma, Tennessee. Lee A. Wallace, *A Guide to Virginia Military Organizations, 1861–1865* (Lynchburg, VA: H. E. Howard, 1986), 23; O. V. Anderson, "Capt. Pierce B. Anderson's Sword," *CV* 19 (1911): 544.
12. These were actually two batteries: Company D, 5th U.S. Artillery, commanded by Capt. Charles Griffin, and Company I, 1st U.S. Artillery, commanded by Capt. James B. Ricketts.
13. The Federals reported a loss of twenty-five guns, while the Confederates claimed the capture of twenty-eight. *The War of the Rebellion: The Official Records of the Union and Confederate Armies* (hereafter cited as *O.R.;* Harrisburg, PA: National Historical Society, 1971), ser. 1, vol. 2, 328, 503.
14. John Horace Forney (August 12, 1829–September 13, 1902) commanded the 10th Alabama Infantry, which was in Brig. Gen. Kirby Smith's Brigade. Forney later became a major general. He is buried not far from Pelham in City Cemetery, Jacksonville, Alabama. "Maj. Gen. John H. Forney," *CV* 15 (1907): 488.
15. Pelham was wrong concerning one of the officers. Col. Egbert J. Jones (1820–September 2, 1861), commanding the regiment, was shot through both hips and died from his wound. The lieutenant colonel was Evander M. Law (August 7, 1836–October 31, 1920), who became colonel of the regiment and went on to be a brigadier general. Maj. Charles Lewis Scott (January 23, 1827–April 30, 1899) survived a leg wound, but when it would not heal, he was forced to resign from the service. Krick, *Lee's Colonels,* 213, 336; Ezra J. Warner, *Generals in Gray* (Baton Rouge: Louisiana State University Press, 1959), 174–75.
16. *Jacksonville Republican,* August 8, 1861. Copy courtesy of Calhoun County War Memorial Library, Anniston, Alabama.

17. *O.R.,* ser. 1, vol. 2, 481.
18. Roger Preston Chew File, VMIA.
19. Rouss File, VMIA.
20. One source stated that the battery's armament consisted of the Blakely, a howitzer, and a six-inch gun. Avis Mary Cusuis Cauley, "The Confederacy in the Lower Shenandoah Valley as Illustrated by the Career of Colonel Roger Preston Chew" (Master's thesis, University of Pittsburgh, Pennsylvania, 1937), 22–23.
21. Chew, *Stonewall Jackson, Roger Preston Chew Papers,* Jefferson County Historical Society, 15.
22. *O.R.,* ser. 1, vol. 5, 390, 396–97.
23. James H. Williams to Cora DeMovelle (Pritchartt) Williams, December 14, 1861, Williams Family Papers, Virginia Historical Society (hereafter cited as VHS).
24. *O.R.,* ser. 1, vol. 5, 390.
25. Ibid, 399.
26. William P. Palmer, H. W. Flournoy, and Sherwin McRae, eds., *Calendar of Virginia State Papers: January 1, 1836–April 15, 1869* (Richmond, 1893), 11: 197–98.
27. In a letter to his wife, Flora, on November 24, 1861, Stuart mentioned that Pelham wanted and might be given the position. This indicates that two days before Pelham was drawing guns and supplies for his battery and signing as commander of the Stuart Horse Artillery, Stuart had no knowledge of the fact that Pelham was to receive the appointment. Adele H. Mitchell, ed., *The Letters of Major General James E. B. Stuart* (Stuart-Mosby Historical Society, 1990), 225.
28. *Compiled Service Records of Confederate General and Staff Officers, and Non-Regimental Enlisted Men* (hereafter cited as *C.S.R.;* Washington, DC, 1961), microcopy M331, roll 195.
29. Manuscript Department, William R. Perkins Library, Duke University, Durham, North Carolina.
30. Mitchell, *Stuart,* 225.
31. Ibid.
32. Lt. Chiswell Dabney, one of Stuart's aides-de-camp, wrote to his father on December 17, 1861, and mentioned that a scout was made toward Annandale that day. He further stated that Captain Pelham and one gun accompanied the cavalry. The scouting expedition does not appear in the Official Records, but this does not mean it did not occur. Dabney did not record the result of the scout, as he finished the letter before the cavalry's return. If Pelham fired on the enemy, it would be the first known engagement of the Stuart Horse Artillery. But since no other record of the action has been found, it cannot be confirmed as such. Evidently Pelham was being called a captain by some because he commanded a battery, even though he did not officially hold the rank. Chiswell Dabney to Rev. John Blair Dabney, December 17, 1861, Saunders Family Papers, VHS.
33. *C.S.R.,* microcopy M331, roll 195.
34. Wallace, *Virginia Military Organizations,* 2, 83.
35. H. H. Matthews, "Organization of the Pelham-Breathed Battery of Stuart's Horse Artillery Operating with Stuart's Cavalry, Army of Northern Virginia, including the Battle of Williamsburg, May 5, 1862," *St. Mary's Beacon,* November 3, 1904.
36. Gary W. Gallagher, ed., *Fighting for the Confederacy: The Personal Recollections of General Edward Porter Alexander* (Chapel Hill: University of North Carolina Press, 1989), 76.
37. Brown's rank was only temporary. He never actually held a commission as a lieutenant in the battery and was not elected in March 1862 to any of the officer positions.

38. "Mounted Flying Artillery," *Cannoneer* 8, 3 (November 1989): 6–7; *Jacksonville Republican,* December 19, 1861.
39. Records show that Pelham enlisted Ashton Chichester in Culpeper Court House on March 10, 1862. *Compiled Service Records of Confederate Soldiers Who Served in Organizations from the State of Virginia* (hereafter cited as *C.S.R.V.;* Washington, DC, 1961), microcopy M324, roll 267.
40. George M. Neese, *Three Years in the Confederate Horse Artillery* (Dayton: Press of Morningside Bookshop, 1983), 11.
41. Ibid.
42. Diary of James H. Williams, Williams Family Papers, VHS.
43. Ibid.
44. Ibid.; Neese, *Confederate Horse Artillery,* 17.
45. Williams Diary.
46. James H. Williams to Cora DeMovelle (Pritchartt) Williams, January 11, 1862, Williams Papers.
47. Williams Diary.
48. Neese, *Confederate Horse Artillery,* 18–20.
49. Jackson's report of the campaign is found in *O.R.,* ser. 1, vol. 5, 390–95.
50. Neese, *Confederate Horse Artillery,* 21.
51. Francis Henney Smith (October 12, 1812–March 21, 1890) had graduated from West Point with the Class of 1833. He served as a lieutenant in the U.S. Army for three years, before becoming a professor of mathematics at Hampden-Sidney College. He came to VMI as its first superintendent in 1839 and remained there for the next fifty years. He had a distinguished career that included serving on the Board of Visitors for the United States Military Academy and as a major general of Virginia Volunteers during the war. Smith is buried in Stonewall Jackson Cemetery, Lexington, Virginia. Wentz, *1989 Register,* 27.
52. Chew File, VMIA.
53. Williams Diary.
54. James H. Williams to Cora DeMovelle (Pritchartt) Williams, March 10, 1862, Williams Papers.
55. *C.S.R.,* microcopy M331, roll 195.

Chapter 3

1. Neese, *Confederate Horse Artillery,* 25–27.
2. Ibid., 27–29.
3. James H. Williams to Cora DeMovelle (Pritchartt) Williams, March 15, 1862, Williams Papers.
4. Neese, *Confederate Horse Artillery,* 29–30.
5. Williams Diary.
6. There was no report of these actions, and Neese, who gave the only account, did not mention any casualties. However, there are many men from the battery whose records indicate that they were wounded but for which no date is given. It is possible that some may have been wounded in these actions. Neese, *Confederate Horse Artillery,* 30–31.
7. *O.R.,* ser. 1, vol. 12, part 1, 339.
8. Ibid., 385; Neese, *Confederate Horse Artillery,* 31–33.
9. Robert G. Tanner, *Stonewall in the Valley* (Garden City, NY: Doubleday & Company, 1976), 118.
10. The brush with Ashby and Chew caused Shields to push more troops toward Winchester. One of the units ordered forward was commanded by Col. Nathan Kim-

ball, who would command the entire division in the coming battle. *O.R.*, ser. 1, vol. 12, part 1, 339.

11. Neese's diary is the only account that states that one gun went into position at this location. All other sources claim that all three of Chew's guns were unlimbered. In their reports, Col. Samuel S. Carroll and Lt. Col. Franklin Sawyer, who commanded the Federal skirmishers of the 8th Ohio Infantry, maintained that they faced a battery of artillery that was driven from its first position to a second one in front of some woods. On the Confederate side, both Ashby and Nadenbousch mentioned "guns" or "battery" in their reports. All versions state that two positions were held by Chew's battery. Neese, *Confederate Horse Artillery,* 33; Rev. James B. Avirett, *The Memoirs of General Turner Ashby and His Compeers* (Baltimore: Selby & Dulany, 1867), 159–60; *O.R.*, ser. 1, vol. 12, part 1, 368, 369, 385, 389.
12. Neese, *Confederate Horse Artillery,* 34; *O.R.*, ser. 1, vol. 12, part 1, 385.
13. This was probably a section of Battery B, 1st West Virginia Artillery, commanded by Capt. John Jenks. *O.R.*, ser. 1, vol. 12, part 1, 359.
14. Neese recorded that it was a four-gun battery, but the Federal chief of artillery, Lt. Col. Philip Daum, did not mention in his report that he had ordered Jenks to withdraw or any casualties to this battery. He simply stated that the section, meaning two guns, "did good service." Commanding the Union infantry on that flank was Col. Jeremiah C. Sullivan, who confirms that he had just two guns with him. Neese, *Confederate Horse Artillery,* 34; *O.R.*, ser. 1, vol. 12, part 1, 359.
15. Not all sources agree as to who saved Chew's Battery on this occasion. Neese gave all the credit to the fire of the artillery, while two other sources cited Ashby's cavalry charge. One of these sources stated that the Federals "seemed in no degree checked by it [Chew's Battery], and passed on." In all probability, it was a combination of Chew's fire and Ashby's charge that decided the issue. Neese, *Confederate Horse Artillery,* 37; Avirett, *Memoirs of Ashby,* 167; Capt. William N. McDonald, *A History of the Laurel Brigade* (Arlington, VA: R. W. Beatty, 1969), 148.
16. Neese, *Confederate Horse Artillery,* 37–39; Avirett, *Memoirs of Ashby,* 168; Edward A. Moore, *The Story of a Cannoneer under Stonewall Jackson* (New York: Neale Publishing Company, 1907), 35.
17. Capt. William McLaughlin commanded the Rockbridge Artillery, and Capt. James H. Waters the West Augusta Battery. As Williams recorded, both batteries did lose a gun because of the horses being shot. *O.R.*, ser. 1, vol. 12, part 1, 396–99.
18. James H. Williams to Cora DeMovelle (Pritchartt) Williams, March 25, 1862, Williams Papers.
19. Williams Diary.
20. Neese, *Confederate Horse Artillery,* 39.
21. Ibid., 40; *O.R.*, ser. 1, vol. 12, part 1, 418–20.
22. Neese, *Confederate Horse Artillery,* 40; *O.R.*, ser. 1, vol. 12, part 1, 419.
23. *O.R.*, ser. 1, vol. 12, part 1, 418.
24. Neese, *Confederate Horse Artillery,* 40; *O.R.*, ser. 1, vol. 12, part 1, 418–20; Tanner, *Stonewall in the Valley,* 138.
25. Neese, *Confederate Horse Artillery,* 41.
26. Moore, *Cannoneer under Jackson,* 38.
27. Neese, *Confederate Horse Artillery,* 43–44.
28. McDonald, *Laurel Brigade,* 49.
29. These men were Capt. Hugh R. T. Koontz and Pvt. Harry Hatcher. Richard L. Armstrong, *7th Virginia Cavalry* (Lynchburg, VA: H. E. Howard, 1992), 26, 160, 178; Avirett, *Memoirs of Ashby,* 173–74; Neese, *Confederate Horse Artillery,* 45; McDonald, *Laurel Brigade,* 49.

30. Neese, *Confederate Horse Artillery,* 46.
31. Ibid., 46.
32. Ibid., 48.
33. *O.R.,* ser. 1, vol. 12, part 1, 446.
34. Ibid.
35. Ibid., part 3, 446.
36. Williams Diary.
37. James H. Williams to Cora DeMovelle (Pritchartt) Williams, April 24, 1862, Williams Papers.
38. Neese, *Confederate Horse Artillery,* 49–50.
39. Ibid., 51–52.
40. Tanner, *Stonewall in the Valley,* 162–63.
41. Moore, *Cannoneer under Jackson,*45–46.
42. Neese, *Confederate Horse Artillery,* 52.
43. Tanner, *Stonewall in the Valley,* 162–63; *O.R.,* ser. 1, vol. 12, part 3, 893–94.
44. Neese, *Confederate Horse Artillery,* 52.
45. The election of Williams to a lieutenancy on April 23 could have been negated by this election, since the army had ordered this one. He made no reference to this election in his diary and in fact was not present. His father had passed away, and Williams had left the battery on the seventeenth to go home. Williams Diary.
46. Neese, *Confederate Horse Artillery,* 55.
47. Ibid., 55–56; Moore, *Cannoneer under Jackson,* 53.
48. Jennings Cropper Wise, *The Long Arm of Lee* (Lynchburg, VA: J. P. Bell Company, 1915), 166–67.
49. Ibid., 167.
50. Neese, *Confederate Horse Artillery,* 58.
51. Williams Diary.
52. Neese, *Confederate Horse Artillery,* 60–62.
53. *O.R.,* ser. 1, vol. 12, part 1, 738.
54. Ibid., 739.
55. Williams stated that he fell back to Middletown, which was below Newtown. Neese recorded that he struck the Valley Pike at Newtown. Williams Diary; Neese, *Confederate Horse Artillery,* 62–63.
56. Neese, *Confederate Horse Artillery,* 63–64.
57. Ibid., 64.
58. Williams Diary.
59. Neese, *Confederate Horse Artillery,* 64–65.
60. In his report, Col. Owen Jones of the 1st Pennsylvania Cavalry stated that his orderly, Private Teagarden, was killed at his side by a shell. It could only have been Neese's shot that caused the casualty. *O.R.,* ser. 1, vol. 12, part 1, 581.
61. Williams Diary; Neese, *Confederate Horse Artillery,* 65.
62. Williams Diary; Neese, *Confederate Horse Artillery,* 65–66.
63. In his report of the campaign from May 23 to June 9, Col. Stapleton Crutchfield, Jackson's chief of artillery, recorded that Chew's best gun was damaged during the retreat, which forced other batteries to act with Ashby as the artillery of the rear guard. Neither Williams nor Neese mentioned any of Chew's guns being disabled during this time. Williams Diary; Neese, *Confederate Horse Artillery,* 65–66; *O.R.,* ser. 1, vol. 12, part 1, 727.
64. The unit was also designated the 42nd Regiment of the Line. O. R. Howard Thompson and William H. Rauch, *History of the "Bucktails"* (Philadelphia: Electric Printing Company, 1906), title page, 11, 153.

65. *O.R.,* ser. 1, vol. 12, part 1, 782, 817; Thompson and Rauch, *"Bucktails,"* 154–55; W. W. Goldsborough, *The Maryland Line in the Confederate Army* (Gaithersburg, MD: Olde Soldier Books, 1987), 50–53; "The 'Bucktail' Flag," *St. Mary's Beacon,* January 19, 1888; Edward G. Longacre, *Jersey Cavaliers* (Hightstown, NJ: Longstreet House, 1992), 60–65; Tanner, *Stonewall in the Valley,* 280–81.
66. Neese, *Confederate Horse Artillery,* 70.
67. James H. Williams to Cora DeMovelle (Pritchartt) Williams, June 21, 1862, Williams Papers.
68. Daniel Murray Lee was the son of Sidney Smith Lee, brother of Robert E. Lee.
69. John S. Wise, "A Modern Greek," *Bob Taylor's Magazine* 4, no. 3 (December 1906): 267.
70. The reports of Brig. Gen. Charles S. Winder, Capt. Joseph Carpenter, and Capt. William T. Poague of the Rockbridge Artillery did not mention Chew's Battery being on the hill at any time during the engagement or after. Neither Williams nor Neese recorded that the battery was engaged. In fact, Williams specifically stated that the battery was not engaged. Neese seemed to indicate that Chew arrived after the engagement was almost over and remained in a supporting position. Williams Diary; Neese, *Confederate Horse Artillery,* 72; *O.R.,* ser. 1, vol. 12, part 1, 739–40, 759, 762.
71. Neese, *Confederate Horse Artillery,* 72.
72. *O.R.,* ser. 1, vol. 12, part 1, 742.
73. Williams Diary.
74. James H. Williams to Cora DeMovelle (Pritchartt) Williams, June 17, 1862, Williams Papers.
75. McDonald, *Laurel Brigade,* 75–76; Armstrong, *7th Virginia Cavalry,* 37–38.

Chapter 4

1. One source stated that the Floyd County men were assigned to Pelham's Battery about April 9, but a letter written by William P. Walters on the twelfth made no mention of his being in the horse artillery at that time. He was still in Camp Winder in Richmond. Stuart's quartermaster, Philip H. Powers, wrote to his wife on the twenty-first, stating that the cavalry had left Richmond on the sixteenth and arrived at Yorktown on the eighteenth. The battery would have accompanied Stuart's command. In addition, the battery's records show that at least eighteen Floyd County men enlisted on either the fifteenth or sixteenth. There is no enlistment date for Walters, but he most likely joined at the same time. Milham, *Gallant Pelham,* 73; Robert J. Trout, *With Pen and Saber: The Letters and Diaries of J. E. B. Stuart's Staff Officers* (Mechanicsburg, PA: Stackpole Books, 1995), 61; *C.S.R.V.,* microcopy M324, rolls 267, 336, 337.
2. William A. Simpson to James Simpson, April 22, 1862, William P. Walters Papers.
3. *O.R.*, ser. 1, vol. 11, part 3, 484.
4. *C.S.R.,* microcopy M331, roll 195.
5. Not all the men from Floyd County had volunteered for service in the battery at this time. A number had been attached as conscripts and, like Walters, were hoping that they would be allowed to go home or into another unit once the battery had filled up its roster with volunteers.
6. William P. Walters to Matilda E. Walters, April 30, 1862, Walters Papers.
7. *O.R.,* ser. 1, vol. 11, part 1, 574.
8. Ibid., 444.
9. According to his record, Corp. Moses A. Febrey, gunner to the Blakely, was also wounded in this action. *C.S.R.V.,* microcopy M324, roll 336.

10. *O.R.,* ser. 1, vol. 11, part 1, 574–75.
11. This was Battery H of the 1st U.S. Artillery commanded by Capt. Charles H. Webber, which lost four guns, one caisson, and forty horses. *O.R.,* ser. 1, vol. 11, part 1, 471.
12. *O.R.,* ser. 1, vol. 11, part 1, 571–72.
13. Mitchell, *Letters of Stuart,* 253–54.
14. Matthews, "Organization of Pelham-Breathed Battery."
15. *O.R.,* ser. 1, vol. 11, part 1, 436, 575.
16. Ibid., 628.
17. William P. Walters to Matilda E. Walters, May ?, 1862 (first part of letter missing but second half dated May 13), Walters Papers.
18. Ibid., May 13, 1862.
19. George W. Shreve, "Reminiscences in the History of the Stuart Horse Artillery, C.S.A.," Chew Papers, 1.
20. Matthews, "Organization of Pelham-Breathed Battery."
21. The letter includes sections written on May 20, 22, and 23.
22. William P. Walters to Matilda E. Walters, May 23, 1862, Walters Papers.
23. *O.R.,* ser. 1, vol. 11, part 1, 641–48.
24. The exact location of the horse artillery's camp is unknown. Two sources gave it as being northwest of Richmond, while one stated it was at the one-mile tollgate on the Williamsburg Turnpike. There is the possibility that the battery stopped for a day or so at the tollgate and then moved to the camp northeast of the city. William P. Walters to Matilda E. Walters, May 25, 1862, Walters Papers; Milham, *Gallant Pelham,* 82; Matthews, "Organization of Pelham-Breathed Battery."
25. William P. Walters to Matilda E. Walters, May 25, 1862, Walters Papers; *O.R.,* ser. 1, vol. 11, part 1, 663–64.
26. Though it is possible that the recruiting records are incomplete, all evidence suggests that Lieutenant Shepherd was the recruiting officer for the battery at this time, enlisting fifty-nine men from May 1 to September 9. During the same period, Pelham enlisted two. *C.S.R.V,* microcopy M324, rolls 267, 336, 337.

    In his book, *Gallant Pelham,* Charles G. Milham stated that after the "Ride Around McClellan" Pelham was most likely on recruiting duty, offering as evidence that a reorganization of the battery occurred. He mentioned that part of that reorganization was the addition of new men from Maryland, a shuffling of other personnel, and an election of officers in which Daniel Shanks became third lieutenant and Moses A. Febrey became fourth lieutenant. Most of what was asserted here is in error. While many Marylanders did join the battery the majority enlisted in July. Of those who joined the battery before the raid only three enlisted before June 17. Additionally, Daniel Shanks only enlisted in the battery on July 10 and was promoted to lieutenant on January 9, 1863. Moses A. Febrey was commissioned lieutenant on September 22, 1862. No evidence for an election held at this time could be found. Milham, *Gallant Pelham,* 88; *C.S.R.,* microcopy M324, rolls 336, 337.
27. This may have been jaundice. William P. Walters to Matilda E. Walters, June 11, 1862, Walters Papers.
28. *O.R.,* ser. 1, vol. 11, part 1, 1045.
29. Ibid.
30. *C.S.R.,* microcopy M331, roll 195.
31. The Napoleon had been captured from the Union army at the battle of Fair Oaks and turned over to Pelham sometime in June. Milham, *Gallant Pelham,* 88.
32. *O.R.,* ser. 1, vol. 11, part 2, 515.
33. Ibid., 556.

34. William P. Walters to Matilda E. Walters, July 5, 1862, Walters Papers.
35. *O.R.*, ser. 1, vol. 11, part 2, 354.
36. Ibid., 245.
37. Ibid., 560.
38. Stuart wrote at the end of his report, "Capt. John Pelham, of the Horse Artillery, displayed such signal ability as an artillerist, such heroic example and devotion in danger, and indomitable energy under difficulties in the movement of his battery, that, reluctant as I am at the chance of losing such a valuable limb from the brigade, I feel bound to ask for his promotion, with the remark that in either cavalry or artillery no field grade is too high for his merit and capacity." Ibid., 522.
39. Col. William T. Martin of the Jeff Davis Legion stated in his report that two guns were brought up. Ibid., 529.
40. Ibid., 201.
41. Ibid., 234–35.
42. Ibid., 517–18.
43. Ibid., 529–30.
44. Pelham might simply have been conserving his fire and not replying to Stone's guns.
45. Department of Rare Books, William R. Perkins Library, Duke University.
46. In *Four Years with General Lee,* Walter H. Taylor, Lee's adjutant general, wrote that had it not been for the firing of the artillery, the infantry would have reached and taken possession of the heights before the enemy was aware of their presence. Conversely, then, it was reasonable for Stuart to presume that having sent word to Lee in the middle of the night (Pelham's note was dated the second), the Confederate infantry would arrive and take possession of the plateau while he kept the enemy in a state of disarray. What the Federals would or would not have done should have no bearing on deciding whether Stuart's action was precipitate. Longstreet's losing his way could not have been foreseen by Lee, Longstreet, or Stuart and would not have figured into Stuart's decision. What did was his past experience. Even had the infantry arrived in time, its success could not have been guaranteed. Walter H. Taylor, *Four Years with General Lee* (New York: Bonanza Books, 1957), 41–44.
47. *O.R.,* ser. 1, vol. 11, part 2, 925–26.
48. Ibid., 924–27.
49. Pelham's report of the action at Williamsburg remains the only official source for casualties in the horse artillery during the campaign. Even these were not included in the Confederate return of casualties. The sole fatality, Pvt. George Brown, is known only through William P. Walters's letter. The possibility that there were others cannot be disregarded.

Chapter 5

1. William P. Walters to Matilda E. Walters, July 12, 1862, Walters Papers.
2. Ibid., July 16, 1862.
3. Ibid., July 18, 1862.
4. Milham, *Gallant Pelham,* 109.
5. J. W., Jesse, and Ennis Altizer and Edward and Rufus Nolly.
6. No individual with the name of Wall appears on any roster of Pelham's Battery.
7. William P. Walters to Matilda E. Walters, July 22, 1862, Walters Papers.
8. Maj. Heros von Borcke, Stuart's adjutant and inspector general, wrote in his rollicking memoir that a section of artillery was "ordered to turn to the left in pursuit of the column." Capt. W. W. Blackford, Stuart's engineer officer, wrote that "Stuart

instantly charged down the road after them with the main body, holding some in reserve, the horse artillery under Pelham charging through the fields on either side." Heros von Borcke, *Memoirs of the Confederate War for Independence* (Dayton: Morningside House, 1985), 96; W. W. Blackford, *War Years with Jeb Stuart* (New York: Charles Scribner's Sons, 1945), 95.

9. This second disabling of the Blakely for the same reason would seem to indicate a design flaw in an otherwise fine artillery piece.
10. Trout, *With Pen and Saber,* 88.
11. Henry Lane (January 9, 1826–August 9, 1862) was from Floyd County. A lawyer and newspaper editor before the war, Lane had been captain of Company B, 42nd Virginia Infantry, known as the Floyd Guards. He had been promoted to major in April 1862. He was killed in action at Cedar Mountain. Krick, *Lee's Colonels,* 228.
12. William P. Walters to Matilda E. Walters, August 15, 1862, Walters Papers.
13. Neese, *Confederate Horse Artillery,* 77–80.
14. Ibid., 81–91.
15. Ibid., 91–94.
16. William P. Walters to Matilda E. Walters, August 22, 1862, Walters Papers.
17. Neither Fitz Lee nor Pelham filed a report of this action. Stuart mentioned that Lee's report had not been received and so said little about what occurred. Longstreet, who followed after Lee, reported only that he crossed the Rapidan at Raccoon Ford. The little information that is available concerning the horse artillery's role comes from the reminiscences of Sgt. George W. Shreve, written after the war. Shreve also stated that the battery suffered one casualty, an Alabamian, killed. There is no confirmation of this from any other source. Shreve, "Stuart Horse Artillery," 2.
18. *Supplement to the Official Records of the Union and Confederate Armies* (hereafter cited *Supp. to O.R.;* Wilmington, NC: Broadfoot Publishing Company, 1994) part 1, vol. 2, 715; *O.R.,* ser. 1, vol. 12, part 2, 330, 382.
19. As to which batteries supported Rosser, Brig. Gen. William B. Taliaferro stated that the guns were from Brockenbrough's and Wooding's Batteries, whereas Capt. James K. Boswell gave credit to Poague's Battery. *O.R.,* ser. 1, vol. 12, part 2, 649, 655.
20. Three Federal batteries were in the vicinity of the railroad bridge on the twenty-first, any one of which could have exchanged shots with Chew: Capt. Michael Wiedrich's Battery I, 1st New York Light Artillery; Capt. William L. De Beck's Battery K, 1st Ohio Light Artillery; and Capt. George F. Leppien's 5th Battery (E), Maine Light Artillery. *Supp. to O.R.,* part 1, vol. 2, 723.
21. *O.R.,* ser. 1, vol. 12, part 2, 730.
22. Ibid., 316.
23. Stuart reported that Pelham's Battery suffered casualties. While this may have been the case, only McCaffrey was listed as being wounded in the battery's records. However, these records are incomplete, so additional casualties may have occurred and either were not reported or were lost. Ibid., 730; *C.S.R.V.,* microcopy M324, rolls 267, 336, 337.
24. While both Pelham and Chew were engaged in the same general area, it does not appear that they were in immediate proximity of each other. The Federal artillery, as many as four batteries, was spread out along the northern bank of the river, providing Pelham and Chew with numerous targets throughout the engagement. There is no evidence that the two Confederate batteries were ever fighting side by side. Indeed, Milroy's report suggests that at least Pelham, who engaged first, changed position several times.

25. Neese, *Confederate Horse Artillery,* 98.
26. Ibid., 99–100.
27. *C.S.R.V.,* microcopy M324, roll 273.
28. At least two guns (and probably the third as well) of Chew's Battery were replaced by some of Jackson's artillery sometime around 10:00. How long Pelham's Battery remained engaged is not known, but it would be safe to say that he was probably withdrawn before noon because of low ammunition. Jackson's guns undoubtedly inflicted some of the Federal casualties, but by the time they were effectively engaged Pelham and Chew had turned the tide.
29. *O.R.,* ser. 1, vol. 12, part 2, 303–4.
30. There is no record that either Pelham or Chew accompanied the artillery on this raid. The name of the officer in command of the section is unknown.
31. Neese, *Confederate Horse Artillery,* 101.
32. Ibid., 102.
33. *O.R.,* ser. 1, vol. 12, part 2, 317.
34. Neese, *Confederate Horse Artillery,* 102.
35. *O.R.,* ser. 1, vol. 12, part 2, 706–7.
36. Neese, *Confederate Horse Artillery,* 104.
37. Ibid., 104–5.
38. William P. Walters to Matilda E. Walters, August 24 and 26, 1862, Walters Papers.
39. Ibid., August 26, 1862.
40. The Blakely was manufactured in England, and its ammunition had to be imported. There were relatively few of these guns with the army in comparison with the other types of ordnance, except the Whitworth gun and a few other exotic pieces. The wagons carrying the ammunition would have been fewer in number and more difficult to locate with the army on the move.
41. No officer mentioned Chew's Battery as having participated in the battle, but the muster roll lists one casualty at Second Manassas, although whether it occurred on the twenty-ninth or the thirtieth is unclear. In his report, Pelham stated that his was the only battery of horse artillery available on the thirtieth, which would indicate that if Chew participated in the battle, it was probably on the twenty-ninth. However, Chew may have been engaged on the thirtieth without Pelham's knowledge. Neese, *Confederate Horse Artillery,* 106; *C.S.R.V.,* microcopy M324, roll 337; *O.R.,* ser. 1, vol. 12, part 2, 755.
42. In his reminiscences, Sgt. George W. Shreve stated, "Some of our guns were engaged, under Fitz Lee." However, he did not indicate exactly when this occurred. Considering that Pelham is not mentioned as having reunited with Stuart until the evening of the twenty-seventh, and that Fitz Lee was dispatched to Fairfax Court House prior to Pelham's arrival, it would seem that Shreve was mistaken if he was referring to the twenty-sixth or the twenty-seventh. Additionally, Stuart did not mention any of Pelham's guns being in action on these days, only that, "Captain Pelham, arriving late [on the twenty-seventh], was indefatigable in his efforts to get away the captured guns." Stuart did report that on the twenty-sixth, after he had rendezvoused with Jackson, he protected the infantry's flanks above and below Gainesville with cavalry and artillery. This could not have been the horse artillery, as it had been left at Salem to follow in the wake of Jackson's wagons, artillery, and ambulances and could not have been at Gainesville when the action occurred. Shreve, "Stuart Horse Artillery," 2; *O.R.,* ser. 1, vol. 12, part 2, 734–35.
43. In his biography of Pelham, Charles G. Milham wrote that the horse artillery under Pelham was engaged in repulsing Brig. Gen. George W. Taylor's New Jersey Brigade, which had been sent by train to secure the Manassas Junction supply

depot. Pelham supposedly fired on the Federal infantry from ambush and, with some assistance from the Confederate infantry, chased Taylor's men all over the countryside. Milham may have based his account in part on that of Lt. Col. R. L. T. Beale, who named Pelham as the commander of the artillery. However, though exciting and dramatic, the incident never occurred. As stated in note 42, Pelham did not arrive until late in the day. According to Federal accounts, the action began with Confederate artillery fire about 8:30 A.M. Furthermore, Jackson's report made no mention of Pelham being engaged, but it did mention that Capt. John C. Carpenter's Allegheny Battery and Capt. William T. Poague's Rockbridge Battery were engaged with Taylor, along with infantry from Hill's division. Stuart also reported the clash with Taylor but did not refer to Pelham as having participated in the repulse of the Federals. Milham, *Gallant Pelham,* 131; R. L. T. Beale, *History of the 9th Virginia Cavalry in the War Between the States* (Amissville, VA: American Fundamentalist, 1981), 34; Moore, *Cannoneer under Jackson,* 103–5; *O.R.,* ser. 1, vol. 12, part 2, 405–8, 539–44, 643–44, 734–35.

44. Shreve, "Stuart Horse Artillery," 2.
45. *O.R.,* ser. 1, vol. 12, part 2, 753–54.
46. In his report, Stuart's only mention of Pelham's action following the fight in Jackson's rear was to refer to Pelham's report. Jackson failed to mention Pelham's having reported to him in his official account of the battle. A. P. Hill's report was equally silent concerning Pelham's role in the day's battle, though he does mention Braxton's, Pegram's, McIntosh's, and Crenshaw's Batteries. The only record of what Pelham did on the twenty-ninth comes from his own report, which gives little detail. *O.R.,* ser. 1, vol. 12, part 2, 755.
47. Shreve recorded that a "Lt. Hoxie of Alexandria" was killed. He was unsure of the name, but there was no lieutenant by that name in the battery then or later. Sgt. William Hoxton was born in Alexandria and was wounded in the battle. He later went on to become a lieutenant. Shreve was most likely thinking of him. Shreve, "Stuart Horse Artillery," 3.
48. Pelham's report gave Burwell's name as R. T. Burwell. However, no individual by that name appears in any roster of the battery. The only Burwell serving at that time was Robert. *O.R.,* ser. 1, vol. 12, part 2, 755.
49. There is no way of knowing exactly when all of these casualties occurred. Turner was killed and Hoxton wounded during the fight with the Federal artillery. It is also known that Private Evans and Sergeant Thomas suffered their wounds on the twenty-ninth.
50. While it could be argued that the entire battery remained behind at Gaines's Cross Roads, every gun was needed in the coming battle. Only the Blakely lacked ammunition. Stuart would not have left two guns behind because a third was out of ammunition.
51. Neese, *Confederate Horse Artillery,* 106–7.
52. Von Borcke stated that the horse artillery shelled the wagon train. However, Stuart's report mentioned only a section of the Washington Artillery as having been present. Von Borcke, *Memoirs,* vol. 1, 167; *O.R.,* ser. 1, vol. 12, part 2, 744.
53. R. L. T. Beale asserted that Pelham's guns opened the battle of Chantilly, but neither Jackson nor Stuart, or any other officer, made any reference to Pelham in his report. The Rockbridge Artillery was there early in the fight but did not fire. Col. Stapleton Crutchfield, Jackson's artillery commander, stated that no artillery from Jackson's Corps was engaged, though several batteries were posted at key locations to bolster the Confederate infantry should the Federals break through. Beale, *9th Virginia Cavalry,* 36; Moore, *Cannoneer under Jackson,* 126–27; *O.R.,* ser. 1, vol. 12, part 2, 647, 654, 744.

54. Hart had reported to Hampton on August 10 with six guns: two six-pound brass howitzers and four twelve-pound howitzers. Six horses pulled each gun and caisson, but because of a lack of horses, only half of the cannoneers were mounted. Maj. James F. Hart, Dr. L. C. Stephens, Louis Sherfesee, and Charles H. Schwing, "History of Hart's Battery" (Manuscript, South Carolina Library, University of South Carolina, Columbia) 4, 20.
55. The exact time this action began cannot be determined from Stuart's report. However, he does state that the pursuit was cut short by darkness, which would indicate that the skirmish had begun sometime in the afternoon. The Federals engaged were troops of Maj. Gen. Edwin V. Sumner's Corps. Sumner's orders to withdraw into the entrenchments protecting Washington City had come from Pope, who had received them from Washington around noon. These orders would have reached the troops facing Stuart sometime in the afternoon. As to which batteries' guns were engaged in this first action at Flint Hill, the evidence would seem to indicate that they were Hart's, which began shelling the enemy position at 4:00. Pelham got into action when Hampton advanced. Hart apparently did not follow, perhaps concentrating his fire in another direction, and again when Stuart called on him. One source (Brooks) states that Hart's Battery accompanied Hampton in his pursuit and maintained its fire until near sunset. However, Hampton reported that during his pursuit, he had no horse artillery. *O.R.,* ser. 1, vol. 12, part 2, 46, 86, 744; *O.R.,* ser. 1, vol. 19, part 1, 822; U. R. Brooks, ed., *Stories of the Confederacy* (Columbia, SC: State Company, 1912), 76.
56. Stuart Wright, ed., *Colonel Heros von Borcke's Journal* (Palaemon Press, 1981), 145.
57. Union Maj. Gen. Fitz John Porter reported that on the afternoon of September 2, Confederate cavalry and two guns took a position on Barnett's (Barrett's) Hill and shelled Brig. Gen. Alfred Pleasonton's cavalry at Falls Church. The exact time was not given, but this could only have been the section of Pelham's Battery with a portion of Hampton's Brigade following up their success at Flint Hill. *O.R.,* ser. 1, vol. 12, part 3, 803, and vol. 19, part 1, 822.
58. Ibid., vol. 19, part 2, 176–77.
59. Ibid., 176.
60. Neese, *Confederate Horse Artillery,* 111.

Chapter 6

1. The 6th Virginia had been left behind on the Manassas battlefield, and the 17th Battalion had been ordered on detached service. McDonald, *Laurel Brigade,* 90; Michael P. Musick, *6th Virginia Cavalry* (Lynchburg, VA: H. E. Howard, 1990), 21.
2. *O.R.,* ser. 1, vol. 19, part 1, 825.
3. Dennis E. Frye, *12th Virginia Cavalry* (Lynchburg, VA: H. E. Howard, 1988), 14.
4. *O.R.,* ser. 1, vol. 19, part 1, 815, 825.
5. Neese, *Confederate Horse Artillery,* 114.
6. Ibid.
7. Ibid., 115.
8. Munford stated in his report that Chew's guns assisted in repulsing the enemy's charge by firing two rounds of canister from the howitzer. Neese does not mention this, nor is there any evidence that the 3rd Indiana was repulsed by anything other than the countercharges of the 7th and 12th Virginia Cavalry, which were sustained only long enough to extract the guns. *O.R.,* ser. 1, vol. 19, part 1, 825.

9. The battery apparently suffered no casualties in men or horses during the action. Neese made no mention of any member of the battery being killed or wounded, and the muster rolls do not report any casualties for the engagement. However, these records are incomplete, and a large number of men are reported as having been wounded without giving any specific dates. Considering the accurate fire from Chapin's guns and the wild melee around the battery, it would be presumptuous to assume the battery escaped completely unscathed. More likely, there were some minor injuries that were not reported.
10. William H. Beach, *The First New York (Lincoln) Cavalry* (Annandale, VA: Bacon Race Books, 1988), 168.
11. Heros von Borcke's account of this incident included descriptions of a charge made by several Confederate regiments and of Pelham "pouring a rapid fire" on the enemy. This "charge" was not recorded in any official report of the action, Union or Confederate; it appeared only in von Borcke's memoirs. Beach's account mentioned nothing about a charge, and his only reference to artillery was on the ninth. Von Borcke's "many killed and wounded, and a considerable number of prisoners" translated to no casualties on the 1st New York's casualty lists. Milham wrote that Pelham commanded a section of Hart's Battery during the action. However, Hart's own history of the battery recorded that his battery's first action in the campaign occurred on the twelfth. Milham obviously based his account on von Borcke's and added Hart's Battery for good measure. There is no evidence that any horse artillery was involved at any time. While it makes for exciting reading, the "charge" and the horse artillery's participation were apparently fictitious. *O.R.,* ser. 1, vol. 19, part 1, 815, 822; Beach, *First New York Cavalry,* 168–69, 538; Milham, *Gallant Pelham,* 131; von Borcke, *Memoirs,* 196; James F. Hart, *Record of Hart's Battery*; Chew Papers, 5.
12. Neese, *Confederate Horse Artillery,* 116.
13. Beach, *First New York Cavalry,* 169.
14. *O.R.,* ser. 1, vol. 19, part 1, 209; *Supp. to the O.R.,* part 1, vol. 3, 522.
15. Neese, *Confederate Horse Artillery,* 116.
16. Pvt. Samuel Gilpin of the 3rd Indiana wrote that the Federal artillery silenced the Confederate artillery. However, Neese, who was very accurate in recording the actions of his battery, did not mention firing once the battery reached the scene of the fight. If the Federal guns had "silenced" the Confederates, it could only have been through very accurate fire. As he had previously, Neese would have commented on being driven from a position by such accurate fire. Neese, *Confederate Horse Artillery,* 116; John Michael Priest, *Before Antietam: The Battle for South Mountain* (Shippensburg, PA: White Mane Publishing Company, 1992), 68.
17. Priest, *Before Antietam,* 76–79.
18. Neese, *Confederate Horse Artillery,* 117.
19. William P. Walters to Matilda E. Walters, September 12, 1862, Walters Papers.
20. Priest, *Before Antietam,* 88; Neese, *Confederate Horse Artillery,* 117–18.
21. *O.R.,* ser. 1, vol. 19, part 1, 822.
22. Priest, *Before Antietam,* 91–92.
23. Just when Hart was sent to the pass is unknown. Two sources stated that the section was stationed there with Martin as Hampton passed through on his way to Middletown. However, Hampton's report states that "Captain Hart, with a section of rifled guns, had been sent to Colonel Martin." This would indicate that Hart had not been left with the cavalry but was dispatched sometime during the night. Brooks, *Confederacy,* 83; Priest, *Before Antietam,* 102; *O.R.,* ser. 1, vol. 19, part 1, 823.
24. Von Borcke, *Memoirs,* 206.
25. Priest, *Before Antietam,* 111.

26. Pleasonton's report of the fight consisted of three sentences in which he gave the impression that the action was very brief and was fought with only a few squadrons of the 8th Illinois and 3rd Indiana and the sections of Robertson's and Hains's Batteries. According to him, "a severe cannonading and several warm volleys with carbines" caused the Confederates to retreat rapidly. The eight-hour delay (Hampton recorded the fight began at daylight—around 6 A.M.) the Rebels caused him somehow failed to make it into the report. *O.R.,* ser. 1, vol. 19, part 1, 209, 823. One source stated that the fight began about 9:00 A.M., which would reduce the length of the contest to five hours. Brooks, *Confederacy,* 84.
27. One source identified the Federal artillery as being Robertson and Hains, but Pleasonton himself named Gibson's as the battery in this engagement. Priest, *Before Antietam,* 114; *O.R.,* ser. 1, vol. 19, part 1, 209.
28. Hart et al., "Hart's Battery," 22–23.
29. There is no record of Hart's Battery having sustained casualties in any of these actions.
30. Neese, *Confederate Horse Artillery,* 118.
31. Ibid.
32. Ibid., 119.
33. As to which Pennsylvania regiment was attached to McReynolds's Brigade, the *O.R.* gave the unit as the 12th Pennsylvania, Beach the 8th Pennsylvania. *O.R.,* ser. 1, vol. 19, part 1, 180; Beach, *First New York Cavalry,* 170.
34. Only von Borcke mentioned this incident. He did not make it clear whether Pelham was alone or with some of his guns. Von Borcke, *Memoirs,* 212–13.
35. The wartime spelling was Boonsborough.
36. Rosser must have had a section of Pelham's Battery with him while he operated independently of Fitz Lee. If he did not, then it must be assumed, considering von Borcke's statement, that when Pelham became separated from Fitz Lee, he had with him a part of his battery. His being at Boonsboro in the early morning would have required him to march with these guns through the night over unfamiliar roads, heedless of the threat of encountering the enemy, to arrive in time for Stuart to assign him to accompany Rosser. Fitz Lee did not arrive at Boonsboro until late on the afternoon of the fourteenth. Even for Pelham alone, the ride would have been phenomenal, but with artillery in tow, it would have been miraculous.
37. According to George D. Grattan, an aide to Colonel Colquitt, who was present at a conference that took place between Stuart and Colquitt, Stuart stated that the only Union forces following him were cavalry, and a single brigade of infantry could hold the pass. Hill wrote in his report, however, that Stuart told him that "two brigades" were pursuing him. Hill did not say whether Stuart distinguished between cavalry or infantry, but the fact that Hill subsequently sent two infantry brigades, instead of the one Stuart suggested, and brought his remaining three brigades up to Boonsboro would indicate he thought the threat greater than that from cavalry alone. George D. Grattan, "The Battle of Boonsboro Gap or South Mountain," *Southern Historical Society Papers* (hereafter cited as *SHSP*) 39 (1914): 34; *O.R.,* ser. 1, vol. 19, part 1, 1019.
38. Hill believed that Stuart was ordered to support him at Turner's and Fox's Gaps with his entire division. He even quoted Robert E. Lee's report of the battle to support his statement. However, Lee's report used the words "passes," which included not only Turner's and Fox's, but also Crampton's to the south. Once Colquitt arrived to support Rosser, Stuart felt obligated by his orders to check on the situation at Crampton's Gap. With Colquitt's Brigade on the mountain, Garland's Brigade on the way, and the remainder of Hill's division close at hand, Stuart obviously thought he would be of greater use where the majority of his command was

stationed—Crampton's Gap. Daniel H. Hill, "The Battle of South Mountain, or Boonsboro'," *Battles and Leaders of the Civil War* (hereafter cited as *BLCW*) 2 (soft-cover reprint of original *Century Magazine* in thirty-two parts), part 14 (1884): 560–61.

39. Grattan wrote that Stuart sent Rosser to Fox's Gap without informing Hill. Hill also made this same statement in an article that appeared after the war, adding that Rosser was not directed to report to him. However, Hill noted in his report of the battle, which was written sometime in late 1862, that Rosser did report to him. This would have been the proper action, since Stuart had left for Crampton's Gap and may not have had the opportunity to see Hill. The accusation has also been made that Stuart never informed Hill of the existence of the Old Sharpsburg Road, which ran through Fox's Gap. Neither Grattan nor Hill makes any statements concerning this, so it is apparently without substance. Grattan, "Boonsboro Gap," 39; Hill, "South Mountain," 562; *O.R.,* ser. 1, vol. 19, part 1, 1019–20; Priest, *Before Antietam,* 127.
40. Priest, *Before Antietam,* 131.
41. *O.R.,* ser. 1, vol. 19, part 1, 1032.
42. Neese, *Confederate Horse Artillery,* 120–21.
43. William B. Franklin, "Notes on Crampton's Gap and Antietam," *BLCW* 2: part 15 (1884): 595.
44. Priest, *Before Antietam,* 396.
45. Neese, *Confederate Horse Artillery,* 121–22.
46. According to Munford's report, Thompson's guns were not effective because of their limited range. They evidently fired several rounds until this was determined. He made no further mention of their subsequent role in the action. *O.R.,* ser. 1, vol. 19, part 1, 826.
47. Munford stated that he moved only two pieces to the crest of the mountain. This was Chew's Battery. Thompson evidently had withdrawn earlier or did so at this time. Ibid.
48. Priest, *Before Antietam,* 283.
49. *O.R.,* ser. 1, vol. 19, part 1, 827.
50. Ibid., 828.
51. Thomas P. Nanzig, *3rd Virginia Cavalry* (Lynchburg, VA: H. E. Howard, 1989), 20–21; Robert K. Krick, *9th Virginia Cavalry* (Lynchburg, VA: H. E. Howard, 1982), 10–11; Beale, *9th Virginia Cavalry,* 40–41; Milham, *Gallant Pelham,* 156–57; Priest, *Before Antietam,* 315–18.
52. According to Brig. Gen. William N. Pendleton, Robert E. Lee's artillery chief, Pelham had four guns (two sections)—two rifled and two Napoleons—with him at this time. One section was still in Orange County, Virginia. Pendleton did not give the location of the other section. However, Sterling Murray, a member of the battery, remembered that Pelham had six guns: four three-inch rifles, a Napoleon, and a Blakely. He recalled that a section under Breathed was with Longstreet near Hagerstown and obviously arrived at the battlefield with that command. Additionally, Pendleton also failed to take the batteries of Chew and Hart into his accounting of the cavalry's artillery. *O.R.,* ser. 1, vol. 19, part 1, 835; Letter of Sterling Murray, July 25, 1898, Antietam National Military Park Archives.
53. Blackford, *War Years,* 145; von Borcke, *Memoirs,* 220–21; Priest, *Before Antietam,* 305–7.
54. Milham wrote that Chew had virtually no ammunition because of the capture of Longstreet's wagon train by Col. Benjamin F. "Grimes" Davis of the 8th New York Cavalry, following his breakout from Harpers Ferry. Because of the route the battery took to Sharpsburg, however, there would have been ample opportunity to

resupply the battery from either Confederate wagons south of the Potomac or Federal stores captured at Harpers Ferry. As was stated in the text, Chew had expended all his ammunition at Crampton's Gap. Without ammunition, he most likely would not have recrossed the Potomac and certainly would not have been put in support of Munford's Brigade during the early stages of the battle at Sharpsburg. Milham, *Gallant Pelham,* 159; Neese, *Confederate Horse Artillery,* 124; Frye, *12th Virginia Cavalry,* 17.

55. *O.R.,* ser. 1, vol. 19, part 1, 824; Hart, *Hart's Battery,* 5.
56. While Milham gave credit to Pelham for participating in this action, the evidence to support this claim is lacking. Stuart does not mention that Pelham was engaged. Milham, *Gallant Pelham,* 159; *O.R.,* ser. 1, vol. 19, part 1, 824.
57. Neese, *Confederate Horse Artillery,* 124.
58. Only one source located Chew's Battery at the Antietam Iron Works. Munford failed to note in his report anything about his brigade's or Chew's Battery's role during the battle. Stuart stated that Munford was on the right but does not specifically name Chew as being with him. Neese limited his writing to what happened to the Blakely. Wise, *Long Arm of Lee,* 296; *O.R.,* ser. 1, vol. 19, part 1, 819, 827; Neese, *Confederate Horse Artillery,* 124–26.
59. While in Harpers Ferry, Hart exchanged his two six-pound howitzers for two rifled brass pieces. Stuart also directed the battery to take two one-pound smooth-bore rapid-fire guns. After a brief trial, they were abandoned as worthless. Hart et al., "Hart's Battery," 20.
60. *O.R.,* ser. 1, vol. 19, part 1, 857.
61. Various sources gave these batteries as those placed under Pelham at some time during the fighting: Capt. John B. Brockenbrough's Baltimore Light Artillery, Capt. John C. Carpenter's Alleghany Artillery, Capt. James Carrington's Charlottesville Artillery; Capt. William H. Caskie's Hampden Artillery, Capt. Louis E. D'Aquin's Louisiana Guard Artillery, Lt. William Elliot's South Carolina Battery (Rhett's or Brooks Artillery), Capt. Ashur W. Garber's Staunton Artillery, Capt. John R. Johnson's Bedford Artillery, Capt. William W. Parker's Richmond Battery, Capt. William J. Pegram's Purcell Battery, Capt. William T. Poague's Rockbridge Artillery, Capt. Charles J. Raine's Lee Battery, Capt. George W. Wooding's Danville Artillery, Capt. Pichegru Woolfolk, Jr.'s, Ashland Battery, and Pelham's own Stuart Horse Artillery. Curt Johnson and Richard C. Anderson, Jr., *Artillery Hell: The Employment of Artillery at Antietam* (College Station: Texas A&M University Press, 1995), 48; James V. Murfin, *The Gleam of Bayonets* (New York: Bonanza Books, 1965), 220; Peggy Vogtsberger, "Pelham in the Maryland Campaign, Part II: The Battle of Antietam," *Cannoneer* 3, no. 1 (July 1984): 4; *O.R.,* ser. 1, vol. 19, part 1, 821.

    The number of guns that Pelham actually commanded is conjectured. Estimates range from nineteen to twenty-five. Vogtsberger, "Battle of Antietam," 4; John Michael Priest, *Antietam: The Soldiers' Battle* (New York: Oxford University Press, 1989), 97.
62. *O.R.,* ser. 1, vol. 19, part 1, 820.
63. In his book, *The Long Arm of Lee,* Jennings C. Wise gave the credit for the maneuver to Pelham. In Stuart's report, however, he stated: "The enemy had advanced too far into the woods near the Dunkard church for the fire to be continued without danger of harming our own men. I accordingly withdrew the batteries to a position farther to the rear." Jackson's report corroborated this. Pelham most certainly commanded the guns before and after the movement, but it is doubtful that he would have ordered it, since Stuart was actually in command at that end of the line. Stuart never missed an opportunity to praise Pelham, which he did in his

report, but he did not credit Pelham with the idea of the movement, nor did he state that he even consulted Pelham about it. Jackson made no reference to Pelham at all in his report of the battle. Wise, *Long Arm of Lee,* 301–2; *O.R.,* ser. 1, vol. 19, part 1, 820, 956.

64. Wise gives the number of guns moved as thirteen. Wise, *Long Arm of Lee,* 301.
65. Robert J. Driver, Jr., *The Staunton Artillery—McClanahan's Battery* (Lynchburg, VA: H. E. Howard, 1988), 25.
66. William Thomas Poague, *Gunner with Stonewall* (Jackson, TN: McCowat-Mercer Press, 1957), 47.
67. Neese, *Three Years,* 124–26.
68. One source inferred that Hart fought with Pelham on the army's left, but there is nothing to confirm this. Manly Wade Wellman, *Giant in Gray* (New York: Charles Scribner's Sons, 1949), 93.
69. Two of Hart's pieces were Blakelys. They were probably the two brass rifled pieces he had exchanged at Harpers Ferry, and his inability to replenish his ammunition for these guns may be for the same reason that prevented Chew's Blakely from participating in the Second Manassas campaign. The lack of ammunition for the howitzers was indicative of the state of the army's ammunition supply in general. There just wasn't enough for all. Hart et al., "Hart's Battery," 24.
70. Neither Hampton's nor Stuart's report elaborated on what role Hampton's Brigade played in the battle after reaching Sharpsburg.
71. Murfin, *Bayonets,* 291.
72. Neese, *Confederate Horse Artillery,* 126.
73. Part of the brigade crossed directly opposite Shepherdstown, but the rest crossed at Boteler's Ford. Milham and Hassler asserted that Pelham with his guns crossed at Boteler's and went into battery, assisting Brig. Gen. W. N. Pendleton's massed artillery in firing on the Federal force that eventually arrived at the ford in pursuit of the Confederates. In Pendleton's report, however, he listed all the batteries he placed at Boteler's, and Pelham's was not among them. In his reminiscences, George W. Shreve says nothing of fighting once he crossed the river. There is no support for Milham's or Hassler's claims that Pelham was engaged at Boteler's Ford on the nineteenth. Milham, *Gallant Pelham,* 168; Hassler, *Colonel John Pelham,* 97; *O.R.,* ser. 1, vol. 19, part 1, 830–31; Shreve, "Reminiscences," 4.
74. Von Borcke wrote in his memoirs that the cavalry force Stuart took with him included Robertson's (Munford's) Brigade. Though Stuart's report mentioned that the 12th Virginia was with him, Munford's report is silent on his brigade's participation. A communication sent on the nineteenth from Col. James G. Hodges, then commanding Brig. Gen. Lewis Armistead's Brigade, to Gen. William N. Pendleton stated that Munford requested Hodges to dispatch the 9th Virginia Infantry to a ford below Hodges's position, which was in the vicinity of Boteler's Ford. This would indicate that Munford was still near the ford and not off with Stuart, who had left on the eighteenth. The part of the 12th that was with Stuart may have been under the command of Maj. Thomas B. Massie, who was operating independently of Munford. Von Borcke, *Memoirs,* 242; Frye, *12th Virginia Cavalry,* 17; *O.R.,* ser. 1, vol. 19, part 1, 820, 827, and part 2, 612.
75. Neese, *Confederate Horse Artillery,* 126.
76. Ibid.
77. William P. Walters to Matilda E. Walters, September 19, 1862, Walters Papers.
78. Von Borcke, *Memoirs,* 250–51.
79. Neese, *Confederate Horse Artillery,* 126–27.
80. Shreve, "Stuart Horse Artillery," 4.
81. Wright, *Von Borcke's Journal,* 189, 191.

Chapter 7

1. *O.R.,* ser. 1, vol. 19, part 2, 647.
2. William P. Walters to Matilda E. Walters, September 26, 1862, Walters Papers.
3. The battery's movements during this time span probably were motivated in part as a response to a Federal reconnaissance to Ashby's Gap on the twenty-second, during which the 6th Virginia Cavalry was roughly handled by the 1st Vermont Cavalry. Musick, *6th Virginia Cavalry,* 22–23; *O.R.,* ser. 1, vol. 19, part 2, 3.
4. Some evidence indicates that one gun of the battery was left behind. In a letter he wrote on October 2, Lt. James H. Williams recounted his actions on August 30 and 31, stating that on the 30th he went to Berryville and only returned on the night of the 31st. He also mentioned that the rest of the battery was in Loudoun County. Williams obviously did not accompany Chew, who must have taken only two guns on the raid. Additional support for this comes from a letter written by the 6th Virginia's chaplain, Rev. Richard T. Davis, who recorded that about 1,000 cavalry and two guns reached Leesburg. James H. Williams to Cora DeMovelle (Pritchartt) Williams, October 2, 1862, Williams Papers; Musick, *6th Virginia Cavalry,* 23; Rev. Richard T. Davis Letters, Davis-Preston-Saunders Collection, Manuscript Department, Alderman Library, University of Virginia.
5. Neese, *Confederate Horse Artillery,* 127–28.
6. Fitz Lee had been kicked by a mule and was incapacitated. Wright, *Von Borcke's Journal,* 198.
7. Henry's Battery was camped too far south to have participated in the engagement. One source gave its location as between Strasburg and White Post, while a second said it was near Millwood, which is about two miles northeast of White Post. Juliette Burwell Henry Jones, "Major Mathis Winston Henry, C.S.A. of Bowling Green, Ky.," *Journal of the Clarke County Historical Association* 6, (1946): 55; Shreve, "Stuart Horse Artillery," 4.
8. Pleasonton stated in his report that he was fired on by a battery of artillery before he crossed the bridge. According to Hampton's report, he did not reach the bridge until after the Federals were across and did not mention that his lone gun fired a single round or even that it went into position, only that he recalled the squadron and the gun and sent them into Martinsburg. Robert E. Lee's report of the action mentioned W. H. F. Lee's artillery as having gone into position on the west bank. He did not record whether Pelham fired. *O.R.,* ser. 1, vol. 19, part 2, 11–13.
9. Von Borcke stated that Hampton withdrew on the road to Hainesville, which was north of Martinsburg. This is in direct contradiction of both Hampton's and R. E. Lee's reports and would have meant that he was moving away from Lee and his wagon train. Von Borcke was obviously in error. Wright, *Von Borcke's Journal,* 199.
10. William P. Walters to Matilda E. Walters, October 2, 1862, Walters Papers.
11. Neese, *Confederate Horse Artillery,* 128–29.
12. Milham, *Gallant Pelham,* 238.
13. Jones, "Major Henry," 55; John Flournoy Henry, *A History of the Henry Family* (Louisville, KY: Press of John P. Morton & Co., 1900), 80.
14. H. H. Matthews, "Pelham-Breathed Battery: The Chambersburg Raid," *St. Mary's Beacon,* February 2, 1905.
15. The idea for the raid does not appear to have originated with Stuart. How much it was discussed prior to the October 8 order is not known. H. B. McClellan wrote that for a few days prior to October 9, "a more than usual stir at cavalry headquarters aroused suspicion," which could indicate that Lee-Stuart talks were taking place and everyone was cranking out rumors about what they portended. Douglas Southall Freeman, *Lee's Lieutenants* (New York: Charles Scribner's Sons, 1943),

Vol. 2, 284; H. B. McClellan, *I Rode with Jeb Stuart* (Bloomington: Indiana University Press, 1958), 136; William R. Brooksher and David K. Snyder, "Around McClellan Again," *Civil War Times Illustrated* (hereafter cited as *CWTI*) 13, no. 5 (August 1974): 5.

16. *O.R.*, ser. 1, vol. 19, part 2, 55.
17. Lee and Jones received their commissions as brigadier generals on October 3, the former to date from September 15 and the latter from September 19. Nevertheless, Stuart specifically referred to them as colonels in his report of the raid. Furthermore, Lee did not actually receive his brigade until November 12, when a reshuffling of the cavalry took place. Freeman, *Lee's Lieutenants,* vol. 2, 281; *O.R.*, ser. 1, vol. 19, part 2, 52.
18. H. H. Matthews claimed that all four guns were from Breathed's Battery and that Breathed and P. P. Johnston were in command of the two sections. Breathed was certainly on the expedition, and Johnston may have been as well, but with only two guns. The other section, Lt. Frank M. Bamberg's two rifled guns, was most definitely from Hart's Battery, as Hampton's report and Hart's history of the battery state. Louis Sherfesee's reminiscences of his service in the battery also recount Hart's participation in the raid, as does the battery's unpublished history. *O.R.*, ser. 1, vol. 19, part 2, 57; Hart, *Hart's Battery,* 5; Louis Sherfesee, "Reminiscences of a Color-Bearer" (Manuscript, South Carolina Relic Room and Museum, Columbia), 29–37; Hart et al., "Hart's Battery," 25.
19. *O.R.*, ser. 1, vol. 19, part 2, 57.
20. Sherfesee, "Color-Bearer," 29–32.
21. Matthews, "Chambersburg Raid."
22. Sherfesee, "Color-Bearer," 32.
23. Matthews, "Chambersburg Raid."
24. Apparently the troopers sent to destroy the bridge, Capt. Thomas Whitehead and a detachment of Company B, 2nd Virginia Cavalry, never reached it. The bridge was actually wooden (Brig. Gen. Albert G. Jenkins burned it during the Gettysburg campaign), but before Whitehead reached it, some enterprising civilian told him that it was iron. The trusting captain didn't question the information and, not having explosives, returned and made his report. Samuel L. Daihl, "1865—Our Johnnies Come Marching Home," *Kittochtinny Historical Society, Papers Read before the Society* 15 (1970): 129–30.
25. Matthews, "Chambersburg Raid."
26. *O.R.*, ser. 1, vol. 19, part 2, 53.
27. Matthews, "Chambersburg Raid."
28. Ibid.
29. Ibid.
30. Biles's report did not include his receiving any demand for surrender from Lee. He indicated that the main factors contributing to his decision to retreat were his lack of reinforcement and the two artillery pieces he faced. *O.R.*, ser. 1, vol. 19, part 2, 50.
31. Ibid., 58.
32. Blackford, *War Years,* 177.
33. A prolonge is a three-and-a-half-inch-thick hemp cable, twenty-six feet, seven inches long, that enabled the gun to be drawn rearward, eliminating limbering and unlimbering, while continuing to fire.
34. Hart et al., "Hart's Battery," 27.
35. In a letter to his mother dated October 15, 1862, Price specifically wrote that Stuart had ordered him to bring off Breathed and his gun, which was the last to leave. Yet Blackford recalled seeing Pelham standing by the piece. The order from Stuart may have been sent to Breathed rather than Pelham out of professional cour-

tesy. Breathed was now the battery commander. Richard Channing Price to Mrs. Thomas Randolph Price, Sr., October 15, 1862, R. Channing Price Papers (#2571), Southern Historical Collection, Wilson Library, University of North Carolina at Chapel Hill.

36. Sherfesee, "Color-Bearer," 35.
37. Matthews's and Sherfesee's accounts of the crossing make for fascinating reading but unfortunately are incompatible. Each man wrote as if his battery was the only one present and gave no credit to the other. The version presented here took a few facts from their stories that could be substantiated and combined them with the reports of various officers involved and with other sources. The actual locations of Captains Breathed and Hart during the action are unknown, although toward the end of the fight, Channing Price placed Breathed at the gun on the towpath. I made the assumption that Pelham would have sent Breathed, as the next ranking officer, to the ford with Lee. It is also my opinion that Hart was probably with Butler and the rear guard, though there is no evidence for this. Matthews, "Chambersburg Raid"; Sherfesee, "Color-Bearer," 35–36; Col. Wilbur S. Nye, "How Stuart Got Back across the Potomac," *CWTI* 4, no. 9 (January 1966): 45–48; Brooksher and Snyder, "Around McClellan Again," 5–6, 8, 39–48; Blackford, *War Years,* 175–78; Richard Channing Price to Mrs. Thomas Randolph Price, Sr., October 15, 1862, Price Papers; *O.R.,* ser. 1, vol. 19, part 2, 49–54, 57–58.
38. The only casualty in horse artillery was Pvt. Frederick W. Arnholter of Hart's Battery, who was wounded.
39. Sherfesee, "Color-Bearer," 36.
40. James H. Williams to Cora DeMovelle (Pritchartt) Williams, October 14, 1862, Williams Papers.
41. Watson was not present. His gun was under Smith's command. *O.R.,* ser. 1, vol. 19, part 2, 97.
42. Munford's report credited the Confederate artillery for holding up the Federal advance into Charles Town for four hours. Neese supports Munford's claim concerning the exhausting of the artillery's ammunition. The various Union reports failed to denote the time at which Charles Town was occupied. However, the reports of Hancock and the other officers indicated that their entry was not immediate and that time was lost in bringing up the infantry and additional artillery. Neese, *Confederate Horse Artillery,* 129; *O.R.,* ser. 1, vol. 19, part 2, 90–97.
43. The casualties in the artillery were two killed and three wounded. Except for Carter, no other casualties to Chew's Battery are known. The Confederates also lost one limber. The Federal horse artillery, a battery from the 4th U.S. Artillery under Lt. George Dickenson, suffered one killed and three wounded, with one gun disabled. Ibid., 91, 96–97.
44. William P. Walters to Matilda E. Walters, October 19, 1862, Walters Papers.

Chapter 8

1. Grease heel is an uncommon dermatitis, a form of eczema also known as scratches, mud fever, or cracked heels. A serum oozes from scratchlike lesions at the heel and pastern area, drying and becoming crusty. Lameness can result in severe cases. The condition may be caused by standing in dirty stables; constant contact with dung and urine; or working in deep, irritating mud, dry limestone or sandy dust in dry weather, or snow and freezing mud. U.S. Department of Agriculture, *Diseases of the Horse* (1942), 441; *Veterinary Treatments and Medication for Horsemen* (Equine Research, 1974), 309.

2. *O.R.,* ser. 1, vol. 19, part 2, 141.
3. H. H. Matthews, "Pelham-Breathed Battery: From the Valley to Fredericksburg," *St. Mary's Beacon,* February 9, 1905.
4. One solution attempted was to quarantine the animals. The horse artillery established a hospital for its horses at Culpeper Court House. The assignment fell to Lt. Moses A. Febrey of Breathed's Battery. Ibid.
5. Hampton received orders to reunite with Stuart at Upperville on November 3. *O.R.,* ser. 1, vol. 19, part 2, 141.
6. Fitz Lee was disabled.
7. According to Milham, Pelham left The Bower to personally pick up Henry's and Breathed's Batteries at Millwood. This presumes that both batteries were at that location. However, Breathed's Battery was encamped near The Bower, whereas Henry's was encamped at or near Millwood. Pelham obviously picked up Breathed's on the way to Millwood. The total number of guns in the two batteries was eight. Stuart stated that he took only six. Just which battery's guns were left behind and what they did is unknown. The cause was most likely a shortage of horses. Milham, *Gallant Pelham,* 190; *O.R.,* ser. 1, vol. 19, part 2, 141.
8. *O.R.,* ser. 1, vol. 19, part 2, 141.
9. Frederic Denison, *Sabres and Spurs: The First Regiment Rhode Island Cavalry in the Civil War, 1861–1865* (Baltimore: Butternut and Blue, 1994), 169.
10. Pelham was engaged initially from only one position, based on information from historian John Divine. Letter from John Divine to writer, September 6, 1995.
11. Longacre, Jersey Cavaliers, 112–14; Denison, *Sabres and Spurs,* 168–70; *O.R.,* ser. 1, vol. 19, part 2, 141.
12. John Esten Cooke, *Wearing of the Gray* (Millwood, NY: Krause Reprint Co., 1959), 280.
13. Stuart might have been somewhat frustrated by the inability of Pelham to keep his guns toward the front of the column. In his report, he wrote, "Our pursuit had been too rapid for the artillery to keep pace, but it finally came up." The word "finally" was the closest Stuart had ever come to saying something negative about his gallant artillery commander. *O.R.,* ser. 1, vol. 19, part 2, 141.
14. Both Stuart and Cooke claimed that Pelham's fire forced the Federal artillery to change its position. H. H. Matthews went one better, claiming that one of Gibson's guns was disabled. For his part, Bayard reported on the evening of the thirty-first that Stuart had two guns with him. On November 1, Bayard's estimate grew to four guns. Cooke, *Wearing of the Gray,* 280; Matthews, "Valley to Fredericksburg"; *O.R.,* ser. 1, vol. 19, part 2, 136, 141.
15. *O.R.,* ser. 1, vol. 19, part 2, 125.
16. Now called Unison.
17. *O.R.,* ser. 1, vol. 19, part 2, 125, 129, 141–42.
18. Ibid., 142.
19. Ibid., 125, 131.
20. Von Borcke, *Memoirs,* vol. 2, 18–19; *O.R.,* ser. 1, vol. 19, part 2, 142.
21. Matthews recorded that these men were killed at the battery's first position by Pennington's fire, and not by the exploding caisson at the second position. Matthews, "Valley to Fredericksburg."
22. Another of the wounded was Pvt. Henry "Hal" Hopkins. The third man cannot be identified.
23. Milham, *Gallant Pelham,* 198.
24. *O.R.,* ser. 1, vol. 19, part 2, 142.

25. Ibid., 142–43.
26. This impressive show of distance and accuracy may have been a strong contributing factor in Stuart's attempt to secure a Whitworth for the horse artillery later in the year.
27. The day's fighting almost exhausted Breathed's remaining ammunition but caused no further casualties. Fortunately, Lt. Col. Edward Porter Alexander's ordnance train had been marching to Culpeper Court House via Sperryville on the third. He had issued 300 rounds of three-inch ammunition and 500 friction primers to the horse artillery. It would arrive just when needed most. Matthews, "Valley to Fredericksburg"; *Supp. to the O.R.,* part 1, vol. 3, 493.

    Henry's Battery does not seem to have been engaged very much, if at all, during the previous day's fighting. Stuart's report mentions it for the first time in conjunction with Rosser's move. *O.R.,* ser. 1, vol. 19, part 2, 144.
28. Ibid., 143.
29. Now Hume.
30. *O.R.,* ser. 1, vol. 19, part 2, 115–16.
31. Ibid., 144.
32. Brooks, *Confederacy,* 114.
33. Von Borcke, *Memoirs,* vol. 2, 43.
34. Beale, *9th Virginia Cavalry,* 51.
35. The number of guns present on the Confederate side varies according to which account is consulted. Henry definitely had two pieces at the crossroads. Von Borcke wrote that Hampton had two fifteen-pound brass guns with him. But he also stated that Hampton held Stuart's right, when in actuality Hampton was on the left, so his memory must be questioned. U. R. Brooks placed the number of guns at six—one section each at the left, center, and right of the line. From the Federal side, Col. David McM. Gregg of the 8th Pennsylvania Cavalry indicated in his report that he was opposed by more than one section. The location of Hart's and Breathed's Batteries, as well as the other section of Henry's Battery, cannot be determined from currently available accounts and records, but it is possible that one or more sections of these batteries were engaged. Von Borcke, *Memoirs,* vol. 2, 45; Brooks, *Confederacy,* 115; *O.R.,* ser. 1, vol. 19, part 2, 130.
36. The units that made up the enemy force are unknown. Lt. Col. William H. F. Payne of the 4th Virginia, for reasons unknown, led the 2nd North Carolina. *O.R.,* ser. 1, vol. 19, part 2, 144.
37. Alexander recorded that on the seventh, Cooke returned the nine wagons, with five of them untouched. He did not elaborate on what type of ammunition they contained. Cooke showed up again on the tenth with a requisition for three wagonloads, but he returned them the next day with two loads intact. At that time, he asked for three additional loads. Cooke's vacillation prompted a complaint by one of Alexander's lieutenants that the horse artillery's ordnance officer didn't know what he wanted. On the twelfth, Hart's Battery was issued Blakely ammunition while stationed at Sperryville. *Supp. to the O.R.,* part 1, vol. 3, 494–95.
38. Pleasonton reported the capture of two guns from Stuart's force during the brief engagement near Jeffersonton. Stuart does not mention the loss of any of his artillery. However, von Borcke wrote that two guns were buried because of the horses' inability to move them along the muddy roads. These may have been the guns Pleasonton claimed to have captured. Maj. Henry B. McClellan, Stuart's adjutant, who investigated Pleasonton's claim to some degree, stated that the officers of the Stuart Horse Artillery he consulted denied the loss of any guns. If Stuart had been forced to bury some of his artillery, the incident never found its way

into his report. Von Borcke, *Memoirs,* vol. 2, 52; McClellan, *I Rode with Jeb Stuart,* 184; *O.R.,* ser. 1, vol. 19, part 2, 127.

Pleasonton also stated in a dispatch dated November 8 that his command found a twelve-pound gun abandoned by Stuart's cavalry, along with a caisson filled with six-pounder ammunition. He added that the gun was the third he had captured that day. In contrast, Pleasonton indicated in his report that the two guns were captured on the seventh, not the eighth, and made no mention of the lone gun captured on the eighth. As with the evidence for the capture of the two guns on the seventh, Pleasonton's claim of this additional gun cannot be substantiated in any other source. *O.R.,* ser. 1, vol. 19, part 2, 118.

39. Hart et al., "Hart's Battery," 30–31; Brooks, *Confederacy,* 115; *O.R.,* ser. 1, vol. 19, part 2, 127, 144–45.
40. Brooks, *Confederacy,* 117–18.
41. Hart, *Hart's Battery,* 6.
42. Pvt. Jesse A. Adams was also wounded in the fighting on the tenth.
43. Von Borcke, *Memoirs,* vol. 2, 58.
44. *O.R.,* ser. 1, vol. 19, part 2, 557.
45. Ibid., 145.
46. The location of the third gun cannot be determined. Neese, *Confederate Horse Artillery,* 131.
47. John W. Schildt, *Stonewall Jackson Day by Day* (Chewsville, MD: Antietam Publications, n.d.), 82.
48. Neese, *Confederate Horse Artillery,* 131–32.
49. Ibid., 132.
50. James H. Williams to Cora DeMovelle (Pritchartt) Williams, November 9, 1862, Williams Papers.
51. Ibid.
52. Summit Point is now in Jefferson County, West Virginia.
53. Neese, *Confederate Horse Artillery,* 133–35.
54. The 17th Battalion became the 11th Virginia Cavalry on February 5, 1863, when two companies were added, bringing its strength up to ten companies. Richard L. Armstrong, *11th Virginia Cavalry* (Lynchburg, VA: H. E. Howard, 1989), 22.
55. Robert J. Driver, Jr., *1st Virginia Cavalry* (Lynchburg, VA: H. E. Howard, 1991), 51.
56. John J. Shoemaker, *Shoemaker's Battery* (Gaithersburg, MD: Butternut Press, n.d.), 22.
57. Lt. Edmund H. Moorman loaned his diary to Shoemaker to help that officer with the writing of the battery's history. The personal observations could be either Moorman's or Shoemaker's. Ibid., 24.
58. These gunboats were the *Anacostia, Cœur de Lion, Currituck,* and *Jacob Bell. O.R.,* ser. 1, vol. 21, 36.
59. Lewis T. Nunnelee, *History of a Famous Company of the War of Rebellion (So Called) Between the States,* Lewis T. Nunnelee Papers, Museum of the Confederacy, 60; courtesy of Lewis T. Nunnelee II.
60. Diary of Helen Struan Bernard Robb, Robb-Bernard Collection, College of William and Mary.
61. Milledge's Battery had been assigned to augment the horse artillery on November 28. Moorman's Battery, which was attached to W. H. F. Lee's Brigade, of which the 9th Virginia was a part, apparently was not involved in this action. Shoemaker made no mention of any section moving to support Waller. Instead, he stated that on December 1, the battery's two sections were still in the positions they had been

occupying since November 24. *O.R.*, ser. 1, vol. 21, 564; Shoemaker, *Shoemaker's Battery*, 25.

62. There is some confusion as to exactly when this action took place. D. H. Hill gave the date as the fifth. W. H. F. Lee, who wrote his report on the fifth, stated that the engagement occurred "yesterday," meaning the fourth. Col. David McM. Gregg of the 8th Pennsylvania Cavalry reported the withdrawal of the gunboats at 10:00 the night of the fourth. The date of the fourth has been used here, since both Lee's and Gregg's accounts give that date. *O.R.*, ser. 1, vol. 21, 36–37, 826–27.
63. Charles R. Phelps, December 8, 1862, Charles R. Phelps Letters (#2920), Albert H. Small Special Collections Library, University of Virginia.
64. *O.R.*, ser. 1, vol. 21, 37.
65. William A. Simpson to James Simpson, December 1, 1862, Walters Papers.
66. William P. Walters to Matilda E. Walters, December 2, 1862, Walters Papers.

Chapter 9

1. *O.R.*, ser. 1, vol. 21, 84–87.
2. Ibid., 87.
3. The batteries were Capt. John G. Simpson's 1st Pennsylvania Light Artillery, Battery A; Capt. James H. Cooper's 1st Pennsylvania Light Artillery, Battery B; Capt. Frank P. Amsden's 1st Pennsylvania Light Artillery, Battery G; and Capt. Dunbar R. Ransom's 5th United States, Battery C. Ibid., 140.
4. Ibid., 511.
5. Lt. R. Channing Price, one of Stuart's aides-de-camp, wrote in a letter that Pelham took only the Napoleon to the road junction and that the Blakely came up later and occupied a position nearer the railroad. From Richard Channing Price to Mrs. Thomas Randolph Price, Sr., December 17, 1862, Price Papers.
6. *O.R.*, ser. 1, vol. 21, 511.
7. Simpson had four guns. Cooper probably had four as well. The U.S. batteries normally had six guns. This gives a total of fourteen. Certainly there were not less than twelve.
8. *O.R.*, ser. 1, vol. 21, 458.
9. Ibid., 484.
10. Ibid., 458.
11. The official losses for Henry's Battery during the battle were given as six wounded, but another source recorded that there were up to ten men killed and wounded. The lack of reports from Stuart, Pelham, or Henry makes it impossible to be accurate. Ibid., 558; William P. Walters to Matilda E. Walters, December 17, 1862, Walters Papers.
12. Very little information exists on the "Napoleon Detachment." Pvt. Jean Bacigalupo appears only on postwar rosters. A highly romanticized account of his mortal wounding and death is recorded in John Esten Cooke's novel, *Surry of Eagle's Nest.*

    A Pvt. James McNelis is listed on one postwar roster as having been killed in action at Fredericksburg, while another source states that he was captured on June 30, 1863, at Westminster, Maryland. However, he was from Breathed's Battery, not Henry's. The role of Breathed's Battery in the battle is unknown.
13. Von Borcke, *Memoirs,* vol. 2, 118.
14. Two versions of this order have appeared in print, but the sources were not given, making them suspect. Philip Mercer, *The Gallant Pelham* (Wilmington, NC: Broadfoot Publishing Company, 1995), 138; Hassler, *Colonel John Pelham,* 148.

15. In his copy of John Esten Cooke's *Life of Stonewall Jackson,* Nathaniel Burwell, the father of Henry's wife, wrote in the margin "P. [Pelham] told me H. [Henry] was entitled to all the credit." Ever modest, Pelham was never one to brag about his actions or even claim his fair share of the glory associated with them. His comment is worthy of note in that it ably illustrates that he was well aware that his performance was dependent on that of his men, and that he desired that they should receive their fair share of the credit. Jones, "Major Henry," 57.
16. If Shreve is correct, the rapid return of fire by Union guns so quickly after Pelham's first discharge can be explained only if it had been from the guns in position on the north bank of the river. Simpson, Cooper, and Ransom could not have put their pieces into battery that quickly, and the other batteries on the south side did not come into position until after these three batteries commenced fire.
17. Shreve, "Stuart Horse Artillery," 4–5.
18. William P. Walters to Matilda E. Walters, December 17, 1862, Walters Papers.
19. Brooks, *Confederacy,* 120.
20. Matthews, "Valley to Fredericksburg."
21. Shoemaker, *Shoemaker's Battery,* 26; Charles R. Phelps, December 8, 1862, Phelps Letters.
22. William P. Walters to Matilda E. Walters, December 17, 1862, Walters Papers.
23. Matthews, "Valley to Fredericksburg."
24. The exact date of Johnston's departure is unknown, but from November 11, 1862, to March 25, 1863, he enlisted thirty-four men for the battery. *C.S.R.V.,* microcopy M324, rolls 336, 337.
25. Charles R. Phelps, December 22, 1862, Phelps Letters.
26. *O.R.,* ser. 1, vol. 21, 690–91.
27. Ibid., 696.
28. Lt. Francis M. Bamberg commanded the section from Hart's Battery. The section commanders from Breathed's Battery were Lt. Philip P. Johnston, who was on recruiting duty, and probably Sgt. William Hoxton, as Lt. Moses A. Febrey had resigned on December 10. Hoxton would be promoted to lieutenant on January 9. Henry's section commanders were Lt. William M. McGregor, who was absent wounded, and Lt. Charles E. Ford. Lt. G. Wilmer Brown probably took over for McGregor, since Lt. William C. Elston had resigned on December 22. Burwell would be promoted to lieutenant on January 9. Which of these sections went on the raid is unknown. Ibid., 736.
29. Ibid., 731.
30. Ibid., 723, 730–31.
31. Matthews, "Valley to Fredericksburg."
32. The length of time that Breathed's Battery was engaged must have been considerably longer than that of Henry's. Depending what type or types of guns had been brought, Breathed had between sixty-four and seventy-eight rounds in his limber chests. It can be surmised that since he used his entire supply, or a sufficient amount to render his remaining with the command superfluous, his rate of fire must have been rapid or he fired for a long time. Colonel Candy reported that the enemy on his right did not engage until 3:00. Stuart pulled back at dark, which at this time of the year could not have been later than 6:00. The artillery fire must have been rather intense for some time, which would indicate that Stuart seriously contemplated making a major assault. Henry's fire must have been much slower during the first encounter with the enemy, and he may not have continued for very long once Breathed opened fire. Candy did state that Lieutenant Rogers's guns were under a crossfire for part of the engagement. Ordnance Bureau, *The Field Manual for the Use of the Officers on Ordnance Duty* (Richmond, VA: Ritchie & Dunnavant, 1862), 90; *O.R.,* ser. 1, vol. 21, 724–26.

33. *O.R.,* ser. 1, vol. 21, 708, 733.
34. Though Price gave the doctor's last name only, this undoubtedly was Dr. William A. Herndon, who would attend Pelham when he fell at Kelly's Ford in March the following year. Richard Channing Price to Miss Ellen Price, January 2, 1863, Price Papers.
35. Some of the cavalry was from the 3rd Pennsylvania, and the remainder from a squadron sent by Brig. Gen. William W. Averell. *O.R.,* ser. 1, vol. 21, 742–44.
36. Hart, *Hart's Battery,* 7.
37. Barnes's command did not include the 6th New York Cavalry but did include a detachment of 100 troopers from the 3rd Pennsylvania Cavalry, under the command of Lt. William Baughman. Hart's reference to the 6th New York and Captain Van Buren as participating in this encounter cannot be substantiated from the records. *O.R.,* ser. 1, vol. 21, 743.
38. The battery would maintain its picket duty role until February 1863, when it was sent to the Valley to recruit its horses. Hart, *Hart's Battery,* 7.
39. Charles R. Phelps, January 20, 1863, Phelps Letters.
40. Francis Halsey Wigfall to Mrs. Louis T. Wigfall, January 22, 1863, Francis Halsey Wigfall Papers, Manuscript Division, Library of Congress.
41. The addition of this gun to the horse artillery poses an interesting question: Did this gun replace one of the other guns in one of the batteries? Pelham's comment that it was entirely detached would indicate that it was not a part of any, but was independent of them. Crew members were selected from Breathed's Battery to man the piece, but their names still appeared on Breathed's muster rolls. Breathed appears to have kept his four guns, at least for the moment. The Whitworth acted apart from the other batteries, and its participation in engagements has been difficult to document outside of a few direct references. At this time, the Whitworth should be listed as part of the horse artillery battalion but separate from any battery.

    However, at some time between the death of Pelham and the battle of Aldie, the status of the Whitworth gun appears to have changed. Lt. Francis H. Wigfall, who commanded the gun in that fight, wrote that the Whitworth gun was detached from "his section" of the battery. This would mean that the Whitworth eventually became attached to Breathed's Battery, more than likely replacing one of the other pieces, and was detached from it when required. Francis Halsey Wigfall to Mrs. Louis T. Wigfall, June 18, 1863, Wigfall Papers.
42. Letter appears with the kind permission of A. R. Hoxton.
43. William Hoxton to Mrs. Sarah Randolph, February 17, 1863, Randolph Family Papers, VHS.
44. William A. Simpson to James Simpson, February 22, 1863, Walters Papers.
45. William P. Walters to Matilda E. Walters, February 22, 1863, Walters Papers.
46. *O.R.,* ser. 1, vol. 25, part 1, 20, and part 2, 649.
47. Fitz Lee did not record Breathed's artillery as among the troops he took on the raid. Likewise, the Federal reports fail to mention that they encountered any artillery. That Breathed accompanied the raiders is recorded in Pvt. H. H. Matthews's reminiscences. Ibid., part 1, 21–26; H. H. Matthews, "Pelham-Breathed Battery: Death of John Pelham," *St. Mary's Beacon,* February 16, 1905.
48. *O.R.,* ser. 1, vol. 25, part 2, 640.
49. Stuart had written to General Cooper on February 10, 1863, shortly before Pendleton's request, urging Pelham's promotion to colonel. His praise was extensive and with such a recommendation, it would have been difficult for Stuart to have stopped the promotion even if he had wanted to. *C.S.R.,* microcopy M331, roll 195.

50. Gallagher, *Fighting for the Confederacy,* 193.
51. Francis Halsey Wigfall to Louis T. Wigfall, February 7, 1863, Wigfall Papers.
52. Henry's promotion probably was linked to his performance at Fredericksburg under Pelham.

Chapter 10

1. *O.R.,* ser. 1, vol. 21, 31–32.
2. Neese, *Confederate Horse Artillery,* 138–39.
3. Ibid., 139–40.
4. James H. Williams to Cora DeMovelle (Pritchartt) Williams, December 15, 1862, Williams Papers.
5. Ibid., December 26, 1862.
6. Neese, *Confederate Horse Artillery,* 141.
7. At this time, the Baltimore Light Artillery was part of the Maryland Line, which had been encamped around New Market. The battery had not yet been converted to horse artillery. Why Chew was not with his battery is unknown. *O.R.,* ser. 1, vol. 21, 747; Goldsborough, *Maryland Line,* 283; Wise, *Long Arm of Lee,* 446.
8. Jones attributed the lack of his artillery's success on defective ammunition. This accusation brought a fiery response from Col. Josiah Gorgas, the Confederate ordnance chief. He threw the blame back on the artillerists, intimating it was more likely that they were incompetent than that his ammunition was defective. Chew does not appear to have been involved in the exchange, and Neese made no mention of defective ammunition, only the extreme range. Jones was undoubtedly trying to cover up the reasons for the expedition's outcome, which did not end in the success that had been anticipated. *O.R.,* ser. 1, vol. 21, 747–48; Neese, *Confederate Horse Artillery,* 144.
9. Neese, *Confederate Horse Artillery,* 145.
10. *O.R.,* ser. 1, vol. 21, 747–48; Neese, *Confederate Horse Artillery,* 148–49.
11. Ada Bruce Bradshaw, ed., *The Civil War Diary of Charles William McVicar* (1977), 2. Courtesy of the Winchester-Frederick County Historical Society Collection.
12. *O.R.,* ser. 1, vol. 25, part 2, 634.
13. Ibid., 633.
14. Report of inspection of Jones's Brigade, February 14, 1863, Hairston and Wilson Papers (#3149), Southern Historical Collection, Wilson Library, University of North Carolina at Chapel Hill.
15. Rev. L. G. Potts, "Recollections of the Civil War," *Randolph Enterprise,* 1921–22.
16. McVicar recorded in his diary that the alarm was given at 3:00 A.M. on the twenty-fifth and that the battery marched to Narrow Passage that day, returning to its camp that evening. The reason for this discrepancy between McVicar and Neese is unknown but could indicate that the battery was called out twice, once on February 25 and again on March 1. Bradshaw, *Diary of McVicar,* 2; Neese, *Confederate Horse Artillery,* 150.
17. Bradshaw, *Diary of McVicar,* 2; Neese, *Confederate Horse Artillery,* 150–51.
18. McVicar and Neese again disagree as to the date of arrival at Luray. McVicar gave the twentieth, Neese the nineteenth. Considering the weather and the condition of the roads, the twentieth seems more probable. Bradshaw, *Diary of McVicar,* 2; Neese, *Confederate Horse Artillery,* 152.
19. Bradshaw, *Diary of McVicar,* 3; Neese, *Confederate Horse Artillery,* 153.
20. Bradshaw, *Diary of McVicar,* 3–4.
21. Ibid., 3–4; Neese, *Confederate Horse Artillery,* 154–55.
22. *O.R.,* ser. 1, vol. 25, part 2, 622.

23. Ibid., 684–85.
24. Ibid., 710–12.
25. Ibid., part 1, 98–99.
26. This "battery" was actually one section (a ten-pound Parrott and a six-pound brass smoothbore) belonging to Capt. Chatham T. Ewing's West Virginia Battery. Ibid., 94.
27. Benjamin F. Potts was Lantz G. Potts's brother.
28. According to Col. George R. Latham of the 2nd West Virginia Infantry, who commanded the Federal force, the engagement lasted from 2:00 to 4:00, with his artillery fire commencing at 2:00. There is no official record of how many times McClanahan fired, but the Federal retreat was prompted by the threat of being cut off from Buckhannon and not by McClanahan's fire. As to the capture of a cannon, Latham did not admit to losing one, nor did Imboden claim to have captured one. *O.R.,* ser. 1, vol. 25, part 1, 94, 100; Potts, "Recollections."
29. Thomas J. Arnold, "Beverly in the Civil War," *Randolph Enterprise,* November 22, 1923.
30. *O.R.,* ser. 1, vol. 25, part 1, 100–102.
31. Ibid., 113.
32. The battery left one of its four guns behind in its camp at Harrisonburg. Bradshaw, *Diary of McVicar,* 7.
33. Wise, *Long Arm of Lee,* 446.
34. Neese, *Confederate Horse Artillery,* 157.
35. *O.R.,* ser. 1, vol. 25, part 1, 123–24.
36. Ibid., 103.
37. Ibid.
38. Ibid.
39. Ibid., 120.
40. This force was composed of the 110th, 122nd, and 123rd Ohio Volunteer Infantry, and the 10th West Virginia Infantry under the command of Brig. Gen. Washington L. Elliot. Ibid., 143.
41. Though no evidence can be found to support it, Griffin's Battery, which was encamped nearby, probably accompanied Chew.
42. Neese, *Confederate Horse Artillery,* 162–63.
43. James H. Williams to Cora DeMovelle (Pritchartt) Williams, May 12, 1863, Williams Papers.
44. Bradshaw, *Diary of McVicar,* 8.
45. At this time, Jenkins's Brigade consisted of the 8th, 14th, 16th, 17th, and 19th Virginia Cavalry and the 34th, 36th, and 37th Virginia Cavalry Battalions.
46. In a letter he wrote in 1909, Micajah Woods, a lieutenant in the battery, gave the date of organization as April 1, 1863, but this was when Jackson began to sign men for service in the battery. The official organization was not until May 2. Micajah Woods to Roger P. Chew, July 5, 1909, Chew Papers.
47. No individual named Harman appears on any roster for Jackson's Battery. He apparently did not enlist once he was defeated for a lieutenancy. There were fourteen Harmans in the 8th Virginia Cavalry, ten in the 16th Virginia Cavalry, and one each in the 17th Virginia Cavalry and 37th Virginia Cavalry Battalion. More than likely the candidate came from one of these units.
48. Micajah Woods to Dr. John R. Woods, May 3, 1863, Papers of Micajah Woods (#10279), Albert H. Small Special Collections Library, University of Virginia Library.
49. *C.S.R.V.,* microcopy M324, roll 310.
50. Micajah Woods to Dr. John R. Woods, May 7, 1863, Woods Papers.

Chapter 11

1. The battery's captain, Walter M. Bramhall, had resigned on February 3. His successor would be Joseph W. Martin, who was the battery's senior first lieutenant. Why Martin was not present with the battery is unknown, although it probably had something to do with Bramhall's resignation. Browne was the battery's junior first lieutenant.
2. The 4th New York, 6th Ohio, and 1st Rhode Island made up Duffié's Brigade. McIntosh led the 3rd, 4th, and 16th Pennsylvania. Reno commanded the 1st and 5th U.S. Cavalry. *O.R.,* ser. 1, vol. 25, part 1, 48, 53, 59.
3. Ibid., 60–61.
4. The battery was encamped near Culpeper Court House on the north bank of Mountain Run. Matthews, "Death of Pelham."
5. Peggy Vogtsberger, "The Mysteries of Kelly's Ford," *Cannoneer* 5, no. 5 (July 1985), 2–4; Milham, *Gallant Pelham,* 226–27.
6. Lt. Col. Henry Clay Pate of the 5th Virginia Cavalry was being court-martialed on charges brought by Stuart.
7. In his report, Averell stated that he did not reach the ford until 8:00 A.M., though he may have meant that he did not secure the ford until that time. However, Lieutenant Browne's and Colonel McIntosh's reports stated that the ford was reached at 6:30 and 6:00 A.M., respectively. Fitz Lee wrote that he first heard of the crossing at 7:30 A.M. Obviously, this could not have occurred if Averell had arrived at 8:00 A.M. Browne and McIntosh would appear to have been more accurate in recording the time of the attack on Lee's pickets. *O.R.,* ser. 1, vol. 25, part 1, 48, 54, 56, 61.
8. Robert J. Driver, Jr., and H. E. Howard, *2nd Virginia Cavalry* (Lynchburg, VA: H. E. Howard, 1995), 74.
9. Matthews, "Death of Pelham."
10. The exact time at which Averell's column moved out from the ford is difficult to determine. Averell wrote that it was at noon. The historian for the 1st Rhode Island stated it was at 10:00 A.M. Colonel McIntosh reported that his men were in position and were attacked shortly after noon. If the Confederate pickets were attacked between 6:00 and 6:30 and repulsed one or two attempts at crossing, as Lieutenant Browne related, the ford probably was captured by 7:00 A.M. Giving three hours to clear the ford of obstructions and water the horses of the column as it moved through the ford, the advance should have moved out at about 10:00. *O.R.,* ser. 1, vol. 25, part 1, 48, 54, 61; Denison, *Sabres and Spurs,* 210.
11. *O.R.,* ser. 1, vol. 25, part 1, 51, 54.
12. Ibid., 49, 61; Nanzig, *3rd Virginia Cavalry,* 30; Garland C. Hudgins and Richard B. Kleese, eds., *Recollections of an Old Dominion Dragoon* (Orange, VA: Publisher's Press, 1993), 64–65.
13. At least three sources place Pelham with Breathed's guns when they first arrived on the field, which was sometime between the 3rd Virginia's first and second charges. Milham, *Gallant Pelham,* 230-31; Matthews, "Death of Pelham"; Freeman, *Lee's Lieutenants,* vol. 2, 462. Freeman's source was Jed Hotchkiss, who had received the information directly from Stuart.
14. Depending on whose account you read, this was done by Capt. Harry Gilmor, Pvt. James Bailey, Lt. Charles Minnigerode, or Lt. Henry B. McClellan.
15. Denison, *Sabres and Spurs,* n.p.
16. He was first taken to the home of Dr. William A. Herndon in Culpeper, then to the Shackelford's. Vogtsberger, "Kelly's Ford," 8.
17. Henry Haw Matthews, "Major John Pelham, Confederate Hero," *SHSP* 38 (1910): 382–83.

18. *Jacksonville Republican,* April 2, 1863.
19. *O.R.,* ser. 1, vol. 25, part 1, 60.
20. Capt. John H. McClanahan's Staunton Battery and Capt. Wiley H. Griffin's 2nd Maryland Battery were not in the battalion at this time.
21. There were allegations that non-West Point graduates or that non-Virginians frequently were bypassed for promotions in the Army of Northern Virginia. Stuart's decision may have reflected this phenomenon. This does not mean that Stuart was unwilling to nominate an individual who was not a graduate of the U.S. Military Academy or who was not a Virginian, only that he realized the higher authorities who could accept or reject his choice might look unfavorably on such a nomination. Coupled with the facts that several officers in the battalion had seniority over Breathed and that Stuart previously had attempted to have Breathed appointed commander of the horse artillery when it first was being formed, Stuart could have felt that to nominate Breathed might bring about the appointment of someone he did not want or that he might have to search for another candidate. If the latter were to occur, the battalion would be without a commander for an even longer period of time. In the end, Stuart probably realized he would not be able to push Breathed's nomination through and so decided to look elsewhere. He might also have had other reasons that will never be known.
22. Stuart underestimated Terrell's desire for a combat command. The young officer decided to leave the staff and confronted Stuart. The situation was discussed, but Terrell was not satisfied. He requested and received a furlough. Stuart tried to placate Terrell with an appointment to the horse artillery. Whether this would have been in an administrative capacity, as ordnance officer, or as Beckham's second in command is unknown. In any event, Terrell, who wrote he was "heartily sick" of his place on the staff, handed in his resignation just five days after his appointment to the battalion. For once, Stuart's ability to appraise and judge a man had failed. He lost a fine officer. *C.S.R.,* microcopy M331, roll 244, S.V. "Lewis F. Terrell"; Robert J. Trout, *They Followed the Plume* (Mechanicsburg, PA: Stackpole Books, 1993), 256–60.
23. Thomas Henry Carter (June 13, 1831–June 2, 1908) graduated from VMI in the class of 1849. He then attended the University of Virginia and graduated with a degree in medicine. He was appointed captain of the King William Artillery on June 1, 1861, and promoted to major and chief of Hill's artillery on December 12, 1862. He successively held the ranks of lieutenant colonel (March 2, 1863) and colonel (February 27, 1864) when he was chief of artillery in Lt. Gen. Jubal Early's Valley Army. He was a farmer and physician postwar. Carter is buried in Hollywood Cemetery, Richmond. Krick, *Lee's Colonels,* 86.
24. The information that Stuart offered command to Carter and the reason for his failure to accept appear in a letter Carter later wrote to John W. Daniel in which he stated that he declined the proffered command because the guns were not fought as a complete unit as most battalions were. Thomas H. Carter to John W. Daniel, October 11, 1904, William E. Peters Papers, Lewis Leigh Collection, U.S. Army Military History Institute.
25. J. E. B. Stuart to Gen. Samuel Cooper, March 26, 1863; *C.S.R.,* microcopy M331, roll 20, S.V. "Robert F. Beckham."
26. Gustavus W. Smith, *Confederate War Papers* (New York: Atlantic Publishing and Engraving Company, 1884), 340.
27. *O.R.,* ser. 1, vol. 25, part 2, 858.
28. From Richard Channing Price to Mrs. Thomas R. Price, Sr., March 25, 1863, Price Papers.

The Beckham Era

Chapter 12

1. William A. Simpson to James Simpson, April 10, 1863, Walters Papers.
2. William P. Walters to Matilda E. Walters, April 10, 1863, Walters Papers.
3. *O.R.,* ser. 1, vol. 25, part 1, 1066–67.
4. The corps strength at this time was given as 9,895 men and twenty-two guns manned by 427 artillerymen. Ibid., 1067.
5. Lee's Brigade had only four of its six regiments (2nd North Carolina and 5th, 9th, and 13th Virginia). Two (10th and 15th Virginia) had been detached for picket duty near Beaver Dam and below Fredericksburg. The total force available to Lee was 1,200 cavalry and eight guns, with about 150 artillerymen. John Bigelow, Jr., *Chancellorsville* (New York: Konecky & Konecky, 1995), 145–46.

   At this time, Hart's Battery was in the Valley recruiting its horses. Lieutenant Hoxton and the Whitworth gun were stationed on the road a mile beyond Brandy Station. Breathed's Battery was either with Fitz Lee's Brigade on a scout in Fauquier County or at Culpeper Court House. According to H. H. Matthews's and H. B. McClellan's accounts, Breathed had one gun in the fight at Rappahannock Bridge. However, only two guns were engaged there, and Moorman claimed in his report that both were his. This is supported by the report of Capt. J. W. Strange, whose company was support for the guns. Breathed's Battery probably did not participate in the action. Hart, *Hart's Battery,* 7; *O.R.,* ser. 1, vol. 25, part 1, 87; Driver, *1st Virginia Cavalry,* 56; H. H. Matthews, "Pelham-Breathed Battery: Movements of Breathed's Battery after the Engagement at Kelly's Ford, 17th March, 1863, up to and including Chancellorsville, May 1st and 2nd, 1863," *St. Mary's Beacon,* February 23, 1905; McClellan, *I Rode with Stuart,* 221.
6. Nunnelee, *Famous Company,* 68.
7. Elder stated in his report that he was opposed by two guns. Moorman's account placed only one gun at the ford. *O.R.,* ser. 1, vol. 25, part 1, 83, 89.
8. In his history of Moorman's Battery, Shoemaker stated that three guns of the battery were stationed at the ford. Moorman's report gives the number as two. Shoemaker, *Shoemaker's Battery,* 30; *O.R.,* ser. 1, vol. 25, part 1, 89.
9. This action probably began sometime around 10:00 A.M. R. Channing Price, Stuart's adjutant, wrote that at 11:00 A.M., Stuart received word at Brandy Station of Gregg's crossing. From Richard Channing Price to Mrs. Thomas R. Price, Sr., April 16, 1863, Price Papers.
10. There may have been only two companies charging across the bridge. The history of the 1st Maine Cavalry names only Companies A and B as making the attack led by Maj. Stephen Boothby. These troops did retire under fire from artillery on the hills behind the rifle pits. Edward P. Tobie, *History of the First Maine Cavalry, 1861–1865* (Boston: Press of Emery & Hughes, 1887), 128.
11. *O.R.,* ser. 1, vol. 25, part 1, 89.
12. Ibid.
13. Ibid., 84, 89.
14. Shoemaker, *Shoemaker's Battery,* 30–31.
15. Lieutenant Ford reported that he fired about 100 rounds on the fourteenth and fifteenth. The action on the second day was brief, so most of the ammunition, probably around eighty rounds, was used on the fourteenth. Moorman would have used a proportional amount. *O.R.,* ser. 1, vol. 25, part 1, 89.

16. William A. Simpson to James Simpson, April 16, 1863, Walters Papers.
17. William P. Walters to Matilda E. Walters, April 16, 1863, Walters Papers.
18. Charles R. Phelps, April 16, 1863, Phelps Letters.
19. Ibid., April 18, 1863.
20. Francis Halsey Wigfall to Miss Louise Wigfall, April 21, 1863, Wigfall Papers.
21. William A. Simpson to James Simpson, April 26, 1863, Walters Papers.
22. William P. Walters to Matilda E. Walters, April 26, 1863, Walters Papers.
23. Francis Halsey Wigfall to Mrs. Louis T. Wigfall, April 26, 1863, Wigfall Papers.
24. Maj. Robert F. Beckham to Maj. R. Channing Price, April 28, 1863, Price Papers.
25. Lee still had only two regiments with him, the 9th and 13th Virginia Cavalry. McClellan, *I Rode with Stuart,* 227.
26. At this time, the section commanded by Shoemaker may have contained only one piece. Shoemaker claimed to have two guns, but Nunnelee recorded that only one gun from the battery, his rifled piece, went in pursuit of the raiders, though he was not present. Rooney Lee reported having just one gun with him at Kelly's Ford, so Nunnelee was probably correct. Shoemaker, *Shoemaker's Battery,* 32; Nunnelee, *Famous Company,* 70; *O.R.,* ser. 1, vol. 25, part 1, 1098.
27. In his report, Lee makes little mention of the artillery that accompanied him. He failed to mention that Hart's Battery joined him in the vicinity of Kelly's Ford during his withdrawal to Culpeper. Other sources recorded that Shoemaker's section (one gun) and Hart's Battery (three guns) rode with Lee as he shadowed the Federal cavalry. *O.R.,* ser. 1, vol. 25, part 1, 1098; Shoemaker, *Shoemaker's Battery,* 32; Nunnelee, *Famous Company,* 70; Hart, *Hart's Battery,* 7; Bigelow, Chancellorsville, 210.

    The reason that Shoemaker's section and Hart's Battery were short one gun each may have been a lack of horses or a lack of men. Sgt. Lewis T. Nunnelee was off on furlough, and it is possible that men from the other batteries were also absent, leaving the batteries short-handed. The possibility also exists that Shoemaker's other gun was with Moorman and that Hart's missing piece was on picket duty elsewhere, as was the case with Lt. G. W. Brown and one gun from McGregor's Battery.
28. Just where Beckham was at this time is unknown. In all probability he was with Stuart, but no evidence exists to confirm this. Beckham's report sheds little light on what he or the horse artillery did up to May 1.
29. Matthews, "Movements after Kelly's Ford."
30. *O.R.,* ser. 1, vol. 25, part 1, 744.
31. In his history of the battery, Shoemaker mistakenly recorded that a courier from W. H. F. Lee rode passed Phelps's section and reported that Shoemaker's section had fought at Raccoon Ford. This was not possible, as Shoemaker was at Rapidan Station with Hart. The only explanation for this is that Shoemaker based his book on the diary of Lt. E. H. Moorman, who was undoubtedly with Phelps and heard the erroneous report. Time apparently clouded Shoemaker's memory in regard to where he was on this occasion. Shoemaker, *Shoemaker's Battery,* 34.
32. *O.R.,* ser. 1, vol. 25, part 1, 1088, 1092.
33. The names of four of the men captured are known: Pvt. George S. Freeman, Pvt. William Scarborough, Pvt. Edward Sully, and Pvt. William Tapp. One man was thought to have been mortally wounded, but the records fail to give his name. Brown's subsequent movements and whereabouts are unknown. Bigelow indicated that Brown rejoined McGregor and was with him on May 1, but there is no evidence to support this. In fact, Beckham reported that he had only three of McGregor's guns with him during his engagement on the first. Ibid., 1050, 1088, 1092; Bigelow, *Chancellorsville,* 245.

34. Three of these guns were from McGregor's Battery, two from Moorman's, and one from Breathed's. The whereabouts of Breathed's fourth gun and the Whitworth under Hoxton are unknown. McGregor's fourth gun under Lieutenant Brown probably had not yet returned. *O.R.,* ser. 1, vol. 25, part 1, 1049.
35. Just which guns went forward is a point of conjecture. Matthews claimed that they were two of McGregor's and two of Breathed's. However, Beckham stated that he only had one of Breathed's guns with him. Shoemaker alluded to the fact that Phelps's section was engaged, but there is no support for this claim from other sources. In a postwar article, Moorman wrote that he had six men wounded without being able to unlimber his guns. Lt. Lewis T. Nunnelee recorded one man, Pvt. John McMasters, as being wounded at Chancellorsville. Beckham did mention several officers in his report, and this combined with other information would seem to indicate that McGregor's three pieces and Breathed's lone piece were the ones engaged. Matthews, "Movements after Kelly's Ford"; Shoemaker, *Shoemaker's Battery,* 33; Marcellus N. Moorman, "Narrative of Events and Observations Connected with the Wounding of General T. J. (Stonewall) Jackson," *SHSP* 30 (1902): 111; Nunnelee, *Famous Company,* 71; *O.R.,* ser. 1, vol. 25, part 1, 1049.
36. These were six guns of Battery M, 1st New York Artillery, under Lt. Charles E. Winegar and four guns of Battery F, 4th U.S. Artillery. Two guns of this battery were with Winegar, and two under Lt. Franklin B. Crosby were in position at Hazel Grove. *O.R.,* ser. 1, vol. 25, part 1, 723.
37. The name of this second man is unknown. Two other men besides Walters were reported killed at Chancellorsville, one on May 1 and one on May 2. A Private Corbin and Pvt. J. E. Duval were listed on a postwar roster as having been killed at Chancellorsville, but it is not clear which was killed during the action on May 1.
38. *O.R.,* ser. 1, vol. 25, part 1, 413.
39. H. H. Matthews, "Appendix," *St. Mary's Beacon,* June 22, 1905.
40. There was some controversy and no little amount of bitterness after the war when an article by Maj. Marcellus N. Moorman appeared in the *Southern Historical Society Papers,* which in effect claimed that Moorman's Battery was the one that fought with Jackson at Chancellorsville. Pvt. H. H. Matthews vehemently disputed Moorman's claim in newspapers and in a letter to Lt. Col. Roger P. Chew, last commander of the horse artillery. Moorman died two years after the article appeared, and the controversy died with him. Moorman, "Wounding of Jackson," 112; H. H. Matthews to Roger P. Chew, October 21, 1908, Chew Papers.
41. Francis Halsey Wigfall to Mrs. Louis T. Wigfall, May 2, 1863, Wigfall Papers.
42. H. H. Matthews, "Movements of Breathed's Battery After the Engagement at Kelly's Ford, 17th March, 1863, up to and including Chancellorsville, May 1st and 2nd, 1863," *St. Mary's Beacon,* March 2, 1905.
43. This was either Private Corbin or Pvt. J. E. Duval.
44. Matthews, "Movement of Breathed's Battery." McClellan's version did not include "and the brave men under you." McClellan, *I Rode with Stuart,* 234.
45. Moorman claimed that his guns did fire that night and in fact opened the action. To support his contention, he quoted from a postwar letter written by Brig. Gen. James H. Lane, who was on the ground with his brigade. However, Lane never mentioned Moorman or his guns in his report of the battle, stating only that Confederate batteries answered the Federal artillery. He undoubtedly did not know which batteries responded to the enemy's barrage. Additionally, Beckham recorded that Moorman's guns were not used because of their inferior range. Shoemaker wrote that Phelps's section was under fire from the enemy but gave no indication that it responded. Moorman, "Wounding of Jackson," 112; *O.R.,* ser. 1, vol. 25, part 1, 916, 1050; Shoemaker, *Shoemaker's Battery,* 34.

46. Hart et al., "Hart's Battery," 34.
47. The horse artillery's poor showing may have been caused by several factors. The Confederate cavalry may have been too close to the Federals to risk firing, or the enemy simply may have been out of range. Also, the Confederates may have been conserving ammunition. In any event, Beale was critical of the horse artillery for not performing up to its usual standards. Beale, *9th Virginia Cavalry,* 63.
48. Tobie, *First Maine Cavalry,* 136.
49. Hart et al., "Hart's Battery," 34–35.
50. Shoemaker claimed that his section fought at Gordonsville and at Columbia. There is no reference either by Lee or by any Federal officer that the artillery of either side played a part in the engagement at Gordonsville, and since Wyndham had evacuated Columbia before Lee ever arrived, Shoemaker could scarcely have been involved in any fighting there. It does not appear that Shoemaker had the opportunity to use his guns after the fighting at Rapidan Station on May 1. Shoemaker, *Shoemaker's Battery,* 36.
51. In their histories of the battery, both Hart and Sherfesee recorded that their battery (and presumably Shoemaker's section as well) was separated from Lee when he supposedly charged through a division of the enemy that closed in behind him. The battery, which had been trailing behind Lee, was cut off and was unable to rejoin the cavalry. Hart and Sherfesee claimed the battery eluded the Federals with a combination of ruse and good luck and made its way back to Gordonsville.

    The only charge made by Lee was executed on May 4 by one squadron of the 9th Virginia Cavalry, against what turned out to be about eighty men of the 5th U.S. Cavalry, picketing Shannon's Crossroads below Louisa Court House. The Federals were driven back, and several were killed, wounded, and taken prisoner. Lee determined that his force was too spent to pursue further and returned to Gordonsville.

    Hart's and Sherfesee's accounts are difficult to prove or disprove. That the battery failed to keep up with Lee's troopers is certain. What happened after they separated cannot be determined from existing records. That Lee would completely abandon his artillery seems unlikely, but then, he failed to record that he had any artillery at all with him. Apparently, Hart and Shoemaker found themselves falling farther and farther behind. When they reached the scene of the fighting, Lee was already heading back to Gordonsville. Trailing after the column, the artillery may have received a scare from nearby Federal cavalry that was equally too exhausted to take much interest. If Hart did execute a ruse, the performance was given before an audience too sleepy to watch. Hart, *Hart's Battery,* 7; Hart et al., "Hart's Battery," 36; *O.R.,* ser. 1, vol. 25, part 1, 1061–62, 1098.
52. Shoemaker, *Shoemaker's Battery,* 36.

Chapter 13

1. *O.R.,* ser. 1, vol. 25, part 1, 818.
2. Stuart claimed that Baldwin had used the phrase "appropriated by the Stuart Horse Artillery" in his report. However, in writing to Stuart about the guns, Lee accepted the blame for the statement and assured Stuart that nothing objectionable was intended. Ibid., part 2, 836.
3. *C.S.R.,* microcopy M331, roll 20, S.V. "Robert F. Beckham."
4. H. H. Matthews, "Pelham-Breathed Battery: The Great Cavalry Fight of the War, Fleetwood Hill or Brandy Plains, June 9, 1863," *St. Mary's Beacon,* Thursday, March 9, 1905.
5. Hart et al., "Hart's Battery," 36.

6. Matthews, "Fleetwood Hill."
7. Nunnelee, *Famous Company,* 72.
8. William A. Simpson to James Simpson, May 24, 1863, Walters Papers.
9. William A. Simpson to Matilda E. Walters, May 24, 1863, Walters Papers.
10. William Hoxton to Mrs. Sarah Randolph, May (?), 1863, Randolph Papers.
11. Now Delaplane.
12. *O.R.,* ser. 1, vol. 25, 138, 145.
13. Francis Halsey Wigfall to Miss Louise Wigfall, June 4, 1863, Wigfall Papers.
14. James H. Williams to Cora DeMovelle (Pritchartt) Williams, June 6, 1863, Williams Papers.
15. Phelps meant Ellis' Ford on the Rappahannock, which is almost due north of Ely's Ford on the Rapidan.
16. Charles R. Phelps, June 6, 1863, Phelps Letters.
17. Nunnelee, *Famous Company,* 72.
18. Bradshaw, *Diary of McVicar,* 9–10.
19. If Neese is correct, then four guns of the battalion did not participate in the review. They may have been assigned to picket duty.
20. Neese, *Confederate Horse Artillery,* 166–69.
21. Bradshaw, *Diary of McVicar,* 9–10.
22. Neese, *Confederate Horse Artillery,* 169–70.
23. Ibid., 170.

Chapter 14

1. Just who ordered the horse artillery to camp in this location is unknown, but Stuart has been blamed for the placement of his units on the evening of the eighth. He has also been accused of a lack of vigilance, in that he failed to discern Pleasonton's approach. Since the orders to the various brigades and the horse artillery regarding their camp locations for the night of the eighth are not available for study, one can say only that the placement of the horse artillery so close to the ford without proper support was an error on someone's part. As commander, however, Stuart must bear the responsibility, whether or not he knew of the battalion's location. As to the lack of vigilance charge, Stuart had often been surprised by Federal cavalry and infantry crossing a river unexpectedly. While there were times he was somewhat aware of their coming, he was by no means omniscient. His talent lay in dealing with the enemy after they penetrated his picket lines. A study of the cavalry operations up to and after this time will illustrate this fact effectively.

   There are those critics of Stuart and Beckham who state that Pelham would not have made the mistake of locating his camp so close to the river without support. Such comments are irrelevant, since they cannot be proven.
2. At least three sources stated that there were some tents standing when the Federals attacked in the morning. Bradshaw, *Diary of McVicar,* 10; Sherfesee, "Color-Bearer," 40; Hart, *Hart's Battery,* 8.
3. Just when the artillery became aware of the opening of the battle remains unclear. Neese stated that the alarm occurred before sunrise, McVicar at daylight, Hart at dawn, and Beckham just before sunrise. Neese, *Confederate Horse Artillery,* 171; Bradshaw, *Diary of McVicar,* 10; Hart, *Hart's Battery,* 8; *O.R.,* ser. 1, vol. 27, 772.
4. Neese, *Confederate Horse Artillery,* 171.
5. Sherfesee, "Color-Bearer," 40; Hart, *Hart's Battery,* 8.
6. Sherfesee, "Color-Bearer," 40.
7. Beckham reported that he ordered one of Hart's pieces into the road. Hart did not remember whether it was one or two, nor did he admit to Beckham giving him the

order to deploy. He intimated that he had placed the gun on his own initiative. Sherfesee stated that there was one gun in the road and that it was already being loaded when he arrived. He wrote that Beckham rode up and ordered Hart to remain where he was to provide covering fire for the rest of the battalion. Sherfesee added that the guns, meaning at least two, were retreated by pieces. Hart corroborated this. What evidently occurred was that one piece was placed in the road and opened fire, and another gun joined it prior to the retreat to St. James Church. *O.R.,* ser. 1, vol. 27, 772; James F. Hart, "Battle of Brandy Station," *Philadelphia Weekly Times* 4, no. 18 (June 26, 1880); Sherfesee, "Color-Bearer," 40–41.

8. Hart et al., "Hart's Battery," 38.
9. These two guns were from Halsey's section and were being commanded by Hart. The two gunners were James R. Blount and Benjamin B. Cox. Ibid., 39.
10. Sherfesee, "Color-Bearer," 41.
11. Bradshaw, *Diary of McVicar,* 10; Edward G. Longacre, *The Cavalry at Gettysburg* (Cranbury, NJ: Associated University Presses, 1986), 85.
12. Sherfesee, "Color-Bearer," 41.
13. Another account stated that one of Hart's two guns was limbered and retreated. The last gun was retired by prolonge, firing as it withdrew. Its retreat was covered in part by the fire from the guns at St. James Church. Hart et al., "Hart's Battery," 39.
14. Edward G. Longacre, ed., "A Race for Life at Brandy Station," *CWTI* 17, no. 9 (January 1979): 34.
15. Ibid.
16. One source recorded that when the Federals came within 200 yards of the guns, Lt. Col. Elijah V. White's 35th Battalion of Virginia Cavalry charged into them. In the resulting melee, White was pushed back until he was only twenty yards from Hart's guns. The artillery fired canister into both friend and foe alike in an attempt to stem the enemy's charge, but to no avail. The Yanks swept through the guns. This incident is not supported by any other accounts. White did charge, but on the left and before the artillery was fully in position at St. James Church. Hart et al., "Hart's Battery," 40; John Divine, *35th Battalion Virginia Cavalry* (Lynchburg, VA: H. E. Howard, 1985), 28.
17. Hart et al., "Hart's Battery," 40.
18. Hart, *Hart's Battery,* 8.
19. Vincent's section was commanded by Sgt. Elijah Spencer. *Supp. to the O.R.,* part 1, vol. 5, 295.
20. Ibid., 277.
21. Ibid., 233.
22. Ibid., 277.
23. Ibid., 233.
24. Col. Thomas C. Devin, who commanded the 6th New York Cavalry, reported that Maynadier fired only one or two rounds before retiring. Though Devin did not give a reason for this, it is apparent that Johnston's guns were still dominating the field at this time. Ibid., 234.
25. Robertson made no mention of any artillery accompanying him or reaching him during the battle. Apparently, Chew's section reached the Kellysville Road near the railroad and before it could move on to Robertson was recalled to defend Fleetwood Hill. *O.R.,* ser. 1, vol. 27, part 2, 733–36.
26. Wise, *Long Arm of Lee,* 587.
27. *O.R.,* ser. 1, vol. 27, part 2, 730.
28. U. R. Brooks, *Butler and His Cavalry in the War of Secession, 1861–1865* (Camden, SC: J. J. Fox, 1989), 154.

29. McClellan, *I Rode with Stuart,* 269.
30. There is some confusion concerning how many guns Carter had with him. Beckham stated, "The pieces first placed on Pettis' [Fleetwood] hill were under the command of Lieutenant [John W.] Carter, of Chew's battery, and had been repeatedly charged by the enemy and retaken by our cavalry." At first glance, this appears to indicate that Carter had at least two guns with him, but Beckham's reference to Carter being charged repeatedly is erroneous. Carter was at no time charged by the Federal cavalry. Beckham may have been referring to those guns that arrived after Carter's withdrawal. Captain Martin stated in his report that he faced a full battery from the outset. Lt. Moses P. Clark of Martin's Battery wrote only that he dueled with "the enemy's artillery" and did not indicate the number of guns. Neither Neese nor McVicar shed any light on the subject, as they were not under Carter's command. Jennings Wise offered the best solution. He claimed that a section was with Carter but that only one gun opened fire on Gregg. Unfortunately, he failed to give the source of this information.

    In his book on Stuart's campaigns, McClellan wrote that it was a six-pounder howitzer that fired on the approaching Federals. He was, other than Carter, the only officer present, and his view has seldom been questioned. However, there is the possibility that Carter did not have a six-pounder howitzer. On April 9, 1864, less than a year from the battle of Brandy Station, McClellan wrote an endorsement supporting a request by Chew to have Carter promoted to captain. In it, McClellan recounted the action on Fleetwood Hill and stated that Carter had a twelve-pounder howitzer. To add to the confusion, the inspection report for Chew's Battery at the end of February 1863 listed the battery's composition as two Blakelys and a twenty-four-pounder howitzer. A Napoleon was expected at any time. Unless one of the guns was disabled, there was no reason to use a six-pounder, with its limited range. McClellan was not an artilleryman and may have been mistaken as to the caliber of the gun. McClellan, *I Rode with Stuart,* 269; *C.S.R.V.,* microcopy M324, roll 273; *O.R.,* ser. 1, vol. 27, part 2, 772–73; *Supp. to the O.R.,* part 1, vol. 5, 280–81; Wise, *Long Arm of Lee,* 588.
31. There is no evidence that the artillery's ammunition wagons were at Fleetwood Hill. Why Carter was there is unknown.
32. *Supp. to the O.R.,* part 1, vol. 5, 280–81.
33. Beckham supposedly had sixteen guns with him at St. James Church. However, in his report of what happened with the guns under his command, only thirteen are accounted for. The missing pieces would appear to have been from Hart's Battery.

    Concerning which battery's guns went where, one source recorded that the gun sent to Butler was from Moorman's Battery, though Shoemaker did not mention it in his history of the battery. Nunnelee's account of the fight also failed to include the detaching of a gun from the battery. The same source stated that the two pieces on the Kellysville Road were from Chew's Battery. Beckham did not say which battery's guns were sent to these locations. Another source claimed that Moorman's piece was sent to support Robertson, but this does not agree with the known facts. Fairfax Downey, *Clash of Cavalry: The Battle of Brandy Station* (New York: David McKay Company, 1959), 108; Shoemaker, *Shoemaker's Battery,* 39; Nunnelee, *Famous Company,* 74–75; Neese, *Confederate Horse Artillery,* 173; Wise, *Long Arm of Lee,* 587.
34. Neese, *Confederate Horse Artillery,* 173.
35. Hart wrote that he was ordered to "ride back and see what this foolishness was all about," and that he saw Federal cavalry "forming to the right and upon Fleetwood Hill." While he may have observed the enemy forming south of the hill, he could

not have seen them to the right of the hill (toward Brandy Station) due to the intervening high ground. Neither did he see them on the hill itself, because by all other accounts, the Confederate and Federal cavalry met on the top, charging up opposite sides, to decide the issue of possession. Hart was probably guilty of embellishing his recollections concerning this point. Hart, "Brandy Station."

36. Frank Robertson Reade, L. Minor Blackford, and Robert J. Trout, *In the Saddle with Stuart: The Story of Frank S. Robertson of Stuart's Staff* (Gettysburg, PA: Thomas Publications, 1998), 60.
37. Hart, *Hart's Battery,* 9; Hart et al., "Hart's Battery," 41.
38. Hart recorded that all four of his guns were with him, whereas Beckham reported that Hart had only one gun. This is evidently where the discrepancy lies between the number of guns accounted for in Beckham's report and the actual number of pieces engaged. Hart, *Hart's Battery,* 9; *O.R.,* ser. 1, vol. 27, part 2, 773.
39. The delay caused by Hart's pause to fire allowed Ford's section to attain the summit slightly ahead of Hart.
40. *O.R.,* ser. 1, vol. 27, part 2, 772.
41. Hart, *Hart's Battery,* 9–10.
42. Beckham's report stated that each officer killed one of the enemy. *O.R.,* ser. 1, vol. 27, part 2, 773.
43. Shreve, "Stuart Horse Artillery," 9.
44. *O.R.,* ser. 1, vol. 27, part 2, 773.
45. In his history of the battery, Hart claimed that when he reached the top of Fleetwood Hill, he saw a line of Federal cavalry scarcely thirty yards away. He raised his saber as a signal to halt, but his gunners misunderstood it and charged the enemy. The blue cavalry did not hang around to fight but ran for it, leaving a battery of artillery (Martin's) unprotected. Hart's cannoneers then captured the battery. That Hart had the nerve to write, in all sincerity, that his men captured Martin's Battery demonstrates the tendency for officers and men on both sides to add to their unit's glory by claiming acts committed by another. No such action by Hart or his battery took place. Hart, *Hart's Battery,* 9.

    A second version of this incident recounted that Hart had two of his guns out of action and that he sent their teams down the slope to recover two of Martin's guns. Bringing them to the crest of Fleetwood, Hart turned these two guns on the retreating Federals. Since Martin had spiked his guns, and in the midst of battle there would have been little time to undo this, the claim that Hart used these pieces should be disregarded. Hart et al., "Hart's Battery," 43.

    Col. Hampton S. Thomas of the 1st Pennsylvania Cavalry asserted that one of Martin's guns had been advanced to the crest of Fleetwood but only managed to fire two rounds of canister before it was pulled back and placed with the other two pieces at the base of the hill. Lt. Moses P. Clark stated in his report that he put his gun "in battery upon the very ground vacated by the enemy's pieces." After a few rounds, Captain Martin joined him with the other section. Apparently Clark was moved up on the crest of the hill, fired, and then withdrew to the base of the hill, where he was joined by Martin. At no time did the Federals have more than one gun on Fleetwood's crest. McClellan, *I Rode with Stuart,* 276; *O.R.,* ser. 1, vol. 27, part 1, 1024–25; *Supp. to the O.R.,* part 1, vol. 5, 281.
46. Out of thirty-six men, only six came out safely. The rest were killed, wounded, or missing.
47. *Supp. to the O.R.,* part 1, vol. 5, 229.
48. Matthews, "Fleetwood Hill."
49. *O.R.,* ser. 1, vol. 27, part 2, 738.

50. The casualties in Chew's Battery were Pvt. George Longerbeam, mortally wounded; Pvt. George Hooff, wounded; and Pvt. John Proctor, captured. *C.S.R.V.,* microcopy M324, roll 273.
51. The knob on the end of the breech (rear) of a gun.
52. Bradshaw, *Diary of McVicar,* 10–13.
53. Williams, a brother of Lieutenant Williams, was a private in the 12th Virginia Cavalry. Frye, *12th Virginia Cavalry,* 178.
54. Lieutenant Williams wrote in greater detail concerning his brother's death on June 16. Chew's Battery was at the time camped about nine miles from Culpeper Court House on the Warrenton Road. He wrote, in part: "The flood gates of grief have been turned loose upon my soul. . . . George, brave fellow is gone. He had charged ahead of his company, taken a prisoner, who was on foot, took his arms, and was hurrying him to the rear and had gone some 10 yards when in sight of the enemy (our men had fallen back) the cowardly prisoner drew a pocket pistol and killed him instantly." James H. Williams to Cora DeMovelle (Pritchartt) Williams, June 16, 1863, Williams Papers.
55. Ibid., June 10, 1863.
56. Moorman's Battery as a whole lost Anthony E. Dornin, killed; William D. Nowlin, Robert Saunders, and William M. Shoemaker, wounded; and Samuel T. Kessler, captured. Shoemaker, *Shoemaker's Battery,* 39–40; *C.S.R.V.,* microcopy M324, rolls 337, 338.
57. Charles R. Phelps, June 11, 1863, Phelps Letters.
58. The wounded were Privates Harry Wagner, Henry F. Wegner, and Harry Wickes. *C.S.R.V.,* microcopy M324, roll 337.
59. Francis Halsey Wigfall to Miss Louise Wigfall, June 13, 1863, Wigfall Papers.
60. *O.R.,* ser. 1, vol. 27, part 2, 683.
61. The horse artillery's total loss was one killed, ten wounded, and one missing. In addition to those already mentioned, Jacob Belitzer of Hart's Battery was also wounded.

Chapter 15

1. Micajah Woods to Dr. John R. Woods, May 22, 1863, Woods Papers.
2. Micajah Woods to Roger P. Chew, July 5, 1909, Chew Papers.
3. *O.R.,* ser. 1, vol. 27, part 3, 865.
4. Ibid., 865–66.
5. Wilbur S. Nye speculated that Lee may have purposely kept Stuart south of the Rappahannock to deceive Hooker as to his actual intentions. This allowed Ewell to slip away into the Valley. Wilbur S. Nye, *Here Come the Rebels* (Baton Rouge: Louisiana State University Press, 1965), 165–66.
6. Edward G. Longacre, "Target: Winchester, Virginia," *CWTI* 15, no. 3 (June 1976): 25.
7. *O.R.,* ser. 1, vol. 27, part 3, 50–51.
8. Goldsborough, *Maryland Line,* 283.
9. Pvt. Washington Hands, a member of Griffin's Battery, contended that Griffin actually opened the bombardment. This is not corroborated by any other source, but it is within the realm of possibility if Griffin had been acting under orders of Herbert, Gordon, or Ewell in an attempt to draw Milroy's attention away from the west, where Early was forming. Ibid., 283.
10. *O.R.,* ser. 1, vol. 27, part 3, 878.
11. Ibid., part 2, 442.
12. Micajah Woods to Dr. John R. Woods, June 16, 1863, Woods Papers.

13. Goldsborough, *Maryland Line,* 284.
14. The battery was assigned to Ewell's artillery reserve, commanded by Col. J. Thompson Brown. *O.R.,* ser. 1, vol. 27, part 2, 455.
15. Col. J. Thompson Brown reported that Griffin was attached to Jenkins's Brigade on June 14. Ibid., 450.
16. Goldsborough, *Maryland Line,* 284.
17. Potts, "Recollections."
18. Driver, *Staunton Artillery,* 75.
19. *O.R.,* ser. 1, vol. 27, part 3, 905–6.
20. Potts, "Recollections."
21. Roger U. Delauter, *18th Virginia Cavalry* (Lynchburg, VA: H. E. Howard, 1985), 7; *O.R.,* ser. 1, vol. 27, part 3, 947–48.
22. Goldsborough, *Maryland Line,* 284–85.
23. Micajah Woods to Dr. John R. Woods, June 25, 1863, Woods Papers.
24. Micajah Woods to Mrs. Sabina Lewis Stuart Creigh Woods, June 30, 1863, Woods Papers.
25. Nye, *Here Come the Rebels,* 329–30.
26. Woods wrote this letter on the thirtieth. This does not agree with all other accounts, which state that the battery arrived on the twenty-eighth and moved with Jenkins to Mechanicsburg. The reason for this discrepancy is unknown. Micajah Woods to Mrs. Sabina Lewis Stuart Creigh Woods, June 30, 1863, Woods Papers; Nye, *Here Come the Rebels,* 329–30; Longacre, *Cavalry at Gettysburg,* 145.
27. Micajah Woods to Mrs. Sabina Lewis Stuart Creigh Woods, June 30, 1863, Woods Papers.
28. Nye, *Here Come the Rebels,* 330.
29. Ibid., 333.
30. The actual name of the church was the Den Freidens Church, founded by the Lutherans in the eighteenth century. Ibid.
31. The hotel stood in the angle of the intersection of the Trindle Spring Road and the Carlisle Pike. Ibid., 341.
32. Micajah Woods to Mrs. Sabina Lewis Stuart Creigh Woods, June 30, 1863, Woods Papers.

Chapter 16

1. Chew's Battery probably had a complement of just three guns, having lost the famous "Ashby gun" at Brandy Station when it burst at the cascabel. Neither Neese nor McVicar mentioned the gun being replaced. The dispute between Stuart and Lt. Col. Brisco G. Baldwin, the army's chief of ordnance, was still fresh in both men's minds. In all likelihood, the three guns of the 6th New York Battery captured by Stuart were turned over to Baldwin. Stuart had little time to fight both Lee's ordnance chief and the Yankees.
2. One of these batteries was Moorman's. The identity of the other is unknown. Neese, *Confederate Horse Artillery,* 180; Nunnelee, *Famous Company,* 76.
3. *O.R.,* ser. 1, vol. 27, part 3, 172.
4. Kilpatrick's Brigade consisted of the 2nd and 4th New York, 6th Ohio, 1st Massachusetts Cavalry, and the absent 1st Rhode Island.
5. The turnpike is called the Ashby's Gap Turnpike west of Aldie and the Little River Turnpike east of the town. To avoid confusion, it will be referred to as the Little River Turnpike in all instances.
6. The intersection is present-day Gilbert's Corner. The Old Carolina Road went north to Leesburg.

7. Matthews wrote that Breathed's Battery accompanied Munford and the 2nd and 3rd Virginia to locate forage, but Wickham's report stated that the battery was with him. Munford does not state that the battery accompanied him. H. H. Matthews, "Pelham-Breathed Battery: On the Way to Gettysburg, Pa., Engagements at Aldie, Upperville and Middleburg," *St. Mary's Beacon,* April 13, 1905; *O.R.,* ser. 1, vol. 27, part 2, 739, 745.
8. Exactly where Wigfall placed his gun is in dispute. Fragments of a Whitworth shell found in rear of Boston's position would indicate that it may have been some distance to the rear, along the Little River Turnpike. Munford's report stated that he took only one gun from the battery over to the Snickersville Gap Road, but Wigfall was independent of the battery and given free rein as to where he fought his piece. He could have followed Munford and attempted to support Boston from a position along the Snickersville Gap Road. The Whitworth had the range to make such positioning possible.
9. H. H. Matthews recorded that this gun crew consisted of Sgt. J. W. Cosgrave; Corp. Joseph Warro, gunner; Pvt. Michael Garigan at no. 1 position; Pvt. James Mann, no. 2; Pvt. Henry H. Matthews, no. 3; Pvt. James C. Kane, no. 4; Pvt. John Fay, no. 5; Pvt. "Mississippi" Smith, no. 6; Rev. George H. Zimmerman, no. 7; and Pvt. John Culbreth, no. 8. Behind the gun, Privates John M. Bollman and Frank Neal manned the limber. Privates Henry Neal and Patrick Stanley were the caisson drivers. This is the only recorded position-by-position gun crew for the entire battalion. However, the evidence suggests that Matthews was claiming to be somewhere he was not. The casualties for Breathed's Battery as given by Munford were two killed (Privates Thomas W. Herb "Hebb" Greenwell and Thomas Parker) and three wounded (Privates John Francis Key, Elijah Tarleton Russell, and George R. Terry). Additionally, one other casualty appears on the roster—Pvt. J. Franklin A. Arnold, listed as killed. As can be seen, none of these men were in the gun crew Matthews claimed fought the action.

   Arnold's addition to the list of killed raises another problem. Lt. Francis H. Wigfall wrote in his letter of June 18 that one man from each of the other pieces was killed. If Wigfall was referring to the two other pieces that were on the Little River Turnpike, that would confirm the number of killed as two. However, if he was referring to the rest of the entire battery, three more guns, it would place the number of killed at three, meaning that Arnold would be included. In the Sharon Baptist Churchyard at Middleburg are two tombstones. One has "W. Parker Stew. Hos. Art." and the other "F. H. G. Breathed Stew. Hos. Art." The first is undoubtedly Thomas Parker, the "W" being a mistake. The second is most likely Greenwell. The "F" is probably an error and should be a "T." The "H" and "G" fit, and the "Breathed" is obviously a reference to Breathed's Battery. If Arnold was killed, he did not show up in the cemetery with his comrades or on Munford's casualty list. Matthews, "Aldie, Upperville and Middleburg"; *O.R.,* ser. 1, vol. 27, part 2, 741; Francis Halsey Wigfall to Mrs. Louis T. Wigfall, June 18, 1863, Wigfall Papers.
10. Matthews testified, "That gun used more canister on that occasion than was ever used by the entire section in any previous engagement." Again, Matthews's words must be taken with caution, since he was in all likelihood not with the gun on the Snickersville Gap Road. Matthews, "Aldie, Upperville and Middleburg."
11. Ibid.
12. The pole is that part of the limber that extends between the horses.
13. The pintle hook is that part of the limber to which the lunette, the circular ring at the end of the gun carriage, is attached in order to haul the gun.
14. Francis Halsey Wigfall to Mrs. Louis T. Wigfall, June 18, 1863, Wigfall Papers.

15. The scouts Chambliss sent to Thoroughfare Gap returned and reported that they had seen nothing. As officers of the 9th Virginia settled down to a meal in a house along the road about a mile from the gap, a sentry sounded the alarm. Maj. Thomas Waller quickly formed the regiment, but the enemy disappeared before he could come to grips with them. Chambliss did nothing to hinder Duffié's march, allowing the Federals to reach Middleburg. Beale, *9th Virginia Cavalry,* 70; G. W. Beale, *A Lieutenant of Cavalry in Lee's Army* (Baltimore: Butternut and Blue, 1994), 100.
16. Shoemaker stated that the battery arrived at Rector's Crossroads on the seventeenth but only reached Middleburg to participate in the fight of the twenty-first. Lt. Charles R. Phelps wrote that the battery arrived at Middleburg on the eighteenth. Nunnelee recorded that the battery reached the vicinity of Middleburg after dark on the seventeenth. Since Nunnelee did not give a time and the battery could have arrived close to midnight, a compromise between Phelps and Nunnelee has been used here. Shoemaker, *Shoemaker's Battery,* 41; Charles R. Phelps, June 25, 1863, Phelps Letters; Nunnelee, *Famous Company,* 77.
17. *O.R.,* ser. 1, vol. 27, part 3, 208.
18. Just which battery or batteries participated in this fight has been a subject of conjecture. Hart's Battery has often been given the credit, but the records show that Hampton's Brigade, to which the battery was attached, did not arrive until the twentieth. H. H. Matthews claimed that Breathed was on the field when in reality he was with Munford at Union, opposing Buford. Moorman's Battery was available, and at least one source inferred that they were engaged that day, though another failed to confirm the claim. Nunnelee recorded that Moorman's Battery was put into position early in the morning but was withdrawn, except for one gun, at 9:00 A.M. At 1:00 P.M., the rest of the battery returned to the same position, where it remained until dark. It did not fire a round the whole day. Stuart's staff officer, Maj. Heros von Borcke, wrote that he placed more than one battery into position due to Beckham's absence but did not name the batteries. George W. Shreve of McGregor's Battery recounted his participation in the fighting on the nineteenth but did not allude to any other artillery being present. Col. R. L. T. Beale, in his history of the 9th Virginia Cavalry, wrote that only one battery took position on the hill. It would appear that Moorman's and McGregor's Batteries were present, but only McGregor's was engaged. Longacre, *Cavalry at Gettysburg,* 122; Nye, *Here Come the Rebels,* 190; *O.R.,* ser. 1, vol. 27, part 2, 690; Matthews, "Aldie, Upperville and Middleburg"; Charles R. Phelps, June 25, 1863, Phelps Letters; Shoemaker, *Shoemaker's Battery,* 41; Nunnelee, *Famous Company,* 77–78; von Borcke, *Memoirs,* 290; Shreve, "Stuart Horse Artillery," 9–10; Beale, *9th Virginia Cavalry,* 72.
19. *O.R.,* ser. 1, vol. 27, part 1, 1034.
20. Ibid., 953.
21. Tobie, *First Maine Cavalry,* 165.
22. Beale, *9th Virginia Cavalry,* 72–73.
23. Shreve, "Stuart Horse Artillery," 10.
24. Neese, *Confederate Horse Artillery,* 181.
25. Ibid.
26. Ibid., 181–82.
27. The positioning of Bamberg's section comes from a letter written by Alexander Wood, a member of Hart's Battery. Wood wrote that his section took position on the left of the road. Except for the piece that was captured, the exact location of the other guns of the battery is unknown. Bamberg could have been north of the pike, and Halsey, once he came up, south of the pike. The possibility also exists

that once Wood's gun left, Bamberg could have moved his remaining piece to the south side of the road to link with Halsey. While no evidence of such a move has been uncovered, the fact that it could have taken place should not be discounted. G. N. Saussy, "Campaigning with Jeb Stuart," *Watson's Magazine* 13, no. 2 (June 1911): 156–57.

28. Hart stated that both of the guns that were saved left riding on their caissons. Wood recorded that the first piece was carried over the mountains the next day. Hart, *Hart's Battery,* 11; Saussy, "Campaigning with Stuart," 156–57.
29. Saussy, "Campaigning with Stuart," 156–57.
30. Ibid.
31. Several sources recorded that Hart retired by sections. While technically correct, the truth is that he could only retire one gun while keeping the other firing because of the loss of his other two pieces. The time between Bamberg's departure from the ridge and Halsey's attempt to follow could not have been more than a few minutes. Halsey may have had time for one or two shots, but the situation deteriorated around him so quickly that it is doubtful that Bamberg had reached a new position and unlimbered in time to cover Halsey's withdrawal. One source stated that Hampton's line had fallen back behind the guns before Hart received the order to withdraw his pieces. If so, Halsey's escape window was extremely small once Bamberg had gone. Hart's attempt to "retire by sections" does not appear to have happened on this occasion. James F. Hart to John B. Bachelder, March 3, 1886, Bachelder Papers, New Hampshire Historical Society.

    Some accounts of the fighting record that Hart still had three guns when he unlimbered at the Goose Creek Bridge. However, Alexander Wood's recollection that he passed Halsey's section going into the fight at the creek 600 yards to the rear is more detailed than any other source. While he could be in error concerning the second gun being damaged by recoil in this location, he certainly would have a clear memory of where his own piece was damaged. Except for the piece captured by the Federals, Hart's history sheds no light as to where the other guns were disabled. Wood's account has been used here. Hart, *Hart's Battery,* 10; Saussy, "Campaigning with Stuart," 156–57.
32. Wood wrote that the explosion killed the three off horses. Saussy, "Campaigning with Stuart," 157.
33. Hart et al., "Hart's Battery," 48.
34. Historians previously were unsure whether McGregor's Battery was present at all or, if it was, whether only a section participated. Matthews recalled that McGregor's Battery was with Breathed's north of Goose Creek and retreated with it toward Upperville. Though this appears possible, Breathed's Battery was attached to Munford, not Chambliss or Jones, and probably was with Munford's Brigade on the Snickersville Gap Road. McGregor could have had one section at Goose Creek Bridge while the other was with Chambliss, but more likely the battery was united and in the fight along with Hart and Moorman. Nunnelee recorded that McGregor went forward with Moorman's Battery and that McGregor unlimbered his guns at the first position with Moorman's. Shoemaker also confirmed McGregor's presence before the retreat to Rector's Crossroads. Shreve related that he was wounded at the "Stone Bridge near Rector's," which adds evidence that McGregor's Battery fought here. All three writers stated that McGregor's Battery was engaged, meaning all four guns. Matthews, "Aldie, Upperville and Middleburg"; Nunnelee, *Famous Company,* 78; Shoemaker, *Shoemaker's Battery,* 41; Shreve, "Stuart Horse Artillery," 10.
35. Stuart reported that his first position was before Middleburg, meaning the ridge west of Mount Defiance, and that his second position was on the west bank of

Goose Creek. In Stuart's mind, this may well have been the case because he made no determined stand with the cavalry between those points. However, there was constant skirmishing, and the horse artillery most definitely retired in its customary leapfrog manner. Each ridge offered an opportunity for at least one section or battery to unlimber and fire on the enemy while the cavalry and other sections of the artillery withdrew. On the next ridge, another section or battery unlimbered to cover the withdrawal of the first. Between Hart's first position and Goose Creek, the horse artillery held at least two other ridges: the first position of McGregor and Moorman behind Cromwell's Run, and then Moorman's position at the crossroads.

36. Lieutenant Fuller reported that when his battery reached the Confederates' position (at Rector's Crossroads), he found "one man dead on the ground, horribly mangled, and traces of blood where they had carried off their wounded, to testify to the accuracy of our fire." Fuller's next statement was that his battery also fought at Goose Creek. This supports the fact that Moorman participated in the battle prior to the action at Goose Creek Bridge. *O.R.,* ser. 1, vol. 27, part 1, 1035.
37. Nunnelee, *Famous Company,* 79.
38. *Supp. to the O.R.,* part 1, vol. 5, 254.
39. Shreve, "Stuart Horse Artillery," 10.
40. Ibid.
41. Nunnelee also reported that two horses were killed at this location. Nunnelee, *Famous Company,* 79.
42. Hart wrote that all of his guns were disabled in the fighting of the twenty-first. He failed to record just when and under what circumstances his last piece was damaged. James F. Hart to John B. Bachelder, March 3, 1886, Bachelder Papers.
43. The fact that Shoemaker was sent to Chambliss supports the view that McGregor was fighting on the Little River Turnpike with Stuart. Shoemaker, *Shoemaker's Battery,* 42; Nunnelee, *Famous Company,* 79.
44. The third section, under Lt. Theophilus B. von Michalowski, remained with Buford and was deployed frequently against the Confederate skirmishers. *O.R.,* ser. 1, vol. 27, part 1, 932, 1029.
45. Ibid., 920–21.
46. Ibid., 921.
47. Just which guns were involved in the fighting is still a topic of controversy. Matthews stated that both Breathed and McGregor were present, but Matthews frequently claimed participation in actions when his guns were never on the field. This would appear to be the case here. Breathed in all probability was with Munford on the Snickersville Gap Road. McGregor was on the Little River Turnpike fighting Gregg. Hart was reduced to one gun. One of Moorman's sections was still battling beside McGregor and Hart. That leaves Shoemaker's section from Moorman's Battery and Chew's Battery facing Buford. The two guns that went into position to the right of the Trappe Road, as mentioned by Beale, belonged to Shoemaker. Gamble reported that his regiments encountered the fire of five guns. These would have been the two under Shoemaker and three from Chew's Battery. Matthews, "Aldie, Upperville and Middleburg"; Shoemaker, *Shoemaker's Battery,* 42; *O.R.,* ser. 1, vol. 27, part 1, 933; Beale, *9th Virginia Cavalry,* 74.
48. Abner Hard, *History of the Eighth Cavalry Regiment Illinois Volunteers* (Dayton: Morningside Bookshop, 1996), 251.
49. Bradshaw, *Diary of McVicar,* 14.
50. Shoemaker wrote that he ran out of ammunition and had to go to Ashby's Gap for more. Beale recorded that his regiment, the 9th Virginia, was marching in rear of the guns when it was called back to the field to relieve the 2nd North Carolina. Since the 9th had been in support of the two guns that went into position to the

right of the Trappe Road, they were the same guns it was accompanying at the time the regiment received its new orders. In the fighting, Shoemaker had one man, Corp. Radford H. Padgett, wounded in the finger. Shoemaker, *Shoemaker's Battery,* 42; Beale, *9th Virginia Cavalry,* 74; Nunnelee, *Famous Company,* 80.

51. O'Ferrall was only a captain at this time.
52. Bradshaw, *Diary of McVicar,* 14–15.
53. McDonald, *Laurel Brigade,* 150–51.
54. Beale, *A Lieutenant in Lee's Army,* 104–5.
55. Gregg reported that when the Confederates made their final stand outside Upperville, they had no artillery. Nunnelee wrote that the Confederate artillery did not unlimber after leaving the position at the bridge. His reasons for this are given in the text. *O.R.,* ser. 1, vol. 27, part 1, 954; Nunnelee, *Famous Company,* 79.
56. *O.R.,* ser. 1, vol. 27, part 1, 1029–30, 1035.
57. Gregg reported that the 1st Maine charged into Upperville and encountered an artillery piece, which fired on them. The crew then abandoned the gun, described in the regimental history as a "small mountain howitzer," which was then captured. Stuart admitted to losing only one piece, and that was from Hart's Battery at the first position of the day. No other Confederate account mentions the loss of a second gun, and as far as is known, none of the batteries had a "small mountain howitzer" as part of its ordnance. *O.R.,* ser. 1, vol. 27, part 1, 912, 954, and part 2, 687–710; Tobie, *First Maine Cavalry,* 171.
58. If any of these guns fired, McVicar failed to record it. Cabell reported Fraser's presence, but not whether his battery participated in turning back Gregg's column. Fraser was mortally wounded at Gettysburg.
59. *O.R.,* ser. 1, vol. 27, part 1, 911.
60. Beckham's role in the battles of Aldie, Middleburg, and Upperville is unknown. His name failed to appear in any account of the horse artillery in these actions. If he filed a report, it has been lost. Whereas Pelham seemed always center stage, Beckham does not even appear to be in the play. This became the norm throughout Beckham's tenure as commander of the battalion. The few occasions that he garnered mention in reports provide few details of his command techniques or his personal involvement with the batteries in battle. It appears that he allowed the captains to do the fighting while he coordinated their efforts. The reorganization of the horse artillery when Beckham took command contributed considerably to the necessity of this approach. How much Pelham would have been affected by it remains an intriguing question that can never be answered. Both men had talent as artillerists, but Pelham's command style may have been cramped by the battalion reorganization, which would have left him without a battery to command directly. Beckham made the adjustment. Unfortunately, in doing so, his contributions in battle have been lost.
61. Nunnelee, *Famous Company,* 80; Neese, *Confederate Horse Artillery,* 184; Bradshaw, *Diary of McVicar,* 16.
62. Neese and McVicar confirmed their battery's participation. Nunnelee testified to Moorman's and McGregor's involvement in the firing, though only one section of Moorman's took part. This may have been the case with the other batteries as well. Neese, *Confederate Horse Artillery,* 184; Bradshaw, *Diary of McVicar,* 16; Nunnelee, *Famous Company,* 80.
63. Nunnelee, *Famous Company,* 80.
64. Ibid., 81.

Chapter 17

1. John was Saunders's servant.
2. Dornin was killed at Brandy Station.
3. Charles R. Phelps, June 25, 1863, Phelps Letters.
4. Stuart's report stated that six guns accompanied his column on the march. However, as is so common in regard to the horse artillery, he failed to tell which batteries the guns belonged to. Despite this, in some accounts of the ride and in the actions fought along the way, notably the battle of Hanover, Stuart has been credited with having as many as twelve guns. The batteries usually connected with the ride are Chew's, Hart's, and McGregor's. Information from various sources confirms that Stuart had only six guns and that they were from Breathed's and McGregor's Batteries. H. H. Matthews, "Pelham-Breathed Battery: The Road into Maryland, Hanover and Carlisle, Pa. up to and including Gettysburg," *St. Mary's Beacon,* April 20, 1905; Francis Halsey Wigfall to Louis T. Wigfall, July 7, 1863, Wigfall Papers; Shoemaker, *Shoemaker's Battery,* 43; Hart, *Hart's Battery,* 11; Neese, *Confederate Horse Artillery,* 184–85; Bradshaw, *Diary of McVicar,* 16–17.

   Beckham's participation in Stuart's ride cannot be confirmed. While it is difficult to imagine that he was left behind with Chew, Moorman, and Hart, there is that possibility. These batteries were in rough shape after the fighting at Aldie, Middleburg, and Upperville, and Beckham may have remained with them to assist in whatever way he could in their rehabilitation.
5. In his history of Breathed's Battery, H. H. Matthews recorded that Sgt. Sterling Murray was captured while enjoying a meal in the town. Actually, nine men from the battery, Privates Julius E. Bates, Thomas Burger, Martin Cahill, Stephen Mays, James McNelis, John Murphy, Thomas Rudden, and Charles L. Seymour and Sergeant Murray, are listed in the battery's roster as having been captured at Westminster on June 30, 1863. The commanding officer of the 1st Delaware Cavalry, Maj. Napoleon B. Knight, did not claim to have captured any Confederates and in fact reported sixty-seven of his own men killed, wounded, and captured. The last of Stuart's column left Westminster the morning of the thirtieth. Federal forces, elements of Gregg's cavalry division and Maj. Gen. John Sedgwick's VI Corps, reoccupied the town shortly after Stuart vacated it. Sergeant Murray and company had to have been captured by these troops, as there were no other Federal troops near the town. Matthews stated that it was the returning 1st Delaware that took his batterymates prisoner. However, there is no evidence that the 1st Delaware returned to Westminster on the thirtieth. Matthews probably assumed they did. Matthews, "Road into Maryland"; *C.S.R.V.,* microcopy M324, rolls 336, 337.
6. Francis Halsey Wigfall to Miss Louise Wigfall, July 18, 1863, Wigfall Papers.
7. No records indicate which battery of horse artillery rode with Chambliss's Brigade. McGregor is given here based upon several facts. The capture of the men from Breathed's Battery on the morning of the thirtieth in Westminster, when Gregg's cavalry arrived in town, would seem to suggest that Breathed was with the rear brigade, Hampton's. It is very doubtful that the men could or would have remained behind if their battery had left with Chambliss, who had the advance. Additionally, one account of the battle stated that Hampton placed four guns in position in Mount Olivet Cemetery. It is far more likely that Breathed's complete battery was with Hampton, as opposed to one section of Breathed's and McGregor's section. Finally, in his account of the battle, John Esten Cooke, Stuart's ordnance officer, referred to Breathed's presence on the field only after recording Hampton's arrival. Prior to that, when Cooke wrote of the artillery, he did not give the name of its commander. Though the evidence is circumstantial, it does appear

more likely that McGregor's section opened the battle, with Breathed entering the fight upon Hampton's arrival. It should also be noted that Fitz Lee did not have any horse artillery with him that day. William F. Fox, *New York at Gettysburg* (Albany, NY: J. B. Lyon Company, Printers, 1900), 117; William Anthony, *History of the Battle of Hanover, Tuesday, June 30, 1863* (Hanover, PA: The Historical Publication Committee of the Hanover Chamber of Commerce, 1945), 66; Beale, *Lieutenant in Lee's Army,* 104–5; Cooke, *Wearing of the Gray,* 240–42.

8. The first shell Breathed fired fell into the town, striking the house of Henry Winebrenner on Frederick Street. It passed through a balcony door, smashed a bureau, penetrated both the floor and the ceiling, and struck the brick wall of the northeast corner of the sitting room, where Winebrenner's family had taken shelter. The shell failed to explode. Unafraid, Mr. Winebrenner picked up the twelve-pound projectile and tossed it into the yard. The only casualties were the family's nerves. *Encounter at Hanover: Prelude to Gettysburg* (Hanover, PA: Historical Publication Committee of the Hanover Chamber of Commerce, 1985), 50–51.
9. Nye, *Here Come the Rebels,* 190; *Encounter at Hanover,* 62.
10. *Encounter at Hanover,* 61–62.
11. J. H. Kidd, *Personal Recollections of a Cavalryman* (Ionia, MI: Sentinel Printing Company, 1908), 127.
12. If Breathed had indeed been at Dover to do this, he would have had to have left Hanover with Fitz Lee's Brigade, which moved out first and reached Dover hours before Hampton. The only source for this fact is a short article titled "Four Hours Till Noon," by an unknown author.
13. Ibid.
14. Breathed is given here for several reasons. He was probably still accompanying Fitz Lee when that officer's command left Dover. Stuart's assistant engineer officer, Lt. Frank S. Robertson, wrote in his memoirs that "a battery" was run up to fire on the town. Finally, the roster for Breathed's Battery shows one private wounded at Carlisle. Reade, Blackford, and Trout, *In the Saddle with Stuart,* 78; *C.S.R.V.,* microcopy M324, roll 337.

    McGregor's participation in the bombardment cannot be verified. Shreve wrote in his reminiscences that his brother, Richard, who had graduated from the cavalry school in 1860, was at Carlisle and "pointed out the various localities" with which he was familiar. This could mean that McGregor's guns were there, either firing or for support, or that Richard rode to Carlisle to render whatever assistance he could. Considering that McGregor had been in action at Hanover hours longer than Breathed and that he must have expended a considerable amount of his ammunition supply, it is doubtful that he participated in the shelling of Carlisle. As has been suggested, he may have been in support of Breathed. Shreve, "Stuart Horse Artillery," 10.
15. There is confusion as to whether the Confederate artillery fired before Lee sent in his officers to demand Smith's surrender. Some sources stated that Lee had a few shells lobbed in the town's general direction to rattle nerves, in the hope that he would not have to face a prolonged engagement. Other sources recorded that Lee fired only after Smith rejected his offer. In his report, Stuart wrote that the offer of surrender preceded his shelling of the town. Longacre, *Cavalry at Gettysburg,* 196; Nye, *Here Come the Rebels,* 325; Reade, Blackford, and Trout, *In the Saddle with Stuart,* 78; Lt. Woodruff Jones, "Defending Pennsylvania against Lee," *CWTI* 5, no. 6 (October 1966): 41; Beale, *9th Virginia Cavalry,* 72; Beale, *Lieutenant in Lee's Army,* 114; Cooke, *Wearing of the Gray,* 245; *O.R.,* ser. 1, vol. 27, part 2, 696–97.
16. Jones, "Defending Pennsylvania," 43.

17. Yates is the only casualty listed on the battery's roster. As with other casualty reports, there may have been others. Lieutenant Jones of the Philadelphia Battery wrote that a Federal who had been a prisoner and a contraband reported the Confederate battery had eight men killed or wounded and its horses scattered. There is nothing to support this claim. *C.S.R.V.*, microcopy M324, roll 337; Jones, "Defending Pennsylvania," 43.
18. Francis Halsey Wigfall to Miss Louise Wigfall, July 18, 1863, Wigfall Papers.
19. These dates are from the history of the battery by Hart, Stephens, Sherfesee, and Schwing. In his short history of the battery, Hart gave the date on which the battery reached Martinsburg as the twenty-fourth and the date it reached Lee near Chambersburg as the twenty-sixth. This is an error. Lee was not at Chambersburg until the twenty-eighth. Hart et al., "Hart's Battery," 50; Hart, *Hart's Battery,* 11.

    Alexander Wood of Hart's Battery claimed that his gun, the first one disabled in the fighting on the twenty-first, was taken over the mountains and repaired on the twenty-second. Saussy, "Campaigning with Stuart," 157.
20. There is no evidence to suggest that Hart received a replacement for the lost gun at this time.
21. Artificers were blacksmiths.
22. In his history of the battery, Hart wrote that three disabled guns were repaired at this time. This is a contradiction of his earlier statement in the same history that "every piece but one was disabled and two were dismounted and borne off on the caissons" and is undoubtedly an error unless the last gun of the battery was damaged at the fight at Goose Creek. Hart, *Hart's Battery,* 11.
23. The manner in which the guns were repaired is worth recording: "For new axles, heavy bars of 'U' railroad rail, taken from the B & O track, were cut the required lengths, and the spindles of the old axles welded on to those. The convex surface of this hollow rail was inserted in the new axle boxes, the bands and straps readjusted to fit; broken spokes and fellies in the wheels replaced, and other repairs completed after several hours of arduous work." Hart et al., "Hart's Battery," 50.
24. Neese, *Confederate Horse Artillery,* 184; Bradshaw, *Diary of McVicar,* 16.
25. Chew's Battery actually camped three miles south of Martinsburg. Moorman's Battery, and very likely McGregor's section, was about two miles outside of town on the farm of the Hon. Charles James Faulkner. Charles McVicar to Miss Katie McVicar, July 11, 1863, Letters of Charles McVicar, with permission of Mrs. Ada Bruce Desper Bradshaw and courtesy of the Winchester-Frederick County Historical Society Collection; Neese, *Confederate Horse Artillery,* 185; Bradshaw, *Diary of McVicar,* 17; Shoemaker, *Shoemaker's Battery,* 43; Nunnelee, *Famous Company,* 83.
26. Chew undoubtedly was taking a side trip to his own home in Charles Town.
27. James H. Williams to Cora DeMovelle (Pritchartt) Williams, July 1, 1863, Williams Papers.
28. Shoemaker recorded that the crossing at Williamsport was opposed by Federal artillery on the north bank and that his battery only crossed the river on July 2 after the enemy had gone. This is not supported by any other source. Nunnelee stated that the battery crossed on the first and made no reference to meeting any resistance. Jones made no mention of it in his report, and neither did Neese or McVicar in their diaries. Shoemaker, *Shoemaker's Battery,* 44; *O.R.,* ser. 1, vol. 27, part 2, 752; Nunnelee, *Famous Company,* 83; Neese, *Confederate Horse Artillery,* 186; Bradshaw, *Diary of McVicar,* 17.
29. Bradshaw, *Diary of McVicar,* 17; Nunnelee, *Famous Company,* 83.
30. Charles McVicar to Miss Katie McVicar, July 11, 1863, McVicar Letters.
31. Bradshaw, *Diary of McVicar,* 17.

32. Shoemaker, *Shoemaker's Battery,* 44; Nunnelee, *Famous Company,* 84.
33. In his report of the campaign, Jones stated that on June 29, he had detached the 12th Virginia Cavalry to picket toward Harpers Ferry. This was the only regiment separated from his brigade. Therefore, Robertson must have used part of his brigade to execute Lee's orders. As far as can be determined, no artillery was sent with this detachment. *O.R.,* ser. 1, vol. 27, part 2, 751–52.
34. Ibid., 752.
35. Ibid.; Paul M. Shevchuk, "The Cavalry Fight at Fairfield, Pennsylvania, July 3, 1863," *Gettysburg Magazine,* no. 1 (July 1989): 110–11; McDonald, *Laurel Brigade,* 154–55; Longacre, *Cavalry at Gettysburg,* 235–37.
36. There is the possibility that Chew's guns were not engaged. In a letter to his sister, Charles McVicar wrote that the battery was not engaged because of the hand-to-hand fighting between the two forces. Support for this view comes from Jones himself. His report does not credit Chew with firing on the Federals and seems to indicate that the charge of the 7th Virginia was followed rapidly by the charge of the 6th, which succeeded. Capt. William N. McDonald, in his history of the Laurel Brigade, also claimed that the charge of the 6th Virginia came almost immediately after the repulse of the 7th. Neither Maj. Cabell E. Flournoy, commanding the 6th, nor Lt. Col. Thomas Marshall, who led the 7th, mentioned his regiment engaging in small-arms skirmishing. In fact, Flournoy wrote that his regiment was in column of squadrons, hardly a skirmishing formation. Both recorded that the charge of the 6th Virginia was made upon the heels of the 7th's retreat. No Federal officer filed a report. A history of the 6th U.S. Cavalry written in 1896 does state that the Federals faced artillery fire. If Chew did fire his guns during this occasion, it was only a handful of rounds. Neese, *Confederate Horse Artillery,* 188; Charles McVicar to Miss Katie McVicar, July 11, 1863, McVicar Letters; McDonald, *Laurel Brigade,* 154–55; *O.R.,* ser. 1, vol. 27, part 2, 752, 756, 760; William H. Carter, "The Sixth Regiment of Cavalry," *Maine Bugle* 3 (October 1896): 299.
37. Nunnelee recorded that Moorman's Battery camped on the site of the battle. Nunnelee, *Famous Company,* 85.
38. Nunnelee reported hearing it while grazing the battery's horses near Cashtown. Ibid.
39. Neese, *Confederate Horse Artillery,* 188.

Chapter 18

1. Griffin's and Jackson's Batteries had marched from Carlisle, trailing after Ewell's infantry. On the morning of June 30, one of Jackson's guns had been sent to Mechanicsburg with a company of the 14th Virginia Cavalry to hold the town and to tear up railroad track until ordered otherwise. Federal skirmishers annoyed the workers, and Jackson, who was with the gun, was ordered to lob a few shells into the woods to disperse the enemy. These were the last artillery shots fired in the vicinity of Harrisburg. That evening, orders came to pull back to Carlisle. Jackson's Battery was assigned the rear guard, along with Maj. Vincent A. Witcher's 34th Virginia Battalion. Griffin was with the main body of Jenkins's cavalry and therefore reached Gettysburg in advance of Jackson. Paul M. Shevchuk, "The Wounding of Albert Jenkins, July 2, 1863," *Gettysburg Magazine,* no. 3 (July 1990): 56; Lt. Hermann Schuricht, "Jenkins's Brigade in the Gettysburg Campaign," *SHSP* 24 (1896): 343–44.
2. Shevchuk, "Wounding of Jenkins," 58.
3. Hart et al., "Hart's Battery," 51; David L. Ladd and Aubrey J. Ladd, *The Bachelder Papers: Gettysburg in Their Own Words* (Dayton: Morningside House, 1994–95), vol. 2, 1215.

4. Ladd and Ladd, *Bachelder Papers,* vol. 2, 1215.
5. This hill is now known as Barlow's Knoll.
6. Shevchuk, "Wounding of Jenkins," 60–61.
7. Petersburg is now York Springs.
8. Schuricht, "Jenkins's Brigade," 344–45.
9. Griffin and Jackson were in the area, but at the time, Jenkins's Brigade had not been placed under Stuart's command. Furthermore, Stuart may not have known that these batteries were with Jenkins or their location.
10. *O.R.,* ser. 1, vol. 27, part 2, 495, 497, 724.
11. Ibid., 697.
12. Ibid.
13. Ibid., 497.
14. McGregor still had only one section with him. The other was with Jones and Robertson.
15. In describing his participation in the cavalry fight on the third, Woods never claimed that he was in command of the battery. In fact, he confirmed Jackson's presence. Micajah Woods to Dr. John R. Woods, July 16, 1863, Woods Papers.
16. Matthews, "Road into Maryland."
17. Stuart's adjutant, H. B. McClellan, is the main source for this action, but he credits Griffin's Battery with firing the shots. H. H. Matthews of Breathed's Battery claimed that the gun belonged to Jackson's Battery and was under the command of Lieutenant Woods. Matthews was not present, being back with Breathed's Battery refilling the ammunition chests, and Woods, the officer mentioned by Matthews, provided a detailed account of his battery's participation in the battle but did not claim that a gun from his battery fired these shots. Nevertheless, it does appear that the gun was from Jackson's Battery. McClellan, *I Rode with Stuart,* 338; Matthews, "Road into Maryland."
18. *O.R.,* ser. 1, vol. 27, part 2, 724.
19. Ibid., part 1, 956.
20. Woods's guns were near the end of the woods overlooking the Rummel farm. Blain was most likely somewhat north and a bit separated from Woods, as Blain suffered no damage from the bombardment that devastated Woods. When he arrived, Green occupied Jackson's original position.
21. Kevin E. O'Brien, "'Glory Enough for All': Lt. William Brooke-Rawle and the 3rd Pennsylvania Cavalry at Gettysburg," *Gettysburg Magazine,* no. 13 (July 1995): 96; Micajah Woods to Dr. John R. Woods, July 10, 1863, Woods Papers; *O.R.,* ser. 1, vol. 27, part 2, 497.
22. *O.R.,* ser. 1, vol. 27, part 1, 1051.
23. Woods claimed that his gun alone suffered casualties. Blain may have been withdrawn simply because he could not respond to the Federal artillery. Micajah Woods to Dr. John R. Woods, July 10, 1863, Woods Papers.
24. In his book, H. B. McClellan does not credit Jackson's Battery with participating in this action. He instead names Griffin's Battery. However, after the war, McClellan admitted mistaking Griffin's Battery for Jackson's. McClellan, *I Rode with Stuart,* 338; Ladd and Ladd, *Bachelder Papers,* vol. 3, 1384–85.
25. This infantry was probably the dismounted skirmishers of Custer's and McIntosh's Brigade.
26. Maj. Lewis Frank Terrell had been a member of Stuart's staff. He had been assigned to court-martial duty but longed for a post in the horse artillery. He expected to be selected as the replacement for Pelham. When this did not happen, Terrell asked to be transferred. One source claimed that he was assigned as chief of artillery to Maj. Gen. Isaac R. Trimble, which was a hollow position, since at the time Trimble had no command. Why Woods referred to Terrell as a battalion commander is unknown. Trout, *They Followed the Plume,* 259.

27. Micajah Woods to Dr. John R. Woods, July 10, 1863, Woods Papers.
28. Woods was mistaken. Bragg did command Ringgold's Battery (Battery C, 3rd U.S. Artillery) in Mexico. However, that battery was under the command of Lt. William D. Fuller at the time of the battle of Gettysburg and was in Manchester, Maryland, on July 3. It did not participate in the battle at all. *O.R.,* ser. 1, vol. 27, part 1, 1035.
29. Micajah Woods to Dr. John R. Woods, July 16, 1863, Woods Papers.
30. Hampton was emphatic in his report that the three Confederate cavalry brigades had only two pieces of artillery supporting them. He may not have known that Jackson had been engaged earlier, but it is apparent that for most of the battle in the middle and late afternoon, only Green's section was on the field. *O.R.,* ser. 1, vol. 27, part 2, 724.
31. Ladd and Ladd, *Bachelder Papers,* vol. 3, 1381–83.
32. Matthews, "Road into Maryland."
33. Just when Breathed and McGregor arrived is a point of conjecture. Certainly the earlier artillery duel was long over, and the cavalry fighting was either in full fury or beginning to taper off.
34. The battery's roster lists only one man, Samuel J. Shaffer, wounded. *C.S.R.V.,* microcopy M324, rolls 336, 337.
35. Matthews overly dramatized his battery's participation in the fight. Breathed and McGregor did reach the field. However, their involvement was minimal, being relegated to the closing firing between the opposing batteries. Lt. Francis H. Wigfall of McGregor's Battery recorded, "We were engaged on the third only of the fight at Gettysburg with a battery of the enemy at long range." Matthews, "Road into Maryland"; Francis Halsey Wigfall to Louis T. Wigfall, July 7, 1863, Wigfall Papers.
36. *Supp. to the O.R.,* part 1, vol. 5, 285.
37. Micajah Woods to Dr. John R. Woods, July 10, 1863, Woods Papers.
38. Edwin B. Coddington, *The Gettysburg Campaign: A Study in Command* (New York, Charles Scribner's Sons, 1968), 524; Hart et al., "Hart's Battery," 51; Ladd and Ladd, *Bachelder Papers,* vol. 2, 1215.
39. Longacre, *Cavalry at Gettysburg,* 240.
40. Hart et al., "Hart's Battery," 51.
41. Hart wrote two letters to John B. Bachelder. In his first correspondence, he recalled that his battery took position on the southeastern slope of a hill "just beyond the Kern House." In his second letter, Hart was more exact and recorded that he passed the Kern and the Currens houses, unlimbering just beyond. Ladd and Ladd, *Bachelder Papers,* vol. 2, 1215–17.
42. Hart was himself confused about who gave the order. In one source he stated that Law gave this order, and in another that Black gave it. Hart et al., "Hart's Battery," 51; Ladd and Ladd, *Bachelder Papers,* vol. 2, 1215.
43. Black stated that Hart had only two guns. Hart wrote nothing that would support or refute this, but it is highly unlikely that Hart left his third piece behind when sent to the right. Ladd and Ladd, *Bachelder Papers,* vol. 2, 1241.
44. Ibid., 1217.
45. *O.R.,* ser. 1, vol. 27, part 2, 402–3.
46. Some sources credit Hart with firing on Farnsworth, but he did not claim to have done so. Both Hart and Black agree that they were off to the west facing Merritt. Kathy Georg Harrison, "Ridges of Grim War," *Blue and Gray Magazine* 5, no. 6 (July 1988): 32; James F. Hart to John B. Bachelder, March 3 and 5, 1886, Bachelder Papers; Ladd and Ladd, *Bachelder Papers,* vol. 2, 1241.
47. Ladd and Ladd, *Bachelder Papers,* vol. 2, 1217.
48. Micajah Woods to Dr. John R. Woods, July 16, 1863, Woods Papers.

Chapter 19

1. One source stated that Imboden claimed to have only 200 men, including McClanahan's Battery. This would appear to be in error. McClanahan had about 100 men himself, which would have left Imboden with a cavalry force of the same number. Harold R. Woodward, Jr., *Defender of the Valley: Brigadier General John Daniel Imboden, C.S.A.* (Berryville, VA: Rockbridge Publishing Company, 1996), 79.
2. Woodward, *Defender of the Valley,* 79–80; John D. Imboden, "The Confederate Retreat from Gettysburg," *BLCW,* part 21 (1884): 422.
3. In his recollection of the retreat, Imboden incorrectly named Col. Pierce M. B. Young as commander of Hampton's Brigade. Imboden, "Confederate Retreat," 422.
4. Nunnelee, *Famous Company,* 85.
5. Neese, *Confederate Horse Artillery,* 190.
6. Bradshaw, *Diary of McVicar,* 18.
7. Neese, *Confederate Horse Artillery,* 191–92.
8. Stuart referred to Smithsburg as Smithtown. *O.R.,* ser. 1, vol. 27, part 2, 700.
9. W. W. Goldsborough's account of this action credits Griffin with participating in a heavy artillery duel at "point blank range," which saved a column of infantry and a wagon train. Stuart's report was much closer to the truth. There is no record of Jackson's Battery's role in this phase of the retreat. However, it probably accompanied Ferguson's column, since Griffin was with Chambliss. Goldsborough, *Maryland Line,* 285; *O.R.,* ser. 1, vol. 27, part 2, 700.
10. Imboden wrote that the axes were wielded by civilians, who were either driven off or captured. Dahlgren supposedly took the axes his men used from nearby farmers. Imboden, *Confederate Retreat,* 425.
11. One source claimed that the guns were from Eshleman's Battery, but the major's own report states that he tried to push forward a section under Capt. Joseph Norcom but failed to arrive in time. Imboden recorded that the guns were from McClanahan's Battery. Longacre, *Cavalry at Gettysburg,* 254; *O.R.,* ser. 1, vol. 27, part 2, 437; Imboden, "Confederate Retreat," 425.
12. This may have been the same incident as that related by General Imboden. Driver, *Staunton Artillery,* 77.
13. During the march, Hart's Battery received an unexpected addition to its complement of guns. Just before the battery passed through the gap in the South Mountain on July 5, two U.S. three-inch rifled pieces that had been abandoned by Capt. Victor Maurin's Donaldsonville (Louisiana) Artillery, the horses having broken down, were hitched to Hart's spare horses. How Hart had managed to retain some spare horses is a mystery. The guns were used at Williamsport on July 6. *O.R.,* ser. 1, vol. 27, part 2, 654–55; Hart et al., "Hart's Battery," 51.
14. The troops that attacked at Williamsport were actually from Buford's Cavalry Division. They only slightly outnumbered the Confederates, having about 3,500 men to about 3,000. *O.R.,* ser. 1, vol. 27, part 1, 928, 943; Longacre, *Cavalry at Gettysburg,* 255–56.
15. Imboden had much more cavalry than Hart credited him, though it may not all have been available.
16. Capt. J. B. Richardson of Maj. Benjamin F. Eshleman's Artillery Battalion acknowledged Sergeant Newton's gallantry in his report to his commanding officer, who included it in his account of the action. *O.R.,* ser. 1, vol. 27, part 2, 438.
17. Imboden cited Hart and Eshleman with providing much-needed assistance in bringing the Federal attack to a halt. Imboden, "Confederate Retreat," 427.
18. Hampton's Brigade was commanded by Col. Laurence S. Baker, not Young.
19. Hart et al., "Hart's Battery," 52–56.

20. The dispositions of the horse artillery batteries are based on reports and accounts of participants. No official record of the assignments of these batteries to specific brigades is extant. The routes of the various brigades appear in Stuart's report. *O.R.,* ser. 1, vol. 27, part 2, 701.
21. Shoemaker, *Shoemaker's Battery,* 46. Nunnelee recorded only that the enemy made a charge and retreated immediately. He gave no indication that he felt any of the guns threatened. However, he may not have been in a position to see how close the Federals came. Nunnelee, *Famous Company,* 87.
22. Shoemaker mistakenly credited Breathed's Battery with participating in this action. Breathed was with Fitz Lee's Brigade north of Williamsport.
23. Both McVicar and Neese called Leitersburg by different names: McVicar, Littlestown, and Neese, Lighterstown. Bradshaw, *Diary of McVicar,* 19; Neese, *Confederate Horse Artillery,* 193.
24. Bradshaw, *Diary of McVicar,* 18–19.
25. Colonel Richmond reported that the fire from Elder's Battery exploded one of Chew's caissons or limber chests. However, neither Neese nor McVicar mentioned any explosion as a result of this action. *O.R.,* ser. 1, vol. 27, part 1, 1006.
26. The participation of these batteries can be verified. Jackson's Battery probably was engaged as well, but no record exists to support this. Bradshaw, *Diary of McVicar,* 18–19; Neese, *Confederate Horse Artillery,* 193–96; Goldsborough, *Maryland Line,* 285; Shoemaker, *Shoemaker's Battery,* 46.
27. As he did on many occasions, Matthews claimed for Breathed what was actually accomplished by others. Stuart reported that a section of the Stuart Horse Artillery accompanied Robertson and Jenkins (Ferguson) as they rode parallel to Chambliss toward Williamsport. This was undoubtedly the section from McGregor's Battery that had been with Robertson and Jones. Further evidence to support this view comes from a letter written by Lt. Francis H. Wigfall to his father on July 7, 1863. He confirms his battery's arrival at Williamsport on the sixth during the fighting. However, he emphatically stated that his battery—Breathed's—was not engaged. This writer has altered Matthews's account, which appears to be accurate otherwise, by replacing McGregor's name for Breathed's. *O.R.,* ser. 1, vol. 27, part 2, 702; Francis Halsey Wigfall to Mr. Louis T. Wigfall, July 7, 1863, Wigfall Papers.
28. This change of position by Elder was similar to that of the Confederate horse artillery at the battles of Middleburg and Upperville. Elder was not forced to change his position by McGregor's fire but did so as a stratagem to cover Richmond's retreat.
29. H. H. Matthews, "From Gettysburg to Hagerstown, Williamsport and back to the Rappahannock," *St. Mary's Beacon,* April 27, 1905.
30. McVicar was with that part of the battery that went with Jones. Neese stayed in Williamsport, where his horses were shod. He did not reach Hagerstown until the eighth. Bradshaw, *Diary of McVicar,* 19; Neese, *Confederate Horse Artillery,* 196.
31. Nunnelee, *Famous Company,* 87.
32. One source stated that McGregor's Battery opened the fight at 5:00 A.M. This is a possibility, because a section of that battery had accompanied Robertson and Jones to Williamsburg. However, there is a greater probability that it was McVicar's section of Chew's Battery. McVicar recorded in his diary that the fighting opened "ugly and early" on the eighth. There is documentation that Chew's Battery did have a section with Jones the day before. Longacre, *Cavalry at Gettysburg,* 260; Bradshaw, *Diary of McVicar,* 19.
33. The participation of these batteries is documented. *O.R.,* ser. 1, vol. 27, part 2, 701–2; Hart et al., "Hart's Battery," 58; Micajah Woods to Dr. John R. Woods, July 10, 1863, Woods Papers.

Neese recorded that the Confederates had ten guns in action during the day: three from Chew's Battery, three from Hart's, two from McGregor's, and two from Jackson's. This division of guns is derived from the fact that Chew had three guns in his battery and both McVicar and Neese were engaged, that a section of McGregor's Battery had been with Jones and Robertson, that Hart had three guns with him ever since the fighting at Middleburg, and that Jackson's Battery had been reduced to two effective pieces. Neese, *Confederate Horse Artillery,* 197; Micajah Woods to Dr. John R. Woods, July 10, 1863, Woods Papers.

34. The identity of this section is unknown. Stuart mentions only two batteries in his report—McGregor's and Chew's—as having participated in this action. However, neither can be linked positively with this incident, and it could just as easily have been a section of Hart's or Jackson's battery. *O.R.,* ser. 1, vol. 27, part 2, 701–2, and part 1, 935.
35. Not surprisingly, none of the Confederates who kept diaries or wrote histories of their batteries admitted to changing position during the battle for any other reason than to pursue a retreating foe or because of a lack of ammunition.
36. This incident could not have happened close to nightfall, because the Federals counterattacked Stuart late in the afternoon and regained all the ground they had lost during the day.
37. Hart et al., "Hart's Battery," 58–59. Stuart may have been referring to this episode in his report when he wrote, "His [Buford's] batteries had been driven away from the hill by the Napoleons of McGregor's battery, which for close fighting, evinced this day their great superiority over rifled guns of greater number." *O.R.,* ser. 1, vol. 27, part 2, 703.
38. The identity of this battery is also unknown.
39. *O.R.,* ser. 1, vol. 27, part 1, 1033.
40. Ferguson retreated along the Williamsport Road.
41. Neither McVicar nor Neese wrote of this part of the fighting on the eighth. However, Stuart included it in his report and was undoubtedly a witness. *O.R.,* ser. 1, vol. 27, part 2, 704.
42. As far as can be determined, Breathed's, Moorman's, McClanahan's, and Griffin's Batteries and the other section of McGregor's Battery remained in the vicinity of Williamsport during the eighth. Nunnelee verifies Moorman's location there. Nunnelee, *Famous Company,* 87–88.
43. The only one in the battery named Bird was William M. Bird, whose service record does not indicate that he was wounded or taken prisoner during the Gettysburg campaign. *C.S.R.V,* microcopy M324, roll 273.
44. The only one in the battery with a similar name was Fountain D. Johnson, whose records do not show his capture during the Gettysburg campaign. Ibid.
45. James H. Williams to Cora DeMovelle (Pritchartt) Williams, July 8, 1863, Williams Papers.
46. McVicar wrote that he was "on picket in full view of the enemy" when the fighting began. Bradshaw, *Diary of McVicar,* 20.
47. Stuart failed to report this action, but the reports filed by Gamble, Devin, and others, in addition to McVicar's and Neese's accounts, confirm that it took place.
48. Neese, *Confederate Horse Artillery,* 197.
49. The locations of Breathed, Griffin, McClanahan, and the section of McGregor cannot be given with any certainty. Their participation in the cavalry fighting from the eighth to the twelfth is unverifiable due to the paucity of records. Those sources that are available, including letters, diaries, reminiscences, and battery histories, do not mention them as having fought with Stuart. Jennings C. Wise credited Breathed and Griffin with fighting on those dates but did not provide the source on

which he based his claim. Wise, *Long Arm of Lee,* 701; Shoemaker, *Shoemaker's Battery,* 47; Nunnelee, *Famous Company,* 88.

50. Phelps gives the wrong date here. The battery arrived at Cashtown on the third with the rest of Robertson's command, which included Chew's Battery. Pvt. George M. Neese of that battery confirmed that they reached Cashtown on the third, not the second. Neese, *Confederate Horse Artillery,* 187.
51. Charles R. Phelps, July 9, 1863, Phelps Letters.
52. The casualties to Calef's Battery were one man wounded and one horse killed. This indicates either poor firing on the part of Moorman or that the Confederates concentrated more on the enemy's dismounted skirmishers. *O.R.,* ser. 1, vol. 27, part 1, 1033.
53. Shoemaker, *Shoemaker's Battery,* 47–48.
54. Calef reported that at one point he faced eight enemy guns. *O.R.,* ser. 1, vol. 27, part 1, 1033.
55. White's report stated that the fire came from the Stuart Horse Artillery. This general reference could have meant Breathed's or McGregor's Battery or any of those in the battalion, since it was known as the Stuart Horse Artillery. *O.R.,* ser. 1, vol. 27, part 2, 398.
56. The only record that McClanahan's Battery was engaged in this skirmish is in a listing of the battery's engagements. Fox's report is the sole source of what happened. Ibid., 274–75.
57. "Res gestæ" means "things done."
58. Micajah Woods to Dr. John R. Woods, July 10, 1863, Woods Papers.
59. Chew's and Moorman's Battery can be placed in Williamsport on the eleventh. A section of Moorman's Battery returned to the front that same day, but Chew remained there until the thirteenth. Shoemaker, *Shoemaker's Battery,* 48; Bradshaw, *Diary of McVicar,* 20; Neese, *Confederate Horse Artillery,* 198; Nunnelee, *Famous Company,* 89.

Chapter 20

1. *O.R.,* ser. 1, vol. 27, part 2, 705; Hart et al., "Hart's Battery," 59.
2. Driver, *Staunton Artillery,* 80.
3. Driver, *1st Virginia Cavalry,* 68; Beale, *Lieutenant in Lee's Army,* 118; *O.R.,* ser. 1, vol. 27, part 2, 706.
4. McDonald, *Laurel Brigade,* 165.
5. Bradshaw, *Diary of McVicar,* 20; Neese, *Confederate Horse Artillery,* 199.
6. Shoemaker, *Shoemaker's Battery,* 49; Nunnelee, *Famous Company,* 91.
7. There is no documentation to place these batteries in this location. However, they had been serving with Fitz Lee's and Chambliss's Brigades and were probably still with them.
8. Goldsborough, *Maryland Line,* 285; Washington Hands, *Washington Hands Civil War* Notebook, Maryland Historical Society, 103.
9. In this, Woods reinforces Pelham's findings during the Chambersburg Raid. The big Pennsylvania farm horses were wonderfully strong and built for plowing. However, they failed miserably at withstanding the rigors of service in the horse artillery.
10. Micajah Woods to Dr. John R. Woods, July 16, 1863, Woods Papers.
11. Neese, *Confederate Horse Artillery,* 199–200; Tobie, *First Maine Cavalry,* 181; *O.R.,* ser. 1, vol. 27, part 1, 978.
12. *O.R.,* ser. 1, vol. 27, part 1, 955.

13. Neese, *Confederate Horse Artillery,* 200.
14. Only Shoemaker's section can be documented as having fought in this action. Breathed and McGregor most likely accompanied Lee and Chambliss, but only indirect references support this. Lt. G. W. Beale recalled seeing the artillery fire by the piece and then by sections, implying more than one section. The *Richmond Times Dispatch* credited Fitz Lee with only three pieces in the fight. A Federal account places the number of Confederate guns at eight, as does Colonel Gregg's report of the engagement. Shoemaker, *Shoemaker's Battery,* 49; Nunnelee, *Famous Company,* 91; Beale, *Lieutenant in Lee's Army,* 122; *Richmond Times Dispatch,* July 18, 1863; Tobie, *First Maine Cavalry,* 184; *O.R.,* ser. 1, vol. 27, part 1, 978.

    Breathed's Battery probably had only a section in the fight. Lt. Francis H. Wigfall recorded in a letter dated July 18, 1863, that the section under his immediate command was without ammunition since crossing the Potomac. It could not have participated in the engagement of the sixteenth. Francis Halsey Wigfall to Miss Louise Wigfall, July 18, 1863, Wigfall Papers.
15. The historian of the 1st Maine claimed that at one point, Lt. William P. Coleman led Companies B and K in a charge that drove some of the Confederate cannoneers from their guns. The scanty Confederate sources say nothing about this incident. Tobie, *First Maine Cavalry,* 182–84.
16. Beale, *Lieutenant in Lee's Army,* 122.
17. *O.R.,* ser. 1, vol. 27, part 1, 979, and part 2, 706.
18. Micajah Woods to Dr. John R. Woods, July 17, 1863, Woods Papers.
19. Francis Halsey Wigfall to Miss Louise Wigfall, July 18, 1863, Wigfall Papers.
20. *O.R.,* ser. 1, vol. 27, part 2, 534.
21. Micajah Woods to Mrs. Sabina Lewis Stuart Creigh Woods, July 20, 1863, Woods Papers.
22. *O.R.,* ser. 1, vol. 27, part 3, 743.
23. Bradshaw, *Diary of McVicar,* 21; Neese, *Confederate Horse Artillery,* 200.
24. Bradshaw, *Diary of McVicar,* 21; Neese, *Confederate Horse Artillery,* 200–202.
25. Though this letter is not dated, the events discussed are of this time period.
26. George W. Stewart was a member of Chew's Battery.
27. Charles McVicar to Mrs. Catherine Thatcher McVicar, n.d., Letters of Charles McVicar, with permission of Mrs. Ada Bruce Desper Bradshaw and courtesy of the Winchester-Frederick County Historical Society Collection.
28. The battery camped near Smithfield on the Nicholas Shaw farm from the seventeenth through twenty-first. On the twenty-second, it moved through Summit Point, Berryville, and Millwood, turned toward Ashby Gap, and camped on the farm of Walter Bowen about a mile and a half beyond Stone Bridge. Nunnelee declared the march "disagreeable." Nunnelee, *Famous Company,* 92.
29. Shoemaker, *Shoemaker's Battery,* 50; Nunnelee, *Famous Company,* 92.
30. Shoemaker, *Shoemaker's Battery,* 50. Nunnelee recorded that half of the battery and the battalion continued to march toward Gaines's Cross Roads on the twenty-fourth, not the twenty-fifth, as Shoemaker reported. Nunnelee, *Famous Company,* 93.
31. This division is based on several sources. In his history of the battery, Shoemaker wrote that his section and part of the battalion were sent to Gaines's Cross Roads, while Phelps's section and the remainder of the battalion rode on to Culpeper County, through Thornton's Gap. According to Nunnelee, Phelps reached the vicinity of Culpeper on July 26. In a letter dated July 30, Lieutenant Wigfall of Breathed's Battery wrote that his battery arrived in Culpeper on July 26. On this evidence, it would appear that the batteries marched as suggested. Shoemaker, *Shoemaker's Battery,* 50; Nunnelee, *Famous Company,* 93; Francis Halsey Wigfall to Mrs. Louis T. Wigfall, July 30, 1863, Wigfall Papers.

The horse artillery's use of Thornton's Gap also meant that Fitz Lee's, Chambliss's, and Ferguson's Brigades had no artillery with them when they crossed the mountains at Chester Gap. There is evidence to support this view. Stuart's report stated that the cavalry reached Chester Gap only by taking a bypath and then, "with great difficulty and a forced march, that night bivouacked below Gaines's Cross Roads." The order for Shoemaker's section and a part of the battalion to ride to Gaines's Cross Roads was given to reunite at least part of the horse artillery with the cavalry. *O.R.*, ser. 1, vol. 27, part 2, 707.

Sgt. George W. Shreve mentioned in his reminiscences that his battery, McGregor's, crossed the Blue Ridge at Luray Gap. This is an error of location, as Luray Gap penetrates the Massanutten Mountain west of Luray. Shreve obviously meant Thornton's Gap, which lies east of Luray. Shreve, "Stuart Horse Artillery," 10.

32. Shoemaker recorded that Phelps's contingent crossed the mountains at Thoroughfare Gap. There is a Thoroughfare Gap in the Blue Ridge, but it is well north and east of Oak Hill and would have required considerable countermarching and time to reach it. Furthermore, what is there today is little more than a trail or farm road. No road may have existed at all during the war. Shoemaker undoubtedly was mistaken when he wrote that Phelps crossed over the mountains via this route. Shoemaker, *Shoemaker's Battery,* 50.
33. Ibid.
34. The history of the battery by Hart et al. states that it crossed the Blue Ridge at Chester Gap. While not impossible, this is highly unlikely, as it would have required the battery to ride from Luray back up the Page Valley almost to Front Royal, when it easily could have crossed the Blue Ridge at Thornton Gap just east of Luray, bringing it considerably closer to Culpeper Court House, its ultimate destination. The route taken by the battery was the same as that of Early's division until it crossed the Massanutten, when the infantry swung south to cross the Blue Ridge at Fisher's Gap. Hart et al., "Hart's Battery," 60; *O.R.,* ser. 1, vol. 27, part 2, 473.
35. The Rossers had been married on May 28, 1863.
36. Cunningham was on Hood's staff. The general had been severely wounded at Gettysburg.
37. Francis Halsey Wigfall to Mrs. Louis T. Wigfall, July 30, 1863, Wigfall Papers.

Chapter 21

1. Bradshaw, *Diary of McVicar,* 21; Neese, *Confederate Horse Artillery,* 202.
2. Francis Halsey Wigfall to Mrs. Louis T. Wigfall, August 13, 1863, Wigfall Papers.
3. Though the guns were moved around during this time, their camp remained in the vicinity of Salem Church. Nunnelee thought the entire movement was due to a rumor about a possible Federal crossing of the Rappahannock. He took time to visit Fredericksburg and the grave of George Washington's mother, amply illustrating that the report was without substance. Shoemaker, *Shoemaker's Battery,* 50–51; Nunnelee, *Famous Company,* 93–97.
4. Hart et al., "Hart's Battery," 60.
5. Ibid.
6. McGregor's Battery may have been with Hart on Fleetwood Hill. There are five accounts or references to the fighting of August 1, written by men of the three batteries involved—Hart's, McGregor's, and Chew's—but each writer only gives credit to his own battery. Sgt. George W. Shreve's version hints that McGregor's Battery was in the fight from the beginning. More likely, it was encamped on the Botts farm and came into the fight at this point. Shreve, "Stuart Horse Artillery," 11.

7. Buford's report is the only official account of this fight. He failed to mention what artillery accompanied him. The history of Hart's Battery placed the enemy artillery at three batteries. Neese recorded that he saw two Federal batteries when his gun entered the fight. *O.R.*, ser. 1, vol. 27, part 1, 932; Hart et al., "Hart's Battery," 61; Neese, *Confederate Horse Artillery,* 203.
8. Hart et al., "Hart's Battery," 61–62.
9. Shreve, "Stuart Horse Artillery," 11.
10. McVicar's section was relieved from picket duty along the Hazel River sometime after 10:00 A.M. At 1:00 P.M., his section was moving toward Culpeper. Since Baker was still responsible for picketing the river, it is doubtful that he brought his whole brigade. He probably left at least one regiment and a section of Chew's Battery on watch. Bradshaw, *Diary of McVicar,* 21.
11. Ibid., 21–22.
12. *O.R.*, ser. 1, vol. 27, part 1, 932.
13. Hart et al., "Hart's Battery," 62.
14. Shreve recorded that he stayed with Burwell in a house in Culpeper the night of the first. According to Shreve, Burwell had every hope of "getting well and returning to us [the battery] soon." Shreve gave Burwell's place of death as his family's home, Glenvin, near Millwood in Clarke County. Two other sources gave the location as a hospital in Staunton, which seems more likely, as his home would have been behind enemy lines. Shreve, "Stuart Horse Artillery," 11; J. E. Norris, ed., *History of the Lower Shenandoah Valley Counties of Frederick, Berkeley, Jefferson, and Clarke* (Chicago: A. Warner & Co., 1890), 649; Jones, "Major Henry," 56.
15. Hart et al., "Hart's Battery," 62.
16. Phelps's recollection of the days on which the fighting at Brandy Station took place is somewhat confusing when compared with other accounts. The dates of the Monday, Thursday, and Saturday actions would have been August 3, 6, and 8. No fighting, except for possible picket exchanges, took place on those dates in the vicinity of Brandy Station. Phelps's reference to the fight of Tuesday, August 4, however, is accurate. Charles R. Phelps, August 10, 1863, Phelps Letters.
17. Ibid.
18. Evidently, the Whitworth that had been damaged at Aldie had been repaired and was again ready for service. In the fighting on August 4, the Federals reported that the enemy had a Whitworth gun that was in the action. *O.R.*, ser. 1, vol. 29, part 1, 21.
19. Moorman's lone gun was commanded by Lieutenant Shoemaker, Moorman being absent from the battery.
20. If Buford's report that he faced six guns is accurate, then Griffin had two. *O.R.*, ser. 1, vol. 29, part 1, 22.
21. Hoxton was a member of Breathed's Battery, which was not engaged. His duties as battalion adjutant would have placed him in the fight. This is also an indication that Beckham was probably there as well.
22. Francis Halsey Wigfall to Mrs. Louis T. Wigfall, August 13, 1863, Wigfall Papers.
23. Shoemaker recorded that Poindexter was killed outright, but Phelps's version is probably the more accurate. Shoemaker, *Shoemaker's Battery,* 51.
24. Bradshaw, *Diary of McVicar,* 23.
25. Williams was speaking of having a photograph taken of him, which Miss Pritchartt had requested.
26. James H. Williams to Cora DeMovelle (Pritchartt) Williams, August 6, 1863, Williams Papers.
27. Hart et al., "Hart's Battery," 62.
28. Apparently, this was the time when the gun lost on June 21 was replaced.

29. At least part of Breathed's Battery was downriver near Fredericksburg. Hart's location is unknown. Bradshaw, *Diary of McVicar,* 23–24; Neese, *Confederate Horse Artillery,* 206–7; Shoemaker, *Shoemaker's Battery,* 52.
30. Stewart was a fellow private in the battery.
31. This exchange took place before August 9. On that date, the 8th Illinois was pulled back across the Rappahannock. Hard, *Eighth Illinois,* 269.
32. Charles McVicar to Miss Katie McVicar, August 18, 1863, McVicar Letters.
33. Charles McVicar to Miss Annie Campbell, August 29, 1863, McVicar Letters.
34. Lt. Edmond H. Moorman.
35. Charles R. Phelps, August 30, 1863, Phelps Letters.
36. If this number includes the guns of all six batteries, the battalion was ten pieces under its full complement. This seems most unlikely. A more probable explanation would be that Beckham was counting only the pieces of those batteries that were available for duty at the time. *O.R.,* ser. 1, vol. 29, part 2, 61.
37. All of the batteries were encamped in Culpeper County at this time. Why Breathed's and Hart's Batteries do not appear to have stood picket duty is unknown. They may have been stationed elsewhere than on Fleetwood Hill. Hart was requisitioning enough corn to feed 118 horses, so his battery was certainly mobile. At the same time, he was requisitioning shoes, jackets, pants, and caps for his men. *Compiled Service Records of Confederate Soldiers Who Served in Organizations from the State of South Carolina* (Washington, DC, 1961), microcopy M267, roll 98.

    The horse returns for the other batteries are interesting as well. Breathed reported having 35 horses and 8 mules on August 26. Chew had 120 on the fourteenth. McGregor received 36 horses and 21 mules on the twenty-sixth, which illustrates how few he had previously. Moorman reported on the thirty-first that his battery had 80 horses. The report for Griffin's Battery is missing. *C.S.R.V,* microcopy M324, rolls 267, 273, 336, 337, and 338.
38. Charles McVicar to Miss Katie McVicar, September 1, 1863, McVicar Letters.
39. Llewellyn Griffith Hoxton had attended the U.S. Military Academy before the war. He served as an artillery officer in the western armies and rose to the rank of lieutenant colonel.
40. William Hoxton to Llewellyn G. Hoxton, September 5, 1863, Randolph Papers.
41. *O.R.,* ser. 1, vol. 29, part 1, 401–2.
42. Maj. Gen. Alfred Pleasonton commanded the Cavalry Corps of the Army of the Potomac. He had the divisions of Brig. Gen. John Buford, Brig. Gen. David McM. Gregg, Brig. Gen. H. Judson Kilpatrick, and Brig. Gen. Wesley Merritt's Reserve Brigade. His horse artillery consisted of Lt. Albert O. Vincent's Battery B/L, 2nd U.S. Artillery, and Lt. Edward B. Williston's Battery D, 2nd U.S. Artillery, attached to Buford's division; Capt. Joseph W. Martin's 6th New York Light Battery and Lt. Horatio B. Reed's Battery A, 4th U.S. Artillery, attached to Gregg's division; and Lt. Alexander C. M. Pennington's Battery M, 2nd U.S. Artillery, and Capt. Samuel S. Elder's Battery E, 4th U.S. Artillery, attached to Kilpatrick's division. *O.R.,* ser. 1, vol. 29, part 1, 224–25.
43. B. T. Holliday, *The Account of My Capture,* Chew Papers.
44. Kilpatrick reported that he had encountered a battery of three guns near Brandy Station. Sgt. George W. Shreve recorded that his battery had been engaged in an artillery duel on Fleetwood Hill during the opening stage of the fight. If Shreve is correct in his recollection and Kilpatrick in the number of guns that he faced, then McGregor probably had just one section on the hill with Chew's single piece. This would be in keeping with sending only one section of a battery at a time to do picket duty while the second section rested. *O.R.,* ser. 1, vol. 29, part 1, 118; Shreve, "Stuart Horse Artillery," 11; Holliday, *My Capture.*

45. In his reminiscences, Pvt. Washington Hands wrote that Beckham was ordered to put his guns in position near Muddy Run. Unfortunately, the only battery Hands mentioned was Griffin's. Hands Notebook, 103.
46. Holliday's failure to mention any artillery exchange does not negate either Shreve's or Kilpatrick's statements. It just could mean that McGregor's section was stationed elsewhere on Fleetwood Hill and engaged with another portion of Kilpatrick's force.
47. Despite having attended VMI for two years, Holliday does not appear to have had a working knowledge of artillery equipment. As his tenure with Chew's Battery lasted only eight days, he did not have time to learn much about the equipment, either. He could not have been holding on to the trunnions while riding on the limber chest. The trunnions are part of the gun tube. Holliday was probably holding on to the handles of the limber chest.
48. Holliday, *My Capture.*
49. *O.R.,* ser. 1, vol. 29, part 1, 124.
50. Holliday, *My Capture.*
51. *O.R.,* ser. 1, vol. 29, part 1, 118. Capt. Willard Glazier, who led one of the charges that day near Brandy Station, wrote, "Three men and four horses were killed and wounded in this [Glazier's] company by the first discharge of the enemy's artillery, whose fire was terribly accurate." Willard Glazier, *Three Years in the Federal Cavalry* (New York: R. H. Ferguson & Company, 1874), 321.
52. *C.S.R.V,* microcopy M324, roll 273.
53. Ibid., rolls 337, 338.
54. Hands Notebook, 103–4.
55. *O.R.,* ser. 1, vol. 29, part 1, 118–19, 129.
56. *Compiled Service Records of Confederate Soldiers Who Served in Organizations from the State of Maryland* (Washington, DC, 1961), microcopy M321, rolls 10, 11.
57. Captain McGregor was not in command of the battery at this time. The wound he had received on November 10, 1862, was not healing. He had returned to his home in Talledaga, Alabama, to recuperate. The granting of his application for an extension of his medical furlough dated September 18, 1863, provides proof of this. *C.S.R.V,* microcopy M324, roll 267.
58. Shreve, "Stuart Horse Artillery," 11–12.
59. *C.S.R.V,* microcopy M324, roll 267.
60. One source claimed that Hart's Battery did not cross the river until the morning of the fourteenth. This is very possible, since most of the Federal cavalry encamped around Pony Mountain. *O.R.,* ser. 1, vol. 29, part 1, 121, 124, 126–28, 130.
61. These probably were from Griffin's and McGregor's Batteries.
62. Nunnelee, *Famous Company,* 103–4.
63. James H. Williams to Cora DeMovelle (Pritchartt) Williams, September 15, 1863, Williams Papers.

Chapter 22

1. Bradshaw, *Diary of McVicar,* 25; Charles R. Phelps, September 18, 1863, Phelps Letters.
2. The battery would remain here until the nineteenth, when Griffin's Battery replaced it. There was a short engagement on the eighteenth with the enemy cavalry. Nunnelee reported that a few shots dispersed them, and another fifteen to twenty convinced them that they had little to gain in trying to force the ford. Shoemaker, *Shoemaker's Battery,* 54; Nunnelee, *Famous Company,* 104–5.
3. Charles R. Phelps, September 18, 1863, Phelps Letters.

4. The official returns for the cavalry corps on September 20, the day before the campaign opened, stated that the horse artillery battalion had sixteen guns. This is eight pieces below the regular strength of four guns per battery or twenty-four guns in the battalion. Obviously, the losses of the thirteenth had not been rectified. However, besides those three pieces, five others were not available. A number of reasons could account for this; lack of horses, lack of personnel (only 261 men and 14 officers were present for duty), or unrepaired damage are the most likely. Whatever the cause, Beckham was about to enter a campaign with just sixty percent of his guns available. *O.R.,* ser. 1, vol. 29, part 1, 404.
5. Lt. Edwin L. Halsey commanded Hart's Battery during this entire campaign. Captain Hart left on furlough after the battery had been pulled back from its position at Morton's Ford to rest and recuperate at Orange Court House. This occurred between September 16 and 20. Hart et al., "Hart's Battery," 64.
6. McGregor's Battery supplied one section. Moorman's Battery sent one gun under Lieutenants Shoemaker and Phelps. Lt. Edmund H. Moorman was left at Barnett's Ford with one gun. Another piece was in Richmond for repairs, and one piece had been captured on the thirteenth. Hart's entire battery was engaged. Shreve, "Stuart Horse Artillery," 12; Shoemaker, *Shoemaker's Battery,* 54–55; Hart et al., "Hart's Battery," 64.
7. Shoemaker, *Shoemaker's Battery,* 55; Nunnelee, *Famous Company,* 106.
8. Shoemaker, *Shoemaker's Battery,* 55.
9. Hart et al., "Hart's Battery," 64. Lt. William T. Adams was wounded during the fighting. Ibid., 67.
10. *O.R.,* ser. 1, vol. 29, part 1, 147.
11. Ibid.
12. Nunnelee, *Famous Company,* 107.
13. A section of Moorman's Battery had picket duty near Locust Dale from September 28 to 30, when a section from Griffin's Battery relieved it. A section of Moorman's Battery also had picket duty on October 8 and 9. The other batteries' assignments to picket duty are unknown. Ibid., 107–8.
14. Sgt. Maj. John Williams Green of Company D, 11th Virginia Cavalry, had been a member of Chew's Battery until August 31, 1863, when he transferred to the cavalry.
15. James H. Williams to Cora DeMovelle (Pritchartt) Williams, September 24, 1863, Williams Papers.
16. James H. Williams to Sallie Pritchartt, October 1, 1863, Williams Papers.
17. McVicar is referring to the battle of Chickamauga, which was fought on September 19–20.
18. Charles McVicar to Miss Katie McVicar, October 4, 1863, McVicar Letters.
19. *Soldier's Paper* 1, no. 7 (November 1, 1863).
20. Charles R. Phelps, October 8, 1863, Phelps Letters.
21. Butler's Brigade was commanded by Col. Pierce M. B. Young. Gordon was given Brig. Gen. Laurence Baker's Brigade, as that officer was absent due to wounds. Jones's Brigade was led by Col. Oliver R. Funsten.
22. *O.R.,* ser. 1, vol. 29, part 1, 439–40.
23. Ibid., 384, 440.
24. Ibid., 385–440.
25. *Supp. to the O.R.,* part 1, vol. 5, 589.
26. In his sketch of the battery, Washington Hands recounted that Young's Brigade approached James City unobserved and announced its presence by having Sgt. Harry A. Marston of the battery drop a shell among the members of a Federal band, who were serenading the local citizenry. Unfortunately, this colorful account

could not have occurred, simply because the Federals were well aware of Stuart's approach, and it was Elder's guns who opened fire first. Hands Notebook, 104.

27. Stuart reported that Griffin had two guns "occasionally engaging their [the Federal] batteries from a position near the village." Obviously, Griffin did not fire continually. He may have been conserving his ammunition. On one occasion, Griffin's cessation of fire caused Davies to credit Elder with silencing an entire enemy battery with one section. *O.R.,* ser. 1, vol. 29, part 1, 385, 440.
28. Ibid., 440.
29. Hands Notebook, 104.
30. *O.R.,* ser. 1, vol. 29, part 1, 390.
31. In Stuart's account of this incident, the name of the battery is omitted, though the 1st South Carolina receives mention. The battery's identity is revealed in the history of the battery. Ibid., 440; Hart et al., "Hart's Battery," 65.
32. *O.R.,* ser. 1, vol. 29, part 1, 390.
33. Ibid., 385.
34. McGregor's role in this campaign is undocumented up until Stuart's entrapment at Auburn on the evening of the thirteenth. Undoubtedly, the battery accompanied the cavalry prior to this, but its actions are unknown.
35. Bradshaw, *Diary of McVicar,* 27; Neese, *Confederate Horse Artillery,* 216.
36. Neese, *Confederate Horse Artillery,* 217.
37. This was probably Lt. Edward B. Heaton's Battery B/L, 2nd U.S. Artillery, which was attached to Devin's Brigade. Buford reported that as Devin made good his escape, both Heaton's Battery and Lt. Edward B. Williston's Battery D, 2nd U.S. Artillery, attached to Chapman's Brigade, were in position north of the river and were engaged. *O.R.,* ser. 1, vol. 29, part 1, 348.
38. Bradshaw, *Diary of McVicar,* 27–28.
39. *O.R.,* ser. 1, vol. 29, part 1, 348.
40. Ibid., 471.
41. Ibid.
42. Francis Halsey Wigfall to Mrs. Louis T. Wigfall, October 13, 1863, Wigfall Papers.
43. Bradshaw, *Diary of McVicar,* 28–29.
44. *O.R.,* ser. 1, vol. 29, part 1, 471.
45. Ibid., 381; *Supp. to the O.R.,* part 1, vol. 5, 589–90.
46. Hart and Moorman were with Young at James City, leaving only Griffin's Battery to accompany Stuart, who had yet to link up with Fitz Lee. Hart et al., "Hart's Battery," 65; Charles R. Phelps, October 13, 1863, Phelps Letters.
47. *O.R.,* ser. 1, vol. 29, part 1, 381.
48. Ibid., 442–43.
49. Ibid.
50. These were either Pennington's or Elder's.
51. Neese, *Confederate Horse Artillery,* 220.
52. Rosser probably did not remain with Young through the night. Neese and McVicar both claimed that they left an hour after the last shots were fired and camped at Rixeyville for the night. Rosser most likely accompanied them. Moorman's Battery remained with Young. The exact location of Hart's Battery, under Lieutenant Halsey, is a point of conjecture. The two histories of the battery claim that it was with Stuart at Auburn. However, in one of the accounts, Hart said his battery fought with Young at Culpeper. This was true. For the battery then to be trapped with Stuart at Auburn, it would have had to cross two rivers, the Hazel and the Rappahannock, and rendezvous with Stuart at Warrenton before 10:00 A.M. on the thirteenth, when he rode out on his reconnaissance to Catlett's Station. Though not

entirely impossible, that such a feat occurred is improbable. The battery had marched with Young from James City and fought on the twelfth. The additional miles and fording of the rivers during the night of the twelfth would have taxed the horses beyond their capacities. Furthermore, at this time, Hart's service seems to have been linked with Young's (Butler's) Brigade, which did not cross the river until the morning of the fourteenth and only rejoined Stuart near Manassas Junction on the night of the fifteenth. Also, the guns accompanying Stuart could not keep up and were unavailable for the forced crossing of the Rappahannock on the thirteenth. Neese, *Confederate Horse Artillery,* 220; Bradshaw, *Diary of McVicar,* 30; Hart et al., "Hart's Battery," 65; Hart, *Hart's Battery,* 13; *O.R.,* ser. 1, vol. 29, part 1, 447, 459.

53. Charles R. Phelps, October 13, 1863, Phelps Letters.
54. McGregor's Battery ended up with Stuart at Auburn on the thirteenth. Griffin had accompanied Stuart through the fighting around Culpeper and probably remained with him on his move to the Rappahannock. Only one gun of Chew's Battery had been left with Rosser. The other section rode with Stuart's columns, a fact confirmed by Neese. Beckham, who rode with Stuart, had seven guns in all. How many from each battery is debatable, but a close estimate would be three from McGregor's, two from Griffin's, and two from Chew's. Neese, *Confederate Horse Artillery,* 225.
55. *O.R.,* ser. 1, vol. 29, part 1, 417, 422, 447.
56. The list of known casualties for Breathed's Battery for October 10–21 shows three killed, one mortally wounded, and seven wounded. Those killed were Privates Vaughn, Ham Mintner, and Alfred C. Muth. Pvt. John Dorsey was mortally wounded. Lieutenants Philip P. Johnston and Daniel Shanks, Bugler Martin Burke, and Privates Frank Hart, William G. Lewis, Haywood F. Tripplett, and Milton B. Young were wounded.
57. Francis Halsey Wigfall to Mrs. Louis T. Wigfall, October 13, 1863, Wigfall Papers.
58. Lomax did not mention having artillery with him, and Breathed was not employed by Lee before Lomax was ordered to withdraw. *O.R.,* ser. 1, vol. 29, part 1, 463, 466.
59. Ibid., 453.
60. Dorsey was the only member of the battery to be mortally wounded during this time period. While Wigfall doesn't mention him by name, he could have only been referring to Dorsey. Francis Halsey Wigfall to Miss Louise Wigfall, October 16, 1863, Wigfall Papers.
61. Shoemaker recorded that his battery was engaged with Federal cavalry under Kilpatrick at Warrenton Springs on the fourteenth. However, no other record supports this claim. Young had been ordered to Bealton Station, and Warrenton Springs was miles out of his way. Furthermore, Kilpatrick was engaged in the vicinity of Gainesville on the fourteenth. Nunnelee did record passing Warrenton Springs on the march but did not refer to any fighting taking place there. Shoemaker would seem to be in error as to the timing of this event. *O.R.,* ser. 1, vol. 29, part 1, 376, 459; Shoemaker, *Shoemaker's Battery,* 56–57; Nunnelee, *Famous Company,* 110.
62. Stuart reported that Young joined him with four pieces of artillery, probably a section of two guns each from Hart's and Moorman's Batteries. *O.R.,* ser. 1, vol. 29, part 1, 450.
63. One gun from Chew's Battery was also with Hart and Moorman.
64. Stuart had seven guns with him at Auburn; Breathed had three with him, according to McVicar; and Chew's remaining gun had come up. Bradshaw, *Diary of McVicar,* 30.

65. Francis Halsey Wigfall to Miss Louise Wigfall, October 16, 1863, Wigfall Papers.
66. *C.S.R.,* microcopy M331, roll 20, S.V. "Robert F. Beckham."
67. McVicar claimed that his gun lost a wheel and seven men were wounded in this engagement. There are no records that support this contention. Once again, either the wounds were superficial or the date was not recorded in the records of the men wounded. Bradshaw, *Diary of McVicar,* 30.
68. Shoemaker, *Shoemaker's Battery,* 58–59. One source claims that Hart's Battery also accompanied Stuart. Hart et al., "Hart's Battery," 67.
69. Francis Halsey Wigfall to Miss Louise Wigfall, October 16, 1863, Wigfall Papers.
70. Bradshaw, *Diary of McVicar,* 30; Neese, *Confederate Horse Artillery,* 228.
71. *Supp. to the O.R.,* part 1, vol. 5, 591.
72. Shreve, "Stuart Horse Artillery," 13.
73. H. H. Matthews, "From Gettysburg to Hagerstown, Williamsport and Back to the Rappahannock," *St. Mary's Beacon,* May 11, 1905.
74. Francis Halsey Wigfall to Louis T. Wigfall, October 19, 1863, Wigfall Papers.
75. Lissa was Amanda Melissa Lewis, who became McVicar's wife in 1869.
76. Charles McVicar to Miss Katie McVicar, October 22, 1863, McVicar Letters.
77. Francis Halsey Wigfall to Louis T. Wigfall, October 23, 1863, Wigfall Papers.
78. Charles R. Phelps, October 26, 1863, Phelps Letters.

Chapter 23

1. Nunnelee, *Famous Company,* 113–14.
2. The locations of Griffin's, McGregor's and Breathed's Batteries, except for Lieutenant Wigfall's reference to Beverly's Ford in his letter of October 23, are unknown.
3. The battery became part of the "Maryland Line," which was under the command of Col. Bradley T. Johnson. The Baltimore Light Artillery was christened the 2nd Maryland Artillery but did not lose its status as horse artillery. It was eventually attached to the Department of Richmond, commanded by Maj. Gen. Arnold Elzey. As of April 20, 1864, the battery consisted of 4 officers and 104 men (66 effectives) with four guns. *O.R.,* ser. 1, vol. 33, 1076, 1089, 1299.
4. Ibid., vol. 29, part 2, 816.
5. Bradshaw, *Diary of McVicar,* 32.
6. *O.R.,* ser. 1, vol. 29, part 2, 820–21.
7. Trout, *They Followed the Plume,* 160.
8. Neese, *Confederate Horse Artillery,* 234–35.
9. Nunnelee indicated that Fleetwood Hill had artillery on it when he arrived. He did not take up position on the hill, but went directly to the Kennedy farm. Whether Nunnelee was referring to his gun, his section, or the entire battery is unknown. Certainly the possibility that only a portion of the battery unlimbered on Fleetwood Hill should be considered. Shoemaker, *Shoemaker's Battery,* 60; Nunnelee, *Famous Company,* 114; Bradshaw, *Diary of McVicar,* 32.
10. Nunnelee gave no account of this fight. Nunnelee, *Famous Company,* 114–15; Shoemaker, *Shoemaker's Battery,* 60.
11. Hart et al., "Hart's Battery," 68.
12. Shoemaker, *Shoemaker's Battery,* 60–61; Nunnelee, *Famous Company,* 115.
13. Neese, *Confederate Horse Artillery,* 236–38; Hart et al., "Hart's Battery," 68.
14. Hart et al., "Hart's Battery," 68.
15. Charles R. Phelps, November 17, 1863, Phelps Letters.
16. Dr. Jay Luvas and Col. Wilbur S. Nye, "The Campaign That History Forgot," *CWTI* 8, no. 7 (November 1969): 18.

17. Ibid.; *O.R.,* ser. 1, vol. 29, part 1, 903.
18. *O.R.,* ser. 1, vol. 29, part 1, 898.
19. Ibid.
20. Hart et al., "Hart's Battery," 68; Shoemaker, *Shoemaker's Battery,* 61–62; Neese, *Confederate Horse Artillery,* 239–40.
21. Shreve claimed that McGregor's Battery saw no action after the Rappahannock Station fight, and Matthews, who was not shy in claiming what his battery accomplished, did not mention Breathed's Battery as having taken part in the brief campaign. Wigfall wrote that his battery, Breathed's, left camp but never took up a position. Shreve, "Stuart Horse Artillery," 13; H. H. Matthews, "Winter of 1863 and Spring of 1864, including the Charlottesville Raid," *St. Mary's Beacon,* May 18, 1905; Francis Halsey Wigfall to Mrs. Louis T. Wigfall, December 13, 1863, Wigfall Papers.
22. Shoemaker, *Shoemaker's Battery,* 61–62; Nunnelee, *Famous Company,* 116; Neese, *Confederate Horse Artillery,* 240.
23. *O.R.,* ser. 1, vol. 29, part 1, 806.
24. Ibid., 898; Chris J. Hartley, *Stuart's Tarheels: James B. Gordon and His North Carolina Cavalry* (Baltimore: Butternut & Blue, 1996), 304; Luvas and Nye, "Campaign History Forgot," 22.
25. *O.R.,* ser. 1, vol. 29, part 1, 899.
26. *Supp. to the O.R.,* part 1, vol. 5, 634.
27. This was the same battery that lost three guns at Brandy Station in June. *O.R.,* ser. 1, vol. 29, part 1, 807.
28. *Supp. to the O.R.,* part 1, vol. 5, 634; *O.R.,* ser. 1, vol. 29, part 1, 899.
29. Neese, *Confederate Horse Artillery,* 241.
30. *O.R.,* ser. 1, vol. 29, part 1, 816.
31. Neese, *Confederate Horse Artillery,* 241–42.
32. Shoemaker, *Shoemaker's Battery,* 62; Nunnelee, *Famous Company,* 116.
33. *O.R.,* ser. 1, vol. 29, part 1, 899.
34. Ibid., 905–6.
35. Shoemaker claimed to have three guns in this engagement. Stuart, Hampton, Gordon, Rosser, and Young did not mention Shoemaker's participation in the movement and fighting, although this does not preclude the possibility that he was there. Shoemaker's details as to the route taken and the location of that night's camp lend credence to his claims. The remaining gun of the battery, under Lieutenant Phelps, was reported by Shoemaker to have been engaged elsewhere. Nunnelee was with Shoemaker on this occasion and recorded the same movements. He did not mention engaging the enemy. The battery most likely was in the rear of the column and not engaged. Shoemaker, *Shoemaker's Battery,* 62; Nunnelee, *Famous Company,* 117.
36. *O.R.,* ser. 1, vol. 29, part 1, 902–3.
37. Shoemaker, *Shoemaker's Battery,* 63–64; Nunnelee, *Famous Company,* 117.
38. *O.R.,* ser. 1, vol. 29, part 1, 900; Hart et al., "Hart's Battery," 69–70.
39. *O.R.,* ser. 1, vol. 29, part 1, 900.
40. Charles R. Phelps, December 12, 1863, Phelps Letters.
41. Francis Halsey Wigfall to Mrs. Louis T. Wigfall, December 13, 1863, Wigfall Papers.
42. Neese, *Confederate Horse Artillery,* 244.
43. In Brig. Gen. William N. Pendleton's report to Robert E. Lee dated November 20, 1863, Beckham was indeed recommended for a lieutenant colonelcy. Moorman, Chew, and Breathed were to be promoted to majors. It was months before this was implemented, but in the end it led to two of these men leaving the battalion. *O.R.,* ser. 1, vol. 29, part 2, 840–41.
44. Francis Halsey Wigfall to Louis T. Wigfall, December 20, 1863, Wigfall Papers.

45. Brown was only a lieutenant at this time and as such commanded one of the sections. He was promoted to captain in December 1864.
46. David Cardwell, "A Horse Battery," *CV* 27 (1919): 7.
47. Neese, *Confederate Horse Artillery,* 245.

Chapter 24

1. As part of that recovery, the battery was issued a three–inch rifled gun manufactured in Rome, Georgia, sometime in mid-August. *O.R.,* ser. 1, vol. 51, part 2, 758–59.
2. Micajah Woods to Mrs. Sabina Lewis Stuart Creigh Woods, August 25, 1863, Woods Papers.
3. Ibid., August 26, 1863.
4. Micajah Woods to Dr. John R. Woods, August 29, 1863, Woods Papers.
5. "Et id genus omne" means "and everything of the sort."
6. Woods may have been referring to Rev. Samuel Wilson Blain, Lieutenant Blain's father.
7. Micajah Woods to Dr. John R. Woods, September 4, 1863, Woods Papers.
8. Micajah Woods to Mrs. Sabina Lewis Stuart Creigh Woods, September 9, 1863, Woods Papers.
9. On September 7 at Bath, September 11 at Moorefield, and September 25 at Seneca Trace Crossing on the Cheat River. *O.R.,* ser. 1, vol. 29, part 2, 105–6, 197–98.
10. F. Carter Berkeley, "Imboden's Dash into Charlestown," *SHSP* 31 (1903): 14.
11. The man was not a field officer but Lt. Charles H. Richardson, the 9th Maryland's adjutant. Ibid., 18.
12. Ibid., 14.
13. C. C. Hart, "The Charles Town Raid," *CV* 25 (1917): 21.
14. Ibid.
15. Berkeley, "Imboden's Dash," 14.
16. Ibid.
17. *O.R.,* ser. 1, vol. 29, part 1, 492.
18. Micajah Woods to Mrs. Sabina Lewis Stuart Creigh Woods, September 9, 1863, Woods Papers.
19. Ibid., September 29, 1863.
20. Ibid.
21. Ibid., October 7, 1863.
22. *O.R.,* ser. 1, vol. 29, part 1, 481.
23. Latin for "for our altars and hearths."
24. Micajah Woods to Dr. John R. Woods, October 12, 1863, Woods Papers.
25. Micajah Woods to Mrs. Sabina Lewis Stuart Creigh Woods, October 14, 1863, Woods Papers.
26. Randolph H. Blain to Mrs. Susan Isham Harrison Blain, October 17, 1863, Blain Papers, Special Collections, Leyburn Library, Washington and Lee University.
27. Micajah Woods to Dr. John R. Woods, October 18, 1863, Woods Papers.
28. Ibid., October 29, 1863.
29. Ibid.
30. Terry Lowry, *Last Sleep: The Battle of Droop Mountain* (Charleston, WV: Pictorial Histories Publishing Co., 1996), 65; *O.R.,* ser. 1, vol. 29, part 1, 536.
31. *O.R.,* ser. 1, vol. 29, part 1, 528.
32. Ibid., 537.
33. Ibid., 508.
34. Ibid., 546.

35. Ibid., 546–47.
36. Lowry, *Last Sleep,* 191.
37. Micajah Woods to Dr. John R. Woods, November 8, 1863, Woods Papers.
38. Confederate casualties were 33 killed, 100 wounded, and 122 captured or missing. The Federals lost 30 killed, 88 wounded, and 1 captured or missing. Lowry, *Last Sleep,* 260, 269.
39. Randolph H. Blain to Mrs. Susan Isham Harrison Blain, November 8, 1863, Blain Papers.
40. Micajah Woods to Mrs. Sabina Lewis Stuart Creigh Woods, November 11, 1863, Woods Papers.
41. Ibid., November 15, 1863.
42. The strength of the battery as of November 30 was given as four officers and forty-five men present for duty, with sixty-seven aggregate present and absent. *O.R.,* ser. 1, vol. 29, part 2, 857.
43. The strength of the battery as of November 30 was given as five officers and forty-three men present for duty, with seventy-seven aggregate present and absent. Ibid.
44. McClanahan was at Harrisonburg by December 9. Driver, *Staunton Artillery,* 83.
45. *O.R.,* ser. 1, vol. 29, part 1, 968–69.
46. Ibid., 930.
47. Micajah Woods to Dr. John R. Woods, December 21, 1863, Woods Papers.
48. *O.R.,* ser. 1, vol. 29, part 1, 940.
49. Diary of Micajah Woods, Woods Papers.
50. Robert H. Moore II, *Graham's Petersburg, Jackson's Kanawha, and Lurty's Roanoke Horse Artillery* (Lynchburg, VA: H. E. Howard, 1996), 97.
51. Latin for "a partaker of the crime."
52. Micajah Woods to Mrs. Sabina Lewis Stuart Creigh Woods, February 29, 1864, Woods Papers.

Chapter 25

1. Wigfall may have been referring to his application for a transfer.
2. Francis Halsey Wigfall to Miss Louise Wigfall, January 3, 1864, Wigfall Papers.
3. Hart et al., "Hart's Battery," 71.
4. Matthews, "Winter of 1863 and Spring of 1864, including the Charlottesville Raid".
5. The "Doc" probably was Assistant Surgeon Alexander T. Bell.
6. Charles R. Phelps, January 29, 1864, Phelps Letters.
7. J. E. B. Stuart to R. F. Beckham, February 15, 1864; *C.S.R.,* microcopy M331, roll 20, S.V. "Robert F. Beckham."
8. *O.R.,* ser. 1, vol. 33, 172.
9. This is Fuqua's account of that morning. Shoemaker wrote that Fuqua, L. W. Moorman, and Captain Moorman rode to the river to go fishing and that Captain Moorman galloped back to the camp to give the alarm. Moorman's own report refutes Shoemaker's account. Mark B. Fuqua to John J. Shoemaker, April 15, 1910, Chew Papers; Shoemaker, *Shoemaker's Battery,* 66; *O.R.,* ser. 1, vol. 33, 167.
10. *O.R.,* ser. 1, vol. 33, 162.
11. Ibid.
12. Mark B. Fuqua to John J. Shoemaker, April 15, 1910, Chew Papers.
13. Ibid.
14. *O.R.,* ser. 1, vol. 33, 162.
15. Ibid., 168.
16. *C.S.R.,* microcopy M324, roll 273, S.V. "R. Preston Chew."
17. Neese, *Confederate Horse Artillery,* 250.
18. Charles R. Phelps, March 2, 1864, Phelps Letters.
19. Wise, *Long Arm of Lee,* 728–29.

20. Just who was presented the flag was a topic that caused considerable controversy after the war. Henry H. Matthews championed Breathed and insisted that the flag was presented to his battery alone. However, the fact is that Chew ended up with the flag. At the end of the war, it was a member of Chew's Battery who carried the flag and hid it to prevent its surrender at Appomattox. Chew apparently believed that the flag belonged to the battalion as a whole and not to any individual battery.
21. Hart et al., "Hart's Battery," 73.
22. Abraham or George Nicewander.
23. Charles McVicar to Miss Katie McVicar, March 7, 1864, McVicar Letters.
24. Charles R. Phelps, March 22, 1864, Phelps Letters.

The Chew Era

Chapter 26

1. *O.R.*, ser. 1, vol. 29, 841–42.
2. Ibid., vol. 33, 1264.
3. Ibid., vol. 29, part 2, 895–96.
4. Ibid., vol. 33, 1083.
5. Mitchell, *Letters of Stuart,* 379–80.
6. *C.S.R.V.,* microcopy M331, roll 74, S.V. "James Dearing."
7. Mitchell, *Letters of Stuart,* 379–80.
8. The promotions of Moorman, Chew, and Breathed opened three battery captaincies, which needed to be filled. Lt. John J. Shoemaker was promoted and assumed command of the Lynchburg Battery in place of Moorman. Lt. James W. Thomson became captain of Chew's Ashby Battery, and Lt. Philip P. Johnston replaced Breathed as captain of the 1st Stuart Horse Artillery. All three of these officers were talented men and well suited to replace their old commanders.
9. Stuart had to fight not only to secure Breathed's promotion, but to keep him in the horse artillery at all. Stuart's letter to Gen. Samuel Cooper on May 4, 1864, the opening day of the campaign, testifies to how much he thought of Breathed:

> GENERAL: I have the honor to request that the inclosed extracts from paragraph II, Special Orders, No. 93, and paragraph II, Special Orders, No. 100, Adjutant and Inspector General's Office, current series, relative to the transfers of men from Breathed's battery, horse artillery, to the Maryland Line, be revoked, and that these men remain in their present company. This battery as well as McGregor's was, during the first year of the war, organized under the auspices of the Governor of Virginia as a part of the State troops, and enlisted for the war, the officers receiving their commissions from the Governor of the State. Under the immortal Pelham it received large accessions by recruits from Maryland, and while Captain Breathed remained with it, 3 of its 4 officers were natives of that State. Thus have these men, though enlisted for the war in a Virginia organization, been under officers from their own State, and this will continue to be the case, as the officer who succeeds Major Breathed in the command of this battery is also a native of Maryland.

> But the most weighty reason why this transfer should not be consummated is that at the very commencement of a momentous campaign a battery which has won for itself a name second to none in this army, whose services cannot be dispensed with without great injury to the cause, will be disorganized and rendered almost entirely useless, and this great injury to the battalion of horse artillery will be without any corresponding gain to our service in any other direction, for these men will probably remain in camp of instruction for a considerable portion of the coming campaign, and in lieu of the distinguished service they might render in the field, will consume their time in the monotonous duties of the camp. I visited this battery yesterday, and find that many of the men are changing their opinions, and, desiring to remain in that company, are requesting that the order for their transfer be revoked. I inclose two of those applications. If this transfer is still insisted upon, I would earnestly request that it may be made gradually as dismounted cavalry are transferred to the company.

Stuart's request was granted, and Breathed's place in the horse artillery was secure. *O.R.,* ser. 1, vol. 36, part 2, 948–49.

10. William Hoxton to Mrs. Sarah Randolph, April 9, 1864, Randolph Papers.
11. *O.R.,* ser. 1, vol. 33, 1267.
12. Charles R. Phelps, April 22, 1864, Phelps Letters.
13. Shoemaker's Battery had waited for new horses for about a month but received only 38, not nearly the amount it needed. The horse situation was critical to the efficiency of the battalion. Breathed's Battery reported having 77 on March 31; Hart's Battery had 124 on February 29; and McGregor's Battery had 80 on March 31.
14. Charles R. Phelps, May 4, 1864, Phelps Letters.
15. McGregor's Battery joined with Rooney Lee as ordered and remained with him through the battles that followed. On May 6, Lee was at Pisgah Church west of the Old Turnpike, guarding the army's extreme left flank. There are no records of the battery's movements or activities, but it presumably marched with Chambliss's Brigade from Lee's left to the vicinity of Massaponax Church on the ninth. The battery did not see any action until the twelfth, when it was engaged on the army's right flank near Spotsylvania Court House.
16. *O.R.,* ser. 1, vol. 36, part 2, 955.
17. Neese, *Confederate Horse Artillery,* 259–60.
18. Lieutenant Nunnelee of Shoemaker's Battery reported that Thomson had eight men wounded. Nunnelee, *Famous Company,* 126.
19. Benjamin W. Crowninshield, *A History of the First Regiment of Massachusetts Cavalry Volunteers* (Boston: Houghton, Mifflin and Company, 1891), 204.
20. McDonald, *Laurel Brigade,* 228.
21. *O.R.,* ser. 1, vol. 36, part 1, 860.
22. This was probably the 16th Pennsylvania Cavalry. Ibid., 871.
23. Hart with Bamberg's section remained with Hampton in front of Spotsylvania Court House and was not engaged. Hart, *Hart's Battery,* 15.
24. There is no reason to doubt that a single gun opened the contest, but McDonald's insistence that this was the only gun on the field for the Confederates is not borne out by the facts. McDonald, *Laurel Brigade,* 228.
25. Neese, *Confederate Horse Artillery,* 261.
26. By contrast, Thomson had only one man, Pvt. Amos Shaffer, wounded.

27. Lieutenant Nunnelee commented that his battery was "too much annoyed by sharpshooters." Nunnelee, *Famous Company,* 127.
28. Neese recorded that Thomson's Battery bivouacked for the night behind Confederate infantry. The battery's movement to the left of Rosser's line had brought it near Robert E. Lee's flank. Shoemaker was with Rosser. Neese, *Confederate Horse Artillery,* 262.
29. *Supp. to O.R.,* part 1, vol. 6, 787–88.
30. The Federals claimed to have killed and wounded several of their opponents' men. Breathed admitted to losing a few horses but suffered no known casualties among the men. There are no records concerning casualties in Halsey's section. *O.R.,* ser. 1, vol. 36, part 1, 846; Breathed Report.
31. There is the possibility that Bamberg's section of Hart's Battery was engaged on the Catharpin Road, though no records exist to support this. Shoemaker would be out of action for a few days due to the losses he had suffered on the sixth. McGregor supposedly was with Rooney Lee, but evidence of his participation in the fighting is lacking.
32. Neese, *Confederate Horse Artillery,* 262–63.
33. Two sources stated that Halsey's section fought with Breathed on the eighth. Just where and under what circumstances are unknown. Halsey is not mentioned by any source as having fought at the Alsop house with Johnston. *Supp. to O.R.,* part 1, vol. 6, 819; Hart et al., "Hart's Battery," 74.
34. H. H. Matthews, "Sheridan's Raid to Yellow Tavern and Mortal Wounding of Major General J. E. B. Stuart, May 11, 1864," *St. Mary's Beacon,* May 25, 1905.
35. Philip P. Johnston, "Worn Suit of Gray: Tribute to Breathed," *CV* 17 (1909): 267.
36. E. A. Pollard, *The Lost Cause* (New York: E. B. Treat & Co., 1867), 595.
37. Breathed's own account of the incident was brief, and he claimed no credit for saving the gun (Breathed Report).
38. Nunnelee, *Famous Company,* 128.
39. Neese, *Confederate Horse Artillery,* 264.
40. Nunnelee, *Famous Company,* 128.
41. Ibid.
42. Neese, *Confederate Horse Artillery,* 265.
43. *Supp. to O.R.,* part 1, vol. 6, 819.
44. *O.R.,* ser. 1, vol. 36, part 1, 533.
45. One source stated that Confederate artillery was engaged at Mitchell's Shop late on the ninth, but whose guns they were is unknown. In his report, Breathed made no reference to any action having occurred on the ride prior to Yellow Tavern. Gordon C. Rhea, *The Battles for Spotsylvania Court House and the Road to Yellow Tavern* (Baton Rouge: Louisiana State University Press, 1997), 117; Breathed Report.
46. Bradley T. Johnson, "A Striking War Incident," *SHSP* 19 (1901): 227–28.
47. Ibid.
48. Garnett, *Riding with Stuart,* 66–67.
49. One source stated that Griffin first held a position near Yellow Tavern. Shortly after the fighting began, the battery was withdrawn about half a mile, and it did not go into its final position until Stuart himself called Griffin up and placed him. There is no corroborating evidence to support the idea that Griffin was at any time at Yellow Tavern. Garnett does record that the battery had unlimbered to the rear and was brought into position a second time, but the inference is that it reoccupied the same position as before. He also intimated that all four of the battery's guns were placed in position, not just three. This view would seem to be more accurate. Hands Notebook, 105; Garnett, *Riding with Stuart,* 68, 70.
50. H. H. Matthews once again had his battery take center stage, placing it in the position actually held by Griffin. Most likely Matthews just switched Shanks and

Griffin. This would place Shanks on Lomax's left. The battery on the left was the farthest away from the Federals and suffered the least damage. Breathed's report stated that Johnston's Battery (Shanks's) came away almost unscathed as the enemy targeted Griffin. H. H. Matthews, "Yellow Tavern—Mortal Wounding of Major General J. E. B. Stuart, May 11, 1864," *St. Mary's Beacon,* June 1, 1905; Breathed Report.

51. Goldsborough, *Maryland Line,* 287–88.
52. Stuart's aide-de-camp, Garnett, saw the attack that overran Griffin's Battery. He attempted to bring up reinforcements to support and protect the guns. As the squadron, led by General Lomax himself, came up, McNulty's gun plowed into the column, trying to escape the onrushing Federals. Lomax and the other officers could not rally the men in time to retake the guns that were captured. Garnett, *Riding with Stuart,* 69–70.
53. Matthews, "Yellow Tavern—Mortal Wounding of Major General J. E. B. Stuart, May 11, 1864."
54. Goldsborough, *Maryland Line,* 288.
55. Garnett, *Riding with Stuart,* 70.
56. Hands Notebook, 106–7.
57. McNulty and the two guns remaining of the Baltimore Light rode to Old Church following his brief stand at Half Sink. Ibid., 107.
58. Which Confederate battery or batteries were engaged in either of these actions is unknown. Shanks's was most likely, as it had not played a significant role at Yellow Tavern and was in relatively good condition.
59. Hands Notebook, 107.
60. Nunnelee, *Famous Company,* 129.
61. Neese, *Confederate Horse Artillery,* 265–66.
62. Nunnelee, *Famous Company,* 129.
63. Roger P. Chew Report, Lewis Leigh Collection, U.S. Army Military History Institute.
64. Nunnelee, *Famous Company,* 129.
65. Neese, *Confederate Horse Artillery,* 267–68.
66. *O.R.,* ser. 1, vol. 36, part 1, 643.
67. Nunnelee, *Famous Company,* 130.
68. Chew reported that McGregor was engaged on the thirteenth, but Shreve gave the twelfth. The battery's roster lists casualties only for the twelfth, not the thirteenth. Chew Report; Shreve, "Stuart Horse Artillery," 14; *C.S.R.V.,* microcopy M324, roll 267.
69. Only the movement of Thomson can be confirmed, but since these batteries were operating together at this time, it is likely that they moved at the same time. Neese, *Confederate Horse Artillery,* 269.
70. Charles R. Phelps, May 16, 1864, Phelps Letters.
71. *O.R.,* ser. 1, vol. 36, part 2, 824–25; Shreve, "Stuart Horse Artillery," 14.
72. *O.R.,* ser. 1, vol. 36, part 1, 892; Shreve, "Stuart Horse Artillery," 14.
73. Nunnelee gave the camp's location as the Gabriel Long farm. Nunnelee, *Famous Company,* 131.
74. Charles R. Phelps, May 19, 1864, Phelps Letters.

Chapter 27

1. Shreve, "Stuart Horse Artillery," 14.
2. Neese, *Confederate Horse Artillery,* 274–75.
3. Breathed Report.
4. Nunnelee, *Famous Company,* 133.

5. Wilson's Wharf is located on the James River southeast of Charles City Court House. The remainder of the battery spent the time from the twenty-second through the twenty-sixth shifting its camp between Atlee's Station and the Wickham farm. William J. Black, "Shoemaker's Battery," September 1, 1864, VMIA; Nunnelee, *Famous Company,* 132–33.
6. *Supp. to O.R.,* part 1, vol. 6, 796.
7. Black, "Shoemaker's Battery," September 1, 1864.
8. Micajah Woods to Dr. John R. Woods, May 25, 1864, Woods Papers.
9. *O.R.,* ser. 1, vol. 36, part 3, 830–31.
10. Butler was not present. He was still recuperating from his wound suffered at Brandy Station.
11. Robert A. Williams, "Haw's Shop: A 'Storm of Shot and Shell,'" *CWTI* 9 (January 1971): 15.
12. There is little information concerning which of the three batteries was engaged. Gregg's report stated that he faced more than one battery. Since only Shoemaker's Battery reported a loss, it would seem that it occupied the position on the left flank. Shoemaker reported that only one section of his battery fought in the battle. The battery's other section had been ordered to Atlee's Station and returned late in the day. George W. Shreve wrote that McGregor was engaged but did not indicate the battery's location, though most likely it was with Shoemaker. H. H. Matthews did not mention Johnston's Battery as having been in the fight. It may have accompanied Rooney Lee's Division. *O.R.,* ser. 1, vol. 36, part 1, 854; Black, "Shoemaker's Battery," September 1, 1864; Nunnelee, *Famous Company,* 133–34; Shreve, "Stuart Horse Artillery," 14; H. H. Matthews, "Trevilian Station Fight," *St. Mary's Beacon,* June 8, 1905.
13. Sergeant Neese of Thomson's Battery wrote that his command was in the area of the fighting and under fire but did not fire in return. Neese, *Confederate Horse Artillery,* 277–78.
14. *O.R.,* ser. 1, vol. 36, part 3, 847.
15. Woods Diary.
16. David Cardwell, "When the Gallant Lieutenant Ford Was Killed," *CV* 26 (1918): 207–8.
17. Ibid.
18. There were three crewmen with the name Antonio: Antonio Constantini, a member of the famous "Napoleon Detachment," C. Antonio, and Antonio E. H. Friechien.
19. Cardwell, "When Ford Was Killed," 207–8.
20. Hart et al., "Hart's Battery," 76.
21. McGregor's move to Meadow's Bridge on the second is intimated in Shreve's reminiscences. Shreve, "Stuart Horse Artillery," 15.
22. Nunnelee, *Famous Company,* 135.
23. William Hoxton to Mrs. Sarah Randolph, June 6, 1864, Randolph Papers.
24. Nunnelee, *Famous Company,* 136.
25. Breathed Report.
26. Black, "Shoemaker's Battery," September 1, 1864; Nunnelee, *Famous Company,* 136.
27. *Supp. to O.R.,* part 1, vol. 6, 799.
28. Nunnelee, *Famous Company,* 137.
29. Woods Diary.
30. Ibid.
31. Hart's Battery was the only battery in the battalion that was not engaged on June 3. It remained with Hampton's division near Ashland.
32. The Federal battery cannot be identified beyond belonging to Capt. Dunbar R. Ransom's 2nd Horse Artillery Brigade. *O.R.,* ser. 1, vol. 36, part 1, 882.
33. Black, "Shoemaker's Battery," September 1, 1864.

34. *O.R.,* ser. 1, vol. 36, part 1, 806.
35. Ibid., part 3, 883–84.
36. Nunnelee, *Famous Company,* 137–38.
37. William Hoxton to Mrs. Sarah Randolph, June 6, 1864, Randolph Papers.
38. Shoemaker's Battery received its orders to march about midnight of June 8–9. Nunnelee, *Famous Company,* 138.
39. The gun had been left on picket duty at Long Bridge. Black, "Shoemaker's Battery," September 1, 1864.
40. Lieutenant Halsey commanded the battery, as Hart was ill. He returned to the battery and fought on the twelfth. Hart et al., "Hart's Battery," 77.
41. Sherfesee, "Color-Bearer," 49.
42. R. P. Chew, *The Battle of Trevilians,* Chew Papers; Neese, *Confederate Horse Artillery,* 284.
43. Chew reported that only Adams's section was engaged against the Federals along the Trevilian Station/Clayton's Store Road. However, other sources indicate that the entire battery moved with Butler. Chew Report; Hart et al., "Hart's Battery," 77; Sherfesee, "Color-Bearer," 49.
44. According to Nunnelee, the guns were in position on the farm of a Mr. Vanliew. Nunnelee, *Famous Company,* 140.
45. Left of the road when moving toward Trevilian Station along the Gordonsville Road. D. M. Deck, "Captured at Trevilian Station," *CV* 24 (1916): 123.
46. Chew believed that the position "is what saved our led horses and caissons, and defeated Custer." Chew, *Trevilians.*
47. Sherfesee, "Color-Bearer," 49–50.
48. Major Barker was Hampton's assistant adjutant general.
49. Sherfesee, "Color-Bearer," 50–51.
50. Deck, "Captured," 123.
51. McVicar claimed that Chew had seven guns on the hill. No other source stated how many Chew had with him. Figuring that Thomson had two and Hart four, Chew probably had only six guns with him at that time. Bradshaw, *Diary of McVicar,* 40.
52. Chew, *Trevilians.*
53. Among the liberated wagons was the hospital wagon of Dr. Alexander T. Bell of Shoemaker's Battery. It had been captured, along with Hospital Steward John H. Everett and driver Madison C. Porter. Everett had refused to surrender and had caught a saber blow meant for his head on his wrist. The steward also retrieved his splendid broad-brimmed hat, which had been confiscated by a Federal trooper, who in turn was made a prisoner. Nunnelee, *Famous Company,* 140–41.
54. Nunnelee indicated that all the guns of both batteries were engaged. Nunnelee, *Famous Company,* 140; Black, "Shoemaker's Battery," September 1, 1864.
55. Matthews, "Trevilian Station Fight."
56. Nunnelee, *Famous Company,* 141.
57. *O.R.,* ser. 1, vol. 36, part 1, 1095; Neese, *Confederate Horse Artillery,* 286.
58. Bradshaw, *Diary of McVicar,* 41–42.
59. Ibid.; Hart et al., "Hart's Battery," 77.
60. M. C. Butler, "The Cavalry Fight at Trevilian Station," *BLCW* part 27 (1884): 238.
61. Bradshaw, *Diary of McVicar,* 43.
62. Butler, "Trevilian Station," 238.
63. McVicar was referring to Pvt. Raleigh Powell. There was no Robert Powell in the battery.
64. Beale lived for about five hours but never regained consciousness.
65. Bradshaw, *Diary of McVicar,* 43–44.

66. McVicar wrote that it was Fitz Lee who gave the order, whereas Sherfesee claimed it was Hampton. McVicar's claim seems unlikely, as Lee was off to the right and would have had no reason to visit Butler's part of the line. Hampton could have given the order, but Butler's own account confirms that he gave the order, though he does not mention either Neese or the battery to which he gave it. Ibid., 44; Sherfesee, "Color-Bearer," 54; Butler, "Trevilian Station," 239.
67. Neese, *Confederate Horse Artillery,* 290.
68. Both Hart's and Sherfesee's records of the battery claimed that the man who fired the shot that set the house on fire was Corp. D. Paul Sojourner, using one of Thomson's "three inch rifle" guns. There are difficulties with this view of the events, not the least of which is that according to Butler, the guns put in this position were brass. Additionally, Hart's account does not agree with the history of the battery by Hart et al., who recorded that Halsey unlimbered both his guns, rather than one crew taking over Thomson's abandoned piece. With so many versions of the same feat, for which everyone wanted credit, it becomes difficult to separate truth from fiction. However, Neese's claim seems legitimate and agrees substantially with McVicar's, though the latter does not name the gunner who sighted the shot. Hart, *Hart's Battery,* 17; Sherfesee, "Color-Bearer," 54; Butler, "Trevilian Station," 239; Hart et al., "Hart's Battery," 78–79; Bradshaw, *Diary of McVicar,* 44–45.
69. Breathed wrote that Phelps was sent to Chew with only one gun. Shoemaker's report recorded that a section was sent and that he took the remaining piece and accompanied Breathed in the attack on Sheridan's right. Certainly Shoemaker would know how many guns he had with him during the attack. Nunnelee does not give the number of guns sent and wrote only of the fight at the Ogg house. Breathed Report; Black, a "Shoemaker's Battery," September 1, 1864; Nunnelee, *Famous Company,* 142.
70. Bamberg's section was left on the right flank, where it remained throughout the battle.
71. Hart et al. stated in their history of Hart's Battery that when Halsey arrived, Thomson's guns were abandoned, and Halsey put his two guns on the line and saved the day. No mention is made of a gun being disabled or of Shoemaker's section. In his report, Chew mentioned only Shoemaker's section and that a crew from a disabled gun in Hart's Battery remanned one of Thomson's guns. Shoemaker's report did not refer to any other battery moving to the angle. What actually happened probably was a combination of all three scenarios. Shoemaker's and Hart's sections arrived within minutes of each other, since both accounts set the time at 5:00. On the way, one of Halsey's guns was damaged. Thomson had one gun in action, not having the men to man two. Chew assigned the disabled gun's crew to Thomson's piece, while Halsey's other gun joined Shoemaker's and Thomson's guns on the line. Hart et al., "Hart's Battery," 77; Chew's Report; Black, "Shoemaker's Battery," September 1, 1864.
72. Pvt. William H. Magruder, who was acting as a courier for Major Chew, was mortally wounded in the abdomen at about 7:00. Bradshaw, *Diary of McVicar,* 45.
73. From the casualties, it would appear that Phelps's section took up the position closest to the railroad cut, which caused it to draw more fire from the Federals located there.
74. Just how many guns were in action at any one time is unknown. Chew reported that all the batteries participated but did not mention whether all the guns were in action at once. Neese wrote that eight guns were deployed at one time. This seems the most reasonable: half of the battalion fighting while the other half rested. Since the barrage lasted the entire day, the men would have needed to be relieved from time to time. Nunnelee recorded that Shoemaker's Battery took position with all of

the Stuart Horse Artillery. Chew Report; Neese, *Confederate Horse Artillery,* 296; Nunnelee, *Famous Company,* 149.

75. McVicar was referring to the cavalry. There is no record of any of the horse artillery being engaged from the thirteenth through the nineteenth.
76. McVicar is in error. The battery involved was Hart's. As for the infantry, McVicar may have seen elements of Butler's South Carolina Brigade, which were armed with Enfield rifled muskets. Riding as fast as he was, McVicar may have only glimpsed what he thought was infantry. Hart et al., "Hart's Battery," 81.
77. This was probably Assistant Surgeon Alexander T. Bell of Shoemaker's Battery.
78. Bradshaw, *Diary of McVicar,* 49–50.
79. Nunnelee, *Famous Company,* 150; Black, "Shoemaker's Battery," September 1, 1864.
80. Neese, *Confederate Horse Artillery,* 298; Nunnelee, *Famous Company,* 150.
81. Shreve wrote that the fight took place on the twelfth and that Breckinridge's troops relieved his battery, but other sources indicate that the fight occurred on the morning of the thirteenth. Also, by that time, Breckinridge was well on his way to the Valley. Shreve, "Stuart Horse Artillery," 15; *O.R.,* ser. 1, vol. 36, part 1, 883–84, 1051–52.
82. There is no record of what Shoemaker's gun did during this time, but it most likely remained at Long Bridge.
83. *O.R.,* ser. 1, vol. 40, part 2, 663.
84. Freeman, *Lee's Lieutenants,* 536.
85. The piece from Shoemaker's Battery that had remained on picket duty along the Chickahominy River when the rest of the battery set out after Sheridan does not appear to have crossed the James with Lee and McGregor.
86. *O.R.,* ser. 1, vol. 40, part 2, 669.
87. Ibid., 663.
88. Ibid.
89. Neese, *Confederate Horse Artillery,* 300.
90. Black, "Shoemaker's Battery," September 1, 1864.
91. Nunnelee finally found "Company Q" at Manakin Town in charge of his friend Lieutenant Moorman. Nunnelee, *Famous Company,* 151.

Chapter 28

1. Micajah Woods to Dr. John R. Woods, March 7, 1864, Woods Papers.
2. Ibid., March 15, 1864.
3. Ibid., March 24, 1864.
4. Woods Diary.
5. Micajah Woods to Dr. John R. Woods, April 22, 1864, Woods Papers.
6. Woods Diary.
7. *O.R.,* ser. 1, vol. 37, part 1, 71.
8. William C. Davis, *The Battle of New Market* (Baton Rouge: Louisiana University Press, 1975), 17.
9. Woods Diary.
10. Hart's recollection that McClanahan had only two sections, four guns, in action at Rude's Hill contradicts Imboden's account, which stated that there were six guns. There is a possibility that two sections were in one position while the third was in another. Hart may have been referring to the guns in his immediate vicinity. Calvin C. Hart, "A Confederate Veteran Tells the Story of the Battle of New Market in the

Valley of Virginia Nearly Sixty Years Ago," *Randolph Enterprise* (n.d.); John D. Imboden, "The New Market, Va., May 15th, 1864," *BLCW,* part 30 (1884), 482.

11. On the disabling of the two guns, Lt. Carter Berkeley supports Hart. This would mean that unless the battery had been able to repair the damage, which is highly unlikely, McClanahan's Battery went into the battle of New Market with four guns, not six, as has previously been thought. Susan R. Hull, *Boy Soldiers of the Confederacy,* (New York: Neale Publishing Co., 1905), 119.
12. Imboden gave the time as two hours before daylight. Imboden, "New Market," 482.
13. Hart, "New Market."
14. Imboden, "New Market," 483.
15. This was the section Imboden had taken with him and that had fired on Stahel's cavalry.
16. Hull, *Boy Soldiers,* 118–20.
17. Davis, *New Market,* 157.
18. With these replacements, the battery had two ten-pounder Parrotts, two three-inch Rifles, and two twelve-pounder Napoleons. Micajah Woods to Roger P. Chew, July 5, 1909, Chew Papers.
19. Pvt. Estel Campbell Mustard died of his wound on June 20.
20. The identity of this individual is unknown. The records of the battery do not reveal his name. It is possible that no charges were ever filed.
21. Breckinridge's losses were 43 killed, 474 wounded, and 3 missing. Sigel lost 96 killed, 520 wounded, and 225 missing. Davis, *New Market,* 200–201.
22. Micajah Woods to Dr. John R. Woods, May 16, 1864, Woods Papers.
23. Davis, *New Market,* 157.
24. Col. William H. French's report of May 10 stated that he expected Jackson's command, numbering 1,000 men and two guns, to arrive that morning. While Lurty was not mentioned, his was the only artillery Jackson had. The number of guns is probably correct also, as in April the battery could muster only 4 officers and 57 men, hardly enough to operate a full complement of four guns. *O.R.,* ser. 1, vol. 37, part 1, 62.
25. Ibid., 738.
26. Calvin C. Hart, *Battle of Piedmont—64,* written for the Randolph Chapter, U.D.C. Copy provided by Virgil S. Hart, grandson of Calvin.
27. Hull, *Boy Soldiers,* 132; S. T. Shanks, "Visiting Battlefield of Piedmont," *CV* 11 (1903): 40.
28. John D. Imboden, "The Battle of Piedmont," *CV* 32 (1924): 18.
29. Corp. Newton C. Kestor and Pvt. John R. Kunkel were captured, though at what point in the battle this occurred is unknown. Most likely it was during Berkeley's and Fultz's rapid retreat, when they were being pursued by enemy cavalry.
30. Hart, *Piedmont.*
31. One source stated that Pvt. George W. Crickenberger fired the shot that halted the Federal cavalry and that he destroyed the gun carriage before retreating. If so, then McClanahan lost one gun at Piedmont. However, this is not supported by other accounts.
32. Hull, *Boy Soldiers,* 133–35.
33. Hart, *Piedmont.*
34. *O.R.,* ser. 1, vol. 37, part 1, 96.
35. The wartime spelling was Waynesborough.
36. Micajah Woods to Dr. John R. Woods, June 28, 1864, Woods Papers.
37. Driver, *Stauton Artillery,* 99.
38. Woods Diary.

39. Jubal A. Early, "Early's March on Washington in 1864," *BLCW* 4, part 30 (1884) 492.
40. Micajah Woods to Dr. John R. Woods, June 28, 1864, Woods Papers.
41. The battery continued to be designated as Griffin's Battery, as the captain was not dead but only a prisoner.

Chapter 29

1. *O.R.,* ser. 1, vol. 37, part 1, 175.
2. Washington Hands recorded that Johnson and the Baltimore Light advanced on Martinsburg and entered the town on the fourth, after driving away about 600 enemy cavalry. Lieutenant Bean was credited with dispersing the Federals with a few rounds of spherical case. Hands's account is the only one that places Johnson at Martinsburg. Other sources, including Early's own account, state that Johnson marched from Winchester directly to Leetown on the third and fought Mulligan there. Bean undoubtedly was engaged at Leetown, if only to counter the Federal artillery. Hands Notebook, 107; Early, "March on Washington," 492.
3. *O.R.,* ser. 1, vol. 37, part 1, 175.
4. Ibid., 541.
5. Early, "March on Washington," 495.
6. The disposition of Jackson's Brigade and Lurty's Battery is unknown, but it does not appear that they accompanied McCausland to Hagerstown.
7. *O.R.,* ser. 1, vol. 37, part 1, 223; Hands Notebook, 107.
8. *O.R.,* ser. 1, vol. 37, part 1, 219–20.
9. Captain Alexander's report places the number of Confederate pieces at three. Ibid.
10. According to Alexander, his fire managed to dismount one of the Confederate guns. There is no corroboration of this from Confederate sources. Ibid.
11. Hands Notebook, 108.
12. Driver, *Staunton Artillery,* 100.
13. Goldsborough, *Maryland Line,* 204–6; Hands Notebook, 108; *O.R.,* ser. 1, vol. 37, part 1, 249.
14. Hands Notebook, 108; *O.R.,* ser. 1, vol. 37, part 1, 267, 282–83.
15. S. T. Shanks, "Heroism like That of John Pelham," *CV* 9 (1901): 157.
16. Clement A. Evans, *Confederate Military History* (Dayton: Press of Morningside Bookshop, 1975), 3: 486.
17. It is unclear just how many guns accompanied the column. It is known that Griffin's Battery had only two. If all the guns of the other batteries participated, a total of twelve crossed the Potomac with McCausland. However, this seems high. Most likely a section from each battery was selected, giving a total of six. *O.R.,* ser. 1, vol. 37, part 1, 356.
18. Which battery fired these shots is a point of conjecture.
19. *O.R.,* ser. 1, vol. 37, part 1, 188.
20. The Federals claimed that they picked up two caissons the next morning. From which battery or batteries these came is unknown. Ibid., 189.
21. Goldsborough, *Maryland Line,* 290–91.
22. Lieutenant Woods calculated that the battery lost fourteen men but failed to name them. Micajah Woods to Dr. John R. Woods, August 24, 1864, Woods Papers.
23. Ted Alexander, "McCausland's Raid and the Burning of Chambersburg," *Blue and Gray* 11, no. 6 (August 1994): 60.
24. The attachment of Lurty's Battery to Jackson is conjectural. However, the battery was previously attached to Jackson, and there is no reason to assume that it was not present with him at this time.

25. If, as has been suggested, McCausland only took a section each of Griffin's, Jackson's, and McClanahan's Batteries, then it is possible that the remainder of these batteries participated with Imboden's and Vaughn's cavalry during Early's show of force.

Chapter 30

1. James G. Scott and Edward A. Wyatt IV, *Petersburg's Story* (Petersburg, VA: Titmus Optical Company, 1960), 178.
2. George E. Robertson to Capt. Carter, adjutant general of the A. P. Hill Camp of Confederate Veterans, November 30, 1909, Grinnan Family Papers (Mss1G8855a), VHS.
3. P. H. Drewy, "The Ninth of June, 1864," *CV* 35 (1927): 292; Scott and Wyatt, *Petersburg's Story,* 180.
4. One report stated that during this wild race, one of Graham's guns slid off its wheels but was quickly replaced by the crew. Such a thing is possible, even if the observer meant that the gun came off its carriage or, in other words, was dismounted. Since all four guns were used in the battle that followed, the gun must have remained intact. Moore, *Graham's Petersburg,* 19.
5. *O.R.,* ser. 1, vol. 36, part 2, 308.
6. George E. Robertson to Capt. Carter, November 30, 1909, Grinnan Papers.
7. Kautz reported that the artillery fire from the hill passed over his men without doing any damage. *O.R.,* ser. 1, vol. 36, part 2, 309.
8. Ibid., vol. 40, part 1, 325.
9. One source intimated that all of McGregor's guns opened fire, but another stated that it was only one section (two guns). Walter Clark, ed., *Histories of the Several Regiments and Battalions from North Carolina in the Great War, 1861–'65* (Raleigh, NC: E. M. Uzzell, Printer and Binder, 1901), 3: 610; *O.R.,* ser. 1, vol. 40, part 2, 275.
10. *O.R.,* ser. 1, vol. 40, part 1, 330.
11. The information concerning this little-known engagement was supplied by Don Richard Lauter from his work, *Winslow Homer and Friends in Prince George and Dinwiddie County Virginia, 1864–1865* (n.p., n.d.).
12. Dearing and Graham were attached to Lee's division by Special Order No. 26 on June 19. *O.R.,* ser. 1, vol. 40, part 2, 669.
13. The fact that Graham suffered so many casualties and was forced to abandon his pieces would seem to indicate that Dearing with Graham was the first to strike Chapman.
14. The only account of this comes from Sgt. George W. Shreve, who mistakenly identified the guns as being from Hart's Battery. Shreve, "Stuart Horse Artillery," 16.
15. Ibid.
16. Shreve recorded that the cavalry with a section of McGregor's Battery reached Stony Creek on June 25 and, with the assistance of A. P. Hill's infantry, defeated a large Federal force. Since Hampton reported that he had only two guns and named Graham as the commander, Shreve probably was confusing the fighting of June 25 with the battle on August 25, when McGregor's Battery and A. P. Hill were involved. Ibid.
17. This was the section that had accompanied Rooney Lee in his pursuit of Wilson after the fight at Nottoway Court House. The other section, which suffered heavy casualties there, was sent back to Petersburg. A letter written by Pvt. John E.

Horner and sent from Petersburg on June 26 concerning the mortal wounding of Walter H. Saunders on the twenty-third confirms this. Saunders died on July 3.

18. One account recorded that Graham opened fire at about 4:00 A.M. Another stated that Graham arrived about midnight, placed two Napoleons into position, and opened fire twenty minutes later when the Federals launched another attack. Beale, *9th Virginia Cavalry,* 134; John Z. H. Scott, *Memoirs of J. Z. H. Scott,* VHS, 18–19.
19. *O.R.,* ser. 1, vol. 40, part 1, 808.
20. Beale, *9th Virginia Cavalry,* 135.
21. Matthews was a member of Johnston's Battery, which would have been with Fitz Lee if it had been able to keep up. Breathed never came near Stony Creek Depot on June 29 and could not have parked Johnston's Battery there, since the guns were left far behind. Chew, who was with Hampton, may have parked McGregor's Battery at Stony Creek Depot and moved with the cavalry and Graham's Battery toward Reams's Station. This part of Matthews's account would seem to be another attempt to credit Breathed with an action taken by another officer in order to enhance Breathed's record.
22. This probably was senior brigade surgeon for Brig. Gen. Williams C. Wickham's Brigade, John Randolph Leigh.
23. H. H. Matthews, "Expedition of Gens. Wilson and Kautz against the Richmond and Weldon Railroad," *St. Mary's Beacon,* June 15, 1905.
24. The captured artillery proved a boon for at least one of the Confederate horse batteries. Hart's Battery traded in its worn-out guns, including the last two Blakelys, for four three-inch ordnance rifles. The battery also acquired a number of horses. The tough campaigning had reduced the battery's complement of men to 112, but fresh recruits from South Carolina brought the number up to 140 during the following weeks. Undoubtedly, some of the other batteries profited from the bounty left behind by Wilson and Kautz. Hart et al., "Hart's Battery," 82.
25. *O.R.,* ser. 1, vol. 40, part 1, 809.
26. Ibid., part 2, 712.
27. Neese, *Confederate Horse Artillery,* 303.
28. Ibid.; Bradshaw, *Diary of McVicar,* 51–52.
29. Charles McVicar to Mrs. Catherine Thatcher McVicar, June 28, 1864, Charles McVicar Letters.
30. Neese, *Confederate Horse Artillery,* 303–5; Bradshaw, *Diary of McVicar,* 52.
31. Charles McVicar to Mrs. Catherine Thatcher McVicar, July 18, 1864, McVicar Letters.
32. Charles R. Phelps, July 10, 1864, Phelps Letters.
33. McGregor remained here until July 27 when he received orders to move his camp to the Jones farm near the Boydton Plank Road. Report of Maj. William M. McGregor, December 7, 1864, courtesy of Lewis Leigh.
34. Nunnelee, *Famous Company,* 133; McGregor Report.
35. Nunnelee, *Famous Company,* 133; McGregor Report.
36. David Cardwell, "They Got the Watermelons," *CV* 2 (1894): 24.
37. Bradshaw, *Diary of McVicar,* 53; Neese, *Confederate Horse Artillery,* 307–8.

Chapter 31

1. As senior in rank, Johnston was to be in command of the minibattalion. However, as the batteries passed through Richmond, Maj. James Breathed joined them, having declared himself sufficiently recovered from his wound of June 29. *O.R.,* ser. 1, vol. 42, part 1, 858; Breathed Report.
2. Shoemaker reported that he set out from his camp below Petersburg on August 5. Brig. Gen. William N. Pendleton's report gives the date as "about August 10." Lieutenant Nunnelee recorded that he learned of his battery's movement toward the Valley on August 6. He was in a Richmond hospital at the time, suffering from neuralgia. In light of this, the August 5 date would seem to be correct. Black, "Shoemaker's Battery," September 1, 1864; *O.R.,* ser. 1, vol. 42, part 1, 858; Nunnelee, *Famous Company,* 157.
3. Hart et al., "Hart's Battery," 83; Bradshaw, *Diary of McVicar,* 53.
4. *O.R.,* ser. 1, vol. 42, part 2, 1171–72.
5. Ibid., 1171.
6. Hart et al., "Hart's Battery," 83; Neese, *Confederate Horse Artillery,* 310.
7. Neese, *Confederate Horse Artillery,* 311.
8. One source attributed this to the belief that Hampton's return to Lee's army was only temporary and that he would eventually move on to Culpeper. Hart et al., "Hart's Battery," 83.
9. Ibid., 83–84.
10. Neese, *Confederate Horse Artillery,* 313.
11. Bradshaw, *Diary of McVicar,* 54.
12. Neese, *Confederate Horse Artillery,* 314–16; Bradshaw, *Diary of McVicar,* 55–56.
13. McGregor Report.
14. Brig. Gen. J. Irvin Gregg reported the capture of only four prisoners. *O.R.,* ser. 1, vol. 42, part 1, 637.
15. This is obviously not the same Jones that McGregor referred to along the Boydton Plank Road southwest of Petersburg. McGregor Report.
16. Beale, *9th Virginia Cavalry,* 137.
17. The only casualty recorded for this action is Pvt. Robert W. Hunter, who was wounded in his left hand. Pvt. John C. Phillip is listed as killed on this date, but the location is given as Front Royal. This could have occurred only if Phillip were transferred to Johnston's Battery, but the records do not support this. The man killed on this date would appear to have been Pvt. Phillip Corneau, as mentioned in David Cardwell's postwar roster of the battery.
18. Col. Charles S. Wainwright reported that his Massachusetts Battery faced only a section (two) guns. *O.R.,* ser. 1, vol. 42, part 1, 540.
19. Graham's participation in the ensuing battle cannot be ruled out. With only the four guns from Letcher's Battery accompanying him, Heth may have requested that Graham remain on the field. Brig. Gen. William N. Pendleton failed to mention Graham's part in the opening phase of the battle. Federal accounts state that the battery or section they first encountered (Graham) took up a second position after it had retreated from the Davis house. This was before Heth attacked. This reference to a second position could indicate Graham's further involvement after Dearing pulled out his cavalry. Ibid., 474, 540, 858.
20. Ibid., part 2, 391.
21. Barlow's deteriorating physical condition forced him to relinquish his command to Brig. Gen. Nelson A. Miles on August 24. Ibid., part 1, 222.
22. Ibid., 408; Beale, *9th Virginia Cavalry,* 137.
23. *O.R.,* ser. 1, vol. 42, part 1, 607.

24. Edward L. Wells, *Hampton and His Cavalry in '64* (Richmond, VA: Owens Publishing Co., 1991), 277–78.
25. Minus Col. Thomas J. Simmons's Brigade.
26. Dearing's Brigade and Graham's Battery did not accompany Lee's division and were not engaged.
27. At this time Rooney Lee was incapacitated with a severe case of poison oak. Reade, Blackford, and Trout, *In the Saddle with Stuart,* 97.
28. U. R. Brooks wrote that Hart's and Thomson's Batteries were also present at Reams's Station. However, as has been shown, they were actually many miles away. Brooks's account is grossly inaccurate when discussing the participation of these batteries in this battle. Brooks, *Butler and His Cavalry,* 304–5; U. R. Brooks, "Battle of Reams Station," *CV* 22 (1914): 554.
29. McGregor stated in his report that he accompanied Barringer's Brigade. However, he also recorded that he reached Malone's Crossing about 11:00. Since Barringer did not reach the crossing until the afternoon, just as Hampton was pulling back to that point, McGregor could not have been with Barringer. Further evidence for this view comes from Hampton, who greatly complimented McGregor for his part in driving the enemy back to Reams's Station. This was prior to Hampton's withdrawal. It is possible that McGregor set out with Barringer's Brigade but when he rendezvoused with Hampton was ordered to accompany Davis and Butler. Hampton rode with this column and would have seen McGregor's performance firsthand. McGregor Report; *O.R.,* ser. 1, vol. 42, part 1, 943.
30. *O.R.,* ser. 1, vol. 42, part 1, 942.
31. Spear gave the time as 8:00 A.M. Hampton put the opening of the fight at 9:00 A.M. Ibid., 834–35, 943.
32. McGregor Report.
33. McGregor used words that indicated the gun's discharge caused it to break loose from its mounting. By now the cannoneers should have been accustomed to this all-to-frequent problem that seemed to plague the guns of the horse artillery. Ibid.
34. Ibid.
35. Shreve, "Stuart Horse Artillery," 17.
36. The identity of this casualty is unknown. Ibid.
37. Ibid.
38. *O.R.,* ser. 1, vol. 42, part 1, 944.
39. Chew Report.
40. In all probability, Graham's section did so too. David Cardwell, "A Brilliant Cavalry Coup," *CV* 26 (1918): 474.
41. McGregor stated that he encamped at Stony Creek. McGregor Report.
42. Cardwell, "Cavalry Coup," 475.
43. The advance elements of Lee's division were in position well before dawn. The fact that McGregor only reached Prince George Court House at dawn would indicate that the guns were bringing up the rear of the column.
44. Brig. Gen. August V. Kautz put the time of the Confederate withdrawal from the vicinity of Prince George Court House at 9:00 A.M. *O.R.,* ser. 1, vol. 42, part 1, 822.
45. Ibid.
46. The disposition of Graham's Battery at this time is unknown, but in all likelihood it accompanied Dearing's Brigade, to which it had been attached.
47. Chew Report.
48. *O.R.,* ser. 1, vol. 42, part 1, 946.
49. George E. Robertson to Captain Carter, November 30, 1909, Grinnan Papers.
50. In all probability, these two men deserted. McGregor Report.

51. These totals as of September 30. *O.R.,* ser. 1, vol. 42, part 2, 1309.
52. Richard J. Sommers, *Richmond Redeemed* (Garden City, NY: Doubleday & Company, 1981), 196.
53. Hart et al., "Hart's Battery," 84.
54. Longacre, *Jersey Cavaliers,* 226.
55. This unit was made up of dismounted cavalry.
56. Sommers, *Richmond Redeemed,* 200–1.
57. Ibid., 202.
58. Ibid., 246.
59. Ibid., 249.
60. Moore, *Graham's Petersburg,* 31; Sommers, *Richmond Redeemed,* 251.
61. George E. Robertson to Captain Carter, November 30, 1909, Grinnan Papers.
62. Ibid.
63. Sommers, *Richmond Redeemed,* 254.
64. Robertson contended that the battery lost eleven horses but not the gun. George E. Robertson to Captain Carter, November 30, 1909, Grinnan Papers.
65. Sommers, *Richard Redeemed,* 272.
66. *O.R.,* ser. 1, vol. 42, part 1, 947.
67. Sommers, *Richmond Redeemed,* 288–89; Beale, *9th Virginia Cavalry,* 146.
68. Wells, *Hampton and His Cavalry,* 320.
69. *O.R.,* ser. 1, vol. 42, part 1, 948.
70. Sommers, *Richmond Redeemed,* 300.
71. McGregor Report.
72. Ibid.
73. Sommers, *Richmond Redeemed,* 331.
74. *O.R.,* ser. 1, vol. 42, part 1, 948.
75. One source stated that Graham's Battery was brought up to join Hart. If so, it probably did not arrive until after 3:00 P.M. due to the conditions of the roads, which were very muddy from the recent rains. Sommers, *Richmond Redeemed,* 339.
76. *O.R.,* ser. 1, vol. 42, part 1, 948.
77. Ibid., 142.
78. Ibid., 949.
79. Brooks, *Butler and His Cavalry,* 367; Hart et al., "Hart's Battery," 86.
80. One source gave the time as 7:00 A.M., while another stated it was 8:00 A.M. Hart et al., "Hart's Battery," 83; Chew Report.
81. Hart, *Hart's Battery,* 18.
82. *O.R.,* ser. 1, vol. 42, part 1, 608–9.
83. Ibid., 949.
84. McGregor Report.

    At least one Federal was not overly impressed with McGregor's marksmanship. Sgt. Edward P. Tobie of the 1st Maine wrote in his history of the regiment, "The brigade [Smith's] had two Napoleon guns of Reynolds's battery, and Gen. [*sic*] Smith kept them throwing canister into Hampton's [Rooney Lee's] line, paying no attention to his guns [McGregor], as they hurt no one." Tobie, *First Main Cavalry,* 364.
85. Just when and where Graham's Battery fought is undetermined. It had probably been somewhere in the vicinity of Dearing's Brigade, which was manning trenches north of Hatcher's Run. There was some fighting north of the run, but nothing like that around Burgess Tavern. Graham's Battery probably moved south with the infantry sent by A. P. Hill.
86. In honor of Captain Hart, the battery did not change its name, even when Halsey was promoted to captain.

87. *O.R.,* ser. 1, vol. 42, part 1, 950.
88. Shreve, "Stuart Horse Artillery," 18.
89. Ibid.
90. *O.R.,* ser. 1, vol. 42, part 1, 951.
91. Dearing's Brigade did participate in Hampton's pursuit, but there is no record of Graham's Battery being involved. Hampton did not mention them in his report. Ibid., 950–52.
92. Shreve, "Stuart Horse Artillery," 19; Hart et al., "Hart's Battery," 92.
93. At least part of the winter was spent here. Records reveal that several men deserted while encamped here.
94. The armament of the batteries at this time was Graham, two three-inch rifles and two twelve-pound howitzers; Hart, four three-inch rifles; and McGregor, four three-inch rifles. George E. Robertson to Captain Carter, November 30, 1909, Grinnan Papers; Wise, *Long Arm of Lee,* 916.

Chapter 32

1. Micajah Woods to Dr. John R. Woods, August 24, 1864, Woods Papers.
2. Jackson's section probably was attached to either Vaughn's or Imboden's Brigade and Lurty's section to Jackson's Brigade.
3. Breathed Report.
4. Lt. William Bennett Bean was under arrest for refusing to execute an order given to him by General Early to confiscate shoes from a shoe factory in northern Maryland during the march on Washington.
5. The battery received a number of Marylanders from Johnston's Battery, who were disenchanted that a Virginian, Capt. Philip P. Johnston, was in command. McNulty was able to rebuild his ranks much sooner. Hands Notebook, 110; Matthews, *St. Mary's Beacon,* Thursday, June 15, 1905.
6. Neese, *Confederate Horse Artillery,* 311.
7. One section of the battery had suffered some loss at Moorefield. The strain of the raid and the march back to the army undoubtedly took their toll on the men and horses. This section probably was not ready for active campaigning for a few days.
8. *O.R.,* ser. 1, vol. 43, part 1, 993.
9. Maj. Gen. Robert Ransom, Lomax's predecessor, put the total strength of these brigades at about 4,000 men. This must have included both mounted and dismounted men. Certainly, the mounted portion only numbered a little over 1,500. Ibid., 1003–4.
10. When Breathed arrived, he would have been the senior horse artillery officer present and, as such, could have been placed in command of all the batteries. This does not seem to have been the case, even though many accounts and listings include these batteries as part of "Breathed's Battalion." Breathed's Battalion actually consisted of Johnston's, Shoemaker's, and Thomson's Batteries, when the third joined the army in early October. Griffin's, Jackson's, Lurty's, and McClanahan's Batteries were never grouped together officially as a battalion under any one field officer. Ibid., vol. 42, part 3, 1342.
11. Freeman, *Lee's Lieutenants,* 568.
12. *O.R.,* ser. 1, vol. 43, part 1, 568.
13. Ibid., 439; Jeffry D. Wert, *From Winchester to Cedar Creek: The Shenandoah Campaign of 1864* (Carlisle, PA: South Mountain Press, 1987), 33–34; Breathed Report.
14. *O.R.,* ser. 1, vol. 43, part 1, 473.

15. Ibid., 439.
16. While there is no documented evidence to support this, apart from the wounding of Captain Jackson's horse, the batteries would not have been left behind at Fisher's Hill, and since they were attached to these brigades, they most likely accompanied them.
17. *O.R.,* ser. 1, vol. 43, part 1, 424, 569.
18. Col. Thomas T. Munford of the 2nd Virginia Cavalry attributed the death of Sgt. William B. Cross to "friendly fire," which, under such conditions and with the inferiority of Confederate ammunition, is entirely possible. Gen. T. T. Munford, "Reminiscences of Cavalry Operations," *SHSP* 12 (1884): 349.
19. Lowell reported that his men "were thrown into confusion for a time, but held the ridge till ordered back." *O.R.,* ser. 1, vol. 43, part 1, 486.
20. In his book, Shoemaker wrote that following this engagement, the battery marched back to Winchester, where they remained until the battle on September 19. However, in his report, he stated that after the fight of the twenty-first, he moved on to Charles Town on the twenty-second and did not return to Winchester until September 5. Shoemaker, *Shoemaker's Battery,* 77; Black, "Shoemaker's Battery," September 1, 1864, and December 25, 1864.
21. Imboden's Brigade probably was operating with McCausland.
22. *O.R.,* ser. 1, vol. 43, part 1, 570, 1025.
23. Micajah Woods to Dr. John R. Woods, August 24, 1864, Woods Papers.
24. Wert, *Winchester to Cedar Creek,* 38.
25. Breathed reported that after forty minutes, the enemy was driven from their works. Brig. Gen. William W. Averell, whose troops opposed Breathed, made no mention in his report of being driven from his position. He did state, "He [the Confederate force] was prevented [from crossing] and suffered loss without any casualties worth mentioning in my command." *O.R.,* ser. 1, vol. 43, part 1, 497; Breathed Report.
26. No reason was given for this order. Either Jackson's and Lurty's Batteries had been pulled back to Bunker Hill, or it was felt that they could not contend with the enemy's artillery and needed assistance. No records exist concerning the disposition of either of these batteries during this time. Breathed Report.
27. McCausland, with his and Imboden's Brigades, joined Lomax either at Leetown or Smithfield prior to Merritt's advance. One source stated that the pickets of the 18th Virginia Cavalry of Imboden's Brigade were driven in toward Smithfield on the twenty-eighth. Delauter, *18th Virginia Cavalry,* 31.
28. *O.R.,* ser. 1, vol. 43, part 1, 571, 1025.
29. A large number of Johnston's gunners were dismounted cavalrymen in their first engagement as artillerymen. Most of the Marylanders in the battery had transferred to the Maryland Line. This performance refutes in part the allegation made by H. H. Matthews, who wrote that after the Marylanders left, the battery descended into obscurity. Breathed Report; *St. Mary's Beacon,* Thursday, June 15, 1905.
30. Black, "Shoemaker's Battery," September 1, 1864.
31. Ibid., December 25, 1864.
32. The section, under the command of Lt. Edmund H. Moorman, actually camped on the farm of John G. Meem across the river about one mile from Mount Jackson. Nunnelee, *Famous Company,* 160.
33. One source stated that Johnston's Battery left the Valley sometime around September 1 on a similar mission but traveled to Gordonsville. It returned about the

middle of the month. Robert H. Moore II, *The 1st and 2nd Stuart Horse Artillery* (Lynchburg, VA: H. E. Howard, 1985), 107.

34. There is evidence to suggest that Woods's section rejoined the army prior to Winchester. Micajah Woods to Dr. John R. Woods, September 23, 1864, Woods Papers.
35. Ibid., September 5, 1864.
36. The battery to which the forge belonged is unknown. *O.R.,* ser. 1, vol. 43, part 1, 497.
37. Ibid.
38. Ibid., part 2, 69.
39. McClanahan's Battery may have been split between McCausland's and Imboden's commands.
40. Jackson's Battery had previously been attached to McCausland's Brigade and may have been with either that brigade or Imboden's north of Winchester. However, in a postwar letter, Lt. Micajah Woods listed the engagements in which the battery participated. He made no mention of the battle of Winchester but did list Fisher's Hill. In light of this, the possibility exists that no portion of Jackson's Battery was present during the battle. Micajah Woods to Col. R. P. Chew, July 5, 1909, Chew Papers.
41. Fitz Lee was given command of all the cavalry, so Wickham moved up to command the division. Munford then took over Wickham's Brigade.
42. Only evidence for Shoemaker's section making this move is available. However, the battalion fought together with the division until later in the day, when Munford and Shoemaker were detached. Since there is no record for the position of Johnston's Battery for the hours up to about 10:00 A.M., it would seem likely that it accompanied the division at this time. Shoemaker, *Shoemaker's Battery,* 78.
43. Ibid., 79.
44. *O.R.,* ser. 1, vol. 43, part 1, 443.
45. Jeffrey C. Weaver, *22nd Virginia Cavalry* (Lynchburg, VA: H. E. Howard, 1991), 47–48; Kidd, *Recollections of a Cavalryman,* 385–89; *O.R.,* ser. 1, vol. 43, part 1, 455.
46. Munford, "Cavalry Operations," 447.
47. Col. Edmund M. Atkinson commanded the brigade in Evans's absence.
48. The "battery" actually was Johnston's four guns and Shoemaker's two.
49. Munford, "Cavalry Operations," 447–48.
50. Ibid.
51. Shoemaker's section definitely rode with Munford's Brigade. Johnston's Battery probably remained with Fitz Lee and Payne's Brigade north of Red Bud Run. Shoemaker, *Shoemaker's Battery,* 79.
52. Wert, *Winchester to Cedar Creek,* 77.
53. Averell reported that he captured one piece of artillery west of the Martinsburg Pike. This undoubtedly was from the horse artillery, but which battery is unknown. *O.R.,* ser. 1, vol. 43, part 1, 498.
54. The position of Johnston's Battery at this time is unknown.
55. The battery suffered one other casualty. Louis Lenoir, a volunteer from a Louisiana infantry regiment, had been staying with some members of the battery while recuperating from an arm wound. He chose to accompany his new friends into the battle and was killed almost instantly by an exploding shell while serving as number four on one of the guns. Shoemaker, *Shoemaker's Battery,* 80–81.
56. Later, Herley was badly wounded in the arm and leg. Nunnelee, *Famous Company,* 161.

57. Munford, "Cavalry Operations," 450.
58. Shoemaker, *Shoemaker's Battery,* 79–80.
59. Wise, *Long Arm of Lee,* 888.
60. Captain Shoemaker had remained with the cavalry when the section, under Lieutenant Phelps, retreated from Fort Hill. He mistakenly thought that it had gone with Wickham's cavalry toward Front Royal and rode in that direction. He rejoined the battery on the twenty-second, much to the relief of his men. Shoemaker, *Shoemaker's Battery,* 81–82; Nunnelee, *Famous Company,* 161.
61. Munford, "Cavalry Operations," 455.
62. *O.R.,* ser. 1, vol. 43, part 1, 428, 441.
63. Ibid., 611.
64. Actually, only one section was present; the other was still in camp near Mount Jackson.
65. Micajah Woods to Dr. John R. Woods, September 23, 1864, Woods Papers.
66. *O.R.,* ser. 1, vol. 43, part 1, 576, 1028.
67. Kershaw's division reached Early on the twenty-fifth.
68. Sheridan replaced Averell with Powell on September 23. *O.R.,* ser. 1, vol. 43, part 1, 505.
69. Munford, "Cavalry Operations," 457–58.
70. Denison, *Sabres and Spurs,* 397–98.
71. Micajah Woods to Dr. John R. Woods, September 30, 1864, Woods Papers.

Chapter 33

1. Nunnelee, *Famous Company,* 162, 165.
2. McClanahan's attachment to Smith is speculation, but since this was the brigade with which the battery normally served, the probability is high that this occurred.
3. Lurty's Battery is completely absent from the records during this entire campaign. However, since McCausland's Brigade was split between these gaps and Jackson's Battery was stationed at Brown's, in all likelihood artillery was also assigned to Swift Run Gap. Lurty's Battery would have been a logical choice for this duty.
4. Wickham had left the army to prepare to take his seat in the Confederate Congress. Munford had been commanding the division in his absence.
5. Neese, *Confederate Horse Artillery,* 318.
6. *O.R.,* ser. 1, vol. 43, part 1, 520.
7. Ibid.
8. Gen. T. T. Munford, "Reminiscences of Cavalry Operations," *SHSP* 13 (1885): 137.
9. *O.R.,* ser. 1, vol. 43, part 1, 520–521.
10. Neese, *Confederate Horse Artillery,* 323; *O.R.,* ser. 1, vol. 43, part 1, 549–50.
11. This was either Pvt. Bayly R. Brown or Pvt. Louis B. Morel.
12. Charles F. Conrad to Col. R. P. Chew, n.d., John Warwick Daniels Papers, University of Virginia Library.
13. Goldsborough, *Maryland Line,* 291–92.
14. *O.R.,* ser. 1, vol. 43, part 1, 613.
15. The exact role of Thomson's other section is obscure. In his report, Brig. Gen. William N. Pendleton placed it with Lomax's cavalry as a guard for the cavalry's wagon train on the pike. It does not appear to have marched with Shoemaker's Battery, as that battery's members make no mention in any of the accounts. Ibid., vol. 42, part 1, 864.
16. Nunnelee, *Famous Company,* 165.

17. Ibid.
18. Somewhere in the chaos, Thomson's Battery lost a third gun. Merritt's troopers captured it in the headlong pursuit of Lomax through the area where the wagon train had been parked. Shoemaker remembered seeing "one battery, without horses or men, parked with the wagons, and, of course, left standing." This could have been the third piece Thomson's Battery lost. McVicar wrote that the enemy took "one gun, one caisson, wagons of forage, and thirteen men." He may have been referring to the same gun Shoemaker mentioned. Lomax, in his report, made no reference to losing a fifth gun. Shoemaker, *Shoemaker's Battery,* 85; Bradshaw, *Diary of McVicar,* 58; *O.R.,* ser. 1, vol. 43, part 1, 448, 612–13.
19. Shoemaker, *Shoemaker's Battery,* 87.
20. Nunnelee, *Famous Company,* 165–66.
21. The men were Privates James C. Cullen, Isaac Curry, and Joseph H. Torrence. The latter returned to the battery on October 24, having escaped on the night of the ninth. Nunnelee, *Famous Company,* 171.
22. Hands Notebook, 112.
23. Bradshaw, *Diary of McVicar,* 58.
24. Not a single officer of the horse artillery was killed, wounded, or captured during the fighting at Tom's Brook and Woodstock—a singular circumstance that requires some comment. Knowing the fighting qualities of Breathed, Thomson, Johnston, McNulty, and the others, this cannot be attributed to a lapse in the performance of their duty or to cowardice. The answer would seem to lie in horseflesh. Once the officers had done all they could to get their guns up and running, a point was reached when it became clear that nothing more could be accomplished. The guns were going to be captured, and the time had come to try to save as many of the men as possible. Though it cannot be proven, the greatest loss among the men undoubtedly came from those who rode the limbers and caissons and the outriders. The horses pulling the equipment would have been the first to become exhausted. The officers and those men mounted on their own horses had a much better chance of escaping when it became every man for himself.
25. Nunnelee, *Famous Company,* 168.
26. McVicar stated that the "guns" were sent back. However, since Thomson only had one, this was probably just an error on his part. He also wrote that he and two other men, Corp. Carthage Kendall and Pvt. George W. Stewart, received permission from Major Chew to remain with the cavalry. If McVicar was correct, then Chew may have been visiting Breathed's Battalion at this time. Bradshaw, *Diary of McVicar,* 59.
27. There is reason to believe that Johnston joined Thomson at Mount Solon to refit and wait for new guns. At least some of these were received by early November. As to why these batteries were outfitted and Griffin's was not, an answer may lie in the service records of Johnston's and Thomson's, the oldest horse batteries in the army (along with McGregor's); the fact that Griffin's Battery had already been completely or partially outfitted twice before; that Griffin's was a Maryland battery as compared with two Virginia batteries; or a combination of all three. Also, it certainly didn't hurt that Chew, now the commander of the battalion, had once been captain of Thomson's Battery and that Breathed had once commanded Johnston's. Rank doth have its privileges.
28. *O.R.,* ser. 1, vol. 43, part 1, 524.
29. Ibid.
30. Some accounts state that it did help defend the rear of the army during the retreat. Part of the brigade is known to have camped at Little Washington east of the Blue Ridge on the seventeenth. For it to reach Early by the nineteenth would have been

most remarkable. Lomax with Jackson and Johnson was in the Luray Valley and did not manage to make it to Cedar Creek. According to his own report, he did not cover Early's retreat, not being able to make contact with the army. Instead, he retreated to Front Royal. Robert J. Driver, *14th Virginia Cavalry* (Lynchburg, VA: H. E. Howard, 1988), 53; Jack L. Dickinson, *16th Virginia Cavalry* (Lynchburg, VA: H. E. Howard, 1989), 60; *O.R.*, ser. 1, vol. 43, part 1, 613.

31. Some of these pieces were captured Federal artillery. Early put his loss in guns at twenty-three. *O.R.*, ser. 1, vol. 43, part 1, 564.
32. Lieutenants Robert D. Lurty and Lorenzo D. Lorentz of Lurty's Battery were captured on October 29 during an abortive attack on the 8th Ohio Volunteer Cavalry's camp at Beverly, West Virginia. The Confederate force, which numbered about 350, led by Maj. Samuel Houston Hall of the 25th Virginia Cavalry, was composed of men from eleven different regiments and batteries (one source said twenty-one). Since there was no artillery involved in the fight, the reason for Lurty's and Lorentz's presence is unknown. Lieutenant Lorentz was wounded three times, and he and Lieutenant Lurty were out of the war. Additionally, Lt. Parkison Collett led a contingent from McClanahan's Battery into the fight. According to one source, Collett served as Hall's second in command. The lieutenant was wounded, and Sgt. Thomas H. Neilson was taken prisoner. Pvt. Abel Garletts (or Goedetz) took the opportunity to desert to the enemy. Ibid., 646–48; Krick, *Lee's Colonels,* 173; *Elkins Inter-Mountain,* May 15, 1911.
33. Micajah Woods to Dr. John R. Woods, October 26, 1864, Woods Papers.
34. *O.R.,* ser. 1, vol. 43, part 1, 510.
35. Shoemaker gives the date of their leaving Lomax as the fifth, but Nunnelee's account is much more accurate, giving the time of departure, 1:00 P.M., and route of march. His date has been accepted as correct. Black, "Shoemaker's Battery," September 1, and December 25, 1864; Nunnelee, *Famous Company,* 171–72.
36. Charles R. Phelps, November 4, 1864, Phelps Letters.
37. Bradshaw, *Diary of McVicar,* 60–61.
38. Ibid., 61; Nunnelee, *Famous Company,* 174.
39. What had reduced Shoemaker's Battery by one gun is unknown. William J. Black Diary, October 1864–January 1865, VMI.
40. *O.R.,* ser. 1, vol. 43, part 1, 533; Bradshaw, *Diary of McVicar,* 62; Nunnelee, *Famous Company,* 174.
41. *O.R.,* ser. 1, vol. 43, part 1, 614.
42. Command of the battery fell to Lt. John J. Dunnington.
43. Bradshaw, *Diary of McVicar,* 62–63; Nunnelee, *Famous Company,* 174–75.
44. Micajah Woods to Dr. John R. Woods, November 17, 1864, Woods Papers.
45. Ibid., November 30, 1864, Woods Papers.
46. This was either Pvt. James L. Green or Pvt. Zachariah W. Green.
47. Nunnelee, *Famous Company,* 175–76.
48. Bradshaw, *Diary of McVicar,* 63–64.
49. Nunnelee, *Famous Company,* 177.
50. Ibid., 178.
51. The best horses in the battalion were taken to haul the guns, leaving the rest, "Company Q," behind. Lieutenant Phelps took two three-inch rifles from Shoemaker's Battery; Lieutenant Carter took one three-inch rifle and one howitzer from Thomson's; and Captain Johnston took three three-inch rifles from his own battery. Ibid.; Black Diary.
52. Nunnelee, *Famous Company,* 178–79.
53. Bradshaw, *Diary of McVicar,* 63–66.
54. *O.R.,* ser. 1, vol. 43, part 1, 677–78.

55. Micajah Woods to Mrs. Sabina Lewis Stuart Creigh Woods, December 27, 1864, Woods Papers.
56. Black Diary.
57. Nunnelee, *Famous Company,* 180.
58. Micajah Woods to Col. R. P. Chew, July 5, 1909, Chew Papers.
59. *O.R.,* ser. 1, vol. 46, part 2, 1184.

Chapter 34

1. *O.R.,* ser. 1, vol. 46, part 2, 1084.
2. Ibid., 1101.
3. Hart et al., "Hart's Battery," 100.
4. Ibid., 94.
5. Ibid.
6. *O.R.,* ser. 1, vol. 46, part 2, 1266.
7. Captain McClanahan had been on duty in Staunton and had moved with the army to Waynesboro. His service with the army there is unknown.
8. Pvt. George Pforr, Jr., had deserted McClanahan's Battery and on February 22, 1864, had joined Company K, 1st New York (Lincoln) Cavalry, under the name of Charles W. Anderson. He captured a Confederate battle flag at Waynesboro and earned a Medal of Honor.
9. William Hoxton to Mrs. Sarah Randolph, March 9, 1865, Randolph Papers.
10. Griffin's and Lurty's Batteries had not been issued guns and, in fact, had so few men they could not have manned more than three altogether. McClanahan's Battery had just lost its guns at Waynesboro. Griffin's, Lurty's, and McClanahan's Batteries had no captains appointed as yet. Griffin's was sent to Petersburg about the time that the reorganization became effective. Shoemaker's and Thomson's Batteries still were disbanded.
11. Lt. Edwin L. Halsey, who was promoted to captain, would command Hart's Battery.
12. Lt. George Wilmer Brown, who was promoted to captain, would command McGregor's Battery. At this time, Pendleton was unaware that Captain McClanahan had resigned and had been captured, and that the battery had lost its guns.
13. Lt. John W. Goodman would command Griffin's Battery.
14. Lt. Daniel Shanks, who was promoted to captain, would command Johnston's Battery.
15. Lt. John W. Carter, who was promoted to captain, would command Thomson's Battery. Lurty's Battery would be commanded by Breathed's former adjutant, William R. Lyman, also promoted to captain.
16. *O.R.,* ser. 1, vol. 46, part 3, 1327–28.
17. Pendleton undoubtedly was referring to the guns of Johnston's Battery, which were under the command of Lt. William Hoxton. Custer sent a dispatch to Sheridan, stating that he had captured three guns with seventy-five prisoners. Ibid., part 2, 792.
18. Ibid., part 3, 1328.
19. Ibid., 1329, 1334.
20. Ibid., 1336.
21. Ibid., 1340–41.
22. This battery had an advantage over Thomson's Battery. Raised in the Lynchburg area, Shoemaker's was able to reunite much faster than Thomson's, whose men were from farther north in the Valley.
23. Nunnelee, *Famous Company,* 185.
24. *O.R.,* ser. 1, vol. 47, part 2, 1300.

25. After the war, the battery's standard bearer, Louis Sherfesee, related an incident that occurred while the battery was awaiting its orders ("Color-Bearer," 59–60):

> The boys were lounging around—some with white collars, others with well greased boots and nearly all wore nice artillery jackets, when one of General [Joseph] Wheeler's cavalry regiments passed and the men began [to taunt] us by saying: "Come up out of those collars!" and "You needn't hide. I see you in those boots," and some of them would kindly offer to snap a cap on their rifles if we would give them five cents, etc., etc. The boys did not reply. We knew they took us for some militia company and thought it best to say nothing.
>
> A few days afterwards we passed the same regiment on the road. In the meantime we had been in two engagements with them, one between Fayetteville and Bentonville and the other the battle of Bentonville.
>
> When the head of their column met the battery and they recognized us, they took off their hats and said, "Boys, we take back all we said the other day. You will do to tie to."

26. *O.R.*, ser. 1, vol. 47, part 2, 1415.
27. Wade Hampton, "The Battle of Bentonville," *BLCW* 4, Part 32 (1884) 702.
28. Earle's Battery was armed with one Napoleon, two twelve-pounder howitzers, and one ten-pounder Parrott. Hart's had four three-inch rifled guns.
29. Chew and Cohen had fought a duel against each other earlier that morning. The two had fired every chamber of their pistols at each other without result. The seconds in the contest were Privates William J. Verdier and Leonidas M. Raysor. They had loaded the pistols with blanks. Strangely, both duelists were killed and one of the seconds severely wounded in the battle that followed. Sherfesee, "Color-Bearer," 60–61.
30. Ibid., 61–62.
31. *O.R.*, ser. 1, vol. 47, part 1, 575, 579–80.
32. The history of the battery by Hart et al. confirms that Halsey did lead the battery in a charge on the 19th Indiana Battery and assisted in capturing the guns when they were overrun. Hart et al., "Hart's Battery," 96.
33. Micajah Woods to Col. R. P. Chew, July 5, 1909, Chew Papers.
34. *O.R.*, ser. 1, vol. 46, part 1, 1156–57.
35. The position given for Brown's Battery (referred to as McGregor's in all of the campaign records) at the beginning of the battle has always been on the left, immediately in rear or slightly north of the "Return." This view seems to have originated with Colonel Munford. In his testimony on May 29, 1880, before the Warren Commission, which was investigating the conduct of Maj. Gen. Gouverneur K. Warren during the Five Forks campaign, Munford stated that he requested artillery be sent to him from the "Return" or at least open fire on the enemy. The guns supposedly were under the command of Brig. Gen. Matthew W. Ransom, who, according to Munford, refused the request. Munford probably was aware that McGregor's Battery had been encamped near the "Return" in the early morning. However, he does not appear to have known of its movement to the right and assumed that it was still in position at the "Return" later in the day when he requested artillery support. Munford testified that he did not have any horse artillery with him, stating that it was in reserve with the wagon trains, because "the country was so bad." He then added that the battery he requested from Ransom,

referring to it as "his," meaning Ransom's, was McGregor's. Munford was obviously very confused. McGregor's Battery was horse artillery. Furthermore, it was unlikely that it would have been placed under Ransom's command if it had been available for Munford's use. Munford's lack of knowledge of the actual deployment of the horse artillery was evident when he stated that it was with the wagon train. There was no horse artillery with Rosser. David Cardwell, *The State Columbia,* n.d.; *Supp. to O.R.,* part 1, vol. 8, 442.

The only other reference to McGregor's Battery being on the left came from Capt. William Gordon McCabe, adjutant to Lt. Col. William J. Pegram. On June 7, 1880, in answer to a question concerning artillery other than Pegram's at Five Forks, McCabe stated, "I have heard since—that I know nothing of—that McGregor had a couple of guns, horse artillery, somewhere on the left." By his own admission, his testimony was based on hearsay evidence. *Supp. to O.R.,* part 1, vol. 8, 515.

There was additional testimony concerning the position of McGregor's Battery. Rooney Lee testified on June 8, 1880, that McGregor's Battery, possibly minus a section with Roberts, was with him on the right. (There is no evidence that Roberts had artillery with him.) Ibid., 8, 532, 536.

Samuel Y. Gilliam, who was the sixteen-year-old son of the owner of the farm that Lee's troopers fronted, testified on June 29, 1880, that he saw three of McGregor's guns in position near a barn on the right of the line with Lee's troopers. He added that the guns retreated from the field by moving west along the White Oak Road and up Roper's Road. It is important to note that this testimony also refutes the long-held claim that all four of McGregor's guns were captured on Ford's Road north of Five Forks late in the battle. Ibid., 671–72, 681.

In regard to guns being placed in or near the "Return" on the Confederate left, Lt. James H. Blakemore, who served as ordnance officer on Ransom's staff, gave testimony on November 19, 1880, as to the disposition of the troops defending the "Return." He made no mention of any artillery being there at any time. Maj. Gen. Romeyn B. Ayers, whose troops took the "Return," gave a detailed description of the work but made no mention of any artillery present or of his troops encountering any artillery fire whatsoever in their advance. Ibid., vol. 9, 1187–97, 1680.

Concerning the supposed position of McGregor's Battery along the Ford Road at the south edge of the Boisseau/Young field, Col. Joseph Mayo, who commanded the infantry sent to confront the Federals advancing from that direction, testified on June 7, 1880, that he never deployed in the open field, but in the woods. He further stated that his brigade was not overwhelmed or captured at this time. He did not mention that any artillery accompanied him, met him, or was in position near him during this time. Ibid., vol. 8, 499–500.

Finally, the Federals claimed to have captured five pieces of artillery along the Ford Road near the crossroads. No claim was made concerning capturing guns in or near the Boisseau/Young field. Maj. West Funk, whose command was credited with capturing three guns (Pegram's), testified on May 28, 1880, that he was within fifty or sixty yards of the forks when he overran the guns and had never even seen the Boisseau/Young field, which was at least 600 yards from the forks. Three of the five guns captured belonged to Lt. Col. William J. Pegram's Battalion, and two to Graham's Battery of horse artillery. McGregor stated in a letter to Munford in 1906 that none of his guns were captured at Five Forks. Ibid., vol. 9, 1186; Ibid., 435–36; *O.R.,* ser. 1, vol. 46, part 1, 1100; George E. Robertson to Captain Carter, November 30, 1909, Grinnan Papers; W. M. McGregor to Gen. Thomas T. Munford, March 14, 1906, Munford-Ellis Papers, William R. Perkins Library, Duke University.

The possibility that McGregor's Battery could have moved to the right in the morning and back to the left later in the day would seem to be ruled out by an account of the fighting around "Burnt Quarter" by Miss Albeena Gilliam. She was present in the house and stated that the fighting began about 3:00 P.M. The Confederate position was in the peach orchard behind the house. Miss Gilliam recalled that grapeshot struck the back of the house as the Confederate artillery tried to stop the advancing Federals. This could only have come from McGregor's Battery, which was, according to the testimony of Samuel Y. Gilliam, in position near the tobacco barn northwest of the house. Pegram's guns were too far away to have used grapeshot. It is inconceivable that McGregor's Battery would have been withdrawn from a sector where the enemy was active and moved the entire length of the line over muddy roads to a sector where there was as yet no activity, or that Rooney Lee would have allowed such a move. *Progress Index,* January 31, 1926; *Supp. to O.R.,* part 1, vol. 8, 671.

36. Pvt. George E. Robertson recorded that the guns, two Napoleons, moved to the left in their attempt to reach Steuart, meaning that they were somewhere on the right behind the line. Who gave the order is unknown. Rooney Lee did not mention having this battery with him in his testimony to the Warren Commission, and in fact, he may not have known it was present, as it was not assigned to his division. The order could have come from Pickett around the same time he sent for Mayo. George E. Robertson to Captain Carter, November 30, 1909, Grinnan Papers.

    Brig. Gen. Montgomery D. Corse, who gave testimony to the Warren Commission on May 28, 1880, first stated that three guns from his front were moved to the left but later changed the number to two. He believed they were from Pegram's Battalion and that they accompanied Pegram when he rode over to the forks at the beginning of the battle. However, Capt. William Gordon McCabe, Pegram's adjutant, offered testimony on June 7, 1880, that refuted the movement to the left of Pegram's guns on Corse's front. He also stated that those three guns were not captured. *Supp. to O.R.,* part 1, vol. 8, 423, 428, 512, 514.

    Though he was mistaken as to what command the guns belonged to, Corse's recollection of guns being moved from his front to the left supports Robertson's account of Graham's two Napoleons moving in that direction to reinforce Steuart. McCabe certainly knew which of his guns were captured that day and which escaped. There is ample evidence to conclude that Pegram lost three guns and Graham two at Five Forks.
37. George W. Shreve stated that the battery "took only a small part" in the fighting at Five Forks. Shreve, "Stuart Horse Artillery," 19.
38. Cardwell, *State Columbia.*
39. W. M. McGregor to Gen. Thomas T. Munford, March 14, 1906, Munford-Ellis Papers.
40. *O.R.,* ser. 1, vol. 46, part 1, 1280.
41. Shreve, "Stuart Horse Artillery," 19–20.
42. *O.R.,* ser. 1, vol. 46, part 1, 1140; Chris Calkins, "With Shouts of Triumph and Trumpets Blowing," *Blue and Gray* 7, no. 6 (August 1990): 32–36; W. M. McGregor to Gen. Thomas T. Munford, March 14, 1906, Munford-Ellis Papers.
43. Nunnelee, *Famous Company*, 190.
44. From a booklet, *Letters and Papers Relating to Services of Lieutenant-Colonel R. P. Chew, C.S.A.,* n.d., Chew Papers.
45. George E. Robertson to Captain Carter, November 30, 1909, Grinnan Papers.
46. The identity of Breathed's savior is in question. One source claims it was Lt. William B. Conrad of the 12th Virginia Cavalry, another a Sergeant Scruggs of Munford's staff. This was probably Corp. James E. Scruggs of the 2nd Virginia Cavalry, who retrieved General Read's sword as a souvenir of the battle. R. P. Chew, "Defense of High Bridge, Near Farmville," *CV* 16 (1908): 394; Bradley T.

Johnston, "Major James Breathed," *Confederate Military History*, vol. 2, *Maryland* (Wilmington, NC: Broadfoot Publishing Company, 1988) 213.

47. George E. Robertson to Captain Carter, November 30, 1909, Grinnan Papers.
48. Shreve, "Stuart Horse Artillery," 21–22.
49. McGregor stated that the guns were left on the fairgrounds. W. M. McGregor to Gen. Thomas T. Munford, March 14, 1906, Munford-Ellis Papers.
50. Shreve, "Stuart Horse Artillery," 22–23.
51. Wartime spelling was Greensborough.
52. George E. Robertson to Captain Carter, November 30, 1909, Grinnan Papers.
53. Jennings C. Wise wrote that Shoemaker's Battery surrendered at Appomattox, but this was not the case. The source for his estimate of the battery's strength, which he placed at ninety men, is unknown. However, the number probably was fairly accurate, as the battery had been reorganized over a month earlier. Wise, *Long Arm of Lee,* 954.
54. Shoemaker claimed that Nunnelee joined him at Lynchburg and rode south with the men of the battery. However, Nunnelee's own account of his actions refutes this. Shoemaker, *Shoemaker's Battery,* 94–95; Nunnelee, *Famous Company,* 186–90.
55. Charles W. McVicar, "Chew's Battery—Reunion of October, 1890," *SHSP* 18 (1890): 283–84.
56. Roger Preston Chew to Thomas T. Munford, March 26, 1906, and July 11, 1911, Thomas T. Munford Papers, Manuscript Department, William R. Perkins Library, Duke University.
57. Micajah Woods to Col. R. P. Chew, July 5, 1909, Chew Papers.
58. Now Burlington.
59. Hart et al., "Hart's Battery," 97; Sherfesee, "Color-Bearer," 63–64.
60. Sherfesee, "Color-Bearer," 65–66.

Appendix I

1. McClellan, *I Rode with Stuart,* 210–11.
2. Matthews, "Death of Pelham"; Matthews, "Major John Pelham," 382.
3. Col. Harry Gilmor, *Four Years in the Saddle* (New York: Harper & Brothers, 1866), 70–71.
4. Averell's report names the 4th Pennsylvania and the 4th New York as the regiments he ordered deployed before ordering up a section of Browne's Battery. Another source states that a platoon of the 1st Rhode Island, a squadron of the 6th Ohio, supported by the remainder of the 1st Rhode Island, formed the advance guard. Denison, *Sabres and Spurs,* 210; *O.R.,* ser. 1, vol. 25, part 1, 49.
5. Browne stated in his report: "Owing, however, to the narrow and extremely muddy and impracticable condition of the road, I could bring but one piece into battery, sending the others to the rear. The enemy now appeared in such force as to momentarily check the advance of our cavalry, which, however, soon rallied, and drove them from the woods, their left flank being turned by our cavalry on the right, with which was posted two of my pieces, commanded by Lieutenant Clark, and which did good service."

   If he sent his other guns to the rear, they could not have been in position to fire on the 3rd Virginia during its first charge. When they were brought forward again, it was to support McIntosh's Brigade, which occupied the Wheatley farm buildings before the Confederates could seize them. *O.R.,* ser. 1, vol. 25, part 1, 54, 56–57.
6. Ibid., 49.

7. Ibid., 55.
8. Ibid., 57.
9. Hudgins and Kleese, *Old Dominion Dragoon,* 65.
10. Matthews, "Death of Pelham."
11. *Supp. to O.R.,* part 1, vol. 4, 504.

Appendix II

1. Ladd and Ladd, *Bachelder Papers,* vol. 2, 1250–51, 1288–89.
2. McClellan, *I Rode with Stuart,* 338.
3. Ladd and Ladd, *Bachelder Papers,* vol. 3, 1384–85.
4. Davis recorded that the battery arrived on the first and that it was asked the next morning to participate in the attacks. While his route has never been questioned, his timetable has. The "next morning" was conveniently interpreted to mean July 3 so as to be able to place the battery in the bombardment preceding Pickett's Charge. Ibid., 1250; *O.R.,* ser. 1, vol. 27, part 2, 675.
5. Ladd and Ladd, *Bachelder Papers,* vol. 2, 1289.
6. Nye, *Here Come the Rebels,* 270.
7. *O.R.,* ser. 1, vol. 27, part 2, 675.
8. Ladd and Ladd, *Bachelder Papers,* vol. 2, 1250, 1289.
9. Both Davis and Hayden agree that the battery arrived on the field on July 2. Ibid., 1251, 1289.
10. Ibid., 1289.
11. Ibid., 1250.
12. *O.R.,* ser. 1, vol. 27, part 2, 543; Wise, *Long Arm of Lee,* 636.
13. Ladd and Ladd, *Bachelder Papers,* vol. 2, 1289.
14. Goldsborough, *Maryland Line,* 285.
15. Ladd and Ladd, *Bachelder Papers,* vol. 2, 1289.
16. *O.R.,* ser. 1, vol. 27, part 2, 602–4.
17. Ibid., 604–5.

BIBLIOGRAPHY

MANUSCRIPTS

Anniston and Calhoun County Public Library
- Fred Martin Papers
- Stuart to "My Dear Sir" (Dr. Atkinson Pelham): March 29, 1863

College of William and Mary
- Robb-Bernard Collection

Duke University
- Munford-Ellis Papers
- Thomas T. Munford Papers

Jefferson County Museum
- Roger Preston Chew Papers

Library of Congress
- Louis Trezevant Wigfall Papers

Maryland Historical Society
- Washington Hands Civil War Notebook

Museum of the Confederacy
- Lewis T. Nunnelee Papers

National Archives (Compiled Service Records)
- Compiled Service Records of Confederate General and Staff Officers, and Non-Regimental Enlisted Men
- Microcopy M331, Rolls 20, 74, 195, and 244
- Compiled Service Records of Confederate Soldiers Who Served in Organizations from the State of Maryland
- Microcopy M321, Rolls 10 and 11
- Compiled Service Records of Confederate Soldiers Who Served in Organizations from the State of South Carolina
- Microcopy M267, Roll 98
- Compiled Service Records of Confederate Soldiers Who Served in Organizations from the State of Virginia
- Microcopy M324, Rolls 4, 65, 77, 120, 267, 273, 304, 310, 319, 336, 337, and 338
- Unfiled Slips and Papers, Confederate Records

New Hampshire Historical Society
- Bachelder Papers

South Carolina Relic Room
- Louis Sherfesee Papers

Tulane University
William R. Lyman, "Cross Keys and Port Republic: A Speech Read before A.N.V. Camp No. 1, November 12, 1892."
United States Army Military History Institute
Lewis Leigh Collection
William E. Peters Papers
University of North Carolina at Chapel Hill
Hairston-Wilson Papers
Edwin L. Halsey Papers
R. Channing Price Papers
University of Virginia
Berkeley Papers
John Warwick Daniel Papers
Charles R. Phelps Papers
Davis-Preston-Saunders Collection
Micajah Woods Papers
Virginia Historical Society
Philip Preston Johnston Papers
Randolph Family Papers
Grinnan Family Papers
Saunders Family Papers
John Zachary Holladay Scott Letter
Williams Family Papers
Virginia Military Institute Archives
George Wilmer Brown File
William J. Black Papers
Roger Preston Chew File
Charles Edward Ford File
Marcellus Newton Moorman File
Milton Rouss File
James Walton Thomson File
Edward Duke Yancy File
Privately Owned Papers
Mr. Sharon Bell
William P. Walters Papers
Virgil S. Hart
Calvin C. Hart Papers
Mrs. Anne E. Inglis
William B. Bean Papers
Lewis Leigh
Report of Maj. William M. McGregor

NEWSPAPERS

Elkins Inter-Mountain
Jacksonville Republican
Progress Index
Randolph Enterprise
Soldier's Paper
The State Columbia
St. Mary's Beacon

ARTICLES AND UNPUBLISHED MANUSCRIPTS

Alexander, Ted. "McCausland's Raid and the Burning of Chambersburg." *Blue and Gray* 11, no. 6 (August 1994): 11–18, 46–64.

Anderson, O. V. "Capt. Pierce B. Anderson's Sword." *Confederate Veteran* 19 (1911): 544.

"Beauregard Rifles." *Southern Historical Society Papers* 30 (1902): 323–25.

Berkeley, F. Carter. "Imboden's Dash into Charlestown." *Southern Historical Society Papers* 31 (1903): 11–18.

Bowmaster, Patrick A. "Confederate Brig. Gen. B. H. Robertson and the 1863 Gettysburg Campaign." Master's thesis. Virginia Polytechnic Institute and State University, Blacksburg, Virginia.

Breathed, Frank. "In Memoriam—Maj. James Breathed." *Confederate Veteran* 16 (1908): 574–75.

Brooks, U. R. "Battle of Reams Station." *Confederate Veteran* 22 (1914): 554–55.

Brooksher, William R., and David K. Snyder. "Around McClellan Again." *Civil War Times Illustrated* 13, no. 5 (August 1974): 5–8, 39–48.

Butler, M. C. "The Cavalry Fight at Trevilian Station." *Battles and Leaders of the Civil War* part 27 (1884): 4: 237–39.

Calkins, Chris. "With Shouts of Triumph and Trumpets Blowing." *Blue and Gray* 7, no. 6 (August 1990): 32–36.

Cardwell, David. "A Brilliant Cavalry Coup." *Confederate Veteran* 26 (1918): 474–76.

———. "A Horse Battery." *Confederate Veteran* 27 (1919): 6–7.

———. "They Got the Watermelons." *Confederate Veteran* 2 (1894): 24.

———. "When the Gallant Lieutenant Ford Was Killed." *Confederate Veteran* 26 (1918): 207–8.

Carter, William H. "The Sixth Regiment of Cavalry." *Maine Bugle* 3 (October 1896): 299.

Cauley, Avis Mary Cusuis. "The Confederacy in the Lower Shenandoah Valley as Illustrated by the Career of Colonel Roger Preston Chew." Master's thesis. University of Pittsburgh, Pennsylvania.

Chew, R. P. "Defense of High Bridge, Near Farmville." *Confederate Veteran* 16 (1908): 394.

Cooke, John Esten. "Gallant John Pelham." *Philadelphia Weekly Times* 5, no. 10 (April 30, 1881).

Daihl, Samuel L. "1865—Our Johnnies Come Marching Home." *Kittochtinny Historical Society, Papers Read before the Society* 15 (1970): 129–30.

Davis, Jacob. "Index Miscellaneous Deaths, 1855 to 1875." *Jacob Davis Notebook.* Danville Public Library Genealogical Room.

Deck, D. M. "Captured at Trevilian Station." *Confederate Veteran* 24 (1916): 123–24.

Drewy, P. H. "The Ninth of June, 1864." *Confederate Veteran* 35 (1927): 290–93.

Early, Jubal A. "Early's March on Washington in 1864." *Battles and Leaders of the Civil War* part 30 (1884): 4: 492–98.

Elmore, Thomas L. "The Grand Cannonade: A Confederate Perspective." *Gettysburg Magazine* 19: 100–111.

Franklin, William B. "Notes on Crampton's Gap and Antietam." *Battles and Leaders of the Civil War* part 15 (1884): 2: 591–97.

Grattan, George D. "The Battle of Boonsboro Gap or South Mountain." *Southern Historical Society Papers* 39 (1914): 31–44.

Hall, Clark B. "Robert F. Beckham: The Man Who Commanded Stuart's Horse Artillery after Pelham Fell." *Blue and Gray Magazine* (December 1991): 34–37.

Hampton, Wade. "The Battle of Bentonville." *Battles and Leaders of the Civil War* part 32 (1884): 700–705.

Harrison, Kathy Georg. "Ridges of Grim War." *Blue and Gray Magazine* 5, no. 6 (July 1988): 10–52.

Hart, C. C. "The Charles Town Raid." *Confederate Veteran* 25 (1917): 21.

———. *Battle of Piedmont—64,* written for the Randolph Chapter United Daughters of the Confederacy. Copy provided by Virgil S. Hart, grandson of Calvin C. Hart.

Hart, James F. "Battle of Brandy Station." *Philadelphia Weekly Times* 4, no. 18 (June 26, 1880).

Hart, Maj. James F., Dr. L. C. Stephens, Louis Sherfesee, and Charles H. Schwing. "History of Hart's Battery." Manuscript. South Carolina Library, University of South Carolina, Columbia.

Hill, Daniel H. "The Battle of South Mountain, or Boonsboro'." *Battles and Leaders of the Civil War* part 14 (1884): 559–81.

Imboden, John D. "The Battle of New Market, Va., May 15th, 1864." *Battles and Leaders of the Civil War* part 30 (1884): 480–86.

———. "The Battle of Piedmont." *Confederate Veteran* 32 (1924): 18–20.

———. "The Confederate Retreat from Gettysburg." *Battles and Leaders of the Civil War* part 21 (1884): 420–29.

"John Pelham's Academic Record at West Point." *Cannoneer: Newsletter of the John Pelham Historical Association* 4, no. 1 (July 1985): 6.

Johnson, Bradley T. "A Striking War Incident." *Southern Historical Society Papers* 29 (1901): 227–29.

Johnston, Philip P. "Worn Suit of Gray: Tribute to Breathed." *Confederate Veteran* 17 (1909): 267.

Jones, Juliette Burwell Henry. "Major Mathis Winston Henry, C.S.A. of Bowling Green, Ky." *Journal of the Clarke County Historical Association* 6 (1946): 53–60.

Jones, Lt. Woodruff. "Defending Pennsylvania against Lee." *Civil War Times Illustrated* 5, no. 6 (October 1966): 36–43.

Longacre, Edward G. "Target: Winchester, Virginia." *Civil War Times Illustrated* 15, no. 3 (June 1976): 22–31.

———, ed. "A Race for Life at Brandy Station." *Civil War Times Illustrated* 17, no. 9 (January 1979): 32–38.

Luvas, Dr. Jay, and Col. Wilbur S. Nye. "The Campaign That History Forgot." *Civil War Times Illustrated* 8, no. 7 (November 1969): 11–42.

"Maj. Gen. John H. Forney, *Confederate Veteran* 15 (1907): 488.

Matthews, Henry Hau. "Major John Pelham, Confederate Hero." *Southern Historical Society Papers* 38 (1910): 379–84.

McDonald, Capt. William N. "The Confederate Dead in Stonewall Cemetery, Winchester, VA." *Southern Historical Society Papers* 22 (1894): 41–48.

McVicar, Charles W. "Chew's Battery—Reunion of October, 1890." *Southern Historical Society Papers* 18 (1890): 28–86.

Moorman, Marcellus N. "Narrative of Events and Observations Connected with the Wounding of General T. J. (Stonewall) Jackson." *Southern Historical Society Papers* 30 (1902): 110–17.

"Mounted Flying Artillery." *Cannoneer* 8, no. 3 (November 1989): 6–7.

Munford, Gen. T. T. "Reminiscences of Cavalry Operations." *Southern Historical Society Papers* 12 (1884): 342–50.

———. "Reminiscences of Cavalry Operations." *Southern Historical Society Papers* 13 (1885): 133–44.

Nye, Col. Wilbur S. "How Stuart Got Back across the Potomac." *Civil War Times Illustrated* 4, no. 9 (January 1966): 45–48.

O'Brien, Kevin E. "'Glory Enough for All': Lt. William Brooke-Rawle and the 3rd Pennsylvania Cavalry at Gettysburg." *Gettysburg Magazine,* no. 13, (July 1995): 89–107.

Proceedings of the Clarke County Historical Association. 11 (1951–53): 57.

Proceedings of the Clarke County Historical Association. 12 (1951–53): 85.

Rhea, Gordon C. "They Fought Confounded Plucky." *North and South* 3, no. 1 (November 1999): 48–66.

Rollins, Richard. "Lee's Artillery Prepares for Pickett's Charge." *North and South* 2, no. 7 (September 1999): 41–55.

Saussy, G. N. "Campaigning with Jeb Stuart." *Watson's Magazine* 13, no. 2 (June 1911): 152–57.

Schultz, Fred L. "A Cavalry Fight Was On." *Civil War Times Illustrated* 23, no. 10 (February 1985): 14–17, 44–47.

Schuricht, Lt. Hermann. "Jenkins's Brigade in the Gettysburg Campaign." *Southern Historical Society Papers* 24 (1896): 339–51.

Scott, John Z. H. *Memoirs of J. Z. H. Scott,* Virginia Historical Society.

Shanks, S. T. "Heroism like That of John Pelham." *Confederate Veteran* 9 (1901): 157.

———. "Visiting Battlefield of Piedmont." *Confederate Veteran* 11 (1903): 40.

Sherfesee, Louis. "Reminiscences of a Color-Bearer." Manuscript. South Carolina Relic Room and Museum, Columbia, SC.

Shevchuk, Paul M. "The Cavalry Fight at Fairfield, Pennsylvania, July 3, 1863." *Gettysburg Magazine* no. 1 (July 1989): 105–17.

———. "The Wounding of Albert Jenkins, July 2, 1863." *Gettysburg Magazine* no. 3 (July 1990): 51–63.

Smith, J. C. "Roll of the Stuart Horse Artillery, (McGregor's Battery) Army of Northern Virginia." *Southern Historical Society Papers* 19 (1891): 281–83.

Vogtsberger, Peggy. "The Mysteries of Kelly's Ford." *Cannoneer* 5, no. 5 (July 1985): 2–8.

———. "Pelham in the Maryland Campaign, Part II: The Battle of Antietam." *Cannoneer* 3, no. 1 (July 1984): 2–6.

———. "The Ten Days." *Cannoneer* 1, no. 4 (January 1983): 4–6.

Williams, Robert A. "Haw's Shop: A 'Storm of Shot and Shell.'" *Civil War Times Illustrated* 9 (January 1971): 12–19.

Wise, John S. "A Modern Greek." *Bob Taylor's Magazine* 4, no. 3 (December 1906): 260–72.

BOOKS AND PAMPHLETS

Alexander, Gen. Edward Porter. *Military Memoirs of a Confederate.* New York: Da Capo Press, 1993.

Alexander, Ted, Jin Neitzel, Virginia Stake, and William P. Conrad. *Southern Revenge.* Shippensburg, PA: White Mane Publishing Company, 1989.

Andrews, R. Snowden. *Andrews' Mounted Artillery Drill.* Charleston: Evans and Cogswell, 1863.

Anthony, William. *History of the Battle of Hanover, Tuesday, June 30, 1863.* Hanover, PA: Hanover B. P. O. E. 1945.

Armstrong, Richard L. *7th Virginia Cavalry.* Lynchburg, VA: H. E. Howard, 1992.

———. *11th Virginia Cavalry.* Lynchburg, VA: H. E. Howard, 1989.

Avirett, Rev. James B. *The Memoirs of General Turner Ashby and His Compeers.* Baltimore: Selby and Dulany, 1867.

Balfour, Daniel T. *13th Virginia Cavalry.* Lynchburg VA: H. E. Howard, 1986.
Barefoot, Daniel W. *General Robert F. Hoke: Lee's Modest Warrior.* Winston-Salem, NC: John F. Blair Publisher, 1996.
Barrett, John G. *The Civil War in North Carolina.* Chapel Hill: University of North Carolina Press, 1963.
Beach, William H. *The First New York (Lincoln) Cavalry.* Annandale,VA: Bacon Race Books, 1988.
Beale, G. W. *A Lieutenant of Cavalry in Lee's Army.* Baltimore: Butternut and Blue, 1994.
Beale, R. L. T. *History of the 9th Virginia Cavalry in the War Between the States.* Amissville, VA: American Fundamentalist, 1981.
Bearss, Ed, and Chris Calkins. *The Battle of Five Forks.* Lynchburg, VA: H. E. Howard, 1985.
Bigelow, John, Jr. *Chancellorsville.* New York: Konecky and Konecky, 1995.
Blackford, W. W. *War Years with Jeb Stuart.* New York: Charles Scribner's Sons, 1945.
Boykin, Edward. *Beefsteak Raid.* New York: Funk and Wagnells Company, 1960.
Bradshaw, Ada Bruce Despe, ed. *Civil War Diary of Charles McVicar.* 1977.
Brooks, U. R. *Butler and His Cavalry in the War of Secession, 1861–1865.* Camden, SC: J. J. Fox, 1989.
———, ed. *Stories of the Confederacy.* Columbia, SC: State Company, 1912.
Capers, Ellison. *Confederate Military History.* Vol. 6, *South Carolina.* Wilmington, NC: Broadfoot Publishing Company, 1987.
Catton, Bruce. *Grant Takes Command.* Boston: Little, Brown and Company, 1969.
Chew, Roger Preston. *Stonewall Jackson: Address of R. P. Chew Delivered at the Virginia Military Institute, Lexington, Virginia, on the Unveiling of Ezekiel's Statue of General T. J. Jackson, June 12, 1912.* Lexington, VA: Rockbridge County News Print, 1912.
Clark, Walter, ed. *Histories of the Several Regiments and Battalions from North Carolina in the Great War 1861–'65.* Raleigh, NC: E. M. Uzzell, Printer and Binder, 1901.
Coddington, Edwin B. *The Gettysburg Campaign: A Study in Command.* New York, Charles Scribner's Sons, 1968.
Cohen, Stan. *The Civil War in West Virginia.* Charleston, WV: Pictorial Histories Publishing Company, 1976.
Cooke, John Esten. *Mohun.* Charlottesville: Historical Publishing Co., 1936.
———. *Surry of Eagle's-Nest.* New York: G. W. Dillingham Co., Publisher, 1894.
———. *Wearing of the Gray.* Millwood: Krause Reprint Co., 1959.
Copland, D. Graham. *Many Years After.* n.p., n.d.

Crowninshield, Benjamin W. *A History of the First Regiment of Massachusetts Cavalry Volunteers.* Boston: Houghton, Mifflin and Company, 1891.

Davis, Burke. *Jeb Stuart: The Last Cavalier.* New York: Bonanza Books, 1957.

Davis, William C. *The Battle of New Market.* Baton Rouge: Louisiana University Press, 1975.

Delauter, Roger U. *18th Virginia Cavalry.* Lynchburg, VA: H. E. Howard, 1985.

Denison, Frederic. *Sabres and Spurs: The First Regiment Rhode Island Cavalry in the Civil War, 1861–1865.* Baltimore: Butternut and Blue, 1994.

Dickinson, Jack L. *16th Virginia Cavalry.* Lynchburg, VA: H. E. Howard, 1989.

Dimitry, John. *Confederate Military History.* Vol. 13, *Louisiana.* Wilmington, NC: Broadfoot Publishing Company, 1988.

Divine, John. *35th Battalion Virginia Cavalry.* Lynchburg, VA: H. E. Howard, 1985.

Douglas, Henry Kyd. *I Rode with Stonewall.* Greenwich, CT: Fawcett Publications, 1961.

Downey, Fairfax. *Clash of Cavalry: The Battle of Brandy Station.* New York: David McKay Company, 1959.

Driver, Robert J., Jr., *The Staunton Artillery—McClanahan's Battery.* Lynchburg, VA: H. E. Howard, 1988.

———. *1st Virginia Cavalry.* Lynchburg, VA: H. E. Howard, 1991.

———. *14th Virginia Cavalry.* Lynchburg, VA: H. E. Howard, 1988.

Driver, Robert J., Jr., and H. E. Howard. *2nd Virginia Cavalry.* Lynchburg, VA: H. E. Howard, 1995.

Encounter at Hanover: Prelude to Gettysburg. Hanover, PA: Historical Publication Committee of the Hanover Chamber of Commerce, 1985.

Fox, William F. *New York at Gettysburg.* Albany, NY: J. B. Lyon Company, Printers, 1900.

Freeman, Douglas Southall. *Lee's Lieutenants.* New York: Charles Scribner's Sons, 1942.

French, William H., William F. Barry, and Henry J. Hunt. *Instruction for Field Artillery.* Philadelphia: J. B. Lippincott and Co., 1861.

Frye, Dennis E. *12th Virginia Cavalry.* Lynchburg, VA: H. E. Howard, 1988.

Gallagher, Gary W., ed. *Fighting for the Confederacy: The Personal Recollections of General Edward Porter Alexander.* Chapel Hill: University of North Carolina Press, 1989.

Garnett, Theodore Stanford. *Riding with Stuart: Reminiscences of an Aide-de-Camp.* Edited by Robert J. Trout. Shippensburg, PA: White Mane Publishing Company, 1994.

Gibbon, John. *The Artillerist's Manual.* Glendale: Benchmark Publishing Company, 1970.

Gilmor, Col. Harry. *Four Years in the Saddle.* New York: Harper and Brothers, 1866.

Glazier, Willard. *Three Years in the Federal Cavalry.* New York: R. H. Ferguson and Company, 1874.

Goldsborough, W. W. *The Maryland Line in the Confederate Army.* Gaithersburg, MD: Olde Soldier Books, 1987.

Griess, Col. Thomas E., and Jay Luvas, eds. *Instruction for Field Artillery.* New York: Greenwood Press, 1968.

Hard, Abner. *History of the Eighth Cavalry Regiment Illinois Volunteers.* Dayton: Morningside Bookshop, 1996.

Hartley, Chris J. *Stuart's Tarheels: James B. Gordon and His North Carolina Cavalry.* Baltimore: Butternut and Blue, 1996.

Hartzler, Daniel D. *Marylanders in the Confederacy.* Westminster: Family Line Publications, 1986.

Hassler, William Woods. *Colonel John Pelham: Lee's Boy Artillerist.* Chapel Hill: University of North Carolina Press, 1960.

Hennessy, John J. *Return to Bull Run.* New York: Simon and Schuster, 1993.

Henry, John Flournoy. *A History of the Henry Family.* Louisville, KY: Press of John P. Morton & Co., 1900.

Hewett, Janet B., Noah Andre Trudeau, and Bryce A. Suderow. *Supplement to the Official Records of the Union and Confederate Armies.* Wilmington, NC: Broadfoot Publishing Company, 1994.

History of Roanoke County. n.p. 1902.

Horn, John. *The Destruction of the Weldon Railroad.* Lynchburg, VA: H. E. Howard, 1991.

Hotchkiss, Maj. Jed, and Clement A. Evans, eds. *Confederate Military History.* Vol. 3, *Virginia.* Dayton: Press of Morningside Bookshop, 1975.

Hudgins, Garland C., and Richard B. Kleese, eds. *Recollections of an Old Dominion Dragoon.* Orange, VA: Publisher's Press, 1993.

Hull, Susan R. *Boy Soldiers of the Confederacy.* New York: Neale Publishing Co., 1905.

Johnson, Curt, and Richard C. Anderson, Jr. *Artillery Hell: The Employment of Artillery at Antietam.* College Station: Texas A&M University Press, 1995.

Johnston, Bradley T. *Confederate Military History.* Vol. 2, *Maryland.* Wilmington, NC: Broadfoot Publishing Company, 1988.

Kidd, J. H. *Personal Recollections of a Cavalryman.* Ionia, MI: Sentinel Printing Company, 1908.

Krick, Robert K. *Conquering the Valley.* New York: William Morrow and Company, 1996.

———. *Lee's Colonels.* Dayton, OH: Morningside House, 1991.

———. *9th Virginia Cavalry.* Lynchburg, VA: H. E. Howard, 1982.

Ladd, David L. and Aubrey J., eds. *The Bachelder Papers: Gettysburg in Their Own Words.* Vol. 2. Dayton, OH: Morningside House, 1994.

Laidley, T. T. S. *The Ordnance Manual for the Use of the Officers of the United States Army.* Philadelphia: J. B. Lippincott and Co., 1861.

Lauter, Don Richard. *Winslow Homer and Friends in Prince George and Dinwiddie County Virginia, 1864–1865.* n.p., n.d.

Leech, Margaret. *Reveille in Washington, 1860–1865.* New York: Harper and Brothers Publishers, 1941.

Longacre, Edward G. *The Cavalry at Gettysburg.* Cranbury, NJ: Associated University Presses, 1986.

———. *Jersey Cavaliers.* Hightstown, NJ: Longstreet House, 1992.

———. *Mounted Raids of the Civil War.* Lincoln: University of Nebraska Press, 1994.

Lowry, Terry. *Last Sleep: The Battle of Droop Mountain.* Charleston: Pictorial Histories Publishing Co., 1996.

McClellan, H. B. *I Rode with Jeb Stuart.* Bloomington: Indiana University Press, 1958.

McDonald, William N. *A History of the Laurel Brigade.* Arlington, VA: R. W. Beatty, 1969.

Manucy, Albert. *Artillery through the Ages.* Washington, DC: U.S. Government Printing Office, 1962.

Mercer, Philip. *The Gallant Pelham.* Kennesaw, GA: Continental Book Company, 1958.

Milham, Charles G. *Gallant Pelham: American Extraordinary.*Wilmington, DE: Broadfoot Publishing Company, 1985.

Mitchell, Adele H., ed. *The Letters of Major General James E. B. Stuart.* Stuart-Mosby Historical Society, 1990.

Moore, Edward A. *The Story of a Cannoneer under Stonewall Jackson.* New York: Neale Publishing Company, 1907.

Moore, Robert H., II. *Chew's Ashby, Shoemaker's Lynchburg and the Newtown Artillery.* Lynchburg, VA: H. E. Howard, 1995.

———. *Graham's Petersburg, Jackson's Kanawha, and Lurty's Roanoke Horse Artillery.* Lynchburg, VA: H. E. Howard, 1996.

———. *The 1st and 2nd Stuart Horse Artillery.* Lynchburg, VA: H. E. Howard, 1985.

Morris, George, and Susan Foutz. *Lynchburg in the Civil War: The City—The People—The Battle.* Lynchburg, VA: H. E. Howard, 1984.

Murfin, James V. *The Gleam of Bayonets.* New York: Bonanza Books, 1965.

Musick, Michael P. *6th Virginia Cavalry.* Lynchburg, VA: H. E. Howard, 1990.

Nanzig, Thomas P. *3rd Virginia Cavalry.* Lynchburg, VA: H. E. Howard, 1989.

Neese, George M. *Three Years in the Confederate Horse Artillery.* Dayton: Press of Morningside Bookshop, 1983.

Norris, J. E., ed. *History of the Lower Shenandoah Valley Counties of Frederick, Berkeley, Jefferson, and Clarke.* Chicago: A. Warner & Co., 1890.

Nye, Wilbur S. *Here Come the Rebels.* Baton Rouge: Louisiana State University Press, 1965.

O'Neill, Robert F., Jr. *The Cavalry Battles of Aldie, Middleburg, and Upperville.* Lynchburg, VA: H. E. Howard, 1993.

Opie, John N. *A Rebel Cavalryman.* Chicago: W. B. Conkey Company, 1899.

Ordnance Bureau. *The Field Manual for the Use of the Officers on Ordnance Duty.* Richmond, VA: Ritchie and Dunnavant, 1862.

Palmer, William P., H. W. Flournoy, and Sherwin McRae, eds. *Calendar of Virginia State Papers: January 1, 1836–April 15, 1869.* Richmond, VA: 1893.

Pleasants, Henry, Jr., and George H. Straley. *Inferno at Petersburg.* Philadelphia: Chilton Company, 1961.

Poague, William Thomas. *Gunner with Stonewall.* Jackson, TN: McCowat-Mercer Press, 1957.

Pollard, E. A. *The Lost Cause.* New York: E. B. Treat and Co., 1867.

Priest, John Michael. *Antietam: The Soldiers' Battle.* New York: Oxford University Press, 1989.

———. *Before Antietam: The Battle for South Mountain.* Shippensburg, PA: White Mane Publishing Company, 1992.

Reade, Frank Robertson, L. Minor Blackford, and Robert J. Trout. *In the Saddle with Stuart: The Story of Frank S. Robertson of Stuart's Staff.* Gettysburg, PA: Thomas Publications, 1998.

Rhea, Gordon C. *The Battle of the Wilderness.* Baton Rouge, LA: Louisiana State University Press, 1994.

———. *The Battles for Spotsylvania Court House and the Road to Yellow Tavern.* Baton Rouge, LA: Louisiana State University Press, 1997.

Schenck, Martin. *Up Came Hill.* Harrisburg, PA: Stackpole Company, 1958.

Schildt, John W. *Stonewall Jackson Day by Day.* Chewsville, MD: Antietam Publications, n.d.

Scott, James G., and Edward A. Wyatt IV. *Petersburg's Story.* Petersburg, VA: Titmus Optical Company, 1960.

Sergent, Mary Elizabeth. *They Lie Forgotten.* Middletown, NY: Prior King Press, 1986.

Shoemaker, John J. *Shoemaker's Battery.* Gaithersburg, MD: Butternut Press, n.d.

Smith, Gustavus W. *Confederate War Papers.* New York: Atlantic Publishing and Engraving Company, 1884.

Sommers, Richard J. *Richmond Redeemed.* Garden City, NY: Doubleday & Company, 1981.

Stackpole, Edward J. *The Fredericksburg Campaign.* Harrisburg, PA: Stackpole Company, 1957.

———. *Sheridan in the Shenandoah.* Harrisburg, PA: Stackpole Company, 1961.

Supplement to the Official Records of the Union and Confederate Armies. Wilmington, NC: Broadfoot Publishing Company, 1994.

Switlik, M. C. *The Complete Cannoneer.* Rochester, MI: Ray Russell Books, 1979.

Tanner, Robert G. *Stonewall in the Valley.* Garden City, NY: Doubleday & Company, 1976.

Taylor, Walter H. *Four Years with General Lee.* New York: Bonanza Books, 1957.

Thomas, Emory M. *Bold Dragoon.* New York: Harper and Row Publishers, 1986.

Thomason, John W., Jr. *Jeb Stuart.* New York: Charles Scribner's Sons, 1930.

Thompson, O. R. Howard, and William H. Rauch. *History of the "Bucktails."* Philadelphia: Electric Printing Company, 1906.

Tobie, Edward P. *History of the First Maine Cavalry, 1861–1865.* Boston: Press of Emery & Hughes, 1887.

Trout, Robert J. *They Followed the Plume.* Mechanicsburg, PA: Stackpole Books, 1993.

———. *With Pen and Saber: The Letters and Diaries of J. E. B. Stuart's Staff Officers.* Mechanicsburg, PA: Stackpole Books, 1995.

U.S. Department of Agriculture. *Diseases of the Horse.* 1942.

U.S. War Department. *The War of the Rebellion: The Official Records of the Union and Confederate Armies.* Harrisburg, PA: National Historical Society, 1971.

Veterinary Treatments and Medication for Horsemen. Equine Research, 1974.

Von Borcke, Heros. *Memoirs of the Confederate War for Independence.* Dayton, OH: Morningside House, 1985.

Von Borcke, Heros, and Justus Scheibert. *Die Grosse Reiterschlacht bei Brandy Station, 9. Juni 1863.* Gaithersburg, MD: Olde Soldier Books Company, 1976.

Walker, Charles D. *Biographical Sketches of the Graduates and Élèves of the Virginia Military Institute Who Fell during the War Between the States.* Philadelphia: J. B. Lippincott and Co., 1875.

Wallace, Lee A. *A Guide to Virginia Military Organizations, 1861–1865.* Lynchburg, VA: H. E. Howard, 1986.

The War of the Rebellion: The Official Records of the Union and Confederate Armies. Harrisburg, PA: National Historical Society, 1971.

Warner, Ezra J. *Generals in Gray.* Baton Rouge: Louisiana State University Press, 1959.

Weaver, Jeffrey C. *22nd Virginia Cavalry.* Lynchburg, VA: H. E. Howard, 1991.

Wellman, Manly Wade. *Giant in Gray.* New York: Charles Scribner's Sons, 1949.

Wells, Edward L. *Hampton and His Cavalry in '64.* Richmond, VA: Owens Publishing Co., 1991.

Wentz, Robert W., ed. *The 1989 Register & Former Cadets of the Virginia Military Institute.* Lexington, VA: VMI Alumni Association, 1989.

Wert, Jeffry D. *From Winchester to Cedar Creek: The Shenandoah Campaign of 1864.* Carlisle, PA: South Mountain Press, 1987.

Wise, Jennings Cropper. *The Long Arm of Lee.* Lynchburg, VA: J. P. Bell Company, 1915.

Wittenberg, Eric J. *Gettysburg's Forgotten Cavalry Actions.* Gettysburg, PA: Thomas Publications, 1998.

Woodward, Harold R., Jr. *Defender of the Valley: Brigadier General John Daniel Imboden, C.S.A.* Berryville, VA: Rockbridge Publishing Company, 1996.

Wright, Stuart. *Colonel Heros von Borcke's Journal.* Palaemon Press Limited, 1981.

INDEX